P9-CLP-591

ENCYCLOPEDIA OF
AMERICAN HISTORICAL
DOCUMENTS

VOLUME II

LIBRARY
MILWAUKEE AREA TECHNICAL COLLEGE
Milwaukee Campus

ENCYCLOPEDIA OF AMERICAN HISTORICAL DOCUMENTS

VOLUME II

Edited by Susan Rosenfeld

R
973.03
E 56
V. 2

☑®
Facts On File, Inc.

MILWAUKEE AREA TECHNICAL COLLEGE

Encyclopedia of American Historical Documents

Copyright © 2004 by Susan Rosenfeld

All rights reserved. No part of this book may be reproduced or utilized in any form or by any means, electronic or mechanical, including photocopying, recording, or by any information storage or retrieval systems, without permission in writing from the publisher. For information contact:

Facts On File, Inc.
132 West 31st Street
New York NY 10001

Library of Congress Cataloging-in-Publication Data

Encyclopedia of American Historical Documents / edited by Susan Rosenfeld
p. cm.
Includes bibliographical references and index.
ISBN 0-8160-4995-5 (set)—ISBN 0-8160-5993-4 (vol. 1)—
ISBN 0-8160-5994-2 (vol. 2)—ISBN 0-8160-5995-0 (vol. 3)
1. United States—History—Sources—Encyclopedias. I. Rosenfeld, Susan C.
E173.E54 2004
973'.03—dc21   2003051610

Facts On File books are available at special discounts when purchased in bulk quantities for businesses, associations, institutions, or sales promotions. Please call our Special Sales Department in New York at (212) 967-8800 or (800) 322-8755.

You can find Facts On File on the World Wide Web at http://www.factsonfile.com

Text adaptation by Theresa Montoya and Cathy Rincon
Cover design by Cathy Rincon

Printed in the United States of America

VB FOF 10 9 8 7 6 5 4 3 2 1

This book is printed on acid-free paper.

Contents

ERAS 4 TO 6

ERA 4

Expansion and Reform

(1800–1860)

The major themes of this era, expansion and reform, encompass a multitude of developments. The United States expanded in many ways. Geographically, the 16 eastern states that elected Thomas Jefferson president in 1800 (Vermont [1791], Kentucky [1792], and Tennessee [1796], plus the original 13) had grown to 33 in the election of 1860; the boundaries of the "Lower Forty-eight" were set pretty much as they stand today. However, the move west also resulted in the ousting of eastern Indians from their tribal lands. Their relocation resulted in many deaths as they trekked to new territories and reservations. In 1800 the nation's foreign interests had been limited to Europe, Africa, and the Caribbean; by 1860 they extended to Central and South America, China, and Japan. The population expanded as well. Not only in numbers but in the varieties of people, as refugees from the European upheavals and Irish famine of the 1840s emigrated to the United States.

Politically the nation had also expanded. Property and religious qualifications still limited who could hold an office or vote in several states in 1800. By 1860 the United States had what for many years textbooks called "universal suffrage," ignoring the fact that while almost all white men could vote, most blacks and all women were denied the franchise regardless of their other qualifications.

Forced by the War of 1812 to develop indigenous manufactures and bolstered by a commerce-oriented Supreme Court, the nation also expanded economically. The discovery of gold in the West spurred the growth of railroads, while an expansive view of federal responsibilities enabled the development of other modes of interstate transportation, such as roads and canals.

Sectional divisions, obvious from the Constitutional Convention, if not earlier, laid behind every "expansion" category. Where size—small states versus large states—seemed the major distinction in the late 18th century, the major distinction for the 19th begins as an exporting economy (North) versus an importing economy (South) and soon turned on whether or not a state depended on slavery. The major expansion themes of this 60-year period are extremely intermingled.

The other parts cover religious and social reform movements and intellectual and cultural developments. Although the interests of women and slaves were quite different, many women found a voice through antislavery activities. Because the antislavery and the women's movements become intertwined, these two reform groups—and the reaction to antislavery—are handled together in the second part. The next part covers religious and educational developments, and the final part concerns intellectual and cultural matters.

Beginning in 1850, sectional divisions become even more pronounced and will be treated in the next era as a prelude to the Civil War.

513

Territorial Expansion, Political and Economic Developments, and International Relations

Land Act of 1800 (Harrison Land Act)

Federal legislation enacted on May 10, 1800, designed to reduce the national debt and to encourage the settlement of the West by making the purchase of public lands easier than it had been under the Land Act of 1796. The 1800 Land Act, sponsored by William Henry Harrison, retained the minimum price of two dollars per acre from the previous act but authorized minimum purchases of 320 acres, granted buyers four years to pay, and gave a discount of 8 percent for cash payment. Administrative processes were revised to help the small purchaser. Though modified several times, the act served as the basis for federal land policy until the passage of a new Land Act on April 24, 1820. It abolished the liberal credit system that had allowed purchasers of public lands to pay for their property over a period of several years. The credit system, established by the Land Act of 1796 and extended by the Land Act of 1800, had encouraged widespread land speculation, and many settlers were unable or unwilling to make the required deferred payments. The 1820 reform, intended to help settlers and hinder speculators, reduced the minimum price from $2 to $1.25 per acre, set the minimum purchase at 80 acres, and required that the entire amount be paid at the time of purchase. Payments were still too high for most settlers, and speculators benefitted once again.

_____◦⟨∞⟩◦_____

An Act

To amend the act intituled "An act providing for the sale of the lands of the United States, in the territory northwest of the Ohio, and above the mouth of Kentucky river."

Section 1. *Be it enacted by the Senate and House of Representatives of the United States of America in Congress assembled,* That for the disposal of the lands of the United States, directed to be sold by the act, intituled "An act providing for the sale of the lands of the United States, in the territory northwest of the Ohio, and above the mouth of Kentucky river," there shall be four land offices established in the said territory: one at Cincinnati, for lands below the Little Miami, which have not heretofore been granted; one at Chilicothe, for lands east of the Scioto, south of the lands appropriated for satisfying military bounties to the late army of the United States, and west of the fifteenth range of townships, one at Marietta, for the lands east of the sixteenth range of townships, south

of the before mentioned military lands; and south of a line drawn due west from the northwest corner of the first township of the second range, to the said military lands; and one at Steubenville, for the lands north of the last mentioned line, and east or north of the said military lands. Each of the said offices shall be under the direction of an officer, to be called "The Register of the Land Office," who shall be appointed by the President of the United States, by and with the advice and consent of the Senate, and shall give bond to the United States, with approved security, in the sum of ten thousand dollars, for the faithful discharge of the duties of his office; and shall reside at the place where the land office is directed to be kept.

Sec. 2. *And be it further enacted,* That it shall be the duty of the surveyor-general, and he is hereby expressly enjoined, to prepare and transmit to the registers of the several land offices, before the days herein appointed for commencing sales, general plats of the lands hereby directed to be sold at the said offices respectively, and also to forward copies of each of the said plats to the Secretary of the Treasury.

Sec. 3. *And be it further enacted,* That the surveyor-general shall cause the townships west of the Muskingum, which by the above-mentioned act are directed to be sold in quarter townships, to be subdivided into half sections of three hundred and twenty acres each, as nearly as may be, by running parallel lines through the same from east to west, and from south to north, at the distance of one mile from each other, and marking corners, at the distance of each half mile on the lines running from east to west, and at the distance of each mile on those running from south to north, and making the marks, notes and descriptions, prescribed to surveyors by the above-mentioned act: And the interior lines of townships intersected by the Muskingum, and of all the townships lying east of that river, which have not been heretofore actually subdivided into sections, shall also be run and marked in the manner prescribed by the said act, for running and marking the interior lines of townships directed to be sold in sections of six hundred and forty acres each. And in all cases where the exterior lines of the townships, thus to be subdivided into sections or half sections, shall exceed or shall not extend six miles, the excess or deficiency shall be specially noted, and added to or deducted from the western and northern ranges of sections or half sections in such township, according as the error may be in running the lines from east to west, or from south to north; the sections and half sections bounded on the northern and western lines of such townships shall be sold as containing only the quantity expressed in the returns and plats respectively, and all others as containing the complete legal quantity. And the President of the United States shall fix the compensation of the deputy surveyors, chain carriers, and axemen: *Provided,* the whole expense of surveying and marking the lines, shall not exceed three dollars for every mile that shall be actually run, surveyed and marked.

Sec. 4. *And be it further enacted,* That the lands thus subdivided (excluding the sections reserved by the above-mentioned act) shall be offered for sale in sections and half sections, subdivided as before directed at the following places and times, that is to say: Those below the Little Miami shall be offered at public vendue, in the town of Cincinnati, on the first Monday of April one thousand eight hundred and one, under the direction of the register of the land office there established, and of either the governor or secretary of the northwestern territory. The lands east of Scioto, south of the military lands, and west of the fifteenth range of townships, shall be offered in like manner for sale at Chilicothe, on the first Monday of May, one thousand eight hundred and one, under the direction of the register of the land office there established, and of either the governor or secretary of the said territory. The lands east of the sixteenth range of townships, south of the military lands and west of the Muskingum, including all the townships intersected by that river, shall be offered for sale in like manner at Marietta, on the last Monday of May, one thousand eight hundred and one, under the direction of the governor or secretary, or surveyor-general of the said territory. The sales shall remain open at each place for three weeks, and no longer. The superintendents shall observe the rules and regulations of the above-mentioned act, in classing and selling fractional with entire sections, and in keeping and transmitting accounts of the sales. All lands remaining unsold, at the closing of either of the public sales, may be disposed of at private sale by the registers of these respective land offices, in the manner herein after prescribed; and the register of the land office at Steubenville, after the first day of July next, may proceed to sell, at private sale, the lands situate within the district assigned to his direction as herein before described, disposing of the same in sections, and classing fractional with entire sections, according to the provisions and regulations of the above-mentioned act and of this act: And the register of the land office at Marietta, after the said first day of July next, may proceed to sell at private sale, any of the lands within the district assigned to his direction as aforesaid, which are east of the river Muskingum, excluding the townships intersected by the river, disposing of the same in sections, and classing fractional with entire sections as aforesaid.

Sec. 5. *And be it further enacted,* That no lands shall be sold by virtue of this act, at either public or private sale, for less than two dollars per acre, and payment may be made for the same by all purchasers, either in specie, or in evidences of the public debt of the United States, at the rates prescribed by the act, intituled, "An act to authorize the receipt of evidences of the public debt in payment for the lands of the United States;" and shall be made in the following manner, and under the following conditions, to wit:

1. At the time of purchase, every purchaser shall, exclusively of the fees hereafter mentioned, pay six dollars for every section, and three dollars for every half section, he may have purchased, for surveying expenses, and deposit one twentieth part of the amount of purchase money, to be forfeited, if within forty days one fourth part of the purchase money, including the said twentieth part, is not paid.

2. One fourth part of the purchase money shall be paid within forty days after the day of sale as aforesaid; another fourth part shall be paid within two years; another fourth part within three years; and another fourth part within four years after the day of sale.

3. Interest, at the rate of six per cent. a year from the day of sale, shall be charged upon each of the three last payments, payable as they respectively become due.

4. A discount at the rate of eight per cent. a year, shall be allowed on any of the three payments, which shall be paid before the same shall become due, reckoning this discount always upon the sum, which would have been demandable by the United States, on the day appointed for such payment.

5. If the first payment of one fourth part of the purchase money shall not be made within forty days after the sale, the deposit, payment and fees, paid and made by the purchaser, shall be forfeited, and the lands shall and may, from and after the day, when the payment of one fourth part of the purchase money should have been made, be disposed of at private sale, on the same terms and conditions, and in the same manner as the other lands directed by this act to be disposed of at private sale: *Provided ,* that the lands which shall have been sold at public sale, and which shall, on account of such failure of payment, revert to the United States, shall not be sold at private sale, for a price less than the price that shall have been offered for the same at public sale.

6. If any tract shall not be completely paid for within one year after the date of the last payment, the tract shall be advertised for sale by the register of the land office within whose district it may lie, in at least five of the most public places in the said district, for at least thirty days

before the time of sale. And he shall sell the same at public vendue, during the sitting of the court of quarter sessions of the country in which the land office is kept, for a price not less than the whole arrears due thereon, with the expenses of sale; the surplus, if any, shall be returned to the original purchaser, or to his legal representative; but if the sum due, with interest, be not bidden and paid, then the land shall revert to the United States. All monies paid therefor shall be forfeited, and the register of the land office may proceed to dispose of the same to any purchaser, as in case of other lands at private sale.

Sec. 6. *And be it further enacted,* That all and every the payments, to be made by virtue of the preceding section, shall be made either to the treasurer of the United States, or to such person or officer as shall be appointed by the President of the United States, with the advice and consent of the Senate, receiver of public monies for lands of the United States, at each of the places respectively where the public and private sales of the said lands are to be made; and the said receiver of public monies shall, before he enters upon the duties of his office, give bond with approved security, in the sum of ten thousand dollars, for the faithful discharge of his trust; and it shall be the duty of the said treasurer and receiver of public monies to give receipts for the monies by them received, to the persons respectively paying the same; to transmit within thirty days in case of public sale, and quarterly, in case of private sale, an account of all the public monies by them received, specifying the amount received from each person, and distinguishing the sums received for surveying expenses, and those received for purchase money, to the Secretary of the Treasury, and to the registers of the land office, as the case may be. The said receivers of public monies shall, within three months after receiving the same, transmit the monies by them received to the treasurer of the United States; and the receivers of public monies for the said sales, and also the receivers of public monies for the sales which have taken place at Pittsburg under the act, intituled "An act providing for the sale of the lands of the United States in the territory northwest of the Ohio, and above the mouth of Kentucky river," shall receive one per cent. on the money received, as a compensation for clerk hire, receiving, safe keeping, and transmitting it to the treasury of the United States.

Sec. 7. *And be it further enacted,* That it shall be the duty of the registers of the land offices respectively, to receive and enter on books kept for that purpose only, and on which no blank leaves or space shall be left between the different entries, the applications of any person or persons who may apply for the purchase of any section or half section, and who shall pay him the fee hereafter mentioned, and produce a receipt from the treasurer of the United States, or from the receiver of public monies appointed for that purpose, for three dollars for each half section such person or persons may apply for, and for at least one twentieth part of the purchase money, stating carefully in each entry the date of the application, the date of the receipt to him produced, the amount of monies specified in the said receipt, and the number of the section or half section, township and range applied for. If two or more persons shall apply at the same time for the same tract, the register shall immediately determine by lot, in presence of the parties, which of them shall have preference. He shall file the receipt for monies produced by the party, and give him a copy of his entry, and if required, a copy of the description of the tract, and a copy of the plat of the same, or either of them; and it shall be his duty to inform the party applying for any one tract, whether the same has already been entered, purchased, or paid for, and at his request to give him a copy of the entry or entries concerning the same. He shall, three months after the date of each application, if the party shall not have, within that time, produced to him a receipt of the payment of one fourth part of the purchase money, including the twentieth part above mentioned, enter under its proper date, in the said book of entries, that the payment has not been made, and that the land has reverted to the United States, and he shall make a note of the same in the margin of the book opposite to the original entry. And if the party shall, either at the time of making the original entry, or at any time within three months thereafter, produce a receipt to him, for the fourth part of the purchase money, including the twentieth part aforesaid, he shall file the receipt, make an entry of the same, under its proper date, in the said book of entries, make a note of the same in the margin of the book, opposite to the original entry, and give to the party a certificate, describing the land sold, the sum paid on account, the balance remaining due, the time and times when such balance shall become due, and that if it shall be duly discharged, the purchaser or his assignee or other legal representative, shall be entitled to a patent for the said lands; he shall also, upon any subsequent payment being made, and a receipt from the receiver being produced to him, file the original receipt, give a receipt for the same to the party, and enter the same to the credit of the party, in a book kept for that purpose, in which he shall open an account in the name of each purchaser, for each section or half section that may be sold either at public or private sale, and in which he shall charge the party for the whole purchase money, and give him credit for all his payments; making the proper charges and allowances for interest or discount, as the case may be, according to the provisions of the fourth section of this act; and upon the payment being completed and the account finally settled, he shall give a certificate of the same to the party; and on producing to the Secretary of the Treasury, the same final certificate, the President of the United

States is hereby authorized to grant a patent for the lands to the said purchaser, his heirs or assigns; and all patents shall be countersigned by the Secretary of State, and recorded in his office.

Sec. 8. *And be it further enacted,* That the registers of the land offices respectively, shall also note on the book of surveys, or original plat transmitted to them, every tract which may be sold, by inserting the letter A on the day when the same is applied for, and the letter P on the day when a receipt for one fourth part of the purchase money is produced to them, and by crossing the said letter A on the day when the land shall revert to the United States, on failure of the payment of one fourth part of the purchase money within three months after the date of application. And the said book of surveys or original plat shall be open at all times, in presence of the register, for the inspection of any individual, applying for the same and paying the proper fee.

Sec. 9. *And be it further enacted,* That it shall be the duty of the registers of the land offices to transmit quarterly to the Secretary of the Treasury, and to the surveyor-general, an account of the several tracts applied for, of the several tracts for which the payment of one fourth part of the purchase money has been made, of the several tracts which have reverted to the United States on failure of the said payment; and also an account of all the payments of monies by them entered, according to the receipts produced to them, specifying the sums of money, the names of the persons paying the same, the names of the officers who have received the same, and the tracts for which the same have been paid.

Sec. 10. *And be it further enacted,* That the registers aforesaid shall be precluded from entering on their books any application for lands in their own name, and in the name of any other person in trust for them; and if any register shall wish to purchase any tract of land, he may do it by application in writing to the surveyor-general, who shall enter the same on books kept for that purpose by him, who shall proceed in respect to such applications, and to any payments made for the same, in the same manner which the registers by this act are directed to follow, in respect to applications made to them for lands by other persons. The registers shall, nevertheless, note on the book of surveys, or original plat, the applications and payments thus by them made, and their right to the pre-emption of any tract shall bear date from the day, when their application for the same shall have been entered by the surveyor-general in his own book. And if any person applying for any tract shall, notwithstanding he shall have received information from the register, that the same has already been applied for by the said register, or by any other person, insist to make the application, it shall be the duty of the register to enter the same, noting in the margin that the same tract is already

purchased, but upon application of the party made in writing, and which he shall file, he may and shall at any future time enter under its proper date, that the party withdraws his former application, and applies in lieu thereof for any other tract: *Provided always,* that the party shall never be allowed thus to withdraw his former application, and to apply in lieu thereof for another tract, except when the tract described in his former application shall have been applied for previous to the date of that his former application.

Sec. 11. *And be it further enacted,* That the Secretary of the Treasury shall and may prescribe such further regulations, in the manner of keeping books and accounts, by the several officers in this act mentioned, as to him may appear necessary and proper, in order fully to carry into effect the provisions of this act.

Sec. 12. *And be it further enacted,* That the registers of the land offices, respectively, shall be entitled to receive from the treasury of the United States, one half per cent. on all the monies expressed in the receipts by them filed and entered, and of which they shall have transmitted an account to the Secretary of the Treasury, as directed by this act; and they shall further be entitled to receive, for their own use, from the respective parties, the following fees for services rendered, that is to say; for every original application for land, and a copy of the same, for a section three dollars, for a half section two dollars; for every certificate stating that the first fourth part of the purchase money is paid, twenty-five cents; for every subsequent receipt for monies paid, twenty-five cents; for the final settlement of account and giving the final certificate of the same, one dollar; for every copy, either of an application or of the description of any section or half section, or of the plat of the same, or of any entry made on their books, or of any certificate heretofore given by them, twenty-five cents for each; and for any general inspection of the book of surveys, or general plat, made in their presence, twenty-five cents.

Sec. 13. *And be it further enacted,* That the superintendents of the public sales, to be made by virtue of this act, and the superintendents of the sales which have taken place by virtue of the act, intituled "An act providing for the sale of the lands of the United States in the territory northwest of the river Ohio, and above the mouth of Kentucky river," shall receive five dollars a day for every day whilst engaged in that business; and the accounting officers of the treasury are hereby authorized to allow a reasonable compensation for books, stationery and clerk hire, in settling the accounts of the said superintendents.

Sec. 14. *And be it further enacted,* That the fee to be paid for each patent for half a section shall be four dollars, and for every section five dollars, to be accounted for by the receiver of the same.

Sec. 15. *And be it further enacted,* That the lands of the United States reserved for future disposition, may be let upon leases by the surveyor-general, in sections or half sections, for terms not exceeding seven years, on condition of making such improvements as he shall deem reasonable.

Sec. 16. *And be it further enacted,* That each person who, before the passing of this act, shall have erected, or begun to erect, a grist-mill or saw-mill upon any of the lands herein directed to be sold, shall be entitled to the pre-emption of the section including such mill, at the rate of two dollars per acre: *Provided,* the person or his heirs, claiming such right of pre-emption, shall produce to the register of the land office satisfactory evidence that he or they are entitled thereto, and shall be subject to and comply with the regulations and provisions by this act prescribed for other purchasers.

Sec. 17. *And be it further enacted,* That so much of the act, providing for the sale of the lands of the United States in the territory northwest of the river Ohio, and above the mouth of Kentucky river, as comes within the purview of this act, be, and the same is hereby repealed.

Source:

Statutes at Large of the United States of America, 1789–1873. 17 vols. Washington, D.C. 1850–73. Vol. 5, pp. 73–78.

Louisiana Purchase Treaty, 1803

Agreement signed on April 30, 1803, by which the United States purchased from France a vast territory north and west of New Orleans, from the Mississippi River to the Rocky Mountains, for $15 million. The purchase of the 828,000-square-mile area, which Napoleonic France had only recently acquired from Spain, doubled the size of the United States. Suspicious of the French and wary of losing access to the Mississippi from the Gulf of Mexico, President Thomas Jefferson initially sought to purchase only New Orleans, but Napoleon Bonaparte, occupied by the slave revolt in Haiti and the impending war with Great Britain, offered to sell the entire Louisiana Territory. Despite the dubious constitutionality of the purchase, the U.S. Senate approved the treaty in October 1803, and the United States took possession of the territory in December. The precise boundaries of the purchase, which were not defined in the treaty, were disputed for many years. All or part of 15 states were eventually created from this area.

The Adams-Onís Treaty, signed at Washington, D.C., on February 22, 1819, and ratified on February 22, 1821, settled some of the difficulties with Spain while setting the stage for new ones. Spain abandoned all claims to West Florida (which had been seized by U.S. troops under Andrew Jackson the previous year), ceded East Florida to the United States, and gave up its claims to the Pacific Northwest. In exchange, the United States renounced its rights to Texas and agreed to pay up to $5 million to settle disputes of American citizens with Spain. The treaty was negotiated by President James Monroe's secretary of state John Quincy Adams.

No specific authority in the U.S. Constitution authorized the executive to purchase territory. By acquiring the Louisiana Territory, Jefferson switched from being a "strict constructionist," the position previously associated with the Democratic-Republicans, to becoming a "loose constructionist."

Treaty

Between the United States of America and the French Republic.

The President of the United States of America, and the First Consul of the French Republic, in the name of the French people, desiring to remove all source of misunderstanding relative to objects of discussion mentioned in the second and fifth articles of the convention of the 8th Vendemiaire, an. 9 (30th September, 1800) relative to the rights claimed by the United States, in virtue of the treaty concluded at Madrid, the 27th of October, 1795, between his Catholic Majesty and the said United States, and willing to strengthen the union and friendship which at the time of the said convention was happily re-established between the two nations, have respectively named their plenipotentiaries, to wit: the President of the United States [of America,] by and with the advice and consent of the Senate of the said states, Robert R. Livingston, minister plenipotentiary of the United States, and James Monroe, minister plenipotentiary and envoy extraordinary of the said states, near the government of the French Republic; and the First Consul, in the name of the French people, citizen Francis Barbe Marbois, minister of the public treasury, who, after having respectively exchanged their full powers, have agreed to the following articles.

Article I. Whereas, by the article the third of the treaty concluded at St. Ildelfonso, the 9th Vendemiaire, an. 9 (1st October, 1800) between the First Consul of the French Republic and his Catholic Majesty, it was agreed as follows: "His Catholic Majesty promises and engages on his part, to cede to the French Republic, six months after the full and entire execution of the conditions and stipulations herein relative to his royal highness the duke of Parma, the colony or province of Louisiana, with the same extent that it now has in the hands of Spain, and that it had when France possessed it; and such as it should be after the treaties subsequently entered into between Spain and other states." *And whereas,* in pursuance of the treaty, and particularly of the third article, the French Republic has an incontestible title to the domain and to the possession of the said territory: The First Consul of the French Republic desiring to give to the United States a strong proof of his friendship, doth hereby cede to the said United States, in the name of the

French Republic, forever and in full sovereignty, the said territory with all its rights and appurtenances, as fully and in the same manner as they have been acquired by the French Republic, in virtue of the above-mentioned treaty, concluded with his Catholic Majesty.

Art. II. In the cession made by the preceding article are included the adjacent islands belonging to Louisiana, all public lots and squares, vacant lands, and all public buildings, fortifications, barracks and other edifices which are not private property.—The archives, papers, and documents, relative to the domain and sovereignty of Louisiana, and its dependencies, will be left in the possession of the commissaries of the United States, and copies will be afterwards given in due form to the magistrates and municipal officers, of such of the said papers and documents as may be necessary to them.

Art. III. The inhabitants of the ceded territory shall be incorporated in the Union of the United States, and admitted as soon as possible, according to the principles of the Federal constitution, to the enjoyment of all the rights, advantages and immunities of citizens of the United States; and in the mean time they shall be maintained and protected in the free enjoyment of their liberty, property, and the religion which they profess.

Art. IV. There shall be sent by the government of France a commissary to Louisiana, to the end that he do every act necessary, as well to receive from the officers of his Catholic Majesty and said country and its dependences, in the name of the French Republic, if it has not been already done, as to transmit it in the name of the French Republic to the commissary or agent of the United States.

Art. V. Immediately after the ratification of the present treaty by the President of the United States, and in case that of the First Consul shall have been previously obtained, the commissary of the French Republic shall remit all the military posts of New Orleans, and other parts of the ceded territory, to the commissary or commissaries named by the President to take possession; the troops, whether of France or Spain, who may be there, shall cease to occupy any military post from the time of taking possession, and shall be embarked as soon as possible, in the course of three months after the ratification of this treaty.

Art. VI. The United States promise to execute such treaties and articles as may have been agreed between Spain and the tribes and nations of Indians, until, by mutual consent of the United States and the said tribes or nations, other suitable articles shall have been agreed upon.

Art. VII. As it is reciprocally advantageous to the commerce of France and the United States to encourage the communication of both nations for a limited time in the country ceded by the present treaty, until general arrangements relative to the commerce of both nations may be agreed on; it has been agreed between the contracting parties, that the French ships coming directly from France or any of her colonies, loaded only with the produce and manufactures of France or her said colonies; and the ships of Spain coming directly from Spain or any of her colonies, loaded only with the produce or manufactures of Spain or her colonies, shall be admitted during the space of twelve years in the ports of New Orleans, and in all other legal ports of entry within the ceded territory, in the same manner as the ships of the United State coming directly from France or Spain, or any of their colonies, without being subject to any other or greater duty on merchandize, or other or greater tonnage than that paid by the citizens of the United States.

During the space of time above mentioned, no other nation shall have a right to the same privileges in the ports of the ceded territory: the twelve years shall commence three months after the exchange of ratifications, if it shall take place in France, or three months after it shall have been notified at Paris to the French government, if it shall take place in the United States; it is however well understood that the object of the above article is to favor the manufactures, commerce, freight and navigation of France and of Spain, so far as relates to the importations that the French and Spanish shall make into the said ports of the United States, without in any sort affecting the regulations that the United States may make concerning the exportation of the produce and merchandize of the United States, or any right they may have to make such regulations.

Art. VIII. In future and forever after the expiration of the twelve years, the ships of France shall be treated upon the footing of the most favored nations in the ports above mentioned.

Art. IX. The particular convention signed this day by the respective ministers, having for its object to provide for the payment of debts due to the citizens of the United States by the French Republic, prior to the 30th of September, 1800, (8th Vendemiaire, an. 9,) is approved, and to have its execution in the same manner as if it had been inserted in this present treaty; and it shall be ratified in the same form and in the same time, so that the one shall not be ratified distinct from the other.

Another particular convention signed at the same date as the present treaty relative to a definitive rule between the contracting parties is in the like manner approved, and will be ratified in the same form, and in the same time, and jointly.

Art. X. The present treaty shall be ratified in good and due form, and the ratifications shall be exchanged in the space of six months after the date of the signature by the ministers plenipotentiary, or sooner, if possible.

In faith whereof, the respective plenipotentiaries have signed these articles in the French and English languages; declaring nevertheless that the present treaty was originally agreed to in the French language; and have thereunto affixed their seals.

Done at Paris, the tenth day of Floreal, in the eleventh year of the French Republic, and the 30th of April, 1803.

Source:

Charles I. Bevans, comp. *Treaties and Other Agreements of the United States of America, 1776–1949.* Washington, D.C.: Government Printing Office, 1968–76.

The Meriwether Lewis and William Clark Expedition, 1804–1806

After purchasing the Louisiana Territory in 1803, President Thomas Jefferson asked Congress to finance an expedition to explore and map the land and possibly to find a water route to the Pacific Ocean. In addition, Jefferson wanted samples of the flora and fauna, especially if they represented species previously unknown. He appointed his private secretary and relative Meriwether Lewis to lead the expedition, which started from Pittsburgh in August 1803. William Clark joined him two months later, in Indiana. Several members of the party kept journals. The excerpts here provide descriptions of the land, the Indians they encountered, wild animals, and some of their travel experiences.

September 07, 1804, William Clark:
. . . [I] discovered a Village of Small animals that burrow in the grown (those animals are Called by the french Petite Chien [little dogs; today called prairie dogs or gophers]) Killed one and Caught one a live by poreing a great quantity of Water in his hole we attempted to dig to the beds of one of those animals, . . . [the "village"] contains great numbers of holes on the top of which those little animals Set erect make a Whistleing noise and whin allarmed Step into their hole.

September 14, 1804, John Ordway:
. . . Capt Clark joined us had killed a curious annamil resembling a Goat Willard brought it on board. [I]t was 3 feet high resembles a Deer in some parts the legs like a Deer. feet like a Goat. horns like a Goat only forked . . . Such an anamil was never yet known in U.S. States. the Capt had the Skins of the hair & Goat Stuffed in order to send back to the city of Washington. [T]he bones and all.

April 04, 1805, Patrick Gass:
We packed the boxes full of skins, buffaloe robes, and horns of the Mountain ram, of a great size for the president; and began to load the boat.

April 05, 1805, Patrick Gass:
If this brief Journal should happen to be preserved, and be ever thought worthy of appearing in print: some readers will perhaps expect, that, after our long friendly intercourse with these Indians, among whom we have spent the winter; . . . we ought to be prepared now, when we are about to renew our voyage, to give some account of the fair sex of the Missouri: and entertain them with narratives of feats of love as well as of arms. Though we could furnish a sufficient number of entertaining stories and pleasant anecdotes, we do not think it prudent to swell our Journal with them; as our views are directed to more useful information. . . .

It may be observed generally that chastisty is not very high esteemed by these people, and that the severe and loathsome effects of certain French principles are not uncommon among them. The fact is, that the women are generally considered an article of traffic and indulgencies are sold at a very moderate price. As a proof of this I will just mention, that for an old tobacco box, one of our men was granted the honour of passing a night with the daughter of the headchief of the Mandan nation.

April 08, 1805, Patrick Gass:
The woman that is with us [Sacagawea] is a squaw of the Snake nation of Indians, and wife to our interpreter. We expect she will be of service to us, when passing through that nation.

April 10, 1805, Meriwether Lewis:
The country on both sides of the missouri from the tops of the river hills, is one continued level fertile plain as far as the eye can reach, in which there is not even a solitary tree or shrub to be seen, except such as from their moist situations or the steep declivities of hills are sheltered from the ravages of the fire.

April 10, 1805, John Ordway:
[W]e Saw a nomber of large Eagles which had nested on large cottonwood trees. . . . [O]ne of our men Shot a bald Eagle. I took the quills to write.

April 17, 1805, Meriwether Lewis:
There were three beaver taken this morning by the party. [T]he men prefer the flesh of this anamal, to that of any other which we have, or are able to procure at this moment. I eat very heartily of the beaver myself, and think it excellent; particularly the tale, and liver. . . .

April 22, 1805, John Ordway:
Passed a high bluff . . . and a handsom bottom and plains . . . which was covered with buffaloe & buffaloe calfs, Elk deer . . . and large gangs on the opposite Shore I think that

we Saw at one view nearly one thousand animels. they are not to day verry wild for we could go within a 100 yards of them in open view of them before they would run off and then they would go but a Short distance before they would Stop and feed again, . . . Saw a buffaloe Calf which had fell down the bank & could not git up again. [W]e helped it up the bank and it followed us a Short distance.

December 08, 1805, Patrick Gass:
The country towards the south is mountainous at some distance off; and there is some snow on the mountains. Near our camp, the country is closely timbered with spruce-pine, the soil rich, but not deep; and there are numerous springs of running water.

December 11, 1805, William Clark:
Wwe are all employed putting up huts or Cabins for our winters quarters, Sergeant Pryor unwell from a dislocation of his sholder, Gibson with the disentary, Jo. Fields with biles on his legs, & Werner with a Strained Knee. The rain Continued moderately all day.

December 12, 1805, William Clark:
The flees were so troublesom last night that I made but a broken nights rest, we find great dificuelty in getting those trouble[some] insects out of our robes and blankets. . . . [I] can readily discover that they [the local Indians] are close deelers, & Stickle for a verry little, never close a bargin except they think they have the advantage Value Blue beeds highly, white they also prise but no other Colour do they Value in the least.

December 18, 1805, William Clark:
[It] rained and Snowed. . . . The men being thinly Dressed and mockersons without Socks is the reason that but little can be done at the Houses to day. [A]t 12 the Hail & Snow seased, and rain Suckceeded for the latter part of the day

Source:
American Studies at the University of Virginia. "The Journals of Lewis and Clark." Available on-line. URL: http://xroads. virginia.edu/~HYPER/JOURNALS/toc.html. Accessed October 2003.

Trade Prohibitions by Great Britain and France (French Continental System and British Orders in Council), 1806–1807

Decrees issued by French emperor Napoleon I and Great Britain during the Napoleonic Wars. In the Berlin Decree (November 1806) Napoleon forbade any trade to or from the British Isles. Napoleon enforced this decree in retaliation for a British blockade of commercial ports, claiming it was contrary to international law. The Berlin Decree initiated the French Continental System, Napoleon's plan to prevent Britain from exporting or re-exporting goods to continental Europe. Britain retaliated through the British Order in Council, which forbade nearly all trade between Britain and any nation obeying the Continental System. The specific British regulations were issued by the king of England on the advice of the Privy Council and promulgated by the British government starting January 7, 1807, with an order that forbade neutral ships from trading between French ports. Two other British orders (November 11 and 25, 1807) declared that any ship with a cargo bound for France or a French-controlled port would first be required to unload its cargo and pay a duty and then obtain a special license from the British before being allowed to continue to its destination. Napoleon responded with the Milan Decree, stating that ships complying with these orders lost their neutral status and would be treated as British vessels, in December 1807. In an attempt to strengthen the Berlin Decree, the Milan Decree authorized French warships and privateers to capture neutral vessels sailing from any British port or from countries occupied by British armies. Such vessels were deemed British property and liable to seizure by the French as prizes of war. Through these decrees, Napoleon hoped to destroy Great Britain's credit and break its stranglehold over American shipping. The Americans were caught in the middle and responded with the Embargo of 1807.

───────── ⌇⌇ ─────────

Berlin Decree, 1806

ART. I
The British islands are declared in a state of blockade.

II
All commerce and correspondence with the British islands are prohibited. In consequence, letters or packets, addressed either to England, to an Englishman, or in the English language, shall not pass through the post-office and shall be seized.

III
Every subject of England, of whatever rank and condition soever, who shall be found in the countries occupied by our troops, or by those of our allies, shall be made a prisoner of war.

IV
All magazines, merchandise, or property whatsoever, belonging to a subject of England, shall be declared lawful prize.

V

The trade in English merchandise is forbidden; all merchandise belonging to England, or coming from its manufactories and colonies, is declared lawful prize.

VI

One half of the proceeds of the confiscation of the merchandise and property, declared good prize by the preceding articles, shall be applied to indemnify the merchants for the losses which they have suffered by the capture of merchant vessels by English cruisers.

VII

No vessel coming directly from England, or from the English colonies, or having been there since the publication of the present decree, shall be received into any port.

VIII

Every vessel contravening the above clause, by means of a false declaration, shall be seized, and the vessel and cargo confiscated, as if they were English property.

IX

Our tribunal of prizes at Paris is charged with the definitive adjudication of all the controversies, which by the French army, relative to the execution of the present decree. Our tribunal of prizes at Milan shall be charged with the definitive adjudication of the said controversies, which may arise within the extent of our kingdom of Italy.

X

The present decree shall be communicated by our minister of exterior relations, to the kings of Spain, of Naples, of Holland, and of Etruria, and to our allies, whose subjects, like ours, are the victims of the injustice and the barbarism of the English maritime laws. Our finances, our police, and our post masters general, are charged each, in what concerns him, with the execution of the present decree.

Source:

Henry Steele Commager, ed. *Documents of American History.* New York: F.S. Crofts & Co., 1934.

British Order in Council, 1807

Whereas the French Government has issued certain orders, which, in violation of the usages of war, purport to prohibit the commerce of all neutral nations with His Majesty's dominions, and also to prevent such nations from trading with any other country in any articles, the growth, produce, or manufacture of His Majesty's dominions; and whereas the said Government has also taken upon itself to declare all His Majesty's dominions to be in a state of blockade, at the time when the fleets of France and her allies are themselves confined within their own ports by the superior valor and discipline of the British navy; and whereas such attempts, on the part of the enemy, would give to His Majesty an unquestionable right of retaliation, and would warrant His Majesty in enforcing the same prohibition of all commerce with France, which that power vainly hopes to effect against the commerce of His Majesty's subjects, a prohibition which the superiority of His Majesty's naval forces might enable him to support by actually investing the ports and coasts of the enemy with numerous squadrons and cruisers, so as to make the entrance or approach thereto manifestly dangerous; and whereas His Majesty, though unwilling to follow the example of his enemies by proceeding to an extremity so distressing to all nations not engaged in the war, and carrying on their accustomed trade, yet feels himself bound, by due regard to the just defense of the rights and interests of his people not to suffer such measures to be taken by the enemy, without taking some steps on his part to restrain this violence, and to retort upon them the evils of their own injustice; His Majesty is thereupon pleased, by and with the advice of his privy council, to order, and it is hereby ordered, that no vessel shall be permitted to trade from one port to another, both which ports shall belong to or be in the possession of France or her allies, or shall be so far under their control as that British vessels may not trade freely thereat; and the commanders of His Majesty's ships of war and privateers shall be, and are hereby, instructed to warn every neutral vessel coming from any such port, and destined to another such port, to discontinue her voyage, and not to proceed to any such port; and any vessel, after being so warned, or any vessel coming from any such port, after a reasonable time shall have been afforded for receiving information of this His Majesty's order, which shall be found proceeding to another such port, shall be captured and brought in, and together with her cargo shall be condemned as lawful prize; and His Majesty's principal Secretaries of State, the Lords Commissioners of the Admiralty, and the Judges of the High Court of Admiralty, and the Courts of Vice-admiralty, are to take the necessary measures herein as to them shall respectively appertain.

Source:

Henry Steele Commager, ed. *Documents of American History.* New York: F.S. Crofts & Co., 1934.

Milan Decree, 1807

Napoleon, emperor of the French, king of Italy, and protector of the Rhenish confederation.

Observing the measures adopted by the British government, on the 11th November last, by which vessels belonging to neutral, friendly, or even powers the allies of England, are made liable, not only to be searched by English cruisers, but to be compulsorily detailed in England, and to have a tax laid on them of so much per cent on the cargo, to be regulated by the British legislature.

Observing that by these acts the British government *denationalizes* ships of every nation in Europe, that it is not competent for any government to detract from its own independence and rights, all the sovereigns of Europe having in trust the sovereignties and independence of the flag; that if by an unpardonable weakness, and which in the eyes of posterity would be an indelible stain, if such a tyranny was allowed to be established into principles, and consecrated by useage, the English would avail themselves of it to assert it as a right, as they have availed themselves of the tolerance of government to establish the infamous principle, that the flag of a nation does not cover goods, and to have their right of blockade an arbitrary extension, and which infringes on the sovereignty of every state; we have decreed and do decree as follows:

ART. I

Every ship, to whatever nation it may belong, that shall have submitted to be searched by an English ship, or to a voyage to England, or shall have paid any tax whatsoever to the English government, is thereby and for that alone, declared to be *denationalized*, to have forfeited the protection of its king, and to have become English property.

ART. II

Whether the ships thus *denationalized* by the arbitrary measures of the English government, enter into our ports, or those of our allies, or whether they fall into the hands of our ships of war, or of our privateers, they are declared to be good and lawful prize.

ART. III

The British islands are declared to be in a state of blockade, both by land and sea. Every ship, of whatever nation, or whatsoever the nature of its cargo may be, that sails from the ports of England, or those of the English colonies, and of the countries occupied by English troops, and proceeding to England or to the English colonies, or to countries occupied by English troops, is good and lawful prize, as contrary to the present decree, and may be captured by our ships of war, or our privateers, and adjudged to the captor.

ART. IV

These measures, which are resorted to only in just retaliation of the barbarous system adopted by England, which assimilates its legislation to that of Algiers, shall cease to have any effect with respect to all nations who shall have

the firmness to compel the English government to respect their flag. They shall continue to be rigorously in force as long as that government does not return to the principle of the law of nations, which regulates the relations of civilized states in a state of war. The provisions of the present decree shall be abrogated and null, in fact, as soon as the English abide again by the principles of the law of nations, which are also the principles of justice and of honour.

All our ministers are charged with the execution of the present decree, which shall be inserted in the bulletin of the laws.

Napoleon.

Source:

Henry Steele Commager, ed. *Documents of American History.* New York: F.S. Crofts & Co., 1934, pp. 201–202.

Non-Intercourse Act of 1809

Federal legislation signed by President Thomas Jefferson on March 1, 1809, and effective on March 15, repealing the U.S. Embargo Act of 1807. The Embargo Act, passed by Congress on December 22, 1807, prohibited all international trade to and from U.S. ports. It, in turn, supplanted the Non-Importation Act of April 18, 1806, which prohibited the importation of certain British goods. The purpose of this act was to force Great Britain, then at war with France, to cease its practices of seizing neutral American commercial vessels engaged in trade with the French and of impressing (forcing into royal service) American sailors under the claim that they were deserters from the British navy or were British subjects. The 1807 Embargo Act was designed to deny raw materials to both Great Britain and France and to persuade them to cease practices that were damaging American commerce. Rather than achieving its goal, the act dramatically lowered American exports, denied merchants and producers their income from raw materials, cost sailors their jobs, and forced the closure of American ports. This unpopular and unsuccessful legislation was repealed on March 1, 1809. The U.S. Non-Intercourse Act replaced it. The Non-Intercourse Act of 1809 restored trade with all foreign countries except Great Britain and France, which were still at war with each other. The act authorized the president to allow trade to resume between the United States and Britain and France when those two nations stopped seizing American commercial ships, impressing American sailors, and otherwise violating U.S. neutrality rights. When this act failed to end French and British interference with U.S. shipping, it was replaced in 1810 by the Macon Act, also known as Macon's Bill #2 after its sponsor, Senator Nathaniel Macon. The Macon Act reopened trade with both nations but provided that if either France or Britain recognized American neutrality and ceased violations of American shipping, the United States would cease trading with the other nation. Trade was restored with France, and nonintercourse was reimposed on Great Britain in 1811, a prelude to the War of 1812.

──────────────────⟡──────────────────

An Act

To interdict the commercial intercourse between the United States and Great Britain and France, and their dependencies; and for other purposes.

Be it enacted by the Senate and House of Representatives of the United States of America in Congress assembled, That from and after the passing of this act, the entrance of the harbors and waters of the United States and of the territories thereof, be, and the same is hereby interdicted to all public ships and vessels belonging to Great Britain or France, excepting vessels only which may be forced in by distress, or which are charged with despatches or business from the government to which they belong, and also packets having no cargo nor merchandise on board. And if any public ship or vessel as aforesaid, not being included in the exception above mentioned, shall enter any harbor or waters within the jurisdiction of the United States, or of the territories thereof, it shall be lawful for the President of the United States, or such other person as he shall have empowered for that purpose, to employ such part of the land and naval forces, or of the militia of the United States, or the territories thereof, as he shall deem necessary, to compel such ship or vessel to depart.

Sec. 2. *And be it further enacted,* That it shall not be lawful for any citizen or citizens of the United States or the territories thereof, nor for any person or persons residing or being in the same, to have any intercourse with, or to afford any aid or supplies to any public ship or vessel as aforesaid, which shall, contrary to the provisions of this act, have entered any harbor or waters within the jurisdiction of the United States or the territories thereof; and if any person shall, contrary to the provisions of this act, have any intercourse with such ship or vessel, or shall afford any aid to such ship or vessel, either in repairing the said vessel or in furnishing her, her officers or crew with supplies of any kind or in any manner whatever, or if any pilot or other person shall assist in navigating or piloting such ship or vessel, unless it be for the purpose of carrying her beyond the limits and jurisdiction of the United States, every person so offending, shall forfeit and pay a sum not less than one hundred dollars, nor exceeding ten thousand dollars; and shall also be imprisoned for a term not less than one month, nor more than one year.

Sec. 3. *And be it further enacted,* That from and after the twentieth day of May next, the entrance of the harbors and waters of the United States and the territories thereof

be, and the same is hereby interdicted to all ships or vessels sailing under the flag of Great Britain or France, or owned in whole or in part by any citizen or subject of either; vessels hired, chartered or employed by the government of either country, for the sole purpose of carrying letters or despatches, and also vessels forced in by distress or by the dangers of the sea, only excepted. And if any ship or vessel sailing under the flag of Great Britain or France, or owned in whole or in part by any citizen or subject of either, and not excepted as aforesaid, shall after the said twentieth day of May next, arrive either with or without a cargo, within the limits of the United States or of the territories thereof, such ship, or vessel, together with the cargo, if any, which may be found on board, shall be forfeited, and may be seized and condemned in any court of the United States or the territories thereof, having competent jurisdiction, and all and every act and acts heretofore passed, which shall be within the purview of this act, shall be, and the same are hereby repealed.

Sec. 4. *And be it further enacted,* That from and after the twentieth day of May next, it shall not be lawful to import into the United States or the territories thereof, any goods, wares or merchandise whatever, from any port or place situated in Great Britain or Ireland, or in any of the colonies or dependencies of Great Britain, nor from any port or place situated in France, or in any of her colonies or dependencies, nor from any port or place in the actual possession of either Great Britain or France. Nor shall it be lawful to import into the United States, or the territories thereof, from any foreign port or place whatever, any goods, wares or merchandise whatever, being of the growth, produce or manufacture of France, or of any of her colonies or dependencies, or being of the growth, produce or manufacture of Great Britain or Ireland, or of any of the colonies or dependencies of Great Britain, or being of the growth, produce or manufacture of any place or country in the actual possession of either France or Great Britain: *Provided,* that nothing herein contained shall be construed to affect the cargoes of ships or vessels wholly owned by a citizen or citizens of the United States, which had cleared for any port beyond the Cape of Good Hope, prior to the twenty-second day of December, one thousand eight hundred and seven, or which had departed for such port by permission of the President, under the acts supplementary to the act laying an embargo on all ships and vessels in the ports and harbors of the United States.

Sec. 5. *And be it further enacted,* That whenever any article or articles, the importation of which is prohibited by this act, shall, after the twentieth of May, be imported into the United States, or the territories thereof, contrary to the true intent and meaning of this act, or shall, after the said twentieth of May, be put on board of any ship or vessel, boat, raft or carriage, with intention of importing the same into the United States, or the territories thereof, all such articles, as well as all other articles on board the same ship or vessel, boat, raft or carriage, belonging to the owner of such prohibited articles, shall be forfeited; and the owner thereof shall moreover forfeit and pay treble the value of such articles.

Sec. 6. *And be it further enacted,* That if any article or articles, the importation of which is prohibited by this act, shall, after the twentieth of May, be put on board of any ship or vessel, boat, raft or carriage, with intention to import the same into the United States, or the territories thereof, contrary to the true intent and meaning of this act, and with the knowledge of the owner or master of such ship or vessel, boat, raft or carriage, such ship or vessel, boat, raft or carriage shall be forfeited, and the owner and master thereof shall moreover each forfeit and pay treble the value of such articles.

Sec. 7. *And be it further enacted,* That if any article or articles, the importation of which is prohibited by this act, and which shall nevertheless be on board of any ship or vessel, boat, raft or carriage, arriving after the said twentieth of May next, in the United States, or the territories thereof, shall be omitted in the manifest, report or entry of the master, or the person having the charge or command of such ship or vessel, boat, raft or carriage, or shall be omitted in the entry of the goods owned by the owner or consigned to the consignee of such articles, or shall be imported, or landed, or attempted to be imported or landed without a permit, the same penalties, fines, and forfeitures, shall be incurred, and may be recovered, as in the case of similar omission or omissions, landing, importation, or attempt to land or import in relation to articles liable to duties on their importation into the United States.

Sec. 8. *And be it further enacted,* That every collector, naval officer, surveyor, or other officer of the customs, shall have the like power and authority to seize goods, wares and merchandise imported contrary to the intent and meaning of this act, to keep the same in custody until it shall have been ascertained whether the same have been forfeited or not, and to enter any ship or vessel, dwelling-house, store, building or other place, for the purpose of searching for and seizing any such goods, wares and merchandise which he or they now have by law in relation to goods, wares and merchandise subject to duty; and if any person or persons shall conceal or buy any goods, wares or merchandise, knowing them to be liable to seizure by this act, such person or persons shall, on conviction thereof, forfeit and pay a sum double the amount or value of the goods, wares and merchandise so concealed or purchased.

Sec. 9. *And be it further enacted,* That the following additions shall be made to the oath or affirmation taken by the masters or persons having the charge or command of any ship or vessel arriving at any port of the United States,

or the territories thereof, after the twentieth of May, viz: "I further swear (or affirm) that there are not, to the best of my knowledge and belief, on board, (*insert the denomination and name of the vessel*) any goods, wares or merchandise, the importation of which into the United States, or the territories thereof, is prohibited by law: and I do further swear (or affirm) that if I shall hereafter discover or know of any such goods, wares or merchandise, on board the said vessel, or which shall have been imported in the same, I will immediately, and without delay, make due report thereof to the collector of the port of this district."

Sec. 10. *And be it further enacted,* That the following addition be made, after the twentieth of May, to be oath or affirmation taken by importers, consignees, or agents, at the time of entering goods imported into the United States, or the territories thereof, viz. "I also swear, (or affirm) that there are not, to the best of my knowledge and belief, amongst the said goods, wares and merchandise, imported or consigned as aforesaid, any goods, wares or merchandise, the importation of which into the United States, or the territories thereof, is prohibited by law; and I do further swear (or affirm) that if I shall hereafter discover or know of any such goods, wares or merchandise, amongst the said goods, wares and merchandise, imported or consigned as aforesaid, I will immediately and without delay report the same to the collector of this district."

Sec. 11. *And be it further enacted,* That the President of the United States be, and he hereby is authorized, in case either France or Great Britain shall so revoke or modify her edicts, as that they shall cease to violate the neutral commerce of the United States, to declare the same by proclamation; after which the trade of the United States, suspended by this act, and by the act laying an embargo on all ships and vessels in the ports and harbors of the United States, and the several acts supplementary thereto, may be renewed with the nation so doing: *Provided,* that all penalties and forfeitures which shall have been previously incurred, by virtue of this or of any other act, the operation of which shall so cease and determine, shall be recovered and distributed, in like manner as if the same had continued in full force and virtue: and vessels bound thereafter to any foreign port or place, with which commercial intercourse shall by virtue of this section be again permitted, shall give bond to the United States, with approved security, in double the value of the vessel and cargo, that they shall not proceed to any foreign port, nor trade with any country other than those with which commercial intercourse shall have been or may be permitted by this act.

Sec. 12. *And be it further enacted,* That so much of the act laying an embargo on all ships and vessels in the ports and harbors of the United States, and of the several acts supplementary thereto, as forbids the departure of vessels owned by citizens of the United States, and the exportation of domestic and foreign merchandise to any foreign port or place, be, and the same as hereby repealed, after the fifteenth day of March, one thousand eight hundred and nine, except so far as they relate to Great Britain or France, or their colonies or dependencies, or places in the actual possession of either: *Provided,* that all penalties and forfeitures which shall have been previously incurred by virtue of so much of the said acts as is repealed by this act, or which have been or may hereafter be incurred by virtue of the said acts, on account of any infraction of so much of the said acts as is not repealed by this act, shall be recovered and distributed in like manner as if the said acts had continued in full force and virtue.

Sec. 13. *And be it further enacted,* That during the continuance of so much of the act laying an embargo on all ships and vessels in the ports and harbors of the United States, and of the several acts supplementary thereto, as is not repealed by this act, no ship or vessel bound to a foreign port, with which commercial intercourse shall, by virtue of this act, be again permitted, shall be allowed to depart for such port, unless the owner or owners, consignee or factor of such ship or vessel shall, with the master, have given bond with one or more sureties to the United States, in a sum double the value of the vessel and cargo, if the vessel is wholly owned by a citizen or citizens of the United States; and in a sum four times the value, if the vessel is owned in part or in whole by any foreigner or foreigners, that the vessel shall not leave the port without a clearance, nor shall, when leaving the port, proceed to any port or place in Great Britain or France, or in the colonies or dependencies of either, or in the actual possession of either, nor be directly or indirectly engaged during the voyage in any trade with such port, nor shall put any article on board of any other vessel; nor unless every other requisite and provision of the second section of the act, intituled "An act to enforce and make more effectual an act, intituled An act laying an embargo on all ships and vessels in the ports and harbors of the United States, and the several acts supplementary thereto," shall have been complied with. And the party or parties to the above mentioned bond shall, within a reasonable time after the date of the same, to be expressed in the said bond, produce to the collector of the district, from which the vessel shall have been cleared, a certificate of the landing of the same, in the same manner as is provided by law for the landing of goods exported with the privilege of drawback; on failure whereof, the bond shall be put in suit; and in every such suit judgment shall be given against the defendant or defendants, unless proof shall be produced of such relanding, or of loss at sea.

Sec. 14. *And be it further enacted,* That so much of the act laying an embargo on all ships and vessels in the ports and harbors of the United States, and of the several acts

supplementary thereto, as compels vessels owned by citizens of the United States, bound to another port of the said States, or vessels licensed for the coasting trade, or boats, either not masted or not decked, to give bond, and to load under the inspection of a revenue officer, or renders them liable to detention, merely on account of the nature of their cargo, (such provisions excepted as relate to collection districts adjacent to the territories, colonies or provinces of a foreign nation, or to vessels belonging or bound to such districts) be, and the same is hereby repealed, from and after the fifteenth day of March, one thousand eight hundred and nine: *Provided however,* that all penalties and forfeitures which shall have been previously incurred by any of the said acts, or which may hereafter be incurred by virtue of the said acts, on account of any infraction of so much of the said acts, as is not repealed by this act, shall be recovered and distributed in like manner as if the same had continued in full force and virtue.

Sec. 15. *And be it further enacted,* That during the continuance of so much of the act laying an embargo on all ships and vessels in the ports and harbors of the United States, and of the several acts supplementary thereto, as is not repealed by this act, no vessel owned by citizens of the United States, bound to another port of the said States or licensed for the coasting trade, shall be allowed to depart from any port of the United States, or shall receive a clearance, nor shall it be lawful to put on board any such vessel any specie or goods, wares, or merchandise, unless a permit shall have been previously obtained from the proper collector, or from a revenue officer, authorized by the collector to grant such permits; nor unless the owner, consignee, agent, or factor shall, with the master, give bond with one or more sureties, to the United States, in a sum double the value of the vessel and cargo, that the vessel shall not proceed to any foreign port or place, and that the cargo shall be relanded in some port of the United States: *Provided,* that it shall be lawful and sufficient in the case of any such vessel, whose employment has been uniformly confined to rivers, bays and sounds within the jurisdiction of the United States, to give bond in an amount equal to one hundred and fifty dollars, for each ton of said vessel, with condition that such vessel shall not, during the time limited in the condition of the bond, proceed to any foreign port or place, or put any article on board of any other vessel, or be employed in any foreign trade.

Sec. 16. *And be it further enacted,* That if any ship of vessel shall, during the continuance of so much of the act laying an embargo on all ships and vessels in the ports and harbors of the United States, and of the several acts supplementary thereto, as is not repealed by this act, depart from any port of the United States without a clearance or permit, or having given bond in the manner provided by law, such ship or vessel, together with her cargo, shall be wholly forfeited; and the owner or owners, agent, freighter or factors, master or commander of such ship or vessel shall, moreover, severally forfeit and pay a sum equal to the value of the ship or vessel, and of the cargo put on board the same.

Sec. 17. *And be it further enacted,* That the act to prohibit the importation of certain goods, wares and merchandise, passed the eighteenth of April, one thousand eight hundred and six, and the act supplementary thereto, be, and the same are hereby repealed, from and after the said twentieth day of May next: *Provided,* that all penalties and forfeitures which shall have been previously incurred by virtue of the said acts shall be recovered and distributed in like manner as if the said acts had continued in full force and virtue.

Sec. 18. *And be it further enacted,* That all penalties and forfeitures arising under or incurred by virtue of this act, may be sued for, prosecuted and recovered, with costs of suit, by action of debt, in the name of the United States of America, or by indictment or information, in any court having competent jurisdiction to try same; and shall be distributed and accounted for in the manner prescribed by the act, intituled "An act to regulate the collection of duties on imports and tonnage," passed the second day of March, one thousand seven hundred and ninety-nine; and such penalties and forfeitures may be examined, mitigated or remitted, in like manner, and under the like conditions, regulations and restrictions, as are prescribed, authorized and directed by the act, intituled "An act to provide for mitigating or remitting the forfeitures, penalties and disabilities, accruing in certain cases therein mentioned," passed the third day of March, one thousand seven hundred and ninety-seven, and made perpetual by an act passed the eleventh day of February, one thousand eight hundred.

Sec. 19. *And be it further enacted,* That this act shall continue and be in force until the end of the next session of Congress, and no longer; and that the act laying an embargo on all ships and vessels in the ports and harbors of the United States, and the several acts supplementary thereto, shall be, and the same are hereby repealed from and after the end of the next session of Congress.

Source:

Statutes at Large of the United States of America, 1789–1873. 17 vols. Washington, D.C. 1850–73. Vol. 9, pp. 528–533.

War Message of 1812

Message delivered by President James Madison to Congress on June 1, 1812, urging Congress to declare war on Great Britain following the failure of other attempts to end British interference with American shipping. Madison cited as grounds for war the British impressment of American sailors, the violation of American territorial waters and neutral shipping rights, and the blockade of U.S. ports. The House of Representatives approved a declaration of war on June 4; the Senate passed the measure on June 18, and Madison signed it the same day, thus beginning the War of 1812.

———————————— ⁓∞⁓ ————————————

To the Senate and House of Representatives of the United States:

I communicate to Congress certain documents, being a continuation of those heretofore laid before them on the subject of our affairs with Great Britain.

Without going back beyond the renewal in 1803 of the war in which Great Britain is engaged, and omitting unrepaired wrongs of inferior magnitude, the conduct of her Government presents a series of acts hostile to the United States as an independent and neutral nation.

British cruisers have been in the continued practice of violating the American flag on the great highway of nations, and of seizing and carrying off persons sailing under it, not in the exercise of a belligerent right founded on the law of nations against an enemy, but of a municipal prerogative over British subjects. British jurisdiction is thus extended to neutral vessels in a situation where no laws can operate but the law of nations and the laws of the country to which the vessels belong, and a self-redress is assumed which, if British subjects were wrongfully detained and alone concerned, is that substitution of force for a resort to the responsible sovereign which falls within the definition of war. Could the seizure of British subjects in such cases be regarded as within the exercise of a belligerent right, the acknowledged laws of war, which forbid an article of captured property to be adjudged without a regular investigation before a competent tribunal, would imperiously demand the fairest-trial where the sacred rights of persons were at issue. In place of such a trial these rights are subjected to the will of every petty commander.

The practice, hence, is so far from affecting British subjects alone that, under the pretext of searching for these, thousands of American citizens, under the safeguard of public law and of their national flag, have been torn from their country and from everything dear to them; have been dragged on board ships of war of a foreign nation and exposed, under the severities of their discipline, to be exiled to the most distant and deadly climes, to risk their lives in the battles of their oppressors, and to be the melancholy instruments of taking away those of their own brethren.

Against this crying enormity, which Great Britain would be so prompt to avenge if committed against herself, the United States have in vain exhausted remonstrances and expostulations, and that no proof might be wanting of their conciliatory dispositions, and no pretext left for a continuance of the practice, the British Government was formally assured of the readiness of the United States to enter into arrangements such as could not be rejected if the recovery of British subjects were the real and the sole object. The communication passed without effect.

British cruisers have been in the practice also of violating the rights and the peace of our coasts. They hover over and harass our entering and departing commerce. To the most insulting pretensions they have added the most lawless proceedings in our very harbors, and have wantonly spilt American blood within the sanctuary of our territorial jurisdiction. The principles and rules enforced by that nation, when a neutral nation, against armed vessels of belligerents hovering near her coasts and disturbing her commerce are well known. When called on, nevertheless, by the United States to punish the greater offenses committed by her own vessels, her Government has bestowed on their commanders additional marks of honor and confidence.

Under pretended blockades, without the presence of an adequate force and sometimes without the practicability of applying one, our commerce has been plundered in every sea, the great staples of our country have been cut off from their legitimate markets, and a destructive blow aimed at our agricultural and maritime interests. In aggravation of these predatory measures they have been considered as in force from the dates of their notification, a retrospective effect being thus added, as has been done in other important cases, to the unlawfulness of the course pursued. And to render the outrage the more signal these mock blockades have been reiterated and enforced in the face of official communications from the British Government declaring as the true definition of a legal blockade "that particular ports must be actually invested and previous warning given to vessels bound to them not to enter."

Not content with these occasional expedients for laying waste our neutral trade, the cabinet of Britain resorted at length to the sweeping system of blockades, under the name of orders in council, which has been molded and managed as might best suit its political views, its commercial jealousies, or the avidity of British cruisers.

To our remonstrances against the complicated and transcendent injustice of this innovation the first reply was that the orders were reluctantly adopted by Great Britain as a necessary retaliation on decrees of her enemy proclaiming a general blockade of the British Isles at a time when the naval force of that enemy dared not issue from his own ports. She was reminded without effect that her own prior blockades, unsupported by an adequate naval force actually applied and continued, were a bar to this plea; that executed edicts against millions of our property

could not be retaliation on edicts confessedly impossible to be executed; that retaliation, to be just, should fall on the party setting the guilty example, not on an innocent party which was not even chargeable with an acquiescence in it.

When deprived of this flimsy veil for a prohibition of our trade with her enemy by the repeal of his prohibition of our trade with Great Britain, her cabinet, instead of a corresponding repeal or a practical discontinuance of its orders, formally avowed a determination to persist in them against the United States until the markets of her enemy should be laid open to British products, thus asserting an obligation on a neutral power to require one belligerent to encourage by its internal regulations the trade of another belligerent, contradicting her own practice toward all nations, in peace as well as in war, and betraying the insincerity of those professions which inculcated a belief that, having resorted to her orders with regret, she was anxious to find an occasion for putting an end to them.

Abandoning still more all respect for the neutral rights of the United States and for its own consistency, the British Government now demands as prerequisites to a repeal of its orders as they relate to the United States that a formality should be observed in the repeal, of the French decrees nowise necessary to their termination nor exemplified by British usage, and that the French repeal besides including that portion of the decrees which operates within a territorial jurisdiction, as well as that which operates on the high seas, against the commerce of the United States should not be a single and special repeal in relation to the United States, but should be extended to whatever other neutral nations unconnected with them may be affected by those decrees. And as an additional insult, they are called on for a formal disavowal of conditions and pretensions advanced by the French Government for which the United States are so far from having made themselves responsible that, in official explanations which have been published to the world, and in a correspondence of the American minister at London with the British minister for foreign affairs such a responsibility was explicitly and emphatically disclaimed.

It has become, indeed, sufficiently certain that the commerce of the United States is to be sacrificed, not as interfering with the belligerent rights of Great Britain; not as supplying the wants of her enemies, which she herself supplies; but as interfering with the monopoly which she covets for her own commerce and navigation. She carries on a war against the lawful commerce of a friend that she may the better carry on a commerce with an enemy—a commerce polluted by the forgeries and perjuries which are for the most part the only passports by which it can succeed.

Anxious to make every experiment short of the last resort of injured nations, the United States have withheld from Great Britain, under successive modifications, the benefits of a free intercourse with their market, the loss of which could not but outweigh the profits accruing from her restrictions of our commerce with other nations. And to entitle these experiments to the more favorable consideration they were so framed as to enable her to place her adversary under the exclusive operation of them. To these appeals her Government has been equally inflexible, as if willing to make sacrifices of every sort rather than yield to the claims of justice or renounce the errors of a false pride. Nay, so far were the attempts carried to overcome the attachment of the British cabinet to its unjust edicts that it received every encouragement within the competency of the executive branch of our Government to expect that a repeal of them would be followed by a war between the United States and France, unless the French edicts should also be repealed. Even this communication, although silencing forever the plea of a disposition in the United States to acquiesce in those edicts originally the sole plea for them, received no attention.

If no other proof existed of a predetermination of the British Government against a repeal of its orders, it might be found in the correspondence of the minister plenipotentiary of the United States at London and the British secretary for foreign affairs in 1810, on the question whether the blockade of May, 1806, was considered as in force or as not in force. It had been ascertained that the French Government, which urged this blockade as the ground of its Berlin decree, was willing in the event of its removal, to repeal that decree, which, being followed by alternate repeals of the other offensive edicts, might abolish the whole system on both sides. This inviting opportunity for accomplishing an object so important to the United States, and professed so often to be the desire of both the belligerents, was made known to the British Government. As that Government admits that an actual application of an adequate force is necessary to the existence of a legal blockade, and it was notorious that if such a force had ever been applied its long discontinuance had annulled the blockade in question, there could be no sufficient objection on the part of Great Britain to a formal revocation of it, and no imaginable objection to a declaration of the fact that the blockade did not exist. The declaration would have been consistent with her avowed principles of blockade, and would have enabled the United States to demand from France the pledged repeal of her decrees, either with success, in which case the way would have been opened for a general repeal of the belligerent edicts, or without success, in which case the United States would have been justified in turning their measures exclusively against France. The British Government would, however, neither rescind the blockade nor declare its nonexistence, nor permit its non-existence to be inferred

and affirmed by the American plenipotentiary. On the contrary, by representing the blockade to be comprehended in the orders in council, the United States were compelled so to regard it in their subsequent proceedings.

There was a period when a favorable change in the policy of the British cabinet was justly considered as established. The minister plenipotentiary of His Britannic Majesty here proposed an adjustment of the differences more immediately endangering the harmony of the two countries. The proposition was accepted with the promptitude and cordiality corresponding with the invariable professions of this Government. A foundation appeared to be laid for a sincere and lasting reconciliation. The prospect, however, quickly vanished. The whole proceeding was disavowed by the British Government without any explanations which could at that time repress the belief that the disavowal proceeded from a spirit of hostility to the commercial rights and prosperity of the United States; and it has since come into proof that at the very moment when the public minister was holding the language of friendship and inspiring confidence in the sincerity of the negotiation with which he was charged a secret agent of his Government was employed in intrigues having for their object a subversion of our Government and a dismemberment of our happy union.

In reviewing the conduct of Great Britain toward the United States our attention is necessarily drawn to the warfare just renewed by the savages on one of our extensive frontiers—a warfare which is known to spare neither age nor sex and to be distinguished by features peculiarly shocking to humanity. It is difficult to account for the activity and combinations which have for some time been developing themselves among tribes in constant intercourse with British traders and garrisons without connecting their hostility with that influence and without recollecting the authenticated examples of such interpositions heretofore furnished by the officers and agents of that Government.

Such is the spectacle of injuries and indignities which have been heaped on our country, and such the crisis which its unexampled forbearance and conciliatory efforts have not been able to avert. It might at least have been expected that an enlightened nation, if less urged by moral obligations or invited by friendly dispositions on the part of the United States, would have found its true interest alone a sufficient motive to respect their rights and their tranquillity on the high seas; that an enlarged policy would have favored that free and general circulation of commerce in which the British nation is at all times interested, and which in times of war is the best alleviation of its calamities to herself as well as to other belligerents; and more especially that the British cabinet would not, for the sake of a precarious and surreptitious intercourse with hostile markets, have persevered in a course of measures which necessarily put at hazard the invaluable market of a great and growing country, disposed to cultivate the mutual advantages of an active commerce.

Other counsels have prevailed. Our moderation and conciliation have had no other effect than to encourage perseverance and to enlarge pretensions. We behold our seafaring citizens still the daily victims of lawless violence, committed on the great common and highway of nations, even within sight of the country which owes them protection. We behold our vessels, freighted with the products of our soil and industry, or returning with the honest proceeds of them, wrested from their lawful destinations, confiscated by prize courts no longer the organs of public law but the instruments of arbitrary edicts, and their unfortunate crews dispersed and lost, or forced or inveigled in British ports into British fleets, whilst arguments are employed in support of these aggressions which have no foundation but in a principle equally supporting a claim to regulate our external commerce in all cases whatsoever.

We behold, in fine, on the side of Great Britain, a state of war against the United States, and on the side of the United States a state of peace toward Great Britain.

Whether the United States shall continue passive under these progressive usurpations and these accumulating wrongs, or, opposing force to force in defense of their national rights, shall commit a just cause into the hands of the Almighty Disposer of Events, avoiding all connections which might entangle it in the contest or views of other powers, and preserving a constant readiness to concur in an honorable re-establishment of peace and friendship, is a solemn question which the Constitution wisely confides to the legislative department of the Government. In recommending it to their early deliberations I am happy in the assurance that the decision will be worthy the enlightened and patriotic councils of a virtuous, a free, and a powerful nation.

Having presented this view of the relations of the United States with Great Britain and of the solemn alternative growing out of them. I proceed to remark that the communications last made to Congress on the subject of our relations with France will have shewn that since the revocation of her decrees, as they violated the neutral rights of the United States, her Government has authorized illegal captures by its privateers and public ships, and that other outrages have been practised on our vessels and our citizens. It will have been seen also that no indemnity had been provided or satisfactorily pledged for the extensive spoliations committed under the violent and retrospective orders of the French Government against the property of our citizens seized within the jurisdiction of France. I abstain at this time from recommending to the consideration of Congress definitive measures with respect

to that nation, in the expectation that the result of unclosed discussions between our minister plenipotentiary at Paris and the French Government will speedily enable Congress to decide with greater advantage on the course due to the rights, the interests, and the honor of our country.

Proclamation

Whereas the Congress of the United States, by virtue of the constituted authority vested in them, have declared by their act bearing date the 18th day of the present month that war exists between the United Kingdom of Great Britain and Ireland and the dependencies thereof and the United States of America and their Territories:

Now, therefore, I, James Madison, President of the United States of America, do hereby proclaim the same to all whom it may concern; and I do specially enjoin on all persons holding offices, civil or military, under the authority of the United States that they be vigilant and zealous in discharging the duties respectively incident thereto; and I do moreover exhort all the good people of the United States, as they love their country, as they value the precious heritage derived from the virtue and valor of their fathers, as they feel the wrongs which have forced on them the last resort of injured nations, and as they consult the best means under the blessing of Divine Providence of abridging its calamities, that they exert themselves in preserving order, in promoting concord, in maintaining the authority and efficacy of the laws, and in supporting and invigorating all the measures which may be adopted by the constituted authorities for obtaining a speedy, a just, and an honorable peace.

Source:

Gaillard Hunt, ed. *The Writings of James Madison.* Vol. 8. New York: Putnam's Sons, 1900–1910, pp. 192–200.

Treaty of Fort Jackson, 1814

Treaty signed on August 9, 1814, ending the Creek War of 1813–14 and ceding to the U.S. government 23 million acres in Mississippi Territory, two-thirds of the lands belonging to the Creek tribe. The war, initiated by the Upper Creek of "Red Sticks," was fought largely in Tennessee. It was brought to a close after a decisive victory led by Major General Andrew Jackson, who became president in 1829, and the Tennessee militia at Horseshoe Bend. The treaty, signed by only some of the Creek, forced the tribe to give up lands rich in cotton in southern Georgia and central and southern Alabama. It marked the end of Native American resistance in this area and opened it to white settlement after the War of 1812.

Articles of Agreement and Capitulation

Made and concluded this ninth day of August, one thousand eight hundred and fourteen, between major general Andrew Jackson, on behalf of the President of the United States of America, and the chiefs, deputies, and warriors of the Creek Nation.

Whereas an unprovoked, inhuman, and sanguinary war, waged by the hostile Creeks against the United States, hath been repelled, prosecuted and determined, successfully, on the part of the said States, in conformity with principles of national justice and honorable warfare—And whereas consideration is due to the rectitude of proceeding dictated by instructions relating to the re-establishment of peace: Be it remembered, that prior to the conquest of that part of the Creek nation hostile to the United States, numberless aggressions had been committed against the peace, the property, and the lives of citizens of the United States, and those of the Creek nation in amity with her, at the mouth of Duck river, Fort Mimms, and elsewhere, contrary to national faith, and the regard due to an article of the treaty concluded at New-York, in the year seventeen hundred ninety, between the two nations: That the United States, previously to the perpetration of such outrages, did, in order to ensure future amity and concord between the Creek nation and the said states, in conformity with the stipulations of former treaties, fulfil, with punctuality and good faith, her engagements to the said nation: that more than two-thirds of the whole number of chiefs and warriors of the Creek nation, disregarding the genuine spirit of existing treaties, suffered themselves to be instigated to violations of their national honor, and the respect due to a part of their own nation faithful to the United States and the principles of humanity, by impostures [impostors,] denominating themselves Prophets, and by the duplicity and misrepresentation of foreign emissaries, whose governments are at war, open or understood, with the United States. Wherefore,

1st—The United States demand an equivalent for all expenses incurred in prosecuting the war to its termination, by a cession of all the territory belonging to the Creek nation within the territories of the United States, lying west, south, and south-eastwardly, of a line to be run and described by persons duly authorized and appointed by the President of the United States—Beginning at a point on the eastern bank of the Coosa river, where the south boundary line of the Cherokee nation crosses the same; running from thence down the said Coosa river with its eastern bank according to its various meanders to a point one mile above the mouth of Cedar creek, at Fort Williams, thence east two miles, thence south two miles, thence west to the eastern bank of the said Coosa river, thence down the eastern bank thereof according to its various meanders to a point opposite the upper end of the great falls, (called by the natives Woetumka,) thence east from a true meridian line to a point due north of the mouth of Ofucshee, thence south by a like meridian line to the mouth of Ofucshee on the south side of the Tallapoosa river, thence up the same, according to its various meanders, to a point where a direct course will cross the same at the distance of ten miles from the mouth thereof, thence a direct line to the mouth of Summochico creek, which empties into the Chatahouchie river on the east side thereof below the Eufaulau town, thence east from a true meridian line to a point which shall intersect the line now dividing the lands claimed by the said Creek nation from those claimed and owned by the state of Georgia: Provided, nevertheless, that where any possession of any chief or warrior of the Creek nation, who shall have been friendly to the United States during the war, and taken an active part therein, shall be within the territory ceded by these articles to the United States, every such person shall be entitled to a reservation of land within the said territory of one mile square, to include his improvements as near the centre thereof as may be, which shall inure to the said chief or warrior, and his descendants, so long as he or they shall continue to occupy the same, who shall be protected by and subject to the laws of the United States; but upon the voluntary abandonment thereof, by such possessor or his descendants, the right of occupancy or possession of said lands shall devolve to the United States, and be identified with the right of property ceded hereby.

2nd—The United States will guarantee to the Creek nation, the integrity of all their territory eastwardly and northwardly of the said line to be run and described as mentioned in the first article.

3d—The United States demand, that the Creek nation abandon all communication, and cease to hold any intercourse with any British or Spanish post, garrison, or town; and that they shall not admit among them, any agent or trader, who shall not derive authority to hold commercial, or other intercourse with them, by license from the President or authorised agent of the United States.

4th—The United States demand an acknowledgment of the right to establish military posts and trading houses, and to open roads within the territory, guaranteed to the Creek nation of the second article, and a right to the free navigation of all its waters.

5th—The United States demand, that a surrender be immediately made, of all the persons and property, taken from the citizens of the United States, the friendly part of the Creek nation, the Cherokee, Chickasaw, and Choctaw nations, to the respective owners; and the United States will cause to be immediately restored to the formerly hostile Creeks, all the property taken from them since their submission, either by the United States, or by any Indian nation in amity with the United States, together with all the prisoners taken from them during the war.

6th—The United States demand the caption and surrender of all the prophets and instigators of the war, whether foreigners or natives, who have not submitted to the arms of the United States, and become parties to these articles of capitulation, if ever they shall be found within the territory guaranteed to the Creek nation by the second article.

7th—The Creek nation being reduced to extreme want, and not at present having the means of subsistence, the United States, from motives of humanity, will continue to furnish gratuitously the necessaries of life, until the crops of corn can be considered competent to yield the nation a supply, and will establish trading houses in the nation, at the discretion of the President of the United States, and at such places as he shall direct, to enable the nation, by industry and economy, to procure clothing.

8th—A permanent peace shall ensue from the date of these presents forever, between the Creek nation and the United States, and between the Creek nation and the Cherokee, Chickasaw, and Choctaw nations.

9th—If in running east from the mouth of Summochico creek, it shall so happen that the settlement of the Kennards, fall within the lines of the territory hereby ceded, then, and in that case, the line shall be run east on a true meridian to Kitchofoonee creek, thence down the middle of said creek to its junction with Flint River, immediately below the Oakmulgee town, thence up the middle of Flint river to a point due east of that at which the above line struck the Kitchofoonee creek, thence east to the old line herein before mentioned, to wit: the line dividing the lands claimed by the Creek nation, from those claimed and owned by the state of Georgia.

The parties to these presents, after due consideration for themselves and their constituents, agree to, ratify and confirm the preceding articles, and constitute them the basis of a permanent peace between the two nations; and they do hereby solemnly bind themselves, and all the parties concerned and interested, to a faithful performance of every stipulation contained therein. In testimony whereof, they have hereunto interchangeably set their hands and affixed their seals, the day and date above written.

Source:
Charles J. Kappler, *Indian Affairs: Laws and Treaties.* Vol. 2. Washington, D.C.: Government Printing Office, 1904.

Treaty of Ghent, 1814

Compromise settlement ending the indecisive War of 1812 between the United States and Great Britain, signed in Ghent,

Belgium, on December 24, 1814. Both the Americans and the British receded from demands that would have prolonged the war and agreed to a mutual restoration of conquests. Britain gave up territorial gains in what was then known as the American Northwest, and the United States agreed to respect Native American rights. In addition, the treaty provided for joint arbitral commissions to settle fishing rights and boundary disputes between the United States and Canada and for cooperation between the United States and Britain in suppressing the international slave trade. Issues left hanging in this treaty were resolved in the Convention of London, 1818. Also called the London Convention of 1818, it established the northern border of the Louisiana Territory (between the United States and Canada) at the 49th parallel, running between the Lake of the Woods in northern Minnesota to the Rocky Mountains. The Oregon Territory was to be occupied jointly by the United States and Britain and open to the citizens of both countries for a 10-year, renewable period. The treaty also awarded the United States fishing rights in certain areas off the coasts of Labrador and Newfoundland.

***

Treaty of Peace and Amity
Between his Britannic Majesty and the United States of America

His Britannic Majesty and the United States of America, desirous of terminating the war which has unhappily subsisted between the two countries, and of restoring, upon principles of perfect reciprocity, peace, friendship, and good understanding between them, have, for that purpose, appointed their respective plenipotentiaries, that is to say: His Britannic Majesty, on his part, has appointed the right honorable James Lord Gambier, late admiral of the white, now admiral of the red squadron of His Majesty's fleet, Henry Goulburn Esquire, a member of the Imperial Parliament, and under Secretary of State, and William Adams, Esquire, Doctor of Civil Laws:—And the President of the United States, by and with the advice and consent of the Senate thereof, has appointed John Quincy Adams, James A. Bayard, Henry Clay, Jonathan Russell and Albert Gallatin, citizens of the United States, who, after a reciprocal communication of their respective full powers, have agreed upon the following articles:

Article the First
There shall be a firm and universal peace between His Britannic Majesty and the United States, and between their respective countries, territories, cities, towns, and people, of every degree, without exception of places or persons. All hostilities, both by sea and land, shall cease as soon as this treaty shall have been ratified by both parties, as hereinafter mentioned. All territory, places, and possessions whatsoever, taken by either party from the other, during

the war, or which may be taken after the signing of this treaty, excepting only the islands hereinafter mentioned, shall be restored without delay, and without causing any destruction, or carrying away any of the artillery or other public property originally captured in the said forts or places, and which shall remain therein upon the exchange of the ratifications of this treaty, or any slaves or other private property. And all archives, records, deeds, and papers, either of a public nature, or belonging to private persons, which, in the course of the war, may have fallen into the hands of the officers of either party, shall be, as far as may be practicable, forthwith restored and delivered to the proper authorities and persons to whom they respectively belong. Such of the islands in the Bay of Passama quoddy as are claimed by both parties, shall remain in the possession of the party in whose occupation they may be at the time of the exchange of the ratifications of this treaty, until the decision respecting the title to the said islands shall have been made in conformity with the fourth article of this treaty. No disposition made by this treaty, as to such possession of the islands and territories claimed by both parties, shall, in any manner whatever, be construed to affect the right of either.

Article the Second

Immediately after the ratifications of this treaty by both parties, as hereinafter mentioned, orders shall be sent to the armies, squadrons, officers, subjects and citizens, of the two powers, to cease from all hostilities. And to prevent all causes of complaint which might arise on account of the prizes which may be taken at sea after the said ratifications of this treaty, it is reciprocally agreed, that all vessels and effects which may be taken after the space of twelve days from the said ratifications, upon all parts of the coast of North America, from the latitude of twenty-three degrees north, to the latitude of fifty degrees north, and as far eastward in the Atlantic ocean, as the thirty-sixth degree of west longitude from the meridian of Greenwich, shall be restored on each side: That the time shall be thirty days in all other parts of the Atlantic ocean, north of the equinoctial line or equator, and the same time for the British and Irish channels, for the Gulf of Mexico and all parts of the West Indies: Forty days for the North seas, for the Baltic, and for all parts of the Mediterranean: Sixty days for the Atlantic ocean south of the equator, as far as the latitude of the Cape of Good Hope: Ninety days for every other part of the world south of the equator: And one hundred and twenty days for all other parts of the world, without exception.

Article the Third

All prisoners of war taken on either side, as well by land as by sea, shall be restored as soon as practicable after the rat-ifications of this treaty, as hereinafter mentioned, on their paying the debts which they may have contracted during their captivity. The two contracting parties respectively engage to discharge, in specie, the advances which may have been made by the other for the sustenance and maintenance of such prisoners.

Article the Fourth

Whereas it was stipulated by the second article in the treaty of peace, of one thousand seven hundred and eighty-three, between His Britannic Majesty and the United States of America, that the boundary of the United States should comprehend all islands within twenty leagues of any part of the shores of the United States, and lying between lines to be drawn due east from the points where the aforesaid boundaries, between Nova Scotia, on the one part, and East Florida on the other, shall respectively touch the bay of Fundy, and the Atlantic ocean, excepting such islands as now are, or heretofore have been, within the limits of Nova Scotia; and whereas the several islands in the Bay of Passamaquoddy, which is part of the Bay of Fundy, and the island of Grand Menan in the said Bay of Fundy, are claimed by the United States as being comprehended within their aforesaid boundaries, which said islands are claimed as belonging to his Britannic Majesty, as having been at the time of, and previous to, the aforesaid treaty of one thousand seven hundred and eighty-three, within the limits of the province of Nova Scotia: In order, therefore, finally to decide upon these claims, it is agreed that they shall be referred to two commissioners to be appointed in the following manner, viz: one commissioner shall be appointed by his Britannic Majesty, and one by the president of the United States, by and with the advice and consent of the Senate thereof, and the said two commissioners so appointed shall be sworn impartially to examine and decide upon the said claims according to such evidence as shall be laid before them on the part of his Britannic Majesty and of the United States respectively. The said commissioners shall meet at Saint Andrews, in the province of New Brunswick, and shall have power to adjourn to such other place or places as they shall think fit. The said commissioners shall, by a declaration or report under their hands and seals, decide to which of the two contracting parties the several islands aforesaid do respectively belong, in conformity with the true intent of the said treaty of peace of one thousand seven hundred and eighty-three. And if the said commissioners shall agree in their decision, both parties shall consider such decision as final and conclusive. It is further agreed, that in the event of the two commissioners differing upon all or any of the matters so referred to them, or in the event of both or either of the said commissioners refusing, or declining, or wilfully omitting, to act as such, they shall make jointly or separately, a report or reports, as well to the Government of his Britannic majesty as to that of the United States, stating in detail the points on which they differ, and the grounds upon which their respective opinions have been formed, or the grounds upon which they, or either of them, have so refused, declined, or omitted to act. And his Britannic majesty, and the government of the United States, hereby agree to refer the report or reports of the said commissioners, to some friendly sovereign or state, to be then named for that purpose, and who shall be requested to decide on the differences which may be stated in the said report or reports, or upon the report of one commissioner, together with the grounds upon which the other commissioner shall have refused, declined, or omitted to act, as the case may be. And if the commissioner so refusing, declining, or omitting to act, shall also wilfully omit to state the grounds upon which he has so done, in such manner that the said statement may be referred to such friendly sovereign or state, together with the report of such other commissioner, then such sovereign or state shall decide ex parte upon the said report alone. And his Britannic majesty and the government of the United States engage to consider the decision of such friendly sovereign or state to be final and conclusive on all the matters so referred.

Article the Fifth

Whereas neither that point of the high lands lying due north from the source of the river St. Croix, and designated in the former treaty of peace between the two powers as the northwest angle of Nova- Scotia, nor the northwesternmost head of Connecticut river, has yet been ascertained; and whereas that part of the boundary line between the dominions of the two powers which extends from the source of the river St. Croix directly north to the abovementioned northwest angle of Nova-Scotia, thence along the said highlands which divide those rivers that empty themselves into the river St. Lawrence from those which fall into the Atlantic ocean to the northwesternmost head of Connecticut river, thence down along the middle of that river to the forty-fifth degree of north latitude; thence by a line due west on said latitude until it strikes the river Iroquois or Cataraguy, has not yet been surveyed: it is agreed, that for these several purposes two commissioners shall be appointed, sworn, and authorized to act exactly in the manner directed with respect to those mentioned in the next preceding article, unless otherwise specified in the present article. The said commissioners shall meet at St. Andrews, in the province of New-Brunswick, and shall have power to adjourn to such other place or places as they shall think fit. The said commissioners shall have power to ascertain and determine the points abovementioned, in conformity with the provisions of the said treaty of peace of one thousand seven hundred and eighty three, and shall

cause the boundary aforesaid, from the source of the river St. Croix to the river Iroquois or Cataraguy, to be surveyed and marked according to the said provisions. The said commissioners shall make a map of the said boundary, and annex to it a declaration under their hands and seals, certifying it to be the true map of the said boundary, and particularizing the latitude and longitude of the northwest angle of Nova-Scotia, of the northwesternmost head of Connecticut river, and of such other points of the said boundary as they may deem proper. And both parties agree to consider such map and declaration as finally and conclusively fixing the said boundary. And in the event of the said two commissioners differing, or both, or either, of them, refusing, declining, or wilfully omitting to act, such reports, declarations, or statements, shall be made by them, or either of them, and such reference to a friendly sovereign or state, shall be made, in all respects, as in the latter part of the fourth article is contained, and in as full a manner as if the same was herein repeated.

Article the Sixth

Whereas, by the former treaty of peace that portion of the boundary of the United States from the point where the forty-fifth degree of north latitude strikes the river Iroquois or Cataraguy to the lake Superior, was declared to be "along the middle of said river into lake Ontario, through the middle of said lake until it strikes the communication by water between that lake and lake Erie, thence along the middle of said communication into lake Erie, through the middle of said lake until it arrives at the water communication into the lake Huron, thence through the middle of said lake to the water communication between that lake and lake Superior." And whereas doubts have arisen what was the middle of the said river, lakes and water communications, and whether certain islands lying in the same were within the dominions of his Britannic majesty or of the United States: In order, therefore, finally to decide these doubts, they shall be referred to two commissioners, to be appointed, sworn, and authorized to act exactly in the manner directed with respect to those mentioned in the next preceding article, unless otherwise specified in this present article. The said commissioners shall meet, in the first instance, at Albany, in the state of New-York, and shall have power to adjourn to such other place or places as they shall think fit: The said commissioner shall, by a report or declaration, under their hands and seals, designate the boundary through the said river, lakes, and water communications, and decide to which of the two contracting parties the several islands lying within the said rivers, lakes, and water communications, do respectively belong, in conformity with the true intent of the said treaty of one thousand seven hundred and eighty-three. And both parties agree to consider such designation and decision as final and conclusive. And in the event of the said two commissioners differing, or both, or either of them, refusing, declining, or wilfully omitting to act, such reports, declarations or statements, shall be made by them, or either of them, and such reference to a friendly sovereign or state shall be made in all respects as in the latter part of the fourth article is contained, and in as full a manner as if the same was herein repeated.

Article the Seventh

It is further agreed that the said two last-mentioned commissioners, after they shall have executed the duties assigned to them in the preceding article, shall be, and they are hereby authorized, upon their oaths impartially to fix and determine, according to the true intent of the said treaty of peace, of one thousand seven hundred and eighty-three, that part of the boundary between the dominions of the two powers, which extends from the water communication between lake Huron, and lake Superior, to the most north-western point of the lake of the Woods, to decide to which of the two parties the several islands lying in the lakes, water communications, and rivers, forming the said boundary, do respectively belong, in conformity with the true intent of the said treaty of peace, of one thousand seven hundred and eighty-three; and to cause such parts of the said boundary, as require it, to be surveyed and marked. The said commissioners shall, by a report or declaration under their hands and seals, designate the boundary aforesaid, state their decision on the points thus referred to them, and particularize the latitude and longitude of the most north-western point of the lake of the Woods, and of such other parts of the said boundary as they may deem proper. And both parties agree to consider such designation and decision as final and conclusive. And, in the event of the said two commissioners differing, or both, or either of them refusing, declining, or wilfully omitting to act, such reports, declarations, or statements, shall be made by them, or either of them and such reference to a friendly sovereign or state, shall be made in all respects, as in the latter part of the fourth article is contained, and in as full a manner as if the same was herein repeated.

Article the Eighth

The several boards of two commissioners mentioned in the four preceding articles, shall respectively have power to appoint a secretary, and to employ such surveyors or other persons as they shall judge necessary. Duplicates of all their respective reports, declarations, statements and decisions, and of their accounts, and of the journal of their proceedings, shall be delivered by them to the agents of his Britannic majesty, and to the agents of the United States, who may be respectively appointed and authorized to manage the business on behalf of their respective governments. The said commissioners shall be respectively paid in such manner as shall be agreed between the two contracting parties, such agreement being to be settled at the time of the exchange of the ratifications of this treaty. And all other expenses attending the said commissions shall be defrayed equally by the two parties. And in the case of death, sickness, resignation, or necessary absence, the place of every such commissioner, respectively, shall be supplied in the same manner as such commissioner was first appointed, and the new commissioner shall take the same oath or affirmation, and do the same duties. It is further agreed between the two contracting parties, that in case any of the islands mentioned in any of the preceding articles, which were in the possession of one of the parties prior to the commencement of the present war between the two countries, should, by the decision of any of the boards of commissioners aforesaid, or of the sovereign or state so referred to, as in the four next preceding articles contained, fall within the dominions of the other party, all grants of land made previous to the commencement of the war, by the party having had such possession, shall be as valid as if such island or islands had, by such decision or decisions, been adjudged to be within the dominions of the party having had such possession.

Article the Ninth

The United States of America engage to put an end, immediately after the ratification of the present treaty, to hostilities with all the tribes or nations of Indians with whom they may be at war at the time of such ratification; and forthwith to restore to such tribes or nations, respectively, all the possessions, rights, and privileges, which they may have enjoyed or been entitled to in one thousand eight hundred and eleven, previous to such hostilities: *Provided always,* That such tribes or nations shall agree to desist from all hostilities, against the United States of America, their citizens and subjects, upon the ratification of the present treaty being notified to such tribes or nations, and shall so desist accordingly. And his Britannic majesty engages, on his part, to put an end immediately after the ratification of the present treaty, to hostilities with all the tribes or nations of Indians with whom he may be at war at the time of such ratification, and forthwith to restore to such tribes or nations, respectively, all the possessions, rights, and privileges, which they may have enjoyed or been entitled to, in one thousand eight hundred and eleven, previous to such hostilities:

Provided always, That such tribes or nations shall agree to desist from all hostilities against his Britannic majesty, and his subjects, upon the ratification of the present treaty being notified to such tribes or nations, and shall so desist accordingly.

Article the Tenth

Whereas the traffic in slaves is irreconcileable with the principles of humanity and justice, and whereas both his Majesty and the United States are desirous of continuing their efforts to promote its entire abolition, it is hereby agreed that both the contracting parties shall use their best endeavors to accomplish so desirable an object.

Article the Eleventh

This treaty, when the same shall have been ratified on both sides, without alteration by either of the contracting parties, and the ratifications mutually exchanged, shall be binding on both parties, and the ratifications shall be exchanged at Washington, in the space of four months from this day, or sooner, if practicable.

Source:

Hunter Miller, ed. *Treaties and Other International Acts of the United States of America.* Vol. 2. Washington, D.C.: Government Printing Office, 1931.

Hartford Convention Resolutions of 1815

Report issued on January 4, 1815, summarizing the conclusions and resolutions of the Hartford Convention, staged in December 1814. The convention, a gathering of New England Federalists, protested the trampling of states' rights by the Madison administration's policies concerning the War of 1812 and the admission of western states into the Union.

───────────── ⌒⋙⋘⌒ ─────────────

The Delegates from the Legislatures of the States of Massachusetts, Connecticut, and Rhode- Island, and from the Counties of Grafton and Cheshire in the State of New-Hampshire and the county of Windham in the State of Vermont, assembled in Convention, beg leave to report the following result of their conference.

The Convention is deeply impressed with a sense of the arduous nature of the commission which they were appointed to execute, of devising the means of defense against dangers, and of relief from oppressions proceeding from the act of their own Government, without violating constitutional principles, or disappointing the hopes of a suffering and injured people. To prescribe patience and firmness to those who are already exhausted by distress, is sometimes to drive them to despair, and the progress towards reform by the regular road, is irksome to those whose imaginations discern, and whose feelings prompt, to a shorter course.—But when abuses, reduced to system and accumulated through a course of years, have pervaded every department of Government, and spread corruption through every region of the State; when these are clothed with the forms of law, and enforced by an Executive whose will is their source, no summary means of relief can be applied without recourse to direct and open resistance. This experiment, even when justifiable, cannot fail to be painful to the good citizen; and the success of the effort will be no security against the danger of the example. Precedents of resistance to the worst administration, are eagerly seized by those who are naturally hostile to the best. Necessity alone can sanction a resort to this measure; and it should never be extended in duration or degree beyond the exigency, until the people, not merely in the fervor of sudden excitement, but after full deliberation, are determined to change the Constitution.

It is a truth, not to be concealed, that a sentiment prevails to no inconsiderable extent, that Administration have given such constructions to that instrument, and practiced so many abuses under color of its authority, that the time for a change is at hand. Those who so believe, regard the evils which surround them as intrinsic and incurable defects in the Constitution. They yield to a persuasion, that no change, at any time, or on any occasion, can aggravate the misery of their country. This opinion may ultimately prove to be correct. But as the evidence on which it rests is not yet conclusive, and as measures adopted upon the assumption of its/ certainty might be irrevocable, some general considerations are submitted, in the hope of reconciling all to a course of moderation and firmness, which may save them from the regret incident to sudden decisions, probably avert the evil, or at least insure consolation and success in the last resort.

The Constitution of the United States, under the auspices of a wise and virtuous Administration, proved itself competent to all the objects of national prosperity, comprehended in the views of its framers. No parallel can be found in history, of a transition so rapid as that of the United States from the lowest depression to the highest felicity—from the condition of weak and disjointed republics, to that of a great, united, and prosperous nation.

Although this high state of public happiness has undergone a miserable and afflicting reverse, through the prevalence of a weak and profligate policy, yet the evils and afflictions which have thus been induced upon the country, are not peculiar to any form of Government. The lust and caprice of power, the corruption of patronage, the oppression of the weaker interests of the community by the stronger, heavy taxes, wasteful expenditures, and unjust and ruinous wars, are the natural offspring of bad Administrations, in all ages and countries. It was indeed to be hoped, that the rulers of these States would not make such disastrous haste to involve their infancy in the embarrassments of old and rotten institutions. Yet all this have they done; and their conduct calls loudly for their dismission and disgrace. But to attempt upon every abuse of power to change the Constitution, would be to perpetuate the evils of revolution.

Again, the experiment of the powers of the Constitution, to regain its vigor, and of the people to recover from their delusions, has been hitherto made under the greatest possible disadvantages arising from the state of the world. The fierce passions which have convulsed the nations of Europe, have passed the Ocean, and finding their way to the bosoms of our citizens, have afforded to Administration the means of perverting public opinion, in respect to our foreign relations, so as to acquire its aid in the indulgence of their animosities, and the increase of their adherents. Further, a reformation of public opinion, resulting from dear bought experience, in the Southern Atlantic States, at least, is not to be despaired of. They will have felt, that the Eastern States cannot be made exclusively the victims of a capricious and impassioned policy.—They will have seen that the great and essential interests of the people, are common to the South and to the East. They will realize the fatal errors of a system, which seeks revenge for commercial injuries in the sacrifice of commerce, and aggravates by needless wars, to an immeasurable extent, the injuries it professes to redress. They may discard the influence of visionary theorists, and recognize the benefits of a practical policy. Indications of this desirable revolution of opinion, among our brethren in those States, are already manifested.—While a hope remains of its ultimate completion, its progress should not be retarded or stopped, by exciting fears which must check these favorable tendencies, and frustrate the efforts of the wisest and best men in those States, to accelerate this propitious change.

Finally, if the Union be destined to dissolution, by reason of the multiplied abuses of bad administrations, it should, if possible, be the work of peaceable times, and deliberate consent.—Some new form of confederacy should be substituted among those States, which shall intend to maintain a federal relation to each other.—Events may prove that the causes of our calamities are deep and permanent. They may be found to proceed, not merely from the blindness of prejudice, pride of opinion, violence of party spirit, or the confusion of the times; but they may be traced to implacable combinations of individuals, or of States, to monopolize power and office, and to trample without remorse upon the rights and interests of commercial sections of the Union. Whenever it shall appear that these causes are radical and permanent, a separation by equitable arrangement, will be preferable to an alliance by constraint, among nominal friends, but real enemies, inflamed by mutual hatred and jealousies, and inviting by intestine divisions, contempt, and aggression from abroad. But a severance of the Union by one or more

States, against the will of the rest, and especially in a time of war, can be justified only by absolute necessity. These are among the principal objections against precipitate measures tending to disunite the States, and when examined in connection with the farewell address of the Father of his country, they must, it is believed, be deemed conclusive.

Under these impressions, the Convention have proceeded to confer and deliberate upon the alarming state of public affairs especially as affecting the interests of the people who have appointed them for this purpose, and they are naturally led to a consideration, in the first place, of the dangers and grievances which menace an immediate or speedy pressure, with a view of suggesting means of present relief; in the next place, of such as are of a more remote and general description, in the hope of attaining future security.

Among the subjects of complaint and apprehension, which might be comprised under the former of these propositions, the attention of the Convention has been occupied with the claims and pretensions advanced, and the authority exercised over the militia, by the executive and legislative departments of the National Government. Also, upon the destitution of the means of defense in which the Eastern States are left; while at the same time they are doomed to heavy requisitions of men and money for national objects.

The authority of the National Government over the militia is derived from those clauses in the Constitution which give power to Congress "to provide for calling forth the militia, to execute the laws of the Union, suppress insurrections and repel invasions"—Also, "to provide for organizing, arming and disciplining the militia, and for governing such parts of them as may be employed in the service of the United States, reserving to the States respectively the appointment of the officers, and the authority of training the militia according to the discipline prescribed by Congress." Again, "The President shall be Commander in Chief of the army and navy of the United States, and of the militia of the several States, *when called into the actual service of the United States.*" In these specified cases only, has the National Government any power over the militia; and it follows conclusively, that for all general and ordinary purposes, this power belongs to the States respectively, and to them alone. It is not only with regret, but with astonishment, the Convention perceive that under color of an authority conferred with such plain and precise limitations, a power is arrogated by the executive government, and in some instances sanctioned by the two Houses of Congress, of control over the militia, which if conceded, will render nugatory the rightful authority of the individual States over that class of men, and by placing at the disposal of the National Government the lives and services of the great body of the people, enable it at pleasure to destroy their liberties, and erect a military despotism on the ruins.

An elaborate examination of the principles assumed for the basis of these extravagant pretensions, of the consequences to which they lead, and of the insurmountable objections to their admission, would transcend the limits of this Report. A few general observations, with an exhibition of the character of these pretensions, and a recommendation of a strenuous opposition to them, must not however be omitted.

It will not be contended, that by the terms used in the constitutional compact, the power of the National Government to call out the militia is other than a power expressly limited to three cases. One of these must exist as a condition precedent to the exercise of that power—Unless the laws shall be opposed, or an insurrection shall exist, or an invasion shall be made, Congress, and of consequence the President as their organ, has no more power over the militia than over the armies of a foreign nation.

But if the declaration of the President should be admitted to be an unerring test of the existence of these cases, this important power would depend, not upon the truth of the fact, but upon executive infallibility; and the limitation of the power would consequently be nothing more than merely nominal, as it might always be eluded. It follows therefore that the decision of the President in this particular cannot be conclusive. It is as much the duty of the State authorities to watch over the rights *reserved,* as of the United States to exercise the powers which are *delegated.*

The arrangement of the United States into military districts, with a small portion of the regular force, under an officer of high rank of the standing army, with power to call for the militia, as circumstances in his judgment may require; and to assume the command of them, is not warranted by the Constitution or any law of the United States. It is not denied that Congress may delegate to the President of the United States the power to call forth the militia in the cases which are within their jurisdiction—But he has no authority to substitute military prefects throughout the Union, to use their own discretion in such instances. To station an officer of the army in a military district without troops corresponding to his rank, for the purpose of taking command of the militia that may be called into service, is a manifest evasion of that provision of the Constitution which expressly reserves to the States the appointment of the officers of the militia; and the object of detaching such officer cannot be well conceived to be any other, than that of superseding the Governor or other officers of the militia in their right to command.

The power of dividing the militia of the States into classes, and obliging such classes to furnish by contract or draft, able bodied men, to serve for one or more years for the defense of the frontier, is not delegated to Congress. If a claim to draft the militia for one year for such general object be admissible, no limitation can be assigned to it, but the discretion of those who make the law. Thus with a power in Congress to authorize such a draft or conscription, and in the Executive to decide conclusively upon the existence and continuance of the emergency, the whole militia may be converted into a standing army disposable at the will of the President of the United States.

The power of compelling the militia and other citizens of the United States, by a forcible draft or conscription to serve in the regular armies, as proposed in a late official letter of the Secretary of War, is not delegated to Congress by the Constitution, and the exercise of it would be not less dangerous to their liberties, than hostile to the sovereignty of the States. The effort to deduce this power from the right of raising armies, is a flagrant attempt to pervert the sense of the clause in the Constitution which confers that right, and is incompatible with other provisions in that instrument. The armies of the United States have always been raised by contract, never by conscription, and nothing more can be wanting to a Government, possessing the power thus claimed, to enable it to usurp the entire control of the militia, in derogation of the authority of the State, and to convert it by impressment into a standing army.

It may be here remarked, as a circumstance illustrative of the determination of the Executive to establish an absolute control over all descriptions of citizens, that the right of impressing seamen into the naval service is expressly asserted by the Secretary of the Navy in a late report. Thus a practice, which in a foreign government has been regarded with great abhorrence by the people, finds advocates among those who have been the loudest to condemn it.

The law authorizing the enlistment of minors and apprentices into the armies of the United States, without the consent of parents and guardians, is also repugnant to the spirit of the Constitution. By a construction of the power to raise armies, as applied by our present rulers, not only persons capable of contracting are liable to be impressed into the army, but those who are under legal disabilities to make contracts, are to be invested with this capacity, in order to enable them to annul at pleasure contracts made in their behalf by legal guardians. Such an interference with the municipal laws and rights of the several States, could never have been contemplated by the framers of the Constitution. It impairs the salutary control and influence of the parent over his child—the master over his servant—the guardian over his ward—and thus destroys the most important relations in society, so that by the conscription of the father, and the seduction of the son, the power of the Executive over all the effective male population of the United States is made complete.

Such are some of the odious features of the novel system proposed by the rulers of a free country, under the limited powers derived from the Constitution. What portion of them will be embraced in acts finally to be passed, it is yet impossible to determine. It is, however, sufficiently alarming to perceive, that these projects manate from the highest authority; nor should it be forgotten, that by the plan of the Secretary of War, the classification of the militia embraced the principle of direct taxation upon the white population only; and that, in the House of Representatives, a motion to apportion the militia among the white population exclusively, which would have been in its operation a direct tax, was strenuously urged and supported.

In this whole series of devices and measures for raising men, this Convention discern a total disregard for the Constitution, and a disposition to violate its provisions, demanding from the individual States a firm and decided opposition. An iron despotism can impose no harder servitude upon the citizen, than to force him from his home and his occupation, to wage offensive wars, undertaken to gratify and pride or passions of his master. The example of France has recently shewn that a cabal of individuals assuming to act in the name of the people, may transform the great body of citizens into soldiers, and deliver them over into the hands of a single tyrant. No war, not held in just abhorrence by a people, can require the aid of such stratagems to recruit an army. Had the troops already raised, and in great numbers sacrificed upon the frontier of Canada, been employed for the defense of the country, and had the millions which have been squandered with shameless profusion, been appropriated to their payment, to the protection of the coast, and to the naval service, there would have been no occasion for unconstitutional expedients. Even at this late hour, let Government leave to New-England the remnant of her resources, and she is ready and able to defend her territory, and to resign the glories and advantages of the border war, to those who are determined to persist in its prosecution.

That acts of Congress in violation of the Constitution are absolutely void, is an undeniable position. It does not, however, consist with the respect and forbearance due from a confederate State towards the General Government, to fly to open resistance upon every infraction of the Constitution. The mode and the energy of the opposition should always conform to the nature of the violation, the intention of its authors, the extent of the injury inflicted, the determination manifested to persist in it, and the danger of delay. But in cases of deliberate, dangerous, and palpable infractions of the Constitution, affecting the sovereignty of a State, and liberties of the people; it is not only the right but the duty of such a State to interpose its authority for their protection, in the manner best calculated to secure that end. When emergencies occur which are either beyond the reach of the judicial tribunals, or too pressing to admit of the delay incident to their forms, States, which have no common umpire, must be their own judges, and execute their own decisions. It will thus be proper for the several States to await the ultimate disposal of the obnoxious measures, recommended by the Secretary of War, or pending before Congress, and so to use their power according to the character these measures shall finally assume, as effectually to protect their own sovereignty, and the rights and liberties of their citizens.

The next subject which has occupied the attention of the Convention, is the means of defense against the common enemy. This naturally leads to the inquiries, whether any expectation can be reasonably entertained, that adequate provision for the defense of the Eastern States will be made by the National Government? Whether the several States can, from their own resources, provide for self-defense and fulfill the requisitions which are to be expected for the national Treasury? and, generally, what course of conduct ought to be adopted by those States, in relation to the great object of defense?

Without pausing at present to comment upon the causes of the war, it may be assumed as a truth, officially announced, that to achieved the conquest of Canadian territory, and to hold it as a pledge for peace, is the deliberate purpose of Administration. This enterprise, commenced at a period when Government possessed the advantage of selecting the time and occasion for making a sudden descent upon an unprepared enemy, now languishes in the third year of the war. It has been prosecuted with various fortune, and occasional brilliancy of exploit, but without any solid acquisition. The British armies have been recruited by veteran regiments. Their navy commands Ontario. The American ranks are thinned by the casualties of war. Recruits are discouraged by the unpopular character of the contest, and by the uncertainty of receiving their pay.

In the prosecution of this favorite warfare, Administration have left the exposed and vulnerable parts of the country destitute of all efficient means of defense. The main body of the regular army has been marched to the frontier.—The navy has been stripped of a great part of its sailors for the service of the Lakes. Meanwhile the enemy scours the sea-coast, blockades our ports, ascends our bays and rivers, makes actual descents in various and distant places, holds some by force, and threatens all that are assailable with fire and sword. The sea-board of four of the New-England States, following its curvatures, presents an extent of more than seven hundred miles, generally occupied by a compact population, and accessible by a naval force, exposing a mass of people and property to the devastation of the enemy, which bears a great proportion to the residue of the maritime frontier of the United States. This extensive shore has been exposed to frequent attacks, repeated contributions. and constant alarms. The regular forces detached by the national Government for its defense, are mere pretexts for placing officers of high rank in command. They are besides confined to a few places, and are too insignificant in number to be included in any computation.

These States have thus been left to adopt measures for their own defense. The militia have been constantly kept on the alert, and harassed by garrison duties, and other hardships, while the expenses, of which the National Government decline the reimbursement, threaten to absorb all the resources of the States. The President of the United States has refused to consider the expense of the militia detached by state authority, for the indispensable defense of the State, as chargeable to the Union, on the ground of a refusal by the Executive of the State, to place them under the command of officers of the regular army. Detachments of militia placed at the disposal of the General Government, have been dismissed either without pay, or with depreciated paper. The prospect of the ensuing campaign is not enlivened by the promise of any alleviation of these grievances. From authentic documents, extorted by necessity from those whose inclination might lead them to conceal the embarrassments of the Government, it is apparent that the treasury is bankrupt, and its credit prostrate. So deplorable is the state of the finances, that those who feel for the honor and safety of the country, would be willing to conceal the melancholy spectacle, if those whose infatuation has produced this state of fiscal concerns, had not found themselves compelled to unveil it to public view.

If the war be continued, there appears no room for reliance upon the national government for the supply of those means of defense, which must become indispensable to secure these States from desolation and ruin. Nor is it possible that the States can discharge this sacred duty from their own resources, and continue to sustain the burden of the national taxes. The Administration, after a long perseverance in plans to baffle every effort of commercial enterprise, had fatally succeeded in their attempts at the epoch of the war. Commerce, the vital spring of New-England's prosperity, was annihilated. Embargoes, restrictions, and the rapacity of revenue officers, had completed its destruction. The various objects for the employment of productive labor, in the branches of business dependent on commerce, have disappeared. The fisheries have shared its fate. Manufactures, which Government has professed an intention to favor and to cherish, as an indemnity

for the failure of these branches of business, are doomed to struggle in their infancy with taxes and obstructions, which cannot fail most seriously to affect their growth. The specie is withdrawn from commerce arose from the furious collisions of the powers at war, yet the great and good men of that time conformed to the force of circumstances which they could not control, and preserved their country in security from the tempests, which overwhelmed the old world, and threw the wreck of their fortunes on these shores.—Respect abroad, prosperity at home, wise laws made by honored legislators, and prompt obedience yielded by a contended people, had silenced the enemies of republican institutions.—The arts flourished—the sciences were cultivated—the comforts and conveniences of life were universally diffused—and nothing remained for succeeding administrations, but to reap the advantages, and cherish the resources, flowing from the policy of their predecessors.

But no sooner was a new administration established in the hands of the party opposed to the Washington policy, than a fixed determination was perceived and avowed of changing a system which had already produced these substantial fruits. The consequences of this change, for a few years after its commencement, were not sufficient to counteract the prodigious impulse towards prosperity, which had been given to the nation. But a steady perseverance in the new plans of administration at length developed their weakness and deformity, but not until a majority of the people had been deceived by flattery, and inflamed by passion, into blindness to their defects. Under the withering influence of this new system, the declension of the nation has been uniform and rapid. The richest advantages for securing the great objects of the Constitution have been wantonly rejected. While Europe reposes from the convulsions that had shaken down her ancient institutions, she beholds with amazement this remote country; once so happy and so envied, involved in a ruinous war, and excluded from intercourse with the rest of the world. To investigate and explain the means whereby this fatal reverse has been effected, would require a voluminous discussion. Nothing more can be attempted in this Report, than a general allusion to the principal outlines of the policy which has produced this vicissitude. Among these may be enumerated—

First.—A deliberate and extensive system for effecting a combination among certain States, by exciting local jealousies and ambition, so as to secure to popular leaders in one section of the Union, the control of public affairs, in perpetual succession. To which primary object most other characteristics of the system may be reconciled.

Secondly.—The political intolerance displayed and avowed, in excluding from office men of unexceptionable merit, for want of adherence to the executive creed.

Thirdly.—The infraction of the judiciary authority and rights, by depriving judges of their offices in violation of the Constitution.

Fourthly.—The abolition of existing Taxes, requisite to prepare the Country for those charges to which nations are always exposed, with a view to the acquisition of popular favor.

Fifthly.—The influence of patronage in the distribution of offices, which in these states has been almost invariably made among men the least entitled to such distinction, and who have sold themselves as ready instruments for distracting public opinion, and encouraging administration to hold in contempt the wishes and remonstrance's of a people thus apparently divided.

Sixthly.—The admission of new States into the Union, formed at pleasure in the western region, has destroyed the balance of power which existed among the original States, and deeply affected their interest.

Seventhly.—The easy admission of naturalized foreigners to places of trust, honor or profit, operating as an inducement to the malcontent subjects of the old world to come to these States, in quest of executive patronage, and to repay it by an abject devotion to executive measures.

Eighthly.—Hostility to Great-Britain, and partiality to the date government of France, adopted as coincident with popular prejudice, and subservient to the main object, party power, Connected with these must be ranked erroneous and distorted estimates of the power and resources of those nations, of the probable of their controversies, and of our political relations to them respectively.

Lastly and principally.—A visionary and superficial theory in regard to commerce, accompanied by a real hatred but a feigned regard to its interests, and a ruinous perseverance in efforts to render it an instrument of coercion and war.

But it is not conceivable that the obliquity of any administration could, in so short a period, have so nearly consummated the work of national ruin, unless favored by defects in the Constitution. To enumerate all the improvements of which that instrument is susceptible, and to propose such amendments as might render it in all respects perfect, would be a task, which this Convention has not thought proper to assume.—They have confined their attention to such as experience has demonstrated to be essential, and even among these, some are considered entitled to a more serious attention than others. They are suggested without any intentional disrespect to other States, and are meant to be such as all shall find an interest in promoting. Their object is to strengthen, and if possible to perpetuate, the Union of the States, by removing the grounds of existing jealousies, and providing for a fair and equal representation, and a limitation of powers which have been misused.

The first amendment proposed, relates to the apportionment of Representatives among the slave- holding States. This cannot be claimed as a right. Those States are entitled to the slave representation, by a constitutional compact. It is therefore merely a subject of agreement, which should be conducted upon principles of mutual interest and accommodation, and upon which no sensibility on either side should be permitted to exist. It has proved unjust and unequal in its operation. Had this effect been foreseen, the privilege would probably not have been demanded; certainly not conceded. Its tendency in future will be adverse to that harmony and mutual confidence, which are more conducive to the happiness and prosperity of every confederated State, than a mere preponderance of power, the prolific source of jealousies and controversy, can be to any one of them. The time may therefore arrive, when a sense of magnanimity and justice will reconcile those States to acquiesce in a revision of this article, especially as a fair equivalent would result to them in the apportionment of taxes.

The next amendment relates to the admission of new States into the union.

This amendment is deemed to be highly important, and in fact indispensable. In proposing it, it is not intended to recognize the right of Congress to admit new States without the original limits of the United States, nor is any idea entertained of disturbing the tranquillity of any State already admitted into the union. The object is merely to restrain the constitutional power of Congress in admitting new States. At the adoption of the Constitution, a certain balance of power among the original parties was considered to exist, and there was at that time, and yet is among those parties, a strong affinity between their great and general interests.—By the admission of these States, that balance has been materially affected, and unless the practice be modified, must ultimately be destroyed. The Southern States will first avail themselves of their new confederates to govern the East, and finally the Western States multiplied in number, and augmented in population, will control the interests of the whole. Thus for the sake of present power, the Southern States will be common sufferers with the East, in the loss of permanent advantages. None of the old States can find an interest in creating prematurely an overwhelming Western influence, which may hereafter discern (as it has heretofore) benefits to derived to them by wars and commercial restrictions.

The next amendments proposed by the convention, relate to the powers of Congress, in relation to Embargo and the interdiction of commerce.

Whatever theories upon the subject of commerce have hitherto divided the opinions of statesmen, experience has at last shewn, that it is a vital interest in the United States, and that its success is essential to the encouragement of agriculture and manufactures, and to the wealth, finances, defense, and liberty of the nation. Its welfare can never interfere with the other great interests of the State, but must promote and uphold them. Still, those who are immediately concerned in the prosecution of commerce, will of necessity be always a minority of the nation. They are, however, best qualified to manage and direct its course by the advantages of experience, and the sense of interest. But they are entirely unable to protect themselves against the sudden and injudicious decisions of bare majorities, and the mistaken or oppressive projects of those who are not actively concerned in its pursuits. Of consequence, this interest is always exposed to be harassed, interrupted, and entirely destroyed, upon pretense of securing other interests. Had the merchants of this nation been permitted, by their own government, to pursue an innocent and lawful commerce, how different would have been the state of the treasury and of public credit! How shortsighted and miserable is the policy which has annihilated this order of men, and doomed their ships to rot in the docks, their capital to waste unemployed, and their affections to be alienated from the Government which was formed to protect them! What security for an ample and unfailing revenue can ever be had, comparable to that which once was realized in the good faith, punctuality, and sense of honor, which attached the mercantile class to the interests of the Government? Without commerce, where can be found the aliment for a navy; and without a navy, what is to constitute the defense, and ornament, and glory of this nation? No union can be durably cemented, in which every great interest does not find itself reasonably secured against the encroachment and combinations of other interests. When, therefore, the past system of embargoes and commercial restrictions shall have been reviewed—when the fluctuation and inconsistency of public measures, betraying a want of information as well as feeling in the majority, shall have been considered, the reasonableness of some restrictions upon the power of a bare majority to repeat these oppressions, will appear to be obvious.

The next amendment proposes to restrict the power of making offensive war. In the consideration of this amendment, it is not necessary to inquire into the justice of the present war. But one sentiment now exists in relation to its expediency, and regret for its declaration is nearly universal. No indemnity can ever be attained for this terrible calamity, and its only palliation must be found in obstacles to its future recurrence. Rarely can the state of this country call for or justify offensive war. The genius of our institutions is unfavorable to its successful prosecution; the felicity of our situation exempts us from its necessity.—In this case, as in the former, those more immediately exposed to its fatal effects are a minority of the nation. The

commercial towns, the shores of our seas and rivers, contain the population, whose vital interests are most vulnerable by a foreign enemy. Agriculture, indeed, must feel at last, but this appeal to its sensibility comes too late. Again, the immense population which has swarmed into the West, remote from immediate danger, and which is constantly augmenting, will not be averse from the occasional disturbances of the Atlantic States. Thus interest may not infrequently combine with passion and intrigue, to plunge the nation into needless wars, and compel it to become a military, rather than a happy and flourishing people. These considerations, which it would be easy to augment, call loudly for the limitation proposed in the amendment.

Another amendment, subordinate in importance, but still in a high degree expedient, relates to the exclusion of foreigners, hereafter arriving in the United States, from the capacity of holding offices of trust, honor or profit.

That the stock of population already in these States, is amply sufficient to render this nation in due time sufficiently great and powerful, is not a controvertible question—Nor will it be seriously pretended, that the national deficiency in wisdom, arts, science, arms or virtue, needs to be replenished from foreign countries. Still, it is agreed, that a liberal policy should offer the rights of hospitality, and the choice of settlement, to those who are disposed to visit the country.—But why admit to a participation in the government aliens who were no parties to the compact—who are ignorant of the nature of our institutions, and have no stake in the welfare of the country, but what is recent and transitory? It is surely a privilege sufficient, to admit them after due probation to become citizens, for all but political purposes.—To extend it beyond these limits, is to encourage foreigners to come to these states as candidates for preferment. The Convention forbear to express their opinion upon the inauspicious effects which have already resulted to the honor and peace of this nation, from this misplaced and indiscriminate liberality.

The last amendment respects the limitation of the office of President to a single constitutional term, and his eligibility from the same State two terms in succession.

Upon this topic it is superfluous to dilate. The love of power is a principle in the human heart, which too often impels to the use of all practicable means to prolong its duration. The office of President has charms and attractions which operate as powerful incentives to this passion. The first and most natural exertion of a vast patronage is directed towards the security of a new election. The interest of the country, the welfare of the people, even honest fame and respect for the opinion of posterity, are secondary considerations. All the engines of intrigue, all the means of corruption, are likely to be employed for this object. A President, whose political career is limited to a single election, may find not other, interest than will be promoted by making it glorious to himself, and beneficial to his country. But the hope of re-election is prolific of temptations, under which these magnanimous motives are deprived of their principal force. The repeated election of the President of the United States from any one State, affords inducements and means for intrigue, which tend to create an undue local influence, and to establish the domination of particular States. The justice, therefore, of securing to every State a fair and equal chance for the election of this officer from its own citizens, is apparent, and this object will be essentially promoted by preventing an election from the same State twice in succession.

Such is the general view which this Convention has thought proper to submit, of the situation of these States, of their dangers and their duties. Most of the subjects which it embraces have separately received an ample and luminous investigation, by the great and able assertors of the rights of their Country, in the National Legislature; and nothing more could be attempted on this occasion, than a digest of general principles, and of recommendations, suited to the present state of public affairs. The peculiar difficulty and delicacy of performing, even this undertaking, will be appreciated by all who think seriously upon the crisis. Negotiations for Peace are at this hour supposed to be pending, the issue of which must be deeply interesting to all. No measures should be adopted, which might unfavorably affect that issue; none which should embarrass the Administration, if their professed desire for peace is sincere; and none, which on supposition of their insincerity, should afford them pretexts for prolonging the war, or relieving themselves from the responsibility of a dishonorable peace. It is also devoutly to be wished, that an occasion may be afforded to all friends of the country, of all parties, and in all places, to pause and consider the awful state, to which pernicious counsels, and blind passions, have brought this people. The number of those who perceive, and who are ready to retrace errors, must, it is believed, be yet sufficient to redeem the nation. It is necessary to rally and unite them by the assurance, that no hostility to the Constitution is meditated, and to obtain their aid, in placing it under guardians, who alone can save it from destruction. Should this fortunate change be effected, the hope of happiness and honor may once more dispel the surrounding gloom. Our nation may yet be great, our union durable. But should this prospect be utterly hopeless, the time will not have been lost, which shall have ripened a general sentiment of the necessity of more mighty efforts to rescue from ruin, at least some portion of our beloved Country.

Therefore Resolved—

That it be and hereby is recommended to the Legislatures of the several States represented in this Convention, to adopt all such measures as may be necessary effectually to protect the citizens of said States from the operation and effects to all acts which have been or may be passed by the Congress of the United States, which shall contain provisions, subjecting the militia or other citizens to forcible drafts, conscription's, or impressments, not authorized by the Constitution of the United States.

Resolved, That it be and hereby is recommended to the said Legislatures, to authorize an immediate and earnest application to be made to the Government of the United States, requesting their consent to some arrangement, whereby the said States may, separately or in concert, be empowered to assume upon themselves the defense of their territory against the enemy; and a reasonable portion of the taxes, collected within said States, may be paid into the respective treasuries thereof, and appropriated to the payment of the balance due said States, and to the future defense of the same. The amount so paid into the said treasuries to be credited, and the disbursements made as aforesaid to be charged to the United States.

Resolved, That it be, and it hereby is, recommended to the Legislatures of the aforesaid States, to pass laws (where it has not already been done) authorizing the Governors or Commanders in Chief of their militia to make detachments from the same, or to form voluntary corps, as shall be most convenient and conformable to their Constitutions, and to cause the same to be well armed, equipped and disciplined, and held in readiness for service; and upon the request of the Governor of either of the other States, to employ the whole of such detachment or corps, as well as the regular forces of the State, or such part thereof as may be required and can be spared consistently with the safety of the State, in assisting the State, making such request to repel any invasion thereof which shall be made or attempted by the public enemy.

Resolved, That the following amendments of the Constitution of the United States, be recommended to the States represented as aforesaid, to be proposed by them for adoption by the State Legislatures, and, in such cases as may be deemed expedient, by a Convention chosen by the people of each State.

And it is further recommended, that the said States shall persevere in their efforts to obtain such amendments, until the same shall be effected.

First. Representatives and direct taxes shall be apportioned among the several States which may be included within this union, according to their respective numbers of free persons, including those bound to serve for a term of years, and excluding Indians not taxed, and all other persons.

Second. No new State shall be admitted into the union by Congress in virtue of the power granted by the Constitution, without the concurrence of two thirds of both Houses.

Third. Congress shall not have power to lay any embargo on the ships or vessels of the citizens of the United States, in the ports or harbors thereof, for more than sixty days.

Fourth. Congress shall not have power, without the concurrence of two thirds of both Houses, to interdict the commercial intercourse between the United States and any foreign nation or the dependencies thereof.

Fifth. Congress shall not make or declare war, or authorize acts of hostility against any foreign nation, without the concurrence of two thirds of both Houses, except such acts of hostility be in defense of the territories of the United States when actually invaded.

Sixth. No person who shall hereafter be naturalized, shall be eligible as a member of the Senate or House of Representatives of the United States, nor capable of holding any civil office under the authority of the United States.

Seventh. The same person shall not be elected President of the United States a second time; nor shall the President be elected from the same State two terms in succession.

Resolved, That if the application of these States to the government of the United States, recommended in a foregoing Resolution, should be unsuccessful, and peace should not be concluded, and the defense of these States should be neglected, as it has been since the commencement of the war, it will in the opinion of this Convention be expedient for the Legislatures of the several States to appoint Delegates to another Convention, to meet at Boston, in the State of Massachusetts, on the third Thursday of June next, with such powers and instructions as the exigency of a crisis so momentous may require.

Resolved, That the Hon. George Cabot, the Hon. Chauncey Goodrich, and the Hon. Daniel Lyman, or any two of them, be authorized to call another meeting of this Convention, to be holden in Boston, at any time before new Delegates shall be chosen, as recommended in the above Resolution, if in their judgment the situation of the Country shall urgently require it.

Source:
William Smith Porter. *Historical Notices of Connecticut.* Hartford: E. Geer's Press, 1842, pp. 4–22.

Tariff Act, 1816

Legislation enacted on April 27, 1816, that established the first protective tariff in the United States. (The first tariff for revenue was passed in 1789, although it had protectionist aspects.)

Passed to protect "infant industries" that had developed when the United States could not import British manufactured goods during the War of 1812, the tariff placed a duty of 25 percent on most woolen, cotton, and iron manufactures. It set a minimum valuation of 25 cents per square yard on cotton cloth, virtually eliminating cheap cotton imports. An ad valorem rate of 30 percent was applied to certain paper and leather goods and hats; a 15 percent rate applied to other commodities. (Ad valorem rates are based on an estimated value of a product.) The tariff was opposed by New England shipping and commercial interests.

Federal legislation enacted on May 22, 1824, increased tariff protection on wool, iron, lead, glass, silk, linens, cutlery, hemp, and cotton bagging. The levy on cotton and woolens set by the Tariff Act of 1816 was increased to 33.3 percent. The 1824 measure, favored by American manufacturers seeking protection from foreign competition, was opposed by New England shippers and commercial interests, as well as by those in the South. Agitation for even greater protection led to the Tariff Act of 1828, which provided the impetus for John C. Calhoun's theorizing about nullification and strong expressions of southern sectionalism.

Other tariff acts were passed in 1833 (a compromise meant to placate southerners), 1842 (sponsored by Whigs and raising import duties), and 1846 (the Democrat-sponsored Walker Tariff of 1846, which lowered duties and divided imports into several tariff classes). The Democrat-supported tariff of March 3, 1857, made possible by excess government income, lowered protectionist tariffs to a general level of about 20 percent, the lowest rate since 1850, and enlarged the free list.

An Act
To regulate the duties on imports and tonnage.

Be it enacted by the Senate and House of Representatives of the United States of America, in Congress assembled, That from and after the thirtieth day of June, one thousand eight hundred and sixteen, the duties heretofore laid by law, on goods, wares and merchandise, imported into the United States, shall cease and determine, and there shall be levied, and collected, and paid, the several duties hereinafter mentioned, that is to say:

First. A duty of seven and a half per centum ad valorem, on all dyeing drugs and materials for composing dyes, not subject to other rates of duty; gum arabic, gum senegal, saltpetre; jewelry, gold, silver, and other watches, and parts of watches; gold and silver lace, embroidery and epaulettes; precious stones and pearls of all kinds, set or not set; bristol stones or paste work, and all articles composed wholly or chiefly of gold, silver, pearl and precious stones; and laces, lace veils, lace shawls, or shades, of thread on silk.

Second. A duty of fifteen per centum ad valorem on gold leaf, and on all articles not free, and not subject to any other rate of duty.

Third. A duty of twenty per centum ad valorem on hempen cloth or sail cloth, (except Russian and German linens, Russia and Holland duck) stockings, or wool or cotton; printing types; all articles manufactured from brass, copper, iron, steel, pewter, lead or tin, or of which these metals, or either of them, is the material of chief value; brass wire, cutlery, pins, needles, buttons, button moulds and buckles of all kinds; gilt, plated and japanned wares of all kinds: cannon, muskets, fire arms and side arms; Prussian blue, china ware, earthen ware, stone ware, porcelain and glass manufactures, other than window glass and black glass quart bottles.

Fourth. A duty of twenty-five per centum ad valorem, on woollen manufactures of all description, or of which wool is the material of chief value, excepting blankets, woollen rugs and worsted or stuff goods, shall be levied, collected and paid, from and after the thirtieth day of June next, until the thirtieth day of June, one thousand eight hundred and nineteen, and after that day, twenty per centum on the said articles; and on cotton manufactures of all descriptions, or of which cotton is the material of chief value, and on cotton twist, yarn or thread, as follows, viz: for three years next ensuing the thirtieth day of June next, a duty of twenty-five per centum ad valorem; and after the expiration of the three years aforesaid, a duty of twenty per centum ad valorem: *Provided,* That all cotton cloths, or cloths of which cotton is the material of chief value, (excepting nankeens, imported directly from China) the original cost of which at the place whence imported, with the addition of twenty per centum, if imported from the cape of Good Hope, or from places beyond it, and of ten per cent, if imported from any other place, shall be less than twenty-five cents per square yard, shall, with such addition, be taken and deemed to have cost twenty-five cents per square yard, and shall be charged with duty accordingly: *Provided also,* that all unbleached and uncoloured cotton twist, yarn or thread, the original cost of which shall be less than sixty cents per pound, shall be deemed and taken to have cost sixty cents per pound, and shall be charged with duty accordingly; and all bleached or coloured yarn, the original cost of which shall have been less than seventy-five cents per pound, shall be taken and deemed to have cost seventy-five cents per pound, and shall be charged with duty accordingly: *And provided further,* that cotton piece goods imported in ships or vessels of the United States which shall have sailed from the United States before the passage of this act, and shall arrive therein between the thirtieth day of June, one thousand eight hundred and sixteen, and the first day of June, one thousand eight hundred and seventeen, the original cost of

which cotton piece goods, at the place whence imported, shall have been less than twenty-five cents per square yard, shall be admitted to entry, subject only to a duty of thirty-three and a third per centum on the cost of the said cotton piece goods in India, and on the usual addition of twenty per centum on that cost.

Fifth. A duty of thirty per centum ad valorem on umbrellas, parasols, of whatever materials made, and sticks or frames for umbrellas or parasols; bonnets and caps for women, fans, feather ornaments for headdresses, artificial flowers, millinery of all sorts; hats or caps of wool, fur, leather, chip, straw or silk; cosmetics, washes, balsams, perfumes; painted floor cloths; mats, of grass or flags; salad oil, pickles, capers, olives, mustard, comfits or sweetmeats, preserved in sugar or brandy, wafers, cabinet wares, and all manufactures of wood; carriages of all descriptions, and parts thereof; leather, and all manufactures of leather, or of which leather is the material of chief value; saddles, bridles, harness; paper of every description, paste-board, paper hangings, blank books, parchment, vellum; brushes, canes, walking sticks, whips; and clothing ready made. And in all cases where an ad valorem duty shall be charged, it shall be calculated on the net cost of the article, at the place whence imported (exclusive of packages, commissions and all charges) with the usual addition established by law, of twenty per cent, on all merchandise, imported from places beyond the cape of Good Hope, and of ten per centum on articles imported from all other places.

Sixth. The following duties, severally and specifically: on ale, beer and porter, in bottles, fifteen cents per gallon; on ale, beer and porter, imported otherwise than in bottles, ten cents per gallon; on alum, one dollar per hundred weight; on almonds, three cents per pound; on black glass quart bottles, one hundred and forty-four cents per groce; on boots, one dollar and fifty cents per pair; on bristles, three cents per pound; on playing cards, thirty cents per pack; on tarred cables and cordage, three cents per pound; on untarred cordage, yarns, twine, packthread, and seines, four cents per pound; on tallow candles, three cents per pound: on wax and spermaceti candles, six cents per pound; on Chinese cassia, six cents per pound; on cinnamon, twenty-five cents per pound; on cloves, twenty-five cents per pound: on cheese, nine cents per pound; on chocolate, three cents per pound; on cocoa, two cents per pound; on coal, five cents per heaped bushel: on copperas, one dollar per hundred weight; on copper rods, bolts, spikes or nails, and composition rods, bolts, spikes or nails, four cents per pound; on coffee, five cents per pound; on cotton, three cents per pound: on currants, three cents per pound; on figs, three cents per pound; on foreign caught fish, one dollar per quintal; on mackerel, one dollar and fifty cents per barrel; on salmon, two dollars per barrel, and on all other pickled fish, one dollar per barrel: on window glass, not above eight inches by ten inches in size, two dollars and fifty cents per hundred square feet; on the same, not above ten inches by twelve inches in size, two dollars and seventy-five cents per hundred square feet; on the same, if above ten inches by twelve inches in size, three dollars and twenty-five cents per hundred square feet; on glue, five cents per pound; on gunpowder, eight cents per pound; on hemp, one dollar and fifty cents per hundred weight; on iron or steel wire not exceeding number eighteen, five cents per pound, and over number eighteen, nine cents per pound; on iron, in bars and bolts, excepting iron manufactured by rolling, forty-five cents per hundred weight; on iron in sheets, rods and hoops, two dollars and fifty cents per hundred weight, and in bars or bolts, when manufactured by rolling, and on anchors, one dollar and fifty cents per hundred weight; on indigo, fifteen cents per pound; on lead, in pigs, bars or sheets, one cent per pound; on shot manufactured of lead, two cents per pound; on red and white lead, dry or ground in oil, three cents per pound; on mace, one dollar per pound; on molasses, five cents per gallon; on nails, three cents per pound: on nutmegs, sixty cents per pound; on pepper, eight cents per pound; on pimento, six cents per pound; on plums, and prunes, three cents per pound; on muscatel raisins, and raisins in jars and boxes, three cents per pound; on all other raisins, two cents per pound; on salt, twenty cents per bushel of fifty-six pounds; on ochre, dry, one cent per pound, in oil, one and a half cents per pound; on steel, one dollar per hundred weight; on segars, two dollars and fifty cents per thousand; on spirits, from grain of first proof, forty-two cents per gallon; of second proof, forty-five cents per gallon; of third proof, forty-eight cents per gallon; of fourth proof, fifty-two cents per gallon; of fifth proof, sixty cents per gallon; above fifth proof, seventy-five cents per gallon; on spirits from other materials than grain, of first and second proof, thirty-eight cents per gallon; of third proof, forty-two cents per gallon; of fourth proof, forty-eight cents per gallon; of fifth proof, fifty-seven cents per gallon; above fifth proof, seventy cents per gallon; on shoes, and slippers of silk, thirty cents per pair; on shoes, and slippers of leather, twenty-five cents per pair; on shoes and slippers for children, fifteen cents per pair; on spikes, two cents per pound; on soap, three cents per pound; on brown sugar, three cents per pound; on white clayed or powdered sugar, four cents per pound; on lump sugar, ten cents per pound; on loaf sugar and on sugar candy, twelve cents per pound; (a) on snuff, twelve cents per pound; on tallow, one cent per pound; on tea, from China, in ships or vessels of the United States, as follows, viz. bohea, twelve cents per pound; souchong and other black, twenty-five cents per pound; imperial, gunpowder, and gomee, fifty cents per pound; hyson and young hyson, forty cents per pound: hyson skin and other green, twenty-eight cents per pound; on teas, from any other place, or in any other than ships or vessels of the United States, as follows, viz. bohea, fourteen cents per pound; souchong and other black, thirty-four cents per pound; imperial, gunpowder and gomee, sixty- eight cents per pound; hyson and young hyson, fifty-six cents per pound; hyson skin and other green, thirty-eight cents per pound; on manufactured tobacco, other than snuff and segars, ten cents per pound; on whiting and Paris white, one cent per pound; on wine, as follows, viz. on Madeira, Burgundy, Champaign, Rhenish and Tokay, one dollar per gallon; on Sherry and St. Lucar, sixty cents per gallon; on other wine, not enumerated, when imported in bottles or cases, seventy cents per gallon; or Lisbon, Oporto and other wines of Portugal, and on those of Sicily, fifty cents per gallon; on the Teneriffe, Fayal, and other wines of the western islands, forty cents per gallon; on all other wines when imported otherwise than in cases and bottles, twenty-five cents per gallon; on Russia duck, (not exceeding fifty-two archeens each piece,) two dollars; on ravens duck, (not exceeding fifty-two archeens each piece,) one dollar and twenty-five cents; on Holland duck, (not exceeding fifty-two archeens each piece,) two dollars and fifty cents; on spermaceti oil of foreign fishing, twenty-five cents per gallon; on whale and other fish oil, of foreign fishing, fifteen cents per gallon; and on olive oil in casks, at twenty-five cents per gallon.

Sec. 2. *And be it further enacted,* That the following articles shall be imported into the United States free of duties; that is to say, all articles imported for the use of the United States; philosophical apparatus, instruments, books, maps, charts, statues, busts, casts, paintings, drawings, engravings, specimens of sculpture, cabinets of coins, gems, medals, and all other collections of antiquities, statuary, modelling, painting, drawing, etching or engraving, specially imported by order and for the use of any society incorporated for philosophical or literary purposes, or for the encouragement of the fine arts, or by order, and for the use of any seminary of learning; specimens in natural history, mineralogy, botany, and anatomical preparations, models of machinery and other inventions, plants and trees; wearing apparel and other personal baggage in actual use, and the implements or tools of trade of persons arriving in the United States; regulus of antimony, bark of the cork tree, unmanufactured; animals imported for breed; burr stones, unwrought; gold coin, silver coin, and bullion; clay; unwrought copper, imported in any shape for the use of the mint; copper and brass, in pigs, bars, or plates, suited to the sheathing of ships; old copper and brass, and old pewter, fit only to be re-manufactured; tin, in pigs or bars; furs, undressed, of all kinds; raw hides and skins; lapis calaminaris; plaster of Paris; rags of any kind of cloth; sulphur or brimstone; barilla; Brazil wood, brazilletto, red wood, camwood, fustic, logwood, Nicaragua, and other dye woods; wood, unmanufactured, of any kind; zinc, teutenague or spelter.

Sec. 3. *And be it further enacted,* That an addition of ten per centum shall be made to the several rates of duties above specified and imposed, in respect to all goods, wares, and merchandise, on the importation of which in American or foreign vessels a specific discrimination has not been herein already made, which, after the said thirtieth day of June, one thousand eight hundred and sixteen, shall be imported, in ships or vessels not of the United States: *Provided,* That this additional duty shall not apply to goods, wares and merchandise, imported in ships or vessels not of the United States, entitled by treaty, or by any act or acts of Congress, to be centered in the ports of the United States, on the payment of the same duties as are paid on goods, wares and merchandise, imported in ships or vessels of the United States.

Sec. 4. *And be it further enacted,* That there shall be allowed a drawback of the duties, by this act imposed, on goods, wares and merchandise imported into the United States, upon the exportation thereof within the time, and in the manner prescribed by the existing laws, subject to the following provisions, that is to say: that there shall not be an allowance of the drawback of duties in the case of goods imported in foreign vessels from any of the dominions, colonies or possessions of any foreign power, to and with which the vessels of the United States are not permitted to go and trade; that there shall not be an allowance of the drawback of duties for the amount of the additional duties by this act imposed on goods imported in vessels not of the United States; that there shall not be an allowance of the drawback in case of foreign dried and pickled fish, and other salted provisions, fish oil, or playing cards; that there shall be deducted and retained from the amount of the duties on goods exported, with the benefit of drawback, (other than spirits) two and a half per centum; and that there shall be retained in the case of spirits exported with the benefit of drawback, two cents per gallon upon the quantity of spirits, and also three per centum on the amount of duties payable on the importation thereof. But, nevertheless, the provisions of this act shall not be deemed in any wise to impair any rights and privileges, which have been or may be acquired by any foreign nation, under the laws and treaties of the United States, upon the subject of exporting goods from the United States, with the benefit of a drawback of the duties payable upon the importation thereof.

Sec. 5. *And be it further enacted,* That after the thirtieth day of June next, in all cases of entry of mer-

chandise for the benefit of drawback, the time of twenty days shall be allowed from the date of the entry, for giving the exportation bonds for the same: *Provided,* That the exporter shall, in every other particular, comply [with] the regulations and formalities heretofore established for entries of exportation for the benefit of drawback.

Sec. 6. *And be it further enacted,* That the duty on the tonnage of vessels, and the boundaries, advances, and drawbacks in the case of exporting pickled fish, of the fisheries of the United States, in the case of American vessels employed in the fisheries, and in the case of exporting sugar, refined within the United States, shall be and continue the same as the existing law provides. *Provided always,* That this provision shall not be deemed in anywise to impair any rights and privileges, which have been, or may be acquired by any foreign nation, under the laws and treaties of the United States, relative to the duty of tonnage on vessels.

Sec. 7. *And be it further enacted,* That the existing laws shall extend to, and be in force for the collection of the duties imposed by this act, on goods, wares, and merchandise, imported into the United States; and for the recovery, collection, distribution and remission of all fines, penalties, and forfeitures; and for the allowance of the drawbacks and bounties by this act authorized, as fully and effectually as if every regulation, restriction, penalty, forfeiture, provision, clause, matter and thing, in the existing laws contained, had been inserted in, and re-enacted by this act. And that all acts, and parts of acts, which are contrary to this act, and no more, shall be, and the same are hereby repealed.

Sec. 8. *And be it further enacted,* That the act passed the third day of March, one thousand eight hundred and fifteen, entitled "An act to repeal so much of the several acts imposing duties on the tonnage of ships and vessels, and on goods, wares and merchandise imported into the United States, as imposes a discriminating duty on tonnage between foreign vessels and vessels of the United States, and between goods imported into the United States in foreign vessels and vessels of the United States," shall apply and be in full force as to the discriminating duties established by this act on the tonnage of foreign vessels, and the goods, wares, and merchandise therein imported.

See also TARIFF ACT, 1789; THE TARIFF ACT OF 1824, THE TARIFF ACT OF 1828, THE TARIFF OF 1833, THE WALKER TARIFF OF 1846, AND THE TARIFF ACT OF 1857.

Source:
United States Statutes at Large, Vol. 3, pp. 310–314.

James Monroe's
First Inaugural Address, 1817

Speech delivered by James Monroe on March 4, 1817, at his inauguration as the fifth president of the United States. Following the successful conclusion of the War of 1812, Monroe took office at a time of unprecedented American nationalistic pride. Even though he was a Virginian, the warmth with which Monroe was greeted in New England (the home turf of his political rivals) led one newspaper to dub the commencement of his presidency the "Era of Good Feelings." Monroe reflected that sentiment in his inaugural address, praising "the happy Government under which we live . . . which contains within it no cause of discord." He went on to list the goals of his presidency, which included fortifying the nation's frontiers, strengthening its militia, improving roads and canals, cultivating friendly relations with Indian tribes, and paying off the national debt.

―――――――――⎯⎯∞⎯⎯―――――――――

I should be destitute of feeling if I was not deeply affected by the strong proof which my fellow-citizens have given me of their confidence in calling me to the high office whose functions I am about to assume. As the expression of their good opinion of my conduct in the public service, I derive from it a gratification which those who are conscious of having done all that they could to merit it can alone feel. My sensibility is increased by a just estimate of the importance of the trust and of the nature and extent of its duties, with the proper discharge of which the highest interests of a great and free people are intimately connected. Conscious of my own deficiency, I cannot enter on these duties without great anxiety for the result. From a just responsibility I will never shrink, calculating with confidence that in my best efforts to promote the public welfare my motives will always be duly appreciated and my conduct be viewed with that candor and indulgence which I have experienced in other stations.

In commencing the duties of the chief executive office it has been the practice of the distinguished men who have gone before me to explain the principles which would govern them in their respective Administrations. In following their venerated example my attention is naturally drawn to the great causes which have contributed in a principal degree to produce the present happy condition of the United States. They will best explain the nature of our duties and shed much light on the policy which ought to be pursued in future.

From the commencement of our Revolution to the present day almost forty years have elapsed, and from the establishment of this Constitution twenty-eight. Through this whole term the Government has been what may emphatically be called self-government. And what has been the effect? To whatever object we turn our attention, whether it relates to our foreign or domestic concerns, we find abundant cause to felicitate ourselves in the excellence of our institutions. During a period fraught with difficulties and marked by very extraordinary events the United States have flourished beyond example. Their citizens individually have been happy and the nation prosperous.

Under this Constitution our commerce has been wisely regulated with foreign nations and between the States; new States have been admitted into our Union; our territory has been enlarged by fair and honorable treaty, and with great advantage to the original States; the States, respectively protected by the National Government under a mild, parental system against foreign dangers, and enjoying within their separate spheres, by a wise partition of power, a just proportion of the sovereignty, have improved their police, extended their settlements, and attained a strength and maturity which are the best proofs of wholesome laws well administered. And if we look to the condition of individuals what a proud spectacle does it exhibit! On whom has oppression fallen in any quarter of our Union? Who has been deprived of any right of person or property? Who restrained from offering his vows in the mode which he prefers to the Divine Author of his being? It is well known that all these blessings have been enjoyed in their fullest extent; and I add with peculiar satisfaction that there has been no example of a capital punishment being inflicted on anyone for the crime of high treason.

Some who might admit the competency of our Government to these beneficent duties might doubt it in trials which put to the test its strength and efficiency as a member of the great community of nations. Here too experience has afforded us the most satisfactory proof in its favor. Just as this Constitution was put into action several of the principal States of Europe had become much agitated and some of them seriously convulsed. Destructive wars ensued, which have of late only been terminated. In the course of these conflicts the United States received great injury from several of the parties. It was their interest to stand aloof from the contest, to demand justice from the party committing the injury, and to cultivate by a fair and honorable conduct the friendship of all. War became at length inevitable, and the result has shown that our Government is equal to that, the greatest of trials, under the most unfavorable circumstances. Of the virtue of the people and of the heroic exploits of the Army, the Navy, and the militia I need not speak. Such, then, is the happy Government under which we live—a Government adequate to every purpose for which the social compact is formed; a Government elective in all its branches, under which every citizen may by his merit obtain the highest trust recognized by the Constitution; which contains within it no cause of discord, none to put at variance one portion of the community with another; a Government which protects every citizen in the full enjoyment of his rights, and is able to protect the nation against injustice from foreign powers.

Other considerations of the highest importance admonish us to cherish our Union and to cling to the Government which supports it. Fortunate as we are in our political institutions, we have not been less so in other circumstances on which our prosperity and happiness essentially depend. Situated within the temperature zone, and extending through many degrees of latitude along the Atlantic, the United States enjoy all the varieties of climate, and every production incident to that portion of the globe. Penetrating internally to the Great Lakes and beyond the sources of the great rivers which communicate through our whole interior, no country was ever happier with respect to its domain. Blessed, too, with a fertile soil, our produce has always been very abundant, leaving, even in years the least favorable, a surplus for the wants of our fellow-men in other countries. Such is our peculiar felicity that there is not a part of our Union that is not particularly interested in preserving it. The great agricultural interest of the nation prospers under its protection. Local interests are not less fostered by it. Our fellow-citizens of the North engaged in navigation find great encouragement in being made the favored carriers of the vast productions of the other portions of the United States, while the inhabitants of these are amply recompensed, in their turn, by the nursery for seamen and naval force thus formed and reared up for the support of our common rights. Our manufacturers find a generous encouragement by the policy which patronizes domestic industry, and the surplus of our produce a steady and profitable market by local wants in less-favored parts at home.

Such, then, being the highly favored condition of our country, it is the interest of every citizen to maintain it. What are the dangers which menace us? If any exist they ought to be ascertained and guarded against.

In explaining my sentiments on this subject it may be asked, What raised us to the present happy state? How did we accomplish the Revolution? How remedy the defects of the first instrument of our Union, by infusing into the National Government sufficient power for national purposes, without impairing the just rights of the States or affecting those of individuals? How sustain and pass with glory through the late war? The Government has been in the hands of the people. To the people, therefore, and to the faithful and able depositaries of their trust is the credit due. Had the people of the United States been educated in different principles, had they been less intelligent, less independent, or less virtuous, can it be believed that we should have maintained the same steady and consistent career or been blessed with the same success? While, then, the constituent body retains its present sound and healthful state everything will be safe. They will choose competent and faithful representatives for every department. It is only when the people become ignorant and corrupt, when they degenerate into a populace, that they are incapable of exercising the sovereignty. Usurpation is then an easy attainment, and an usurper soon found. The people themselves become the willing instruments of their own debasement and ruin. Let us, then, look to the great cause, and endeavor to preserve it in full force. Let us by all wise and constitutional measures promote intelligence among the people as the best means of preserving our liberties.

Dangers from abroad are not less deserving of attention. Experiencing the fortune of other nations, the United States may be again involved in war, and it may in that event be the object of the adverse party to overset our Government, to break our Union, and demolish us as a nation. Our distance from Europe and the just, moderate, and pacific policy of our Government may form some security against these dangers, but they ought to be anticipated and guarded against. Many of our citizens are engaged in commerce and navigation, and all of them are in a certain degree dependent on their prosperous state. Many are engaged in the fisheries. These interests are exposed to invasion in the wars between other powers, and we should disregard the faithful admonition of experience if we did not expect it. We must support our rights or lose our character, and with it, perhaps, our liberties. A people who fail to do it can scarcely be said to hold a place among independent nations. National honor is national property of the highest value. The sentiment in the mind of every citizen is national strength. It ought therefore to be cherished.

To secure us against these dangers our coast and inland frontiers should be fortified, our Army and Navy, regulated upon just principles as to the force of each, be kept in perfect order, and our militia be placed on the best practicable footing. To put our extensive coast in such a state of defense as to secure our cities and interior from invasion will be attended with expense, but the work when finished will be permanent, and it is fair to presume that a single campaign of invasion by a naval force superior to our own, aided by a few thousand land troops, would expose us to greater expense, without taking into the estimate the loss of property and distress of our citizens, than would be sufficient for this great work. Our land and naval forces should be moderate, but adequate to the necessary purposes—the former to garrison and preserve our fortifications and to meet the first invasions of a foreign foe, and, while constituting the elements of a greater force, to preserve the science as well as all the necessary implements of war in a state to be brought into activity in the event of war; the latter, retained within the limits proper in a state of peace, might aid in maintaining the neutrality of the United States with dignity in the wars of other powers and in saving the property of their citizens from spoliation. In time of war, with the enlargement of which the great naval resources of the county render it susceptible, and which should be duly fostered in time of peace, it would contribute essentially, both as an auxiliary of defense and as a powerful engine of annoyance, to diminish the calamities of war and to bring the war to a speedy and honorable termination.

But it ought always to be held prominently in view that the safety of these States and of everything dear to a free people must depend in an eminent degree on the militia. Invasion may be made too formidable to be resisted by any land and naval force which it would comport either with the principles of our Government or the circumstances of the United States to maintain. In such cases recourse must be had to the great body of the people, and in a manner to produce the best effect. It is of the highest importance, therefore, that they be so organized and trained as to be prepared for any emergency. The arrangement should be such as to put at the command of the Government the ardent patriotism and youthful vigor of the country. If formed on equal and just principles, it can not be oppressive. It is the crisis which makes the pressure, and not the laws which provide a remedy for it. This arrangement should be formed, too, in time of peace, to be the better prepared for war. With such an organization of such a people the United States have nothing to dread from foreign invasion. At its approach an overwhelming force of gallant men might always be put in motion.

Other interests of high importance will claim attention, among which the improvement of our country by roads and canals, proceeding always with a constitutional sanction, holds a distinguished place. By thus facilitating the intercourse between the States we shall add much to the convenience and comfort of our fellow-citizens, much to the ornament of the country, and, what is of greater importance, we shall shorten distances, and, by making each part more accessible to and dependent on the other, we shall bind the Union more closely together. Nature has done so much for us by intersecting the country with so many great rivers, bays, and lakes, approaching from distant points so near to each other, that the inducement to complete the work seems to be peculiarly strong. A more interesting spectacle was perhaps never seen than is exhibited within the limits of the United States—a territory so vast and advantageously situated, containing objects so grand, so useful, so happily connected in all their parts! Our manufacturers will likewise require the systematic and fostering care of the Government. Possessing as we do all the raw materials, the fruit of our own soil and industry,

we ought not to depend in the degree we have done on supplies from other countries. While we are thus dependent the sudden event of war, unsought and unexpected, can not fail to plunge us into the most serious difficulties. It is important, too, that the capital which nourishes our manufacturers should be domestic, as its influence in that case instead of exhausting, as it may do in foreign hands, would be felt advantageously on agriculture and every other branch of industry. Equally important is it to provide at home a market for our raw materials, as by extending the competition it will enhance the price and protect the cultivator against the casualties incident to foreign markets.

With the Indian tribes it is our duty to cultivate friendly relations and to act with kindness and liberality in all our transactions. Equally proper is it to persevere in our efforts to extend to them the advantages of civilization.

The great amount of our revenue and the flourishing state of the Treasury are a full proof of the competency of the national resources for any emergency, as they are of the willingness of our fellow-citizens to bear the burdens which the public necessities require. The vast amount of vacant lands, the value of which daily augments, forms an additional resource of great extent and duration. These resources, besides accomplishing every other necessary purpose, put it completely in the power of the United States to discharge the national debt at an early period. Peace is the best time for improvement and preparation of every kind; it easily paid, and that the revenue is most productive.

The Executive is charged officially in the Departments under it with the disbursement of the public money, and is responsible for the faithful application of it to the purposes for which it is raised. The Legislature is the watchful guardian over the public purse. it is its duty to see that the disbursement has been honestly made. To meet the requisite responsibility every facility should be afforded to the Executive to enable it to bring the public agents intrusted with the public money strictly and promptly to account. Nothing should be presumed against them; but if, with the requisite facilities, the public money is suffered to lie long and uselessly in their hands, they will not be the only defaulters, nor will the demoralizing effect be confined to them. It will evince a relaxation and want of tone in the Administration which will be felt by the whole community. I shall do all I can to secure economy and fidelity in this important branch of the Administration, and I doubt not that the Legislature will perform its duty with equal zeal. A thorough examination should be regularly made, and I will promote it.

It is particularly gratifying to me to enter on the discharge of these duties at a time when the United States are blessed with peace. It is a state most consistent with their prosperity and happiness. It will be my sincere desire to preserve it, so far as depends on the Executive, on just principles with all nations, claiming nothing unreasonable of any and rendering to each what is its due.

Equally gratifying is it to witness the increased harmony of opinion which pervades our Union. Discord does not belong to our system. Union is recommended as well by the free and benign principles of our Government, extending its blessings to every individual, as by the other eminent advantages attending it. The American people have encountered together great dangers and sustained severe trials with success. They constitute one great family with a common interest. Experience has enlightened us on some questions of essential importance to the country. The progress has been slow, dictated by a just reflection and a faithful regard to every interest connected with it. To promote this harmony in accord with the principles of our republican Government and in a manner to give them the most complete effect, and to advance in all other respects the best interests of our Union, will be the object of my constant and zealous exertions.

Never did a government commence under auspices so favorable, nor ever was success so complete. If we look to the history of other nations, ancient or modern, we find no example of a growth so rapid, so gigantic, of a people so prosperous and happy. In contemplating what we have still to perform, the heart of every citizen must expand with joy when he reflects how near our Government has approached to perfection; that in respect to it we have no essential improvement to make; that the great object is to preserve it in the essential principles and features which characterize it, and that that is to be done by preserving the virtue and enlightening the minds of the people; and as a security against foreign dangers to adopt such arrangements as are indispensable to the support of our independence, our rights and liberties. If we persevere in the career in which we have advanced so far and in the path already traced, we can not fail, under the favor of a gracious Providence, to attain the high destiny which seems to await us.

In the Administrations of the illustrious men who have preceded me in this high station, with some of whom I have been connected by the closest ties from early life, examples are presented which will always be found highly instructive and useful to their successors. From these I shall endeavor to derive all the advantages which they may afford. Of my immediate predecessor, under whom so important a portion of this great and successful experiment has been made, I shall be pardoned for expressing my earnest wishes that he may long enjoy in his retirement the affections of a grateful country, the best reward of exalted talents and the most faithful and meritorious service. Relying on the aid to be derived from the other departments of the Government, I enter on the trust to which I have been called by the suffrages of my fellow-citizens with my fervent prayers to the Almighty that He will be graciously pleased to continue to us that protection which He has already so conspicuously displayed in our favor.

See also FIRST ANNUAL MESSAGE TO CONGRESS, 1825; ANDREW JACKSON, FIRST INAUGURAL ADDRESS, 1829.

Source:
Inaugural Addresses of the Presidents of the United States, 1789–1965. Washington, D.C.: Government Printing Office, 1965.

Rush-Bagot Agreement of 1817

Convention for mutual disarmament on the Great Lakes and Lake Champlain concluded in Washington, D.C., on April 28–29, 1817, between Great Britain and the United States. The correspondence between acting U.S. secretary of state Richard Rush and British minister to the United States Charles Bagot brought about the agreement, under which their respective countries consented to restrict their construction and use of naval forces on these inland waters (each side agreed to maintain only three armed ships in the Great Lakes and only one on Lake Champlain). The agreement could be annulled by either side by giving the other a six-month advance notice to that effect. The U.S. Senate approved the agreement about a year later, thus beginning a policy of a relatively unfortified U.S.-Canadian border that was later extended to the land along the border.

Nevertheless, borders remained in contention for many years. The Webster-Ashburton Treaty, signed August 9, 1842, settled the northeastern border. Negotiated by U.S. secretary of state Daniel Webster and British minister Alexander Baring, the treaty set the present boundary between Maine and New Brunswick, giving the United States 7,000 of the 12,000 square miles of disputed territory; adjusted the boundaries of Vermont and New York; settled a border conflict in the Great Lakes region; and assured U.S. navigation rights along the St. John River. It also provided for joint efforts in suppressing the African slave trade and for mutual extradition of criminals. The treaty led to greatly improved relations between Great Britain and the United States. Four years later, on June 15, 1846, the Senate ratified the Oregon Boundary Treaty, settling border problems in the Northwest. The boundary was set at the 49th parallel. The compromise treaty replaced an 1818 agreement for joint occupancy of the area between the 42nd and 54th parallels. The treaty also provided for free navigation rights for both nations in the channel between Vancouver Island and the mainland and in Fuca's Straits; it also gave the British navigation rights in the Columbia River, south of the boundary.

⌒⌒⌒

Arrangement

Between the United States and Great Britain, between Richard Rush, Esq., acting as Secretary of the Department of State, and Charles Bagot, His Britannic Majesty's Envoy Extraordinary, &c.

The naval force to be maintained upon the American lakes, by his majesty and the government of the United States, shall henceforth be confined to the following vessels on each side; that is—

On lake Ontario, to one vessel not exceeding one hundred tons burden, and armed with one eighteen pound cannon.

On the upper lakes, to two vessels, not exceeding like burden, each, and armed with like force.

On the waters of lake Champlain, to one vessel not exceeding like burden, and armed with like force.

All other armed vessels on these lakes shall be forthwith dismantled, and no other vessels of war shall be there built or armed.

If either party should hereafter be desirous of annulling this stipulation, and should give notice to that effect to the other party, it shall cease to be binding after the expiration of six months from the date of such notice.

The naval force so to be limited shall be restricted to such services as will, in no respect, interfere with the proper duties of the armed vessels of the other party.

Source:

Landmark Documents in American History, Facts On File, Inc.

McCulloch v. Maryland, 1819

Decision of the U.S. Supreme Court in favor of the plaintiff, James W. McCulloch, finding that the tax imposed by the state of Maryland on the Bank of the United States was unconstitutional, and that Congress did have the power to incorporate a federal bank. In a carefully argued opinion, Chief Justice John Marshall found that although the Constitution does not specifically give the government the right to create a federal bank, it nevertheless implies the granting of such a power. This argument confirmed the constitutional right of implied powers. Chief Justice Marshall also found the tax unconstitutional, since a state did not have the right to exercise its powers over the federal government.

State banks that issued their own currency were already in existence when Congress incorporated the second Bank of the United States in 1816 (the first had been incorporated from 1791 to 1811). Many states resented having to compete with the federal bank, which operated branches within the several states. In an effort to discourage Marylanders from doing business with banks other than the Bank of Maryland, the state legislature in 1818 decided to tax all transactions not conducted through the state bank. When James McCulloch, a cashier for the Baltimore branch of the Bank of the United States, refused to pay the tax, the state of Maryland sued him for lack of compliance with state law. The case went to the Supreme Court the following year, where it was heard over the course of nine days. Among the distinguished lawyers who argued on behalf of the plaintiff were William Pinkney and Daniel Webster.

The Court's opinion is divided into two parts. First, in considering whether Congress can legally incorporate a bank, Chief Justice Marshall treated the problem of determining the extent and breadth of the powers the Constitution grants to Congress in respect to those granted to the individual states, taking into account the further delineation of states' rights as set forth in the Tenth Amendment. Marshall applied the doctrine of "implied powers," concluding that while the Constitution imposes limits, it "must allow to the national legislature that discretion . . . which will enable that body to perform the high duties assigned to it, in the manner most beneficial to the people." The state of Maryland had argued that the Constitution does not grant Congress the right to form a corporation. Chief Justice Marshall countered that, if the "end" Congress seeks is "legitimate" and "within the scope of the constitution," then "all means which are appropriate, which are plainly adapted to that end, which are not prohibited, but consist with the letter and spirit of the constitution, are constitutional."

To the extent that *McCulloch* considered the broader issue of federal power, it illustrates the political debate that took shape after the Revolution between the Federalists and the Anti-Federalists (later the Democratic-Republicans). Federalists, such as Alexander Hamilton, the man behind the creation of a federal bank, favored a strong central government, while Anti-Federalists, such as Thomas Jefferson, promoted the rights of the individual states against a national government that could potentially exceed the powers granted to it by the Constitution. Within this political context the very issue of a national bank had already been raised 28 years earlier, when Hamilton first proposed the idea in Congress in 1791. (See FIRST REPORT ON PUBLIC CREDIT, 1790.) In deciding *McCulloch*, the Supreme Court, led by Chief Justice Marshall, who was himself a Federalist, opened the door for the expansion of government that the Anti-Federalists wanted to prevent.

⌒⌒⌒

McCulloch v. State of Maryland et al.
March 7th, 1819

Marshall, Ch. J., delivered the opinion of the court.—In the case now to be determined, the defendant, a sovereign state, denies the obligation of a law enacted by the legislature of the Union, and the plaintiff, on his part, contests the validity of an act which has been passed by the legislature of that state. The constitution of our country, in its most interesting and vital parts, is to be considered; the conflicting powers of the government of the Union and of its members, as marked in that constitution, are to be discussed; and an opinion given, which may essentially influence the great operations of the government. No tribunal can approach such a question without a deep sense of its important, and of the awful responsibility involved in its decision. But it must be decided peacefully, or remain a source of hostile legislation, perhaps, of hostility of a still more serious nature; and if it is to be so decided, by this tribunal alone can the decision be made. On the supreme court of the United States has the constitution of our country devolved this important duty.

The first question made in the cause is—has congress power to incorporate a bank? It has been truly said, that this can scarcely be considered as an open question, entirely unprejudiced by the former proceedings of the nation respecting it. The principle now contested was introduced at a very early period of our history, has been recognised by many successive legislatures, and has been acted upon by the judicial department, in cases of peculiar delicacy, as a law of undoubted obligation.

It will not be denied, that a bold and daring usurpation might be resisted, after an acquiescence still longer and more complete that this. But it is conceived, that a doubtful question, one on which human reason may pause, and the human judgment be suspended, in the decision of which the great principles of liberty are not concerned, but the respective powers of those who are equally the representatives of the people, are to be adjusted; if not put at rest by the practice of the government, ought to receive a considerable impression from that practice. An exposition of the constitution, deliberately established by legislative acts, on the faith of which an immense property has been advanced, ought not to be lightly disregarded.

The power now contested was exercised by the first congress elected under the present constitution. The bill for incorporating the Bank of the United States did not steal upon an unsuspecting legislature, and pass unobserved. Its principle was completely understood, and was opposed with equal zeal and ability. After being resisted, first, in the fair and open field of debate, and afterwards, in the executive cabinet, with as much persevering talent as any measure has ever experienced, and being supported by arguments which convinced minds as pure and as intelligent as this country can boast, it became a law. The original act was permitted to expire; but a short experience of the embarrassments to which the refusal to revive it exposed the government, convinced those who were most

prejudiced against the measure of its necessity, and induced the passage of the present law. It would require no ordinary share of intrepidity, to assert that a measure adopted under these circumstances, was a bold and plain usurpation, to which the constitution gave no countenance. These observations belong to the cause; but they are not made under the impression, that, were the question entirely new, the law would be found irreconcilable with the constitution.

In discussing this question, the counsel for the state of the Maryland have deemed it of some importance, in the construction of the constitution, to consider that instrument not as emanating from the people, but as the act of sovereign and independent states. The powers of the general government, it has been said, are delegated by the states, who alone are truly sovereign; and must be exercised in subordination to the states, who alone possess supreme dominion. It would be difficult to sustain this proposition. The convention which framed the constitution was indeed elected by the state legislatures. But the instrument, when it came from their hands, was a mere proposal, without obligation, or pretensions to it. It was reported to the then existing congress of the United States, with a request that it might "be submitted to a convention of delegates, chosen in each state by the people thereof, under the recommendation of its legislature, for their assent and ratification." This mode of proceeding was adopted; and by the convention by congress, and by the state legislatures, the instrument was submitted to the *people*. They acted upon it in the only manner in which they can act safely, effectively and wisely, on such a subject, by assembling in convention. It is true, they assembled in their several states—and where else should they have assembled? No political dreamer was ever wild enough to think of breaking down the lines which separate the states, and of compounding the American people into one common mass. Of consequence, when they act, they act in their states. But the measures they adopt do not, on that account, cease to be the measures of the people themselves, or become the measures of the state governments. From these conventions, the constitution derives its whole authority. The government proceeds directly from the people; is "ordained and established," in the name of the people; and is declared to be ordained, "in order to form a more perfect union, establish justice, insure domestic tranquillity, and secure the blessings of liberty to themselves and to their posterity." The assent of the states, in their sovereign capacity, is implied, in calling a convention, and thus submitting the instrument to the people. But the people were at perfect liberty to accept or reject it; and their act was final. It required not the affirmance, and could not be negatived, by the state governments. The constitution, when thus adopted, was of complete obligation, and bound the state sovereignties.

It has been said, that the people had already surrendered all their powers to the state sovereignties, and had nothing more to give. But, surely, the question whether they may resume and modify the powers granted to government, does not remain to be settled in this country. Much more might the legitimacy of the general government be doubted, had it been created by the states. The powers delegated to the state sovereignties were to be exercised by themselves, not by a distinct and independent sovereignty, created by themselves. To the formation of a league, such as was the confederation, the state sovereignties were certainly competent. But when, "in order to form a more perfect union," it was deemed necessary to change this alliance into an effective government, possessing great and sovereign powers and acting directly on the people, the necessity of referring it to the people, and of deriving its powers directly from them, was felt and acknowledged by all. The government of the Union, then (whatever may be the influence of this fact on the case), is emphatically and truly, a government of the people. In form, and in substance, it emanates from them. Its powers are granted by them, and are to be exercised directly on them, and for their benefit.

This government is acknowledged by all, to be one of enumerated powers. The principle, that it can exercise only the powers granted to it, would seem to apparent, to have required to be enforced by all those arguments, which its enlightened friends, while it was depending before the people, found it necessary to urge; that principle is now universally admitted. But the question respecting the extent of the powers actually granted, is perpetually arising, and will probably continue to arise, so long as our system shall exist. In discussing these questions, the conflicting powers of the general and state governments must be brought into view, and the supremacy of their respective laws, when they are in opposition, must be settled.

If any one proposition could command the universal assent of mankind, we might expect it would be this—that the government of the Union, though limited in its powers, is supreme within its sphere of action. This would seem to result, necessarily, from its nature. It is the government of all; its powers are delegated by all; it represents all, and acts or all. Though any one state may be willing to control its operations, no state is willing to allow others to control them. The nation, on those subjects on which it can act, must necessarily bind its component parts. But this question is not left to mere reason: the people have, in express terms, decided it by saying, this constitution, and the laws of the United States, which shall be made in pursuance thereof," "shall be the supreme law of the land," and by

requiring that the members of the state legislatures, and the officers of the executive and judicial departments of the states, shall take the oath of fidelity to it. The government of the United States, then, though limited in its powers, is supreme; and its laws, when made in pursuance of the constitution, form the supreme law of the land, "anything in the constitution or laws of any state to the contrary notwithstanding."

Among the enumerated powers, we do not find that of establishing a bank or creating a corporation. But there is no phrase in the instrument which, like the articles of confederation, excludes incidental or implied powers; and which requires that everything granted shall be expressly and minutely described. Even the 10th amendment, which was framed for the purpose of quieting the excessive jealousies which had been excited omits the word "expressly," and declares only, that the powers "not delegated to the United States, nor prohibited to the states, are reserved to the state or to the people;" thus leaving the question, whether the particular power which may become the subject of contest, has been delegated to the one government, or prohibited to the other, to depend on a fair construction of the whole instrument. The men who drew and adopted this amendment had experienced the embarrassments resulting from the insertion of this word in the articles of confederation, and probably omitted it, to avoid those embarrassments. A constitution, to contain an accurate detail of all the subdivisions of which its great powers will admit, and of all the means by which they may be carried into execution, would partake of the prolixity of a legal code, and could scarcely be embraced by the human mind. It would, probably, never be understood by the public. Its nature, therefore, requires, that only its great outlines should be marked, its important objects designated, and the minor ingredients which compose those objects, be deduced from the nature of the objects themselves. That this idea was entertained by the framers of the American constitution, is not only to be inferred from the nature of the instrument, but from the language. Why else were some of the limitations, found in the 9th section of the 1st article, introduced? It is also, in some degree, warranted, by their having omitted to use any restrictive term which might prevent its receiving a fair and just interpretation. In considering this question, then, we must never forget that it is a *constitution* we are expounding.

Although, among the enumerated powers of government, we do not find the word "bank" or "incorporation," we find the great powers, to lay and collect taxes; to borrow money; to regulate commerce; to declare and conduct a war; and to raise and support armies and navies. The sword and the purse, all the external relations, and no inconsiderable portion of the industry of the nation, are intrusted to its government. It can never be pretended, that these vast powers draw after them others of inferior importance, merely because they are inferior. Such an idea can never be advanced. But it may with great reason be contended, that a government, intrusted with such ample powers, on the due execution of which the happiness and prosperity of the nation so vitally depends, must also be intrusted with ample means for their execution. The power being given, it is the interest of the nation to facilitate its execution. It can never be their interest, and cannot be presumed to have been their intention, to clog and embarrass its execution, by withholding the most appropriate means. Throughout this vast republic, from the St. Croix to the Gulf of Mexico, from the Atlantic to the Pacific, revenue is to be collected and expended, armies are to be marched and supported. The exigencies of the nation may require, that the treasure raised in the north should be transported to the south, that raised in the east, conveyed to the west, or that this order should be reversed. Is that construction of the constitution to be preferred, which would render these operations difficult, hazardous and expensive? Can we adopt that construction (unless the words imperiously require it), which would impute to the framers of that instrument, when granting these powers for the public, the intention of impeding their exercise, by withholding a choice of means? If, indeed, such be the mandate of the constitution, we have only to obey; but that instrument does not profess to enumerate the means by which the powers it confers may be executed; nor does it prohibit the creation of a corporation, if the existence of such being be essential, to he beneficial exercise of those powers. It is, then, the subject of fair inquiry, how far such means may be employed.

It is not denied, that the powers given to the government imply the ordinary means of execution. That, for example, of raising revenue, and applying it to national purposes, is admitted to imply the power of conveying money from place to place, as the exigencies of the nation may require, and of employing the usual means of conveyance. But it is denied, that the government has its choice of means; or, that it may employ the most convenient means, if, to employ them, it be necessary to erect a corporation. On what foundation does this argument rest? On this alone: the power of creating a corporation, is one appertaining to sovereignty, and is not expressly conferred on congress. This is true. But all legislative powers appertain to sovereignty. The original power of giving the law on any subject whatever, is a sovereign power; and if the government of the Union is restrained from creating a corporation, as a means for performing its functions, on the single reason that the creation of a corporation is an act of sovereignty; if the sufficiency of this reason be acknowledged, there would be some difficulty in sustaining the authority of congress to pass other laws for the accomplishment of the same objects. The government which has a right to do an act, and has imposed on it, the duty of performing that act, must, according to the dictates of reason, be allowed to select the means; and those who contend that it may not select any appropriate means, that one particular mode of effecting the object is excepted, take upon themselves the burden of establishing that exception.

The creation of a corporation, it is said, appertains to sovereignty. This is admitted. But to what portion of sovereignty does it appertain? Does it belong to one more than to another? In America, the powers of sovereignty are divided between the government of the Union, and those of the states. They are each sovereign, with respect to the objects committed to it, and neither sovereign, with respect to the objects committed to the other. We cannot comprehend that train of reasoning, which would maintain, that the extent of power granted by the people is to be ascertained, not by the nature and terms of the grant, but by its date. Some state constitutions were formed before, some since that of the United States. We cannot believe, that their relation to each other is in any degree dependent upon this circumstance. Their respective powers must, we think, be precisely the same, as if they had been formed at the same time. Had they been formed at the same time, and had the people conferred on the general government the power contained in the constitution, and on the states the whole residuum of power, would it have been asserted, that the government of the Union was not sovereign, with respect to those objects which were intrusted to it, in relation to which its laws were declared to be supreme? If this could not have been asserted, we cannot well comprehend the process of reasoning which maintains, that a power appertaining to sovereignty cannot be connected with that vast portion of it which is granted to the general government, so far as it is calculated to subserve the legitimate objects of that government. The power of creating a corporation, though appertaining to sovereignty, is not, like the power of making war, or levying taxes, or of regulating commerce, a great substantive and independent power, which cannot be implied as incidental to other powers, or used as a means of executing them. It is never the end of which other powers are exercised, but a means by which other objects are accomplished. No contributions are made to charity, for the sake of an incorporation, but a corporation is created to administer the charity; no seminary of learning is instituted, in order to be incorporated, but the corporate character is conferred to subserve the purposes of education. No city was ever built, with the sole object of being incorporated, but is incorporated as affording the best means of being well governed. The power of creating a corporation is never used for its own sake, but for the purpose of effecting something else. No sufficient reason is, therefore, perceived, why it may not pass as incidental to those powers which are expressly given, if it be a direct mode of executing them.

But the constitution of the United States has not left the right of congress to employ the necessary means, for the execution of the powers conferred on the government, to general reasoning. To its enumeration of powers is added, that of making "all laws which shall be necessary and proper, for carrying into execution the foregoing powers, and all other powers vested by this constitution, in the government of the United States, or in any department thereof." The counsel for the state of Maryland have urged various arguments, to prove that this clause, though, in terms, a grant of power, is not so, in effect; but is really restrictive of the general right, which might otherwise be implied, of selecting means for executing the enumerated powers. In support of this proposition, they have found it necessary to contend, that this clause was inserted for the purpose of conferring on congress the power of making laws. That, without it, doubts might be entertained, whether congress could exercise its powers in the form of legislation.

But could this be the object for which it was inserted? A government is created by the people, having legislative, executive and judicial powers. Its legislative powers are vested in a congress, which is to consist of a senate and house of representatives. Each house may determine the rule of its proceedings; and it is declared, that every bill which shall have passed both houses, shall, before it becomes a law, be presented to the president of the United States. The 7th section describes the course of proceedings, by which a bill shall become a law; and, then, the 8th section enumerates the powers of congress. Could it be necessary to say, that a legislature should exercise legislative powers, in the shape of legislation? After allowing each house to prescribe its own course of proceeding, after describing the manner in which a bill should become a law, would it have entered into the mind of a single member of the convention, that an express power to make laws was necessary, to enable the legislature to make them? That a legislature, endowed with legislative powers, can legislate, is a proposition too self-evident to have been questioned.

But the argument on which most reliance is placed, is drawn from that peculiar language of this clause. Congress is not empowered by it to make all laws, which may have relation to the powers confered on the government, but such only as may be *"necessary and proper"* for carrying them into execution. The word *"necessary"* is considered as controlling the whole sentence, and as limiting the right to pass laws for the execution of the granted powers, to such as are indispensable, and without which the power would be nugatory. That it excludes the choice of means, and leaves to congress, in each case, that only which is most direct and simple.

Is it true, that this is the sense in which the word "necessary" is always used? Does it always import an absolute physical necessity, so strong, that one thing to which another may be termed necessary, cannot exist without that other? We think it does not. If reference be had to its use, in the common affairs of the word, or in approved authors, we find that it frequently imports no more than that one thing is convenient, or useful, or essential to another. To employ the means necessary to an end, is generally understood as employing any means calculated to produce the end, and not as being confined to those single means, without which the end would be entirely unattainable. Such is the character of human language, that no word conveys to the mind, in all situations, one single definite idea; and nothing is more common than to use words in a figurative sense. Almost all compositions contain words, which, taken in a their rigorous sense, would convey a meaning different from that which is obviously intended. It is essential to just construction, that many words which import something excessive, should be understood in a more mitigated sense—in that sense which common usage justifies. The word "necessary" is of this description. It has not a fixed character, peculiar to itself. It admits of all degrees of comparison; and is often connected with other words, which increase or diminish the impression the mind receives of the urgency it imports. A thing may be necessary, very necessary, absolutely or indispensably necessary. To no mind would the same idea be conveyed by these several phrases. The comment on the word is well illustrated by the passage cited at the bar, from the 10th section of the 1st article of the constitution. It is, we think, impossible to compare the sentence which prohibits a state from laying "imposts, or duties on imports or exports, except what may be *absolutely* necessary for executing its inspection laws," with that which authorizes congress" to make all laws which shall be necessary and proper for carrying into execution" the powers of the general government, without feeling a conviction, that the convention understood itself to change materially the meaning of the word "necessary," by prefixing the word "absolutely." This word, then, like others, is used in various senses; and, in its construction, the subject, the context, the intention of the person using them are all to be taken into view.

Let this be done in the case under consideration. The subject is the execution of those great powers on which the welfare of a nation essentially depends. It must have been the intention of those who gave these powers, to insure, so far as human prudence could insure, their beneficial execution. This could not be done, by confiding the choice of means to such narrow limits as not to leave it in the power of congress to adopt any which might be appropriate, and which were conducive to the end. This provision is made in a constitution, intended to endure for ages to come, and consequently, to be adapted to the various *crises* of human affairs. To have prescribed the means by which government should, in all future time, execute its powers, would have been to change, entirely, the character of the instrument, and give it the properties of a legal code. It would have been an unwise attempt to provide, by immutable rules, for exigencies which, if foreseen at all, must have been seen dimly, and which can be best provided for as they occur. To have declared, that the best means shall not be used, but those alone, without which the power given would be nugatory, would have been to deprive the legislature of the capacity to avail itself of experience, to exercise its reason, and to accommodate its legislation to circumstances.

If we apply this principle of construction to any of the powers of the government, we shall find it so pernicious in its operation that we shall be compelled to discard it. The powers vested in congress may certainly be carried into execution, without prescribing an oath of office. The power to exact this security for the faithful performance of duty, is not given, nor is it indispensably necessary. The different departments may be established; taxes may be imposed and collected; armies and navies may be raised and maintained; and money may be borrowed, without requiring an oath of office. It might be argued, with as much plausibility as other incidental powers have been assailed, that the convention was not unmindful of this subject. The oath which might be exacted—that of fidelity to the constitution—is prescribed, and no other can be required. Yet, he would be charged with insanity, who should contend, that the legislature might not superadd, to the oath directed by the constitution, such other oath of office as its wisdom might suggest.

So, with respect to the whole penal code of the United States: whence arises the power to punish, in cases not prescribed by the constitution? All admit, that the government may, legitimately, punish any violation of its laws; and yet, this is not among the enumerated powers of congress. The right to enforce the observance of law, by punishing its infraction, might be denied, with the more plausibility, because it is expressly given in some cases.

Congress is empowered "to provide for the punishment of counterfeiting the securities and current coin of the United States," and "to define and punish piracies and felonies committed on the high seas, and offences against the law of nations." The several powers of congress may exist, in a very imperfect state, to be sure, but they may exist and be carried into execution, although no punish-

ment should be inflicted, in cases where the right to punish is not expressly given.

Take, for example, the power "to establish post-offices and post-roads." This power is executed, by the single act of making the establishment. But, from this has been inferred the power and duty of carrying the mail along the post-road, from one post-office to another. And from this implied power, has again been inferred the right to punish those who steal letters from the post-office, or rob the mail. It may be said, with some plausibility, that the right to carry the mail, and to punish those who rob it, is not indispensably necessary to the establishment of a post-office and post-road. This right is indeed essential to the beneficial exercise of the power, but not indispensably necessary to its existence. So, of the punishment of the crimes of stealing or falsifying a record or process of a court of the United States, or of perjury in such court. To punish these offences, is certainly conducive to the due administration of justice. But court may exist, and may decide the causes brought before them, though such crimes escape punishment.

The baneful influence of this narrow construction on all the operations of the government, and the absolute impracticability of maintaining it, without rendering the government incompetent to its great objects, might be illustrated by numerous examples drawn from the constitution, and from our laws. The good sense of the public has pronounced, without hesitation, that the power of punishment appertains to sovereignty, and may be exercised, whenever the sovereign has a right to act, as incidental to his constitutional powers. It is a means for carrying into execution all sovereign powers, and may be used, although not indispensably necessary. It is a right incidental to the power, and conducive to its beneficial exercise.

If this limited construction of the word "necessary" must be abandoned, in order to punish, whence is derived the rule which would reinstate it, when the government would carry its powers into execution, by means not vindictive in their nature? If the word "necessary" means "needful," "requisite," "essential," "conducive to," in order to let in the power of punishment for the infraction of law; why is it not equally comprehensive, when required to authorize the use of means which facilitate the execution of the powers of government, without the infliction of punishment?

In ascertaining the sense in which the word "necessary" is used in this clause of the constitution, we may derive some aid from that with which it is associated. Congress shall have power "to make all laws which shall be necessary and proper to carry into execution" the powers of the government. If the word "necessary" was used in that strict and rigorous sense for which the counsel for the state of Maryland contend, it would be an extraordinary departure from the usual course of the human mind, as exhibited in composition, to add a word, the only possible offect of which is, to qualify that strict and rigorous meaning; to present to the mind the idea of some choice of means of legislation, not strained and compressed within the narrow limits for which gentlemen contend.

But the argument which most conclusively demonstrates the error of the construction contended for by the counsel for the state of Maryland, is founded on the intention of the convention, as manifested in the whole clause. To waste time and argument in proving that, without it, congress might carry its powers into execution, would be not much less idle, than to hold a lighted taper to the sun. As little can it be required to prove, that in the absence of this clause, congress would have some choice of means. That it might employ those which, in its judgment, would most advantageously effect the object to be accomplished. That any means adapted to the end, any means which tended directly to the execution of the constitutional powers of the government, were in themselves constitutional. This clause, as construed by the state of Maryland, would abridge, and almost annihilate, this useful and necessary right of the legislature to select its means. That this could not be intended, is, we should think, had it not been already controverted, too apparent for controversy.

We think so for the following reasons: 1st. The clause is placed among the powers of congress, not among the limitations on those powers. 2d. Its terms purport to enlarge, not to diminish the powers vested in the government. It purports to be an additional power, not a restriction on those already granted. No reason has been, or can be assigned, for thus concealing an intention to narrow the discretion of the national legislature, under words which purport to enlarge it. The framers of the constitution wished its adoption, and well knew that it would be endangered by its strength, not by its weakness. Had they been capable of using language which would convey to the eye one idea, and, after deep reflection, impress on the mind, another, they would rather have disguised the grant of power, than its limitation. If, then, their intention had been, by this clause, to restrain the free use of means which might otherwise have been implied, that intention would have been inserted in another place, and would have been expressed in terms resembling these. "In carrying into execution the foregoing powers, and all others," &c., "no laws shall be passed but such as are necessary and proper." Had the intention been to make this clause restrictive, it would unquestionably have been so in form as well as in effect.

The result of the most careful and attentive consideration bestowed upon this clause is, that if it does not enlarge, it cannot be construed to restrain the powers of congress, or to impair the right of the legislature to exercise its best judgment in the selection of measures to carry into execution the constitutional powers of the government. If no other motive for its insertion can be suggested, a sufficient one is found in the desire to remove all doubts respecting the right to legislate on that vast mass of incidental powers which must be involved in the constitution, if that instrument be not a splendid bauble. We admit, as all must admit, that the powers of the government are limited, and that its limits are not to be transcended. But we think the sound construction of the constitution must allow to the national legislature that discretion, with respect to the means by which the powers it confers are to be carried into execution, which will enable that body to perform the high duties assigned to it, in the manner most beneficial to the people. Let the end be legitimate, let it be within the scope of the constitution, and all means which are appropriate, which are plainly adapted to that end, which are not prohibited, but consist with the letter and spirit of the constitution, are constitutional.

That a corporation must be considered as a means not less usual, not of higher dignity, not more requiring a particular specification than other means, has been sufficiently proved. If we look to the origin of corporations, to the manner in which they have been framed in that government from which we have derived most of our legal principles and ideas, or to the uses to which they have been applied, we find no reason to suppose, that a constitution, omitting, and wisely omitting, to enumerate all the means for carrying into execution the great powers vested in government, ought to have specified this. Had it been intended to grant this power, as one which should be distinct and independent, to be exercised in any case whatever, it would have found a place among the enumerated powers of the government. But being considered merely as a means, to be employed only for the purpose of carrying into execution the given powers, there could be no motive for particularly mentioning it.

The propriety of this remark would seem to be generally acknowledged, by the universal acquiescence in the construction which has been uniformly put on the 3d section of the 4th article of the constitution. The power to "make all needful rules and regulations respecting the territory or other property belonging to the United States," is not more comprehensive, than the power "to make all laws which shall be necessary and proper for carrying into execution" the powers of the government. Yet all admit the constitutionality of a territorial government, which is a corporate body.

If a corporation may be employed, indiscriminately with other means, to carry into execution the powers of the government, no particular reason can be assigned for excluding the use of a bank, if required for its fiscal operations. To use one, must be within the discretion of congress, if it be an appropriate mode of executing the powers of government. That it is a convenient, a useful, and essential instrument in the prosecution of its fiscal operations, is not now a subject of controversy. All those who have been concerned in the administration of our finances, have concurred in representing its importance and necessity; and so strongly have they been felt, that statesmen of the first class, whose previous opinions against it had been confirmed by every circumstances which can fix the human judgment, have yielded those opinions to the exigencies of the nation. Under the confederation, congress, justifying the measure by its necessity; transcended, perhaps, its powers, to obtain the advantage of a bank; and our own legislation attests the universal conviction of the utility of this measure. The time has passed away, when it can be necessary to enter into any discussion, in order to prove the importance of this instrument, as a means to effect the legitimate objects of the government.

But were its necessity less apparent, none can deny its being an appropriate measure; and if it is, the decree of its necessity, as has been very justly observed, is to be discussed in another place. Should congress, in the execution of its powers, adopt measures which are prohibited by the constitution; or should congress, under the pretext of executing its powers, pass laws for the accomplishment of objects not intrusted to the government; it would become the painful duty of this tribunal, should a case requiring such a decision come before it, to say, that such an act was not the law of the land. But where the law is not prohibited, and is really calculated to effect any of the objects intrusted to the government, to undertake here to inquire into the decree of its necessity, would be to pass the line which circumscribes the judicial department, and to tread on legislative ground. This court disclaims all pretensions to such a power.

After this declaration, it can scarcely be necessary to say, that the existence of state banks can have no possible influence on the question. No trace is to be found in the constitution, of an intention to create a dependence of the government of the Union on those of the states, for the execution of the great powers assigned to it. Its means are adequate to its ends; and on those means alone was it expected to rely for the accomplishment of its ends. To impose on it the necessity of resorting to means which it cannot control, which another government may furnish or withhold, would render its course precarious, the result of its measures uncertain, and create a dependence on other governments, which might disappoint its most important

designs, and is incompatible with the language of the constitution. But were it otherwise, the choice of means implies a right to choose a national bank in preference to state banks, and congress alone can make the election.

After the most deliberate consideration, it is the unanimous and decided opinion of this court, that the act to incorporate the Bank of the United States is a law made in pursuance of the constitution, and is a part of the supreme law of the land.

The branches, proceeding from the same stock, and being conducive to the complete accomplishment of the object, are equally constitutional. It would have been unwise, to locate them in the charter, and it would be unnecessarily inconvenient, to employ the legislative power in making those subordinate arrangements. The great duties of the bank are prescribed; those duties require branches; and the bank itself may, we think, be safely trusted with the selection of places where those branches shall be fixed; reserving always to the government the right to require that a branch shall be located where it may be deemed necessary.

It being the opinion of the court, that the act incorporating the bank is constitutional; and that the power of establishing a branch in the state of Maryland might be properly exercised by the bank itself, we proceed to inquire—

2. Whether the state of Maryland may, without violating the constitution, tax that branch? That the power of taxation is one of vital importance; that it is retained by the states; that it is not abridged by the grant of a similar power to the government of the Union; that it is to be concurrently exercised by the two governments—are truths which have never been denied. But such is the paramount character of the constitution, that its capacity to withdraw any subject from the action of even this power, is admitted. The states are expressly forbidden to lay any duties on imports or exports, except what may be absolutely necessary for executing their inspection laws. If the obligation of this prohibition must be conceded—if it may restrain a state from the exercise of its taxing power on imports and exports—the same paramount character would seem to restrain, as it certainly may restrain, a state from such other exercise of this power, as is in its nature incompatible with, and repugnant to, the constitutional laws of the Union. A law, absolutely repugnant to another, as entirely repeals that other as if express terms of repeal were used. On this ground, the counsel for the bank place its claim to be exempted from the power of a state to tax its operations. There is no express provision for the case, but the claim has been sustained on a principle which so entirely pervades the constitution, is so intermixed with the materials which compose it, so interwoven with its web, so blended

with its texture, as to be incapable of being separated from it, without rending it into shreds. This great principle, is, that the constitution and the laws made in pursuance thereof are supreme; that they control the constitution and laws of the respective states, and cannot be controlled by them. From this, which may be almost termed an axiom, other propositions are deduced as corollaries, on the truth or error of which, and on their application to this case, the cause has been supposed to depend. These are, 1st. That a power to create implies a power to preserve: 2d. That a power to destroy, if wielded by a different hand, is hostile to, and incompatible with these powers to create and to preserve: 3d. That where this repugnancy exists, that authority which is supreme must control, not yield to that over which it is supreme.

These propositions, as abstract truths, would, perhaps, never be converted. Their application to this case, however, has been denied; and both in maintaining the affirmative and the negative, a splendor of eloquence, and strength of argument, seldom, if ever, surpassed, have been displayed. The power of congress to create, and of course, to continue, the bank, was the subject of the preceding part of this opinion; and is no longer to be considered as questionable. That the power of taxing it by the states may be exercised so as to destroy it, is too obvious to be denied. But taxation is said to be an absolute power, which acknowledges no other limits than those expressly prescribed in the constitution, and like sovereign power of every other description, is intrusted to the discretion of those who use it. But the very terms of this argument admit, that the sovereignty of the state, in the article of taxation itself, is subordinate to, and may be controlled by the constitution of the United States. How far it has been controlled by that instrument, must be a question of construction. In making this construction, no principle, not declared, can be admissible, which would defeat the legitimate operations of a supreme government. It is of the very essence of supremacy, to remove all obstacles to its action within its own sphere, and so to modify every power vested in subordinate governments, as to exempt its own operations from their own influence. This effect need not be stated in terms. It is so involved in the declaration of supremacy, so necessarily implied in it, that the expression of it could not make it more certain. We must, therefore, keep it in view, while construing the constitution.

The argument on the part of the state of Maryland, is, not that the states may directly resist a law of congress, but that they may exercise their acknowledged powers upon it, and that the constitution leaves them this right, in the confidence that they will not abuse it. Before we proceed to examine this argument, and to subject it to test of the constitution, we must be permitted to bestow a few considerations on the nature and extent of this original right of taxation, which is acknowledged to remain with the states. It is admitted, that the power of taxing the people and their property, is essential to the very existence of government, and may be legitimately exercised on the objects to which it is applicable, to the utmost extent to which the government may choose to carry it. The only security against the abuse of this power, is found in the structure of the government itself. In imposing a tax, the legislature acts upon its constituents. This is, in general, a sufficient security against erroneous and oppressive taxation. The people of a state, therefore, give to their government a right of taxing themselves and their property, and as the exigencies of government cannot be limited, they prescribe no limits to the exercise of this right, resting confidently on the interest of the legislator, and on the influence of the constituent over their representative, to guard them against its abuse. But the means employed by the government of the Union have no such security, nor is the right of a state to tax them sustained by the same theory. Those means are not given by the people of a particular state, not given by the constituents of the legislature, which claim the right to tax them, but by the people of all the states. They are given by all, for the benefit of all—and upon theory, should be subjected to that government only which belongs to all.

It may be objected to this definition, that the power of taxation is not confined to the people and property of a state. It may be exercised upon every object brought within its jurisdiction. This is true. But to what source do wo trace this right? It is obvious, that it is an incident of sovereignty, and is co-extensive with that to which it is an incident. All subjects over which the sovereign power of a state extends, are objects of taxation; but those over which it does not extend, are, upon the soundest principles, exempt from taxation. This proposition may almost be pronounced self-evident.

The sovereignty of a state extends to everything which exists by its own authority, or is introduced by its permission; but does it extend to those means which are employed by congress to carry into execution powers conferred on that body by the people of the United States? We think it demonstrable, that it does not. Those powers are not given by the people of a single state. They are given by the people of the United States, to a government whose laws, made in pursuance of the constitution, are declared to be supreme. Consequently, the people of a single state cannot confer a sovereignty which will extend over them.

If we measure the power of taxation residing in a state, by the extent of sovereignty which the people of a single state possess, and can confer on its government, we have an intelligible standard, applicable to every case to which the power may be applied. We have a principle which leaves the power of taxing the people and property of a state unimpaired; which leaves to a state the command of all its resources, and which places beyond its reach, all those powers which are conferred by the people of the United States on the government of the Union, and all those means which are given for the purpose of carrying those powers into execution. We have a principle which is safe for the states, and safe for the Union. We are relieved, as we ought to be, from clashing sovereignty; from interfering powers; from a repugnancy between a right in one government to pull down, what there is an acknowledged right in another to build up; from the incompatibility of a right in one government to destroy, what there is a right in another to preserve. We are not driven to the perplexing inquiry, so unfit for the judicial department, what degree of taxation is the legitimate use, and what degree may amount to the abuse of the power. The attempt to use it on the means employed by the government of the Union, in pursuance of the constitution, is itself an abuse, because it is the usurpation of a power which the people of a single state cannot give. We find, then, on just theory, a total failure of this original right to tax the means employed by the government of the Union, for the execution of its powers. The right never existed, and the question whether it has been surrendered, cannot arise.

But, waiving this theory for the present, let us resume the inquiry, whether this power can be exercised by the respective states, consistently with a fair construction of the constitution? That the power to tax involves the power to destroy; that the power to destroy may defeat and render useless the power to create; that there is a plain repugnance in conferring on one government a power to control the constitutional measures of another, which other, with respect to those very measures, is declared to be supreme over that which exerts the control, are propositions not to be denied. But all inconsistencies are to be reconciled by the magic of the word *confidence*. Taxation, it is said, does not necessarily and unavoidably destroy. To carry it to the excess of destruction, would be an abuse, to presume which, would banish that confidence which is essential to all government. But is this a case of confidence? Would the people of any one state trust those of another with a power to control the most insignificant operations of their state government? We know they would not. Why, then, should we suppose, that the people of any one state should be willing to trust those of another with a power to control the operations of a government to which they have confided their most important and most valuable interests? In the legislature of the Union alone, are all represented. The legislature of the Union alone, therefore, can be trusted by the people with the power of controlling measures which concern all, in the confidence that it will not be abused. This, then, is not a case of confidence, and we must consider it is as it really is.

If we apply the principle for which the state of Maryland contends, to the constitution, generally, we shall find it capable of changing totally the character of that instrument. We shall find it capable of arresting all the measures of the government, and of prostrating it at the foot of the states. The American people have declared their constitution and the laws made in pursuance thereof, to be supreme; but this principle would transfer the supremacy, in fact, to the states. If the states may tax one instrument, employed by the government in the execution of its powers, they may tax any and every other instrument. They may tax the mail; they may tax the mint; they may tax patent-rights; they may tax the papers of the custom-house; they may tax judicial process; they may tax all the means employed by the government, to an excess which would defeat all the ends of government. This was not intended by the American people. They did not design to make their government dependent on the states.

Gentlemen says, they do not claim the right to extend state taxation to these objects. They limit their pretensions to property. But on what principle, is this distinction made? Those who make it have furnished no reason for it, and the principle for which they contend denies it. They contend, that the power of taxation has no other limit than is found in the 10th section of the 1st article of the constitution; that, with respect to everything else, the power of the states is supreme, and admits of no control. If this be true, the distinction between property and other subjects to which the power of taxation is applicable, is merely arbitrary, and can never be sustained. This is not all. If the controlling power of the states be established; if their supremacy as to taxation be acknowledged; what is to restrain their exercising control in any shape they may please to give it? Their sovereignty is not confined to taxation; that is not the only mode in which it might be displayed. The question is, in truth, a question of supremacy; and if the right of the states to tax the means employed by the general government be conceded, the declaration that the constitution, and the laws made in pursuance thereof, shall be the supreme law of the land, is empty and unmeaning declamation.

In the course of the argument, the Federalist has been quoted; and the opinions expressed by the authors of that work have been justly supposed to be entitled to great respect in expounding the constitution. No tribute can be paid to them which exceeds their merit; but in applying their opinions to the cases which may arise in the progress of our government, a right to judge of their correctness must be retained; and to understand the argument, we must examine the proposition it maintains, and the objections against which it is directed. The subject of those numbers, from which passages have been cited, is the unlimited power of taxation which is vested in the general government. The objection to this unlimited power, which the argument seeks to remove, is stated with fulness and clearness. It is, "that an indefinite power of taxation in the latter (the government of the Union) might, and probably would, in time, deprive the former (the government of the states) of the means of providing for their own necessities; and would subject them entirely to the mercy of the national legislature. As the laws of the Union are to become the supreme law of the land; as it is to have power to pass all laws that may be necessary for carrying into execution the authorities with which it is proposed to vest it; the national government might, at any time, abolish the taxes imposed for state objects, upon the pretence of an interference with its own. It might allege a necessity for doing this, in order to give efficacy to the national revenues; and thus, all the resources of taxation might, by degrees, become the subjects of federal monopoly, to the entire exclusion and destruction of the state governments."

The objections to the constitution which are noticed in these numbers, were to the undefined power of the government to tax, not to the incidental privilege of exempting its own measures from state taxation. The consequences apprehended from this undefined power were, that it would absorb all the objects of taxation, "to the exclusion and destruction of the state governments." The arguments of the Federalist are intended to prove the fallacy of these apprehensions; not to prove that the government was incapable of executing any of its powers, without exposing the means it employed to the embarrassments of state taxation. Arguments urged against these objections, and these apprehensions, are to be understood as relating to the points they mean to prove. Had the authors of those excellent essays been asked, whether they contended for that construction of the constitution, which would place within the reach of the states those measures which the government might adopt for the execution of its powers; no man, who has read their instructive pages, will hesitate to admit, that their answer must have been in the negative.

It has also been insisted, that, as the power of taxation in the general and state governments is acknowledged to be concurrent, every argument which would sustain the right of the general government to tax banks chartered by the states, will equally sustain the right of the states to tax banks chartered by the general government. But the two cases are not on the same reason. The people of all the states have created the general government, and have conferred upon it the general power of taxation. The people of all the states, and the states themselves, are represented in congress, and, by their representatives, exercise this power. When they tax the chartered institutions of the states, they tax their constituents; and these taxes must be uniform. But when a state taxes the operations of the government of the United States, it acts upon institutions created, not by their own constituents, but by people over whom they claim on control. It acts upon the measures of a government created by others as well as themselves, for the benefit of others in common with themselves. The difference is that which always exists, and always must exist, between the action of the whole on a part, and the action of a part of the whole—between the laws of a government declared to be supreme, and those of a government which, when in opposition to those laws, is not supreme.

But if the full application of this argument could be admitted, it might bring into question the right of congress to tax the state banks, and could not prove the rights of the states to tax the Bank of the United States.

The court has bestowed on this subject it most deliberate consideration. The result is a conviction that the states have no power, by taxation or otherwise, to retard, impede, burden, or in any manner control, the operations of the constitutional laws enacted by congress to carry into execution the powers vested in the general government. This is, we think, the unavoidable consequence of that supremacy which the constitution has declared. We are unanimously of opinion, that the law passed by the legislature of Maryland, imposing a tax on the Bank of the United States, is unconstitutional and void.

This opinion does not deprive the states of any resources which they originally possessed. It does not extend to a tax paid by the real property of the bank, in common with the other real property within the state, nor to a tax imposed on the interest which the citizens of Maryland may hold in this institution, in common with other property of the same description throughout the state. But this is a tax on the operations of the bank, and is, consequently, a tax on the operation of an instrument employed by the government of the Union to carry its powers into execution. Such a tax must be unconstitutional. Judgment.—This cause came on to be heard, on the transcript of the record of the court of appeals of the state of Maryland, and was argued by counsel: on consideration whereof, it is the opinion of this court, that the act of the legislature of Maryland is contrary to the constitution of the United States, and void; and therefore, that the said court of appeals of the state of Maryland erred, in affirming the judgment of the Baltimore country court, in which judgment was rendered against James W. McCulloch; but that the said court of appeals of Maryland ought to have reversed the said judgment of the said Baltimore country court, and ought to have given judgment for the said appellant, McCulloch: It is, therefore, adjudged and ordered, that the said judgement of the said court of appeals of the state of Maryland in this case, be, and the same hereby is, reversed and annulled. And this court, proceeding to render such judgment as the said court of appeals should have rendered; it is further adjudged and ordered, that the judgment of the said Baltimore county court be reversed and annulled, and that judgment be entered in the said Baltimore country court for the said James W. McCulloch.

Source:

Radford University. "McCulloch v. Maryland." Available on-line. URL: www.radford.edu/~mfranck/images/438%20fall% 202003/McCulloch.pdf. Accessed October 2003.

Missouri Compromise (Missouri Enabling Act), 1820

Legislation enacted by Congress on March 3, 1820, that admitted Maine to the Union as a free state and authorized Missouri to adopt a constitution with no restrictions on slavery. Missouri (acquired as part of the Louisiana Purchase) was admitted as a slaveholding state in 1821. The compromise prohibited slavery in the remaining territory of the Louisiana Purchase north of 36° 30′ east latitude. The measure, engineered by Speaker of the House Henry Clay, was designed to maintain the political balance between free and slave states, which had been equal in number in 1819. The Thomas Amendment provided for the return of fugitive slaves from above the compromise line, and the Taylor Amendment added that the civil rights and condition of servitude extant before the act's passage would remain unchanged. The compromise marked the beginning of the great national debate over slavery; it postponed the issue but failed to resolve it. The law was repealed in 1854 by the Kansas-Nebraska Act.

———————⌘———————

An Act

To authorize the people of the Missouri territory to form a constitution and state government, and for the admission of such state into the Union on an equal footing with the original states, and to prohibit slavery in certain territories.

Be it enacted That the inhabitants of that portion of the Missouri territory included within the boundaries hereinafter designated, be, and they are hereby, authorized to form for themselves a constitution and state government, and to assume such name as they shall deem proper; and the said state, when formed, shall be admitted into the Union, upon an equal footing with the original states, in all respects whatsoever.

Sec. 2. That the said state shall consist of all the territory included within the following boundaries, to wit: Beginning in the middle of the Mississippi river, on the parallel of thirty-six degrees of north latitude; thence west, along that parallel of latitude, to the St. Francois river;

thence up, and following the course of that river, in the middle of the main channel thereof, to the parallel of latitude of thirty-six degrees and thirty minutes; thence west, along the same, to a point where the said parallel is intersected by a meridian line passing through the middle of the mouth of the Kansas river, where the same empties into the Missouri river, thence, from the point aforesaid north, along the said meridian line, to the intersection of the parallel of latitude which passes through the rapids of the river Des Moines, making the said line to correspond with the Indian boundary line; thence east, from the point of intersection last aforesaid, along the said parallel of latitude, to the middle of the channel of the main fork of the said river Des Moines; thence down and along the middle of the main channel of the said river Des Moines, to the mouth of the same, where it empties into the Mississippi river; thence, due east, to the middle of the main channel of the Mississippi river; thence down, and following the course of the Mississippi river, in the middle of the main channel thereof, to the place of beginning: . . .

Sec. 3. That all free white male citizens of the United States, who shall have arrived at the age of twenty-one years, and have resided in said territory three months previous to the day of election, and all other persons qualified to vote for representatives to the general assembly of the said territory, shall be qualified to be elected, and they are hereby qualified and authorized to vote, and choose representatives to form a convention: . . .

✳   ✳   ✳

. . . Sec. 8. That in all that territory ceded by France to the United States, under the name of Louisiana, which lies north of thirty-six degrees and thirty minutes north latitude, not included within the limits of the state, contemplated by this act, slavery and involuntary servitude, otherwise than in the punishment of crimes, whereof the parties shall have been duly convicted, shall be, and is hereby, forever prohibited: *Provided always,* That any person escaping into the same, from whom labour or service is lawfully claimed, in any state or territory of the United States, such fugitive may be lawfully reclaimed and conveyed to the person claiming his or her labour or service as aforesaid.

Source:

Henry Steele Commager, ed. *Documents of American History.* New York: F.S. Crofts & Co., 1934.

James Kent, "Universal Suffrage," 1821

Speech delivered to the New York Constitutional Convention of 1821 by Chancellor James Kent, one of the most able jurists of his time, arguing against the extension of male suffrage. The convention was considering a proposal to abolish the property ownership requirement for suffrage. Kent argued that "the tendency of universal suffrage is to jeopardize the rights of property, and the principles of liberty." Despite such fierce criticism, the proposal was approved.

I am in favor of the amendment which has been submitted by my honorable colleague from Albany; and I must beg leave to trespass for a few moments upon the patience of the committee, while I state the reasons which have induced me to wish, that the senate should continue, as heretofore, the representative of the landed interest, and exempted from the control of universal suffrage. I hope what I may have to say will be kindly received, for it will be well intended. But, if I thought otherwise, I should still prefer to hazard the loss of the little popularity which I might have in this house, or out of it, than to hazard the loss of the approbation of my own conscience.

I have reflected upon the report of the select committee with attention and with anxiety. We appear to be disregarding the principles of the constitution, under which we have so long and so happily lived, and to be changing some of its essential institutions. I cannot but think that the considerate men who have studied the history of republics, or are read in lessons of experience, must look with concern upon our apparent disposition to vibrate from a well balanced government, to the extremes of the democratic doctrines. Such a broad proposition as that contained in the report, at the distance of ten years past, would have struck the public mind with astonishment and terror. So rapid has been the career of our vibration.

Let us recall our attention, for a moment, to our past history.

This state has existed for forty-four years under our present constitution, which was formed by those illustrious sages and patriots who adorned the revolution. It has wonderfully fulfilled all the great ends of civil government. During that long period, we have enjoyed in an eminent degree, the blessings of civil and religious liberty. We have had our lives, our privileges, and our property, protected. We have had a succession of wise and temperate legislatures. The code of our statute law has been again and again revised and corrected, and it may proudly bear a comparison with that of any other people. We have had, during that period, (though I am, perhaps, not the fittest person to say it) a regular, stable, honest, and enlightened administration of justice. All the peaceable pursuits of industry, and all the important interests of education and science, have been fostered and encouraged. We have trebled our numbers within the last twenty-five years, have displayed mighty resources, and have made unexampled progress in

the career of prosperity and greatness. Our financial credit stands at an enviable height; and we are now successfully engaged in connecting the great lakes with the ocean by stupendous canals, which excite the admiration of our neighbors, and will make a conspicuous figure even upon the map of the United States. These are some of the fruits of our present government; and yet we seem to be dissatisfied with our condition, and we are engaged in the bold and hazardous experiment of remodeling the constitution. Is it not fit and discreet: I speak as to wise men; is it not fit and proper that we should pause in our career, and reflect well on the immensity of the innovation in contemplation? Discontent in the midst of so much prosperity, and with such abundant means of happiness, looks like ingratitude, and as if we were disposed to arraign the goodness of Providence. Do we not expose ourselves to the danger of being deprived of the blessings we have enjoyed?—When the husbandman has gathered in his harvest, and has filled his barns and his granaries with the fruits of his industry, if he should then become discontented and unthankful, would he not have reason to apprehend, that the Lord of the harvest might come in his wrath, and with his lightning destroy them?

The senate has hitherto been elected by the farmers of the state—by the free and independent lords of the soil, worth at least $250 in freehold estate, over and above all debts charged thereon. The governor has been chosen by the same electors, and we have hitherto elected citizens of elevated rank and character. Our assembly has been chosen by freeholders, possessing a freehold of the value of $50, or by persons renting a tenement of the yearly value of $5, and who have been rated and actually paid taxes to the state. By the report before us, we propose to annihilate, at one stroke, all those property distinctions and to bow before the idol of universal suffrage. That extreme democratic principle, when applied to the legislative and executive departments of government, has been regarded with terror, by the wise men of every age because in every European republic, ancient and modern, in which it has been tried, it has terminated disastrously, and been productive of corruption, injustice, violence, and tyranny. And dare we flatter ourselves that we are a peculiar people, who can run the career of history, exempted from the passions which have disturbed and corrupted the rest of mankind? If we are like other races of men, with similar follies and vices, then I greatly fear that our posterity will have reason to deplore in sackcloth and ashes, the delusion of the day.

It is not my purpose at present to interfere with the report of the committee, so far as respects the qualifications of electors for governor and members of assembly. I shall feel grateful if we may be permitted to retain the stability and security of a senate, bottomed upon the freehold property of the state. Such a body, so constituted, may prove a sheet anchor amidst the future factions and storms of the republic. The great leading and governing interest of this state, is, at present, the agricultural; and what madness would it be to commit that interest to the winds. The great body of the people, are now the owners and actual cultivators of the soil. With that wholesome population we always expect to find moderation, frugality, order, honesty, and a due sense of independence, liberty, and justice. It is impossible that any people can lose their liberties by internal fraud or violence, so long as the country is parceled out among freeholders of moderate possessions, and those freeholders have a sure and efficient control in the affairs of the government. Their habits, sympathies, and employments, necessarily inspire them with a correct spirit of freedom and justice; they are the safest guardians of property and the laws: We certainly cannot too highly appreciate the value of the agricultural interest: It is the foundation of national wealth and power. According to the opinion of her ablest political economists, it is the surplus produce of the agriculture of England, that enables her to support her vast body of manufacturers, her formidable fleets and armies, and the crowds of persons engaged in the liberal professions, and the cultivation of the various arts.

Now, sir, I wish to preserve our senate as the representative of the landed interest. I wish those who have an interest in the soil, to retain the exclusive possession of a branch in the legislature, as a strong hold in which they may find safety through all the vicissitudes which the state may be destined, in the course ,of Providence, to experience. I wish them to be always enabled to say that their freeholds cannot be taxed without their consent. The men of no property, together with the crowds of dependents connected with great manufacturing and commercial establishments, and the motley and undefinable population of crowded ports, may, perhaps, at some future day, under skillful management, predominate in the assembly, and yet we should be perfectly safe if no laws could pass without the free consent of the owners of the soil. That security we at present enjoy; and it is that security which I wish to retain.

The apprehended danger from the experiment of universal suffrage applied to the whole legislative department, is no dream of the imagination. It is too mighty an excitement for the moral constitution of men to endure. The tendency of universal suffrage, is to jeopardize the rights of property, and the principles of liberty. There is a constant tendency in human society, and the history of every age proves it; there is a tendency in the poor to covet and to share the plunder of the rich; in the debtor to relax or avoid the obligation of contracts; in the majority to tyrannize over the minority, and trample down their rights; in

the indolent and the profligate, to cast the whole burthens of society upon the industrious and the virtuous; and *there is a tendency in ambitious and wicked men, to inflame these combustible materials*. It requires a vigilant government, and a firm administration of justice, to counteract that tendency. Thou shalt not covet; thou shalt not steal; are divine injunctions induced by this miserable depravity of our nature. Who can undertake to calculate with any precision, how many millions of people, this great state will contain in the course of this and the next century, and who can estimate the future extent and magnitude of our commercial ports? The disproportion between the men of property, and the men of no property, will be in every society in a ratio to its commerce, wealth, and population. We are no longer to remain plain and simple republics of farmers, like the New-England colonists, or the Dutch settlements on the Hudson. We are fast becoming a great nation, with great commerce, manufactures, population, wealth, luxuries, and with the vices and miseries that they engender. One seventh of the population of the city of Paris at this day subsists on charity, and one third of the inhabitants of that city die in the hospitals; what would become of such a city with universal suffrage? France has upwards of four, and England upwards of five millions of manufacturing and commercial laborers without property. Could these kingdoms sustain the weight of universal suffrage" The radicals in England, with the force of that mighty engine, would at once sweep away the property, the laws, and the liberties of that island like a deluge.

The growth of the city of New-York is enough to startle and awaken those who are pursuing the *ignis fatuus* of universal suffrage.

In 1773 it had 21,000 souls. 1801 " 60,000 do. 1806 " 76,000 do. 1820 " 123,000 do.

It is rapidly swelling into the unwieldly population, and with the burdensome pauperism, of an European metropolis. New-York is destined to become the future London of America; and in less than a century, that city, with the operation of universal suffrage, and under skillful direction, will govern this state. The notion that every man that works a day on the road, or serves an idle hour in the militia, is entitled as of right to an equal participation in the whole power of the government, is most unreasonable, and has no foundation in justice. We had better at once discard from the report such a nominal test of merit. If such persons have an equal share in one branch of the legislature, it is surely as much as they can in justice or policy demands. Society is an association for the protection of property as well as of life, and the individual who contributes only one cent to the common stock, ought not to have the same power and influence in directing the property concerns of the partnership, as he who contributes his thousands. He will not have the same inducements to care, and diligence, and fidelity. His inducements and his temptation would be to divide the whole capital upon the principles of an agrarian law.

Liberty, rightly understood, is an inestimable blessing, but liberty without wisdom, and without justice, is no better than wild and savage licentiousness. The danger which we have hereafter to apprehend, is not the want, but the abuse, of liberty. We have to apprehend the oppression of minorities, and a disposition to encroach on private right—to disturb chartered privileges—and to weaken, degrade, and overawe the administration of justice; we have to apprehend this establishment of unequal, and consequently, unjust systems of taxation, and all the mischiefs of a crude and mutable legislation. A stable senate, exempted from the influence of universal suffrage, will powerfully check these dangerous propensities, and such a check becomes the more necessary, since this Convention has already determined to withdraw the watchful eye of the judicial department from the passage of laws. We are destined to become a great manufacturing as well as commercial state. We have already numerous and prosperous factories of one kind or another, and one master capitalist with his one hundred apprentices, and journeymen, and agents, and dependents, will bear down at the polls, an equal number of farmers of small estates in his vicinity, who cannot safely unite for their common defense. Large manufacturing and mechanical establishments, can act in an instant with the unity and efficacy of disciplined troops. It is against such combinations, among others, that I think we ought to give to the freeholders, or those who have interest in land, one branch of the legislature for their asylum and their comfort. Universal suffrage once granted, is granted forever, and never can be recalled. There is no retrograde step in the rear of democracy. However mischievous the precedent may be in its consequences, or however fatal in its effects, universal suffrage never can be recalled or checked, but by the strength of the bayonet. We stand, therefore, this moment, on the brink of fate, on the very edge of the precipice. If we let go our present held on the senate, we commit our proudest hopes and our most precious interests to the waves.

It ought further to be observed, that the senate is a court of justice in the last resort. It is the last depository of public and private rights; of civil and criminal justice. This gives the subject an awful consideration, and wonderfully increases the importance of securing that house from the inroads of universal suffrage. Our country freeholders are exclusively our jurors in the administration of justice, and there is equal reason that none but those who have an interest in the soil, should have any concern in the composition of that court. As long as the senate is safe, justice is safe, property is safe, and our liberties are safe. But when the wisdom, the integrity, and the independence of that court is lost, we may be certain that the freedom and happiness of this state, are fled forever.

I hope, sir, we shall not carry desolation through all the departments of the fabric erected by our fathers. I hope we shall not put forward to the world a new constitution, as will meet with the scorn of the wise, and the tears of the patriot.

Source:

Reports of the Proceedings and Debates of the Convention of 1821, Assembled for the Purpose of Amending the Constitution of the State of New York. Albany: E. and E. Hosford, 1821.

Resolves of the Nashville Convention of 1823

Resolutions issued by the General Assembly of the state of Tennessee on November 1, 1823, condemning the party caucus method used to elect the president. This protest declared that "the practice of congressional nominations is a violation of the spirit of the Constitution of the United States." Tennessee resolved that the president should be elected by "the people themselves, through the medium of electors chosen by them." Following the 1824 election and the controversial victory of John Quincy Adams, the caucus system was abandoned and replaced by nominations by state legislatures.

Mr. Grundy offered the following resolutions, which were read and laid on the table, under the rule of the house, which requires all resolutions to lie on the table for one day:

The general assembly of the state of Tennessee has taken into consideration the practice which, on former occasions, has prevailed at the city of Washington, of members of the congress of the United States meeting in Caucus, and nominating persons to be voted for as president and vice-president of the United States: and, upon the best view of the subject which this general assembly has been enabled to take, it is believed that the practice of congressional nominations is a violation of the spirit of the constitution of the United States.

That instrument provides that there shall be three separate and distinct departments of the government and great care and caution seems of have been exercised by its framers to prevent any one department from exercising the smallest degree of influence over another; and such solicitude was felt on this subject, that, in the second section of the second article, it is expressly declared, "That no *senator or representative,* or person holding an office of trust or profit under the United States, shall be appointed an elector. From this provision, it is apparent that the convention intended that the members of congress should not be the principal and primary agents or actors in electing the president and vice- president of the United States—so far from it, they are expressly disqualified from being placed in a situation to vote for those high officers. Is there not more danger of undue influence to be apprehended, when the members of congress meet in caucus and mutually and solemnly pledge themselves to support the individuals who may have the highest number of votes in such meeting, than there would be in permitting them to be eligible to the appointment of electors? In the latter case, a few characters, rendered ineligible by the constitution, might succeed; but, in the former, a powerful combination of influential men is formed, who may fix upon the American people their highest officers against the consent of a clear majority of the people themselves; and this may be done by the very men whom the constitution intended to prohibit from acting on the subject. Upon an examination of the constitution of the United States, there is but one case in which the members of congress are permitted to act, which is in the event of a failure to make an election by the electoral colleges: and then the members of the house of representatives vote by states. With that propriety the same men, who, in the year 1825, may be called on to discharge a constitutional duty, can, in the year 1824, go into a caucus and pledge themselves to support the men then nominated, cannot be discerned, especially when it might so happen that the persons thus nominated, could, under any circumstances, obtain a single vote from the state whose members stand pledged to support them.

It said that an election by the house of representatives would be a dangerous occurrence, which ought to be avoided. If so, let the constitution be so changed as to avoid it; but so long as the constitution directs one mode of electing officers, let not a different mode prevail in practice. When the history of the American government is looked into, with an eye to this subject, the apprehended danger disappears. Experience long since pointed out the inconveniences of the original provision in the constitution on this subject. An amendment, calculated, as was supposed, to remove every obstacle, was proposed by our wisest statesmen—it was adopted by the American people, and no difficulty has presented itself in subsequent practice. Shall a fear, that the amendment made may fail to answer the end proposed by it, induce us to adopt a course, or persist in a practice, which is manifestly an evasion of the constitution and a direct infraction of the spirit of one of its most important provisions?

It has been said, that the members of congress in caucus only recommend to the people for whom to vote, and that such recommendation is not obligatory. This is true, and clearly proves that it is a matter which does not belong to them—that, in recommending candidates, they go beyond the authority committed to them as members of congress, and thus transcend the trust delegated to them by their constituents. If their acts had any obligatory force, then the authority must be derived from some part of the constitution of the United States, and might be rightfully exercised; but when they say the only *recommend,* it is admission, on their part, that they are acting without authority and are attempting, by an usurped influence, to effect an objects not confided to them, and not within their powers, even by implication. It cannot be admitted that there is any weight in the argument drawn from the fact, that both the parties, heretofore contending for the superiority in the United States, have, in former times, resorted to this practice. The actions of public or private men, heated by party zeal and struggling for ascendency and power, ought not to be urged as precedents, when circumstances have entirely changed. All political precedents are of doubtful authority, and should never be permitted, to pass unquestioned, unless made in good times and for laudable purposes. In palliation of the practice of resorting to caucus nominations in former times, it was said that each party must of necessity consult together in the best practicable way, and select the most suitable persons from their respective parties, so that the united efforts of all those composing it might be brought to bear upon their opponents. It is to be recollected that there is no danger of a departure from, or violation of the constitution, except when strong temptations are presented, and this will seldom occur, except when parties are arrayed against each other, and their feelings violently excited. The state of things, however, in the United States is entirely changed it is no longer a selection made by members of congress of different parties, but it is an election by the two houses of congress, in which all the members must be permitted to attend and vote. It is not difficult to perceive that this practice may not promote and place men in office, who could not be elected were the constitutional mode pursued. It is placing the election of president and vice president of the United States—an election in which all the states have an equal interest and equal rights, more in the power of a few of the most populous states that was contemplated by the constitution. This practice is considered objectionable on other accounts: so long as congress is considered as composed of the individuals on whom the election depends, the executive will is subjected to the control of that body, and it ceases, in some degree, to be separate and independent branch of the government; and an expectation of executive patronage may have an unhappy influence on the deliberations of congress.

Upon a review of the whole question, the following reasons, which admit of much amplification and enlargement, more than has been urged in the foregoing, might be conclusively relied on, to prove the impolicy and unconstitutionally of the congressionally nominations of candidates for the presidency and vice presidency of the United States.

1st. A caucus nomination is against the spirit of the constitution. 2d. It is both inexpedient and impolitic. 3d Members of congress may become the final electors, and therefore ought not to prejudge the case of pledging themselves previously to support particular candidates. 4th. It violates the equality intended to be secured by the constitution to the weaker states. 5th Caucus nominations may, in time, (by the interference of the states), acquire the force of precedents and become authoritive, and thereby endanger the liberties of the American people.

This general assembly, believing that the true spirit of the constitution will be best preserved by leaving the election of president and vice president to the *people themselves*, through the medium of electors chosen by them, uninfluenced by any previous nomination, made by members of congress, have adopted the following resolutions:

1st. *Resolved,* That the senators in congress from this state, be instructed, and our representatives be requested to use their exertions to prevent a nomination being made during the next session of congress, by the members thereof in caucus, of persons to fill the offices of president and vice president of the United States.

2d. *Resolved,* That the general assembly will, at its present session, divide the state into as many districts, in convenient form, as this state is entitled to electoral votes, for the purpose of closing an elector in each, to vote for president and vice president of the United States.

3d. *Resolved,* That the governor of this state transmit a copy of the foregoing preamble and resolutions to the executive of each of the United States, with a request that the same be laid before each of their respective legislatures.

4th. *Resolved,* That the governor transmit a copy to each of the senators and representatives in congress from this state.

On the reading this preamble and resolutions, some debate insued, running into the merits of the first resolution, which was, after presentation, amended by the mover, so as to read as above, and the whole was made the order of the day for Wednesday next.

Source:
Tennessee State Library and Archives. Nashville, Tenn.

Monroe Doctrine, 1823

Principles of U.S. foreign policy stated in a message to Congress by President James Monroe on December 2, 1823. In his doctrine, Monroe declared U.S. opposition to any further colonization of the Americas by European powers and to any European intervention in political affairs of the Western Hemisphere; he also stated the U.S. policy of noninterference in existing colonies and in European affairs. The doctrine was prompted by American concern with Russian expansion along the northwest coast of North America and fear that some European powers would seek to reassert colonial control in newly independent Latin American republics. It was modified in 1904 by the Roosevelt Corollary. Although it rarely influenced policy during the 19th century, the Monroe Doctrine has often been used to justify U.S. actions in 20th-century Latin America.

———————————⌇✥⌇———————————

Fellow-Citizens of the Senate and House of Representatives:

Many important subjects will claim your attention during the present session, of which I shall endeavor to give, in aid of your deliberations, a just idea in this communication. I undertake this duty with diffidence, from the vast extent of the interests on which I have to treat and of their great importance to every portion of our Union. I enter on it with zeal from a thorough conviction that there never was a period since the establishment of our Revolution when, regarding the condition of the civilized world and its bearing on us, there was greater necessity for devotion in the public servants to their respective duties, or for virtue, patriotism, and union in our constituents.

Meeting in you a new Congress, I deem it proper to present this view of public affairs in greater detail than might otherwise be necessary. I do it, however, with peculiar satisfaction, from a knowledge that in this respect I shall comply more fully with the sound principles of our Government. The people being with us exclusively the sovereign, it is indispensable that full information be laid before them on all important subjects, to enable them to exercise that high power with complete effect. If kept in the dark, they must be incompetent to it. We are all liable to error, and those who are engaged in the management of public affairs are more subject to excitement and to be led astray by their particular interests and passions than the great body of our constituents, who, living at home in the pursuit of their ordinary avocations, are calm but deeply interested spectators of events and of the conduct of those who are parties to them. To the people every department of the Government and every individual in each are responsible, and the more full their information the better they can judge of the wisdom of the policy pursued and of the conduct of each in regard to it. From their dispassionate judgment much aid may always be obtained, while their approbation will form the greatest incentive and most gratifying reward for virtuous actions, and the dread of their censure the best security against the abuse of their confidence. Their interests in all vital questions are the same, and the bond, by sentiment as well as by interest, will be proportionably strengthened as they are better informed of the real state of public affairs, especially in difficult conjunctures. It is by such knowledge that local prejudices and jealousies are surmounted, and that a national policy, extending its fostering care and protection to all the great interests of our Union, is formed and steadily adhered to.

A precise knowledge of our relations with foreign powers as respects our negotiations and transactions with each is thought to be particularly necessary. Equally necessary is it that we should form a just estimate of our resources, revenue, and progress is every kind of improvement connected with the national prosperity and public defense. It is by rendering justice to other nations that we may expect it from them. It is by our ability to resent injuries and redress wrongs that we may avoid them. The commissioners under the fifth article of the treaty of Ghent, having disagreed in their opinions respecting that portion of the boundary between the Territories of the United States and of Great Britain the establishment of which had been submitted to them, have made their respective reports in compliance with that article, that the same might be referred to the decision of a friendly power. It being manifest, however, that it would be difficult, if not impossible, for any power to perform that office without great delay and much inconvenience to itself, a proposal has been made by this Government, and acceded to by that of Great Britain, to endeavor to establish that boundary by amicable negotiation. It appearing from long experience that no satisfactory arrangement could be formed of the commercial intercourse between the United States and the British colonies in this hemisphere by legislative acts while each party pursued its own course without agreement or concert with the other, a proposal has been made to the British Government to regulate his commerce by treaty, as it has been to arrange in like manner the just claim of the citizens of the United States inhabiting the States and Territories bordering on the lakes and rivers which empty into the St. Lawrence to the navigation of that river to the ocean. For these and other objects of high importance to the interests of both parties a negotiation has been opened with the British Government which it is hoped will have a satisfactory result.

The commissioners under the sixth and seventh articles of the treaty of Ghent having successfully closed their labors in relation to the sixth, have proceeded to the discharge of those relating to the seventh. Their progress in the extensive survey required for the performance of their duties justifies the presumption that it will be completed in the ensuing year.

The negotiation which had been long depending with the French Government on several important subjects, and particularly for a just indemnity for losses sustained in the late wars by the citizens of the United States under unjustifiable seizures and confiscations of their property, has not as yet had the desired effect. As this claim rests on the same principle with others which have been admitted by the French Government, it is not perceived on what just ground it can be rejected. A minister will be immediately appointed to proceed to France and resume the negotiation on this and other subjects which may arise between the two nations.

At the proposal of the Russian Imperial Government, made through the minister of the Emperor residing here, a full power and instructions have been transmitted to the minister of the United States at St. Petersburg to arrange by amicable negotiation the respective rights and interest of the two nations on the northwest coast of this continent. A similar proposal had been made by His Imperial Majesty to the Government of Great Britain, which has likewise been acceded to. The Government of the United States has been desirous by this friendly proceeding of manifesting the great value which they have invariably attached to the friendship of the Emperor and their solicitude to cultivate the best understanding with his Government. In the discussions to which this interest has given rise and in the arrangements by which they may terminate the occasion has been judged proper for asserting, as a principle in which the rights and interests of the United States are involved, that the American continents, by the free and independent condition which they have assumed and maintain, are henceforth not to be considered as subjects for future colonization by any European powers.)

Since the close of the last session of Congress the commissioners and arbitrators for ascertaining and determining the amount of indemnification which may be due to citizens of the United States under the decision of His Imperial Majesty the Emperor of Russia, in conformity to the convention concluded at St. Petersburg on the 12th of July, 1822, have assembled in this city, and organized themselves as a board for the performance of the duties assigned to them by that treaty. The commission constituted under the eleventh article of the treaty of the 22d of February, 1819, between the United States and Spain is also in session here, and as the term of three years limited by the treaty for the execution of the trust will expire before the period of the next regular meeting of Congress, the attention of the Legislature will be drawn to the measures which may be necessary to accomplish the objects for which the commission was instituted. In compliance with a resolution of the House of Representatives adopted at their last session, instructions have been given to all the ministers of the United States accredited to the powers of Europe and America to propose the proscription of the African slave trade by classing it under the denomination, and inflicting on its perpetrators the punishment, of piracy. Should this proposal be acceded to, it is not doubted that this odious and criminal practice will be promptly and entirely suppressed. It is earnestly hoped that it will be acceded to, from the firm belief that it is the most effectual expedient that can be adopted for the purpose.

At the commencement of the recent war between France and Spain it was declared by the French Government that it would grant no commissions to privateers, and that neither the commerce of Spain herself nor of neutral nations should be molested by the naval force of France, except in the breach of a lawful blockade. This declaration, which appears to have been faithfully carried into effect, concurring with principles proclaimed and cherished by the United States from the first establishment of their independence, suggested the hope that the time had arrived when the proposal for adopting it as a permanent and invariable rule in all future maritime wars might meet the favorable consideration of the great European powers. Instructions have accordingly been given to our ministers with France, Russia, and Great Britain to make those proposals to their respective Governments, and when the friends of humanity reflect on the essential amelioration to the condition of the human race which would result from the abolition of private war on the sea and on the great facility by which it might by accomplished, requiring only the consent of a few sovereigns, a earnest hope is indulged that these overtures will meet with an attention animated by the spirit in which they were made, and that they will ultimately be successful.

The ministers who were appointed to the Republics of Colombia and Buenos Ayres during the last session of Congress proceeded shortly afterwards to their destinations. Of their arrival there official intelligence has not yet been received. The minister appointed to the Republic of Chile will sail in a few days. An early appointment will also be made to Mexico. A minister has been received from Colombia, and the other Governments have been informed that ministers, or diplomatic agents of inferior grade, would be received from each, accordingly as they might prefer the one or the other.

The minister appointed to Spain proceeded soon after his appointment for Cadiz, the residence of the Sovereign to whom he was accredited. In approaching that port the frigate which conveyed him was warned off by the commander of the French squadron by which it was blockaded and not permitted to enter, although

appraised by the captain of the frigate of the public character of the person whom he had on board, the landing of whom was the sole object of his proposed entry. This act, being considered an infringement of the rights of ambassadors and of nations, will form a just cause of complaint to the Government of France against the officer by whom it was committed.

The actual condition of the public finances more than realizes the favorable anticipations that were entertained of it at the opening of the last session of Congress. On the 1st of January there was a balance in the Treasury of $4,237,427.55. From that time to the 30th September the receipts amounted to upward of $16,100,000, and the expenditures to $11,400,000. During the fourth quarter of the year it is estimated that the receipts will at least equal the expenditures, and that there will remain in the Treasury on the 1st day of January next a surplus of nearly $9,000,000.

On the 1st of January, 1825, a large amount of the war debt and a part of the Revolutionary debt become redeemable. Additional portions of the former will continue to become redeemable annually until the year 1835. It is believed, however, that if the United States remain at peace the whole of that debt may be redeemed by the ordinary revenue of those years during that period under the provision of the act of March 3, 1817, creating the sinking fund, and in that case the only part of the debt that will remain after the year 1835 will be the $7,000,000 of 5 per cent stock subscribed to the Bank of the United States, and the 3 per cent Revolutionary debt, amounting to $13,296,099.06, both of which are redeemable at the pleasure of the Government.

The state of the Army in its organization and discipline has been gradually improving for several years, and has now attained a high degree of perfection. The military disbursements have been regularly made and the accounts regularly and promptly rendered for settlement. The supplies for various descriptions have been of good quality, and regularly issued at all of the posts. A system of economy and accountability has been introduced into every branch of the service which admits of little additional improvement. This desirable state has been attained by the act reorganizing the staff of the Army, passed on the 14th of April, 1818.

The moneys appropriated for fortifications have been regularly and economically applied, and all the works advanced as rapidly as the amount appropriated would admit. Three important works will be completed in the course of this year—that is, Fort Washington, Fort Delaware, and the fort at the Rigolets, in Louisiana.

The Board of Engineers and the Topographical Corps have been in constant and active service in surveying the coast and projecting the works necessary for its defense.

The Military Academy, has attained a degree of perfection in its discipline and instruction equal, as is believed, to any institution of its kind in any country.

The money appropriated for the use of the Ordnance Department has been regularly and economically applied. The fabrication of arms at the national armories and by contract with the Department has been gradually improving in quality and cheapness. It is believed that their quality is now such as to admit of but little improvement.

The completion of the fortifications renders it necessary that there should be a suitable appropriation for the purpose of fabricating the cannon and carriages necessary for those works.

Under the appropriation of $5,000 for exploring the Western waters for the location of a site for a Western armory, a commission was constituted, consisting of Colonel McRee, Colonel Lee, and Captain Talcott, who have been engaged in exploring the country. They have not yet reported the result of their labors, but it is believed that they will be prepared to do it at an early part of the session of Congress.

During the month of June last General Ashley and his party, who were trading under a license from the Government, were attacked by the Ricarees while peaceably trading with the Indians at their request. Several of the party were killed and wounded and their property taken or destroyed.

Colonel Leavenworth, who commanded Fort Atkinson, at the Council, Bluffs, the most western post, apprehending that the hostile spirit of the Ricarees would extend to other tribes in that quarter, and that thereby the lives of the traders on the Missouri and the peace of the frontier would be endangered, took immediate measures to check the evil.

With a detachment of the regiment stationed at the Bluffs he successfully attacked the Ricaree village, and it is hoped that such an impression has been made on them as well as on the other tribes on the Missouri as will prevent a recurrence of future hostility.

The report of the Secretary of War, which is herewith transmitted, will exhibit in greater detail the condition of the Department in its various branches, and the progress which has been made in its administration during the three first quarters of the year.

I transmit a return of the militia of the several States according to the last reports which have been made by the proper officers in each to the Department of War. By reference to this return it will be seen that it is not complete, although great exertions have been made to make it so. As the defense and even the liberties of the country must depend in times of imminent danger on the militia, it is of the highest importance that it be well organized, armed, and disciplined throughout the Union. The report of the

Secretary of War shews the progress made during the three first quarters of the present year by the application of the fund appropriated for arming the militia. Much difficult is found in distributing the arms according to the act of Congress providing for it from the failure of the proper departments in many of the States to make regular returns. The act of May 12, 1820, provides that the system of tactics and regulations of the various corps of the Regular Army shall be extended to the militia. This act has been very imperfectly executed from the want of uniformity in the organization of the militia, proceeding from the defects of the system itself, and especially in its application to that main arm of the public defense. It is thought that this important subject in all its branches merits the attention of Congress.

The report of the Secretary of the Navy, which is now communicated, furnishes an account of the administration of that Department for the three first quarters of the present year, with the progress made in augmenting the Navy, and the manner in which the vessels in commission have been employed.

The usual force has been maintained in the Mediterranean Sea, the Pacific Ocean, and along the Atlantic coast, and has afforded the necessary protection to our commerce in those seas.

In the West Indies and the Gulf of Mexico our naval force has been augmented by the addition of several small vessels provided for by the "act authorizing an additional naval force for the suppression of piracy," passed by Congress at their last session. That armament has been eminently successful in the accomplishment of its object. The piracies by which our commerce in the neighborhood of the island of Cuba had been afflicted have been repressed and the confidence of our merchants in a great measure restored.

The patriotic zeal and enterprise of Commodore Porter, to whom the command of the expedition was confided, has been fully seconded by the officers and men under his command. And in reflecting with high satisfaction on the honorable manner in which they have sustained the reputation of their country and its Navy, the sentiment is alloyed only by a concern that in the fulfillment of that arduous service the diseases incident to the season and to the climate in which it was discharged have deprived the nation of many useful lives, and among them of several officers of great promise.

In the month of August a very malignant fever made its appearance at Thompsons Island, which threatened the destruction of our station there. Many perished, and the commanding officer was severely attacked. Uncertain as to his fate and knowing that most of the medical officers had been rendered incapable of discharging their duties, it was thought expedient to send to that post an officer of rank and experience, with several skillful surgeons, to ascertain the origin of the fever and the probability of its recurrence there in future seasons; to furnish every assistance to those who were suffering, and, if practicable, to avoid the necessity of abandoning so important a station. Commodore Rodgers, with a promptitude which did him honor, cheerfully accepted that trust, and has discharged it in the manner anticipated from his skill and patriotism. Before his arrival Commodore Porter, with the greater part of the squadron, had removed from the island and returned to the United States in consequence of the prevailing sickness. Much useful information has, however, been obtained as to the state of the island and great relief afforded to those who had been necessarily left there.

Although our expedition, cooperating with an invigorated administration of the government of the island of Cuba, and with the corresponding active exertions of a British naval force in the same seas, have almost entirely destroyed the unlicensed piracies from that island, the success of our exertions has not been equally effectual to suppress the same crime, under other pretenses and colors, in the neighboring island of Porto Rico. They have been committed there under the abusive issue of Spanish commissions. At an early period of the present year remonstrances were made to the governor of that island, by an agent who was sent for the purpose, against those outrages on the peaceful commerce of the United States, of which many had occurred. That officer, professing his own want of authority to make satisfaction for our just complaints, answered only by a reference of them to the Government of Spain. The minister of the United States to that court was specially instructed to urge the necessity of the immediate and effectual interposition of that Government, directing restitution and indemnity for wrongs already committed and interdicting the repetition of them. The minister, as has been seen, was debarred access to the Spanish Government, and in the meantime several new cases of flagrant outrage have occurred, and citizens of the United States in the island of Porto Rico have suffered, and others been threatened with assassination for asserting their unquestionable rights even before the lawful tribunals of the country.

The usual orders have been given to all our public ships to seize American vessels engaged in the slave in the trade and bring them in for adjudication, and I have the gratification to state that not one so employed has been discovered, and there is good reason to believe that our flag is now seldom, if at all, disgraced by that traffic.

It is a source of great satisfaction that we are always enabled to recur to the conduct of our Navy with pride and commendation. As a means of national defense it enjoys the public confidence, and is steadily assuming additional importance. It is submitted whether a more efficient and equally economical organization of it might not in several respects be effected. It is supposed that higher grades than now exist by law would be useful. They would afford well-merited rewards to those who have long and faithfully served their country, present the best incentives to good conduct, and the best means of insuring a proper discipline: destroy the inequality in that respect between military and naval services, and relieve our officers from many inconveniences and mortifications which occur when our vessels meet those of other nations, ours being the only service in which such grades do not exist.

A report of the Postmaster-General, which accompanies this communication, will shew the present state of the Post-Office Department and its general operations for some years past.

There is established by law 88,600 miles of post-roads, on which the mail is now transported 85,700 miles, and contracts have been made for its transportation on all the established routes, with one or two exceptions. There are 5,240 post-offices in the Union, and as many postmasters. The gross amount of postage which accrued from the 1st July, 1822, to the 1st July, 1823, was $1,114,345.12. During the same period the expenditures of the Post-Office Department amounted to $1,169,885.51, and consisted of the following items, viz: Compensation to postmasters, $353,995.98; incidental expenses, $30,866.37; transportation of the mail, $784,600.08; payments into the Treasury, $423.08. On the 1st of July last there was due to the Department from postmasters $135,245.28; from *late* postmasters and contractors, $256,749.31; making a total amount of balances due to the Department of $391,994.59. These balances embrace all delinquencies of postmasters and contractors which have taken place since the organization of the Department. There was due by the Department to contractors on the 1st of July last $26,548.64.

The transportation of the mail within five years past has been greatly extended, and the expenditures of the Department proportionably increased. Although the postage which has accrued within the last three years has fallen short of the expenditures $262,821.46, it appears that collections have been made from the outstanding balances to meet the principal part of the current demands.

It is estimated that not more than $250,000 of the above balances can be collected, and that a considerable part of this sum can only be realized by a resort to legal process. Some improvement in the receipts for postage is expected. A prompt attention to the collection of moneys received by postmasters, it is believed, will enable the Department to continue its operations without aid from the Treasury, unless the expenditures shall be increased by the establishment of new mail routes.

A revision of some parts of the post-office law may be necessary; and it is submitted whether it would not be proper to provide for the appointment of postmasters, where the compensation exceeds a certain amount, by nomination to the Senate, as other officers of the General Government are appointed. Having communicated my views to Congress at the commencement of the last session respecting the encouragement which ought to be given to our manufactures and the principle on which it should be founded, I have only to add that those views remain unchanged, and that the present state of those countries with which we have the most immediate political relations and greatest commercial intercourse tends to confirm them. Under this impression I recommend a review of the tariff for the purpose of affording such additional protection to those articles which we are prepared to manufacture, or which are more immediately connected with the defense and independence of the country.

The actual state of the public accounts furnishes additional evidence of the efficiency of the present system of accountability in relation to the public expenditure. Of the moneys drawn from the Treasury since the 4th March, 1817, the sum remaining unaccounted for on the 30th of September last is more than a million and a half of dollars less than on the 30th of September preceding; and during the same period a reduction of nearly a million of dollars has been made in the amount of the unsettled accounts for moneys advanced previously to the 4th of March, 1817. It will be obvious that in proportion as the mass of accounts of the latter description is diminished by settlement the difficulty of settling the residue is increased from the consideration that in many instances it can be obtained only by legal process. For more precise details on this subject I refer to a report from the First Comptroller of the Treasury.

The sum which was appropriated at the last session for the repairs of the Cumberland road has been applied with good effect to that object. A final report has not yet been received from the agent who was appointed to superintend it. As soon as it is received it shall be communicated to Congress.

Many patriotic and enlightened citizens who have made the subject an object of particular investigation have suggested an improvement of still greater importance. They are of opinion that the waters of the Chesapeake and Ohio may be connected together by one continued canal, and at an expense far short of the value and importance of the object to be obtained. If this could be accomplished it is impossible to calculate the beneficial consequences which would result from it. A great portion of the produce of the very fertile country through which it would pass would find a market through that channel. Troops might be moved with great facility in war, with cannon and every kind of munition, and in either direction. Connecting the Atlantic with the Western country in a line passing through the seat of the National Government, it would contribute essentially to strengthen the bond of union itself. Believing as I do that Congress possess the right to appropriate money for such a national object (the jurisdiction remaining to the States through which the canal would pass), I submit it to your consideration whether it may not be advisable to authorize by an adequate appropriation the employment of a suitable number of the officers of the Corps of Engineers to examine the unexplored ground during the next season and to report their opinion thereon. It will likewise be proper to extend their examination to the several routes through which the waters of the Ohio may be connected by canals with those of Lake Erie.

As the Cumberland road will require annual repairs, and Congress have not thought it expedient to recommend to the States an amendment to the Constitution for the purpose of vesting in the United States a power to adopt and execute a system of internal improvement, it is also submitted to your consideration whether it may not be expedient to authorize the Executive to enter into an arrangement with the several States through which the road passes to establish tolls, each within its limits, for the purpose of defraying the expense of future repairs and of providing also by suitable penalties for its protection against future injuries.

The act of Congress of the 7th of May, 1822, appropriated the sum of $22,700 for the purpose of erecting two piers as a shelter for vessels from ice near Cape Henlopen, Delaware Bay. To effect the object of the act the officers of the Board of Engineers, with Commodore Bainbridge, were directed to prepare plans and estimates of piers sufficient to answer the purpose intended by the act. It appears by their report, which accompanies the documents from the War Department, that the appropriation is not adequate to the purpose intended; and as the piers would be of great service both to the navigation of the Delaware Bay and the protection of vessels on the adjacent parts of the coast, I submit for the consideration of Congress whether additional and sufficient appropriation should not be made.

The Board of Engineers were also directed to examine and survey the entrance of the harbor of the port of Presquille, in Pennsylvania, in order to make an estimate of the expense of removing the obstructions to the entrance, with a plan of the best mode of effecting the same, under the appropriation for that purpose by act of Congress passed 3d of March last. The report of the Board accompanies the papers from the War Department, and is submitted for the consideration of Congress.

A strong hope has been long entertained, founded on the heroic struggle of the Greeks, that they would succeed in their contest and resume their equal station among the nations of the earth. It is believed that the whole civilized world take a deep interest in their welfare. Although no power has declared in their favor, yet none, according to our information, has taken part against them. Their cause and their name have protected them from dangers which might ere this have overwhelmed any other people. The ordinary calculations of interest and of acquisition with a view to aggrandizement, which mingles so much in the transactions of nations, seem to have had no effect in regard to them. From the facts which have come to our knowledge there is good cause to believe that their enemy has lost forever all dominion over them; that Greece will become again an independent nation. That she may obtain that rank is the object of our most ardent wishes.

It was stated at the commencement of the last session that a great effort was then making in Spain and Portugal to improve the condition of the people of those countries, and that it appeared to be conducted with extraordinary moderation. It need scarcely be remarked that the result has been so far very different from what was then anticipated. Of events in that quarter of the globe, with which we have so much intercourse and from which we derive our origin, we have always been anxious and interested spectators. The citizens of the United States cherish sentiments the most friendly in favor of the liberty and happiness of their fellow-men on that side of the Atlantic. In the wars of the European powers in matters relating to themselves we have never taken any part, nor does it comport with our policy so to do. It is only when our rights are invaded or seriously menaced that we resent injuries or make preparation for our defense. With the movements in this hemisphere we are of necessity more immediately connected, and by causes which must be obvious to all enlightened and impartial observers. The political system of the allied powers is essentially different in this respect from that of America. This difference proceeds from that which exists in their respective Governments; and to the defense of our own, which has been achieved by the loss of so much blood and treasure, and matured by the wisdom of their most enlightened citizens, and under which we have enjoyed unexampled felicity, this whole nation is devoted. We owe it, therefore, to candor and to the amicable relations existing between the United States and those powers to declare that we should consider any attempt on their part to extend their system to any portion of this hemisphere as dangerous to our peace and safety. With the existing colonies or dependencies of any European power we have not interfered and shall not interfere. But with the Governments who have declared their independence and maintained it, and whose independence we have, on great consideration and on just principles, acknowledged, we could not view any interposition for the purpose of oppressing them, or controlling in any other manner their destiny, by any European power in any other light than as the manifestation of an unfriendly disposition toward the United States. In the war between those new Governments and Spain we declared our neutrality at the time of their recognition, and to this we have adhered, and shall continue to adhere, provided no change shall occur which, in the judgment of the competent authorities of this Government, shall make a corresponding change on the part of the United States indispensable to their security.

The late events in Spain and Portugal shew that Europe is still unsettled. Of this important fact no stronger proof can be adduced than that the allied powers should have thought it proper, on any principle satisfactory to themselves, to have interposed by force in the internal concerns of Spain. To what extent such interposition may be carried, on the same principle, is a question in which all independent powers whose governments differ from theirs are interested, even those most remote, and surely none more so than the United States. Our policy in regard to Europe, which was adopted at an early stage of the wars which, have so long agitated that quarter of the globe, nevertheless remains the same, which is, not to interfere in the internal concerns of any of its powers; to consider the government *de facto* as the legitimate government for us; to cultivate friendly relations with it, and to preserve those relations by a frank, firm, and manly policy, meeting in all instances the just claims of every power, submitting to injuries from none. But in regard to those continents circumstances are eminently and conspicuously different. It is impossible that the allied powers should extend their political system to any portion of either continent without endangering our peace and happiness; nor can anyone believe that our southern brethren, if left to themselves, would adopt it of their own accord. It is equally impossible, therefore, that we should behold such interposition in any form with indifference. If we look to the comparative strength and resources of Spain and those new Governments, and their distance from each other, it must be obvious that she can never subdue them. It is still the true policy of the United States to leave the parties to themselves, in the hope that other powers will pursue the same course.

If we compare the present condition of our Union with its actual state at the close of our Revolution, the history of the world furnishes no example of a progress in improvement in all the important circumstances which constitute the happiness of a nation which bears any resemblance to it. At the first epoch our population did not exceed 3,000,000. By the last census it amounted to about 10,000,000, and, what is more extraordinary, it is almost altogether native, for the immigration from other countries has been inconsiderable. At the first epoch half the territory within our acknowledged limits was uninhabited and a wilderness. Since then new territory has been acquired of vast extent, comprising within it many rivers, particularly the Mississippi, the navigation of which to the ocean was of the highest importance to the original States. Over this territory our population has expanded in every direction, and new States have been established almost equal in number to those which formed the first bond of our Union. This expansion of our population and accession of new States to our Union have had the happiest effect on all its highest interests. That it has eminently augmented our resources and added to our strength and respectability as a power is admitted by all. But it is not in these important circumstances only that this happy effect is felt. It is manifest that by enlarging the basis of our system and increasing the number of States the system itself has been greatly strengthened in both its branches. Consolidation and disunion have thereby been rendered equally impracticable. Each Government, confiding in its own strength, has less to apprehend from the other, and in consequence each, enjoying a greater freedom of action, is rendered more efficient for all the purposes for which it was instituted. It is unnecessary to treat here of the vast improvement made in the system itself by the adoption of this Constitution and of its happy effect in elevating the character and in protecting the rights of the nation as well as of individuals. To what, then, do we owe these blessings? It is known to all that we derive them from the excellence of our institutions. Ought we not, then, to adopt every measure which may be necessary to perpetuate them?

Source:

James D. Richardson, ed. *A Compilation of the Messages and Papers of the Presidents, 1789–1897.* Washington, D.C.: Government Printing Office, 1896–99.

Henry Clay, "On Internal Improvement," 1824

Speech delivered by Henry Clay to the House of Representatives on January 16, 1824. Clay was addressing the debate concerning the role of the federal government in constructing works of internal improvement, such as surveying for roads and canals. With the rapid westward expansion, the need for a national transportation infrastructure was a hotly debated issue. Supporters of federal sponsorship, such as Clay, claimed the government should create, control, and fund such improvements because the benefits went to the entire nation. Opponents, fearful of big government and its invasion upon

states' rights, argued that each leg of the transportation network was a local municipal issue and should be approved and controlled by the locality it ran through.

President James Madison, as the last official act of his presidency, had vetoed federal legislation passed by Congress on March 3, 1817, to create a permanent fund for internal transportation improvements by using profits from the recently established second Bank of the United States. Madison argued that the U.S. Constitution did not authorize Congress to construct roads or canals or to improve waterways and suggested a constitutional amendment.

I cannot enter on the discussion of the subject before me, without first asking leave to express my thanks for the kindness of the committee, in so far accommodating me as to agree unanimously to adjourn its sitting to the present time, in order to afford me the opportunity of exhibiting my views; which, however, I fear I shall do very unacceptably. As a requital for this kindness, I will endeavor, as far as is practicable, to abbreviate what I have to present to your consideration. Yet, on a question of this extent and moment, there are so many topics which demand a deliberate examination, that, from the nature of the case, it will be impossible, I am afraid, to reduce the argument to any thing that the committee will consider a reasonable compass.

It is known to all who hear me, that there has now existed for several years a difference of opinion between the executive and legislative branches of this government, as to the nature and extent of certain powers conferred upon it by the constitution. Two successive Presidents have returned to Congress bills which had previously passed both houses of that body, with a communication of the opinion that Congress, under the constitution, possessed no power to enact such laws. High respect, personal and official, must be felt by all, as it is due, to those distinguished officers, and to their opinions, thus solemnly announced; and the most profound consideration belongs to our present Chief Magistrate, who has favored this House with a written argument, of great length and labor, containing not less than sixty or seventy pages, in support of his exposition of the constitution. From the magnitude of the interests involved in the question, all will readily concur, that, if the power is granted, and does really exist, it ought to be vindicated, upheld, and maintained, that the country may derive the great benefits which may flow from its prudent exercise. If it has not been communicated to Congress, then all claim to it should be at once surrendered. It is a circumstance of peculiar regret to me, that one more competent than myself has not risen to support the course which the legislative department has heretofore felt itself bound to pursue on this great question. Of all the trusts which are created by human agency, that is the highest, most solemn, and most responsible, which involves the exercise of political power. Exerted when it has not been intrusted, the public functionary is guilty of usurpation. And his infidelity to the public good is not, perhaps, less culpable, when he neglects or refuses to exercise a power which has been fairly conveyed, to promote the public prosperity. If the power, which he thus forbears to exercise, can only be exercised by him—if no other public functionary can employ it, and the public good requires its exercise, his treachery is greatly aggravated. It is only in those cases where the object of the investment of power is the personal ease or aggrandizement of the public agent, that his forbearance to use it is praiseworthy, gracious, or magnanimous.

I am extremely happy to find, that, on many of the points of the argument of the honorable gentleman from Virginia, there is entire concurrence between us, widely as we differ in our ultimate conclusions. On this occasion, (as on all others on which that gentleman obliges the House with an expression of his opinions,) he displays great ability and ingenuity; and, as well from the matter as from the respectful manner of his argument, it is deserving of the most thorough consideration. I am compelled to differ from that gentleman at the very threshhold. He commenced by laying down, as a general principle, that, in the distribution of powers among our federal and State governments, those which are of a municipal character are to be considered as appertaining to the State governments, and those which relate to external affairs, to the general government. If I may be allowed to throw the argument of the gentleman into the form of a syllogism, (a shape which I presume will be quite agreeable to him,) it amounts to this: Municipal powers belong exclusively to the State governments; but the power to make internal improvements is municipal; therefore it belongs to the State governments alone. I deny both the premises and the conclusion. If the gentleman had affirmed that certain municipal powers, and the great mass of them, belong to the State governments, his proposition would have been incontrovertible. But, if he had so qualified it, it would not have assisted the gentleman at all in his conclusion. But surely the power of taxation—the power to regulate the value of coin—the power to establish a uniform standard of weights and measures—to establish post-offices and post-roads—to regulate commerce among the several States—that in relation to the judiciary—besides many other powers indisputably belonging to the federal government, are strictly municipal. If, as I understood the gentleman in the course of the subsequent part of his argument to admit, some municipal powers belong to the one system, and some to the other, we shall derive, very little aid from the gentleman's princi-

ple, in making the discrimination between the two. The question must ever remain open—whether any given power, and, of course, that in question, is or is not delegated to this government, or retained by the States?

The conclusion of the gentleman is, that all internal improvements belong to the State governments; that they are of a limited and local character, and are not comprehended within the scope of the federal powers, which relate to external or general objects. That many, perhaps most internal improvements, partake of the character described by the gentleman, I shall not deny. But it is no less true that there are others, emphatically national, which neither the policy, nor the power, nor the interests of any State will induce it to accomplish, and which can only be effected by the application of the resources of the nation. The improvement of the navigation of the Mississippi furnishes a striking example. This is undeniably a great and important object. The report of a highly scientific and intelligent officer of the engineer corps, (which I hope will be soon taken up and acted upon,) shows that the cost of any practicable improvements in the navigation of that river, in the present state of the inhabitants of its banks, is a mere trifle in comparison to the great benefits which would accrue from it. I believe that about double the amount of the loss of a single steamboat and cargo, (the Tennessee,) would effect the whole improvement in the navigation of that river which ought to be at this time attempted. In this great object twelve States and two Territories are, in different degrees, interested. The power to effect the improvement of that river is surely not municipal, in the sense in which the gentleman uses the term. If it were, to which of the twelve States and two Territories concerned does it belong? It is a great object, which can only be effected by a confederacy. And here is existing that confederacy, and no other can lawfully exist; for the constitution prohibits the States, immediately interested, from entering into any treaty or compact with each other. Other examples might be given to show that, if even the power existed, the inclination to exert it would not be felt, to effectuate certain improvements eminently calculated to promote the prosperity of the Union. Neither of the three States, nor all of them united, through which the Cumberland road passes, would ever have erected that road. Two of them would have thrown in every impediment to its completion in their power. Federative in its character, it could only have been executed so far by the application of federative means. Again: the contemplated canal through New Jersey; that to connect the waters of the Chesapeake and Delaware; that to unite the Ohio and the Potomac, are all objects of a general and federative nature, in which the States through which they may severally pass cannot be expected to feel any such special interest as will lead to their execution. Tending, as undoubtedly they would do, to promote the good of the whole, the power and the treasure of the whole must be applied to their execution, if they are ever consummated.

I do not think, then, that we should be at all assisted in expounding the constitution of the United States, by the principle which the gentleman from Virginia has suggested in respect to municipal powers. The powers of both governments are undoubtedly municipal, often operating upon the same subject. I think a better rule than that which the gentleman furnished for interpreting the, constitution, might be deduced from an attentive consideration of the peculiar character of the articles of confederation, as contrasted with that of the present constitution. By those articles, the powers of the thirteen United States were exerted collaterally. They operated through an intermediary. They were addressed to the several States, and their execution depended upon the pleasure and the co-operation of the States individually. The States seldom fulfilled the expectations of the general government in regard to its requisitions, and often wholly disappointed them. Languor and debility, in the movement of the old confederation, were the inevitable consequence of that arrangement of power. By the existing constitution, the powers of the general government act directly on the persons and things within its scope, without the intervention or impediments incident to an intermediary. In executing the great trust which the constitution of the United States creates, we must, therefore, reject that interpretation of its provisions which would make the general government dependant upon those of the States for the execution of any of its powers, and may safely conclude that the only genuine construction would be that which should enable this government to execute the great purposes of its institution, without the co-operation, and, if indispensably necessary, even against the will of any particular State. This is the characteristic difference between the two systems of government, of which we should never lose sight. Interpreted in the one way, we shall relapse into the feebleness and debility of the old confederacy. In the other, we shall escape from its evils, and fulfil the great purposes which the enlightened framers of the existing constitution intended to effectuate. The importance of this essential difference in the two forms of government, will be shown in the future progress of the argument.

Before I proceed to comment on those parts of the constitution which appear to me to convey the power in question, I hope I shall be allowed to disclaim, for my part, several sources whence others have deduced the authority. The gentleman from Virginia seemed to think it remarkable that the friends of the power should disagree so much among themselves; and to draw a conclusion against its existence from the fact of this discrepancy. But I can see nothing extraordinary in this diversity of views. What is more common than for different men to contemplate the same subject under various aspects? Such is the nature of the human mind, that enlightened men, perfectly upright in their intentions, differ in their opinions on almost every topic that can be mentioned. It is rather a presumption in favor of the cause which I am humbly maintaining, that the same result is attained by so many various modes of reasoning. But, it contrariety of views might be pleaded with any effect against the advocates of the disputed power, it is equally available against our opponents. There is, for example, not a very exact coincidence in opinion between the President of the United States and the gentleman from Virginia. The President says, (page 25 of his book,)

"The use of the existing road, by the stage, mail-carrier, or post-boy, in passing over it, as others do, is all that would be thought of; the jurisdiction and soil remaining to the State, with a right in the State, or *those authorized by its legislature*, to *change* the road at *pleasure.*"

Again, page 27, the President asks:

"If the United States possessed the power contended for under this grant, might they not, in adopting the roads of the individual States, for the carriage of the mail, ?s has been done, assume jurisdiction over them, and preclude a right to interfere with or *alter* them?"

They both agree that the general government does not possess the power. The gentleman from Virginia admits, if I understood him correctly, that the designation of a State road as a post-road, so far withdraws it from the jurisdiction of the State, that it cannot be afterwards put down or closed by the State; and in this he claims for the general government more power than the President concedes to it. The President, on the contrary, pronounces, that "the absurdity of such a pretension" (that is, preventing, by the designation of a post-road, the power of the State from altering or changing, it) "must be apparent to all who examine it!" The gentleman thinks that the designation of a post-road withdraws it entirely, so far as it is used for that purpose, from the power of the whole State; whilst the President thinks it absurd to assert that a mere county court may not defeat the execution of a law of the United States! The President thinks that, under the power of appropriating the money of the United States, Congress may apply it to any object of internal improvement, provided it does not assume any territorial jurisdiction; and, in this respect, he claims for the general government more power than the gentleman from Virginia assigns to it. And I must own, that I so far coincide with the gentleman from Virginia. If the power can be traced to no more legitimate source than to that of appropriating the public treasure, I will yield the question.

The truth is, that there is no specific grant, in the constitution, of the power of appropriation; nor is any such requisite. It is a resulting power. The constitution vests in Congress the power of taxation, with but few limitations, to raise a public revenue. It then enumerates the powers of Congress. And it follows, of necessity that Congress has the right to apply the money, so raised, to the execution of the powers so granted. The clause which concludes the enumeration of the granted powers, by authorizing the passage of all laws, "necessary and proper" to effectuate them, comprehends the power of appropriation. And the framers of the constitution recognise it by the restriction that no money shall be drawn from the treasury but in virtue of a previous appropriation by law. It is to me wonderful how the President could have brought his mind to the conclusion, that, under the power of appropriation, thus incidentally existing, a right could be set up, in its nature almost without limitation, to employ the public money. He combats with great success and much ability, any deduction of power from the clause relating to the general welfare. He shows that the effect of it would be to overturn, or render useless and nugatory, the careful enumeration of our powers; and that it would convert a cautiously limited government into one without limitations. The same process of reasoning by which his mind was brought to this just conclusion, one would have thought, should have warned him against his claiming, under the power of appropriation, such a vast latitude of authority. He reasons strongly against the power, as claimed by us, harmless, and beneficent, and limited as it must be admitted to be, and yet he sets up a power boundless in its extent, unrestrained to the object of internal improvements, and comprehending the whole scope of human affairs! For, if the power exists, as he asserts it, what human restraint is there upon it? He does, indeed, say, that it cannot be exerted so as to interfere with the territorial jurisdiction of the States. But this is a restriction altogether gratuitous, flowing from the bounty of the President, and not found in the prescriptions of the constitution. If we have a right, indefinitely, to apply the money of the government to internal improvements, or to any other object, what is to prevent the application of it to the purchase of the sovereignty itself of a State if a State were mean enough to sell its sovereignty—to the purchase of kingdoms, empires, the globe itself? With an almost unlimited power of taxation, and, after the revenue is raised, with a right to apply it under no other limitations than those which the President's caution has suggested, I cannot see what other human power is needed. It has been said, by Caesar or Bonaparte, no doubt thought by both, that with soldiers enough, they could get money enough; and, with money enough, they could command soldiers enough. According to the President's interpretation of the constitution, one of these great levers of public force and power is possessed by this government. The President seems to contemplate, as fraught with great danger, the power, humbly as it is claimed, to effect the internal improvement of the country, and, in his attempt to overthrow it, sets up one of infinitely greater magnitude. The quantum of power which we claim over the subject of internal improvement, is, it is true, of greater amount and force than that which results from the President's view of the constitution; but then it is *limited* to the object of internal improvements; whilst the power set up by the President has no such limitation; and, in effect, as I conceive, has no limitation whatever, but that of the ability of the people to bear taxation.

With the most profound respect for the President, and after the most deliberate consideration of his argument, I cannot agree with him. I cannot think that any political power accrues to this government, from the mere authority which it possesses to appropriate the public revenue. The power to make internal improvements draws after it, most certainly, the right to appropriate money to consummate the object. But I cannot conceive that this right of appropriation draws after it the power of internal improvements. The appropriation of money is consequence, not cause. It follows; it does not precede. According to the order of nature, we first determine upon the object to be accomplished, and then appropriate the money necessary to its consummation. According to the order of the constitution, the power is defined, and the application, that is, the appropriation of the money requisite to its effectuation, follows as a necessary and proper means. The practice of congressional legislation is conformable to both. We first inquire what we may do, and provide by law for its being done, and we then appropriate, by another act of legislation, the money necessary to accomplish the specified object. The error of the argument lies in its beginning to soon. It supposes the money to be in the treasury, and then seeks to disburse it. But how came it there? Congress cannot impose taxes without an object. Their imposition must be in reference to the whole mass of our powers, to the general purposes of government, or with the view to the fulfilment of some of those powers, or to the attainment of some of those purposes. In either case, we consult the constitution, and ascertain the extent of the authority which is confided to us. We cannot, constitutionally, lay the taxes without regard to the extent of our powers; and then, having acquired the money or the public, appropriate it, because we have got it, to any object indefinitely.

Nor do I claim the power in question, from the consent or grant of any particular State or States, through which an object of internal improvement may pass. It might, indeed, be prudent to consult a State, through which an improvement might happen to be carried, from considerations of deference and respect to its sovereign power; and from a disposition to maintain those relations of perfect am? which are ever desirable, between the general and State governments. But the power to establish the improvement must be found in the constitution, or it does not exist. And what is granted by all, it can not be necessary to obtain the consent of some to perform.

The gentleman from Virginia, in speaking of incidental powers, has used a species of argument which I entreat him candidly to reconsider. He has said, that the chain of cause and effect is without end; that if we argue from a power expressly granted to all others, which might be convenient or necessary to its execution, there are no bounds to the power of this government; that, for example, under the power "to provide and maintain a navy," the right might be assumed to the timber necessary to its construction, and the soil on which it grew. The gentleman might have added, the acorns from which it sprang. What, upon the gentleman's own hypothesis, ought to have been his conclusion? That Congress possessed no power to provide and maintain a navy. Such a conclusion would have been quite as logical, as that Congress has no power over internal improvements, from the *possible* lengths to which this power may be pushed. No one ever has, or can, controvert the existence of incidental powers. We may apply different rules for their extraction, but all must concur in the necessity of their actual existence. They result from the imperfections of our nature, and from the utter impossibility of foreseeing all the turns and vicissitudes in human affairs. They cannot be defined. Much is attained when the power, the end is specified and guarded. Keeping that constantly in view, the means necessary to its attainment must be left to the sound and responsible discretion of the public functionary. Intrench him as you please, employ what language you may, in the constitutional instrument, "necessary and proper," "indispensably necessary," or any other, and the question is still left open. Does the proposed measure fall within the scope of the incidental power, circumscribed as it may be? Your safety against abuse must rest in his intesest, his integrity, his responsibility to the exercise of the elective franchise; finally, in the ultimate right, when all other redress fails, of an appeal to the remedy, to be used only in extreme cases, of forcible resistance against intolerable oppression.

Doubtless, by an extravagant and abusive enlargement of incidental powers, the State governments may be reduced within too narrow limits. Take any power, however incontestably granted to the general government, and employ that kind of process of reasoning in which the gentleman from Virginia is so skilful, by tracing it to its remotest effects, you may make it absorb the powers of the State governments. Pursue the opposite course; take any incontestable power belonging to the State governments, and follow it out into all its possible ramifications, and you make it thwart and defeat the great operations of the government of the whole. This is the consequence of our systems. Their harmony is to be preserved only by forbearance, liberality, practical good sense, and mutual concession. Bring these dispositions into the administrations of our various institutions, and all the dreaded conflicts of authorities will be found to be perfectly imaginary.

I disclaim, for myself, several sources to which others have ascended, to arrive at the power in question. In making this disclaimer, I mean to cast no imputation on them. I am glad to meet them by whatever road they travel, at the point of a constitutional conclusion. Nor do their positions weaken mine; on the contrary, if correctly taken, and mine also are justified by fair interpretation, they add strength to mine. But I feel it my duty, frankly and sincerely, to state my own views of the constitution. In coming to the ground on which I make my stand to maintain the power, and where I am ready to meet its antagonist, I am happy, in the outset, to state my hearty concurrence with the gentleman from Virginia, in the old 1798 republican principles—now become federal also—by which the constitution is to be interpreted. I agree with him, that this is a limited government, that it has no powers but the granted powers; and that the granted powers are those which are expressly enumerated, or such as, being implied, are necessary and proper to effectuate the enumerated powers. And, if I do not show the power over federative, national, internal improvements, to be fairly deducible, after the strictest application of these principles, I entreat the committee unanimously to reject the bill. The gentleman from Virginia has rightly anticipated, that, in regard to roads, I claim the power under the grant to *establish* post offices and post roads. The whole question, on this part of the subject, turns upon the true meaning of this clause, and that again upon the genuine signification of the word *"establish."* According to my understanding of it, the meaning of it is, to fix, to make firm, to build. According to that of the gentleman from Virginia, it is to designate, to adopt. Grammatical criticism was to me always unpleasant, and I do not profess to be any proficient in it. But I will confidently appeal, in support of my definition, to any vocabulary whatever, of respectable authority, and to the common use of the word. That it cannot mean only adoption is to me evident, for *adoption* presupposes establishment, which is precedent in its very nature. That which does not exist, which is not established, cannot be adopted. There is, then, an essential difference between the gentleman from Virginia and me. I consider the power as original and creative; he as derivative, adoptive. But I will show, out of the mouth of the President himself, who agrees with the gentleman from Virginia, as to the sense of this word, that what I contend for is its genuine meaning. The President, in almost the first lines of his message to this House, of the fourth of May, 1822, returning the Cumberland bill with his veto, says, "a power to *establish* turnpikes, with gates and tolls, &c., implies a power to adopt and execute a complete system of internal improvement." What is the sense in which the word "establish" is here used? Is it not creative? Did the President mean to adopt or designate some pre-existing turnpikes, with gates, &c., or for the first time to set them up, under the authority of Congress? Again, the President says, "If it exist as to one road, (that is, the power to lay duties of transit, and to take the land on a valuation,) it exists as to any other, and to as many roads as Congress may think proper to *"establish."* In what sense does he here employ the word? The truth is, that the President could employ no better than the constitutional word, and he is obliged to use it in the precise sense for which I contend. But I go to a higher authority than that of the chief magistrate—to that of the constitution itself. In expounding that instrument, we must look at all its parts; and if we find a word, the meaning of which it is desirable to obtain, we may safely rest upon the use which has been made of the same word in other parts of the instrument. The word "establish" is one of frequent recurrence in the constitution; and I venture to say that it will be found uniformly to express the same idea. In the clause enumerating our powers "Congress has power to *establish* a uniform rule of naturalization," &c.; in the preamble, "We, the people of the United States, in order to form a more perfect union, *establish* justice, &c., do ordain and *establish* this constitution," &c.; what pre-existing code of justice was adopted? Did not the people of the United States, in this high sovereign act, contemplate the construction of a code adapted to their federal condition? The sense of the word, as contended for, is self-evident when applied to the constitution.

But let us look at the nature, object, and purposes of the power. The trust confided to Congress is one of the most beneficial character. It is the diffusion of information among all the parts of this republic. It is the transmission and circulation of intelligence; it is to communicate knowledge of the laws and acts of government, and to promote the great business of society in all its relations. This is a great trust, capable of being executed in a highly salutary manner. It can be executed only by Congress, and it should be as well performed as it can be, considering the wants and exigencies of government. And here I beg leave to advert to the principle which I some time ago laid down, that the powers granted to this government are to be carried into execution by its own inherent force and energy, without necessary dependance upon the State governments. If my construction secures this object; and if that of my opponents places the execution of this trust at the pleasure and mercy of the State governments, we must reject theirs, and assume mine. But the construction of the President does make it so dependent. He contends that we can

only use as post roads those which the States shall have previously established; that they are at liberty to alter, to change, and of course to shut them up at pleasure. It results from this view of the President, that any of the great mail routes now existing that, for example, from south to north, may be closed at pleasure or by caprice, by any one of the States, or its authorities, through which it passes—by that of Delaware, or any other. Is it possible that that construction of the constitution can be correct, which allows a law of the United States, enacted for the good of the whole, to be obstructed or defeated in its operation by any one of twenty-four sovereigns. The gentleman from Virginia, it is true, denies the right of a State to close a road which has been designated as a post road. But suppose the State, no longer having occasion to use it for its own separate and peculiar purposes, withdraws all care and attention from its preservation. Can the State be compelled to repair it? No! the gentleman from Virginia must say; and I will say, May not the general government repair this road which is abandoned by the State power? May it not repair it in the most efficacious manner? And may it not protect and defend that which it has thus repaired, and which there is no longer an interest or inclination in the State to protect and defend? Or does the gentleman mean to contend that a road may exist in the statute book, which a State will not, and the general government cannot, repair and improve? And what sort of an account should we render to the people of the United States, of the execution of the high trust confided for their benefit to us, if we were to tell them that we had failed to execute it, because a State would not make a road for us?

The roads, and other internal improvements of States, are made in reference to their individual interests. It is the eye only of the whole, and the power of the whole, that can look to the interests of all. In the infancy of the government, and in the actual state of the public treasury, it may be the only alternative left us to use those roads, which are made for State purposes, to promote the national object, ill as they may be adapted to it. It may never be necessary to make more than a few great national arteries of communication, leaving to the States the lateral and minor ramifications. Even these should only be executed, without pressure upon the resources of the country, and according to the convenience and ability of government. But, surely, in the performance of a great national duty imposed upon this government, which has for its object the distribution of intelligence, civil, commercial, literary, and social, we ought to perform the substance of the trust, and not content ourselves with a mere inefficient naper execution of it. If I am right in these views, the power to establish post roads being in its nature original and creative, and the government having adopted the roads made by State means only from its inability to exert the whole extent of its authority, the controverted power is *expressly* granted to Congress, and there is an end of the question.

It ought to be borne in mind, that this power over roads was not, contained in the articles of confederation, which limited Congress to the establishment of post-offices; and that the general character of the present constitution, as contrasted with those articles, is that of an enlargement of power. But, if the construction of my opponents be correct, we are left precisely where the articles of confederation left us, notwithstanding the additional words contained in the present constitution. What, too, will the gentleman do with the first member of the clause to establish post *offices*? Must Congress adopt, designate, some pre-existing office, established by State authority? But there is none such. May it not then fix, build, create, *establish* offices of its own?

The gentleman from Virginia sought to alarm us by the awful emphasis with which he set before us the total extent of post roads in the Union. Eighty thousand miles of post roads! exclaimed the gentleman; and you will assert for the general government jurisdiction, and erect turnpikes, on such an immense distance? Not to-day, nor to-morrow; but this government is to last, I trust, for ever; we may at least hope it will endure until the wave of population, cultivation, and intelligence shall have washed the Rocky mountains, and have mingled with the Pacific. And may we not also hope that the day will arrive when the improvements and the comforts of social life shall spread over the wide surface of this vast continent? All this is not to be suddenly done. Society must not be burdened or oppressed. Things must be gradual and progressive. The same species of formidable array which the gentleman makes, might be exhibited in reference to the construction of a navy, or any other of the great purposes of government. We might be told of the fleets and vessels of great maritime powers, which whiten the ocean; and triumphantly asked if we should vainly attempt to cope with or rival that tremendous power? And we should shrink from the effort, if we were to listen to his counsels, in hopeless despair. Yes, sir, it is a subject of peculiar delight to me to look forward to the proud and happy period, distant as it may be, when circulation and association between the Atlantic and the Pacific, and the Mexican gulf, shall be as free and perfect as they are at this moment in England, or in any other the most highly improved country on the globe. In the mean time, without bearing heavily upon any of our important interests, let us apply ourselves to the accomplishment of what is most practicable, and immediately necessary.

But what most staggers my honorable friend, is the jurisdiction over the sites of roads, and other internal improvements, which he supposes Congress might assume; and he considers the exercise of such a jurisdiction as furnishing the just occasion for serious alarm. Let us analyze the subject. Prior to the erection of a road under the authority of the general government, there existed, in the State throughout which it passes, no actual exercise of jurisdiction over the ground which it traverses *as a road.* There was only the possibility of the exercise of such a jurisdiction, when the State should, if ever erect such a road. But the road is made by the authority of Congress, and out of the *fact* of its erection arises a necessity for its preservation and protection. The road is some thirty, or fifty, or sixty feet in width, and with that narrow limit passes through a part of the territory of the State. The capital expended in the making of the road incorporates itself with and becomes a part of the permanent and immoveable property of the State. The jurisdiction which is claimed for the general government, is that only which relates to the necessary defence, protection, and preservation of the road. It is of a character altogether conservative. Whatever does not relate to the existence and protection of the road, remains with the State. Murders, trespasses, contracts—all the occurrences and transactions of society upon the road, not affecting its actual existence, will fall within the jurisdiction of the civil or criminal tribunals of the State, as if the road had never been brought into existence. How much remains to the State! How little is claimed for the general government! Is it possible that a jurisdiction so limited, so harmless, so unambitious, can be regarded as seriously alarming to the sovereignty of the States? Congress now asserts and exercises, without contestation, a power to protect the mail in its transit, by the sanction of all suitable penalties. The man who violates it is punished with death, or otherwise, according to the circumstances of the case. This power is exerted as incident to that of establishing post offices and post roads. Is the protection of the thing *in transitu* a power more clearly deducible from the grant, than that of facilitating, by means of a practical road, its actual transportation? Mails certainly imply roads, roads imply their own preservation, their preservation implies the power to preserve them, and the constitution tells us, in express terms, that we shall establish the one and the other.

In respect to cutting canals, I admit the question is not quite so clear as in regard to roads. With respect to these, as I have endeavored to show, the power is expressly granted. In regard to canals, it appears to me to be fairly comprehended in, or deducible from, certain granted powers. Congress has power to regulate commerce with foreign nations and among the several States. Precisely the same measure of power which is granted in the one case is conferred in the other. And the uniform practical exposition of the constitution, as to the regulation of foreign commerce, is equally applicable to that among the several States. Suppose, instead of directing the legislation of this government constantly, as heretofore, to the object of foreign commerce, to the utter neglect of the interior commerce among the several States, the fact had been reversed, and now, for the first time, we were about to legislate for our foreign trade. Should we not, in that case, hear all the controverted objections made to the erection of buoys, beacons, light-houses, the surveys of coasts, and the other numerous facilities accorded to the foreign trade, which we now hear to the making of roads and canals? Two years ago, a seawall, or in other words, a marine canal, was authorized by an act of Congress in New Hampshire, and I doubt not that many of those voted for it who have now conscientious scruples on this bill. Yes, any thing, every thing may be done for foreign commerce; any thing, every thing on the margin of the ocean; but nothing for domestic trade; nothing for the great interior of the country! Yet, the equity and the beneficence of the constitution equally comprehena both. The gentleman does, indeed, maintain that there is a difference as to the character of the facilities in the two cases. But I put it to his own candor, whether the only difference is not that which springs from the nature of the two elements on which the two species of commerce are conducted—the difference between land and water. The principle is the same, whether you promote commerce by opening for it an artificial channel where now there is none, or by increasing the ease or safety with which it may be conducted through a natural channel which the bounty of Providence has bestowed. In the one case, your object is to facilitate arrival and departure from the ocean to the land. In the other, it is to accomplish the same object from the land to the ocean. Physical obstacles may be greater in the one case than in the other, but the moral or constitutional power equally includes both. The gentleman from Virginia has, to be sure, contended that the power to make these commercial facilities was to be found in another clause of the constitution—that which enables Congress to obtain cessions of territory for specific objects, and grants to it an exclusive jurisdiction. These cessions may be obtained for the "erection of forts, magazines, arsenals, dock-yards, or other needful buildings." It is apparent that it relates altogether to military or naval affairs, and not to the regulation of commerce. How is the marine canal covered by this clause? Is it to be considered as a "needful building?" The object of this power is perfectly obvious. The convention saw that, in military or naval posts, such as are indicated, it was indispensably necessary, for their proper government, to vest in Congress the power of exclusive legislation. If we claimed over objects of internal improvement an exclusive jurisdiction, the gentleman might urge, with much force, the clause in question. But the claim of concurrent jurisdiction only is asserted. The gentleman professes himself unable to comprehend how concurrent jurisdiction can be exercised by two different governments at the same time over the same persons and things. But, is not this the fact, with respect to the State and federal governments? Does not every person and every thing, within our limits, sustain a two-fold relation to the State and to the federal authority? The power of taxation, as exerted by both governments, that over the militia, besides many others, is concurrent. No doubt embarrassing cases may be conceived and stated by gentlemen of acute and ingenious minds. One was put tb me yesterday Two canals are desired, one by the federal, and the other by a State government; and there is not a supply of water but for the feeder of one canal—which is to take it? The constitution which ordains the supremacy of the laws of the United States, answers the question. The good of the whole is paramount to the good of a part. The same difficulty might possibly arise in the exercise of the incontestable power of taxation. We know that the imposition of taxes has its limits. There is a maximum which cannot be transcended. Suppose the citizen to be taxed by the general government to the utmost extent of his ability, or a thing as much as it can possibly beat and the State imposes a tax at the same time, which authority is to take it: Extreme cases of this sort may serve to amuse and to puzzle; but they will hardly ever arise in practice. And we may safely confide in the moderation, good sense, and mutual good dispositions of the two governments, to guard against the imagined conflicts.

It is said by the President, that the power to regulate commerce merely authorizes the laying of imposts and duties. But Congress has no power to lay imposts and duties on the trade among the several States. The grant must mean, therefore, something else. What is it? The power to regulate commerce among the several States, if it have any meaning, implies authority to foster it, to promote it, to bestow on it facilities similar to those which have been conceded to our foreign trade. It cannot mean only an empty authority to adopt regulations, without the capacity to give practical effect to them All the powers of this government should be interpreted in reference to its first, its best, its greatest object, the union of these States. And is not that union best invigorated by an intimate, social, and commercial connexion between all the parts of the confederacy? Can that be accomplished, that is, can the federative objects of this government be attained, but by the application of federative resources?

Of all the powers bestowed on this government, none are more clearly vested, than that to regulate the distribution of the intelligence, private and official, of the country; to regulate the distribution of commerce; and to regulate the distribution of the physical force of the Union. In the execution of the high and solemn trust which these beneficial powers imply, we must look to the great ends which the framers of our admirable constitution had in view. We must reject, as wholly incompatible with their enlightened and beneficent intentions, that construction of these powers which would resuscitate all the debility and inefficiency of the ancient confederacy. In the vicissitudes of human affairs, who can foresee all the possible cases, in which it may be necessary to apply the public force, within or without the Union? This government is charged with the use of it, to repel invasions, to suppress insurrections, to enforce the laws of the Union; in short, for all the unknown and undefinable purposes of war, foreign or intestine, wherever and however it may rage. During its existence, may not government, for its effectual prosecution, order a road to be made, or a canal to be cut to relieve for example an exposed point of the Union? If, when the emergency comes, there is a power to provide for it, that power must exist in the constitution, and not in the emergency. A wise, precautionary, and parental policy, anticipating danger, will beforehand provide for the hour of need. Roads and canals are in the nature of fortifications, since if not the deposites of military resources, they enable you to bring into rapid action the military resources of the country, whatever they may be. They are better than any fortifications, because they serve the double purposes of peace and of war. They dispense in a great degree with fortifications, since they have all the effect of that concentration at which fortifications aim. I appeal from the precepts of the President to the practice of the President. While he denies to Congress the power in question, he does not scruple, upon his sole authority, as numerous instances in the statute book will testify, to order, at pleasure, the opening of roads by the military, and then come here to ask us to pay for them. Nay, more, sir; a subordinate but highly respectable officer of the executive government I believe would not hesitate to provide a boat or cause a bridge to be erected over an inconsiderable stream, to ensure the regular transportation of the mail. And it happens to be within my personal knowledge, that the head of the post-office department, as a prompt and vigilant officer should do, has recently despatched an agent to ascertain the causes of the late frequent vexatious failures of the great northern mail, and to inquire if a provision of a boat or bridge over certain small streams in Maryland, which have produced them, would not prevent their recurrence.

I was much surprised at one argument of the honorable gentleman. He told the House, that the constitution had carefully guarded against inequality, among the several States, in the public burdens, by certain restrictions upon taxation; that the effect of the adoption of a system of internal improvements would be to draw the resources from one part of the Union, and to expend them in the improvements of another; and that the spirit, at least, of the constitutional equality would be thus violated. From the nature of things, the constitution could not specify the theatre of the expenditure of the public treasure That expenditure, guided by and looking to the public good, must be made, necessarily, where it will most subserve the interests of the whole Union. The argument is, that the *locale* of the collection of the public contributions, and the *locale* of their disbursement, should be the same. Now, sir, let us carry this argument out; and no man is more capable than the ingenious gentleman from Virginia, of tracing an argument to its utmost consequences. The *locale* of the collection of the public revenue is the pocket of the citizen; and, to abstain from the violation of the principle of equality adverted to by the gentleman, we should restore back into each man's pocket precisely what was taken from it. If the principle contended for be true, we are habitually violating it. We raise about twenty millions of dollars, a very large revenue, considering the actual distresses of the country. And, sir, notwithstanding all the puffing, flourishing statements of its prosperity, emanating from printers who are fed upon the pap of the public treasury, the whole country is in a condition of very great distress. Where is this vast revenue expended? Boston, New York, the great capitals of the north, are the theatres of its disbursement. There the interest upon the public debt is paid. There the expenditure in the building, equipment, and repair of the national vessels takes place. There all the great expenditures of the government necessarily concentrate. This is no cause of just complaint. It is inevitable, resulting from the accumulation of capital, the state of the arts, and other circumstances belonging to our great cities. But sir, if there be a section of this Union having more right than any other to complain of this transfer of the circulating medium from one quarter of the Union to another, the west, the poor west—

[Here Mr. Barbour explained. He had meant that the constitution limited Congress as to the proportions of revenue to be drawn from the several States; but the principle of this provision would be vacated by internal improvements of immense expense, and yet of a local character. Our public ships, to be sure, are built at the seaports, but they do not remain there. Their home is the mountain wave; but internal improvements are essentially local; they touch the soil of the States, and their benefits, at least the largest part of them, are confined to the States where they exist.]

The explanation of the gentleman has not materially varied the argument. He says the home of our ships is the mountain wave. Sir, if the ships go to sea, the money with which they are built, or refitted, remains on shore, and the cities where the equipment takes place derive the benefit of the expenditure. It requires no stretch of the imagination to conceive the profitable industry—the axes, the hammers, the saws—the mechanic arts, which are put in motion by this expenditure. And all these, and other collateral advantages, are enjoyed by the seaports. The navy is built for the interest of the whole Internal improvements of that general, federative character, for which we contend, would also be for the interest of the whole. And I should think their abiding with us, and not going abroad on the vast deep, was rather cause of recommendation than objection.

But, Mr. Chairman, if there be any part of this Union more likely than all others to be benefited by the adoption of the gentleman's principle, regulating the public expenditure, it is the west. There is a perpetual drain, from that embarrassed and highly distressed portion of our country, of its circulating medium to the east. There, but few and inconsiderable expenditures of the public money take place. There we have none of those public works, no magnificent edifices, forts, armories, arsenals, dockyards, &c., which, more or less, are to be found in every Atlantic State. In at least seven States beyond the Alleghany, not one solitary public work of this government is to be found. If, by one of those awful and terrible dispensations of Providence which sometimes occur, this government should be annihilated, everywhere on the seaboard traces of its former existence would be found; whilst we should not have, in the west, a single monument remaining, on which to pour out our affections and our regrets. Yet, sir, we do not complain. No portion of your population is more loyal to the Union, than the hardy freemen of the west Nothing can weaken or eradicate their ardent desire for its lasting preservation. None are more prompt to vindicate the interests and rights of the nation from all foreign aggression. Need I remind you of the glorious scenes in which they participated during the late war—a war in which they had no peculiar or direct interest, waged for no commerce, no seamen of theirs. But it was enough for them that it was a war demanded by the character and the honor of the nation. They did not stop to calculate its cost of blood or of treasure. They flew to arms; they rushed down the valley of the Mississippi, with all the impetuosity of that noble river. They sought the enemy. They found him at the beach. They fought, they bled; they covered themselves and their country with immortal glory. They enthusiastically shared in all the transports occasioned by our victories, whether won on the ocean or on the land. They felt, with the keenest distress, whatever disaster befell us. No, sir, I repeat it, neglect, injury itself, cannot alienate the affections of the west from this government. They cling to it, as to their best, their greatest, their last hope. You may

impoverish them, reduce them to ruin, by the mistakes of your policy, and you cannot drive them from you. They do not complain of the expenditure of the public money where the public exigencies require its disbursement. But, I put it to your candor, if you ought not, by a generous and national policy, to mitigate, if not prevent, the evils resulting from the perpetual transfer of the circulating medium from the west to the east. One million and a half of dollars annually is transferred for the public lands alone; and almost every dollar goes, like him who goes to death—to a bourne from which no traveller returns. In ten years it will amount to fifteen millions; in twenty, to—but I will not pursue the appalling results of arithmetic. Gentlemen who believe that these vast sums are supplied by emigrants from the east, labor under great error. There was a time when the tide of emigration from the east bore along with it the means to effect the purchase of the public domain. But that tide has, in a great measure, now stopped. And, as population advances farther and farther west, it will entirely cease. The greatest migrating States in the Union, at this time, are Kentucky first, Ohio next, and Tennessee. The emigrants from those States carry with them, to the States and Territories lying beyond them, the circulating medium, which, being invested in the purchase of the public land, is transmitted to the points where the wants of government require it. If this debilitating and exhausting process were inevitable, it must be borne with manly fortitude. But we think that a fit exertion of the powers of this government would mitigate the evil. We believe that the government incontestably possesses the constitutional power to execute such internal improvements as are called for by the good of the whole. And we appeal to your equity, to your parental regard, to your enlightened policy, to perform the high and beneficial trust thus sacredly reposed. I am sensible of the delicacy of the topic to which I have reluctantly adverted, in consequence of the observations of the honorable gentleman from Virginia. And I hope there will be no misconception of my motives in dwelling upon it. A wise and considerate government should anticipate and prevent, rather than wait for the operation of causes of discontent.

Let me ask, Mr. Chairman, what has this government done on the great subject of internal improvements, after so many years of its existence, and with such an inviting field before it? You have made the Cumberland road, only. Gentlemen appear to have considered that a western road. They ought to recollect that not one stone has yet been broken, not one spade of earth has been yet removed in any western State. The road begins in Maryland, and it terminates at Wheeling. It passes through the States of Maryland, Pennsylvania, and Virginia. All the direct benefit of the expenditure of the public money on that road, has accrued to those three States; not one cent in any western State. And yet we have had to beg, entreat, supplicate you, session after session, to grant the necessary appropriations to complete the road. I have myself toiled until my powers have been exhausted and prostrated, to prevail on you to make the grant. We were actuated to make these exertions for the sake of the collateral benefit only to the west; that we might have a way by which we should be able to continue and maintain an affectionate intercourse with our friends and brethren—that we might have a way to reach the capital of our country, and to bring our counsels, humble as they may be, to consult and mingle with yours in the advancement of the national prosperity. Yes, sir, the Cumberland road has only reached the margin of a western State; and, from some indications which have been given during this session, I should apprehend it would there pause for ever, if my confidence in you were not unbounded; if I had not before witnessed that appeals were never unsuccessful to your justice, to your magnanimity, to your fraternal affection.

But, sir, the bill on your table is no western bill. It is emphatically a national bill, comprehending all, looking to the interests of the whole. The people of the west never thought of, never desired, never asked for, a system exclusively for their benefit. The system contemplated by this bill looks to great national objects, and proposes the ultimate application to their accomplishment of the only means by which they can be effected, the means of the nation—means which, if they be withheld from such objects, the Union, I do most solemnly believe, of these now happy and promising States, may, at some distant (I trust a far, far distant) day, be endangered and shaken at its centre.

Source:

Clay, Henry. *The Works of Henry Clay, Comprising His Life, Correpsondence and Speeches of Henry Clay*, ed. by Calvin Colton. 10 vols. New York: G. P. Putnam's Sons, 1904.

Gibbons v. Ogden, 1824

A case dealing with the power of the federal government to regulate interstate commerce. Aaron Ogden, having been assigned an official monopoly by the state of New York to operate steamboats in that state's waters, sought and obtained a state court injunction against Thomas Gibbons, who was operating steamboats between New Jersey and New York. Since Gibbons was operating legally and had registered with the federal government as an interstate transport service, he appealed to the Supreme Court for removal of the New York

injunction. Speaking for the Court in a unanimous opinion, Chief Justice John Marshall held that Gibbons's federal license was valid and constitutional, as a legitimate exercise of the regulation of commerce provided in Article 1, Section 8 of the Constitution. The New York State law creating a commercial monopoly was therefore void, since it conflicted with the regulatory power of the federal government in the performance of its constitutional responsibilities, and Gibbons must be allowed to operate within the waters of the state of New York. This decision was of great significance for the development of a free national economy; since state laws that interfered with interstate commerce were seen as a de facto invasion of federal regulatory power, it would not even be necessary for a state law to be in conflict with a specific federal act to be declared void. The way was therefore cleared for the federal judiciary to intervene in all levels of commerce and to strike down state laws that were seen, even indirectly, as an obstruction of interstate trade.

Gibbons, Appellant, v. Ogden, respondent

Mr. Chief Justice Marshall delivered the opinion of the Court, and, after stating the case, proceeded as follows:

The appellant contends that this decree is erroneous, because the laws which purport to give the exclusive privilege it sustains, are repugnant to the constitution and laws of the United States.

They are said to be repugnant—

1st. To that clause in the constitution which authorizes Congress to regulate commerce.

2d. To that which authorizes Congress to promote the progress of science and useful arts.

The State of New-York maintains the constitutionality of these laws; and their Legislature, their Council of Revision, and their Judges, have repeatedly concurred in this opinion. It is supported by great names—by names which have all the titles to consideration that virtue, intelligence, and office, can bestow. No tribunal can approach the decision of this question, without feeling a just and real respect for that opinion which is sustained by such authority; but it is the province of this Court, while it respects, not to bow to it implicitly; and the Judges must exercise, in the examination of the subject, that understanding which Providence has bestowed upon them, with that independence which the people of the United States expect from this department of the government.

As preliminary to the very able discussions of the constitution, which we have heard from the bar, and as having some influence on its construction, reference has been made to the political situation of these States, anterior to its formation. It has been said, that they were sovereign, were completely independent, and were connected with each other only by a league. This is true. But, when these allied sovereigns converted their league into a government, when they converted their Congress of Ambassadors, deputed to deliberate on their common concerns, and to recommend measures of general utility, into a Legislature, empowered to enact laws on the most interesting subjects, the whole character in which the States appear, underwent a change, the extent of which must be determined by a fair consideration of the instrument by which that change was effected.

This instrument contains an enumeration of powers expressly granted by the people to their government. It has been said, that these powers ought to be construed strictly. But why ought they to be so construed? Is there one sentence in the constitution which gives countenance to this rule? In the last of the enumerated powers, that which grants, expressly, the means for carrying all others into execution, Congress is authorized "to make all laws which shall be necessary and proper" for the purpose. But this limitation on the means which may be used, is not extended to the powers which are conferred; nor is there one sentence in the constitution, which has been pointed out by the gentlemen of the bar, or which we have been able to discern, that prescribes this rule. We do not, therefore, think ourselves justified in adopting it. What do gentlemen mean, by a strict construction? If they contend only against that enlarged construction, which would extend words beyond their natural and obvious import, we might question the application of the term, but should not controvert the principle. If they contend for that narrow construction which, in support of some theory not to be found in the constitution, would deny to the government those powers which the words of the grant, as usually understood, import, and which are consistent with the general views and objects of the instrument; for that narrow construction, which would cripple the government, and render it unequal to the object for which it is declared to be instituted, and to which the powers given, as fairly understood, render it competent; then we cannot perceive the propriety of this strict construction, nor adopt it as the rule by which the constitution is to be expounded. As men, whose intentions require no concealment, generally employ the words which most directly and aptly express the ideas they intend to convey, the enlightened patriots who framed our constitution, and the people who adopted it, must be understood to have employed words in their natural sense, and to have intended what they have said. If, from the imperfection of human language, there should be serious doubts respecting the extent of any given power, it is a well settled rule, that the objects for which it was given, especially when those objects are expressed in the instrument itself, should have great influence in the construction. We know of no reason for excluding this rule from the present case. The grant does not convey power which might be beneficial to the grantor, if retained by himself, or which can endure solely to the benefit of the grantee; but is an investment of power for the general advantage, in the hands of agents selected for that purpose; which power can never be exercised by the people themselves, but must be placed in the hands of agents, or lie dormant. We know of no rule for construing the extent of such powers, other than is given by the language of the instrument which confers them, taken in connection with the purposes for which they were conferred.

The words are, "Congress shall have power to regulate commerce with foreign nations, and among the several States, and with the Indian tribes."

The subject to be regulated is commerce; and our constitution being, as was aptly said at the bar, one of enumeration, and not of definition, to ascertain the extent of the power, it becomes necessary to settle the meaning of the word. The counsel for the appellee would limit it to traffic, to buying and selling, or the interchange of commodities, and do not admit that it comprehends navigation. This would restrict a general term, applicable to many objects, to one of its signification's. Commerce, undoubtedly, is traffic, but it is something more: it is intercourse. It describes the commercial intercourse between nations, and parts of nations, in all its branches, and is regulated by prescribing rules for carrying on that intercourse. The mind can scarcely conceive a system for regulating commerce between nations, which shall exclude all laws concerning navigation, which shall be silent on the admission of the vessels of the one nation into the ports of the other, and be confined to prescribing rules for the conduct of individuals, in the actual employment of buying and selling, or of barter.

If commerce does not include navigation, the government of the Union has no direct power over that subject, and can make no law prescribing what shall constitute American vessels, or requiring that they shall be navigated by American seamen. Yet this power has been exercised from the commencement of the government, has been exercised with the consent of all, and has been understood by all to be a commercial regulation. All America understands, and has uniformly understood, the word "commerce," to comprehend navigation. It was so understood, and must have been so understood, when the constitution was framed. The power over commerce, including navigation, was one of the primary objects for which the people of America adopted their government, and must have been contemplated in forming it. The convention must have used the word in that sense, because all have understood it in that sense; and the attempt to restrict it comes too late.

If the opinion that "commerce," as the word is used in the constitution, comprehends navigation also, requires any additional confirmation, that additional confirmation is, we think, furnished by the words of the instrument itself.

It is a rule of construction, acknowledged by all, that the exceptions from a power mark its extent; for it would be absurd, as well as useless, to except from a granted power, that which was not granted—that which the words of the grant could not comprehend. If, then, there are in the constitution plain exceptions from the power over navigation, plain inhibitions to the exercise of that power in a particular way, it is a proof that those who made these exceptions, and prescribed these inhibitions, understood the power to which they applied as being granted.

The 9th section of the 1st article declares, that "no preference shall be given, by any regulation of commerce or revenue, to the ports of one State over those of another." This clause cannot be understood as applicable to those laws only which are passed for the purposes of revenue, because it is expressly applied to commercial regulations; and the most obvious preference which can be given to one port over another, in regulating commerce, relates to navigation. But the subsequent part of the sentence is still more explicit. It is, "nor shall vessels bound to or from one State, be obliged to enter, clear, or pay duties, in another." These words have a direct reference to navigation.

The universally acknowledged power of the government to impose embargoes, must also be considered as showing, that all America is united in that construction which comprehends navigation in the word commerce. Gentlemen have said, in argument, that this is a branch of the war-making power, and that an embargo is an instrument of war, not a regulation of trade.

That it may be, and often is, used as an instrument of war, cannot be denied. An embargo may be imposed for the purpose of facilitating the equipment or manning of a fleet, or for the purpose of concealing the progress of an expedition preparing to sail from a particular port. In these, and in similar cases, it is a military instrument, and partakes of the nature of war. But all embargoes are not of this description. They are sometimes resorted to without a view to war, and with a single view to commerce. In such case, an embargo is no more a war measure, than a merchantman is a ship of war, because both are vessels which navigate the ocean with sails and seamen.

When Congress imposed that embargo which, for a time, engaged the attention of every man in the United States, the avowed object of the law was, the protection of commerce, and the avoiding of war. By its friends and its enemies it was treated as a commercial, not as a war measure. The persevering earnestness and zeal with which it was opposed, in a part of our country which supposed its interests to be vitally affected by the act, cannot be forgot-

ten. A want of acuteness in discovering objections to a measure to which they felt the most deep rooted hostility, will not be imputed to those who were arrayed in opposition to this. Yet they never suspected that navigation was no branch of trade, and was, therefore, not comprehended in the power to regulate commerce. They did, indeed, contest the constitutionality of the act, but, on a principle which admits the construction for which the appellant contends. They denied that the particular law in question was made in pursuance of the constitution, not because the power could not act directly on vessels, but because a perpetual embargo was the annihilation, and not the regulation of commerce. In terms, they admitted the applicability of the words used in the constitution to vessels; and that, in a case which produced a degree and an extent of excitement, calculated to draw forth every principle on which legitimate resistance could be sustained. No example could more strongly illustrate the universal understanding of the American people on this subject.

The word used in the constitution, then, comprehends, and has been always understood to comprehend, navigation within its meaning; and a power to regulate navigation, is as expressly granted, as if that term had been added to the word "commerce."

To what commerce does this power extend? The constitution informs us, to commerce "with foreign nations, and among the several States, and with the Indian tribes."

It has, we believe, been universally admitted, that these words comprehend every species of commercial intercourse between the United States and foreign nations. No sort of trade can be carried on between this country and any other, to which this power does not extend. It has been truly said, the commerce, as the word is used in the constitution, is a unit, every part of which is indicated by the term. If this be the admitted meaning of the word, in its application to foreign nations, it must carry the same meaning throughout the sentence, and remain unit, unless there be some plain intelligible cause which alters it.

The subject to which the power is next applied, is to commerce "among the several States." The word "among" means intermingled with. A thing which is among others, is intermingled with them. Commerce among the States, cannot stop at the external boundary line of each State, but may be introduced into the interior.

It is not intended to say that these words comprehend that commerce, which is completely internal, which is carried on between man and man in a State, or between different parts of the same State, and which does not extend to or affect other States. Such a power would be inconvenient, and is certainly unnecessary.

Comprehensive as the word "among" is, it may very properly be restricted to that commerce which concerns more States than one. The phrase is not one which would probably have been selected to indicate the completely interior traffic of a State, because it is not an apt phrase for that purpose and the enumeration of the particular classes of commerce to which the power was to be extended, would not have been made, had the intention been to extend the power to every description. The enumeration presuppose something not enumerated; and that something, if we regard the language or the subject of the sentence, must be the exclusively internal commerce of a State. The genius and character of the whole government seem to be, that its action is to be applied to all the external concerns of the nation, and to those internal concerns which affect the States generally; but not to those which are completely within a particular State, which do not affect other States, and with which it is not necessary to interfere, for the purpose of executing some of the general powers of the government. The completely internal commerce of a State, then, may be considered as reserved for the State itself.

But, in regulating commerce with foreign nations, the power of Congress does not stop at the jurisdictional lines of the several States. It would be a very useless power, if it could not pass those lines. The commerce of the United States with foreign nations, is that of the whole United States. Every district has a right to participate in it. The deep streams which penetrate our country in every direction, pass through the interior of almost every State in the Union, and furnish the means of exercising this right. If Congress has the power to regulate it, that power must be exercised whenever the subject exists. If it exists within the States, if a foreign voyage may commence or terminate at a port within a State, then the power or Congress may be exercised with a State.

This principles is, if possible, still more clear, when applied to commerce "among the several States." They either join each other, in which case they are separated by a mathematical line, or they are remote from each other, in which case other States lie between them. What is commerce "among" them; and how is it to be conducted" Can a trading expedition between two adjoining States, commence and terminate outside of each? And if the trading intercourse be between two States remote from each other, must it not commence in one, terminate in the other, and probably pass through a third? Commerce among the States must, of necessity, be commerce with the States. In the regulation of trade with the Indian tribes, the action of the law, especially when the constitution was made, was chiefly within a State. The power of Congress, then, whatever it may be, must be exercised within the territorial jurisdiction of the several States. The sense of the nation on this subject, is unequivocally manifested by the provisions made in the laws for transporting goods, by

land, between Baltimore and Providence, between New-York and Philadelphia, and between Philadelphia and Baltimore.

We are now arrived at the inquiry—What is this power?

It is the power to regulate; that is, to prescribe the rule by which commerce is to be governed. This power, like all others vested in Congress, is complete in itself, may be exercised to its utmost extent and acknowledge no limitations, other than are prescribed in the constitution. These are expressed in plain terms, and do not affect the questions which arise in this case, or which have been discussed at the bar. If, as has always been understood, the sovereignty of Congress, though limited to specified objects, is plenary as to those objects, the power over commerce with foreign nations, and among the several States, is vested in Congress as absolutely as it would be in a single government, having in its constitution the same restrictions on the exercise of the power as are found in the constitution of the United States. The wisdom and the discretion of Congress, their identity with the people, and the influence which their constituents possess of elections, are, in this, as in many other instances, as that, for example, of declaring war, the sole restraints on which they have relied, to secure them from its abuse. They are the restraints on which the people must often rely solely, in all representative governments.

The power of Congress, then, comprehends navigation, within the limits of every State in the Union; so far as that navigation may be, in any manner, connected with "commerce with foreign nations, or among the several States, or with the Indian tribes." It may, of consequence, pass the jurisdictional line of New York, and act upon the very waters to which the prohibition now under consideration applies.

But it has been urged with great earnestness, that, although the power of Congress to regulate commerce with foreign nations, and among the several States, be coextensive with the subject itself, and have no other limits than are prescribed in the constitution, yet the States may severally exercise the same power, within their respective jurisdiction. In support of this argument, it is said, that they possessed it as an inseparable attribute of sovereignty, before the formation of the constitution, and still retain it, except so far as they have surrendered it by that instrument; that this principle results from the nature of the government, and is secured by the tenth amendment; that an affirmative grant of power is no exclusive, unless in its own nature it be such that the continued exercise of it by the former possessor is inconsistent with the grant, and that this is not of that description.

The appellant, conceding these postulates, except the last, contends, that full power to regulate a particular subject, implies the whole power, and leaves no residuum; that a grant of the whole is incompatible with the existence of a right in another to any part of it.

Both parties have appealed to the constitution, to legislative acts, and judicial decisions; and have drawn arguments from all these sources, to support and illustrate the propositions they respectively maintain.

The grant of the power to lay and collect taxes is, like the power to regulate commerce, made in general terms, and has never been understood to interfere with the exercise of the same power by the States; and hence has been drawn an argument which has been applied to the question under consideration. But the two grants are not, it is conceived, similar in their terms or their nature. Although many of the powers formerly exercised by the States, are transferred to the government of the Union, yet the State governments remain, and constitute a most important part of our system. The power of taxation is indispensable to their existence, and is a power which, in its own nature, is capable of residing in, and being exercised by, different authorities at the same time. We are accustomed to see it placed, for different purposes, in different hands. Taxation is the simple operation of taking small portions from a perpetually accumulating mass, susceptible of almost infinite division; and a power in one to take what is necessary for certain purposes, is not, in its nature, incompatible with a power in another to take what is necessary for other purposes. Congress is authorized to lay and collect taxes, &c. to pay the debts, and provide for the common defense and general welfare of the United States. This does not interfere with the power of the States to tax for the support of their own governments; nor is the exercise of that power by the States, an exercise of any portion of the power that is granted to the United States. In imposing taxes for State purposes, they are not doing what Congress is empowered to do. Congress is not empowered to tax for those purposes which are within the exclusive province of the States. When, then, each government exercises the power of taxation, neither is exercising the power of the other. But, when a State proceeds to regulate commerce with foreign nations, or among the several States, it is exercising the very power that is granted to Congress, and is doing the very thing which Congress is authorized to do. There is no analogy, then, between the power of taxation and the power of regulating commerce.

In discussing the question, whether this power is still in the States, in the case under consideration, we may dismiss from it the inquiry, whether it is surrendered by the mere grant to Congress, or is retained until Congress shall exercise the power. We may dismiss that inquiry, because it has been exercised, and the regulations which Congress deemed it proper to make, are now in full operation. The sole question is, can a State regulate commerce with for-

eign nations and among the States, while Congress is regulating it?

The counsel for the respondent answer this question in the affirmative, and rely very much on the restrictions in the 10th section, as supporting their opinion. They say, very truly, that limitations of a power, furnish a strong argument in favor of the existence of that power, and that the section which prohibits the States from laying duties on imports or exports, proves that this power might have been exercised, had it not been expressly forbidden; and, consequently, that any other commercial regulation, not expressly forbidden, to which the original power of the State was competent, may still be made.

That this restriction shows the opinion of the Convention, that a State might impose duties on exports and imports, if not expressly forbidden, will be conceded; but that it follows as a consequence, from this concession, that a State may regulate commerce with foreign nations and among the States, cannot be admitted.

We must first determine whether the act of laying "duties or imposts on imports or exports," is considered in the constitution as a branch of the taxing power, or of the power to regulate commerce. We think it very clear, that it is considered as a branch of the taxing power. It is so treated in the first clause of the 8th section: "Congress shall have power to lay and collect taxes, duties, imposts, and excises;" and, before commerce is mentioned, the rule by which the exercise of this power must be governed, is declared. It is, that all duties, imposts, and excises, shall be uniform. In a separate clause' of the enumeration, the power to regulate commerce is given, as being entirely distinct from the right to levy taxes and imposts, and as being a new power, not before conferred. The constitution, then, considers these powers as substantive, and distinct from each other; and so places them in the enumeration it contains. The power of imposing duties on imports is classed with the power to levy taxes, and that seems to be its natural place. But the power to levy taxes could never be considered as abridging the right of the States on that subject; and they might, consequently, have exercised it by levying duties on imports or exports, had the constitution contained no prohibition on this subject. This prohibition, then, is an exception from the acknowledged power of the States to levy taxes, not from the questionable power to regulate commerce.

"A duty of tonnage" is as much a tax, as a duty on imports or exports; and the reason which induced the prohibition of those taxes, extends to this also. This tax may be imposed by a State, with the consent of Congress; and it may be admitted, that Congress cannot give a right to a State, in virtue of its own powers. But a duty of tonnage being part of the power of imposing taxes, its prohibition may certainly be made to depend on Congress, without affording any implication respecting a power to regulate commerce. It is true, that duties may often be, and in fact often are, imposed on tonnage, with a view to the regulation of commerce; but they may be also imposed with a view to revenue; and it was, therefore, a prudent precaution, to prohibit the States from exercising this power. The idea that the same measure might, according to circumstances, be arranged with different classes of power, was no novelty to the framers of our constitution. Those illustrious statesmen and patriots had been, many of them, deeply engaged in the discussions which preceded the war of our revolution, and all of them were well read in those discussions. The right to regulate commerce, even by the imposition of duties, was not controverted; but the right to impose a duty for the purpose of revenue, produced a war as important, perhaps, in its consequences to the human race, as any the world has ever witnessed.

These restrictions, then, are on the taxing power, not on that to regulate commerce; and presuppose the existence of that which they restrain, not of that which they do not purport to restrain. But, the inspection laws are said to be regulations of commerce, and are certainly recognized in the constitution, as being passed in the exercise of a power remaining with the States.

That inspection laws may have a remote and considerable influence on commerce, will not be denied; but that a power to regulate commerce is the source from which the right to pass them is derived, cannot be admitted. The object of inspection laws, is to improve the quality of articles produced by the labor of a country; to fit them for exportation; or, it may be, for domestic use. They act upon the subject before it becomes an article of foreign commerce, or of commerce among the States, and prepare it for that purpose. They form a portion of that immense mass of legislation, which embraces every thing within the territory of a State, not surrendered to the general government: all which can be most advantageously exercised by the States themselves. Inspection laws, quarantine laws, health laws of every description, as well as laws for regulating the internal commerce of a State, and those which respect turnpike roads, ferries, &c., are component parts of this mass.

No direct general power over these objects is granted to Congress; and, consequently, they remain subject to State legislation. If the legislative power of the Union can reach them, it must be for national purposes; it must be where the power is expressly given for a special purpose, or is clearly incidental to some power which is expressly given. It is obvious, that the government of the Union, in the exercise of its express powers, that, for example, of regulating commerce with foreign nations and among the States, may use means that may also be employed by a State, in the exercise of its acknowledged powers; that, for example, of regulating commerce within the State. If Congress license vessels to sail from one port to another, in the same State, the act is supposed to be, necessarily, incidental to the power expressly granted to Congress, and implies no claim of a direct power to regulate the purely internal commerce of a State, or to act directly on its system of police. So, if a State, in passing laws on subjects acknowledge to be within its control, and with a view to those subjects, shall adopt a measure of the same character with one which Congress may adopt, it does not derive its authority from the particular power which has been granted, but from some other, which remains with the State, and may be executed by the same means. All experience shows, that the same measures, or measures scarcely distinguishable from each other, may flow from distinct powers; but this does not prove that the powers themselves are identical. Although the means used in their execution may sometimes approach each other so nearly as to be confounded, there are other situations in which they are sufficiently distinct to establish their individuality.

In our complex system, presenting the rare and difficult scheme of one general government, whose action extends over the whole, but which possesses only certain enumerated powers; and of numerous State governments, which retain and exercise all powers not delegated to the Union, contests respecting power must arise. Were it even otherwise, the measures taken by the respective governments to execute their acknowledge powers, would often be of the same description, and might, sometimes, interfere. This, however, does not prove that the one is exercising, or has a right to exercise, the powers of the other.

The acts of Congress, passed in 1796 and 1799, empowering and directing the officers of the general government to conform to, and assist in the execution of the quarantine and health laws of a State, proceed, it is said, upon the idea that these laws are constitutional. It is undoubtedly true, that they do proceed upon that idea; and the constitutionally of such laws has never, so far as we are informed, been denied. But they do not imply an acknowledgment that a State may rightfully regulate commerce with foreign nations, or among the States; for they do not imply that such laws are an exercise of that power, or enacted with a view to it. On the contrary, they are treated as quarantine and health laws, are so denominated in the acts of Congress, and are considered as flowing from the acknowledged power of a State, to provide for the health of its citizens. but, as it was apparent that some of the provisions made for this purpose, and in virtue of this power, might interfere with, and be affected by the laws of the United States, made for the regulation of commerce, Congress, in that spirit of harmony and conciliation, which ought always to characterize the conduct of governments standing in the relation which that of the

Union and those of the States bear to each other, has directed its officers to aid in the execution of these laws; and has, in some measure, adapted its own legislation to this object, by making provisions in aid of those of the States. But, in making these provisions, the opinion is unequivocally manifested, that Congress may control the State laws, so far as it may be necessary to control them, for the regulation of commerce.

The act passed in 1803, prohibiting the importation of slaves into any State which shall itself prohibit their importation, implies, it is said, an admission that the States possessed the power to exclude or admit them; from which it is inferred, that they possess the same power with respect to other articles.

If this inference were correct; if this power was exercised, not under any particular clause in the constitution, but in virtue of a general right over the subject of commerce, to exist as long as the constitution itself, it might now be exercised. Any State might now import African slaves into its own territory. But it is obvious, that the power of the States over this subject, previous to the year 1808, constitutes an exception to the power of Congress to regulate commerce, and the exception is expressed in such words, as to manifest clearly the intention to continue the pre-existing right of the States to admit or exclude, for a limited period. The words are, "the migration or importation of such persons as any of the States, now existing, *shall* think proper to admit, shall ~~~ prohibited by the Congress prior to the year 1808. The whole object of the exception is, to preserve the power to those States which might be disposed to exercise it; and its language seems to the Court to convey this idea unequivocally. The possession of this particular power, then, during the time limited in the constitution, cannot be admitted to prove the possession of any other similar power.

It has been said, that the act of August 7, 1789, acknowledges a concurrent power in the States to regulate the conduct of pilots, and hence is inferred an admission of their concurrent right with Congress to regulate commerce with foreign nations, and amongst the States. But this inference is not, we think, justified by the fact.

Although Congress cannot enable a State to legislate, Congress may adopt the provisions of a State on any subject. When the government of the Union was brought into existence, it found a system for the regulation of its pilots in full force in every State. The act which has been mentioned, adopts this system, and gives it the same validity as if its provisions had been specially made by Congress. But the act, it may be said, is prospective also, and the adoption of laws to be made in future, presupposes the right in the maker to legislate on the subject.

The act unquestionably manifests an intention to leave this subject entirely to the States, until Congress should think proper to interpose; but the very enactment of such a law indicates an opinion that it was necessary; that the existing system would not be applicable to the new state of things, unless expressly applied to it by Congress. But this section is confined to pilots within the "bays, inlets, rivers, harbors, and ports of the United States," which are, of course, in whole or in part, also within the limits of some particular state. The acknowledged power of a State to regulate its police, its domestic trade, and to govern its own citizens, may enable it to legislate on this subject, to a considerable extent; and the adoption of its system by Congress, and the application of it to the whole subject of commerce, does not seem to the Court to imply a right in the States so to apply it of their own authority. But the adoption of the State system being temporary, being only "until further legislative provision shall be made by Congress," shows, conclusively, an opinion that Congress could control the whole subject, and might adopt the system of the States, or provide one of its own.

A State, it is said, or even a private citizen, may construct light houses. But gentlemen must be aware, that if this proves a power in a State to regulate commerce, it proves that the same power is in the citizen. States, or individuals who own lands, may, if not forbidden by law, erect on those lands what buildings they please; but this power is entirely distinct from that of regulating commerce, and may, we presume, be restrained, if exercised so as to produce a public mischief.

These acts were cited at the bar for the purpose of showing an opinion in Congress, that the States possess, concurrently with the Legislature of the Union, the power to regulate commerce with foreign nations and among the States. Upon reviewing them, we think they do not establish the proposition they were intended to prove. They show the opinion, that the States retain powers enabling them to pass the laws to which allusion has been made, not that those laws proceed from the particular power which has been delegated to Congress.

It has been contended by the counsel for the appellant, that, as the word "to regulate" implies in its nature, full power over the thing to be regulated, it excludes, necessarily, the action of all others that would perform the same operation on the same thing. That regulation is designed for the entire result, applying to those parts which remain as they were, as well as to those which are altered. It produces a uniform whole, which is as much disturbed and deranged by changing what the regulating power designs to leave untouched, as that on which it has operated.

There is great force in this argument, and the Court is not satisfied that it has been refuted. Since, however, in exercising the power of regulating their own purely internal affairs, whether of trading or police, the States may sometimes enact laws, the validity of which depends on their interfering with, and being contrary to, an act of Congress passed in pursuance of the constitution, the Court will enter upon the inquiry, whether the laws of New-York, as expounded by the highest tribunal of that State, have, in their application to this case, come into collision with an act of Congress, and deprived a citizen of a right to which that act entitles him. Should this collision exist, it will be immaterial whether those laws were passed in virtue of a concurrent power "to regulate commerce with foreign nations and among the several States," or, in virtue of a power to regulate their domestic trade and police. In one case and the other, the acts of New-York must yield to the law of Congress; and the decision sustaining the privilege they confer, against a right given by a law of the Union, must be erroneous.

This opinion has been frequently expressed in this Court, and is founded, as well on the nature of the government as on the words of the constitution. In argument, however, it has been contended, that if a law passed by a State, in the exercise of its acknowledged sovereignty, comes into conflict with a law passed by Congress in pursuance of the constitution, they affect the subject, and each other, like equal opposing powers.

But the framers of our constitution foresaw this state of things, and provided for it, by declaring the supremacy not only of itself, but of the laws made in pursuance of it. The nullity of any act, inconsistent with the constitution, is produced by the declaration, that the constitution is the supreme law. The appropriate application of that part of the clause which confers the same supremacy on laws and treaties, is to such acts of the State Legislatures as do not transcend their powers, but, though enacted in the execution of acknowledged State powers, interfere with, or are contrary to the laws of Congress, made in pursuance of the constitution, or some treaty made under the authority of the United States. In every such case, the act of Congress, or the treaty, is supreme; and the law of the State, though enacted in the exercise of powers not controverted, must yield to it.

In pursuing this inquiry at the bar, it has been said, that the constitution does not confer the right of intercourse between State and State. That right derives its source from those laws whose authority is acknowledged by civilized man throughout the world. This is true. The constitution found it an existing right, and gave to Congress the power to regulate it. In the exercise of this power, Congress has passed "an act for enrolling or licensing ships or vessels to be employed in the coasting trade and fisheries, and for regulating the same." The counsel for the respondent contend, that this act does not give the right to sail from port to port, but confines itself to regulating a pre-existing right, so far only as to confer certain privileges on enrolled and licensed vessels in its exercise.

It will at once occur, that, when a Legislature attaches certain privileges and exemptions to the exercise of a right over which its control is absolute, the law must imply a power to exercise the right. The privileges are gone, if the right itself be annihilated. It would be contrary to all reason, and to the course of human affairs, to say that a State is unable to strip a vessel of the particular privileges attendant on the exercise of a right, and yet may annul the right itself; that the State of New-York cannot prevent an enrolled and licensed vessel, proceeding from Elizabethtown, in New-Jersey, to New-York, from enjoying, in her course, and on her entrance into port, all the privileges conferred by the act of Congress; but can shut her up in her own port, and prohibit altogether her entering the waters and ports of another State. To the Court it seems very clear, that the whole act on the subject of the coasting trade, according to those principles which govern the construction of statutes, implies, unequivocally, an authority to licensed vessels to carry on the coasting trade.

But we will proceed briefly to notice those sections which bear more directly on the subject. The first section declares, that vessels enrolled by virtue of a previous law, and certain other vessels, enrolled as described in that act, and having a license in force, as is by the act required, "and no others, shall be deemed ships or vessels of the United States, entitled to the privileges of ships or vessels employed in the coasting trade."

This section seems to the Court to contain a positive enactment, that the vessels it describes shall be entitled to the privileges of ships or vessels employed in the coasting trade. These privileges cannot be separated from the trade, and cannot be enjoyed, unless the trade may be prosecuted. The grant of the privilege is an idle, empty form, conveying nothing, unless it convey the right to which the privilege is attached, and in the exercise of which its whole value consists. To construe these words otherwise than as entitling the ships or vessels described, to carry on the coasting trade, would be, we think, to disregard the apparent intent of the act.

The fourth section directs the proper officer to grant to a vessel qualified to receive it, "a license for carrying on the coasting trade;" and prescribes its form. After reciting the compliance of the applicant with the previous requisites of the law, the operative words of the instrument are, "license is hereby granted for the said steam-boat, Bellona, to be employed in carrying on the coasting trade for one year from the date hereof, and no longer."

These are not the words of the officer; they are the words of the legislature; and convey as explicitly the authority the act intended to give, and operate as effectually, as if they had been inserted in any other part of the act, than in the license itself.

The word "license," means permission, or authority; and a license to do any particular thing, is a permission or authority to do that thing; and if granted by a person having power to grant it, transfers to the grantee the right to do whatever it purports to authorize. It certainly transfers to him all the right which the grantor can transfer, to do what is within the terms of the license.

Would the validity or effect of such an instrument be questioned by the respondent, if executed by persons claiming regularly under the laws of New-York?

The license must be understood to be what it purports to be, a legislative authority to the steamboat Bellona, "to be employed in carrying on the coasting trade, for one year from this date."

It has been denied that these words authorize a voyage from New-Jersey to New-York. It is true, that no ports are specified; but it is equally true, that the words used are perfectly intelligible, and do confer such authority as unquestionably, as if the ports had been mentioned. The coasting trade is a term well understood. The law has defined it; and all know its meaning perfectly. The act describes, with great minuteness, the various operations of a vessel engaged in it; and it cannot, we think, be doubted, that a voyage from New-Jersey to New-York, is one of those operations.

Notwithstanding the decided language of the license, it has also been maintained, that it gives no right to trade; and that its sole purpose is to confer the American character.

The answer given to this argument, that the American character is conferred by the enrollment, and not by the license, is, we think, founded too clearly in the words of the law, to require the support of any additional observations. The enrollment of vessels designed for the coasting trade, corresponds precisely with the registration of vessels designed for the foreign trade, and requires every circumstance which can constitute the American character. The license can be granted only to vessels already enrolled, if they be of the burthen of twenty tons and upwards; and requires no circumstance essential to the American character. The object of the license, then, cannot be to ascertain the character of the vessel, but to do what it professes to do—that is, to give permission to a vessel already proved by her enrollment to be American, to carry on the coasting trade.

But, if the license be a permit to carry on the coasting trade, the respondent denies that these boats were engaged in that trade, or that the decree under consideration has restrained them from prosecuting it. The boats of the appellant were, we are told, employed in the transportation of passengers; and this is no part of that commerce which Congress may regulate.

If, as our whole course of legislation on this subject shows, the power of Congress has been universally understood in America, to comprehend navigation, it is a very persuasive, if not a conclusive argument, to prove that the construction is correct; and, if it be correct, no clear distinction is perceived between the power to regulate vessels employed in transporting men for hire, and property for hire. The subject is transferred to Congress, and no exception to the grant can be admitted, which is not proved by the words or the nature of the thing. A coasting vessel employed in the transportation of passengers, is as much a portion of the American marine, as one employed in the transportation of a cargo; and no reason is perceived why such vessel should be withdrawn from the regulating power of that government, which has been thought best fitted for the purpose generally. The provisions of the law respecting native seamen, and respecting ownership, are as applicable to vessels carrying men, as to vessels carrying manufactures; and no reason is perceived why the power over the subject should not be placed in the same hands. The argument urged at the bar, rest on the foundation, that the power of Congress does not extend to navigation, as a branch of commerce, and can only be applied to that subject incidentally and occasionally. But if that foundation be removed, we must show some plain, intelligible distinction, supported by the constitution, or by reason, for discriminating between the power of Congress over vessels employed in navigating the same seas. We can perceive no such distinction.

If we refer to the constitution, the inference to be drawn from it is rather against the distinction. The section which restrains Congress from prohibiting the migration or importation of such persons as any of the States may think proper to admit, until the year 1808, has always been considered as an exception from the power to regulate commerce, and certainly seems to class migration with importation. Migration applies as appropriately to voluntary, as importation does to involuntary, arrivals; and, so far as an exception from a power proves its existence, this section proves that the power to regulate commerce applies equally to the regulation of vessels employed in transporting men, who pass from place to place voluntarily, and to those who pass involuntarily.

If the power reside in Congress, as a portion of the general grant to regulate commerce, them acts applying that power to vessels generally, must be construed as comprehending all vessels. If none appear to be excluded by the language of the act, none can be excluded by construction. Vessels have always been employed to a greater or less extent in the transportation of passengers, and have never been supposed to be, on that account, withdrawn from the control or protection of Congress. Packets which ply along the coast, as well as those which make voyages between Europe and America, consider the transportation of passengers as an important part of their business. Yet it has never been suspected that the general laws of navigation did not apply to them.

The duty act, sections 23 and 46, contains provisions respecting passengers, and shows, that vessels which transport them, have the same rights, and must perform the same duties, with other vessels. They are governed by the general laws of navigation.

In the progress of things, this seems to have grown into a particular employment, and to have attracted the particular attention of government. Congress was no longer satisfied with comprehending vessels engaged specially in this business, within those provisions which were intended for vessels generally; and, on the 2d of March, 1819 passed "an act regulating passenger ships and vessels." This wise and humane law provides for the safety and comfort of passengers, and for the communication of every thing concerning them which may interest the government, to the Department of State, but makes no provision concerning the entry of the vessel, or her conduct in the waters of the United States. This, we think, shows conclusively the sense of Congress, (if, indeed, any evidence to that point could be required,) that the pre-existing regulations comprehended passenger ships among others; and, in prescribing the same duties, the Legislature must have considered them as possessing the same rights.

If, then, it were even true, that the Bellona and the Stoudinger were employed exclusively in the conveyance of passengers between New-York and New-Jersey, it would not follow that this occupation did not constitute a part of the coasting trade of the United States, and was not protected by the license annexed to the answer. But we cannot perceive how the occupation of these vessels can be drawn into question, in the case before the Court. The laws of New-York, which grant the exclusive privilege set up by the respondent, take no notice of the employment of vessels, and relate only to the principle by which they are propelled. Those laws do not inquire whether vessels are engaged in transporting men or merchandise, but whether they are moved by steam or wind. If by he former, the waters of New-York are closed against them, though their cargoes be dutiable goods, which the laws of the United States permit them to enter and deliver in New-York. If by the latter, those waters are free to them, though they should carry passengers only. In conformity with the law, is the bill of the plaintiff in the State Court. The bill does not complain that the Bellona and the Stoudinger carry passengers, but that they are moved by steam. This is the injury of which he complains, and is the sole injury against the continuance of which he asks relief. The bill does not even allege, specially, that those vessels were employed in the transportation of passengers, but says, generally, that they were employed "in the transportation of passengers, or otherwise." The answer avers, only, that they were employed in the coasting trade, and insists on the right to carry on any trade authorized by the license. No testimony is taken, and the writ of injunction and decree restrain these licensed vessels, nor from carrying passengers, but from being moved through the waters of New-York by steam, for any purpose whatever.

The questions, then, whether the conveyance of passengers be a part of the coasting trade, and whether a vessel can be protected in that occupation by a coasting license, are not, and cannot be, raised in this case. The real and sole question seems to be, whether a steam machine, in actual use, deprives a vessel of the privileges conferred by a license.

In considering this question, the first idea which presents itself, is, that the laws of Congress for the regulation of commerce, do not look to the principle by which vessels are moved. That subject is left entirely to individual discretion; and, in that vast and complex system of legislative enactment concerning it, which embraces every thing that the Legislature thought it necessary to notice, there is not, we believe, one word respecting the peculiar principle by which vessels are propelled through the water, except what may be found in a single act, granting a particular privilege to steam boats. With this exception, every act, either prescribing duties, or granting privileges, applies to every vessel, whether navigated by the instrumentality of wind or fire, of sails or machinery. The whole weight of proof, then, is thrown upon him who would introduce a distinction to which the words of the law give no countenance.

If a real difference could be admitted to exist between vessels carrying passengers and others, it has already been observed, that there is no fact in this case which can bring up that question. And, if the occupation of steam boats be a matter of such general notoriety, that the Court may be presumed to know it, although not specially informed by the record, then we deny that the transportation of passengers is their exclusive occupation. It is a matter of general history, that, in our western waters, their principal employment is the transportation of merchandise; and all know, that in the waters of the Atlantic they are frequently so employed.

But all inquiry into this subject seems to the Court to be put completely at rest, by the act already mentioned, entitled, "An act for the enrolling and licensing of steam boats."

This act authorizes a steam boat employed, or intended to be employed, only in a river or bay of the United States, owned wholly or in part by an alien, resident within the United States, to be enrolled and licensed as if the same belonged to a citizen of the United States.

This act demonstrates the opinion of Congress, that steam boats may be enrolled and licensed, in common with vessels using sails. They are, of course, entitled to the same privileges, and can no more be restrained from navigating waters, and entering ports which are free to such vessels, than if they were wafted on their voyage by the winds, instead of being propelled by the agency of fire. The one element may be as legitimately used as the other, for every commercial purpose authorized by the laws of the Union; and the act of a State inhibiting the use of either to any vessel having a license under the act of Congress, comes, we think, in direct collision with that act.

As this decides the cause, it is unnecessary to enter in an examination of that part of the constitution which empowers Congress to promote the progress of science and the useful arts.

The Court is aware that, in stating the train of reasoning by which we have been conducted to this result, much time has been consumed in the attempt to demonstrate propositions which may have been thought axioms. It is felt that the tediousness inseparable from the endeavour to prove that which is already clear, is imputable to a considerable part of this opinion. But it was unavoidable. The conclusion to which we have come, depends on a chain of principles which it was necessary to preserve unbroken; and, although some of them were thought nearly self-evident, the magnitude of the question, the weight of character belonging to those from whose judgment we dissent, and the argument at the bar, demanded that we should assume nothing.

Powerful and ingenious minds, taking, as postulates, that the powers expressly granted to the government of the Union, are to be contracted by construction, into the narrowest possible compass, and that the original powers of the States are retained, if any possible construction will retain them, may, by a course of well digested, but refined and metaphysical reasoning, founded on these premises, explain away the constitution of our country, and leave it, a magnificent structure, indeed, to look at, but totally unfit for use. They may so entangle and perplex the understanding, as to obscure principles, which were before thought quite plain, and induce doubts where, if the mind were to pursue its own course, none would be perceived. In such a case, it is peculiarly necessary to recur to safe and fundamental principles to sustain those principles, and when sustained, to make them the tests of the arguments to be examined.

Source:

United States Reports, Cases Argued and Adjudged in the Supreme Court of the United States. Vol, 9, 824, pp. 185–222.

John Quincy Adams, First Annual Message to Congress, 1825

Address delivered by President John Quincy Adams, the real author of the Monroe Doctrine, to Congress on December 6, 1825, near the end of his first year in office. In this message, Adams introduced a crucial issue for his administration when he referred to the Panama Congress, a meeting of Latin American nations to which he later urged the U.S. Congress to send representatives. The message also discussed Adams's policies of governmental support for internal improvements not only of roads and canals but also of educational and scientific institutions. He also urged further exploration of the American continent.

———————————⟨∞⟩———————————

Fellow-Citizens of the Senate and of the House of Representatives:

In taking a general survey of the concerns of our beloved country, with reference to subjects interesting to the common welfare, the first sentiment which impresses itself upon the mind is of gratitude to the Omnipotent Disposer of All Good for the continuance of the signal blessings of His providence, and especially for that health which to an unusual extent has prevailed within our borders, and for that abundance which in the vicissitudes of the seasons has been scattered with profusion over our land. Nor ought we less to ascribe to Him the glory that we are permitted to enjoy the bounties of His hand in peace and tranquillity—in peace with all the other nations of the earth, in tranquillity among ourselves. There has, indeed, rarely been a period in the history of civilized man in which the general condition of the Christian nations has been marked so extensively by peace and prosperity.

Europe, with a few partial and unhappy exceptions, has enjoyed ten years of peace, during which all her Governments, whatever the theory of their constitutions may have been, are successively taught to feel that the end of their institution is the happiness of the people, and that the exercise of power among men can be justified only by the blessings it confers upon those over whom it is extended.

During the same period our intercourse with all those nations has been pacific and friendly; it so continues. Since the close of your last session no material variation has occurred in our relations with any one of them. In the commercial and navigation system of Great Britain important changes of municipal regulation have recently been sanctioned by acts of Parliament, the effect of which upon the interests of other nations, and particularly upon ours, has not yet been fully developed. In the recent renewal of the diplomatic missions on both sides between the two Governments assurances have been given and received of the continuance and increase of the mutual confidence and cordiality by which the adjustment of many points of difference had already been effected, and which affords the surest pledge for the ultimate satisfactory adjustment of those which still remain open or may hereafter arise.

The policy of the United States in their commercial intercourse with other nations has always been of the most liberal character. In the mutual exchange of their respective productions they have abstained altogether from prohibitions; they have interdicted themselves the power of laying taxes upon exports, and whenever they have favored their own shipping by special preferences or exclusive privileges in their own ports it has been only with a view to countervail similar favors and exclusions granted by the nations with whom we have been engaged in traffic to their own people or shipping, and to the disadvantage of ours. Immediately after the close of the last war a proposal was fairly made by the act of Congress of the 3d of March, 1815, to all the maritime nations to lay aside the system of retaliating restrictions and exclusions, and to place the shipping of both parties to the common trade on a footing of equality in respect to the duties of tonnage and impost. This offer was partially and successively accepted by Great Britain, Sweden, the Netherlands, the Hanseatic cities, Prussia, Sardinia, the Duke of Oldenburg, and Russia. It was also adopted, under certain modifications, in our late commercial convention with France, and by the act of Congress of the 8th January, 1824, it has received a new confirmation with all the nations who had acceded to it, and has been offered again to all those who are or may hereafter be willing to abide in reciprocity by it. But all these regulations, whether established by treaty or by municipal enactments, are still subject to one important restriction.

The removal of discriminating duties of tonnage and of impost is limited to articles of the growth, produce, or manufacture of the country to which the vessel belongs or to such articles as are most usually first shipped from her ports. It will deserve the serious consideration of Congress whether even this remnant of restriction may not be safely abandoned, and whether the general tender of equal competition made in the act of 8th January, 1824, may not be extended to include all articles of merchandise not prohibited, of what country soever they may be the produce or manufacture. Propositions to this effect have already been made to us by more than one European Government, and it is probable that if once established by legislation or compact with any distinguished maritime state it would recommend itself by the experience of its advantages to the general accession of all.

The convention of commerce and navigation between the United States and France, concluded on the 24th of June, 1822, was, in the understanding and intent of both parties, as appears upon its face, only a temporary arrangement of the points of difference between them of the most immediate and pressing urgency. It was limited in the first instance to two years from the 1st of October, 1822, but with a proviso that it should further continue in force till the conclusion of a general and definitive treaty of commerce, unless terminated by a notice, six months in advance, of either of the parties to the other. Its operation so far as it extended has been mutually advantageous, and it still continues in force by common consent. But it left unadjusted several objects of great interest to the citizens and subjects of both countries, and particularly a mass of claims to considerable amount of citizens of the United States upon the Government of France of indemnity for property taken or destroyed under circumstances of the most aggravated and outrageous character. In the long period during which continual and earnest appeals have been made to the equity and magnanimity of France in behalf of these claims their justice has not been, as it could not be, denied. It was hoped that the accession of a new Sovereign to the throne would have afforded a favorable opportunity for presenting them to the consideration of his Government. They have been presented and urged hitherto without effect. The repeated and earnest representations of our minister at the Court of France remain as yet even without an answer. Were the demands of nations upon the justice of each other susceptible of adjudication by the sentence of an impartial tribunal, those to which I now refer would long since have been settled and adequate indemnity would have been obtained. There are large amounts of similar claims upon the Netherlands, Naples and Denmark. For those upon Spain prior to 1819 indemnity was, after many years of patient forbearance, obtained; and those upon Sweden have been lately compromised by a private settlement, in which the claimants themselves have acquiesced. The Governments of Denmark and of Naples have been recently reminded of those yet existing against them, nor will any of them be forgotten while a hope may be indulged of obtaining justice by the means within the constitutional power of the Executive, and without resorting to those means of self-redress which, as well as the time, circumstances, and occasion which may require them, are within the exclusive competency of the Legislature.

It is with great satisfaction that I am enabled to bear witness to the liberal spirit with which the Republic of Colombia has made satisfaction for well-established claims of a similar character, and among the documents now communicated to Congress will be distinguished a treaty of commerce and navigation with that Republic, the ratifications of which have been exchanged since the last recess of the Legislature. The negotiation of similar treaties with all the independent South American States has been contemplated and may yet be accomplished. The basis of them all, as proposed by the United States, has been laid in two principles—the one of entire and unqualified reciprocity, the other the mutual obligation of the parties to place each other permanently upon the footing of the most favored nation. These principles are, indeed, indispensable to the effectual emancipation of the American hemisphere from the thraldom of colonizing monopolies and exclusions, an event rapidly realizing in the progress of human affairs, and which the resistance still opposed in certain parts of Europe to the acknowledgment of the Southern American Republics as independent States will, it is believed, contribute more effectually to accomplish. The time has been, and that not remote, when some of those States might, in their anxious desire to obtain a nominal recognition, have accepted of a nominal independence, clogged with burdensome conditions, and exclusive commercial privileges granted to the nation from which they have separated to the disadvantage of all others. They are all now aware that such concessions to any European nation would be incompatible with that independence which they have declared and maintained.

Among the measures which have been suggested to them by the new relations with one another, resulting from the recent changes in their condition, is that of assembling at the Isthmus of Panama a congress, at which each of them should be represented, to deliberate upon objects important to the welfare of all. The Republics of Colombia, of Mexico, and of Central America have already deputed plenipotentiaries to such a meeting, and they have invited the United States to be also represented there by their ministers. The invitation has been accepted, and ministers on the part of the United States will be commissioned to attend at those deliberations, and to take part in them so far as may be compatible with that neutrality from which it is neither our intention nor the desire of the other American State that we should depart.

The commissioners under the seventh article of the treaty of Ghent have so nearly completed their arduous labors that, by the report recently received from the agent on the part of the United States, there is reason to expect that the commission will be closed at their next session, appointed for the 22d of May of the ensuring year.

The other commission, appointed to ascertain the indemnities due for slaves carried away from the United States after the close of the late war, have met with some difficulty, which has delayed their progress in the inquiry. A reference has been made to the British Government on the subject, which, it may be hoped, will tend to hasten the decision of the commissioners, or serve as a substitute for it.

Among the powers specifically granted to Congress by the Constitution are those of establishing uniform laws on the subject of bankruptcies throughout the United States and of providing for organizing, arming, and disciplining the militia and for governing such part of them as may be employed in the service of the United States. The magnitude and complexity of the interests affected by legislation upon these subjects may account for the fact that, long and often as both of them have occupied the attention and animated the debates of Congress, no systems have yet been devised for fulfilling to the satisfaction of the community the duties prescribed by these grants of power. To conciliate the claim of the individual citizen to the enjoyment of personal liberty, with the effective obligation of private contracts, is the difficult problem to be solved by a law of bankruptcy. These are objects of the deepest interest to society, affecting all that is precious in the existence of multitudes of persons, many of them in the classes essentially dependent and helpless, of the age requiring nurture, and of the sex entitled to protection from the free agency of the parent and the husband. The organization of the militia is yet more indispensable to the liberties of the country. It is only by an effective militia that we can at once enjoy the repose of peace and bid defiance to foreign aggression; it is by the militia that we are constituted an armed nation, standing in perpetual panoply of defense in the presence of all the other nations of the earth. To this end it would be necessary, if possible, so to shape its organization as to give it a more united and active energy. There are laws for establishing an uniform militia throughout the United States and for arming and equipping its whole body. But it is a body of dislocated members, without the vigor of unity and having little of uniformity but the name. To infuse into this most important institution the power of which it is susceptible and to make it available for the defense of the Union at the shortest notice and at the smallest expense possible of time, of life, and of treasure are among the benefits to be expected from the persevering deliberations of Congress.

Among the unequivocal indications of our national prosperity is the flourishing state of our finances. The revenues of the present year, from all their principal sources, will exceed the anticipations of the last. The balance in the Treasury on the 1st of January last was a little short of $2,000,000, exclusive of two millions and a half, being the moiety of the loan of five millions authorized by the act of 26th of May, 1824. The receipts into the Treasury from the 1st of January to the 30th of September, exclusive of the other moiety of the same loan, are estimated at $16,500,000, and it is expected that those of the current quarter will exceed $5,000,000, forming an aggregate of receipts of nearly twenty-two millions, independent of the loan. The expenditures of the year will not exceed that sum more than two millions. By those expenditures nearly eight millions of the principal of the public debt have been discharged. More than a million and a half has been devoted to the debt of gratitude to the warriors of the Revolution; a nearly equal sum to the construction of fortifications and the acquisition of ordnance and other permanent preparations of national defense; half a million to the gradual increase of the Navy; an equal sum for purchase of territory from the Indians and payment of annuities to them; and upward of a million for objects of internal improvement authorized by special acts of the last Congress. If we add to these $4,000,000 for payment of interest upon the public debt, there remains a sum of about seven millions, which have defrayed the whole expense of the administration of Government in its legislative, executive, and judiciary departments, including the support of the military and naval establishments and all the occasional contingencies of a government coextensive with the Union.

The amount of duties secured on merchandise imported since the commencement of the year is about twenty-five millions and a half, and that which will accrue during the current quarter is estimated at five millions and a half; from these thirty-one millions, deducting the drawbacks, estimated at less than seven millions, a sum exceeding twenty-four millions will constitute the revenue of the year, and will exceed the whole expenditures of the year. The entire amount of the public debt remaining due on the 1st of January next will be short of $81,000,000.

By an act of Congress of the 3d of March last a loan of $12,000,000 was authorized at 4 1/2 per cent, or an exchange of stock to that amount of 4 1/2 per cent for a stock of 6 per cent, to create a fund for extinguishing an equal amount of the public debt, bearing an interest of 6 per cent, redeemable in 1826. An account of the measures taken to give effect to this act will be laid before you by the Secretary of the Treasury. As the object which it had in view has been but partially accomplished, it will be for the consideration of Congress whether the power with which it clothed the Executive should not be renewed at an early day of the present session, and under what modifications.

The act of Congress of the 3d of March last, directing the Secretary of the Treasury to subscribe, in the name and for the use of the United States, for 1,500 shares of the capital stock of the Chesapeake and Delaware Canal Company, has been executed by the actual subscription for the amount specified; and such other measures have been adopted by that officer, under the act, as the fulfillment of its intentions requires. The latest accounts received of this important undertaking authorize the belief that it is in successful progress.

The payments into the Treasury from the proceeds of the sales of the public lands during the present year were estimated at $1,000,000. The actual receipts of the first two quarters have fallen very little short of that sum; it is not expected that the second half of the year will be equally productive, but the income of the year from that source may now be safely estimated at a million and a half. The act of Congress of 18th May, 1824, to provide for the extinguishment of the debt due to the United States by the purchasers of public lands, was limited in its operation of relief to the purchaser to the 10th of April last. Its effect at the end of the quarter during which it expired was to reduce that debt from ten to seven millions. By the operation of similar prior laws of relief, from and since that of 2d March, 1821, the debt had been reduced from upward of twenty-two millions to ten. It is exceedingly desirable that it should be extinguished altogether; and to facilitate that consummation I recommend to Congress the revival for one year more of the act of 18th May, 1824, with such provisional modification as may be necessary to guard the public interests against fraudulent practices in the resale of the relinquished land. The purchasers of public lands are among the most useful of our fellow-citizens, and since the system of sales for cash alone has been introduced great indulgence has been justly extended to those who had previously purchased upon credit. The debt which had been contracted under the credit sales had become unwieldy, and its extinction was alike advantageous the purchaser and to the public. Under the system of sales, matured as it has been by experience, and adapted to the exigencies of the times, the lands will continue as they have become, an abundant source of revenue; and when the pledge of them to the public creditor shall have been redeemed by the entire discharge of the national debt, to the swelling tide of wealth with which they replenish the common Treasury may be made to reflow in unfailing streams of improvement from the Atlantic to tie Pacific Ocean.

The condition of the various branches of the public service resorting from the Department of War, and their administration during the current year, will be exhibited in the report of the Secretary of War and the accompanying documents herewith communicated. The organization and discipline of the Army are effective and satisfactory. To counteract the prevalence of desertion among the troops it has been suggested to withhold from the men a small portion of their monthly pay until the period of their discharge; and some expedient appears to be necessary to preserve and maintain among the officers so much of the art of horsemanship as could scarcely fail to be found wanting on the possible sudden eruption of a war, which should take us unprovided with a single corps of cavalry. The Military Academy at West Point, under the restrictions of a severe but paternal superintendence, recommends itself more and more to the patronage of the nation, and the numbers of meritorious officers which it forms and introduces to the public service furnishes the means of multiplying the undertakings of public improvements to which their acquirements at that institution are peculiarly adapted. The school of artillery practice established at Fortress Monroe is well suited to the same purpose, and may need the aid of further legislative provision to the same end. The reports of the various officers at the head of the administrative branches of the military service, connected with the quartering, clothing, subsistence, health, and pay of the Army, exhibit the assiduous vigilance of those officers in the performance of their respective duties, and the faithful accountability which has pervaded every part of the system.

Our relations with the numerous tribes of aboriginal natives of this country, scattered over its extensive surface and so dependent even for their existence upon our power, have been during the present year highly interesting. An act of Congress of 25th of May, 1824, made an appropriation to defray the expenses of making treaties of trade and friendship with the Indian tribes beyond the Mississippi. An act of 3d of March, 1825, authorized treaties to be made with the Indians for their consent to the making of a road from the frontier of Missouri to that of New Mexico, and another act of the same date provided for defraying the expenses of holding treaties with the Sioux, Chippeways, Menomenees, Sauks, Foxes, etc., for the purpose of establishing boundaries and promoting peace between said tribes. The first and the last objects of these acts have been accomplished, and the second is yet in a process of execution. The treaties which since the last session of Congress have been concluded with the several tribes will be laid before the Senate for their consideration conformably to the Constitution. They comprise large and valuable acquisition of territory, and they secure an adjustment of boundaries and give pledges of permanent peace between several tribes which had been long waging bloody wars against each other. On the 12th of February last a treaty was signed at the Indian Springs between commissioners appointed on the part of the United States and certain chiefs and individuals of the Creek Nation of Indians, which was received at the seat of Government only a very few days before the close of the last session of Congress and of the late Administration. The advice and consent of the Senate was given to it on the 3d of March, too late for it to receive the ratification of the then President of the United States; it was ratified on the 7th of March, under the unsuspecting impression that it had been negotiated in good faith and in the confidence inspired by the recommendation of the Senate. The subsequent transactions is in relation to this treaty will form the subject of a separate communication.

The appropriations made by Congress for public works, as well in the construction of fortifications as for purposes of internal improvement, so far as they have been expended, have been faithfully applied. Their progress has been delayed by the want of suitable officers for superintending them. An increase of both the corps of engineers, military and topographical, was recommended by my predecessor at the last session of Congress. The reasons upon which that recommendation was founded subsist in all their force and have acquired additional urgency since that time. It may also be expedient to organize the topographical engineers into a corps similar to the present establishment of the Corps of Engineers. The Military Academy at West Point will furnish from the cadets annually graduated there officers well qualified for carrying this measure into effect.

The Board of Engineers for Internal Improvement, appointed for carrying into execution the act of Congress of 30th of April, 1824, "to procure the necessary surveys, plans, and estimates on the subject of roads and canals," have been actively engaged in that service from the close of the last session of Congress. They have completed the surveys necessary for ascertaining the practicability of a canal from the Chesapeake Bay to the Ohio River, and are preparing a full report on that subject, which, when completed, will be laid before you. The same observation is to be made with regard to the two other objects of national importance upon which the Board have been occupied, namely, the accomplishment of a national road from this city to New Orleans, and the practicability of uniting the waters of Lake Memphramagog with Connecticut River and the improvement of the navigation of that river. The surveys have been made and are nearly completed. The report may be expected at an early period during the present session of Congress.

The acts of Congress of the last session relative to the surveying, marking, or laying out roads in the Territories of Florida, Arkansas, and Michigan, from Missouri to Mexico, and for the continuation of the Cumberland road, are, some of them, fully executed, and others in the process of execution. Those for completing or commencing fortifications have been delayed only so far as the Corps of Engineers has been inadequate to furnish officers for the necessary superintendence of the works. Under the act confirming the statutes of Virginia and Maryland incorporating the Chesapeake and Ohio Canal Company, three commissioners on the part of the United States have been appointed for opening books and receiving subscriptions, in concert with a like number of commissioners appointed on the part of each of those States. A meeting of the commissioners has been postponed, to await the definitive report of the board of engineers. The light-houses and monuments for the safety of our commerce and mariners, the works for the security of Plymouth Beach and for the preservation of the islands in Boston Harbor, have received the attention required by the laws relating to those objects respectively. The continuation of the Cumberland road, the most important of them all, after surmounting no inconsiderable difficulty in fixing upon the direction of the road, has commenced under the most promising auspices, with the improvements of recent invention in the mode of construction, and with the advantage of a great reduction in the comparative cost of the work.

The operation of the laws relating to the Revolutionary pensioners may deserve the renewed consideration of Congress. The act of the 18th of March, 1818, while it made provision for many meritorious and indigent citizens who had served in the War of Independence, opened a door to numerous abuses and impositions. To remedy this the act of 1st May, 1820, exacted proofs of absolute indigence, which many really in want were unable and all susceptible of that delicacy which is allied to many virtues must be deeply reluctant to give. The result has been that some among the least deserving have been retained, and some in whom the requisites both of worth and want were combined have been stricken from the list. As the numbers of these venerable relics of an age gone by diminish; as the decays of body, mind, and estate of those that survive must in the common course of nature increase, should not a more liberal portion of indulgence be dealt out to them? May not the want in most instances be inferred from the demand when the service can be proved, and may not the last days of human infirmity be spared the mortification of purchasing a pittance of relief only by the exposure of its own necessities? I submit to Congress the expediency of providing for individual cases of this description by special enactment, or of revising the act of the 1st of May, 1820, with a view to mitigate the rigor of its exclusions in favor of persons to whom charity now bestowed can scarcely discharge the debt of justice.

The portion of the naval force of the Union in actual service has been chiefly employed on three stations—the Mediterranean, the coasts of South America bordering on the Pacific Ocean, and the West Indies. An occasional cruiser has been sent to range along the African shores most polluted by the traffic of slaves; one armed vessel has been stationed on the coast of our eastern boundary, to cruise along the fishing grounds in Hudsons Bay and on the coast of Labrador, and the first service of a new frigate has been performed in restoring to his native soil and domestic enjoyments the veteran hero whose youthful blood and treasure had freely flowed in the cause of our country's independence, and whose whole life has been a series of services and sacrifices to the improvement of his fellow-men. The visit of General Lafayette, alike honorable to himself and to our country, closed, as it had commenced, with the most affecting testimonials of devoted attachment on his part, and of unbounded gratitude of this people to him in return. It will form hereafter a pleasing incident in the annals of our Union, giving to real history

the intense interest of romance and signally marking the unpurchasable tribute of a great nation's social affections to the disinterested champion of the liberties of humankind.

The constant maintenance of a small squadron in the Mediterranean is a necessary substitute for the humiliating alternative of paying tribute for the security of our commerce in that sea, and for a precarious peace, at the mercy of every caprice of four Barbary States, by whom it was liable to be violated. An additional motive for keeping a respectable force stationed there at this time is found in the maritime war raging between the Greeks and the Turks, and in which the neutral navigation of this Union is always in danger of outrage and depredation. A few instances have occurred of such depredations upon our merchant vessels by privateers or pirates wearing the Grecian flag, but without real authority from the Greek or any other Government. The heroic struggles of the Greeks themselves, in which our warmest sympathies as freemen and Christians have been engaged, have continued to be maintained with vicissitudes of success adverse and favorable.

Similar motives have rendered expedient the keeping of a like force on the coasts of Peru and Chile on the Pacific. The irregular and convulsive character of the war upon the shores has been extended to the conflicts upon the ocean. An active warfare has been kept up for years with alternate success, though generally to the advantage of the American patriots. But their naval forces have not always been under the control of their own Governments. Blockades, unjustifiable upon any acknowledged principles of international law, have been proclaimed by officers in command, and though disavowed by the supreme authorities, the protection of our own commerce against them has been made cause of complaint and erroneous imputations against some of the most gallant officers of our Navy. Complaints equally groundless have been made by the commanders of the Spanish royal forces in those seas; but the most effective protection to our commerce has been the flag and the firmness of our own commanding officers. The cessation of the war by the complete triumph of the patriot cause has removed, it is hoped, all cause of dissension with one party and all vestige of force of the other. But an unsettled coast of many degrees of latitude forming a part of our own territory and a flourishing commerce and fishery extending to the islands of the Pacific and to China still require that the protecting power of the Union should be displayed under its flag as well upon the ocean as upon the land.

The objects of the West India Squadron have been to carry into execution the laws for the suppression of the African slave trade; for the protection of our commerce against vessels of piratical character, though bearing commissions from either of the belligerent parties; for its protection against open and unequivocal pirates. These objects during the present year have been accomplished more effectually than at any former period. The African slave trade has long been excluded from the use of our flag, and if some few citizens of our country have continued to set the laws of the Union as well as those of nature and humanity at defiance by persevering in that abominable traffic, it has been only by sheltering themselves under the banners of other nations less earnest for the total extinction of the trade than ours. The irregular privateers have within the last year been in a great measure banished from those seas, and the pirates for months past appear to have been almost entirely swept away from the borders and the shores of the two Spanish islands in those regions. The active, persevering, and unremitted energy of Captain Warrington and of the officers and men under his command on that trying and perilous service have been crowned with Signal success, and are entitled to the approbation of their country. But experience has shown that not even a temporary suspension or relaxation from assiduity can be indulged on that station without reproducing piracy and murder in all their horrors; nor is it probable that for years to come our immensely valuable commerce in those seas can navigate in security without the steady continuance of an armed force devoted to its protection.

It were, indeed, a vain and dangerous illusion to believe that in the present or probable condition of human society a commerce so extensive and so rich as ours could exist and be pursued in safety without the continual support of a military marine-the only arm by which the power of this Confederacy can be estimated or felt by foreign nations, and the only standing military force which can never be dangerous to our own liberties at home. A permanent naval peace establishment, therefore, adapted to our present condition, and adaptable to that gigantic growth with which the nation is advancing in its career, is among the subjects which have already occupied the foresight of the last Congress, and which will deserve your serious deliberations. Our Navy, commenced at an early period of our present political organization upon a scale commensurate with the incipient energies, the scanty resources, and the comparative indigence of our infancy, was even then found adequate to cope with all the powers of Barbary, save the first, and with one of the principal maritime powers of Europe.

At a period of further advancement, but with little accession of strength, it not only sustained with honor the most unequal of conflicts, but covered itself and our country with unfading glory. But it is only since the close of the late war that by the numbers and force of the ships of which it was composed it could deserve the name of a navy. Yet it retains nearly the same organization as when it consisted only of five frigates. The rules and regulations by which it is governed earnestly call for revision, and the want of a naval school of instruction, corresponding with the Military Academy at West Point, for the formation of scientific and accomplished officers, is felt with daily increasing aggravation.

The act of Congress of 26th of May, 1824, authorizing an examination and survey of the harbor of Charleston, in South Carolina, of St. Marys, in Georgia, and of the coast of Florida, and for other purposes, has been executed so far as the appropriation would admit. Those of the 3d of March last, authorizing the establishment of a navy-yard and depot on the coast of Florida, in the Gulf of Mexico, and authorizing the building of the sloops of war, and for other purposes, are in the course of execution, for the particulars of which and other objects connected with this Department I refer to the report of the Secretary of the Navy, herewith communicated.

A report from the Postmaster-General is also submitted, exhibiting the present flourishing condition of that Department. For the first time for many years the receipts for the year ending on the 1st of July last exceeded the expenditures during the same period to the amount of more than $45,000. Other facts equally creditable to the administration of this Department are that in two years from the 1st of July, 1823, an improvement of more than $185,000 in its pecuniary affairs has been realized; that in the same interval the increase of the transportation of the mail has exceeded 1,500,000 miles annually, and that 1,040 new post-offices have been established. It hence appears that under judicious management the income from this establishment may be relied on as fully adequate to defray its expenses, and that by the discontinuance of post-roads altogether unproductive others of more useful character may be opened, till the circulation of the mail shall keep pace with the spread of our population, and the comforts of friendly correspondence, the exchanges of internal traffic, and the lights of the periodical press shall be distributed to the remotest corners of the Union, at a charge scarcely perceptible to any individual, and without the cost of a dollar to the public Treasury.

Upon this first occasion of addressing the Legislature of the Union, with which I have been honored, in presenting to their view the execution so far as it has been effected of the measures sanctioned by them for promoting the internal improvement of our country, I can not close the communication without recommending to their calm and persevering consideration the general principle in a more enlarged extent. The great object of the institution of civil government is the improvement of the condition of those who are parties to the social compact, and no government, in whatever form constituted, can accomplish the lawful ends of its institution but in proportion as it improves the condition of those over whom it is established. Roads and canals, by multiplying and facilitating the communications and intercourse between distant regions and multitudes of men, are among the most important means of improvement. But moral, political, intellectual improvement are duties assigned by the Author of Our Existence to social no less than to individual man. For the fulfillment of those duties governments are invested with power, and to the attainment of the end—the progressive improvement of the condition of the governed—the exercise of delegated powers is a duty as sacred and indispensable as the usurpation of powers not granted is criminal and odious. Among the first, perhaps the very first, instrument for the improvement of the condition of men is knowledge, and to the acquisition of much of the knowledge adapted to the wants, the comforts, and enjoyments of human life public institutions and seminaries of learning are essential. So convinced of this was the first of my predecessors in this office, now first in the memory, as, living, he was first in the hearts, of our countrymen, that once and again in his addresses to the Congresses with whom he cooperated in the public service he earnestly recommended the establishment of seminaries of learning, to prepare for all the emergencies of peace and war—a national university and a military academy. With respect to the latter, had he lived to the present day, in turning his eyes to the institution at West Point he would have enjoyed the gratification of his most earnest wishes; but in surveying the city which has been honored with his name he would have seen the spot of earth which he had destined and bequeathed to the use and benefit of his country as the site for an university still bare and barren.

In assuming her station among the civilized nations of the earth it would seem that our country had contracted the engagement to contribute her share of mind, of labor, and of expense to the improvement of those parts of knowledge which lie beyond the reach of individual acquisition, and particularly to geographical and astronomical science. Looking back to the history only of the half century since the declaration of our independence, and observing the generous emulation with which the Governments of France, Great Britain, and Russia have devoted the genius, the intelligence, the treasures of their respective nations to the common improvement of the species in these branches of science, is it not incumbent upon us to inquire whether we are not bound by obligations of a high and honorable character to contribute our portion of energy and exertion to the common stock? The voyages of discovery prosecuted in the course of that time at the expense of those nations have not only redounded to their glory, but to the improvement of human knowledge. We have been partakers of that improvement and owe for it a sacred debt, not only of gratitude, but of equal or proportional exertion in the same

common cause. Of the cost of these undertakings, if the mere expenditures of outfit, equipment, and completion of the expeditions were to be considered the only charges, it would be unworthy of a great and generous nation to take a second thought. One hundred expeditions of circumnavigation like those of Cook and La Perouse would not burden the exchequer of the nation fitting them out so much as the ways and means of defraying a single campaign in war. But if we take into the account the lives of those benefactors of mankind of which their services in the cause of their species were the purchase, how shall the cost of those heroic enterprises be estimated, and what compensation can be made to them or to their countries for them? Is it not by bearing them in affectionate remembrance? Is it not still more by imitating their example—by enabling countrymen of our own to pursue the same carrier and to hazard their lives in the same cause?

In inviting the attention of Congress to the subject of internal improvements upon a view thus enlarged it is not my design to recommend the equipment of an expedition for circumnavigating the globe for purposes of scientific research and inquiry. We have objects of useful investigation nearer home, and to which our cares may be more beneficially applied. The interior of our own territories has yet been very imperfectly explored. Our coasts along many degrees of latitude upon the shores of the Pacific Ocean, though much frequented by our spirited commercial navigators, have been barely visited by our public ships. The River of the West, first fully discovered and navigated by a countryman of our own, still bears the name of the ship in which he ascended its waters, and claims the protection of our armed national flag at its mouth. With the establishment of a military post there or at some other point of that coast, recommended by my predecessor and already matured in the deliberations of the last Congress, I would suggest the expediency of connecting the equipment of a public ship for the exploration of the whole northwest coast of this continent.

The establishment of an uniform standard of weights and measures was one of the specific objects contemplated in the formation of our Constitution, and to fix that standard was one of the powers delegated by express terms in that instrument to Congress. The Governments of Great Britain and France have scarcely ceased to be occupied with inquiries and speculations on the same subject since the existence of our Constitution, and with them it has expanded into profound, laborious, and expensive researches into the figure of the earth and the comparative length of the pendulum vibrating seconds in various latitudes from the equator to the pole. These researches have resulted in the composition and publication of several works highly interesting to the cause of science. The experiments are yet in the process of performance. Some of them have recently been made on our own shores, within the walls of one of our own colleges, and partly by one of our own fellow-citizens. It would be honorable to our country if the sequel of the same experiments should be countenanced by the patronage of our Government, as they have hitherto been by those of France and Britain.

Connected with the establishment of an university, or separate from it, might be undertaken the erection of an astronomical observatory, with provision for the support of an astronomer, to be in constant attendance of observation upon the phenomena of the heavens, and for the periodical publication of his observations. It is with no feeling of pride as an American that the remark may be made that on the comparatively small territorial surface of Europe there are existing upward of 130 of these light-houses of the skies, while throughout the whole American hemisphere there is not one. If we reflect a moment upon the discoveries which in the last four centuries have been made in the physical constitution of the universe by the means of these buildings and of observers stationed in them, shall we doubt of their usefulness to every nation? And while scarcely a year passes over our heads without bringing some new astronomical discovery to light, which we must fain receive at second hand from Europe, are we not cutting ourselves off from the means of returning light for light while we have neither observatory nor observer upon our half of the globe and the earth revolves in perpetual darkness to our unsearching eyes?

When, on the 25th of October, 1791, the first President of the United States announced to Congress the result of the first enumeration of the inhabitants of this Union, he informed them that the returns gave the pleasing assurance that the population of the United States bordered on 4,000,000 persons. At the distance of thirty years from that time the last enumeration, five years since completed, presented a population bordering upon 10,000,000. Perhaps of all the evidences of a prosperous and happy condition of human society the rapidity of the increase of population is the most unequivocal. But the demonstration of our prosperity rests not alone upon this indication. Our commerce, our wealth, and the extent of our territories have increased in corresponding proportions, and the number of independent communities associated in our Federal Union has since that time nearly doubled. The legislative representation of the States and people in the two Houses of Congress has grown with the growth of their constituent bodies. The House, which then consisted of 65 members, now numbers upward of 200. The Senate, which consisted of 26 members, has now 48. But the executive and, still more, the judiciary departments are yet in a great measure confined to their primitive organization, and are now not adequate to the urgent wants of a still growing community.

The naval armaments, which at an early period forced themselves upon the necessities of the Union, soon led to the establishment of a Department of the Navy. But the Departments of Foreign Affairs and of the Interior, which early after the formation of the Government had been united in one, continue so united to this time, to the unquestionable detriment of the public service. The multiplication of our relations with the nations and Governments of the Old World has kept pace with that of our population and commerce, while within the last ten years a new family of nations in our own hemisphere has arisen among the inhabitants of the earth, with whom our intercourse, commercial and political, would of itself furnish occupation to an active and industrious department. The constitution of the judiciary, experimental and imperfect as it was even in the infancy of our existing Government, is yet more inadequate to the administration of national justice at our present maturity. Nine years have elapsed since a predecessor in this office, now not the last, the citizen who, perhaps, of all others throughout the Union contributed most to the formation and establishment of our Constitution, in his valedictory address to Congress, immediately preceding his retirement from public life, urgently recommended the revision of the judiciary and the establishment of an additional executive department. The exigencies of the public service and its unavoidable deficiencies, as now in exercise, have added yearly cumulative weight to the considerations presented by him as persuasive to the measure, and in recommending it to your deliberations I am happy to have the influence of his high authority in aid of the undoubting convictions of my own experience.

The laws relating to the administration of the Patent Office are deserving of much consideration and perhaps susceptible of some improvement. The grant of power to regulate the action of Congress upon this subject has specified both the end to be obtained and the means by which it is to be effected, "to promote the progress of science and useful arts by securing for limited times to authors and inventors the exclusive right to their respective writings and discoveries." If an honest pride might be indulged in the reflection that on the records of that office are already found inventions the usefulness of which has scarcely been transcended in the annals of human ingenuity, would not its exultation be allayed by the inquiry whether the laws have effectively insured to the inventors the reward destined to them by the Constitution—even a limited term of exclusive right to their discoveries?

On the 24th of December, 1799, it was resolved by Congress that a marble monument should be erected by the United States in the Capitol at the city of Washington; that the family of General Washington should be requested to permit his body to be deposited under it, and that the monument be so designed as to commemorate the great events of his military and political life. In reminding Congress of this resolution and that the monument contemplated by it remains yet without execution, I shall indulge only the remarks that the works at the Capitol are approaching to completion; that the consent of the family, desired by the resolution, was requested and obtained; that a monument has been recently erected in this city over the remains of another distinguished patriot of the Revolution, and that a spot has been reserved within the walls where you are deliberating for the benefit of this and future ages, in which the mortal remains may be deposited of him whose spirit hovers over you and listens with delight to every act of the representatives of his nation which can tend to exalt and adorn his and their country.

The Constitution under which you are assembled is a charter of limited powers. After full and solemn deliberation upon all or any of the objects which, urged by an irresistible sense of my own duty, I have recommended to your attention should you come to the conclusion that, however desirable in themselves, the enactment of laws for effecting them would transcend the powers committed to you by that venerable instrument which we are all bound to support, let no consideration induce you to assume the exercise of powers not granted to you by the people. But if the power to exercise exclusive legislation in all cases whatsoever over the District of Columbia; if the power to lay and collect taxes, duties, imposts, and excises, to pay the debts and provide for the common defense and general welfare of the United States; if the power to regulate commerce with foreign nations and among the several States and with the Indian tribes, to fix the standard of weights and measures, to establish post-offices and post-roads, to declare war, to raise and support armies, to provide and maintain a navy, to dispose of and make all needful rules and regulations respecting the territory or other property belonging to the United States, and to make all laws which shall be necessary and proper for carrying these powers into execution—if these powers and others enumerated in the Constitution may be effectually brought into action by laws promoting the improvement of agriculture, commerce, and manufactures, the cultivation and encouragement of the mechanic and of the elegant arts, the advancement of literature, and the progress of the sciences, ornamental and profound, to refrain from exercising them for the benefit of the people themselves would be to hide in the earth the talent committed to our charge—would be treachery to the most sacred of trusts.

The spirit of improvement is abroad upon the earth. It stimulates the hearts and sharpens the faculties not of our fellow-citizens alone, but of the nations of Europe and of their rulers. While dwelling with pleasing satisfaction upon the superior excellence of our political institutions, let us

not be unmindful that liberty is power; that the nation blessed with the largest portion of liberty must in proportion to its numbers be the most powerful nation upon earth, and that the tenure of power by man is, in the moral purposes of his Creator, upon condition that it shall be exercised to ends of beneficence, to improve the condition of himself and his fellowmen. While foreign nations less blessed with that freedom which is power than ourselves are advancing with gigantic strides in the career of public improvement, were we to slumber in indolence or fold up our arms and proclaim to the world that we are palsied by the will of our constituents, would it not be to cast away the bounties of Providence and doom ourselves to perpetual inferiority? In the course of the year now drawing to its close we have beheld, under the auspices and at the expense of one State of this Union, a new university unfolding its portals to the sons of science and holding up the torch of human improvement to eyes that seek the light. We have seen under the persevering and enlightened enterprise of another State the waters of our Western lakes mingled with those of the ocean. If undertakings like these have been accomplished in the compass of a few years by the authority of single members of our Confederation, can we, the representative authorities of the whole Union, fall behind our fellow-servants in the exercise of the trust committed to us for the benefit of our common sovereign by the accomplishment of works important to the whole and to which neither the authority nor the resources of any one State can be adequate?

Finally, fellow-citizens, I shall await with cheering hope and faithful cooperation the result of your deliberations, assured that, without encroaching upon the powers reserved to the authorities of the respective States or to the people, you will, with a due sense of your obligations to your country and of the high responsibilities weighing upon yourselves, give efficacy to the means committed to you for the common good. And may He who searches the hearts of the children of men prosper your exertions to secure the blessings of peace and promote the highest welfare of our country.

Source:

James D. Richardson, ed. *A Compilation of the Messages and Papers of the Presidents, 1789–1897.* Washington, D.C.: Government Printing Office, 1896–99.

Constitution of the Southern Cherokee Nation, 1827

Constitution drafted by the Cherokee Constitutional Convention on July 26, 1827. The document formed the basis for the foundation of the Cherokee Nation and outlined a system of government with an elected principal chief, a senate, and a house of representatives. A full-blood faction led by White Path had formed a rebel council to oppose the convention in February 1827. The mixed-blood leader John Ross, who later chaired the convention, defused White Path's rebellion by assuring the rebels that their views would be taken into consideration at the convention.

———————————⟨❦⟩———————————

We, the Representatives of the people of the Cherokee Nation in Convention assembled, in order to establish justice, ensure tranquility, promote our common welfare, and secure to ourselves and our posterity the blessings of liberty; acknowledging with humility and gratitude the goodness of the sovereign Ruler of the Universe, in offering us an opportunity so favorable to the design, and imploring his aid and direction in its accomplishment, do ordain and establish this Constitution for the Government of the Cherokee Nation.

Article I

Sec. 1. The Boundaries of this nation, embracing the lands solemnly guarantied and reserved forever to the Cherokee Nation by the Treaties concluded with the United States, are as follows; and shall forever hereafter remain unalterably the same to wit. Beginning on the North Bank of Tennessee River at the upper part of the Chickasaw old fields: then following the main channel of said river, including all the Islands therein, to the mouth of the Hiwassee river, thence up the main channel of said river including Islands, to the first hill which closes in on said river, about two miles above Hiwassee old Town; thence along the ridge which divides the waters of the Hiwassee and little Tellico, to the Tennessee river at Tallassee; thence along the main channel, including Islands, to the junction of the Cowee and Nanteyalee; thence along the ridge in the fork of said river, to the top of the blue ridge; thence along the blue ridge to the Unicoy Turnpike road; thence by a straight line to the main source of the Chestatee; thence along its main channel, including Islands, to the Chattahoocky; and thence down the same to the Creek boundary at Buzzard Roost, thence along the boundary line which separates this and the Creek Nation, to a point on the Coosa river opposite the mouth of Wills Creek; thence readmission. *Moreover* the Legislature shall have power to adopt such laws and regulations, as its wisdom may deem expedient and proper, to prevent the citizens from monopolizing improvements with the view of speculation.

Article II

Sec. 1. The Power of this Government shall be divided into three distinct departments;—the Legislative, the Executive, and the Judicial.

Sec. 2. No person or persons, belonging to one of these Departments, shall exercise any of the powers properly belonging to either of the others, except in the cases hereinafter expressly directed or permitted.

Article III

Sec. 1. The Legislative Power shall be vested in two distinct branches; a Committee, and a Council, each to shave a negative on the other, and both to be styled the General Council of the Cherokee Nation; and the style of their acts and laws shall be,

"Resolved by the Committee and Council in General Council convened."

Sec. 2. The Cherokee Nation, as laid off into eight Districts, shall so remain.

Sec. 3. The Committee shall consist of two members from each District, and the Council shall consist of three members from each District, to be chosen by the qualified electors of their respective Districts for two years; and the elections to be held in every District on the first Monday in August for the year 1828, and every succeeding two years thereafter; and the General Council shall be held once a year, to be convened on the second Monday of October in each year, at New Echota.

Sec. 4. No person shall be eligible to a seat in the General Council, but a free Cherokee Male citizen, who shall have attained to the age of twenty-five years. The descendants of Cherokee men by all free women, except the African race, whose parents may be or have been living together as man and wife, according to the customs and laws of this Nation, shall be entitled to all the rights and privileges of this Nation, as well as the posterity of Cherokee women by all free men. No person who is of negro or mulatto parentage, either by the father or mother side, shall be eligible to hold any office of profit, honor or trust, under this Government.

Sec. 5. The Electors, and members of the General Council shall, in all cases except those of treason, felony, or breach of the peace, be privileged from arrest during their attendance at election, and at the General Council, and in going to, and returning from, the same.

Sec. 6. In all elections by the people, the electors shall vote *viva voce.* Electors for members to the General Council for 1828, shall be held at the places of holding the several courts, and at the other two precincts in each District which are designated by the law under which the members of this Convention were elected; and the District Judges shall superintend the elections within the precincts of their respective Court Houses, and the Marshals & Sheriffs shall superintend within the precincts which may be assigned them by the Circuit Judges of their respective Districts, together with one other person, who shall be appointed by the Circuit Judges for each precinct within their respective Districts; and the Circuit Judges shall also appoint a clerk to each precinct.—The superintendents and clerks shall, on the Wednesday morning succeeding the election, assemble at their respective Court Houses and proceed to examine and ascertain the true state of the polls, and shall issue to each member, duly elected, a certificate and also make an official return of the state of the polls of election to the principal Chief, and it shall be the duty of the Sheriffs to deliver the same to the Executive Office; *Provided, nevertheless.* The General Council shall have power, after the election of 1828, to regulate by law the precincts and superintendents and clerks of elections in the several Districts.

Sec. 7. All free Male citizens, (excepting negroes, and descendants of white and Indian men by negro women, who may have been set free.) who shall have attained to the age of eighteen years shall be equally entitled to vote at all public elections.

Sec. 8. Each House of the General Council shall Judge of the qualifications, elections, and returns, of its own members.

Sec. 9. Each House of the General Council may determine the rules of its proceedings, punish a member for disorderly behaviour, and, with the concurrence of two thirds, expel a member; but not a second time for the same cause.

Sec. 10. Each House of the General Council, when assembled, shall choose its own officers; a majority of each house shall constitute a quorum to do business, but a smaller number may adjourn from day to day, and compel the attendance of absent members in such manner and under such penalty, as each house may prescribe.

Sec. 11. The members of the Committee shall each receive from the public Treasury a compensation for their services which shall be *two dollars* and *fifty cents* per day during their attendance at the General Council; and the members of the Council shall each receive *two dollars* per day, for their services during their attendance at the General Council:— *Provided,* That the same may be increased or diminished by law, but no alteration shall take effect during the period of service of the members of the General Council, by whom such alteration shall have been made.

Sec. 12. The General Council shall regulate by law, by whom and in what manner, writs of elections shall be issued to fill the vacancies which may happen in either branch thereof.

Sec. 13. Each member of the General Council, before he takes his seat, shall take the following oath, or affirmation; to wit: "I, A. B. do solemnly swear (or affirm as the ease may be) that I have not obtained my election by Bribery, Treaties, of any undue and unlawful means used by himself, or others by my desire or approbation, for that purpose; that I consider myself Constitutionally qualified as a member of . . . ; and that, on all questions and measures which may come before me, I will so give my vote, and so conduct myself, as may, in my judgment, appear most conducive to the interest and prosperity of this Nation; and that I will bear true faith and allegiance to the same, and to the utmost of my ability and power observe, conform to, support, and defend the Constitution thereof."

Sec. 14. No person who may be convicted of felony before any court of this Nation, shall be eligible to any office or appointment of honor, profit or trust, within this Nation.

Sec. 15. The General Council shall have power to make all laws and regulations, which they shall deem necessary and proper for the good of the Nation, which shall not be contrary to this Constitution.

Sec. 16. It shall be the duty of the General Council to pass such laws as may be necessary and proper, to decide differences by arbitrators to be appointed by the parties, who may choose that summary mode of adjustment.

Sec. 17. No power of suspending the laws of this Nation shall be exercised, unless by the Legislature or its authority.

Sec. 18. No retrospective law, nor any law impairing the obligations of contracts shall be passed.

Sec. 19. The Legislature shall have power to make laws for laying and collecting taxes, for the purpose of raising a revenue.

Sec. 20. All bills making appropriations shall originate in the Committee, but the Council may propose amendments or reject the same.

Sec. 21. All other bills may originate in either house, a subject to the concurrence or rejection of the other.

Sec. 22. All acknowledged Treaties shall be the Supreme law of the land.

Sec. 23. The General Council shall have the solo power of deciding on the construction of all Treaty stipulations.

Article IV

Sec. 1. The Supreme Executive Power of this Nation shall be vested in a Principal Chief, who shall be chosen by the General Council, and shall hold his office four years; to be elected as follows,—The General Council, by a joint vote, shall, at their second annual session, after the rising of this Convention, and at every fourth annual session thereafter, on the second day after the Houses shall be organized, and competent to proceed to business, elect a Principal Chief.

Sec. 2. No person except a natural born citizen shall be eligible to the office of Principal Chief; neither shall any person be eligible to that office, who shall not have attained to the age of thirty-five years.

Sec. 3. There shall also be chosen at the same time, by the General Council, in the same manner, for four years, an assistant Principal Chief.

Sec. 4. In case of the removal of the Principal Chief from office, or of his death resignation, or inability to discharge the powers and duties of the said office, the same shall devolve on the assistant principal Chief, until the inability be removed or the vacancy filled by the General Council.

Sec. 5. The General Council may, by law, provide for the case of removal, death, resignation or inability of both the Principal and assistant Principal Chiefs, declaring what officer shall then act as Principal Chief until the disability be removed, or a Principal Chief shall be elected.

Sec. 6. The Principal Chief and assistant Principal Chief, shall, at stated times, receive for their services, a compensation, which shall neither be increased nor diminished during the period for which they shall have been elected; and they shall not receive, within that period, any other emolument from the Cherokee Nation, or any other government.

Sec. 7. Before the Principal Chief enters on the execution of his office, he shall take the following oath, or affirmation; I do solemnly swear (or affirm) that I will faithfully execute the office of Principal Chief of the Cherokee Nation, and will, to the best of my ability, preserve, protect and defend the Constitution of the Cherokee Nation."

Sec. 8. He may, on extraordinary occasions, convene the General Council at the Seat of Government.

Sec. 9. He shall from time to time give to the General Council information of the State of the Government, and recommend to their consideration such measures as he may think expedient.

Sec. 10. He shall take care that the laws be faithfully executed.

Sec. 11. It shall be his duty to visit the different districts, at least once in two years, to inform himself of the general condition of the Country.

Sec. 12. The assistant Principal Chief shall, by virtue of his office, aid and advise the Principal Chief in the Administration of the Government, at all times during his continuance in office.

Sec. 13. Vacancies that may happen in offices, the appointment on which is vested in the General Council shall be filled by by the Principal Chief during the recess of the General Council, by granting Commissions which shall expire at the end of the next Session.

Sec. 14. Every Bill which shall have passed both Houses of the General Council shall, before it becomes a law, be presented to the Principal Chief of the Cherokee Nation. If he approve, he shall sign it, but if not, he shall return it, with his objections, to that house in which it shall have originated, who shall enter the objections at large on their journals, and proceed to reconsider it. If, after such reconsideration, two thirds of that House shall agree to pass the bill, it shall be sent, together with the objections, to the other house, by which it shall likewise be reconsidered, and if approved by two thirds of that house, it shall become a law. If any bill shall not be returned by the Principal Chief within five days (Sunday's excepted) after it shall have been presented to him, the same shall be a law, in like manner as if he had signed it; unless the General Council by their adjournment prevent its return, in which case it shall be a law, unless sent back within three days after their next meeting.

Sec. 15. Members of the General Council and all officers, Executive and Judicial, shall be bound by oath to support the Constitution of this Nation, and to perform the duties of their respective offices, with fidelity.

Sec. 16. In case of disagreement between the two houses with respect to the time of adjournment, the Principal Chief shall have power to adjourn the General Council to such a time as he thinks proper, *provided,* it be not to a period beyond the next Constitutional meeting of the same.

Sec. 17. The Principal Chief shall during the sitting of the General Council attend at the Seat of Government.

Sec. 18. There shall be a Council to consist of three men to be appointed by the joint vote of both Houses, to advise the Principal Chief in the Executive part of the Government, whom the Principal Chief shall have full power, at his discretion, to assemble; and he, together with the assistant Principal Chief, and the Counsellors, or a majority of them, may, from time to time, hold and keep a Council for ordering and directing the affairs of the Nation according to law.

Sec. 19. The members of the Council shall chosen for the term of one year.

Sec. 20. The resolutions and advice of the Council shall be recorded in a register and signed by the members agreeing thereto, which may be called for by either house of the General Council; and any counsellor may enter his dissent to the resolution of the majority.

Sec. 21. The Treasurer of the Cherokee Nation shall be chosen by the joint vote of both Houses of the General Council for the term of two years.

Sec. 22. The Treasurer shall, before entering on the duties of his office, give bond to the Nation with sureties to the satisfaction of the Legislature, for the faithful discharge of his trust.

Sec. 23. No money shall be drawn from the Treasury, but by warrant from the Principal Chief, and in consequence of appropriations made by law.

Sec. 25. It shall be the duty of the Treasurer to receive all public moneys, the joint vote of both Houses, to advise the Principal Chief in the Executive part of the Government, whom the Principal Chief shall have full power, at his discretion, to assemble; and be, together with the assistant Principal Chief, and the Counsellors, or a majority of them, may, from time to time, hold and keep a Council for ordering and directing the affairs of the Nation according to law.

Article V

Sec. 1. The Judicial Powers shall be vested in the Supreme Court, and such Circuit and Inferior Courts, as the General Council may, from time to time, ordain and establish.

Sec. 2. The Supreme Court shall consist of three Judges, any two of whom shall be a quorum.

Sec. 3. The two Judges of each shall hold their Commissions four years, but any of them may be removed from office on the address of two thirds of each house of the General Council to the Principal Chief, for that purpose.

Sec. 4. The Judges of the Supreme and Circuit Courts shall, at stated times, receive a compensation, which shall not be diminished during their continuance in office, but they shall receive no fees or perquisites of office, nor hold any other office of profit or trust, under this Nation or any other power.

Sec. 5. No person shall be appointed a Judge of any of the Courts before he shall have attained to the age of thirty years, nor shall any person continue to execute the duties of any of the said offices after he shall have attained to the age of seventy years.

Sec. 6. The Judges of the Supreme and Circuit Courts shall be appointed by a joint vote of both houses of the General Council.

Sec. 7. There shall be appointed in each District, under the legislative authority, as many Justices of the Peace as it may be deemed the public good requires, whose powers, duties and duration in office, shall be clearly designated.

Sec. 8. The Judges of the Supreme Court and Circuit Courts shall have complete criminal Jurisdiction in such cases & in such manner as may be pointed out by law.

Each Court shall choose its own Clerks for the term of four years; but such Clerks shall not be continued in office unless their qualifications shall be adjudged and approved of, by the Judges of the Supreme Court, and they shall be removable for breach of good behaviour of any time, by the Judges of their respective courts.

Sec. 10. No Judge shall sit on trial of any cause, where the parties shall be connected with him by affinity or consanguinity, except by consent of the parties. In case all the Judges of the Supreme court shall be interested in the event of any cause, or related to all, or either, of the parties, the Legislature may provide by law for the selection of three men, of good character and knowledge, for the determination thereof, who shall be specially commissioned by the Principal Chief for the case.

Sec. 11. All writs and other process shall run, in the name of the Cherokee Nation, and bear test, and be signed by the respective clerks.

Sec. 12. Indictments shall conclude, "against the peace & dignity of the Cherokee Nation."

Sec. 13. The Supreme Court shall hold its Session annually at the Seat of Government to be convened on the second Monday of October in each year.

Sec. 14. In all criminal prosecutions, the accused shall have the right of being heard, of demanding the nature and cause of the accusation against him, of meeting the witnesses face to face, of having compulsory process for obtaining witness in his favour; and, in prosecutions by indictment or information, a speedy public trial by an impartial jury of the vicinage; nor shall be be compelled to give evidence against himself.

Sec. 15. The people shall be secure in their persons, houses, papers and possessions from unreasonable seisures and searches, and no warrant to search any place or to seize any person or things shall issue without describing them as nearly as may be, nor without good cause, supported by oath, or affirmation. all prisoners shall be bailable by sufficient securities, unless for capital offences, where the proof is evident, or presumption great.

Source:

Laws of the Cherokee Nation, from a facsimile of the 1852 edition, produced by Legal Classics Library, a division of Gryphon Editions, New York.

John C. Calhoun, South Carolina Exposition Speech, 1828

Essay protesting the Tariff Act of 1828, drafted secretly, but not signed, by U.S. vice president John C. Calhoun of South Carolina, and issued by that state's legislature.

Supporters of President John Quincy Adams had proposed a high duty on foreign manufactures to protect New England industries; the South opposed the plan. Adams's opponents—supporters of Andrew Jackson—hoped to defeat the bill and discredit Adams by adding a high duty to the tariff on imported raw materials, an addition that New England was expected to oppose. The bill nonetheless passed, with support from New England and the West, but it proved very unpopular and contributed to Jackson's victory over Adams in the presidential election of 1828.

Calhoun argued that the tariff was "unconstitutional, oppressive, and unjust." He declared that the U.S. Constitution gave Congress the power to tax only to raise revenues, not the power to protect manufactures, and that the tariff violated these principles. Moreover, he claimed that a state could declare null and void a federal statute that it considered unconstitutional; such nullification could be overridden only by a constitutional amendment. South Carolina adopted an ordinance of nullification in response to the tariff passed by the U.S. Congress on July 14, 1832, that lowered somewhat the high protective tariff rates that had been established by the 1828 act. The 1832 act eliminated some features that eastern manufacturers and commercial interests disliked. It also increased the levy on woolens but allowed free admission to cheap raw wool and flax.

The Senate and House of Representatives of South Carolina, now met, and sitting in General Assembly, through the Hon. William Smith and the Hon. Robert Y. Hayne, their representatives in the Senate of the United States, do, in the name and on behalf of the good people of the said commonwealth, solemnly Protest against the system of protecting duties, lately adopted by the federal government, for the following reasons:—

1st. *Because* the good people of this commonwealth believe that the powers of Congress were delegated to it in trust for the accomplishment of certain specified objects which limit and control them, and that every exercise of them for any other purposes, is a violation of the Constitution as unwarrantable as the undisguised assumption of substantive, independent powers not granted or expressly withheld.

2d. *Because* the power to lay duties on imports is, and in its very nature can be, only a means of effecting objects specified by the Constitution; since no free government, and least of all a government of enumerated powers, can of right impose any tax, any more than a penalty, which is not at once justified by public necessity, and clearly within the scope and purview of the social compact; and since the right of confining appropriations of the public money to such legitimate and constitutional objects is as essential to the liberty of the people as their unquestionable privilege to be taxed only by their consent.

3d. *Because* they believe that the tariff law passed by Congress at its last session, and all other acts of which the principal object is the protection of manufactures, or any other branch of domestic industry, if they be considered as the exercise of a power in Congress to tax the people at its own good will and pleasure, and to apply the money raised to objects not specified in the Constitution, is a violation of these fundamental principles, a breach of a well-defined trust, and a perversion of the high powers vested in the federal government for federal purposes only.

4th. *Because* such acts, considered in the light of a regulation of commerce, are equally liable to objection; since, although the power to regulate commerce may, like all other powers, be exercised so as to protect domestic manufactures, yet it is clearly distinguishable from a power to do so *eo nomine*, both in the nature of the thing and in the common acception of the terms; and because the confounding of them would lead to the most extravagant results, since the encouragement of domestic industry implies an absolute control over all the interests, resources, and pursuits of a people, and is consistent with the idea of any other than a simple, consolidated government.

5th. *Because*, from the contemporaneous exposition of the Constitution in the numbers of the *Federalist*, (which is cited only because the Supreme Court has recognized its authority), it is clear that the power to regulate commerce was considered by the Convention as only incidentally connected with the encouragement of agriculture and manufactures; and because the power of laying imposts and duties on imports was not understood to justify in any case, a prohibition of foreign commodities, except as a means of extending commerce, by coercing foreign nations to a fair reciprocity in their intercourse with us, or for some *bona fide* commercial purpose.

6th. *Because*, whilst the power to protect manufactures is nowhere expressly granted to Congress, nor can be considered as necessary and proper to carry into effect any specified power, it seems to be expressly reserved to the states, by the 10th section of the 1st article of the Constitution.

7th. *Because* even admitting Congress to have a constitutional right to protect manufactures by the imposition of duties, or by regulations of commerce, designed principally for that purpose, yet a tariff of which the operation is grossly unequal and oppressive, is such an abuse of power as is incompatible with the principles of a free government and the great ends of civil society, justice, and equality of rights and protection.

8th. *Finally*, because South Carolina, from her climate, situation, and peculiar institutions, is, and must ever continue to be, wholly dependent upon agriculture and commerce, not only for her prosperity, but for her very existence as a state; because the valuable products of her soil—the blessings by which Divine Providence seems to have designed to compensate for the great disadvantages under which she suffers in other respects—are among the very few that can be cultivated with any profit by slave labor; and if, by the loss of her foreign commerce, these products should be confined to an inadequate market, the fate of this fertile state would be poverty and utter desolation; her citizens, in despair, would emigrate to more fortunate regions, and the whole frame and constitution of her civil policy be impaired and deranged, if not dissolved entirely.

Deeply impressed with these considerations, the representatives of the good people of this commonwealth, anxiously desiring to live in peace with their fellow-citizens, and to do all that in them lies to preserve and perpetuate the union of the states, and liberties of which it is the surest pledge, but feeling it to be their bounden duty to expose and resist all encroachments upon the true spirit of the Constitution, lest an apparant acquiescence in the system of protecting duties should be drawn into precedent—do, in the name of the commonwealth of South Carolina, claim to enter upon the Journal of the Senate their *protest* against it as unconstitutional, oppressive, and unjust.

Source:

Henry Steele Commager, ed. *Documents of American History.* New York: F.S. Crofts & Co., 1934.

Andrew Jackson, First Inaugural Address, 1829

Speech delivered by Andrew Jackson upon his inauguration as the seventh president of the United States on March 4, 1829, in Washington, D.C. Democrat Jackson expressed himself with an earnestness befitting a figure beheld as a man of the people and a symbol of their potential to attain political power. Outlining the principles he expected to follow in his tenure, Jackson vowed to respect limitations on presidential authority in administering federal legislation and pledged proper regard for states' rights. He promised economy and simplicity in his management of the public treasury, advocating a policy dedicated to eliminating the national debt. Jackson voiced federal support for internal improvements but offered no clear policy statement on the tariff, currency, or the Bank of the United States. Invoking the danger to free governments posed by peacetime standing armies, he forswore any increase in the existing U.S. force and trumpeted the state militias as the bulwark of the nation's defense. He called for a just and liberal policy toward Native American tribes within U.S. territorial claims. In closing, Jackson pledged to reform the federal civil service system that, he said, was corrupted by political patronage.

Fellow-Citizens:

About to undertake the arduous duties that I have been appointed to perform by the choice of a free people, I avail myself of this customary and solemn occasion to express the gratitude which their confidence inspires and to acknowledge the accountability which my situation enjoins. While the magnitude of their interests convinces me that no thanks can be adequate to the honor they have conferred, it admonishes me that the best return I can make is the zealous dedication of my humble abilities to their service and their good.

As the instrument of the Federal Constitution it will devolve on me for a stated period to execute the laws of the United States, to superintend their foreign and their confederate relations, to manage their revenue, to command their forces, and, by communications to the Legislature, to watch over and to promote their interests generally. And the principles of action by which I shall endeavor to accomplish this circle of duties it is now proper for me briefly to explain.

In administering the laws of Congress I shall keep steadily in view the limitations as well as the extent of the Executive power, trusting thereby to discharge the functions of my office without transcending its authority. With foreign nations it will be my study to preserve peace and to cultivate friendship on fair and honorable terms, and in the adjustment of any differences that may exist or arise to exhibit the forbearance becoming a powerful nation rather than the sensibility belonging to a gallant people.

In such measures as I may be called on to pursue in regard to the rights of the separate States I hope to be animated by a proper respect for those sovereign members of our Union, taking care not to confound the powers they have reserved to themselves with those they have granted to the Confederacy.

The management of the public revenue—that searching operation in all governments—is among the most delicate and important trusts in ours, and it will, of course, demand no inconsiderable share of my official solicitude. Under every aspect in which it can be considered it would appear that advantage must result from the observance of a strict and faithful economy. This I shall aim at the more anxiously both because it will facilitate the extinguishment of the national debt, the unnecessary duration of which is incompatible with real independence, and because it will counteract that tendency to public and private profligacy which a profuse expenditure of money by the Government is but too apt to engender. Powerful auxiliaries to the attainment of this desirable end are to be found in the regulations provided by the wisdom of Congress for the specific appropriation of public money and the prompt accountability of public officers.

With regard to a proper selection of the subjects of impost with a view to revenue, it would seem to me that the spirit of equity, caution, and compromise in which the Constitution was formed requires that the great interests of agriculture, commerce, and manufactures should be equally favored, and that perhaps the only exception to this rule should be consist in the peculiar encouragement of any products of either of them that may be found essential to our national independence.

Internal improvement and the diffusion of knowledge, so far as they can be promoted by the constitutional acts of the federal Government, are of high importance.

Considering standing armies as dangerous to free governments in time of peace, I shall not seek to enlarge our present establishment, nor disregard that salutary lesson of political experience which teaches that the military should be held subordinate to the civil power. The gradual increase of our Navy, whose flag has displayed in distant climes our skill in navigation and our fame in arms; the preservation of our forts, arsenals, and dockyards, and the introduction of progressive improvements in the discipline and science of both branches of our military service are so plainly prescribed by prudence that I should be excused for omitting their mention sooner than for enlarging on their importance. But the bulwark of our defense is the national militia, which in the present state of our intelligence and population must render us invincible. As long as our Government is administered for the good of the people, and is regulated by their will; as long as it secures to us the rights of person and of property, liberty of conscience and of the press, it will be worth defending; and so long as it is worth defending a patriotic militia will cover it with an impenetrable aegis. Partial injuries and occasional mortifications we may be subjected to, but a million of armed freemen, possessed of the means of war, can never be conquered by a foreign foe. To any just system, therefore, calculated to strengthen this natural safeguard of the country I shall cheerfully lend all the aid in my power.

It will be my sincere and constant desire to observe toward the Indian tribes within our limits a just and liberal policy, and to give that humane and considerate attention to their rights and their wants which is consistent with the habits of our Government and the feelings of our people.

The recent demonstration of public sentiment inscribes on the list of Executive duties, in characters too legible to be overlooked, the task of *reform*, which will require particularly the correction of those abuses that have brought the patronage of the Federal Government into conflict with the freedom of elections, and the counteraction of those causes which have disturbed the rightful course of appointment and have placed or continued power in unfaithful or incompetent hands.

In the performance of a task thus generally delineated I shall endeavor to select men whose diligence and talents will insure in their respective stations able and faithful cooperation, depending for the advancement of the public service more on the integrity and zeal of the public officers than on their numbers.

A diffidence, perhaps too just, in my own qualifications will teach me to look with reverence to the examples of public virtue left by my illustrious predecessors, and

with veneration to the lights that flow from the mind that founded and the mind that reformed our system. The same diffidence induces me to hope for instruction and aid from the coordinate branches of the Government, and for the indulgence and support of my fellow-citizens generally. And a firm reliance on the goodness of that Power whose providence mercifully protected our national infancy, and has since upheld our liberties in various vicissitudes, encourages me to offer up my ardent supplications that He will continue to make our beloved country the object of His divine care and gracious benediction.

Source:

Inaugural Addresses of the Presidents of the United States, 1789–1965. Washington, D.C.: Government Printing Office, 1896–99.

Daniel Webster's Second Reply to Robert Y. Hayne, 1830

Senators Robert Y. Hayne of South Carolina and Daniel Webster of Massachusetts debated nationalism versus states' rights in January 1830. The cause was a resolution sponsored by Senator Samuel A. Foot of Connecticut on December 29, 1829, halting the sale of public land. For two weeks the Senate debated in speeches ranging broadly over the issues of tariff, slavery, sectionalism, state nullification of federal statutes, the U.S. Constitution, and the nature of the Union.

The climax came with Webster's second reply (January 26–27) to Hayne. In it, the Massachusetts senator declared that the Union was the creation of the American people, not the states, and that the government was answerable only to the people. Samuel E. Morrison and Henry S. Commager in their history of the United States, *Growth of the American Republic,* consider Webster's speech "the greatest recorded American oration." It contains his call for nationalism: "Liberty and Union, now and for ever, one and inseparable." The following excerpts are from the concluding remarks, in which Webster argues against Haynes' position regarding states rights: "I understand him to insist, that if the exigency of the case, in the opinion of any State Government, require it, such State Government may, by its own sovereign authority, annul an act of the General Government, which it deems plainly and palpably unconstitutional."

―――――――― ⌒⟨∞⟩⌒ ――――――――

Direct collision, therefore, between force and force, is the unavoidable result of that remedy for the revision of unconstitutional laws which the gentleman contends for. It must happen in the very first case to which it is applied. Is not this the plain result? To resist, by force, the execution of a law, generally, is treason. Can the Courts of the United

States take notice of the indulgence of a State to commit treason? The common saying, that a State cannot commit treason herself, is nothing to the purpose. Can she authorize others to do it? If John Fries had produced an act of Pennsylvania, annulling the law of Congress, would it have helped his case? Talk about it as we will, these doctrines go the length of revolution. They are incompatible with any peaceable administration of the Government. They lead directly to disunion and civil commotion; and, therefore, it is, that at their commencement, when they are first found to be maintained by respectable men, and in a tangible form, I enter my public protest against them all.

The honorable gentleman argues, that if this Government be the sole judge of the extent of its own powers, whether that right of judging be in Congress, or the Supreme Court, it equally subverts State sovereignty. This the gentleman sees, or thinks he sees, although he cannot perceive how the right of judging, in this matter, if left to the exercise of State Legislatures, has any tendency to subvert the Government of the Union. The gentleman's opinion may be, that the right *ought not* to have the lodged with the General Government; he may like better such a Constitution, as we should have under the right of State interference; but I ask him to meet me on the plain matter of fact—I ask him to meet me on the Constitution itself—I ask him if the power is not found there—clearly and visibly found there?—Note 3.

But, sir, what is this danger, and what the grounds of it? Let it be remembered, that the Constitution of the United States is not unalterable. It is to continue in its present form no longer than the People who established it shall choose to continue it. If they shall become convinced that they have made an injudicious or inexpedient partition and distribution of power, between the State Governments and the General Government, they can alter that distribution at will.

If any thing be found in the National Constitution, either by original provision, or subsequent interpretation, which ought not to be in it, the People know how to get rid of it. If any construction be established, unacceptable to them, so as to become, practically, a part of the Constitution, they will amend it, at their own sovereign pleasure. But while the people chuse to maintain it, as it is; while they are satisfied with it, and refuse to change it; who has given, or who can give, to the State Legislatures a right to alter it, either by interference, construction, or otherwise? Gentlemen do not seem to recollect that the People have any power to do any thing for themselves; they imagine there is no safety for them, any longer than they are under the close guardianship of the State Legislatures. Sir, the People have not trusted their safety, in regard to the general Constitution, to these hands. They have required other security, and taken other bonds. They have chosen in trust themselves, first, to the plain words of the instru-

ment, and to such construction as the Government itself, in doubtful cases, should put on its own powers, under their oaths of office, and subject to their responsibility to them; just as the People of a State trust their own State Governments with a similar power. Secondly, they have reposed their trust in the efficacy of frequent elections, and in their own power to remove their own servants and agents, whenever they see cause. Thirdly, they have reposed trust in the Judicial power, which, in order that it might be trust-worthy, they have made as respectable, as disinterested, and as independent as was practicable. Fourthly, they have seen fit to rely, in case of necessity, or high expediency, on their known and admitted power, to alter or amend the Constitution, peaceably and quietly, whenever experience shall point out defects or imperfections. And, finally, the People of the United States have, at not time, in no way, directly or indirectly, authorized any State Legislature to construe or interpret *their* high instrument of Government; much less to interfere, by their own power, to arrest its course and operation.

If, sir, the People, in these respects, had done otherwise than they have done, their Constitution could neither have been preserved, nor would it have been worth preserving. And, if its plain provisions shall now be disregarded, and these new doctrines interpolated in it, it will become as feeble and helpless a being as its enemies, whether early or more recent, could possibly desire. It will exist in every State, but as a poor dependent on State permission. It must borrow leave to be; and will be, no longer than State pleasure, or State discretion, sees fit to grant the indulgence, and to prolong its poor existence.

But, sir, although there are fears, there are hopes also. The People have preserved this, their own chosen Constitution, for forty years, and have seen their happiness, prosperity, and renown, grow with its growth, and strengthen with its strength. They are now, generally, strongly attached to it. Overthrown by direct assault, it cannot be; evaded, undermined, Nullified it will not be, if we, and those who shall succeed us here, as agents and representatives of the People, shall conscientiously and vigilantly discharge the two great branches of our public trust—faithfully to preserve, and wisely to administer it.

Mr. President, I have thus stated the reasons of my dissent to the doctrines which have been advanced and maintained. I am conscious of having detained you and the Senate much too long. I was drawn into the debate, with no previous deliberation such as is suited to the discussion of so grave and important a subject. But it is a subject of which my heart is full, and I have not been willing to suppress the utterance of its spontaneous sentiments. I cannot, even now, persuade myself to relinquish it, without expressing, once more, my deep conviction, that, since it respects nothing less than the Union of the States, it is of most vital essential importance to the public happiness. I profess, sir, in my career, hitherto, to have kept steadily in view the prosperity and honor of the whole country, and preservation of our Federal Union. It is to that Union we owe our safety at home, and our consideration and dignity abroad. It is to that Union that we are chiefly indebted for whatever makes us most proud of our country. That Union we reached only by the discipline of our virtues in the severe school of adversity. It had its origin in the necessities of disordered finance, prostrate commerce, and ruined credit. Under its benign influences, these great interests immediately awoke, as from the dead, and sprang forth with newness of life. Every year of its duration has teemed with fresh proofs of its utility and its blessings; and, although our territory has stretched out wider and wide, and our population spread farther and farther, they have not outrun its protection or its benefits. It has been to us all a copious fountain of national, social, and personal happiness. I have not allowed myself, sir, to look beyond the Union, to see what might lie hidden in the dark recess behind. I have not cooly weighed the chances of preserving liberty, when the bonds that unite us together shall be broken asunder. I have not accustomed myself to hang over the precipice of disunion, to see whether, with my short sight, I can fathom the depth of the abyss below; nor could I regard him as a safe counsellor in the affairs of this Government, whose thoughts should be mainly bent on considering, not how the Union should be best preserved, but how tolerable might be the condition of the People when it shall be broken up and destroyed. While the Union lasts, we have high, exciting, gratifying prospects spread out before us, for us, and our children. Beyond that I seek not to penetrate the veil. God grant that, in my day, at least, that curtain may not rise. God grant that on my vision never may be opened what lies behind. When my eyes shall be turned to behold, for the last time, the sun in Heaven, may I not see him shining on the broken and dishonored fragments of a once glorious Union; on States dissevered, discordant, belligerent; on a land rent with civil feuds, or drenched, it may be, in fraternal blood! Let their last feeble and lingering glance, rather behold the gorgeous Ensign of the Republic, now known and honored throughout the earth, still high advanced, its arms and trophies streaming in their original lustre, not a stripe erased or polluted, nor a single star obscured—bearing for its motto, no such miserable interrogatory as, *What is all this worth?* Nor those other words of delusion and folly, *Liberty, first, and Union, afterwards*—but every where, spread all over in characters of living light, blazing on all its ample folds, as they float over the sea and over the land, and in every wind under the whole Heavens, that other sentiment, dear to every true American heart—Liberty *and* Union, now and forever, one and inseparable!

Source:

Charles M. Wiltse, ed. *The Papers of Daniel Webster*. Ser. 4, Vol. 1. Hanover, N.H.: Dartmouth College University Press of New England, 1974.

Indian Removal Act of 1830

Federal legislation enacted on May 28, 1830, authorizing the president to exchange land west of the Mississippi River for eastern lands held by the Indians. The act codified a policy proposed by President Andrew Jackson to allow increased white settlement in the East. In the subsequent decade, approximately 100,000 Native Americans were removed to the Great Plains, where whites were not interested in settling at that time. Under this act, many northern tribes were removed from their homes and the land they had inhabited for thousands of years. The southeastern Cherokee appealed to the Supreme Court and won, only to have President Jackson ignore the decision, stating, "John Marshall has made his decision; let him enforce it now if he can." (John Marshall was the chief justice of the Supreme Court.) Consequently, the Cherokee were forcibly deported to the West by the U.S. military in what came to be known as the "Trail of Tears."

─────────────────── ⌬ ───────────────────

An Act

To provide for an exchange of lands with the Indians residing in any of the states or territories, and for their removal west of the river Mississippi.

Be it enacted by the Senate and House of Representatives of the United States of America, in Congress assembled, That it shall and may be lawful for the President of the United States to cause so much of any territory belonging to the United States, west of the river Mississippi, not included in any state or organized territory, and to which the Indian title has been extinguished, as he may judge necessary, to be divided into a suitable number of districts, for the reception of such tribes or nations of Indians as may choose to exchange the lands where they now reside, and remove there; and to cause each of said districts to be so described by natural or artificial marks, as to be easily distinguished from every other.

Sec. 2. *And be it further enacted,* That it shall and may be lawful for the President to exchange any or all of such districts, so to be laid off and described, with any tribe or nation of Indians now residing within the limits of any of the states or territories, and with which the United States have existing treaties, for the whole or any part or portion of the territory claimed and occupied by such tribe or nation, within the bounds of any one or more of the states or territories, where the land claimed and occupied by the Indians, is owned by the United States, or the United

States are bound to the state within which it lies to extinguish the Indian claim thereto.

Sec. 3. *And be it further enacted,* That in the making of any such exchange or exchanges, it shall and may be lawful for the President solemnly to assure the tribe or nation with which the exchange is made, that the United States will forever secure and guaranty to them, and their heirs or successors, the country so exchanged with them; and if they prefer it, that the United States will cause a patent or grant to be made and executed to them of the same: *Provided always,* That such lands shall revert to the United States, if the Indians become extinct, or abandon the same.

Sec. 4. *And be it further enacted,* That if, upon any of the lands now occupied by the Indians, and to be exchanged for, there should be such improvements as add value to the land claimed by any individual or individuals of such tribes or nations, it shall and may be lawful for the President to cause such value to be ascertained by appraisement or otherwise, and to cause such ascertained value to be paid to the person or persons rightfully claiming such improvements. And upon the payment of such valuation, the improvements so valued and paid for, shall pass to the United States, and possession shall not afterwards be permitted to any of the same tribe.

Sec. 5. *And be it further enacted,* That upon the making of any such exchange as is contemplated by this act, it shall and may be lawful for the President to cause such aid and assistance to be furnished to the emigrants as may be necessary and proper to enable them to remove to, and settle in, the country for which they may have exchanged; and also, to give them such aid and assistance as may be necessary for their support and subsistence for the first year after their removal.

Sec. 6. *And be it further enacted,* That it shall and may be lawful for the President to cause such tribe or nation to be protected, at their new residence, against all interruption or disturbance from any other tribe or nation of Indians, or from any other person or persons whatever.

Sec. 7. *And be it further enacted,* That it shall and may be lawful for the President to have the same superintendence and care over any tribe or nation in the country to which they may remove, as contemplated by this act, that he is now authorized to have over them at their present places of residence: *Provided,* That nothing in this act contained shall be construed as authorizing or directing the violation of any existing treaty between the United States and any of the Indian tribes.

Sec. 8. *And be it further enacted,* That for the purpose of giving effect to the provisions of this act, the sum of five hundred thousand dollars is hereby appropriated, to be paid out of any money in the treasury, not otherwise appropriated.

See also CHEROKEE CASES AND ANDREW JACKSON, MESSAGE ON REMOVAL OF SOUTHERN INDIANS.

Source:
Statutes at Large. Vol. 4, pp. 411–412.

Worcester v. Georgia, 1832

Two cases derived from Georgia's attempts to take over lands held by the Cherokees according to prior treaties. The first decision, *Cherokee Nation v. Georgia,* was issued by the U.S. Supreme Court on March 18, 1831. It defined the legal status of Native Americans as "domestic dependent nations," not foreign nations. *Worcester v. Georgia* in 1832 eventually led to the Cherokee removal from Georgia to Oklahoma. In the early 19th century, the rich Cherokee lands in Georgia were coveted by white settlers. When the Georgia legislature in 1828 passed statutes claiming ownership of all Cherokee territory and annulling all Cherokee laws and customs, the Native Americans sought a U.S. Supreme Court injunction to prevent the execution of these laws. Writing for the majority, Chief Justice John Marshall ruled that the Court had no jurisdiction over the case because the Cherokees did not constitute a foreign nation with sovereignty rights over their own lands.

A year later, in *Worcester v. Georgia,* the Supreme Court declared that the Cherokee Nation was under the jurisdiction of the United States government, not the Georgia state government. The case arose when missionary Samuel A. Worcester and others violated a Georgia statute requiring white men who lived in Cherokee territory to take an oath of allegiance to the state and to obtain a license. Their conviction was reversed in this decision, but Georgia refused to obey the decision. The ruling also angered President Andrew Jackson, who refused to enforce it. This case was part of Georgia's effort to secure sovereignty over Cherokee lands.

Efforts to remove Indians were continued in Florida. On May 9, 1832, the United States and the Seminole Indians concluded a treaty that provided for the tribe's removal from Florida to the Indian Territory west of the Mississippi River. The Seminole, as one of the Five Civilized Tribes of the American Southeast, were a target of the federal Native American removal policy initiated in the late 1820s in response to worsening frontier clashes between white settlers and the Native tribes upon whose lands they were encroaching. By terms of the treaty, negotiated at Payne's Landing between U.S. representative James Gadsden and Seminole chiefs, the Seminole ceded all their land in Florida to the United States and agreed to emigrate to an allocated area west of the Mississippi. Consent to removal was contingent upon the tribe being able to send a deputation to judge the quality of the designated lands. The United States pledged to cover the costs of relocation and of feeding the tribe for one year after their arrival in the Indian Territory. The tribal deputation raised no objection to relocation, and the Payne's Landing Treaty was effectively ratified by a follow-up treaty of March 28, 1833.

———————————— ⌒⧓⌒ ————————————

Mr. Chief Justice Marshall delivered the opinion of the Court.

This cause, in every point of view in which it can be placed, is of the deepest interest.

The defendant is a state, a member of the union, which has exercised the powers of government over a people who deny its jurisdiction, and are under the protection of the United States.

The plaintiff is a citizen of the state of Vermont, condemned to hard labour for four years in the penitentiary of Georgia; under colour of an act which he alleges to be repugnant to the constitution, laws, and treaties of the United States.

The legislative power of a state, the controlling power of the constitution and laws of the United States, the rights, if they have any, the political existence of a once numerous and powerful people, the personal liberty of a citizen, are all involved in the subject now to be considered.

It behoves this court, in every case, more especially in this, to examine into its jurisdiction with scrutinizing eyes; before it proceeds to the exercise of a power which is controverted.

The first step in the performance of this duty is the inquiry whether the record is properly before the court.

It is certified by the clerk of the court, which pronounced the judgment of condemnation under which the plaintiff in error is imprisoned; and is also authenticated by the seal of the court. It is returned with, and annexed to, a writ of error issued in regular form, the citation being signed by one of the associate justices of the supreme court, and served on the governor and attorney-general of the state, more than thirty days before the commencement of the term to which the writ of error was returnable.

The judicial act . . . so far as it prescribes the mode of proceeding, appears to have been literally pursued.

❖   ❖   ❖

The record, then, according to the judiciary act, and the rule and the practice of the court, is regularly before us. The more important inquiry is, does it exhibit a case cognizable by this tribunal?

The indictment charges the plaintiff in error, and others, being white persons, with the offence of "residing within the limits of the Cherokee nation without a license," and "without having taken the oath to support and defend the constitution and laws of the state of Georgia."

The defendant in the state court appeared in proper person, and filed the following plea:

"And the said Samuel A. Worcester, in his own proper person, comes and says, that this court ought not to take further cognizance of the action and prosecution aforesaid, because, he says, that, on the 15th day of July in the year 1831, he was, and still is, a resident in the Cherokee nation; and that the said supposed crime or crimes, and each of them, were committed, if committed at all, at the town of New Echota, in the said Cherokee nation, out of the jurisdiction of this court, and not in the county Gwinnett, or elsewhere, within the jurisdiction of this court: and this defendant saith, that he is a citizen of the state of Vermont, one of the United States of America, and that he entered the aforesaid Cherokee nation in the capacity of a duly authorised missionary of the American Board of Commissioners for Foreign Missions, under the authority of the president of the United States, and has not since been required by him to leave it: that he was, at the time of his arrest, engaged in preaching the gospel to the Cherokee Indians, and in translating the sacred scriptures into their language, with the permission and approval of the said Cherokee nation, and in accordance with the humane policy of the government of the United States for the civilization and improvement of the Indians; and that his residence there, for this purpose, is the residence charged in the aforesaid indictment: and this defendant further saith, that this prosecution the state of Georgia ought not to have or maintain, because, he saith, that several treaties have, from time to time, been entered into between the United States and the Cherokee nation of Indians . . . by which treaties, the United States of America acknowledge the said Cherokee nation to be a sovereign nation, authorised to govern themselves, and all persons who have settled within their territory, free from any right of legislative interference by the several states composing the United States of America. . . . That the laws of the state of Georgia, which profess to add the said territory to the several adjacent counties of the said state, and to extend the laws of Georgia over the said territory, and persons inhabiting the same; and, in particular, the act on which this indictment against this defendant is grounded . . . are repugnant to the aforesaid treaties; which, according to the constitution of the United States, compose a part of the supreme law of the land; and that these laws of Georgia are, therefore, unconstitutional, void, and of no effect; that the said laws of Georgia are also unconstitutional and void, because they impair the obligation of the various contracts formed by and between the aforesaid Cherokee nation and the said United States of America...and because the said laws are repugnant to the statute of the United States, passed on the—day of March 1802, entitled 'an act to regulate trade and intercourse with the Indian tribes, and to preserve peace on the frontiers:' and that, therefore, this court has no jurisdiction . . . and, therefore, this defendant prays judgment whether he shall be held bound to answer further to said indictment."

This plea was overruled by the court. And the prisoner, being arraigned, plead not guilty. The jury found a verdict against him, and the court sentenced him to hard labour, in the penitentiary, for the term of four years.

By overruling this plea, the court decided that the matter it contained was not a bar to the action. The plea, therefore, must be examined, for the purpose of determining whether it makes a case which brings the party within the provisions of the twenty-fifth section of the "act to establish the judicial courts of the United States."

✻   ✻   ✻

The indictment and plea in this case draw in question, we think, the validity of the treaties made by the United States with the Cherokee Indians; if not so, their construction is certainly drawn in question; and the decision has been, if not against their validity, "against the right, privilege or exemption, specially set up and claimed under them." They also draw into question the validity of a statute of the state of Georgia, "on the ground of its being repugnant to the constitution, treaties and laws of the United States, and the decision is in favour of its validity."

It is, then, we think, too clear for controversy, that the act of congress, by which this court is constituted, has given it the power, and of course imposed on it the duty, of exercising jurisdiction in this case. This duty, however unpleasant, cannot be avoided. . . .

It has been said at the bar, that the acts of the legislature of Georgia seize on the whole Cherokee country, parcel it out among the neighbouring counties of the state, extend her code over the whole country, abolish its institutions and its laws, and annihilate its political existence.

If this be the general effect of the system, let us inquire into the effect of the particular statute and section on which the indictment is founded.

It enacts that "all white persons, residing within the limits of the Cherokee nation on the 1st day of March next, or at any time thereafter, without a license or permit from his excellency the governor, or from such agent as his excellency the governor shall authorise to grant such permit or license, and who shall not have taken the oath hereinafter required, shall be guilty of a high misdemeanour, and, upon conviction thereof, shall be punished by confinement to the penitentiary, at hard labour, for a term not less than four years."

The eleventh section authorises the governor, should be deem it necessary for the protection of the mines, or the enforcement of the laws in force within the Cherokee nation, to raise and organize a guard," &c.

The thirteenth section enacts, "that the said guard or any member of them, shall be, and they are hereby authorised and empowered to arrest any person legally charged with or detected in a violation of the laws of this state, and to convey, as soon as practicable, the person so arrested, before a justice of the peace, judge of the superior, or justice of inferior court of this state, to be dealt with according to law."

The extra-territorial power of every legislature being limited in its action, to its own citizens or subjects, the very passage of this act is an assertion of jurisdiction over the Cherokee nation, and of the rights and powers consequent on jurisdiction.

The first step, then, in the inquiry, which the constitution and laws impose on this court, is an examination of the rightfulness of this claim.

✻   ✻   ✻

The same stipulation entered into with the United States, is undoubtedly to be construed in the same manner. They receive the Cherokees nation into their favour and protection. The Cherokee acknowledge themselves to be under the protection of the United States, and of no other power. Protection does not imply the destruction of the protected. The manner in which this stipulation was understood by the American government, is explained by the language and acts of our first president.

✻   ✻   ✻

The treaties and laws of the United States contemplate the Indian territory as completely separated from that of the states; and provide that all intercourse with them shall be carried on exclusively by the government of the union.

Is this rightful exercise of power, or is it usurpation?

The Indian nations had always been considered as distinct, independent political communities, retaining their original natural rights, as the undisputed possessors of the soil, from time immemorial, with the single exception of that imposed by irresistible power, which excluded them from intercourse with any other European potentate than the first discover of the coast of the particular region claimed: and this was a restriction which those European potentates imposed on themselves, as well as on the Indians. The very term "nation," so generally applied to them, means "a people distinct from others." The constitution, by declaring treaties already made, as well as those to be made, to be the supreme law of the land, has adopted and sanctioned the previous treaties with the Indian nations, and consequently admits their rank among those powers who are capable of making treaties. The words "treaty" and "nation" are words of our own language, selected in our diplomatic and legislative proceedings, by ourselves, having each a definite and well understood meaning. We have applied them to Indians, as we have applied them to the other nations of the earth. They are applied to all in the same sense.

Georgia, herself, has furnished conclusive evidence that her former opinions on this subject concurred with those entertained by her sister states, and by the government of the United States. Various acts of her legislature have been cited in the argument, including the contract of cession made in the year 1802, all tending to prove her acquiescence in the universal conviction that the Indian nations possessed a full right to the lands they occupied, until the right should be extinguished by the United States, with their consent: that their territory was separated from that of any state within whose chartered limits they might reside, by a boundary line, established by treaties: that, within their boundary, they possessed rights with which no state could interfere: and that the whole power of regulating the intercourse with them, was vested in the United States. A review of these acts, on the part of Georgia, would occupy too much time, and is the less necessary, because they have been accurately detailed in the argument at the bar. Her new series of laws, manifesting her abandonment of these opinions, appears to have commenced in December 1828.

In opposition to this original right, possessed by the undisputed occupants of every country; to this recognition of that right, which is evidenced by our history, in every change through which we have passed; is placed the charters granted by the monarch of a distant and distinct region, parcelling out a territory in possession of others whom he could not remove and did not attempt to remove, and the cession made of his claims by the treaty of peace.

* * *

The Cherokee nation, then, is a distinct community occupying its own territory, with boundaries accurately described, in which the law of Georgia can have no force, and which the citizens of Georgia have no right to enter, but with the assent of the Cherokees themselves, or in conformity with treaties, and with the acts of congress. The whole intercourse between the United States and this nation, is, by our constitution and laws, vested in the government of the United States.

The act of the state of Georgia, under which the plaintiff in error was prosecuted, is consequently void, and the judgment a nullity. Can this court revise, and reverse it?

If the objection to the system of legislation, lately adopted by the legislature of Georgia, in relation to the Cherokee nation, was confined to its extra-territorial operation, the objection, though complete, so far as respected mere right, would give this court no power over the subject. But it goes much further. If the review which has been taken be correct, and we think it is, the acts of Geor-

gia are repugnant to the constitution, laws, and treaties of the United States.

They interfere forcibly with the relations established between the United States and the Cherokee nation, the regulation of which, according to the settled principles of our constitution, are committed exclusively to the government of the union.

They are in direct hostility with treaties, repeated in a succession of years, which mark out the boundary that separates the Cherokee country from Georgia; guaranty to them all the land within their boundary; solemnly pledge the faith of the United States to restrain their citizens from trespassing on it; and recognize the pre-existing power of the nation to govern itself.

They are in equal hostility with the acts of congress for regulating this intercourse, and giving effect to the treaties.

The forcible seizure and abduction of the plaintiff in error, who was residing in the nation with its permission, and by authority of the president of the United States, is also a violation of the acts which authorise the chief magistrate to exercise this authority.

Will these powerful considerations avail the plaintiff in error? We think they will. He was seized, and forcibly carried away, while under guardianship of treaties guarantying the country in which he resided, and taking it under the protection of the United States. He was seized while performing, under the sanction of the chief magistrate of the union, those duties which the humane policy adopted by congress had recommended. He was apprehended, tried, and condemned, under colour of a law which has been shown to be repugnant to the constitution, laws, and treaties of the United States. Had a judgment, liable to the same objections, been rendered for property, none would question the jurisdiction of this court. It cannot be less clear when the judgment affects personal liberty, and inflicts disgraceful punishment, if punishment could disgrace when inflicted on innocence. The plaintiff in error is not less interested in the operation of this unconstitutional law than if it affected his property. He is not less entitled to the protection of the constitution, laws, and treaties of his country.

* * *

It is the opinion of this court that the judgment of the superior court for the county of Gwinnett, in the state of Georgia, condemning Samuel A. Worcester to hard labour, in the penitentiary of the state of Georgia, for four years, was pronounced by that court under colour of a law which is void, as being repugnant to the constitution, treaties, and laws of the United States, and ought, therefore, to be reversed and annulled.

Source:
Supreme Court Reports, Vol. 5, p.1.

Andrew Jackson, Nullification Proclamation, 1832

Proclamation issued by President Andrew Jackson on December 10, 1832, concerning states' powers to nullify federal statutes. Prepared in response to South Carolina's Ordinance of Nullification, which declared the Tariff Acts of 1828 and 1832 to be null and void, Jackson's proclamation called nullification unconstitutional and an "impractical absurdity." The president maintained the supremacy of the federal government and declared that no state could refuse to obey federal laws. He warned that state governments should not consider using state troops to oppose federal legislation, stating that "disunion by armed force" constituted treason.

The South Carolina legislature on December 20, 1832, issued a series of resolutions asserting that the president had no constitutional authority to interfere in the affairs of a state or to proclaim the repeal of state statutes, and that states had the right to secede peaceably from the Union. South Carolina called Jackson's proclamation "subversive to the rights of the states and liberties of the people."

Congress backed up Jackson with federal legislation; the Force Act passed by Congress on March 2, 1833, at the request of Jackson. It granted the federal government the authority to enforce its revenue laws with military action if necessary. At the same time that Congress passed the Force Act, however, it also approved the compromise Tariff Act of 1833, which reduced the levies that South Carolina had found objectionable. While accepting the compromise tariff, South Carolina continued to assert its sovereignty by declaring on March 18, 1833, that the Force Act was null and void.

Proclamation to the People of the United States
I

Whereas a convention assembled in the State of South Carolina have passed an ordinance by which they declare "that the several acts and parts of acts of the Congress of the United States purporting to be laws for the imposing of duties and imposts on the importation of foreign commodities, and now having actual operation and effect within the United States, and more especially" two acts for the same purposes passed on the 29th of May, 1828, and on the 14th of July, 1832, "are unauthorized by the Constitution of the United States, and violate the true meaning and intent thereof, and are null and void and no law," nor binding on the citizens of that State or its officers; and by the said ordinance it is further declared to be unlawful for any of the constituted authorities of the State or of the United States to enforce the payment of the duties imposed by the said acts within the same State, and that it is the duty of the legislature to pass such laws as may be necessary to give full effect to the said ordinance; and

Whereas by the said ordinance it is further ordained that in no case of law or equity decided in the courts of said State wherein shall be drawn in question the validity of the said ordinance, or of the acts of the legislature that may be passed to give it effect, or of the said laws of the United States, no appeal shall be allowed to the Supreme Court of the United States, nor shall any copy of the record be permitted or allowed for that purpose, and that any person attempting to take such appeal shall be punished as for contempt of court; and, finally, the said ordinance declares that the people of South Carolina will maintain the said ordinance at every hazard, and that they will consider the passage of any act by Congress abolishing or closing the ports of the said State or otherwise obstructing the free ingress or egress of vessels to and from the said ports, or any other act of the Federal Government to coerce the State, shut up her ports, destroy or harass her commerce, or to enforce the said acts otherwise than through the civil tribunals of the country, as inconsistent with the longer continuance of South Carolina in the Union, and that the people of the said State will thenceforth hold themselves absolved from all further obligation to maintain or preserve their political connection with the people of the other States, and will forthwith proceed to organized a separate government and do all other acts and things which sovereign and independent states may of right do; and

Whereas the said ordinance prescribes to the people of South Carolina a course of conduct in direct violation of their duty as citizens of the United States, contrary to the laws of their country, subversive of its Constitution, and having for its object the destruction of the Union—that Union which, coeval with our political existence, led our fathers, without any other ties to unite them than those of patriotism and a common cause, through a sanguinary struggle to a glorious independence; that sacred Union, hitherto inviolate, which, perfected by our happy Constitution, has brought us, by the favor of Heaven, to a state of prosperity at home and high consideration abroad rarely, if ever, equaled in the history of nations:

To preserve this bond of our political existence from destruction, to maintain inviolate this state of national honor and prosperity, and to justify the confidence my fellow-citizens have reposed in me, I, Andrew Jackson, President of the United States, have thought proper to issue this my proclamation, stating my views of the Constitution and laws applicable to the measures adopted by the convention of South Carolina and to the reasons they have put forth to sustain them, declaring the course which duty will require me to pursue, and, appealing to the understanding and patriotism of the people, warn them of the consequences that must inevitably result from an observance of the dictates of the convention.

II

Strict duty would require of me nothing more than the exercise of those powers with which I am now or may be hereafter invested for preserving the peace of the Union and for the execution of the laws; but the imposing aspect which opposition has assumed in this case, by clothing itself with State authority, and the deep interest which the people of the United States must all feel in preventing a resort to stronger measures while there is a hope that anything will be yielded to reasoning and remonstrance, perhaps demand, and will certainly justify, a full exposition to South Carolina and the nation of the views I entertain of this important question, as well as a distinct enunciation of the course which my sense of duty will require me to pursue.

The ordinance is founded, not on the indefeasible right of resisting acts which are plainly unconstitutional and too oppressive to be endured, but on the strange position that any one State may not only declare an act of Congress void, but prohibit its execution; that they may do this consistently with the Constitution; that the true construction of that instruments permits a State to retain its place in the Union and yet be bound by no other of its laws than those it may choose to consider as constitutional. It is true, they add, that to justify this abrogation of a law it must be palpably contrary to the Constitution; but it is evident that to give the right of resisting laws of that description, coupled with the uncontrolled right to decide what laws deserve that character, is to give the power of resisting all laws; for as by the theory there is no appeal, the reasons alleged by the State, good or bad, must prevail. If it should be said that public opinion is a sufficient check against the abuse of this power, it may be asked why it is not deemed a sufficient guard against the passage of an unconstitutional act by Congress?

There is, however, a restraint in this last case which makes the assumed power of a State more indefensible, and which does not exist in the other. There are two appeals from an unconstitutional act passed by Congress— one to the judiciary, the other to the people and the States. There is no appeal from the State decision in theory, and the practical illustration shows that the courts are closed against an application to review it, both judges and jurors being sworn to decide in its favor. But reasoning on this subject is superfluous when our social impact, in express terms, declares that the laws of the United States, its Constitution, and treaties made under it are the supreme law of the land, and, for greater caution, adds "that the judges in every State shall be bound thereby, anything in the constitution or laws of any State to the contrary notwithstand-

ing." And it may be asserted without fear of refutation that no federative government could exist without a similar provision. Look for a moment to the consequence. If South Carolina considers the revenue laws unconstitutional and has a right to prevent their execution in the port of Charleston, there would be a clear constitutional objection to their collection in every other port; and no revenue could be collected anywhere, for all imposts must be equal. It is no answer to repeat that an unconstitutional law is no law so long as the question of its legality is to be decided by the State itself, for every law operating injuriously upon any local interest will be perhaps thought, and certainly represented, as unconstitutional, and, as has been shown, there is no appeal.

If this doctrine had been established at an earlier day, the Union would have been dissolved in its infancy. The excise law in Pennsylvania, the embargo and nonintercourse law in the Eastern States, the carriage tax in Virginia, were all deemed unconstitutional, and were more unequal in their operation than any of the laws now complained of; but, fortunately, none of those States discovered that they had the right now claimed by South Carolina. The war into which we were forced to support the dignity of the nation and the rights of our citizens might have ended in defeat and disgrace, instead of victory and honor, if the States who supposed it a ruinous and unconstitutional measure had thought they possessed the right of nullifying the act by which it was declared and denying supplies for its prosecution. Hardly and unequally as those measures bore upon several members of the Union, to the legislatures of none did this efficient and peaceable remedy, as it is called, suggest itself. The discovery of this important feature in our Constitution was reserved to the present day. To the statesmen of South Carolina belongs the invention, and upon the citizens of the State will unfortunately fall the evils of reducing it to practice.

If the doctrine of a State veto upon the laws of the Union carries with it internal evidence of its impracticable absurdity, our constitutional history will also afford abundant proof that it would have been repudiated with indignation had it been proposed to form a feature in our Government.

In our colonial state, although dependent on another power, we very early considered ourselves as connected by common interest with each other. Leagues were formed for common defense, and before the declaration of independence we were known in our aggregate character as *the United Colonies of America*. That decisive and important step was taken jointly. We declared ourselves a nation by a joint, not by several acts, and when the terms of our Confederation were reduced to form, it was in that of a solemn league of several States, by which they agreed that they would collectively form one nation for the purpose of conducting some certain domestic concerns and all foreign relations. In the instrument forming that Union is found an article which declares that "every State shall abide by the determinations of Congress on all questions which by that Confederation should be submitted to them."

Under the Confederation, then, no State' could legally annul a decision of the Congress or refuse to submit to its execution; but no provision was made to enforce these decisions, Congress made requisitions, but they were not complied with. The Government could not operate on individuals. They had no judiciary, no means of collecting revenue.

But the defects of the Confederation need not be detailed. Under its operation we could scarcely be called a nation. We had neither prosperity at home nor consideration abroad. This state of things could not be endured, and our present happy Constitution was formed, but formed in vain if this fatal doctrine prevails. It was formed for important objects that are announced in the preamble, made in the name and by the authority of the people of the United States, whose delegates framed and whose conventions approved it. The most important among these objects— that which is placed first in rank, on which all the others rest—is *to form a more perfect union.* Now, is it possible that even if there were no express provision giving supremacy to the Constitution and laws of the United States over those of the States, can it be conceived that an instrument made for the purpose of *forming a more perfect union* "than that of the Confederation could be so constructed by the assembled wisdom of our country as to substitute for that Confederation a form of government dependent for its existence on the local interest, the party spirit, of a State, or of a prevailing faction in a State? Every man of plain, unsophisticated understanding who hears the question will give such an answer as will preserve the Union. Metaphysical subtlety, in pursuit of an impracticable theory, could alone have devised one that is calculated to destroy it.

I consider, then, the power to annul a law of the United States, assumed by one State, *incompatible with the existence of the Union, contradicted expressly by the letter of the Constitution, unauthorized by its spirit, inconsistent with every principle on which it was founded, and destructive of the great object for which it was formed.*

After this general view of the leading principle, we must examine the particular application of it which is made in the ordinance.

III

The preamble rests its justification on these grounds: It assumes as a fact that the obnoxious laws, although they purport to be laws for raising revenue, were in reality intended for the protection of manufactures, which purpose it asserts to be unconstitutional; that the operation of these laws is unequal; that the amount raised by them is greater than is required by the wants of the Government; and, finally, that the proceeds are to be applied to objects unauthorized by the Constitution. These are the only causes alleged to justify an open opposition to the laws of the country and a threat of seceding from the Union if any attempt should be made to enforce them. The first virtually acknowledges that the law in question was passed under a power expressly given by the Constitution to lay and collect imposts; but its constitutionality is drawn in question from the *motives* of those who passed it. However apparent this purpose may be in the present case, nothing can be more dangerous than to admit the position that an unconstitutional purpose entertained by the members who assent to a law enacted under a constitutional power shall make that law void. For how is that purpose to be ascertained? Who is to make the scrutiny? How often may bad purposes be falsely imputed, in how many cases are they concealed by false professions, in how many is no declaration of motive made? Admit this doctrine, and you give to the States an uncontrolled right to decide, and every law may be annulled under this pretext. If, therefore, the absurd and dangerous doctrine should be admitted that a State may annul an unconstitutional law, or one that it deems such, it will not apply to the present case.

The next objection is that the laws in question operate unequally. This objection may be made with truth to every law that has been or can be passed. The wisdom of man never yet contrived a system of taxation that would operate with perfect equality. If the unequal operation of a law makes it unconstitutional, and if all laws of that description may be abrogated by any State for that cause, then, indeed, is the Federal Constitution unworthy of the slightest effort for its preservation. We have hitherto relied on it as the perpetual bond of our Union; we have received it as the work of the assembled wisdom of the nation; we have trusted to it as to the sheet anchor of our safety in the stormy times of conflict with a foreign or domestic foe; we have looked to it with sacred awe as the palladium of our liberties, and with all the solemnities of religion have pledged to each other our lives and fortunes here and our hopes of happiness hereafter in its defense and support. Were we mistaken, my countrymen, in attaching this importance to the Constitution of our country? Was our devotion paid to the wretched, inefficient, clumsy contrivance which this new doctrine would make it? Did we pledge ourselves to the support of an airy nothing—a bubble that must be blown away by the first breath of disaffection? Was this self-destroying, visionary theory the work of the profound statesmen, the exalted patriots, to whom the task of constitutional reform was intrusted? Did the name of Washington sanction, did the States deliberately ratify, such an anomaly in the history of fundamental legislation? No; we were not mistaken. The letter of this great instrument is free from this radical fault. Its language directly contradicts the imputation; its spirit, its evident intent, contradicts it. No; we did not err. Our Constitution does not contain the absurdity of giving power to make laws and another to resist them. The sages whose memory will always be reverenced have given us a practical and, as they hoped, a permanent constitutional compact. The father of his country did not affix his revered name to so palpable an absurdity. Nor did the States, when they severally ratified it, do so under the impression that a veto on the laws of the United States was reserved to them or that they could exercise it by implication. Search the debates in all their conventions, examine the speeches of the most zealous opposers of Federal authority, look at the amendments that were proposed; they are all silent—not a syllable uttered, not a vote given, not a motion made to correct the explicit supremacy given to the laws of the Union over those of the States, or to show that implication, as is now contended, could defeat it. No; we have not erred. The Constitution is still the object of our reverence, the bond of our Union, our defense in danger, the source of our prosperity in peace. It shall descend, as we have received it, uncorrupted by sophistical construction, to our posterity; and the sacrifices of local interest, of State prejudices, of personal animosities, that were made to bring it into existence, will again be patriotically offered for its support.

The two remaining objections made by the ordinance to these laws are that the sums intended to be raised by them are greater than are required and that the proceeds will be unconstitutionally employed. The Constitution has given, expressly, to Congress the right of raising revenue and of determining the sum the public exigencies will require. The States have no control over the exercise of this right other than that which results from the power of changing the representatives who abuse it, and thus procure redress. Congress may undoubtedly abuse this discretionary power; but the same may be said of others with which they are vested. Yet the discretion must exist somewhere. The Constitution has given it to the representatives of all the people, checked by the representatives of the States and by the Executive power. The South Carolina construction gives it to the legislature or the convention of a single State, where neither the people of the different States, nor the States in their separate capacity, nor the Chief Magistrate elected by the people have any representation. Which is the most discreet disposition of the power? I do not ask you, fellow-citizens, which is the constitutional disposition; that instrument speaks a language

not to be misunderstood. But if you were assembled in general convention, which would you think the safest depository of this discretionary power in the last resort? Would you add a clause giving it to each of the States, or would you sanction the wise provisions already made by your Constitution? If this should be the result of your deliberations when providing for the future, are you, can you, be ready to risk all that we hold dear, to establish for a temporary and a local purpose, that which you must acknowledge to be destructive, and even absurd, as a general provision? Carry out the consequences of this right vested in the different States, and you must perceive that the crisis your conduct presents at this day would recur whenever any law of the United States displeased any of the States, and that we should soon cease to be a nation.

The ordinance, with the same knowledge of the future that characterizes a former objection, tells you that the proceeds of the tax will be unconstitutionally applied. If this could be ascertained with certainty, the objection would with more propriety be reserved for the law so applying the proceeds, but surely cannot be urged against the laws levying the duty.

These are the allegations contained in the ordinance. Examine them seriously, my fellow-citizens; judge for yourselves. I appeal to you to determine whether they are so clear, so convincing, as to leave no doubt of their correctness; and even if you should come to this conclusion, how far they justify the reckless, destructive course which you are directed to pursue. Review these objections and the conclusions drawn from them once more. What are they? Every law, then, for raising revenue according to the South Carolina ordinance, may be rightfully annulled, unless it be so framed as no law ever will or can be framed. Congress have a right to pass laws for raising revenue and each State have a right to oppose their execution—two rights directly opposed to each other; and yet is this absurdity supposed to be contained in an instrument drawn for the express purpose of avoiding collisions between the States and the General Government by an assembly of the most enlightened statesmen and purest patriots ever embodied for a similar purpose.

In vain have these sages declared that Congress shall have power to lay and collect taxes, duties, imposts, and excises; in vain have they provided that they shall have power to pass laws which shall be necessary and proper to carry those powers into execution, that those laws and that Constitution shall be the "supreme law of the land, and that the judges in every State shall be bound thereby, anything in the constitution or laws of any State to the contrary notwithstanding"; in vain have the people of the several States solemnly sanctioned these provisions, made them their paramount law, and individually sworn to support them whenever they were called on to execute any office. Vain provisions! ineffectual restrictions! vile profanation of oaths! miserable mockery of legislation! if a bare majority of the voters in any one State may, on a real or supposed knowledge of the intent with which a law has been passed, declare themselves free from its operation; say, here it gives too little, there, too much, and operates unequally; here it suffers articles to be free that ought to be taxed; there it taxes those that ought to be free; in this case the proceeds are intended to be applied to purposes which we do not approve; in that, the amount raised is more than is wanted. Congress, it is true, are invested by the Constitution with the right of deciding these questions according to their sound discretion. Congress is composed of the representatives of all the States and of all the people of all the States. But *we*, part of the people of one State, to whom the Constitution has given no power on the subject, from whom it has expressly taken it away: *we*, who have solemnly agreed that this Constitution shall be our law; *we*, most of whom have sworn to support it— *we* now abrogate this law and swear, and force others to swear, that it shall not be obeyed; and we do this not because Congress have no right to pass such laws—this we do not allege—but because they have passed them with improper views. They are unconstitutional from the motives of those who passed them, which we can never with certainty know; from their unequal operation, although it is impossible, from the nature of things, that they should be equal; and from the disposition which we presume may be made of their proceeds, although that disposition has not been declared. This is the plain meaning of the ordinance in relation to laws which it abrogates for alleged unconstitutionality. But it does not stop there. It repeals in express terms an important part of the Constitution itself and of laws passed to give it effect, which have never been alleged to be unconstitutional.

The Constitution declares that the judicial powers of the United States extend to cases arising under the laws of the United States, and that such laws, the Constitution, and treaties shall be paramount to the State constitutions and laws. The judiciary act prescribes the mode by which the case may be brought before a court of the United States by appeal when a State tribunal shall decide against this provision of the Constitution. The ordinance declares there shall be no appeal—makes the State law paramount to the Constitution and laws of the United States, forces judges and jurors to swear that they will disregard their provisions, and even makes it penal in a suitor to attempt relief by appeal. It further declares that it shall not be lawful for the authorities of the United States or of that State to enforce the payment of duties imposed by the revenue laws within its limits.

Here is a law of the United States, not even pretended to be unconstitutional, repealed by the authority of a small majority of the voters of a single State. Here is a provision of the Constitution which is solemnly abrogated by the same authority.

On such expositions and reasonings the ordinance grounds not only an assertion of the right to annual the laws of which it complains, but to enforce it by a threat of seceding from the Union if any attempt is made to execute them.

This right to secede is deduced from the nature of the Constitution, which, they say, is a compact between sovereign States who have preserved their whole sovereignty and therefore are subject to no superior; that because they made the compact they can break it when in their opinion it has been departed from by the other States. Fallacious as this course of reasoning is, it enlists State pride and finds advocates in the honest prejudices of those who have not studied the nature of our Government sufficiently to see the radical error on which it rests.

The people of the United States formed the Constitution, acting through the State legislatures in making the compact, to meet and discuss its provisions, and acting in separate conventions when they ratified those provisions; but the terms used in its construction show it to be a Government in which the people of all the States, collectively, are represented. We are *one people* in the choice of President and Vice-President. Here the States have no other agency than to direct the mode in which the votes shall be given. The candidates having the majority of all the votes are chosen. The electors of a majority of States may have given their votes for one candidate, and yet another may be chosen. The people, then, and not the States, are represented in the executive branch.

In the House of Representatives there is this difference, that the people of one State do not, as in the case of President and Vice-President, all vote for the same officers. The people of all the States do not vote for all the members, each State electing only its own representatives. But this creates no material distinction. When chosen, they are all representatives of the United States, not representatives of the particular State from which they come. They are paid by the United States, not by the State; nor are they accountable to it for any act done in the performance of their legislative functions; and however they may in practice, as it is their duty to do, consult and prefer the interests of their particular constituents when they come in conflict with any other partial or local interest, yet it is their first and highest duty, as representatives of the United States, to promote the general good.

The Constitution of the United States, then, forms a *government*, not a league; and whether it be formed by compact between the States or in any other manner, its character is the same. It is a Government in which all the people are represented, which operates directly on the people individually, not upon the States; they retained all the power they did not grant. But each State, having expressly parted with so many powers as to constitute, jointly with the other States, a single nation, cannot, from that period, possess any right to secede, because such secession does not break a league, but destroys the unity of a nation; and any injury to that unity is not only a breach which would result from the contravention of a compact, but it is an offense against the whole Union. To say that any State may at pleasure secede from the Union is to say that the United States are not a nation, because it would be a solecism to contend that any part of a nation might dissolve its connection with the other parts, to their injury or ruin, without committing any offense. Secession, like any other revolutionary act, may be morally justified by the extremity of oppression; but to call it a constitutional right is confounding the meaning of terms, and can only be done through gross error or to deceive those who are willing to assert a right, but would pause before they made a revolution or incur the penalties consequent on a failure.

Because the Union was formed by a compact, it is said the parties to that compact may, when they feel themselves aggrieved, depart from it; but it is precisely because it is a compact that they cannot. A compact is an agreement or binding obligation. It may by its terms have a sanction or penalty for its breach, or it may not. If it contains no sanction, it may be broken with no other consequence than moral guilt; if it have a sanction, then the breach incurs the designated or implied penalty. A league between independent nations generally has no sanction other than a moral one; or if it should contain a penalty, as there is no common superior it cannot be enforced. A government, on the contrary, always has a sanction, express or implied; and in our case it is both necessarily implied and expressly given. An attempt, by force of arms, to destroy a government is an offense, by whatever means the constitutional compact may have been formed; and such government has the right by the law of self-defense to pass acts for punishing the offender, unless that right is modified, restrained, or resumed by the constitutional act. In our system, although it is modified in the case of treason, yet authority is expressly given to pass all laws necessary to carry its powers into effect, and under this grant provision has been made for punishing acts which obstruct the due administration of the laws.

It would seem superfluous to add anything to show the nature of that union which connects us, but as erroneous opinions on this subject are the foundation of doctrines the most destructive to our peace, I must give some further development to my views on this subject. No one, fellow-citizens, has a higher reverence for the reserved rights of the States than the Magistrate who now addresses you. No one would make greater personal sacrifices or official exertions to defend them from violation; but equal care must be taken to prevent, on their part, an improper interference with or resumption of the rights they have vested in the nation. The line has not been so distinctly drawn as to avoid doubts in some cases of the exercise of power. Men of the best intentions and soundest views may differ in their construction of some parts of the Constitution; but there are others on which dispassionate reflection can leave no doubt. Of this nature appears to be the assumed right of secession. It rests, as we have seen, on the alleged undivided sovereignty of the States and on their having formed in this sovereign capacity a compact which is called the Constitution, from which, because they made it, they have the right to secede. Both of these positions are erroneous, and some of the arguments to prove them have been anticipated.

The States severally have not retained their entire sovereignty. It has been shown that in becoming parts of a nation, not members of a league, they surrendered many of their essential parts of sovereignty. The right to make treaties, declare war, levy taxes, exercise exclusive judicial and legislative powers, were all of them functions of sovereign power. The States, then, for all these important purposes were no longer sovereign. The allegiance of their citizens was transferred, in the first instance, to the Government of the United States; they became American citizens and owed obedience to the Constitution of the United States and to laws made in conformity with the powers it vested in Congress. This last position has not been and cannot be denied. How, then, can that State be said to be sovereign and independent whose citizens owe obedience to laws not made by it and whose magistrates are sworn to disregard those laws when they come in conflict with those passed by another? What shows conclusively that the States cannot be said to have reserved an undivided sovereignty is that they expressly ceded the right to punish treason—not treason against their separate power, but treason against the United States. Treason is an offense against *sovereignty*, and sovereignty must reside with the power to punish it. But the reserved rights of the States are not less sacred because they have, for their common interest, made the General Government the depository of these powers. The unity of our political character (as has been shown for another purpose) commenced with its very existence. Under the royal Government we had no separate character; our opposition to its oppressions began as *united colonies*. We were the *United States* under the Confederation, and the name was perpetuated and the Union rendered more perfect by the Federal Constitution. In none of these stages did we consider ourselves in any other light as forming one nation. Treaties and alliances were made in the name of all. Troops were raised for the joint defense. How, then, with all these proofs that under all changes of our position we had, for designated purposes and with defined powers, created national governments, how is it that the most perfect of those several modes of union should now be considered as a mere league that may be dissolved at pleasure? It is from an abuse of terms. Compact is used as synonymous with league, although the true term is not employed, because it would at once show the fallacy of the reasoning. It would not do to say that our Constitution was only a league, but it is labored to prove it a compact (which in one sense it is) and then to argue that as a league is a compact every compact between nations must of course be a league, and that from such an engagement every sovereign power has a right to secede. But it has been shown that in this sense the States are not sovereign, and that even if they were, and the national Constitution had been formed by compact, there would be no right in any one State to exonerate itself from its obligations.

So obvious are the reasons which forbid this secession that it is necessary only to allude to them. The Union was formed for the benefit of all. It was produced by mutual sacrifices of interests and opinions. Can those sacrifices be recalled? Can the States who magnanimously surrendered their title to the territories of the West recall the grant? Will the inhabitants of the inland States agree to pay the duties that may be imposed without their assent by those on the Atlantic or the Gulf for their own benefit? Shall there be a free port in one State and onerous duties in another? No one believes that any right exists in a single State to involve all the others in these and countless other evils contrary to engagements solemnly made. Everyone must see that the other States, in self-defense, must oppose it at all hazards.

These are the alternatives that are presented by the convention—a repeal of all the acts for raising revenue, leaving the Government without the means of support, or an acquiescence in the dissolution of our Union by the secession of one of its members. When the first was proposed, it was known that it could not be listened to for a moment. It was known, if force was applied to oppose the execution of the laws, that it must be repelled by force; that Congress could not, without involving itself in disgrace and the country in ruin, accede to the proposition; and yet if this is not done in a given day, or if any attempt is made to execute the laws, the State is by the ordinance declared to be out of the Union. The majority of a convention assembled for the purpose have dictated these terms, or rather this rejection of all terms, in the name of the people of South Carolina. It is true that the governor of the State speaks of the submission of their grievances to a convention of all the States, which, he says, they "sincerely and anxiously seek and desire." Yet this obvious and constitutional mode of obtaining the sense of the other States on the construction of the federal compact, and amending it if necessary, has never been attempted by those who have urged the State on to this destructive measure. The State might have proposed the call for a general convention to the other States, and Congress, if a sufficient number of them concurred, must have called it. But the first magistrate of South Carolina, when he expressed a hope that "on a review by Congress and the functionaries of the General Government of the merits of the controversy" such a convention will be accorded to them, must have known that neither Congress nor any functionary of the General Government has authority to call such a convention unless it be demanded by two-thirds of the States. This suggestion, then, is another instance of the reckless inattention to the provisions of the Constitution with which this crisis has been madly hurried on, or of the attempt to persuade the people that a constitutional remedy had been sought and refused. If the legislature of South Carolina "anxiously desire" a general convention to consider their complaints, why have they not made application for it in the way the Constitution points out? The assertion that they "earnestly seek" it is completely negatived by the omission.

This, then, is the position in which we stand: A small majority of the citizens of one State in the Union have elected delegates to a State convention; that convention has ordained that all the revenue laws of the United States must be repealed, or that they are no longer a member of the Union. The governor of that State has recommended to the legislature the raising of an army to carry the secession into effect, and that he may be empowered to give clearances to vessels in the name of the State. No act of violent opposition to the laws has yet been committed, but such a state of things is hourly apprehended. And it is the intent of this instrument to *proclaim,* not only that the duty imposed on me by the Constitution "to take care that the laws be faithfully executed" shall be performed to the extent of the powers already vested in me by law, or of such others as the wisdom of Congress shall devise and intrust to me for that purpose, but to warn the citizens of South Carolina who have been deluded into an opposition to the laws of the danger they will incur by obedience to the illegal and disorganizing ordinance of the convention; to exhort those who have refused to support it to preserve in their determination to uphold the Constitution and laws of their country; and to point out to all the perilous situation into which the good people of that State have been led, and that the course they are urged to pursue is one of ruin disgrace to the very State whose rights they affect to support.

IV

Fellow-citizens of my native State, let me not only admonish you, as the First Magistrate of our common country, not to incur the penalty of its laws, but use the influence that a father would over his children whom he saw rushing to certain ruin. In that paternal language, with that paternal feeling, let me tell you, my countrymen, that you are deluded by men who are either deceived themselves or wish to deceive you. Mark under what pretenses you have been led on to the brink of insurrection and treason on which you stand. First, a diminution of the value of your staple commodity, lowered by overproduction in other quarters, and the consequent diminution in the value of your lands were the sole effect of the tariff laws. The effect of those laws was confessedly injurious, but the evil was greatly exaggerated by the unfounded theory you were taught to believe—that its burthens were in proportion to your exports, not to your consumption of imported articles. Your pride was roused by the assertion that a submission to those laws was a state of vassalage and that resistance to them was equal in patriotic merit to the opposition our fathers offered to the oppressive laws of Great Britain. You were told that this opposition might be peaceably, might be constitutionally, made; that you might enjoy all the advantages of the Union and bear none of its burthens. Eloquent appeals to your passions, to your State pride, to your native courage, to your sense of real injury, were used to prepare you for the period when the mask which concealed the hideous features of *disunion* should be taken off. It fell, and you were made to look with complacency on objects which not long since you would have regarded with horror. Look back to the arts which have brought you to this state; look forward to the consequences to which it must inevitably lead! Look back to what was first told you as an inducement to enter into this dangerous course. The great political truth was repeated to you that you had the revolutionary right of resisting all laws that were palpably unconstitutional and intolerably oppressive. It was added that the right to nullify a law rested on the same principle, but that it was a peaceable remedy. This character which was given to it made you receive with too much confidence the assertions that were made of the unconstitutionality of the law and its oppressive effects. Mark, my fellow-citizens, that by the admission of your leaders the unconstitutionality must be *palpable*, or it will not justify either resistance or nullification. What is the meaning of the word *palpable* in the sense in which it is here used? That which is apparent to everyone; that which no man or ordinary intellect will fail to perceive. Is the unconstitutionality of these laws of that description? Let those among your leaders who once approved and advocated the principle of protective duties answer the question; and let them choose whether they will be considered as incapable then of per-

ceiving that which must have been apparent to every man of common understanding, or as imposing upon your confidence and endeavoring to mislead you now. In either case they are unsafe guides in the perilous path they urge you to tread.

Ponder well on this circumstance, and you will know how to appreciate the exaggerated language they address to you. They are not champions of liberty, emulating the fame of our Revolutionary fathers, nor are you an oppressed people, contending, as they repeat to you, against worse than colonial vassalage. You are free members of a flourishing and happy Union. There is no settled design to oppress you. You have indeed felt the unequal operation of laws which may have been unwisely, not unconstitutionally, passed; but that inequality must necessarily be removed. At the very moment when you were madly urged on to the unfortunate course you have begun, a change in public opinion had commenced. The nearly approaching payment of the public debt and the consequent necessity of a dimunition of duties had already produced a considerable reduction, and that, too, on some articles of general consumption in your State. The importance of this change was underrated, and you were authoritatively told that no further alleviation of your burthens was to be expected at the very time when the condition of the country imperiously demanded such a modification of the duties as should reduce them to a just and equitable scale. But, as if apprehensive of the effect of this change in allaying your discontents, you were precipitated into the fearful state in which you now find yourselves.

I have urged you to look back to the means that were used to hurry you on to the position you have now assumed and forward to the consequences it will produce. Something more is necessary. Contemplate the condition of that country of which you still form an important part. Consider its Government, uniting in one bond of common interest and general protection so many different States, giving to all their inhabitants the proud title of *American citizen*, protecting their commerce, securing their literature and their arts, facilitating their intercommunication, defending their frontiers, and making their name respected in the remotest parts of the earth. Consider the extent of its territory, its increasing and happy population, its advance in arts which render life agreeable, and the sciences which elevate the mind! See education spreading the lights of religion, morality, and general information into every cottage in this wide extent of our Territories and States. Behold it as the asylum where the wretched and the oppressed find a refuge and support. Look on this picture of happiness and honor and say, *We too are citizens of America.* Carolina is one of these proud States; her arms have defended, her best blood has cemented, this happy Union. And then add, if you can, without horror and remorse, *This happy Union we will dissolve; this picture of peace and prosperity we will deface; this free intercourse we will interrupt; these fertile fields we will deluge with blood; the protection of that glorious flag we renounce; the very name of Americans we discard.*

And for what, mistaken men? For what do you throw away these inestimable blessings? For what would you exchange your share in the advantages and honor of the Union? For the dream of a separate independence—a dream interrupted by bloody conflicts with your neighbors and a vile dependence on a foreign power? If your leaders could succeed in establishing a separation, what would be your situation? Are you united at home? Are you free from the apprehension of civil discord, with all its fearful consequences? Do our neighboring republics, every day suffering some new revolution or contending with some new insurrection, do they excite your envy? But the dictates of a high duty oblige me solemnly to announce that you can not succeed. The laws of the United States must be executed. I have no discretionary power on the subject; my duty is emphatically pronounced in the Constitution. Those who told you that you might peaceably prevent their execution deceived you; they could not have been deceived themselves. They know that a forcible opposition could alone prevent the execution of the laws, and they know that such opposition must be repelled. Their object is disunion. But be not deceived by names. Disunion by armed force is *treason.* Are you really ready to incur its guilt? If you are, on the heads of the instigators of the act be the dreadful consequences; on their heads be the dishonor, but on yours may fall the punishment. On your unhappy State will inevitably fall all the evils of the conflict you force upon the Government of your country. It can not accede to the mad project of disunion, of which you would be the first victims. Its First Magistrate can not, if he would, avoid the performance of his duty.

The consequence must be fearful for you, distressing to your fellow-citizens here and to the friends of good government throughout the world. Its enemies have beheld our prosperity with a vexation they could not conceal; it was a standing refutation of their slavish doctrines, and they will point to our discord with the triumph of malignant joy. It is yet in your power to disappoint them. There is yet time to show that the descendants of the Pinckneys, the Sumpters, the Rutledges, and of the thousand other names which adorn the pages of your Revolutionary history will not abandon that Union to support which so many of them fought and bled and died. I adjure you, as you honor their memory, as you love the cause of freedom, to which they dedicated their lives, as you prize the peace of your country, the lives of its best citizens, and your own fair name, to retrace your steps. Snatch from the archives of your State the disorganizing edict of its convention; bid its members to reassemble and promulgate the decided expressions of your will to remain in the path which alone can conduct you to safety, prosperity, and honor. Tell them that compared to disunion all other evils are light, because that brings with it an accumulation of all. Declare that you will never take the field unless the star-spangled banner of your country shall float over you; that you will not be stigmatized when dead, and dishonored and scorned while you live, as the authors of the first attack on the Constitution of your country. Its destroyers you cannot be. You may disturb its peace, you may interrupt the course of its prosperity, you may cloud its reputation for stability; but its tranquillity will be restored, its prosperity will return, and the stain upon its national character will be transferred and remain an eternal blot on the memory of those who caused the disorder.

Fellow-citizens of the United States, the threat of unhallowed disunion, the names of those once respected by whom it is uttered, the array of military force to support it, denote the approach of a crisis in our affairs on which the continuance of our unexampled prosperity, our political existence, and perhaps that of all free governments may depend. The conjuncture demanded a free, a full, and explicit enunciation, not only of my intentions, but of my principles of action; and as the claim was asserted of a right by a State to annul the laws of the Union, and even to secede from it at pleasure, a frank exposition of my opinions in relation to the origin and form of our Government and construction I give to the instrument by which it was created seemed to be proper. Having the fullest confidence in the justness of the legal and constitutional opinion of my duties which has been expressed, I rely with equal confidence on your undivided support in my determination to execute the laws, to preserve the Union by all constitutional means, to arrest, if possible, by moderate and firm measures the necessity of a recourse to force; and if it be the will of Heaven that the recurrence of its primeval curse on man for the shedding of a brother's blood should fall upon our land, that it be not called down by any offensive act on the part of the United States.

Fellow-citizens, the momentous case is before you. On your undivided support of your Government depends the decision of the great question it involves—whether your sacred Union will be preserved and the blessings it secures to us as one people shall be perpetuated. No one can doubt that the unanimity with which that decision will be expressed will be such as to inspire new confidence in republican institutions, and that the prudence, the wisdom, and the courage which it will bring to their defense will transmit them unimpaired and invigorated to our children.

May the Great Ruler of Nations grant that the signal blessings with which He has favored ours may not, by the madness of party or personal ambition, be disregarded and lost; and may His wise providence bring those who have produced this crisis to see the folly before they feel the misery of civil strife, and inspire a returning veneration for that Union which, if we may dare to penetrate His designs, He has chosen as the only means of attaining the high destinies to which we may reasonably aspire.

In testimony whereof I have caused the seal of the United States to be hereunto affixed, having signed the same with my hand.

Source:

John Scott, ed. *Living Documents in American History*. New York: Washington Square Press, 1964-68.

Andrew Jackson, Message on Removal of Southern Indians, 1835

Section of President Andrew Jackson's seventh annual message to Congress, delivered on December 7, 1835, promoting the removal of the Cherokee and other Native tribes from their lands in the southern United States and proposing their resettlement west of the Mississippi. Jackson's support for Native American removal was evident when he refused to enforce the U.S. Supreme Court's decision in *Worcester v. Georgia,* which ruled that the Cherokee were subject to federal, not state, jurisdiction. In order to convince the people that he was justified in removing the Native Americans from their homes so that their desirable land could be settled by whites, Jackson claimed that the removal of the Native Americans was "dictated by a spirit of enlarged liberality," and falsely stated that his aim was to "protect and . . . preserve and perpetuate the scattered remnants of this race." A more accurate reason was probably the discovery of gold on Cherokee land in Georgia.

The removal was codified in the Treaty of New Echota. With this agreement, signed on December 29, 1835, the Cherokee gave up their capital at New Echota, Georgia, and ceded all their lands east of the Mississippi River to the United States in exchange for $5 million and seven million acres of land in the Indian Territory. The treaty, although signed by only a small faction of the Cherokee and repudiated by the majority, bound the entire nation to move west of the Mississippi within three years. Thousands of Cherokee perished during the removal, which was accomplished by military force in 1838 and 1839 and became known as the "Trail of Tears."

───────────◈───────────

Fellow-Citizens of the Senate and House of Representatives:

In the discharge of my official duty the task again devolves upon me of communicating with a new Congress. The reflection that the representation of the Union has been recently renewed, and that the constitutional term of its service will expire with my own, heightens the solicitude with which I shall attempt to lay before it the state of our national concerns and the devout hope which I cherish that its labors to improve them may be crowned with success.

You are assembled at a period of profound interest to the American patriot. The unexampled growth and prosperity of our country having given us a rank in the scale of nations which removes all apprehension of danger to our integrity and independence from external foes, the career of freedom is before us, with an earnest from the past that if true to ourselves there can be no formidable obstacle in the future to its peaceful and uninterrupted pursuit. Yet, in proportion to the disappearance of those apprehensions which attended our weakness, as once contrasted with the power of some of the States of the Old World, should we now be solicitous as to those which belong to the conviction that it is to our own conduct we must look for the preservation of those causes on which depend the excellence and the duration of our happy system of government.

In the example of other systems founded on the will of the people we trace to internal dissension the influences which have so often blasted the hopes of the friends of freedom. The social elements, which were strong and successful when united against external danger, failed in the more difficult task of properly adjusting their own internal organization, and thus gave way the great principle of self-government. Let us trust that this admonition will never be forgotten by the Government or the people of the United States, and that the testimony which our experience thus far holds out to the great human family of the practicability and the blessings of free government will be confirmed in all time to come.

We have but to look at the state of our agriculture, manufactures, and commerce and the unexampled increase of our population to feel the magnitude of the trust committed to us. Never in any former period of our history have we had greater reason than we now have to be thankful to Divine Providence for the blessings of health and general prosperity. Every branch of labor we see crowned with the most abundant rewards. In every element of national resources and wealth and of individual comfort we witness the most rapid and solid improvements. With no interruptions to this pleasing prospect at home which will not yield to the spirit of harmony and good will that so strikingly pervades the mass of the people in every quarter, amidst all the diversity of interest and pursuits to which they are attached, and with no cause of solicitude in regard to our external affairs which will not, it is hoped, disappear before the principles of simple justice and the forbearance that mark our intercourse with foreign powers, we have every reason to feel proud of our beloved country.

The general state of our foreign relations has not materially changed since my last annual message. In the settlement of the question of the northeastern, boundary little progress has been made. Great Britain has declined acceding to the proposition of the United States, presented in accordance with the resolution of the Senate, unless certain preliminary conditions were admitted, which I deemed incompatible with a satisfactory and rightful adjustment of the controversy. Waiting for some distinct proposal from the Government of Great Britain, which has been invited, I can only repeat the expression of my confidence that, with the strong mutual disposition which I believe exists to make a just arrangement, this perplexing question can be settled with a due regard to the well-founded pretensions and pacific policy of all the parties to it. Events are frequently occurring on the northeastern frontier of a character to impress upon all the necessity of a speedy and definitive termination of the dispute. This consideration, added to the desire common to both to relieve the liberal and friendly relations so happily existing between the two countries from all embarrassment, will no doubt have its just influence upon both.

Our diplomatic intercourse with Portugal has been renewed, and it is expected that the claims of our citizens, partially paid, will be fully satisfied as soon as the condition of the Queen's Government will permit the proper attention to the subject of them. That Government has, I am happy to inform you, manifested a determination to act upon the liberal principles which have marked our commercial policy. The happiest effects upon the future trade between the United States and Portugal are anticipated from it, and the time is not thought to be remote when a system of perfect reciprocity will be established. The installments due under the convention with the King of the Two Sicilies have been paid with that scrupulous fidelity by which his whole conduct has been characterized, and the hope is indulged that the adjustment of the vexed question of our claims will be followed by a more extended and mutually beneficial intercourse between the two countries.

The internal contest still continues in Spain. Distinguished as this struggle has unhappily been by incidents of the most sanguinary character, the obligations of the late treaty of indemnification with us have been nevertheless, faithfully executed by the Spanish Government.

No provision having been made at the last session of Congress for the ascertainment of the claims to be paid and the apportionment of the funds under the convention made with Spain, I invite your early attention to the subject. The public evidences of the debt have, according to the terms of the convention and in the forms prescribed by it, been placed in the possession of the United States, and the interest as it fell due has been regularly paid upon them. Our commercial intercourse with Cuba stands as regulated by the act of Congress. No recent information has been received as to the disposition of the Government of Madrid on this subject, and the lamented death of our recently appointed minister on his way to Spain, with the pressure of their affairs at home, renders it scarcely probable that any change is to be looked for during the coming year. Further portions of the Florida archives have been sent to the United States, although the death of one of the commissioners at a critical moment embarrassed the progress of the delivery of them. The higher officers of the local government have recently shewn an anxious desire, in compliance with the orders from the parent Government, to facilitate the selection and delivery of all we have a right to claim.

Negotiations have been opened at Madrid for the establishment of a lasting peace between Spain and such of the Spanish American Governments of this hemisphere as have availed themselves of the intimation given to all of them of the disposition of Spain to treat upon the basis of their entire independence. It is to be regretted that simultaneous appointments by all of ministers to negotiate with Spain had not been made. The negotiation itself would have been simplified, and this long-standing dispute, spreading over a large portion of the world, would have been brought to a more speedy conclusion.

Our political and commercial relations with Austria, Prussia, Sweden, and Denmark stand on the usual favorable bases. One of the articles of our treaty with Russia in relation to the trade on the northwest coast of America having expired, instructions have been given to our minister at St. Petersburg to negotiate a renewal of it. The long and unbroken amity between the two Governments gives every reason for supposing the article will be renewed, if stronger motives do not exist to prevent it than with our view of the subject can be anticipated here.

I ask your attention to the message of my predecessor at the opening of the second session of the Nineteenth Congress, relative to our commercial intercourse with Holland, and to the documents connected with that subject, communicated to the House of Representatives on the 10th of January, 1825, and 18th of January, 1827. Coinciding in the opinion of my predecessor that Holland is not, under the regulations of her present system, entitled to have her vessels and their cargoes received into the United States on the footing of American vessels and cargoes as regards duties of tonnage and impost, a respect for his reference of it to the Legislature has alone prevented me from acting on the subject. I should still have waited without comment for the action of Congress, but recently a claim has been made by Belgian subjects to admission into our ports for their ships and cargoes on the same footing as American, with the allegation we could not dispute that our vessels received in their ports the identical treatment shewn to them in the ports of Holland, upon whose vessels no discrimination is made in the ports of the United States. Giving the same privileges the Belgians expected the same benefits—benefits that were, in fact, enjoyed when Belgium and Holland were united under one Government. Satisfied with the justice of their pretension to be placed on the same footing with Holland, I could not, nevertheless, without disregard to the principle of our laws, admit their claim to be treated as Americans, and at the same time a respect for Congress, to whom the subject had long since been referred, has prevented me from producing a just equality by taking from the vessels of Holland privileges conditionally granted by acts of Congress, although the condition upon which the grant was made has, in my judgment, failed since 1822. I recommend, therefore, a review of the act of 1824, and such a modification of it as will produce an equality on such terms as Congress shall think best comports with our settled policy and the obligations of justice to two friendly powers.

With the Sublime Porte and all the Governments on the coast of Barbary our relations continue to be friendly. The proper steps have been taken to renew our treaty with Morocco.

The Argentine Republic has again promised to send within the current year a minister to the United States. A convention with Mexico for extending the time for the appointment of commissioners to run the boundary line has been concluded and will be submitted to the Senate. Recent events in that country have awakened the liveliest solicitude in the United States. Aware of the strong temptations existing and powerful inducements held out to the citizens of the United States to mingle in the dissensions of our immediate neighbors, instructions have been given to the district attorneys of the United States where indications warranted it to prosecute without respect to persons all who might attempt to violate the obligations of our neutrality, while at the same time it has been thought necessary to apprise the Government of Mexico that we should require the integrity of our territory to be scrupulously respected by both parties.

From our diplomatic agents in Brazil, Chile, Peru, Central America, Venezuela, and New Granada constant assurances are received of the continued good understanding with the Governments to which they are severally accredited. With those Governments upon which our citizens have valid and accumulating claims, scarcely an advance toward a settlement of them is made, owing mainly to their distracted state or to the pressure of imperative domestic questions. Our patience has been and will probably be still further severely tried, but our fellow-citizens whose interests are involved may confide in the determination of the Government to obtain for them eventually ample retribution.

Unfortunately, many of the nations of this hemisphere are still self-tormented by domestic dissensions. Revolution succeeds revolution; injuries are committed upon foreigners engaged in lawful pursuits; much time elapses before a government sufficiently stable is erected to justify expectation of redress; ministers are sent and received, and before the discussions of past injuries are fairly begun fresh troubles arise; but too frequently new injuries are added to the old, to be discussed together with the existing government after it has proved its ability to sustain the assaults made upon it, or with its successor if overthrown. If this unhappy condition of things continues much longer, other nations will be under the painful necessity of deciding whether justice to their suffering citizens does not require a prompt redress of injuries by their own power, without waiting for the establishment of a government competent and enduring enough to discuss and to make satisfaction for them.

Since the last session of Congress the validity of our claims upon France, as liquidated by the treaty of 1831, has been acknowledged by both branches of her legislature, and the money has been appropriated for their discharge; but the payment is, I regret to inform you, still withheld.

A brief recapitulation of the most important incidents in this protracted controversy will shew how utterly untenable are the grounds upon which this course is attempted to be justified.

On entering upon the duties of my station I found the United States an unsuccessful applicant to the justice of France for the satisfaction of claims the validity of which was never questionable, and has now been most solemnly admitted by France herself. The antiquity of these claims, their high justice, and the aggravating circumstances out of which they arose are too familiar to the American people to require description. It is sufficient to say that for a period of ten years and upward our commerce was, with but little interruption, the subject of constant aggressions on the part of France—aggressions the ordinary features of which were condemnations of vessels and cargoes under arbitrary decrees, adopted in contravention as well of the laws of nations as of treaty stipulations, burnings on the high seas, and seizures and confiscations under special imperial rescripts in the ports of other nations occupied by the armies or under the control of France. Such it is now conceded is the character of the wrongs we suffered—wrongs in many cases so flagrant that even their authors never denied our right to reparation. Of the extent of these injuries some conception may be formed from the fact that after the burning of a large amount at sea and the necessary deterioration in other cases by long detention the American property so seized and sacrificed at forced sales, excluding what was adjudged to privateers before or without condemnation, brought into the French treasury upward of 24,000,000 francs, besides large custom-house duties.

The subject had already been an affair of twenty years' uninterrupted negotiation, except for a short time when France was overwhelmed by the military power of united Europe. During this period, whilst other nations were extorting from her payment of their claims at the point of the bayonet, the United States intermitted their demand for justice out of respect to the oppressed condition of a gallant people to whom they felt under obligations for fraternal assistance in their own days of suffering and of peril. The bad effects of these protracted and unavailing discussions, as well upon our relations with France as upon our national character, were obvious, and the line of duty was to my mind equally so. This was either to insist upon the adjustment of our claims within a reasonable period or to abandon them altogether. I could not doubt that by this course the interests and honor of both countries would be best consulted. Instructions were therefore given in this spirit to the minister who was sent out once more to demand reparation. Upon the meeting of Congress in December, 1829, I felt it my duty to speak of these claims and the delays of France in terms calculated to call the serious attention of both countries to the subject. The then French ministry took exception to the message on the ground of its containing a menace, under which it was not agreeable to the French Government to negotiate. The American minister of his own accord refuted the construction which was attempted to be put upon the message and at the same time called to the recollection of the French ministry that the President's message was a communication addressed, not to foreign governments, but to the Congress of the United States, in which it was enjoined upon him by the Constitution to lay before that body information of the state of the Union, comprehending its foreign as well as its domestic relations, and that if in the discharge of this duty he felt it incumbent upon him to summon the attention of Congress in due time to what might be the possible consequences of existing difficulties with any foreign government, he might fairly be supposed to do so under a sense of what was due from him in a frank communication with another branch of his own Government, and not from any intention of holding a menace over a foreign power. The views taken by him received my approbation, the French Government was satisfied, and the negotiation was continued. It terminated in the treaty of July 4, 1831, recognizing the justice of our claims in part and promising payment to the amount of 25,000,000 francs in six annual installments.

The ratifications of this treaty were exchanged at Washington on the 2d of February, 1832, and in five days thereafter it was laid before Congress, who immediately passed the acts necessary on our part to secure to France the commercial advantages conceded to her in the compact. The treaty had previously been solemnly ratified by the King of the French in terms which are certainly not mere matters of form, and of which the translation is as follows:

We, approving the above convention in all and each of the dispositions which are contained in it, do declare, by ourselves as well as by our heirs and successors, that it is accepted, approved, ratified, and confirmed, and by these presents, signed by our hand, we do accept, approve, ratify, and confirm it; promising, on the faith and word of a king, to observe it and to cause it to be observed inviolably, without ever contravening it or suffering it to be contravened, directly or indirectly, for any cause or under any pretense whatsoever.

Official information of the exchange of ratifications in the United States reached Paris whilst the Chambers were in session. The extraordinary and to us injurious delays of the French Government in their action upon the subject of its fulfillment have been heretofore stated to Congress, and I have no disposition to enlarge upon them here. It is sufficient to observe that the then pending session was allowed to expire without even an effort to obtain the necessary appropriations; that the two succeeding ones were also suffered to pass away without anything like a serious attempt to obtain a decision upon the subject, and that it was not until the fourth session, almost three years after the conclusion of the treaty and more than two years after the exchange of ratifications, that the bill for the execution of the treaty was pressed to a vote and rejected.

In the meantime the Government of the United States, having full confidence that a treaty entered into and so solemnly ratified by the French King would be executed in good faith, and not doubting that provision would be made for the payment of the first installment which was to become due on the 2d day of February, 1833, negotiated a draft for the amount through the Bank of the United States. When this draft was presented by the holder with the credentials required by the treaty to authorize him to receive the money, the Government of France allowed it to be protested. In addition to the injury in the nonpayment of the money by France, conformably to her engagement, the United States were exposed to a heavy claim on the part of the bank under pretense of damages, in satisfaction of which that institution seized upon and still retains an equal amount of the public money. Congress was in session when the decision of the Chambers reached Washington, and an immediate communication of this apparently final decision of France not to fulfill the stipulations of the treaty was the course naturally to be expected from the President. The deep tone of dissatisfaction which pervaded the public mind and the correspondent excitement produced in Congress by only a general knowledge of the result rendered it more than probable that a resort to immediate measures of redress would be the consequence of calling the attention of that body to the subject. Sincerely desirous of preserving the pacific relations which had so long existed between the two countries, I was anxious to avoid this course if I could be satisfied that by doing so neither the interests nor the honor of my country would be compromitted. Without the fullest assurances upon that point, I could not hope to acquit myself of the responsibility to be incurred suffering Congress to adjourn without laying the subject before them. Those received by me were believed to be of that character.

That the feelings produced in the United States by the news of the rejection of the appropriation would be such as I have described them to have been was foreseen by the French Government, and prompt measures were taken by it to prevent the consequences. The King in person expressed through our minister at Paris his profound regret at the decision of the Chambers, and promised to send forthwith a national ship with dispatches to his minister here authorizing him to give such assurances as would satisfy the Government and people of the United States that the treaty would yet be faithfully executed by France. The national ship arrived, and the minister received his instructions. Claiming to act under the authority derived from them, he gave to this Government in the name of his the most solemn assurances that as soon after the new elections as the charter would permit the French Chambers would be convened and the attempt to procure the necessary appropriations renewed; that all the constitutional powers of the King and his ministers should be put in requisition to accomplish the object, and he was understood, and so expressly informed by this Government at the time, to engage that the question should be pressed to a decision at a period sufficiently early to permit information of the result to be communicated to Congress at the commencement of their next session. Relying upon these assurances, I incurred the responsibility, great as I regarded it to be, of suffering Congress to separate without communicating with them upon the subject.

The expectations justly founded upon the promises thus solemnly made to this Government by that of France were not realized. The French Chambers met on the 31st of July, 1834, soon after the election, and although our minister in Paris urged the French ministry to bring the subject before them, they declined doing so. He next insisted that the Chambers, if prorogued without acting on the subject, should be reassembled at a period so early that their action on the treaty might be known in Washington prior to the meeting of Congress. This reasonable request was not only declined, but the Chambers were prorogued to the 29th of December, a day so late that their decision, however urgently pressed, could not in all probability be obtained in time to reach Washington before the necessary adjournment of Congress by the Constitution. The reasons given by the ministry for refusing to convoke the Chambers at an earlier period were afterwards shewn not to be insuperable by their actual convocation on the 1st of December under a special call for domestic purposes, which fact, however, did not become known to this Government until after the commencement of the last session of Congress.

Thus disappointed in our just expectations, it became my imperative duty to consult with Congress in regard to the expediency of a resort to retaliatory measures in case the stipulations of the treaty should not be speedily complied with, and to recommend such as in my judgment the occasion called for. To this end all unreserved communication of the case in all its aspects became indispensable. To have shrunk in making it from saying all that was necessary to its correct understanding, and that the truth would justify, for fear of giving offense to others, would have been unworthy of us. To have gone, on the other hand, a single step further for the purpose of wounding the pride of a Government and people with whom we had so many motives for cultivating relations of amity and reciprocal advantage would have been unwise and improper. Admonished by the past of the difficulty of making even the simplest statement of our wrongs without disturbing the sensibilities of those who had by their position become responsible for their redress, and earnestly desirous of preventing further obstacles from that source, I went out of my way to preclude a construction of the message by which the recommendation that was made to Congress might be regarded as a menace to France in not only disavowing such a design, but in declaring that her pride and her power were too well known to expect anything from her fears. The message did not reach Paris until more than a month after the Chambers had been in session, and such was the insensibility of the ministry to our rightful claims and just expectations that our minister had been informed that the matter when introduced would not be pressed as a cabinet measure.

Although the message was not officially communicated to the French Government, and notwithstanding the declaration to the contrary which it contained, the French ministry decided to consider the conditional recommendation of reprisals a menace and an insult which the honor of the nation made it incumbent on them to resent. The measures resorted to by them to evince their sense of the supposed indignity were the immediate recall of their minister at Washington, the offer of passports to the American minister at Paris, and a public notice to the legislative Chambers that all diplomatic intercourse with the United States had been suspended. Having in this manner vindicated the dignity of France, they next proceeded to illustrate her justice. To this end a bill was immediately introduced into the Chamber of Deputies proposing to make the appropriations necessary to carry into effect the treaty. As this bill subsequently passed into a law, the provisions of which now constitute the main subject of difficulty between the two nations, it becomes my duty, in order to place the subject before you in a clear light, to trace the history of its passage and to refer with some particularly to the proceedings and discussions in regard to it.

The minister of finance in his opening speech alluded to the measures which had been adopted to resent the supposed indignity, and recommended the execution of the treaty as a measure required by the honor and justice of France. He as the organ of the ministry declared the message, so long as it had not received the sanction of Congress, a mere expression of the personal opinion of the President, for which neither the Government nor people of the United States were responsible, and that an engagement had been entered into for the fulfillment of which the honor of France was pledged. Entertaining these views, the single condition which the French ministry proposed to annex to the payment of the money was that it should not be made until it was ascertained that the Government of the United States had done nothing to injure the interests of France, or, in other words, that no steps had been authorized by Congress of a hostile character toward France.

What the disposition or action of Congress might be was then unknown to the French cabinet; but on the 14th of January the Senate resolved that it was at that time inexpedient to adopt any legislative measures in regard to the state of affairs between the United States and France, and no action on the subject had occurred in the House of Representatives. These facts were known in Paris prior to the 28th of March, 1835, when the committee to whom the bill of indemnification had been referred reported it to the Chamber of Deputies. That committee substantially reechoed the sentiments of the ministry, declared that Congress had set aside the proposition of the President, and recommended the passage of the bill without any other restriction than that originally proposed. Thus was it known to the French ministry and Chambers that if the position assumed by them, and which had been so frequently and solemnly announced as the only one compatible with the honor of France, was maintained and the bill passed as originally proposed, the money would be paid and there would be an end of this unfortunate controversy.

But this cheering prospect was soon destroyed by an amendment introduced into the bill at the moment of its passage, providing that the money should not be paid until the French Government had received satisfactory explanations of the President's message of the 2nd December, 1834, and, what is still more extraordinary, the president of the council of ministers adopted this amendment and consented to its incorporation in the bill. In regard to a supposed insult which had been formally resented by the recall of their minister and the offer of passports to ours, they now for the first time proposed to ask explanations. Sentiments and propositions which they had declared could not justly be imputed to the Government or people of the United States are set up as obstacles to the performance of an act of conceded justice to that Government and people. They had declared that the honor of France required the fulfillment of the engagement into which the King had entered, unless Congress adopted the recommendations of the message. They ascertained that Congress did not adopt them, and yet that fulfillment is refused unless they first obtain from the President explanations of an opinion characterized by themselves as personal and inoperative.

The conception that it was my intention to menace or insult the Government of France is as unfounded as the attempt to extort from the fears of that nation what her sense of justice may deny would be vain and ridiculous. But the Constitution of the United States imposes on the President the duty of laying before Congress the condition of the country in its foreign and domestic relations, and of recommending such measures as may in his opinion be required by its interests. From the performance of this duty he can not be deterred by the fear of wounding the sensibilities of the people or government of whom it may become necessary to speak; and the American people are incapable of submitting to an interference by any government on earth, however powerful, with the free performance of the domestic duties which the Constitution has imposed on their public functionaries. The discussions which intervene between the several departments of our Government belong to ourselves, and for anything said in them our public servants are only responsible to their own constituents and to each other. If in the course of their consultations facts are erroneously stated or unjust deductions are made, they require no other inducement to correct them, however informed of their error, than their love of justice and what is due to their own character; but they can never submit to be interrogated upon the subject as a matter of right by a foreign power. When our discussions terminate in acts, our responsibility to foreign powers commences, not as individuals, but as a nation. The principle which calls in question the President for the language of his message would equally justify a foreign power in demanding explanation of the language used in the report of a committee or by a member in debate.

This is not the first time that the Government of France has taken exception to the messages of American Presidents. President Washington and the first President Adams in the performance of their duties to the American people fell under the animadversions of the French Directory. The objection taken by the ministry of Charles X, and removed by the explanations made by our minister upon the spot, has already been adverted to. When it was understood that the ministry of the present King took exception to my message of last year, putting a construction upon it which was disavowed on its face, our late minister at Paris, in answer to the note which first announced a dissatisfaction with the language used in the message, made a communication to the French Government under date of the 29th of January, 1835, calculated to remove all impressions which an unreasonable susceptibility had created. He repeated and called the attention of the French Government to the disavowal contained in the message itself of any intention to intimidate by menace; he truly declared that it contained and was intended to contain no charge of ill faith against the King of the French, and properly distinguished between the right to complain in unexceptionable terms of the omission to execute an agreement and an accusation of bad motives in withholding such execution, and demonstrated that the necessary use of that right ought not to be considered as an offensive imputation. Although this communication was made without instructions and entirely on the minister's own responsibility, yet it was afterwards made the act of this Government by my full approbation, and that approbation was officially made known on the 25th of April, 1835, to the French Government. It, however, failed to have any effect. The law, after this friendly explanation, passed with the obnoxious amendment, supported by the King's ministers, and was finally approved by the King.

The people of the United States are justly attached to a pacific system in their intercourse with foreign nations. It is proper, therefore, that they should know whether their Government has adhered to it. In the present instance it has been carried to the utmost extent that was consistent with a becoming self-respect. The note of the 29th of January, to which I have before alluded, was not the only one which our minister took upon himself the responsibility of presenting on the same subject and in the same spirit. Finding that it was intended to make the payment of a just debt dependent on the performance of a condition which he knew could never be complied with, he thought it a duty to make another attempt to convince the French Government that whilst self-respect and regard to the dig-

nity of other nations would always prevent us from using any language that ought to give offense, yet we could never admit a right in any foreign government to ask explanations of or to interfere in any manner in the communications which one branch of our public councils made with another; that in the present case no such language had been used, and that this had in a former note been fully and voluntarily stated, before it was contemplated to make the explanation a condition; and that there might be no misapprehension he stated the terms used in that note, and he officially informed them that it had been approved by the President, and that therefore every explanation which could reasonably be asked or honorably given had been already made; that the contemplated measure had been anticipated by a voluntary and friendly declaration, and was therefore not only useless, but might be deemed offensive, and certainly would not be complied with if annexed as a condition.

When this latter communication, to which I especially invite the attention of Congress, was laid before me, I entertained the hope that the means it was obviously intended to afford of an honorable and speedy adjustment of the difficulties between the two nations would have been accepted, and I therefore did not hesitate to give it my sanction and full approbation. This was due to the minister who had made himself responsible for the act, and it was published to the people of the United States and is now laid before their representatives to shew how far their Executive has gone in its endeavors to restore a good understanding between the two countries. It would have been at any time communicated to the Government of France had it been officially requested.

The French Government having received all the explanation which honor and principle permitted, and which could in reason be asked, it was hoped it would no longer hesitate to pay the installments now due. The agent authorized to receive the money was instructed to inform the French minister of his readiness to do so. In reply to this notice he was told that the money could not then be paid, because the formalities required by the act of the Chambers had not been arranged.

Not having received any official information of the intentions of the French Government, and anxious to bring, as far as practicable, this unpleasant affair to a close before the meeting of Congress, that you might have the whole subject before you, I caused our charge d'affaires at Paris to be instructed to ask for the final determination of the French Government, and in the event of their refusal to pay the installments now due, without further explanations to return to the United States.

The result of this last application has not yet reached us, but is daily expected. That it may be favorable is my sincere wish. France having now, through all the branches of her Government, acknowledged the validity of our claims and the obligation of the treaty of 1831 , and there really existing no adequate cause for further delay, will at length, it may be hoped, adopt the course which the interests of both nations, not less than the principles of justice, so imperiously require. The treaty being once executed on her part, little will remain to disturb the friendly relations of the two countries—nothing, indeed, which will not yield to the suggestions of a pacific and enlightened policy and to the influence of that mutual good will and of those generous recollections which we may confidently expect will then be revived in all their ancient force. In any event, however, the principle involved in the new aspect which has been given to the controversy is so vitally important to the independent administration of the Government that it can neither be surrendered nor compromitted without national degradation. I hope it is unnecessary for me to say that such a sacrifice will not be made through any agency, of mine. The honor of my country shall never be stained by an apology from me for the statement of truth and the performance of duty; nor can I give any exploitation of my official act except such as is due to integrity and justice and consistent with the principles on which our institutions have been framed. This determination will, I am confident, be approved by my constituents. I have, indeed, studied their character to but little purpose if the sum of 25,000,000 francs will have the weight of a feather in the estimation of what appertains to their national independence, and if, unhappily, a different impression should at any time obtain in any quarter, they will, I am sure, rally round the Government of their choice with alacrity and unanimity, and silence forever the degrading imputation.

Having thus frankly presented to you the circumstances which since the last session of Congress have occurred in this interesting and important matter, with the views of the Executive in regard to them, it is at this time only necessary to add that whenever the advices now daily expected from our charge d'affaires shall have been received they will be made the subject of a special communication.

The condition of the public finances was never more flattering than at the present period.

Since my last annual communication all the remains of the public debt have been redeemed, or money has been placed in deposit for this purpose whenever the creditors choose to receive it. All the other pecuniary engagements of the Government have been honorably and promptly fulfilled, and there will be a balance in the Treasury at the close of the present year of about $19,000,000. It is believed that after meeting all outstanding and unexpended appropriations there will remain near eleven millions to be applied to any new objects which Congress may designate or to the more rapid execution of the works already in progress. In aid of these objects, and to satisfy the current expenditures of the ensuing year, it is estimated that there will be received from various sources twenty millions more in 1836.

Should Congress make new appropriations in conformity with the estimates which will be submitted from the proper Departments, amounting to about twenty-four millions, still the available surplus at the close of the next year, after deducting all unexpended appropriations, will probably not be less than six millions. This sum can, in my judgment, be now usefully applied to proposed improvements in our navy-yards, and to new national works which are not enumerated in the present estimates or to the more rapid completion of those already begun. Either would be constitutional and useful, and would render unnecessary any attempt in our present peculiar condition to divide the surplus revenue or to reduce it any faster than will be effected by the existing laws. In any event, as the annual report from the Secretary of the Treasury will enter into details, shewing the probability of some decrease in the revenue during the next seven years and a very considerable deduction in 1842, it is not recommended that Congress should undertake to modify the present tariff so as to disturb the principles on which the compromise act was passed. Taxation on some of the articles of general consumption which are not in competition with our own productions may be no doubt so diminished as to lessen to some extent the source of this revenue, and the same object can also be assisted by more liberal provisions for the subjects of public defense, which in the present state of our prosperity and wealth may be expected to engage your attention. If, however, after satisfying all the demands which can arise from these sources the unexpended balance in the Treasury should still continue to increase, it would be better to bear with the evil until the great changes contemplated in our tariff laws have occurred and shall enable us to revise the system with that care and circumspection which are due to so delicate and important a subject.

It is certainly our duty to diminish as far as we can the burdens of taxation and to regard all the restrictions which are imposed on the trade and navigation of our citizens as evils which we shall mitigate whenever we are not prevented by the adverse legislation and policy of foreign nations or those primary duties which the defense and independence of our country enjoin upon us. That we have accomplished much toward the relief of our citizens by the changes which have accompanied the payment of the public debt and the adoption of the present revenue laws is manifest from the fact that compared with 1833 there is a diminution of near twenty-five millions in the last two years, and that our expenditures, independently of those for the public debt, have been reduced near nine millions during the same period. Let us trust that by the continued observance of economy and by harmonizing the great interests of agriculture, manufactures, and commerce much more may be accomplished to diminish the burdens of government and to increase still further the enterprise and the patriotic affection of all classes of our citizens and all the members of our happy Confederacy. As the data which the Secretary of the Treasury will lay before you in regard to our financial resources are full and extended, and will afford a safe guide in your future calculations, I think it unnecessary to offer any further observations on that subject here.

Among the evidences of the increasing prosperity of the country, not the least gratifying is that afforded by the receipts from the sales of the public lands, which amount in the present year to the unexpected sum of $11,000,000. This circumstance attests the rapidity with which agriculture, the first and most important occupation of man, advances and contributes to the wealth and power of our extended territory. Being still of the opinion that it is our best policy, as far as we can consistently with the obligations under which those lands were ceded to the United States, to promote their speedy settlement, I beg leave to call the attention of the present Congress to the suggestions I have offered respecting it in my former messages.

The extraordinary receipts from the sales of the public lands invite you to consider what improvements the land system, and particularly the condition of the General Land Office, may require. At the time this institution was organized, near a quarter of a century ago, it would probably have been thought extravagant to anticipate for this period such an addition to its business as has been produced by the vast increase of those sales during the past and present years. It may also be observed that since the year 1812 the land offices and surveying districts have been greatly multiplied, and that numerous legislative enactments from year to year since that time have imposed a great amount of new and additional duties upon that office, while the want of a timely application of force commensurate with the care and labor required has caused the increasing embarrassment of accumulated arrears in the different branches of the establishment.

These impediments to the expedition of much duty in the General Land Office induce me to submit to your judgment whether some modification of the laws relating to its organization, or an organization of a new character, be not called for at the present juncture, to enable the office to accomplish all the ends of its institution with a greater degree of facility and promptitude than experience has proved to be practicable under existing regulations. The variety of the concerns and the magnitude and complexity of the details occupying and dividing the attention of the Commissioner appear to render it difficult, if not impracticable, for that officer by any possible assiduity to

bestow on all the multifarious subjects upon which he is called to act the ready and careful attention due to their respective importance, unless the Legislature shall assist him by a law providing, or enabling him to provide, for a more regular and economical distribution of labor, with the incident responsibility among those employed under his direction. The mere manual operation of affixing his signature to the vast number of documents issuing from his office subtracts so largely from the time and attention claimed by the weighty and complicated subjects daily accumulating in that branch of the public service as to indicate the strong necessity of revising the organic law of the establishment. It will be easy for Congress hereafter to proportion the expenditure on account of this branch of the service to its real wants by abolishing from time to time the offices which can be dispensed with.

The extinction of the public debt having taken place, there is no longer any use for the offices of Commissioners of Loans and of the Sinking Fund. I recommend, therefore, that they be abolished, and that proper measures be taken for the transfer to the Treasury Department of any funds, books, and papers connected with the operations of those offices, and that the proper power be given to that Department for closing finally any portion of their business which may remain to be settled.

It is also incumbent on Congress in guarding the pecuniary interests of the country to discontinue by such a law as was passed in 1812 the receipt of the bills of the Bank of the United States in payment of the public revenue, and to provide for the designation of an agent whose duty it shall be to take charge of the books and stock of the United States in that institution, and to close all connection with it after the 3d of March, 1836, when its charter expires. In making provision in regard to the disposition of this stock it will be essential to define clearly and strictly the duties and powers of the officer charged with that branch of the public service.

It will be seen from the correspondence which the Secretary of the Treasury will lay before you that notwithstanding the large amount of the stock which the United States hold in that institution no information has yet been communicated which will enable the Government to anticipate when it can receive any dividends or derive any benefit from it.

Connected with the condition of the finances and the flourishing state of the country in all its branches of industry, it is pleasing to witness the advantages which have been already derived from the recent laws regulating the value of the gold coinage. These advantages will be more apparent in the course of the next year, when the branch mints authorized to be established in North Carolina, Georgia, and Louisiana shall have gone into operation. Aided, as it is hoped they will be, by further reforms in the banking systems of the States and by judicious regulations on the part of Congress in relation to the custody of the public moneys, it may be confidently anticipated that the use of gold and silver as a circulating medium will become general in the ordinary transactions connected with the labor of the country. The great desideratum in modern times is an efficient check upon the power of banks, preventing that excessive issue of paper whence arise those fluctuations in the standard of value which render uncertain the rewards of labor. It was supposed by those who established the Bank of the United States that from the credit given to it by the custody of the public moneys and other privileges and the precautions taken to guard against the evils which the country had suffered in the bankruptcy of many of the State institutions of that period we should derive from that institution all the security and benefits of a sound currency and every good end that was attainable under that provision of the Constitution which authorizes Congress alone to coin money and regulate the value thereof. But it is scarcely necessary now to say that these anticipations have not been realized.

After the extensive embarrassment and distress recently produced by the Bank of the United States, from which the country is now recovering, aggravated as they were by pretensions to power which defied the public authority, and which if acquiesced in by the people would have changed the whole character of our Government, every candid and intelligent individual must admit that for the attainment of the great advantages of a sound currency we must look to a course of legislation radically different from that which created such an institution.

In considering the means of obtaining so important an end we must set aside all calculations of temporary convenience, and be influenced by those only which are in harmony with the true character and the permanent interests of the Republic. We must recur to first principles and see what it is that has prevented the legislation of Congress and the States on the subject of currency from satisfying the public expectation and realizing results corresponding to those which have attended the action of our system when truly consistent with the great principle of equality upon which it rests, and with that spirit of forbearance and mutual concession and generous patriotism which was originally, and must ever continue to be, the vital element of our Union.

On this subject I am sure that I can not be mistaken in ascribing our want of success to the undue countenance which has been afforded to the spirit of monopoly. All the serious dangers which our system has yet encountered may be traced to the resort to implied powers and the use of corporations clothed with privileges, the effect of which is to advance the interests of the few at the expense of the many. We have felt but one class of these dangers exhib-

ited in the contest waged by the Bank of the United States against the Government for the last four years. Happily they have been obviated for the present by the indignant resistance of the people, but we should recollect that the principle whence they sprung is an ever-active one, which will not fail to renew its efforts in the same and in other forms so long as there is a hope of success, founded either on the inattention of the people or the treachery of their representatives to the subtle progress of its influence. The bank is, in fact, but one of the fruits of a system at war with the genius of all our institutions—a system founded upon a political creed the fundamental principle of which is a distrust of the popular will as a safe regulator of political power, and whose great ultimate object and inevitable result, should it prevail, is the consolidation of all power in our system in one central government. Lavish public disbursements and corporations with exclusive privileges would be its substitutes for the original and as yet sound checks and balances of the Constitution—the means by whose silent and secret operation a control would be exercised by the few over the political conduct of the many by first acquiring that control over the labor and earnings of the great body of the people. Wherever this spirit has effected an alliance with political power, tyranny, and despotism have been the fruit. If it is ever used for the ends of government, it has to be incessantly watched, or it corrupts the sources of the public virtue and agitates the country with questions unfavorable to the harmonious and steady pursuit of its true interests.

We are now to see whether, in the present favorable condition of the country, we can not take an effectual stand against this spirit of monopoly, and practically prove in respect to the currency as well as other important interests that there is no necessity for so extensive a resort to it as that which has been heretofore practiced. The experience of another year has confirmed the utter fallacy of the idea that the Bank of the United States was necessary as a fiscal agent of the Government. Without its aid as such, indeed, in despite of all the embarrassment it was in its power to create, the revenue has been paid with punctuality by our citizens, the business of exchange, both foreign and domestic, has been conducted with convenience, and the circulating medium has been greatly improved. By the rise of the State banks, which do not derive their charters from the General Government and are not controlled by its authority, it is ascertained that the moneys of the United States can be collected and disbursed without loss or inconvenience, and that all the wants of the community in relation to exchange and currency are supplied as well as they have ever been before. If under circumstances the most unfavorable to the steadiness of the money market it has been found that the considerations on which the Bank of the United States rested its claims to the public favor were imaginary and groundless, it can not be doubted that the experience of the future will be more decisive against them.

It has been seen that without the agency of a great moneyed monopoly the revenue can be collected and conveniently and safely applied to all the purposes of the public expenditure. It is also ascertained that instead of being necessarily made to promote the evils of an unchecked paper system, the management of the revenue can be made auxiliary to the reform which the legislatures of several of the States have already commenced in regard to the suppression of small bills, and which has only to be fostered by proper regulations on the part of Congress to secure a practical return to the extent required for the security of the currency to the constitutional medium. Severed from the Government as political engines, and not susceptible of dangerous extension and combination, the State banks will not be tempted, nor will they have the power, which we have seen exercised, to divert the public funds from the legitimate purposes of the Government. The collection and custody of the revenue, being, on the contrary, a source of credit to them, will increase the security which the States provide for a faithful execution of their trusts by multiplying the scrutinies to which their operations and accounts will be subjected. Thus disposed, as well from interest as the obligations of their charters, it can not be doubted that such conditions as Congress may see fit to adopt respecting the deposits in these institutions, with a view to the gradual disuse, of the small bills will be cheerfully complied with, and that we shall soon gain in place of the Bank of the United States a practical reform in the whole paper system of the country. If by this policy we can ultimately witness the suppression of all bank bills below $20, it is apparent that gold and silver will take their place and become the principal circulating medium in the common business of the farmers and mechanics of the country. The attainment of such a result will form an era in the history of our country which will be dwelt upon with delight by every true friend of its liberty and independence. It will lighten the great tax which our paper system has so long collected from the earnings of labor, and do more to revive and perpetuate those habits of economy and simplicity which are so congenial to the character of republicans than all the legislation which has yet been attempted.

To this subject I feel that I can not too earnestly invite the special attention of Congress, without the exercise of whose authority the opportunity to accomplish so much public good must pass unimproved. Deeply impressed with its vital importance, the Executive has taken all the steps within his constitutional power to guard the public revenue and defeat the expectation which the Bank of the United States indulged of renewing and perpetuating its monopoly on the ground of its necessity as a fiscal agent and as affording a sounder currency than could be obtained without such an institution. In the performance of this duty much responsibility was incurred which would have been gladly avoided if the stake which the public had in the question could have been otherwise preserved. Although clothed with the legal authority and supported by precedent, I was aware that there was in the act of the removal of the deposits a liability to excite that sensitiveness to Executive power which it is the characteristic and the duty of freemen to indulge; but I relied on this feeling also, directed by patriotism and intelligence, to vindicate the conduct which in the end would appear to have been called for by the best interests of my country. The apprehensions natural to this feeling that there may have been a desire, through the instrumentality of that measure, to extend the Executive influence, or that it may have been prompted by motives not sufficiently free from ambition, were not overlooked. Under the operation of our institutions the public servant who is called on to take a step of high responsibility should feel in the freedom which gives rise to such apprehensions his highest security. When unfounded the attention which they arouse and the discussions they excite deprive those who indulge them of the power to do harm; when just they but hasten the certainty with which the great body of our citizens never fail to repel an attempt to procure their sanction to any exercise of power inconsistent with the jealous maintenance of their rights. Under such convictions, and entertaining no doubt that my constitutional obligations demanded the steps which were taken in reference to the removal of the deposits, it was impossible for me to be deterred from the path of duty by a fear that my motives could be misjudged or that political prejudices could defeat the just consideration of the merits of my conduct. The result has shewn how safe is this reliance upon the patriotic temper and enlightened discernment of the people. That measure has now been before them and has stood the test of all the severe analysis which its general importance, the interests it affected, and the apprehensions it excited were calculated to produce, and it now remains for Congress to consider what legislation has become necessary in consequence.

I need only add to what I have on former occasions said on this subject generally that in the regulations which Congress may prescribe respecting the custody of the public moneys it is desirable that as little discretion as may be deemed consistent with their safe-keeping should be given to the executive agents. No one can be more deeply impressed than I am with the soundness of the doctrine which restrains and limits, by specific provisions, executive discretion, as far as it can be done consistently with the preservation of its constitutional character. In respect to the control over the public money this doctrine is peculiarly applicable, and is in harmony with the great principle which I felt I was sustaining in the controversy with the Bank of the United States, which has resulted in severing to some extent a dangerous connection between a moneyed and political power. The duty of the Legislature to define, by clear and positive enactments, the nature and extent of the action which it belongs to the Executive to superintend springs out of a policy analogous to that which enjoins upon all the branches of the Federal Government an abstinence from the exercise of powers not clearly granted.

In such a Government, possessing only limited and specific powers, the spirit of its general administration can not be wise or just when it opposes the reference of all doubtful points to the great source of authority, the States and the people, whose number and diversified relations, securing them against the influences and excitements which may mislead their agents, make them the safest depository of power. In its application to the Executive, with reference to the legislative branch of the Government, the same rule of action should make the President ever anxious to avoid the exercise of any discretionary authority which can be regulated by Congress. The biases which may operate upon him will not be so likely to extend to the representatives of the people in that body.

In my former messages to Congress I have repeatedly urged the propriety of lessening the discretionary authority lodged in the various Departments, but it has produced no effect as yet, except the discontinuance of extra allowances in the Army and Navy and the substitution of fixed salaries in the latter. It is believed that the same principles could be advantageously applied in all cases, and would promote the efficiency and economy of the public service, at the same time that greater satisfaction and more equal justice would be secured to the public officers generally.

The accompanying report of the Secretary of War will put you in possession of the operations of the Department confided to his care in all its diversified relations during the past year.

I am gratified in being able to inform you that no occurrence has required any movement of the military force, except such as is common to a state of peace. The services of the Army have been limited to their usual duties at the various garrisons upon the Atlantic and inland frontier, with the exceptions stated by the Secretary of War. Our small military establishment appears to be adequate to the purposes for which it is maintained, and it forms a nucleus around which any additional force may be collected should the public exigencies unfortunately require any increase of our military means.

The various acts of Congress which have been recently passed in relation to the Army have improved its condition, and have rendered its organization more useful and efficient. It is at all times in a state for prompt and vigorous action, and it contains within itself the power of extension to any useful limit, while at the same time it preserves that knowledge, both theoretical and practical, which education and experience alone can give, and which, if not acquired and preserved in time of peace, must be sought under great disadvantages in time of war.

The duties of the Engineer Corps press heavily upon that branch of the service, and the public interest requires an addition to its strength. The nature of the works in which the officers are engaged renders necessary professional knowledge and experience, and there is no economy in committing to them more duties than they can perform or in assigning these to other persons temporarily employed, and too often of necessity without all the qualifications which such service demands. I recommend this subject to your attention, and also the proposition submitted at the last session of Congress and now renewed, for a reorganization of the Topographical Corps. This reorganization can be effected without any addition to the present expenditure and with much advantage to the public service. The branch of duties which devolves upon these officers is at all times interesting to the community, and the information furnished by them is useful in peace and war.

Much loss and inconvenience have been experienced in consequence of the failure of the bill containing the ordinary appropriations for fortifications which passed one branch of the National Legislature at the last session, but was lost in the other. This failure was the more regretted not only because it necessarily interrupted and delayed the progress of a system of national defense, projected immediately after the last war and since steadily pursued, but also because it contained a contingent appropriation, inserted in accordance with the views of the Executive, in aid of this important object and other branches of the national defense, some portions of which might have been most usefully applied during the past season. I invite your early attention to that part of the report of the Secretary of War which relates to this subject, and recommend an appropriation sufficiently liberal to accelerate the armament of the fortifications agreeably to the proposition submitted by him, and to place our whole Atlantic seaboard in a complete state of defense. A just regard to the permanent interests of the country evidently requires this measure, but there are also other reasons which at the present juncture give it peculiar force and make it my duty to call to the subject your special consideration.

The present system of military education has been in operation sufficiently long to test its usefulness, and it has given to the Army a valuable body of officers. It is not alone in the improvement, discipline, and operation of the troops that these officers are employed. They are also extensively engaged in the administrative and fiscal concerns of the various matters confided to the War Department; in the execution of the staff duties usually appertaining to military organization; in the removal of the Indians and in the disbursement of the various expenditures growing out of our Indian relations; in the formation of roads and in the improvement of harbors and rivers; in the construction of fortifications, in the fabrication of much of the *material* required for the public defense, and in the preservation, distribution, and accountability of the whole, and in other miscellaneous duties not admitting of classification.

These diversified functions embrace very heavy expenditures of public money, and require fidelity, science, and business habits in their execution, and a system which shall secure these qualifications is demanded by the public interest. That this object has been in a great measure obtained by the Military Academy is shewn by the state of the service and by the prompt accountability which has generally followed the necessary advances. Like all other political systems, the present mode of military education no doubt has its imperfections, both of principle and practice; but I trust these can be improved by rigid inspections and by legislative scrutiny without destroying the institution itself.

Occurrences to which we as well as all other nations are liable, both in our internal and external relations, point to the necessity of an efficient organization of the militia. I am again induced by the importance of the subject to bring it to your attention. To suppress domestic violence and to repel foreign invasion, should these calamities overtake us, we must rely in the first instance upon the great body of the community whose will has instituted and whose power must support the Government. A large standing military force is not consonant to the spirit of our institutions nor to the feelings of our countrymen, and the lessons of former days and those also of our own times shew the danger as well as the enormous expense of these permanent and extensive military organizations. That just medium which avoids an inadequate preparation on one hand and the danger and expense of a large force on the other is what our constituents have a right to expect from their Government. This object can be attained only by the maintenance of a small military force and by such an organization of the physical strength of the country as may bring this power into operation whenever its services are required. A classification of the population offers the most obvious means of effecting this organization. Such a division may be made as will be just to all by transferring each at a proper period of life from one class to another and by calling first for the services of that class, whether for instruction or action, which from age is qualified for the duty and may be called

to perform it with least injury to themselves or to the public. Should the danger ever become so imminent as to require additional force, the other classes in succession would be ready for the call. And if in addition to this organization voluntary associations were encouraged and inducements held out for their formation, our militia would be in a state of efficient service. Now, when we are at peace, is the proper time to digest and establish a practicable system. The object is certainly worth the experiment and worth the expense. No one appreciating the blessings of a republican government can object to his share of the burden which such a plan may impose. Indeed, a moderate portion of the national funds could scarcely be better applied than in carrying into effect and continuing such an arrangement, and in giving the necessary elementary instruction. We are happily at peace with all the world. A sincere desire to continue so and a fixed determination to give no just cause of offense to other nations furnish, unfortunately, no certain grounds of expectation that this relation will be uninterrupted. With this determination to give no offense is associated a resolution, equally decided, tamely to submit to none. The armor and the attitude of defense afford the best security against those collisions which the ambition, or interest, or some other passion of nations not more justifiable is liable to produce. In many countries it is considered unsafe to put arms into the hands of the people and to instruct them in the elements of military knowledge. That fear can have no place here when it is recollected that the people are the sovereign power. Our Government was instituted and is supported by the ballot box, not by the musket. Whatever changes await it, still greater changes must be made in our social institutions before our political system can yield to physical force. In every aspect, therefore, in which I can view the subject I am impressed with the importance of a prompt and efficient organization of the militia.

The plan of removing the aboriginal people who yet remain within the settled portions of the United States to the country west of the Mississippi River approaches its consummation. It was adopted on the most mature consideration of the condition of this race, and ought to be persisted in till the object is accomplished, and prosecuted with as much vigor as a just regard to their circumstances will permit, and as fast as their consent can be obtained. All preceding experiments for the improvement of the Indians have failed. It seems now to be an established fact that they can not live in contact with a civilized community and prosper. Ages of fruitless endeavors have at length brought us to a knowledge of this principle of intercommunication with them. The past we can not recall, but the future we can provide for. Independently of the treaty stipulations into which we have entered with the various tribes for the usufructuary rights they have ceded to us, no one can doubt the moral duty of the Government of the United States to protect and if possible to preserve and perpetuate the scattered remnants of this race which are left within our borders. In the discharge of this duty an extensive region in the West has been assigned for their permanent residence. It has been divided into districts and allotted among them. Many have already removed and others are preparing to go, and with the exception of two small bands living in Ohio and Indiana, not exceeding 1,500 persons, and of the Cherokees, all the tribes on the east side of the Mississippi, and extending from Lake Michigan to Florida, have entered into engagements which will lead to their transplantation.

The plan for their removal and reestablishment is founded upon the knowledge we have gained of their character and habits, and has been dictated by a spirit of enlarged liberality. A territory exceeding in extent that relinquished has been granted to each tribe. Of its climate, fertility, and capacity to support an Indian population the representations are highly favorable. To these districts the Indians are removed at the expense of the United States, and with certain supplies of clothing, arms, ammunition, and other indispensable articles; they are also furnished gratuitously with provisions for the period of a year after their arrival at their new homes. In that time, from the nature of the country and of the products raised by them, they can subsist themselves by agricultural labor, if they choose to resort to that mode of life; if they do not they are upon the skirts of the great prairies, where countless herds of buffalo roam, and a short time suffices to adapt their own habits to the changes which a change of the animals destined for their food may require. Ample arrangements have also been made for the support of schools; in some instances council houses and churches are to be erected, dwellings constructed for the chiefs, and mills for common use. Funds have been set apart for the maintenance of the poor; the most necessary mechanical arts have been introduced, and blacksmiths, gunsmiths, wheelwrights, millwrights, etc., are supported among them. Steel and iron, and sometimes salt, are purchased for them, and plows and other farming utensils, domestic animals, looms, spinning wheels, cards, etc., are presented to them. And besides these beneficial arrangements, annuities are in all cases paid, amounting in some instances to more than $30 for each individual of the tribe, and in all cases sufficiently great, if justly divided and prudently expended, to enable them, in addition to their own exertions, to live comfortably. And as a stimulus for exertion, it is now provided by law that "in all cases of the appointment of interpreters or other persons employed for the benefit of the Indians a preference shall be given to persons of Indian descent, if such can be found who are properly qualified for the discharge of the duties."

Such are the arrangements for the physical comfort and for the moral improvement of the Indians. The necessary measures for their political advancement and for their separation from our citizens have not been neglected. The pledge of the United States has been given by Congress that the country destined for the residence of this people shall be forever "secured and guaranteed to them." A country west of Missouri and Arkansas has been assigned to them, into which the white settlements are not to be pushed. No political communities can be formed in that extensive region, except those which are established by the Indians themselves or by the United States for them and with their concurrence. A barrier has thus been raised for their protection against the encroachment of our citizens, and guarding the Indians as far as possible from those evils which have brought them to their present condition. Summary authority has been given by law to destroy all ardent spirits found in their country, without waiting the doubtful result and slow process of a legal seizure. I consider the absolute and unconditional interdiction of this article among these people as the first and great step in their melioration. Halfway measures will answer no purpose. These can not successfully contend against the cupidity of the seller and the overpowering appetite of the buyer. And the destructive effects of the traffic are marked in every page of the history of our Indian intercourse.

Some general legislation seems necessary for the regulation of the relations which will exist in this new state of things between the Government and people of the United States and these transplanted Indian tribes, and for the establishment among the latter, and with their own consent, of some principles of intercommunication which their juxtaposition will call for; that moral may be substituted for physical force, the authority of a few and simple laws for the tomahawk, and that an end may be put to those bloody wars whose prosecution seems to have made part of their social system.

After the further details of this arrangement are completed, with a very general supervision over them, they ought to be left to the progress of events. These, I indulge the hope, will secure their prosperity and improvement, and a large portion of the moral debt we owe them will then be paid.

The report from the Secretary of the Navy, shewing the condition of that branch of the public service, is recommended to your special attention. It appears from it that our naval force at present in commission, with all the activity which can be given to it, is inadequate to the protection of our rapidly increasing commerce. This consideration and the more general one which regards this arm of the national defense as our best security against foreign aggressions strongly urge the continuance of the measures which promote its gradual enlargement and a speedy increase of the force which has been heretofore employed abroad and at home. You will perceive from the estimates which appear in the report of the Secretary of the Navy that the expenditures necessary to this increase of its force, though of considerable amount, are small compared with the benefits which they will secure to the country.

As a means of strengthening this national arm I also recommend to your particular attention the propriety of the suggestion which attracted the consideration of Congress at its last session, respecting the enlistment of boys at a suitable age in the service. In this manner a nursery of skillful and able-bodied seamen can be established, which will be of the greatest importance. Next to the capacity to put afloat and arm the requisite number of ships is the possession of the means to man them efficiently, and nothing seems better calculated to aid this object than the measure proposed. As an auxiliary to the advantages derived from our extensive commercial marine, it would furnish us with a resource ample enough for all the exigencies which can be anticipated. Considering the state of our resources, it can not be doubted that whatever provision the liberality and wisdom of Congress may now adopt with a view to the perfect organization of this branch of our service will meet the approbation of all classes of our citizens.

By the report of the Postmaster-General it appears that the revenue of the Department during the year ending on the 30th day of June last exceeded its accruing responsibilities $236,206, and that the surplus of the present fiscal year is estimated at $476,227. It further appears that the debt of the Department on the 1st day of July last, including the amount due to contractors for the quarter then just expired, was about $1,064,381, exceeding the available means about $23,700; and that on the 1st instant about $597,077 of this debt had been paid—$409,991 out of postages accruing before July and $187,086 out of postages accruing since. In these payments are included $67,000 of the old debt due to banks. After making these payments the Department had $73,000 in bank on the 1st instant. The pleasing assurance is given that the Department is entirely free from embarrassment, and that by collection of outstanding balances and using the current surplus the remaining portion of the bank debt and most of the other debt will probably be paid in April next, leaving thereafter a heavy amount to be applied in extending the mail facilities of the country. Reserving a considerable sum for the improvement of existing mail routes, it is stated that the Department will be able to sustain with perfect convenience an annual charge of $300,000 for the support of new routes, to commence as soon as they can be established and put in operation.

The measures adopted by the Postmaster-General to bring the means of the Department into action and to effect a speedy extinguishment of its debt, as well as to produce an efficient administration of its affairs, will be found detailed at length in his able and luminous report. Aided by a reorganization on the principles suggested and such salutary provisions in the laws regulating its administrative duties as the wisdom of Congress may devise or approve, that important Department will soon attain a degree of usefulness proportioned to the increase of our population and the extension of our settlements.

Particular attention is solicited to that portion of the report of the Postmaster-General which relates to the carriage of the mails of the United States upon railroads constructed by private corporations under the authority of the several States. The reliance which the General Government can place on those roads as a means of carrying on its operations and the principles on which the use of them is to be obtained can not too soon be considered and settled. Already does the spirit of monopoly begin to exhibit its natural propensities in attempts to exact from the public, for services which it supposes can not be obtained on other terms, the most extravagant compensation. If these claims be persisted in, the question may arise whether a combination of citizens, acting under charters of incorporation from the States, can, by a direct refusal or the demand of an exorbitant price, exclude the United States from the use of the established channels of communication between the different sections of the country, and whether the United States can not, without transcending their constitutional powers, secure to the Post-Office Department the use of those roads by an act of Congress which shall provide within itself some equitable mode of adjusting the amount of compensation. To obviate, if possible, the necessity of considering this question, it is suggested whether it be not expedient to fix by law the amounts which shall be offered to railroad companies for the conveyance of the mails, graduated according to their average weight, to be ascertained and declared by the Postmaster-General. It is probable that a liberal proposition of that sort would be accepted.

In connection with these provisions in relation to the Post-Office Department, I must also invite your attention to the painful excitement produced in the South by attempts to circulate through the mails inflammatory appeals addressed to the passions of the slaves, in prints and in various sorts of publications, calculated to stimulate them to insurrection and to produce all the horrors of a servile war. There is doubtless no respectable portion of our countrymen who can be so far misled as to feel any other sentiment than that of indignant regret at conduct so destructive of the harmony and peace of the country, and so repugnant to the principles of our national compact and to the dictates of humanity and religion. Our happiness and prosperity essentially depend upon peace within our borders, and peace depends upon the maintenance in good faith of those compromises of the Constitution upon which the Union is founded. It is fortunate for the country that the good sense, the generous feeling, and the deep-rooted attachment of the people of the non-slaveholding States to the Union and to their fellow-citizens of the same blood in the South have given so strong and impressive a tone to the sentiments entertained against the proceedings of the misguided persons who have engaged in these unconstitutional and wicked attempts, and especially against the emissaries from foreign parts who have dared to interfere in this matter, as to authorize the hope that those attempts will no longer be persisted in. But if these expressions of the public will shall not be sufficient to effect so desirable a result, not a doubt can be entertained that the nonslaveholding States, so far from countenancing the slightest interference with the constitutional rights of the South, will be prompt to exercise their authority in suppressing so far as in them lies whatever is calculated to produce this evil.

In leaving the care of other branches of this interesting subject to the State authorities, to whom they properly belong, it is nevertheless proper for Congress to take such measures as will prevent the Post-Office Department, which was designed to foster an amicable intercourse and correspondence between all the members of the Confederacy, from being used as an instrument of an opposite character. The General Government, to which the great trust is confided of preserving inviolate the relations created among the States by the Constitution, is especially bound to avoid in its own action anything that may disturb them. I would therefore call the special attention of Congress to the subject, and respectfully suggest the propriety of passing such a law as will prohibit, under severe penalties, the circulation in the Southern States, through the mail, of incendiary publications intended to instigate the slaves to insurrection.

I felt it to be my duty in the first message which I communicated to Congress to urge upon its attention the propriety of amending that part of the Constitution which provides for the election of the President and the Vice-President of the United States. The leading object which I had in view was the adoption of some new provisions which would secure to the people the performance of this high duty without any intermediate agency. In my annual communications since I have enforced the same views, from a sincere conviction that the best interests of the country would be promoted by their adoption. If the subject were an ordinary one, I should have regarded the failure of Congress to act upon it as an indication of their judgment that the disadvantages which belong to the present system were not so great as those which would result from any attainable substitute that had been submitted to

their consideration. Recollecting, however, that propositions to introduce a new feature in our fundamental laws can not be too patiently examined, and ought not to be received with favor until the great body of the people are thoroughly impressed with their necessity and value as a remedy for real evils, I feel that in renewing the recommendation I have heretofore made on this subject I am not transcending the bounds of a just deference to the sense of Congress or to the disposition of the people. However much we may differ in the choice of the measures which should guide the administration of the Government, there can be but little doubt in the minds of those who are really friendly to the republican features of our system that one of its most important securities consists in the separation of the legislative and executive powers at the same time that each is held responsible to the great source of authority, which is acknowledged to be supreme, in the will of the people constitutionally expressed. My reflection and experience satisfy me that the framers of the Constitution, although they were anxious to mark this feature as a settled and fixed principle in the structure of the Government, did not adopt all the precautions that were necessary to secure its practical observance, and that we can not be said to have carried into complete effect their intentions until the evils which arise from this organic defect are remedied.

Considering the great extent of our Confederacy, the rapid increase of its population, and the diversity of their interests and pursuits, it can not be disguised that the contingency by which one branch of the Legislature is to form itself into an electoral college can not become one of ordinary occurrence without producing incalculable mischief. What was intended as the medicine of the Constitution in extreme cases can not be frequently used without changing its character and sooner or later producing incurable disorder.

Every election by the House of Representatives is calculated to lessen the force of that security which is derived from the distinct and separate character of the legislative and executive functions, and while it exposes each to temptations adverse to their efficiency as organs of the Constitution and laws, its tendency will be to unite both in resisting the will of the people, and thus give a direction to the Government antirepublican and dangerous. All history tells us that a free people should be watchful or delegated power, and should never acquiesce in a practice which will diminish their control over it. This obligation, so universal in its application to all the principles of a republic, is peculiarly so in ours, where the formation of parties founded on sectional interests is so much fostered by the extent of our territory. These interests, represented by candidates for the Presidency, are constantly prone, in the zeal of party and selfish objects, to generate influences unmindful of the general good and forgetful of the restraints which the great body of the people would enforce if they were in no contingency to lose the right of expressing their will. The experience of our country from the formation of the Government to the present day demonstrates that the people can not too soon adopt some stronger safeguard for their right to elect the highest officers known to the Constitution than is contained in that sacred instrument as it now stands.

It is my duty to call the particular attention of Congress to the present condition of the District of Columbia. From whatever cause the great depression has arisen which now exists in the pecuniary concerns of this District, it is proper that its situation should be fully understood and such relief or remedies provided as are consistent with the powers of Congress. I earnestly recommend the extension of every political right to the citizens of this District which their true interests require, and which does not conflict with the provisions of the Constitution. It is believed that the laws for the government of the District require revisal and amendment, and that much good may be done by modifying the penal code so as to give uniformity to its provisions.

Your attention is also invited to the defects which exist in the judicial system of the United States. As at present organized the States of the Union derive unequal advantages from the Federal judiciary, which have been so often pointed out that I deem it unnecessary to repeat them here. It is hoped that the present Congress will extend to all the States that equality in respect to the benefits of the laws of the Union which can only be secured by the uniformity and efficiency of the judicial system.

With these observations on the topics of general interest which are deemed worthy of your consideration, I leave them to your care, trusting that the legislative measures they call for will be met as the wants and the best interests of our beloved country demand.

Source:

James D. Richardson, ed. *A Compilation of the Messages and Papers of the Presidents, 1789–1897.* Washington, D.C.: Government Printing Office, 1896–99.

Alexis de Tocqueville, *Democracy in America*, 1835

Democracy in America is a book written by Frenchman Alexis de Tocqueville to explain democracy, which he sees as an inevitable development in Europe, to his compatriots. His analysis of the American political system is considered a classic of political literature. Most influential is his disquisition on what he calls "the absolute sovereignty of the majority." The introduction to that chapter is reproduced here. The book was drawn from de Tocqueville's observations made during a working tour of the United States to study the penal system. The two-volume French edition was first published in 1835. The book's popularity and de Tocqueville's insights have endured. The first English translation was published between 1835 and 1840; three different English translations were published again in 2000. The following excerpts are from the 1961 publication.

Introductory Chapter

Amongst the novel objects that attracted my attention during my stay in the United States, nothing struck me more forcibly than the general equality of conditions. I readily discovered the prodigious influence which this primary fact exercises on the whole course of society, by giving a certain direction to public opinion, and a certain tenor to the laws; by imparting new maxims to the governing powers, and peculiar habits to the governed.

I speedily perceived that the influence of this fact extends far beyond the political character and the laws of the country, and that it has no less empire over civil society than over the Government; it creates opinions, engenders sentiments, suggests the ordinary practices of life, and modifies whatever it does not produce.

The more I advanced in the study of American society, the more I perceived that the equality of conditions is the fundamental fact from which all others seem to be derived, and the central point at which all my observations constantly terminated.

❋   ❋   ❋

Chapter IV. The Principle of the Sovereignty of the People in America

It predominates over the whole of society in America.—Application made of this principle by the Americans even before their Revolution.—Development given to it by that Revolution.—Gradual and irresistible extension of the elective qualification.

Whenever the political laws of the United States are to be discussed, it is with the doctrine of the sovereignty of the people that we must begin.

The principle of the sovereignty of the people, which is to be found, more or less, at the bottom of almost all human institutions, generally remains concealed from view. It is obeyed without being recognised, or if for a moment it be brought to light, it is hastily cast back into the gloom of the sanctuary.

"The will of the nation" is one of those expressions which have been most profusely abused by the wily and the despotic of every age. To the eyes of some it has been represented by the venal suffrages of a few of the satellites of power; to others, by the votes of a timid or an interested minority; and some have even discovered it in the silence of a people, on the supposition that the fact of submission established the right of command.

In America, the principle of the sovereignty of the people is not either barren or concealed, as it is with some other nations; it is recognised by the customs and proclaimed by the laws; it spreads freely, and arrives without impediment at its most remote consequences. If there be a country in the world where the doctrine of the sovereignty of the people can be fairly appreciated, where it can be studied in its application to the affairs of society, and where its dangers and its advantages may be foreseen, that country is assuredly America.

I have already observed that, from their origin, the sovereignty of the people was the fundamental principle of the greater number of British colonies in America. It was far, however, from then exercising as much influence on the government of society as it now does.

❀   ❀   ❀

The American revolution broke out, and the doctrine of the sovereignty of the people, which had been nurtured in the townships and municipalities, took possession of the State: every class was enlisted in its cause; battles were fought, and victories obtained for it; until it became the law of laws.

A no less rapid change was effected in the interior of society, where the law of descent completed the abolition of local influences.

At the very time when this consequence of the laws and of the revolution was apparent to every eye, victory was irrevocably pronounced in favour of the democratic cause. All power was, in fact, in its hands, and resistance was no longer possible. The higher orders submitted without a murmur and without a struggle to an evil which was thenceforth inevitable. The ordinary fate of falling powers awaited them; each of their several members followed his own interest; and as it was impossible to wring the power from the hands of a people which they did not detest sufficiently to brave, their only aim was to secure its good-will at any price. The most democratic laws were consequently voted by the very men whose interests they impaired: and thus, although the higher classes did not excite the passions of the people against their order, they accelerated the triumph of the new state of things; so that, by a singular change, the democratic impulse was found to be most irresistible in the very States where the aristocracy had the firmest hold.

Chapter XV. Power of the Majority in the United States, and Its Consequences

❀   ❀   ❀

The very essence of democratic government consists in the absolute sovereignty of the majority; for there is nothing in democratic states which is capable of resisting it. Most of the American Constitutions have sought to increase this natural strength of the majority by artificial means. The legislature is, of all political institutions, the one which is most easily swayed by the wishes of the majority. The Americans determined that the members of the legislature should be elected by the people immediately, and for a very brief term, in order to subject them, not only to the general convictions, but even to the daily passions of their constituents. The members of both Houses are taken from the same class in society, and are nominated in the same manner; so that the modifications of the legislative bodies are almost as rapid and quite as irresistible as those of a single assembly. It is to a legislature thus constituted, that almost all the authority of the government has been entrusted.But whilst the law increased the strength of those authorities which of themselves were strong, it enfeebled more and more those which were naturally weak. It deprived the representatives of the executive of all stability and independence; and by subjecting them completely to the caprices of the legislature, it robbed them of the slender influence which the nature of a democratic government might have allowed them to retain. In several States, the judicial power was also submitted to the elective discretion of the majority; and in all of them its existence was made to depend on the pleasure of the legislative authority, since the representatives were empowered annually to regulate the stipend of the judges.

Custom, however, has done even more than law. A proceeding which will in the end set all the guarantees of representative government at naught, is becoming more and more general in the United States: it frequently happens that the electors, who choose a delegate, point out a certain line of conduct to him, and impose upon him a certain number of positive obligations which he is pledged to fulfil. With the exception of the tumult, this comes to the same thing as if the majority of the populace held its deliberations in the market-place.

Several other circumstances concur in rendering the power of the majority in America not only preponderant, but irresistible. The moral authority of the majority is partly based upon the notion, that there is more intelligence and more wisdom in a great number of men collected together than in a single individual, and that the quantity of legislators is more important than their quality. The theory of equality is in fact applied to the intellect of man; and human pride is thus assailed in its last retreat, by a doctrine which the minority hesitate to admit, and in which they very slowly concur. Like all other powers, and perhaps more than all other powers, the authority of the many requires the sanction of time; at first it enforces obedience by constraint; but its laws are not respected until they have long been maintained. The right of governing society, which the majority supposes itself to derive from its superior intelligence, was introduced into the United States by the first settlers; and this idea, which would be sufficient of itself to create a free nation, has now been amalgamated with the manners of the people, and the minor incidents of social intercourse.

The French, under the old monarchy, held it for a maxim, (which is still a fundamental principle of the English Constitution), that the King could do no wrong; and if he did do wrong, the blame was imputed to his advisers. This notion was highly favourable to habits of obedience; and it enabled the subject to complain of the law, without ceasing to love and honour the lawgiver. The Americans entertain the same opinion with respect to the majority.

The moral power of the majority is founded upon yet another principle, which is, that the interests of the many are to be preferred to those of the few. It will readily be perceived that the respect here professed for the rights of the majority must naturally increase or diminish according to the state of parties. When a nation is divided into several irreconcilable factions, the privilege of the majority is often overlooked, because it is intolerable to comply with its demands.

If there existed in America a class of citizens whom the legislating majority sought to deprive of exclusive privileges, which they had possessed for ages, and to bring down from an elevated station to the level of the ranks of the multitude, it is probable that the minority would be less ready to comply with its laws. But as the United States were colonized by men holding equal rank amongst themselves, there is as yet no natural or permanent source of dissension between the interests of its different inhabitants.

There are certain communities in which the persons who constitute the minority can never hope to draw over the majority to their side, because they must then give up the very point which is at issue between them. Thus, an aristocracy can never become a majority whilst it retains its exclusive privileges, and it cannot cede its privileges without ceasing to be an aristocracy.

In the United States, political questions cannot be taken up in so general and absolute a manner; and all parties are willing to recognize the rights of the majority, because they all hope to turn those rights to their own advantage at some future time. The majority therefore in that country exercises a prodigious actual authority, and a moral influence which is scarcely less preponderant; no obstacles exist which can impede, or so much as retard its *progress, or which can induce it to heed the complaints of those whom it crushes upon its path. This state of things is fatal in itself and dangerous for the future.*

Source:

Alexis de Tocqueville, *Democracy in America*. Vols. 1 and 2. New York: Schocken Books, 1961.

Specie Circular of 1836

Circular issued by President Andrew Jackson on July 11, 1836, requiring the U.S. Treasury to accept only specie (gold or silver), not paper money, as payment in the sale of public lands. The circular was intended to protect federal revenues and to curb high inflation and rampant land speculation in the West. It resulted in an increased demand for specie that many banks could not accommodate, which, in turn, caused bank failures, reduction of credit, and increased unemployment in an economic crisis known as the panic of 1837. The circular was repealed on May 21, 1838.

Circular from the Treasury that gold and silver only be received in payment for public lands
Communicated to the Senate, December 14, 1836.
Treasury Department, July 11, 1836.

In consequence of complaints which have been made of frauds speculations, and monopolies, in the purchase of the public lands, and the aid which is said to be given to effect these objects by excessive bank credits, and dangerous if not partial facilities, through bank drafts and bank deposits, and the general evil influence likely, to result to the public interests, and especially the safety of the great amount of money in the Treasury, and the sound condition of the currency of the country, from the further exchange of the national domain in this manner, and chiefly for bank credits and paper money, the President of the United States has given directions, and you are hereby instructed, after the 15th day of August next, to receive in payment of the public lands nothing except what is directed by the existing laws, viz.: gold and silver, and in the proper cases, Virginia land scrip; provided that, till the 15th of December next, the same indulgences heretofore extended as to the kind of money received, may be continued for any quantity of land not exceeding 320 acres to each purchaser who is an actual settler, or bonafide resident in the State where the sales are made.

In order to insure the faithful execution of these instructions, all receiver are strictly prohibited from accepting for land sold, and draft, certificate, or other evidence of money or deposit, though for specie, unless signed by the Treasurer of the United States, in conformity to the act of April 24, 1820. And each of those officers is required to annex to his monthly returns to this department, the amount of gold and of silver respectively, as well as the bill received under the foregoing exception; and each deposit bank is required to annex to every certificate given upon a deposit of money, the proportions of it actually paid in gold, in silver, and in banknotes. All former instructions on this subjects, except as now modified, will be considered as remaining in full force.

The principal objects of the President, in adopting this measure, being to repress alleged frauds, and to withhold any countenance or facilities in the power of the government from the monopoly of the public lands in the hands of speculators and capitalists, to the injury of the actual settlers in the new States, and of emigrants in search of new homes, as well as to discourage the ruinous extension of bank issues and bank credits, by which those results are generally supposed to be promoted, your utmost vigilance is required, and relied on, to carry this order into complete execution.

Source:
American State Papers: Documents of the Congress of the United States in Relation to Public Lands, 1835–37, Vol. 8, p. 910.

Charles River Bridge
v. Warren Bridge, 1837

U.S. Supreme Court decision issued on February 14, 1837, establishing the principle that legislative grants are to be interpreted narrowly and that any ambiguity must be resolved in favor of the public, not the corporation. The decision modified the ruling in *Dartmouth College v. Woodward (1819)*, which protected private contracts against legislative inference. Here the Charles River Bridge Company, which held a state charter for a toll bridge and claimed monopoly rights, sued to prevent the Warren Bridge Company from constructing a competing free bridge. Chief Justice Roger Taney rejected the monopolistic claim because it was not specified in the original charter and would injure the public welfare.

Two years later, in *Bank of Augusta v. Earle*, 1839, the Supreme Court established that in the absence of specific state action to the contrary, a corporation chartered by one state was presumed to have the right to do business, under interstate comity, in other states, and a state did have the right to exclude a corporation by positive action. Chief Justice Roger Taney also ruled that a corporation did not possess all the U.S. constitutional rights of a natural person.

Mr. Chief Justice Taney delivered the opinion of the Court.

The questions involved in this case are of the gravest character, and the Court have given to them the most anxious and deliberate consideration. The value of the right claimed by the plaintiffs is large in amount; and many persons many no doubt be seriously affected in their pecuniary interests by any decision which, the Court may pronounce; and the questions which have been raised as to the power of the several states, in relation to the corporations they have chartered, are pregnant with important consequences; not only to the individuals who are concerned in the corporate franchises, but to the communities in which they exist. The Court are fully sensible that it is their duty, in exercising the high powers conferred on them by the constitution of the United States, to deal with these great and extensive interests with the utmost caution; guarding, as far as they have the power to do so, the rights of property, and at the same time carefully abstaining from any encroachment on the rights reserved to the states.

It appears, from the record, that in the year 1650, the legislature of Massachusetts, granted to the president of Harvard college "the liberty and power," to dispose of the ferry from Charlestown to Boston, by lease or otherwise, in the behalf and for the behalf of the college: and that, under that grant, the college continued to hold and keep the ferry by its lessees or agents, and to receive the profits of it until 1785. In the last mentioned year, a petition was presented to the legislature, by Thomas Russell and others, stating the inconvenience of the transportation be ferries, over Charles river, and the public advantages that would result from a bridge; and praying to be incorporated for the purpose of erecting a bridge in the place where the ferry between Boston and Charlestown was then kept. Pursuant to this petition, the legislature, on the 9th of March, 1785, passed an act incorporating a company, by the name of "The Proprietors of the Charles River Bridge," for the purpose mentioned in the petition. Under this charter the company were empowered to erect a bridge, in "the place where the ferry was then kept;" certain tolls were granted, and the charter was limited to forty years, from the first opening of the bridge for passengers; and from the time the toll commenced, until the expiration of this term, the company were to pay two hundred pounds, annually, to Harvard college; and at the expiration of the forty years the bridge was to be the property of the commonwealth; "saving (as the law expresses it) to the said college or university, a reasonable annual compensation, for the annual income of the ferry, which they might have received had not the said bridge been erected."

The bridge was accordingly built, and was opened for passengers on the 17th of June, 1786. In 1792, the charter was extended to seventy years, from the opening of the bridge; and at the expiration of that time it was to belong to the commonwealth. The corporation have regularly paid to the college the annual sum of two hundred pounds, and have performed all of the duties imposed on them by the terms of their charter.

In 1828, the legislature of Massachusetts incorporated a company by the name of "The Proprietors of the Warren Bridge," for the purpose of erecting another bridge over Charles river. This bridge is only sixteen rods, at its commencement, on the Charlestown side, form the commencement of the bridge of the plaintiffs; and they are about fifty rods apart at their termination on the Boston side. The travelers who pass over either bridge, proceed from Charlestown square, which receives the travel of many great public roads leading from the country; and the passengers and travelers who go to and from Boston, used to pass over the Charles River Bridge, from and through this square, before the erection of the Warren Bridge.

The Warren Bridge, by the terms of its charter, was to be surrendered to the state, as soon as the expenses of the proprietors in building and supporting it should be reimbursed; but this period was not, in any event, to exceed six years from the time the company commenced receiving toll.

When the original bill in this case was filed, the Warren Bridge had not been built; and the bill was filed after the passage of the law, in order to obtain an injunction to prevent its erection, and for general relief. The bill, among other things, charged as a ground for relief, that the act for the erection of the Warren Bridge impaired the obligation of the contract between the commonwealth and the proprietors of the Charles River Bridge; and was therefore repugnant to the constitution of the United States. Afterwards, a supplemental bill was filed, stating that the bridge had then been so far completed, that it had been opened for travel, and that divers persons had passed over, and thus avoided the payment of the toll, which would otherwise have been received by the plaintiffs. The answer to the supplemental bill admitted that the bridge had been so far completed, that foot passengers could pass; but denied that any persons but the workmen and the superintendents had passed over with their consent. In this state of the pleadings, the cause came on for hearing in the supreme judicial court for the county of Suffolk, in the commonwealth of Massachusetts, at November term, 1829; and the court decided that the act incorporating the Warren Bridge, did not impair the obligation of the contract with the proprietors of the Charles River Bridge, and dismissed the complainants' bill: and the case is brought here by writ of error from that decision. It is, however,

proper to state, that it is understood that the state court was equally divided upon the question; and that the decree dismissing the bill upon the ground above stated, was pronounced by a majority of the court, for the purpose of enabling the complainants to bring the question for decision before this Court.

In the argument here, it was admitted, that since the filing of the supplemental bill, a sufficient amount of toll had been received by the proprietors of the Warren Bridge to reimburse all their expenses, and that the bridge is now the property of the state, and has been made a free bridge; and that the value of the franchise granted to the proprietors of the Charles River Bridges; has by this means been entirely destroyed.

If the complainants deemed these facts material, they ought to have been brought before the state court, by a supplemental bill; and this Court, in pronouncing its judgment, cannot regularly notice them. But in the view which the Court take of this subject, these additional circumstances would not in any degree influence their decision. And as they are conceded to be true, and the case has been argued on that ground, and the controversy has been for a long time depending, and all parties desire a final end of it; and as it is of importance to them, that the principles on which this Court decide should not be misunderstood; the case will be treated in the opinion now delivered, as if these admitted facts were regularly before us.

A good deal of evidence has been offered to show the nature and extent of the ferry right granted to the college; and also to show the rights claimed by the proprietors of the bridges at different times, by virtue of their charter; and the opinions entertained by committees of the legislature, and others, upon that subject. But as these circumstances do not affect the judgment of this Court, it is unnecessary to recapitulate them.

The plaintiffs in error insist, mainly, upon two grounds: 1st. That by virtue of the grant of 1650, Harvard college was entitled, in perpetuity, to the right of keeping a ferry between Charlestown and Boston; that this right was exclusive; and that the legislature had not the power to establish another ferry on the same line of travel, because it would infringe the rights of the college; and that these rights, upon the erection of the bridge in the place of the ferry, under the charter of 1785, were transferred to, and became vested in "the proprietors of the Charles River Bridge;" and that under, and by virtue of this transfer of the ferry right, the rights of the bridge company were as exclusive in that line of travel, as the rights of the ferry. 2d. That independently of the ferry right, the acts of the legislature of Massachusetts of 1785, and 1792, by their true construction, necessarily implied that the legislature would not authorize another bridge, and especially a free one, by the side of this, and placed in the same line of travel, whereby the franchise granted to the "proprietors of the Charles River Bridge" should be rendered of no value; and the plaintiffs in error contend, that the grant of the ferry to the college, and of the charter to the proprietors of the bridge, are both contracts on the part of the state; and that the law authorizing the erection of the Warren Bridge in 1828, impairs the obligation of one or both of these contracts.

It is very clear, that in the form in which this case comes before us; being a writ of error to a state court; the plaintiffs in claiming under either of these rights, must place themselves on the ground of contract, and cannot support themselves upon the principle, that the law divests vested rights. It is well settled by the decisions of this Court, that a state law may be retrospective in its character, and may divest vested rights; and yet not violate the constitution of the United States, unless it also impairs the obligation of a contract. In 2 Peters, 413; Satterlee v. Mathewson; this Court, in speaking of the state law then before them, and interpreting the article in the constitution of the United States which forbids the states to pass laws impairing the obligation of contracts, uses the following language. "It (the state law) is said to be retrospective; be it so. But retrospective laws which do not impair the obligation of contracts, or partake of the character of ex post facto laws, are not condemned or forbidden by any part of that instrument," (the constitution of the United States). And in another passage in the same case, the Court say; "the objection, however, most pressed upon the Court, and relied upon by the counsel for the plaintiff in error, was, that the effect of this act was to divest rights which were vested by law in Satterlee. There is certainly no part of the constitution of the United States, which applies to a state law of this description; nor are we aware of any decision of this, or of any circuit court, which has condemned such a law upon this ground, provided its effect be not to impair the obligation of a contract." The same principles were reaffirmed in this Court, in the late case of Watson and others v. Mercer, decided in 1834, 8 Pet. 110; "as to the first point, (say the Court,) it is clear that this Court has no right to pronounce an act of the state legislature void, as contrary to the constitution of the United States, from the mere fact that it divests antecedent vested rights of property. The constitution of the United States does not prohibit the states from passing retrospective laws, generally; but only ex post facto laws."

After these solemn decisions of this Court, it is apparent that the plaintiffs in error cannot sustain themselves here, either upon the ferry right, or the charter to the bridge; upon the ground that vested rights of property have been divested by the legislature. And whether they claim under the ferry right, or the charter to the bridge, they must show that the title which they claim, was acquired by contract, and that the terms of that contract, have been violated by the charter to the Warren Bridge. In other words, they must show that the state had entered into a contract with them, or those under whom they claim, not to establish a free bridge at the place where the Warren Bridge is erected. Such, and such only, are the principles upon which the plaintiffs in error can claim relief in this case.

The nature and extent of the ferry right granted to Harvard college, in 1650, must depend upon the laws of Massachusetts; and the character and extent of this right has been elaborately discussed at the bar. But in the view which the Court take of the case before them, it is not necessary to express any opinion on these questions. For assuming that the grant to Harvard college, and the charter to the Bridge company, were both contracts, and that the ferry right was as extensive and exclusive as the plaintiffs contend for; still they cannot enlarge the privileges granted to the bridge, unless it can be shown, that the rights of Harvard college in this ferry-have, by assignment, or in some other way, been transferred to the proprietors of the Charles River Bridge, and still remain in existence, vested in them, to the same extent with that in which they were held and enjoyed by the college before the bridge was built.

It has been strongly pressed upon the Court, by the plaintiffs in error, that these rights are still existing, and are now held by the proprietors of the bridge. If this franchise still exists, there must be somebody possessed of authority to use it, and to keep the ferry. Who could now lawfully set up a ferry where the old one was kept? The bridge was built in the same place, and its abutments occupied the landings of the ferry. The transportation of passengers in boats, from landing to landing, was no longer possible; and the ferry was as effectually destroyed, as if a convulsion of nature had made there a passage of dry land. The ferry then, of necessity, ceased to exist, as soon as the bridge was erected; and when the ferry itself was destroyed, how can rights which were incident to it, be supposed to survive? The exclusive privileges, if they had such, must follow the fate of the ferry, and can have no legal existence without it—and if the ferry right had been assigned by the college, in due and legal form, to the proprietors of the bridge, they themselves extinguished that right, when they erected the bridge in its place. It is not supposed by any one, that the Bridge company have a right to keep a ferry. No such right is claimed for them, nor can be claimed for them, under their charter to erect a bridge—and it is difficult to imagine how ferry rights can be held by a corporation, or an individual, who have no right to keep a ferry. It is clear, that the incident must follow the fate of the principal, and the privilege connected with property, cannot survive the destruction of the property; and if the ferry right in Harvard college was exclusive, and had been assigned to the proprietors of the bridge, the privilege of exclusion could not remain in the hands of their assignees, if those assignees destroyed the ferry.

But upon what ground can the plaintiffs in error contend that the ferry rights of the college have been transferred to the proprietors of the bridge? If they have been thus transferred, it must be by some mode of transfer known to the law; and the evidence relied on to prove it, can be pointed out in the record. How was it transferred? It is not suggested that there ever was, in point of fact, a deed of conveyance executed by the college to the Bridge company. Is there any evidence in the record from which such a conveyance may, upon legal principle, be presumed? The testimony before the Court, so far from laying the foundation for such a presumption, repels it in the most positive terms. The petition to the legislature, in 1785, on which the charter was granted, does not suggest an assignment, nor any agreement or consent on the part of the college; and the petitioners do not appear to have regarded the wishes of that institution, as by any means necessary to ensure their success. They place their application entirely on considerations of public interest and public convenience, and the superior advantages of a communication across Charles river by a bridge, instead of a ferry. The legislature, in granting the charter, show, by the language of the law, that they acted on the principle assumed by the petitioners. The preamble recites that the bridge "will be of great public utility;" and that is the only reason they assign, for passing the law which incorporates this company. The validity of the charter is not made to depend on the consent of the college, nor of any assignment or surrender on their part; and the legislature deal with the subject, as if it were one exclusively within their own power, and as if the ferry right were not to be transferred to the Bridge company, but to be extinguished and they appear to have acted on the principle, that the state by virtue of its sovereign powers and eminent domain, had a right to take away the franchise of the ferry; because, in their judgment, the public interest and convenience would be better promoted by a bridge in the same place; and upon that principle they proceed to make a pecuniary compensation to the college, for the franchise thus taken away: and as there is an express reservation of a continuing pecuniary compensation to the college, when the bridge shall become the property of the state, and no provision whatever for the restoration of the ferry right, it is evident that no such right was intended to be reserved or continued. The ferry, with all its privileges was intended to be forever at an end, and a compensation in money was given in lieu of it. The college acquiesced in this arrangement, and there is proof, in the record, that it was all done with their consent. Can a deed of assignment to the Bridge

company which would keep alive the ferry rights in their hands, be presumed under such circumstances? Do not the petition, the law of incorporation, and the consent of the college to the pecuniary provision made for it in perpetuity, all repel the notion of an assignment of its rights to the Bridge company, and prove that every party to this proceeding, intended that its franchises, whatever they were, should be resumed by the state, and be no longer held by any individual, or corporation? With such evidence before us, there can be no ground for presuming a conveyance to the plaintiffs. There was no reason for such a conveyance. There was every reason against it; and the arrangements proposed by the charter to the bridge, could not have been carried into full effect, unless the rights of the ferry were entirely extinguished.

It is however said, that the payment of the two hundred pounds a year to the college, as provided for in the law, gives to the proprietors of the bridge an equitable claim to be treated as the assignees of their interest; and by substitution, upon chancery principles, to be clothed with all their rights.

The answer to this argument is obvious. This annual sum was intended to be paid out of the proceeds of the tolls, which the company were authorized to collect. The amount of the tolls, it must be presumed, was graduated with a view to this encumbrance, as well as to every other expenditure to which the company might be subjected, under the provisions of their charter. The tolls were to be collected from the public, and it was intended that the expense of the annuity to Harvard college should be borne by the public; and it is manifest that it was so borne, from the amount which it is admitted they received, until the Warren Bridge was erected. Their agreement, therefore, to pay that sum, can give them no equitable right to be regarded as the assignees of the college, and certainly can furnish no foundation for presuming a conveyance; and as the proprietors of the bridge are neither the legal nor equitable assignees of the college, it is not easy to perceive how the ferry franchise can be invoked in aid of their claims, if it were even still a subsisting privilege; and had not been resumed by the state, for the purpose of building a bridge in its place.

Neither can the extent of the pre-existing ferry right, whatever it may have been, have any influence upon the construction of the written charter for the bridge. It does not, by any means, follow, that because the legislative power in Massachusetts, in 1650, may have granted to a justly favored seminary of learning, the exclusive right of ferry between Boston and Charlestown, they would, in 1785, give the same extensive privilege to another corporation, who were about to erect a bridge in the same place. The fact that such a right was granted to the college, cannot by any sound rule of construction, be used to extend the privileges of the Bridge company beyond what the words of the charter naturally and legally import. Increased population longer experienced in legislation, the different character of the corporations which owned the ferry from that which owned the bridge, might well have induced a change in the policy of the state in this respect; and as the franchise of the ferry, and that of the bridge, are different in their nature, and were each established by separate grants, which have no words to connect the privileges of the one with the privileges of the other; there is no rule of legal interpretation, which would authorize the Court to associate these grants together, and to infer that any privilege was intended to be given to the Bridge company, merely because it had been conferred on the ferry. The charter to the Bridge is a written instrument which must speak for itself, and be interpreted by its own terms.

This brings us to act of the legislature of Massachusetts, of 1785, by which the plaintiffs were incorporated by the name of "The Proprietors of the Charles River Bridge;" and it is here, and in the law of 1792, prolonging their charter, that we must look for the extent and nature of the franchise conferred upon the plaintiffs.

Much has been said in the argument of the principles of construction by which this law is to be expounded, and what undertakings, on the part of the state, may be implied. The Court think there can be no serious difficulty on that head. It is the grant of certain franchises by the public to a private corporation, and in a matter where the public interest is concerned. The rule of construction in such cases is well settled, both in England, and by the decisions of our own tribunals. In 2 Barn. & Adol. 793, in the case of the Proprietors of the Stourbridge Canal against Wheely and others, the court say, "the canal having been made under an act of parliament, the rights of the plaintiffs are derived entirely from that act. This, like many other cases, is a bargain between a company of adventurers and the public, the terms of which are expressed in the statute; and the rule of construction in all such cases, is now fully established to be this; that any ambiguity in the terms of the contract, must operate against the adventurers, and in favor of the public, and the plaintiffs can claim nothing that is not clearly given them by the act." And the doctrine thus laid down in abundantly sustained by the authorities referred to in this decision. The case itself was as strong a one, as could well be imagined, for giving to the canal company, by implication, a right to the tolls they demanded. Their canal had been used by the defendants, to a very considerable extent, in transporting large quantities of coal. The rights of all persons to navigate the canal, were expressly secured by the act of parliament; so that the company could not prevent them from using it, and the toll demanded was admitted to be reasonable. Yet, as they only used one of the levels of the canal, and did not pass

through the locks; and the statute, in giving the right to exact toll, had given if for articles which passed *"through any one or more of the locks,"* and had said nothing as to toll for navigating one of the levels; the court held that the right to demand toll, in the latter case, could not be implied, and that the company were not entitled to recover it. This was a fair case for an equitable construction of the act of incorporation, and for an implied grant; if such a rule of construction could ever be permitted in a law of that description. For the canal had been made at the expense of the company; the defendants had availed themselves of the fruits of their labors, and used the canal freely and extensively for their own profit. Still the right to exact toll could not be implied, because such a privilege was not found in the charter.

Borrowing, as we have done, our system of jurisprudence from the English law; and having adopted, in every other case, civil and criminals, its rules for the construction of statutes; is there any thing in our local situation, or in the nature of our political institutions, which should lead us to depart from the principle where corporations are concerned? Are we to apply to acts of incorporation, a rule of construction differing from that of the English law, and, by implication, make the terms of a charter in one of the states, more unfavorable to the public, than upon an act of parliament, framed in the same words, would be sanctioned in an English court? Can any good reason be assigned for excepting this particular class of cases from the operation of the general principle; and for introducing a new and adverse rule of construction in favor of corporations, while we adopt and adhere to the rules of construction known to the English common law, in every other case, without exception? We think not; and it would present a singular spectacle, if, while the courts in England are restraining, within the strictest limits, the spirit of monopoly, and exclusive privileges in nature of monopolies, and confining corporations to the privileges plainly given to them in their charter; the courts of this country should be found enlarging these privileges by implication; and construing a statute more unfavorably to the public, and to the rights of the community, than would be done in a like case in an English court of justice.

But we are not now left to determine, for the first time, the rules by which public grants are to be construed in this country. The subject has already been considered in this Court; and the rule of construction, above stated, fully established. In the case of the United States v. Arredondo, 9 Pet. 738, the leading cases upon this subject are collected together by the learned judge who delivered the opinion of the Court; and the principle recognized, that in grants by the public, nothing passes by implication.

The rule is still more clearly and plainly stated in the case of Jackson v. Lamphire, in 3 Pet. 289. That was a grant of land by the state; and in speaking of this doctrine if implied covenants in grants by the state, the Court use the following language, which is strikingly applicable to the case at bar:—"The only contract made by the state, is the grant to John Cornelius, his heirs and assigns, of the land in question. The patent contains no covenant to do, or not to do any further act in relation to the land; and we do not feel ourselves at liberty, in this case, to create one by implication. The state has not, by this act, impaired the force of the grant; it does not profess or attempt to take the land from the assigns of Cornelius, and give it to one not claiming under him; neither does the award produce that effect; the grant remains in full force; the property conveyed is held by his grantee, and the state asserts no claim to it."

The same rule of construction is also stated in the case of Beatty v. The Lessee of Knowles, 4 Pet. 168; decided in this Court in 1830. In delivering their opinion in that case, the Court say:— "That a corporation is strictly limited to the exercise of those powers which are specially conferred on it, will not be decided. The exercise of the corporate franchise being restrictive of individual rights, cannot be extended beyond the letter and spirit of the act incorporation."

But the case most analogous to this, and in which the question came more directly before the Court, is the case of the Providence Bank v. Billings & Pittmann, 4 Pet. 514; and which was decided in 1830. In that case, it appeared that the legislature of Rhode Island had chartered the bank, in the usual form of such acts of incorporation. The charter contained no stipulation on the part of the state, that it would not impose a tax on the bank, nor any reservation of the right to do so. It was silent on this point. Afterwards, a law was passed, imposing a tax on all banks in the state; and the right to impose this tax was resisted by the Providence Bank, upon the ground, that if the state could impose a tax, it might tax so heavily as to render the franchise of no value, and destroy the institution; that the charter was a contract, and that a power which may in effect destroy the charter is inconsistent with it, and is impliedly renounced by granting it. But the Court said that the taxing power was of vital importance, and essential to the existence of government; and that the relinquishment of such a power is never to be assumed. And in delivering the opinion of the Court, the late Chief Justice states the principle, in the following clear and emphatic language. Speaking of the taxing power, he says, "as the whole community is interested in retaining it undiminished, that community has a right to insist that its abandonment ought to be presumed, in a case in which the deliberate purpose of the state to abandon it does not appear." The case now before the Court, is, in principle, precisely the same. It is a charter from a state. The act of incorporation is silent in relation to the contested power. The argument in favor of

the proprietors of the Charles River Bridge, is the same, almost in words, with that used by the Providence bank; that is, that the power claimed by the state, if it exists, may be so used as to destroy the value of the franchise they have granted to the corporation. The argument must receive the same answer; and the fact that the power has been already exercised so as to destroy the value of the franchise, cannot in any degree affect the principle. The existence of the power does not, and cannot depend upon the circumstance of its having been exercised or not.

It may, perhaps, be said, that in the case of the Providence Bank, this Court were speaking of the taxing power; which is of vital importance to the very existence of every government. But the object and end of all government is to promote the happiness and prosperity of the community by which it is established; and it can never be assumed, that the government intended to diminish its power of accomplishing the end for which it was created. And in a country like ours, free, active and enterprising, continually advancing in numbers and wealth; new channels of communication are daily found necessary, both for travel and trade; and are essential to the comfort, convenience, and prosperity of the people. A state ought never to be presumed to surrender this power, because, like the taxing power, the whole community have an interest in preserving it undiminished. And when a corporation alleges, that a state has surrendered for seventy years, its power of improvement and public accommodation, in a great and important line of travel, along which a vast number of its citizens must daily pass; the community have a right to insist, in the language of this Court above quoted, "that its abandonment ought not to be presumed, in a case, in which the deliberate purpose of the state to abandon it does not appear." The continued existence of a government would be of no great value, if by implications and presumptions, it was disarmed of the powers necessary to accomplish the ends of its creation; and the functions it was designed to perform, transferred to the hands of privileged corporations. The rule of construction announced by the Court, was not confined to the taxing power; nor is it so limited in the opinion delivered. On the contrary, it was distinctly placed on the ground that the interests of the community were concerned in preserving, undiminished, the power then in question; and whenever any power of the state is said to be surrendered or diminished, whether it be the taxing power or any other affecting the public interest, the same principle applies, and the rule of construction must be the same. No one will question that the interests of the great body of the people of the state, would, in this instance, be affected by the surrender of this great line of travel to a single corporation, with the right to exact toll, and exclude competition for seventy years. While the rights of private property are sacredly guarded, we must not forget that the community also have rights, and that the happiness and well being of every citizen depends on their faithful preservation.

Adopting the rule of construction above stated as the settled one, we proceed to apply it to the charter of 1785, to the proprietors of the Charles River Bridge. This act of incorporation is in the usual form, and the privileges such as are commonly given to corporations of that kind. It confers on them the ordinary faculties of a corporation, for the purpose of building the bridge; and establishes certain rates of toll, which the company are authorized to take. This is the whole grant. There is no exclusive privilege given to them over the waters of Charles river, above or below their bridge. No right to erect another bridge themselves, nor to prevent other persons from erecting one. No engagement from the state, that another shall not be erected; and no undertaking not to sanction competition, nor to make improvements that may diminish the amount of its income. Upon all these subjects the charter is silent; and no thing is said in it about a line of travel, so much insisted on in the argument, in which they are to have exclusive privileges. No words are used, from which an intention to grant any of these rights can be inferred. If the plaintiff is entitled to them, it must be implied, simply, from the nature of the grant; and cannot be inferred from the words by which the grant is made.

The relative position of the Warren Bridge has already been described. It does not interrupt the passage over the Charles River Bridge, nor make the way to it or from it less convenient. None of the faculties or franchises granted to that corporation, have been revoked by the legislature; and its right to take the tolls granted by the charter remains unaltered. In short, all the franchises and rights of property enumerated in the charter, and there mentioned to have been granted to it, remain unimpaired. But its income is destroyed by the Warren Bridge; which, being free, draws off the passengers and property which would have gone over it, and renders their franchise of no value. This is the gist of the complaint. For it is not pretended, that the erection of the Warren Bridge would have done them any injury, or in any degree affected their right of property; if it had not diminished the amount of their tolls. In order then to entitle themselves to relief, it is necessary to show, that the legislature contracted not to do the act of which they complain; and that they impaired, or in other words, violated that contract by the erection of the Warren Bridge.

The inquiry then is, done the charter contain such a contract on the part of the state? is there any such stipulation to be found in that instrument? I must be admitted on all hands, that there is none—no words that even relate to another bridge, or to the diminution of their tolls, or to the line of travel. If a contract on the subject can be gathered from the charter, it must be by implication; and cannot be found in the words used. Can such an agreement be implied? The rule of construction before stated is an answer to the question. In charters of this description, no rights are taken from the public, or given to the corporation, beyond those which the words of the charter, by their natural and proper construction, purport to convey. There are no words which import such a contract as the plaintiffs in error contend for, and none can be implied; and the same answer must be given to them that was given by this Court to the Providence Bank. The whole community are interested in this inquiry, and they have a right to require that the power of promoting their comfort and convenience, and of advancing the public prosperity, by providing safe, convenient, and cheap ways for the transportation of produce, and the purposes of travel, shall not be construed to have been surrendered or diminished by the state; unless it shall appear by plain words, that it was intended to be done.

But the case before the Court is even still stronger against any such implied contract, as the plaintiffs in error contend for. The Charles River Bridge was completed in 1786. The time limited for the duration of the corporation by their original charter, expired in 1826. When, therefore, the law passed authorizing the erection of the Warren Bridge, the proprietors of Charles River Bridge held their corporate existence under the law of 1792, which extended their charter for thirty years; and the rights, privileges, and franchises of the company, must depend upon the construction of the last mentioned law, taken in connection with the act of 1785.

The act of 1792, which extends the charter of this bridge, incorporates another company to build a bridge over Charles river; furnishing another communication with Boston, and distant only between one and two miles from the old bridge.

The first six sections of this act incorporate the proprietors of the West Boston Bridge, and define the privileges, and describe the duties of that corporation. In the seventh section there is the following recital: "And whereas the erection of Charles River Bridge was a work of hazard and public utility, and another bridge in the place of West Boston bridge may diminish the emoluments of Charles River Bridge; therefore, for the encouragement of enterprise," they proceed to extend the charter of the Charles River Bridge, and to continue it for the term of seventy years from the day the bridge was completed; subject to the conditions prescribed in the original act, and to be entitled to the same tolls. It appears, then, that by the same act that extended this charter, the legislature established another bridge, which they knew would lessen its profits; and this, too, before the expiration of the first charter, and only seven years after it was granted; thereby showing, that the state did not suppose that, by the terms it had used in the first law, it had deprived itself of the power of making such public improvements as might impair the profits of the Charles River Bridge; and from the language used in the clauses of the law by which the charter is extended, it would seem, that the legislature were especially careful to exclude any inference that the extension was made upon the ground of compromise with the Bridge Company, or as a compensation for rights impaired.

On the contrary, words are cautiously employed to exclude that conclusion; and the extension is declared to be granted as a reward for the hazard they had run, and "for the encouragement of enterprise." The extension was given because the company had undertaken and executed a work of doubtful success; and the improvements which the legislature then contemplated, might diminish the emoluments they had expected to receive from it. It results from this statement, that the legislature in the very law extending the charter, asserts its rights to authorize improvements over Charles river which would take off a portion of the travel from this bridge and diminish its profits; and the Bridge Company accept the renewal thus given, and thus carefully connected with this assertion of the right on the part of the state. Can they, when holding their corporate existence under this law, and deriving their franchises altogether from it; add to the privileges expressed in their charter an implied agreement, which is in direct conflict with a portion of the law from which they derive their corporate existence? Can the legislature be presumed to have taken upon themselves an implied obligation, contrary to its own acts and declarations contained in the same law? It would be difficult to find a case justifying such an implication, even between individuals; still less will it be found where sovereign rights are concerned, and where the interests of a whole community would be deeply affected by such an implication. It would, indeed, be a strong exertion of judicial power, acting upon its own views of what justice required, and the parties ought to have done; to raise, by a sort of judicial coercion, an implied contract, and infer it from the nature of the very instrument in which the legislature appear to have taken pains to use words which disavow and repudiate any intention, on the part of the state, to make such a contract.

Indeed, the practice and usage of almost every state in the Union, old enough to have commenced the work of internal improvement, is opposed to the doctrine contended for on the part of the plaintiffs in error. Turnpike roads have been made in succession, on the same line of travel; the later ones interfering materially with the profits of the first. These corporations have, in some instances, been utterly ruined by the introduction of newer and better modes of transportation, and traveling. In some cases,

rail roads have rendered the turnpike roads on the same line of travel so entirely useless, that the franchise of the turnpike corporation is not worth preserving. Yet in none of these cases have the corporations supposed that their privileges were invaded, or any contract violated on the part of the state. Amid the multitude of cases which have occurred, and have been daily occurring for the last forty or fifty years, this is the first instance in which such an implied contract has been contended for, and this Court called upon to infer it from an ordinary act of incorporation, containing nothing more than the usual stipulations and provisions to be found in every such law. The absence of any such controversy, when there must have been so many occasions to give rise to it, proves that neither states, nor individuals, nor corporations, ever imagined that such a contract could be implied from such charters. It shows that the men who voted for these laws, never imagined that they were forming such a contract; and if we maintain that they have made it, we must create it by a legal fiction, in opposition to the truth of the fact, and the obvious intention of the party. We cannot deal thus with the rights reserved to the states; and by legal intendments and mere technical reasoning, take away from them any portion of that power over their own internal police and improvement, which is so necessary to their well being and prosperity.

And what would be the fruits of this doctrine of implied contracts on the part of the states, and of property in a line of travel by a corporation, if it should now be sanctioned by this Court? To what results would it lead us? If it is to be found in the charter to this bridge, the same process of reasoning must discover it, in the various acts which have been passed, within the last forty years, for turnpike companies. And what is to be the extent of the privileges of exclusion on the different sides of the road? The counsel who have so ably argued this case, have not attempted to define it by any certain boundaries. How far must the new improvement be distant from the old one? How near may you approach without invading its rights in the privileged line? If this Court should establish the principles now contended for, what is to become of the numerous rail roads established on the same line of travel with turnpike companies; and which have rendered the franchises of the turnpike corporations of no value? Let it once be understood that such charters carry with them these implied contracts, and give this unknown and undefined property in a line of traveling; and you will soon find the old turnpike corporations awakening from their sleep, and calling upon this Court to put down the improvements which have taken their place. The millions of property which have been invested in rail roads and canals, upon lines of travel which had been before occupied by turnpike corporations, will be put in jeopardy. We shall be thrown back to the improvements of the last century, and obliged to stand still, until the claims of the old turnpike corporations shall be satisfied; and they shall consent to permit these states to avail themselves of the lights of modern science, and to partake of the benefit of those improvements which are now adding to the wealth and prosperity, and the convenience and comfort, of every other part of the civilized world. Nor is this all. This Court will find itself compelled to fix, by some arbitrary rule, the width of this new kind of property in a line of travel; for if such a right of property exists, we have no lights to guide us in marking out its extent, unless, indeed, we resort to the old feudal grants, and to the exclusive rights of ferries, by prescription, between towns; and are prepared to decide that when a turnpike road from one town to another, had been made, no rail road or canal, between these two points, could afterwards be established. This Court are not prepared to sanction principles which must lead to such results.

Many other questions, of the deepest importance, have been raised and elaborately discussed in the argument. It is not necessary, for the decision of this case, to express our opinion upon them; and the Court deem it proper to avoid volunteering an opinion on any question, involving the construction of the constitution, where the case itself does not bring the question directly before them, and make it their duty to decide upon it.

Some questions, also, of a purely technical character, have been made and argued, as to the form of proceeding and the right to relief. But enough appears on the record to bring out the great question in contest; and it is the interest of all parties concerned, that the real controversy should be settled without further delay: and as the opinion of the Court is pronounced on the main question in dispute here, and disposes of the whole case, it is altogether unnecessary to enter upon the examination of the forms of proceeding, in which the parties have brought it before the Court.

The judgment of the supreme judicial court of the commonwealth of Massachusetts, dismissing the plaintiffs' bill, must, therefore, be affirmed, with costs.

Source:

Reports of Cases Argued and Adjudged in the Supreme Court of the United States. Vol. 12, 1837, pp. 536–553.

Pre-Emption Act of 1841

Federal legislation enacted on September 4, 1841, that permitted western settlers to claim up to 160 acres of surveyed public lands and, after a period of residence, to purchase that land from the U.S. government at a minimum price of $1.25 per acre before it was put up for public auction. That act was favored by western states to encourage settlement, rather than land speculation, but was opposed by the eastern states, who feared a loss of its labor supply. Eastern support was gained with the addition of a plan to distribute revenues from the sale of public lands among the states, based on population. Though the distribution provisions were repealed in 1842, the Pre-Emption Act remained in effect until 1891, when abuses led to its repeal.

An Act

To appropriate the proceeds of the sales of the public lands, and to grant pre-emption rights.

Be it enacted by the Senate and House of Representatives of the United States of America in Congress assembled, That from and after the thirty-first day of December, in the year of our Lord one thousand eight hundred and forty-one, there be allowed and paid to each of the States of Ohio, Indiana, Illinois, Alabama, Missouri, Mississippi, Louisiana, Arkansas, and Michigan, over and above what each of the said States is entitled to by the terms of the compacts entered into between them and the United States, upon their admission into the Union, the sum of ten per centum upon the nett proceeds of the sales of the public lands, which, subsequent to the day aforesaid, shall be made within the limits of each of said States, respectively: *Provided,* That the sum so allowed to the said States, respectively, shall be in no wise affected or diminished on account of any sums which have been heretofore, or shall be hereafter, applied to the construction or continuance of the Cumberland road, but that the disbursements for the said road shall remain, as heretofore, chargeable on the two per centum fund provided for by compacts with several of the said States.

Sec. 2. *And be it further enacted,* That after deducting the said ten per centum, and what, by the compacts aforesaid, has heretofore been allowed to the States aforesaid, the residue of the nett proceeds, which nett proceeds shall be ascertained by deducting from the gross proceeds all the expenditures of the year for following objects: salaries and expenses on account of the General Land Office; expenses for surveying public lands; salaries and expenses in the surveyor general's offices; salaries, commissions, and allowances to the registers and receivers; the five per centum to new States, of all the public lands of the United States, wherever situated, which shall be sold subsequent to the said thirty-first day of December, shall be divided among the twenty-six States of the Union and the District of Columbia, and the Territories of Wisconsin, Iowa, and Florida, according to their respective federal representative population as ascertained by the last census, to be applied by the Legislatures of the said States to such purposes as the said Legislatures may direct: *Provided,* That the distributive share to which the District of Columbia shall be entitled, shall be applied to free schools, or education in some other form, as Congress may direct: *And provided, also,* That nothing herein contained shall be construed to the prejudice of future applications for a reduction of the price of the public lands, or to the prejudice of applications for a transfer of the public lands, on reasonable terms, to the States within which they lie, or to make such future disposition of the public lands, or any part thereof, as Congress may deem expedient.

Sec. 3. *And be if further enacted,* That the several sums of money received in the Treasury as the nett proceeds of the sales of the public lands shall be paid at the Treasury half yearly on the first day of January and July in each year, during the operation of this act, to such person or persons as the respective Legislatures of the said States and Territories, or the Governors thereof, in case the Legislatures shall have made no such appointment, shall authorize and direct to receive the same.

Sec. 4. *And be it further enacted,* That any sum of money, which at any time may become due, and payable to any State of the Union, or to the District of Columbia, by virtue of this act, as the portion of the said State or District, of the proceeds of the sales of the public lands, shall be first applied to the payment of any debt, due, and payable from the said State or District, to the United States: *Provided,* That this shall not be construed to extend to the sums deposited with the States under the act of Congress of twenty-third June, eighteen hundred and thirty-six, entitled "an act to regulate the deposits of the public money," nor to any sums apparently due to the United States as balances of debts growing out of the transactions of the Revolutionary war.

Sec. 5. *And be it further enacted* That this act shall continue and be in force until otherwise provided by law, unless the United States shall become involved in war with any foreign Power, in which event, from the commencement of hostilities, this act shall be suspended during the continuance of such war: *Provided, nevertheless,* That if, prior to the expiration of this act, any new State or States shall be admitted into the Union, there be assigned to such new State or States, the proportion of the proceeds accruing after their admission into the Union, to which such State or States may be entitled, upon the principles of this act, together with what such State or States may be entitled to by virtue of compacts to be made on their admission into the Union.

Sec. 6. *And be it further enacted,* That there shall be annually appropriated for completing the surveys of said lands, a sum not less than one hundred and fifty thousand dollars; and the minimum price at which the public lands are now sold at private sale shall not be increased, unless Congress shall think proper to grant alternate sections

along the line of any canal or other internal improvement, and at the same time to increase the minimum price of the sections reserved; and in case the same shall be increased by law, except as aforesaid, at any time during the operation of this act, then so much of this act as provides that the nett proceeds of the sales of the public lands shall be distributed among the several States, shall, from and after the increase of the minimum price thereof, cease and become utterly null and of no effect, any thing in this act to the contrary notwithstanding: *Provided,* That if, at any time during the existence of this act, there shall be an imposition of duties on imports inconsistent with the provisions of the act of March second one thousand eight hundred and thirty-three, entitled, "An act to modify the act of the fourteenth of July one thousand eight hundred and thirty-two, and all other acts imposing duties on imports," and beyond the rate of duty fixed by that act, to wit: twenty per cent on the value of such imports, or any of them, then the distribution provided in this act shall be suspended and shall so continue until this cause of its suspension shall be removed, and when removed, if not prevented by other provisions of this act, such distribution shall be resumed.

Sec. 7. *And be it further enacted,* That the Secretary of the Treasury may continue any land district in which is situated the seat of government of any one of the States, and may continue the land office in such district, notwithstanding the quantity of land unsold in such district may not amount to one hundred thousand acres, when, in his opinion, such continuance may be required by public convenience, or in order to close the land system in such State at a convenient point, under the provisions of the act on that subject, approved twelfth June, one thousand eight hundred and forty.

Sec. 8. *And be it further enacted,* That there shall be granted to each State specified in the first section of this act five hundred thousand acres of land for purposes of internal improvement: *Provided,* that to each of the said States which has already received grants for said purposes, there is hereby granted no more than a quantity of land which shall, together with the amount such State has already received as aforesaid, make five hundred thousand acres, the selections in all of the said States, to be made within their limits respectively in such manner as the Legislatures thereof shall direct; and located in parcels conformably to sectional divisions and subdivisions, of not less than three hundred and twenty acres in any one location, on any public land except such as is or may be reserved from sale by any law of Congress or proclamation of the President of the United States, which said locations may be made at any time after the lands of the United States in said States respectively, shall have been surveyed according to existing laws. And there shall be and hereby is, granted to each new State that shall be hereafter admitted into the Union, upon such admission, so much land as, including such quantity as may have been granted to such State before its admission, and while under a Territorial Government, for purposes of internal improvement as aforesaid, as shall make five hundred thousand acres of land, to be selected and located as aforesaid.

Sec. 9. *And be it further enacted* That the lands herein granted to the States above named shall not be disposed of at a price less than one dollar and twenty-five cents per acre, until otherwise authorized by a law of the United States; and the nett proceeds of the sales of said lands shall be faithfully applied to objects of internal improvement within the States aforesaid, respectively, namely: Roads, railways, bridges, canals and improvement of water-courses, and draining of swamps; and such roads, railways, canals, bridges and water-courses, when made or improved, shall be free for the transportation of the United States mail, and munitions of war, and for the passage of their troops, without the payment of any toll whatever.

Sec. 10. *And be it further enacted,* That from and after the passage of this act, every person being the head of a family, or widow, or single man, over the age of twenty-one years, and being a citizen of the United States, or having filed his declaration of intention to become a citizen, as required by the naturalization laws, who since the first day of June, A.D. eighteen hundred and forty, has made or shall hereafter make a settlement in person on the public lands to which the Indian title had been at the time of such settlement extinguished, and which has been, or shall have been, surveyed prior thereto, and who shall inhabit and improve the same, and who has or shall erect a dwelling thereon, shall be, and is hereby, authorized to enter with the register of the land office for the district in which such land may lie, by legal subdivisions, any number of acres not exceeding one hundred and sixty, or a quarter section of land, to include the residence of such claimant, upon paying to the United States the minimum price of such land, subject, however, to the following limitations and exceptions: No person shall be entitled to more than one pre-emptive right by virtue of this act; no person who is the proprietor of three hundred and twenty acres of land in any State or Territory of the United States, and no person who shall quit or abandon his residence on his own land to reside on the public land in the same State or Territory, shall acquire any right of pre-emption under this act; no lands included in any reservation, by any treaty, law, or proclamation of the President of the United States, or reserved for salines, or for other purposes; no lands reserved for the support of schools, nor the lands acquired by either of the two last treaties with the Miami tribe of Indians in the State of Indiana, or which may be acquired of the Wyandot tribe of Indians in the State of Ohio, or

other Indian reservation to which the title has been or may be extinguished by the United States at any time during the operation of this act; no sections of land reserved to the United States alternate to other sections granted to any of the States for the construction of any canal, railroad, or other public improvement; no sections or fractions of sections included within the limits of any incorporated town; no portions of the public lands which have been selected as the site for a city or town; no parcel or lot of land actually settled and occupied for the purposes of trade and not agriculture; and no lands on which are situated any known salines or mines, shall be liable to entry under and by virtue of the provisions of this act. And so much of the proviso of the act of twenty-second of June, eighteen hundred and thirty-eight, or any order of the President of the United States, as directs certain reservations to be made in favor of certain claims under the treaty of Dancing-rabbit creek, be, and the same is hereby, repealed: *Provided,* That such repeal shall not affect any title to any tract of land secured in virtue of said treaty.

Sec. 11. *And be it further enacted,* That when two or more persons shall have settled on the same quarter section of land, the right of pre-emption shall be in him or her who made the first settlement, provided such persons shall conform to the other provisions of this act; and all questions as to the right of pre-emption arising between different settlers shall be settled by the register and receiver of the district within which the land is situated, subject to an appeal to and a revision by the Secretary of the Treasury of the United States.

Sec. 12. *And be it further enacted,* That prior to any entries being made under and by virtue of the provisions of this act, proof of the settlement and improvement thereby required, shall be made to the satisfaction of the register and receiver of the land district in which such lands may lie, agreeably to such rules as shall be prescribed by the Secretary of the Treasury, who shall each be entitled to receive fifty cents from each applicant for his services, to be rendered as aforesaid; and all assignments and transfers of the right hereby secured, prior to the issuing of the patent, shall be null and void.

Sec. 13. *And be it further enacted,* That before any person claiming the benefit of this act shall be allowed to enter such lands, he or she shall make oath before the receiver or register of the land district in which the land is situated, (who are hereby authorized to administer the same,) that he or she has never had the benefit of any right of pre-emption under this act; that he or she is not the owner of three hundred and twenty acres of land in any State or Territory of the United States, nor hath he or she settled upon and improved said land to sell the same on speculation, but in good faith to appropriate it to his or her own exclusive use or benefit; and that he or she has not, directly or indirectly, made any agreement or contract, in any way or manner, with any person or persons whatsoever, by which the title which he or she might acquire from the Government of the United States, should ensure in whole or in part, to the benefit of any person except himself or herself; and if any person taking such oath shall swear falsely in the premises, he or she shall be subject to all the pains and penalties of perjury, and shall forfeit the money which he or she may have paid for said land, and all right and title to the same; and any grant or conveyance which he or she may have made, except in the hands of bona fide purchasers, for a valuable consideration, shall be null and void. And it shall be the duty of the officer administering such oath to file a certificate thereof in the public land office of such district, and to transmit a duplicate copy to the General Land Office, either of which shall be good and sufficient evidence that such oath was administered according to law.

Sec. 14. *And be it further enacted,* That this act shall not delay the sale of any of the public lands of the United States beyond the time which has been, or may be, appointed by the proclamation of the President, nor shall the provisions of this act be available to any person or persons who shall fail to make the proof and payment, and file the affidavit required before the day appointed for the commencement of the sales as aforesaid.

Sec. 15. *And be it further enacted,* That whenever any person has settled or shall settle and improve a tract of land, subject at the time of settlement to private entry, and shall intend to purchase the same under the provisions of this act, such person shall in the first case, within three months after the passage of the same, and in the last within thirty days next after the date of such settlement, file with the register of the proper district a written statement, describing the land settled upon, and declaring the intention of such person to claim the same under the provisions of this act; and shall, where such settlement is already made, within twelve months after the passage of this act, and where it shall hereafter be made, within the same period after the date of such settlement, make the proof, affidavit, and payment herein required; and if he or she shall fail to file such written statement as aforesaid, or shall fail to make such affidavit, proof, and payment, within the twelve months aforesaid, the tract of land so settled and improved shall be subject to the entry of any other purchaser.

Sec. 16. *And be it further enacted,* That the two per cent. of the nett proceeds of the lands sold, or that may hereafter be sold, by the United States in the State of Mississippi, since the first day of December, eighteen hundred and seventeen, and by the act entitled "An act to enable the people of the western part of the Mississippi Territory to form a constitution and State government, and for the admission of such State into the Union on an equal footing with the original States," and all acts supplemental thereto reserved for the making of a road or roads leading to said State, be, and the same is hereby relinquished to the State of Mississippi, payable in two equal instalments; the first to be paid on the first of May, eighteen hundred and forty-two, and the other on the first of May, eighteen hundred and forty-three, so far as the same may then have accrued, and quarterly, as the same may accrue, after said period: *Provided,* That the Legislature of said State shall first pass an act, declaring their acceptance of said relinquishment in full of said fund, accrued and accruing, and also embracing a provision, to be unalterable without the consent of Congress, that the whole of said two per cent. fund shall be faithfully applied to the construction of a railroad, leading from Brandon, in the State of Mississippi, to the eastern boundary of said State, in the direction, as near as may be, of the towns of Selma, Cahaba, and Montgomery, in the State of Alabama.

Sec. 17. *And be it further enacted,* That the two per cent. of the nett proceeds of the lands sold by the United States, in the State of Alabama, since the first day of September, eighteen hundred and nineteen, and reserved by the act entitled "An act to enable the people of the Alabama Territory to form a constitution and State government, and for the admission of such State into the Union on an equal footing with the original States," for the making of a road or roads leading to the said State, be, and the same is hereby, relinquished to the said State of Alabama, payable in two equal instalments, the first to be paid on the first day of May, eighteen hundred and forty-two, and the other on the first day of May, eighteen hundred and forty-three, so far as the same may then have accrued, and quarterly, as the same may thereafter accrue: *Provided,* That the Legislature of said State shall first pass an act, declaring their acceptance of said relinquishment, and also embracing a provision, to be unalterable without the consent of Congress, that the whole of said two per cent. fund shall be faithfully applied, under the direction of the Legislature of Alabama, to the connection, by some means of internal improvement, of the navigable waters of the bay of Mobile with the Tennessee river, and to the construction of a continuous line of internal improvements from a point on the Chattahoochie river, opposite West Point, in Georgia, across the State of Alabama, in a direction to Jackson in the State of Mississippi.

Source:
Statutes at Large. Vol. 5, pp. 453–458.

Treaty of Wanghia, 1844

Treaty signed on July 3, 1844, at Wanghia, China (near Macao), between the United States and China, opening certain Chinese ports to American trade and granting Americans the right of extraterritoriality, or exemption from the jurisdiction of Chinese laws and courts (Americans accused of crimes were to be tried by American consular officials). The treaty was negotiated by U.S. commissioner Caleb Cushing, and the U.S. Senate consented to it on January 8, 1845. As in other treaties concluded with Great Britain and France during this period, China therein granted a foreign power most-favored-nation status, guaranteeing trading equality. The Wanghia agreement led to increased American trade and an influx of Christian missionaries into China.

At Tientsin on June 18, 1858, after the Anglo-French War against China (1857–58), U.S. minister to China William B. Reed signed a new treaty. China opened up 11 additional treaty ports to foreign trade and residence and provided for extraterritorial protection of foreign nationals traveling and trading throughout China. In the treaty, Reed secured the same treatment for U.S. citizens as other foreigners had obtained through earlier treaties with China.

Treaty with China

The United States of America and the Ta Tsing Empire, desiring to establish firm, lasting, and sincere friendship between the two nations, have resolved to fix, in a manner clear and positive, by means of a treaty or general convention of peace, amity, and commerce, the rules which shall in future be mutually observed in the intercourse of their respective countries:—For which most desirable object, the President of the United States has conferred full powers on their Commissioner Caleb Cushing, Envoy Extraordinary and Minister Plenipotentiary of the United States to China; and the August Sovereign of the Ta Tsing Empire on his Minister and Commissioner Extraordinary Tsiyeng, of the Imperial House, a vice Guardian of the Heir Apparent, Governor-general of the Two Kwang, and Superintendent General of the trade and foreign intercourse of the five ports.

And the said Commissioners, after having exchanged their said full powers, and duly considered the premises, have agreed to the following articles:

Article I

There shall be a perfect, permanent, universal peace, and a sincere and cordial amity, between the United States of America on the one part, and the Ta Tsing Empire on the other part, and between their people respectively, without exception of persons or places.

Article II

Citizens of the United States resorting to China for the purposes of commerce will pay the duties of import and export prescribed in the Tariff, which is fixed by and made a part of this Treaty. They shall, in no case, be subject to other or higher duties than are or shall be required of the people of any other nation whatever. Fees and charges of every sort are wholly abolished, and officers of the revenue, who may be guilty of exaction, shall be punished according to the laws of China. If the Chinese Government desire to modify, in any respect, the said Tariff, such modification shall be made only in consultation with consuls or other functionaries thereto duly authorized in behalf of the United States, and with consent thereof. And if additional advantages or privileges of whatever description, be conceded hereafter by China to any other nation, the United States, and the citizens thereof, shall be entitled thereupon, to a complete, equal, and impartial participation in the same.

Article III

The citizens of the United States are permitted to frequent the five ports of Kwang-chow, Amoy, Fuchow, Ningpo, and Shanghai, and to reside with their families and trade there, and to proceed at pleasure with their vessels and merchandize to and from any foreign port and either of the said five ports, and from either of the said five ports to any other of them. But said vessels shall not unlawful enter the other ports of China, nor carry on a clandestine and fraudulent trade along the coasts thereof. And any vessel belonging to a citizen of the United States, which violates this provision, shall, with her cargo, be subject to confiscation to the Chinese Government.

Article IV

For the superintendence and regulation of the concerns of the citizens of the United States doing business at the said five ports, the Government of the United States may appoint consuls, or other officers, at the same, who shall be duly recognized as such by the officers of the Chinese Government, and shall hold official intercourse and correspondence with the latter, either personal or in writing, as occasions may require, on terms of equality and reciprocal respect. If disrespectfully treated or aggrieved in any way by the local authorities, said officers on the one hand shall have the right to make representation of the same to the superior officers of the Chinese Government, who will see that full inquiry and strict justice be had in the premises; and on the other hand, the said consuls will carefully avoid all acts of unnecessary offence to, or collision with, the officers and people of China.

Article V

At each of the said five ports, citizens of the United States lawfully engaged in commerce, shall be permitted to import from their own or any other ports into China, and sell there, and purchase therein, and export to their own or any other ports, all manner of merchandize, of which the importation or exportation is not prohibited by this Treaty, paying the duties which are prescribed by the Tariff here-inbefore established, and no other charges whatsoever.

Article VI

Whenever any merchant vessel belonging to the United States shall enter either of the said five ports for trade, her papers shall be lodged with the consul, or person charged with affairs, who will report the same to the Commissioner of Customs; and tonnage duty shall be paid on said vessel at the rate of five mace per ton, if she be over one hundred and fifty tons burden; and one mace per ton if she be of the burden of one hundred and fifty tons or under, according to the amount of her tonnage as specified in the register; said payment to be in full of the former charges of measurement and other fees, which are wholly abolished. And if any vessel, which having anchored at one of the said ports, and there paid tonnage duty, shall have occasion to go to any others of the said ports to complete the disposal of her cargo, the consul, or person charged with affairs, will report the same to the Commissioner of Customs, who, on the departure of the said vessel, will note in the port-clearance that the tonnage duties have been paid, and report the same to the other custom-houses; in which case on entering another port the said vessel will only pay duty there on her cargo, but shall not be subject to the payment of tonnage duty a second time.

Article VII

No tonnage duty shall be required on boats belonging to citizens of the United States, employed in the conveyance of passengers, baggage, letters, and articles of provision, or others not subject to duty, to or from any of the five ports. All cargo-boats, however, conveying merchandize subject to duty, shall pay the regular tonnage duty of one mace per ton, provided they belong to citizens of the United States, but not if hired by them from subjects of China.

Article VIII

Citizens of the United States, for their vessels bound in, shall be allowed to engage pilots, who will report said vessels at the passes, and take them into port; and, when the lawful duties have all been paid, they may engage pilots to leave port. It shall also be lawful for them to hire, at pleasure, servants, compradors, linguists, and writers, and passage or cargo boats, and to employ laborers, seamen, and persons for whatever necessary service, for a reasonable compensation, to be agreed on by the parties, or settled by application to the consular officer of their government, without interference on the part of the local officers of the Chinese government.

Article IX

Whenever merchant vessels belonging to the United States shall have entered port, the superintendent of customs will, if he see fit, appoint custom-house officers to guard said vessels, who may live on board the ship or their own boats, at their convenience; but provision for the subsistence of said officers shall be made by the superintendent of customs, and they shall not be entitled to any allowance from the vessel or owner thereof; and they shall be subject to suitable punishment for any exaction practised by them in violation of this regulation.

Article X

Whenever a merchant vessel belonging to the United States shall cast anchor in either of said ports, the supercargo, master, or consignee, will, within forty-eight hours, deposit the ship's papers in the hands of the consul or person charged with the affairs of the United States, who will cause to be communicated to the superintendent of customs a true report of the name and tonnage of such vessel, the names of her men, and of the cargo on board; which being done, the superintendent will give a permit for the discharge of her cargo.

And the master, supercargo, or consignee, if he proceed to discharge the cargo without such permit, shall incur a fine of five hundred dollars; and the goods so discharged without permit shall be subject to forfeiture to the Chinese government. But if the master of any vessel in port desire to discharge a part only of the cargo, it shall be lawful for him to do so, paying duties on such part only, and to proceed with the remainder to any other ports.

Or, if the master so desire, he may, within forty-eight hours after the arrival of the vessel, but not later, decide to depart without breaking bulk; in which case he will not be subject to pay tonnage or other duties or charges, until, on his arrival at another port, he shall proceed to discharge cargo, when he will pay the duties on vessel and cargo, according to law. And the tonnage duties shall be held to be due after the expiration of said forty-eight hours.

Article XI

The superintendent of customs, in order to the collection of the proper duties, will, on application made to him through the consul, appoint suitable officers, who shall proceed, in the presence of the captain, supercargo, or consignee, to make a just and fair examination of all goods in the act of being discharged for importation, or laden for exportation on board any merchant vessel of the United States. And if dispute occur in regard to the value of goods subject to an ad valorem duty, or in regard to the amount of tare, and the same cannot be satisfactorily arranged by the parties, the question may, within twenty-four hours, and not afterwards, be referred to the said consul to adjust with the superintendent of customs.

Article XII

Sets of standard balances, and also weights and measures, duly prepared, stamped, and sealed, according to the standard of the custom at Canton, shall be delivered by the superintendents of customs to the consuls at each of the five ports, to secure uniformity, and prevent confusion in measures and weights of merchandize.

Article XIII

The tonnage duty on vessels belonging to citizens of the United States shall be paid on their being admitted to entry. Duties of import shall be paid on the discharge of the goods, and duties of export on the lading of the same. When all such duties shall have been paid, and not before, the superintendent of customs shall give a port-clearance, and the consul shall return the ship's papers, so that she may depart on her voyage. The duties shall be paid to the shroffs authorized by the Chinese government to receive the same in its behalf. Duties payable by merchants of the United States shall be received either in sycee silver or in foreign money, at the rate of exchange as ascertained by the regulations now in force. And imported goods, on their resale or transit in any part of the empire, shall be subject to the imposition of no other duty than they are accustomed to pay at the date of this treaty.

Article XIV

No goods on board any merchant vessel of the United States in port are to be transhipped to another vessel, unless there be particular occasion therefor; in which case, the occasion shall be certified by the consul to the superintendant of customs, who may appoint officers to examine into the facts, and permit the transhipment. And if any goods be transhipped without such application, inquiry, and permit, they shall be subject to be forfeited to the Chinese government.

Article XV

The former limitation of the trade of foreign nations to certain persons appointed at Canton by the Government, and commonly called hong-merchants, having been abolished, citizens of the United States engaged in the purchase or sale of goods of import or export, the admitted to trade with any and all subjects of China without distinc-

tion; they shall not be subject to any new limitations, nor impeded in their business by monopolies or other injurious restrictions.

Article XVI

The Chinese Government will not hold itself responsible for any debts which may happen to be due from subjects of China to citizens of the United States, or for frauds committed by them: but citizens of the United States may seek redress in law; and on suitable representation being made to the Chinese local authorities through the consul, they will cause due examination in the premises, and take all proper steps to compel satisfaction. But in case the debtor be dead, or without property, or have absconded, the creditor cannot be indemnified according to the old system of the co-hong so called. And if citizens of the United States be indebted to subjects of China, the latter may seek redress in the same way through the consul, but without any responsibility for the debt on the part of the United States.

Article XVII

Citizens of the United States residing or sojourning at any of the ports open to foreign commerce, shall enjoy all proper accommodation in obtaining houses and places of business, or in hiring sites from the inhabitants on which to construct houses and places of business, and also hospitals, churches and cemeteries. The local authorities of the two Governments shall select in concert the sites for the foregoing objects, having due regard to the feelings of the people in the location thereof: and the parties interested will fix the rent by mutual agreement, the proprietors on the one hand not demanding any exorbitant price, nor the merchants on the other unreasonably insisting on particular spots, but each conducting with justice and moderation. And any desecration of said cemeteries by subjects of China shall be severely punished according to law.

At the places of anchorage of the vessels of the United States, the citizens of the United States, merchants, seamen, or others sojourning there, may pass and repass in the immediate neighbourhood; but they shall not at their pleasure make excursions into the country among the villages at large, nor shall they repair to public marts for the purpose of disposing of goods unlawfully and in fraud of the revenue. And, in order to the preservation of the public peace, the local officers of government at each of the five ports, shall, in concert with the consuls, define the limits beyond which it shall not be lawful for citizens of the United States to go.

Article XVIII

It shall be lawful for the officers or citizens of the United States to employ scholars and people of any part of China without distinction of persons, to teach any of the languages of the empire, and to assist in literary labors; and the persons so employed shall not, for that cause, be subject to any injury on the part either of the government or of individuals: and it shall in like manner be lawful for citizens of the United States to purchase all manner of books in China.

Article XIX

All citizens of the United States in China, peaceably attending to their affairs, being placed on a common footing of amity and goodwill with subjects of China, shall receive and enjoy, for themselves and every thing appertaining to them, the special protection of the local authorities of Government, who shall defend them from all insult or injury of any sort on the part of the Chinese. If their dwellings or property be threatened or attacked by mobs, incendiaries, or other violent or lawless persons, the local officers, on requisition of the consul, will immediately despatch a military force to disperse the rioters, and will apprehend the guilty individuals, and punish them with the utmost rigor of the law.

Article XX

Citizens of the United States who may have imported merchandize into any of the free ports of China, and paid the duty thereon, if they desire to re-export the same, in part or in whole, to any other of the said ports, shall be entitled to make application, through their consul, to the superintendant of Customs, who, in order to prevent frauds on the revenue, shall cause examination to be made by suitable officers to see that the duties paid on such goods, as entered on the custom-house books, correspond with the representation made, and that the goods remain with their original marks unchanged, and shall then make a memorandum in the port-clearance, of the goods, and the amount of duties paid on the same, and deliver the same to the merchant; and shall also certify the facts to the officers of customs of the other ports. All which being done, on the arrival in port of the vessel in which the goods are laden, and every thing being found on examination there to correspond, she shall be permitted to break bulk and land the said goods, without being subject to the payment of any additional duty thereon. But if, on such examination, the superintendent of customs shall detect any fraud on the revenue in the case, then the goods shall be subject to forfeiture and confiscation to the Chinese Government.

Article XXI

Subjects of China who may be guilty of any criminal act towards citizens of the United States, shall be arrested and punished by the Chinese authorities according to the laws of China: and citizens of the United States, who may commit any crime in China, shall be subject to be tried and punished only by the consul, or other public functionary of the United States, thereto authorized according to the laws of the United States. And in order to the prevention of all controversy and disaffection, justice shall be equitably and impartially administered on both sides.

Article XXII

Relations of peace and amity between the United States and China being established by this treaty, and the vessels of the United States being admitted to trade freely to and from the five ports of China open to foreign commerce, it is further agreed that in case at any time hereafter, China should be at war with any foreign nation whatever, and for that cause should exclude such nation from entering her ports, still the vessels of the United States shall not less continue to pursue their commerce in freedom and security, and to transport goods to and from the ports of the belligerent parties, full respect being paid to the neutrality of the flag of the United States: Provided that the said flag shall not protect vessels engaged in the transportation of officers or soldiers in the enemy's service; nor shall said flag be fraudulently used to enable the enemy's ships with their cargoes to enter the ports of China; but all such vessels so offending shall be subject to forfeiture and confiscation to the Chinese Government.

Article XXIII

The consuls of the United States at each of the five ports open to foreign trade, shall make annually to the respective Governors-general thereof, a detailed report of the number of vessels belonging to the United States which have entered and left said ports during the year, and of the amount and value of goods imported or exported in said vessels, for transmission to and inspection of the Board of Revenue.

Article XXIV

If citizens of the United States have special occasion to address any communication to the Chinese local officers of Government, they shall submit the same to their consul, or other officer, to determine if the language be proper and respectful, and the matter just and right; in which event he shall transmit the same to the appropriate authorities for their consideration and action in the premises. In like manner, if subjects of China have special occasion to address the consul of the United States, they shall submit the communication to the local authorities of their own Government, to determine if the language be respectful and proper, and the matter just and right; in which case the said authorities will transmit the same to the consul, or other officer, for his consideration and action in the premises. And if controversies arise between citizens of the United States and subjects of China, which cannot be amicably settled otherwise, the same shall be examined and decided conformably to justice and equity by the public officers of the two nations acting in conjunction.

Article XXV

All questions in regard to rights, whether of property or person, arising between citizens of the United States in China, shall be subject to the jurisdiction and regulated by the authorities of their own Government. And all controversies occurring in China between citizens of the United States and the subjects of any other Government, shall be regulated by the treaties existing between the United States and such Governments, respectively, without interference on the part of China.

Article XXVI

Merchant vessels of the United States lying in the waters of the five ports of China open to foreign commerce, will be under the jurisdiction of the officers of their own Government; who, with the masters and owners thereof, will manage the same without control on the part of China. For injuries done to the citizens or the commerce of the United States by any foreign power, the Chinese Government will not hold itself bond to make reparation. But if the merchant-vessels of the United States, while within the waters over which the Chinese Government exercise jurisdiction, be plundered by robbers or pirates, then the Chinese local authorities, civil and military, on receiving information thereof, will arrest the said robbers or pirates, and punish them according to law, and will cause all the property which can be recovered, to be placed in the hands of the nearest consul, or other officer of the United States, to be by him restored to the true owner. But if, by reason of the extent of territory and numerous population of China, it should, in any case, happen that the robbers cannot be apprehended, or the property only in part recovered, then the law will take its course in regard to the local authorities, but the Chinese Government will not make indemnity for the goods lost.

Article XXVII

If any vessel of the United States shall be wrecked or stranded on the coast of China, and be subjected to plunder or other damage, the proper officers of Government on receiving information of the fact, will immediately adopt measures for their relief and security; and the persons on board shall receive friendly treatment, and be enabled at once to repair to the most convenient of the free ports, and shall enjoy all facilities for obtaining supplies of provisions and water. And if a vessel shall be forced in whatever way to take refuge in any port other than one of the free ports, then in like manner the persons on board

shall receive friendly treatment, and the means of safety and security.

Article XXVIII

Citizens of the United States, their vessels and property, shall not be subject to any embargo; nor shall they be seized or forcibly detained for any pretense of the public service; but they shall be suffered to prosecute their commerce in quiet, and without molestation or embarrassment.

Article XXIX

The local authorities of the Chinese Government will cause to be apprehended all mutineers or deserters from on board the vessels of the United States in China, and will deliver them up to the consuls or other officers for punishment. And if criminals, subjects of China, take refuge in the houses or on board the vessels of citizens of the United States, they shall not be harbored or concealed, but shall be delivered up to justice, on due requisition by the Chinese local officers addressed to those of the United States.

The merchants, seamen, and other citizens of the United States shall be under the superintendance of the appropriate officers of their government. If individuals of either nation commit acts of violence and disorder, use arms to the injury of others, or create disturbances endangering life, the officers of the two governments will exert themselves to enforce order, and to maintain the public peace, by doing impartial justice in the premises.

Article XXX

The superior authorities of the United States and of China, in corresponding together, shall do so in terms of equality, and in the form of mutual communication, (*chau hwui.*) The consuls, and the local officers, civil and military, in corresponding together, shall likewise employ the style and form of mutual communication, (*chau hwui.*) When inferior officers of the one government address superior officers of the other, they shall do so in the style and form of memorial, (*shin chin.*) Private individuals, in addressing superior officers, shall employ the style of petition, (*pin ching.*) In no case shall any terms or style be suffered which shall be offensive or disrespectful to either party. And it is agreed that no presents, under any pretext or form whatever, shall ever be demanded of the United States by China, or of China by the United States.

Article XXXI

Communications from the government of the United States to the court of China shall be transmitted through the medium of the Imperial Commissioner charged with the superintendence of the concerns of foreign nations with China, or through the Governor-general of the Liang Kwang, that of Min and Cheh, or that of the Liang Kiang.

Article XXXII

Whenever ships of war of the United States, in cruizing for the protection of the commerce of their country, shall arrive at any of the ports of China, the commanders of said ships and the superior local authorities of Government, shall hold intercourse together in terms of equality and courtesy, in token of the friendly relations of their respective nations. And the said ships of war shall enjoy all suitable facilities on the part of the Chinese Government in the purchase of provisions, procuring water, and making repairs if occasion require.

Article XXXIII

Citizens of the United States, who shall attempt to trade clandestinely with such of the ports of China as are not open to foreign commerce, or who shall trade in opium or any other contraband article of merchandize, shall be subject to be dealt with by the Chinese Government, without being entitled to any countenance or protection from that of the United States; and the United States will take measures to prevent their flag from being abused by the subjects of other nations, as a cover for the violation of the laws of the Empire.

Article XXXIV

When the present convention shall have been definitively concluded, it shall be obligatory on both Powers, and its provisions shall not be altered without grave cause; but, inasmuch as the circumstances of the several ports of China open to foreign commerce are different, experience may show that inconsiderable modifications are requisite in those parts which relate to commerce and navigation: in which case, the two Governments will, at the expiration of twelve years from the date of said convention, treat amicably concerning the same, by the means of suitable persons appointed to conduct such negotiation.

And when ratified, this Treaty shall be faithfully observed in all its parts by the United States and China, and by every citizen and subject of each. And no individual State of the United States can appoint or send a minister to China to call in question the provisions of the same.

The present treaty of peace, amity, and commerce, shall be ratified and approved by the President of the United States, by and with the advice and consent of the Senate thereof, and by the August Sovereign of the Ta Tsing Empire, and the ratifications shall be exchanged,

within eighteen months from the date of the signature thereof, of sooner if possible.

In faith whereof, We, the respective Plenipotentiaries of the United States of America, and of the Ta Tsing Empire, as aforesaid, have signed and sealed these presents.

Done at Wang Hiya, this third day of July, in the year of our Lord Jesus Christ, one thousand eight hundred and forty-four; and of Taoukwang, the twenty-fourth year, fifth month, and eighteenth day.

Tsiyeng, *(in Manchu)* (L.S.)
C. Cushing, (L.S.)

The tariff of duties to be levied on imported and exported merchandize at the five ports.

The duties which it is agreed shall be paid upon goods imported and exported by the United States, at the Custom Houses of Canton, Amoy, Fuchow, Ningpo, and Shanghai, are as follows; the articles being arranged in classes, viz.

Class 17.

Rice and other grains, duty free. *Contraband.* — Opium.

Shipping dues. —These have been hitherto charged on the measurement of the ship's length and breadth, at so much per *chang*, but it is now agreed to alter the system and charge according to the registered statement of the number of tons of the ship's burden. On each ton (reckoned equal to the cubic contents of 122 tows), a shipping charge of five mace is to be levied; and all the old charges of measurement, entrance and port-clearance fees, daily and monthly fees, &c., are abolished.

Source:
Landmark Documents in American History, Facts On File, Inc.

Annexation of Texas, 1845

Joint resolution of Congress enacted on March 1, 1845, by which the United States annexed Texas, which had been an independent republic since 1836.

Texas had first declared its independence from Mexico in November 1835. On March 2, 1836, in a convention held in Washington, Texas, it issued a formal declaration and a constitution based on the U.S. Constitution. The Texas Declaration of Independence described the Mexican government as despotic and proclaimed the country in a state of anarchy, giving Texas the right to create a new government. Independence was actually achieved after the decisive Battle of San Jacinto on April 21, 1836.

The annexation of Texas culminated a decade-long drive by American expansionists to acquire the Lone Star Republic and thereby preempt rival Britain's suspected imperial designs on Texas. The resolution approved terms of an unratified 1844 annexation treaty between the United States and Texas. It stipulated that Texas skip territorial status and be admitted immediately as a state, that Texas keep its public lands and pay its own debt, that at most four more states be formed from its territory, and that slavery in Texas be safeguarded by extending the Missouri Compromise line to Texas. The resolution passed over the objection of northern antislavery elements that viewed annexation as a conspiracy by southern slaveholding interests to shift the political balance in Congress on the slavery issue in their favor. Its enactment further inflamed America's relations with Mexico, which continued to claim Texas as part of its national domain. Texas was admitted to the Union as the 28th state on December 29, 1845.

───────────── ⸎ ─────────────

An Act

To extend the Laws of the United States over the State of Texas, and for other Purposes.

Be it enacted by the Senate and House of Representatives of the United States of America in Congress assembled, That all the laws of the United States are hereby declared to extend to and over, and to have full force and effect within, the State of Texas, admitted at the present session of Congress into the Confederacy and Union of the United States.

Sec. 2. *And be it further enacted,* That the said State of Texas shall constitute one judicial district, to be called the District of Texas, for which one judge shall be appointed, who shall reside therein, and who shall receive a salary of two thousand dollars per annum, and who shall hold the first term of said court at Galveston, on the first Monday of February next, and at such other times and places in said district as may be provided by law, or as said judge may order; and that said court shall have and exercise the same powers and jurisdiction as have been conferred by law on the District Courts of the United States; and, also, shall have and exercise the powers and jurisdiction of a Circuit Court of the United States; and appeals and writs of error shall lie from the decisions of said District and Circuit Courts for the District of Texas to the Supreme Court of the United States, in the same cases as from a Circuit Court of the United States to said Supreme Court, and under the same regulations.

Sec. 3. *And be it further enacted,* That there shall be appointed in and for said district a person learned in the law, to act as attorney of the United States for said district, and also a person to act as marshal of the United States for said district, each of whom shall receive an annual salary of two hundred dollars, and also such compensation and fees for official services as have been or may be provided by law for United States district attorneys and marshals; and the judge of said court shall appoint a clerk therefor, who shall receive like compensation and fees as have been or may be allowed by law to clerks of the District and Circuit Courts of the United States.

Source:
Statutes at Large, Vol. 9, pp. 1–2.

Message on War with Mexico, 1846

Message from President James K. Polk, dated May 11, 1846, to the U.S. Congress, requesting a declaration of war against Mexico due to the dispute over the U.S. annexation of Texas. In his message, Polk traced the origins of the conflict and claimed that Mexico had invaded American territory "and shed American blood upon the American soil" in its April 24 attack on U.S. troops in the area between the Rio Grande and the Nueces River. Although this territory was not indisputedly part of the United States (despite Polk's claim), Congress declared war two days later.

───────────── ⸎ ─────────────

To the Senate and House of Representatives:

The existing state of the relations between the United States and Mexico renders it proper that I should bring the subject to the consideration of Congress. In my message at the commencement of your present session the state of these relations, the causes which led to the suspension of diplomatic intercourse between the two countries in March, 1845, and the long-continued and unredressed wrongs and injuries committed by the Mexican Government on citizens of the United States in their persons and property were briefly set forth.

As the facts and opinions which were then laid before you were carefully considered, I can not better express my present convictions of the condition of affairs up to that time than by referring you to that communication.

The strong desire to establish peace with Mexico on liberal and honorable terms, and the readiness of this Government to regulate and adjust our boundary and other causes of difference with that power on such fair and equitable principles as would lead to permanent relations of the most friendly nature, induced me in September last to seek the reopening of diplomatic relations between the two countries. Every measure adopted on our part had for its object the furtherance of these desired results. In communicating to Congress a succinct statement of the injuries which we had suffered from Mexico, and which have been accumulating during a period of more than twenty years, every expression that could tend to inflame the people of Mexico or defeat or delay a pacific result was carefully avoided. An envoy of the United States repaired to Mexico with full powers to adjust every existing difference. But though present on the Mexican soil by agreement between the two Governments, invested with full powers, and bearing evidence of the most friendly dispositions, his mission has been unavailing. The Mexican Government not only refused to receive him or listen to his propositions, but after a long-continued series of menaces have at least invaded our territory and shed the blood of our fellow-citizens on our own soil.

It now becomes my duty to state more in detail the origin, progress, and failure of that mission. In pursuance of the instructions given in September last, an inquiry was made on the 13th of October, 1845, in the most friendly terms, through our consul in Mexico, of the minister for foreign affairs, whether the Mexican Government "would receive an envoy from the United States intrusted with full powers to adjust all the questions in dispute between the two Governments," with the assurance that "should the answer be in the affirmative such an envoy would be immediately dispatched to Mexico." The Mexican minister on the 15th of October gave an affirmative answer to this inquiry, requesting at the same time that our naval force at Vera Cruz might be withdrawn, lest its continued presence might assume the appearance of menace and coercion pending the negotiations. This force was immediately withdrawn. On the 10th of November, 1845; Mr. John Slidell, of Louisiana, was commissioned by me as envoy extraordinary and minister plenipotentiary of the United States to Mexico, and was intrusted with full powers to adjust both the questions of the Texas boundary and of indemnification to our citizens. The redress of the wrongs of our citizens naturally and inseparably blended itself with the question of boundary. The settlement of the one question in any correct view of the subject involves that of the other. I could not for a moment entertain the idea that the claims of our much-injured and long-suffering citizens, many of which had existed for more than twenty years, should be postponed or separated from the settlement of the boundary question.

Mr. Slidell arrived at Vera Cruz on the 30th of November, and was courteously received by the authorities of that city. But the Government of General Herrera was then tottering to its fall. The revolutionary party had seized upon the Texas question to effect or hasten its overthrow. Its determination to restore friendly relations with the United States, and to receive our minister to negotiate for the settlement of this question, was violently assailed, and was made the great theme of denunciation against it. The Government of General Herrera, there is good reason to believe, was sincerely desirous to receive our minister; but it yielded to the storm raised by its enemies, and on the 21st of December refused to accredit Mr. Slidell upon the most frivolous pretexts. These are so fully and ably exposed in the note of Mr. Slidell of the 24th of December last to the Mexican minister of foreign relations, herewith transmitted, that I deem it unnecessary to enter into further detail on this portion of the subject.

Five days after the date of Mr. Slidell's note General Herrera yielded the Government to General Paredes without a struggle, and on the 30th of December resigned the Presidency. This revolution was accomplished solely by the army, the people having taken little part in the contest; and thus the supreme power in Mexico passed into the hands of a military leader.

Determined to leave no effort untried to effect an amicable adjustment with Mexico, I directed Mr. Slidell to present his credentials to the Government of General Paredes and ask to be officially received by him. There would have been less ground for taking this step had General Paredes come into power by a regular constitutional succession. In that event his administration would have been considered but a mere constitutional continuance of the Government of General Herrera, and the refusal of the latter to receive our minister would have been deemed conclusive unless an intimation had been given by General Paredes of his desire to reverse the decision of his predecessor. But the Government of General Paredes owes its existence to a military revolution, by which the subsisting constitutional authorities had been subverted. The form of government was entirely changed, as well as all the high functionaries by whom it was administered.

Under these circumstances, Mr. Slidell, in obedience to my direction, addressed a note to the Mexican minister of foreign relations, under date of the 1st of March last, asking to be received by that Government in the diplomatic character to which he had been appointed. This minister in his reply, under date of the 12th of March, reiterated the arguments of his predecessor, and in terms that may be considered as giving just grounds of offense to the Government and people of the United States denied the application of Mr. Slidell. Nothing therefore remained for our envoy but to demand his passports and return to his own country.

Thus the Government of Mexico, though solemnly pledged by official acts in October last to receive and accredit an American envoy, violated their plighted faith and refused the offer of a peaceful adjustment of our difficulties. Not only was the offer rejected, but the indignity of its rejection was enhanced by the manifest breach of faith in refusing to admit the envoy who came because they had bound themselves to receive him. Nor can it be said that the offer was fruitless from the want of opportunity of discussion it; our envoy was present on their own soil. Nor can it be ascribed to a want of sufficient powers;

our envoy had full powers to adjust every question of difference. Nor was there room for complaint that our propositions for settlement were unreasonable; permission was not even given our envoy to make any proposition whatever. Nor can it be objected that we, on our part, would not listen to any reasonable terms of their suggestion; the Mexican Government refused all negotiation, and have made no proposition of any kind.

In my message at the commencement of the present session I informed you that upon the earnest appeal both of the Congress and convention of Texas I had ordered an efficient military force to take a position "between the Nueces and the Del Norte." This had become necessary to meet a threatened invasion of Texas by the Mexican forces, for which extensive military preparations had been made. The invasion was threatened solely because Texas had determined, in accordance with a solemn resolution of the Congress of the United States, to annex herself to our Union, and under these circumstances it was plainly our duty to extend our protection over her citizens and soil.

This force was concentrated at Corpus Christi, and remained there until after I had received such information from Mexico as rendered it probable, if not certain, that the Mexican Government would refuse to receive our envoy.

Meantime Texas, by the final action of our Congress, had become an integral part of our Union. The Congress of Texas, by its act of December 19, 1836, had declared the Rio del Norte to be the boundary of that Republic. its jurisdiction had been extended and exercised beyond the Nueces. The country between that river and the Del Norte had been represented in the Congress and in the convention of Texas, had thus taken part in the act of annexation itself, and is now included within one of our Congressional districts. Our own Congress had, moreover, with great unanimity, by the act approved December 31, 1845, recognized the country beyond the Nueces as a part of our territory by including it within our own revenue system, and a revenue officer to reside within that district has been appointed by and with the advice and consent of the Senate. it became, therefore, of urgent necessity to provide for the defense of that portion of our country. Accordingly, on the 13th of January last instructions were issued to the general in command of these troops to occupy the left bank of the Del Norte. This river, which is the southwestern boundary of the State of Texas, is an exposed frontier. From this quarter invasion was threatened; upon it and in its immediate vicinity, in the judgment of high military experience, are the proper stations for the protecting forces of the Government. In addition to this important consideration, several others occurred to induce this movement. Among these are the facilities afforded by the ports at Brazos Santiago and the mouth of the Del Norte

for the reception of supplies by sea, the stronger and more healthful military positions, the convenience for obtaining a ready and a more abundant supply of provisions, water, fuel, and forage, and the advantages which are afforded by the Del Norte in forwarding supplies to such posts as may be established in the interior and upon the Indian frontier.

The movement of the troops to the Del Norte was made by the commanding general under positive instructions to abstain from all aggressive acts toward Mexico or Mexican citizens and to regard the relations between that Republic and the United States as peaceful unless she should declare war or commit acts of hostility indicative of a state of war. he was specially directed to protect private property and respect personal rights.

The Army moved from Corpus Christi on the 11th of March, and on the 28th of that month arrived on the left bank of the Del Norte opposite to Matamoras, where it encamped on a commanding position, which has since been strengthened by the erection of fieldworks. A depot has also been established at Point Isabel, near the Brazos Santiago, 30 miles in rear of the encampment. The selection of his position was necessarily confided to the judgment of the general in command.

The Mexican forces at Matamoras assumed a belligerent attitude, and on the 12th of April General Ampudia, then in command, notified General Taylor to break up his camp within twenty-four hours and to retire beyond the Nueces River, and in the event of his failure to comply with these demands announced that arms, and arms alone, must decide the question. But no open act of hostility was committed until the 24th of April. On that day General Arista, who had succeeded to the command of the Mexican forces, communicated to General Taylor that "he considered hostilities commenced and should prosecute them." A party of dragoons of 63 men and officers were on the same day dispatched from the American camp up the Rio del Norte, on its left bank, to ascertain whether the Mexican troops had crossed or were preparing to cross the river, "became engaged with a large body of these troops, and after a short affair, in which some 16 were killed and wounded, appear to have been surrounded and compelled to surrender."

The grievous wrongs perpetrated by Mexico upon our citizens throughout a long period of years remain unredressed, and solemn treaties pledging her public faith for this redress have been disregarded. A government either unable or unwilling to enforce the execution of such treaties fails to perform one of its plainest duties.

Our commerce with Mexico has been almost annihilated. It was formerly highly beneficial to both nations, but our merchants have been deterred from prosecuting it by the system of outrage and extortion which the Mexican authorities have pursued against them, whilst their appeals through their own Government for indemnity have been made in vain. Our forbearance has gone to such an extreme as to be mistaken in its character. Had we acted with vigor in repelling the insults and redressing the injuries inflicted by Mexico at the commencement, we should doubtless have escaped all the difficulties in which we are now involved.

Instead of this, however, we have been exerting our best efforts to propitiate her good will. Upon the pretext that Texas, a nation as independent as herself, thought proper to unite its destinies with our own she has affected to believe that we have severed her rightful territory, and in official proclamations and manifestoes has repeatedly threatened to make war upon us for the purpose of reconquering Texas. In the meantime we have tried every effort at reconciliation. The cup of forbearance had been exhausted even before the recent information from the frontier of the Del Norte. But now, after reiterated menaces, Mexico has passed the boundary of the United States, has invaded our territory and shed American blood upon the American soil. She has proclaimed that hostilities have commenced, and that the two nations are now at war.

As war exists, and, notwithstanding all our efforts to avoid it, exists by the act of Mexico herself, we are called upon by every consideration of duty and patriotism to vindicate with decision the honor, the rights, and the interests of our country.

Anticipating the possibility of a crisis like that which has arrived, instructions were given in August last, "as a precautionary measure" against invasion or threatened invasion, authorizing General Taylor, if the emergency required, to accept volunteers, not from Texas only, but from the States of Louisiana, Alabama, Mississippi, Tennessee, and Kentucky, and corresponding letters were addressed to the respective governors of those States. These instructions were repeated, and in January last, soon after the incorporation of "Texas into our Union of States," General Taylor was further "authorized by the President to make a requisition upon the executive of that State for such of its militia force as may be needed to repel invasion or to secure the country against apprehended invasion." On the 2d day of March he was again reminded, "in the event of the approach of any considerable Mexican force, promptly and efficiently to use the authority with which he was clothed to call to him such auxiliary force as he might need." War actually existing and our territory having been invaded, General Taylor, pursuant to authority vested in him by my direction, has called on the governor of Texas for four regiments of State troops, two to be mounted and two to serve on foot, and on the governor of Louisiana for four regiments of infantry to be sent to him as soon as practicable.

In further vindication of our rights and defense of our territory, I invoke the prompt action of Congress to recognize the existence of the war, and to place at the disposition of the Executive the means of prosecuting the war with vigor, and thus hastening the restoration of peace. To this end I recommend that authority should be given to call into the public service a large body of volunteers to serve for not less than six or twelve months unless sooner discharged. A volunteer force is beyond question more efficient than any other description of citizen soldiers, and it is not to be doubted that a number far beyond that required would readily rush to the field upon the call of their country. I further recommend that a liberal provision be made for sustaining our entire military force and furnishing it with supplies and munitions of war. The most energetic and prompt measures and the immediate appearance in arms of a large and overpowering force are recommended to Congress as the most certain and efficient means of bringing the existing collision with Mexico to a speedy and successful termination.

In making these recommendations I deem it proper to declare that it is my anxious desire not only to terminate hostilities speedily, but to bring all matters in dispute between this Government and Mexico to an early and amicable adjustment; and in this view I shall be prepared to renew negotiations whenever Mexico shall be ready to receive propositions or to make propositions of her own.

I transmit herewith a copy of the correspondence between our envoy to Mexico and the Mexican minister for foreign affairs, and so much of the correspondence between that envoy and the Secretary of State and between the Secretary of War and the general in command on the Del Norte as is necessary to a full understanding of the subject.

Source:

James D. Richardson, ed. *A Compilation of the Messages and Papers of the Presidents, 1789–1897*. Washington, D.C.: Government Printing Office, 1896–99.

Independent Treasury Act of 1846

Federal legislation enacted on August 8, 1846, that established an independent treasury—separate from the national banking and financial system—in Washington, D.C., as well as subtreasuries in various U.S. cities. This system replaced the national Bank of the United States. A similar act, passed in 1840, had been repealed the following year. According to the 1846 measure, the federal treasury would store all public funds and would receive and disburse all federal payments. The act required that such payments be made in gold or silver coin or treasury notes, an effort to remove from circulation unsecured currencies. The act remained in effect until the Civil War (1861–65).

An Act

To provide for the better Organization of the Treasury, and for the Collection, Safe-Keeping, Transfer, and Disbursement of the public Revenue.

Whereas, by the fourth section of the act entitled "An Act to establish the Treasury Department," approved September two, seventeen hundred and eighty-nine, it was provided that it should be the duty of the treasurer to receive and keep the moneys of the United States, and to disburse the same upon warrants drawn by the Secretary of the Treasury, countersigned by the comptroller, and recorded by the register, and not otherwise: and whereas it is found necessary to make further provisions to enable the treasurer the better to carry into effect the intent of the said section in relation to the receiving and disbursing the moneys of the United States: Therefore—

Be it enacted by the Senate and House of Representatives of the United States of America in Congress assembled, That the rooms prepared and provided in the new treasury building at the seat of government for the use of the treasurer of the United States, his assistants, and clerks, and occupied by them, and also the fireproof vaults and safes erected in said rooms for the keeping of the public moneys in the possession and under the immediate control of said treasurer, and such other apartments as are provided for in this act as places of deposit of the public money, are hereby constituted and declared to be treasury of the United States. And all moneys paid into the same shall be subject to the draft of the treasurer, drawn agreeably to appropriations made by law.

Sec. 2. *And be it further enacted,* That the mint of the United States in the city of Philadelphia, in the State of Pennsylvania, and the branch mint in the city of New Orleans, in the State of Louisiana, and the vaults and safes thereof, respectively, shall be places of deposit and safe-keeping of the public moneys at those points, respectively; and the treasurer of the said mint and branch mint, respectively, for the time being, shall be assistant treasurers under the provisions of this act, and shall have the custody and care of all public moneys deposited within the same, and shall perform all the duties required to be performed by them, in reference to the receipt, safe-keeping, transfer, and disbursements of all such moneys, according to the provisions hereinafter contained.

Sec. 3. *And be it further enacted,* That the rooms which were directed to be prepared and provided within the custom-houses in the city of New York, in the State of New York, and in the city of Boston, in the State of Massachusetts, for the use of receivers-general of public moneys, under the provisions of the act entitled "An Act to provide for the Collection, Safe-Keeping, Transfer, and Disbursement, of the public Revenue," approved July fourth, eighteen hundred and forty, shall be for the use of the assistant treasurers hereinafter directed to be appointed at those places respectively; as shall be also the fire-proof vaults and safe prepared and provided within said rooms for the keeping of the public moneys collected and deposited with them respectively; and the assistant treasurers, from time to time appointed at those points, shall have the custody and care of the said rooms, vaults, and safes, respectively, and of all the public moneys deposited within the same, and shall perform all the duties required to be performed by them, in reference to the receipt, safe-keeping, transfer, and disbursement, of all such moneys, according to the provisions of this act.

Sec. 4. *And be it further enacted,* That the offices, with suitable and convenient rooms, which were directed to be erected, prepared, and provided, for the use of receivers-general of public money, at the expense of the United States, at the city of Charleston, in the State of South Carolina, and at the city of St. Louis, in the State of Missouri, under the act entitled "An Act to provide for the Collection, Safe-Keeping, Transfer, and Disbursement, of the public Revenue," approved July fourth, eighteen hundred and forty, shall be for the use of the assistant treasurers hereinafter directed to be appointed at the places above-named; as shall be also the fire-proof vaults and safes erected within the said offices and rooms form the keeping of the public money collected and deposited at those points respectively; and the said assistant treasurers, from time to time appointed at those places, shall have the custody and care of the said offices, vaults, and safes, erected, prepared, and provided, as aforesaid, and of all the public moneys deposited within the same, and shall perform all the duties required to be performed by them, in reference to the receipt, safe-keeping, transfer, and disbursement, of all such moneys, according to the provisions hereinafter contained.

Sec. 5. *And be it further enacted,* That the President shall nominate, and by and with the advice and consent of the Senate appoint, four officers to be denominated "assistant treasurers of the United States," which said officers shall hold their respective officers for the term of four years, unless sooner removed therefrom; one of which shall be located at the city of New York, in the State of New York; one other of which shall be located at the city of Boston, in the State of Massachusetts; one other of which shall be located at the city of Charleston, in the State of South Carolina; and one other at St. Louis, in the State of Missouri. And all of which said officers shall give bonds to the United States, with sureties, according to the provisions hereinafter contained, for the faithful discharge of the duties of their respective offices.

Sec. 6. *And be it further enacted,* That the treasurer of the United States, the treasurer of the mint of the United States, the treasurers, and those acting as such, of the various branch mints, all collectors of the customs, all surveyors of the customs acting also as collectors, all assistant treasurers, all receivers of public moneys at the several land offices, all postmasters, and all public officers of whatsoever character, be, and they are hereby, required to keep safely, without loaning, using, depositing in banks, or exchanging for other funds than as allowed by this act, all the public money collected by them, or otherwise at any time placed in their possession and custody, till the same is ordered, by the proper department or officer of the government, to be transferred or paid out; and when such orders for transfer or payment are received, faithfully and promptly to make the same as directed, and to do and perform all other duties as fiscal agents of the government which may be imposed by this or any other acts of Congress, or by any regulation of the treasury department made in conformity to law; and also to do and perform all acts and duties required by law, or by direction of any of the Executive departments of the government, as agents for paying pensions, or for making any other disbursements which either of the heads of those departments may be required by law to make, and which are of a character to be made by the depositaries hereby constituted, consistently with the other official duties imposed upon them.

Sec. 7. *And be it further enacted,* That the treasurer of the United States, the treasurer of the mint of the United States, the treasurer of the branch mint at New Orleans, and all the assistant treasurers hereinbefore directed to be appointed, shall respectively give bonds to the United States faithfully to discharge the duties of their respective offices according to law, and for such amounts as shall be directed by the Secretary of the Treasury, with sureties to the satisfaction of the solicitor of the treasury; and shall, from time to time, renew, strengthen, and increase, their official bonds as the Secretary of the Treasury may direct, any law in reference to any of the official bonds of any of the said officers to the contrary notwithstanding.

Sec. 8. *And be it further enacted,* That it shall be the duty of the Secretary of the Treasury, at as early a day as possible after the passage of this act, to require from the several depositaries hereby constituted, and whose official bonds are not hereinbefore provided for, to execute bonds, new and suitable in their terms, to meet the new and increased duties imposed upon them respectively by this act, and with sureties and in sums such as shall seem reasonable and safe to the solicitor of the treasury; and from time to time to require such bonds to be renewed and increased in amount, and strengthened by new sureties, to meet any increasing responsibility which may grow out of

accumulations of money in the hands of the depositary, or out of any other duty or responsibility arising under this or any other law of Congress.

Sec. 9. *And be it further enacted,* That all collectors and receivers of public money, of every character and description, within the District of Columbia, shall, as frequently as they may be directed by the Secretary of the Treasury, or the Postmaster-General so to do, pay over to the treasurer of the United States, at the treasury, all public moneys collected by them, or in their hands; that all such collectors and receivers of public moneys within the cities of Philadelphia and New Orleans shall, upon the same direction, pay over to the treasurers of the mints in their respective cities, at the said mints, all public moneys collected by them, or in their hands; and that all such collectors and receivers of public moneys within the cities of New York, Boston, Charleston, and St. Louis, shall, upon the same direction, pay over to the assistant treasurers in their respective cities, at their offices, respectively, all the public moneys collected by them, or in their hands, to be safely kept by the said respective depositaries until otherwise disposed of according to law; and it shall be the duty of the said Secretary and Postmaster-General respectively to direct such payments by the said collectors and receivers at all the said places, at least as often as once in each week, and as much more frequently, in all cases, as they in their discretion may think proper.

Sec. 10. *And be it further enacted.* That it shall be lawful for the Secretary of the Treasury to Transfer the moneys in the hands of any depositary hereby constituted to the treasury of the United States, to be there safely kept, to the credit of the treasurer of the United States, according to the provisions of this act; and also to transfer moneys in the hands of any one depositary constituted by this act to any other depositary constituted by the same, at his discretion, and as the safety of the public moneys, and the convenience of the public service, shall seem to him to require; which authority to transfer the moneys belonging to the post-office department is also hereby conferred upon the Postmaster-General, so far as its exercise by him may be consistent with the provisions of existing laws; and every depositary constituted by this act shall keep his account of the money paid to or deposited with him, belonging to the post-office department, separate and distinct from the account kept by him of other public moneys so paid or deposited. And for the purpose of payments on the public account, it shall be lawful for the treasurer of the United States to draw upon any of the said depositaries, as he may think most conducive to the public interest, or to the convenience of the public creditors, or both. And each depositary so drawn upon shall make returns to the treasury and post-office departments of all moneys received and paid by him, at such times and in such form as shall be directed by the Secretary of the Treasury or the Postmaster-General.

Sec. 11. *And be it further enacted,* That the Secretary of the Treasury shall be, and he is hereby, authorized to cause examinations to be made of the books, accounts, and money on hand, of the several depositaries constituted by this act; and for that purpose to appoint special agents, as occasion may require, with such compensation, not exceeding six dollars per day and travelling expenses, as he may think reasonable, to be fixed and declared at the time of each appointment. The agents selected to make these examinations shall be instructed to examine as well the books, accounts, and returns, of the officer, as the money on hand, and the manner of its being kept, to the end that uniformity and accuracy in the accounts, as well as safety to the public moneys, may be secured thereby.

Sec. 12. *And be it further enacted,* That, in addition to the examinations provided for in the last preceding section, and as a further guard over the public moneys, it shall be the duty of each naval officer and surveyor, as a check upon the assistant treasurers, or the collector of the customs, of their respective districts; of each register of a land office, as a check upon the receiver of his land office; and of the director and superintendent of each mint and branch mint, when separate offices, as a check upon the treasurers, respectively, of the said mints, or the persons acting as such, at the close of each quarter of the year, and as much more frequently as they shall be directed by the Secretary of the Treasury to do so, to examine the books, accounts, returns, and money on hand, of the assistant treasurers, collectors, receivers of land offices, treasurers of the mint, and each branch mint, and persons acting as such, and to make a full, accurate, and faithful return to the treasury department of their condition.

Sec. 13. *And be it further enacted,* That the said officers, respectively, whose duty it is made by this act to receive, keep, and disburse, the public moneys, as the fiscal agents of the government, may be allowed any necessary additional expenses for clerks, fire-proof chests or vaults, or other necessary expenses of sake-keeping, transferring, and disbursing, said moneys; all such expenses of every character to be first expressly authorized by the Secretary of the Treasury, whose directions upon all the above subjects, by way of regulation and other, wise, so far as authorized by law, are to be strictly followed by all the said officers: *Provided,* That the whole number of clerks to be appointed by virtue of this section of this act shall not exceed ten; and that the aggregate compensations of the whole number shall not exceed eight thousand dollars; nor shall the compensation of any one clerk so appointed exceed eight hundred dollars per annum.

Sec. 14. *And be it further enacted,* That the Secretary of the Treasury may, at his discretion, transfer the balances remaining with any of the present depositaries to any other of the present depositaries, as he may deem the safety of the public money or the public convenience may require: *Provided,* That nothing in this act shall be so construed as to authorize the Secretary of the Treasury to transfer the balances remaining with any of the present depositaries to the depositaries constituted by this act before the first day of January next: *And provided* That, for the purpose of payments on public account, out of balances remaining with the present depositaries, it shall be lawful for the treasurer of the United States to draw upon any of the said depositaries as he may think most conducive to the public interests, or to the convenience of the public creditors, or both.

Sec. 15. *And be it further enacted,* That all marshals, district attorneys, and others having public money to pay to the United States, and all patentees wishing to make payment for patents to be issued, may pay all such moneys to the treasurer of the United States, to the treasurer of either of the mints in Philadelphia or New Orleans, to either of the other assistant treasurers, or to such other depositary constituted by this act as shall be designated by the Secretary of the Treasury in other parts of the United States to receive such payments, and give receipts or certificates of deposit therefor.

Sec. 16. *And be it further enacted,* That all officers and other persons, charged by this act, or any other act, with the safe-keeping, transfer, and disbursement, of the public moneys, other than those connected with the post-office department, are hereby required to keep an accurate entry of each sum received, and of each payment or transfer; and that if any one of the said officers, or of those connected with the post-office department, shall convert to his own use, in any way whatever, or shall use, by way of investment in any kind of property or merchandise, or shall loan, with or without interest, or shall deposit in any bank, or shall exchange for other funds, except as allowed by this act, any portion of the public moneys intrusted to him for safe-keeping, disbursement, transfer, or for any other purpose, every such act shall be deemed and adjudged to be an embezzlement of so much of the said moneys as shall be thus taken, converted, invested, used, loaned, deposited, or exchanged, which is hereby declared to be a felony; and any failure to pay over or to produce the public moneys intrusted to such person shall be held and taken to be *prima facie* evidence of such embezzlement; and if any officer charged with the disbursements of public moneys shall accept, or receive, or transmit to the treasury department to be allowed in his favor, any receipt or voucher from a creditor of the United States, without having paid to such creditor, in such funds as the said officer may have received for disbursement, or such other funds as he may be authorized by this act to take in exchange, the full amount specified in such receipt or voucher, every such act shall be deemed to be a conversion by such officer to his own use of the amount specified in such receipt or voucher; and any officer or agent of the United States, and all persons advising or participating in such act, being convicted thereof before any court of the United States of competent jurisdiction, shall be sentenced to imprisonment for a term of not less than six months nor more than ten years, and to a fine equal to the amount of the money embezzled. And, upon the trial of any indictment against any person for embezzling public money under the provisions of this act, it shall be sufficient evidence, for the purpose of showing a balance against such person, to produce a transcript from the books and proceedings of the treasury, as required in civil cases, under the provisions of the act entitled "An Act to provide more effectually for the Settlement of Accounts between the United States and Receivers of public Money," approved March third, one thousand seven hundred and ninety-seven; and the provisions of this act shall be so construed as to apply to all persons charged with the safe-keeping, transfer, or disbursement, of the public money, whether such persons be indicted as receivers or depositaries of the same; and the refusal of such person, whether in or out of office, to pay any draft, order, or warrant, which may be drawn upon him by the proper officer of the treasury department, for any public money in his hands belonging to the United States, no matter in what capacity the same may have been received or may be held, or to transfer or disburse any such money promptly, upon the legal requirement of any authorized officer of the United States, shall be deemed and taken, upon the trial of any indictment against such person for embezzlement, as *prima facie* evidence of such embezzlement.

Sec. 17. *And be it further enacted,* That, until the rooms, offices, vaults, and safes, directed by the first four sections of this act to be constructed and prepared for the use of the treasurer of the United States, the treasurers of the mints at Philadelphia and New Orleans, and the assistant treasurers at New York, Boston, Charleston, and St. Louis, can be constructed and prepared for use, it shall be the duty of the Secretary of the Treasury to procure suitable rooms for offices for those officers at their respective locations, and to contract for such use of vaults and safes as may be required for the safe-keeping of the public moneys in the charge and custody of those officers respectively, the expense to be paid by the United States.

And whereas, by the thirtieth section of the act entitled "An Act to regulate the Collection of Duties imposed by Law on the Tonnage of Ships or Vessels, and on Goods, Wares, and Merchandises, imported into the United States," approved July thirty-one, seventeen hundred and eighty-nine, it was provided that all fees and dues collected by virtue of that act should be received in gold and silver coin only; and whereas, also, by the fifth section of the act approved May ten, eighteen hundred, entitled "An Act to amend the Act entitled 'An Act providing for the Sale of the Lands of the United States in the Territory North-west of the Ohio, and above the Mouth of Kentucky River,'" it was provided that payment for the said lands shall be made by all purchasers in specie, or in evidences of the public debt; and whereas, experience has proved that said provisions ought to be revived and enforced, according to the true and wise intent of the constitution of the United States.—

Sec. 18. *Be it further enacted,* That on the first day of January, in the year one thousand eight hundred and forty-seven, and thereafter, all duties, taxes, sales of public lands, debts, and sums of money accruing or becoming due to the United States, and also all sums due for postages or otherwise, to the general post-office department, shall be paid in gold and silver coin only, or in treasury notes issued under the authority of the United States: *Provided,* That the Secretary of the Treasury shall publish, monthly, in two newspapers at the city of Washington, the amount of specie at the several places of deposit, the amount of treasury notes or drafts issued, and the amount outstanding on the last day of each month.

Sec. 19. *And be it further enacted,* That on the first day of April, one thousand eight hundred and forty-seven, and thereafter, every officer or agent engaged in making disbursements on account of the United States, or of the general post-office, shall make all payments in gold and silver coin, or in treasury notes, if the creditor agree to receive said notes in payment; and any receiving or disbursing officer or agent who shall neglect, evade, or violate, the provisions of this and the last preceding section of this act, shall, by the Secretary of the Treasury, be immediately reported to the President of the United States, with the facts of such neglect, evasion, or violation; and also to Congress, if in session; and if not in session, at the commencement of its session next after the violation takes place.

Sec. 20. *And be it further enacted,* That no exchange of funds shall be made by any disbursing officers or agents of the government, of any grade or denomination whatsoever, or connected with any branch of the public service, other than an exchange for gold and silver; and every such disbursing officer, when the means for his disbursements are furnished to him in gold and silver, shall make his payments in the money so furnished; or when those means are furnished to him in drafts, shall cause those drafts to be presented at their place of payment, and properly paid according to the law, and shall make his payments in the money so received for the drafts furnished, unless, in either case, he can exchange the means in his hands for gold and silver at par. And it shall be and is hereby made the duty of the head of the proper department immediately to suspend from duty any disbursing officer who shall violate the provisions of this section, and forthwith to report the name of the officer or agent to the President, with the fact of the violation, and all the circumstances accompanying the same, and within the knowledge of the said Secretary, to the end that such officer or agent may be promptly removed from office, or restored to his trust and the performance of his duties, as to the President may seem just and proper: *Provided, however,* That those disbursing officers having at present credits in the banks shall, until the first day of January next, be allowed to check on the same, allowing the public creditors to receive their pay from the banks either in specie or bank notes.

Sec. 21. *And be it further enacted,* That it shall be the duty of the Secretary of the Treasury to issue and publish regulations to enforce the speedy presentation of all government drafts for payment at the place where payable, and to prescribe the time, according to the different distances of the depositaries from the seat of government, within which all drafts upon them, respectively, shall be presented for payment; and, in default of such presentation, to direct any other mode and place of payment which he may deem proper; but, in all these regulations and directions, it shall be the duty of the Secretary of the Treasury to guard, as far as may be, against those drafts being used or thrown into circulation as a paper currency or medium of exchange. And no officer of the United States shall, either directly or indirectly, sell or dispose to any person or persons, or corporations, whatsoever, for a premium, any treasury note, draft, warrant, or other public security, not his private property, or sell or dispose of the avails or proceeds of such note, draft, warrant, or security, in his hands for disbursement, without making return of such premium, and accounting therefor by charging the same in his accounts to the credit of the United States; and any officer violating this section shall be forthwith dismissed from office.

Sec. 22. *And be it further enacted,* That the assistant treasurers directed by this act to be appointed shall receive, respectively, the following salaries per annum, to be paid quarter-yearly at the treasury of the United States, to wit: the assistant treasurer at New York shall be paid a salary of four thousand dollars per annum; the assistant treasurer at Boston shall be paid a salary of two thousand five hundred dollars per annum; the assistant treasurer at Charleston shall be paid a salary of two thousand five hundred dollars per annum; the assistant treasurer at St. Louis shall be paid a salary of two thousand five hundred dollars per annum; the treasurer of the mint at Philadelphia shall, in addition to his present salary, receive five hundred dol-

lars annually, for the performance of the duties imposed by this act; the treasurer of the branch mint at New Orleans shall also receive five hundred dollars annually, for the additional duties created by this act; and these salaries, respectively, shall be in full for the services of the respective officers; nor shall either of them be permitted to charge or receive any commission, pay, or perquisite, for any official service, of any character or description whatsoever; and the making of any such charge, or the receipt of any such compensation, is hereby declared to be a misdemeanor, for which the officer convicted thereof, before any court of the United States of competent jurisdiction, shall be subject to punishment by fine or imprisonment, or both, at the discretion of the court before which the offence shall be tried.

Sec. 23. *And be it further enacted,* That there shall be and hereby is appropriated, to be paid out of any money in the treasury not otherwise appropriated, the sum of five thousand dollars, to be expended, under the direction of the Secretary of the Treasury, in such repairs or additions as may be necessary to put in good condition for use, with as little delay as may be consistent with the public interests, the offices, rooms, vaults, and safes, herein mentioned, and in the purchase of any necessary additional furniture and fixtures, in the purchase of necessary books and stationery, and in defraying any other incidental expenses necessary to carry this act into effect.

Sec. 24. *And be it further enacted,* That all acts, or parts of acts, which come in conflict with the provisions of this act be, and the same are hereby, repealed.

Source:
Statutes at Large, Vol. 9, pp. 59–66.

Treaty of Guadalupe-Hidalgo, 1848

Treaty signed in Guadalupe-Hidalgo, Mexico, on February 2, 1848, ending the 1846–48 Mexican-American War between the United States and Mexico. Under the terms of the treaty, Mexico relinquished the land occupied by current-day California, Nevada, Arizona, New Mexico, and Utah. Mexico was also forced to recognize Texas—which had declared itself independent of Mexico in 1836 and had been admitted as a U.S. state in 1845, precipitating the Mexican-American War—as U.S. territory, with its border at the Rio Grande. The United States, in turn, withdrew troops from Mexican soil and paid an indemnity of $15 million for Mexico's loss of roughly half of its territory; the United States also agreed to assume U.S. citizens' claims against Mexico, which amounted to $3.25 million. The vast territory acquired by the United States as a result of this treaty is known as the "Mexican Cession."

In the name of Almighty God:

The United States of America, and the United Mexican States, animated by a sincere desire to put an end to the calamities of the war which unhappily exists between the two Republics, and to establish upon a solid basis relations of peace and friendship, which shall confer reciprocal benefits upon the citizens of both, and assure the concord, harmony and mutual confidence, wherein the two Peoples should live, as good Neighbours, have for that purpose appointed their respective Plenipotentiaries: that is to say, the President of the United States has appointed Nicholas P. Trist, a citizen of the United States, and the President of the Mexican Republic has appointed Don Luis Gonzaga Cuevas, Don Bernardo Couto, and Don Miguel Atristain, citizens of the said Republic; who, after a reciprocal communication of their respective full powers, have under the protection of Almighty God, the author of Peace, arranged, agreed upon, and signed the following
Treaty of peace, friendship, limits and settlement between the United States of America and the Mexican Republic

Article I

There shall be firm and universal peace between the United States of America and the Mexican Republic, and between their respective Countries, territories, cities, towns and people, without exception of places or persons.

Article II

Immediately upon the signature of this Treaty, a convention shall be entered into between a Commissioner or Commissioners appointed by the General in Chief of the forces of the United States, and such as may be appointed by the Mexican Government, to the end that a provisional suspension of hostilities shall take place, and that, in the places occupied by the said forces, constitutional order may be reestablished, as regards the political, administrative and judicial branches, so far as this shall be permitted by the circumstances of military occupation.

Article III

Immediately upon the ratification of the present treaty by the Government of the United States, orders shall be transmitted to the Commanders of their land and naval forces, requiring the latter, (provided this Treaty shall then have been ratified by the Government of the Mexican Republic and the ratifications exchanged) immediately to desist from blockading any Mexican ports; and requiring the former (under the same condition) to commence, at the earliest moment practicable, withdrawing all troops of the United States then in the interior of the Mexican Republic, to points, that shall be selected by common agreement, at a distance from the sea-ports, not exceeding thirty leagues; and such evacuation of the interior of the Republic shall be completed with the least possible delay: the Mexican Government hereby binding itself to afford every facility in it's power for rendering the same convenient to the troops, on their march and in their new positions, and for promoting a good understanding between them and the inhabitants. In like manner, orders shall be despatched to the persons in charge of the custom houses at all ports occupied by the forces of the United States, requiring them (under the same condition) immediately to deliver possession of the same to the persons authorized by the Mexican Government to receive it, together with all bonds and evidences of debt for duties on importations and on exportations, not yet fallen due. Moreover, a faithful and exact account shall be made out, showing the entire amount of all duties on imports and on exports, collected at such Custom Houses, or elsewhere in Mexico, by authority of the United States, from and after the day of ratification of this Treaty by the Government of the Mexican Republic; and also an account of the cost of collection; and such entire amount, deducting only the cost of collection, shall be delivered to the Mexican Government, at the City of Mexico, within three months after the exchange of ratifications.

The evacuation of the Capital of the Mexican Republic by the Troops of the United States, in virtue of the above stipulation, shall be completed in one month after the orders there stipulated for shall have been received by the commander of said troops, or sooner if possible.

Article IV

Immediately after the exchange of ratifications of the present treaty, all castles, forts, territories, places and possessions, which have been taken or occupied by the forces of the United States during the present war, within the limits of the Mexican Republic, as about to be established by the following Article, shall be definitively restored to the said Republic, together with all the artillery, arms, apparatus of war, munitions, and other public property, which were in the said castles and forts when captured, and which shall remain there at the time when this treaty shall be duly ratified by the Government of the Mexican Republic. To this end, immediately upon the signature of this treaty, orders shall be despatched to the American officers commanding such castles and forts, securing against the removal or destruction of any such artillery, arms, apparatus of war, munitions, or other public property. The city of Mexico, within the inner line of intrenchments surrounding the said city, is comprehended in the above stipulations, as regards the restoration of artillery, apparatus of war, &c.

The final evacuation of the territory of the Mexican Republic, by the forces of the United States, shall be completed in three months from the said exchange of ratifications, or sooner, if possible: the Mexican Government hereby engaging, as in the foregoing Article, to use all means in its power for facilitating such evacuation, and rendering it convenient to the troops, and for promoting a good understanding between them and the inhabitants.

If, however, the ratification of this treaty by both parties should not take place in time to allow the embarkation of the troops of the United States to be completed before the commencement of the sickly season, at the Mexican ports on the Gulf of Mexico; in such case a friendly arrangement shall be entered into between the General in Chief of the said troops and the Mexican Government, whereby healthy and otherwise suitable places at a distance from the ports not exceeding thirty leagues shall be designated for the residence of such troops as may not yet have embarked, until the return of the healthy season. And the space of time here referred to, as comprehending the sickly season, shall be understood to extend from the first day of May to the first day of November.

All prisoners of war taken on either side, on land or on sea, shall be restored as soon as practicable after the exchange of ratifications of this treaty. It is also agreed that if any Mexicans should now be held as captives by any savage tribe within the limits of the United States, as about to be established by the following Article, the Government of the said United States will exact the release of such captives, and cause them to be restored to their country.

Article V
The Boundary line between the two Republics shall commence in the Gulf of Mexico, three leagues from land, opposite the mouth of the Rio Grande, otherwise called Rio Bravo del Norte, or opposite the mouth of it's deepest branch, if it should have more than one branch emptying directly into the sea; from thence, up the middle of that river, following the deepest channel, where it has more than one to the point where it strikes the Southern boundary of New Mexico; thence, westwardly along the whole Southern Boundary of New Mexico (which runs north of the town called *Paso*) to its western termination; thence, northward, along the western line of New Mexico, until it intersects the first branch of the river Gila; (or if it should not intersect any branch of that river, then, to the point on the said line nearest to such branch, and thence in a direct line to the same;) thence down the middle of the said branch and of the said river, until it empties into the Rio Colorado; thence, across the Rio Colorado, following the division line between Upper and Lower California to the Pacific Ocean.

The southern and western limits of New Mexico, mentioned in this Article, are those laid down in the Man, entitled *"Map of the United Mexican States, as organized and defined by various acts of the Congress of said Repub-lic, and constructed according to the best authorities. Revised edition. Published at New York in 1847 by J. Dis-turnell:"* Of which Map a Copy is added to this Treaty, bearing the signatures and seals of the Undersigned Plenipotentiaries. And, in order to preclude all difficulty in tracing upon the ground the limit separating Upper from Lower California, it is agreed that the said limit shall consist of a straight line, drawn from the middle of the Rio Gila, where it unites with the Colorado, to a point on the Coast of the Pacific Ocean, distant one marine league due south of the southernmost point of the Port of San Diego, according to the plan of said port, made in the year 1782, by Don Juan Pantoja, second sailing-Master of the Spanish fleet, and published at Madrid in the year 1802, in the Atlas to the voyage of the schooners *Sutil* and *Mexicana:* of which plan a Copy is hereunto added, signed and sealed by the respective Plenipotentiaries.

In order to designate the Boundary line with due precision, upon authoritative maps, and to establish upon the ground landmarks which shall show the limits of both Republics, as described in the present Article, the two Governments shall each appoint a Commissioner and a Surveyor, who, before the expiration of one year from the date of the exchange of ratifications of this treaty, shall meet at the Port of San Diego, and proceed to run and mark the said Boundary in its whole course to the mouth of the Rio Bravo del Norte. They shall keep journals and make out plans of their operations; and the result, agreed upon by them, shall be deemed a part of this treaty, and shall have the same force as if it were inserted therein. The two Governments will amicably agree regarding what may be necessary to these persons, and also as to their respective escorts, should such be necessary.

The Boundary line established by this Article shall be religiously respected by each of the two Republics, and no change shall ever be made therein, except by the express and free consent of both nations, lawfully given by the General Government of each, in conformity with its own constitution.

Article VI
The vessels and citizens of the United States shall, in all time, have a free and uninterrupted passage by the Gulf of California, and by the river Colorado below its confluence with the Gila, to and from their possessions situated north of the Boundary line defined in the preceding Article: it being understood that this passage is to be by navigating the Gulf of California and the river Colorado, and not by land, without the express consent of the Mexican Government.

If, by the examinations which may be made, it should be ascertained to be practicable and advantageous to construct a road, canal or railway, which should, in whole or in part, run upon the river Gila, or upon it's right or its left bank, within the space of one marine league from either margin of the river, the Governments of both Republics will form an agreement regarding its construction, in order that it may serve equally for the use and advantage of both countries.

Article VII

The river Gila, and the part of the Rio Bravo del Norte lying below the southern boundary of New Mexico, being, agreeably to the fifth Article, divided in the middle between the two Republics, the navigation of the Gila and the Bravo below said boundary shall be free and common to the vessels and citizens of both countries; and neither shall, without the consent of the other, construct any work that may impede or interrupt, in whole or in part, the exercise of this right: not even for the purpose of favoring new methods of navigation. Nor shall any tax or contribution, under any denomination or title, be levied upon vessels or persons navigating the same, or upon merchandise or effects transported thereon, except in the case of landing upon one of their shores. If, for the purpose of making the said rivers navigable, or for maintaining them in such state, it should be necessary or advantageous to establish any tax or contribution, this shall not be done without the consent of both Governments.

The stipulations contained in the present Article shall not impair the territorial rights of either Republic, within its established limits.

Article VIII

Mexicans now established in territories previously belonging to Mexico, and which remain for the future within the limits of the United States, as defined by the present Treaty, shall be free to continue where they now reside, or to remove at any time to the Mexican Republic, retaining the property which they possess in the said territories, or disposing thereof and removing the proceeds wherever they please; without their being subjected, on this account, to any contribution, tax or charge whatever.

Those who shall prefer to remain in the said territories, may either retain the title and rights of Mexican citizens, or acquire those of citizens of the United States. But, they shall be under the obligation to make their election within one year from the date of the exchange of ratifications of this treaty: and those who shall remain in the said territories, after the expiration of that year, without having declared their intention to retain the character of Mexicans, shall be considered to have elected to become citizens of the United States.

In the said territories, property of every kind, now belonging to Mexicans not established there, shall be inviolably respected. The present owners, the heirs of these, and all Mexicans who may hereafter acquire said property

by contract, shall enjoy with respect to it, guaranties equally ample as if the same belonged to citizens of the United States.

Article IX (11)

The Mexicans who, in the territories aforesaid, shall not preserve the character of citizens of the Mexican Republic, conformably with what is stipulated in the preceding article, shall be incorporated into the Union of the United States and be admitted, at the proper time (to be judged of by the Congress of the United States) to the enjoyment of all the rights of citizens of the United States according to the principles of the Constitution; and in the mean time shall be maintained and protected in the free enjoyment of their liberty and property, and secured in the free exercise of their religion without restriction.

(11) The United States amendment of article IX substituted a new text. The text of article IX as signed reads as follows:

"The Mexicans who, in the territories aforesaid, shall not preserve the character of citizens of the Mexican Republic, conformably with what is stipulated in the preceding Article, shall be incorporated into the Union of the United States, and admitted as soon as possible, according to the principles of the Federal Constitution, to the enjoyment of all the rights of citizens of the United States. In the mean time, they shall be maintained and protected in the enjoyment of their liberty, their property, and the civil rights now vested in them according to the Mexican laws. With respect to political rights, their condition shall be on an equality with that of the inhabitants of the other territories of the United States; and at least equally good as that of the inhabitants of Louisiana and the Floridas, when these provinces, by transfer from the French Republic and the Crown of Spain, became territories of the United States.

"The same most ample guaranty shall be enjoyed by all ecclesiastics and religious corporations or communities, as well in the discharge of the offices of their ministry, as in the enjoyment of their property or every kind, whether individual or corporate. This guaranty shall embrace all temples, houses and edifices dedicated to the Roman Catholic worship; as well as all property destined to it's support, or to that of schools, hospitals and other foundations for charitable or beneficent purposes. No property of this nature shall be considered as having become the property of the American Government, or as subject to be, by it, disposed of or diverted to other uses.

"Finally, the relations and communication between the Catholics living in the territories aforesaid, and their respective ecclesiastical authorities, shall be open, free and exempt from all hindrance whatever, even although such authorities should be reside within the limits of the Mexican Republic, as defined by this treaty; and this freedom shall continue, so long as a new demarcation of ecclesiastical districts shall not have been made, conformably with the laws of the Roman Catholic Church."

Article X (12)

(12) article X, stricken out by the United States amendments, reads as follows:

"All grants of land made by the Mexican Government or by the competent authorities, in territories previously appertaining to Mexico, and remaining for the future within the limits of the United States, shall be respected as valid, to the same extent that the same grants would be valid, if the said territories had remained the limits of Mexico. But the grantees of lands in Texas, put in possession thereof, who, by reason by the circumstances of the country since the beginning of the troubles between Texas and the Mexican Government, may have been prevented from fulfilling all the conditions of their grants, shall be under the obligation to fulfill the said conditions within the periods limited in the same respectively; such periods to be now counted from the date of the exchange of ratifications of this treaty: in default of which the said grants shall not be obligatory upon the State of Texas, in virtue of the stipulations contained in this Article.

"The foregoing stipulation in regard to grantees of land in Texas, is extended to all grantees of land in the territories aforesaid, elsewhere than in Texas, put in possession under such grants; and, in default of the fulfilment of the conditions of any such grant, within the new period, which, as is above stipulated, begins with the day of the exchange of ratifications of this treaty, the same shall be null and void.

"The Mexican Government declares that no grant whatever of lands in Texas has been made since the second day of March one thousand eight hundred and thirty six; and that no grant whatever of lands in any of the territories aforesaid has been made since the thirteenth day of May one thousand eight hundred and forty-six."

Article XI

Considering that a great part of the territories which, by the present treaty, are to be comprehended for the future within the limits of the United States, is now occupied by savage tribes, who will hereafter be under the exclusive control of the Government of the United States, and whose incursions within the territory of Mexico would be prejudicial in the extreme; it is solemnly agreed that all such incursions shall be forcibly restrained by the Government of the United States, whensoever this may be necessary; and that when they cannot be prevented, they shall be punished by the said Government, and satisfaction for the same shall be exacted: all in the same way, and with

equal diligence and energy, as if the same incursions were meditated or committed within its own territory against it's own citizens.

It shall not be lawful, under any pretext whatever, for any inhabitant of the United States, to purchase or acquire any Mexican or any foreigner residing in Mexico, who may have been captured by Indians inhabiting the territory of either of the two Republics; nor to purchase or acquire horses, mules, cattle or property of any kind, stolen within Mexican territory by such Indians;

And, in the event of any person or persons, captured within Mexican territory by Indians, being carried into the territory of the United States, the Government of the latter engages and binds itself, in the most solemn manner, so soon as it shall know of such captives being within it's territory, and shall be able so to do, through the faithful exercise of it's influence and power, to rescue them, and return them to their country, or deliver them to the agent or representative of the Mexican Government. The Mexican Authorities will, as far as practicable, give to the Government of the United States notice of such captures; and it's agent shall pay the expenses incurred in the maintenance and transmission of the rescued captives; who, in the mean time, shall be treated with the utmost hospitality by the American Authorities at the place where they may be. But if the Government of the United States, before receiving such notice from Mexico, should obtain intelligence through any other channel, of the existence of Mexican captives within its territory, it will proceed forthwith to effect their release and delivery to the Mexican agent, as above stipulated.

For the purpose of giving to these stipulations the fullest possible efficacy, thereby affording the security and redress demanded by their true spirit and intent, the Government of the United States will now and hereafter pass, without unnecessary delay, and always vigilantly enforce, such laws as the nature of the subject may require. And finally, the sacredness of this obligation shall never be lost sight of by the said Government, when providing for the removal of the Indians from any portion of the said territories, or for its being settled by citizens of the United States; but on the contrary, special care shall then be taken not to place it's Indian occupants under the necessity of seeking new homes, by committing those invasions which the United States have solemnly obliged themselves to restrain.

Article XII

In consideration of the extension acquired by the boundaries of the United States, as defined in the fifth Article of the present treaty, the Government of the United States engages to pay to that of the Mexican Republic the sum of fifteen Millions of Dollars.

Immediately after this Treaty shall have been duly ratified by the Government of the Mexican Republic, the sum of three Millions of Dollars shall be paid to the said Government by that of the United States at the city of Mexico, in the gold or silver coin of Mexico. The remaining twelve Millions of Dollars shall be paid at the same place, and in the same coin, in annual instalments of three Millions of Dollars each, together with interest on the same at the rate of six per centum per annum. This interest shall begin to run upon the whole sum of twelve millions, from the day of the ratification of the present treaty by the Mexican Government, and the first of the instalments shall be paid at the expiration of one year from the same day. Together with each annual instalment, as it falls due, the whole interest accruing on such instalment from the beginning shall also be paid.

Article XIII

The United States engage moreover, to assume and pay to the claimants all the amounts now due them, and those hereafter to become due, by reason of the claims already liquidated and decided against the Mexican Republic, under the conventions between the two Republics, severally concluded on the eleventh day of April eighteen hundred and thirty-nine, and on the thirtieth day of January eighteen hundred and forty three: so that the Mexican Republic shall be absolutely exempt for the future, from all expense whatever on account of the said claims.

Article XIV

The United States do furthermore discharge the Mexican Republic from all claims of citizens of the United States, not heretofore decided against the Mexican Government, which may have arisen previously to the date of the signature of this treaty: which discharge shall be final and perpetual, whether the said claims be rejected or to be allowed by the Board of Commissioners provided for in the following Article, and whatever shall be the total amount of those allowed.

Article XV

The United States, exonerating Mexico from all demands on account of the claims of their citizens mentioned in the preceding Article, and considering them entirely and forever cancelled, whatever their amount may be, undertake to make satisfaction for the same, to an amount not exceeding three and one quarter millions of dollars. To ascertain the validity and amount of those claims, a Board of Commissioners shall be established by the Government of the United States, whose awards shall be final and conclusive: provided that in deciding upon the validity of each claim, the board shall be guided and governed by the principles and rules of decision described by the first and fifth Articles of the unratified convention, concluded at the city of Mexico on the twentieth day of November one thousand eight hundred and forty-three; and in no case shall an award be made in favor of any claim not embraced by these principles and rules.

If, in the opinion of the said Board of Commissioners, or of the claimants, any books, records or documents in the possession or power of the Government of the Mexican Republic, shall be deemed necessary to the just decision of any claim, the Commissioners or the claimants, through them, shall within such period as Congress may designate, make an application in writing for the same, addressed to the Mexican Minister for Foreign Affairs, to be transmitted by the Secretary of State of the United States; and the Mexican Government engages, at the earliest possible moment after the receipt of such demand, to cause any of the books, records or documents, so specified, which shall be in their possession or power, (or authenticated copies or extracts of the same) to be transmitted to the said Secretary of State, who shall immediately deliver them over the said Board of Commissioners: *Provided* That no such application shall be made, by, or at the instance of, any claimant, until the facts which it is expected to prove by such books, records or documents, shall have been stated under oath or affirmation.

Article XVI

Each of the contracting parties reserves to itself the entire right to fortify whatever point within its territory, it may judge proper so to fortify, for its security.

Article XVII

The Treaty of Amity, Commerce and Navigation, concluded at the city of Mexico on the fifth day of April A.D. 1831, between the United States of America and the United Mexican States, except the additional Article, and except so far as the stipulations of the said treaty may be incompatible with any stipulation contained in the present treaty, is hereby revived for the period of eight years from the day of the exchange of ratifications of this treaty, with the same force and virtue as if incorporated therein; it being understood that each of the contracting parties reserves to itself the right, at any time after the said period of eight years shall have expired, to terminate the same by giving one year's notice of such intention to the other party.

Article XVIII

All supplies whatever for troops of the United States in Mexico, arriving at ports in the occupation of such troops, previous to the final evacuation thereof, although subsequently to the restoration of the Custom Houses at such ports, shall be entirely exempt from duties and charges of any kind: the Government of the United States hereby engaging and pledging its faith to establish and vigilantly to enforce, all possible guards for securing the revenue of

Mexico, by preventing the importation, under cover of this stipulation, of any articles, other than such, both in kind and in quantity, as shall really be wanted for the use and consumption of the forces of the United States during the time they may remain in Mexico. To this end, it shall be the duty of all officers and agents of the United States to denounce to the Mexican Authorities at the respective ports, any attempts at a fraudulent abuse to this stipulation, which they may know of or may have reason to suspect, and to give to such authorities all the aid in their power with regard thereto: and every such attempt, when duly proved and established by sentence of a competent tribunal, shall be punished by the confiscation of the property so attempted to be fraudulently introduced.

Article XIX

With respect to all merchandise, effects and property whatsoever, imported into ports of Mexico, whilst in the occupation of the forces of the United States, whether by citizens of either republic, or by citizens or subjects of any neutral nation, the following rules shall be observed:

I. All such merchandise, effects and property, if imported previously to the restoration of the Custom Houses to the Mexican Authorities, as stipulated for in the third Article of this treaty, shall be exempt from confiscation, although the importation of the same be prohibited by the Mexican tariff.

II. The same perfect exemption shall be enjoyed by all such merchandise, effects and property, imported subsequently to the restoration of the Custom Houses, and previously to the sixty days fixed in the following Article for the coming into force of the Mexican tariff at such ports respectively: the said merchandise, effects and property being, however, at the time of their importation, subject to the payment of duties as provided for in the said following Article.

III. All merchandise, effects and property, described in the two rules foregoing, shall, during their continuance at the place of importation, and upon their leaving such place for the interior, be exempt from all duty, tax or impost of every kind, under whatsoever title or denomination. Nor shall they be there subjected to any charge whatsoever upon the sale thereof.

IV. All merchandise, effects and property, described in the first and second rules, which shall have been removed to any place in the interior, whilst such place was in the occupation of the forces of the United States, shall, during their continuance therein, be exempt from all tax upon the sale or consumption thereof, and from every kind of impost or contribution, under whatsoever title or denomination.

V. But if any merchandise, effects or property, described in the first and second rules, shall be removed to any place not occupied at the time by the forces of the United States, they shall, upon their introduction into such place, or upon their sale or consumption there, be subject to the same duties which, under the Mexican laws, they would be required to pay in such cases, if they had been imported in time of peace through the Maritime Custom Houses, and had there paid the duties, conformably with the Mexican tariff.

VI. The owners of all merchandise, effects or property, described in the first and second rules, and existing in any port of Mexico, shall have the right to reship the same, exempt from all tax, impost or contribution whatever.

With respect to the metals, or other property, exported from any Mexican port, whilst in the occupation of the forces of the United States, and previously to the restoration of the Custom House at such port, no person shall be required by the Mexican Authorities, whether General or State, to pay any tax, duty or contribution upon any such exportation, or in any manner to account for the same to the said Authorities.

Article XX

Through consideration for the interests of commerce generally, it is agreed, that if less than sixty days should elapse between the date of the signature of this treaty and the restoration of the Custom Houses, conformably with the stipulation in the third Article, in such case, all merchandise, effects and property whatsoever, arriving at the Mexican ports after the restoration of the said Custom Houses, and previously to the expiration of sixty days after the day of the signature of this treaty, shall be admitted to entry; and no other duties shall be levied thereon than the duties established by the tariff found in force at such Custom Houses at the time of the restoration of the same. And to all such merchandise, effects and property, the rules established by the preceding Article shall apply.

Article XXI

If unhappily any disagreement should hereafter arise between the Governments of the two Republics, whether with respect to the interpretation of any stipulation in this treaty, or with respect to any other particular concerning the political or commercial relations of the two Nations, the said Governments, in the name of those Nations, do promise to each other, that they will endeavour, in the most sincere and earnest manner, to settle the differences so arising, and to preserve the state of peace and friendship, in which the two countries are now placing themselves: using, for this end, mutual representations and pacific negotiations. And if, by these means, they should not be enabled to come to an agreement, a resort shall not, on this account, be had to reprisals, aggression or hostility of any kind, by the one Republic against the other, until the Government of that which deems itself aggrieved, shall have maturely considered, in the spirit of peace and good neighbourship, whether it would not be better that such difference should be settled by the arbitration of Commissioners appointed on each side, or by that of a friendly nation. And should such course be proposed by either party, it shall be acceded to by the other, unless deemed by it altogether incompatible with the nature of the difference, or the circumstances of the case.

Article XXII

If (which is not to be expected, and which God forbid!) war should unhappily break out between the two Republics, they do now, with a view to such calamity, solemnly pledge themselves to each other and to the world, to observe the following rules: absolutely, where the nature of the subject permits, and as closely as possible in all cases where such absolute observance shall be impossible.

I. The merchants of either Republic, then residing in the other, shall be allowed to remain twelve months (for those dwelling in the interior) and six months (for those dwelling at the sea-ports) to collect their debts and settle their affairs; during which periods they shall enjoy the same protection, and be on the same footing, in all respects, as the citizens or subjects of the most friendly nations; and, at the expiration thereof, or at any time before, they shall have full liberty to depart, carrying off all their effects, without molestation or hinderance: conforming therein to the same laws, which the citizens or subjects of the most friendly nations are required to conform to. Upon the entrance of the armies of either nation into the territories of the other, women and children, ecclesiastics, scholars of every faculty, cultivators of the earth, merchants, artisans, manufacturers, and fishermen, unarmed and inhabiting unfortified towns, villages or places, and in general all persons whose occupations are for the common subsistence and benefit of mankind, shall be allowed to continue their respective employments, unmolested in their persons. Nor shall their houses or goods be burnt, or otherwise destroyed; nor their cattle taken, nor their fields wasted, by the armed force, into whose power, by the events of war, they may happen to fall; but if the necessity arise to take anything from them for the use of such armed force, the same shall be paid for at an equitable price. All churches, hospitals, schools, colleges, libraries, and other establishments for charitable and beneficent purposes, shall be respected, and all persons connected with the same protected in the discharge of their duties and the pursuit of their vocations.

II. In order that the fate of prisoners of war may be alleviated, all such practices as those of sending them into distant, inclement or unwholesome districts, or crowding them into close and noxious places, shall be studiously avoided. They shall not be confined in dungeons, prison-ships, or prisons; nor be put in irons, or bound, or other-

wise restrained in the use of their limbs. The officers shall enjoy liberty on their paroles, within convenient districts, and have comfortable quarters; and the common soldier shall be disposed in cantonments, open and extensive enough for air and exercise, and lodged in barracks as roomy and good as are provided by the party in whose power they are for its own troops. But, if any officer shall break his parole by leaving the district so assigned him, or any other prisoner shall escape from the limits of his cantonment, after they shall have been designated to him, such individual, officer or other prisoner, shall forfeit so much of the benefit of this article as provides for his liberty on parole or in cantonment. And if any officer so breaking his parole, or any common soldier so escaping from the limits assigned him, shall afterwards be found in arms, previously to his being regularly exchanged, the person so offending shall be dealt with according to the established laws of war. The officers shall be daily furnished by the party in whose power they are, with as many rations, and of the same articles as are allowed either in kind or by communication, to officers of equal rank in its own army; and all others shall be daily furnished with such ration as is allowed to a common soldier in its own service: the value of all which supplies shall, at the close of the war, or at periods to be agreed upon between the respective commanders, be paid by the other party on a mutual adjustment of accounts for the subsistence of prisoners; and such accounts shall not be mingled with or set off against any others, nor the balance due on them be withheld, as a compensation of reprisal for any cause whatever, real or pretended. Each party shall be allowed to keep a commissary of prisoners, appointed by itself, with every cantonment of prisoners, in possession of the other: which commissary shall see the prisoners as often as he pleases; shall be allowed to receive, exempt from all duties or taxes, and to distribute whatever comforts may be sent to them by their friends; and shall be free to transmit his reports in open letters to the party by whom he is employed.

And it is declared that neither the pretence that war dissolves all treaties, nor any other whatever shall be considered as annulling or suspending the solemn covenant contained in this article. On the contrary, the state of war is precisely that for which it is provided; and during which it's stipulations are to be as sacredly observed as the most acknowledged obligations under the law of nature or nations.

Article XXIII

This treaty shall be ratified by the President of the United States of America, by and with the advice and consent of the Senate thereof; and by the President of the Mexican Republic, with the previous approbation of it's General Congress: and the ratifications shall be exchanged in the

City of Washington, or at the seat of government of Mexico, in four months from the date of the signature hereof, or sooner if practicable.

In faith whereof, we, the respective Plenipotentiaries, have signed this Treaty of Peace, Friendship, Limits and Settlement, and have hereunto affixed our seals respectively. Done in Quintuplicate, at the City of Guadalupe Hidalgo, on the second day of February in the year of Our Lord one thousand eight hundred and forty eight.

Source:

Charles I. Bevans. *Treaties and Other Agreements of the United States of America, 1776–1949.* Washington, D.C.: Government Printing Office, 1968–76.

Irish Immigration to America, 1850

Between 1840 and 1860, the United States experienced a wave of European immigration. More than a million Germans immigrated, and a million and a half Irish came. In addition, more than 35,000 Chinese entered the country, mainly to California.

The following article describing Irish immigration to the United States is from *The Illustrated London News.*

———————— ⟨❧⟩ ————————

The great tide of Emigration flows steadily westward. The principle emigrants are Irish peasants and labourers. It is calculated that at least four out of every five persons who leave the shores of the old country to try their fortunes in the new, are Irish. Since the fatal years of the potato famine and the cholera, the annual numbers of emigrants have gone on increasing, until they have become so great as to suggest the idea, and almost justify the belief, of a graduate depopulation of Ireland. The colonies of Great Britain offer powerful attractions to the great bulk of the English and Scottish emigrants who forsake their native land to make homes in the wilderness. But the Irish emigration flows with full force upon the United States. Though many of the Irish emigrants are, doubtless, persons of small means, who have been hoarding and saving for years, and living in rags and squalor, in order to amass sufficient money to carry themselves and families across the Atlantic, and to beg their way to the western states, where they may "squat" or purchase cheap lands, the great bulk appear to be people of the most destitute class, who go to join their friends and relatives, previously established in America. Large sums of money reach this country annually from the United States. Through Liverpool houses alone, near upon a million sterling, in small drafts, varying from L2 to L3 to L10 each, are annually forwarded from America, for poor persons in Ireland, to enable them to emigrate; and the passage-money of many thousands, in addition, is paid in New York. Before the fatal year 1847, the emigration was very considerable; but since that time, it has very rapidly increased.

Source:

The Illustrated London News, 1850. University of Virginia Health System website. Available on-line. URL: hsc.virginia.edu/~eas5e/Irish/Emigration2.html

Treaties of Fort Laramie of 1851

Two agreements between the United States government and the Sioux, Shoshone, Cheyenne, and Arapaho tribes that assigned reservations to each tribe of the northern Great Plains area, granted each an annuity of $50,000, and established certain roads and forts within the allotted Native American lands. This effort to ensure peace as whites expanded west of the Mississippi River and across the Indian Territory later failed; Sioux uprisings began in 1862, continuing until the resolution of another Treaty of Fort Laramie in 1868.

———————— ⟨❧⟩ ————————

First Treaty of Fort Laramie (1851)
Millard Fillmore,
President of the United States of America:

To All and Singular to Whom These Presents Shall Come, Greeting,

Whereas a treaty was made and concluded at Traverse des Sioux, in the Territory of Minnesota, on the twenty-third day of July, one thousand eight hundred and fifty-one, between the United States of America, by Luke Lea, Commissioner of Indian Affairs, and Alexander Ramsey, Governor and *ex-officio* Superintendent of Indian Affairs in said Territory, acting as Commissioners, and the See-see-toan and Wah-pay-toan bands of Dakota or Sioux Indians, which treaty is in the words following, to wit:

Articles of a treaty made and concluded at Traverse des Sioux, upon the Minnesota River, in the Territory of Minnesota, on the twenty-third day of July, eighteen hundred and fifty-one, between the United States of America, by Luke Lea, Commissioner of Indian Affairs, and Alexander Ramsey, Governor and *ex-officio* Superintendent of Indian Affairs in said Territory, commissioners duly appointed for that purpose, and the See-see-toan and Wah-pay-toan bands of Dakota or Sioux Indians.

Article 1. It is stipulated and solemnly agreed, that the peace and friendship now so happily existing between the United States and the aforesaid bands of Indians, shall be perpetual.

Article 2. The said See-see-toan and Wah-pay-toan bands of Dakota or Sioux Indians, agree to cede, and do hereby cede, sell, and relinquish to the United States, all their lands in the State of Iowa; and, also, all their lands in the Territory of Minnesota, lying east of the following line, to wit: Beginning at the junction of the Buffalo River with the Red River of the north; thence along the western bank of said Red River of the north, to the mouth of the Sioux Wood River; thence along the western bank of said Sioux Wood River to Lake Traverse; thence, along the western shore of said lake, to the southern extremity thereof; thence in a direct line, to the junction of Kampeska Lake with the Tchan-kas-an-data or Sioux River; thence along the Western bank of said river to its point of intersection with the northern line of the State of Iowa; including all the islands in said rivers and lake.

Article 3. In part consideration of the foregoing cession, the United States do hereby set apart for the future occupancy and home of the Dakota Indians, parties to this treaty, to be held by them as Indian lands are held, all that tract of country on either side of the Minnesota River from the Western boundary of the lands herein ceded, east to the Tchay-tam-bay River on the north, and to the Yellow Medicine River on the south side, to extend, on each side, a distance of not less than ten miles from the general course of said river; the boundaries of said tract to be marked out by as straight lines as practicable, whenever deemed expedient by the President, and in a such manner as he shall direct.

Article 4. In further and full consideration of said cession, the United States agree to pay to said Indians, the sum of one million, six hundred and sixty-five thousand dollars ($1,665,000) at the several times, in the manner and for the purposes following, to wit:

1st. To the Chiefs of the said bands, to enable them to settle their affairs and comply with their present just engagement; and in consideration of their removing themselves to the country set apart for them as above, which they agree to do within two years or sooner, if required by the President, without further cost or expense to the United States, and in consideration of their subsisting themselves the first year after their removal, which they agree to do without further cost or expense on the part of the United States, the sum of two hundred and seventy-five thousand dollars ($275,000): *Provided,* That said sum shall be paid to the Chiefs in such manner, as they, hereafter, in open Council shall request, and as soon after the removal of said Indians to the home set apart for them, as the necessary appropriation therefor shall be made by Congress.

2d. To be laid out under the direction of the President, for the establishment of manual labor schools; the erection of mills and blacksmith shops, opening farms, fencing and breaking land, and for such other beneficial objects as may be deemed most conducive to the prosperity and happiness of said Indians, thirty thousand dollars ($30,000.)

The balance of said sum of one million six hundred and sixty-five thousand dollars ($1,665,000) to wit: One million, three hundred and sixty thousand dollars ($1,360,000,) to remain in trust with the United States, and five per cent. interest thereon to be paid, annually, to said Indians for the period of fifty years, commencing the first day of July, eighteen hundred and fifty-two (1852,) which shall be in full payment of said balance, principal and interest, the said payment to be applied under the direction of the President, as follows to wit:

3d. For a general agricultural improvement and civilization fund, the sum of twelve thousand dollars ($12,000.)

4th. For educational purposes, the sum of six thousand dollars, ($6,000.)

5th. For the purchase of goods and provisions, the sum of ten thousand dollars, ($10,000.)

6th. For money annuity, the sum of forty thousand dollars ($40,000.)

Article 5. The laws of the United States prohibiting the introduction and sale of spirituous liquors in the Indian country shall be in full force and effect throughout the Territory hereby ceded and lying in Minnesota until otherwise directed by Congress or the President of the United States.

Article 6. Rules and regulations to protect the rights of persons and property among the Indians, parties to this Treaty, and adapted to their conditions and wants, may be prescribed and enforced in such manner as the President or the Congress of the United States, from time to time, shall direct.

In testimony whereof, the said Commissioners, Luke Lea and Alexander Ramsey, and the undersigned Chiefs and Headmen of the aforesaid See-see-toan and Wah-pay-toan bands of Dakota or Sioux Indians, have hereunto subscribed their names and affixed their seals, in duplicate, at Traverse des Sioux, Territory of Minnesota, this twenty-third day of July, one thousand eight hundred and fifty-one.

Second Treaty of Fort Laramie (1851)
Millard Fillmore,
President of the United States of America:

To All and Singular to Whom These Presents Shall Come, Greeting:

Whereas a Treaty was made and concluded at Mendota, in the Territory of Minnesota, on the fifth day of August, one thousand eight hundred and fifty-one, between the United States of America, by Luke Lea, Commissioner of Indian Affairs, and Alexander Ramsey, Governor and ex-officio Superintendent of Indian Affairs in aid territory, acting as commissioners, and the Med-ay-wa-kan-toan and Wah-pay-koo-tay bands of Dakota or Sioux Indians, which treaty is in the words following, to wit:

Articles of a treaty made and concluded at Mendota, in the Territory of Minnesota, on the fifth day of August, eighteen hundred and fifty-one, between the United States of America, by Luke Lea, Commissioner of Indian Affairs, and Alexander Ramsey, Governor and ex-officio Superintendent of Indian Affairs in said territory, commissioners duly appointed for that purpose, and the Med-ay-wa-kan-toan and Way-pay-koo-tay bands of Dakota and Sioux Indians.

Article 1. The peace and friendship existing between the United States and the Med-ay-wa-kan-toan and Wah-pay-koo-tay bands of Dakota or Sioux Indians, shall be perpetual.

Article 2. The said Med-ay-wa-kan-toan and Wah-pay-koo-tay bands of Indians do hereby cede and relinquish all their lands and all their right, title and claim to any land whatever, in the Territory of Minnesota, or in the State of Iowa.

Article 3. In part consideration of the foregoing cession and relinquishment, the United States do hereby set apart for the future occupancy and home of the Dakota Indians, parties to this treaty, to be held by them, as Indian lands are held, a tract of country of the average width of ten miles on either side of the Minnesota River, and bounded on the West by the Tchay-tam-bay and Yellow Medicine Rivers, and on the East by the Little Rock River, and a line running due South from its mouth to the Waraju River; the boundaries of said tract to be marked our by as straight lines as practicable, whenever and in such manner as the President of the United States shall direct: *Provided,* That said tract shall be held and occupied by said bands in common, and that they shall hereafter participate equally and alike, in all the benefits derived from any former treaty between said bands or either of them, and the United States.

Article 4. In further and full consideration of said cession and relinquishment, the United States agree to pay to said Indians the sum of one million four hundred and ten thousand dollars, ($1,410,000) at the several times, in the manner and for the purposes following, to wit:

1st. To the Chiefs of the said bands, to enable them to settle their affairs and comply with their present just engagements; and in consideration of their removing themselves to the country set apart for them as above, (which they agree to do within one year after the ratification of this treaty, without further cost or expense to the United States,) and in consideration of their subsisting themselves the first year after their removal, (which they agree to do without further cost or expense on the part of the United States,) the sum of two hundred and twenty thousand dollars ($220,000.) *Provided,* That said shall be paid, one half to the

Chiefs of the Med-ay-wa-kan-toan band, and one half to the Chief and Headmen of the Wah-pay-koo-tay band, in such manner as they, hereafter, in open Council, shall respectively request, and as soon after the removal of said Indians to the home set apart for them as the necessary appropriations therefor shall be made by Congress.

2d. To be laid out, under the direction of the President, for the establishment of manual labor schools; the erection of mills and blacksmith shops, opening farms, fencing and breaking land, and for such other beneficial objects as may be deemed most conducive to the prosperity and happiness of said Indians, thirty thousand dollars ($30,000.)

The balance of said sum of one million four hundred and ten thousand dollars, ($1,410,000) to wit: One million, one hundred and sixty thousand dollars ($1,160,000) to remain in trust with the United States, and five per cent. interest thereon to be paid annually to said Indians for the period of fifty years, commencing on the first day of July, eighteen hundred and fifty two (1852,) which shall be in full payment of said balance, principal and interest: said payments to be made and applied, under the direction of the President as follows, to wit:

3d. For a general agricultural improvement and civilization fund, the sum of twelve thousand dollars, ($12,000.)

4th. For educational purposes, the sum of six thousand dollars, ($6,000.)

5th. For the purchase of goods and provisions, the sum of ten thousand dollars, ($10,000.)

6th. For money annuity, the sum of thirty thousand dollars, ($30,000.)

Article V. The entire annuity, provided for in the first section of the second article of the treaty of September twenty-ninth, eighteen hundred and thirty seven (1837,) including any unexpended balance that may be in the treasury on the first of July, eighteen hundred and fifty-two, (1852,) shall thereafter be paid in money.

Article VI. The laws of the United States prohibiting the introduction and sale of spirituous liquors in the Indian country shall be in full force and effect throughout the Territory hereby ceded and lying in Minnesota, until otherwise directed by Congress or the President of the United States.

Article VII. Rules and Regulations to protect the rights of persons and property among the Indians parties to this Treaty, and adapted to their condition and wants, may be prescribed and enforced in such manner as the President or the Congress of the United States, from time to time, shall direct.

Article VIII. The Half-Breeds of the Sioux Nation having failed and refused to avail themselves of the provisions for their benefit in the ninth and tenth articles of the treaty concluded at Prairie du Chien on the fifteenth of

July, eighteen hundred and thirty, it is hereby agreed at their request, that, in lieu of the tract of land set apart for the occupancy of said Half-Breeds there shall be paid to them, by the United States, under the direction of the President, the sum of one hundred and fifty thousand dollars ($150,000): *Provided,* That the non-ratification of this article shall, in no manner affect the other provisions of this Treaty.

In witness whereof, the said Luke Lea and Alexander Ramsey, Commissioners on the part of the United States and the undersigned Chiefs and Headmen of the Med-ay-wa-kan-toan and Wah-pay-koo-tay bands of Dakota or Sioux Indians, have hereunto set their hands, at Mendota, in the Territory of Minnesota, this fifth day of August, Anno Domini, one thousand eight hundred and fifty-one.

Source:
Statutes at Large, Vol. 10, pp. 949–959.

Gadsden Purchase Treaty of 1853

Agreement negotiated in 1853 by James Gadsden to settle boundary issues between the United States and Mexico arising from the Treaty of Guadalupe-Hidalgo. Mexico agreed to cede territory in what is now southern Arizona and southern New Mexico in exchange for $15 million. The United States wanted that area for a southern transcontinental railroad route and to protect private U.S. concessions there. The treaty (signed on December 30, 1853) met strong opposition in the Senate, which cut the payment to Mexico to $10 million and the size of the new territory to about 30,000 square miles before ratifying the treaty in 1854.

The treaty did not contain a clause prohibiting slavery. Such a proposal, the Wilmot Proviso, named after Democratic congressman David Wilmot of Pennsylvania, had passed the House of Representatives in 1846 and 1847; however, the Senate rejected it. The proviso stated that a fundamental condition of any such territorial acquisition was a ban on slavery and involuntary servitude within that territory. It sparked a national debate and fueled the sectional dispute over slavery.

―――――――――――――⸰✖⸰―――――――――――――

A Proclamation
Whereas a treaty between the United States of America and the Mexican Republic was concluded and signed at the City of Mexico on the thirtieth day of December, one thousand eight hundred and fifty- three; which treaty, as amended by the Senate of the United States, and being in the English and Spanish languages, is word for word as follows:

In the name of Almighty God:

The Republic of Mexico and the United States of America, desiring to remove every cause of disagreement which might interfere in any manner with the better friend-ship and intercourse between the two countries, and especially in respect to the true limits which should be established, when, notwithstanding what was covenanted in the treaty of Guadalupe Hidalgo in the year 1848, opposite interpretations have been urged, which might give occasion to questions of serious moment: to avoid these, and to strengthen and more firmly maintain the peace which happily prevails between the two republics, the President of the United States has, for this purpose, appointed James Gadsden, Envoy Extraordinary and Minister Plenipotentiary of the same, near the Mexican government, and the President of Mexico has appointed as Plenipotentiary *"ad hoc"* his excellency Don Manuel Diez de Bonilla, cavalier grand cross of the national and distinguished order of Guadalupe, and Secretary of State, and of the office of Foreign Relations, and Don Jose Salazar Ylarregui and General Mariano Monterde as scientific commissioners, invested with full powers for this negotiation, who, having communicated their respective full powers, and finding them in due and proper form, have agreed upon the articles following:

Article I
The Mexican Republic agrees to designate the following as her true limits with the United States for the future: retaining the same dividing line between the two Californias as already defined and established, according to the 5th article of the treaty of Guadalupe Hidalgo, the limits between the two republics shall be as follows: Beginning in the Gulf of Mexico, three leagues from land, opposite the mouth of the Rio Grande, as provided in the 5th article of the treaty of Guadalupe Hidalgo; thence, as defined in the said article, up the middle of that river to the point where the parallel of 31 degree 47 degree north latitude crosses the same; thence due west one hundred miles; thence south to the parallel of 31 degree 20 degree north latitude; thence along the said parallel of 31 degree 20 degree to the 111th meridian of longitude west of Greenwich; thence in a straight line to a point on the Colorado River twenty English miles below the junction of the Gila and Colorado Rivers; thence up the middle of the said river Colorado until it intersects the present line between the United States and Mexico.

For the performance of this portion of the treaty, each of the two governments shall nominate one commissioner, to the end that, by common consent the two thus nominated, having met in the city of Paso del Norte, three months after the exchange of the ratifications of this treaty, may proceed to survey and mark out upon the land the dividing line stipulated by this article, where it shall not have already been surveyed and established by the mixed commission, according to the treaty of Guadalupe, keeping a journal and making proper plans of their operations. For this purpose, if they should judge it necessary, the contracting parties shall be at liberty each to unite to its respective commissioner, scientific or other assistants, such as astronomers and surveyors, whose concurrence shall not be considered necessary for the settlement and ratification of a true line of division between the two Republics; that line shall be alone established upon which the commissioners may fix, their consent in this particular being considered decisive and an integral part of this treaty, without necessity of ulterior ratification or approval, and without room for interpretation of any kind by either of the parties contracting.

The dividing line thus established shall, in all time, be faithfully respected by the two governments, without any variation therein, unless of the express and free consent of the two, given in conformity to the principles of the law of nations, and in accordance with the constitution of each country respectively. In consequence, the stipulation in the 5th article of the treaty of Guadalupe upon the boundary line therein described is no longer of any force, wherein it may conflict with that here established, the said line being considered annulled and abolished wherever it may not coincide with the present, and in the same manner remaining in full force where in accordance with the same.

Article II

The government of Mexico hereby releases the United States from all liability on account of the obligations contained in the eleventh article of the treaty of Guadalupe Hidalgo; and the said article and the thirty-third article of the treaty of amity, commerce, and navigation between the United States of America and the United Mexican States concluded at Mexico, on the fifth day of April, 1831, are hereby abrogated.

Article III

In consideration of the foregoing stipulations, the Government of the United States agrees to pay to the government of Mexico, in the city of New York, the sum of ten millions of dollars, of which seven millions shall be paid immediately upon the exchange of the ratifications of this treaty, and the remaining three millions as soon as the boundary line shall be surveyed, marked, and established.

Article IV

The provisions of the 6th and 7th articles of the treaty of Guadalupe Hidalgo having been rendered nugatory, for the most part, by the cession of territory granted in the first article of this treaty, the said articles are hereby abrogated and annulled, and the provisions as herein expressed substituted therefor. The vessels, and citizens of the United States shall, in all time, have free and uninterrupted passage through the Gulf of California, to and from their possessions situated north of the boundary line of the two countries. It being understood that this passage is to be by navigating the Gulf of California and the river Colorado, and not by land, without the express consent of the

Mexican government; and precisely the same provisions, stipulations, and restrictions, in all respects, are hereby agreed upon and adopted, and shall be scrupulously observed and enforced by the two contracting governments in reference to the Rio Colorado, so far and for such distance as the middle of that river is made their common boundary line by the first article of this treaty.

The several provisions, stipulations, and restrictions contained in the 7th article of the treaty of Guadalupe Hidalgo shall remain in force only so far as regards the Rio Bravo del Norte, below the initial of the said boundary provided in the first article of this treaty; that is to say, below the intersection of the 31 degree 47'30" parallel of latitude, with the boundary line established by the late treaty dividing said river from its mouth upwards, according to the fifth article of the treaty of Guadalupe.

Article V

All the provisions of the eight and ninth, sixteenth and seventeenth articles of the treaty of Guadalupe Hidalgo, shall apply to the territory ceded by the Mexican Republic in the first article of the present treaty, and to all the rights of persons and property, both civil and ecclesiastical, within the same, as fully and as effectually as if the said articles were herein again recited and set forth.

Article VI

No grants of land within the territory ceded by the first article of this treaty bearing date subsequent to the day—twenty-fifth of September—when the minister and subscriber to this treaty on the part of the United States, proposed to the Government of Mexico to terminate the question of boundary, will be considered valid or be recognized by the United States, or will any grants made previously be respected or be considered as obligatory which have not been located and duly recorded in the archives of Mexico.

Article VII

Should there at any future period (which God forbid) occur any disagreement between the two nations which might lead to a rupture of their relations and reciprocal peace, they bind themselves in like manner to procure by every possible method the adjustment of every difference; and should they still in this manner not succeed, never will they proceed to a declaration of war, without having previously paid attention to what has been set forth in article twenty-one of the treaty of Guadalupe for similar cases; which article, as well as the twenty-second, is here reaffirmed.

Article VIII

The Mexican Government having on the 5th of February, 1853, authorized the early construction of a plank and railroad across the Isthmus of Tehuantepec, and, to secure the stable benefits of said transit way to the persons and merchandise of the citizens of Mexico and the United States, it is stipulated that neither government will interpose any obstacle to the transit of persons and merchandise of both nations; and at no time shall higher charges be made on the transit of persons and property of citizens of the United States, than may be made on the persons and property of other foreign nations, nor shall any interest in said transit way, nor in the proceeds thereof, be transferred to any foreign government.

The United States, by its agents, shall have the right to transport across the isthmus, in closed bags, the mails of the United States not intended for distribution along the line of communication; also the effects of the United States government and its citizens, which may be intended for transit, and not for distribution on the isthmus, free of custom-house or other charges by the Mexican government. Neither passports nor letters of security will be required of persons crossing the isthmus and not remaining in the country. When the construction of the railroad shall be completed, the Mexican government agrees to open a port of entry in addition to the port of Vera Cruz, at or near the terminus of said road on the Gulf of Mexico.

The two governments will enter into arrangements for the prompt transit of troops and munitions of the United States, which that government may have occasion to send from one part of its territory to another, lying on opposite sides of the continent.

The Mexican government having agreed to protect with its whole power the prosecution, preservation, and security of the work, the United States may extend its protection as it shall judge wise to it when it may feel sanctioned and warranted by the public or international law.

Article IX

This treaty shall be ratified, and the respective ratifications shall be exchanged at the city of Washington within the exact period of six months from the date of its signature, or sooner, if possible.

In testimony whereof, we, the plenipotentiaries of the contracting parties, have hereunto affixed our hands and seals at Mexico, the thirtieth (30th) day of December, in the year of our Lord one thousand eight hundred and fifty-three, in the thirty-third year of the independence of the Mexican republic, and the seventy-eighth of that of the United States.

James Gadsden, [l. s.]
Manuel Diez De Bonilla [l. s.]
Jose Salazar Ylarregui [l. s.]
J. Mariano Monterde, [l. s.]

And whereas the said treaty, as amended, has been duly ratified on both parts, and the respective ratifications of the same have this day been exchanged at Washington, by William L. Marcy, Secretary of State of the United States, and Senor General Don Juan N. Almonte, Envoy Extraordinary and Minister Plenipotentiary of the Mexican Republic, on the part of their respective Governments:

Now, therefore, be it known that I, Franklin Pierce, President of the United States of America, have caused the said treaty to be made public, to the end that the same, and every clause and article thereof, may be observed and fulfilled with good faith by the United States and the citizens thereof.

In witness whereof I have hereunto set my hand and caused the seal of the United States to be affixed.

Done at the city of Washington, this thirtieth day of June, in the year of our Lord one thousand eight hundred and fifty-four, and of the Independence of the United States the seventy-eight.

Source:

Charles I. Bevans, comp. *Treaties and Other Agreements of the United States of America, 1776–1949.* Washington, D.C.: Government Printing Office, 1968–76.

Harris Treaty of 1858

First commercial treaty between Japan and the United States, signed on July 29, 1858. It was negotiated by Townsend Harris, acting as consul general (the first U.S. diplomatic representative to Japan,1855–61). His arrival was a result of the Treaty of Kanagawa of 1854. This pact of peace, friendship, and commerce was negotiated by U.S. commodore Matthew C. Perry, and it ended Japan's isolation from the West. In 1853 Perry sailed into Tokyo Bay with a fleet of warships as a show of force to deliver proposals from President Millard Fillmore on establishing commercial relations. When Perry returned the following year with a larger fleet, Japanese officials decided to abandon their policy of seclusion. Signed on March 31, 1854, the treaty opened the Japanese ports of Shimoda and Hakodate to U.S. trade, allowed the United States to establish a consulate at Shimoda, and provided for the protection of shipwrecked U.S. nationals. Three years later, an 1857 agreement opened Nagasaki to U.S. commerce. The Harris Treaty of 1858 then opened additional ports, granted Americans residence rights, and established diplomatic representatives at the capitals of the two nations. The U.S. Senate consented to the treaty on December 15, 1858.

Treaty

The President of the United States of America and his Majesty the Ty-Coon of Japan, desiring to establish on firm and lasting foundations the relations of peace and friendship now happily existing between the two countries, and to secure the best interest of their respective citizens and subjects by encouraging, facilitating, and regulating their industry and trade, have resolved to conclude a treaty of amity and commerce for this purpose, and have, therefore, named as their plenipotentiaries, that is to say: The President of the United States, his excellency Townsend Harris, Consul General of the United States of America for the Empire of Japan, and his Majesty the Ty-Coon of Japan, their excellencies Jno-oo-ye, Prince of Sinano, and Iwasay, Prince of Hego, who, after having communicated to each other their respective full powers, and found them to be in good and due form, have agreed upon and concluded the following articles:

Article I

There shall henceforward be perpetual peace and friendship between the United States of America and his Majesty the Ty-Coon of Japan and his successors.

The President of the United States may appoint a diplomatic agent to reside at the city of Yedo, and consuls or consular agents to reside at any or all of the ports in Japan which are opened for American commerce by this treaty. The diplomatic agent and consul general of the United States shall have the right to travel freely in any part of the empire of Japan from the time they enter on the discharge of their official duties.

The government of Japan may appoint a diplomatic agent to reside at Washington, and consuls or consular agents for any or all of the ports of the United States. The diplomatic agent and consul general of Japan may travel freely in any part of the United States from the time they arrive in the country.

Article II

The President of the United States, at the request of the Japanese government, will act as a friendly mediator in such matters of difference as may arise between the government of Japan and any European power.

The ships of war of the United States shall render friendly aid and assistance to such Japanese vessels as they may meet on the high seas, so far as can be done without a breach of neutrality; and all American consuls residing at ports visited by Japanese vessels shall also give them such friendly aid as may be permitted by the laws of the respective countries in which they reside.

Article III

In addition to the ports of Simoda and Hakodadi, the following ports and towns shall be opened on the dates respectively appended to them, that is to say: Kanagawa, on the (4th of July, 1859) fourth day of July, one thousand eight hundred and fifty-nine; Nagasaki, on the (4th of July,

1859) fourth day of July, one thousand eight hundred and fifty-nine; Nee-e-gata, on the (1st of January, 1860) first day of January, one thousand eight hundred and sixty; Hiogo, on the (1st of January 1863) first day of January, one thousand and eight hundred and sixty-three.

In Nee-e-gata is found to be unsuitable as a harbor, another port on the west coast of Nipon shall be selected by the two governments in lieu thereof. Six months after the opening of Kanagawa the port of Simoda shall be closed as a place of residence and trade for American citizens. In all the foregoing ports and towns American citizens may permanently reside; they shall have the right to lease ground, and purchase the buildings thereon, and may erect dwellings and warehouses. But no fortification or place of military strength shall be erected under pretence of building dwellings or warehouses; and to see that this article is observed, the Japanese authorities shall have the right to inspect, from time to time, any buildings which are being erected, altered, or repaired. The place which the Americans shall occupy for their buildings, and the harbor regulations, shall be arranged by the American consul and the authorities of each place, and if they cannot agree the matter shall be referred to and settled by the American diplomatic agent and the Japanese government.

No wall, fence, or gate shall be erected by the Japanese around the place of residence of the Americans, or anything done which may prevent a free egress and ingress to the same.

From the (1st of January, 1862) first day of January, one thousand eight hundred and sixty-two, Americans shall be allowed to reside in the city of Yedo; and from the (1st of January, 1863) first day of January, one thousand eight hundred and sixty-three, in the city of Osaca, for the purposes of trade only. In each of these two cities a suitable place within which they may hire houses, and the distance they may go, shall be arranged by the American diplomatic agent and the government of Japan. Americans may freely buy from Japanese and sell to them any articles that either may have for sale, without the intervention of any Japanese officers in such purchase or sale, or in making or receiving payment for the same; and all classes of Japanese may purchase, sell, keep, or use any articles sold to them by the Americans.

The Japanese government will cause this clause to be made public in every part of the empire as soon as the ratifications of this treaty shall be exchanged.

Munitions of war shall only be sold to the Japanese government and foreigners.

No rice or wheat shall be exported from Japan as cargo, but all Americans resident in Japan, and ships, for their crews and passengers, shall be furnished with sufficient supplies of the same. The Japanese government will sell, from time to time, at public auction, any surplus quantity of copper that may be produced. Americans residing in

Japan shall have the right to employ Japanese as servants or in any other capacity.

Article IV

Duties shall be paid to the government of Japan on all goods landed in the country, and on all articles of Japanese production that are exported as cargo, according to the tariff hereunto appended.

If the Japanese custom-house officers are dissatisfied with the value placed on any goods by the owner, they may place a value thereon, and offer to take the goods at that valuation. If the owner refuses to accept the offer, he shall pay duty on such valuation. If the offer be accepted by the owner, the purchase money shall be paid to him without delay, and without any abatement or discount.

Supplies for the use of the United States navy may be landed at Kanagawa, Hakodadi, and Nagasaki, and stored in warehouse, in the custody of an officer of the American government, without the payment of any duty. But, if any such supplies are sold in Japan, the purchaser shall pay the proper duty to the Japanese authorities.

The importation of opium is prohibited, and any American vessel coming to Japan for the purposes of trade, having more than three (3) catties (four pounds avoirdupois) weight of opium on board, such surplus quantity shall be seized and destroyed by the Japanese authorities. All goods imported into Japan, and which have paid the duty fixed by this treaty, may be transported by the Japanese into any part of the empire without the payment of any tax, excise, or transit duty whatever.

No higher duties shall be paid by Americans on goods imported into Japan that are fixed by this treaty, nor shall any higher duties be paid by Americans than are levied on the same description of goods if imported in Japanese vessels, or the vessels of any other nation.

Article V

All foreign coin shall be current in Japan and pass for its corresponding weight of Japanese coin of the same description. Americans and Japanese may freely use foreign or Japanese coin in making payments to each other.

As some time will elapse before the Japanese will be acquainted with the value of foreign coin, the Japanese government will, for the period of one year after the opening of each harbor, furnish the Americans with Japanese coin, in exchange for theirs, equal weight being given and no discount taken for recoinage. Coins of all description (with the exception of Japanese copper coin) may be exported from Japan, and foreign gold and silver uncoined.

Article VI

Americans committing offences against Japanese shall be tried in American consular courts, and when guilty shall be punished according to American law. Japanese committing offences against Americans shall be tried by the Japanese authorities and punished according to Japanese law. The consular courts shall be open to Japanese creditors, to enable them to recover their just claims against American citizens, and the Japanese courts shall in like manner be open to American citizens for the recovery of their just claims against Japanese.

All claims for forfeitures or penalties for violations of this treaty, or of the articles regulating trade which are appended hereunto, shall be sued for in the consular courts, and all recoveries shall be delivered to the Japanese authorities.

Neither the American or Japanese governments are to be held responsible for the payment of any debts contracted by their respective citizens or subjects.

Article VII

In the opened harbors of Japan Americans shall be free to go, where they please, within the following limits:

At Kanagawa, the River Logo, (which empties into the Bay of Yedo between Kawasaki and Sinagawa,) and (10) ten ri in another direction.

At Hakodadi, (10) ten ri in any direction.

At Hiogo, (10) ten ri in any direction, that of Kioto excepted, which city shall not be approached nearer than (10) ten ri. The crews of vessels resorting to Hiogo shall not cross the River Enagawa, which empties into the Bay between Hiogo and Asaca. The distances shall be measured inland from Goyoso, or town hall, of each of the foregoing harbors, the ri being equal to (4,275) four thousand two hundred and seventy-five yards, American measure.

At Nagasaki Americans may go into any part of the imperial domain in its vicinity. The boundaries of Nee-e-gata, or the place that may be substituted for it, shall be settled by the American diplomatic agent and the government of Japan. Americans who have been convicted of felony, or twice convicted of misdemeanors, shall not go more than (1) one Japanese ri inland from the places of their respective residences, and all persons so convicted shall lose their right of permanent residence in Japan, and the Japanese authorities may require them to leave the country.

A reasonable time shall be allowed to all such persons to settle their affairs, and the American consular authority shall, after an examination into the circumstances of each case, determine the time to be allowed, but such time shall not in any case exceed one year, to be calculated from the time the person shall be free to attend to his affairs.

Article VIII

Americans in Japan shall be allowed the free exercise of their religion, and for this purpose shall have the right to erect suitable places of worship. No injury shall be done to such buildings, nor any insult be offered to the religious worship of the Americans. American citizens shall not injure any Japanese temple or mia, or offer any insult or injury to Japanese religious ceremonies, or to the objects of their worship.

The Americans and Japanese shall not do anything that may be calculated to excite religious animosity. The government of Japan has already abolished the practice of trampling on religious emblems.

Article IX

When requested by the American consul, the Japanese authorities will cause the arrest of all deserters and fugitives from justice, receive in jail all persons held as prisoners by the consul, and give to the consul such assistance as may be required to enable him to enforce the observance of the laws by the Americans who are on land, and to maintain order among the shipping. For all such service, and for the support of prisoners kept in confinement, the consul shall in all cases pay a just compensation.

Article X

The Japanese government may purchase or construct in the United States ships of war, steamers, merchant ships, whale ships, cannon, munitions of war, and arms of all kinds, and any other things it may require. It shall have the right to engage in the United States scientific, naval and military men, artizans of all kinds, and mariners to enter into its service. All purchases made for the government of Japan may be exported from the United States, and all persons engaged for its service may freely depart from the United States: *Provided,* That no articles that are contraband of war shall be exported, nor any persons engaged to act in a naval or military capacity, while Japan shall be at war with any power in amity with the United States.

Article XI

The articles for the regulation of trade, which are appended to this treaty, shall be considered as forming a part of the same, and shall be equally binding on both the contracting parties to this treaty, and on their citizens and subjects.

Article XII

Such of the provisions of the treaty made by Commodore Perry, and signed at Kanagawa, on the 31st of March, 1854, as conflict with the provisions of this treaty are hereby revoked; and as all the provisions of a convention executed by the consul general of the United States and the governors of Simoda, on 17th of June, 1857, are incorporated in this treaty, that convention is also revoked.

The person charged with the diplomatic relations of the United States in Japan, in conjunction with such person or persons as may be appointed for that purpose by the Japanese government, shall have power to make such rules and regulations as may be required to carry into full and complete effect the provisions of this treaty, and the provisions of the articles regulating trade appended thereunto.

Article XIII

After the (4th of July, 1872) fourth day of July, one thousand eight hundred and seventy-two, upon the desire of either the American or Japanese governments, and on one year's notice given by either party, this treaty, and such portions of the treaty of Kanagawa as remain unrevoked by this treaty, together with the regulations of trade hereunto annexed, or those that may be hereafter introduced, shall be subject to revision by commissioners appointed on both sides for this purpose, who will be empowered to decide on, and insert therein, such amendments as experience shall prove to be desirable.

Article XIV

This treaty shall go into effect on the (4th of July, 1859) fourth day of July, in the year of our Lord one thousand eight hundred and fifty-nine, on or before which day the ratifications of the same shall be exchanged at the city of Washington; but if, from any unforseen cause, the ratifications cannot be exchanged by that time, the treaty shall still go into effect at the date above mentioned.

The act of ratification on the part of the United States shall be verified by the signature of the President of the United States, countersigned by the Secretary of State, and sealed with the seal of the United States.

The act of ratification on the part of Japan shall be verified by the name and seal of his Majesty the Ty-Coon, and by the seals and signatures of such of his high officers as he may direct.

This treaty is executed in quadruplicate, each copy being written in the English, Japanese, and Dutch languages, all the versions having the same meaning and intention, but the Dutch version shall be considered as being the original.

In witness whereof, the above named plenipotentiaries have hereunto set their hands and seals, at the city of Yedo, this twenty-ninth day of July, in the year of our Lord one thousand eight hundred and fifty-eight, and of the independence of the United States of America the eighty-third, corresponding to the Japanese era, the nineteenth day of the sixth month of the fifth year of Ansei Mma.

Townsend Harris [seal]

Regulations under which American trade is to be conducted in Japan

Regulation First

Within (48) forty-eight hours (Sunday excepted) after the arrival of an American ship in Japanese port, the captain or commander shall exhibit to the Japanese custom-house authorities the receipt of the American consul, showing that he has deposited the ship's register and other papers, as required by the laws of the United States, at the American consulate, and he shall then make an entry of his ship, by giving a written paper, stating the name of the ship, and the name of the port from which she comes, her tonnage, the name of her captain or commander, the names of her passengers, (if any,) and the number of her crew, which paper shall be certified by the captain or commander to be a true statement, and shall be signed by him; he shall at the same time deposit a written manifest of his cargo, setting forth the marks and numbers of the packages and their contents, as they are described in his bills of lading, with the names of the person or persons to whom they are consigned. A list of the stores of the ship shall be added to the manifest. The captain or commander shall certify the manifest to be a true account of all the cargo and stores on board the ship, and shall sign his name to the same. If any error is discovered in the manifest, it may be corrected within (24) twenty-four hours (Sundays excepted) without the payment of any fee; but for any alteration or post entry to the manifest made after that time, a fee of ($15) fifteen dollars shall be paid. All goods not entered on the manifest shall pay double duties on being landed. Any captain or commander that shall neglect to enter his vessel at the Japanese custom-house within the time prescribed by this regulation shall pay a penalty of ($60) sixty dollars for each day that he shall so neglect to enter his ship.

Regulation Second

The Japanese government shall have the right to place custom-house officers on board any ship in their ports (men-of-war excepted.) All custom-house officers shall be treated with civility, and such reasonable accommodation shall be allotted to them as the ship affords. No goods shall be unladen from any ship between the hours of sunset and sunrise, except by special permission of the custom-house authorities, and the hatches, and all other places of entrance into that part of the ship where the cargo is stowed, may be secured by Japanese officers, between the hours of sunset and sunrise, by affixing seals, locks, or other fastenings; and if any person shall, without due permission, open any entrance that has been so secured, or shall break or remove any seal, lock, or other fastening that has been affixed by the Japanese custom-house officers, every person so offending shall pay a fine of ($60) sixty

dollars for each offence. Any goods that shall be discharged or attempted to be discharged from any ship, without having been duly entered at the Japanese custom-house, as hereinafter provided, shall be liable to seizure and confiscation.

Packages of goods made up with an attempt to defraud the revenue of Japan, by concealing therein articles of value which are not set forth in the invoice, shall be forfeited.

American ships that shall smuggle, or attempt to smuggle, goods in any of the non-opened harbors of Japan, all such goods shall be forfeited to the Japanese government, and the ship shall pay a fine of ($1,000) one thousand dollars for each offence. Vessels needing repairs may land their cargo for that purpose without the payment of duty. All goods so landed shall remain in charge of the Japanese authorities, and all just charges for storage, labor, and supervision shall be paid thereon. But if any portion of such cargo be sold, the regular duties shall be paid on the portion so disposed of. Cargo may be transhipped to another vessel in the same harbor without the payment of duty; but all transhipments shall be made under the supervision of Japanese officers, and after satisfactory proof has been given to the custom-house authorities of the *bona fide* nature of the transaction, and also under a permit to be granted for that purpose by such authorities. The importation of opium being prohibited, if any person or persons shall smuggle, or attempt to smuggle, any opium, he or they shall pay a fine of ($15) fifteen dollars for each catty of opium so smuggled or attempted to be smuggled; and if more than one person shall be engaged in the offence, they shall collectively be held responsible for the payment of the foregoing penalty.

Regulation Third

The owner or consignee of any goods, who desires to land them, shall make an entry of the same at the Japanese custom-house. The entry shall be in writing, and shall set forth the name of the person making the entry, and the name of the ship in which the goods were imported, and the marks, numbers, packages, and the contents thereof, with the value of each package extended separately in one amount, and at the bottom of the entry shall be placed the aggregate value of all the goods contained in the entry. On each entry the owner or consignee shall certify, in writing, that the entry then presented exhibits the actual cost of the goods, and that nothing has been concealed whereby the customs of Japan would be defrauded; and the owner or consignee shall sign his name to such certificate.

The original invoice or invoices of the goods so entered shall be presented to the custom-house authorities, and shall remain in their possession until they have examined the goods contained in the entry.

The Japanese officers may examine any or all of the packages so entered, and for this purpose may take them to the custom-house, but such examination shall be without expense to the importer or injury to the goods, and after examination, the Japanese shall restore the goods to their original condition in the packages, (so far as may be practicable,) and such examination shall be made without any unreasonable delay.

If any owner or importer discovers that his goods have been damaged on the voyage of importation before such goods have been delivered to him, he may notify the custom-house authorities of such damage, and he may have the damaged goods appraised by two or more competent and disinterested persons, who, after due examination, shall make a certificate setting forth the amount per cent. of damage on each separate package, describing it by its mark and number, which certificates shall be signed by the appraisers in presence of the custom-house authorities, and the importer may attach the certificate to his entry, and make a corresponding deduction from it. But this shall not prevent the custom-house authorities from appraising the goods in the manner provided in article fourth of the treaty, to which these regulations are appended.

After the duties have been paid, the owner shall receive a permit authorizing the delivery to him of the goods, whether the same are at the custom-house or on ship-board. All goods intended to be exported shall be entered at the Japanese custom-house before they are placed on ship-board. The entry shall be in writing, and shall state the name of the ship by which the goods are to be exported, with the marks and numbers of the packages, and the quantity, description, and value of their contents. The exporter shall certify in writing that the entry is a true account of all the goods contained therein, and shall sign his name thereto. Any goods that are put on board of a ship for exportation before they have been entered at the custom-house, and all packages which contain prohibited articles, shall be forfeited to the Japanese government.

No entry at the custom-house shall be required for supplies for the use of ships, their crews and passengers, nor for the clothing, &c., of passengers.

Regulation Fourth

Ships wishing to clear shall give (24) twenty-four hours' notice at the custom-house, and at the end of that time they shall be entitled to their clearance; but if it be refused, the custom-house authorities shall immediately inform the captain or consignee of the ship of the reasons why the clearance is refused, and they shall also give the same notice to the American consul.

Ships of war of the United States shall not be required to enter or clear at the custom-house, nor shall they be visited by Japanese custom-house or police officers. Steamers carrying the mails of the United States may enter and clear on the same day, and they shall not be required to make a manifest, except for such passengers and goods as are to be landed in Japan; but such steamers shall, in all cases, enter and clear at the custom-house.

Whale ships touching for supplies, or ships in distress, shall not be required to make a manifest of their cargo; but if they subsequently wish to trade, they shall then deposit a manifest, as required in regulation first.

The word ship, wherever it occurs in these regulations, or in the treaty to which they are attached, is to be held as meaning ship, barque, brig, schooner, sloop, or steamer.

Regulation Fifth

Any person signing a false declaration or certificate with the intent to defraud the revenue of Japan shall pay a fine of ($125) one hundred and twenty-five dollars for each offence.

Regulation Sixth

No tonnage duties shall be levied on American ships in the ports of Japan, but the following fees shall be paid to the Japanese custom-house authorities: For the entry of a ship ($15) fifteen dollars; for the clearance of a ship ($7) seven dollars; for each permit ($1 1/2) one dollar and a half; for each bill of health ($1 1/2) one dollar and a half; for any other document ($1 1/2) one dollar and a half.

Regulation Seventh

Duties shall be paid to the Japanese government on all goods landed in the country according to the following tariff:

Class One.—All articles in this class shall be free of duty.

Gold and silver, coined or uncoined.

Wearing apparel in actual use.

Household furniture and printed books not intended for sale, but the property of persons who come to reside in Japan.

Class Two.—A duty of (5) five per cent. shall be paid on the following articles: All articles used for the purpose of building, rigging, repairing, or fitting out of ships; whaling gear of all kinds; salted provisions of all kinds; bread and breadstuffs; living animals of all kinds; coals; timber for building houses; rice; paddy; steam machinery; zinc; lead; tin; raw silk.

Class Three.—A duty of (35) thirty-five per cent shall be paid on all intoxicating liquors, whether prepared by distillation, fermentation, or in any other manner.

Class Four.—All goods not included in any of the preceding classes shall pay a duty of (20) twenty per cent.

All articles of Japanese production, which are exported as cargo, shall pay a duty of (5) five per cent, with the exception of gold and silver coin and copper in bars. (5) Five years after the opening of Kanagawa the import and export duties shall be subject to revision if the Japanese government desires it.

Source:

Charles I. Bevans, comp. *Treaties and Other Agreements of the United States of America, 1776–1949.* Washington, D.C.: Government Printing Office, 1968–76.

The Slavery Debate and the Rights of Women

Liberator Editorial, 1831

Weekly antislavery newspaper published by militant American abolitionist William Lloyd Garrison between January 1, 1831, and December 29, 1865. This periodical, issued in Boston, decried slavery as a national sin and promoted the immediate, unconditional emancipation of slaves in the United States. Although its paid circulation never exceeded 3,000 subscribers, the *Liberator* had a wide influence, persuading many northern abolitionists to abandon proposals for more gradual, compensated emancipation and encouraging southerners to defend the institution of slavery. Few copies reached the South between January and August of 1831. Nevertheless, when Nat Turner instigated a rebellion that month in Virginia, southerners blamed the *Liberator*. The paper ceased publication after ratification of the Thirteenth Amendment, ending slavery. The editorial below, from the paper's first issue, illustrates the anger, passion, and eloquence behind the movement.

———— ⚬❦⚬ ————

In the month of August, I issued proposals for publishing 'The Liberator' in Washington city; but the enterprise, though hailed approvingly in different sections of the country, was palsied by public indifference. Since that time, the removal of the 'Genius of Universal Emancipation' to the Seat of Government has rendered less imperious the establishment of a similar periodical in that quarter.

During my recent tour for the purpose of exciting the minds of the people by a series of discourses on the subject of slavery, every place that I visited gave fresh evidence of the fact, that a greater revolution in public sentiment was to be effected in the free States—and particularly in New England—than at the South. I found contempt more bitter, opposition more active, detraction more relentless, prejudice more stubborn, and apathy more frozen, than among slave owners themselves. Of course, there were individual exceptions to the contrary. This state of things afflicted, but did not dishearten me. I determined, at every hazard, to lift up the standard of emancipation in the eyes of the nation, within sight of Bunker Hill, and in the birth-place of liberty. That standard is now unfurled; and long may it float, unhurt by the spoliations of time or the missiles of a desperate foe; yea, till every chain be broken, and every bondman set free! Let Southern oppressors tremble; let their secret abettors tremble; let their Northern apologists tremble; let all the enemies of the persecuted blacks tremble.

Assenting to the 'self-evident truths' maintained in the American Declaration of Independence, 'that all men are created equal, and endowed by their Creator with certain inalienable rights—among which are life, liberty, and the pursuit of happiness,' I shall strenuously contend for the immediate enfranchisement of our slave population. In Park Street Church, on the Fourth of July, 1829, in an address on slavery, I unreflectingly assented to the popular but pernicious doctrine of gradual abolition. I seize this opportunity to make a full and unequivocal recantation, and thus publicly to ask pardon of my God, of my country, and of my brethren, the poor slaves, for having uttered a sentiment so full of timidity, injustice and absurdity. A similar recantation, from my pen, was published in the 'Genius of Universal Emancipation,' at Baltimore, in September, 1829. My conscience is now satisfied.

I am aware, that many object to the severity of my language; but is there not cause for severity? I will be as harsh as truth, and as uncompromising as justice. On this subject, I do not wish to think, or speak, or write, with moderation. No! no! Tell a man, whose house is on fire, to give a moderate alarm; tell him to moderately rescue his wife from the hands of the ravisher; tell the mother to gradually extricate her babe from the fire into which it has fallen; but urge me not to use moderation in a cause like the present! I am in earnest. I will not equivocate—I will not excuse—I will not retreat a single inch—and I will be heard. The apathy of the people is enough to make every statue leap from its pedestal, and to hasten the resurrection of the dead.

It is pretended, that I am retarding the cause of emancipation by the coarseness of my invective, and the precipitancy of my measures. The charge is not true. On this question, my influence, humble as it is, is felt at this moment to a considerable extent, and shall be felt in coming years—not perniciously, but beneficially—not as a curse, but as a blessing; and posterity will bear testimony that I was right. I desire to thank God, that he enables me to disregard 'the fear of man which bringeth a snare,' and to speak his truth in its simplicity and power. And here I close with this fresh dedication:—

'Oppression! I have seen thee, face to face, And met thy cruel eye and cloudy brow; But thy soul-withering glance I fear not now—For dread to prouder feelings doth give place, Of deep abhorrence! Scorning the disgrace Of slavish knees that at thy footstool bow, I also kneel—but with far other vow Do hail thee and thy herd of hirelings base:—I swear, while life-blood warms my throbbing veins, Still to oppose and thwart, with heart and hand, Thy brutalizing sway—till Africa's chains Are burst, and Freedom rules the rescued land, Trampling Oppression and his iron rod:—Such is the vow I take—so help me, God!'

Source:

Writings and Speeches of William Lloyd Garrison. Boston: R.F. Walcott, p. 62–64.

Constitution of the American Anti-Slavery Society, The Declaration of Sentiments of the American Anti-Slavery Convention, 1833

Basic principles and rules, prepared by William Lloyd Garrison and issued in Philadelphia on December 4, 1833, by the founding convention of the militant, abolitionist American Anti-Slavery Society. The constitution condemned the institution of slavery as a danger to prosperity, peace, and national unity, as well as contrary to "natural justice," republican government, and Christian belief; it called for immediate emancipation of all slaves and abolition of the domestic slave trade and opposed expatriation of the freed slaves. The society also declared as goals the elimination of prejudice and the "intellectual, moral and religious improvement" of people of color in order to secure their civil rights and religious equality with whites.

Constitution of the American Anti-Slavery Society
Article I

This Society shall be called the American Anti-Slavery Society.

Article II

The objects of this Society are the entire abolition of slavery in the United States. While it admits that each State, in which slavery exists, has, by the Constitution of the United States, the exclusive rights to *legislate* in regard to its abolition in this State, it shall *aim* to convince all our fellow-citizens, by arguments addressed to their understandings and consciences, that slave-holding is a heinous crime in the sight of God, and that the duty, safety, and best interests of all concerned, require its *immediate abandonment*, without expatriation. The Society will also endeavor, in a constitutional way, to influence Congress to put an end to the domestic slave-trade, and to abolish slavery in all those portions of our common country, which come under its control, especially in the District of Columbia, and likewise to prevent the extension of it to any State that may be hereafter admitted to the Union.

Article III

This Society shall aim to elevate the character and condition of the people of color, by encouraging their intellectual, moral, and religious improvement, and by removing public prejudice, that thus they may, according to their intellectual and moral worth, share an equality with the whites, of civil and religious privileges; but this Society will never, in any way, countenance the oppressed in vindicating their rights by resorting to physical force.

Article IV

Any person who consents to the principles of this Constitution, who contributes to the funds of this Society, and is not a slave-holder, may be a member of this Society, and shall be entitled to vote at the meetings.

Article V

The officers of this Society shall be a President, Vice-Presidents, a Secretary of Foreign Correspondence, a Secretary of Domestic Correspondence, a Recording Secretary, a Treasurer, and a Board of Mangers, composed of the above, and not less than ten other members of the Society. They shall be annually elected by the members of the Society, and five shall constitute a quorum.

Article VI

The Board of Managers shall annually elect an Executive Committee, to consist of not less than five, nor more than twelve members, which shall be located in New York, who shall have power to enact their own by-laws, fill any vacancy in their body, employ agents, determine what compensation shall be paid to agents, and to the Corresponding Secretaries, direct the Treasurer in the application of all moneys, and call special meetings of the Society. They shall make arrangements for all meetings of the Society, make an annual written report of their doings, the income, expenditures, and funds of the Society, and shall hold stated meetings, and adopt the most energetic measures in their power to advance the objects of the Society.

Article VII

The President shall preside at all meetings of the Society, or, in his absence, one of the Vice-Presidents, or, in their absence, a President pro tem. The Corresponding Secretaries shall conduct the correspondence of the Society. The Recording Secretary shall notify all meetings of the Society, and of the Executive Committee, and shall keep records of the same in separate books. The Treasurer shall collect the subscriptions, make payments at the direction of the Executive Committee, and present a written and audited account to accompany the annual report.

Article VIII

The annual meeting of the Society shall be held each year, at such time and place as the Executive Committee may direct, when the accounts of the Treasurer shall be presented, the annual report read, appropriate addresses delivered, the officers chosen, and such other business transacted as shall be deemed expedient. A special meeting shall always be held on the Tuesday immediately preceding the second Thursday in May, in the City of New York, at 10 o'clock, A. M., provided the annual meeting be not held there at that time.

Article IX

Any Anti-Slavery Society, or association, founded on the same principles, may become auxiliary to this Society. The officers of each Auxiliary Society shall be ex-officio members of the Parent Institution, and shall be entitled to deliberate and vote in the transaction of its concerns.

Article X

This Constitution may be amended at any annual meeting of the Society, by a vote of two-thirds of the members present, provided the amendments proposed have been previously submitted, in writing, to the Executive Committee.

Source:

The Constitution of the American Anti-Slavery Society . . . New York: American Anti-Slavery Society, 1838.

South Carolina Resolutions on Abolitionist Propaganda, 1835

Censorious resolutions against abolitionist propaganda passed by the South Carolina legislature on December 16, 1835. South Carolina, among other southern states, acted to crack down on activities of abolitionist societies in free northern states directed at the slaveholding South. State lawmakers issued a severe warning against printing or voicing anything that condemned slavery or that might incite insurrection among the slaves. The resolutions, fixing responsibility on the northern states within whose borders the abolitionists organized and operated, denounced the antislavery societies as incendiary and asserted that their activities violated the compact of union among the several states. The northern states must not, if they valued their own peace and security, abide within their limits the fomenting of antislavery conspiracy aimed at fellow states in the Union. The legislature appealed to northern state governments to suppress abolitionist societies within their borders by harshly penalizing publication and distribution of antislavery literature. It asserted that interference by northern states with slavery in the South would be considered unlawful and resolutely resisted. Northern states were called on to pass laws disclaiming their or the federal government's right to interfere with domestic slavery, and the U.S. post office was urged to close the mail to abolitionist literature.

---

1. *Resolved,* That the formation of the abolition societies, and the acts and doings of certain fanatics, calling themselves abolitionists, in the non-slaveholding states of this confederacy, are in direct violation of the obligations of the compact of the union, dissocial, and incendiary in the extreme.

2. *Resolved,* That no state having a just regard for her own peace and security can acquiesce in a state of things by which such conspiracies are engendered within the limits of a friendly state, united to her by the bonds of a common league of political association, without either surrendering or compromising her most essential rights.

3. *Resolved,* That the Legislature of South Carolina, having every confidence in the justice and friendship of the non-slaveholding states, announces to her co-states her confident expectation, and she earnestly requests that the governments of these states will promptly and effectually suppress all those associations within their respective limits, purporting to be abolition societies, and that they will make it highly penal to print, publish, and distribute newspapers, pamphlets, tracts and pictorial representations calculated and having an obvious tendency to excite the slaves of the southern states to insurrection and revolt.

4. *Resolved,* That, regarding the domestic slavery of the southern states as a subject exclusively within the control of each of the said states, we shall consider every interference, by any other state of the general government, as a direct and unlawful interference, to be resisted at once, and under every possible circumstance.

5. *Resolved,* In order that a salutary negative may be put on the mischievous and unfounded assumption of some of the abolitionists—the non-slaveholding states are requested to disclaim by legislative declaration, all right, either on the part of themselves or the government of the United States, to interfere in any manner with domestic slavery, either in the states, or in the territories where it exists.

6. *Resolved,* That we should consider the abolition of slavery in the District of Columbia, as a violation of the rights of the citizens of that District, derived from the implied conditions on which that territory was ceded to the general government, and as an usurpation to be at once resisted as nothing more than the commencement of a scheme of much more extensive and flagrant injustice.

7. *Resolved,* That the legislature of South Carolina, regards with decided approbation, the measures of security adopted by the Post Office Department of the United States, in relation to the transmission of incendiary tracts. But if this highly essential and protective policy, be counteracted by congress, and the United States mail becomes a vehicle for the transmission of the mischievous documents, with which it was recently freighted we, in this contingency, expect that the Chief Magistrate of our state, will forthwith call the legislature together, that timely measures may be taken to prevent its traversing our territory.

Source:

Henry Steele Commager, ed. *Documents of American History.* New York: F.S. Crofts & Co., 1934.

Proceedings of the Anti-Slavery Convention of American Women, 1838

Minutes of the Anti-Slavery Convention of American Women, held in Philadelphia in May 1838. The participants were female abolitionist groups from several different states. This account of the proceedings includes the participants' resolutions and letters of support. Lists of donations received, a list of delegates, additional letters of support, some resolutions, all adjournments and other administrative actions are omitted here.

The minutes show that the women resolved to petition the government, to boycott churches sympathetic to slaveholders, and to educate their children according to abolitionist beliefs. The convention stated that slavery opposes the laws of God

and called on churches to take action against it. Upholding the First Amendment right to petitioning the government had become especially important regarding slavery. In 1836 Congress passed a "gag resolution" in order to stifle debate over eliminating the slave trade in the District of Columbia. Some 500,000 petitions, more than half the signers women, arrived in Congress between 1836 and 1840. The rule was repealed in 1844. The night after the first meeting, a mob stormed the convention hall and burned it.

Female abolitionist organizations such as those represented at this convention became more prominent in the early 1830s, after the Anti-Slavery Society excluded women from its proceedings. These organizations would serve as the first steps in the creation of the women's rights movement. South Carolinians Sarah M. Grimké and Angelina E. Grimké (Weld) were among the most notable female abolitionists.

Proceeding of an Anti-Slavery Convention of Women, assembled from various parts of the United States, in Pennsylvania Hall, in the city of Philadelphia, on Tuesday, the 15th of May, 1838. At 10 o'clock, A. M. the Convention was called to order. On the nomination of a committee, appointed at preliminary meeting, on Monday, May 14th, the following officers were appointed: Mary S. Parker, of Boston, *President;* [ten vice-presidents; four secretaries]; Sarah M. Douglass, *Treasurer.*

Wednesday Morning, May 16

The 94th Psalm was read by the President and prayer offered by Margaret Prior.

On Motion of Juliana A. Tappan, *Resolved,* That whatever may be the sacrifice, and whatever other rights may be yielded or denied, we will maintain practically the right of petition, until the slave shall go free, or our energies, like Loveyjoy's, are paralyzed in death.

Resolved, That for every petition by the National Legislature, during their late session, we will endeavor to send *five* the present year; and that we will not cease our efforts until the prayers of every woman within the sphere of our influence shall be heard in the halls of Congress on this subject.

On motion of Mary Spencer, *Resolved,* That we regard the right of petition as clear and inalienable, and so far from glamouring a dictatorial spirit, it is the refuge of the most humble and powerless, and *true greatness* would never turn away from such appeals.

Mary Grew offered the following resolution, *Whereas,* The principles of Christ are commanded to have no fellowship with the "unfruitful works of darkness;" and, whereas, union in His church is the strongest expression of fellowship between men; therefore,

Resolved, That it is our duty to keep ourselves separate from those churches which receive to their pulpits and their communion tables, those who buy, or sell, or hold as property, the image of the living God. This resolution was adopted. [Those who voted in the negative on the above resolution, fully concur with their sisters, in the belief that slaveholders and their apologists are guilty before God, and that, with the former, Northern Christian should hold no fellowship; but as it is their full belief that there is still moral power sufficient in the church, if rightly applied, to purify it, they cannot feel it their duty to withdraw until the utter inefficiency of the means used, shall constrain them to believe the church totally corrupt.]

Thursday Morning, May 17

Lucretia Mott made some impressive remarks respecting the riot of the preceding evening [in which the hall in which they had been meeting was burned], and exhorted the members of the Convention to be steadfast and solemn in the prosecution of the business for which they were assembled.

On motion of Margaret Dye, *Resolved,* That the Anti-Slavery enterprise presents one of the most appropriate fields for the exertion of the influence of woman, and that we pledge ourselves, with divine assistance, never to desert the work, while an American slave groans in bondage.

On motion of Abigail B. Ordway, *Resolved,* That every mother is bound by imperative obligations, to instruct her children in the principles abolition, by teaching them the nature and sanctity of human rights, and the claims of the great law of office, as binding alike on every member of the human family.

On motion of Mary Grew, *Resolved,* That in view of unparalleled sufferings of the slave, and also in relation to the oppression of the nominally free people of color in the United States, it becomes us, as women and as christians, to invoke the special aid of Almighty God for the speedy deliverance of this people from their oppressions, in that way which will most glorify Himself.

On motion of Henrietta Willcox, *Resolved,* That in view of the exigencies of the times, and the loud call for money to aid in the dissemination of truth, this Convention recommend to Female Anti-Slavery Societies to take immediate measures for the formation of cent-a-week societies, on the plan proposed by the Executive Committee of the American Anti-Slavery Society.

On motion of Margaret Dye, *Resolved,* That the system of American slavery is contrary to the laws of God, and the spirit of true religion, and that the church is deeply implicated in this sin, and that it therefore becomes the imperative duty of all her members to petition their ecclesiastical bodies to enter their decided protests against it,

and exclude slaveholders from their pulpits and communion tables.

❋   ❋   ❋

Thursday Afternoon, May 17

The President read the 6th chapter of 2d Cor., and Sarah M. Grimké offered prayer.

On motion of Thankful Southwick, *Resolved,* That it is the duty of all those who call themselves abolitionists to make the *most vigorous efforts* to procure for the use of their families the products of *free labor,* so that their hands may be clean, in this particular, when inquisition is made for blood.

Friday Morning, May 18

The Convention met pursuant to adjournment at Temperance hall, but found the doors closed by order of the managers [. . . Much excitement still prevailing, the managers of Temperance Hall, fearing for the safety of their building, refused to open the doors.] A member of the Convention offered the use of a school-room. . . .

The President read the 4th chapter of 2d Cor., and prayer was offered by Juliana A. Tappan, and Mary E. Smith.

On motion of Sarah R. Ingraham, *Resolved,* That in view of the manifestation of public sentiment, as recently exhibited in the outbreakings of a lawless mob, resulting in insult and abuse towards all abolitionists, and personal injury to some of our colored friends, the case of the latter be earnestly commended to God, and prayer be offered that He will redress their wrongs, and protect them from the dangers to which they may be in future exposed.

Abby Kelly offered the following resolution, which was adopted:

Whereas, A vast portion of the wealth of the North has accrued, and is still accruing, from the slave system, either directly in the holding of slaves, by Northern citizens, or indirectly by our social and commercial intercourse with slaveholding communities; therefore,

Resolved, That we are very deeply implicated in the sin of using our brother's service without wages, and of holding in our hands the gains of oppression; consequently it is our duty to bring forth fruits meet for repentance, by laboring devotedly in the service of the spoiled, and by contributing with unsparing liberality to the treasury of the slave.

On motion of Sarah M. Grimké,

Resolved, That prejudice against color is the very spirit of slavery, sinful in those who indulge it, and is the fire which is consuming the happiness and energies of the free people of color.

That it is, therefore, the duty of abolitionists to identify themselves with these oppressed Americans, by sitting with them in places of worship, by appearing with them in our streets, by giving them our countenance in steamboats and stages, by visiting them at their homes and encouraging them to visit us, receiving them as we do our white fellow citizens. [Not unanimous—a number voted in the negative, believing that a resolution couched in such phraseology, might, by being misapprehended, injure the abolition cause.]

On motion of Sarah M. Grimké, *Resolved,* That those of our Southern brethren and sisters who feel and mourn over the guilt of slavery, while circumstances impose on them the necessity of remaining witnesses of its evils and its horrors, are entitled to our sympathy and prayers, and that we encourage them to walk with weeping and supplication before God, that His judgments may be averted from our beloved country. . . .

Catherine M. Sullivan offered the following resolution, which was adopted: Believing the principles of the Anti-Slavery cause to be identical with those on which the whole gospel rests, and that the constant and vigorous propagation of them will equally advance the kingdom of Christ, in the hearts and outward lives of men; therefore,

Resolved, That we increase our efforts for the spiritual and temporal salvation of the slave, knowing that such labors will involve the salvation of the master, the good of our own souls, the general promotion of peace, moral reform, temperance; the circulation of the Scriptures, the education of youth, and the exaltation of our country to so high a standard of morals and religion, that its example shall go forth unto all the earth and recommend the gospel to every creature.

On motion of Sarah M. Grimké,

Resolved, That we regard the insult and scorn, manifest on our leaving the Hall on the 16th instant, as identical with the spirit of slavery at the South, and the spirit exhibited by the Reform Convention, who have recommended that the people of Pennsylvania should wrest from the free people of color the right of suffrage.

On motion of Angelina E. G. Weld,

Resolved, That we have heard, with grief and shame, of the burning of Pennsylvania Hall, last evening, but rejoice in fulness of hope that God will overrule evil for good, by causing the flames which consumed that beautiful Hall, dedicated to virtue, liberty, and independence, to light up the fires of freedom on every hill-top and in every valley in the state of Pennsylvania, and our country at large.

Resolved, That the delegates from different states be now called upon, in order to pledge sums on behalf of their respective societies, to defray the expenses of the Convention.

[List of contributions and list of the 75 attendees follows.]

To the Anti-Slavery Convention of American Women:—

Dear Sisters:—With the deepest emotions of gratitude to our Almighty Father, we congratulate you upon your assemblage, for the second time, as a Convention. While we rejoice in the wisdom and love that we trust will overshadow you in your deliberations, we cannot but contemplate with awe the sublime results that may emanate from your councils.

Arduous and responsible labor is before you:-the iron shackle that drags heavily along the plains of the South, and the golden fetter hugged by so many of our sex, are alike to be broken!

And this allegiance to *Truth* and unfaltering trust to its power of guidance, is to yourselves an *emancipation act:* from the servile degradation of ages, you arise in the moral accountability and dignity of womanhood, and at the feet of Jesus, imbued with the uncompromising spirit of his teachings, declare the truths that have made you free! Thus strong in the freedom of his giving, true to the faith of his sustaining, the applause or contumely of the world is hushed by the overpowering presence of the "still small voice." Earthly ambition vanishes, before the glorious smile of an approving God; and worldly policy dares not seek an entrance where it is met at every corner by the "flaming sword" of truth.

Our whole souls are with you at this eventful time, and we would fain all join the delegation that leaves us to be with you at this glorious era—to move in concert upon these first waves of a mighty revolution that is to sweep away the strong foundations of prejudice and custom. We feel an assurance that the same unflinching stand of principle, the like unshaken determination of action, which characterized your measures a year since, will mark your decisions at the present time. May the Father of light and love in your midst; then, indeed, all will be well.

On behalf of the Providence
Female Anti-Slavery Society.
Eliza J. Davis, Cor. Secretary.

To the Anti-Slavery Convention of American Women:—

✿   ✿   ✿

—At an Anti-Slavery meeting a clergyman, who had travelled South, said he was forbidden, when there, to preach to slaves: a slaveholder said to him, it is not safe for the slaves to be enlightened, he could not permit them to hear the sermon upon the mount, and said that the precept, "Whatsoever ye would that men should do unto you, do ye even so unto them," would open their eyes to their situation,"Therefore I forbid you to preach to them." This clergyman observed that they could not be taught the Lord's prayer without witnessing its denial all around them. What an avowal is this of the bondage of both master and slave! The sermon upon the mount would create insurrection! Truly the divine aspirations commencing, "Our Father who art in heaven," [*that* Father who hath made of one blood all nations of the earth, and commanded all to love as brethren,] are virtually denied.

We should be unjust to our feelings, did we not take this opportunity to tender our grateful tribute of respect and love to those friends of humanity, Misses Sarah M. and Angelina E. Grimke, for their noble exertions in our vicinity the past year; we think many a Felix has trembled, and many a jailor, himself in bonds, has cried out, "What shall I do to be saved?"

There are those, and the number is neither few nor small, who think that slavery is a political affair, and women have no concern in it; but deluded or callous must be that heart which acknowledges that woman inflicts an injury, but should be powerless in redressing it. "We have not so learned Christ!" We think that to woman is committed the precious trust of rearing our lawgivers; as she is pure and elevated, so may she infuse her spirit into the laws of country; and heaven grant that politics may not be another name for corruption. When statesman and philanthropist, philanthropist and statesman, are identical terms, then may we hope that "righteousness will flow down our streets, and prosperity be within our walls." May the women of this country so purge their hearts of all ambitious views, of all selfish aims, as to be fit and honored instruments for doing the Lord's work; and to be able to say, "Not unto us, O Lord, but to thy name be glory." May we so learn Christ that, in the spirit of his might, we may "bind up the broken-hearted, proclaim liberty to the captives, and the opening of the prison to them that are bound; give unto them beauty for ashes, the oil of joy for mourning, the garment of praise for the spirit of heaviness." To the ladies of the Anti-Slavery Convention we say, may God guide your counsels, and may you do all to his glory.

On behalf of the Society,
L. Willard, *Cor. Secretary*

Source:
Library of Congress. Rare Book and Special Collections Division. National American Woman Suffrage Association Collection.

United States v. Libellants and Claimants of the Schooner Amistad, 1841

In February 1839, Portuguese slave hunters, violating all treaties of the time, illegally abducted a group of Africans from Sierra Leone. The group was then taken to Havana, Cuba, a major center of the slave trade. In Cuba the group was sold to two Spanish plantation owners, who boarded its members onto a schooner called the *Amistad*, which was bound for a Caribbean plantation. On July 1, 1839, the Africans, under the leadership of a man called Cinque, revolted and seized the vessel, killing the captain and the cook. Two months later the vessel was seized off the shore of Long Island by the United States ship *Washington,* and the Africans were brought to Connecticut to stand trial. Murder charges against them were dropped, but they were kept in custody because certain issues of property rights had yet to be resolved. President Martin Van Buren made arguments for their extradition to Cuba.

The *Amistad* mutineers, however, became a cause célèbre for abolitionists, led by financier Lewis Tappan. Yale students taught them how to read, write, and speak English. Roger Baldwin, future governor of Connecticut, defended them in the lower courts. In the Supreme Court, Baldwin was joined by former president John Quincy Adams to defend the prisoners. The decision was written by Justice Joseph Story, who declared that the mutineers had been free men kidnaped by pirates and that the United States had no jurisdiction to try them for murder. Unlike the lower courts, it also refused to hold that they had to be returned to Africa. The case turned not on questions of slavery but of international law. However, it was considered a great victory for the abolitionists, and it is now considered one of the most significant Supreme Court cases involving slavery.

Thirty-five of the original 53 people enslaved returned home to Africa. The remaining 18 died either in prison awaiting trial or at sea returning to Africa. One of the mutineers, Sarah, later returned to the United States and attended Oberlin College. The following is the opinion of the Court delivered by Justice Story.

This is the case of an appeal from the decree of the Circuit Court of the District of Connecticut, sitting in admiralty. The leading facts, as they appear upon the transcript of the proceedings, are as follows: On the 27th of June, 1839, the schooner L'Amistad, being the property of Spanish subjects, cleared out from the port of Havana, in the island of Cuba, for Puerto Principe, in the same island. On board of the schooner were the captain, Ransom Ferrer, and Jose Ruiz, and Pedro Montez, all Spanish subjects. The former had with him a negro boy, named Antonio, claimed to be his slave. Jose Ruiz had with him forty-nine negroes, claimed by him as his slaves, and stated to be his property, in a certain pass or document, signed by the Governor General of Cuba. Pedro Montez had with him four other negroes, also claimed by him as his slaves, and stated to be his property, in a similar pass or document, also signed by the Governor General of Cuba. On the voyage, and before the arrival of the vessel at her port of destination, the negroes rose, killed the captain, and took possession of her. On the 26th of August, the vessel was discovered by Lieutenant Gedney, of the United States brig Washington, at anchor on the high seas, at the distance of half a mile from the shore of Long Island. A part of the negroes were then on shore at Culloden Point, Long Island; who were seized by Lieutenant Gedney, and brought on board. The vessel, with the negroes and other persons on board, was brought by Lieutenant Gedney into the district of Connecticut, and there libelled for salvage in the District Court of the United States. A libel for salvage was also filed by Henry Green and Pelatiah Fordham, of Sag Harbour, Long Island. On the 18th of September, Ruiz and Montez filed claims and libels, in which they asserted their ownership of the negroes as their slaves, and of certain parts of the cargo, and prayed that the same might be "delivered to them, or to the representatives of her Catholic majesty, as might be most proper." On the 19th of September, the Attorney of the United States, for the district of Connecticut, filed an information or libel, setting forth, that the Spanish minister had officially presented to the proper department of the government of the United States, a claim for the restoration of the vessel, cargo, and slaves, as the property of Spanish subjects, which had arrived within the jurisdictional limits of the United States, and were taken possession of by the said public armed brig of the United States; under such circumstances as made it the duty of the United States to cause the same to be restored to the true proprietors, pursuant to the treaty between the United States and Spain: and praying the Court, on its being made legally to appear that the claim of the Spanish minister was well founded, to make such order for the disposal of the vessel, cargo, and slaves, as would best enable the United States to comply with their treaty stipulations. But if it should appear, that the negroes were persons transported from Africa, in violation of the laws of the United States, and brought within the United States contrary to the same laws; he then prayed the Court to make such order for their removal to the coast of Africa, pursuant to the laws of the United States, as it should deem fit.

On the 19th of November, the Attorney of the United States filed a second information or libel, similar to the first, with the exception of the second prayer above set forth in his former one. On the same day, Antonio G. Vega, the vice-consul of Spain, for the state of Connecticut, filed his libel, alleging that Antonio was a slave, the property of the representatives of Ramon Ferrer, and praying the Court to cause him to be delivered to the said vice-consul, that he might be returned by him to his lawful owner in the island of Cuba.

On the 7th of January, 1840, the negroes, Cinque and others, with the exception of Antonio, by their counsel,

filed an answer, denying that they were slaves, or the property of Ruiz and Montez, or that the Court could, under the Constitution or laws of the United States, or under any treaty, exercise any jurisdiction over their persons, by reason of the premises; and praying that they might be dismissed. They specially set forth and insist in this answer, that they were native born Africans; born free, and still of right ought to be free and not slaves; that they were, on or about the 15th of April, 1839, unlawfully kidnapped, and forcibly and wrongfully carried on board a certain vessel on the coast of Africa, which was unlawfully engaged in the slave trade, and were unlawfully transported in the same vessel to the island of Cuba, for the purpose of being there unlawfully sold as slaves; that Ruiz and Montez, well knowing the premises, made a pretended purchase of them: that afterwards, on or about the 28th of June, 1839, Ruiz and Montez, confederating with Ferrer, (captain of the Amistad,) caused them, without law or right, to be placed on board of the Amistad, to be transported to some place unknown to them, and there to be enslaved for life; that, on the voyage, they rose on the master, and took possession of the vessel, intending to return therewith to their native country, or to seek an asylum in some free state; and the vessel arrived, about the 26th of August, 1839, off Montauk Point, near Long Island. . . .

On the same day, all the libellants and claimants, by their counsel, except Jose Ruiz and Pedro Montez, (whose libels and claims, as stated of record, respectively, were pursued by the Spanish minister, the same being merged in his claims,) appeared, and the negroes also appeared by their counsel; and the case was heard on thie libels, claims, answers, and testimony of witnesses.

On the 23d day of January, 1840, the District Court made a decree. By that decree, the Court rejected the claim of Green and Fordham for salvage, but allowed salvage to Lieutenant Gedney and others, on the vessel and cargo, of one-third of the value thereof, but not on the negroes, Cinque and others; it allowed the claim of Tellincas, and Aspe and Laca with the exception of the above-mentioned salvage; it dismissed the libels and claims of Ruiz and Montez, with costs, as being included under the claim of the Spanish minister; it allowed the claim of the Spanish vice-consul for Antonio, on behalf of Ferrer's representatives; it rejected the claims of Ruiz and Montez for the delivery of the negroes, but admitted them for the cargo, with the exception of the above-mentioned salvage; it rejected the claim made by the Attorney of the United States on behalf of the Spanish minister, for the restoration of the negroes under the treaty; but it decreed that they should be delivered to the President of the United States, to be transported to Africa, pursuant to the act of 3d March, 1819.

From this decree the District Attorney, on behalf of the United States, appealed to the Circuit Court, except so

far as related to the restoration of the slave Antonio. . . .
The Circuit Court, by a mere pro forma decree, affirmed
the decree of the District Court, reserving the question of
salvage upon the claims of Tellincas, and Aspe and Laca.
And from that decree the present appeal has been brought
to this Court.

The cause has been very elaborately argued, as well
upon the merits, as upon a motion on behalf of the
appellees to dismiss the appeal. On the part of the United
States, it has been contended, 1. That due and sufficient
proof concerning the property has been made to authorize
the restitution of the vessel, cargo, and negroes to the
Spanish subjects on whose behalf they are claimed pursuant to the treaty with Spain, of the 27th of October,
1795. 2. That the United States had a right to intervene in
the manner in which they have done, to obtain a decree for
the restitution of the property, upon the application of the
Spanish minister. These propositions have been strenuously denied on the other side. . . .

. . . The only parties now before the Court on one side,
are the United States, intervening for the sole purpose of
procuring restitution of the property as Spanish property,
pursuant to the treaty, upon the grounds stated by the
other parties claiming the property in their respective
libels. The United States do not assert any property in
themselves, or any violation of their own rights, or
sovereignty, or laws, by the acts complained of. They do
not insist that these negroes have been imported into the
United States, in contravention of our own slave trade acts.
They do not seek to have these negroes delivered up for
the purpose of being transported to Cuba as pirates or robbers, or as fugitive criminals against the laws of Spain.
They do not assert that the seizure, and bringing the vessel, and cargo, and negroes into port, by Lieutenant Gedney, for the purpose of adjudication, is a tortious [legally
wrongful] act. They simply confine themselves to the right
of the Spanish claimants to the restitution of their property, upon the facts asserted in their respective allegations.

In the next place, the parties before the Court on the
other side as appellees, are Lieutenant Gedney, on his libel
for salvage, and the negroes, (Cinque, and others,) asserting themselves, in their answer, not to be slaves, but free
native Africans, kidnapped in their own country, and illegally transported by force from that country; and now entitled to maintain their freedom.

No question has been here made, as to the proprietary
interests in the vessel and cargo. It is admitted that they
belong to Spanish subjects, and that they ought to be
restored. The only point on this head is, whether the restitution ought to be upon the payment of salvage or not? The
main controversy is, whether these negroes are the property of Ruiz and Montez, and ought to be delivered up; and
to this, accordingly, we shall first direct our attention.

It has been argued on behalf of the United States, that
the Court are bound to deliver them up, according to the
treaty of 1795, with Spain, which has in this particular
been continued in full force, by the treaty of 1819, ratified
in 1821. . . . The ninth article provides, "that all ships and
merchandise, of what nature soever, which shall be rescued out of the hands of any pirates or robbers, on the high
seas, shall be brought into some port of either state, and
shall be delivered to the custody of the officers of that port,
in order to be taken care of and restored entire to the true
proprietor, as soon as due and sufficient proof shall be
made concerning the property thereof." This is the article
on which the main reliance is placed on behalf of the
United States, for the restitution of these negroes. To bring
the case within the article, it is essential to establish, First,
That these negroes, under all the circumstances, fall within
the description of merchandise, in the sense of the treaty.
Secondly, That there has been a rescue of them on the
high seas, out of the hands of the pirates and robbers;
which, in the present case, can only be, by showing that
they themselves are pirates and robbers; and, Thirdly, That
Ruiz and Montez, the asserted proprietors, are the true
proprietors, and have established their title by competent
proof.

If these negroes were, at the time, lawfully held as
slaves under the laws of Spain, and recognised by those
laws as property capable of being lawfully bought and sold;
we see no reason why they may not justly be deemed
within the intent of the treaty, to be included under the
denomination of merchandise, and, as such, ought to be
restored to the claimants: for, upon that point, the laws of
Spain would seem to furnish the proper rule of interpretation. But, admitting this, it is clear, in our opinion, that neither of the other essential facts and requisites has been
established in proof; and the onus probandi of both lies
upon the claimants to give rise to the causes. . . . It is plain
beyond controversy, if we examine the evidence, that these
negroes never were the lawful slaves of Ruiz or Montez, or
of any other Spanish subjects. They are natives of Africa,
and were kidnapped there, and were unlawfully transported to Cuba, in violation of the laws and treaties of
Spain, and the most solemn edicts and declarations of that
government. By those laws, and treaties, and edicts, the
African slave trade is utterly abolished; the dealing in that
trade is deemed a heinous crime; and the negroes thereby
introduced into the dominions of Spain, are declared to be
free. Ruiz and Montez are proved to have made the pretended purchase of these negroes, with a full knowledge of
all the circumstances. And so cogent and irresistible is the
evidence in this respect, that the District Attorney has
admitted in open Court, upon the record, that these
negroes were native Africans, and recently imported into
Cuba, as alleged in their answers to the libels in the case.

The supposed proprietary interest of Ruiz and Montez, is completely displaced, if we are at liberty to look at the evidence of the admissions of the District Attorney.

If, then, these negroes are not slaves, but are kidnapped Africans, who, by the laws of Spain itself, are entitled to their freedom, and were kidnapped and illegally carried to Cuba, and illegally detained and restrained on board of the Amistad; there is no pretence to say, that they are pirates or robbers. We may lament the dreadful acts, by which they asserted their liberty, and took possession of the Amistad, and endeavoured to regain their native country; but they cannot be deemed pirates or robbers in the sense of the law of nations, or the treaty with Spain, or the laws of Spain itself; at least so far as those laws have been brought to our knowledge. Nor do the libels of Ruiz or Montez assert them to be such.

This posture of the facts would seem, of itself, to put an end to the Whole inquiry upon the merits. But it is argued, on behalf of the United States, that the ship, and cargo, and negroes were duly documented as belonging to Spanish subjects, and this Court have no right to look behind these documents; that full faith and credit is to be given to them; and that they are to be held conclusive evidence in this cause, even although it should be established by the most satisfactory proofs, that they have been obtained by the grossest frauds and impositions upon the constituted authorities of Spain. To this argument we can, in no wise, assent. There is nothing in the treaty which justifies or sustains the argument. . . . What we proceed upon is this, that although public documents of the government, accompanying property found on board of the private ships of a foreign nation, certainly are to be deemed prima facie evidence of the facts which they purport to state, yet they are always open to be impugned for fraud. . . . Fraud will vitiate any, even the most solemn transactions; and an asserted title to property, founded upon it, is utterly void. . . and it is just as applicable to the transactions of civil intercourse between nations in times of peace. . . . In the solemn treaties between nations, it can never be presumed that either state intends to provide the means of perpetrating or protecting frauds; but all the provisions are to be construed as intended to be applied to bona fide transactions. . . .

It is also a most important consideration in the present case, which ought not to be lost sight of, that, supposing these African negroes not to be slaves, but kidnapped, and free negroes, the treaty with Spain cannot be obligatory upon them; and the United States are bound to respect their rights as much as those of Spanish subjects. The conflict of rights between the parties under such circumstances, becomes positive and inevitable, and must be decided upon the eternal principles of justice and international law. If the contest were about any goods on board of this ship, to which American citizens asserted a title, which

was denied by the Spanish claimants, there could be no doubt of the right of such American citizens to litigate their claims before any competent American tribunal, notwithstanding the treaty with Spain. A fortiori, the doctrine must apply where human life and human liberty are in issue; and constitute the very essence of the controversy. The treaty with Spain never could have intended to take away the equal rights of all foreigners, who should contest their claims before any of our Courts, to equal justice; or to deprive such foreigners of the protection given them by other treaties, or by the general law of nations. Upon the merits of the case, then, there does not seem to us to be any ground for doubt, that these negroes ought to be deemed free; and that the Spanish treaty interposes no obstacle to the just assertion of their rights. There is another consideration growing out of this part of the case, which necessarily rises in judgment. It is observable, that the United States, in their original claim, filed it in the alternative, to have the negroes, if slaves and Spanish property, restored to the proprietors; or, if not slaves, but negroes who had been transported from Africa, in violation of the laws of the United States, and brought into the United States contrary to the same laws, then the Court to pass an order to enable the United States to remove such persons to the coast of Africa, to be delivered there to such agent as may be authorized to receive and provide for them. . . . The decree of the District Court . . . contained an order for the delivery of the negroes to the United States, to be transported to the coast of Africa, under the act of the 3d of March, 1819, ch. 224. The United States do not now insist upon any affirmance of this part of the decree; and, in our judgment, upon the admitted facts, there is no ground to assert that the case comes within the purview of the act of 1819, or of any other of our prohibitory slave trade acts. These negroes were never taken from Africa, or brought to the United States in contravention of those acts. When the Amistad arrived she was in possession of the negroes, asserting their freedom; and in no sense could they possibly intend to import themselves here, as slaves, or for sale as slaves. In this view of the matter, that part of the decree of the District Court is unmaintainable, and must be reversed.

The view which has been thus taken of this case, upon the merits, under the first point, renders it wholly unnecessary for us to give any opinion upon the other point, as to the right of the United States to intervene in this case in the manner already stated. We dismiss this, therefore, as well as several minor points made at the argument.

As to the claim of Lieutenant Gedney for the salvage service, it is understood that the United States do not now desire to interpose any obstacle to the allowance of it, if it is deemed reasonable by the Court. It was a highly meritorious and useful service to the proprietors of the ship and cargo; and such as, by the general principles of maritime law, is always deemed a just foundation for salvage. The rate allowed by the Court, does not seem to us to have been beyond the exercise of a sound discretion, under the very peculiar and embarrassing circumstances of the case.

Upon the whole, our opinion is, that the decree of the Circuit Court, affirming that of the District Court, ought to be affirmed, except so far as it directs the negroes to be delivered to the President, to be transported to Africa . . .and, as to this, it ought to be reversed: and that the said negroes be declared to be free, and be dismissed from the custody of the Court, and go without d[el]ay.

Source:

Cornell Law School. The Legal Information Institute. *The United States Appellants, v. the Libellants and Claimants of the Schooner* Amistad . . . Available on-line. URL: www.law.cornell.edu/background/amistad/opinion.html. Accessed October 2003.

Seneca Falls "Declaration of Rights and Sentiments," 1848

Proclamation issued on July 19, 1848, at the Seneca Falls (New York) Convention on the rights of women; it is also known as the "Seneca Falls Declaration and Resolutions," the "Declaration of Independence for Women," and the "Declaration of Women's Rights." Modeled on the Declaration of Independence, the document outlined the unequal and unjust treatment of women and argued that women had rights to equality under the law in all spheres, including education, religion, free speech, and employment opportunities. Its most controversial resolution called for the enfranchisement of women, thus marking the beginning of the woman suffrage movement in the United States.

―――――――――∽⊗∾――――――――――

1. Declaration of Sentiments

When, in the course of human events, it becomes necessary for one portion of the family of man to assume among the people of the earth a position different from that which they have hitherto occupied, but one to which the laws of nature and of nature's God entitle them, a decent respect to the opinions of mankind requires that they should declare the causes that impel them to such a course.

We hold these truths to be self-evident: that all men and women are created equal; that they are endowed by their Creator with certain inalienable rights; that among these are life, liberty, and the pursuit of happiness; that to secure these rights governments are instituted, deriving their just powers from the consent of the governed. Whenever any form of government becomes destructive of these ends, it is the right of those who suffer from it to refuse allegiance to it, and to insist upon the institution of a new government, laying its foundation on such principles, and organizing its powers in such form, as to them shall seem most likely to effect their safety and happiness. Prudence, indeed, will dictate that governments long established should not be changed for light and transient causes; and accordingly all experience hath shown that mankind are more disposed to suffer while evils are sufferable, than to right themselves by abolishing the forms to which they are accustomed. But when a long train of abuses and usurpations, pursuing invariably the same object, evinces a design to reduce them under absolute despotism, it is their duty to throw off such government, and to provide new guards for their future security. Such has been the patient sufferance of the women under this government, and such is now the necessity which constrains them to demand the equal station to which they are entitled.

The history of mankind is a history of repeated injuries and usurpations on the part of man toward woman, having in direct object the establishment of an absolute tyranny over her. To prove this, let facts be submitted to a candid world.

He has never permitted her to exercise her inalienable right to the elective franchise.

He has compelled her to submit to laws, in the formation of which she had no voice.

He has withheld from her rights which are given to the most ignorant and degraded men—both natives and foreigners.

Having deprived her of this first right of a citizen, the elective franchise, thereby leaving her without representation in the halls of legislation, he has oppressed her on all sides.

He has made her, if married, in the eye of the law, civilly dead.

He has taken from her all right in property, even to the wages she earns.

He has made her, morally, an irresponsible being, as she can commit many crimes with impunity, provided they be done in the presence of her husband. In the covenant of marriage, she is compelled to promise obedience to her husband, he becoming, to all intents and purposes, her master—the law giving him power to deprive her of her liberty, and to administer chastisement.

He has so framed the laws of divorce, as to what shall be the proper causes, and in case of separation, to whom the guardianship of the children shall be given, as to be wholly regardless of the happiness of women—the law, in all cases, going upon a false supposition of the supremacy of man, and giving all power into his hands.

After depriving her of all rights as a married woman, if single, and the owner of property, he has taxed her to support a government which recognizes her only when her property can be made profitable to it.

He has monopolized nearly all the profitable employments, and from those she is permitted to follow, she receives but a scanty remuneration. He closes against her all the avenues to wealth and distinction which he considers most honorable to himself. As a teacher of theology, medicine, or law, she is not known.

He has denied her the facilities for obtaining a thorough education, all colleges being closed against her.

He allows her in Church, as well as State, but a subordinate position, claiming Apostolic authority for her exclusion from the ministry, and, with some exceptions, from any public participation in the affairs of the Church.

He has created a false public sentiment by giving to the world a different code of morals for men and women, by which moral delinquencies which exclude women from society, are not only tolerated, but deemed of little account in man.

He has usurped the prerogative of Jehovah himself, claiming it as his right to assign for her a sphere of action, when that belongs to her conscience and to her God.

He has endeavored, in every way that he could, to destroy her confidence in her own powers, to lessen her self-respect and to make her willing to lead a dependent and abject life.

Now, in view of this entire disfranchisement of one-half the people of this country, their social and religious degradation—in view of the unjust laws above mentioned, and because women do feel themselves aggrieved, oppressed, and fraudulently deprived of their most sacred rights, we insist that they have immediate admission to all the rights and privileges which belong to them as citizens of the United States.

In entering upon the great work before us, we anticipate no small amount of misconception, misrepresentation, and ridicule; but we shall use every instrumentality within our power to effect our object. We shall employ agents, circulate tracts, petition the State and National legislatures, and endeavor to enlist the pulpit and the press in our behalf. We hope this Convention will be followed by a series of Conventions embracing every part of the country.

2. Resolutions

Whereas, The great precept of nature is conceded to be, that "man shall pursue his own true and substantial happiness." Blackstone in his Commentaries remarks, that this law of Nature being coeval with mankind, and dictated by God himself, is of course superior in obligation to any other. It is binding over all the globe, in all countries and at all times; no human laws are of any validity if contrary to this, and such of them as are valid, derive all their force,

and all their validity, and all their authority, mediately and immediately, from this original; therefore,

Resolved, That all laws which prevent woman from occupying such a station in society as her conscience shall dictate, or which place her in a position inferior to that of man, are contrary to the great precept of nature, and therefore of no force or authority.

Resolved, That woman is man's equal—was intended to be so by the Creator, and the highest good of the race demands that she should be recognized as such.

Resolved, That the women of this country ought to be enlightened in regard to the laws under which they live, that they may no longer publish their degradation by declaring themselves satisfied with their present position, nor their ignorance, by asserting that they have all the rights they want.

Resolved, That inasmuch as man, while claiming for himself intellectual superiority, does accord to woman moral superiority, it is pre-eminently his duty to encourage her to speak and teach, as she has an opportunity, in all religious assemblies.

Resolved, That the same amount of virtue, delicacy, and refinement of behavior that is required of woman in the social state, should also be required of man, and the same transgressions should be visited with equal severity on both man and woman.

Resolved, That the objection of indelicacy and impropriety, which is so often brought against woman when she addresses a public audience, comes with a very ill-grace from those who encourage, by their attendance, her appearance on the stage, in the concert, or in feats of the circus.

Resolved, That woman has too long rested satisfied in the circumscribed limits which corrupt customs and a perverted application of the Scriptures have marked out for her, and that it is time she should move in the enlarged sphere which her great Creator has assigned her.

Resolved, That it is the duty of the women of this country to secure to themselves their sacred right to the elective franchise.

Resolved, That the equality of human rights results necessarily from the fact of the identity of the race in capabilities and responsibilities.

Resolved, That the speedy success of our cause depends upon the zealous and untiring efforts of both men and women, for the overthrow of the monopoly of the pulpit, and for the securing to women an equal participation with men in the various trades, professions, and commerce.

Resolved, therefore, That, being invested by the creator with the same capabilities, and the same consciousness of responsibility for their exercise, it is demonstrably the right and duty of woman, equally with man, to promote every righteous cause by every righteous means; and especially in regard to the great subjects of morals and religion, it is self-evidently her right to participate with her brother in teaching them, both in private and in public, by writing and by speaking, by any instrumentalities proper to be used, and in any assemblies proper to be held; and this being a self-evident truth growing out of the divinely implanted principles of human nature, any custom or authority adverse to it, whether modern or wearing the hoary sanction of antiquity, is to be regarded as a self-evident falsehood, and at war with mankind.

Source:

Henry Steele Commager, ed. *Documents of American History.* New York: F.S. Crofts & Co., 1934.

New York Married Women's Property Acts, 1848, 1860

Two landmark pieces of legislation passed in New York State that extended women's rights. The law of 1848, passed on April 7, allowed for the protection of property owned by a woman when she married. She was, however, still barred from inheriting her husband's property. Following the Seneca Falls Declaration of 1848, the embryonic women's movement began to grow. In 1854 Elizabeth Cady Stanton addressed the New York legislature, calling for a further expansion of the property laws. On March 20, 1860, New York passed a law giving women the right to their wages and to the custody of their children. Those rights were repealed, however, in 1862.

———————————— ⟨◈⟩ ————————————

**New York Married Women's Property Act (1848)
An Act**

For the more effectual Protection of the Property of Married Women.
Passed April 7, 1848.

The People of the State of New-York, represented in Senate and Assembly do enact as follows:

Sec. 1. The real and personal property of any female who may hereafter marry, and which she shall own at the time of marriage, and the rents issues and profits thereof shall not be subject to the disposal of her husband, nor be liable for his debts, and shall continue her sole and separate property, as if she were a single female.

Sec. 2. The real and personal property, and the rents issues and profits thereof of any female now married shall not be subject to the disposal of her husband; but shall be her sole and separate property as if she were a single

female except so far as the same may be liable for the debts of her husband heretofore contracted.

Sec. 3. It shall be lawful for any married female to receive, by gift, grant devise or bequest, from any person other than her husband and hold to her sole and separate use, as if she were a single female, real and personal property, and the rents, issues and profits thereof, and the same shall not be subject to the disposal of her husband, nor be liable for his debts.

Sec. 4. All contracts made between persons in contemplation of marriage shall remain in full force after such marriage takes place.

**New York Married Women's Property Act (1860)
An Act**

Concerning the rights and liabilities of husband and wife.
Passed March 20, 1860.

The People of the State of New York, represented in Senate and Assembly, do enact as follows:

Section 1. The property, both real and personal, which any married woman now owns, as her sole and separate property; that which comes to her by decent, devise, bequest, gift or grant; that which she acquires by her trade, business, labor or services, carried on or performed on her sole or separate account; that which a woman married in this state owns at the time of her marriage, and the rents, issues and proceeds of all such property, shall, notwithstanding her marriage, be and remain her sole and separate property, and may be used, collected and invested by her in her own name, and shall not be subject to the interference or control of her husband, or liable for his debts, except such debts as may have been contracted for the support of herself or her children, by her as his agent.

Section 2. A married woman may bargain, sell, assign and transfer her separate personal property, and carry on any trade or business, and perform any labor or services on her sole and separate account, and the earnings of any married woman, from her trade, business, labor or services, shall be her sole and separate property, and may be used or invested by her in her own name.

Section 3. Any married woman possessed of real estate as her separate property, may bargain, sell and convey such property, and enter into any contract in reference to the same, but no such conveyance or contract shall be valid without the assent, in writing, of her husband, except as hereinafter provided.

Section 4. In case any married woman possessed of separate real property, as aforesaid, may desire to sell or convey the same, or to make any contract in relation thereto, and shall be unable to procure the assent of her husband, as in the preceding section provided, in consequence of his refusal, absence, insanity, or other disability, such married woman may apply to the county court in the county where she shall at the time reside, for leave to make such sale, conveyance or contract, without the assent of her husband.

Section 5. Such application may be made by petition, verified by her, and setting forth the grounds of such application. If the husband be a resident of the county, and not under disability, from insanity or other cause, a copy of said petition shall be served upon him, with a notice of the time when the same will be presented to the said court, at least ten days before such application. In all other cases the county court to which such application shall be made, shall, in its discretion, determine whether any notice shall be given, and if any, the mode and manner of giving it.

Section 6. If it shall satisfactorily appear to such court, upon such application, that the husband of such applicant has willfully abandoned his said wife, and lives separate and apart from her, or that he is insane, or imprisoned as a convict in any state prison, or that he is an habitual drunkard, or that he is in any way disabled from making a contract, or that he refuses to give his consent, without good cause therefor, then such court shall cause an order to be entered upon its records, authorizing such married woman to sell and convey her real estate, or contract in regard thereto without the assent of her husband, with the same effect as though such conveyance or contract had been made with his assent.

Section 7. Any married woman may, while married, sue and be sued in all matters having relation to her property, which may be her sole and separate property, or which may hereafter come to her by descent, devise, bequest, or the gift of any person except her husband, in the same manner as if she were sole. And any married woman may bring and maintain an action in her own name, for damages, against any person or body corporate, for any injury to her person or character, the same as if she were sole; and the money received upon the settlement of any such action, or recovered upon a judgment, shall be her sole and separate property.

Section 8. No bargain or contract made by any married woman, in respect to her sole and separate property, or any property which may hereafter come to her by descent, devise, bequest or gift of any person except her husband, and no bargain or contract entered into by any married woman in or about the carrying on of any trade or business under the statutes of this state, shall be binding upon her husband, or render him or his property in any way liable therefor.

Section 9. Every married woman is hereby constituted and declared to be the joint guardian of her children, with her husband, with equal powers, rights and duties in regard to them, with the husband.

Section 10. At the decease of husband or wife, leaving no minor child or children, the survivor shall hold, possess and enjoy a life estate in one-third of all the real estate of which the husband or wife died seized.

Section 11. At the decease of the husband or wife intestate, leaving minor child or children, the survivor shall hold, possess and enjoy all the real estate of which the husband or wife died seized, and all the rents, issues and profits thereof during the minority of the youngest child, and one-third thereof during his or her natural life.

Source:

New York Statutes at Large, 71st Sess., 1848, pp. 307–308; *New York Statutes at Large*, 83rd Sess., Ch. 90, 1860, pp. 157–159.

Sojourner Truth, "A'n't I a Woman?", 1851

Surprise speech given by freed slave Sojourner Truth in 1850 at the second American Women's Rights Convention in Akron, Ohio. Both men and women attended this conference, including women's rights activists Maria Giddings, Emily Robbinson, and Frances D. Gage (whose comments are included in the excerpt below). Speeches were given on the rights of women under the law, and 15 resolutions were eventually adopted. Truth came up to the stand after several clergymen in attendance, who were strongly opposed to women's rights, began to stage attacks against the resolutions already accepted. Some of these arguments claimed "superior rights and privileges for man," on the grounds of "superior intellect" and "the manhood of Christ." Truth gave a poised and eloquent speech, swaying the majority of the crowd to her favor. During the speech, she even showed her muscles from the work she endured as a slave and made a strong argument against each rebuttal she received from the audience.

———————————— ⚬≫⚬ ————————————

"Wall, chilern, whar dar is so much racket dar must be somethin' out o' kilter. I tink dat 'twixt de niggers of de Souf and de womin at de Nork, all talkin' 'bout rights, de white men will be in a fix pretty soon. But what's all dis here talkin' 'bout?"

"Dat man ober dar say dat womin needs to be helped into carriages, and lifted ober ditches, and to hab de best place everywhar. Nobody eber helps me into carriages, or ober mud-puddles, or gibs me any best place!" And raising herself to her full height, and her voice to a pitch like rolling thunders, she asked "And a'n't I a woman? Look at me! Look at me! Look at my arm!" and she bared her right arm to the shoulder, showing her tremendous muscular power. "I have ploughed, and planted, and gathered into barns, and no man could head me! And a'n't I a woman? I could work as much and eat as much as a man—when I could get it—and bear de lash a well! And a'n't I a woman? I have borne thirteen chilern, and seen 'em mos' all sold off to slavery, and when I cried out with my mother's grief, none but Jesus heard me! And a'n't I a woman?"

"Den dey talks 'bout dis ting in de head; what dis dey call it?" "Intellect," whispered some one near. "Dat's it, honey. What's dat got to do wid womin's rights or nigger's rights? If my cup won't hold but a pint, and yourn holds a quart, wouldn't ye be mean not to let me have my little half-measure full?" And she pointed her significant finger, and sent a keen glance at the minister who had made the argument. The cheering was long and loud.

"Den dat little man in black dar, he say women can't have as much rights as men, 'cause Christ wan't a woman! Whar did your Christ come from?" Rolling thunder couldn't have stilled that crowd, as did those deep, wonderful tones, as she stood there with outstretched arms and eyes of fire. Raising her voice still louder, she repeated, "Whar did your Christ come from? From God and a woman! Man had nothin' to do wid Him." Oh, what a rebuke that was to that little man.

Turning again to another objector, she took up the defense of Mother Eve. I can not follow her through it all. It was pointed, and witty, and solemn; eliciting at almost every sentence deafening applause; and she ended by asserting: "If de fust woman God ever made was strong enough to turn de world upside down all alone, dese women togedder (and she glanced her eye over the platform) ought to be able to turn it back, and get it right side up again! And now dey is asking to do it, de men better let 'em." Long-continued cheering greeted this. "Bleeged to ye for hearin' on me, and now old Sojourner han't got nothin' more to say."

Source:

James Andrews and David Zarefsky, eds. *American Voices: Significant Speeches in American History, 1640–1945.* New York: Longman, 1989.

Trial of Mrs. Douglass for Teaching Black Children to Read, 1853

The institution of slavery was supported by a series of slave codes enacted throughout the southern states. In Virginia, whites were forbidden from teaching any "Negro" to read. On May 9, 1853, Mrs. Douglass, a Norfolk Sunday School teacher, was arrested for violating the state statute regarding teaching black children to read. Douglass defended herself at the trial. She told the jury that she was not an abolitionist but "deemed it the duty of every southerner . . . to instruct his slaves, that they may know their duties to their masters, and to their common God." Critical of the treatment of slaves, she

asked the court, "Shall we treat our Slaves with less compassion than we do the cattle in our fields?" Douglass concluded that she was not a convicted felon, but "a single sufferer under the operation of one of the most inhuman and unjust laws that ever disgraced the statute book of a civilized community." The court found Douglass guilty, and she received a one-month jail sentence.

———————— ⌘ ————————

The Defense

Mrs. Douglass. I wish, before examining my witnesses, to make a statement to the Court in reference to my daughter's absence. I beg leave to inform your honor, and you, gentlemen of the jury, that my daughter, whose name is joined with mine in this prosecution, is at present in the city of New York, and was there at the time the summons was issued and served upon me: but, if she were in Norfolk at this time, I do not know that you have any business whatever with her. She is under age, and has been brought up in strict obedience to me in all things. I am alone responsible for any act of hers, as well as for my own. I am here to answer to any charge that may be brought against me. I have been notified to present myself this day before this court to answer to the charge of having been engaged in teaching colored children to read and to write, and I am informed that in so doing I have been acting against the peace and dignity of the Commonwealth. This charge, gentlemen, I do not like, but we shall see who it is that destroys our peace and insults our dignity.

Walter Taylor (sworn.) *Mrs. Douglass.* Were you a teacher in the Christ Church Sunday school? A. For the white children I was, and the school was held in the church. Q. Did you never visit the lecture room? A. I had nothing to do with the school that was kept there? Q. Did you never distribute books to the negro children of that school? A. I attended the library of the school for white children. Q. Did you not instruct colored children to read from those books? A. I did not.

John Williams. Am a lawyer and clerk of the Circuit Court. Myself and daughter teach in the Christ Church Sunday school. We do not teach the negro children to read.

William Sharp (sworn.) *Mrs. Douglass.* Were you a teacher in the school for colored children, held in Christ's Church lecture room? A. No, madam. Q. Did you not attend the Sabbath school held there for the instruction of negro children? A. I went there, occasionally, and lectured to them. Q. Did you not distribute books among them? A. The ladies had all to do with that! Q. When you visited that school, did you not instruct them yourself? A. I did not teach them to read and write, I do not know that the law prohibits religious and moral instructions to negroes.

Mrs. Douglass. If you, sir, who are engaged in the practice of the law, did not know it, how could it be expected that I should?

Mr. Sharp. I ask the Court to allow me to explain. Certain negroes appeared to Rev. Mr. Cummings, the Pastor of Christ's Church, for religious instruction and were allowed by him to meet for that purpose in the lecture room of the church. I occasionally visit the school and lecture to them. I found that some of them could read very well, but that when they came to the hard words, I allow them to skip over them.

Mrs. Douglass. Gentlemen of the Jury: I now deem it right and proper that you should know something of Mrs. Douglass, who stands before you charged with violating your laws. I do not plead guilty to this charge, for, in my opinion, to be a violator of any law or laws, the individual must know that they are such, which I did not, and had abundant precedents among those who should have known it, if they were such, for what I did. I am a Southern woman by birth, education and feeling. I have been a slaveholder myself, and I would be again, if I felt so disposed. I am a native of and have always resided in a Southern slave state. The home of my childhood is as dear to me as my life, and I am as deeply interested in the welfare of Virginia, and of the whole united Southern slave states, as I am in the State of South Carolina; yes, and a great deal more so than very many who call themselves men. I am no abolitionist, neither am I a fanatic, and I am by education as strongly opposed as you are to the interference of Northern anti-slavery men with our institutions, although I believe that their principles are based on a religious foundation. I deem it the duty of every Southerner, morally and religiously, to instruct his slaves, that they may know their duties to their masters, and to their common God. Let the masters first do their duty to them, for they are still our slaves and servants, whether bond or free, and can be nothing else in our community. Let us not quarrel with our neighbors, but rather look around us and see what we have ourselves to do that we have left undone so long. I am a strong advocate for the religious and moral instruction of the whole human family. I have always instructed my own slaves, and will continue to do so as long as I remain in a slave state. Still, I am not disposed to violate the laws of any people or place where I may chance to reside. I cannot believe for a moment that this prosecution is a mere matter of dollars and cents, or that there is not one truly good and noble hearted man among you. Oh no; this I cannot and will not believe. Then let it be the welfare of your people and your country that you seek, and I am with you, heart and soul. This is a matter that calls for the consideration of every true and noble heart—the common welfare of our people. So far as my knowledge of human nature extends, the man who is born a coward, nursed in the lap of ignorance, and brought up a coward, naturally dies a coward. The application of this I leave to yourselves.

The children whom I had for instruction were members of Christ's Church Sunday school. My own little servant was handed a primer by one of the teachers of that school, with the instruction that he must study his book, and attend the Sunday school. He was made ready by myself of daughter, and sent every afternoon with his book, to that school. This was done for two years before I interested myself in these children in the form of a regular day-school. I believe it is not expected that ladies will come to the court house to learn the laws, rules, and regulations of a city in which they may happen to reside. In my opinion, whatever the religious portion of the community is engaged in doing, whether in city, town, or country, is generally considered as lawful and proper. We took care of those children, visited them when sick, and ministered to their wants, and it was a pleasure for us to do so. Was there anything wrong in this?

Let us look into the situation of our colored population in the city of Norfolk, for they are not dumb brutes. If they were, they would be more carefully considered, and their welfare better provided for. For instance, two or three of these people are not allowed to assemble together by themselves, whether in sickness or in health. There is no provision made for them, whatever the circumstances may be, and such meetings are pronounced unlawful and treasonable. Think you, gentlemen, that there is not misery and distress among these people? Yes, indeed, misery enough, and frequently starvation. Even those that are called free are heavily taxed, and their privileges greatly limited; and when they are sick, or in want, on whom does the duty devolve to seek them out and administer to their necessities? Does it fall upon you, gentlemen? Oh no, it is not expected that gentlemen will take the trouble to seek out a negro hut for the purpose of alleviating the wretchedness he may find within it. Why then persecute your benevolent ladies for doing that which you yourselves have so long neglected? Shall we treat our slaves with less compassion than we do the cattle in our fields?

In my opinion, we have nothing to fear from the true blooded negro. It is the half-breed, or those with more or less white blood in their veins, whom I have always found presumptive, treacherous and revengeful. And do you blame them for this? How can you? Ask yourselves the cause. Ask how that white blood got beneath those tawny skins, and let nature herself account for the exhibition of these instincts. Blame the authors of this devilish mischief, but not the innocent victims of it.

As for myself, I shall keep on with my good work; not, however, by continuing to violate what I now know to be your laws, but by endeavoring to teach the colored race humility and a prayerful spirit; how to bear their sufferings as our Savior bore his for us all. I will teach them their duty to their superiors, how to live, and how to die. And now, if ignorance of your peculiar laws is not a sufficient excuse for my violation of the letter of them, surely my good intentions, and the abundant examples set before me by your most worthy and pious citizens, ought to convince you that I was actuated by no improper motives, and had no ulterior designs against the peace and dignity of your Commonwealth. But, if otherwise, there are your laws: enforce them to the letter. You may send me, if you so decide, to that cold and gloomy prison. I can be as happy there as I am in my quiet little home; and, in the pursuit of knowl-edge, and with the resources of a well-stored mind, I shall be, gentlemen, a sufficient companion for myself. Of one consolation you cannot deprive me: I go not as a convicted felon, for I have violated no tittle of any one of the laws that are embodied in the Divine Decalogue; I shall be only a single sufferer under the operation of one of the most inhuman and unjust laws that ever disgraced the statute book of a civilized community.

Source:

John Lawson, ed. *American State Trials*. Vol. 7. Buffalo, N.Y.: W.S. Hein, 2000, pp. 45–60.

Religion and Education

Chief Sagoyewatha, "On the White Man's and Red Man's Religion," 1805

Speech given by the Seneca chief known as Sagoyewatha (Red Jacket) in the summer of 1805. The speech was given at a council of chiefs of the Iroquois Confederacy, in response to an American missionary's attempt to convert the Native Americans to the "white man's religion." Sagoyewatha explained that the Native Americans' trust in whites had already eroded because the colonists took away their land and introduced them to strong liquor. He begged the missionary to give them the freedom to practice their own religion and challenged him to convert them through example, rather than just faith.

Friend and Brother:—It was the will of the Great Spirit that we should meet together this day. He orders all things and has given us a fine day for our council. He has taken His garment from before the sun and caused it to shine with brightness upon us. Our eyes are opened that we see clearly; our ears are unstopped that we have been able to hear distinctly the words you have spoken. For all these favors we thank the Great Spirit, and Him only.

Brother, this council fire was kindled by you, It was at your request that we came together at this time. We have listened with attention to what you have said. You requested us to speak our minds freely. This gives us great joy; for we now consider that we stand upright before you and can speak what we think. All have heard your voice and all speak to you now as one man. Our minds are agreed.

Brother, you say you want an answer to your talk before you leave this place. It is right you should have one, as you are a great distance from home and we do not wish to detain you. But first we will look back a little and tell you what our fathers have told us and what we have heard from the white people.

Brother, listen to what we say. There was a time when our forefathers owned this great island. Their seats extended from the rising to the setting sun. The Great Spirit had made it for the use of Indians. He had created the buffalo, the deer, and other animals for food. He had made the bear and the beaver. Their skins served us for clothing. He had scattered them over the country and taught us how to produce corn for bread. All this He had done for His red children because He loved them. If we had some disputes about our hunting-ground they were generally settled without the shedding of much blood.

But an evil day came upon us. Your forefathers crossed the great water and landed on this island. Their numbers were small. They found friends and not enemies. They told us they had fled from their own country for fear of wicked men and had come here to enjoy their religion. They asked us for a small seat. We took pity on them, granted their request, and they sat down among us. We gave them corn and meat; they gave us poison in return.

The white people, brother, had now found our country. Tidings were carried back and more came among us.

Yet we did not fear them. We took them to be friends. They called us brothers. We believed them and gave them a larger seat. At length their numbers had greatly increased. They wanted more land; they wanted our country. Our eyes were opened and our minds became uneasy. Wars took place. Indians were hired to fight against Indians, and many of our people were destroyed. They also brought strong liquor among us. It was strong and powerful, and has slain thousands.

Brother, our seats were once large and yours were small. You have now become a great people, and we have scarcely a place left to spread our blankets. You have got our country, but are not satisfied; you want to force your religion upon us.

Brother, continue to listen. You say that you are sent to instruct us how to worship the Great Spirit agreeably to His mind; and, if we do not take hold of the religion which you white people teach we shall be unhappy hereafter. You say that you are right and we are lost. How do you know this to be true? We understand that your religion is written in a Book. If it was intended for us, as well as you, why has not the Great Spirit given to us, and not only to us, but why did He not give to our forefathers the knowledge of that Book, with the means of understanding it rightly. We only know what you tell us about it. How shall we know when to believe, being so often deceived by the white people?

Brother, you say there is but one way to worship and serve the Great Spirit. If there is but one religion, why do you white people differ so much about it? Why not all agreed, as you can all read the Book?

Brother, we do not understand these things. We are told that your religion was given to your forefathers and has been handed down from father to son. We also have a religion which was given to our forefathers and has been handed down to us, their children. We worship in that way. It teaches us to be thankful for all the favors we receive, to love each other, and to be united. We never quarrel about religion.

Brother, the Great Spirit has made us all, but He has made a great difference between His white and His red children. He has given us different complexions and different customs. To you He has given the arts. To these He has not opened our eyes. We know these things to be true. Since He has made so great a difference between us in other things, why may we not conclude that He has given us a different religion according to our understanding? The Great Spirit does right. He knows what is best for His children; we are satisfied.

Brother, we do not wish to destroy your religion or take it from you. We only want to enjoy our own.

Brother, you say you have not come to get our land or our money, but to enlighten our minds. I will now tell you that I have been at your meetings and saw you collect money from the meeting. I can not tell what this money was intended for, but suppose that it was for your minister; and, if we should conform to your way of thinking, perhaps you may want some from us.

Brother, we are told that you have been preaching to the white people in this place. These people are our neighbors. We are acquainted with them. We will wait a little while and see what effect your preaching has upon them. If we find it does them good, make them honest, and less disposed to cheat Indians, we will then consider again of what you have said.

Brother, you have now heard our answer to your talk, and this is all we have to say at present. As we are going to part, we will come and take you by the hand, and hope the Great Spirit will protect you on your journey and return you safe to your friends.

Source:

James Andrews and David Zarefsky, eds. *American Voices: Significant Speeches in American History, 1640–1945.* New York: Longman, 1989.

Massachusetts High School Law, 1827

Legislation passed by the Massachusetts legislature in 1827. This law provided the mandatory establishment of high schools throughout the state and was the first such statute enacted in the United States. Although the 1827 law was educationally progressive, Boston maintained by law a segregated school system. (Massachusetts had long outlawed slavery.) It was upheld in *Roberts v City of Boston*). It never got beyond the Massachusetts Supreme Judicial Court and was cited in the 1896 *Plessy v. Ferguson* "separate but equal" decision. However, in 1855, Massachusetts became the first state to abolish segregated education.

An Act

To provide for the Instruction of Youth.

Sec. 1. Be *it enacted by the Senate and House of Representatives in General Court assembled, and by the authority of the same,* That each town or district within this Commonwealth, containing fifty families, or house holders, shall be provided with a teacher or teachers, of good morals, to instruct children in orthography, reading, writing, English grammar, geography, arithmetic, and good behaviour, for such term of time as shall be equivalent to six months for one school in each year: and every town or district, containing one hundred families or house holders, shall be provided with such teacher or teachers, for such term of time as shall be equivalent to twelve months, for one school in each year: and every town or district, containing one hundred and fifty families or house holders, shall be provided with such teacher or teachers, as shall be equivalent to eighteen months, for one school in each year. And every city, town, or district, containing five hundred families, or house holders, shall be provided with such teacher or teachers, for such term of time as shall be equivalent to twenty-four months, for one school in a year, and shall also be provided with a master of good morals, competent to instruct, in addition to the branches of learning aforesaid, the history of the United States, book-keeping by single entry, geometry, surveying, and algebra; and shall employ such master to instruct a school, in such city, town, or district, for the benefit of all the inhabitants thereof, at least ten months in each year, exclusive of vacations, in such convenient place, or alternately at such places in such city, town, or district, as the said inhabitants, at their meeting in March, or April, annually, shall determine; and in every city, or town, containing four thousand inhabitants, such master shall be competent to instruct, in addition to all the foregoing branches, the Latin and Greek languages, history, rhetoric, and logic.

Sec. 2. *Be it further enacted,* That the several towns and districts in this Commonwealth, be, and they hereby are authorized and empowered, in town meetings to be called for that purpose, to determine and define the limits of school districts, within their towns and districts, respectively: *Provided,* that nothing contained in this act, shall be so construed, as to prevent any town from carrying into effect the provisions of this act, in their corporate capacity, and not in school districts, if said town shall so determine.

Sec. 3. *Be it further enacted,* That it shall be, and it hereby is, made the duty of the President, Professors, and Tutors, of the University and Cambridge, and of the several Colleges in this Commonwealth, Preceptors and Teachers of Academies, and all other Instructors of Youth, to take diligent care, and to exert their best endeavours to impress on the minds of children, and youth, committed to their care and instruction, the principles of piety, justice, and sacred regard to truth, love to their country, humanity, and universal benevolence, sobriety, industry, and frugality, chastity, moderation, and temperance, and those other virtues, which are the ornament of human society, and the basis upon which the Republicans Constitution is founded. And it shall be the duty of such Instructors, to endeavor to lead those under their care, as their ages and capacities will admit, into a particular understanding of the tendency of the above mentioned virtues, to preserve and perfect a Republican Constitution, and to secure the blessings of Liberty, as well as to promote their future happiness, and the tendency of the opposite vices to slavery and ruin. And it shall be the duty of the resident Ministers of the Gospel, the Selectmen, and School Committees, in the several towns in this Commonwealth, to exercise their influence, and use their best endeavours, that the youth of their respective towns, and districts, do regularly attend the Schools established and supported as aforesaid for their instruction.

Sec. 4. *Be it further enacted,* That the several towns in this Commonwealth are hereby authorized, empowered and directed, at their annual meetings for the choice of town officers, or at any regular meeting called for that purpose, to vote and raise such sums of money for the support of the schools as aforesaid, as they shall judge necessary for that purpose, which sums, so voted to be raised, shall be assessed and collected in like manner as other town taxes are by law assessed and collected.

Sec. 5. *Be it further enacted,* That each town in this Commonwealth shall, at the annual meeting thereof, for the choice of town officers, choose by written or printed ballots a School Committee, consisting of three, five, or seven persons, who shall have the general charge and superintendence of all the public schools in said town, which are supported at the expense thereof: *Provided,* that any town, containing four thousand inhabitants, and upwards, may choose an additional number, not exceeding five; and it shall be the duty of said committee to require full and satisfactory evidence of the good moral character of all instructors, who may be employed in the several schools in said town, and to satisfy themselves, by personal examination or otherwise, of their literary qualifications and capacity for the government of schools; and no instructor shall be entitled to receive any compensation for his or her service in the instruction of any of the schools aforesaid, without first obtaining from said committee a certificate of his or her qualifications as aforesaid; and it shall furthermore be the duty of said committee to determine the number and qualifications of the scholars, to be admitted into the school kept for the use of the whole town as aforesaid; to visit such school, at least quarter yearly, for the purpose of making a careful examination thereof, and of seeing that the scholars are properly supplied with books; and they shall, at such examination, enquire into the regulation and discipline of such schools, and the habits and proficiency of the scholars therein; and said committee, or some one or more of them, shall visit each of the district schools in said town, for the purposes aforesaid, on some day during the first or second week of the commencement thereof, and also on some day during the two last weeks of the same; and also all the schools kept by said town, once a month for the purpose aforementioned, without giving previous notice thereof to the instructors.

Sec. 6. *Be it further enacted,* That each town in this Commonwealth, which is or may be divided into school districts, at their annual meeting aforesaid, shall, in addition to the committee aforesaid, choose a committee for each school district in said town, consisting of one person, who shall be a resident in the district for which he shall be chosen and be called the prudential committee thereof, whose duty it shall be to keep the school house of such district in good order, at the expense of such district; and in case there be no school house, to provide a suitable place for the school of the district, at the expense thereof; to provide fuel, and all things necessary for the comfort of the scholars therein; to select and contract with a school teacher for his own district, and to give such information and assistance to the said school committee, as may be necessary to aid them in the discharge of the duties required of them by this act: *Provided,* That in any town in the Commonwealth, which shall so determine, the members of said prudential committee may be chosen in the several school districts to which they respectively belong, in such manner as said district may decide.

Sec. 7. *Be it further enacted,* That the school committee of each town, shall direct and determine the class books to be used in the respective classes, in all the several schools kept by said town; and the scholars sent to such schools shall be supplied by their parents, masters or guardians, with the books prescribed for their classes; and the school committee of each town shall procure, at the expense of the town, and to be paid for out of the town treasury, a sufficient supply of such class books for all the schools aforesaid, and give notice of the place or places, where such books may be obtained; and such books shall be supplied to such scholars at such prices as merely to reimburse to the town the expense of the same; and in case any scholars shall not have been furnished by their parent, master or guardian, with the requisite books, all such scholars shall be supplied therewith by the school committee, at the expense of the town; and the school committee shall give notice, in writing, to the assessors of the town, of the names of the scholars so supplied by them with books, of the books so furnished, the prices of the same, and the names of the parents, masters or guardian, who ought to have supplied the same; and said assessors shall add the amount of the books, so supplied, to the next annual tax of the parents, masters or guardians, who ought to have supplied the same; and the amount so added shall be levied, collected, and paid into the town treasury, in the same manner as the public taxes: *Provided, however,* that in case such assessors shall be of opinion, that any of such parents, masters or guardians are not able, and cannot afford to pay the whole expense of the books so supplied on their account respectively, such parents, masters or guardians, shall be exonerated from the payment of the whole or part of such expense, and the said assessors shall omit to add the amount of such books, or shall add only a part thereof to the annual tax of such parent, master or guardian, according to the proportion of such expense, which such

parent, master or guardian shall in their opinion be able and can afford to pay: *Provided, nevertheless,* that in cases where children are already supplied with books, which shall not be considered by the committee as being extremely faulty, in comparison with others, which might be obtained and which may be possessed in such numbers as to admit of the proper and convenient classification of the school, then, and in that case, the committee shall not direct the purchase of new books, without first obtaining the consent of the parents, masters or guardians of a majority of the children, so already provided for, under the term of two years from the passing of this act, unless such books become so worn, as to be unfit for use: *Provided, also,* that said committee shall never direct any school books to be purchased or used, in any of the schools under their superintendence, which are calculated to favour any particular religious sect or tenet,

Sec. 8. *Be it further enacted,* That the school committee, in the City of Boston, and in the several towns in this Commonwealth, be, and they hereby are required to make and return a report to the Secretary of the Commonwealth, on or before the first Monday of June, in the year of our Lord one thousand eight hundred and twenty-eight, and on the first Monday of June of every year thereafter, the amount of money paid by such city or town during the year ending on the first day of May preceding the time of making said report, for the instruction of the schools kept by said city or town; the number of school districts into which said city or towns is divided; the aggregate number of months, that the several schools were kept by such city or town in said year, and what portion thereof was kept by male, and what by female teachers; the whole number of pupils, who have attended any of the schools kept by such city or town during said year; the number of academies and private schools; the number of pupils in the academies and private schools, who have not attended any school kept by such city or town during said year; the estimated amount of the compensation paid to the instructors of academies and private schools during said year; and whether there are any, and what number of persons, over fourteen and under twenty-one years of age, who are unable to read and write.

Sec. 9. *Be it further enacted,* That it shall be the duty of the Secretary of the Commonwealth, in the year of our Lord one thousand eight hundred and twenty-eight, and every year thereafter, to furnish to each city and town a blank form of return, in manner following, viz:—

Sec. 10. *Be it further enacted,* That the inhabitants of the several school districts, within any town, which hath already, or which shall hereafter define the limits of such districts, qualified to vote in town affairs, be, and they hereby are empowered, at any meeting called in the manner hereinafter provided, to raise money for erecting or repairing a school house in their respective districts, or to purchase, or hire, any house or building, to be used as a school house, and also to purchase land for a school house to stand upon, and for the accommodation of the same: to determine in what part of said district such school house shall stand; to choose a committee to superintended the building, repairing, or purchasing of such school house; to choose a clerk, who shall be sworn faithfully to discharge the duties of his office, and whose duty it shall be make a fair record of all votes passed at any meeting of said district, and to certify the same when required, and shall hold such office until another person shall be chosen and sworn in his room; also to raise money at any such meeting, to procure necessary utensils for their respective school houses, to be certified as aforesaid, and assessed in manner as is hereinafter provided: *Provided however,* that any town may carry into effect the provisions of this section, in their corporate capacity, and at the expense of the town, and may at any legal meeting raise and assess taxes, and adopt all necessary and proper measures for providing school houses and sites thereof, for the several school districts in such town.

Sec. 11. *Be it further enacted,* That for the purposes aforesaid, every person shall be taxed in the district in which he lives for all the estate he holds in the town, being under his own actual improvement, and all other of his real estate, in the same town, shall be taxed in the district in which it is included; and lands where the owner thereof lives without the town, shall be taxed in such district as the assessors, having regard to the local situation thereof, shall appoint; and it shall be the duty of the assessors, before they assess a tax for any district, to determine in which district such lands respectively shall be taxed, and to certify in writing their determination to the clerk of the town, who shall record the same; and such land, while owned by any person residing without the limits of the town, shall be taxed in such districts, until the town shall be districted anew: *Provided, however,* that all the lands within any town owned by the same person not living therein, shall be taxed in one and the same district; and the assessors shall assess, in the same manner as town taxes are assessed, on the polls and estates of the inhabitants comprising any school districts defined as aforesaid, and on lands in said town belonging to persons living out of the same, which the assessors shall have directed to be taxed in such district, all monies voted to be raised by the inhabitants of such district for the purposes aforesaid, in thirty days after the clerk of the district shall certify to said assessors the sum voted by the district to be raised as aforesaid; and it shall be the duty of said assessors to make a warrant in due form of law, directed to one of the collectors of the town to which such district belongs, requiring and empowering said collector to levy and collect the tax so assessed, and to

pay the same within a time to be limited in said warrant, to the treasurer of the town, to whom a certificate of the assessment shall be made by the assessors; and the money so collected and paid, shall be at the disposal of the committee of the district, to be by them applied to the building or repairing of a school house, or to the purchase of a house or building, to be used as a school house, or to the purchase of land for the site of a school house, as herein provided for, in the district to which such committee shall belong; and such collector, in collecting such tax, shall have the same powers, and be holden to proceed in the same manner, as is by law provided in collecting town taxes.

Sec. 12. *Be it further enacted,* That the treasurer of any town, to whom a certificate of the assessment of a district tax shall be transmitted as aforesaid, shall have the same authority to enforce the collection and payment of the money so assessed and certified, as if the same had been voted to be raised by the town, for the town's use; and the treasurer and collector shall be paid the same commissions on the money collected and paid for the use of a school district aforesaid; and the assessors for assessing said tax shall be allowed by the district the same sum for each and every day while employed in assessing the same, as is allowed and paid by the town for similar purposes.

Sec. 13. *Be it further enacted,* That the assessors of the several towns and districts in this Commonwealth, be, and they are hereby vested with the same powers to remit sums of money assessed on the inhabitants of every school district, for the purpose of purchasing, building, hiring, repairing, or furnishing school houses, as they have to remit any sums of money assessed on the inhabitants of any town or district, for defraying town or district expenses.

Sec. 14. *Be it further enacted,* That it shall be the duty of the selectmen of the several towns, divided into school districts as aforesaid, upon application made to them in writing by three or more freeholders resident within any school district in their respective towns, "or if there be not so many freeholders resident in such district, then any three of the inhabitants thereof, who pay taxes," to issue their warrant directed to one of the persons making such application, requiring him to warn the inhabitants of such district qualified to vote in town affairs, to meet at such time and place in the same district, as the selectmen shall in their warrant appoint; and the warning aforesaid shall be by notifying personally every person in the district, qualified to vote in town affairs, or by leaving at his last and usual place of abode a written or printed notification, expressing therein, the time, place, and purpose of the meeting, seven days at least, before the time appointed for holding the same: *Provided, however,* that any school district, at any regular meeting thereof, warned as aforesaid, having an article in the warrant of the selectmen, for that purpose, shall have power to prescribe the mode of warning all future meetings of such district, and the mode so prescribed shall be legal until altered by such district at a subsequent meeting thereof; and any vote to raise money for any of the purposes aforesaid, passed by a majority of the inhabitants of a school district, present at a district meeting, warned and held as aforesaid, shall be obligatory on the inhabitants of said school district, to be assessed, levied, and collected, in the manner herein provided.

Sec. 15. *Be it further enacted,* That if the inhabitants of any school district cannot agree where to erect or place a school house for the accommodation of the same, the selectmen of the town to which such district belongs, upon application made to them by the committee of the district, for building or placing a school house, are hereby authorized and empowered to determine the place, where a school house for the accommodation of the district, shall be placed or erected.

Sec. 16. *Be it further enacted,* That whenever a meeting of the inhabitants of any school district, within this Commonwealth, shall be called for the purpose of raising money as aforesaid, and a majority of the voters present are opposed to the raising of money for any of the purposes contemplated in the warrant for calling such meeting, it shall be lawful for any five or more of the freeholders, who are inhabitants of said school district, or if there be not so many freeholders resident in such district, then any five of the inhabitants thereof, who pay taxes, to make application in writing to the selectmen of the town, in which such school district is situated, requesting them to insert in their warrant for calling the next town meeting, an article requiring the opinion of the town relative to the expediency of raising such monies, as are proposed in the warrant for said district meeting: and if the majority of the voters, present in said town meeting, shall think the raising of any of the sums of money proposed in said warrant, to be necessary and expedient, they shall grant such sum or sums as they shall think necessary for the purposes contemplated, and the same shall be assessed on the polls and estates of the inhabitants of said district, and collected and paid over in the manner herein provided.

Sec. 17. *Be it further enacted,* That each and every school district in this Commonwealth, is hereby made a body corporate, so far as to bring and maintain any action, on any agreement made with any person or persons for the non-performance thereof, or for any damage done to their school houses, or other property, and shall be liable to have any action brought and maintained against them, for the non-performance of any contract made by them; and said corporation shall have power to take, and hold, in fee simple, or otherwise, any estate, real or personal, which has been, or may be given, by any person or per-

sons for the purpose of supporting a school or schools in said district, and to apply the same for the purposes aforesaid; and may prosecute and defend any suit or suits relative to the same; and every member of any school district shall and may be admitted as a competent witness, and his deposition be used, in the same manner as inhabitants of towns, districts, precincts, or parishes, or religious societies, are by law now admitted, and their depositions taken and used.

Sec. 18. *Be it further enacted,* That nothing in this act contained, shall be so construed as to affect the right of any corporation, heretofore, or which may be hereafter established in any city, town, or district, in this Commonwealth, to manage any estate, or funds given or obtained for the purpose of supporting schools therein, or in any wise to affect any such estate or funds, given or obtained, for the purpose aforesaid, but such corporate powers, and such estate and funds, shall be, and remain, as if this act had never passed.

Sec. 19. *Be it further enacted,* That any town in this Commonwealth, which shall refuse or neglect, at their annual meeting, for the choice of town officers, to vote and raise money for the support of schools, as provided for in this act, and to choose a school committee to superintend said schools, or if, said town is divided into school districts, prudential committees in the several districts in said town, for the purposes herein before mentioned, every such town shall forfeit and pay, for refusing or neglecting to vote and raise money as aforesaid, upon conviction thereof, a sum equal to twice the highest sum which such town had ever voted to raise for the support of schools therein; and for refusing or neglecting to choose either of the committees aforesaid, on conviction thereof, a sum, of not more than two hundred dollars, nor less than one hundred dollars, to be recovered by information, or indictment, in the Supreme Judicial Court, or Court of Common Pleas, when holden in and for the county within which such town is situated; and the money so recovered shall be paid into the Treasury of said County, one fourth thereof for the use of said County, and three fourths thereof shall be paid by the said Treasurer to the school committee of such town, if any such committee exist, if not, to the Selectmen of such town, for the support of schools therein; and every such school committee, or board of Selectmen, who shall receive notice from the Treasurer of the County, in which they reside, of any money being holden by him for the purpose aforesaid, shall forthwith receive, apportion, and appropriate the same to the support of schools in such town, in the same way and manner it should have been appropriated, if it had been raised by such town, pursuant to the provisions of this Act.

Sec. 20. *Be it further enacted,* That the Secretary of this Commonwealth be instructed to transmit to the Town

Clerk of each and every town in the Commonwealth, as soon as conveniently may be, a sufficient number of printed copies of this act, to supply each school district with one copy; and it shall be the duty of said Town Clerks to deliver to the Prudential Committee of each district, one copy, for the use and benefit of the district.

Sec. 21. *Be it further enacted,* That an act passed on the twenty-fifth day of June, in the year of our Lord one thousand seven hundred and eighty-nine, entitled "An Act to provide for the Instruction of Youth, and for the promotion of good education"—also an Act passed on the twenty-eighth day of February, in the year of our Lord one thousand eight hundred, entitled, "an act in addition to an act, entitled, an act to provide for the Instruction of Youth, and for the promotion of good education"—also an act passed on the twenty-third day of June, in the year of our Lord one thousand eight hundred and two, entitled "an act in addition to an act passed in the year of our Lord one thousand eight hundred, entitled, an act in addition to an act, to provide for the Instruction of Youth, and for the promotion of good education"—and also an act passed on the twenty-first day of June, in the year of our Lord one thousand eight hundred and eleven, entitled, "an act in addition to the several acts respecting School Districts"—also an act passed on the twenty-eighth day of February, in the year of our Lord one thousand eight hundred and fifteen, entitled, "an act in addition to the several acts regulating the building and repairing of school houses"—also an act passed on the thirteenth day of June, in the year of our Lord one thousand eight hundred and seventeen, entitled, "an act in addition to the several laws now in force respecting school districts"—also an act, passed on the twenty-second day of February, in the year of our Lord one thousand eight hundred and twenty-two, entitled, "an act making members of school districts competent witnesses in certain cases"—also an act passed on the eighteenth day of February, in the year of our Lord one thousand eight hundred and twenty four, entitled, "an act to alter and amend an act, entitled, an act to provide for the instruction of Youth, and for the promotion of good education"—also an act passed on the fourth day of March, in the year of our Lord one thousand eight hundred and twenty-six, entitled, "an act further to provide for the instruction of youth," severally be, and they hereby are repealed: *Provided however,* That the several acts aforesaid shall continue and be in force, so far as they or either of them may relate to any suit or suits, or any thing done, in virtue of said acts or either of them.

Source:
Facts On File, Inc. *Landmark Documents in American History.*

Charles Grandison Finney, "A Revival of Religion," 1834

Charles Grandison Finney was considered one of the greatest preachers during the Second Great Awakening, which occurred especially along the American frontier during the 1830s. It was characterized by huge camp meetings that attracted thousands. This Great Awakening not only resulted in converts to traditional and new religious sects like the Latter Day Saints (Mormons) and the short-lived millenialist Millerites but also stimulated a reform movement that lasted to the Civil War.

This sermon was one of Finney's Friday night lectures that was reprinted in the Reverend Joshua Leavitt's *New York Evangelist.* The issues containing the lectures proved so popular that they were reprinted in a book in 1835. Some 12,000 copies of the first edition were sold within three months of publication.

✳   ✳   ✳

A "Revival of Religion" presupposes a declension. Almost all the religion in the world has been produced by revivals. God has found it necessary to take advantage of the excitability there is in mankind, to produce powerful excitements among them, before he can lead them to obey. Men are so sluggish, there are so many things to lead their minds off from religion, and to oppose the influence of the gospel that it is necessary to raise an excitement among them, till the tide rises so high as to sweep away the opposing obstacles. They must be so excited that they will break over these counteracting influences, before they will obey God.

✳   ✳   ✳

There is so little *principle* in the church, so little firmness and stability of purpose, that unless they are greatly excited, they will not obey God. They have so little knowledge, and their principles are so weak, that unless they are excited, they will go back from the path of duty, and do nothing to promote the glory of God. The state of the world is still such, and probably will be till the millennium is fully come, that religion must be mainly promoted by these excitements. . . . As the millennium advances, it is probable that these periodical excitements will be unknown. Then the church will be enlightened, and the counteracting causes removed, and the entire church will be in a state of habitual and steady obedience to God. The entire church will stand and take the infant mind, and cultivate it for God. Children will be trained up in the way they should go, and there will be no such torrents of worldliness, and fashion, and covetousness, to bear away the piety of the church, as soon as the excitement of a revival is withdrawn.

* * *

II. I am to show what a revival is

It presupposes that the church is sunk down in a backslidden state, and a revival consists in the return of the church from her backslidings, and in the conversion of sinners.

1. A revival always includes conviction of sin on the part of the church. Backslidden professors cannot wake up and begin right away in the service of God, without deep searchings of heart.

The fountains of sin need to be broken up. In a true revival, Christians are always brought under such convictions; they see their sins in such a light, that often they find it impossible to maintain a hope of their acceptance with God. It does not always go to that extent; but there are always, in a genuine revival, deep convictions of sin, and often cases of abandoning all hope.

2. Backslidden Christians will be brought to repentance. A revival is nothing else than a new beginning of obedience to God. Just as in the case of a converted sinner, the first step is a deep repentance, a breaking down of heart, a getting down into the dust before God, with deep humility, and forsaking of sin.

3. Christians will have their faith renewed . . . when they enter into a revival, they no longer see men as trees walking, but they see things in that strong light which will renew the love of God in their hearts. This will lead them to labor zealously to bring others to him. They will feel grieved that others do not love God, when they love him so much. And they will set themselves feelingly to persuade their neighbors to give him their hearts. So their love to men will be renewed. . . . They will be in agony for individuals whom they want to have saved; their friends, relations, enemies. They will not only be urging them to give their hearts to God, but they will carry them to God in the arms of faith, and with strong crying and tears beseech God to have mercy on them, and save their souls from endless burnings.

* * *

5. When the churches are thus awakened and reformed, the reformation and salvation of sinners will follow, going through the same stages of conviction, repentance, and reformation. Their hearts will be broken down and changed. Very often the most abandoned profligates are among the subjects. Harlots, and drunkards, and infidels, and all sorts of abandoned characters, are awakened and converted. The worst part of human society are softened and reclaimed, and made to appear as lovely specimens of the beauty of holiness.

* * *

Remarks

1. . . . For a long time, it was supposed by the church, that a revival was a miracle, an interposition of Divine power which they had nothing to do with, and which they had no more agency in producing, than they had in producing thunder, or a storm of hail, or an earthquake. It is only within a few years that ministers generally have supposed revivals were to be promoted, by the use of means designed and adapted specially to that object. Even in New England, it has been supposed that revivals came just as showers do, sometimes in one town, and sometimes in another, and that ministers and churches could do nothing more to produce them, than they could to make showers of rain come on their own town, when they are falling on a neighboring town.

* * *

. . . 3. You see the error of those who are beginning to think that religion can be better promoted in the world without revivals, and who are disposed to give up all efforts to produce religious excitements. Because there are evils arising in some instances out of great excitements on the subject of religion, they are of opinion that it is best to dispense with them altogether. This cannot, and must not be. True, there is danger of abuses. In cases of great *religious* as well as all other excitements, more or less incidental evils may be expected of course. But this is no reason why they should be given up. The best things are always liable to abuses. Great and manifold evils have originated in the providential and moral governments of God. But these *foreseen* perversions and evils were not considered a sufficient reason for giving them up. For the establishment of these governments was on the whole the best that could be done for the production of the greatest amount of happiness. So in revivals of religion, it is found by experience, that in the present state of the world, religion cannot be promoted to any considerable extent without them. The evils which are sometimes complained of, when they are real, are incidental, and of small importance when compared with the amount of good produced by revivals. The sentiment should not be admitted by the church for a moment, that revivals may be given up. It is fraught with all that is dangerous to the interests of Zion, is death to the cause of missions, and brings in its train the damnation of the world.

FINALLY — I have a proposal to make to you who are here present. I have not commenced this course of Lectures on Revivals to get up a curious theory of my own on the subject. I would not spend my time and strength merely to give you instructions, to gratify your curiosity, and furnish you something to talk about. I have no idea of preaching *about* revivals. It is not my design to preach so as to have you able to say at the close, "We *understand* all about revivals now," while you do *nothing*. But I wish to ask you a question. What do you hear lectures on revivals for? Do you mean that whenever you are convinced what your duty is in promoting a revival, you will go to work and practice it?

Will you follow the instructions I shall give you from the word of God, and put them in practice in your own hearts? Will you bring them to bear upon your families, your acquaintances, neighbors, and through the city? Or will you spend the winter in learning *about* revivals, and do nothing *for* them? I want you, as fast as you learn any thing on the subject of revivals, to put it in practice, and go to work and see if you cannot promote a revival among sinners here. If you will not do this, I wish you to let me know at the beginning, so that I need not waste my strength. You ought to decide *now* whether you will do this or not. You know that we call sinners to decide on the spot whether *they* will obey the gospel. And we have no more authority to let you take time to deliberate whether *you* will obey God, than we have to let sinners do so.

We call on you to unite now in a solemn pledge to God, that you will do your duty as fast as you learn what it is, and to pray that He will pour out his Spirit upon this church and upon all the city this winter.

Source:

"What a Revival of Religion Is." American Studies at the University of Virginia. Available on-line. URL: xroads.virginia.edu/~HYPER/DETOC/religion/finney1.html. Accessed October 2003.

Dorothea Dix, Memorial to the Legislature of Massachusetts, 1843

Report on the facilities for the retarded and mentally ill in Massachusetts, written by humanitarian Dorothea Dix and delivered to the state's legislature in January 1843. The result of two years of investigation, the account documented serious abuse and neglect of "the miserable, the desolate, the outcast" in state prisons, almshouses, hospitals, and insane asylums. Dix reported that the mentally ill were often confined—sometimes chained, unwashed, and naked—in cages, closets, and cellars, and beaten or lashed to compel obedience. Few efforts were made to treat even those illnesses deemed remediable. The report and Dix's efforts led to reform in Massachusetts and throughout the United States.

———————————— ⌒⟊⌒ ————————————

Gentlemen,

I respectfully ask to present this Memorial, believing that the *cause,* which actuates to and sanctions so unusual a movement, presents no equivocal claim to public consid-

eration and sympathy. Surrendering to calm and deep convictions of duty my habitual views of what is womanly and becoming, I proceed briefly to explain what has conducted me before you unsolicited and unsustained, trusting, while I do so, that the memorialist will be speedily forgotten in the memorial.

About two years since leisure afforded opportunity, and duty prompted me to visit several prisons and almshouses in the vicinity of this metropolis. I found, near Boston, in the Jails and Asylums for the poor, a numerous class brought into unsuitable connexion with criminals and the general mass of Paupers. I refer to Idiots and Insane persons, dwelling in circumstances not only adverse to their own physical and moral improvement, but productive of extreme disadvantages to all other persons brought into association with them. I applied myself diligently to trace the causes of these evils, and sought to supply remedies. As one obstacle was surmounted, fresh difficulties appeared. Every new investigation has given depth to the conviction that it is only by decided, prompt, and vigorous legislation the evils to which I refer, and which I shall proceed more fully to illustrate, can be remedied. I shall be obliged to speak with great plainness, and to reveal many things revolting to the taste, and from which my woman's nature shrinks with peculiar sensitiveness. But truth is the highest consideration. *I tell what I have seen* —painful and shocking as the details often are—that from them you may feel more deeply the imperative obligation which lies upon you to prevent the possibility of a repetition or continuance of such outrages upon humanity. If I inflict pain upon you, and move you to horror, it is to acquaint you with sufferings which you have the power to alleviate, and make you hasten to the relief of the victims of legalized barbarity.

I come to present the strong claims of suffering humanity. I come to place before the Legislature of Massachusetts the condition of the miserable, the desolate, the outcast. I come as the advocate of helpless, forgotten, insane and idiotic men and women; of beings, sunk to a condition from which the most unconcerned would start with real horror; of beings wretched in our Prisons, and more wretched in our Alms-Houses. And I cannot suppose it needful to employ earnest persuasion, or stubborn argument, in order to arrest and fix attention upon a subject, only the more strongly pressing in its claims, because it is revolting and disgusting in its details.

I must confine myself to few examples, but am ready to furnish other and more complete details, if required. If my pictures are displeasing, coarse, and severe, my subjects, it must be recollected, offer no tranquil, refined, or composing features. The condition of human beings, reduced to the extremest states of degradation and misery, cannot be exhibited in softened language, or adorn a polished page.

I proceed, Gentlemen, briefly to call your attention to the *present* state of Insane Persons confined within its Commonwealth, in *cages, closets, cellars, stalls, pens! Chained, naked, beaten with rods,* and *lashed* into obedience!

As I state cold, severe *facts,* I feel obliged to refer to persons, and definitely to indicate localities. But it is upon my subject, not upon localities or individuals, I desire to fix attention; and I would speak as kindly as possible of all Wardens, Keepers, and other responsible officers, believing that *most* of these have erred not through hardness of heart and wilful cruelty, so much as want of skill and knowledge, and want of consideration. Familiarity with suffering, it is said, blunts the sensibilities, and where neglect once finds a footing other injuries are multiplied. This is not all, for it may justly and strongly be added that, from the deficiency of adequate means to meet the wants of these cases, it has been an absolute impossibility to do justice in this matter. Prisons are not constructed in view of being converted into County Hospitals, and Alms-Houses are not founded as receptacles for the Insane. And yet, in the face of justice and common sense, Wardens are by law compelled to receive, and the Masters of Alms-Houses not to refuse, Insane and Idiotic subjects in all stages of mental disease and privation.

It is the Commonwealth, not its integral parts, that is accountable for most of the abuses which have lately, and do still exist. I repeat it, it is defective legislation which perpetuates and multiplies these abuses.

In illustration of my subject, I offer the following extracts from my Note-Book and Journal:—

Springfield. In the jail, on lunatic woman, furiously mad, a state pauper, improperly situated, both in regard to the prisoners, the keepers, and herself. It is a case of extreme self-forgetfulness and oblivion to all the decencies of life; to describe which, would be to repeat only the grossest scenes. She is much worse since leaving Worcester. In the almshouse of the same town is a woman apparently only needing judicious care, and some well-chosen employment, to make it unnecessary to confine her in solitude, in a dreary unfurnished room. Her appeals for employment and companionship are most touching, but the mistress replied, 'she had no time to attend to her.'

Northampton. In the jail, quite lately, was a young man violently mad, who had not, as I was informed at the prison, come under medical care, and not been returned from any hospital. In the almshouse, the cases of insanity are now unmarked by abuse, and afford evidence of judicious care by the keepers.

Williamsburg. The almshouse has several insane, not under suitable treatment. No apparent intentional abuse.

Rutland. Appearance and report of the insane in the almshouse not satisfactory.

Sterling. A terrible case; manageable in a hospital; at present as well controlled perhaps as circumstances in a case so extreme allow. An almshouse, but wholly wrong in relation to the poor crazy woman, to the paupers generally, and to her keepers.

Burlington. A woman, declared to be very insane; decent room and bed; but not allowed to rise oftener, the mistress said, 'than every other day: it is too much trouble.'

Concord. A woman from the hospital in a cage in the almshouse. In the jail several, decently cared for in general, but not properly placed in a prison. Violent, noisy, unmanageable most of the time.

Lincoln. A woman in a cage.

Medford. One idiotic subject chained, and one in a close stall for 17 years.

Pepperell. One often doubly chained, hand and foot; another violent; several peaceable now.

Brookfield. One man caged, comfortable.

Granville. One often closely confined; now losing the use of his limbs from want of exercise.

Charlemont. One man caged.

Savoy. One man caged.

Lenox. Two in the jail; against whose unfit condition there, the jailor protests.

Dedham. The insane disadvantageously placed in the jail. In the almshouse, two females in stalls, situated in the main building; lie in wooden bunks filled with straw; always shut up. One of these subjects is supposed curable. The overseers of the poor have declined giving her a trial at the hospital, as I was informed, on account of expense.

Franklin. One man chained; decent.

Taunton. One woman caged.

Plymouth. One man stall-caged, from Worcester hospital.

Scituate. One man and one woman stall-caged.

West-Bridgewater. Three idiots; never removed from one room.

Barnstable. Four females in pens and stalls; two chained certainly, I think all. Jail, one idiot.

Welfleet. Three insane; one man and one woman chained, the latter in a bad condition.

Brewster. One woman violently mad, solitary: could not see her, the master and mistress being absent, and the paupers in charge having strict orders to admit no one.

Rochester. Seven insane; at present none caged.

Milford. Two insane, not now caged.

Cohasset. One idiot, one insane; most miserable condition.

Plympton. One insane, three idiots; condition wretched.

Besides the above, I have seen many who, part of the year, are chained or caged. The use of cages all but universal; hardly a town but can refer to some not distant period of using them: chains are less common: negligences frequent: wilful abuse less frequent than sufferings proceeding from ignorance, or want of consideration. I encountered during the last three months many poor creatures wandering reckless and unprotected through the country. Innumerable accounts have been sent me of persons who had roved away unwatched and unsearched after; and I have heard that responsible persons, controlling the almshouses, have not thought themselves culpable in sending away from their shelter, to cast upon the chances of remote relief, insane men and women. These, left on the highways, unfriended and incompetent to control or direct their own movements, sometimes have found refuge in the hospital, and others have not been traced. But I cannot particularize; in traversing the state I have found hundreds of insane persons in every variety of circumstance and condition; many whose situation could not and need not be improved; a less number, but that very large, whose lives are the saddest pictures of human suffering and degradation. I give a few illustrations; but description fades before reality.

Danvers. November; visited the almshouse; a large building, much out of repair; understand a new one is in contemplation. Here are from fifty-six to sixty inmates; one idiotic; three insane; one of the latter in close confinement at all times.

Long before reaching the house, wild shouts, snatches of rude songs, imprecations, and obscene language, fell upon the ear, proceeding from the occupant of a low building, rather remote from the principal building to which my course was directed. Found the mistress, and was conducted to the place, which was called '*the home*' of the *forlorn* maniac, a young woman, exhibiting a condition of neglect and misery blotting out the faintest idea of comfort, and outraging every sentiment of decency. She had been, I learnt, "a respectable person; industrious and worthy; disappointments and trials shook her mind, and finally laid prostrate reason and self-control; she became a maniac for life! She had been at Worcester Hospital for a considerable time, and had been returned as incurable." The mistress told me she understood that, while there, she was "comfortable and decent." Alas! what a change was here exhibited! She had passed from one degree of violence and degradation to another, in swift progress; there she stood, clinging to, or beating upon, the bars of her caged apartment, the contracted size of which afforded space only for increasing accumulations of filth, a *foul* spectacle; there she stood with naked arms and dishevelled hair; the unwashed frame invested with fragments of unclean garments, the air so extremely offensive, though ventilation was afforded on all sides save one, that it was not possible to remain beyond a few moments without retreating for recovery to the outward air. Irritation of body, produced by utter filth and exposure, incited her to the horrid process of tearing off her skin by inches; her face, neck, and person, were thus disfigured to hideousness; she held up a fragment just rent off; to my exclamation of horror, the mistress replied, "oh, we can't help it; half the skin is off sometimes; we can do nothing with her; and it makes no difference what she eats, for she consumes her own filth as readily as the food which is brought her."

It is now January; a fortnight since, two visitors reported that most wretched outcast as "wallowing in dirty straw, in a place yet more dirty, and without clothing, without fire. Worse cared for than the brutes, and wholly lost to consciousness of decency!" Is the whole story told? What was seen, is; what is reported is not. These gross exposures are not for the pained sight of one alone; all, all, coarse, brutal men, wondering, neglected children, old and young, each and all, witness this lowest, foulest state of miserable humanity. And who protects her, that worse than Paria outcast, from other wrongs and blacker outrages? I do not *know* that such *have been*. I do know that they are to be dreaded, and that they are not guarded against.

Some may say these things cannot be remedied; these furious maniacs are not to be raised from these base conditions. I *know* they are; could give *many* examples; let *one* suffice. A young woman, a pauper, in a distant town, *Sandisfield*, was for years a raging maniac. A cage, chains, and *the whip*, were the agents for controlling her, united with harsh tones and profane language. Annually, with others (the town's poor) she was put up at auction, and bid off at the lowest price which was declared for her. One year, not long past, an old man came forward in the number of applicants for the poor wretch; he was taunted and ridiculed; "what would he and his old wife do with such a mere beast?" "My wife says yes," replied he, "and I shall take her." She was given to his charge; he conveyed her home; she was washed, neatly dressed, and placed in a decent bed-room, furnished for comfort and opening into the kitchen. How altered her condition! As yet *the chains* where not off. The first week she was somewhat restless, at times violent, but the quick kind ways of the old people wrought a change; she received her food decently; forsook acts of violence, and no longer uttered blasphemous or indecent language; after a week, the chain was lengthened, and she was received as a companion into the kitchen. Soon she engaged in trivial employments. "After a fortnight," said the old man, "I knocked off the chains and made her a free woman." She is at times excited, but not violently; they are careful of her diet; they keep her very clean; she calls them "father" and "mother." Go there now and you will find her "clothed," and though not perfectly in her "right mind," so far restored as to be a safe and comfortable inmate.

Newburyport. Visited the almshouse in June last; eighty inmates; seven insane, one idiotic. Commodious and neat house; several of the partially insane apparently very comfortable; two very improperly situated, namely, an insane man, not considered incurable, in an out-building, whose room opened upon what was called 'the dead room,' affording in lieu of companionship with the living, a contemplation of corpses! The other subject was a woman in a *cellar.* I desired to see her; much reluctance was shown. I pressed the request; the Master of the House stated that she was *in the cellar;* that she was *dangerous to be approached;* that 'she had lately attacked his wife;' and *was often naked.* I persisted; 'if you will not go with me, give me the keys and I will go alone?' Thus importuned, the outer doors were opened. I descended the stairs from within; a strange, unnatural noise seemed to proceed from beneath our feet; at the moment I did not much regard it. My conductor proceeded to remove a padlock, while my eye explored the wide space in quest of the poor woman. All for a moment was still. But judge my horror and amazement, when a door to a closet *beneath* the *staircase* was opened, revealing in the imperfect light a female apparently wasted to a skeleton, partially wrapped in blankets, furnished for the narrow bed on which she was sitting; her countenance furrowed, not by age, but suffering, was the image of distress; in that contracted space, unlighted, unventilated, she poured forth the wailings of despair: mournfully she extended her arms and appealed to me, "why am I consigned to hell? dark—dark—I used to pray, I used to read the Bible—I have done no crime in my heart; I had friends, why have all forsaken me!—my God! my God! why hast *thou* forsaken me!" Those groans, those wailings come up daily, mingling, with how many others, a perpetual and sad memorial. When the good Lord shall require an account of our stewardship, what shall all and each answer!

Perhaps it will be inquired how long, how many days or hours was she imprisoned in these confined limits? *For years!* In another part of the cellar were other small closets, only better, because higher through the entire length, into one of which she by turns was transferred, so as to afford opportunity for fresh whitewashing, &c.

Saugus. December 24; thermometer below zero; drove to the poorhouse; was conducted to the master's family-room by himself; walls garnished with handcuffs and chains, not less than five pair of the former; did not inquire how or on whom applied; thirteen pauper inmates; one insane man; one woman insane; one idiotic man; asked to see them; the two men were shortly led in; appeared pretty decent and comfortable. Requested to see the other insane subject; was denied decidedly; urged the request, and finally secured a reluctant assent. Was led through an outer passage into a lower room, occupied by the paupers; crowded; not neat; ascended a rather low flight of stairs upon an open entry, through the floor of which was introduced a stove pipe, carried along a *few feet,* about six inches above the floor, through which it was reconveyed below. From this entry opens a room of moderate size, having a sashed-window; floor, I think, painted; apartment entirely unfurnished; no chair, table, nor bed; neither, what is seldom missing, a bundle of straw or lock of hay; cold, very cold; the first movement of my conductor was to throw open a window, a measure imperatively necessary for those who entered. *On the floor* sat a woman, her limbs immovably contracted, so that the knees were brought upward to the chin; the face was concealed; the head rested on the folded arms; for clothing she appeared to have been furnished with *fragments* of many discharged garments; these were folded about her, yet they little benefitted her, if one might judge by the constant shuddering which almost convulsed her poor crippled frame. Woful was this scene; language is feeble to record the misery she was suffering and had suffered! In reply to my inquiry if she could not change her position, I was answered by the master in the negative, and told that the contraction of limbs was occasioned by "neglect and exposure in former years," but *since she had been crazy,* and before she fell under the charge, as I inferred, of her present *guardians.* Poor wretch! she, like may others, was an example of what humanity becomes when the temple of reason falls in ruins, leaving the mortal part to injury and neglect, and showing how much can be endured of privation, exposure, and disease, without extinguishing the lamp of life.

Passing out, the man pointed to a something, revealed to more than one sense, which he called "her bed; and we throw some blankets over her at night." Possibly this is done; others, like myself, might be pardoned a doubt, if they could have seen all I saw, and heard abroad all I heard. The *bed,* so called, was about *three* feet long, and from a half to three-quarters of a yard wide; of old ticking or tow cloth was the case; the contents might have been a *full handful* of hay or straw. My attendant's exclamations on my leaving the house were emphatic, and can hardly be repeated.

The above case recalls another of equal neglect or abuse. Asking my way to the almshouse in Berkeley, which had been repeatedly spoken of as greatly neglected, I was answered as to the direction, and informed that there were "plenty of insane people and idiots there." "Well taken care of?" "Oh, well enough for such sort of creatures?" "Any violently insane?" "Yes; my sister's son is there, a real tiger. I kept him here at my house awhile, but it was too much trouble to go on; so I carried him there." "Is he comfortably provided for?" "Well enough." "Has he decent clothes?" "Good enough; wouldn't wear them if he had more." "Food?" "Good enough; good enough for him."

"One more question, has he the comfort of a fire?" "Fire! fire, indeed! what does a crazy man need of fire? red-hot iron wants fire as much as he!" And such are sincerely the ideas of not a few persons in regard to the actual wants of the insane. Less regarded than the lowest brutes! no wonder they sink even lower.

Ipswich. Have visited the prison three several times; visited the almshouse once. In the latter are several cases of insanity; three especially distressing, situated in a miserable out-building, detached from the family-house, and confined in stalls or pens; three individuals, one of which is apparently very insensible to the deplorable circumstances which surround him, and perhaps not likely to comprehend privations or benefits. Not so the person directly opposite to him, who looks up wildly, anxiously by turns, through those strong bars. Cheerless sight! strange companionship for the mind flitting and coming by turns to some perception of persons and things. He too is one of the returned incurables. His history is a sad one; I have not had all the particulars, but it shows distinctly, what the most prosperous and affluent may come to be. I understand his connexions are excellent and respectable; his natural abilities in youth were superior; he removed from Essex county to Albany, and was established there as the editor of a popular newspaper, in course of time he was chosen a senator for that section of the state, and of course was a Judge in the Court of Errors.

Vicissitudes followed, and insanity closed the scene. He was conveyed to Worcester; after a considerable period, either to give place to some new patient, or because the County objected to the continued expense, he being declared incurable, was removed to Salem jail; thence to Ipswich jail; associated with the prisoners there, partaking the same food, and clad in like apparel. After a time the town complained of the expense of keeping him in jail; it was cheaper in the almshouse; to the almshouse he was conveyed, and there perhaps must abide. How sad a fate! I found him in a quiet state; though at times was told that he is greatly excited; what wonder, with such a companion before him; such cruel scenes within! I perceived in him some little confusion as I paused before the stall, against the bars of which he was leaning; he was not so lost to propriety but that a little disorder of the bed-clothes, &c. embarrassed him. I passed on, but he asked, in a moment, earnestly, "Is the lady gone—gone quite away?" I returned; be gazed a moment without answering my inquiry if he wished to see me? "And have you too lost all your dear friends?" Perhaps my mourning apparel excited his inquiry. 'Not all.' "Have you any dear father and mother to love you?" and then he sighed and then laughed and traversed the limited stall. Immediately adjacent to this stall was one occupied by a *simple* girl, who was "put there to be out of harm's way." A cruel lot! for this priva-

tion of a sound mind. A madman on the one hand, not so much separated as to secure decency, another almost opposite, and no screen! I do not know how it is argued, that mad persons and idiots may be dealt with as if no spark of recollection ever lights up the mind; the observation and experience of those, who have had charge of Hospitals, show opposite conclusions.

Violence and severity do but exasperate the Insane: the only availing influence is kindness and firmness. It is amazing what these will produce. How many examples might illustrate this position: I refer to one recently exhibited in Barre. The town Paupers are disposed of annually to some family who, for a stipulated sum agree to take charge of them. One of them, a young woman, was shown to me will clothed, neat, quiet, and employed at needle-work. Is it possible that this is the same being who, but last year, was a raving madwoman, exhibiting every degree of violence in action and speech; a very tigress wrought to fury; caged, chained, beaten, loaded with injuries, and exhibiting the passions which an iron rule might be expected to stimulate and sustain. It is the same person; another family hold her in charge who better understand human nature and human influences; she is no longer chained, caged, and beaten; but if excited, a pair of mittens drawn over the hands secures from mischief. Where will she be next year, after the annual sale?

It is not the insane subject alone who illustrates the power of the all prevailing law of kindness. A poor idiotic young man, a year or two since, used to follow me at times through the prison as I was distributing books and papers: at first he appeared totally stupid, but cheerful expressions, a smile, a trifling gift, seemed gradually to light up the void temple of the intellect, and by slow degrees some faint images of thought passed before the mental vision. He would ask for books, though he could not read. I indulged his fancy and he would appear to experience delight in examining them; and kept them with a singular care. If I read the Bible, he was reverently, wonderingly attentive; if I talked, he listened with a half-conscious aspect. One morning I passed more hurriedly than usual, and did not speak particularly to him. "Me, me, me a book." I returned; "good morning, Jemmy; so you will have a book today? well, keep it carefully." Suddenly turning aside he took the bread brought for his breakfast, and passing it with a hurried earnestness through the bars of his iron door—"Here's bread, a'nt you hungry?" Never may I forget the tone and grateful affectionate aspect of that poor idiot. How much might we do to bring back or restore the mind, if we but knew how to touch the instrument with a skilful hand!

My first visit to Ipswich prison was in March, 1842. The day was cold and stormy. The Turnkey very obligingly conducted me through the various departments. Pausing before the iron door of a room in the jail, he said, "we have here a crazy man, whose case seems hard, for he has sense enough to know he is in a prison, and associated with prisoners. He was a physician in this county, and was educated at Cambridge, I believe; it was there, or at one of the New-England colleges. Should you like to see him?" I objected that it might be unwelcome to the sufferer; but urged, went in. The apartment was very much out of order, neglected, and unclean; there was no fire; it had been forgotten amidst the press of other duties. A man, a prisoner waiting trial, was sitting near a bed where the Insane man lay, rolled in dirty blankets. The Turnkey told him my name, and he broke forth into a most touching appeal, that I would procure his liberation by prompt application to the highest State authorities. I soon retired, but communicated his condition to an official person before leaving the town, in the hope he might be rendered more comfortable. Shortly I received from this Insane person, through my esteemed friend, Dr. Bell, several letters, from which I venture to make a few extracts. They are written from Ipswich where is the general County receptacle for insane persons. I may remark that he has at different times been under skilful treatment, both at Charlestown and Worcester; but being, long since, pronounced incurable, and his property being expended, he became chargeable to the town or county, and was removed, first to Salem jail, thence to that at Ipswich by the desire of the High Sheriff, who requested the Commissioners to remove him to Ipswich as a more retired spot, where he would be less likely to cause disturbance." In his paroxysms of violence, his shouts and turbulence disturb a whole neighborhood. These still occur. I give the extracts literally:—"Respected lady: since your heavenly visit my time has passed in perfect quietude, and for the last week I have been entirely alone; the room has been cleansed and whitewashed, and is now quite decent. I have read your books and papers with pleasure and profit, and retain them subject to your order. You say, in your note, others shall be sent if desired, and if any particular subject has interest it shall be procured. Your kindness is felt and highly appreciated," &c. In another letter he writes, " You express confidence that I have self-control, and self-respect. I have and were I free and in good circumstances, could command as much as any man." In a third he says, "Your kind note, with more books and papers was received on the 8th, and I immediately addressed to you a letter superscribed to Dr. Bell; but having discovered the letters on your seal, I suppose them the initials of your name, and now address you directly," &c. &c.

The original letters may be seen. I have produced these extracts, and stated facts of personal history, in order that a judgment may be formed from few of many examples, as to the justness of incarcerating lunatics in all and every stage of insanity, for an indefinite period, or for life, in dreary prisons, and in connection with every class of criminals who may be lodged successively under the same roof, and in the same apartments. I have shown, from two examples, to what condition men may be brought, not through crime, but misfortune, and that misfortune embracing the heaviest calamity to which human nature is exposed. In the touching language of scripture may these captives cry out—"Have pity upon me! have pity upon me! for the hand of the Lord hath smitten me." "My kinsfolk have failed, and my own familiar friend hath forgotten me."

The last visit to the Ipswich prison was the third week in December. Twenty-two Insane persons and Idiots: general condition gradually improved within the last year. All suffer for want of air and exercise. The Turnkey, while disposed to discharge kindly the duties of his office, is so crowded with business, as to be positively unable to give any but the most general attention to the Insane department. Some of the subjects are invariably confined in small dreary cells, insufficiently warmed and ventilated. Here one sees them traversing the narrow dens with ceaseless rapidity, or dashing from side to side like caged tigers, perfectly furious, through the invariable condition of unalleviated confinement. The case of one *simple* boy is peculiarly hard. December 6, 1841, he was committed to the house of correction, East Cambridge, from Charlestown, as an *Insane* or *Idiotic* boy. He was unoffending, and competent to perform a variety of light labors under direction, and was often allowed a good deal of freedom in the open air. September 6, 1812, he was directed to pull some weeds, (which indulgence his harmless disposition permitted) without the prison walls, merely, I believe, for the sake of giving him a little employment. He escaped, it was thought, rather through sudden waywardness than any distinct purpose. From that time nothing was heard of him till in the latter part of December, while at Ipswich, in the common room, occupied by a portion of the lunatics not furiously mad, I heard some one say, "I know her, I know her," and with a joyous laugh John hastened towards me. "I'm so glad to see you! so glad to see you! I can't stay here long; I want to go out," &c. It seems he had wandered to Salem, and was committed as an Insane or *Idiot* boy. I cannot but assert that most of the Idiotic subjects in the prisons in Massachusetts are unjustly committed, being wholly incapable of doing harm, and none manifesting any disposition either to injure others or to exercise mischievous propensities. I ask an investigation into this subject for the sake of many whose association with prisoners and criminals, and also with persons in almost every stage of insanity, is as useless and unnecessary, as it is cruel and ill-judged. If it were proper, I might place in your hands a volume, rather than give a page, illustrating these premises.

Sudbury. First week in September last I directed my way to the poor-farm there. Approaching, as I supposed, that place, all uncertainty vanished, as to which, of several dwellings in view, the course should be directed. The terrible screams and imprecations, impure language and amazing blasphemies, of a maniac, now, as often heretofore, indicated the place sought after. I know not how to proceed! the English language affords no combinations fit for describing the condition of the unhappy wretch there confined. In a stall, built under a woodshed on the road, was a naked man, defiled with filth, furiously tossing through the bars and about the cage, portions of straw (the only furnishing of his prison) already trampled to chaff. The mass of filth within, diffused wide abroad the most noisome stench. I have never witnessed paroxysms of madness so appalling; it seemed as if the ancient doctrine of the possession of demons was here illustrated. I hastened to the house overwhelmed with horror. The mistress informed me that ten days since he had been brought from Worcester Hospital, where the town did not choose any longer to meet the expenses of maintaining him; that he had been "dreadful noisy and dangerous to go near," ever since; it was hard work to give him food at any rate, for what was not immediately dashed at those who carried it, was cast down upon the festering mass within. "He's a dreadful care; worse than all the people and work on the farm beside." Have you any other insane persons? "Yes; this man's sister has been crazy here for several years; she does nothing but take on about him; and maybe she'll grown as bad as he." I went into the adjoining room to see this unhappy creature; in a low chair, wearing an air of deepest despondence, sat a female no longer young; her hair fell uncombed upon her shoulders; her whole air revealed woe, unmitigated woe! She regarded me coldly and uneasily; I spoke a few words of sympathy and kindness; she fixed her gaze for a few moments steadily upon me, then grasping my hand, and bursting into a passionate flood of tears, repeatedly kissed it, exclaiming in a voice broken by sobs, "O, my poor brother, my poor brother; hark, hear him! hear him!" then relapsing into apathetic calmness, she neither spoke nor moved, but the tears again flowed fast, as I went away. I avoided passing the maniac's cage; but there, with strange curiosity and eager exclamations, were gathered, at a safe distance; the children of the establishment, little boys and girls, receiving their early lessons in hardness of heart and vice; but the demoralizing influences were not confined to children.

The same day revealed two scenes of extreme exposure and unjustifiable neglect, such as I could not have supposed the whole New-England States could furnish.

Wayland. Visited the almshouse. There, as in Sudbury, caged in a wood-shed, and also *fully exposed* upon the *public* road, was seen a man at that time less violent, but equally debased by exposure and irritation. He then wore a portion of clothing, though the mistress remarked that he was "more likely to be naked than not;" and added that he was "less noisy than usual." I spoke to him, but received no answer; a wild, strange gaze, and impatient movement of the hand, motioned us away; he refused to speak, rejected food, and wrapped over his head a torn coverlet; want of accommodations for the imperative calls of nature has converted the cage into a place of utter offence. "My husband cleans him out once a week or so; but it's a hard matter to master him sometimes. He does better since the last time he was broken in." I learnt that the confinement and cold together, had so affected his limbs that he was often powerless to rise; "you see him," said my conductress, "in his best state." *His best state!* what then was the *worst?*

Westford. Not many miles distant from Wayland is a sad spectacle; was told by the family who kept the poorhouse, that they had twenty-six paupers: one idiot; one simple; and one insane, an incurable case from Worcester hospital. I requested to see her, but was answered that she "wasn't fit to be seen; she was naked, and made so much trouble they did not know how to get along." I hesitated but a moment; I must see her, I said. I cannot adopt descriptions of the condition of the insane secondarily; what I assert for fact, I must see for myself. On this I was conducted above stairs into an apartment of decent size, pleasant aspect from abroad, and tolerably comfortable in its general appearance; but the inmates!—grant I may never look upon another such scene! A young woman, whose person was partially covered with portions of a blanket, sat upon the floor; her hair dishevelled; her naked arms crossed languidly over the breast; a distracted, unsteady eye, and low, murmuring voice, betraying both mental and physical disquiet. *About the waist was a chain,* the extremity of which was fastened into the wall of the house. As I entered she raised her eyes, blushed, moved uneasily, endeavoring at the same time to draw about her the insufficient fragments of the blanket. I knelt beside her and asked if she did not wish to be dressed? "Yes; I want some clothes." "But you'll tear' em all up, you know you will," interposed her attendant. "No, I won't, I won't tear them off;" and she tried to rise, but the waist-encircling chain threw her back, and she did not renew the effort, but bursting into a wild shrill laugh, pointed to it, exclaiming, "see there, see there, nice clothes!" Hot tears might not dissolve that iron bondage, imposed, to all appearance, most needlessly. As I left the room the poor creature said, "I want my gown!" The response from the attendant might have roused to indignation one not dispossesed of reason, and owning self-control.

Groton. A few rods removed from the poorhouse is a wooden building upon the road- side, constructed of heavy board and plank; it contains one room, unfurnished, except so far as a bundle of straw constitutes furnishing. There is not window, save an opening half the size of a sash, and closed by a board shutter; in one corner is some brick-work surrounding an iron stove, which in cold weather serves for warming the room. The occupant of this dreary abode is a young man, who has been declared incurably insane. He can move a measured distance in his prison; that is, so far as a strong, heavy chain, depending from an *iron collar which invests his neck,* permits. In fine whether, and it was pleasant when I was there in June last, the door is thrown open, at once giving admission to light and air, and affording some little variety to the solitary in watching the passers-by. But that portion of the year which allows of open doors in not the chiefest part; and it may be conceived, without drafting much on the imagination, what is the condition of one who, for days, and weeks, and months, sits in darkness and alone, without employment, without object. It may be supposed that paroxysms of frenzy are often exhibited, and that the tranquil state is rare in comparison with that which incites to violence. This I was told is the fact.

I may here remark that severe measures, in enforcing rule, have in many places been openly revealed. I have not seen chastisement administered by stripes, and in but few instances have I seen the *rods* and *whips,* but I have seen blows inflicted, both passionately and repeatedly.

I have been asked if I have investigated the causes of insanity? I have not; but I have been told that this most calamitous overthrow of reason, often is the result of a life of sin; it is sometimes, but rarely, added, they must take the consequences, they deserve no better care! Shall man be more just than God; he who causes his sun, and refreshing rains, and life-giving influence, to fall alike on the good and the evil? Is not the total wreck of reason, a state of distraction, and the loss of all that makes life cherished, a retribution sufficiently heavy, without adding to consequences so appalling, every indignity that can bring still lower the wretched sufferer? Have pity upon those who, while they were supposed to lie hid in secret sins, "have been scattered under *a dark veil of forgetfulness;* over whom is spread a heavy night, and who unto themselves are more grievous than the darkness."

Fitchburg. In November visited the almshouse: inquired the number of insane? was answered, several; but two in close confinement; one idiotic subject. Saw an insane woman in a dreary neglected apartment, unemployed and alone. Idleness and solitude weaken, it is said, the sane mind, much more must it hasten the downfall of that which is already trembling at the foundations. From this apartment I was conducted to an out-building, a portion of which was inclosed, so as to unite shelter, confinement, and solitude. The first space was a sort of entry, in which was a window; beyond, a close partition with doors indicated where was the insane man I had wished to see. He had been returned from the hospital as incurable; I

asked if he was violent or dangerous? `No.' Is he clothed? `Yes.' Why keep him shut in this close confinement? `O my husband is afraid he'll run away, then the overseers won't like it; he'll get to Worcester, and then the town will have money to pay." He must come out, I wish to see him. The opened door disclosed a squalid place, dark, and *furnished* with straw. The crazy man raised himself slowly from the floor upon which he was couched, and with unsteady steps came towards me. His look was feeble and sad, but calm and gentle.

"Give me those books, oh give me those books!" and with trembling eagerness he reached for some books I had carried in my hand: "do give them to me, I want them," said he with kindling earnestness. You could not use them, friend; you cannot see there; "O give them to me, do;" and he raised his hand and bent a little forward, lowering his voice; *"I'll pick a little hole in the plank and let in some of God's light?"*

The master came round. "Why cannot you take this man abroad to work on the farm, he is harmless; air and exercise will help to recover him." The answer was in substance the same as that first given; but he added, "I've been talking with our overseers, and I've proposed getting from the blacksmith an iron collar and chain, then I can have him out by the house." An iron collar and chain! "Yes, I had a cousin up in Vermont, crazy as a wild-cat, and I got a collar made for him, *and he like it."* Liked it! how did he manifest his pleasure? "Why he left off trying to run away. I kept the alms-house at Groton: there was a man there from the Hospital: I built an out-house for him, and the blacksmith made him an iron collar and chain, so we had him fast, and the overseers approved it, and—" I here interrupted him. I have seen that poor creature at Groton in his doubly iron bondage, and you must allow me to say that, as I understand you remain but one year in the same place, and you may find insane subjects in all, I am confident, if overseers permit such a multiplication of collars and chains, that public will not long sanction such barbarities; but if you had Groton any argument for this measure in the violent state of the unfortunate subject, how can you justify such treatment of a person quiet and not dangerous as is this poor man? I beg you to forbear the chains, and treat him as you yourself would like to be treated in like fallen circumstances.

Bolton. Late in December, 1842; thermometer 4 degree above zero; visited the almshouse; neat and comfortable establishment; two insane women, one in the house associated with the family, the other *"out of doors."* The day following was expected a young man from Worcester Hospital, incurably insane; fears were expressed of finding him "dreadful hard to manage." I asked to see the subject who was "out of doors;" and following the mistress of the house through the deep snow, shuddering and benumbed by the piercing cold, several hundred yards, we came in rear of the barn to a small building, which might have afforded a degree of comfortable shelter, but it did not. About two thirds of the interior was filled with wood and peat; the other third was divided into two parts, one about six feet square contained a cylinder stove, in which was no fire, the rusty pipe seeming to threaten, in its decay, either suffocation by smoke, which by and by we nearly realized, or conflagration of the building, together with destruction of its poor crazy inmate. My companion uttered an exclamation at finding no fire, and busied herself to light one, while I explored, as the deficient light permitted, the cage which occupied the undescribed portion of the building. "Oh, I'm so cold, so cold," was uttered in plaintive tones by a woman within the cage; "oh, so cold, so cold!" And well might she be cold; the stout, hardy, driver of the sleigh had declared 'twas too hard for a man to stand the wind and snow that day, yet here was a woman caged and imprisoned without fire or clothes, not naked indeed, for one thin cotton garment partly covered her, and part of a blanket was gathered about the shoulders; there she stood, shivering in that dreary place, the grey locks falling in disorder about the face gave a wild expression to the pallid features; untended and comfortless, she might call aloud, none could hear; she might die, and there be none to close the eye. But death would have been a blessing here. "Well, you shall have a fire, Axey; I've been so busy getting ready for the funeral!" One of the paupers lay dead. "Oh, I want some clothes," rejoined the lunatic; "I'm so cold." "Well, Axey, you shall have some as soon as the children come from school; I've had so much to do." "I want to go out, do let me out!" "Yes, as soon as I get time," answered the respondent. "Why do you keep her here?" I asked, "she appears harmless and quiet." "Well, I mean to take her up to the house pretty soon; the people that used to have care here, kept her shut up all the year; but it *is* cold here, and we take her to the house in hard weather; the only danger is her running away; I've been meaning to, this good while." The poor creature listened eagerly, "oh, I won't run away, do take me out!" "Well, I will in a few days." Now the smoke from the kindling fire became so dense that a new anxiety struck the captive; "oh, I shall smother, I'm afraid; don't fill that up, I'm afraid." Pretty soon I moved to go away; "stop, did you walk?" "No." "Did you ride?" "Yes." "Do take me with you, do, I'm so cold. Do you know my sisters? they live in this town; I want to see them so much; do let me go!" and shivering with eagerness to get out, as with the biting cold, she rapidly tried the bars of the cage.

The mistress seemed a kind person; her tones and manner to the lunatic were kind; but how difficult to unite all the cares of her household, and neglect none! Here was not wilful abuse, but great, very great, suffering through undesigned negligence. We need an Asylum for this class, the incurable, where conflicting duties shall not admit of such examples of privations and misery.

One is continually amazed at the tenacity of life in these persons. In conditions that wring the heart to behold, it is hard to comprehend that days rather than years should not conclude the measure of their griefs and miseries. Picture her condition! place yourselves in that dreary cage, remote from the inhabited dwelling, alone by day and by night, without fire, without clothes, *except when remembered;* without object or employment; weeks and months passing on in drear succession, not a blank, but with keen life to suffering; with kindred, but deserted by them; and you shall not lose the memory of that time when they loved you, and you in turn loved them, but now no act or voice of kindness makes sunshine in the heart. Has fancy realized this to you? It *may* be the state of some of those you cherish! Who shall be sure his own hearth-stone shall not be desolate? nay, who shall say his own mountain stands strong, his lamp of reason shall not go out in darkness! To how many has this become a heart-rending reality! If for selfish ends only, should not effectual Legislation here interpose?

Shelburne. November last; I found no poorhouse, and but few paupers; these were distributed in private families. I had heard, before visiting this place, of the bad condition of a lunatic pauper. The case seemed to be pretty well known throughout the county. Receiving a direction by which I might find him, I reached a house of most respectable appearance; every thing without and within indicating abundance and prosperity. Concluding I must have mistaken my way, I prudently inquired where the insane person might be found? was readily answered, "here." I desired to see him; and after some difficulties raised and set aside, I was conducted into the yard, where was a small building of rough boards imperfectly joined; through these crevices was admitted what portion of heaven's light and air was allowed by man to his fellow-man. This shanty or shell, inclosing a cage, might have been eight or ten feet square, I think it did not exceed; a narrow passage within allowed to pass in front of the cage. It was very cold; the air within was burthened with the most noisome vapors, and Desolation with Misery seemed here to have settled their abode. All was still, save now and then a low groan. The person who conducted me tried, with a stick, to rouse the inmate; I intreated her to desist; the twilight of the place making it difficult to discern any thing within the cage; there at last I saw a human being, partially extended, cast upon his back amidst a mass of filth, the sole furnishing, whether for comfort or necessity which the place afforded; there he lay, ghastly, with upturned, glazed eyes, and fixed gaze, heavy breathings, interrupted only by faint groans, which seemed symptomatic of an approaching termination of his sufferings. Not so, thought the mistress; "he has all sorts of ways; he'll soon rouse up and be noisy enough; he'll scream and beat about the place like any wild beast, half the time." "And cannot you make him more comfortable? can he not have some clean, dry place, and a fine?" "As for clean, it will do no good; he's cleaned out now and then; but what's the use for such a creature" his own brother tried him once, but got sick enough of the bargain?" "But a fire, there is space even here, for a small box stove?" "If he had a fire he'd only pull off his clothes, so it's no use." "But you say your husband takes care of him, and he is shut in here in almost total darkness, so that seems a less evil than that he should lie there to perish in that horrible condition." I made no impression; it was plain that to keep him securely confined from escape was the chief object. "How do you give him his food? I see no means for introducing any thing here?" "O," pointing to the floor, "one of the bars is cut shorter there, we push it through there." "There? impossible! you cannot do that; you would not treat your lowest dumb animals with that disregard *to decency!*" "As for what he eats, or where he eats, it makes no difference to him, he'd as soon swallow one thing as another."

Newton. It was a cold morning in October last, that I visited the almshouse. The building itself is ill adapted for the purposes to which it is appropriated; the town, I understand have in consideration a more advantageous location, and propose to erect more commodious dwellings. The mistress of the house informed me that they had several insane inmates, some of them very bad. In reply to my request to see them, she objected "that they were not fit—that they were not cleaned—that they were very crazy," &c. Urging my request more decidedly, she said they should be got ready, if I would wait. Still no order was given which would hasten my object. I renewed the subject, when, with manifest unwillingness, she called to a colored man, a cripple, who with several others of the poor were employed in the yard, to go and get a woman up— naming her. I waited some time at the kitchen door to see what all this was to produce. The man slowly proceeded to the remote part of the wood-shed where, part being divided from the open space, were two small rooms, in the outer of which he slept and lived, as I understood; there was his furniture; and there his charge! Opening into this room only, was the second, which was occupied by a woman not old, and furiously mad: it contained a wooden bunk filled with filthy straw, the room itself a counterpart to the lodging place; inexpressibly disgusting and loathsome was all: but the inmate herself was even more horribly repelling; she rushed out, as far as the chains would allow, almost in a state of nudity, exposed to a dozen persons, and vociferating at the top of her voice; pouring forth such a flood of indecent language as might corrupt even

Newgate. I entreated the man, who still was there, to go out and close the door. He refused; that was *his place!* Sick, horror-struck, and almost incapable of retreating, I gained the outward air, and hastened to see the outer subject, to remove from a scene so outraging all decency and humanity. In the apartment over that last described was a crazy man, I was told. I ascended the stairs in the wood-shed, and passing through a small room stood at the entrance of the one occupied; occupied with what? The furniture was a wooden box or bunk containing straw, and something I was told was a man, I could not tell, as likely it might have been a wild animal, half buried in the offensive mass that made his bed; his countenance concealed by long tangled hair and unshorn beard. He lay sleeping. Filth, neglect and misery reigned there. I begged he might not be roused. If sleep could visit a wretch so forlorn, how merciless to break the slumber! Protruding from the foot of the box was—, nay, it could not be the feet; yet from these stumps, these maimed members were swinging chains, fastened to the side of the building. I descended; the master of the house briefly stated the history of these two victims of wretchedness. The old man had been crazy above twenty years. As, till within a late period, the town had owned no farm for the poor, this man with others had been annually put up at auction. I hope there is nothing offensive in the idea of these *annual sales* of old men and women, the sick, the infirm, and the helpless, the middle-aged and children; why should we not *sell* people as well as otherwise blot out human rights, it is only being *consistent,* surely not worse than chaining and caging naked Lunatics upon public roads, or burying them in closets and cellars? But, as I was saying, the crazy man was annually sold to some new master, and a few winters since, being kept in an out-house, the people within being warmed and clothed, 'did not reckon how cold it was,' and so his feet froze Were chains now the more necessary? he cannot run. But he might *crawl* forth, and in his transports of frenzy "do some damage."

That young woman; her lot is most appalling! who shall dare describe it! who shall have courage or hardihood to write her history? That young woman was the child of respectable, hard-working parents. The girl became insane; the father, a farmer with small means, from a narrow income had placed her at the State Hospital. There, said my informer, she remained as long as he could by any means pay her expenses. Then, then only, he resigned her to the care of the town, to those who are, in the eye of the law, the guardians of the poor and needy; she was placed with the other town-paupers, and given in charge to a man. I assert boldly, as truly, that I have given but a *faint representation* of what she was, and what was her condition as I saw her last autumn. Written language is weak to declare it.

Could we in fancy place ourselves in the situation of some of these poor wretches, bereft of reason, deserted of friends, hopeless; troubles without, and more dreary troubles within, overwhelming the wreck of the mind as 'a wide breaking in of the waters,'—how should we, as the terrible illusion was cast off, not only offer the thank-offering of prayer, that so mighty a destruction had not overwhelmed our mental nature, but as an offering more acceptable devote ourselves to alleviate that state from which we are so mercifully spared.

It may not appear much more credible than the fact above stated, that a few months since, a young woman in a state of complete insanity, was confined entirely naked in a pen or stall in a barn; there, unfurnished with clothes, without bed, and without fire, she was left—but alone; profligate men and idle boys had access to the den, whenever curiosity or vulgarity prompted. She is now removed into the house with other paupers; and for this humanizing benefit she was indebted to the remonstrances, in the first instance, *of an insane man!*

Another town now owns a poorhouse, which I visited, and am glad to testify to the present comfortable state of the inmates; but there the only provision the house affords for an insane person, should one, as is not improbable, be conveyed there, is a closet in the cellar, formed by the arch upon which the chimney rests; this has a close door, not only securing the prisoner, but excluding what of light and pure air might else find admission.

Abuses assuredly cannot always or altogether be guarded against; but if in the civil and social relations all shall have "done what they could," no ampler justification will be demanded at the Great Tribunal.

Of the dangers and mischiefs sometimes following the location of insane persons in our almhouses, I will record but one more example. In Worcester, has for several years resided a young woman, a lunatic pauper of decent life and respectable family. I have seen her as she usually appeared, listless and silent, almost or quite sunk into a state of dementia, sitting one amidst the family, 'but not of them.' A few weeks since, revisiting that almshouse, judge my horror and amazement to see her negligently bearing in her arms a young infant, of which I was told she was the unconscious parent! Who was the father, none could or would declare. Disqualified for the performance of maternal cares and duties, regarding the helpless little creature with a perplexed, or indifferent gaze, she sat a silent, but O how eloquent, a pleader for the protection of others of her neglected and outraged sex! Details of that black story would not strengthen the cause; needs it a weightier plea, than the sight of that forlorn creature and her wailing infant? Poor little child, more than orphan from birth, in this unfriendly world! a demented Mother—a Father, on whom the sun might blush or refuse to shine!

Men of Massachusetts, I beg, I implore, I demand, pity and protection, for these of my suffering, outraged sex!—Fathers, Husbands, Brothers, I would supplicate you for this boon—but what to I say? I dishonor you, divest you at once of christianity and humanity—does this appeal imply distrust. If it comes burthened with a doubt of your righteousness in this Legislation, then blot it out; while I declare confidence in your honor, not less than your humanity. Here you will put away the cold, calculating spirit of self-ishness and self-seeking; lay off the armor of local strife and political opposition; here and now, for once, forgetful of the earthly and perishable come up to these halls and consecrate them with one heart and one mind to works of righteousness and just judgement. Become the benefactors of your race, the just guardians of the solemn rights you hold in trust. Raise up the fallen; succor the desolate; restore the outcast; defend the helpless; and for your eternal and great reward, receive the benediction. . . . "Well done, good and faithful servants, become rulers over many things!"

But gentlemen, I do not come to quicken your sensibilities into short-lived action, to pour forth passionate exclamation, nor yet to move your indignation against those, whose misfortune, not fault, it surely is to hold in charge these poor demented creatures, and whose whole of domestic economy, or prison discipline, is absolutely overthrown by such proximity of conflicting circumstances, and opposite conditions of mind and character. Allow me to illustrate this position by a few examples; it were easy to produce hundreds.

The master of one of the best regulated almshouses, viz. that of Plymouth, where every arrangement shows that the comfort of the sick, the aged, and the infirm, is suitably cared for, and the amendment of the unworthy is studied and advanced, said, as we stood opposite a latticed stall, where was confined a madman, that the hours of the day were few; when the whole household was not distracted from employment by screams, and turbulent stampings, and every form of violence, which the voice or muscular force could produce. This unfortunate being was one of the "returned incurables," since whose last admission to the almshouse, they were no longer secure of peace for the aged, or decency for the young; it was morally impossible to do justice to the sane and insane in such improper vicinity to each other. The conviction is continually deepened that Hospitals are the only places where insane persons can be at once humanely and properly controlled. Poorhouse, converted into madhouse, cease to effect the purposes for which they were established, and instead of being asylums for the aged, the homeless, and the friendliness, and places of refuge for orphaned or neglected childhood, are transformed into perpetual bedlams.

This crying evil and abuse of institutions, is not confined to our almshouses. The warden of a populous prison near this metropolis, populous, not with criminals only, but with the insane in almost every stage of insanity, and the idiotic in descending states from silly and simple, to helpless and speechless, has declared that, since their admission under the Rev. Stat. of 1835, page 382, "the prison has often more resembled the infernal regions than any place on earth!" and, what with the excitement inevitably produced by the crowded state of the prisons, and multiplying causes, not subject to much modification, there has been neither peace nor order one hour of the twenty-four; if ten were quiet, the residue were probably raving. Almost without interval might, and *must*, these be heard, blaspheming and furious, and to the last degree impure and indecent; uttering language, from which the base and the profligate have turned shuddering aside, and the abandoned have shrunk abashed. I myself, with many beside, can bear sad witness to those things.

Such cases of transcendent madness have not been few in this prison. Admission for a portion of them, not already having been discharged as incurable from the State Hospital, has been sought with importunity, and pressed with obstinate perseverance, often without success or advantage; and it has not been, till application has followed application, and petition succeeded petition, that the Judge of Probate, absolutely wearied by the 'continual coming,' has sometimes granted warrants for removal. It cannot be overlooked that in this delay or refusal was more of just deliberation than hardness, for it is well known that, in the present crowded state of the Hospital, every new patient displaces one who has for a longer or shorter time received the benefit of that noble institution.

A few months since, through exceeding effort, an inmate of this prison, whose contaminating influence for two years had been the dread and curse of all persons who came within her sphere, whether incidentally, or compelled by imprisonment, or by daily duty, was removed or Worcester. She had set at defiance all efforts for controlling the contaminating violence of her excited passions; every variety of blasphemous expression; every form of polluting phraseology, was poured forth in torrents, sweeping away every decent thought, and giving reality to that blackness of darkness, which it is said might convert a heaven into a hell; there, day after day, month after month, were the warden and his own immediate household; the subordinate officials, and casual visitors; young women detained as witnesses; men, women, and children, waiting trial or under sentence; debtors and criminals; the neighborhood, and almost the whole town; subjected to this monstrous offence—*and no help! the law* permitted her there, and there she remained till July last, when, after an application to the Judge, so determined, that all refusal was refused, a warrant was granted for her transfer to the State Hospital. I saw her there two weeks since; what a

change! decent, orderly, neatly dressed; capable of light employment; partaking with others her daily meals. Decorously, and without any manifestation of passion, moving about, not a rational woman by any means, but no longer a nuisance, rending off her garments and tainting the moral atmosphere with every pollution; she exhibited how much could be done for the most unsettled and apparently the most hopeless cases, by being placed in a situation adapted to the wants and necessities of her condition. Transformed from a very Tisiphone, she is now a controllable woman. But this most wonderful change may not be lasting; she is liable to be returned to the prison, as have been others, and then, no question, but in a short time like scenes will distract and torment all in a vicinity so much to be dreaded.

Already has been transferred from Worcester to Concord a furious man, last July conveyed to the Hospital from Cambridge, whose violence is second only to that of the subject above described. While our *Revised Statutes* permit the incarnation of madmen and madwomen, epileptics and idiots in prisons, all responsible officers should, in ordinary justice, be exonerated from obligation to maintain prison discipline. And the fact is conclusive, if the injustice to prison officers is great, it is equally great towards prisoners; an additional penalty to a legal sentence pronounced in a Court of Justice,which might, we should think, in all the prisons we have visited, serve as a sound plea for false imprisonment. If reform is intended to be united with punishment, there never was a greater absurdity then to look for moral restoration under such circumstances; and if that is left out of view, we know no rendering of the law which sanctions such a cruel and oppressive aggravation of the circumstances of imprisonment, as to expose these prisoners day and night to the indescribable horrors of such association.

The greatest evils, in regard to the insane and idiots in the prisons of this Commonwealth, are found at Ipswich and Cambridge, and distinguish these places only, as I believe, because the numbers are larger, being more than twenty in each. Ipswich has the advantage over Cambridge in having fewer furious subjects, and in the construction of the buildings, though these are so bad as to have afforded cause for presentment by the Grand Jury some time since. It is said that the new Country House, in progress of building, will meet the exigencies of the case. If it is meant that the wing in the new prison, to be appropriated-to the insane, will provide accommodation for all the insane and idiotic paupers in the country, I can only say that it could receive no more than can be gathered in the three towns of Salem, Newburyport, and Ipswich, supposing these are to be removed; there being in Ipswich twenty-two in the prison, and eight in the almshouse; in Salem almshouse, seventeen uniformly crazy, and two part of the time deranged; and in that of Newburyport eleven, including idiots. Here at once are sixty. The returns of 1842 exhibit an aggregate of one hundred and thirty-five. Provision is made in the new prison for fifty- seven of this class, leaving seventy-eight unprovided for, except in the alms-houses. From such a fate, so far as Danvers, Saugus, East Bradford, and some other towns in the county, reveal conditions of insane subjects, we pray they may be exempt.

I have the verbal and written testimony of many officers of this Commonwealth, who are respectable alike for their integrity and the fidelity with which they discharge their official duties, and whose opinions, based on experience, are entitled to consideration, that the occupation of prisons for the detention of lunatics and of idiots is, under all circumstances, an evil, subversive alike of good order, strict discipline, and good morals. I transcribe a few passages which will place this mischief in its true light. The Sheriff of Plymouth county writes as follows:—"I am decidedly of the opinion that the county jail is a very improper place for lunatics and idiots. The last summer its bad effects were fully realized here, not only by the prisoners in jail, but the disturbance extended to the inhabitants dwelling in the neighborhood. A foreigner was sentenced by a Justice of the Peace, to thirty days' confinement in the house of correction. He was to all appearance a lunatic, or madman. He destroyed every article in his room, even to his wearing apparel, his noise and disturbance was incessant for hours, day and night. I consider prisons places for the safe keeping of prisoners, and all these are equally entitled to humane treatment from their keepers, without regard to the cause of commitment. We have in jails no conveniences to make the situation of lunatics and idiots much more decent than would be necessary for the brute creation, and impossible to prevent the disturbance of the inmates under the same roof."

In relation to the confinement of the insane in prisons the Sheriff of Hampshire county writes as follows:—

"I concur fully in the sentiments entertained by you in relation to this unwise, not to say inhuman, provision of our law (see Rev. Stat. 382) authorizing the commitment of lunatics to our Jails and Houses of Correction. Our Jails preclude occupation, and our Houses of Correction cannot admit of that variety of pursuit, and its requisite supervision, so indispensable to these unfortunates.

"Indeed this feature of our law seems to me a relic of that ancient barbarism which regarded misfortune as a crime, and those bereft of reason as also bereft of all sensibility; as having forfeited not only all title to compassion but to *humanity,* and consigned them without a tear of sympathy, or twinge of remorse, or even a suspicion of injustice to the companionship of the vicious, the custody of the course and ignorant, and the horrors of the hopeless dungeon. I cannot persuade myself that anything more than a motion

by any member of our Legislature is necessary to effect an immediate repeal of this odious provision."

The Sheriff of Berkshire says, conclusively, that "Jails and Houses of Correction *cannot* be so managed as to render them suitable places of confinement for that unfortunate class of persons, who are the subjects of your inquiries, and who, never having violated the law, should not be ranked with felons, or confined within the same walls with them. Jailors and Oversects of Houses of Correction, whenever well qualified for the management of criminals, do not usually possess those peculiar qualifications required in those to whom should be entrusted the care of lunatics."

A letter from the surgeon and physician of the Prison Hospital at Cambridge, whose observation and experience has laid the foundation of his opinions, and hence has a title to speak with authority, affords the following views:—"On this subject, it seems to me, there can be but one opinion. No one can be more impressed than I am with the great injustice done to the insane by confining them in Jails and Houses of Correction. It must be revolting to the better feelings of every one to see the innocent and unfortunate insane occupying apartments with, or consigned to those occupied by the criminal. Some of the insane are conscious of the circumstances in which they are placed, and feel the degradation. They exclaim sometimes in their ravings, and sometimes in their lucid intervals, "What have *I* done that I must be shut up in Jail?" and "why do you not let met out?" This state of things unquestionably retards the recovery of the few who do recover their reason under such circumstances, and may tender those permanently insane, who under other circumstances might have been restored to their right mind. There is also in our Jails very little opportunity for the classification of the insane. The quiet and orderly must in many cases occupy the same rooms with the restless and noisy, another great hindrance to recovery.

"*Injustice* is also done to the *convicts;* it is certainly very wrong that they should be doomed day after day, and night after night, to listen to the ravings of madmen and madwomen. This is a kind of punishment that is not recognised by our statutes; and is what the criminal ought not to be called upon to undergo. The confinement of the criminal and of the insane in the same building is subversive of that good order and discipline which should be observed in every well-regulated prison. I do most sincerely hope that more permanent provision will be made for the Pauper Insane by the State, either to restore Worcester Insane Asylum to what it was originally designed to be, or else make some just appropriation for the benefit of this very unfortunate class of our 'fellow beings'."

From the efficient Sheriff of Middlesex county, I have a letter upon this subject, from which I make such extracts as my limits permit:—"I do not consider it right, just, or humane, to hold for safe keeping, in the county jails and houses of correction, persons classing as lunatics or idiots. Our prisons are not constructed with a view to the proper accommodation of this class of persons; their interior arrangements are such as to render it very difficult, if not impossible, to extend to such persons that care and constant oversight which their peculiarly unfortunate condition absolutely demands; and besides, the occupation of prisons for lunatics is unquestionably subversive of discipline, comfort, and good order. Prisoners are thereby subjected to unjust aggravation of necessary confinement, be being exposed to an almost constant disquiet from the restless or raving lunatic. You inquire whether "it may not justly be said, that the qualifications for wardenship, or for the offices of overseer, do not usually embrace qualifications for the management of lunatics, whether regarded as curable, or incurably lost to reason?" and also, whether "the government of jails and houses of correction for the detention or punishment of offenders and criminals, can suitably be united with the government and discipline fitted for the most unfortunate and friendless of the human race, viz: pauper lunatics and idiots, a class not condemned by the laws, and I must add not mercifully protected by them?" The first of the preceding questions I answer in the *affirmative;* the last *negatively.*"

A communication from the warden of the Cambridge prison affords the following opinions, results of his experience:—"As to the expediency or propriety of holding for safe keeping, in the jails or houses of correction, insane persons or idiots, I must say that I consider it both inexpedient and decidedly wrong that the insane, or idiots, or any other persons, should be confined in prisons, except those who have been convicted for crimes, or who are so strongly suspected that it is necessary they should be holden for safe keeping until they can be tried for the offences for which they stand charged. Any person having the least experience in prison-keeping, must, I think, be fully sensible of the demoralizing and pernicious influences insane persons must have on the order and discipline of a prison, nor can it be doubted that the punishment of all sane persons is very much enhanced and aggravated by their exposure to the ravings of the insane. Neither can the keepers or other officers of prisons be selected with a view to their fitness to take care of the insane, consequently they are in want of those qualifications which make them suitable for the management of such persons, be they curable or incurable."

From the Sheriff of Dukes county I have testimony, corresponding to that elsewhere received, and from which I am obliged to make extracts, when the entire letters would be valuable: "I beg leave to say that I am decidedly of opinion that such confinement, even if it were in some cases "expedient," is not in accordance with the principles of sound enlightened philanthropy. Humanity shudders at the thought that those whom God in his providence has bereft of the light of reason, should be confined within the narrow bounds of a prison, deprived of the enjoyment of the pure air of heaven; of necessary exercise; of the comforts of which they have been used, comforts which their peculiar circumstances render so necessary; and made companions of felons, and the worthless outcasts of society.

"With proper care and attention, lunatics may not only be made comfortable, but in many instances restored again to society with sound minds. But this care and attention cannot be expected from those who have charge of prisons, worthy men though many of them be; it requires a union of qualifications rarely found in one individual, to manage successfully those from whom that, which chiefly distinguishes man from the brute creation, is taken away.

"I conclude with expressing the hope that the wisdom of our Legislature may devise a remedy for the evils now attending the unfortunate pauper lunatic and idiot."

The warden of one of the best conducted prisons in this or any other country, I refer to that at South Boston, writes:—"I affirm, most decisively, that jails and houses of correction are not fit places for the safe keeping of lunatics and idiots, and, as far as my experience goes, the officers are not qualified to take charge of lunatics."

The master of the Plymouth almshouse writes, in a letter containing many clear views,—"I hope to hear people are awake on this subject, and trust they will not rest till they have compelled the public to provide suitable places for that unfortunate class of demented persons. They should never be received in almshouses."

It is not few but many, it is not a part but the whole, who bear unqualified testimony to this evil. A voice strong and deep comes up from every almshouse and prison in Massachusetts where the insane are or have been, protesting against such evils as have been illustrated in the preceding pages.

Gentlemen, I commit to you this sacred cause. Your action upon this subject will affect the present and future condition of hundreds and of thousands.

In this legislation, as in all things, may you exercise that "wisdom which is the breath of the power of God."

Respectfully submitted,
D. L. Dix.
85 Mt. Vernon Street, Boston. *January,* 1843.

Source:
Landmark Documents in American History, Facts On File, Inc.

Intellectual and Cultural Life in the Early Nineteenth-Century United States

Ralph Waldo Emerson, "American Scholar," 1837

Famous address delivered by American poet and essayist Ralph Waldo Emerson before the Harvard Phi Beta Kappa Society's annual gathering at Cambridge, Massachusetts, on August 31, 1837. Describing the scholar as the "delegated intellect" in the "divided or social state," Emerson observed that when victimized by society, "he tends to become a mere thinker, or still worse, the parrot of other men's thinking." Emerson then examined in great detail the main influences on the scholar: (1) nature, which "becomes to him the measure of his attainments"; (2) "the mind of the Past—in whatever form, whether of literature, of art, of institutions that mind is inscribed"; and (3) action—"Without it, he is not yet man. Without it, thought can never ripen into truth." According to Emerson, the scholar's duties are "to guide men by showing them facts amidst appearances," to "relinquish display and immediate fame," to "resist vulgar prosperity," and to be brave and free. Finally, he challenged the scholar: "It is for you to know all, it is for you to dare all!"

―――――――――――❧――――――――――――

Mr. President and gentlemen,—I greet you on the recommencement of our literary year. Our anniversary is one of hope, and perhaps not enough of labor. We do not meet for games of strength or skill, for the recitation of histories, tragedies, and odes, like the ancient Greeks; for parliaments of love and poesy, like the Troubadours; nor for the advancement of science, like our contemporaries in the British and European capitals. Thus far our holiday has been simply a friendly sign of the survival of the love of letters amongst a people too busy to give to letters any more. As such it is precious as the sign of an indestructible instinct. Perhaps the time has already come when it ought to be and will be something else; when the sluggard intellect of this continent will look from under its iron lids and fill the postponed expectation of the world with something better than the exertions of mechanical skill. Our day of dependence, our long apprenticeship to the learning of other lands, draws to a close. The millions that around us are rushing into life cannot always be fed on the sere remains of foreign harvests. Events, actions arise, that must be sung, that will sing themselves. Who can doubt that poetry will revive and lead in a new age, as the star in the constellation Harp, which now flames in our zenith, astronomers announce, shall one day be the pole-star for a thousand years?

In this hope I accept the topic which not only usage, but the nature of our association, seem to prescribe to this day—the American Scholar. Year by year we come up hither to read one more chapter of his biography. Let us inquire what light new days and events have thrown on his character and his hopes.

It is one of those fables which, out of an unknown antiquity, convey an unlooked-for-wisdom, that the gods in the beginning divided Man into men, that he might be more helpful to himself; just as the hand was divided into fingers, the better to answer its end.

The old fable covers a doctrine ever new and sublime; that there is One Man—present to all particular men only partially, or through one faculty; and that you must take the whole society to find the whole man. Man is not a farmer, or professor, or an engineer, but he is all. Man is priest, and scholar, and statesman, and producer, and soldier. In the divided or social state these functions are parcelled out to individuals, each of whom aims to do his stint of the joint work, whilst each other performs his. The fable implies, that the individual to possess himself must sometimes return from his own labor to embrace all the other laborers. But unfortunately, this original unit, this fountain of power, has been so distributed to multitudes, has been so minutely subdivided and peddled out, that it is spilled into drops, and cannot be gathered. The state of society is one in which the members have suffered amputation from the trunk, and strut about, so many walking monsters—a good finger, a neck, a stomach, an elbow, but never a man.

Man is thus metamorphosed into a thing, into many things. The planter, who is Man sent out into the field to gather food, is seldom cheered by any idea of the true dignity of his ministry. He sees his bushel and his cart, and nothing beyond, and sinks into the farmer, instead of Man on the farm. The tradesman scarcely ever gives an ideal worth to his work, but is ridden by the routine of his craft and the soul is subject to dollars. The priest becomes a form; the attorney, a statute book; the mechanic, a machine; the sailor, a rope of a ship.

In this distribution of functions the scholar is the delegated intellect. In the right state he is Man Thinking. In the degenerate state, when the victim of society, he tends to become a mere thinker, or, still worse, the parrot of other men's thinking.

In this view of him, as Man Thinking, the theory of his office is contained. Him nature solicits with all her placid, all her monitory pictures; him the past instructs; him the future invites. Is not, indeed, every man a student, and do not all things exist for the student's behoof? And finally is not the true scholar the only true master? But the old oracle said, "All things have two handles: beware of the wrong one." In life too often the scholar errs with mankind and forfeits his privilege. Let us see him in his school and consider him in reference to the main influences he receives.

I. The first in time and the first in importance of the influences upon the mind is that of nature. Every day, the sun; and after sunset, night and her stars. Ever the winds blow; ever the grass grows. Every day men and women conversing, beholding and beholden. The scholar is he of all men whom this spectacle most engages. He must settle its value in his mind. What is nature to him? There is never a beginning, there is never an end to the inexplicable continuity of this web of God, but always circular power returning into itself. Therein it resembles his own spirit, whose beginning, whose ending, he never can find—so entire, so boundless. Far, too, as her splendors shine, system on system shooting like rays, upward, downward, without centre, without circumference—in the mass and in the particle nature hastens to render account of herself to the mind. Classification begins. To the young mind everything is individual, stands by itself. By and by it finds how to join two things and see in them one nature, then three, then three thousand; and so, tyrannized over by its own unifying instinct, it goes on tying things together, diminishing anomalies, discovering roots, running under ground, whereby contrary and remote things cohere and flower out from on stem. It presently learns that since the dawn of history there has been a constant accumulation and classifying of facts. But what is classification but the perceiving that these objects are not chaotic and are not foreign, but have a law which is also a law of the human mind? The astronomer discovers that geometry, a pure abstraction of the human mind, is the measure of planetary motion. The chemist finds proportions and intelligible method throughout matter; and science is nothing but the finding of analogy, identity, in the most remote parts. The ambitious soul sits down before each refractory fact; one after another, reduces all strange constitutions, all new powers, to their class and their law, and goes on forever to animate the last fibre of organization, the outskirts of nature, by insight.

Thus to him, to this school-boy under the bending dome of day, is suggested that he and it proceed from one root; one is leaf and one is flower; relation, sympathy, stirring in every vein. And what is that Root? Is not that the soul of his soul?—a thought too bold,—a dream too wild. Yet when this spiritual light shall have revealed the law of more earthly natures,—when he has learned to worship the soul, and to see that the natural philosophy that now is, is only the first gropings of its gigantic hand, he shall look forward to an ever expanding knowledge as to a becoming creator. He shall see that nature is the opposite of the soul, answering to it part for part. One is seal and one is print. Its beauty is the beauty of his own mind. Its laws are the laws of his own mind. Nature then becomes to him the measure of his attainments. So much of nature as he is ignorant of, so much of his own mind does he not yet possess. And in fine the ancient precept, "Know thyself," and the modern precept, "Study nature," become at last one maxim.

II. The next great influence into the spirit of the scholar is the mind of the Past,—in whatever form, whether of literature, of art, of institutions, that mind is inscribed. Books are the best type of the influence of the pasts, and perhaps we shall get at the truth,—learn the amount of this influence more conveniently,—by considering their value alone.

The theory of books is noble. The scholar of the first age received into him the world around; brooded thereon; gave it the new arrangement of his own mind and uttered it again. It came into him, life; it went out from him, truth. It came to him, short-lived actions; it went out from him, immortal thoughts. It came to him, business; it went from him, poetry. It was dead fact; now, it is quick thought. It can stand and it can go. It now endures, it now flies, it now inspires. Precisely in proportion to the depth of mind from which it issued, so high does it soar, so long does it sing.

Or, I might say, it depends on how far the process had gone, of transmuting life into truth. In proportion to the completeness of the distillation, so will the purity and imperishableness of the product be. But none is quite perfect. As no air-pump can by any means make a perfect vacuum, so neither can any artist entirely exclude the conventional, the local, the perishable from his book, or write a book of pure thought, that shall be as efficient, in all respects, to a remote posterity, as to contemporaries, or rather to the second age. Each age, it is found, must write its own books; or rather, each generation for the next succeeding. The books of an older period will not fit this.

Yet hence arises a grave mischief. The sacredness which attaches to the act of creation,—the act of thought,—is transferred to the record. The poet chanting, was felt to be a divine man: henceforth the chant is divine also. The writer was a just and wise spirit: henceforward it is settled, the book is perfect; as love of the hero corrupts into worship of his statue. Instantly the book becomes noxious: the guide is a tyrant. The sluggish and perverted mind of the multitude, slow to open to the incursions of

Reason, having once so opened, having once received this book, stands upon it and makes an outcry if it is disparaged. Colleges are built on it. Books are written on it by thinkers, not by Man Thinking; by men of talent, that is, who start wrong, who set out from accepted dogmas, not from their own sight of principles. Meek young men grow up in libraries, believing it their duty to accept the views which Cicero, which Locke, which Bacon have given, forgetful that Cicero, Locke, and Bacon were only young men in libraries when they wrote these books.

Hence, instead of Man Thinking, we have the bookworm. Hence, the booklearned class who value books, as such; not as related to nature and the human constitution, but as making a sort of Third Estate with the world and the soul. Hence, the restorers of readings, the emendators, the bibliomaniacs of all degrees.

Books are the best of things, well used; abused, among the worst. What is the right use? What is the one end, which all means go to effect? They are for nothing but to inspire. I had better never see a book than to be warped by its attraction clean out of my own orbit and made a satellite instead of a system. The one thing in the world of value is the active soul. This every man is entitled to; this every man contains within him although, in almost all men, obstructed, and as yet unborn. The soul active sees absolute truth; and utters truth, or creates. In this action, it is genius; not the privilege of here and there a favorite, but the sound estate of every man. In its essence, it is progressive. The book, the college, the school of art, the institution of any kind, stop with some past utterance of genius. This is good, say they,—let us hold by this. They pin me down. They look backward and not forward. But genius looks forward: the eyes of man are set in his forehead, not in his hindhead; man hopes, genius creates. Whatever talents may be, if the man create not, the pure efflux of the Deity is not his; cinders and smoke there maybe, but not yet flame. There are creative manners, there are creative actions, and creative words; manners, actions, words, that is, indicative of no custom or authority, but springing spontaneous from the mind's own sense of good and fair.

On the other part, instead of being its own seer, let it receive from another mind its truth, though it were in torrents of light, without periods of solitude, inquest, and self-recovery, and a fatal disservice is done. Genius is always sufficiently the enemy of genius by over-influence. The literature of every nation bear me witness. The English dramatic poets have Shakespearized now for two hundred years.

Undoubtedly there is a right way of reading, so it be sternly subordinated. Man Thinking must not be subdued by his instruments. Books are for the scholar's idle times. When he can read God directly, the hour is too precious to be wasted in other men's transcripts of their readings. But when the intervals of darkness come, as come they must,— when the sun is hid, and the stars withdraw their shining,—we repair to the lamps which were kindled by their ray, to guide our steps to the East again, where the dawn is. We hear, that we may speak. The Arabian proverb says, "A fig-tree, looking on a fig-tree, becomes fruitful." It is remarkable, the character of the pleasure we derive from the best books. They impress us with the conviction, that one nature wrote and the same reads. We read the verses of one of the great English poets, of Chaucer, of Marvell, of Dryden, with the most modern joy,—with a pleasure, I mean, which is in great part caused by the abstraction of all time from their verses. There is some awe mixed with the joy of our surprise, when this poet, who lived in some past world, two or three hundred years ago, says that which lies close to my own soul, that which I also had wellnigh thought and said. But for the evidence thence afforded to the philosophical doctrine of the identity of all minds, we should suppose some pre-established harmony, some foresight of souls that were to be, and some preparation of stores for their future wants, like the fact observed in insects, who lay up food before death for the young grub they shall never see.

I would not be hurried by any love of system, by any exaggeration of instincts, to underrate the Book. We all know that, as the human body can be nourished on any food, though it were boiled grass and the broth of shoes, so the human mind can be fed by any knowledge. And great and heroic men have existed who had almost no other information than by the printed page. I only would say, that it needs a strong head to bear that diet. One must be an inventor to read well. As the proverb says, "He that would bring home the wealth of the Indies, must carry out the wealth of the Indies." There is, then, creative reading as well as creative writing. When the mind is braced by labor and invention, the page of whatever book we read becomes luminous with manifold allusion. Every sentence is doubly significant, and the sense of our author is as broad as the world. We then see, what is always true, that, as the seer's hour of vision is short and rare among heavy days and months, so is its record, perchance, the least part of his volume. The discerning will read, in his Plato or Shakespeare, only that least part,—only the authentic utterances of the oracle; all the rest he rejects, were it never so many times Plato's and Shakespeare's.

Of course there is a portion of reading quite indispensable to a wise man. History and exact science he must learn by laborious reading. Colleges, in like manner, have their indispensable office,—to teach elements. But they can only highly serve us when they aim not to drill, but to create; when they gather from far every ray of various genius to their hospitable halls, and, by the concentrated fires, set the hearts of their youth on flame. Thought and knowledge are natures in which apparatus and pretension avail nothing. Gowns and pecuniary foundations, though of towns of gold, can never countervail the least sentence or syllable of wit. Forget this, and our American colleges will recede in their public importance, whilst they grow richer every year.

III. There goes in the world a notion that the scholar should be a recluse, a valetudinarian,—as unfit for any handiwork or public labor as a penknife for an axe. The so-called "practical men" sneer at speculative men as if, because they speculate or see, they could do nothing. I have heard it said that the clergy,—who are always, more universally than any other class, the scholars of their day,—are addressed as women; that the rough, spontaneous conversation of men they do not hear, but only a mincing and diluted speech. They are often virtually disfranchised; and, indeed, there are advocates for their celibacy. As far as this is true of the studious classes, it is not just and wise. Action is with the scholar subordinate, but it is essential. Without it, he is not yet man. Without it, thought can never ripen into truth. Whilst the world hangs before the eye as a cloud of beauty, we cannot even see its beauty. Inaction is cowardice, but there can be no scholar without the heroic mind. The preamble of thought, the transition through which it passes from the unconscious to the conscious, is action. Only so much do I know as I have lived. Instantly, we know whose words are loaded with life, and whose not.

The world,—this shadow of the soul, or *other me*, lies wide around. Its attractions are the keys which unlock my thoughts and make me acquainted with myself. I run eagerly into this resounding tumult. I grasp the hands of those next me, and take my place in the ring to suffer and to work, taught by an instinct, that so shall the dumb abyss be vocal with speech. I pierce its order; I dissipate its fear; I dispose of it within the circuit of my expanding life. So much only of life as I know by experience, so much of the wilderness have I vanquished and planted, or so far have I extended by being, my dominion. I do not see how any man can afford, for the sake of his nerves and his nap, to spare any action in which he can partake. It is pearls and rubies to his discourse. Drudgery, calamity, exasperation, want, are instructors in eloquence and wisdom. The true scholar grudges every opportunity of action past by as a loss of power.

It is the raw material out of which the intellect moulds her splendid products. A strange process too, this, by which experience is converted into thought, as a mulberry leaf is converted into stain. The manufacture goes forward at all hours.

The actions and events of our childhood and youth are now matters of calmest observation. They lie like fair pictures in the air. Not so with our recent actions,—with the business which we now have in hand. On this we are quite unable to speculate. Our affections as yet circulate through it. We no more feel or know it than we feel the feet or the hand or the brain of our body. The new deed is yet a part of life,—remains for a time immersed in our unconscious life. In some contemplative hour, it detaches itself from the life like a ripe fruit, to become a thought of the mind. Instantly, it is raised, transfigured; the corruptible has put on incorruption. Henceforth it is an object of beauty, however base its origin and neighborhood. Observe, too, the impossibility of antedating this act. In its grub state it cannot fly, it cannot shine, it is a dull grub. But suddenly, without observation, the selfsame thing unfurls beautiful wings and is an angel of wisdom. So is there no fact, no event in our private history, which shall not, sooner or later, lose its adhesive, inert form, and astonish us by soaring from our body into the empyrean. Cradle and infancy, school and playground, the fear of boys, and dogs, and ferules, the love of little maids and berries, and many another fact that once filled the whole sky, are gone already; friend and relative, profession and party, town and country, nation and world, must also soar and sing.

Of course he who has put forth his total strength in fit actions has the richest return of wisdom. I will not shut myself out of this globe of action and transplant an oak into a flower-pot, there to hunger and pine; nor trust the revenue of some single faculty, and exhaust one vein of thought, much like those Savoyards, who, getting their livelihood by carving shepherds, shepherdesses, and smoking Dutchmen, for all Europe, went out one day to the mountain to find stock and discovered that they had whittled up the last of their pine-trees. Authors we have in numbers who have written out their vein, and who, moved by a commendable prudence, sail for Greece or Palestine, follow the trapper into the prairie, or ramble around Algiers, to replenish their merchantable stock.

If it were only for a vocabulary, the scholar would be covetous of action. Life is our dictionary. Years are well spent in country labors; in town, in the insight into trades and manufactures; in frank intercourse with many men and women; in science; in art; to the one end of mastering in all their facts a language by which to illustrate and embody our perceptions. I learn immediately from any speaker how much he has already lived, through the poverty or the splendor of his speech. Life lies behind us as the quarry from whence we get titles and cope-stones for the masonry of to-day. This is the way to learn grammar. Colleges and books only copy the language which the field and the workyard made.

But the final value of action, like that of books, and better than books, is, that it is a resource. That great principle of Undulation in nature that shows itself in the inspiring and expiring of the breath; in desire and satiety; in the ebb and flow of the sea; in day and night; in heat and cold;

and as yet more deeply ingrained in every atom and every fluid, is known to us under the name of Polarity,—these "fits of easy transmission and reflection," as Newton called them, are the law of nature because they are the law of spirit.

The mind now thinks; now acts; and each fit reproduces the other. When the artist has exhausted his materials, when the fancy no longer paints, when thoughts are no longer apprehended, and books are a weariness,—he has always the resource to live. Character is higher than intellect. Thinking is the function. Living is the functionary. The stream retreats to its source. A great soul will be strong to live, as well as strong to think. Does he lack organ or medium to impart his truths? He can still fall back on this elemental force of living them. This is a total act. Thinking is a partial act. Let the grandeur of justice shine in his affairs. Let the beauty of affection cheer his lowly roof. Those "far from fame," who dwell and act with him, will feel the force of his constitution in the doings and passages of the day better than it can be measured by any public and designed display. Time shall teach him that the scholar loses no hour which the man lives. Herein he unfolds the sacred germ of his instinct, screened from influence. What is lost in seemliness is gained in strength. Not out of those on whom systems of education have exhausted their culture comes the helpful giant to destroy the old or to build the new, but out of unhandselled savage nature, out of terrible Druids and berserkirs, come at last Alfred and Shakespeare.

I hear, therefore, with joy whatever is beginning to be said of the dignity and necessity of labor to every citizen. There is virtue yet in the hoe and the spade, for learned as well as for unlearned hands. And labor is everywhere welcome; always we are invited to work; only be this limitation observed, that a man shall not for the sake of wider activity sacrifice any opinion of the popular judgments and modes of action. I have now spoken of the education of the scholar by nature, by books, and by action. It remains to say somewhat of his duties.

They are such as become Man Thinking. They may all be comprised in self-trust. The Office of the scholar is to cheer, to raise, and to guide men by showing them facts amidst appearances. He plies the slow, unhonored, and unpaid task of observation. Flamsteed and Herschel, in their glazed observatories, may catalogue the stars with the praise of all men, and, the results being splendid and useful, honor is sure. But he, in his private observatory, cataloguing obscure and nebulous stars of the human mind, which as yet no man has thought of as such,—watching days and months, sometimes, for a few facts; correcting still his old records;—must relinquish display and immediate fame. In the long period of his preparation he must betray often an ignorance and shiftlessness in popular arts,

incurring the disdain of the able who shoulder him aside. Long he must stammer in his speech; often forego the living for the dead. Worse yet, he must accept,—how often! poverty and solitude. For the ease and pleasure of treading the old road, accepting the fashions, the education, the religion of society, he takes the cross of making his own, and, of course, the self-accusation, the faint heart, the frequent uncertainty and loss of time, which are the nettles and tangling vines in the way of the self-relying and self-directed; and the state of virtual hostility in which he seems to stand to society, and especially to educated society. For all this loss and scorn, what offset? He is to find consolation in exercising the highest functions of human nature. He is one who raises himself from private considerations, and breathes and lives on public and illustrious thoughts. He is the world's eye. He is the world's heart. He is to resist the vulgar prosperity that retrogrades ever to barbarism, by preserving and communicating heroic sentiments, noble biographies, melodious verse, and the conclusions of history. Whatsoever oracles the human heart, in all emergencies, in all solemn hours, has uttered as its commentary on the world of actions,—these he shall receive and impart. And whatsoever new verdict Reason from her inviolable seat pronounces on the passing men and events of to-day,—this he shall hear and promulgate.

These being his functions, it becomes him to feel all confidence in himself, and to defer never to the popular cry. He and he only knows the world. The world of any moment is the merest appearance. Some great decorum, some fetish of a government, some ephemeral trade, or war, or man, is cried up by half mankind and cried down by the other half, as if all depended on this particular up and down. The odds are that the whole question is not worth the poorest thought which the scholar has lost in listening to the controversy. Let him not quit his belief that a popgun is a popgun, though the ancient and honorable of the earth affirm it to be the crack of doom. In silence, in steadiness, in severe abstraction, let him hold by himself; add observation to observation, patient of neglect, patient of reproach; and bide his own time,—happy enough, if he can satisfy himself alone, that this day he has seen something truly. Success treads on every right step. For the instinct is sure that prompts him to tell his brother what he thinks. He then learns that in going down into the streets of his own mind, he has descended into the secrets of all minds. He learns that he who has mastered any law in his private thoughts is master to that extent of all men whose language he speaks and of all into whose language his own can be translated. The poet, in utter solitude remembering his spontaneous thoughts and recording them, is found to have recorded that which men in crowded cities find true for them also. The orator distrusts at first the fitness of his frank confessions,—his want of knowledge of the persons he addresses,—until he finds that he is the complement of his hearers; that they drink his words because he fulfils for them their own nature; the deeper he dives into his privatest, secretest presentiment, to his wonder he finds this is the most acceptable, most public, and universally true. The people delight in it; the better part of every man feels, This is my music; this is myself.

In self-trust all the virtues are comprehended. Free should the scholar be,—free and brave. Free even to the definition of freedom, "without any hindrance that does not arise out of his own constitution." Brave; for fear is a thing which a scholar by his very function puts behind him. Fear always springs from ignorance. It is a shame to him if his tranquillity, amid dangerous times, arise from the presumption that, like children and women, his is a protected class; or if he seek a temporary peace by the diversion of his thoughts from politics or vexed questions, hiding his head like an ostrich in the flowering bushes, peeping into microscopes, and turning rhymes, as a boy whistles to keep his courage up. So is the danger a danger still; so is the fear worse. Manlike let him turn and face it. Let him look into its eye and search its nature, inspect its origin,—see the whelping of this lion, which lies no great way back; he will then find in himself a perfect comprehension of its nature and extent; he will have made his hands meet on the other side, and can henceforth defy it and pass on superior. The world is his who can see through its pretension. What deafness, what stone-blind custom, what overgrown error you behold is there only by sufferance,—by your sufferance. See it to be a lie, and you have already dealt it its mortal blow.

Yes, we are the cowed,—we the trustless. It is a mischievous notion that we are come late into nature; that the world was finished a long time ago. As the world was plastic and fluid in the hands of God, so it is ever to so much of his attributes as we bring to it. To ignorance and sin, it is flint. They adapt themselves to it as they may; but in proportion as man has anything in him divine, the firmament flows before him and takes his signet and form. Not he is great who can alter matter, but he who can alter my state of mind. They are the kings of the world who give the color of their present thought to all nature and all art, and persuade men by the cheerful serenity of their carrying the matter, that this thing which they do is the apple which the ages have desired to pluck, now at last ripe, and inviting nations to the harvest. The great man makes the great thing. Wherever Macdonald sits, there is the head of the table. Linnaeus makes botany the most alluring of studies, and wins it from the farmer and the herb-woman; Davy, chemistry; and Cuvier, fossils. The day is always his who works in it with serenity and great aims. The unstable estimates of men crowd to him whose mind is filled with a truth, as the heaped waves of the Atlantic follow the moon. For this self-trust, the reason is deeper than can be fath-

omed,—darker than can be enlightened. I might not carry with me the feeling of my audience in stating my own belief. But I have already shown the ground of my hope, in adverting to the doctrine that man is one. I believe man has been wronged; he has wronged himself. He has almost lost the light that can lead him back to his prerogatives. Men are become of no account. Men in history, men in the world of to-day are bugs, are spawn, and are called "the mass" and "the herd." In a century, in a millennium, one or two men; that is to say,—one or two approximations to the right state of every man. All the rest behold in the hero or the poet their own green and crude being,—ripened; yes, and are content to be less, so *that* may attain to its full stature. What a testimony,—full of grandeur, full of pity, is borne to the demands of his own nature, by the poor clansman, the poor partisan, who rejoices in the glory of his chief. The poor and the low find some amends to their immense moral capacity, for their acquiescence in a political and social inferiority. They are content to be brushed like flies from the path of a great person, so that justice shall be done by him to that common nature which is the dearest desire of all to see enlarged and glorified. They sun themselves in the great man's light, and feel it to be their own element. They cast the dignity of man from their downtrod selves upon the shoulders of a hero, and will perish to add one drop of blood to make that great heart beat, those giant sinews combat and conquer. He lives for us, and we live in him.

Men such as they are, very naturally, seek money or power; and power because it is as good as money,—the "spoils," so called, "of office." And why not? for they aspire to the highest, and this, in their sleep-walking, they dream is highest. Wake them, and they shall quit the false good and leap to the true, and leave governments to clerks and desks. This revolution is to be wrought by the gradual domestication of the idea of Culture. The main enterprise of the world for splendor, for extent, is the upbuilding of a man. Here are the materials strown along the ground. The private life of one man shall be a more illustrious monarchy,—more formidable to its enemy, more sweet and serene in its influence to its friend, than any kingdom in history. For a man, rightly viewed, comprehendeth the particular natures of all men. Each philosopher, each bard, each actor, has only done for me, as by a delegate, what one day I can do for myself. The books which once we valued more than the apple of the eye we have quite exhausted. What is that but saying that we have come up with the point of view which the universal mind took through the eyes of one scribe; we have been that man, and have passed on. First, one; then, another; we drain all cisterns, and, waxing greater by all these supplies, we crave a better and more abundant food. The man has never lived that can feed us ever. The human mind cannot be enshrined in a person, who shall set a barrier on any one side to this unbounded, unboundable empire. It is one central fire, which, flaming now out of the lips of Etna, lightens the capes of Sicily; and, now out of the throat of Vesuvius, illuminates the towers and vineyards of Naples. It is one light which beams out of a thousand stars. It is one soul which animates all men.

But I have dwelt perhaps tediously upon this abstraction of the Scholar. I ought not to delay longer to add what I have to say, of nearer reference to the time and to this country.

Historically, there is thought to be a difference in the ideas which predominate over successive epochs, and there are data for marking the genius of the Classic, of the Romantic, and now of the Reflective or Philosophical age. With the views I have intimated of the oneness or the identity of the mind through all individuals, I do not much dwell on these differences. In fact, I believe each individual passes through all three. The boy is a Greek; the youth, romantic; the adult, reflective. I deny not, however, that a revolution in the leading idea may be distinctly enough traced.

Our age is bewailed as the age of Introversion. Must that needs be evil? We, it seems, are critical; we are embarrassed with second thoughts; we cannot enjoy anything for hankering to know whereof the pleasure consists; we are lined with eyes; we see with our feet; the time is infected with Hamlet's unhappiness—

Sicklied o'er with the pale cast of thought.

Is it so bad then? Sight is the last thing to be pitied. Would we be blind? Do we fear lest we should outsee nature and God, and drink truth dry? I look upon the discontent of the literary class as a mere announcement of the fact that they find themselves not in the state of mind of their fathers, and regret the coming state as untried, as a boy dreads the water before he has learned that he can swim. If there is any period one would desire to be born in, is it not the age of Revolution; when the old and the new stand side by side, and admit of being compared; when the energies of all men are searched by fear and by hope; when the historic glories of the old can be compensated by the rich possibilities of the new era? This time, like all times, is a very good one, if we but know what to do with it.

I read with joy some of the auspicious signs of the coming days, as they glimmer already through poetry and art, through philosophy and science, through church and state.

One of these signs is the fact that the same movement which effected the elevation of what was called the lowest class in the state assumed in literature a very marked and as benign an aspect. Instead of the sublime and beautiful, the near, the low, the common, was explored and poetized. That which had been negligently trodden under foot by those who were harnessing and provisioning themselves for long journeys into far countries is suddenly found to be richer than all foreign parts. The literature of the poor, the feelings of the child, the philosophy of the street, the meaning of household life, are the topics of the time. It is a great stride. It is a sign, is it not? of new vigor when the extremities are made active, when currents of warm life run into the hands and the feet. I ask not for the great, the remote, the romantic, what is doing in Italy or Arabia, what is Greek art or Provencal minstrelsy; I embrace the common; I explore and sit at the feet of the familiar, the low. Give me insight into to-day, and you may have the antique and future worlds. What would we really know the meaning of? The meal in the firkin, the milk in the pan, the ballad in the street, the news of the boat, the glance of the eye, the form and the gait of the body; show me the ultimate reason of these matters; show me the sublime presence of the highest spiritual cause lurking, as always it does lurk, in these suburbs and extremities of nature; let me see every trifle bristling with the polarity that ranges it instantly on an eternal law; and the shop, the plough, and the ledger, referred to the like cause by which light undulates and poets sing—and the world lies no longer a dull miscellany and lumber-room, but has form and order; there is no trifle; there is no puzzle; but one design unites and animates the farthest pinnacle and the lowest trench.

This idea has inspired the genius of Goldsmith, Burns, Cowper, and, in a newer time, of Goethe, Wordsworth, and Carlyle. This idea they have differently followed and with various success. In contrast with their writing, the style of Pope, of Johnson, of Gibbon, looks cold and pedantic. This writing is blood-warm. Man is surprised to find that things near are not less beautiful and wondrous than things remote. The near explains the far. The drop is a small ocean. A man is related to all nature. This perception of the worth of the vulgar is fruitful in discoveries. Goethe, in this very thing the most modern of the moderns, has shown us, as none ever did, the genius of the ancients.

There is one man of genius who has done much for this philosophy of life, whose literary value has never yet been rightly estimated; I mean Emanuel Swedenborg. The most imaginative of men, yet writing with the precision of a mathematician, he endeavored to engraft a purely philosophical Ethics on the popular Christianity of his time. Such an attempt, of course, must have difficulty which no genius could surmount. But he saw and showed the connection between nature and the affections of the soul. He pierced the emblematic or spiritual character of the visible, audible, tangible world. Especially did his shade-loving muse hover over and interpret the lower parts of nature; he showed the mysterious bond that allies moral evil to the foul material forms, and has given in epical parables a theory of insanity, of beasts, of unclean and fearful things.

Another sign of our times, also marked by an analogous political movement, is the new importance given to the single person. Everything that tends to insulate the individual—to surround him with barriers of natural respect, so that each man shall feel the world in his, and man shall treat with man as a sovereign State with a sovereign State—tends to true union as well as greatness. "I learned," said the melancholy Pestalozzi, "that no man in God's wide earth is either willing or able to help any other man." Help must come from the bosom alone. The scholar is that man who must take up into himself all the ability of the time, all the contributions of the past, all the hopes of the future. He must be an university of knowledges. If there be one lesson more than another which should pierce his ear, it is, The world is nothing, the man is all; in yourself is the law of all nature, and you know not yet how a globule of sap ascends; in yourself slumbers the whole of Reason; it is for you to know all, it is for you to dare all. Mr. President and gentlemen, this confidence in the unsearched might of man belongs, by all motives, by all prophecy, by all preparation, to the American Scholar. We have listened too long to the courtly muses of Europe. The spirit of the American freeman is already suspected to be timid, imitative, tame. Public and private avarice make the air we breathe thick and fat. The scholar is decent, indolent, complaisant. See already the tragic consequence. The mind of this country, taught to aim at low objects, eats upon itself. There is no work for any but the decorous and the complaisant. Young men of the fairest promise, who begin life upon our shores, inflated by the mountain winds, shined upon by all the stars of God, find the earth below not in unison with these, but are hindered from action by the disgust which the principles on which business is managed inspire, and turn drudges, or die of disgust—some of them suicides. What is the remedy? They did not yet see, and thousands of young men as hopeful now crowding to the barriers for the career, do not yet see that if the single man plant himself indomitably on his instincts, and there abide, the huge world will come round to him. Patience—patience; with the shades of all the good and great for company; and for solace, the perspective of your own infinite life; and for work, the study and the communication of principles, the making those instincts prevalent, the conversion of the world. Is it not the chief disgrace in the world not to be an unit; not to be reckoned one character; not to yield that peculiar fruit which each man was created to bear, but to be reckoned in the gross, in the hundred, or the thousand, of the party, the section, to which we belong; and our opinion predicted geographically, as the north, or the south! Not so, brothers and friends; please God ours shall not be so! We will walk on our own feet; we will work with our own hands; we will speak our own minds. The study of letters shall be no longer a name for pity, for doubt, and for sensual indulgence. The dread of man and the love of man shall be a wall of defence and a wreath of joy around all. A nation of men will for the first time exist, because each believes himself inspired by the Divine Soul, which also inspires all men.

Source:

James Andrews and David Zarefsky, eds. *American Voices: Significant Speeches in American History, 1640–1945.* New York: Longman, 1989.

Henry David Thoreau, "Civil Disobedience," 1849

Influential essay written by American author and naturalist Henry David Thoreau, who advocated civil disobedience as a means for an individual to protest governmental actions that he or she considers unjust. The essay was originally given in 1849 as a lecture called "Resistance to Civil Disobedience" and then published that year in his friend Elizabeth Peabody's volume, *Aesthetic Papers.* It was written after Thoreau had spent a night in prison for refusing to pay a poll tax used to finance the Mexican War, which Thoreau opposed as imperialistic and as an attempt to extend slavery. Thoreau argued that there is a higher law than the civil law and that the higher law must be followed, regardless of the penalty: "Under a government which imprisons any unjustly, the true place for a just man is also a prison." The essay, titled "Civil Disobedience" in 1866, influenced many social and political reformers, including Mohandas Gandhi and the Reverend Dr. Martin Luther King, Jr.

———————————— ❧ ————————————

Civil Disobedience

I heartily accept the motto,—"That government is best which governs least;" and I should like to see it acted up to more rapidly and systematically. Carried out, it finally amounts to this, which also I believe,—"That government is best which governs not at all;" and when men are prepared for it, that will be the kind of government which they will have. Government is at best but an expedient; but most governments are usually, and all governments are sometimes, inexpedient. The objections which have been brought against a standing army, and they are many and weighty, and deserve to prevail, may also at last be brought against a standing government. The standing army is only an arm of the standing government. The government itself, which is only the mode which the people have chosen to execute their will, is equally liable to be abused and perverted before the people can act through it. Witness the present Mexican war, the work of comparatively a few individuals using the standing government as their tool; for, in the outset, the people would not have consented to this measure.

This American government,—what is it but a tradition, though a recent one, endeavoring to transmit itself unimpaired to posterity, but each instant losing some of its integrity? It has not the vitality and force of a single living man; for a single man can bend it to his will. It is a sort of wooden gun to the people themselves. But it is not the less necessary for this; for the people must have some complicated machinery or other, and hear its din, to satisfy that idea of government which they have. Governments show thus how successfully men can be imposed on, even impose on themselves, for their own advantage. It is excellent, we must all allow. Yet this government never of itself furthered any enterprise, but by the alacrity with which it got out of its way. *It* does not keep the country free. *It* does not settle the West. *It* does not educate. The character inherent in the American people has done all that has been accomplished; and it would have done somewhat more, if the government had not sometimes got in its way. For government is an expedient by which men would fain succeed in letting one another alone; and, as has been said, when it is most expedient, the governed are most let alone by it. Trade and commerce, if they were not made of India-rubber, would never manage to bounce over the obstacles which legislators are continually putting in their way; and, if one were to judge these men wholly by the effects of their actions and not partly by their intentions, they would deserve to be classed and punished with those mischievous persons who put obstructions on the railroads.

But, to speak practically and as a citizen, unlike those who call themselves no-government men, I ask for, not at once no government, but *at once* a better government. Let every man make known what kind of government would command his respect, and that will be one step toward obtaining it.

After all, the practical reason why, when the power is once in the hands of the people, a majority are permitted, and for a long period continue, to rule is not because they are most likely to be in the right, nor because this seems fairest to the minority, but because they are physically the strongest. But a government in which the majority rule in all cases cannot be based on justice, even as far as men understand it. Can there not be a government in which majorities do not virtually decide right and wrong, but conscience?—in which majorities decide only those questions to which the rule of expediency is applicable? Must the citizen ever for a moment, or in the least degree, resign his conscience to the legislator? Why has every man a conscience, then? I think that we should be men first, and subjects afterward. It is not desirable to cultivate a respect for the law, so much as for the right. The only obligation which I have a right to assume is to do at any time what I think right. It is truly enough said, that a corporation has no conscience; but a corporation of conscientious men is a corporation *with* a conscience. Law never made men a whit more just; and, by means of their respect for it, even the well-disposed are daily made the agents of injustice. A common and natural result of an undue respect for law is, that you may see a file of soldiers, colonel, captain, corporal, privates, powder-monkeys, and all, marching in admirable order over hill and dale to the wars, against their wills, ay, against their common sense and consciences, which makes it very steep marching indeed, and produces a palpitation of the heart. They have no doubt that it is a damnable business in which they are concerned; they are all peaceably inclined. Now, what are they? Men at all? or small movable forts and magazines, at the service of some unscrupulous man in power? Visit the Navy-Yard, and behold a marine, such a man as an American government can make, or such as it can make a man with its black arts,—a mere shadow and reminiscence of humanity, a man laid out alive and standing, and already, as one may say, buried under arms with funeral accompaniments, though it may be,—

"Not a drum was heard, not a funeral note, As his corse to the rampart we hurried;

Not a soldier discharged his farewell shot O'er the grave where our hero we buried."

The mass of men serve the state thus, not as men mainly, but as machines, with their bodies. They are the standing army, and the militia, jailors, constables, posse comitatus, etc. In most cases there is no free exercise whatever of the judgment or of the moral sense; but they put themselves on a level with wood and earth and stones; and wooden men can perhaps be manufactured that will serve the purpose as well. Such command no more respect than men of straw or a lump of dirt. They have the same sort of worth only as horses and dogs. Yet such as these even are commonly esteemed good citizens. Others—as most legislators, politicians, lawyers, ministers, and office-holders— serve the state chiefly with their heads; and, as they rarely make any moral distinctions, they are as likely to serve the Devil, without *intending* it, as God. A very few, as heroes, patriots, martyrs, reformers in the great sense, and *men*, serve the state with their consciences also, and so necessarily resist it for the most part; and they are commonly treated as enemies by it. A wise man will only be useful as a man, and will not submit to be "clay," and "stop a hole to keep the wind away," but leave that office to his dust at least:—

"I am too high-born to be propertied, To be a secondary at control, Or useful serving-man and instrument To any sovereign state throughout the world."

He who gives himself entirely to his fellow-men appears to them useless and selfish; but he who gives himself partially to them is pronounced a benefactor and philanthropist.

How does it become a man to behave toward this American government to-day? I answer, that he cannot without disgrace be associated with it. I cannot for an instant recognize that political organization as *my* government which is the *slave's* government also.

All men recognize the right of revolution; that is, the right to refuse allegiance to, and to resist, the government, when its tyranny or its inefficiency are great and unendurable. But almost all say that such is not the case now. But such was the case, they think, in the Revolution of '75. If one were to tell me that this was a bad government because it taxed certain foreign commodities brought to its ports, it is most probable that I should not make an ado about it, for I can do without them. All machines have their friction; and possibly this does enough good to counterbalance the evil. At any rate, it is a great evil to make a stir about it. But when the friction comes to have its machine, and oppression and robbery are organized, I say, let us not have such a machine any longer. In other words, when a sixth of the population of a nation which has undertaken to be the refuge of liberty are slaves, and a whole country is unjustly overrun and conquered by a foreign army, and subjected to military law, I think that it is not too soon for honest men to rebel and revolutionize. What makes this duty the more urgent is the fact that the country so overrun is not our own, but ours is the invading army.

Paley, a common authority with many on moral questions, in his chapter on the "Duty of Submission to Civil Government," resolves all civil obligation into expediency; and he proceeds to say, "that so long as the interest of the whole society requires it, that is, so long as the established government cannot be resisted or changed without public inconveniency, it is the will of God that the established government be obeyed, and no longer. . . . This principle being admitted, the justice of every particular case of resistance is reduced to a computation of the quantity of the danger and grievance on the one side, and of the probability and expense of redressing it on the other." Of this, he says, every man shall judge for himself. But Paley appears never to have contemplated those cases to which the rule of expediency does not apply, in which a people, as well as an individual, must do justice, cost what it may. If I have unjustly wrested a plank from a drowning man, I must restore it to him though I drown myself. This, according to Paley, would be inconvenient. But he that would save his life, in such a case, shall lose it. This people must cease to hold slaves, and to make war on Mexico, though it cost them their existence as a people. In their practice, nations agree with Paley; but does any one think

that Massachusetts does exactly what is right at the present crisis?

"A drab of state, a cloth-o'-silverslut, To have her train borne up, and her soul trail in the dirt."

Practically speaking, the opponents to a reform in Massachusetts are not a hundred thousand politicians at the South, but a hundred thousand merchants and farmers here, who are more interested in commerce and agriculture than they are in humanity, and are not prepared to do justice to the slave and to Mexico, *cost what it may*. I quarrel not with far-off foes, but with those who, near at home, cooperate with, and do the bidding of, those far away, and without whom the latter would be harmless. We are accustomed to say, that the mass of men are unprepared; but improvement is slow, because the few are not materially wiser or better than the many. It is not so important that many should be as good as you, as that there be some absolute goodness somewhere; for that will leaven the whole lump. There are thousands who are *in opinion* opposed to slavery and to the war, who yet in effect do nothing to put an end to them; who, esteeming themselves children of Washington and Franklin, sit down with their hands in their pockets, and say that they know not what to do, and do nothing; who even postpone the question of freedom to the question of free-trade, and quietly read the prices-current along with the latest advices from Mexico, after dinner, and, it may be, fall asleep over them both. What is the price-current of an honest man and patriot to-day? They hesitate, and they regret, and sometimes they petition; but they do nothing in earnest and with effect. They will wait, well disposed, for others to remedy the evil, that they may no longer have it to regret. At most, they give only a cheap vote, and a feeble countenance and God-speed, to the right, as it goes by them. There are nine hundred and ninety-nine patrons of virtue to one virtuous man. But it is easier to deal with the real possessor of a thing than with the temporary guardian of it.

All voting is a sort of gaming, like checkers or backgammon, with a slight moral tinge to it, a playing with right and wrong, with moral questions; and betting naturally accompanies it. The character of the voters is not staked. I cast my vote, per-chance, as I think right; but I am not vitally concerned that that right should prevail. I am willing to leave it to the majority. Its obligation, therefore, never exceeds that of expediency. Even voting *for the right* is *doing* nothing for it. It is only expressing to men feebly your desire that it should prevail. A wise man will not leave the right to the mercy of chance, nor wish it to prevail through the power of the majority. There is but little virtue in the action of masses of men. When the majority shall at length vote for the abolition of slavery, it will be because they are indifferent to slavery, or because there is but little slavery left to be abolished by their vote. *They* will then be the only slaves. Only *his* vote can hasten the abolition of slavery who asserts his own freedom by his vote.

I hear of a convention to be held at Baltimore, or elsewhere, for the selection of a candidate for the Presidency, made up chiefly of editors, and men who are politicians by profession; but I think, what is it to any independent, intelligent, and respectable man what decision they may come to? Shall we not have the advantage of his wisdom and honesty, nevertheless? Can we not count upon some independent votes? Are there not many individuals in the country who do not attend conventions? But no: I find that the respectable man, so called, has immediately drifted from his position, and despairs of his country, when his country has more reason to despair of him. He forthwith adopts one of the candidates thus selected as the only *available* one, thus proving that he is himself *available* for any purposes of the demagogue. His vote is of no more worth than that of any unprincipled foreigner or hireling native, who may have been bought. O for a man who is a *man,* and, as my neighbor says, has a bone in his back which you cannot pass your hand through! Our statistics are at fault: the population has been returned too large. How many *men* are there to a square thousand miles in this country? Hardly one. Does not America offer any inducement for men to settle here? The American has dwindled into an Odd Fellow,—one who may be known by the development of his organ of gregariousness, and a manifest lack of intellect and cheerful self-reliance; whose first and chief concern, on coming into the world, is to see that the Almshouses are in good repair; and, before yet he has lawfully donned the virile garb, to collect a fund for the support of the widows and orphans that may be; who, in short, ventures to live only by the aid of the Mutual Insurance company, which has promised to bury him decently.

It is not a man's duty, as a matter of course, to devote himself to the eradication of any, even the most enormous wrong; he may still properly have other concerns to engage him; but it is his duty, at least, to wash his hands of it, and, if he gives it no thought longer, not to give it practically his support. If I devote myself to other pursuits and contemplations, I must first see, at least, that I do not pursue them sitting upon another man's shoulders. I must get off him first, that he may pursue his contemplations too. See what gross inconsistency is tolerated. I have heard some of my townsmen say, "I should like to have them order me out to help put down an insurrection of the slaves, or to march to Mexico;—see if I would go;" and yet these very men have each, directly by their allegiance, and so indirectly, at least, by their money, furnished a substitute. The soldier is applauded who refuses to serve in an unjust war by those who do not refuse to sustain the unjust government which makes the war; is applauded by those whose own act and

authority he disregards and sets at naught; as if the state were penitent to that degree that it hired one to scourge it while it sinned, but not to that degree that it left off sinning for a moment. Thus, under the name of Order and Civil Government, we are all made at last to pay homage to and support our own meanness. After the first blush of sin comes its indifference; and from immoral it becomes, as it were, *un* moral, and not quite unnecessary to that life which we have made.

The broadest and most prevalent error requires the most disinterested virtue to sustain it. The slight reproach to which the virtue of patriotism is commonly liable, the noble are most likely to incur. Those who, while they disapprove of the character and measures of a government, yield to it their allegiance and support are undoubtedly its most conscientious supporters, and so frequently the most serious obstacles to reform. Some are petitioning the state to dissolve the Union, to disregard the requisitions of the President. Why do they not dissolve it themselves,—the union between themselves and the state,—and refuse to pay their quota into its treasury? Do not they stand in the same relation to the state that the state does to the Union? And have not the same reasons prevented the state from resisting the Union which have prevented them from resisting the state?

How can a man be satisfied to entertain an opinion merely, and enjoy *it*? Is there any enjoyment in it, if his opinion is that he is aggrieved? If you are cheated out of a single dollar by your neighbor, you do not rest satisfied with knowing that you are cheated, or with saying that you are cheated, or even with petitioning him to pay you your due; but you take effectual steps at once to obtain the full amount, and see that you are never cheated again. Action from principle, the perception and the performance of right, changes things and relations; it is essentially revolutionary, and does not consist wholly with anything which was. It not only divides states and churches, it divides families; ay, it divides the *individual,* separating the diabolical in him from the divine.

Unjust laws exist: shall we be content to obey them, or shall we endeavor to amend them, and obey them until we have succeeded, or shall we transgress them at once? Men generally, under such a government as this, think that they ought to wait until they have persuaded the majority to alter them. They think that, if they should resist, the remedy would be worse than the evil. But it is the fault of the government itself that the remedy *is* worse than the evil. *It* makes it worse. Why is it not more apt to anticipate and provide for reform? Why does it not cherish its wise minority? Why does it cry and resist before it is hurt? Why does it not encourage its citizens to be on the alert to point out its faults, and *do* better than it would have them? Why does it always crucify Christ, and excommunicate Copernicus and Luther, and pronounce Washington and Franklin rebels?

One would think, that a deliberate and practical denial of its authority was the only offense never contemplated by government; else, why has it not assigned its definite, its suitable and proportionate penalty? If a man who has no property refuses but once to earn nine shillings for the state, he is put in prison for a period unlimited by any law that I know, and determined only by the discretion of those who placed him there; but if he should steal ninety times nine shillings from the state, he is soon permitted to go at large again.

If the injustice is part of the necessary friction of the machine of government, let it go, let it go: perchance it will wear smooth,—certainly the machine will wear out. If the injustice has a spring, or a pulley, or a rope, or a crank, exclusively for itself, then perhaps you may consider whether the remedy will not be worse than the evil; but if it is of such a nature that it requires you to be the agent of injustice to another, then, I say, break the law. Let your life be a counter friction to stop the machine. What I have to do is to see, at any rate, that I do not lend myself to the wrong which I condemn.

As for adopting the ways which the state has provided for remedying the evil, I know not of such ways. They take too much time, and a man's life will be gone. I have other affairs to attend to. I came into this world, not chiefly to make this a good place to live in, but to live in it, be it good or bad. A man has not everything to do, but something; and because he cannot do *everything*, it is not necessary that he should do *something* wrong. It is not my business to be petitioning the Governor or the Legislature any more than it is theirs to petition me; and if they should not hear my petition, what should I do then? But in this case the state has provided no way: its very Constitution is the evil. This may seem to be harsh and stubborn and unconciliatory; but it is to treat with the utmost kindness and consideration the only spirit that can appreciate or deserves it. So is all change for the better, like birth and death, which convulse the body. I do not hesitate to say, that those who call themselves Abolitionists should at once effectually withdraw their support, both in person and property, from the government of Massachusetts and not wait till they constitute a majority of one, before they suffer the right to prevail through them. I think that it is enough if they have God on their side, without waiting for that other one. Moreover, any man more right than his neighbors constitutes a majority of one already.

I meet this American government, or its representative, the state government, directly, and face to face, once a year—no more—in the person of its tax-gatherer; this is the only mode in which a man situated as I am necessarily meets it; and it then says distinctly, Recognize me; and the simplest, most effectual, and, in the present posture of affairs, the indispensablest mode of treating with it on this head, of expressing your little satisfaction with and love for it, is to deny it then. My civil neighbor, the tax-gatherer, is the very man I have to deal with,—for it is, after all, with men and not with parchment that I quarrel,—and he has voluntarily chosen to be an agent of the government. How shall he ever know well what he is and does as an officer of the government, or as a man, until he is obliged to consider whether he shall treat me, his neighbor, for whom he has respect, as a neighbor and well-disposed man, or as a maniac and disturber of the peace, and see if he can get over this obstruction to his neighborliness without a ruder and more impetuous thought or speech corresponding with his action. I know this well, that if one thousand, if one hundred, if ten men whom I could name,—if ten *honest* men only,—ay, if *one* honest man, in this State of Massachusetts, *ceasing to hold slaves*, were actually to withdraw from this copartnership, and be locked up in the county jail therefor, it would be the abolition of slavery in America. For it matters not how small the beginning may seem to be: what is once well done is done forever. But we love better to talk about it: that we say is our mission. Reform keeps many scores of newspapers in its service, but not one man. If my esteemed neighbor, the State's ambassador, who will devote his days to the settlement of the question of human rights in the Council Chamber, instead of being threatened with the prisons of Carolina, were to sit down the prisoner of Massachusetts, that State which is so anxious to foist the sin of slavery upon her sister,—though at present she can discover only an act of inhospitality to be the ground of a quarrel with her,—the Legislature would not wholly waive the subject the following winter.

Under a government which imprisons any unjustly, the true place for a just man is also a prison. The proper place to-day, the only place which Massachusetts has provided for her freer and less desponding spirits, is in her prisons, to be put out and locked out of the State by her own act, as they have already put themselves out by their principles. It is there that the fugitive slave, and the Mexican prisoner on parole, and the Indian come to plead the wrongs of his race should find them; on that separate, but more free and honorable ground, where the State places those who are not *with* her, but *against* her,—the only house in a slave State in which a free man can abide with honor. If any think that their influence would be lost there, and their voices no longer afflict the ear of the State, that they would not be as an enemy within its walls, they do not know by how much truth is stronger than error, nor how much more eloquently and effectively he can combat injustice who has experienced a little in his own person. Cast your whole vote, not a strip of paper merely, but your whole influence. A minority is powerless while it conforms to the majority; it is not even a minority then; but it is irresistible when it clogs by its whole weight. If the alternative is to keep all just men in prison, or give up war and slavery, the State will not hesitate which to choose. If a thousand men were not to pay their tax-bills this year, that would not be a violent and bloody measure, as it would be to pay them, and enable the State to commit violence and shed innocent blood. This is, in fact, the definition of a peaceable revolution, if any such is possible. If the tax-gatherer, or any other public officer, asks me, as one has done, "But what shall I do?" my answer is, "If you really wish to do anything, resign your office." When the subject has refused allegiance, and the officer has resigned his office, then the revolution is accomplished. But even suppose blood should flow. Is there not a sort of blood shed when the conscience is wounded? Through this wound a man's real manhood and immortality flow out, and he bleeds to an everlasting death. I see this blood flowing now.

I have contemplated the imprisonment of the offender, rather than the seizure of his goods,—though both will serve the same purpose,—because they who assert the purest right, and consequently are most dangerous to a corrupt State, commonly have not spent much time in accumulating property. To such the State renders comparatively small service, and a slight tax is wont to appear exorbitant, particularly if they are obliged to earn it by special labor with their hands. If there were one who lived wholly without the use of money, the State itself would hesitate to demand it of him. But the rich man—not to make any invidious comparison—is always sold to the institution which makes him rich. Absolutely speaking, the more money, the less virtue; for money comes between a man and his objects, and obtains them for him; and it was certainly no great virtue to obtain it. It puts to rest many questions which he would otherwise be taxed to answer; while the only new question which it puts is the hard but superfluous one, how to spend it. Thus his moral ground is taken from under his feet. The opportunities of living are diminished in proportion as what are called the "means" are increased. The best thing a man can do for his culture when he is rich is to endeavor to carry out those schemes which he entertained when he was poor. Christ answered the Herodians according to their condition. "Show me the tribute-money," said he;—and one took a penny out of his pocket;—if you use money which has the image of Caesar on it and which he has made current and valuable, that is, *if you are men of the State,* and gladly enjoy the advantages of Caesar's government, then pay him back some of his own when he demands it. "Render therefore to Caesar that which is Caesar's, and to God those things which are God's,"—leaving them no wiser than before as to which was which; for they did not wish to know.

When I converse with the freest of my neighbors, I perceive that, whatever they may say about the magnitude and seriousness of the question, and their regard for the public tranquillity, the long and the short of the matter is, that they cannot spare the protection of the existing government, and they dread the consequences to their property and families of disobedience to it. For my own part, I should not like to think that I ever rely on the protection of the State. But, if I deny the authority of the State when it presents its tax-bill, it will soon take and waste all my property, and so harass me and my children without end. This is hard. This makes it impossible for a man to live honestly, and at the same time comfortably, in outward respects. It will not be worth the while to accumulate property; that would be sure to go again. You must hire or squat somewhere, and raise but a small crop, and eat that soon. You must live within yourself, and depend upon yourself always tucked up and ready for a start, and not have many affairs. A man may grow rich in Turkey even, if he will be in all respects a good subject of the Turkish government. Confucius said: "If a state is governed by the principles of reason, poverty and misery are subjects of shame; if a state is not governed by the principles of reason, riches and honors are the subjects of shame." No: until I want the protection of Massachusetts to be extended to me in some distant Southern port, where my liberty is endangered, or until I am bent solely on building up an estate at home by peaceful enterprise, I can afford to refuse allegiance to Massachusetts, and her right to my property and life. It costs me less in every sense to incur the penalty of disobedience to the State than it would to obey. I should feel as if I were worth less in that case.

Some years ago, the State met me in behalf of the Church, and commanded me to pay a certain sum toward the support of a clergyman whose preaching my father attended, but never I myself. "Pay," it said, "or be locked up in the jail." I declined to pay, But, unfortunately, another man saw fit to pay it. I did not see why the schoolmaster should be taxed to support the priest, and not the priest the schoolmaster; for I was not the State's schoolmaster, but I supported myself by voluntary subscription. I did not see why the lyceum should not present its tax-bill, and have the State to back its demand, as well as the Church. However, at the request of the selectmen, I condescended to make some such statement as this in writing:—"Know all men by these presents, that I, Henry Thoreau, do not wish to be regarded as a member of any incorporated society which I have not joined." This I gave to the town clerk; and he has it. The State, having thus learned that I did not wish to be regarded as a member of that church, has never made a like demand on me since; though it said that it must adhere to its original presumption that time. If I had known how to name them, I should then have signed off in detail from all the societies which I never signed on to; but I did not know where to find a complete list.

I have paid no poll-tax for six years. I was put into a jail once on this account, for one night; and, as I stood considering the walls of solid stone, two or three feet thick, the door of wood and iron, a foot thick, and the iron grating which strained the light, I could not help being struck with the foolishness of that institution which treated me as if I were mere flesh and blood and bones, to be locked up. I wondered that it should have concluded at length that this was the best use it could put me to, and had never thought to avail itself of my services in some way. I saw that, if there was a wall of stone between me and my townsmen, there was a still more difficult one to climb or break through before they could get to be as free as I was. I did not for a moment feel confined, and the walls seemed a great waste of stone and mortar. I felt as if I alone of all my townsmen had paid my tax. They plainly did not know how to treat me, but behaved like persons who are underbred. In every threat and in every compliment there was a blunder; for they thought that my chief desire was to stand the other side of that stone wall. I could not but smile to see how industriously they locked the door on my meditations, which followed them out again without let or hindrance, and *they* were really all that was dangerous. As they could not reach me, they had resolved to punish my body; just as boys, if they cannot come at some person against whom they have a spite, will abuse his dog. I saw that the State was half-witted, that it was timid as a lone woman with her silver spoons, and that it did not know its friends from its foes, and I lost all my remaining respect for it, and pitied it.

Thus the State never intentionally confronts a man's sense, intellectual or moral, but only his body, his senses. It is not armed with superior wit or honesty, but with superior physical strength. I was not born to be forced. I will breathe after my own fashion. Let us see who is the strongest. What force has a multitude? They only can force me who obey a higher law than I. They force me to become like themselves. I do not hear of *men* being *forced* to live this way or that by masses of men. What sort of life were that to live? When I meet a government which says to me, "Your money or your life," why should I be in haste to give it my money? It may be in a great strait, and not know what to do: I cannot help that. It must help itself; do as I do. It is not worth the while to snivel about it. I am not responsible for the successful working of the machinery of society. I am not the son of the engineer. I perceive that, when an acorn and a chestnut fall side by side, the one does not remain inert to make way for the other, but both obey their own laws, and spring and grow and flourish as best they can, till one, perchance, over-shadows and

destroys the other. If a plant cannot live according to its nature, it dies; and so a man.

The night in prison was novel and interesting enough. The prisoners in their shirt-sleeves were enjoying a chat and the evening air in the doorway, when I entered. But the jailer said, "Come, boys, it is time to lock up; " and so they dispersed, and I heard the sound of their steps returning into the hollow apartments. My room-mate was introduced to me by the jailer as "a first-rate fellow and a clever man." When the door was locked, he showed me where to hang my hat, and how he managed matters there. The rooms were white-washed once a month; and this one, at least, was the whitest, most simply furnished, and probably the neatest apartment in the town. He naturally wanted to know where I came from, and what brought me there; and, when I had told him, I asked him in my turn how he came there, presuming him to be an honest man, of course; and, as the world goes, I believe he was. "Why," said he, "they accuse me of burning a barn; but I never did it." As near as I could discover, he had probably gone to bed in a barn when drunk, and smoked his pipe there; and so a barn was burnt. He had the reputation of being a clever man, had been there some three months waiting for his trial to come on, and would have to wait as much longer; but he was quite domesticated and contented, since he got his board for nothing, and thought that he was well treated.

He occupied one window, and I the other; and I saw that if one stayed there long, his principal business would be to look out the window. I had soon read all the tracts that were left there, and examined where former prisoners had broken out, and where a grate had been sawed off, and heard the history of the various occupants of that room; for I found that even here there was a history and a gossip which never circulated beyond the walls of the jail. Probably this is the only house in the town where verses are composed, which are afterward printed in a circular form, but not published. I was shown quite a long list of verses which were composed by some young men who had been detected in an attempt to escape, who avenged themselves by singing them.

I pumped my fellow-prisoner as dry as I could, for fear I should never see him again; but at length he showed me which was my bed, and left me to blow out the lamp.

It was like traveling into a far country, such as I had never expected to behold, to lie there for one night. It seemed to me that I never had heard the town-clock strike before, nor the evening sounds of the village; for we slept with the windows open, which were inside the grating. It was to see my native village in the light of the Middle Ages, and our Concord was turned into a Rhine stream, and visions of knights and castles passed before me. They were the voices of old burghers that I heard in the streets. I was an involuntary spectator and auditor of whatever was done and said in the kitchen of the adjacent village-inn,—a wholly new and rare experience to me. It was a closer view of my native town. I was fairly inside of it. I never had seen its institutions before. This is one of its peculiar institutions; for it is a shire town. I began to comprehend what its inhabitants were about.

In the morning, our breakfasts were put through the hole in the door, in small oblong-square tin pans, made to fit, and holding a pint of chocolate, with brown bread, and an iron spoon. When they called for the vessels again, I was green enough to return what bread I had left; but my comrade seized it, and said that I should lay that up for lunch or dinner. Soon after he was let out to work at haying in a neighboring field, whither he went every day, and would not be back till noon; so he bade me good-day, saying that he doubted if he should see me again.

When I came out of prison,—for some one interfered, and paid that tax,—I did not perceive that great changes had taken place on the common, such as he observed who went in a youth and emerged a tottering and gray-headed man; and yet a change had to my eyes come over the scene,—the town, and State, and country,—greater than any that mere time could effect. I saw yet more distinctly the State in which I lived. I saw to what extent the people among whom I lived could be trusted as good neighbors and friends; that their friendship was for summer weather only; that they did not greatly propose to do right; that they were a distinct race from me by their prejudices and superstitions, as the China-men and Malays are; that in their sacrifices to humanity they ran no risks, not even to their property; that after all they were not so noble but they treated the thief as he had treated them, and hoped, by a certain outward observance and a few prayers, and by walking in a particular straight though useless path from time to time, to save their souls. This may be to judge my neighbors harshly; for I believe that many of them are not aware that they have such an institution as the jail in their village.

It was formerly the custom in our village, when a poor debtor came out of jail, for his acquaintances to salute him, looking through their fingers, which were crossed to represent the grating of a jail window, "How do ye do?" My neighbors did not thus salute me, but first looked at me, and then at one another, as if I had returned from a long journey. I was put into jail as I was going to the shoemaker's to get a shoe which was mended. When I was let out the next morning, I proceeded to finish my errand, and, having put on my mended shoe, joined a huckleberry party, who were impatient to put themselves under my conduct; and in half an hour,—for the horse was soon tackled,—was in the midst of a huckleberry field, on one of our highest hills, two miles off, and then the State was nowhere to be seen.

This is the whole history of "My Prisons."

I have never declined paying the highway tax, because I am as desirous of being a good neighbor as I am of being a bad subject; and as for supporting schools, I am doing my part to educate my fellow-countrymen now. It is for no particular item in the tax-bill that I refuse to pay it. I simply wish to refuse allegiance to the State, to withdraw and stand aloof from it effectually. I do not care to trace the course of my dollar, if I could, till it buys a man or a musket to shoot with,—the dollar is innocent,—but I am concerned to trace the effects of my allegiance. In fact, I quietly declare war with the State, after my fashion, though I will still make what use and get what advantage of her I can, as is usual in such cases.

If others pay the tax which is demanded of me, from a sympathy with the State, they do but what they have already done in their own case, or rather they abet injustice to a greater extent than the State requires. If they pay the tax from a mistaken interest in the individual taxed, to save his property, or prevent his going to jail, it is because they have not considered wisely how far they let their private feelings interfere with the public good.

This, then, is my position at present. But one cannot be too much on his guard in such a case, lest his action be biased by obstinacy or an undue regard for the opinions of men. Let him see that he does only what belongs to himself and to the hour.

I think sometimes, Why, this people mean well, they are only ignorant; they would do better if they knew how: why give your neighbors this pain to treat you as they are not inclined to? But I think again, This is no reason why I should do as they do, or permit others to suffer much greater pain of a different kind. Again, I sometimes say to myself, When many millions of men, without heat, without ill will, without personal feeling of any kind, demand of you a few shillings only, without the possibility, such is their constitution, of retracting or altering their present demand, and without the possibility, on your side, of appeal to any other millions, why expose yourself to this overwhelming brute force? You do not resist cold and hunger, the winds and the waves, thus obstinately; you quietly submit to a thousand similar necessities. You do not put your head into the fire. But just in proportion as I regard this as not wholly a brute force, but partly a human force, and consider that I have relations to those millions as to so many millions of men, and not of mere brute or inanimate things, I see that appeal is possible, first and instantaneously, from them to the Maker of them, and, secondly, from them to themselves. But if I put my head deliberately into the fire, there is no appeal to fire or to the Maker of fire, and I have only myself to blame. If I could convince myself that I have any right to be satisfied with men as they are, and to treat them accordingly, and not according, in some respects, to my requisitions and expectations of what they and I ought to be, then, like a good Mussulman and fatalist, I should endeavor to be satisfied with things as they are, and say it is the will of God. And, above all, there is this difference between resisting this and a purely brute or natural force, that I can resist this with some effect; but I cannot expect, like Orpheus, to change the nature of the rocks and trees and beasts.

I do not wish to quarrel with any man or nation. I do not wish to split hairs, to make fine distinctions, or set myself up as better than my neighbors. I seek rather, I may say, even an excuse for conforming to the laws of the land. I am but too ready to conform to them. Indeed, I have reason to suspect myself on this head; and each year, as the tax-gatherer comes round, I find myself disposed to review the acts and position of the general and State governments, and the spirit of the people, to discover a pretext for conformity.

"We must affect our country as our parents, And if at any time we alienate Our love or industry from doing it honor, We must respect effects and teach the soul Matter of conscience and religion, And not desire of rule or benefit."

I believe that the State will soon be able to take all my work of this sort out of my hands, and then I shall be no better a patriot than my fellow-countrymen. Seen from a lower point of view, the Constitution, with all its faults, is very good; the law and the courts are very respectable; even this State and this American government are, in many respects, very admirable, and rare things, to be thankful for, such as a great many have described them; but seen from a point of view a little higher, they are what I have described them; seen from a higher still, and the highest, who shall say what they are, or that they are worth looking at or thinking of at all?

However, the government does not concern me much, and I shall bestow the fewest possible thoughts on it. It is not many moments that I live under a government, even in this world. If a man is thought-free, fancy-free, imagination-free, that which *is not* never for a long time appearing *to be* to him, unwise rulers or reformers cannot fatally interrupt him.

I know that most men think differently from myself; but those whose lives are by profession devoted to the study of these or kindred subjects content me as little as any. States-men and legislators, standing so completely within the institution, never distinctly and nakedly behold it. They speak of moving society, but have no resting-place without it. They may be men of a certain experience and discrimination, and have no doubt invented ingenious and even useful systems, for which we sincerely thank them; but all their wit and usefulness lie within certain not very wide lim-

its. They are wont to forget that the world is not governed by policy and expediency. Webster never goes behind government, and so cannot speak with authority about it. His words are wisdom to those legislators who contemplate no essential reform in the existing government; but for thinkers, and those who legislate for all time, he never once glances at the subject. I know of those whose serene and wise speculations on this theme would soon reveal the limits of his mind's range and hospitality. Yet, compared with the cheap professions of most reformers, and the still cheaper wisdom and eloquence of politicians in general, his are almost the only sensible and valuable words, and we thank Heaven for him. Comparatively, he is always strong, original, and, above all, practical. Still, his quality is not wisdom, but prudence. The lawyer's truth is not Truth, but consistency or a consistent expediency. Truth is always in harmony with herself, and is not concerned chiefly to reveal the justice that may consist with wrong-doing. He well deserves to be called, as he has been called, the Defender of the Constitution. There are really no blows to be given by him but defensive ones. He is not a leader, but a follower. His leaders are the men of '87. "I have never made an effort," he says, "and never propose to make an effort; I have never countenanced an effort, and never mean to countenance an effort, to disturb the arrangement as originally made, by which the various States came into the Union." Still thinking of the sanction which the Constitution gives to slavery, he says, "Because it was a part of the original compact,—let it stand." Notwithstanding his special acuteness and ability, he is unable to take a fact out of its merely political relations, and behold it as it lies absolutely to be disposed of by the intellect,—what, for instance, it behooves a man to do here in America to-day with regard to slavery,—but ventures, or is driven, to make some such desperate answer as the following, while professing to speak absolutely, and as a private man,—from which what new and singular code of social duties might be inferred? "The manner," says he, "in which the governments of those States where slavery exists are to regulate it is for their own consideration, under their responsibility to their constituents, to the general laws of propriety, humanity, and justice, and to God. Associations formed elsewhere, springing from a feeling of humanity, or other cause, have nothing whatever to do with it. They have never received any encouragement from me, and they never will."

They who know of no purer sources of truth, who have traced up its stream no higher, stand, and wisely stand, by the Bible and the Constitution, and drink at it there with reverence and humility; but they who behold where it comes trickling into this lake or that pool, gird up their loins once more, and continue their pilgrimage toward its fountain-head.

No man with a genius for legislation has appeared in America. They are rare in the history of the world. There are orators, politicians, and eloquent men, by the thousand; but the speaker has not yet opened his mouth to speak who is capable of settling the much-vexed questions of the day. We love eloquence for its own sake, and not for any truth which it may utter, or any heroism it may inspire. Our legislators have not yet learned the comparative value of free-trade and of freedom, of union, and of rectitude, to a nation. They have no genius or talent for comparatively humble questions of taxation and finance, commerce and manufactures and agriculture. If we were left solely to the wordy wit of legislators in Congress for our guidance, uncorrected by the seasonable experience and the effectual complaints of the people, America would not long retain her rank among the nations. For eighteen hundred years, though perchance I have no right to say it, the New Testament has been written; yet where is the legislator who has wisdom and practical talent enough to avail himself of the light which it sheds on the science of legislation?

The authority of government, even such as I am willing to submit to,—for I will cheerfully obey those who know and can do better than I, and in many things even those who neither know nor can do so well,—is still an impure one: to be strictly just, it must have the sanction and consent of the governed. It can have no pure right over my person and property but what I concede to it. The progress from an absolute to a limited monarchy, from a limited monarchy to a democracy, is a progress toward a true respect for the individual. Even the Chinese philosopher was wise enough to regard the individual as the basis of the empire. Is a democracy, such as we know it, the last improvement possible in government? Is it not possible to take a step further towards recognizing and organizing the rights of man? There will never be a really free and enlightened State until the State comes to recognize the individual as a higher and independent power, from which all its own power and authority are derived, and treats him accordingly. I please myself with imagining a State at last which can afford to be just to all men, and to treat the individual with respect as a neighbor; which even would not think it inconsistent with its own repose if a few were to live aloof from it, not meddling with it, nor embraced by it, who fulfilled all the duties of neighbors and fellow-men. A State which bore this kind of fruit, and suffered it to drop off as fast as it ripened, would prepare the way for a still more perfect and glorious State, which also I have imagined, but not yet anywhere seen.

Source:

Brooks Atkinson, ed. *Walden and Other Writings of Henry David Thoreau*, New York: The Modern Library, 1992.

Nathaniel Hawthorne, *The Blithedale Romance*, 1852

The reform spirit rampant in parts of the United States (as well as in Europe) in the 1840s produced a number of Utopian communities. They derived their various philosophies from various sources: some, like the Shakers, from religion, others from socialistic Utopians like the Frenchman Charles Fourier, who espoused rewarding workers only for their actual labor and promoted equality of the sexes.

One such Fourieran community was Brooke Farm in Massachusetts. It provided a haven for transcendentalists such as Margaret Fuller; visionaries such as Bronson Alcott, its founder (and father of *Little Women* author Louisa May Alcott); and authors such as Nathaniel Hawthorne. As Hawthorne satirizes in his novel, the members of the real Brooke Farm did not take to agricultural labor, and the experiment, like so many Utopian communities of the time, failed. Hawthorne, a major literary figure at that time, wrote many short stories and five novels, the best known being *The Scarlet Letter* (1850). Steeped in European literature, Hawthorne used his own writings to educate American readers in several ways. His short stories, including a number for children, include Greek mythology and American history. In both his stories and novels, he makes clear that he is employing symbols (like the scarlet letter) and that his tales, which usually have a moral dimension, should be read on several levels. He included something of his philosophy of literature in the parts of the preface excerpted here.

Although Hawthorne stayed at Brooke Farm only a short time, he found inspiration for *The Blithedale Romance*, and characters in the novel are loosely based on the real denizens of Brooke Farm. The flamboyant feminist and transcendental thinker Zenobia was patterned after Fuller. However, the Blithedale character dramatically commits suicide, whereas Fuller, who had married an Italian nobleman, tragically drowned during a transatlantic voyage.

The excerpts here are from Hawthorne's preface and from portions of the novel that illuminate the true state of life on a farm, Utopian or not, and why it failed. Hawthorne speaks about the community through his narrator, Miles Coverdale.

―――――――― ⌒∞⌒ ――――――――

Preface

IN THE BLITHEDALE of this volume, many readers will probably suspect a faint and not very faithful shadowing of BROOK FARM, in Roxbury, which (now a little more than ten years ago) was occupied and cultivated by a company of socialists. The Author does not wish to deny, that he had this Community in his mind, and that (having had the good fortune, for a time, to be personally connected with it) he has occasionally availed himself of his actual reminiscences, in the hope of giving a more lifelike tint to the fancy-sketch in the following pages. He begs it to be understood, however, that he has considered the Institution itself as not less fairly the subject of fictitious handling, than the imaginary personages whom he has introduced there. His whole treatment of the affair is altogether incidental to the main purpose of the Romance; nor does he put forward the slightest pretensions to illustrate a theory, or elicit a conclusion, favorable or otherwise, in respect to Socialism.

In short, his present concern with the Socialist Community is merely to establish a theatre, a little removed from the highway of ordinary travel, where the creatures of his brain may play their phantasmagorical antics, without exposing them to too close a comparison with the actual events of real lives. In the old countries, with which Fiction has long been conversant, a certain conventional privilege seems to be awarded to the romancer; his work is not put exactly side by side with nature; and he is allowed a license with regard to every-day Probability, in view of the improved effects which he is bound to produce thereby. Among ourselves, on the contrary, there is as yet no such Faery Land, so like the real world, that, in a suitable remoteness, one cannot well tell the difference, but with an atmosphere of strange enchantment, beheld through which the inhabitants have a propriety of their own. This atmosphere is what the American romancer needs. In its absence, the beings of imagination are compelled to show themselves in the same category as actually living mortals; a necessity that generally renders the paint and pasteboard of their composition but too painfully discernible. With the idea of partially obviating this difficulty, (the sense of which has always pressed very heavily upon him,) the Author has ventured to make free with his old, and affectionately remembered home, at BROOK FARM, as being, certainly, the most romantic episode of his own life— essentially a daydream, and yet a fact—and thus offering an available foothold between fiction and reality. Furthermore, the scene was in good keeping with the personages whom he desired to introduce.

These characters, he feels it right to say, are entirely fictitious. It would, indeed, (considering how few amiable qualities he distributes among his imaginary progeny,) be a most grievous wrong to his former excellent associates, were the Author to allow it to be supposed that he has been sketching any of their likenesses. Had he attempted it, they would at least have recognized the touches of a friendly pencil. But he has done nothing of the kind. The self-concentrated Philanthropist; the high-spirited Woman, bruising herself against the narrow limitations of her sex; the weakly Maiden, whose tremulous nerves endow her with Sibylline attributes; the Minor Poet, beginning life with strenuous aspirations, which die out with his youthful fervor—all these might have been looked for, at

BROOK FARM, but, by some accident, never made their appearance there . . .

II. Blithedale

. . . Good, comfortable Mrs. Foster (the wife of stout Silas Foster, who was to manage the farm, at a fair stipend, and be our tutor in the art of husbandry) bade us a hearty welcome. At her back—a back of generous breadth— appeared two young women, smiling most hospitably, but looking rather awkward withal, as not well knowing what was to be their position in our new arrangement of the world. We shook hands affectionately, all round, and congratulated ourselves that the blessed state of brotherhood and sisterhood, at which we aimed, might fairly be dated from this moment. Our greetings were hardly concluded, when the door opened, and Zenobia—whom I had never before seen, important as was her place in our enterprise—Zenobia entered the parlor.

This (as the reader, if at all acquainted with our literary biography, need scarcely be told) was not her real name. She had assumed it, in the first instance, as her magazine-signature; and as it accorded well with something imperial which her friends attributed to this lady's figure and deportment, they, half-laughingly, adopted it in their familiar intercourse with her. She took the appellation in good part, and even encouraged its constant use, which, in fact, was thus far appropriate, that our Zenobia— however humble looked her new philosophy—had as much native pride as any queen would have known what to do with.

III. A Knot of Dreamers

. . . "I am the first-comer," Zenobia went on to say, while her smile beamed warmth upon us all; "so I take the part of hostess, for to-day, and welcome you as if to my own fireside. You shall be my guests, too, at supper. Tomorrow, if you please, we will be brethren and sisters, and begin our new life from day-break."

"Have we our various parts assigned?" asked some one.

"Oh, we of the softer sex," responded Zenobia, with her mellow, almost broad laugh—most delectable to hear, but not in the least like an ordinary woman's laugh—"we women (there are four of us here, already) will take the domestic and indoor part of the business, as a matter of course. To bake, to boil, to roast, to fry, to stew—to wash, and iron, and scrub, and sweep, and, at our idler intervals, to repose ourselves on knitting and sewing—these, I suppose, must be feminine occupations for the present. By-and-by, perhaps, when our individual adaptations begin to develop themselves, it may be that some of us, who wear the petticoat, will go afield, and leave the weaker brethren to take our places in the kitchen!"

"What a pity," I remarked, "that the kitchen, and the house-work generally, cannot be left out of our system altogether! It is odd enough, that the kind of labor which falls to the lot of women is just that which chiefly distinguishes artificial life—the life of degenerated mortals—from the life of Paradise. Eve had no dinner-pot, and no clothes to mend, and no washing-day." . . .

. . . It was our purpose—a generous one, certainly, and absurd, no doubt, in full proportion with its generosity—to give up whatever we had heretofore attained, for the sake of showing mankind the example of a life governed by other than the false and cruel principles, on which human society has all along been based.

And, first of all, we had divorced ourselves from Pride, and were striving to supply its place with familiar love. We meant to lessen the laboring man's great burthen of toil, by performing our due share of it at the cost of our own thews and sinews. We sought our profit by mutual aid, instead of wresting it by the strong hand from an enemy, or filching it craftily from those less shrewd than ourselves, (if, indeed, there were any such, in New England,) or winning it by selfish competition with a neighbor; in one or another of which fashions, every son of woman both perpetrates and suffers his share of the common evil, whether he chooses it or no. And, as the basis of our institution, we purposed to offer up the earnest toil of our bodies, as a prayer, no less than an effort, for the advancement of our race . . .

VIII. A Modern Arcadia
. . . But, so long as our union should subsist, a man of intellect and feeling, with a free nature in him, might have sought far and near, without finding so many points of attraction as would allure him hitherward. We were of all creeds and opinions, and generally tolerant of all, on every imaginable subject. Our bond, it seems to me, was not affirmative, but negative. We had individually found one thing or another to quarrel with, in our past life, and were pretty well agreed as to the inexpediency of lumbering along with the old system any farther. As to what should be substituted, there was much less unanimity. We did not greatly care—at least, I never did—for the written constitution under which our millennium had commenced. My hope was, that, between theory and practice, a true and available mode of life might be struck out, and that, even should we ultimately fail, the months or years spent in the trial would not have been wasted, either as regarded passing enjoyment, or the experience which makes men wise.

Arcadians though we were, our costume bore no resemblance to the be-ribboned doublets, silk breeches and stockings, and slippers fastened with artificial roses, that distinguish the pastoral people of poetry and the stage. In outward show, I humbly conceive, we looked rather like a gang of beggars or banditti, than either a company of honest laboring men or a conclave of philosophers. Whatever might be our points of difference, we all of us seemed to have come to Blithedale with the one thrifty and laudable idea of wearing out our old clothes. Such garments as had an airing, whenever we strode afield! Coats with high collars, and with no collars, broad-skirted or swallow-tailed, and with the waist at every point between the hip and armpit; pantaloons of a dozen successive epochs, and greatly defaced at the knees by the humiliations of the wearer before his lady-love; —in short, we were a living epitome of defunct fashions, and the very raggedest presentment of men who had seen better days . . .

. . . Little skill as we boasted in other points of husbandry, every mother's son of us would have served admirably to stick up for a scarecrow. And the worst of the matter was, that the first energetic movement, essential to one downright stroke of real labor, was sure to put a finish to these poor habiliments. So we gradually flung them all aside, and took to honest homespun and linsey-woolsey, as preferable, on the whole, to the plan recommended, I think, by Virgil—'Ara nudes; sere nudes'—which, as Silas Foster remarked when I translated the maxim, would be apt to astonish the women-folks.

After a reasonable training, the yeoman-life throve well with us. Our faces took the sunburn kindly; our chests gained in compass, and our shoulders in breadth and squareness; our great brown fists looked as if they had never been capable of kid gloves. The plough, the hoe, the scythe, and the hayfork, grew familiar to our grasp. The oxen responded to our voices. We could do almost as fair a day's work as Silas Foster himself, sleep dreamlessly after it, and awake at daybreak with only a little stiffness of the joints, which was usually quite gone by breakfast-time . . .

XXIX. Miles Coverdale's Confession
. . . Often, however, in these years that are darkening around me, I remember our beautiful scheme of a noble and unselfish life, and how fair, in that first summer, appeared the prospect that it might endure for generations, and be perfected, as the ages rolled away, into the system of a people, and a world.

. . . More and more, I feel that we had struck upon what ought to be a truth. Posterity may dig it up, and profit by it. The experiment, so far as its original projectors were concerned, proved long ago a failure, first lapsing into Fourierism, and dying, as it well deserved, for this infidelity to its own higher spirit . . .

Source:
The Complete Novels and Selected Tales of Nathaniel Hawthorne, ed. Norman Holmes Pearson. New York: The Modern Library, 1937, pp. 439–440; 444, 446–450; 475–477; 584.

SUGGESTED READING

General

Bruce Collins, *White Society in the Antebellum South.* New York: Longman, 1985.

Hasia Diner, *Erin's Daughters in America.* Baltimore, Md.: Johns Hopkins University Press, 1983.

Territorial Expansion

Stephen E. Ambrose, *Undaunted Courage: Meriwether Lewis, Thomas Jefferson and the Opening of the American West.* New York: Simon and Schuster, 1996.

K. Jack Bauer, *The Mexican-American War, 1846–1848.* Lincoln, Nebr.: University of Nebraska Press, 1993.

Gene M. Brack, *Mexico Views Manifest Destiny, 1821–1846.* Albuquerque, N.Mex.: University of New Mexico Press, 1976.

Patricia Nelson Limerick, *The Legacy of Conquest: The Unbroken Past of the American West.* New York: W.W. Norton, 1987.

Dale Morgan, ed., *Overland in 1846: Diaries and Letters of the California-Oregon Trail.* Lincoln, Nebr.: University of Nebraska Press, 1993.

Michael A. Morison, *Slavery and the American West: The Eclipse of Manifest Destiny and the Coming of the Civil War.* Chapel Hill, N.C.: University of North Carolina Press, 1997.

Glenda Riley, *The Female Frontier.* Lawrence: University Press of Kansas, 1988.

Anthony Wallace, *The Long Bitter Trail: Andrew Jackson and the Indians.* New York: Hill and Wang, 1993.

Economic Developments

Jack N. Rakove, *James Madison and the Creation of the American Republic.* Glenview, Ill.: Scott, Foreman, 1990.

Ronald E. Shaw, *Canals for a Nation: The Canal Era in the United States, 1790–1860.* Lexington, Ky.: University Press of Kentucky, 1990.

Henry L. Watson, *Liberty and Power: The Politics of Jacksonian America.* New York: Hill and Wang, 1990.

David A. Zonderman, *Aspirations and Anxieties: New England Workers and the Mechanized Factory System, 1815–1850.* New York: Oxford University Press, 1992.

Political Developments

Lawrence F. Kohl, *The Politics of Individualism: Parties and the American Character in the Jacksonian Era.* New York: Oxford University Press, 1989.

Edward Pessen, *Jacksonian America: Society, Personality, and Politics.* Homewood, Ill.: Dorsey Press, 1978.

Robert V. Remini, *Henry Clay: Statesman for the Union.* New York: W.W. Norton, 1991.

Merrill D. Peterson, *The Great Triumverate: Webster, Clay, and Calhoun.* New York: Oxford University Press, 1987.

International Relations

James E. Lewis, *The American Union and the Problem of Neighborhood: The United States and the Collapse of the Spanish Empire, 1783–1830.* Chapel Hill, N.C.: University of North Carolina Press, 1998.

Arand Otto Mayr and Robert C. Post, eds., *Yankee Enterprise: The Rise of the American System of Manufactures.* Washington, D.C.: Smithsonian Institution Press, 1981.

J.C.A. Stagg, *Mr. Madison's War: Politics, Diplomacy and Warfare in the Early American Republic, 1783–1830.* Princeton, N.J.: Princeton University Press, 1983.

Reform

Spencer Klaw, *Without Sin: the Life and Death of the Oneida Community,* New York: Allen Lane, 1993.

Steven Mintz, *Moralists and Modernizers: America's Pre-Civil War Reformers.* Baltimore, Md.: Johns Hopkins University Press, 1995.

The Slavery Debate

Ira Berlin, *Slaves Without Masters: The Free Negro in the Antebellum South.* New York: Pantheon Books, 1974.

Catherine Clinton, *The Plantation Mistress: Woman's World in the Old South.* New York: Pantheon Books, 1982.

Frederick Douglass, *The Narrative of the Life of Frederick Douglass: An American Slave.* New York: Fine Creative Media, 2003.

Eugene Genovese, *Roll, Jordan, Roll: The World the Slaves Made.* New York: Pantheon Books, 1974.

J. William Harris, *Slave Folk and Gentry in a Slave Society.* Middleton, Conn.: Wesleyan University Press, 1985.

Lawrence Levine, *Black Culture and Black Consciousness: Afro-American Thought from Slavery to Freedom.* New York: Oxford University Press, 1977.

Ronald G. Walters, *The Antislavery Appeal: American Abolitionism After 1830.* Baltimore, Md.: Johns Hopkins University Press, 1976.

Deborah G. White, *Ar'n't I a Woman? Female Slaves in the Plantation South.* New York: W.W. Norton, 1985.

The Rights of Women

Nancy Cott, *The Bonds of Womanhood: "Women's Sphere" in New England, 1780–1835.* New Haven, Conn.: Yale University Press, 1977.

Kathryn Kish Sklar, *Catherine Beecher: A Study in Domesticity.* New Haven, Conn.: Yale University Press, 1973.

Religion

Keith J. Hardman, *Charles Grandison Finney, 1792–1875: Revivalist and Reformer.* Syracuse, N.Y.: Syracuse University Press, 1987.

Nathan O. Hatch, *The Democratization of American Christianity.* New Haven, Conn.: Yale University Press, 1989.

Education

Carl F. Kaestle, *Pillars of the Republic: Common Schools and American Society, 1780–1860.* New York: Hill and Wang, 1983.

Intellectual and Cultural Life

Karen Halttunen, *Confidence Men and Painted Women: A Study in Middle-Class Culture in America, 1830–1870.* New Haven, Conn.: Yale University Press, 1982.

Jack Larkin, *The Reshaping of Everyday Life, 1790–1849.* New York: Harper & Row, 1988.

Robert D. Richardson, *Emerson: The Mind on Fire.* Berkeley, Calif.: University of California Press, 1995.

———, *Thoreau: A Life of the Mind.* Berkeley, Calif.: University of California Press, 1986.

ERA 5
Civil War and Reconstruction (1850–1877)

No one put the significance of the American Civil War (1861–65) better than President Abraham Lincoln in his Gettysburg Address: It "test[ed] whether" a nation "conceived in Liberty and dedicated to the proposition that all men are created equal . . . can long endure." Whatever its causes, the war pitted family members and close friends against each other and gauged where loyalty—to one's state, one's country, one's view of humanity, or one's economic well-being—lay. Wherever that loyalty lay helps explain the years leading up to the war and the reconstruction that followed it. The legacy of these years remains with Americans in the 21st century.

The slavery question had been splitting the nation from its birth, when Thomas Jefferson, himself a slaveholder, was forced to delete a phrase condemning British support of the slave trade from the list of grievances against George III in the Declaration of Independence. During the Constitutional Convention, the delegates passed a number of compromises in order to placate slaveholders. Although sectional issues like the tariff and federal payment for internal improvements continued, as long as an equal number of slave and free states were in Congress, slaveholding itself remained a major issue only for reformers, especially Northern clergy and women. After the Mexican War brought in new territory and when

sufficient population for statehood loomed in the Louisiana Purchase area, an imbalance in favor of free states became likely. Moreover, abolitionism in one form or another had become a more mainstream issue in the north. The year 1850 marks the last time the slaveholding South was placated by compromise. Yet few in the North were willing to let slavery destroy the Union. Even Lincoln, in his wartime reply to editor Horace Greeley, expressed a willingness to live with slavery if doing so would bring the Union back together: "If I could save the Union without freeing *any* slave, I would do it; and if I could save it by freeing *all* the slaves, I would do it; and if I could do it by freeing some and leaving others alone, I would also do that." (He signed the Emancipation Proclamation several months later.)

If slavery appears to be the major cause of the Civil War, Southern whites and many historians through the 1960s have found other ways to interpret the split—ways that affected the nation's treatment of African Americans that persist into the 21st century. Because most Southern whites owned few if any slaves, other interests had to keep the loyalty of the Confederate troops. One major interpretation is states' rights. Enforcement of the Fugitive Slave Law reversed the traditional Southern support for state over federal power and had the opposite effect in the

North. However, such issues as protectionist tariffs, which favored Northern manufacturing, also loomed large for Southern congressmen and officials. Southerners liked to compare their situation to that of the colonies versus Parliament before the American Revolution. The most significant constitutional questions regarding state versus federal rights could not be solved peacefully through Congress, the courts, or the political party system.

Reconstruction provided continuing divisiveness that split along lines other than sectional ones: between those who wished to punish Southern whites and elevate black men to political equality (which simultaneously punished Southern whites and enhanced the Republican Party) and those who wanted to heal sectional divisions and bring Southern whites back into the Union as quickly as possible. Whether congress or the president dominated the Reconstruction process was also divisive.

Through the Andrew Johnson administration, the "punishment"/congressional Reconstruction group, called Radical Republicans, had the upper hand. But in the long run, those who put Southern white sensibilities above equality for blacks prevailed politically, in the courts, and, until the 1960s, in most history books (a notable exception was the account written in 1935 by the black scholar W. E. B. DuBois, *Black Reconstruction*). Southern whites also claimed the nomenclature victory. *Reconstruction* developed bad connotations, whereas those seeking to restore the "Southern way of life" with its implications for caste and race became the "Redeemers." The vision of Reconstruction these historians brought into the 20th century was one of unrelieved corruption by Northern politicians and uneducated blacks who were pictured as dominating Southern state legislatures. Northern "carpetbaggers" also allegedly corrupted the Southern economy. The historiographical picture was popularized in 1915 by D. W. Griffiths's silent movie *Birth of a Nation*, based on the novel *The Klansmen*, in which the Reconstruction-era Ku Klux Klan were pictured as heroes against predatory blacks. Popular culture, therefore, fed racial prejudices long after Reconstruction ended.

In reality, although blacks held a majority or near majority of voters in the early years after the war when rebel whites were disfranchised, they held comparatively few elective offices. South Carolina was the only state in which blacks constituted a majority of the legislature, and no black governor was ever elected. However, 16 African Americans became congressmen and more than 600 served in state legislatures. The Republican regimes, which lasted only a few months in Virginia but nine years in South Carolina, Florida, and Louisiana, instituted important reforms. They repealed black codes, expanded the number of elective offices, passed antidiscrimination laws, and established the South's first public school systems. They also paved roads and encouraged the railroad. In addition, they instituted public orphanages and asylums. Heavy taxation and corruption attended these reforms, but the good the Reconstruction legislatures accomplished was ignored by most historians until the late 20th century.

Also instructive are the Reconstruction-era debates as to whether women should be included in the Fifteenth Amendment that was to protect the federal franchise. These are placed in the section on women's rights. The question split the feminist organizations between those who preferred to at least grant black men the vote and those who advocated a franchise without regard to gender. Some suggested that an educational requirement applying to both genders and races would be preferable to granting the franchise to all black men but excluding women; of course this requirement would have excluded at least initially the vast majority of blacks and, depending on the level of education, many women as well. In the end only men were included in the Fifteenth Amendment.

The post–Civil War years brought significant economic and political developments, and by 1890 the western frontier had allegedly disappeared, which had particular implications for Native Americans. Because this chapter concentrates on the causes and consequences of the Civil War, these issues will be handled with Era 6.

The Causes of the Civil War

The Compromise of 1850

Set of bills prompted by a speech by Senator Henry Clay and resolutions he introduced. The U.S. Congress passed the bills in September 1850 to settle slavery issues and preserve the Union. By 1850 the United States was divided over the slave trade, fugitive slave laws, and the question of slavery in new U.S. territories and California. The Great Compromiser, Senator Henry Clay of Kentucky, proposed a plan that would admit California as a free state, and admit New Mexico and Utah without determining their slavery status (leaving the matter to popular sovereignty). The Utah Act of 1850 designated as U.S. territory a large part of what today is the state of Utah. In addition, Clay sought to prohibit the slave trade in the District of Columbia and provide the stricter Fugitive Slave Law of 1850. On January 1, 1851, the Act Abolishing the Slave Trade in the District of Columbia went into effect, but the efforts of Clay's compromise merely postponed final settlement of the slavery issue.

Speech by Henry Clay, 1850

Mr. President, never on any former occasion have I risen under feelings of such painful solicitude. I have seen many periods of great anxiety, of peril, and of danger in this country, and I have never before risen to address any assemblage so oppressed, so appalled, and so anxious; and sir, I hope it will not be out of place to do here, what again and again I have done in my private chamber, to implore of Him who holds the destinies of nations and individuals in His hands, to bestow upon our country His blessing, to calm the violence and rage of party, to still passion, to allow reason once more to resume its empire. And may I not ask of Him too, sir, to bestow on his humble servant, now before him, the blessing of his smiles, and of strength and ability to perform the work which now lies before him? Sir, I have said that I have seen other anxious periods in the history of our country, and If I were to venture, Mr. President, to trace to their original source the cause of all our present dangers, difficulties, and distraction, I should ascribe it to the violence and intemperance of party spirit. To party spirit! Sir, in the progress of this session we have had the testimony of two senators here, who, however they may differ on other matters, concur in the existence of that cause in originating the unhappy differences which prevail throughout the country, on the subject of the institution of slavery.

Parties, in their endeavors to obtain, the one ascendency over the other, catch at every passing or floating plank in order to add strength and power to each. We have been told by the two senators to whom I have referred, that each of the parties at the North, in its turn, has moved and endeavored to obtain the assistance of a small party called Abolitionists, in order that the scale in its favor might preponderate against that of its adversary. And all around us, every where, we see too many evidences of the existence of the spirit and intemperance of party. I might go to other legislative bodies than that which is assembled in Congress, and I might draw from them illustrations of the melancholy truth upon which I am dwelling, but I need not pass out of this Capitol itself. I say it, sir, with all deference and respect to that other portion of Congress assembled in the other wing of this Capitol; but what have we seen there? During this very session one whole week has been exhausted—I think about a week—in the vain endeavor to elect a doorkeeper of the House.

And, Mr. President, what was the question in this struggle to elect a doorkeeper? It was not as to the man or the qualities of the man, or who is best adapted to the situation. It was whether the doorkeeper entertained opinions upon certain national measures coincident with this or that side of the House. That was the sole question which prevented the election of a doorkeeper for about the period of a week. Sir, I make no reproaches—none, to either portion of that House; I state the fact; and I state the fact to draw from it the conclusion and to express the hope that there will be an endeavor to check this violence of party.

Sir, what vicissitudes do we not pass through in this short mortal career of ours? Eight years, or nearly eight years ago, I took my leave finally, and, as I supposed, forever, from this body. At that time I did not conceive of the possibility of ever again returning to it. And if my private wishes and particular inclinations, and the desire during the short remnant of my days to remain in repose and quiet, could have prevailed, you would never have seen me occupying the seat which I now occupy upon this floor. The Legislature of the State to which I belong, unsolicited by me, chose to designate me for this station, and I have come here, sir, in obedience to a sense of stern duty, with no personal objects, no private views, now or hereafter, to gratify. I know, sir, the jealousies, the fears, the apprehensions which are engendered by the existence of that party spirit to which I have referred; but if there be in my hearing now, in or out of this Capitol, any one who hopes, in his race for honors and elevation, for higher honors and higher elevation than that which he now occupies, I beg him to believe that I, at least, will never jostle him in the pursuit of those honors or that elevation. I beg him to be perfectly persuaded that, if my wishes prevail, my name shall never be used in competition with his. I beg to assure him that when my service is terminated in this body, my mission, so far as respects the public affairs of this world upon this earth, is closed, and closed, if my wishes prevail, forever.

But, sir, it is impossible for us to be blind to the facts which are daily transpiring before us. It is impossible for us not to perceive that party spirit and future elevation mix more or less in all our affairs, in all our deliberations. At a moment when the White House itself is in danger of conflagration, instead of all hands uniting to extinguish the flames, we are contending about who shall be its next occupant. When a dreadful *crevasse* has occurred, which threatens inundation and destruction to all around it, we are contending and disputing about the profits of an estate which is threatened with total submersion.

Mr. President, it is passion, passion—party, party, and intemperance—that is all I dread in the adjustment of the great questions which unhappily at this time divide our distracted country. Sir, at this moment we have in the legislative bodies of this Capitol and in the States, twenty old furnaces in full blast, emitting heat, and passion, and intemperance, and diffusing them throughout the whole extent of this broad land. Two months ago all was calm in comparison to the present moment. All now is uproar, confusion, and menace to the existence of the Union, and to the happiness and safety of this people. Sir, I implore senators, I entreat them, by all that they expect hereafter, and by all that is dear to them here below, to repress the ardor of these passions, to look to their country, to its interests, to listen to the voice of reason—not as it shall be attempted to be uttered by me, for I am not so presumptuous as to indulge the hope that any thing I may say will avert the effects which I have described, but to listen to their own reason, their own judgment, their own good sense, in determining upon what is best to be done for our country in the actual posture in which we find her. Sir, to this great object have my efforts been directed during the whole session.

I have cut myself off from all the usual enjoyments of social life, I have confined myself almost entirely, with very few exceptions, to my own chamber, and from the beginning of the session to the present time my thoughts have been anxiously directed to the object of finding some plan, of proposing some mode of accommodation, which would once more restore the blessings of concord, harmony and peace to this great country. I am not vain enough to suppose that I have been successful in the accomplishment of this object, but I have presented a scheme, and allow me to say to honorable senators that, if they find in that plan anything that is defective, if they find in it any thing that is worthy of acceptance, but is susceptible of improvement by amendment, it seems to me that the true and patriotic course is not to denounce it, but to improve it—not to reject without examination any project of accommodation having for its object the restoration of harmony in this country, but to look at it to see if it be susceptible of elaboration or improvement, so as to accomplish the object which I indulge the hope is common to all and every one of us, to restore peace and quiet, and harmony and happiness to this country.

Sir, when I came to consider this subject, there were two or three general purposes which it seemed to me to be most desirable, if possible, to accomplish. The one was, to settle all the controverted questions arising out of the subject of slavery. It seemed to me to be doing very little, if we settled one question and left other distracting questions unadjusted, it seemed to me to be doing but little, if we stopped one leak only in the ship of State, and left other leaks capable of producing danger, if not destruction, to the vessel. I therefore turned my attention to every subject connected with the institution of slavery, and out of which controverted questions had sprung, to see if it were possible or practicable to accommodate and adjust the whole of them. Another principal object which attracted my attention was, to endeavor to form such a scheme of accommodation that neither of the two classes of States into which our country is so unhappily divided should make any sacrifice of any great principle. I believe, sir, the series of resolutions which I have had the honor to present to the Senate accomplishes that object.

Sir, another purpose which I had in view was this: I was aware of the difference of opinion prevailing between these two classes of States. I was aware that, while one portion of the Union was pushing matters, as it seemed to me, to the greatest extremity, another portion of the Union was pushing them to an opposite, perhaps not less dangerous extremity. It appeared to me, then, that if any arrangement, any satisfactory adjustment could be made of the controverted questions between the two classes of States, that adjustment, that arrangement, could only be successful and effectual by extracting from both parties some concessions—not of principle, not of principle at all, but of feeling, of opinion, in relation to matters in controversy between them. Sir, I believe the resolutions which I have prepared fulfill that object. I believe, sir, that you will find, upon that careful, rational, and attentive examination of them, which I think they deserve, that neither party in some of them make any concession at all; in others the concessions of forbearance are mutual; and in the third place, in reference to the slaveholding States, there are resolutions making concessions to them by the opposite class of States, without any compensation whatever being rendered by them to the non-slaveholding States. I think every one of these characteristics which I have assigned, and the measures which I proposed, is susceptible of clear and satisfactory demonstration by an attentive perusal and critical examination of the resolutions themselves. Let us take up the first resolution.

The first resolution, Mr. President, as you are aware, relates to California, and it declares that California, with suitable limits, ought to be admitted as a member of this Union, without the imposition of any restriction either to interdict or to introduce slavery within her limits. Well now, is there any concession in this resolution by either party to the other? I know that gentlemen who come from slaveholding States say the North gets all that it desires; but by whom does it get it? Does it get it by any action of Congress? If slavery be interdicted within the limits of California, has it been done by Congress—by this Government? No sir. That interdiction is imposed by California herself. And has it not been the doctrine of all parties that when a State is about to be admitted into the Union, the State has a right to decide for itself whether it will or will not have slavery within its limits?

The great principle, sir, which was in contest upon the memorable occasion of the introduction of Missouri into the Union, was, whether it was competent or not competent for Congress to impose any restriction which should exist after she became a member of the Union. We who were in favor of the admission of Missouri, contended that no such restriction should be imposed. We contented that, whenever she was once admitted into the Union, she had all the rights and privileges of any pre-existing State in the Union, and that among these rights and privileges was one to decide for herself whether slavery should or should not exist within her limits: that she had as much a right to decide upon the introduction of slavery or its abolition as New York had a right to decide upon the introduction or abolition of slavery; and that, although subsequently admitted, she stood among her peers, equally invested with all the privileges that any one of the original thirteen States had a right to enjoy.

Sir, I think that those who have been contending with so much earnestness and perseverance for the Wilmot proviso, ought to reflect that, even if they could carry their object and adopt the proviso, it ceases the moment any State or Territory to which it was applicable came to be admitted as a member of the Union. Why, sir, no one contends now, no one believes, that with regard to those North-western States to which the ordinance of 1787 applied—Ohio, Indiana, Illinois, and Michigan—no one can now believe but that any one of those States, if they thought proper to do it, have just as much right to intro-

duce slavery within their borders, as Virginia has to maintain the existence of slavery within hers. Then, sir, if in the struggle for power and empire between the two classes of States a decision in California has taken place adverse to the wishes of the Southern States, it is a decision not made by the General Government.

It is a decision respecting which they can utter no complaint toward the General Government. It is a decision made by California herself; which California had unquestionably the right to make under the Constitution of the United States. There is, then, in the first resolution, according to the observation which I made some time ago, a case where neither party concedes; where the question of slavery, neither its introduction nor interdiction, is decided in reference to the action of this Government; and if it has been decided, it has been by a different body—by a different power—by California itself, which had a right to make the decision.

Mr. President, the next resolution in the series which I have offered I beg gentlemen candidly now to look at. I was aware, perfectly aware, of the perseverance with which the Wilmot proviso was insisted upon. I knew that every one of the free States in this Union, without exception, had by its Legislative body passed resolutions instructing their Senators and requesting their Representatives to get that restriction incorporated in any Territorial Government which might be established under the auspices of Congress. I knew how much, and I regretted how much, the free States had put their hearts upon the adoption of this measure. In the second resolution I call upon them to waive persisting in it. I ask them, for the sake of peace and in the spirit of mutual forbearance to other members of the Union, to give it up—to no longer insist upon it—to see, as they must see, if their eyes are open, the dangers which lie ahead, if they persevere in insisting upon it.

When I called upon them in this resolution to do this, was I not bound to offer, for a surrender of that favorite principle or measure of theirs, some compensation, not as an equivalent by any means, but some compensation in the spirit of mutual forbearance, which, animating one side, ought at the same time to actuate the other side? Well, sir, what is it that is offered them? It is a declaration of what I characterized, and must still characterize, with great deference to all those who entertain opposite opinions, as two truths, I will not say incontestible, but to me clear, and I think they ought to be regarded as indisputable truths. What are they? The first is, that by law slavery no longer exists in any part of the acquisitions made by us from the Republic of Mexico; and the other is, that in our opinion, according to the probabilities of the case, slavery never will be introduced into any portion of the territories so acquired from Mexico. Now, I have heard it said that this declaration of what I call these two truths is equivalent to the enactment of the Wilmot proviso.

I have heard this asserted, but is that the case? If the Wilmot proviso be adopted in Territorial Governments established over these countries acquired from Mexico, it would be a positive enactment, a prohibition, an interdiction as to the introduction of slavery within them; but with regard to these opinions I had hoped, and I shall still indulge the hope, that those who represent the free States will be inclined not to insist—indeed it would be extremely difficult to give to these declarations the form of positive enactment. I had hoped that they would be satisfied with the simple expression of the opinion of Congress, leaving it upon the basis of that opinion, without asking for what seems to me almost impracticable, if not impossible—for any subsequent enactment to be introduced into the bill by which Territorial Governments should be established.

And I can only say that the second resolution, even without the declaration of these two truths expressed, would be much more acceptable to me than with them—but I could not forget that I was proposing a scheme of arrangement and compromise, and I could not, therefore, depart from the duty which the preparation of such a scheme seems to me to impose, of offering, while we ask the surrender on one side of a favorite measure, of offering to the other side some compensation for that surrender or sacrifice. What are the truths, Mr. President? The first is, that by law slavery does not exist within the Territories ceded to us by the Republic of Mexico. It is a misfortune, sir, in the various weighty and important topics which are connected with the subject that I am now addressing you upon, that any one of the five or six furnishes a theme for a lengthened speech; and I am therefore reduced to the necessity, I think—at least in this stage of the discussion—of limiting myself rather to the expression of opinions, than going at any great length into the discussion of all these various topics.

With respect to the opinion that slavery does not exist in the Territories ceded to the United States by Mexico, I can only refer to the fact of the passage of the law by the Supreme Government of Mexico abolishing it, I think, in 1824; and to the subsequent passage of a law by the Legislative body of Mexico, I forget in what year, by which they proposed—what it is true they have never yet carried into full effect—compensation to the owners of slaves for the property of which they were stripped by the act of abolition. I can only refer to the acquiescence of Mexico in the abolition of slavery, from the time of its extinction down to the time of the treaty by which we acquired these countries. But all Mexico, so far as I know, acquiesced in the non-existence of slavery. Gentlemen, I know, talk about the irregularity of the law by which that act was accomplished; but does it become us, a foreign power, to look

into the mode by which an object has been accomplished by another foreign power, when she herself is satisfied with what she has done; and when, too, she is the exclusive judge whether an object which is local and municipal to herself, has been or has not been accomplished in conformity with her fundamental laws? Why, Mexico upon this subject showed to the last moment, her anxiety in the documents which were laid before the country upon the subject of the negotiation of this treaty, by Mr. Trist.

In the very act, in the very negotiation by which the treaty was concluded, ceding to us the countries in question, the diplomatic representatives of the Mexican Republic urged the abhorrence with which Mexico would view the introduction of slavery into any portion of the Territory which she was about to cede to the United States. The clause of prohibition was not inserted in consequence of the firm ground taken by Mr. Trist, and his declaration that it was an utter impossibility to mention the subject.

I take it then, sir—and availing myself of the benefit of the discussions which took place on a former occasion on this question, and which I think have left the whole country under the impression of the non-existence of slavery within the whole of the Territory in the ceded Territories—I take it for granted that what I have said, aided by the reflection of gentlemen, will satisfy them of that first truth, that slavery does not exist there by law, unless slavery was carried there the moment the treaty was ratified by the two parties, and under the operation of the Constitution of the United States. Now, really, I must say that upon the idea that *eo instanti* upon the consummation of the treaty, the Constitution of the United States spread itself over the acquired Territory, and carried along with it the institution of slavery, the proposition is so irreconcilable with any comprehension or reason that I possess, that I hardly know how to meet it.

Why, these United States consist of thirty States. In fifteen of them there was slavery, in fifteen of them slavery did not exist. Well, how can it be argued that the fifteen slave States, by the operation of the Constitution of the United States, carried into the ceded Territory their institution of slavery, any more than it can be argued on the other side that, by the operation of the same Constitution, the fifteen free States carried into the ceded territory the principle of freedom which they from policy have chosen to adopt within their limits? Why, sir, let me suppose a case. Let me imagine that Mexico had never abolished slavery there at all—let me suppose that it was existing in point of fact and in virtue of law, from the shores of the Pacific to those of the Gulf of Mexico, at the moment of the cession of these countries to us by the treaty in question.

With what patience would gentlemen coming from slaveholding States listen to any argument which should be urged by the free States, that notwithstanding the existence of slavery within those territories, the Constitution of the United States abolished it the moment it operated upon and took effect in the ceded territory? Well, is there not just as much ground to contend that, where a moiety of the States is free, and the other moiety is slaveholding, the principle of freedom which prevails in the one class shall operate as much as the principle of slavery which prevails in the other? Can you come, amid this conflict of interests, principles, and legislation which prevails in the two parts of the Union, to any other conclusion than that which I understand to be the conclusion of the public law of the world, of reason, and justice—that the *status* of law, as it existed at the moment of the conquest or the acquisition, remains until it is altered by the sovereign authority of the conquering or acquiring power? That is the great principle which you can scarcely turn over a page of the public law of the world without finding recognized, and every where established. The laws of Mexico, as they existed at the moment of the cession of the ceded Territories to this country, remained the laws until, and unless, they were altered by that new sovereign power which this people and these Territories come under, in consequence of the treaty of cession to the United States.

I think, then, Mr. President, that without trespassing further, or exhausting the little stock of strength which I have, and for which I shall have abundant use in the progress of the argument, I may leave that part of the subject, with two or three observations only upon the general power which I think appertains to this Government on the subject of slavery.

Sir, before I approach that subject, allow me to say that, in my humble judgment, the institution of slavery presents two questions totally distinct, and resting on entirely different grounds—slavery within the States, and slavery without the States. Congress, the General Government, has no power, under the Constitution of the United States, to touch slavery within the States, except in three specified particulars in that instrument; to adjust the subject of representation; to impose taxes when a system of direct taxation is made; and to perform the duty of surrendering, or causing to be delivered up, fugitive slaves that may escape from service which they owe in slave States, and take refuge in free States. And, sir, I am ready to say that if Congress were to attack, within the States, the institution of slavery, for the purpose of the overthrow or extinction of slavery, then, Mr. President, my voice would be for war; then would be made a case which would justify in the sight of God, and in the presence of the nations of the earth, resistance on the part of the slave States to such an unconstitutional and usurped attempt as would be made on the supposition which I have stated.

Then we should be acting in defense of our rights, our domicils, our property, our safety, our lives; and then, I think, would be furnished a case in which the slaveholding States would be justified by all considerations which pertain to the happiness and security of man, to employ every instrument which God or nature had placed in their hands to resist such an attempt on the part of the free States. And then, if unfortunately civil war should break out, and we should present to the nations of the earth the spectacle of one portion of this Union endeavoring to subvert an institution in violation of the Constitution and the most sacred obligations which can bind men; we should present the spectacle in which we should have the sympathies, the good wishes, and the desire for our success of all men who love justice and truth. Far different, I fear, would be our case—if unhappily we should be plunged into civil war—if the two parts of this country should be placed in a position hostile toward each other, in order to carry slavery into the new Territories acquired from Mexico.

Mr. President, we have heard, all of us have read of the efforts of France to propagate—what, on the continent of Europe? Not slavery, sir; not slavery, but the rights of man; and we know the fate of her efforts in a work of that kind. But if the two portions of this Confederacy should unhappily be involved in civil war, in which the effort on the one side would be to restrain the introduction of slavery into new Territories, and on the other side to force its introduction there, what a spectacle should we present to the contemplation of astonished mankind! An effort not to propagate right, but I must say—though I trust it will be understood to be said with no desire to excite feeling—an effort to propagate wrong in the territories thus acquired from Mexico. It would be a war in which we should have no sympathy, no good wishes, and in which all mankind would be against us, and in which our own history itself would be against us; for, from the commencement of the Revolution down to the present time, we have constantly reproached our British ancestors for the introduction of slavery into this country; and allow me to say that, in my opinion, it is one of the best defenses which can be made to preserve the institution in this country, that it was forced upon us against the wishes of our ancestors, our own colonial ancestors, and by the cupidity of our British commercial ancestors.

The power then, Mr. President, in my opinion—and I will extend it to the introduction as well as the prohibition of slavery in the new territories—I think the power does exist in Congress, and I think there is that important distinction between slavery outside of the States and slavery inside of the States, that all outside is debatable, all inside of the States is undebatable. The Government has no right to touch the institution within the States; but whether she has, and to what extent she has the right or not to touch it outside of the States, is a question which is debatable, and upon which men may honestly and fairly differ, but which, decided however it may be decided, furnishes, in my judgment, no just occasion for breaking up this happy and glorious Union of ours.

Now, I am not going to take up that part of the subject which relates to the power of Congress to legislate either within this District—(I shall have occasion to make some observations upon that when I approach the resolution relating to the District)—either within this District or the Territories. But I must say, in a few words, that I think there are two sources of power, either of which is, in my judgment, sufficient to warrant the exercise of the power, if it was deemed proper to exercise it, either to introduce or to keep out slavery outside the States, within the territories.

Mr. President, I shall not take up time, of which already so much has been consumed, to show that, according to my sense of the Constitution of the United States, or rather according to the sense in which the clause has been interpreted for the last fifty years, the clause which confers on Congress the power to regulate the Territories and other property of the United States conveys the authority.

Mr. President, with my worthy friend from Michigan—and I use the term in the best and most emphatic sense, for I believe he and I have known each other longer that he and I have known any other senator in this hall—I can not concur, although I entertain the most profound respect for the opinions he has advanced upon the subject, adverse to may own; but I must say, when a point is settled by all the elementary writers of our country, by all the departments of our Government, legislative, executive, and judicial—when it has been so settled for a period of fifty years, and never was seriously disturbed until recently, that I think, if we are to regard any thing as fixed and settled under the administration of this Constitution of ours, it is a question which as thus been invariably and uniformly settled in a particular way. Or are we to come to this conclusion that nothing, nothing on earth is settled under this Constitution, but that every thing is unsettled?

Mr. President, we have to recollect it is very possible—sir, it is quite likely—that when that Constitution was framed, the application of it to such Territories as Louisiana, Florida, California, and New Mexico was never within the contemplation of its framers. It will be recollected that when that Constitution was framed the whole country northwest of the river Ohio was unpeopled; and it will be recollected also, that the exercise and the assertion of the power to make governments for Territories in their infant state, are, in the nature of the power, temporary, and to terminate whenever they have acquired a population competent for self-government. Sixty thousand is the number fixed by the ordinance of 1787. Now, sir, recollect that when this Constitution was adopted, and that Territory was unpeopled, is it possible that Congress, to whom it had been ceded by the States for the common benefit of the ceding State and all other members of the Union—is it possible that Congress had no right whatever to declare what description of settlers should occupy the public lands?

Suppose they took up the opinion that the introduction of slavery would enhance the value of the land, and enable them to command for the public treasury a greater amount from that source of revenue than by the exclusion of slaves, would they not have had the right to say, in fixing the rules, regulations, or whatever you choose to call them, for the government of that Territory, that any one that chooses to bring slaves may bring them, if it will enhance the value of the property, in the clearing and cultivation of the soil, and add to the importance of the country? Or take the reverse:—Suppose Congress had thought that a greater amount of revenue would be derived from the waste lands beyond the Ohio river by the interdiction of slavery, would they not have had a right to interdict it? Why, sir, remember how these settlements were made, and what was their progress. They began with a few. I believe that about Marietta the first settlement was made.

It was a settlement of some two or three hundred persons from New England. Cincinnati, I believe, was the next point where a settlement was made. It was settled perhaps by a few persons from New Jersey, or some other State. Did those few settlers, the moment they arrived there, acquire sovereign rights? Had those few persons power to dispose of these territories? Had they even power to govern themselves—the handful of men who established themselves at Marietta or Cincinnati? No, sir, the contemplation of the Constitution no doubt was, that, inasmuch as this power was temporary, as it is applicable to unpeopled territory, and as that territory will become peopled gradually, insensibly, until it reaches a population which may entitle it to the benefit of self-government, in the mean time it is right and proper that Congress, who owns the soil, should regulate the settlement of the soil, and govern the settlers on the soil, until those settlers acquire number and capacity to govern themselves.

Sir, I will not further dwell upon this part of the subject; but I said there is another source of power equally satisfactory, equally conclusive in my mind, as that which relates to the territories, and that is the treaty-making power—the acquiring power. Now, I put it to gentlemen, is there not at this moment a power somewhere existing either to admit or exclude slavery from the ceded territory? It is not an annihilated power. This is impossible. It is a subsisting, actual, existing power; and where does it exist? It existed, I presume no one will controvert, in Mexico prior to the cession of these territories. Mexico could have abolished slavery or introduced slavery either in California or New Mexico. That must be conceded. Who will controvert this position? Well, Mexico has parted from the territory and from the sovereignty over the territory; and to whom did she transfer it? She transferred the territory and the sovereignty of the territory to the Government of the United States.

The Government of the United States acquires in sovereignty and in territory over California and New Mexico, all, either in sovereignty or territory, that Mexico held in California or New Mexico, by the cession of those territories. Sir, dispute that who can. The power exists or it does not; no one will contend for its annihilation. It existed in Mexico. No one, I think, can deny that. Mexico alienates the sovereignty over the territory, and her alience is the Government of the United States. The Government of the United States, then, possesses all power which Mexico possessed over the ceded territories, and the Government of the United States can do in reference to them—within, I admit, certain limits of the Constitution—whatever Mexico could have done. There are prohibitions upon the power of Congress within the Constitution, which prohibitions, I admit, must apply to Congress whenever she legislates, whether for the old States or for new territories; but, within those prohibitions, the powers of the United States over the ceded territories are co-extensive and equal to the powers of Mexico in the ceded territories, prior to the cession.

Sir, in regard to this treaty-making power, all who have any occasion to examine into its character and to the possible extent to which it may be carried, know that it is a power unlimited in its nature, except in so far as any limitation may be found in the Constitution of the United States; and upon this subject there is no limitation which prescribes the extent to which the powers should be exercised. I know, sir, it is argued that there is no grant of power in the Constitution, in specific terms, over the subject of slavery any where; and there is no grant in the Constitution to Congress specifically over the subject of a vast variety of matters upon which the powers of Congress may unquestionably operate. The major includes the minor. The general grant of power comprehends all the particulars and elements of which that power consists. The power of acquisition by treaty draws after it the power of government of the country acquired.

If there be a power to acquire, there must be, to use the language of the tribunal that sits below, a power to govern. I think, therefore, sir, without, at least for the present, dwelling further on this part of the subject, that to the two sources of authority in Congress to which I have referred, and especially to the last, may be traced the power of Congress to act in the territories in question; and, sir, I go to the extent, and I think it is a power in Congress equal to the introduction or exclusion of slavery. I admit the argument in both its forms; I admit if the argument be maintained that the power exists to exclude slavery, it necessarily follows that the power must exist, if Congress choose to exercise it, to tolerate or introduce slavery within the territories.

But, sir, I have been drawn off so far from the second resolution—not from the object of it, but from a particular view of it—that it has almost gone out of my recollection. The resolution asserts—

"That as slavery does not exist by law, and is not likely to be introduced into any of the territory acquired by the United States from the Republic of Mexico, it is inexpedient for Congress to provide by law either for its introduction into or exclusion from any part of the said territory; and that appropriate territorial governments ought to be established by Congress in all of the said territory, not assigned as the boundaries of the proposed State of California, without the adoption of any restriction or condition on the subject of slavery."

The other truth which I respectfully and with great deference conceive to exist, and which is announced in this resolution, is, that slavery is not likely to be introduced into any of these territories. Well, sir, is not that a fact? Is there a member who hears me that will not confirm the fact? What has occurred within the last three months? In California, more than in any other portion of the ceded territory, was it most probable, if slavery was adapted to the interests of the industrial pursuits of the inhabitants, that slavery would have been introduced. Yet, within the space of three or four months, California herself has declared, by a unanimous vote of her convention, against the introduction of slavery within her limits. And, as I remarked on a former occasion, this declaration was not confined to non-slaveholders.

There were persons from the slaveholding States who concurred in that declaration. Thus this fact which is asserted in the resolution is responded to by the act of California. Then, sir, if we come down to those mountain regions which are to be found in New Mexico, the nature of its soil and country, its barrenness, its unproductive character, every thing which relates to it, and every thing which we hear of it and about it, must necessarily lead to the conclusion which I have mentioned, that slavery is not likely to be introduced into them.—Well, sir, if it be true that by law slavery does not now exist in the ceded territories, and that it is not likely to be introduced into the ceded territories—if you, senators, agree to these truths, or a majority of you, as I am persuaded a large majority of you must agree to them—where is the objection or the difficulty to your announcing them to the whole world? Why should you hesitate or falter in the promulgation of incontestable truths? On the other hand, with regard to senators coming from the free States, allow me here to make, with reference to California, one or two observations.

When this feeling within the limits of your States was gotten up; when the Wilmot proviso was disseminated through them, and your people and yourselves attached themselves to that proviso, what was the state of facts? The state of facts at the time was, that you apprehended the introduction of slavery there. You did not know much—very few of us now know much—about those very territories. They were far distant from you. You were apprehensive that slavery might be introduced there. You wanted as a protection to introduce the interdiction called the Wilmot proviso. It was in this state of want of information that the whole North blazed up in behalf of this Wilmot proviso. It was under the apprehension that slavery might be introduced there that you left your constituents. For when you came from home, at the time you left your respective residences, you did not know the fact, which has only reached us since the commencement of the session of Congress, that a constitution has been unanimously adopted by the people of California, excluding slavery from their Territory.

Well, now, let me suppose that two years ago it had been known in the free States that such a constitution would be adopted; let me suppose that it had been believed that in no other portion of these ceded territories would slavery be introduced; let me suppose that upon this great subject of solicitude, negro slavery, the people of the North had been perfectly satisfied that there was no danger; let me also suppose that they had foreseen the excitement, the danger, the irritation, the resolutions which have been adopted by Southern Legislatures, and the manifestations of opinion by the people of the slaveholding States—let me suppose that all this had been known at the North at the time when the agitation was first got up upon the subject of this Wilmot proviso—do you believe that it would have ever reached the height to which it has attained? Do any of you believe it? And if, prior to your departure from your respective homes, you had had an opportunity of conferring with your constituents upon this most leading and important fact—of the adoption of a constitution excluding slavery in California—do you not believe, senators and representatives coming from the free States, that if you had the advantage of that fact told in serious, calm, fire-side conversation with your constituents, they would not have told you to come here and to settle all these agitating questions without danger to this Union?

What do you want? What do you want who reside in the free States? You want that there shall be no slavery introduced into the territories acquired from Mexico. Well, have not you got it in California already, if admitted as a State? Have not you got it in New Mexico, in all

human probability, also? What more do you want? You have got what is worth a thousand Wilmot provisos. You have got nature itself on your side. You have the fact itself on your side. You have the truth staring you in the face that no slavery is existing there. Well, if you are men; if you can rise from the mud and slough of party struggles and elevate yourselves to the height of patriots, what will you do? You will look at the fact as it exists. You will say, this fact was unknown to my people. You will say, they acted on one set of facts, we have got another set of facts here influencing us, and we will act as patriots, as responsible men, as lovers of unity and above all of this Union. We will act on the altered set of facts unknown to our constituents, and we will appeal to their justice, their honor, their magnanimity, to concur with us on this occasion, for establishing concord and harmony, and maintaining the existence of this glorious Union.

Well, Mr. President, I think, entertaining these views, that there was nothing extravagant in the hope in which I indulged when these resolutions were prepared and offered—nothing extravagant in the hope that the North might content itself even with striking out as unnecessary these two declarations. They are unnecessary for any purpose the free States have in view. At all events, if they should insist upon Congress expressing the opinions which are here asserted, they should limit their wishes to the simple assertion of them, without insisting on their being incorporated in any territorial Government which Congress may establish in the territories.

I pass on from the second resolution to the third and fourth, which relate to Texas: and allow me to say, Mr. President, that I approach the subject with a full knowledge of all its difficulties; and of all the questions connected with or growing out of this institution of slavery, which Congress is called upon to pass upon and decide, there are none so difficult and troublesome as those which relate to Texas, because, sir, Texas has a question of boundary to settle, and the question of slavery, or the feelings connected with it, run into the question of boundary. The North, perhaps, will be anxious to contract Texas within the narrowest possible limits, in order to exclude all beyond her to make it a free territory; the South, on the contrary, may be anxious to extend those sources of Rio Grande, for the purpose of creating an additional theater for slavery; and thus, to the question of the limits of Texas, and the settlement of her boundary, the slavery question, with all its troubles and difficulties, is added, meeting us at every step we take.

There is, sir, a third question, also, adding to the difficulty. By the resolution of annexation, slavery was interdicted in all north of 36 degrees 30'; but of New Mexico, that portion of it which lies north of 36 degrees 30' embraces, I think, about one third of the whole of New

Mexico east of the Rio Grande; so that you have free and slave territory mixed, boundary and slavery mixed together, and all these difficulties are to be encountered. And allow me to say, sir, that among the considerations which induced me to think it was necessary to settle all these questions, was the state of things that now exists in New Mexico, and the state of things to be apprehended both there and in other portions of the territories. Why, sir, at this moment—and I think I shall have the concurrence of the two senators from that State when I announce the fact—at this moment there is a feeling approximating to abhorrence on the part of the people of New Mexico at the idea of any union with Texas.

Mr. Rusk. Only, sir, on the part of the office-seekers and army followers, who have settled there, and attempted to mislead the people.

Mr. Clay. Ah! sir, that may be, and I am afraid that New Mexico is not the only place where this class composes a majority of the whole population of the country.— [Laughter.]

Now, sir, if the questions are not settled which relate to Texas, her boundaries, and so forth, and to the territory now claimed by Texas and disputed by New Mexico—the territories beyond New Mexico which are excluded from California—if these questions are not all settled, I think they will give rise to future confusion, disorder and anarchy there, and to agitation here. There will be, I have no doubt, a party still at the North crying out, if these questions are not settled this session, for the Wilmot proviso, or some other restriction upon them, and we shall absolutely do nothing, in my opinion, if we do not accommodate all these difficulties and provide against the recurrence of all these dangers.

Sir, with respect to the state of things in New Mexico, allow me to call the attention of the Senate to what I consider as the highest authority I could offer to them as to the state of things there existing. I mean the acts of their Convention, unless that Convention happens to have been composed altogether of office-seekers, office-holders, and so forth. Now, sir, I call your attention to what they say in depicting their own situation.

Mr. Underwood, at Mr. Clay's request, read the following extract from instructions adopted by the Convention, appended to the journal of the Convention of the Territory of New Mexico, held at the city of Santa Fe, in September, 1849.

"We, the people of New Mexico, in Convention assembled, having elected a delegate to represent this Territory in the Congress of the United States, and to urge upon the Supreme Government a redress of our grievances, and the protection due to us as citizens of our common country, under the Constitution, instruct him as follows: That whereas, for the last three years we have suffered under the paralyzing effects of a government undefined and doubtful in its character, inefficient to protect the rights of the people, or to discharged the high and absolute duty of every Government the enforcement and regular administration of its own laws, in consequence of which, industry and enterprise are paralyzed and discontent and confusion prevail throughout the land. The want of proper protection against the various barbarous tribes of Indians that surround us on every side has prevented the extension of settlements upon our valuable public domain, and rendered utterly futile every attempt to explore or develop the great resources of the territory.

"Surrounded by the Utahs, Camanches, and Apaches, on the North, East and South by the Navajos on the West, with Jicarillas within our limits, and without any adequate protection against their hostile inroads, our flocks and herds are driven off by thousands, our fellow-citizens, men, women, and children, are murdered or carried into captivity. Many of our citizens, of all ages and sexes, are at this moment suffering all the horrors of barbarian bondage, and it is utterly out of our power to obtain their release from a condition to which death would be preferable. The wealth of our territory is being diminished. We have neither the means nor any adopted plan of Government for the education of the rising generation. In fine, with a government temporary, doubtful, uncertain, and inefficient in character and in operation, surrounded and despoiled by barbarous foes, ruin appears inevitably before us, unless speedy and effectual protection be extended to us by the Congress of the United States."

There is a series of resolutions, Mr. President, which any gentleman may look at, if he chooses; but I think it is not worth while to take up the time of the Senate in reading them.

That is the condition, sir, of New Mexico. Well, I suspect that to go beyond it, to go beyond the Rio Grande to the territory which is not claimed by Texas, you will not find a much better state of things. In fact, sir, I can not for a moment reconcile it to my sense of duty to suffer Congress to adjourn without an effort, at least, being made to extend the benefits, the blessings of government to those people who have recently been acquired by us.

Sir, with regard to that portion of New Mexico which lies east of the Rio Grande, undoubtedly, if it is conceded to Texas, while she has two parties, disliking each other as much as those office-holders and office-seekers alluded to by the senator from Texas, if they could possibly be drawn together and governed quietly, peaceably, and comfortably, there might be a remedy, so far as relates to the country east of the Rio Grande; but all beyond it—Deseret and the North of California—would be still open and liable to all the consequences of disunion, confusion and anarchy, without some stable government emanating from the authority of the nation of which they now compose a part, and with which they are but little acquainted. I think, therefore, that all these questions, difficult and troublesome as they may be, ought to be met—met in a spirit of candor and calmness, and decided upon as a matter of duty.

Now these two resolutions which we have immediately under consideration propose a decision of these questions. I have said, sir, that there is scarcely a resolution in the series which I have offered that does not contain some mutual concession or evidence of mutual forbearance, where the concession was not altogether from the non-slaveholding to the slaveholding States.

Now, with respect to this resolution proposing a boundary for Texas, what is it? We know the difference of opinion which has existed in this country with respect to that boundary. We know that a very large portion of the people of the United States have supposed that the western limit of Texas was the Nueces, and that it did not extent to the Rio Grande. We know, by the resolution of annexation, that the question of what is the western limit and the northern limit of Texas was an open question—that it has been all along an open question. It was an open question when the boundary was run, in virtue of the Act of 1838, marking the boundary between the United States and Texas. Sir, at that time the boundary authorized by the Act of 1838 was a boundary commencing at the mouth of the Sabine and running up to its head, thence to Red River, thence westwardly with Red River to, I think, the hundredth degree of west longitude. Well, sir, that did not go so far as Texas now claims, any why? Because it was an open question. War was yet raging between Texas and Mexico; it was not foreseen exactly what might be her ultimate limits. But, sir, we will come to the question of what was done at the time of her annexation.

The whole resolution which relates to the question of boundary, from beginning to end, assumes an open boundary, an unascertained, unfixed boundary to Texas on the West. Sir, what is the first part of the resolution? It is that "Congress doth consent that the Territory properly included within and rightfully belonging to the Republic of Texas may be erected into a new State." Properly including—rightfully belonging to. The resolution specifies no boundary. It could specify none. It has specified no western or northern boundary for Texas. It has assumed in this state of uncertainty what we know in point of fact existed. But then the latter part of it: "Said State to be formed subject to the adjustment of all questions of boundary that may arise with other Governments, and the constitution thereof," &c. That is to say, she is annexed with her rightful and proper boundaries, without a specification of them; but inasmuch as it was known that these boundaries at the west and the north were unsettled, the Government of the

United States retained to itself the power of settling with any foreign nation what the boundary should be.

Now, sir, it is impossible for me to go into the whole question and to argue it fully. I mean to express opinions or impressions, rather than to go into the entire argument. The western and northern limit of Texas being unsettled, and the Government of the United States having retained the power of settling it, I ask, suppose the power had been exercised, and that there had been no cession of territory by Mexico to the United States, but that the negotiations between the countries had been limited simply to the fixation of the western and northern limits of Texas, could it not have been done by the United States and Mexico conjointly? Will any one dispute it? Suppose there had been a treaty of limits of Texas concluded between Mexico and the United States, fixing the Nueces as the western limit of Texas, would not Texas have been bound by it? Why, by the express terms of the resolution she would have been bound by it; or if it had been the Colorado or the Rio Grande, or any other boundary, whatever western limit had been fixed by the joint action of the two powers, would have been binding and obligatory upon Texas by the express terms of the resolution by which she was admitted into the Union. Now, sir, Mexico and the United States conjointly, by treaty, might have fixed upon the western and northern limits of Texas, and if the United States have acquired by treaty all the subjects upon which the limits of Texas might have operated, have not the United States now the power solely and exclusively which Mexico and the United States conjointly possessed prior to the late treaty between the two countries? It seems to me, sir, that this conclusion and reasoning are perfectly irresistible. If Mexico and the United States could have fixed upon any western limit for Texas, and did not do it, and if the United States have acquired to themselves, as acquired by the treaty in question, all the territory upon which the western limit must have been fixed, when it was fixed, it seems to me that no one can resist the logical conclusion, that the United States now have themselves a power to do what the United States and Mexico conjointly could have done.

Sir, I admit it is a delicate power—an extremely delicate power. I admit that it ought to be exercised in a spirit of justice, liberality, and generosity toward this the youngest member of the great American family. But here the power is. Possibly, sir, upon that question—however I offer no positive opinion—possibly, if the United States were to fix it in a way unjust in the opinion of Texas, and contrary to her rights, she might bring the question before the Supreme Court of the United States, and have it there again investigated and decided. I say possibly, sir, because I am not one of that class of politicians who believe that every question is a competent and proper question for the Supreme Court of the United States. There are questions too large for any tribunal of that kind to try; great political questions, national territorial questions, which transcend their limits; for such questions their powers are utterly incompetent. Whether this be one of those questions or not, I shall not decide; but I will maintain that the United States are now invested solely and exclusively with that power which was common to both nations—to fix, ascertain, and settle the western and northern limits of Texas.

Sir, the other day my honorable friend who represents so well the State of Texas aid that we had no more right to touch the limits of Texas than we had to touch the limits of Kentucky. I think that was the illustration he gave us—that a State is one and indivisible, and that the General Government has no right to sever it. I agree with him, sir, in that; where the limits are ascertained and certain, where they are undisputed and indisputable. The General Government has no right, nor has any other earthly power the right, to interfere with the limits of a State whose boundaries are thus fixed, thus ascertained, known, and recognized. The whole power, at least, to interfere with it is voluntary. The extreme case may be put—one which I trust in God may never happen in this nation—of a conquered nation, and of a constitution adapting itself to the state of subjugation or conquest to which it has been reduced; and giving up whole States, as well as parts of States, in order to save from the conquering arms of the invader what remains. I say such a power in case of extremity may exist. But I admit that, short of such extremity, voluntarily, the General Government has no right of separate a State—to take a portion of its territory from it, or to regard it otherwise than as integral, one and indivisible, and not to be affected by any legislation of ours. But, then I assume what does not exist in the case of Texas, and these boundaries must be known, ascertained, and indisputable. With regard to Texas, all was open, all was unfixed; all is unfixed at this moment, with respect to her limits west and north of the Nueces.

But, sir, we gave fifteen millions of dollars for this territory that we bought, and God knows what a costly bargain to this now distracted country it has been! We gave fifteen millions of dollars for the territory ceded to us by Mexico. Can Texas justly, fairly, and honorably come into the Union and claim all that she asserted a right to, without paying any portion of the fifteen millions of dollars which constituted the consideration of the grant by the ceding nation to the United States? She proposes no such thing. She talks, indeed, about the United States having been her agent, her trustee. Why, sir, the United States was no more her agent or her trustee than she was the agent or trustee of the whole people of the United States. Texas involved herself war—(I mean to make this no reproach—none—none—upon the past)—Texas brought herself into a state of war, and when she got into that war,

it was not the war of Texas and Mexico, but it was the war of the whole thirty United States and Mexico; it was a war in which the Government of the United States, which created the hostilities, was as much the trustee and agent of the twenty-nine other States composing the Union as she was the trustee and agent of Texas. And, sir, with respect to all these circumstances—such, for example, as a treaty with a map annexed, as in the case of the recent treaty with Mexico; such as the opinion of individuals highly respected and eminent, like the lamented Mr. Polk, late President of the United States, whose opinion was that he had no right, as President of the United States, or in any character otherwise than as negotiating with Mexico—and in that the Senate would have to act in concurrence with him—that he had no right to fix the boundary; and as to the map attached to the treaty, it is sufficient to say that the treaty itself is silent from beginning to end on the subject of the fixation of the boundary of Texas. The annexation of the map to the treaty was a matter of no utility, for the treaty is not strengthened by it; it no more affirms the truth of any thing delineated upon the map in relation to Texas than it does any thing in relation to any other geographical subject that composed the map.

Mr. President, I have said that I think the power has been concentrated in the Government of the United States to fix upon the limits of the State of Texas. I have said also that this power ought to be exercised in a spirit of great liberality and justice; and I put it to you, sir, to say, in reference to this second resolution of mine, whether that liberality and justice have not been displayed in the resolution which I have proposed. In the resolution, what is proposed? To confine her to the Nueces? No, sir. To extent her boundary to the mouth of the Rio Grande, and thence up that river to the southern limit of New Mexico; and thence along that limit to the boundary between the United States and Spain, as marked under the treaty of 1819.

Why, sir, here is a vast country. I believe—although I have made no estimate about it—that it is inferior in extent of land, of acres, of square miles, to what Texas east of the river Nueces, extending to the Sabine, had before. And who is there can say with truth and justice that there is no reciprocity, nor mutuality, no concession in this resolution, made to Texas, even in reference to the question of boundary alone? You give her a vast country, equal, I repeat, in extent nearly to what she indisputably possessed before; a country sufficiently large, with her consent, hereafter to carve out of it some two or three additional States when the condition of the population may render it expedient to make new States. Sir, is there not in this resolution concession, liberality, justice? But this is not all that we propose to do. The second resolution proposes to pay off a certain amount of the debt of Texas. A blank is left in the resolution, because I have not heretofore been able to ascertain the amount.

Mr. Foote—Will the honorable Senator allow me to suggest that it may be agreeable to him to finish his remarks to-morrow? If such be the case, I will move that the Senate now go into Executive session.

Mr. Clay—I am obliged to the worthy Senator from Mississippi; I do not think it possible for me to conclude to-day, and I will yield with great pleasure if—

Mr. Foote—I now move—

Mr. Clay—If the Senator will permit me to conclude what I have to say in relation to Texas, I will then cheerfully yield the floor for his motion.

I was about to remark that, independently of this most liberal and generous boundary which is tendered to Texas, we propose to offer her in this second resolution a sum which the worthy Senator from Texas thinks will not be less than three millions of dollars—the exact amount neither he nor I can furnish, not having the materials at hand upon which to make a statement. Well, sir, you get this large boundary and three millions of your debt paid. I shall not repeat the argument which I urged upon a former occasion, as to the obligation of the United States to pay a portion of this debt, but was struck the other day, upon reading the treaty of limits, first between the United States and Mexico, and next the treaty of limits between the United States and Texas, to find, in the preamble of both those treaties, a direct recognition of the principle from which I think springs our obligation to pay a portion of this debt, for the payment of which the revenue of Texas was pledged before her annexation. The principle asserted in the treaty of limits with Mexico is that whereas by the treaty of 1819, between Spain and the United States, a limit was fixed between Mexico and the United States, Mexico comprising then a portion of the possessions of the Spanish Government, although Mexico was at the date of the treaty severed from the crown of Spain, yet she, as having been a part of the possessions of the crown of Spain when the treaty of 1819 was made, was bound by that treaty as much as if it had been made by herself instead of Spain—in other words, that the severance of no part of a common empire can exonerate either portion of that empire from the obligations contracted when the empire was entire and unsevered. And, sir, the name principle is asserted in the treaty of 1838, between Texas and the United States. The principle asserted is, that the treaty of 1828 between Mexico and the United States having been made when Texas was a part of Mexico, and that now Texas being dissevered from Mexico, she nevertheless remains bound by that treaty as much as if no such severance had taken place. In other words, the principle is this—that when an independent power creates an obligation or debt, no subsequent political misfortune, no subsequent sever-

ance of the territories of that power, can exonerate it from the obligation that was created while an integral and independent power; in other words, to bring it down and apply it to this specific case—that, Texas being an independent power, and having a right to make loans and to make pledges, having raised a loan and pledged specifically the revenues arising from the customs to the public creditor; the public creditor became invested with a right to that fund; and it is a right of which he could not be divested by any other act than one to which his own consent was given—it could be divested by no political change which Texas might think proper to make. In consequence of the absorption or merging of Texas into the United States, the creditor, being no party to the treaty which was formed, does not lose his right—he retains his right to demand the fulfillment of the pledge that was made upon this specific fund, just as if there had not been any annexation of Texas to the United States.

That was the foundation upon which I arrived at the conclusion expressed in the resolution—that the United States having appropriated to themselves the revenue arising from the imports, which revenue had been pledged to the creditor of Texas, the United States as an honorable and just power ought now to pay the debt for which those duties were solemnly pledged by a power independent in itself, and competent to make the pledge. Well, sir, I think that when you consider the large boundary which is assigned to Texas—and when you take into view the abhorrence, for I think I am warranted in using this expression—with which the people of New Mexico east of the Rio Grande will look upon any political connection with Texas—and when, in addition to this, you take into view the large grant of money that we propose to make, and our liberality in exonerating her from a portion of her public debt, equal to that grant—when we take all these circumstances into consideration, I think I have presented a case in regard to which I confess I shall be greatly surprised if the people of Texas themselves, when they come to deliberate upon these liberal offers, hesitate a moment to accede to them.

I have now got through with what I had to say in reference to this resolution, and if the Senator from Mississippi wishes it, I will give way for a motion for adjournment.

On motion of Mr. Foote the further consideration of the resolution was postponed, and on motion,

The Senate Adjourned.

Wednesday, Feb. 6.

Mr. Clay—Mr. President, if there be in this vast assembly of beauty, grace, elegance, and intelligence, any who have come here under an expectation that the humble individual who now addresses you means to attempt any display, any use of ambitious language, any extraordinary ornament or decoration of speech, they will be utterly disappointed. The season of the year, and my own season of life, both admonish me to abstain from the use of any such ornaments; but, above all, Mr. President, the awful subject upon which it is my duty to address the Senate and the country forbids my saying any thing but what pertains strictly to that subject, and my sole desire is to make myself, in seriousness, soberness, and plainness, understood by you and by those who think proper to listen to me.

When, yesterday, the adjournment of the Senate took place, at that stage of the discussion of the resolutions which I had submitted which related to Texas and her boundary, I thought I had concluded the whole subject, but I was reminded by a friend that perhaps I was not sufficiently explicit on a single point, and that is, the relation of Texas and the Government of the United States, and that portion of the debt of Texas for which I think a responsibility exists on the part of the Government of the United States.

Sir, it was said that perhaps it might be understood, in regard to the proposed grant of three millions, or whatever may be the sum when ascertained, to Texas, in consideration of the surrender of her title to New Mexico this side of the Rio Grande, that we granted nothing—that we merely discharged an obligation which existed upon the Government of the United States, in consequence of the appropriation of the imports receivable in the ports of Texas while she was an independent power. But that is not my understanding, Mr. President. As between Texas and the United States, the obligation on the part of Texas to pay her portion of the debt referred to, is complete and unqualified, and there is, as between these two parties, no obligation on the part of the United States to pay one dollar of the debt of Texas. On the contrary, by an express stipulation in the resolutions of admission, it is declared and provided that in no event do the United States become liable or charged with any portion of the debt or liabilities of Texas.

It is not, therefore, for any responsibility which exists to the State of Texas, on the part of the Government of the United States, that I think provision ought to be made for that debt. No such thing. As between those two parties, the responsibility on the part of Texas is complete to pay the debt, and there is no responsibility on the part of the United States to pay one cent. But there is a third party, who was no party to the annexation whatever—that is to say, the creditor of Texas, who advanced the money on the faith of solemn pledges made by Texas to him, to reimburse the loan by the appropriation of the duties received on foreign imports; and he, and he alone, is the party to whom we are bound, according to the view which I have presented of the subject. Nor can the other creditors of

Texas complain that provision is made only for a particular portion of the debt, leaving the residue of the debt unprovided for by the Government of the United States, because, in so far as we may extinguish any portion of the debt of Texas under which she is now bound, in so far will it contribute to diminish the residue of the debts of Texas, and leave the funds derived from the public lands held by Texas, and what other resources she may have, applicable to the payment of these debts, with more effect than if the entire debt, including the pledged portion as well as the unpledged portion, was obligatory upon her, and she stood bound by it. Nor can the creditors complain, for another reason.

Texas has all the resources which she had when an independent power, with the exception of the duties receivable in her ports upon foreign imports, and she is exempted from certain charges, expenditures, and responsibilities which she would have had to encounter if she had remained a separate and independent power: for example, she would have had to provide for a certain amount of naval force and for a certain amount perhaps of military force, in order to protect herself against Mexico or against any foreign enemy whatever. But by her annexation to the United States she became liberated from all these charges, and, of course, her entire revenues may be applicable to the payment of her debts, those only excepted which are necessary to the support and maintenance of the Government of Texas.

With this explanation upon that part of the subject, I pass to the consideration of the next resolution in the series which I have had the honor to submit, and which relates, if I am not mistaken, to this District.

"*Resolved*, That it is inexpedient to abolish slavery in the District of Columbia, while that institution continues to exist in the State of Maryland, without the consent of that State, without the consent of the people of the District, and without just compensation to the owners of slaves within the District."

Mr. President, an objection at the moment was made to this resolution, by some honorable senator on the other side of the body, that it did not contain an assertion of the unconstitutionality of the exercise of the power of abolition. I said then, as I have uniformly maintained in this body, as I contended for in 1838, and ever have done, that the power to abolish slavery within the District of Columbia has been vested in Congress by language too clear and explicit to admit, in my judgment, of any rational doubt whatever. What, sir, is the language of the Constitution? "To exercise exclusive legislation, in all case whatsoever, over such District (not exceeding ten miles square) as may, by cession of particular States and the acceptance of Congress, become the seat of the Government of the United States." Now, sir, Congress, by this grant of power, is invested with all legislation whatsoever over the District.

Can we conceive of human language more broad and comprehensive than that which invests a legislative body with exclusive power, in all cases whatsoever, of legislation over a given district of territory or country? Let me ask, sir, is there any power to abolish slavery in this District? Let me suppose, in addition to what I suggested the other day, that slavery had been abolished in Maryland and Virginia—let me add to it the supposition that it was abolished in all the States in the Union; is there any power then to abolish slavery within the district of Columbia, or is slavery planted here to all eternity, without the possibility of the exercise of any legislative power for its abolition? It can not be invested in Maryland, because the power with which Congress is invested is exclusive. Maryland, therefore, is excluded, and so all the other States of the Union are excluded. It is here, or it is nowhere.

This was the view which I took in 1838, and I think there it nothing in the resolution which I offered on that occasion incompatible with the view which I now present, and which the resolution contains. While I admitted the power to exist in Congress, and exclusively in Congress, to legislate in all cases whatsoever, and consequently in the case of the abolition of slavery in this District, if it is deemed proper to do so, I admitted on that occasion, as I contend now, that it is a power which Congress can not, in conscience and good faith, exercise while the institution of slavery continues within the State of Maryland. The case, is a good deal altered now from what it was twelve years ago, when the resolution to which I allude was adopted by the Senate.

Upon the occasion Virginia and Maryland both were concerned in the exercise of the power; but, by the retrocession of that portion of the District which lies south of the Potomac, Virginia became no more interested in the question of the abolition of slavery within the residue of the District than any other slaveholding State in the Union is interested in its abolition. The question now is confined to Maryland. I said on that occasion that, although the grant of power is complete, and comprehends the right to abolish slavery within the District, yet it was a thing which never could have entered into the conception of Maryland or Virginia that slavery would be abolished here while slavery continued to exist in either of those two ceding States. I say, moreover, what the grant of power itself indicates, that, although exclusive legislation in all cases whatsoever over the District was vested in Congress within the ten miles square, it was to make it the seat of Government of the United States. That was the great, prominent, substantial object of the grant, and that, in exercising all the powers with which we are invested, complete and full as they may be, yet the great purpose—that of the cession having

been made in order to create a suitable seat of Government—ought to be the leading and controlling idea with Congress in the exercise of this power.

And it is not necessary, in order to render it a proper and suitable seat of Government for the United States, that slavery should be abolished within the limits of the ten miles square. And inasmuch as at the time of the cession—when in spirit of generosity, immediately after the formation of the Constitution—when all was peace, and harmony, and concord—when brotherly affection and fraternal feeling prevailed throughout this whole Union—when Maryland and Virginia, in a moment of generous impulse, and with feelings of high regard toward the members of this Union, chose to make this grant, neither party could have suspected that, at some distant future period, upon the agitation of this unfortunate subject, their generous grant without equivalent was to be turned against them, and that the sword was to be uplifted, as it were, in their bosoms, to strike at their own hearts; thus this implied faith, this honorable obligation, this necessity and propriety of keeping in constant view the great object of cession. Those were considerations which in 1838 governed me, as they now influence me, in submitting the reasons which I have submitted to your consideration.

Now, as then, I do not think Congress ought ever, as an honorable body, acting *bona fide,* in good faith, and according to the nature and purposes, and objects of the cession, at the time it was made—and, looking at the condition of the ceding States at that time, Congress can not, without the forfeiture of all those obligations of honor which men of honor and nations of honor respect as much as if found literally in so many words in the bond itself—Congress can not interfere with the institution of slavery in this District without the violation of all these obligations, not in my opinion less sacred and less binding than if inserted in the constitutional instrument itself.

Well, sir, what does the resolution propose? The resolution neither affirms not disaffirms the constitutionally of the exercise of the power of abolition in this District. It is silent upon the subject. It says it is inexpedient to do it, but upon certain conditions. And what are these considerations? Why, first, that the State of Maryland shall give its consent; in other words, that the State of Maryland shall release the United States from the obligation of the implied faith which I contend is connected with the act of cession by Maryland to the United States. Well, sir, if Maryland, the only state not that ceded any portion of the territory which remains to us, gives us her full consent; in other words, if she releases Congress from all obligations growing out of the cession, with regard to slavery, I consider it is removing one of the obstacles to the exercise of the power, if it were deemed expedient to exercise the power. But it is removing only one of them. There are two other conditions which are inserted in this resolution. The first is the consent of the people of the District.

Mr. President, the condition of the people of this District is anomalous. It is a condition in violation of the great principles which lie at the bottom of our own free institutions, and all free institutions, because it is the case of a people who are acted upon by legislative authority, and taxed by legislative authority, without having any voice or representation in the taxing or legislative body. The Government of the United States, in respect to the people of this District, is a tyranny, an absolute Government—not exercised hitherto, I admit, and I hope it never will be exercised, tyrannically or arbitrarily; but it is in the nature of all arbitrary power, because, if I were to give a definition of arbitrary power, I would say that it is that power which is exercised by an authority over any people who have no voice, no representation in the assembly whose edicts or laws go forth to act upon the unrepresented people to whom I have referred.

Well, sir, that being their condition, and this question of the abolition of slavery affecting them in all the relations which we can imagine—of prosperity, society, comfort, peace, and happiness—I have required as another condition, upon which alone this power should be exercised, the consent of the people of the District. But, sir, I have not stopped there. This resolution requires still another and a third condition, and that is, that slavery shall not be abolished within the District of Columbia, although Maryland consents, although the people of the District themselves consent, without the third condition of making compensation to the owners of the slaves within the District. Sir, it is immaterial to me upon what basis this obligation to compensate for the slaves who may be liberated by the authority of Congress is placed. There is a clause in the Constitution of the United States, of the amendments to the Constitution, which declares that no private property shall be taken for public use, without just compensation being made to the owner of the property.

Well, I think, in a just and liberal interpretation of that clause, we are restrained from taking the property of the people of this District, in slaves, on considerations of any public policy, or for any conceivable or imaginable use of the public, without a full and fair compensation to the people of this District. But, without the obligation of any constitutional restriction, such as is contained in the amendment to which I refer—without that, upon the principles of eternal justice itself, we ought not to deprive those who have property in slaves, in this District, of their property, without compensating them for their full value. Why, sir, no one of the European powers, Great Britain, France, or any other of the powers which undertook to abolish slavery in their respective colonies, has ever ventured to do it without making compensation. They were

under no obligation arising out of any written or other constitution to do it, but under that obligation to which all men ought to bow with homage—that obligation of eternal justice, which declares that no man ought to be deprived of his property without a full and just compensation for its value.

I know it has been argued that the clause of the Constitution which requires compensation for property taken by the public, for its use, would not apply to the case of the abolition of slavery in the District, because the property is not taken for the use of the public. Literally, perhaps, it would not be taken for the use of the public; but it would be taken in consideration of a policy and purpose adopted by the public, as one which it was deemed expedient to carry into full effect and operation; and, by a liberal interpretation of the clause, it ought to be so far regarded as taken for the use of the public, at the instance of the public, as to demand compensation to the extent of the value of the property.

If that is not a restriction as to the power of Congress over the subject of slavery in the District, then the power of Congress stands unrestricted, and that would not be a better condition for the slaveholder in the District than to assume the restriction contained in the amendment. I say it would be unrestricted by constitutional operation or injunction. The great restrictions resulting from the obligations of justice would remain, and they are sufficient to exact from Congress the duty of ascertaining, prior to the abolition of slavery, the value of the property in slaves in the District, and of making full, fair, and just compensation for that property.

Well, Mr. President, I said yesterday there was not a resolution, except the first (which contained no concession by either party), that did not either contain some mutual concession by the two parties, or did not contain concessions altogether from the North to the South.

Now with respect to the resolution under consideration. The North has contended that the power exists under the Constitution to abolish slavery. The South, I am aware, has opposed it, and most, at least a great portion of the South, have contended for the opposite construction. What does the resolution do? It asks of both parties to forbear urging their respective opinions, the one to the exclusion of the other, but it concedes to the South all that the South, it appears to me, upon this subject, ought in reason to demand, in so far as it requires such conditions as amount to an absolute security for property in slaves in the District; such conditions as will probably make the existence of slavery within the District co-eval and co-extensive with its existence in any of the States out of and beyond the District. But, sir, the second clause of this resolution provides "that it is expedient to prohibit within the District the trade in slaves brought into it from States or places beyond the limits of the District, either to be sold therein as merchandise, or to be transported to other markets."

Well, Mr. President, if the concession be made that Congress has the power of legislation, and exclusive legislation, in all cases whatsoever, how can it be doubted that Congress has authority to prohibit what is called the slave-trade in the District of Columbia? Sir, my interpretation of the Constitution is this; that, with regard to all parts of it which operate upon the States, Congress can exercise no power which is not granted, or which is not a necessary implication from a granted power. That is the rule for the action of Congress in relation to its legislation upon the States, but in relation to its legislation upon this District, the reverse. I take it to be the true rule that Congress has all power over the District which is not prohibited by some part of the Constitution of the United States; in other words, that Congress has a power within the District equivalent to, and co-extensive with, the power which any State itself possesses within its own limits. Well, sir, does any one doubt the power and the right of any slaveholding State in this Union to forbid the introduction, as merchandise, of slaves within their limits? Why, sir, almost every slaveholding State in the Union has exercised its power to prohibit the introduction of slaves as merchandise.

It was in the Constitution of my own State; and, notwithstanding all the excitement and agitation upon the subject of slavery which occurred during the past year in the State of Kentucky, the same principle is incorporated in the new Constitution. It is in the Constitution, I know, of Mississippi. That State prohibits the introduction of slaves within its limits as merchandise. I believe it to be in the Constitution or in the laws of Maryland—in the laws of Virginia—in the laws of most of the slaveholding States. It is true that the policy of the different slaveholding States upon this subject has somewhat vacillated—they sometimes adopted it and sometimes excluded it—but there has been no diversity of opinion, no departure from the great principle, that every one of them has the power and authority to prohibit the introduction of slaves within their respective limits, if they choose to exercise it. Well, then, sir, I really do not think that this resolution, which proposes to abolish that trade, ought to be considered as a concession by either class of the States to the other class.

I think it should be regarded as a common object, acceptable to both, and conformable to the wishes and feelings of both; and yet, sir, in these times of fearful and alarming excitement—in these times when every night that I go to sleep and awake up in the morning, it is with the apprehension of some new and fearful and dreadful tidings upon this agitating subject—I have seen in the act of a neighboring State, among the various contingencies which are enumerated, upon the happening of any one of

which delegates are to be sent to the famous Convention which is to assemble at Nashville in June next, that among other substantive grounds for the appointment of delegates to the Convention—of delegates from the State to which I refer—one is, that if Congress abolish the slave-trade in the District of Columbia, that shall be cause for a Convention—in other words, it is cause for considering whether this Union ought to be dissolved or not. Is it possible to portray a greater extent of extravagance to which men may be carried by the indulgence of their passions?

Sir, the power exists; the duty, in my opinion, exists; and there has been no time—as I may say, in language coincident with that used by the honorable senator from Alabama—there has been no time in my public life when I was not willing to concur in the abolition of the slave-trade in this District. I was willing to do it when Virginia's portion of the District was retroceded, that lying south of Potomac. There is still less ground for objection to doing it now, when the District is limited to the portion this side of the Potomac, and when the motive or reason for concentrating slaves here in a depot, for the purpose of transportation to distant foreign markets, is lessened with the diminution of the District, by the retrocession of that portion to Virginia.

Why should slave-traders who buy their slaves in Maryland or Virginia, come here with their slaves in order to transport them to New Orleans or other Southern markets? Why not transport them from the States in which they are purchased? Why are the feelings of citizens here outraged by the scenes exhibited, and the corteges which pass along our avenues, of manacled human beings, not collected at all in our own neighborhood, but brought from distant parts of neighboring States? Why should they be outraged? And who is there, that has a heart, that does not contemplate a spectacle of that kind with horror and indignation? Why should they be outraged by a scene so inexcusable and detestable as this?

Sir, it is no concession, I repeat, from one class of States or from the other. It is an object in which both of them, it seems to me, should heartily unite, and which the one side as much as the other should rejoice in adopting, inasmuch as it lessens one of the causes of inquietude and dissatisfaction which are connected with this District. Abolish the slave-trade in this District; reassert the doctrine of the resolution of 1838, that by an implied assent on the part of Congress slavery ought not to be abolished in the District of Columbia, while it remains in the State of Maryland; reassert the principle of that resolution, and adopt the other healing measures—or other similar or more healing measures—for I am not attached to any thing that is the production of my own hand, if any thing better should be offered by any body else—adopt the other healing measures—which are proposed, and which are required by the distracted condition of the country, and I venture to say that, as we have had peace and quiet for the last twenty years, since the termination of the Missouri controversy, we shall have, in all human probability, peace for a longer period to come upon this unhappy subject of slavery.

The next resolution is:

"That more effectual provision ought to be made by law, according to the requirement of the Constitution, for the restitution and delivery of persons bound to service or labor in any State, who may escape into any other State or Territory in the Union."

Now, Mr. President, upon that subject I go with him who goes furthest in the interpretation of that clause in the Constitution. In my humble opinion, sir, it is a requirement by the Constitution of the United States which is not limited in its operation to the Congress of the United States, but extends to every State in the Union and to the officers of every State in the Union; and I go one step further; it extends to every man in the Union, and devolves upon them all an obligation to assist in the recovery of a fugitive from labor who takes refuge in or escapes into one of the free States. And, sir, I think I can maintain all this by a fair interpretation of the Constitution. It provides—

"That no person held to service or labor in one State, under the laws thereof, escaping into another, shall, in consequence of any law or regulation therein, be discharged from service or labor, but shall be delivered up on claim of the party to whom such service or labor may be due."

It will be observed, Mr. President, that this clause in the Constitution is not among the enumerated powers granted to Congress, for, if that had been the case, it might have been urged that Congress alone could legislate to carry it into effect; but it is one of the general powers, or one of the general rights secured by this constitutional instrument, and it addresses itself to all who are bound by the Constitution of the United States. Now, sir, the officers of the General Government are bound to take an oath to support the Constitution of the United States. All State officers are required by the Constitution to take an oath to support the Constitution of the United States; and all men who love their country and are obedient to its laws, are bound to assist in the execution of those laws, whether they are fundamental or derivative. I do not say that a private individual is bound to make the tour of his State in order to assist an owner of a slave to recover his property; but I do say, if he is present when the owner of a slave is about to assert his rights and endeavor to obtain possession of his property, every man present, whether he be an officer of the General Government or the State Government, or a private individual, is bound to assist, if men are bound at all to assist in the execution of the laws of their country.

Now what is this provision? It is that such fugitives shall be delivered upon claim of the party to whom such service or labor may be due. As has been already remarked in the course of the debate upon the bill upon this subject which is now pending, the language used in regard to fugitives from criminal offenses and fugitives from labor is precisely the same. The fugitive from justice is to be delivered up, and to be removed to the State having jurisdiction; the fugitive from labor is to be delivered up on claim of the party to whom such service is due. Well, has it ever been contended on the part of any State that she is not bound to surrender a fugitive from justice, upon demand from the State from which he fled? I believe not. There have been some exceptions to the performance of this duty, but they have not denied the general right; and if they have refused in any instance to give up the person demanded, it has been upon some technical or legal ground, not at all questioning the general right to have the fugitive surrendered, or the obligation to deliver him up as intended by the Constitution.

I think, then, Mr. President, that with regard to the true interpretation of this provision of the Constitution there can be no doubt. It imposes an obligation upon all the States, free or slaveholding; it imposes an obligation upon all officers of the Government, State, or Federal; and, I will add, upon all the people of the United States, under particular circumstances, to assist in the surrender and recovery of a fugitive slave from his master.

There has been some confusion, and, I think, some misconception, on this subject, in consequence of a recent decision of the Supreme Court of the United States. I think that decision has been entirely misapprehended. There is a vast difference between imposing impediments and affording facilities for the recovery of fugitive slaves. The Supreme Court of the United States has only decided that all laws of impediment are unconstitutional. I know there are some general expressions in the opinion to which I have referred—the case of Maryland against Pennsylvania—that seem to import otherwise; but I think, when you come attentively to read the whole opinion, and the opinion pronounced by all the judges, especially if you take the trouble of doing what I have done, to converse with them as to what their real meaning was, you will find that the whole extent of the authority which they intended to establish was that any laws of impediment enacted by the States were laws that were forbidden by the provision of the Constitution to which I refer; that the General Government has no right, by an act of the Congress of the United States, to impose obligations upon State officers not imposed by the authority of their own Constitution and laws. It is impossible the decision could have been otherwise. It would have been perfectly extrajudicial. The Court had no right to decide the question whether the laws of facility were or were not unconstitutional.

The only question before the Court was the law of impediment passed by the Legislature of Pennsylvania; and if they had gone beyond the case before them, and undertaken to decide upon a case not before them, a principle which was not fairly comprehended within the case before them, it would be what the lawyers term an *obiter dictum,* and is not binding either on that Court itself or any other tribunal. I say it was not possible that, with the case before the Court of a law for giving facility to the holder of the slave to recover his property again, it was utterly impossible that any tribunal should pronounce a decision that such aid and assistance, rendered by the authority of the State, under this provision of the Constitution of the United States, is unconstitutional and void. The Court has not said so, or if they have said so, they have transcended their authority and gone beyond the case which was before them. Laws passed by States, in order to assist the General Government, so far from being laws repugnant to the Constitution, would every where be regarded as laws carrying out, enforcing, and fulfilling the constitutional duties which are created by that instrument.

Why, sir, as well might it be contended that if Congress were to declare war—and no one will doubt the power to declare war is vested exclusively in Congress; no State has the right to do it—no one will contend seriously, I apprehend, that after the declaration of war it would be unconstitutional on the part of any of the States to assist in the vigorous and effective prosecution of that war; and yet it would be just as unconstitutional to lend their aid to the successful and glorious termination of the war in which we might be embarked, as it would be to assist in the performance of a high duty which addresses itself to all the States and all the people of all the States.

Mr. President, I do think that that whole class of Legislation, beginning in the Northern States and extending to some of the Western States, by which obstructions and impediments have been thrown in the way of the recovery of fugitive slaves, is unconstitutional, and has originated in a spirit which I trust will correct itself when those States come calmly to consider the nature and extent of their federal obligations. Of all the States in this Union, unless it be Virginia, the State of which I am a resident suffers most by the escape of their slaves to adjoining States.

I have very little doubt, indeed, that the extent of loss to the State of Kentucky, in consequence of the escape of her slaves is greater, at least, in proportion to the total number of slaves which are held within that commonwealth, even than in Virginia. I know full well, and so does the honorable Senator from Ohio know, that it is at the utmost hazard, and insecurity to life itself, that a Kentuckian can cross the river and go into the interior to take back

his fugitive slave to the place from whence he fled. Recently an example occurred even in the city of Cincinnati, in respect to one of our most respectable citizens. Not having visited Ohio at all, but Covington, on the opposite side of the river, a little slave of his escaped over to Cincinnati. He pursued it; he found it in the house in which it was concealed; he took it out, and it was rescued by the violence and force of a negro mob from his possession—the police of the city standing by, and either unwilling or unable to afford the assistance which was requisite to enable him to recover his property.

Upon this subject I do think that we have just and serious cause of complaint against the free States. I think they fail in fulfilling a great obligation, and the failure is precisely upon one of those subjects which in its nature is the most irritating and inflaming to those who live in the slave States.

Now, sir, I think it is a mark of no good neighborhood, of no kindness, of no courtesy, that a man living in a slave State can not now, with any sort of safety, travel in the free States with his servants, although he has no purpose whatever of stopping there longer than a short time. And on this whole subject, sir, how has the legislation of the free States altered for the worse within the course of the last twenty or thirty years? Why, sir, most of those States, until within a period of the last twenty or thirty years, had laws for the benefit of sojourners, as they were called, passing through or abiding for the moment in the free States, with their servants. Sir, I recollect a case that occurred during the war. My friend, Mr. Cheves, of South Carolina, instead of going home in the vacation, went to Philadelphia, taking his family servants with him. Some of the Abolitionists of that city took out a habeas corpus, seized the slaves, and the question was brought before the Supreme Court of the State of Pennsylvania, where it was argued for days.

It was necessary, during the progress of the arguments, to refer to a great variety of statutes passed from time to time by the Legislature of Pennsylvania, on behalf of the sojourner, guaranteeing and securing to him the possession of his property during his temporary passage or abode within the limits of that commonwealth. Finally, the court gave their opinion *seriatim*— each judge his separate opinion, until it came to Judge Breckenridge to deliver his, who was the youngest judge, I think, on the bench. During the progress of the delivery of their opinions they had frequently occasion to refer to the acts passed for the benefit of sojourners; and each of the judges who preceded Mr. Breckenridge always pronounced the word "sudgeners." When it came to Judge Breckenridge to deliver his opinion, he said, "I agree in all that my learned brethren have pronounced upon this occasion, except in their pronunciation of the word 'sojourner.' They pronounced it 'sudgener;' but I can it 'sojourner.'" [Laughter.] Well, now, sir, all these laws in behalf of these sojourners through the free States are swept away, except I believe in the State of Rhode Island.

Mr. Dayton—And New Jersey.

Mr. Clay—Ay, and in New Jersey. I am happy to hear it; but in most of the large States, in most, if not all, of the New England States, these laws have been abolished, showing the progressive tendency of bad neighborhood and unkind action on the part of the free States toward the slaveholding States.

Mr. President, I do not mean to contest the ground— I am not going to argue the question, whether, if a man carries his slave voluntarily into the free States and he is not a fugitive, whether that slave, by the voluntary action of the master, does or does not become instantly entitled to his freedom. I am not going to argue that question. I know what the decision has been at the North, but I mean to say it is unkind, it is unneighborly, it is not in the spirit of fraternal connection which exists between the members of this confederacy, to execute a strict legal principle in the way suggested, even supposing it to be right so to do. But where there is no purpose of permanent abode, no intention of settling finally and conclusively, and planting his slaves within the commonwealth, it is but right, and a proof of gold neighborhood and kind and friendly feeling, to allow the owner of the slave to pass with his property unmolested through your State.

Allow me to say upon the subject, though it is perhaps going further into detail than is necessary, that of all the existence of power of those who attempt to seduce from their owners their slaves, there is no instance in which it is exercised so injuriously to the objects of their charity and benevolence as in the case of the seduction of family slaves from the service of their owner. The slaves in a family are treated with all the kindness that the children of the family receive. Every thing which they want for their comfort is given them with the most liberal indulgence; and, sir, I have known more instances than one where, by this practice of the seduction of family servants from their owners, they have been rendered wretched and unhappy in the free States; and in my own family, a slave who had been seduced away, addressed her mistress and begged and implored of her the means of getting back from the state of freedom to which she had been seduced, to the state of slavery in which she was so much more happy; and in the case to which I have referred the means were afforded her, and she returned to the State of Kentucky to her mistress.

Then, Mr. President, I think that the existing laws upon the subject, for the recovery of fugitive slaves, and the restoration and delivering of them up to their owners, being found inadequate and ineffective, it is incumbent on Congress—and I hope hereafter, in a better state of feeling, when more harmony and good-will prevail among the members of this confederacy, it will be regarded by the free States themselves as a part of their duty also—to assist in allaying this irritating and disturbing subject to the peace of our Union; but, at all events, whether they do it or not, it is our duty to do it. It is our duty to make the law more effective, and I shall go with the senator from the South who goes furthest in making penal laws and imposing the heaviest sanctions for the recovery of fugitive slaves, and the restoration of them to their owners.

Mr. President, upon this part of the subject, however, allow me to make an observation or two. I do not think the States, as States, ought to be responsible for all the misconduct of particular individuals within those States. I think that the States are only to be held responsible when they act in their sovereign capacity. If there are few persons, indiscreet, mad, if you choose—fanatics, if you choose so to call them—who are for dissolving this Union, as we know there are some at the North, and for dissolving it in consequence of the connection which exists between the free and slaveholding States, I do not think that any State in which such madmen as they are to be found, ought to be held responsible for the doctrines they propagate, unless the State itself adopts those doctrines.

Sir, there have been, perhaps, mutual causes of complaint; and I know, at least I have heard, that Massachusetts, for some of her unfriendly laws on the subject of the recovery of fugitive slaves, urges as the motive for the passage of those laws the treatment which a certain minister of hers experienced in Charleston some years ago. Mr. Hoar, I think, is the name of the individual who was sent to South Carolina to take care of the free negroes of Massachusetts that might pass to Charleston in the vessels of Massachusetts. I think it was a mission that it was hardly worthy of Massachusetts to create. I think she might have omitted to send Mr. Hoar upon any such mission; but she thought it right to send him, and he went there for the purpose of asserting, as he said, the rights of those free people of color before the courts of justice, and of testing the validity of certain laws in South Carolina with regard to the prohibition of free negroes from coming into her ports. I believe that was the object, that was the purpose of his mission. He went there to create no disturbance, as I understand, except so far as asserting those rights and privileges, in the sense in which Massachusetts held them, might create disturbance. He was virtually driven out of Charleston, as I believe he or some other emissary of the same kind was driven out of New Orleans. I do not mean to say whether it was right or wrong to expel him. What I mean to say is, that Massachusetts, or some of her citizens, has said, that, after finding this treatment toward those whom she chooses to consider citizens, on the part of South Carolina, she determined on that course of legislation by which she has withdrawn all aid and assistance for the recovery of fugitives, and interposes obstacles; and then she pleads the treatment of Mr. Hoar as an apology. I think that furnished her with no sufficient apology. If South Carolina treated her ill, it is no reason why she should ill treat Kentucky and Virginia, and other slave-holding States that had done her no wrong. But she thought so.

I mention both cases—the case of the expulsion of Mr. Hoar from Charleston, and the passage of the laws of Massachusetts—not by way of approbation of either, but to show that there have been, unhappily, mutual causes of agitation, furnished by one class of States as well as by the other; though, I admit, not in the same degree by the slave States as by the free States. And I admit, also, that the free States have much less cause for anxiety and solicitude on this subject of slavery than the slave States, and that far more extensive excuses, if not justification, ought to be extended to the slave than the free States, on account of the difference of the condition of the respective parties.

Mr. President, passing from that resolution, I will add only a single observation, that when the bill comes up to be finally acted on, I will vote most cordially and heartily for it.

Mr. Davis, of Massachusetts—Will the honorable Senator permit me to interrupt him for a moment? I want to say one word in behalf of the State of Massachusetts, with his permission.

Mr. Clay—Certainly, certainly.

Mr. Davis—I have never, although most likely he may have, heard the apology stated by the honorable senator for passing the law to which he has referred; but on the contrary I have always understood that the law which Massachusetts had for restoring fugitive slaves, was repealed because the courts below, as they understood it, had pronounced their law unconstitutional. That is the ground which they took; whether they were are in the legislation they adopted I shall not undertake to say. But I wish to say one word in regard to the mission, as it is termed by the honorable senator from Kentucky, to South Carolina.

If I call the facts to my recollection correctly, they are these. We are the owners of much shipping; we employ many sailors, and among them we employ free colored men—men whom we in Massachusetts acknowledge to be citizens of the United States and citizens of the commonwealth, and entitled to the rights of citizens. These citizens were taken from our vessels when they arrived in South Carolina, and were held in custody till the vessels sailed again. This our citizens complained of, whether justly or unjustly, that it was an encroachment, in the first place, upon the rights of citizens, and, in the next place, that it was a great inconvenience to men engaged in commerce. If I remember rightly, and I think I do, the State of Mas-

sachusetts authorized its Governor to propose, at the expense of the State, to some suitable and proper person, who was a citizen of South Carolina, to test the right to hold her citizens in custody in this way, in the courts of the State, or in the courts of the United States. If I remember rightly, that was declined by one or more citizens of South Carolina. Then the mission, to which the honorable Senator refers, was instituted, and the termination of it I believe he has correctly stated.

I wish it to appear that Massachusetts had no aggressive purpose whatever, but simply wished that the judiciary should decide the question existing between them. She wanted nothing more, asked nothing more.

Mr. Clay—Mr. President, I hear with much pleasure this explanation. I have been informed, however, by an eminent citizen of Massachusetts, whose name it is unnecessary to mention—he is not a member of this body—that the motive for the repeal of these laws, or for the passage of these laws, at least one of the motives, was the treatment of Mr. Hoar in Charleston. However, I am glad to hear that it proceeded from another cause, and that is what I conceive to be a misconception of what the true opinion of the judges of the Supreme Court was. When the true exposition of that opinion comes to be known in Massachusetts, I trust that the Legislature of that State will restore the laws facilitating the recovery of fugitive slaves, which she repealed in consequence of that misconception.

Mr. President, I have a great deal yet to say, and I shall, therefore, pass from the consideration of this seventh resolution with the observation, which I believe I have partly made before, that the most stringent provision upon this subject which can be devised will meet with my hearty concurrence and co-operation, in the passage of the bill which is under the consideration of the Senate. The last resolution declares—

"That Congress has no power to prohibit or obstruct the trade in slaves between the slaveholding States; but that the admission or exclusion of slaves brought from one into another of them, depends exclusively upon their own particular laws."

This is a concession, not, I admit, of any real constitutional provision, but a concession from the North to the South of what is understood, I believe, by a great number at the North, to be a constitutional provision. If the resolution should be adopted, take away the decision of the Supreme Court of the United States on this subject, and there is a great deal, I know, that might be said on both sides, as to the right of Congress to regulate the trade between the States, and, consequently, the trade in slaves between the States; but I think the decision of the Supreme Court has been founded upon correct principles, and I trust it will forever put an end to the question whether Congress has or has not the power to regulate the intercourse and trade in slaves between the different States.

Such, Mr. President, is the series of resolutions which in an earnest and anxious desire to present the olive branch to both parts of this distracted, and at the present moment unhappy country, I have thought it my duty to offer. Of all men upon earth I am the least attached to any productions of my own mind. No man upon earth is more ready than I am to surrender any thing which I have proposed, and to accept in lieu of it any thing that is better; but I put it to the candor of honorable senators on the other side and upon all sides of the House, whether their duty will be performed by simply limiting themselves to objections to any one or to all of the series of resolutions that I have offered. If my plan of peace, and accommodation, and harmony, is not right, present us your plan. Let us see the counter project. Let us see how all the questions that have arisen out of this unhappy subject of slavery can be better settled, more fairly and justly settled to all quarters of the Union, than on the plan proposed in the resolutions which I have offered. Present me such a scheme, and I will hail it with pleasure, and will accept it without the slightest feeling of regret that my own was abandoned. Sir, while I was engaged in anxious consideration upon this subject, the idea of the Missouri Compromise, as it has been termed, came under my review, was considered by me, and finally rejected as in my judgment less worthy of the common acceptance of both parts of this Union than the project which I have offered for your consideration.

Before I enter into a particular examination, however, of the Missouri Compromise, I beg to be allowed to correct a great error which is prevailing, not merely in this Senate, but throughout the whole country, in respect to my agency in the Missouri Compromise, or rather in respect to the line of 36 degrees 30' which was established in 1820 by an act of Congress. I do not know whether any thing has excited more surprise in my mind, as to the rapidity with which important historical transactions are obliterated and pass from the mind, than when I understood every where that I had been the author of the line of 36 degrees 30', which was established upon the occasion of the admission of Missouri into the Union. It would take too much time to go over the whole of that important era in the public affairs of the country. I shall not do it, although I have got ample materials before me, derived from a careful examination of the journals of both Houses. I will not occupy your time by going in detail through the whole transaction, but I will content myself with saying that so far from my having presented as a proposition this line of 36 degrees 30', upon the occasion of the consideration whether Missouri should be admitted into the Union or not, it did not originate in the House of which I was a member.

It originated in this body, as those who will cast their recollection back, and I am sure the honorable senator from Missouri, (Mr. Benton), more correctly than any body else, must bring to his recollection the fact that at the Congress when the proposition was first made to admit Missouri—or rather to allow her to hold a convention and frame a constitution and decide whether she should or should not be admitted into the Union—the bill failed by a disagreement between the two Houses, the House insisting on and the Senate dissenting from the provisions contained in the ordinance of 1787. The House insisting on the interdiction of slavery, and the Senate rejecting the proposition of the interdiction of slavery, the bill fell through; it did not pass at that session of Congress. At the next session it was renewed, and at the time of its renewal Maine was knocking at our door to be admitted into the Union. In the House there was a majority for the restriction as to slavery in Missouri; in the Senate there was a majority opposed to all restriction. In the Senate, therefore, in order to carry through the Missouri bill, or the provision for her admission—or rather authorizing her to determine the question of her admission—that bill was coupled with the bill for the admission of Maine. They were connected together and the Senate said to the House, "You want a bill for the admission of Maine passed, but you shall not have it, unless you take along with it a bill for the admission of Missouri also." There was a majority, a very large one, in the Senate, for coupling both together.

Well, sir, the bill went through all the usual stages of disagreement of committees of conference, and there were two committees of conference on the occasion before the matter was finally settled. And it was finally settled to disconnect the two bills—to admit Maine separately, without any connection with Missouri, and to insert in the Missouri bill a clause proposed in the Senate of the United States by Mr. Thomas, Senator from Illinois, restricting slavery north of the line 36 degree 30', and leaving it open south of that line, either to admit it or not to admit it. Well, sir, the bill finally passed. The committees of conference of the two Houses recommended the detachment of the two cases, and the passage of the Missouri bill with the claus 36 degree 30' in it; and so it passed, so it went to Missouri, so it for a moment quieted the country, by means of the introduction of the clause 36 degree 30'. You will find, I repeat, sir, if you will take the trouble to look at the journals, that on as many as three or four different occasions Mr. Thomas in every instance presented the proposition of 36 degree 30'. It was finally agreed to; and I take occasion to say that among those who voted for the 36 degree 30' were the majority of the Southern members—my friend from Alabama (Mr. King), in the Senate, Mr. Pinckney, from Maryland, and indeed the majority of the Southern Senators voted in favor of the line 36 degree 30'; and the majority of the Southern members in the other House, at the head of whom was Mr. Lowndes himself, voted also for that line. I have no doubt I did also; but, as I was Speaker of the House at the time, and the journal does not show how the Speaker votes except in the case of a tie, I was not able to ascertain, by a resort to the records, how I did vote; but I have very little doubt that I voted, in common with my other Southern friends, for the adoption, in a spirit of compromise, it is true, of the line 36 degree 30'.

Well, sir, so the matter ended in 1820. During that year Missouri held her convention, adopted her constitution, sent her delegates to Congress, seeking to be admitted into the Union; but she had inserted a clause in her constitution containing a prohibition of free people of color from that State. She came here with her constitution containing that prohibition, and immediately the Northern members took exception to it. The flame which had been repressed during the previous session now burst forth with double violence throughout the whole Union. Legislative bodies all got in motion to keep out Missouri, in consequence of her interdiction of free people of color from within her limits. I did not arrive at Congress that session till January, and when I got here I found both bodies completely paralyzed in consequence of the struggle to exclude Missouri from the Union on account of that prohibition.

Well, sir, I made the first effort in the House to settle it. I asked for a committee of thirteen, and a committee of thirteen was granted to me, representing all the old States of the Union. The committee met. I presented them a resolution, which was adopted by the committee and reported to the House—not unlike the one to which I will presently call the attention of the Senate—and we should have carried it in the House but for the votes of Mr. Randolph, of Virginia; Mr. Edwards, of North Carolina; and Mr. Burton, of North Carolina—two of the three, I believe, no longer living. These three Southern votes were all cast against the compromise which was prepared by the committee, or rather by myself, as chairman of the committee of thirteen, and defeated it.

Well, sir, in that condition the thing remained for several days. The greatest anxiety pervaded the country—the public mind was unsettled—men were unhappy—there was a large majority of the House then, as I hope and trust there is now a large majority in Congress, in favor of an equitable accommodation or settlement of the question; and the resolution would have been adopted, I believe, but when it came to the vote of yeas and nays, unfortunately then—more unfortunately then, I hope, than now, if there should be occasion for it now—there were few Curtiuses and Leonidases willing to risk themselves for the safety and security of their country. I endeavored to avail myself of that good feeling, as far as I could; and, after a few days had elapsed, I brought forward another proposition; a new

one, perfectly unpracticed in this country, either before or since, as far as I know.

I proposed a joint committee of the two houses; that of the House to consist of twenty-three members (the number of the Senate committee I do not recollect), and that this committee should be appointed by ballot; for at that time Mr. Taylor, of New York, was in the chair, and Mr. Taylor was the very man who had first proposed the restriction upon Missouri. He proposed that she should only be admitted on the principle of the ordinance of 1787; I proposed, therefore, that the committee be appointed by ballot. Well, sir, my motion was carried by a large majority; and members came to me from all quarters of the House, and said, "Whom, Mr. Clay, do you want to have with you on the committee?" I made out my list of twenty-three members, and I venture to say that the happened on that occasion which will hardly ever happen again, eighteen of the twenty-three were elected on the first ballot, and the remaining five on my list having the largest number of votes, but not the majority, I moved to dispense with any further balloting, and that these five should be added to the eighteen, thus completing the committee of twenty-three. One or two gentlemen, Mr. Livermore, of New Hampshire, and one or two others, declined to serve on the committee; and, very much to my regret, and somewhat to my annoyance, the lamented Mr. Randolph and another person were placed in their situation—I forget whether done by ballot or by the Speaker—it is enough to say they were put on the committee.

Well, sir, the Senate immediately agreed to the proposition, appointed its committee, and we met in this hall on the Sabbath day, within two or three days of the close of the session, when the whole nation was waiting with breathless anxiety for some final and healing measure upon the distracting subject which occupied our attention. We met here on that day, and, accordingly, the moment we met, Mr. Randolph made a suggestion which I knew would be attended with the greatest embarrassment and difficulty. He contended that over the two committees of the two houses the chairman of the House committee had a right to preside, and he was about to insist at some length that the two committees should be blended together, and that I should preside over both. I instantly interposed, and said that I did not think that was the correct mode, but that the chairman of the committee of each house should preside over his own committee, and that when the committee of one house matured and adopted a proposition, it should be submitted to the other committee, and if agreed to by them, it should then be reported to the two houses, and its adoption recommended. That course was agreed upon, and Mr. Holmes, I believe, of Maine, presided over the committee of the Senate, and I presided over the committee of the House. I did then, what I have protested I would not do at this session, take too much the lead in the discussion.

I brought forward the proposition which I will refer to presently; and I did more, I took the trouble to ascertain the views of each member of the committee—I polled the committee, if I may use the expression. I said, now, gentlemen, we do not want a proposition carried here by a simple majority and reported to the House, there to be rejected. I am for something practical, something conclusive, something decisive upon this agitating question, and it should be carried by a good majority. How will you vote, Mr. A.? how will you vote, Mr. B.? how will you vote, Mr. C.? and I polled them in that way. Well, sir, to my very great happiness, a sufficient number responded affirmatively, that they would vote for the proposition, to enable me to know that, if they continued to vote that way in the two houses, of which I had not a particle of doubt in the world, the proposition would be carried in the two houses. Accordingly, it having been agreed upon by both committees, and reported to their respective houses, it was finally adopted.

This joint resolution for the admission of Missouri was passed in 1821. (I find I have been furnished with one which was proposed, but not adopted. The right one is contained in the statutes at large; I have seen it there.)

Well, sir, the resolution was finally adopted. I can state, without reading it, what its provisions are. It declares that, if there be any provision in the constitution of Missouri, incompatible with the Constitution of the United States, Missouri shall forbear to enforce the repugnant provisions of her constitution, and that she shall by some solemn and authentic act declare that she will not enforce any provisions of her constitution which are incompatible with the Constitution of the United States; and upon her passage of such a solemn and authentic act, the President of the United States—who was at that time Mr. Monroe—shall make proclamation of the fact; and thereupon, and without any further legislation of Congress, Missouri shall be admitted into the Union.

Now, sir, I want to call your attention to this period of history, and to the transactions which took place during the progress of the discussion upon the resolution.

During the discussion which took place in the House of that time, from day to day, and from night to night—for the discussion frequently ran into the night—we who were for admitting Missouri into the Union said to our brethren from the North, "Why, gentlemen, if there be any provision in the constitution of Missouri which is repugnant to the Constitution of the United States, it is a nullity. The Constitution of the United States, by virtue of its own operation—its own self operation—vacates it. Any tribunal on earth, before which the question may be brought, must pronounce the Constitution of the United States

paramount, and must pronounce invalid the repugnant provisions of the constitution of Missouri." Well, sir, the argument was turned, and twisted, and used in every possible variety of form. All was in vain. An inflexible majority stood out to the last against the admission of Missouri; and yet the resolution—

Mr. Underwood—I have it here.

Mr. Clay—If you will read it, I shall be obliged to you.

Mr. Underwood read the resolution as follows:

"Resolution Providing for the Admission of the State of Missouri into the Union on a Certain Condition.

"Resolved by the Senate and House of Representatives of the United States of America in Congress assembled, That Missouri shall be admitted into this Union on an equal footing with the original States in all respects whatever, upon the fundamental condition that the fourth clause of the 26th section of the third article of the Constitution, submitted on the part of said State to Congress, shall never be construed to authorize the passage of any law, and that no law shall be passed in conformity thereto, by which any citizen of either of the States of this Union shall be excluded from the enjoyment of any of the privileges and immunities to which such citizen is entitled under the Constitution of the United States: *Provided,* That the Legislature of the said State, by a solemn public act, shall declare the assent of the said State to the said fundamental condition, and shall transmit to the President of the United States, on or before the fourth Monday in November next, an authentic copy of the said act; upon the receipt whereof the President, by proclamation, shall announce the fact; whereupon, and without any further proceeding on the part of Congress, the admission of the said State into the Union shall be considered as complete."

Mr. Clay—There is the resolution, sir, and you see it is precisely what I have stated. After all this excitement throughout the country, reaching to such an alarming point that the Union itself was supposed to be in the most imminent peril and danger, the parties were satisfied by the declaration of an incontestable principle of constitutional law, that when the Constitution of a State is violative in its provisions of the Constitution of the United States, the Constitution of the United States is paramount, and the Constitution of the State in that particular is a nullity and void. That was all. They wanted something as a justification, and this appeared, at least, a justification of the course they took. There is a great deal of language there of a high-sounding character—that it shall be a fundamental act, a solemn act, an authentic act; but, after all, when you come to strip it of its verbiage, it is nothing but the announcement of the principle that the Constitution of the United States is paramount over the local Constitution of any one of the States of the Union.

Mr President, I may draw from that transaction in our history which we are now examining, this moral; that now, as then, if we will only suffer our reason to have its scope and sway, and to still and hush the passion and excitement that has been created by the occasion, the difficulty will be more than half removed, in the settlement, upon just and amicable principles, of any questions which unhappily divide us at this moment.

But, sir, I wish to contrast the plan of accommodation which is proposed by met with that which is offered by the Missouri compromise line being extended to the Pacific Ocean, and to ask of gentlemen from the South, and gentlemen from the North, too, which is most proper, which most just, and to which there is the least cause of objection?

Now, sir, what was done by the Missouri line? Slavery was positively interdicted north of that line. The question of the admission or exclusion of slavery south of that line was not settled. There was no provision that slavery should be introduced or established south of that line. In point of fact, it existed in all the territory south of the line of 36 degree 30', embracing Arkansas and Louisiana. It was not necessary then, it is true, to insert a clause admitting slavery at that time. But, sir, if there is a power to interdict, there is a power to admit; and I put it to gentlemen from the South, are they prepared to be satisfied with the line of 36 degree 30', interdicting slavery to the north of it, and giving them no guaranty for the possession of slavery south of that line? The honorable senator from Mississippi told us the other day that he was not prepared to be satisfied with that compromise line. He told us, if I understand him rightly, that nothing short of a positive introduction—

Mr. Foote—Recognition.

Mr. Clay—That nothing short of a positive recognition of slavery south of the line of 36 degree 30' would satisfy him. Well, is there any body who believes that you could get twenty votes in this body, or a proportional number in the other House, to a declaration in favor of the recognition of slavery south of the line of 36 degree 30'? It is impossible. All that you can get, all that you can expect to get, all that was proposed at the last session, was action on the north of the line, and non-action as regards slavery south of that line. It is interdicted on one side, without any corresponding provision for its admission on the other side of the line of 36 degree 30'.

Now, sir, when I came to consider the subject, and to compare the provisions of the line of 36 degree 30'—the Missouri compromise line—with the plan which I propose for the accomodation of this question, what said I to myself? Why, if I offer the line of 36 degree 30', interdicting slavery north of it, and leaving the question open south of that line, I offer that which is illusory to the South; I offer that which will deceive them, if they suppose that slavery will be introduced south of that line. It is better for them, I said to myself—it is better for the whole South, that there should be non-action on both sides, than that there should be action interdicting slavery on one side, without action for the admission of slavery on the other side of the line. Is it not so? What, then, is gained by the South, if the Missouri line is extended to the Pacific, with an interdiction of slavery north of it? Why, sir, one of the very arguments which have been most often and most seriously urged by the South has been this, and we do not want you to legislate upon the subject at all; you ought not to touch it; you have no power over it. I do not concur, as is well known from what I have said upon this occasion, in this view of the subject. But that is the Southern argument. We do not want you to legislate at all on the subject of slavery; but if you adopt the Missouri line and extend it to the Pacific, and interdict slavery north of that line, you do legislate upon the subject of slavery, and you legislate without a corresponding equivalent of legislation on the subject of slavery south of the line. For, if there be legislation interdicting slavery north of the line, the principle of equality would require that there should be legislation admitting slavery south of the line.

Sir, I have said that I never could vote for it, and I repeat that I never can, and never will vote for it; and no earthly power shall ever make me vote to plant slavery where slavery does not exist. Still, if there be a majority—and there ought to be such a majority—for interdicting slavery north of the line, there ought to be an equal majority—if equality and justice be done to the South—to admit slavery south of the line. And if there be a majority ready to accomplish both of these purposes, though I can not concur in the action, yet I would be one of the last to create any disturbance, I would be one of the first to acquiesce in such legislation, though it is contrary to my own judgment and my own conscience. I think, then, it would be better to keep the whole of these territories untouched by any legislation by Congress on the subject of slavery, leaving it open, undecided, without any action of Congress in relation to it; that it would be best for the South, and best for all the views which the South has, from time to time, disclosed to us as correspondent with her wishes.

I know it may be said with regard to these ceded territories, as it is said with regard to California, that non-legislation implies the same thing as the exclusion of slavery. That we can not help. That Congress is not reproachable for. If nature has pronounced the doom of slavery upon those territories—if she has declared, by her immutable laws, that slavery can not and shall not be introduced there, whom can you reproach but nature or nature's God? Congress you can not; Congress abstains; Congress is passive; Congress is non-active in regard to the subject of slavery south and north of the line; or rather Congress, according to the plan which proposes to extend no line, leaves the entire theater of these territories untouched by legislative enactment, either to exclude or admit slavery.

Well, sir, I ask again—if you will listen to the voice of calm and dispassionate reason—I ask of any man from the South to rise and tell me if it is not better for his section of the Union that Congress should remain passive, on both sides of any ideal line, than that it should interdict slavery on one side of the line and be passive in regard to it on the other side of the line.

Sir, I am taxing both the physical and intellectual powers which a kind Providence has bestowed upon me, too much—too much by far—though I beg to be permitted, if the Senate will have patience with me, to conclude what I have to say, for I do not desire to trespass another day upon your time and patience, as I am approaching, though I have not yet nearly arrived at the conclusion.

Mr. Mangum—If the senator will permit me, I will move an adjournment.

Mr. Clay—No, sir, no; I will conclude. I think I can get on better to-day that I shall be able to do if the subject be postponed.

Sir, this Union is threatened with subversion. I want, Mr. President, to take a very rapid glance at the course of public measures in this Union presently. I want, however, before I do that, to ask the Senate to look back upon the career which this country has run since the adoption of this Constitution down to the present day. Was there ever a nation upon which the sun of heaven has shone that has exhibited so much of prosperity? At the commencement of this Government our population amounted to about four millions; it has now reached upward of twenty millions. Our territory was limited chiefly and principally to the border upon the Atlantic ocean, and that which includes the southern shores of the interior lakes of our country.

Our country now extends from the Northern provinces of Great Britain to the Rio Grande and the Gulf of Mexico on one side, and from the Atlantic Ocean to the Pacific on the other side—the largest extent of territory under any Government that exists on the face of the earth, with only two solitary exceptions. Our tonnage, from being nothing, has risen in magnitude and amount so as to rival that of the nation who has been proudly characterized "the mistress of the ocean." We have gone through many wars—wars, too, with the very nation from whom we broke off in 1776, as weak and feeble colonies, and asserted our independence as a member of the family of nations. And, sir, we came out of that struggle, unequal as it was—armed as she was at all points, in consequence of just having come out of her long struggles with other European nations, and unarmed as we were at all points, in consequence of the habits and nature of our country and its institutions—we

came, I say, out of that war without any loss of honor whatever—we emerged from it gloriously.

In every Indian—and we have been engaged in many of them—our armies have triumphed; and without speaking at all as to the causes of the recent war with Mexico, whether it was right of wrong, and abstaining from any expression of opinion as to the justice or property of the war, when once commenced all must admit that, with respect to the gallantry of our armies, the glory of our triumphs, there is no page or pages of history which record more brilliant successes. With respect to one commander of an important portion of our army I need say nothing here; no praise is necessary in behalf of one who has been elevated by the voice of his country to the highest station she could place him in, mainly on account of his glorious military career. And of another, less fortunate in many respects than some other military commanders, I must take the opportunity of saying, that for skill, for science, for strategy, for ability, and daring fighting, for chivalry of individuals and of masses, that portion of the American army which was conducted by the gallant Scott, as the chief commander, stands unrivaled either by the deeds of Cortez himself, or by those of any other commander in ancient or modern times.

Sir, our prosperity is unbounded—nay, Mr. President, I sometimes fear that it is in the wantonness of that prosperity that many of the threatening ills of the moment have arisen. Wild and erratic schemes have sprung up throughout the whole country, some of which have even found their way into legislative halls; and there is a restlessness existing among us which I fear will require the chastisement of Heaven to bring us back to a sense of the immeasurable benefits and blessings which have been bestowed upon us by Providence. At this moment—with the exception of here and there a particular department in the manufacturing business of the country—all is prosperity and peace, and the nation is rich and powerful. Our country has grown to a magnitude, to a power and greatness, such as to command the respect, if it does not awe the apprehensions, of the powers of the earth, with whom we come in contact.

Sir, do I depict with colors too lively the prosperity which has resulted to us from the operations of this Union? Have I exaggerated in any particular her power, her prosperity, or her greatness? And now, sir, let me go a little into detail with respect to sway in the councils of the nation, whether from the North or the South, during the sixty years of unparalleled prosperity that we have enjoyed. During the first twelve years of the administration of the Government Northern counsels rather prevailed; and out of them sprang the Bank of the United States, the assumption of the State debts, bounties to the fisheries, protection to our domestic manufactures—I allude to the act of

1789—neutrality in the wars of Europe, Jay's treaty, the alien and sedition laws, and war with France. I do not say, sir, that these, the leading and prominent measures which were adopted during the administrations of Washington and the elder Adams, were carried exclusively by Northern counsels—they could not have been—but mainly by the ascendency which Northern counsels had obtained in the affairs of the nation. So, sir, of the later period—for the last fifty years.

I do not mean to say the Southern counsels alone have carried the measures which I am about to enumerate. I know they could not exclusively have carried them, but I say that they have been carried by their preponderating influence, with the co-operation, it is true—the large co-operation in some instances—of the Northern section of the Union. And what are those measures? During that fifty years, or nearly that period, in which Southern counsels have preponderated, the embargo and other commercial restrictions of non-intercourse and non-importation were imposed; war with Great Britain, the Bank of the United States overthrown, protection enlarged and extended to domestic manufactures—I allude to the passage of the act of 1815 or 1816—the Bank of the United States re-established, the same bank put down, re-established by Southern counsels and put down by Southern counsels, Louisiana acquired, Florida bought, Texas annexed, war with Mexico, California and other territories acquired from Mexico by conquest and purchase, protection superseded, and free trade established, Indians removed west of the Mississippi, and fifteen new States admitted into the Union. It is very possible, sir, that in this enumeration I may have omitted some of the important measures which have been adopted during this later period of time—the last fifty years—but these I believe to be the most prominent ones.

Now, sir, I do not deduce from the enumeration of the measures adopted by the one side or the other any just cause of reproach either upon one side or the other; though one side or the other has predominated in the two periods to which I have referred. These measures were, to say the least, the joint work of both parties, and neither of them have any just cause to reproach the other. But, sir, I must say, in all kindness and sincerity, that least of all ought the South to reproach the North, when we look at the long list of measures which, under her sway in the counsels of the nation, have been adopted; when we reflect that even opposite doctrines have been from time to time advanced by her; that the establishment of the Bank of the United States, which was done under the administration of Mr. Madison, met with the co-operation of the South—I do not say the whole South—I do not, when I speak of the South or the North, speak of the entire South or the entire North; I speak of the prominent and larger proportion of Southern and Northern men. It was during Mr. Madison's administration that the Bank of the United States was established. My friend, whose sickness—which I very much deplore—prevents us from having his attendance upon this occasion (Mr. Calhoun), was the chairman of the committee, and carried the measure through Congress. I voted for it with all my heart. Although I had been instrumental with other Southern votes in putting down the Bank of the United States, I changed my opinion and co-operated in the establishment of the Bank of 1816. The same bank was again put down by Southern counsels, with General Jackson at their head, at a later period. Again, with respect to the policy of protection. The South in 1815—I mean the prominent Southern men, the lamented Lowndes, Mr. Calhoun, and others—united in extending a certain measure of protection to domestic manufactures as well as the North.

We find a few years afterward the South interposing most serious objections to this policy, and one member of the South, threatening on that occasion, a dissolution of the Union or separation. Now, sir, let us take another view of the question—and I would remark that all these views are brought forward not in a spirit of reproach, but of conciliation—not to provoke or exasperate, but to quiet, to produce harmony and repose, if possible. What have been the territorial acquisitions made by this country, and to what interests have they conduced.? Florida, where slavery exists, has been introduced; Louisiana, or all the most valuable part of that State—for although there is a large extent of territory north of the line 36 degree 30', in point of intrinsic value and importance, I would not give the single State of Louisiana for the whole of it—all Louisiana, I say, with the exception of that which lies north of 36 degree 30', including Oregon, to which we obtained title mainly on the ground of its being a part of the acquisition of Louisiana; all Texas; all the territories which have been acquired by the Government of the United States during its sixty years' operation have been slave territories, the theater of slavery, with the exception that I have mentioned of that lying north of the line 36 degree 30'.

And here, in the case of a war made essentially by the South—growing out of the annexation of Texas, which was a measure proposed by the South in the councils of the country, and which led to the war with Mexico—I do not say all of the South, but the major portion of the South pressed the annexation of Texas upon the country—that measure, as I have said, led to the war with Mexico, and the war with Mexico led to the acquisition of those territories which now constitute the bone of contention between the different members of the Confederacy. And now, sir, for the first time after the three great acquisition of Texas, Florida, and Louisiana have been made and have redounded to the benefit of the South—now, for the first time, when three territories are attempted to be introduced without the institution of slavery, I put it to the hearts of my countrymen of the South, if it is right to press matters to the disastrous consequences which have been indicated no longer ago than this very morning, on the occasion of the presentation of certain resolutions—even extending to a dissolution of the Union. Mr. President, I can not believe it.

Mr. Underwood—Will the Senator give way for an adjournment?

Mr. Clay—Oh, no; if I do not weary the patience of the Senate, I prefer to go on. I think I can begin to see land. I shall soon come to the conclusion of what I have to say. Such is the Union, and such are the glorious fruits which are now threatened with subversion and destruction. Well, sir, the first question which naturally arises is, supposing the Union to be dissolved for any of the causes or grievances which are complained of, how far will dissolution furnish a remedy for those grievances? If the Union is to be dissolved for any existing cause, it will be because slavery is interdicted or not allowed to be introduced into the ceded territories; or because slavery is threatened to be abolished in the District of Columbia; or because fugitive slaves are not restored, as in my opinion they ought to be, to their masters. These, I believe, would be the causes, if there be any causes which can lead to the dreadful event to which I have referred. Let us suppose the Union dissolved; what remedy does it, in a severed state, furnish for the grievances complained of in its united condition? Will you be able at the South to push slavery into the ceded territory? How are you to do it, supposing the North, or all the States north of the Potomac, in possession of the navy and army of the United States? Can you expect, I say, under these circumstances, that if there is a dissolution of the Union you can carry slavery into California and New Mexico? Sir, you can not dream of such an occurrence.

If it were abolished in the District of Columbia and the Union were dissolved, would the dissolution of the Union restore slavery in the District of Columbia? Is your chance for the recovery of your fugitive slaves safer in a state of dissolution or of severance of the Union than when in the Union itself? Why, sir, what is the state of the fact? In the Union you lose some slaves and recover others; but here let me revert to a fact which I ought to have noticed before, because it is highly creditable to the courts and juries of the free States. In every instance, as far as my information extends, in which an appeal has been made to the courts of justice to recover penalties from those who have assisted in decoying slaves from their masters—in every instance, as far as I have heard, the court has asserted the rights of the owner, and the jury has promptly returned an adequate verdict on his behalf. Well, sir, there is then some remedy while you are a part of the Union for the recovery of your slaves, and some indemnification for their loss. What would you have, if the Union was severed? Why, then the several parts would be independent of each other—foreign countries—and slaves escaping from one to the other would be like slaves escaping from the United States to Canada. There would be no right or extradition, no right to demand your slaves; no right to appeal to the courts of justice to indemnify you for the loss of your slaves. Where one slave escapes now by running away from his master, hundreds and thousands would escape if the Union were dissevered—I care not how or where you run the line, or whether independent sovereignties be established. Well, sir, finally, will you, in case of a dissolution of the Union, be safer with your slaves within the separated portions of the States than you are now? Mr. President, that they will escape much more frequently from the border States no one will deny.

And sir, I must take occasion here to say in my opinion there is no right on the part of any one or more of the States to secede from the Union. War and dissolution of the Union are identical and inevitable, in my opinion. There can be a dissolution of the Union only by consent or by war. Consent no one can anticipate, from any existing state of things, is likely to be given, and war is the only alternative by which a dissolution could be accomplished. If consent were given—if it were possible that we were to be separated by one great line—in less than sixty days after such consent was given war would break out between the slaveholding and non-slaveholding portions of this Union—between the two independent parts into which it would be erected in virtue of the act of separation. In less than sixty days, I believe, our slaves from Kentucky, flocking over in numbers to the other side of the river, would be pursued by their owners. Our hot and ardent spirits would be restrained by no sense of the right which appertains to the independence of the other side of the river, should that be the line of separation. They would pursue their slaves into the adjacent free States; they would be repelled, and the consequence would be that, in less than sixty days, war would be blazing in every part of this now happy and peaceful land.

And, sir, how are you going to separate the States of this Confederacy? In my humble opinion, Mr. President, we should begin with at least three separate Confederacies. There would be a Confederacy of the North, a Confederacy of the Southern Atlantic slaveholding States, and a Confederacy of the valley of the Mississippi. My life upon it, that the vast population which has already concentrated and will concentrate on the head-waters and the tributaries of the Mississippi will never give their consent that the mouth of that river shall be held subject to the power of any foreign State or community whatever. Such,

I believe, would be the consequences of a dissolution of the Union, immediately ensuing; but other Confederacies would spring up from time to time, as dissatisfaction and discontent were disseminated throughout the country—the Confederacy of the lakes, perhaps the Confederacy of New England, or of the middle States. Ah, sir, the vail which covers these sad and disastrous events that lie beyond it, is too thick to be penetrated or lifted by any mortal eye or hand.

Mr. President, I am directly opposed to any purpose of secession or separation. I am for staying within the Union, and defying any portion of this Confederacy to expel me or drive me out of the Union. I am for staying within the Union and fighting for my rights, if necessary, with the sword, within the bounds and under the safeguard of the Union. I am for vindicating those rights, not by being driven out of the Union harshly and unceremoniously by any portion of this Confederacy. Here I am within it, and here I mean to stand and die, as far as my individual wishes or purposes can go—within it to protect my property and defend myself, defying all the power on earth to expel me or drive me from the situation in which I am placed. And would there not be more safety in fighting within the Union than out of it? Suppose your rights to be violated, suppose wrong to be done you, aggressions to be perpetrated upon you, can you not better vindicate them—if you have occasion to resort to the last necessity, the sword, for a restoration of those rights—within, and with the sympathies of a large portion of the population of the Union, than by being without the Union, when a large portion of the population have sympathies adverse to your own? You can vindicate your rights within the Union better than if expelled from the Union, and driven from it without ceremony and without authority.

Sir, I have said that I thought there was no right on the part of one or more States to secede from the Union. I think so. The Constitution of the United States was made not merely for the generation that then existed, but for posterity—unlimited, undefined, endless, perpetual posterity. And every State that then came into the Union, and every State that has since come into the Union, came into it binding itself, by indissoluble bands, to remain within the Union itself, and to remain within it by its posterity forever. Like another of the sacred connections, in private life, it is a marriage which no human authority can dissolve or divorce the parties from. And if I may be allowed to refer to some examples in private life, let me say to the North and to the South, what husband and wife say to each other. We have mutual faults; neither of us is perfect; nothing in the form of humanity is perfect; let us, then, be kind to each other—for-bearing, forgiving each other's faults—and above all, let us live in happiness and peace together.

Mr. President, I have said, what I solemnly believe, that dissolution of the Union and war are identical and inevitable; and they are convertible terms; and such a war as it would be, following a dissolution of the Union! Sir, we may search the pages of history, and none so ferocious, so bloody, so implacable, so exterminating—not even the wars of Greece, including those of the Commoners of England and the revolutions of France—none, none of them all would rage with such violence, or be characterized with such bloodshed and enormities as would the war which must succeed, if that event ever happens, the dissolution of the Union. And what would be its termination? Standing armies, and navies, to an extent stretching the revenues of each portion of the dissevered members, would take place. An exterminating war would follow—not, sir, a war of two or three years' duration, but a war of interminable duration—and exterminating wars would ensue, until, after the struggles and exhaustion of both parties, some Philip or Alexander, some Caesar or Napoleon, would arise and cut the Gordian knot, and solve the problem of the capacity of man for self-government, and crush the liberties of both the severed portions of this common empire. Can you doubt it?

Look at all history—consult her pages, ancient or modern—look at human nature; look at the contest in which you would be engaged in the supposition of war following upon the dissolution of the Union, such as I have suggested; and I ask you if it is possible for you to doubt that the final disposition of the whole would be some despot treading down the liberties of the people—the final result would be the extinction of this last and glorious light which is leading all mankind, who are gazing upon it, in the hope and anxious expectation that the liberty which prevails here will sooner or later be diffused throughout the whole of the civilized world. Sir, can you lightly contemplate these consequences? Can you yield yourself to the tyranny of passion, amid dangers which I have depicted in colors far too tame of what the result would be if that direful event to which I have referred should ever occur? Sir, I implore gentlemen, I adjure them, whether from the South or the North, by all that they hold dear in this world—by all their love of liberty—by all their veneration for their ancestors—by all their regard for posterity—by all their gratitude to Him who has bestowed on them such unnumbered and countless blessings—by all the duties which they owe to mankind—and by all the duties which they owe to themselves, to pause, solemnly to pause at the edge of the precipice, before the fearful and dangerous leap be taken into the yawning abyss below, from which none who ever take it shall return in safety.

Finally, Mr. President, and in conclusion, I implore, as the best blessing which Heaven can bestow upon me, upon earth, that if the direful event of the dissolution of this Union is to happen, I shall not survive to behold the sad and heart-rending spectacle.

Source:

Henry Clay, "Compromise Resolutions and Speech." University of Kentucky, Mary I. King Library. *The Life, Correspondence and Speeches of Henry Clay*, Vol 3, ed. Calvin Colton, pp. 301–345.

--------------------- ⟨∞⟩ ---------------------

The Texas and New Mexico Act of 1850

An Act

Proposing to the State of Texas the Establishment of her Northern and Western Boundaries, the Relinquishment by the said State of all Territory claimed by her exterior to said Boundaries, and of all her Claims upon the United States, and to establish a territorial Government for New Mexico.

Be it enacted by the Senate and House of Representatives of the United States of America in Congress assembled, That the following propositions shall be, and the same hereby are, offered to the State of Texas, which, when agreed to by the said State, in an act passed by the general assembly, shall be binding and obligatory upon the United States, and upon the said State of Texas: *Provided,* The said agreement by the said general assembly shall be given on or before the first day of December, eighteen hundred and fifty:

First. The State of Texas will agree that her boundary on the north shall commence at the point at which that meridian of one hundred degrees west from Greenwich is intersected by the parallel of thirty-six degrees thirty minutes north latitude, and shall run from said point due west to the meridian of one hundred and three degrees west from Greenwich; thence her boundary shall run due south to the thirty-second degree of north latitude; thence on the said parallel of thirty-two degrees of north latitude to the Rio Bravo del Norte, and thence with the channel of said river to the Gulf of Mexico.

Second. The State of Texas cedes to the United States all her claim to territory exterior to the limits and boundaries which she agrees to establish by the first article of this agreement.

Third. The State of Texas relinquishes all claim upon the United States for liability of the debts of Texas, and for compensation or indemnity for the surrender to the United States of her ships, forts, arsenals, custom-houses, custom-house revenue, arms and munitions of war and public buildings with their sites, which became the property of the United States at the time of the annexation.

Fourth. The United States, in consideration of said establishment of boundaries, cession of claim to territory, and relinquishment of claims, will pay to the State of Texas the sum of ten millions of dollars in a stock bearing five per cent, interest, and redeemable at the end of fourteen years, the interest payable half-yearly at the treasury of the United States.

Fifth. Immediately after the President of the United States shall have been furnished with an authentic copy of the act of the general assembly of Texas accepting these propositions, he shall cause the stock to be issued in favor of the State of Texas, as provided for in the fourth article of this agreement: *Provided, also,* That no more than five millions of said stock shall be issued until the creditors of the State holding bonds and other certificates of stock of Texas for which duties on imports were specially pledged, shall first file at the treasury of the United States releases of all claim against the United States for or on account of said bonds or certificates in such form as shall be prescribed by the Secretary of the Treasury and approved by the President of the United States: *Provided,* That nothing herein contained shall be construed to impair or qualify any thing contained in the third article of the second section of the "joint resolution for annexing Texas to the United States," approved March first, eighteen hundred and fort-five, either as regards the number of States that may hereafter be formed out of the State of Texas, or otherwise.

Sec. 2. *And be it further enacted,* That all that portion of the Territory of the United States bounded as follows: Beginning at a point in the Colorado River where the boundary line with the republic of Mexico crosses the same; thence eastwardly with the said boundary line to the Rio Grande; thence following the main channel of said river to the parallel of the thirty-second degree of north latitude; thence east with said degree to its intersection with the one hundred and third degree of longitude west of Greenwich; thence north with said degree of longitude to the parallel of thirty-eight degree of north latitude; thence west with said parallel to the summit of the Sierra Madre; thence south with the crest of said mountains to the thirty-seventh parallel of north latitude; thence west with said parallel to its intersection with the boundary line of the State of California; thence with said boundary line to the place of beginning—be, and the same is hereby, erected into a temporary government, by the name of the Territory of New Mexico: *Provided,* That nothing in this act contained shall be construed to inhibit the government of the United States from dividing said Territory into two or more Territories, in such manner and at such times as Congress shall deem convenient and proper, or from attaching any portion thereof to any other Territory or State: *And provided, further,* That, when admitted as a

State, the said Territory, or any portion of the same, shall be received into the Union, with or without slavery, as their constitution may prescribe at the time of their admission.

Sec. 3. *And be it further enacted,* That the executive power and authority in and over said Territory of New Mexico shall be vested in a governor, who shall hold his office for four years, and until his successor shall be appointed and qualified, unless sooner removed by the President of the United States. The governor shall reside within said Territory, shall be commander-in-chief of the militia thereof, shall perform the duties and receive the emoluments of superintendent of Indian affairs, and shall approve all laws passed by the legislative assembly before they shall take effect, he may grant pardons for offences against the laws of said Territory, and reprieves for offenses against the laws of the United States, until the decision of the President can be made known thereon; he shall commission all officers who shall be appointed to office under the laws of the said Territory, and shall take care that the laws be faithfully executed.

Sec. 4. *And be it further enacted,* That there shall be a secretary of said Territory, who shall reside therein, and hold his office for four years, unless sooner removed by the President of the United States; he shall record and preserve all the laws and proceedings of the legislative assembly hereinafter constituted, and all the acts and proceedings of the governor in his executive department; he shall transmit one copy of the laws and one copy of the executive proceedings, on or before the first day of December in each year, to the President of the United States, and, at the same time, two copies of the laws to the Speaker of the House of Representatives and the President of the Senate, for the use of Congress. And, in case of the death, removal, resignation, or other necessary absence of the governor from the Territory, the secretary shall have, and he is hereby authorized and required to execute and perform all the powers and duties of the governor during such vacancy or necessary absence, or until another governor shall be duly appointed to fill such vacancy.

Sec. 5. *And be it further enacted,* That the legislative power and authority of said Territory shall be vested in the governor and a legislative assembly. The legislative assembly shall consist of a Council and House of Representatives. The Council shall consist of thirteen, members, having the qualifications of voters as hereinafter prescribed, whose term of service shall continue two years. The House of Representatives shall consist of twenty-six members, possessing the same qualifications as prescribed for members of the Council, and whose term of service shall continue one year. An apportionment shall be made, as nearly equal as practicable, among the several counties or districts, for the election of the Council and House of Representatives, giving to each section of the Territory representation in the ratio of its population, (Indians excepted,) as nearly as may be. And the members of the Council and of the House of Representatives shall reside in, and be inhabitants of, the district for which they may be elected respectively. Previous to the first election, the governor shall cause a census or enumeration of the inhabitants of the several counties and districts of the Territory to be taken, and the first election shall be held at such time and places, and be conducted in such manner, as the governor shall appoint and direct; and he shall, at the same time, declare the number of the members of the Council and House of Representatives to which each of the counties or districts shall be entitled under this act. The number of persons authorized to be elected having the highest number of votes in each of said Council districts, for members of the Council, shall be declared by the governor to be duly elected to the Council; and the person or persons authorized to be elected having the greatest number of votes for the House of Representatives, equal to the number to which each county or districts shall be entitled, shall be declared by the governor to be duly elected members of the House of Representatives: *Provided,* That in case of a tie between two or more persons voted for, the governor shall order a new election to supply the vacancy made by such tie. And the persons thus elected to the legislative assembly shall meet at such place and on such day as the governor shall appoint; but thereafter, the time, place, and manner of holding and conducting all elections by the people, and the apportioning the representation in the several counties of districts to the Council and House of Representatives according to the population, shall be prescribed by law, as well as the day of the commencement of the regular sessions of the legislative assembly: *Provided,* That no one session shall exceed the term of forty days.

Sec. 6. *And be it further enacted,* That every free white male inhabitant, above the age of twenty-one years, who shall have been a resident of said Territory at the time of the passage of this act, shall be entitled to vote at the first election, and shall be eligible to any office within the said Territory; but the qualifications of voters and of holding office, at all subsequent elections, shall be such as shall be prescribed by the legislative assembly: *Provided,* That the right of suffrage, and of holding office, shall be exercised only by citizens of the United States, including those recognized as citizens by the treaty with the republic of Mexico, concluded February second, eighteen hundred and forty-eight.

Sec. 7. *And be it further enacted,* That the legislative power of the Territory shall extend to all rightful subjects of legislation, consistent with the Constitution of the United States and the provisions of this act; but no law shall be passed interfering with the primary disposal of the soil; not tax shall be imposed upon the property of the United States; nor shall the lands or other property of non-residents be taxed higher than the lands or other property of residents. All the laws passed by the legislative assembly and governor shall be submitted to the Congress of the United States, and, if disapproved, shall be null and of no effect.

Sec. 8. *And be it further enacted,* That all township, district, and county officers, not herein otherwise provided for, shall be appointed or elected, as the case may be, in such manner as shall be provided by the governor and legislative assembly of the Territory of New Mexico. The governor shall nominate, and, by and with the advice and consent of the legislative Council, appoint, all officers not herein otherwise provided for; and in the first instance the governor alone may appoint all said officers, who shall hold their offices until the end of the first session of the legislative assembly, and shall lay off the necessary districts for members of the Council and House of Representatives, and all other officers.

Sec. 9. *And be it further enacted,* That no member of the legislative assembly shall hold, or be appointed to, any office which shall have been created, or the salary or emoluments of which shall have been increased while he was a member, during the term for which he was elected, and for one year after the expiration of such term; and no person holding a commission or appointment under the United States, except postmasters, shall be a member of the legislative assembly, or shall hold any office under the government of said Territory.

Sec. 10. *And be it further enacted,* That the judicial power of said Territory shall be vested in a Supreme Court, District Courts, Probate Courts, and in justices of the peace. The Supreme Court shall consist of a chief justice and two associate justices, any two of whom shall constitute a quorum, and who shall hold a term at the seat of government of said Territory annually, and they shall hold their offices during the period of four years. The said Territory shall be divided into three judicial districts, and a District Court shall be held in each of said districts by one of the justices of the Supreme Court, at such time and place as may be prescribed by law; and the said judges shall, after their appointments, respectively, reside in the districts which shall be assigned them. The jurisdiction of the several courts herein provided for, both appellate and original, and that of the Probate Courts and of justices of the peace, shall be as limited by law: *Provided,* That justices of the peace shall not have jurisdiction of any matter in controversy when the title or boundaries of land may be in dispute, or where the debt or sum claimed shall exceed one hundred dollars; and the said Supreme and District Courts, respectively, shall possess chancery as well as common law jurisdiction. Each District Court, or the judge thereof, shall appoint its clerk, who shall also be the register in chancery, and shall keep his office at the place where the court may be held. Writs of error, bills of exception, and appeals, shall be allowed in all cases from the final decisions of said District Courts to the Supreme Court, under such regulations as may be prescribed by law, but in no case removed to the Supreme Court shall trial by jury be allowed in said court. The Supreme Court, or the justices thereof, shall appoint its own clerk, and every clerk shall hold his office at the pleasure of the court for which he shall have been appointed. Writs of error and appeals from the final decisions of said Supreme Court shall be allowed, and may be taken to the Supreme Court of the United States, in the same manner and under the same regulations as from the Circuit Courts of the United States, where the value of the property or the amount in controversy, to be ascertained by the oath or affirmation of either party, or other competent witness, shall exceed one thousand dollars; except only that in all cases involving title to slaves, the said writs of error or appeals shall be allowed and decided by the said Supreme Court without regard to the value of the matter, property, or title in controversy; and except also that a writ of error or appeal shall also be allowed to the Supreme Court of the United States from the decision of the said Supreme Court created by this act, or of any judge thereof, or of the District Courts corpus involving the question of personal freedom; and each of the said District Courts shall have and exercise the same jurisdiction in all cases arising under the Constitution and laws of the United States as is vested in the Circuit and District Courts of the United States; and the said Supreme and District Courts of the said Territory, and the respective judges thereof, shall and may grant writs of habeas corpus in all cases in which the same are grantable by the judges of the United States in the District of Columbia; and the first six days of every term of said courts, or so much thereof as shall be necessary, shall be appropriated to the trial of causes arising under the said Constitution and laws; and writs of error and appeals in all such cases shall be made to the Supreme Court of said Territory, the same as in other cases. The said clerk shall receive in all such cases the same fees which the clerks of the District Courts of Oregon Territory now receive for similar services.

Sec. 11. *And be it further enacted,* That there shall be appointed an attorney for said Territory, who shall continue in office for four years, unless sooner removed by the President, and who shall receive the same fees and salary as the attorney of the United States for the present Territory of Oregon. There shall also be a marshal for the Territory appointed, who shall hold his offices for four years, unless sooner removed by the President, and who shall execute all processes issuing from the said courts when exercising their jurisdiction as Circuit and District Courts of the United States: he shall perform the duties, be subject to the same regulation and penalties, and be entitled to the same fees as the marshal of the District Court of the United States for the present Territory of Oregon, and shall, in addition, be paid two hundred [dollars] annually as a compensation for extra services.

Sec. 12. *And be it further enacted,* That the governor, secretary, chief justice and associate justices, attorney and marshal, shall be nominated, and, by and with the advice and consent of the Senate, appointed by the President of the United States. The governor and secretary, to be appointed as aforesaid, shall, before they act as such, respectively take an oath or affirmation, before the district judge, or some justice of the peace in the limits of said Territory, duly authorized to administer oaths and affirmations by the laws now in force therein, or before the chief justice or some associate justice of the Supreme Court of the United States, to support the Constitution of the United States, and faithfully to discharge the duties of their respective offices; which said oaths, when so taken, shall be certified by the person by whom the same shall have been taken, and such certificates shall be received and recorded by the said secretary among the executive proceedings; and the chief justice and associate justices, and all other civil officers in said Territory, before they act as such, shall take a like oath or affirmation, before the said governor or secretary, or some judge or justice of the peace of the Territory, who may be duly commissioned and qualified, which said oath or affirmation shall be certified and transmitted, by the person taking the same, to the secretary, to be by him recorded as aforesaid; and afterwards, the like oath or affirmation shall be taken, certified, and recorded, in such manner and form as may be prescribed by law. The governor shall receive an annual salary of fifteen hundred dollars as governor, and one thousand dollars as superintendent of Indian affairs. The chief justice and associate justices shall each receive an annual salary of eighteen hundred dollars. The secretary shall receive an annual salary of eighteen hundred dollars. The said salaries shall be paid quarter-yearly, at the treasury of the United States. The members of the legislative assembly shall be entitled to receive three dollars each per day during their attendance at the sessions thereof, and three dollars each for every twenty miles' travel in going to and returning from the said sessions, estimated according to the nearest usually travelled route. There shall be appropriated annually the sum of one thousand dollars, to be expended by the governor, to defray the contingent expenses of the Territory; there shall also be appropriated annually a sufficient

sum to be expended by the secretary of the Territory, and upon an estimate to be made by the Secretary of the Treasury of the United States, to defray the expenses of the legislative assembly, the printing of the laws, and other incidental expenses; and the secretary of the Territory shall annually account to the Secretary of the Treasury of the United States for the manner in which the aforesaid sum shall have been expended.

Sec. 13. *And be it further enacted,* That the legislative assembly of the Territory of New Mexico shall hold its first session at such time and place in said Territory as the Governor thereof shall appoint and direct; and at said first session, or as soon thereafter as they shall deem expedient, the governor and legislative assembly shall proceed to locate and establish the seat of government for said Territory at such place as they may deem eligible; which place, however, shall thereafter be subject to be changed by the said governor and legislative assembly.

Sec. 14. *And be it further enacted,* That a delegate to the House of Representatives of the United States, to serve during each Congress of the United States, may be elected by the voters qualified to elect members of the legislative assembly, who shall be entitled to the same rights and privileges as are exercised and enjoyed by the delegates from the several other Territories of the United States to the said House of Representatives. The first election shall be held at such time and places, and be conducted in such manner, as the governor shall appoint and direct; and at all subsequent elections, the times, places, and manner of holding the elections shall be prescribed by law. The person having the greatest number of votes shall be declared by the governor to be duly elected, and a certificate thereof shall be given accordingly: *Provided* That such delegate shall receive no higher sum for mileage than is allowed by law to the delegate from Oregon.

Sec. 15. *And be it further enacted,* That when the lands in said Territory shall be surveyed under the direction of the government of the United States, preparatory to bringing the same into market, sections numbered sixteen and thirty-six in each township in said Territory shall be, and the same are hereby, reserved for the purpose of being applied to schools in said Territory, and in the States and Territories hereafter to be erected out of the same.

Sec. 16. *And be it further enacted,* That temporarily and until otherwise provided by law, the governor of said Territory may define the judicial districts of said Territory, and assign the judges who may be appointed for said Territory to the several districts, and also appoint the times and places for holding courts in the several counties or subdivisions in each of said judicial districts, by proclamation to be issued by him; but the legislative assembly, at their first or any subsequent session, may organize, alter, or modify such judicial districts, and assign the judges, and alter the times and places of holding the courts, as to them shall seem proper and convenient.

Sec. 17. *And be it further enacted,* That the Constitution, and all laws of the United States which are not locally inapplicable, shall have the same force and effect within the said Territory of New Mexico as elsewhere within the United States.

Sec. 18. *And be it further enacted,* That the provisions of this act be, and they are hereby, suspended until the boundary between the United States and the State of Texas shall be adjusted; and when such adjustment shall have been effected, the President of the United States shall issue his proclamation, declaring this act to be in full force and operation, and shall proceed to appoint the officers herein provided to be appointed in and for said Territory.

Sec. 19. *And be it further enacted,* That no citizen of the United States shall be deprived of his life, liberty, or property, in said Territory, except by the judgment of his peers and the laws of the land.

Source:

Statutes at Large, Vol. 9, pp. 446–452.

The Utah Act of 1850

An Act
To establish a Territorial Government for Utah.

Be it enacted by the Senate and House of Representatives of the United States of America in Congress assembled, That all part of the territory of the United States included within the following limits, to wit: bounded on the west by the State of California, on the north by the Territory of Oregon, and on the east by the summit of the Rocky Mountains, and on the south by the thirty-seventh parallel of north latitude, be, and the same is hereby, created into a temporary government, by the name of the Territory of Utah; and, when admitted as a State, the said Territory, or any portion of the same, shall be received into the Union, with or without slavery, as their constitution may prescribe at the time of their admission: *Provided,* That nothing in this act contained shall be construed to inhibit the government of the united States from dividing said Territory into two or more Territories, in such manner and at such times as Congress shall deem convenient and proper, or from attaching any portion of said Territory to any other State or Territory of the United States.

Sec. 2. *And be it further enacted,* That the executive power and authority in and over said Territory of Utah shall be vested in a governor, who shall hold his office for four years, and until his successor shall be appointed and qualified, unless sooner removed by the President of the United States. The governor shall reside within said Territory, shall be commander-in-chief of the militia thereof, shall perform the duties and receive the emoluments of superintendent of Indian affairs, and shall approve all laws passed by the legislative assembly before they shall take effect: he may grant pardons for offences against the laws of said Territory, and reprieves for offences against the laws of the United States, until the decision of the President can be made known thereon; he shall commission all officers who shall be appointed to office under the laws of the said Territory, and shall take care that the laws be faithfully executed.

Sec. 3. *And be it further enacted,* That there shall be a secretary of said Territory, who shall reside therein, and hold his office for four years, unless sooner removed by the President of the United States: he shall record and preserve all the laws and proceedings of the legislative assembly hereafter constituted, and all the acts and proceedings of the governor in his executive department; he shall transmit one copy of the laws and one copy of the executive proceedings, on or before the first day of December in each year, to the President of the United States, and, at the same time, two copies of the laws to the Speaker of the House of Representatives, and the President of the Senate, for the use of Congress. And in the case of the death, removal, resignation, or other necessary absence of the governor from the Territory, the secretary shall have, and he is hereby authorized and required to execute and perform, all the powers and duties of the governor during such vacancy or necessary absence, or until another governor shall be duly appointed to fill such vacancy.

Sec. 4. *And be it further enacted,* That the legislative power and authority of said Territory shall be vested in the governor and a legislative assembly. The legislative assembly shall consist of a Council and House of Representatives. The Council shall consist of thirteen members, having the qualifications of voters as hereinafter prescribed, whose term of service shall continue two years. The House of Representatives shall consist of twenty-six members, possessing the same qualifications as prescribed for members of the Council, and whose term of service shall continue one year. An apportionment shall be made, as nearly equal as practicable, among the several counties or districts, for the election of the Council and House of Representatives, giving to each section of the Territory representation in the ratio of its population, Indians excepted, as nearly as may be. And the members of the Council and of the House of Representatives shall reside in, and be inhabitants of, the district for which they may be elected respectively. Previous to the first election, the governor shall cause a census or enumeration of the inhabitants of the several counties and districts of the Territory to be taken, and the first election shall be held at such time and places, and be conducted in such manner, as the governor shall appoint and direct; and he shall, at the same time, declare the number of members of the Council and House of Representatives to which each of the counties or districts shall be entitled under this act. The number of persons authorized to be elected having the highest number of votes in each of said Council districts for members of the Council, shall be declared by the governor to be duly elected to the Council; and the person or persons authorized to be elected having the highest number of votes for the House of Representatives, equal to the number to which each county or district shall be entitled, shall be declared by the governor to be duly elected members of the House of Representatives: *Provide,* That in case of a tie between two or more persons voted for, the governor shall order a new election to supply the vacancy made by such a tie. And the persons thus elected to the legislative assembly shall meet at such place, and on such day, as the governor shall appoint; but thereafter, the time, place, and manner of holding and conducting all elections by the people, and the apportioning the representation in the several counties or districts to the Council and House of Representatives, according to population, shall be prescribed by law, as well as the day of the commencement of the regular sessions of the legislative assembly: *Provided,* That no one session shall exceed the term of forty days.

Sec. 5. *And be it further enacted,* That every free white male inhabitant above the age of twenty-one years, who shall have been a resident of said Territory at the time of the passage of this act, shall be entitled to vote at the first election, and shall be eligible to any office within the said Territory; but the qualifications of voters and of holding office, at all subsequent elections, shall be such as shall be prescribed by the legislative assembly: *Provided,* That the right of suffrage and of holding office shall be exercised only by citizens of the United States, including those recognized as citizens by the treaty with the republic of Mexico, concluded February second, eighteen hundred and forty-eight.

Sec. 6. *And be it further enacted,* That the legislative power of said Territory shall extend to all rightful subjects of legislation, consistent with the Constitution of the United States and the provisions of this act; but no law shall be passed interfering with the primary disposal of the soil; no tax shall be imposed upon the property of the United States; nor shall the lands or other property of non-residents be taxed higher than the lands or other property of residents. All the laws passed by the legislative assembly and governor shall be submitted to the Congress of the United States, and, if disapproved, shall be null and of no effect.

Sec. 7. *And be it further enacted,* That all township, district, and county officers, not herein otherwise provided for, shall be appointed or elected, as the case may be, in such manner as shall be provided by the governor and legislative assembly of the territory of Utah. The governor shall nominate, and, by and with the advice and consent of the legislative Council, appoint all officers not herein otherwise provided for; and in the first instance the governor alone may appoint all said officers, who shall hold their offices until the end of the first session of the legislative assembly, and shall lay off the necessary districts for members of the Council and House of Representatives, and all other offices.

Sec. 8. *And be it further enacted,* That no member of the legislative assembly shall hold or be appointed to any office which shall have been created, or the salary or emoluments of which shall have been increased while he was a member, during the term for which he was elected, and for one year after the expiration of such term; and no person holding a commission or appointment under the United States, except postmasters, shall be a member of the legislative assembly, or shall hold any office under the government of said Territory.

Sec. 9. *And be it further enacted,* That the judicial power of said Territory shall be vested in a Supreme Court, District Courts, Probate Courts, and in justice of the peace. The Supreme Court shall consist of a chief justice and two associate justices, any two of whom shall constitute a quorum, and who shall hold a term at the seat of government of said Territory annually, and they shall hold their offices during the period of four years. The said Territory shall be divided into three judicial districts, and a District Court shall be held in each of said districts by one of the justices of the Supreme Court, at such time and place as may be prescribed by law; and the said judges shall, after their appointments, respectively, reside in the districts which shall be assigned them. The jurisdiction of the several courts herein provided for, both appellate and original, and that of the Probate Courts and of justices of the peace, shall be as limited by law: *Provided,* That justices of the peace shall not have jurisdiction of any matter in controversy when the title or boundaries of land may be in dispute, or where the debt or sum claimed shall exceed one hundred dollars; and the said Supreme and District Courts, respectively, shall possess chancery as well as common law jurisdiction. Each District Court, or the judge thereof, shall appoint its clerk, who shall also be the register in chancery, and shall keep his office at the place where the court may be held. Writs of error, bills of exception, and appeals shall be allowed in all cases from the final decisions of said District Courts to the Supreme Court, under such regulations as may be prescribed by law; but in no case removed to the Supreme Court shall trial by jury be allowed in said court. The Supreme Court, or the justices thereof, shall appoint its own clerk, and every clerk shall hold his office at the pleasure of the court for which he shall have seen appointed. Writs of error, and appeals from the final decisions of said Supreme Court, shall be allowed, and may be taken to the Supreme Court of the United States, in the same manner and under the same regulations as from the Circuit Courts of the United States, where the value of the property or the amount in controversy, to be ascertained by the oath or affirmation of either party, or other competent witness, shall exceed one thousand dollars, except only that, in all cases involving title to slaves, the said writs of error or appeals shall be allowed and decided by the said Supreme Court, without regard to the value of the matter, property, or title in controversy; and except, also, that a writ of error or appeal shall also be allowed to the Supreme Court of the United States, from the decisions of the said Supreme Court created by this act, or of any judge thereof, or of the District Courts created by this act, or of any judge thereof, upon any writ of habeas corpus involving the question of personal freedom; and each of the said District Courts shall have and exercise the same jurisdiction in all cases arising under the Constitution and laws of the United States as is vested in the Circuit and District Courts of the United States; and the said Supreme and District Courts of the said Territory, and the respective judges thereof, shall and may grant writs of habeas corpus in all cases in which the same are granted by the judges of the United States in the District of Columbia; and the first six days of every term of said courts, or so much thereof as shall be necessary, shall be appropriated to the trial of causes arising under the said Constitution and laws; and writs of error and appeal, in all such cases, shall be made to the Supreme Court of said Territory, the same as in other cases. The said clerk shall receive in all such cases the same fees which the clerks of the District Courts of Oregon Territory now receive for similar services.

Sec. 10. *And be if further enacted,* That there shall be appointed an attorney for said Territory, who shall continue in office for four years, unless sooner removed by the President, and who shall receive the same fees and salary as the attorney of the United States for the present Territory of Oregon. There shall also be a marshal for the Territory appointed, who shall hold his office for four years, unless sooner removed by the President, and who shall execute all processes issuing from the said courts, when exercising their jurisdiction as Circuit and District Courts of the United States: he shall perform the duties, be subject to the same regulation and penalties, and be entitled to the same fees as the marshal of the District Court of the United States for the present Territory of Oregon; and shall, in addition, be paid two hundred dollars annually as a compensation for extra services.

Sec. 11. *And be if further enacted,* That the governor, secretary, chief justice and associate justices, attorney and marshal, shall be nominated, and, by and with the advice and consent of the Senate, appointed by the President of the United States. The governor and secretary to be appointed as aforesaid shall, before they act as such, respectively, taken an oath or affirmation, before the district judge, or some justice of the peace in the limits of said Territory, duly authorized to administer oaths and affirmations by the laws now in force therein, or before the chief justice or some associate justice of the Supreme Court of the United States, to support the Constitution of the United States, and faithfully to discharge the duties of their respective offices; which said oaths, when so taken, shall be certified by the person by whom the same shall have been taken, and such certificates shall be received and recorded by the said secretary among the executive proceedings; and the chief justice and associate justices, and all other civil officers in said Territory, before they act as such, shall take a like oath or affirmation, before the said governor or secretary, or some judge or justice of the peace of the Territory who may be duly commissioned and qualified, with said oath or affirmation shall be certified and transmitted, the person taking the same, to the secretary, to be by him recorded as aforesaid; and afterwards, the like oath or affirmations shall be taken, certified, and recorded in such manner and form as may be prescribed by law. The governor shall receive an annual salary of fifteen hundred dollars as governor, and one thousand dollars as superintendent of Indian affairs. The chief justice and associate justices shall each receive an annual salary of eighteen hundred dollars. The secretary shall receive an annual salary of eighteen hundred dollars. The said salaries shall be paid quarterly, at the treasury of the United States. The members of the legislative assembly shall be entitled to receive three dollars each per day during their attendance at the sessions thereof, and three dollars each for twenty miles' travel, in going to and returning from the said sessions, estimated according to the nearest usually travelled route. There shall be appropriated annually the sum of one thousand dollars, to be expended by the governor, to defray the contingent expenses of the Territory. There shall also be appropriated, annually, a sufficient sum, to be expended by the secretary of the Territory, and upon an estimate to be made by the Secretary of the Treasury of the United States, to defray the expenses of the legislative assembly, the printing of the laws, and other incidental expenses; and the secretary of the Territory shall annually account to the Secretary of the Treasury of the United States for the manner in which the aforesaid sum shall have been expended.

Sec. 12. *And be it further enacted,* That the legislative assembly of the Territory of Utah shall hold its first session at such time and place in said Territory as the governor thereof shall appoint and direct; and as said first session, or as soon thereafter as they shall deem expedient, the governor and legislative assembly shall proceed to locate and establish the seat of government for said Territory at such place as they may deem eligible; which place, however, shall thereafter be subject to be changed by the said governor and legislative assembly. And the sum of twenty thousand dollars, out of any money in the treasury not otherwise appropriated, is hereby appropriated and granted to said Territory of Utah to be applied by the governor and legislative assembly to the erection of suitable public buildings at the seat of government.

Sec. 13. *And be it further enacted,* That a delegate to the House of Representatives of the United States, to serve during each Congress of the United States, may be elected by the voters qualified to elect members of the legislative assembly, who shall be entitled to the same rights and privileges as are exercised and enjoyed by the delegates from the several other Territories of the United States to the said House of Representatives. The first election shall be held at such time and places, and be conducted in such manner, as the governor shall appoint and direct; and at all subsequent elections, the times, places, and manner of holding the elections shall be prescribed by law. The person having the greatest number of votes shall be declared by the governor to be duly elected, and a certificate thereof shall be given accordingly: *Provided,* That said delegate shall receive no higher sum for mileage than is allowed by law to the delegate from Oregon.

Sec. 14. *And be it further enacted,* That the sum of five thousand dollars be, and the same is hereby, appropriated out of any moneys in the treasury not otherwise appropriated, to be expended by and under the direction of the said governor of the territory of Utah, in the purchase of a library, to be kept at the seat of government for the use of the governor, legislative assembly, judges of the Supreme Court, secretary, marshal, and attorney of said Territory, and such other persons, and under such regulations, as shall be prescribed by law.

Sec. 15. *And be it further enacted,* That when the lands in the said Territory shall be surveyed under the direction of the government of the United States, preparatory to bringing the same into market, sections numbered sixteen and thirty-six in each township in said Territory shall be, and the same are hereby, reserved for the purpose of being applied to schools in said Territory, and in the States and Territories hereafter to be erected out of the same.

Sec. 16. *And be it further enacted,* That temporarily, and until otherwise provided by law, the governor of said Territory may define the judicial districts of said Territory, and assign the judges who may be appointed for said Territory to the several districts, and also appoint the times and places for holding courts in the several counties or subdivisions in each of said judicial districts, by proclamation to be issued by him, but the legislative assembly, at their first or any subsequent session, may organize, alter, or modify such judicial districts, and assign the judges, and alter the times and places of holding the courts, as to them shall seem proper and convenient.

Sec. 17. *And be it further enacted,* That the Constitution and laws of the United States are hereby extended over and declared to be in force in said Territory of Utah, so far as the same, or any provision thereof, may be applicable.

Source:
Statutes at Large, Vol. 9, pp. 453–458.

The Act Abolishing the Slave Trade in the District of Columbia

An Act
To suppress the Slave Trade in the District of Columbia.

Be it enacted by the Senate and House of Representatives of the United States of America in Congress assembled, That from and after the first day of January, eighteen hundred and fifty-one, it shall not be lawful to bring into the District of Columbia any slave whatever, for the purpose of being sold, or for the purpose of being placed in depot, to be subsequently transferred to any other State or place to be sold as merchandize. And if any slave shall be brought into the said District by its owner, or by the authority or consent of its owner, contrary to the provisions of this act, such slave shall thereupon become liberated and free.

Sec. 2. *And be it further enacted,* That it shall and may be lawful for each of the corporations of the cities of Washington and Georgetown, from time to time, and as often as may be necessary, to abate, break up, and abolish any depot or place of confinement of slaves brought into the said District as merchandize, contrary to the provisions of this act, by such appropriate means as may appear to either of the said corporations expedient and proper. And the same power is hereby vested in the Levy Court of Washington county, if any attempt shall be made, within its jurisdictional limits, to establish a depot or place of confinement for slaves brought into the said District as merchandize for sale contrary to this act.

Source:
Statutes at Large, Vol. 9, pp. 467–468.

Fugitive Slave Act of 1850

Federal law passed on September 18, 1850, as part of the Compromise of 1850. This law required U.S. marshals to seize runaway slaves and imposed severe penalties on anyone who aided fugitives. The law was a response to abolitionist efforts hindering the enforcement of the 1793 Fugitive Slave Act through the Underground Railroad, and it sought to overrule "personal liberty" laws passed by Northern states to protect free blacks that also aided runaway slaves. The 1850 law required that captured runaways be taken before a federal court or commissioner; it also denied fugitives a jury and refused to admit fugitives' testimony, though the masters' claims of ownership were accepted as evidence. The law aroused strong antislavery sentiment in the North, and abolitionists defied it vigorously. The acts of 1793 and 1850 were repealed in 1864. It had the ironic consequence of reversing the states' rights positions of Northern and Southern states. Prior to the enforcement of this act, the South favored states' rights in order to protect slavery. With the federal government behind the Fugitive Slave Act, the Northern states asserted their rights against it, while the South supported federal supremacy over the states.

An Act

To amend, and supplementary to, the Act entitled "An Act respecting Fugitives from Justice, and Persons escaping from the Service of their Masters," approved February twelfth, one thousand seven hundred and ninety-three.

Be it enacted by the Senate and House of Representatives of the United States of America in congress assembled, That the persons who have been, or may hereafter be appointed commissioners, in virtue of any act of Congress, by the Circuit Courts of the United States, and who, in consequence of such appointment, are authorized to exercise the powers that any justice of the peace, or other magistrate of any of the United States, may exercise in respect to offenders for any crime or offence against the United States, by arresting, imprisoning, or bailing the same under and by virtue of the thirty-third section of the act of the twenty-fourth of September seventeen hundred and eighty-nine, entitled "An Act to establish the judicial courts of the United States," shall be, and are hereby, authorized and required to exercise and discharge all the powers and duties conferred by this act.

Sec. 2. *And be it further enacted,* That the Superior Court of each organized Territory of the United States shall have the same power to appoint commissioners to take acknowledgements of bail and affidavits, and to take depositions of witnesses in civil causes, which is now possessed by the Circuit Court of the United States; and all commissioners who shall hereafter be appointed for such purposes by the Superior Court of any organized Territory of the United States, shall possess all the powers, and exercise all the duties, conferred by law upon the commissioners appointed by the Circuit Courts of the United States for similar purposes, and shall moreover exercise and discharge all the powers and duties conferred by this act.

Sec. 3. *And be it further enacted,* That the Circuit Courts of the United States, and the Superior Courts of each organized Territory of the United States, shall from time to time enlarge the number of commissioners, with a view to afford reasonable facilities to reclaim fugitives from labor, and to the prompt discharge of the duties imposed by this act.

Sec. 4. *And be it further enacted,* That the commissioners above named shall have concurrent jurisdiction with the judges of the Circuit and District Courts of the United States, in their respective circuits and districts within the several States, and the judges of the Superior Courts of the Territories, severally and collectively, in term-time and vacation; and shall grant certificates to such claimants, upon satisfactory proof being made, with authority to take and remove such fugitives from service or labor, under the restrictions herein contained, to the State or Territory from which such persons may have escaped or fled.

Sec. 5. *And be it further enacted,* That it shall be the duty of all marshals and deputy marshals to obey and execute all warrants and precepts issued under the provisions of this act, when to them directed; and should any marshal or deputy marshal refuse to receive such warrant, or other process, when tendered, or to use all proper means diligently to execute the same, he shall, on conviction thereof, be fined in the sum of one thousand dollars, to the use of such claimant, on the motion of such claimant, by the Circuit or District Court for the district of such marshal; and after arrest of such fugitive, be such marshal or his deputy, or whilst at any time in his custody under the provisions of this act, should such fugitive escape, whether with or without the assent of such marshal or his deputy, such marshal shall be liable, on his official bond, to be prosecuted for the benefit of such claimant, for the full value of the service or labor of said fugitive in the State, Territory, or District whence he escaped: and the better to enable the said commissioners, when thus appointed, to execute their duties faithfully and efficiently, in conformity with the requirements of the Constitution of the United States and of this act, they are hereby authorized and empowered, within their counties respectively, to appoint, in writing under their hands, any one or more suitable persons, from time to time, to execute all such warrants and other process as may be issued by them in the lawful performance of their respective duties; with authority to such commissioners, or the persons to be appointed by them, to execute process as aforesaid, to summon and call to their aid the bystanders, or *posse comitatus* of the proper county, when necessary to ensure a faithful observance of the clause of the Constitution referred to, in conformity with the provisions of this act; and all good citizens are hereby commanded to aid and assist in the prompt and efficient execution of this law, whenever their services may be required, as aforesaid, for that purpose; and said warrants shall run, and be executed by said officers, any where in the State within which they are issued.

Sec. 6. *And be it further enacted,* That when a person held to service or labor in any State or Territory of the United States, has heretofore or shall hereafter escape into another State or Territory of the United States, the person or persons to whom such service or labor may be due, or his, her, or their agent or attorney, duly authorized, by power of attorney, in writing, acknowledged and certified under the seal of some legal officer or court of the State or Territory in which the same may be executed, may pursue and reclaim such fugitive person, either by procuring a warrant from some one of the courts, judges, or commissioners aforesaid, of the proper circuit, district, or county, for the apprehension of such fugitive from service or labor, or by seizing and arresting such fugitive, where the same can be done without process, and by taking, or causing such person to be taken, forthwith before such court, judge, or commissioner, whose duty it shall be to hear and determine the case of such claimant in a summary manner; and upon satisfactory proof being made, by deposition or affidavit, in writing, to be taken and certified by such court, judge, or commissioner, or by other satisfactory testimony, duly taken and certified by some court, magistrate, justice of the peace, or other legal officer authorized to administer an oath and take depositions under the laws of the State or Territory from which such person owing service or labor may have escaped, with a certificate of such magistracy or other authority, as aforesaid, with the seal of the proper court or officer thereto attached, which seal shall be sufficient to establish the competency of the proof, and with proof, also by affidavit, of the identity of the person whose service or labor is claimed to be due as aforesaid, that the person so arrested does in fact owe service or labor to the person or persons claiming him or her, in the State or Territory from which such fugitive may have escaped as aforesaid, and that said person escaped, to make out and deliver to such claimant, his or her agent or attorney, a certificate setting forth the substantial facts as to the service or labor due from such fugitive to the claimant, and of his or her escape from the State or Territory in which such service or labor was due, to the State or Territory in which he or she was arrested, with authority to such claimant, or his or her agent or attorney, to use such reasonable force and restraint as may be necessary, under the circumstances of the case, to take and remove such fugitive person back to the State or Territory whence he or she may have escaped as aforesaid. In no trial or hearing under this act shall the testimony of such alleged fugitive be admitted in evidence; and the certificates in this and the first [fourth] section mentioned, shall be conclusive of the right of the person or persons in whose favor granted to remove such fugitive to the State or Territory from which he escaped, and shall prevent all molestation of such person or persons by any process issued by any court, judge, magistrate, or other person whomsoever.

Sec. 7. *And be it further enacted,* That any person who shall knowingly and willingly obstruct, hinder, or prevent such claimant, his agent or attorney, or any person or persons lawfully assisting him, her, or them, from arresting such a fugitive from service or labor, either with or without process as aforesaid, or shall rescue, or attempt to rescue, such fugitive from service or labor, from the custody of such claimant, his or her agent or attorney, or other person or persons lawfully assisting as aforesaid, when so arrested, pursuant to the authority herein given and declared; or shall aid, abet, or assist such person so owing service or labor as aforesaid, directly or indirectly, to escape from such claimant, his agent or attorney, or other person or persons legally authorized as aforesaid; or shall harbor or conceal such fugitive, so as to prevent the discovery and arrest of such person, after notice or knowledge of the fact that such person was a fugitive from service or labor as aforesaid, shall, for either of said offences, be subject to a fine not exceeding one thousand dollars, and imprisonment not exceeding six months, by indictment and conviction before the District Court of the United States for the district in which such offence may have been committed, or before the proper court of criminal jurisdiction, if committed within any one of the organized Territories of the United States; and shall moreover forfeit and pay, by way of civil damages to the party injured by such illegal conduct, the sum of one thousand dollars, for each fugitive so lost as aforesaid, to be recovered by action of debt, in any of the District or Territorial Courts aforesaid, within whose jurisdiction the said offence may have been committed.

Sec. 8. *And be it further enacted,* That the marshals, their deputies, and the clerks of the said District and Territorial Courts, shall be paid, for their services, the like fees as may be allowed to them for similar services in other cases; and where such services are rendered exclusively in the arrest, custody, and delivery of the fugitive to the claimant, his or her agent or attorney, or where such supposed fugitive may be discharged out of custody for the want of sufficient proof as aforesaid, then such fees are to be paid in the whole by such claimant, his agent or attorney; and in all cases where the proceedings are before a commissioner, he shall be entitled to a fee of ten dollars in full for his services in each case, upon the delivery of the said certificate to the claimant, his or her agent or attorney; or a fee of five dollars in cases where the proof shall not, in the opinion of such commissioner, warrant such certificate and delivery, inclusive of all services incident to such arrest and examination, to be paid, in either case, by the claimant, his or her agent or attorney. The person or persons authorized to execute the process to be issued by such commissioners for the arrest and detention of fugitives from service or labor as aforesaid, shall also be entitled to a fee of five dollars each for each person he or they may arrest and take before any such commissioner as aforesaid, at the instance and request of such claimant, with such other fees as may be deemed reasonable by such commissioner for such other additional services as may be necessarily performed by him or them; such as attending at the examination, keeping the fugitive in custody, and providing him with food and lodging during his detention, and until the final determination of such commissioner; and, in general, for performing such other duties as may be required by such claimant, his or her attorney or agent, or commissioner in the premises, such fees to be made up in conformity with the fees usually charged by the officers of the courts of justice within the proper district or county, as near as may be practicable, and paid by such claimants, their agents or attorneys, whether such supposed fugitives from service or labor be ordered to be delivered to such claimants by the final determination of such commissioners or not.

Sec. 9. *And be it further enacted,* That, upon affidavit made by the claimant of such fugitive, his agent or attorney, after such certificate has been issued, that he has reason to apprehend that such fugitive will be rescued by force from his or their possession before he can be taken beyond the limits of the State in which the arrest is made, it shall be the duty of the officer making the arrest to retain such fugitive in his custody, and to remove him to the State whence he fled, and there to deliver him to said claimant, his agent, or attorney. And to this end, the officer aforesaid is hereby authorized and required to employ so many persons as he may deem necessary to overcome such force, and to retain them in his service so long as circumstances may require. The said officer and his assistants, while so employed, to receive the same compensation, and to be allowed the same expenses, as are now allowed by law for transportation of criminals, to be certified by the judge of the district within which the arrest is made, and paid out of the treasury of the United States.

Sec. 10. *And be it further enacted,* That when any person held to service or labor in any State or Territory, or in the District of Columbia, shall escape therefrom, the party to whom such service or labor shall be due, his, her, or their agent or attorney, may apply to any court of record therein, or judge thereof in vacation, and make satisfactory proof to such court, or judge in vacation, of the escape aforesaid, and that the person escaping owed service or labor to such party. Whereupon the court shall cause a record to be made of the matters so proved, and also a general description of the person so escaping, with such convenient certainty as may be; and a transcript of such record, authenticated by the attestation of the clerk and of the seal of the said court, being produced in any other State, Territory, or district in which the person so escaping may be found, and being exhibited to any judge, commissioner, or other officer authorized by the law of the United States to cause persons escaping from service or labor to be delivered up, shall be held and taken to be full and conclusive evidence of the fact of escape, and that the service or labor of the person escaping is due to the party in such record mentioned. And upon the production by the said party of other and further evidence if necessary, either oral or by affidavit, in addition to what is contained in the said record of the identity of the person escaping, he or she shall be delivered up to the claimant. And the said court, commissioner, judge, or other person authorized by this act to grant certificates to claimants of fugitives, shall, upon the production of the record and other evidences aforesaid, grant to such claimant a certificate of his right to take any such person identified and proved to be owing service or labor as aforesaid, which certificate shall authorize such claimant to seize or arrest and transport such person to the State or Territory from which he escaped: *Provided,* That nothing herein contained shall be construed as requiring the production of a transcript of such record as evidence as aforesaid. But in its absence the claim shall be heard and determined upon other satisfactory proofs, competent in law.

Source:
Statutes at Large, Vol. 9, pp. 462–465.

Frederick Douglass's Speech on American Slavery, 1850

Speech given by Frederick Douglass in Rochester, New York, as the first of a series of lectures on slavery. Opposition to slavery went back at least as far as 1688 and had become a heated topic between the Northern and Southern states in the first half of the 1800s. Douglass first gained recognition in 1841 as a speaker at the Massachusetts Anti-Slavery Society's convention, and he soon became a living symbol against claims that blacks were inferior. His speech elicited sympathy for the millions of slaves in the South by using the oppression of Ireland for comparison: No matter how badly the Irish were treated, they were still masters of their own body and soul.

Earlier that same year, Congress produced the Great Compromise, which strengthened the Fugitive Slave Law and outraged abolitionists.

———————— ⌒∞⌒ ————————

I come before you this evening to deliver the first lecture of a course which I purpose to give in this city, during the present winter, on the subject of American Slavery.

I make this announcement with no feelings of self-sufficiency. If I do not mistake my own emotions, they are such as result from a profound sense of my incompetency to do justice to the task which I have just announced, and now entered upon.

If any, then, demand of me why I speak, I plead as my apology, the fact that abler and more eloquent men have failed to speak, or what, perhaps, is more true, and therefore more strong, such men have spoken only on the wrong side of the question, and have thus thrown their influence against the cause of liberty, humanity and benevolence.

There are times in the experience of almost every community, when even the humblest member thereof may properly presume to teach—when the wise and great ones, the appointed leaders of the people, exert their powers of mind to complicate, mystify, entangle and obscure the simple truth—when they exert the noblest gifts which heaven has vouchsafed to man to mislead the popular mind, and to corrupt the public heart,— *then* the humblest may stand forth and be excused for opposing even his weakness to the torrent of evil.

That such a state of things exists in this community, I have abundant evidence. I learn it from the Rochester press, from the Rochester pulpit, and in my intercourse with the people of Rochester. Not a day passes over me that I do not meet with apparently good men, who utter sentiments in respect to this subject which would do discredit to savages. They speak of the enslavement of their fellow-men with an indifference and coldness which might be looked for only in men hardened by the most atrocious and villainous crimes.

The fact is, we are in the midst of a great struggle. The public mind is widely and deeply agitated; and bubbling up from its perturbed waters, are many and great impurities, whose poisonous miasma demands a constant antidote.

Whether the contemplated lectures will in any degree contribute towards answering this demand, time will determine.

Of one thing, however, I can assure my hearers—that I come up to this work at the call of duty, and with an honest desire to promote the happiness and well-being of every member of this community, as well as to advance the emancipation of every slave.

The audience will pardon me if I say one word more by way of introduction. It is my purpose to give this subject a calm, candid and faithful discussion. I shall not aim to shock nor to startle my hearers; but to convince their judgment and to secure their sympathies for the enslaved. I shall aim to be as stringent as truth, and as severe as justice; and if at any time I shall fail of this, and do injustice in any respect, I shall be most happy to be set right by any gentleman who shall hear me, subject, of course to order and decorum. I shall deal, during these lectures, alike with individuals and institutions—men shall no more escape me than things. I shall have occasion, at times, to be even personal, and to rebuke sin in high places. I shall not hesitate to arraign either priests or politicians, church or state, and to measure all by the standard of justice, and in the light of truth. I shall not forget to deal with the unrighteous spirit of *caste* which prevails in this community; and I shall give particular attention to the recently enacted fugitive slave bill. I shall keep my eye upon the Congress which is to commence to-morrow, and fully inform myself as to its proceedings. In a word, the whole subject of slavery, in all its bearings, shall have a full and impartial discussion.

A very slight acquaintance with the history of American slavery is sufficient to show that it is an evil of which it will be difficult to rid this country. It is not the creature of a moment, which to-day is, and to-morrow is not; it is not a pigmy, which a slight blow may demolish; it is no youthful upstart, whose impertinent pratings may be silenced by a dignified contempt. No: it is an evil of gigantic proportions, and of long standing.

Its origin in this country dates back to the landing of the pilgrims on Plymouth rock.—It was here more than two centuries ago. The first spot poisoned by its leprous presence, was a small plantation in Virginia. The slaves, at that time, numbered only twenty. They have now increased to the frightful number of three millions; and from that narrow plantation, they are now spread over by far the largest half of the American Union. Indeed, slavery forms an important part of the entire history of the American people. Its presence may be seen in all American affairs. It has become interwoven with all American institutions, and has anchored itself in the very soil of the American Constitution. It has thrown its paralysing arm over freedom of speech, and the liberty of the press; and has created for itself morals and manners favorable to its own continuance. It has seduced the church, corrupted the pulpit, and brought the powers of both into degrading bondage; and now, in the pride of its power, it even threatens to bring down that grand political edifice, the American Union, unless every member of this republic shall so far disregard his conscience and his God as to yield to its infernal behests.

That must be a powerful influence which can truly be said to govern a nation; and that slavery governs the American people, is indisputably true. If there were any doubt on this point, a few plain questions (it seems to me) could not fail to remove it. *What* power has given this nation its Presidents for more than fifty years? *Slavery*. What power is that to which the present aspirants to presidential honors are bowing? *Slavery*. We may call it "Union," "Constitution," "Harmony," or "American institutions," that to which such men as Cass, Dickinson, Webster, Clay and other distinguished men of this country, are devoting their energies, is nothing more nor less than American slavery. It is for this that they are writing letters, making speeches, and promoting the holding of great mass meetings, professedly in favor of *"the Union."* These men know the service most pleasing to their master, and that which is most likely to be richly rewarded. Men may "serve God for nought," as did Job; but he who serves the devil has an eye to his reward. "Patriotism," "obedience to the law," "prosperity to the country," have come to mean, in the mouths of these distinguished statesmen, a mean and servile acquiescence in the most flagitious and profligate legislation in favor of slavery. I might enlarge here on this picture of slave power, and tell of its influence upon the press in the free States, and upon the condition and rights of the free colored people of the North; but I forbear for the present.—Enough has been said, I trust, to convince all that the abolition of this evil will require time, energy, zeal, perseverance and patience; that it will require fidelity, a martyr-like spirit of self-sacrifice, and a firm reliance on Him who has declared Himself to be *"the God of the oppressed."* Having said thus much upon the power and prevalence of slavery, allow me to speak of the nature of slavery itself; and here I can speak, in part, from experience—I can speak with the authority of positive knowledge. . . .

First of all, I will state, as well as I can, the legal and social relation of master and slave. A master is one (to speak in the vocabulary of the Southern States) who claims and exercises a right of property in the person of a fellow man. This he does with the force of the law and the sanction of Southern religion. The law gives the master absolute power over the slave. He may work him, flog him, hire him out, sell him, and, in certain contingencies, *kill* him, with perfect impunity. The slave is a human being, divested of all rights—reduced to the level of a brute—a mere "chattel" in the eye of the law—placed beyond the circle of human brotherhood—cut off from his kind—his name, which the "recording angel" may have enrolled in heaven, among the blest, is impiously inserted in a *master's ledger*, with horses, sheep and swine. In law, the slave has no wife, no children, no country, and no home. He can own nothing, possess nothing, acquire nothing, but what must belong to another. To eat the fruit of his own toil, to clothe his person with the work of his own hands, is considered stealing. He toils that another may reap the fruit;

he is industrious that another may live in idleness; he eats unbolted meal, that another may eat the bread of fine flour; he labors in chains at home, under a burning sun and a biting lash, that another may ride in ease and splendor abroad; he lives in ignorance, that another may be educated; he is abused, that another may be exalted; he rests his toil-worn limbs on the cold, damp ground, that another may repose on the softest pillow; he is clad in coarse and tattered raiment, that another may be arrayed in purple and fine linen; he is sheltered only by the wretched hovel, that a master may dwell in a magnificent mansion; and to this condition he is bound down as by an arm of iron.

From this monstrous relation, there springs an unceasing stream of most revolting cruelties. The very accompaniments of the slave system, stamp it as the offspring of hell itself. To ensure good behavior, the slaveholder relies on *the whip*,; to induce proper humility, he relies on *the whip*,; to rebuke what he is pleased to term insolence, he relies on *the whip*,; to supply the place of wages, as an incentive to toil, he relies on *the whip*,; to bind down the spirit of the slave, to imbrute and to destroy his manhood, he relies on *the whip*, the chain, the gag, the thumb-screw, the pillory, the bowie-knife, the pistol, and the blood-hound. These are the necessary and unvarying accompaniments of the system. . . .

Nor is slavery more adverse to the conscience than it is to the mind.

This is shown by the fact that in every State of the American Union, where slavery exists, except the State of Kentucky, there are laws, *absolutely* prohibitory of education among the slaves. The crime of teaching a slave to read is punishable with severe fines and imprisonment, and, in some instances, with *death itself*.

Nor are the laws respecting this matter, a dead letter. Cases may occur in which they are disregarded, and a few instances may be found where slaves may have learned to read; but such are isolated cases, and only prove the rule. The great mass of slaveholders look upon education among the slaves as utterly subversive of the slave system. I *well* remember when my mistress first announced to my master that she had discovered that I could read. His face colored at once, with surprise and chagrin. He said that "I was ruined, that my value as a slave was destroyed; that a slave should know nothing but to obey his master; that to give a Negro an inch would lead him to take an ell; that having learned how to read, I would soon want to know how to write; and that, bye and bye, I would be running away." I think my audience will bear witness to the correctness of this philosophy, and to the literal fulfilment of this prophecy.

It is perfectly well understood at the South that to educate a slave is to make him discontented with slavery, and to invest him with a power which shall open to him the treasures of freedom; and since the object of the slave-holder is to maintain complete authority over his slave, his constant vigilance is exercised to prevent everything which militates against, or endangers the stability of his authority. Education being among the menacing influences, and, perhaps, the most dangerous, is therefore, the most cautiously guarded against.

It is true that we do not often hear of the enforcement of the law, punishing as crime the teaching of slaves to read, but this in not because of a want of disposition to enforce it. The true reason, or explanation of the matter is this, there is the greatest unanimity of opinion among the white population of the South, in favor of the policy of keeping the slave in ignorance. There is, perhaps, another reason why the law against education is so seldom violated. The slave is *too* poor to be able to offer a temptation sufficiently strong to induce a white man to violate it; and it is not to be supposed that in a community where the moral and religious sentiment is in favor of slavery, many martyrs will be found sacrificing their liberty and lives by violating those prohibitory enactments.

As a general rule, then, darkness reigns over the abodes of the enslaved, and "how great is that darkness!"

We are sometimes told of the contentment of the slaves, and are entertained with vivid pictures of their happiness. We are told that they often dance and sing; that their masters frequently give them wherewith to make merry; in fine, that they have little of which to complain. I admit that the slave *does* sometimes sing, dance, and appear to be merry. But what does this prove? It only proves to my mind, that though slavery is armed with a thousand stings, it is not able entirely to kill the elastic spirit of the bondman. That spirit will rise and walk abroad, despite of whips and chains, and extract from the cup of nature, occasional drops of joy and gladness. No thanks to the slaveholder, nor to slavery, that the vivacious captive may sometimes dance in his chains, his very mirth in such circumstances, stands before God, as an accusing angel against his enslaver.

But *who* tell us of the extraordinary contentment and happiness of the slave? What traveller has explored the balmy regions of our Southern country and brought back "these glad tidings of joy"? Bring him on the platform, and bid him answer a few plain questions, we shall then be able to determine the weight and importance that attach to his testimony. Is he a minister? Yes. Were you ever in a slave State, sir? Yes. May I inquire the object of your mission South? To preach the gospel, sir. Of what denominations are you? A Presbyterian, sir. To whom were you introduced? To the Rev. Dr. Plummer. Is he a slaveholder, sir? Yes, sir. Has slaves about his house? Yes, sir. Were you than the guest of Dr. Plummer? Yes, sir. Waited on by slaves while there? Yes, sir. Did you preach for Dr. Plummer?

Yes, sir. Did you spend your nights at the great house, or at the quarter among the slaves? At the great house. You had, then, no social intercourse with the slaves? No, sir. You fraternized, then, wholly with the *white* portion of the population while there? Yes, sir. This is sufficient, sir; you can leave the platform.

Nothing is more natural than that those who go into slave States, and enjoy the hospitality of slaveholders, should bring back favorable reports of the condition of the slave. If that ultra republican, the Hon. Lewis Cass could not return from the Court of France, without paying a compliment to royalty simply because King Louis Phillippe patted him on the shoulder, called him "friend," and invited him to dinner, it is not to be expected that those hungry shadows of men in the shape of ministers, that go South, can escape a contamination even more beguiling and insidious. Alas! for the weakness of poor human nature! "Pleased with a rattle, tickled with a straw!"

Why is it that all the reports of contentment and happiness among the slaves at the South come to us upon the authority of slaveholders, or (what is equally significant), of slaveholders' friends? *Why* is it that we do not hear from the slaves direct? The answer to this question furnishes the darkest features in the American slave system.

Is is often said, by the opponents of the anti-slavery cause, that the condition of the people of Ireland is more deplorable than that of the American slaves. *Far* be it from me to underrate the sufferings of the Irish people. They have been long oppressed; and the same heart that prompts me to plead the cause of the American bondman, makes it impossible for me *not* to sympathize with the oppressed of all lands. Yet I must say that there is no analogy between the two cases. The Irishman is poor, but he is *not* a slave. He *may* be in rags, but he is *not* a slave. He is still the master of his own body, and can say with the poet, "The hand of Douglass is his own." "The world is all before him, where to choose," and poor as may be my opinion of the British Parliament, I cannot believe that it will ever sink to such a depth of infamy as to pass a law for the recapture of Fugitive Irishmen! The shame and scandal of kidnapping will long remain wholly monopolized by the American Congress! The Irishman has not only the liberty to emigrate from his country, but he has liberty at home. He can write, and speak, and co-operate for the attainment of his rights and the redress of his wrongs.

The multitude can assembly upon all the green hills, and fertile plains of the Emerald Isle—they can pour our their grievances, and proclaim their wants without molestation; and the press, that "swiftwinged messenger," can bear the tidings of their doing to the extreme bounds of the civilized world. They have their "Conciliation Hall" on the banks of the Liffey, their reform Clubs, and the newspapers; they pass resolutions, send forth addresses, and enjoy the right of petition. But how is it with the American slave? *Where* may he assemble? *Where* is his Conciliation Hall? Where are his newspapers? Where is his right of petition? Where is his freedom of speech? his liberty of the press? and his right of locomotion? He is said to be happy; happy men can speak. But ask the slave— *what* is his condition?— *what* his state of mind?— *what* he thinks of this enslavement? and you had as well address your inquiries to the *silent dead.* There comes no *voice* from the enslaved, we are left to gather his feelings by imagining what ours would be, were our souls in his soul's stead.

If there were no other fact descriptive of slavery, than that the slave is dumb, this alone would be sufficient to mark the slave system as a grant aggregation of human horrors.

Most who are present will have observed that leading men, in this country, have been putting forth their skill to secure quiet to the nation. A system of measures to promote this object was adopted a few months ago in Congress.

The result of those measures is known. Instead of quiet, they have produced alarm; instead of peace, they have brought us war, and so must ever be.

While this nation is guilty of the enslavement of three millions of innocent men and women, it is as idle of think of having a sound and lasting peace, as it is to think there is no God, to take cognizance of the affairs of men. There can be no peace to the wicked while slavery continues in the land, it will be condemned, and while it is condemned there will be agitation; Nature must cease to be nature; Men must become monsters; Humanity must be transformed; Christianity must be exterminated; all ideas of justice, and the laws of eternal goodness must be utterly blotted out from the human soul, ere a system so foul and infernal can escape condemnation, or this guilty Republic can have a sound and enduring Peace.

Source:

James Andrews and David Zarefsky, eds. *American Voices: Significant Speeches in American History, 1640–1945.* Reading, Mass.: Longman, 1989.

Harriet Beecher Stowe's *Uncle Tom's Cabin,* 1852

First serialized beginning June 5, 1851, a chapter at a time, in a weekly publication called the *National Era,* and then published in a volume, this book sold more than 350,000 copies when it was first printed and was turned into plays, granting it an even wider audience. Daughter of the famous preacher and abolitionist Henry Ward Beecher, Stowe emphasized the degradation of slave women and the coarsening effect it had on at least some of their mistresses, as well as the horrors of breaking up slave families. Sold abroad as well as in the North, it had a powerful effect on attitudes toward slavery. It has since been translated into more than 20 languages. According to legend, when President Abraham Lincoln was introduced to Stowe, he remarked, "So this is the little lady who made this big war?"

Stowe based her narrative on stories told to her by former slaves and by her observations of plantations in Kentucky. The character of Uncle Tom was allegedly based on a Maryland slave, Josiah Henson. His "cabin" stood into the late 20th century in Montgomery County in the Washington, D.C., suburbs. After working as a slave for 41 years, in 1830 Henson and his family escaped to Ontario, Canada via the Underground Railroad. In 1841 he helped to establish the Dawn Settlement, a refuge providing a new beginning for former slaves. Through his leadership, the British American Institute, one of Canada's first industrial schools, was founded.

The chapter reproduced here describes a slave auction, including the separation of mother and daughter. In the preceding chapter, the widow of Tom's benevolent master disregards the deathbed pleas of her daughter Little Eva and her husband and refuses to grant Tom his freedom. Instead she decides to sell most of the slaves.

CHAPTER XXX The Slave Warehouse A slave warehouse! Perhaps some of my readers conjure up horrible visions of such a place. They fancy some foul, obscure den, some horrible—Tartarus "informis, ingens, cui lumen ademptum."—But no, innocent friend; in these days men have learned the art of sinning expertly and genteelly, so as not to shock the eyes and senses of respectable society. Human property is high in the market; and is, therefore, well fed, well cleaned, tended, and looked after, that it may come to sale sleek, and strong, and shining. A slave-warehouse in New Orleans is a house externally not much unlike many others, kept with neatness; and where every day you may see arranged, under a sort of shed along the outside, rows of men and women, who stand there as a sign of the property sold within. Then you shall be courteously entreated to call and examine, and shall find an abundance of husbands, wives, brothers, sisters, fathers, mothers, and young children, to be "sold separately, or in lots to suit the convenience of the purchaser;" and that soul immortal, once bought with blood and anguish by the Son of God, when the earth shook, and the rocks rent, and the graves were opened, can be sold, leased, mortgaged, exchanged for groceries or dry goods, to suit the phases of trade, or the fancy of the purchaser. It was a day or two after the conversation between Marie and Miss Ophelia, that Tom,

Adolph, and about half a dozen others of the St. Clare estate, were turned over to the loving kindness of Mr. Skeggs, the keeper of a depot on————street, to await the auction, next day. Tom had with him quite a sizable trunk full of clothing, as had most others of them. They were ushered, for the night, into a long room, where many other men, of all ages, sizes, and shades of complexion, were assembled, and from which roars of laughter and unthinking merriment were proceeding. "Ah, ha! that's right. Go it, boys—go it!" said Mr. Skeggs, the keeper. "My people are always so merry! Sambo, I see!" he said, speaking approvingly to a burly negro who was performing tricks of low buffoonery, which occasioned the shouts which Tom had heard. As might be imagined, Tom was in no humor to join these proceedings; and, therefore, setting his trunk as far as possible from the noisy group, he sat down on it, and leaned his face against the wall. The dealers in the human article make scrupulous and systematic efforts to promote noisy mirth among them, as a means of drowning reflection, and rendering them insensible to their condition. The whole object of the training to which the negro is put, from the time he is sold in the northern market till he arrives south, is systematically directed towards making him callous, unthinking, and brutal. The slave-dealer collects his gang in Virginia or Kentucky, and drives them to some convenient, healthy place—often a watering place,—to be fattened. Here they are fed full daily; and, because some incline to pine, a fiddle is kept commonly going among them, and they are made to dance daily; and he who refuses to be merry—in whose soul thoughts of wife, or child, or home, are too strong for him to be gay—is marked as sullen and dangerous, and subjected to all the evils which the ill will of an utterly irresponsible and hardened man can inflict upon him. Briskness, alertness, and cheerfulness of appearance, especially before observers, are constantly enforced upon them, both by the hope of thereby getting a good master, and the fear of all that the driver may bring upon them if they prove unsalable. "What dat ar nigger doin here?" said Sambo, coming up to Tom, after Mr. Skeggs had left the room. Sambo was a full black, of great size, very lively, voluble, and full of trick and grimace. "What you doin here?" said Sambo, coming up to Tom, and poking him facetiously in the side. "Meditatin', eh?" "I am to be sold at the auction, tomorrow!" said Tom, quietly. "Sold at auction—haw! haw! boys, an't this yer fun? I wish't I was gwine that ar way!—tell ye, wouldn't I make em laugh? But how is it,—dis yer whole lot gwine tomorrow?" said Sambo, laying his hand freely on Adolph's shoulder. "Please to let me alone!" said Adolph, fiercely, straightening himself up, with extreme disgust. "Law, now, boys! dis yer's one o' yer white niggers—kind o' cream color, ye know, scented!" said he, coming up to Adolph and snuffing. "O Lor! he'd do for a tobaccer-shop; they could keep him to scent snuff! Lor, he'd keep a whole shope agwine—he would!" "I say, keep off, can't you?" said Adolph, enraged. "Lor, now, how touchy we is—we white niggers! Look at us now!" and Sambo gave a ludicrous imitation of Adolph's manner; "here's de airs and graces. We's been in a good family, I specs." "Yes," said Adolph; "I had a master that could have bought you all for old truck!" "Laws, now, only think," said Sambo, "the gentlemens that we is!" "I belonged to the St. Clare family," said Adolph, proudly. "Lor, you did! Be hanged if they ar'n't lucky to get shet of ye. Spects they's gwine to trade ye off with a lot o' cracked tea-pots and sich like!" said Sambo, with a provoking grin. Adolph, enraged at this taunt, flew furiously at his adversary, swearing and striking on every side of him. The rest laughed and shouted, and the uproar brought the keeper to the door. "What now, boys? Order—order!" he said, coming in and flourishing a large whip. All fled in different directions, except Sambo, who, presuming on the favor which the keeper had to him as a licensed wag, stood his ground, ducking his head with a facetious grin, whenever the master made a dive at him. "Lor, Mas'r, 'tan't us— we 's reglar stiddy,—it's these yer new hands; they's real aggravatin'—kinder pickin' at us, all time!" The keeper, at this, turned upon Tom and Adolph, and distributing a few kicks and cuffs without much inquiry, and leaving general orders for all to be good boys and go to sleep, left the apartment. While this scene was going on in the men's sleeping-room, the reader may be curious to take a peep at the corresponding apartment allotted to the women. Stretched out in various attitudes over the floor, he may see numberless sleeping forms of every shade of complexion, from the purest ebony to white, and of all years, from childhood to old age, lying now asleep. Here is a fine bright girl, of ten years, whose mother was sold out yesterday, and who tonight cried herself to sleep when nobody was looking at her. Here, a worn old negress, whose thin arms and callous fingers tell of hard toil, waiting to be sold tomorrow, as a cast-off article, for what can be got for her; and some forty or fifty others, with heads variously enveloped in blankets or articles of clothing, lie stretched around them. But, in a corner, sitting apart from the rest, are two females of a more interesting appearance than common. One of these is a respectably-dressed mulatto woman between forty and fifty, with soft eyes and a gentle and pleasing physiognomy. She has on her head a high-raised turban, made of a gay red Madras handkerchief, of the first quality, her dress is neatly fitted, and of good material, showing that she has been provided for with a careful hand. By her side, and nestling closely to her, is a young girl of fifteen—her daughter. She is a quadroon, as may be seen from her fairer complexion, though her likeness to her mother is quite discernible. She has the same soft, dark eye, with longer lashes, and her curling hair is of a luxuriant brown. She also is dressed with great neatness, and her white, delicate hands betray very little acquaintance with servile toil. These two are to be sold tomorrow, in the same lot with the St. Clare servants; and the gentleman to whom they belong, and to whom the money for their sale is to be transmitted, is a member of a Christian church in New York, who will receive the money, and go thereafter to the sacrament of his Lord and theirs, and think no more of it. These two, whom we shall call Susan and Emmeline, had been the personal attendants of an amiable and pious lady of New Orleans, by whom they had been carefully and piously instructed and trained. They had been taught to read and write, diligently instructed in the truths of religion, and their lot had been as happy an one as in their condition it was possible to be. But the only son of their protectress had the management of her property; and, by carelessness and extravagance involved it to a large amount, and at last failed. One of the largest creditors was the respectable firm of B. & Co., in New York. B. & Co. wrote to their lawyer in New Orleans, who attached the real estate (these two articles and a lot of plantation hands formed the most valuable part of it), and wrote word to that effect to New York. Brother B., being, as we have said, a Christian man, and a resident in a free State, felt some uneasiness on the subject. He didn't like trading in slaves and souls of men,—of course, he didn't; but, then, there were thirty thousand dollars in the case, and that was rather too much money to be lost for a principle; and so, after much considering, and asking advice from those that he knew would advise to suit him, Brother B. wrote to his lawyer to dispose of the business in the way that seemed to him the most suitable, and remit the proceeds. The day after the letter arrived in New Orleans, Susan and Emmeline were attached, and sent to the depot to await a general auction on the following morning; and as they glimmer faintly upon us in the moonlight which steals through the grated window, we may listen to their conversation. Both are weeping, but each quietly, that the other may not hear. "Mother, just lay your head on my lap, and see if you can't sleep a little," says the girl, trying to appear calm. "I haven't any heart to sleep, Em; I can't; it's the last night we may be together!" "O, mother, don't say so! perhaps we shall get sold together—who knows?" "If 't was anybody's else case, I should say so, too, Em," said the woman; "but I'm so feard of losin' you that I don't see anything but the danger." "Why, mother, the man said we were both likely, and would sell well." Susan remembered the man's looks and words. With a deadly sickness at her heart, she remembered how he had looked at Emmeline's hands, and lifted up her curly hair, and pronounced her a first-rate article. Susan had been trained as a Christian, brought up in the

daily reading of the Bible, and had the same horror of her child's being sold to a life of shame that any other Christian mother might have; but she had no hope—no protection. "Mother, I think we might do first rate, if you could get a place as cook, and I as chambermaid or seamstress, in some family. I dare say we shall. Let's both look as bright and lively as we can, and tell all we can do, and perhaps we shall," said Emmeline. "I want you to brush your hair all back straight, tomorrow," said Susan. "What for, mother? I don't look near so well, that way." "Yes, but you'll sell better so." "I don't see why!" said the child. "Respectable families would be more apt to buy you, if they saw you looked plain and decent, as if you wasn't trying to look handsome. I know their ways better'n you do," said Susan. "Well, mother, then I will." "And, Emmeline, if we shouldn't ever see each other again, after tomorrow—if I'm sold way up on a plantation somewhere, and you somewhere else— always remember how you've been brought up, and all Missis has told you; take your Bible with you, and your hymn-book; and if you're faithful to the Lord, he'll be faithful to you." So speaks the poor soul, in sore discouragement; for she knows that tomorrow any man, however vile and brutal, however godless and merciless, if he only has money to pay for her, may become owner of her daughter, body and soul; and then, how is the child to be faithful? She thinks of all this, as she holds her daughter in her arms, and wishes that she were not handsome and attractive. It seems almost an aggravation to her to remember how purely and piously, how much above the ordinary lot, she has been brought up. But she has no resort but to pray; and many such prayers to God have gone up from those same trim, neatly-arranged, respectable slave-prisons—prayers which God has not forgotten, as a coming day shall show; for it is written, "Who causeth one of these little ones to offend, it were better for him that a millstone were hanged about his neck, and that he were drowned in the depths of the sea." The soft, earnest, quiet moonbeam looks in fixedly, marking the bars of the grated windows on the prostrate, sleeping forms. The mother and daughter are singing together a wild and melancholy dirge, common as a funeral hymn among the slaves: "O, where is weeping Mary? O, where is weeping Mary? 'Rived in the goodly land. She is dead and gone to Heaven; She is dead and gone to Heaven; 'Rived in the goodly land." These words, sung by voices of a peculiar and melancholy sweetness, in an air which seemed like the sighing of earthy despair after heavenly hope, floated through the dark prison rooms with a pathetic cadence, as verse after verse was breathed out: "O, where are Paul and Silas? O, where are Paul and Silas? Gone to the goodly land. They are dead and gone to Heaven; They are dead and gone to Heaven; 'Rived in the goodly land." Sing on poor souls! The night is short, and the morning will part you forever! But now it is morning, and everybody is astir; and the worthy Mr. Skeggs is busy and bright, for a lot of goods is to be fitted out for auction. There is a brisk lookout on the toilet; injunctions passed around to every one to put on their best face and be spry; and now all are arranged in a circle for a last review, before they are marched up to the Bourse. Mr. Skeggs, with his palmetto on and his cigar in his mouth, walks around to put farewell touches on his wares. "How's this?" he said, stepping in front of Susan and Emmeline. "Where's your curls, gal?" The girl looked timidly at her mother, who, with the smooth adroitness common among her class, answers, "I was telling her, last night, to put up her hair smooth and neat, and not havin' it flying about in curls; looks more respectable so." "Bother!" said the man, peremptorily, turning to the girl; in the sale of her." Beneath a splendid dome were men of all nations, moving to and fro, over the marble pave. On every side of the circular area were little tribunes, or stations, for the use of speakers and auctioneers. Two of these, on opposite sides of the area, were now occupied by brilliant and talented gentlemen, enthusiastically forcing up, in English and French commingled, the bids of connoisseurs in their various wares. A third one, on the other side, still unoccupied, was surrounded by a group, waiting the moment of sale to begin. And here we may recognize the St. Clare servants—Tom, Adolph, and others; and there, too, Susan and Emmeline, awaiting their turn with anxious and dejected faces. Various spectators, intending to purchase, or not intending, examining, and commenting on their various points and faces with the same freedom that a set of jockeys discuss the merits of a horse. "Hulloa, Alf! what brings you here?" said a young exquisite, slapping the shoulder of a sprucely-dressed young man, who was examining Adolph through an eye-glass. "Well! I was wanting a valet, and I heard that St. Clare's lot was going. I thought I'd just look at his—" "Catch me ever buying any of St. Clare's people! Spoilt niggers, every one. Impudent as the devil!" said the other. "Never fear that!" said the first. "If I get 'em, I'll soon have their airs out of them; they'll soon find that they've another kind of master to deal with than Monsieur St. Clare. 'Pon my word, I'll buy that fellow. I like the shape of him." "You'll find it'll take all you've got to keep him. He's deucedly extravagant!" "Yes, but my lord will find that he can't be extravagant with me. Just let him be sent to the calaboose a few times, and thoroughly dressed down! I'll tell you if it don't bring him to a sense of his ways! O, I'll reform him, up hill and down—you'll see. I buy him, that's flat!" Tom had been standing wistfully examining the multitude of faces thronging around him, for one whom he would wish to call master. And if you should ever be under the necessity, sir, of selecting, out of two hundred men, one who was to become your absolute owner and disposer, you would, perhaps, realize, just as Tom did, how few there were that

you would feel at all comfortable in being made over to. Tom saw abundance of men—great, burly, gruff men; little, chirping, dried men; long-favored, lank, hard men; and every variety of stubbed-looking, commonplace men, who pick up their fellow-men as one picks up chips, putting them into the fire or a basket with equal unconcern, according to their convenience; but he saw no St. Clare. A little before the sale commenced, a short, broad, muscular man, in a checked shirt considerably open at the bosom, and pantaloons much the worse for dirt and wear, elbowed his way through the crowd, like one who is going actively into a business; and, coming up to the group, began to examine them systematically. From the moment that Tom saw him approaching, he felt an immediate and revolting horror at him, that increased as he came near. He was evidently, though short, of gigantic strength. His round, bullet head, large, light-gray eyes, with their shaggy, sandy eyebrows, and stiff, wiry, sun-burned hair, were rather unprepossessing items, it is to be confessed; his large, coarse mouth was distended with tobacco, the juice of which, from time to time, he ejected from him with great decision and explosive force; his hands were immensely large, hairy, sun-burned, freckled, and very dirty, and garnished with long nails, in a very foul condition. This man proceeded to a very free personal examination of the lot. He seized Tom by the jaw, and pulled open his mouth to inspect his teeth; made him strip up his sleeve, to show his muscle; turned him round, made him jump and spring, to show his paces. "Where was you raised?" he added, briefly, to these investigations. "In Kintuck, Mas'r," said Tom, looking about, as if for deliverance. "What have you done?" "Had care of Mas'r's farm," said Tom. "Likely story!" said the other, shortly, as he passed on. He paused a moment before Dolph; then spitting a discharge of tobacco-juice on his well-blacked boots, and giving a contemptuous umph, he walked on. Again he stopped before Susan and Emmeline. He put out his heavy, dirty hand, and drew the girl towards him; passed it over her neck and bust, felt her arms, looked at her teeth, and then pushed her back against her mother, whose patient face showed the suffering she had been going through at every motion of the hideous stranger. The girl was frightened, and began to cry. "Stop that, you minx!" said the salesman; "no whimpering here—the sale is going to begin." And accordingly the sale begun. Adolph was knocked off, at a good sum, to the young gentlemen who had previously stated his intention of buying him; and the other servants of the St. Clare lot went to various bidders. "Now, up with you, boy! d'ye hear?" said the auctioneer to Tom. Tom stepped upon the block, gave a few anxious looks round; all seemed mingled in a common, indistinct noise—the clatter of the salesman crying off his qualifications in French and English, the quick fire of French and English bids; and almost in a moment came the final thump of the hammer, and the clear ring on the last syllable of the word "dollars," as the auctioneer announced his price, and Tom was made over—He had a master! He was pushed from the block—the short, bullet-headed man seizing him roughly by the shoulder, pushed him to one side, saying, in a harsh voice, "Stand there, you!" Tom hardly realized anything; but still the bidding went on,—ratting, clattering, now French, now English. Down goes the hammer again—Susan is sold! She goes down from the block, stops, looks wistfully back,—her daughter stretches her hands towards her. She looks with agony in the face of the man who has bought her—a respectable middle-aged man, of benevolent countenance. "O, Mas'r, please do buy my daughter!" "I'd like to, but I'm afraid I can't afford it!" said the gentleman, looking, with painful interest, as the young girl mounted the block, and looked around her with a frightened and timid glance. The blood flushes painfully in her otherwise colorless cheek, her eye has a feverish fire, and her mother groans to see that she looks more beautiful than she ever saw her before. The auctioneer sees his advantage, and expatiates volubly in mingled French and English, and bids rise in rapid succession. "I'll do anything in reason," said the benevolent-looking gentleman, pressing in and joining with the bids. In a few moments they have run beyond his purse. He is silent; the auctioneer grows warmer; but bids gradually drop off. It lies now between an aristocratic old citizen and our bullet-headed acquaintance. The citizen bids for a few turns, contemptuously measuring his opponent; but the bullet-head has the advantage over him, both in obstinacy and concealed length of purse, and the controversy lasts but a moment; the hammer falls—he has got the girl, body and soul, unless God help her! Her master is Mr. Legree, who owns a cotton plantation on the Red river. She is pushed along into the same lot with Tom and two other men, and goes off, weeping as she goes. The benevolent gentleman is sorry; but, then, the thing happens every day! One sees girls and mothers crying, at these sales, always! it can't be helped, &c.; and he walks off, with his acquisition, in another direction. Two days after, the lawyer of the Christian firm of B. & Co., New York, send on their money to them. On the reverse of that draft, so obtained, let them write these words of the great Paymaster, to whom they shall make up their account in a future day: "When he maketh inquisition for blood, he forgetteth not the cry of the humble!"

Source:

Harriet Beecher Stowe, *Uncle Tom's Cabin or Life Among the Lowly*, 1852; Kenneth S. Lynne, ed., Harvard Library Classics Edition, 1962. Project Gutenberg Etext. Available online. URL: www.mdarchives.state.md.us./ecp/10/223/0001/html/00010000.html.

Moses Arrives with Six Passengers, 1854

A brief account of Harriet Tubman's career on the Underground Railroad and the stopover in Baltimore, Maryland, of six former slaves whom she was helping to smuggle to freedom. A Maryland-born slave, Tubman escaped in 1849. She changed her name to Harriet but was dubbed "Moses" because of her role in leading black slaves out of bondage to liberation.

"MOSES" ARRIVES WITH SIX PASSENGERS.

"Not allowed to seek a master;"—"Very devilish;"—"father" leaves two little sons;"—"Used hard;"—"Feared falling into the hands of young heirs," etc. John Chase, alias Daniel Floyd; Benjamin Ross, alias James Stewart; Henry Ross, alias Levin Steward; Peter Jackson, alias Staunch Tilghman; Jane Kane, alias Catharine Kane, and Robert Ross.

The coming of these passengers was heralded by Thomas Garrett as follows:

Thomas Garrett's Letter

Wilmington, 12 mo. 29th, 1854.

Esteemed Friend, J. Miller McKim:—We made arrangements last night, and sent away Harriet Tubman, with six men and one women to Allen Agnew's, to be forwarded across the country to the city. Harriet, and one of the men had worn their shoes off their feet, and I gave them two dollars to help fit them out, and directed a carriage to be hired at my expense, to take them out, but do not yet know the expense. I now have two more from the lowest country in Maryland, on the Peninsula, upwards of one hundred miles. I will try to get one of our trusty colored men to take them to-morrow morning to the Anti-slavery office. You can then pass them on.

Thomas Garrett.

Harriet Tubman had been their "Moses," but not in the sense that Andrew Johnson was the "Moses of the colored people." She had faithfully gone down into Egypt, and had delivered these six bondmen by her own heroism. Harriet was a woman of no pretensions, indeed, a more ordinary specimen of humanity could hardly be found among the most unfortunate-looking farm hands of the South. Yet, in point of courage, shrewdness and disinterested exertions to rescue her fellow-men, by making personal visits to Maryland among the slaves, she was without her equal.

Her success was wonderful. Time and again she made successful visits to Maryland on the Underground Rail Road, and would be absent for weeks, at a time, running daily risks while making preparations for herself and passengers. Great fears were entertained for her safety, but she seemed wholly devoid of personal fear. The idea of being captured by slave-hunters or slave-holders, seemed never to enter her mind. She was apparently proof against all adversaries. While she thus manifested such utter personal indifference, she was much more watchful with regard to those she was piloting. Half of her time, she had the appearance of one asleep, and would actually sit down by the road-side and go fast asleep when on her errands of mercy through the South, yet, she would not suffer one of her party to whimper once, about "giving out and going back," however wearied they might be from hard travel day and night. She had a very short and pointed rule or law of her own, which implied death to any who talked of giving out and going back. Thus, in an emergency she would give all to understand that "times were very critical and therefore no foolishness would be indulged in on the road." That several who were rather weak-kneed and faint-hearted were greatly invigorated by Harriet's blunt and positive manner and threat of extreme measures, there could be no doubt.

After having once enlisted, "they had to go to go through or die." Of course Harriet was supreme, and her followers generally had full faith in her, and would back up any word she might utter. So when she said to them that "a live runaway could do great harm by going back, but that a dead one could tell no secrets," she was sure to have obedience. Therefore, none had to die as traitors on the "middle passage." It is obvious enough, however, that her success in going into Maryland as she did, was attributable to her adventurous spirit and utter disregard of consequences. Her like it is probable was never known before or since. On examining the six passengers who came by this arrival they were thus recorded:

December 29th, 1854—John is twenty years of age, chestnut color, of spare build and smart. He fled from a farmer, by the name of John Campbell Henry, who resided at Cambridge, Dorchester Co., Maryland. On being interrogated relative to the character of his master, John gave no very amiable account of him. He testified that he was a "hard man" and that he "owned about one hundred and forty slaves and sometimes he would sell," etc. John was one of the slaves who were "hired out." He "desired to have the privilege of hunting his own master." His desire was not granted. Instead of meekly submitting, John felt wronged, and made this his reason for running away. This looked pretty spirited on the part of one so young as John. The Committee's respect for him was not a little increased, when they heard him express himself.

Benjamin was twenty-eight years of age, chestnut color, medium size, and shrewd. He was the so-called property of Eliza Ann Brodins, who lived near Buckstown, in Maryland. Ben did not hesitate to say, in unqualified terms, that his mistress was "very devilish." He considered his charges, proved by the fact that three slaves (himself on of them) were required to work hard and fare meagerly, to support his mistress' family in idleness and luxury. The Committee paid due attention to his ex parte statement, and was obliged to conclude that this argument, clothed in common and homely language, was forcible, if not eloquent, and that he was well worthy of aid. Benjamin left his parents besides one sister, Mary Ann Williamson, who wanted to come away on the Underground Rail Road.

Henry left his wife, Harriet Ann, to be known in future by the name of "Sophia Brown." He was a fellow-servant of Ben's, and one of the supports of Eliza A. Brodins.

Henry was only twenty-two, but had quite an insight into matters and things going on among slaves and slaveholders generally, in country life. He was the father of two small children, whom he had to leave behind.

Peter was owned by George Wenthrop, a farmer, living near Cambridge, Md. In answer to the question, how he had been used, he said "hard." Not a pleasant thought did he entertain respecting his master, save that he was no longer to demand the sweat of Peter's brow. Peter left parents, who were free; he was born before they were emancipated, consequently, he was retained in bondage.

Jane, aged twenty-two, instead of regretting that she had unadvisedly left a kind mistress and indulgent master, who had afforded her necessary comforts, affirmed that her master, "Rash Jones, was the worst man in the country." The Committee were at first disposed to doubt her sweeping statement, but when they heard particularly how she had been treated, they thought Catherine had good ground for all that she said. Personal abuse and hard usage, were the common lot of poor slave girls.

Robert was thirty-five years of age, of a chestnut color, and well made. His report was similar to that of may others. He had been provided with plenty of hard drudgery—hewing of wood and drawing of water, and had hardly been treated as well as a gentlemen would treat a dumb brute. His feelings, therefore, on leaving his old master and home, were those of an individual who had been unjustly in prison for a dozen years and had at last regained his liberty.

The civilization, religion, and customs under which Robert and his companions had been raised, were, he thought, "very wicked." Although these travelers were all of the field-hand order, they were, nevertheless, very promising, and they anticipated better days in Canada. Good advice was proffered them on the subject of temperance, industry, education, etc. Clothing, food and money were also given them to meet their wants, and they were sent on their way rejoicing.

Source:

William Still. *The Underground Railroad*. Philadelphia: Porter & Coates, 1872, courtesy of Maryland State Archives Library.

Kansas-Nebraska Act, 1854

Bill passed by Congress in 1854 that established the territories of Kansas and Nebraska. It repealed the Missouri Compromise of 1820 and established the principle of popular sovereignty, allowing settlers in the newly organized territories to determine whether to permit slavery there. Although the bill, which was sponsored by Democratic senator Stephen A. Douglas, and signed into law by President Franklin Pierce on May 30, 1854, aimed to reduce the growing national controversy over slavery in the West, it actually intensified the conflict. Its passage contributed to the formation of the Republican Party, which opposed the expansion of slavery into the territories. A period of violence known as Bleeding Kansas erupted between proslavery and antislavery factions. John Brown and his sons participated by viciously murdering five proslavery men. Popular sovereignty led to rival constitutions in Kansas. A constitutional convention held in October–November 1855 at Topeka drafted one establishing Kansas as a free state. The document, prepared in opposition to the proslavery territorial government, prohibited slavery and declared invalid black indentures executed in other U.S. states. It was approved by voters in December. A bill to admit Kansas under this constitution passed the U.S. House of Representatives the following year but failed in the Senate. A period of violence followed.

The Lecompton Constitution represented the next attempt to establish the state, and a constitutional convention adopted it in September 1857. It organized the territory of Kansas as a proslavery state. Free-state supporters boycotted a vote on the document. In October Kansas sought admission to the Union under the Lecompton Constitution. Despite the support of President James Buchanan, the measure failed to win congressional approval and was returned for a territorial referendum. In August 1858 Kansas voters rejected it.

Following the failure of the Lecompton Constitution, a constitutional convention of Republicans and Democrats convened at Wyandotte (now part of Kansas City), Kansas, in July 1859. The document produced there rejected slavery, suffrage for women and blacks, and prohibition, but affirmed property rights for women and established the present boundaries of the state. It was ratified by popular vote on October 4, 1859. Kansas was finally admitted to the Union as a free state on January 29, 1861.

⎯⎯⎯⎯⎯⎯⎯⎯⎯⎯⎯ ⌑ ⎯⎯⎯⎯⎯⎯⎯⎯⎯⎯⎯

An Act
To Organize the Territories of Nebraska and Kansas.

Be it enacted by the Senate and House of Representatives of the United States of America in Congress assembled, That all that part of the territory of the United States included within the following limits, except such portions thereof as are hereinafter expressly exempted from the operations of this act, to wit: beginning at a point in the Missouri River where the fortieth parallel of north latitude crosses the same; thence west on said parallel to the east boundary of the Territory of Utah, on the summit of the Rocky Mountains; thence on said summit northward to the forty-ninth parallel of north latitude; thence east on said parallel to the western boundary of the territory of Minnesota; thence southward on said boundary to the Missouri River; thence down the main channel of said river to the place of beginning, be, and the same is hereby, created into a temporary government by the name of the Territory of Nebraska; and when admitted as a State or States, the said Territory, or any portion of the same, shall be received into the Union with or without slavery, as their constitution may prescribe at the time of their admission: *Provided,* That nothing in this act contained shall be construed to inhibit the government of the United States from dividing said Territory into two or more Territories, in such manner and at such times as Congress shall deem convenient and proper, or from attaching any portion of said Territory to any other State or Territory of the United States: *Provided further,* That nothing in this act contained shall be construed to impair the rights of person or property now pertaining to the Indians in said Territory, so long as such rights shall remain unextinguished by treaty between the United States and such Indians, or to include any territory which, by treaty with any Indian tribe, is not, without the consent of said tribe, to be included within the territorial limits or jurisdiction of any State or Territory; but all such territory shall be excepted out of the boundaries, and constitute no part of the Territory of Nebraska, until said tribe shall signify their assent to the President of the United States to be included within the said Territory of Nebraska, or to affect the authority of the government of the United States to make any regulations respecting such Indians, their lands, property, or other rights, by treaty, law, or otherwise, which it would have been competent to the government to make if this act had never passed.

Sec. 2. *And be it further enacted,* That the executive power and authority in and over said Territory of Nebraska shall be vested in a Governor, who shall hold his office for four years, and until his successor shall be appointed and qualified, unless sooner removed by the President of the United States. The Governor shall reside within said Territory, and shall be commander-in-chief of the militia thereof. He may grant pardons and respites for offences against the laws of said Territory, and reprieves for offences against the laws of the United States, until the decision of the President can be made known thereon; he shall commission all officers who shall be appointed to office under the laws of the said Territory, and shall take care that the laws be faithfully executed.

Sec. 3. *And be it further enacted,* That there shall be a Secretary of said Territory, who shall reside therein, and hold his office for five years, unless sooner removed by the President of the United States; he shall record and preserve all the laws and proceedings of the Legislative Assembly hereinafter constituted, and all the acts and proceedings of the Governor in his executive department; he shall transmit one copy of the laws and journals of the Legislative Assembly within thirty days after the end of each session, and one copy of the executive proceedings and official correspondence semi-annually, on the first days of January and July in each year to the President of the United States, and two copies of the laws to the President of the Senate and to the Speaker of the House of Representatives, to be deposited in the libraries of Congress; and in case of the death, removal, resignation, or absence of the Governor from the Territory, the Secretary shall be, and he is hereby, authorized and required to execute and perform all the powers and duties of the Governor during such vacancy or absence, or until another Governor shall be duly appointed and qualified to fill such vacancy.

Sec. 4. *And be it further enacted,* That the legislative power and authority of said Territory shall be vested in the Governor and a Legislative Assembly. The Legislative Assembly shall consist of a Council and House of Representatives. The Council shall consist of thirteen members, having the qualifications of voters, as hereinafter prescribed, whose term of service shall continue two years. The House of Representatives shall, at its first session, consist of twenty-six members, possessing the same qualifications as prescribed for members of the Council, and whose term of service shall continue one year. The number of representatives may be increased by the Legislative Assembly, from time to time, in proportion to the increase of qualified voters: *Provided,* That the whole number shall never exceed thirty-nine. An apportionment shall be made, as nearly equal as practicable, among the several counties or districts, for the election of the council and representatives, giving to each section of the Territory representation in the ratio of its qualified voters as nearly as may be. And the members of the Council and of the House of Representatives shall reside in, and be inhabitants of, the district or county, or countries for which they may be elected, respectively. Previous to the first election, the Governor shall cause a census, or enumeration of the inhabitants and qualified voters of the several counties and districts of the Territory, to be taken by such persons and in such mode as the Governor shall designate and appoint; and the persons so appointed shall receive a reasonable compensation therefor. And the first election shall be held at such time and places, and be conducted in such manner, both as to the persons who shall superintend such election

and the returns thereof, as the Governor shall appoint and direct; and he shall at the same time declare the number of members of the Council and House of Representatives to which each of the counties or districts shall be entitled under this act. The persons having the highest number of legal votes in each of said council districts for members of the Council, shall be declared by the Governor to be duly elected to the Council; and the persons having the highest number of legal votes for the House of Representatives, shall be declared by the Governor to be duly elected members of said house: *Provided,* That in case two or more persons voted for shall have an equal number of votes, and in case a vacancy shall otherwise occur in either branch of the Legislative Assembly, the Governor shall order a new election; and the persons thus elected to the Legislative Assembly shall meet at such place and on such day as the Governor shall appoint; but thereafter, the time, place, and manner of holding and conducting all elections by the people, and the apportioning the representation in the several counties or districts to the Council and House of Representatives, according to the number of qualified voters, shall be prescribed by law, as well as the day of the commencement of the regular sessions of the Legislative Assembly: *Provided,* That no session in any one year shall exceed the term of forty days, except the first session, which may continue sixty days.

Sec. 5. *And be it further enacted,* That every free white male inhabitant above the age of twenty-one years who shall be an actual resident of said Territory, and shall possess the qualifications hereinafter prescribed, shall be entitled to vote at the first election, and shall be eligible to any office within the said Territory; but the qualifications of voters, and of holding office, at all subsequent elections, shall be such as shall be prescribed by the Legislative Assembly: *Provided,* That the right of suffrage and of holding office shall be exercised only by citizens of the United States and those who shall have declared on oath their intention to become such, and shall have taken an oath to support the Constitution of the United States and the provisions of this act: *And provided further,* That no officer, soldier, seaman, or marine, or other person in the army or navy of the United States, or attached to troops in the service of the United States, shall be allowed to vote or hold office in said Territory, by reason of being on service therein.

Sec. 6. *And be it further enacted,* That the legislative power of the Territory shall extend to all rightful subjects of legislation consistent with the Constitution of the United States and the provisions of this act; but no law shall be passed interfering with the primary disposal of the soil; no tax shall be imposed upon the property of the United States; nor shall the lands or other property of non-residents be taxed higher than the lands or other property of residents. Every bill which shall have passed the Council and House of Representatives of the said Territory shall, before it become a law, be presented to the Governor of the Territory; if he approve, he shall sign it; but if not, he shall return it with his objections to the house in which it originated, who shall enter the objections at large on their journal, and proceed to reconsider it. If, after such reconsideration, two thirds of that house shall agree to pass the bill, it shall be sent, together with the objections, to the other house, by which it shall likewise be reconsidered, and if approved by two thirds of that house, it shall become a law. But in all such cases the votes of both houses shall be determined by yeas and nays, to be entered on the journal of each house respectively. If any bill shall not be returned by the Governor within three days (Sundays excepted) after it shall have been presented to him, the same shall be a law in like manner as if he had signed it, unless the Assembly, by adjournment, prevents its return, in which case it shall not be a law.

Sec. 7. *And be it further enacted,* That all township, district, and county officers, not herein otherwise provided for, shall be appointed or elected, as the case may be, in such manner as shall be provided by the Governor and Legislative Assembly of the Territory of Nebraska. The Governor shall nominate, and, by and with the advice and consent of the Legislative Council, appoint all officers not herein otherwise provided for; and in the first instance the Governor alone appoint all said officers, who shall hold their offices until the end of the first session of the Legislative Assembly; and shall lay off the necessary districts for members of the Council and House of Representatives, and all other officers.

Sec. 8. *And be it further enacted,* That no member of the Legislative Assembly shall hold, or be appointed to, any office which shall have been created, or the salary or emoluments of which shall have been increased, while he was a member, during the term for which he was elected, and for one year after the expiration of such term; but this restriction shall not be applicable to members of the first Legislative Assembly; and no person holding a commission or appointment under the United States, except Postmasters, shall be a member of the Legislative Assembly, or hold any office under the government of said Territory.

Sec. 9. *And be it further enacted,* That the judicial power of said Territory shall be vested in a Supreme Court, District Courts, Probate Courts, and in Justices of the Peace. The Supreme Court shall consist of a chief justice and two associate justices, any two of whom shall constitute a quorum, and who shall hold a term at the seat of government of said Territory annually, and they shall hold their offices during the period of four years, and until their successor shall be appointed and qualified. The said Terri-

tory shall be divided into three judicial districts, and a district court shall be held in each of said districts by one of the justices of the Supreme Court, at such times and places as may be prescribed by law; and the said judges shall, after their appointments, respectively, reside in the districts which shall be assigned them. The jurisdiction of the several courts herein provided for, both appellate and original, and that of the probate courts and of justices of the peace, shall be as limited by law: *Provided,* That justices of the peace shall not have jurisdiction of any matter in controversy when the title or boundaries of land may be in dispute, or where the debt or sum claimed shall exceed one hundred dollars; an the said supreme and district courts, respectively, shall possess chancery as well as common law jurisdiction. Each District Court, or the judge thereof, shall appoint its clerk, who shall also be the register in chancery, and shall keep his office at the place where the court may be held. Writs of error, bills of exception, and appeals, shall be allowed in all cases from the final decisions of said district courts to the Supreme Court, under such regulations as may be prescribed by law; but in no case removed to the Supreme Court shall trial by jury be allowed in said court. The Supreme Court, or the justices thereof, shall appoint its own clerk, and every clerk shall hold his office at the pleasure of the court for which he shall have been appointed. Writs of error, and appeals from the final decisions of said Supreme Court, shall be allowed, and may be taken to the Supreme Court of the United States, in the same manner and under the same regulations as from the circuit courts of the United States, where the value of the property, or the amount in controversy, to be ascertained by the oath or affirmation of either party, or other competent witness, shall exceed one thousand dollars; except only that in all cases involving title to slaves, the said writs of error, or appeals shall be allowed and decided by the said Supreme Court, without regard to the value of the matter, property, or title in controversy; and except also that a writ of error or appeal shall also be allowed to the Supreme Court of the United States, from the decision of the said Supreme Court created by this act, or of any judge thereof, or of the district courts created by this act, or of any judge thereof, upon any writ of *habeas corpus,* involving the question of personal freedom: *Provided,* that nothing herein contained shall be construed to apply to or affect the provisions to the "act respecting fugitives from justice, and persons escaping from the service of their masters," approved February twelfth, seventeen hundred and ninety-three and the "act to amend and supplementary to the aforesaid act," approved September eighteen, eighteen hundred and fifty; and each of the said district courts shall have and exercise the same jurisdiction in all cases arising under the Constitution and Laws of the United States as is vested in the Circuit and District

Courts of the United States; and the said Supreme and District Courts of the said Territory, and the respective judges thereof, shall and may grant writs of *habeas corpus* in all cases in which the same are granted by the judges of the United States in the District of Columbia; and the first six days of every term of said courts, or so much thereof as shall be necessary, shall be appropriated to the trial of causes arising under the said constitution and laws, and writs of error and appeal in all such cases shall be made to the Supreme Court of said Territory, the same as in other cases. The said clerk shall receive in all such cases the same fees which the clerks of the district courts of Utah Territory now receives for similar services.

Sec. 10. *And be it further enacted,* That the provisions of an act entitled "An act respecting fugitives from justice, and persons escaping from the service of their masters," approved February twelve, seventeen hundred and ninety-three, and the provisions of the act entitled "An act to amend, and supplementary to, the aforesaid act," approved September eighteen, eighteen hundred and fifty, be, and the same are hereby, declared to extend to and be in full force within the limits of said Territory of Nebraska.

Sec. 11. *And be it further enacted,* That there shall be appointed an Attorney for said Territory, who shall continue in office for four years, and until his successor shall be appointed and qualified, unless sooner removed by the President, and who shall received the same fees and salary as the Attorney of the United States for the present Territory of Utah. There shall also be a Marshall for the Territory appointed, who shall hold his office for four years, and until his successor shall be appointed and qualified, unless sooner removed by the President, and who shall execute all processes issuing from the said courts when exercising their jurisdiction as Circuit and District Courts of the United States; he shall perform the duties, be subject to the same regulation and penalties, and be entitled to the same fees, as the Marshal of the District Court of the United States for the present Territory of Utah, and shall, in addition, be paid two hundred dollars annually as a compensation for extra services.

Sec. 12. *And be it further enacted,* That the Governor, Secretary, Chief Justice, and Associate Justices, Attorney and Marshal, shall be nominated, and, by and with the advice and consent of the Senate, appointed by the President of the United States. The Governor and Secretary to be appointed as aforesaid, shall, before they act as such, respectively take an oath or affirmation before the District Judge or some Justice of the Peace in the limits of said Territory, duly authorized to administer oaths and affirmations by the laws now in force therein, or before the Chief Justice, or some Associate Justice of the Supreme Court of the United States, to support the Constitution of the United States, and faithfully to discharge the duties of their respective offices, which said oaths, when so taken, shall be certified by the person by whom the same shall have been taken; and such certificates shall be received and recorded by the said Secretary among the Executive proceedings; and the Chief Justice and Associate Justices, and all other civil officers in said Territory, before they act as such, shall take a like oath or affirmation before the said Governor or Secretary, or some Judge or Justice of the Peace of the Territory, who may be duly commissioned and qualified, which said oath or affirmation shall be certified and transmitted by the person taking the same to the Secretary, to be by him recorded as aforesaid; and, afterwards, the like oath or affirmation shall be taken, certified, and recorded, in such manner and form as may be prescribed by law. The Governor shall receive an annual salary of two thousand five hundred dollars. The Chief Justice and Associate Justices shall each receive an annual salary of two thousand dollars. The Secretary shall receive an annual salary of two thousand dollars. The said salaries shall be paid quarter-yearly, from the dates of the respective appointments, at the Treasury of the United States; but no such payment shall be made until said officers shall have entered upon the duties of their respective appointments. The members of the Legislative Assembly shall be entitled to receive three dollars each per day during their attendance at the sessions thereof, and three dollars each for every twenty miles' travel in going to and returning from the said sessions, estimated according to the nearest usually travelled route; and an additional allowance of three dollars shall be paid to the presiding officer of each house for each day he shall so preside. And a chief clerk, one assistant clerk, a sergeant-at-arms, and doorkeeper, may be chosen for each house; and the chief clerk shall receive four dollars per day, and the said other officers three dollars per day, during the session of the Legislative Assembly; but no other officers shall be paid by the United States: *Provided,* That there shall be but one session of the Legislature annually, unless, on an extraordinary occasion, the Governor shall think proper to call the legislature together. There shall be appropriated, annually, the usual sum, to be expended by the Governor, to defray the contingent expenses of the Territory, including the salary of a clerk of the Executive Department; and there shall also be appropriated, annually, a sufficient sum, to be expended by the Secretary of the Territory, and upon an estimate to be made by the Secretary of the Treasury of the United States, to defray the expenses of the Legislative Assembly, the printing of the laws, and other incidental expenses; and the Governor and Secretary of the Territory shall, in the disbursement of all moneys intrusted to them, be governed solely by the instructions of the Secretary of the Treasury of the United States, and shall, semi-annually, account to the said Secretary for the manner in which the aforesaid moneys shall have been expended; and no expenditure shall be made by said Legislative Assembly for objects not specially authorized by the acts of Congress, making the appropriations, nor beyond the sums thus appropriated for such objects.

Sec. 13. *And be it further enacted,* That the Legislative Assembly of the Territory of Nebraska shall hold its first session at such time and place in said Territory as the Governor thereof shall appoint and direct; and at said first session, or as soon thereafter as they shall deem expedient, the Governor and Legislative Assembly shall proceed to locate and establish the seat of government for said Territory at such place as they may deem eligible; which place, however, shall thereafter be subject to be changed by the said Governor and Legislative Assembly.

Sec. 14. *And be it further enacted,* That a delegate to the House of Representatives of the United States, to serve for the term of two years, who shall be a citizen of the United States, may be elected by the voters qualified to elect members of the Legislative Assembly, who shall be entitled to the same rights and privileges as are exercised and enjoyed by the delegates from the several other Territories of the United States to the said House of Representatives, but the delegate first elected shall hold his seat only during the term of the Congress to which he shall be elected. The first election shall be held at such time and places, and be conducted in such manner, as the Governor shall appoint and direct; and at all subsequent elections the times, places, and manner of holding the elections, shall be prescribed by law. The person having the greatest number of votes shall be declared by the Governor to be duly elected; and a certificate thereof shall be given accordingly. That the Constitution, and all Laws of the United States which are not locally inapplicable, shall have the same force and effect within the said Territory of Nebraska as elsewhere within the United States, except the eighth section of the act preparatory to the admission of Missouri into the Union, approved March sixth, eighteen hundred and twenty, which, being inconsistent with the principle of non-intervention by Congress with slavery in the States and Territories, as recognized by the legislation of eighteen hundred and fifty, commonly called the Compromise Measures, is hereby declared inoperative and void; it being the true intent and meaning of this act not to legislate slavery into any Territory or State, nor to exclude it therefrom, but to leave the people thereof perfectly free to form and regulate their domestic institutions in their own way, subject only to the Constitution of the United States: *Provided,* That nothing herein contained shall be construed to revive or put in force any law or regulation which may have existed prior to the act of sixth March, eighteen hundred and twenty, either protecting, establishing, prohibiting, or abolishing slavery.

Sec. 15. *And be it further enacted,* That there shall hereafter be appropriated, as has been customary for the Territorial governments, a sufficient amount, to be expended under the direction of the said Governor of the Territory of Nebraska, not exceeding the sums heretofore appropriated for similar objects, for the erection of suitable public buildings at the seat of government, and for the purchase of a library, to be kept at the seat of government for the use of the Governor, Legislative Assembly, Judges of the Supreme Court, Secretary, Marshal, and Attorney of said Territory, and such other persons, and under such regulations, as shall be prescribed by law.

Sec. 16. *And be it further enacted,* That when the lands in the said Territory shall be surveyed under the direction of the government of the United States, preparatory to bringing the same into market, sections numbered sixteen and thirty-six in each township in said Territory shall be, and the same are hereby, reserved for the purpose of being applied to schools in aid Territory, and in the States and Territories hereafter to be erected out at the same.

Sec. 17. *And be it further enacted,* That, until otherwise provided by law, the Governor of said Territory may define the Judicial Districts of said Territory, and assign the judges who may be appointed for said Territory to the several districts; and also appoint the times and places for holding courts in the several counties or subdivisions in each of said Judicial Districts by proclamation, to be issued by him; but the Legislative Assembly, at their first or any subsequent session, may organize, alter, or modify such Judicial Districts, and assign the judges, and alter the times and places of holding the courts, as to them shall seem proper and convenient.

Sec. 18. *And be it further enacted,* That all officers to be appointed by the President, by and with the advice and consent of the Senate, for the Territory of Nebraska, who, by virtue of the provisions of any law now existing, or which may be enacted during the present Congress, are required to give security for moneys that may be intrusted with them for disbursement, shall give such security, at such time and place, and in such manner, as the Secretary of the Treasury may prescribe.

Sec. 19. *And be it further enacted,* That all that part of the Territory of the United States included within the following limits, except such portions thereof as are hereinafter expressly exempted from the operations of this act, to wit, beginning at a point on the western boundary of the State of Missouri, where the thirty-seventh parallel of north latitude crosses the same; thence west on said parallel to the eastern boundary of New Mexico; thence north on said boundary to latitude thirty-eight; thence following said boundary westward to the east boundary of the Territory of Utah, on the summit of the Rocky Mountains;

thence northward on said summit to the fortieth parallel of latitude; thence east on said parallel to the western boundary of the State of Missouri; thence south with the western boundary of said State to the place of beginning, be, and the same is hereby, created into a temporary government by the name of the Territory of Kansas; and when admitted as a State or States, the said Territory, or any portion of the same, shall be received into the Union with or without slavery, as their Constitution may prescribe at the time of their admission: *Provided,* That nothing in this act contained shall be construed to inhibit the government of the United States from dividing said Territory into two or more Territories, in such manner and at such times as Congress shall deem convenient and proper, or from attaching any portion of said Territory to any other state or Territory of the United States: *Provided further,* That nothing in this act contained shall be construed to impair the rights of person or property now pertaining to the Indians in said Territory, so long as such rights shall remain unextinguished by treaty between the United States and such Indians, or to include any territory which, by treaty with any Indian tribe, is not, without the consent of said tribe, to be included within the territorial limits or jurisdiction of any State or Territory; but all such territory shall be excepted out of the boundaries, and constitute no part of the Territory of Kansas, until said tribe shall signify their assent to the President of the United States to be included within the said Territory of Kansas, or to affect the authority of the government of the United States to make any regulation respecting such Indians, their lands, property, or other rights, by treaty, law, or otherwise, which it would have been competent to the government to make if this act had never passed.

Sec. 20. *And be it further enacted,* That the executive power and authority in and over said Territory of Kansas shall be vested in a Governor, who shall hold his office for four years, and until his successor shall be appointed and qualified, unless sooner removed by the President of the United States. The Governor shall reside within said Territory, and shall be commander-in-chief of the militia thereof. He may grant pardons and respites for offenses against the laws of said Territory, and reprieves for offenses against the laws of the United States, until the decision of the President can be made known thereon; he shall commission all officers who shall be appointed to office under the laws of the said Territory, and shall take care that the laws be faithfully executed.

Sec. 21. *And be it further enacted,* That there shall be a Secretary of said Territory, who shall reside therein, and hold his office for five years unless sooner removed by the President of the United States; he shall record and preserve all the laws and proceedings of the Legislative Assembly hereinafter constituted, and all the acts and proceedings of the Governor in his Executive Department; he shall transmit one copy of the laws and journals of the Legislative Assembly within thirty days after the end of each session, and one copy of the executive proceedings and official correspondence semi-annually, on the first days of January and July in each year, to the President of the United States, and two copies of the laws to the President of the Senate and to the Speaker of the House of Representatives, to be deposited in the libraries of Congress; and, in case of the death, removal, resignation, or absence of the Governor from the Territory, the Secretary shall be, and he is hereby, authorized and required to execute and perform all the powers and duties of the Governor during such vacancy or absence, or until another Governor shall be duly appointed and qualified to fill such vacancy.

Sec. 22. *And be it further enacted,* That the legislative power and authority of said Territory shall be vested in the Governor and a Legislative Assembly. The Legislative Assembly shall consist of a Council and House of Representatives. The Council shall consist of thirteen members, having the qualifications of voters, as hereinafter prescribed, whose term of service shall continue two years. The House of Representatives shall, at its first session, consist of twenty-six members, possessing the same qualifications as prescribed for members of the Council, and whose term of service shall continue one year. The number of representatives may be increased by the Legislative Assembly, from time to time, in proportion to the increase of qualified voters: *Provided,* That the whole number shall never exceed thirty-nine. An apportionment shall be made, as nearly equal as practicable, among the several counties or districts, for the election of the Council and Representatives, giving to each section of the Territory representation in the ratio of its qualified voters as nearly as may be. And the members of the Council and of the House of Representatives shall reside in, and be inhabitants of, the district or county, or counties, for which they may be elected, respectively. Previous to the first election, the Governor shall cause a census, or enumeration of the inhabitants and qualified voters of the several counties and districts of the Territory, to be taken by such persons and in such mode as the Governor shall designate and appoint; and the persons so appointed shall receive a reasonable compensation therefor. And the first election shall be held at such time and places, and be conducted in such manner, both as to the persons who shall superintend such election and the returns thereof, as the Governor shall appoint and direct; and he shall at the same time declare the number of members of the Council and House of Representatives to which each of the counties or districts shall be entitled under this act. The persons having the highest number of legal votes in each of said Council Districts for members of the Council, shall be declared by the Governor to be duly elected to the Council; and the persons having the highest number of legal votes for the House of Representatives, shall be declared by the Governor to be duly elected members of said house: *Provided,* That in case two or more persons voted for shall have an equal number of votes, and in case a vacancy shall otherwise occur in either branch of the Legislative Assembly, the Governor shall order a new election; and the persons thus elected to the Legislative Assembly shall meet at such place and on such day as the Governor shall appoint; but thereafter, the time, place, and manner of holding and conducting all elections by the people, and the apportioning the representation in the several counties or districts to the Council and House of Representatives, according to the number of qualified voters, shall be prescribed by law, as well as the day of the commencement of the regular sessions of the Legislative Assembly: *Provided,* That no session in any one year shall exceed the term of forty days, except the first session, which may continue sixty days.

Sec. 23. *And be it further enacted,* That every free white male inhabitant above the age of twenty-one years, who shall be an actual resident of said Territory, and shall possess the qualifications hereinafter prescribed, shall be entitled to vote at the first election, and shall be eligible to any office within the said Territory; but the qualifications of voters, and of holding office, at all subsequent elections, shall be such as shall be prescribed by the Legislative Assembly: *Provided,* That the right of suffrage and of holding office shall be exercised only by citizens of the United States, and those who shall have declared, on oath, their intention to become such, and shall have taken an oath to support the Constitution of the United States and the provisions of this act: *And, provided further,* That no officer, soldier, seaman, or marine, or other person in the army or navy of the United States, or attached to troops in the service of the United States, shall be allowed to vote or hold office in said Territory by reason of being on service therein.

Sec. 24. *And be it further enacted,* That the legislative power of the Territory shall extend to all rightful subjects of legislation consistent with the Constitution of the United States and the provisions of this act; but no law shall be passed interfering with the primary disposal of the soil; no tax shall be imposed upon the property of the United States; nor shall the lands or other property of nonresidents be taxed higher than the lands or other property of residents. Every bill which shall have passed the Council and House of Representatives of the said Territory shall, before it become a law, be presented to the Governor of the Territory; if he approve, he shall sign it; but if not, he shall return it with his objections to the house in which it originated, who shall enter the objections at large on their journal, and proceed to reconsider it. If, after such

reconsideration, two thirds of that house shall agree to pass the bill, it shall be sent, together with the objections, to the other house, by which it shall likewise be reconsidered, and, if approved by two thirds of that house, it shall become a law. But in all such cases the votes of both houses shall be determined by yeas and nays, to be entered on the journal of each house, respectively. If any bill shall not be returned by the Governor within three days (Sundays excepted) after it shall have been presented to him, the same shall be a law in like manner as if he had signed it, unless the assembly, by adjournment, prevent its return, in which case it shall not be a law.

Sec. 25. *And be it further enacted,* That all township, district, and county officers, not herein otherwise provided for, shall be appointed or elected as the case may be, in such manner as shall be provided by the Governor and Legislative Assembly of the Territory of Kansas. The Governor shall nominate, and, by and with the advice and consent of the Legislative Council, appoint all officers not herein otherwise provided for; and, in the first instance, the Governor alone may appoint all said officers, who shall hold their offices until the end of the first session of the Legislative Assembly; and shall lay off the necessary districts for members of the Council and House of Representatives, and all other officers.

Sec. 26. *And be it further enacted,* That no member of the Legislative Assembly shall hold, or be appointed to, any office which shall have been created, or the salary or emoluments of which shall have been increased, while he was a member, during the term for which he was elected, and for one year after the expiration of such term; but this restriction shall not be applicable to members of the first Legislative Assembly; and no person holding a commission or appointment under the United States, except postmasters, shall be a member of the Legislative Assembly, or shall hold any office under the government of said Territory.

Sec. 27. *And be it further enacted,* That the judicial power of said Territory shall be vested in a supreme court, district courts, probate courts, and in justices of the peace. The Supreme Court shall consist of chief justice and two associate justices, any two of whom shall constitute a quorum, and who shall hold a term at the seat of government of said Territory annually; and they shall hold their offices during the period of four years, and until their successors shall be appointed and qualified. The said Territory shall be divided into three judicial districts, and a district court shall be held in each of said districts by one of the justices of the Supreme Court, at such times and places as may be prescribed by law; and the said judges shall, after their appointments, respectively, reside in the districts which shall be assigned them. The jurisdiction of the several courts herein provided for, both appellate and original, and that of the probate courts and of justices of the peace, shall be as limited by law: *Provided,* That justices of the peace shall not have jurisdiction of any matter in controversy when the title or boundaries of land may be in dispute, or where the debt or sum claimed shall exceed one hundred dollars; and the said supreme and district courts, respectively, shall possess chancery as well as common law jurisdiction. Each District Court, or the judge thereof, shall appoint its clerk, who shall also be the register in chancery, and shall keep his office at the place where the court may be held. Writs of error, bills of exception, and appeals, shall be allowed in all cases from the final decisions of said district courts to the Supreme Court, under such regulations as may be prescribed by law; but in no case removed to the Supreme Court shall trial by jury be allowed in said court. The Supreme Court, or the justices thereof, shall appoint its own clerk, and every clerk shall hold his office at the pleasure of the court for which he shall have been appointed. Writs of error, and appeals from the final decisions of said supreme court, shall be allowed, and may be taken to the Supreme Court of the United States, in the same manner and under the same regulations as from the Circuit Courts of the United States, where the value of the property, or the amount in controversy, to be ascertained by the oath or affirmation of either party, or other competent witness, shall exceed one thousand dollars; except only that in all cases involving title to slaves, the said writs of error or appeals shall be allowed and decided by said supreme court, without regard to the value of the matter, property, or title in controversy; and except also that a writ of error or appeal shall also be allowed to the Supreme Court of the United States, from the decision of the said supreme court created by this act, or of any judge thereof, or of the district courts created by this act, or of any judge thereof, upon any writ of habeas corpus, involving the question of personal freedom: *Provided,* That nothing herein contained shall be construed to apply to or affect the provisions of the "act respecting fugitives from justice, and persons escaping from the service of their masters," approved February twelfth, seventeen hundred and ninety-three, and the "act to amend and supplementary to the aforesaid act," approved September eighteenth, eighteen hundred and fifty; and each of the said district courts shall have and exercise the same jurisdiction in all cases arising under the Constitution and laws of the United States as is vested in the Circuit and District Courts of the United States; and the said supreme and district courts of the said Territory, and the respective judges thereof, shall and may grant writs of habeas corpus in all cases in which the same are granted by the judges of the United States in the District of Columbia; and the first six days of every term of said courts, or so much thereof as may be necessary, shall be appropriated to the trial of causes arising under the said Constitution and laws, and writs of error and appeal in all such cases shall be made to the Supreme Court of said Territory, the same as in other cases. The said clerk shall receive the same fees in all such cases, which the clerks of the district courts of Utah Territory now receive for similar services.

Sec. 28. *And be it further enacted,* That the provisions of the act entitled "An act respecting fugitives from justice, and persons escaping from the service of their masters," approved February twelfth, seventeen hundred and ninety-three, and the provisions of the act entitled "An act to amend, and supplementary to, the aforesaid act," approved September eighteenth, eighteen hundred and fifty, be, and the same are hereby, declared to extend to and be in full force within the limits of the said Territory of Kansas.

Sec. 29. *And be it further enacted,* That there shall be appointed an attorney for said Territory, who shall continue in office for four years, and until his successor shall be appointed and qualified, unless sooner removed by the President, and who shall receive the same fees and salary as the Attorney of the United States for the present Territory of Utah. There shall also be a marshal for the Territory appointed, who shall hold his office for four years, and until his successor shall be appointed and qualified, unless sooner removed by the President, and who shall execute all processes issuing from the said courts when exercising their jurisdiction as Circuit and District Courts of the United States; he shall perform the duties, be subject to the same regulations and penalties, and be entitled to the same fees, as the Marshal of the District Court of the United States for the present Territory of Utah and shall, in addition, be paid two hundred dollars annually as a compensation for extra services.

Sec. 30. *And be it further enacted,* That the Governor, Secretary, Chief Justice, and Associate Justices, Attorney, and Marshal, shall be nominated, and, by and with the advice and consent of the Senate, appointed by the President of the United States. The Governor and Secretary to be appointed as aforesaid shall, before they act as such, respectively take an oath or affirmation before the district judge or some justice of the peace in the limits of said Territory, duly authorized to administer oaths and affirmations by the laws now in therein, or before the Chief Justice or some Associate Justice of the Supreme Court of the United States, to support the Constitution of the United States, and faithfully to discharge the duties of their respective offices, which said oaths, when so taken, shall be certified by the person by whom the same shall have been taken; and such certificates shall be received and recorded by the said secretary among the executive proceedings; and the Chief Justice and Associate Justices, and all other civil officers in said Territory, before they act as such, shall take a like oath or affirmation before the said Governor or Secretary, or some Judge or Justice of the Peace of the Territory who may be duly commissioned and qualified, which said oath or affirmation shall be certified and transmitted by the person taking the same to the Secretary, to be by him recorded as aforesaid; and, afterwards, the like oath or affirmation shall be taken, certified, and recorded, in such manner and form as may be prescribed by law. The Governor shall receive an annual salary of two thousand five hundred dollars. The Chief Justice and Associate Justices shall receive an annual salary of two thousand dollars. The Secretary shall receive an annual salary of two thousand dollars. The said salaries shall be paid quarter-yearly, from the dates of the respective appointments, at the Treasury of the United States; but no such payment shall be made until said officers shall have entered upon the duties of their respective appointments. The members of the Legislative Assembly shall be entitled to receive three dollars each per day during their attendance at the sessions thereof, and three dollars each for every twenty miles' travel in going to and returning from the said sessions, estimated according to the nearest usually travelled route; and an additional allowance of three dollars shall be paid to the presiding officer of each house for each day he shall so preside. And a chief clerk, one assistant clerk, a sergeant-at-arms, and door-keeper, may be chosen for each house; and the chief clerk shall receive four dollars per day, and the said other officers three dollars per day, during the session of the Legislative Assembly; but no other officers shall be paid by the United States: *Provided,* That there shall be but one session of the Legislature annually, unless, on an extraordinary occasion, the Governor shall think proper to call the Legislature together. There shall be appropriated, annually, the usual sum, to be expanded by the Governor, to defray the contingent expenses of the Territory, including the salary of a clerk of the Executive Department and there shall also be appropriated, annually, a sufficient sum, to be expended by the Secretary of the Territory, and upon an estimate to be made by the Secretary of the Treasury of the United States, to defray the expenses of the Legislature Assembly, the printing of the laws, and other incidental expenses; and the Governor and Secretary of the Territory shall, in the disbursement of all moneys intrusted to them, be governed solely by the instructions of the secretary of the Treasury of the United States, and shall, semi-annually, account to the said secretary for the manner in which the aforesaid moneys shall have been expended; and no expenditure shall be made by said Legislative Assembly for objects not specially authorized by the acts of Congress making the appropriations, nor beyond the sums thus appropriated for such objects.

Sec. 31. *And be it further enacted,* That the seat of government of said Territory is hereby located temporarily at Fort Leavenworth; and that such portions of the public buildings as may not be actually used and needed for military purposes, may be occupied and used, under the direction of the Governor and Legislative Assembly, for such public purposes as may be required under the provisions of this act.

Sec. 32. *And be it further enacted,* That a delegate to the House of Representatives of the United States, to serve for the term of two years, who shall be a citizen of the United States, may be elected by the voters qualified to elect members of the Legislative Assembly, who shall be entitled to the same rights and privileges as are exercised and enjoyed by the delegates from the several other Territories of the United States to the said House of Representatives, but the delegate first elected shall hold his seat only during the term of the Congress to which he shall be elected. The first election shall be held at such time and places, and be conducted in such manner, as the Governor shall appoint and direct; and at all subsequent elections, the times, places, and manner of holding the elections shall be prescribed by law. The person having the greatest number of votes shall be declared by the Governor to be duly elected, and a certificate thereof shall be given accordingly. That the Constitution, and all laws of the United States which are not locally inapplicable, shall have the same force and effect within the said Territory of Kansas as elsewhere within the United States, except the eighth section of the act preparatory to the admission of Missouri into the Union, approved March sixth, eighteen hundred and twenty, which, being inconsistent with the principle of non-intervention by Congress with slavery in the States and Territories, as recognized by the legislation of eighteen hundred and fifty, commonly called the Compromise Measures, is hereby declared inoperative and void; it being the true intent and meaning of this act not to legislate slavery into any Territory or State, nor to exclude it therefrom, but to leave the people thereof perfectly free to form and regulate their domestic institutions in their own way, subject only to the Constitution of the United States: *Provided,* That nothing herein contained shall be construed to revive or put in force any law or regulation which may have existed prior to the act of sixth of March, eighteen hundred and twenty, either protecting, establishing, prohibiting, or abolishing slavery.

Sec. 33. *And be it further enacted,* That there shall hereafter be appropriated, as has been customary for the territorial governments, a sufficient amount, to be expended under the direction of the said Governor of the Territory of Kansas, not exceeding the sums heretofore appropriated for similar objects, for the erection of suitable public buildings at the seat of government, and for the purchase of a library, to be kept at the seat of government for the use of the Governor, Legislative Assembly, Judges of the Supreme Court, Secretary, Marshal, and Attorney of said Territory, and such other persons, and under such regulations, as shall be prescribed by law.

Sec. 34. *And be it further enacted,* That when the lands in the said Territory shall be surveyed under the direction of the government of the United States, preparatory to bringing the same into market, sections numbered sixteen and thirty-six in each township in said Territory shall be, and the same are hereby, reserved for the purpose of being applied to schools in said Territory, and in the States and Territories hereafter to be erected out of the same.

Sec. 35. *And be it further enacted,* That, until otherwise provided by law, the Governor of said Territory may define the Judicial Districts of said Territory, and assign the judges who may be appointed for said Territory to the several districts; and also appoint the times and places for holding courts in the several counties or subdivisions in each of said judicial districts by proclamation, to be issued by him; but the Legislative Assembly, at their first or any subsequent session, may organize, alter, or modify such judicial districts, and assign the judges, and alter the times and places of holding the courts as to them shall seem proper and convenient.

Sec. 36. *And be it further enacted,* That all officers to be appointed by the President, by and with the advice and consent of the Senate, for the Territory of Kansas, who, by virtue of the provisions of any law now existing, or which may be enacted during the present Congress, are required to give security for moneys that may be intrusted with them for disbursement, shall give such security, at such time and place, and in such manner as the Secretary of the Treasury may prescribe.

Sec. 37. *And be it further enacted,* That all treaties, laws, and other engagements made by the government of the United States with the Indian tribes inhabiting the territories embraced within this act, shall be faithfully and rigidly observed, notwithstanding any thing contained in this act; and that the existing agencies and superintendencies of said Indians be continued with the same powers and duties which are now prescribed by law, except that the President of the United States may, at his discretion, change the location of the office of superintendent.

See also THE LECOMPTON CONSTITUTION, 1855; CHARLES SUMNER, CRIME AGAINST KANSAS ACT; THE TOPEKA CONSTITUTION, 1855; THE CONSTITUTION OF KANSAS, 1861.

Source:
Statutes at Large, Vol. 10, pp. 277–290.

Dred Scott Decision
(*Scott v. Sandford*[sic]), 1857

Landmark lawsuit decided 7-2 by a Southern-dominated Supreme Court on March 6, 1857, on the status of slavery in federal territories. In 1834 Dred Scott, a black slave, was taken by his owner, Dr. John Emerson, from Missouri, a slave state, to Illinois, a free state, and then to Wisconsin Territory, where slavery was prohibited by the Missouri Compromise; he later returned to Missouri. In the original suit brought in 1846, Scott and his wife, Harriet, sued their owner for freedom on the grounds that he had become free through residence in a free state and a free territory. (To save money, Harriet Scott was dropped from the case and it was stipulated that the decision would also apply to her.) The Supreme Court accepted a newly formed case pitting Scott against the brother of Dr. Emerson's widow, now remarried and living in England. The Court, in a decision by Chief Justice Roger B. Taney, ruled that residence in a free state did not confer freedom on a slave; that a black "whose ancestors were . . . sold as slaves" was not a citizen and could not sue in a federal court; and that Congress had no power to prohibit slavery in the territories, rendering the Missouri Compromise, which had been repealed with the Kansas-Nebraska Act, unconstitutional.

This was only the second time an act of Congress was declared unconstitutional by the Supreme Court. According to one student of the case, "American legal and constitutional scholars consider [it] to be the worst [decision] ever rendered by the Supreme Court." The verdict fueled the ongoing controversy over slavery.

At the time of the ruling, Scott's nominal owner was John F. A. Sanford, whose name was officially misspelled in the court records as "Sandford."

———————————— ⌁ ————————————

DRED SCOTT, PLAINTIFF IN ERROR, v. JOHN F. A. SANDFORD.

Mr. Chief Justice Taney delivered the opinion of the court.

This case has been twice argued. After the argument at the last term, differences of opinion were found to exist among the members of the court; and as the questions in controversy are of the highest importance, and the court was at that time much pressed by the ordinary business of the term, it was deemed advisable to continue the case, and direct a re-argument on some of the points, in order that we might have an opportunity of giving to the whole subject a more deliberate consideration. It has accordingly been again argued by counsel, and considered by the court; and I now proceed to deliver its opinion.

There are two leading questions presented by the record:

1. Had the Circuit Court of the United States jurisdiction to hear and determine the case between these parties? And

2. If it had jurisdiction, is the judgment it has given erroneous or not?

The plaintiff in error, who was also the plaintiff in the court below, was, with his wife and children, held as slaves by the defendant, in the State of Missouri; and he brought this action in the Circuit Court of the United States for that district, to assert the title of himself and his family to freedom.

The declaration is in the form usually adopted in that State to try questions of this description, and contains the averment necessary to give the court jurisdiction; that he and the defendant are citizens of different States; that is, that he is a citizen of Missouri, and the defendant & citizen of New York.

The defendant pleaded in abatement to the jurisdiction of the court, that the plaintiff was not a citizen of the State of Missouri, as alleged in his declaration, being a Negro of African descent, whose ancestors were of pure African blood, and who were brought into this country and sold as slaves.

To this plea the plaintiff demurred, and the defendant joined in demurrer. The court overruled the plea, and gave judgment that the defendant should answer over. And he thereupon put in sundry pleas in bar, upon which issues were joined; and at the trial the verdict and judgment were in his favor. Whereupon the plaintiff brought this writ of error.

Before we speak of the pleas in bar, it will be proper to dispose of the questions which have arisen on the plea in abatement.

That plea denies the right of the plaintiff to sue in a court of the United States , for the reasons therein stated.

If the question raised by it is legally before us, and the court should be of opinion that the facts stated in it disqualify the plaintiff from becoming a citizen, in the sense in which that word is used in the Constitution of the United States, then the judgment of the Circuit Court is erroneous, and must be reversed.

It is suggested, however, that this plea is not before us; and that as the judgment in the court below on this plea was in favor of the plaintiff; he does not seek to reverse it, or bring it before the court for revision by his writ of error; and also that the defendant waived this defense by pleading over, and thereby admitted the jurisdiction of the court.

But, in making this objection, we think the peculiar and limited jurisdiction of courts of the United States has not been adverted to. This peculiar and limited jurisdiction has made it necessary, in these courts, to adopt different rules and principles of pleading, so far as jurisdiction is concerned, from those which regulate courts of common law in England, and in the different States of the Union which have adopted the common-law rules.

In these last-mentioned courts, where their character and rank are analogous to that of a Circuit Court of the United States; in other words, where they are what the law terms courts of general jurisdiction; they are presumed to have jurisdiction, unless the contrary appears. No averment in the pleadings of the plaintiff is necessary, in order to give jurisdiction. If the defendant objects to it, he must plead it specially, and unless the fact on which he relies is found to be true by a jury, or admitted to be true by the plaintiff, the jurisdiction cannot be disputed in an appellate court.

Now, it is not necessary to inquire whether in courts of that description a party who pleads over in bar, when a plea to the jurisdiction has been ruled against him, does or does not waive his plea; nor whether upon a judgment in his favor on the pleas in bar, and a writ of error brought by the plaintiff, the question upon the plea in abatement would be open for revision in the appellate court. Cases that may have been decided in such courts, or rules that may have been laid down by common-law pleaders, can have no influence in the decision in this court. Because, under the Constitution and laws of the United States, the rules which govern the pleadings in its courts, in questions of jurisdiction, stand on different principles and are regulated by different laws.

This difference arises, as we have said, from the peculiar character of the Government of the United States. For although it is sovereign and supreme in its appropriate sphere of action, yet it does not possess all the powers which usually belong to the sovereignty of a nation. Certain specified powers, enumerated in the Constitution, have been conferred upon it; and neither the legislative, executive, nor judicial departments of the Government can lawfully exercise any authority beyond the limits marked out by the Constitution. And in regulating the judicial department, the cases in which the courts of the United States shall have jurisdiction are particularly and specifically enumerated and defined; and they are not authorized to take cognizance of any case which does not come within the description therein specified. Hence, when a plaintiff sues in a court of the United States, it is necessary that he should show, in his pleading, that the suit he brings is within the jurisdiction of the court, and that he is entitled to sue there. And if he omits to do this, and should, by any oversight of the Circuit Court, obtain a judgment in his favor, the judgment would be reversed in the appellate court for want of jurisdiction in the court below. The jurisdiction would not be presumed, as in the case of a common-law English or State court, unless the contrary appeared. But the record, when it comes before the appellate court, must show, affirmatively, that the inferior court had authority, under the Constitution, to hear and determine the case. And if the plaintiff claims a right to sue in a Circuit Court of the United States, under that provision of the Constitution which gives jurisdiction in controversies between citizens of different States, he must distinctly aver in his pleading that they are citizens of different States; and he cannot maintain his suit without showing that fact in the pleadings.

This point was decided in the case of *Bingham v. Cabot* (in 3 Dall., 382) and ever since adhere to by the court. And in Jackson v. Ashton, (8 Pet., 148), it was held that the objection to which it was open could not be waived by the opposite party, because consent of parties could not give jurisdiction.

It is needless to accumulate cases on this subject. Those already referred to, and the cases of *Capron v. Van Noorden* (in 2 Cr., 126,) and *Montalet v. Murray* (4 Cr., 46,) are sufficient to show the rule of which we have spoken. The case of *Capron v. Van Noorden* strikingly illustrates the difference between a common-law court and a court of the United States.

If, however, the fact of citizenship is averred in the declaration, and the defendant does not deny it, and put it in issue by plea in abatement, he cannot offer evidence at the trial to disprove it, and consequently cannot avail himself of the objection in the appellate court, unless the defect should be apparent in some other part of the record. For if there is no plea in abatement, and the want of jurisdiction does not appear in any other part of the transcript brought up by the writ of error, the undisputed averment of citizenship in the declaration must be taken in this court to be true. In this case, the citizenship is averred, but it is denied by the defendant in the manner required by the rules of pleading, and the fact upon which the denial is based is admitted by the demurrer. And, if the plea and demurrer, and judgment of the court below upon it, are before us upon this record, the question to be decided is, whether the facts stated in the plea are sufficient to show that the plaintiff is not entitled to sue as a citizen in a court of the United States.

We think they are before us. The plea in abatement and the judgment of the court upon it, are a part of the judicial proceedings in the Circuit Court, and are there recorded as such; and a writ of error always brings up to the superior court the whole record of the proceedings in the court below. And in the case of the *United States v. Smith*, (11 Wheat., 172,) this court said, that the case being brought up by writ of error, the whole record was under the consideration of this court. And this being the case in

the present instance, the plea in abatement is necessarily under consideration; and it becomes, therefore, our duty to decide whether the facts stated in the plea are or are not sufficient to show that the plaintiff is not entitled to sue as a citizen in a court of the United States.

This is certainly a very serious question, and one that now for the first time has been brought for decision before this court. But it is brought here by those who have a right to bring it, and it is our duty to meet it and decide it.

The question is simply this: Can a Negro, whose ancestors were imported into this country, and sold as slaves, become a member of the political community formed and brought into existence by the Constitution of the United States, and as such become entitled to all the rights, and privileges, and immunities, guarantied by that instrument to the citizen? One of which rights is the privilege of suing in a court of the United States in the cases specified in the Constitution.

It will be observed, that the plea applies to that class of persons only whose ancestors were Negroes of the African race, and imported into this country, and sold and held as slaves. The only matter in issue before the court, therefore, is, whether the descendants of such slaves, when they shall be emancipated, or who are born of parents who had become free before their birth, are citizens of a State, in the sense in which the word citizen is used in the Constitution of the United States. And this being the only matter in dispute on the pleadings, the court must be understood as speaking in this opinion of that class only, that is, of those persons who are the descendants of Africans who were imported into this country, and sold as slaves.

The situation of this population was altogether unlike that of the Indian race. The latter, it is true, formed no part of the colonial communities, and never amalgamated with them in social connections or in government. But although they were uncivilized, they were yet a free and independent people, associated together in nations or tribes, and governed by their own laws. Many of these political communities were situated in territories to which the white race claimed the ultimate right of dominion. But that claim was acknowledged to be subject to the right of the Indians to occupy it as long as they thought proper, and neither the English nor colonial Governments claimed or exercised any dominion over the tribe or nation by whom it was occupied, nor claimed the right to the possession of the territory, until the tribe or nation consented to cede it. These Indian Governments were regarded and treated as foreign Governments, as much so as if an ocean had separated the red man from the white; and their freedom has constantly been acknowledged, from the time of the first emigration to the English colonies to the present day, by the different Governments which succeeded each other. Treaties have been negotiated with them, and their alliance sought for in war; and the people who compose these Indian political communities have always been treated as foreigners not living under our Government. It is true that the course of events has brought the Indian tribes within the limits of the United States under subjection to the white race; and it has been found necessary, for their sake as well as our own, to regard them as in a state of pupilage, and to legislate to a certain extent over them and the territory they occupy. But they may, without doubt, like the subjects of any other foreign Government, be naturalized by the authority of Congress, and become citizens of a State, and of the United States; and if an individual should leave his nation or tribe, and take up his abode among the white population, he would be entitled to all the rights and privileges which would belong to an emigrant from any other foreign people.

We proceed to examine the case as presented by the pleadings.

The words "people of the United States" and "citizens" are synonymous terms, and mean the same thing. The both describe the political body who, according to our republican institutions, form the sovereignty, and who hold the power and conduct the Government through their representatives. They are what we familiarly call the "sovereign people," and every citizen is one of this people, and a constituent member of this sovereignty. The question before us is, whether the class of persons described in the plea in abatement compose a portion of this people, and are constituent members of this sovereignty? We think they are not, and that they are not included, and were not intended to be included, under the word "citizens" in the Constitution, and can therefore claim none of the rights and privileges which that instrument provides for and secures to citizens of the United States. On the contrary, they were at that time considered as a subordinate and inferior class of beings, who had been subjugated by the dominant race, and, whether emancipated or not, yet remained subject to their authority, and had no rights or privileges but such as those who held the power and the Government might choose to grant them.

It is not the province of the court to decide upon the justice or injustice, the policy or impolicy, of these laws. The decision of that question belonged to the political or law-making power; to those who formed the sovereignty and framed the Constitution. The duty of the court is, to interpret the instrument they have framed, with the best lights we can obtain on the subject, and to administer it as we find it, according to its true intent and meaning when it was adopted.

In discussing this question, we must not confound the rights of citizenship which a State may confer within its own limits, and the rights of citizenship as a member of the Union. It does not by any means follow, because he has all the rights and privileges of a citizen of a State, that he must be a citizen of the United States. He may have all of the rights and privileges of the citizen of a State, and yet not be entitled to the rights and privileges of a citizen in any other State. For, previous to the adoption of the Constitution of the United States, every State had the undoubted right to confer on whomsoever it pleased the character of citizen, and to endow him with all its rights. But this character of course was confined to the boundaries of the State, and gave him no rights or privileges in other States beyond those secured to him by the laws of nations and the comity of States. Nor have the several States surrendered the power of conferring these rights and privileges by adopting the Constitution of the United States. Each State may still confer them upon an alien, or any one it thinks proper, or upon any class or description of persons; yet he would not be a citizen in the sense in which that word is used in the Constitution of the United States, nor entitled to sue as such in one of its courts, nor to the privileges and immunities of a citizen in the other States. The rights which he would acquire would be restricted to the State which gave them. The Constitution has conferred on Congress the right to establish an uniform rule of naturalization, and this right is evidently exclusive, and has always been held by this court to be so. Consequently, no State, since the adoption of the Constitution, can by naturalizing an alien invest him with the rights and privileges secured to a citizen of a State under the Federal Government, although, so far as the State alone was concerned, he would undoubtedly be entitled to the rights of a citizen, and clothed with all the rights and immunities which the Constitution and laws of the State attached to that character.

It is very clear, therefore, that no State can, by any act or law of its own, passed since the adoption of the Constitution, introduce a new member into the political community created by the Constitution of the United States. It cannot make him a member of this community by making him a member of its own. And for the same reason it cannot introduce any person, or description of persons, who were not intended to be embraced in this new political family, which the Constitution brought into existence, but were intended to be excluded from it.

The question then arises, whether the provisions of the Constitution, in relation to the personal rights and privileges to which the citizen of a State should be entitled, embraced the Negro African race, at that time in this country, or who might afterwards be imported, who had then or should afterwards be made free in any State; and to put it in the power of a single State to make him a citizen of the United States, and endue him with the full rights of citizenship in every other State without their consent? Does the Constitution of the United States act upon him whenever he shall be made free under the laws of a State, and raised there to the rank of a citizen, and immediately clothe him with all the privileges of a citizen in every other State, and in its own courts?

The court think the affirmative of these propositions cannot be maintained. And if it cannot, the plaintiff in error could not be a citizen of the State of Missouri, within the meaning of the Constitution of the United States, and, consequently, was not entitled to sue in its courts.

It is true, every person, and every class and description of persons, who were at the time of the adoption of the Constitution recognized as citizens in the several States, became also citizens of this new political body; but none other; it was formed by them, and for them and their posterity, but for no one else. And the personal rights and privileges guarantied to citizens of this new sovereignty were intended to embrace those only who were then members of the several State communities, or who should afterwards by birthright or otherwise become members, according to the provisions of the Constitution and the principles on which it was founded. It was the union of those who were at that time members of distinct and separate political communities into one political family, whose power, for certain specified purposes, was to extend over the whole territory of the United States. And it gave to each citizen rights and privileges outside of his State which he did not before possess, and placed him in every other State upon a perfect equality with its own citizens as to rights of person and rights of property; it made him a citizen of the United States.

It becomes necessary, therefore, to determine who were citizens of the several States when the Constitution was adopted. And in order to do this, we must recur to the Governments and institutions of the thirteen colonies, when they separated from Great Britain and formed new sovereignties, and took their places in the family of independent nations. We must inquire who, at that time, were recognized as the people or citizens of a State, whose rights and liberties had been outraged by the English Government; and who declared their independence, and assumed the powers of Government to defend their rights by force of arms.

In the opinion of the court, the legislation and histories of the times, and the language used in the Declaration of Independence, show, that neither the class of persons who had been imported as slaves, nor their descendants, whether they had become free or not, were then acknowledged as a part of the people, nor intended to be included in the general words used in that memorable instrument.

It is difficult at this day to realize the state of public opinion in relation to that unfortunate race, which prevailed in the civilized and enlightened portions of the world at the time of the Declaration of Independence, and when the Constitution of the United States was framed and adopted. But the public history of every European nation displays it in a manner too plain to be mistaken.

They had for more than a century before been regarded as beings of an inferior order, and altogether unfit to associate with the white race, either in social or political relations; and so far inferior, that they had no rights which the white man was bound to respect; and that the Negro might justly and lawfully be reduced to slavery for his benefit. He was bought and sold, and treated as an ordinary article of merchandise and traffic, whenever a profit could be made by it. This opinion was at that time fixed and universal in the civilized portion of the white race. It was regarded as an axiom in morals as well as in politics, which no one thought of disputing, or supposed to be open to dispute; and men in every grade and position in society daily and habitually acted upon it in their private pursuits, as well as in matters of public concern, without doubting for a moment the correctness of this opinion.

And in no nation was this opinion more firmly fixed or more uniformly acted upon than by the English Government and English people. They not only seized them on the coast of Africa, and sold them or held them in slavery for their own use; but they took them as ordinary articles of merchandise to every country where they could make a profit on them, and were far more extensively engaged in this commerce than any other nation in the world.

The opinion thus entertained and acted upon in England was naturally impressed upon the colonies they founded on this side of the Atlantic. And, accordingly, a Negro of the African race was regarded by them as an article of property, and held, and bought and sold as such, in every one of the thirteen colonies which united in the Declaration of Independence, and afterwards formed the Constitution of the United States. The slaves were more or less numerous in the different colonies, as slave labor was found more or less profitable. But of one seems to have doubted the correctness of the prevailing opinion of the time.

The legislation of the different colonies furnishes positive and indisputable proof of this fact.

It would be tedious, in this opinion, to enumerate the various laws they passed upon this subject. It will be sufficient, as a sample of the legislation which then generally prevailed throughout the British colonies, to give the laws of two of them; one being still a large slaveholding State, and the other the first State in which slavery ceased to exist.

The province of Maryland, in 1717, (ch. 13, s. 5,) passed a law declaring "that if any free Negro or mulatto intermarry with any white woman, or if any white man shall intermarry with any Negro or mulatto woman, such Negro or mulatto shall become a slave during life, excepting mulattos born of white women, who, for such intermarriage, shall only become servants for seven years, to be disposed of as the justices of the county court, where such marriage so happens, shall think fit; to be applied by them towards the support of a public school within the said county. And any white man or white woman who shall intermarry as aforesaid, with any Negro or mulatto, such white man or white woman shall become servants during the term of seven years, and shall be disposed of by the justices as aforesaid, and be applied to the uses aforesaid."

The other colonial law to which we refer was passed by Massachusetts in 1705, (chap. 6,) It is entitled "An act for the better preventing of a spurious and mixed issue," &c.; and it provides, that "if any Negro or mulatto shall presume to smite or strike any person of the English or other Christian nation, such Negro or mulatto shall be severely whipped, at the discretion of the justices before whom the offender shall be convicted."

And "that none of her Majesty's English or Scottish subjects, nor of any other Christian nation, within this province, shall contract matrimony with any Negro or mulatto; nor shall any person, duly authorized to solemnize marriage, presume to join any such in marriage, on pain of forfeiting the sum of fifty pounds; one moiety thereof to her Majesty, for and towards the support of the Government within this province, and the other moiety to him or them that shall inform and sue for the same, in any of her Majesty's courts of record within the province, by bill, plaint, or information."

We give both of these laws in the words used by the respective legislative bodies, because the language in which they are framed, as well as the provisions contained in them, show, too plainly to be misunderstood, the degraded condition of this unhappy race. They were still in force when the Revolution began, and are a faithful index to the state of feeling towards the class of persons of whom they speak, and of the position they occupied throughout the thirteen colonies, in the eyes and thoughts of the men who framed the Declaration of Independence and established the State Constitutions and Governments. They show that a perpetual and impassable barrier was intended to be erected between the white race and the one which they had reduced to slavery, and governed as subjects with absolute and despotic power, and which they then looked upon as so far below them in the scale of created beings, that intermarriages between white persons and Negroes or mulattos were regarded as unnatural and immoral, and punished as crimes, not only in the parties, but in the person who joined them in marriage. And no distinction in this respect was made between the free Negro or mulatto

and the slave, but this stigma, of the deepest degradation, was fixed upon the whole race.

We refer to these historical facts for the purpose of showing the fixed opinions concerning that race, upon which the statesmen of that day spoke and acted. It is necessary to do this, in order to determine whether the general terms used in the Constitution of the United States, as to the rights of man and the rights of the people, was intended to include them, or to give to them or their posterity the benefit of any of its provisions.

The language of the Declaration of Independence is equally conclusive:

It begins by declaring that, "when in the course of human events it becomes necessary for one-people to dissolve the political bands which have connected them with another, and to assume among the powers of the earth the separate and equal station to which the laws of nature and nature's God entitle them, a decent respect for the opinions of mankind requires that they should declare the causes which impel them to the separation."

It then proceeds to say: "We hold these truths to be self-evident: that all men are created equal; that they are endowed by their Creator with certain unalienable rights; that among them is life, liberty, and the pursuit of happiness; that to secure these rights, Governments are instituted, deriving their just powers from the consent of the governed."

The general words above quoted would seem to embrace the whole human family, and if they were used in a similar instrument at this day would be so understood. But it is too clear for dispute, that the enslaved African race were not intended to be included, and formed no part of the people who framed and adopted this declaration; for if the language, as understood in that day, would embrace them, the conduct of the distinguished men who framed the Declaration of Independence would have been utterly and flagrantly inconsistent with the principles they asserted; and instead of the sympathy of mankind, to which they so confidently appealed, they would have deserved and received universal rebuke and reprobation.

Yet the men who framed this declaration were great men—high in literary acquirements—high in their sense of honor, and incapable of asserting principles inconsistent with those on which they were acting. They perfectly understood the meaning of the language they used, and how it would be understood by others; and they knew that it would not in any part of the civilized world be supposed to embrace the Negro race, which, by common consent, had been excluded from civilized Governments and the family of nations, and doomed to slavery. They spoke and acted according to the then established doctrines and principles, and in the ordinary language of the day, and no one misunderstood them. The unhappy black race were separated from the white by indelible marks, and laws long before established, and were never thought of or spoken of except as property, and when the claims of the owner or the profit of the trader were supposed to need protection.

This state of public opinion had undergone no change when the Constitution was adopted, as is equally evident from its provisions and language.

The brief preamble sets forth by whom it was formed, for what purposes, and for whose benefit and protection. It declares that it is formed by the *people* for the United States; that is to say, by those who were members of the different political communities in the several States; and its great object is declared to be to secure the blessings of liberty to themselves and their posterity. It speaks in general terms of the *people* of the United States, and of *citizens* of the several States, when it is providing for the exercise of the powers granted or the privileges secured to the citizen. It does not define what description of persons are intended to be included under these terms, or who shall be regarded as a citizen and one of the people. It uses them as terms so well understood, that no further description or definition was necessary.

But there are two clauses in the Constitution which point directly and specifically to the Negro race as a separate class of persons, and show clearly that they were not regarded as a portion of the people or citizens of the Government then formed.

One of these clauses reserves to each of the thirteen States the right to import slaves until the year 1808, if its thinks proper. And the importation which it thus sanctions was unquestionably of persons of the race of which we are speaking, as the traffic in slaves in the United States had always been confined to them. And by the other provision the States pledge themselves to each other to maintain the right of property of the master, by delivering up to him any slave who may have escaped from his service, and be found within their respective territories. By the first above-mentioned clause, therefore, the right to purchase and hold this property is directly sanctioned and authorized for twenty years by the people who framed the Constitution. And by the second, they pledge themselves to maintain and uphold the right of the master in the manner specified, as long as the Government they then formed should endure. And these two provisions show, conclusively, that neither the description of persons therein referred to, nor their descendants, were embraced in any of the other provisions of the Constitution; for certainly these two clauses were not intended to confer on them or their posterity the blessings of liberty, or any of the personal rights so carefully provided for the citizen.

No one of that race had ever migrated to the United States voluntarily; all of them had been brought here as articles of merchandise. The number that had been emancipated at that time were but few in comparison with those held in slavery; and they were identified in the public mind with the race to which they belonged, and regarded as a part of the slave population rather than the free. It is obvious that they were not even in the minds of the framers of the Constitution when they were conferring special rights and privileges upon the citizens of a State in every other part of the Union.

Indeed, when we look to the condition of this race in the several States at the time, it is impossible to believe that these rights and privileges were intended to be extended to them.

It is very true, that in that portion of the Union where the labor of the Negro race was found to be unsuited to the climate and unprofitable to the master, but few slaves were held at the time of the Declaration of Independence; and when the Constitution was adopted, it had entirely worn out in one of them, and measures had been taken for its gradual abolition in several others. But this change had not been produced by any change of opinion in relation to this race; but because it was discovered, from experience, that slave labor was unsuited to the climate and productions of these States: for some of the States, where it had ceased or nearly ceased to exist, were actively engaged in the slave trade, procuring cargoes on the coast of Africa, and transporting them for sale to those parts of the Union where their labor was found to be profitable, and suited to the climate and productions. And this traffic was openly carried on, and fortunes accumulated by it, without reproach from the people of the States where they resided. And it can hardly be supposed that, in the States where it was then countenanced in its worst form—that is, in the seizure and transportation—the people could have regarded those who were emancipated as entitled to equal rights with themselves.

And we may here again refer, in support of this proposition, to the plain and unequivocal language of the laws of the several States, some passed after the Declaration of Independence and before the Constitution was adopted, and some since the Government went into operation.

We need not refer, on this point, particularly to the laws of the present slaveholding States. Their statute books are full of provisions in relation to this class, in the same spirit with the Maryland law which we have before quoted. They have continued to treat them as an inferior class, and to subject them to strict police regulations, drawing a broad line of distinction between the citizen and the slave races, and legislating in relation to them upon the same principle which prevailed at the time of the Declaration of Independence. As relates to these States, it is too plain for argument, that they have never been regarded as a part of the people or citizens of the State, nor supposed to possess any political rights which the dominant race might not withhold or grant at their pleasure. And as long ago as 1822, the Court of Appeals of Kentucky decided that free Negroes and mulattos were not citizens within the meaning of the Constitution of the United States; and the correctness of this decision is recognized, and the same doctrine affirmed, in 1 Meigs's Tenn. Reports, 331.

And if we turn to the legislation of the States where slavery had worn out, or measures taken for its speedy abolition, we shall find the same opinions and principles equally fixed and equally acted upon.

Thus, Massachusetts, in 1786, passed a law similar to the colonial one of which we have spoken. The law of 1786, like the law of 1705, forbids the marriage of any white person with any Negro, Indian, or mulatto, and inflicts a penalty of fifty pounds upon any one who shall join them in marriage; and declares all such marriages absolutely null and void, and degrades thus the unhappy issue of the marriage by fixing upon it the stain of bastardy. And this mark of degradation was renewed, and again impressed upon the race in the careful and deliberate preparation of their revised code published in 1836. This code forbids any person from joining in marriage any white person with any Indian, Negro, or mulatto, and subjects the party who shall offend in this respect, to imprisonment, not exceeding six months, in the common jail, or to hard labor, and to a fine of not less than fifty nor more than two hundred dollars; and, like the law of 1786, it declares the marriage to be absolutely null and void. It will be seen that the punishment is increased by the code upon the person who shall marry them, by adding imprisonment to a pecuniary penalty.

So, too, in Connecticut. We refer more particularly to the legislation of this State, because it was not only among the first to put an end to slavery within its own territory, but was the first to fix a mark of reprobation upon the African slave trade. The law last mentioned was passed in October, 1788, about nine months after the State had ratified and adopted the present Constitution of the United States; and by that law it prohibited its own citizens, under severe penalties, from engaging in the trade, and declared all policies of insurance on the vessel or cargo made in the State to be null and void. But, up to the time of the adoption of the Constitution, there is nothing in the legislation of the State indicating any change of opinion as to the relative rights and position of the white and black races in this country, or indicating that it meant to place the latter, when free, upon a level with its citizens. And certainly nothing which would have led the slaveholding States to suppose, that Connecticut designed to claim for them, under the new Constitution, the equal rights privileges and rank of citizens in every other State.

The first step taken by Connecticut upon this subject was as early as 1774, when it passed an act forbidding the further importation of slave into the State. But the section containing the prohibition is introduced by the following preamble:

"And whereas the increase of slaves in this State is injurious to the poor, and inconvenient."

This recital would appear to have been carefully introduced, in order to prevent any misunderstanding of the motive which induced the Legislature to pass the law, and places it distinctly upon the interest and convenience of the white population—excluding the inference that it might have been intended in any degree for the benefit of the other.

And in the act of 1784, by which the issue of slaves, born after the time therein mentioned, were to be free at a certain age, the section is again introduced by a preamble assigning a similar motive for the act. It is in these words:

"Whereas sound policy requires that the abolition of slavery should be effected as soon as may be consistent with the rights of individuals, and the public safety and welfare"—showing that the right of property in the master was to be protected, and that the measure was one of policy, and to prevent the injury and inconvenience, to the whites, of a slave population in the State.

And still further pursuing its legislation, we find that in the same statute passed in 1774, which prohibited the further importation of slaves into the State, there is also a provision by which any Negro, Indian, or mulatto servant, who was found wandering out of the town or place to which he belonged, without a written pass such as is therein described, was made liable to be seized by any one, and taken before the next authority to be examined and delivered up to his master—who was required to pay the charge which had accrued thereby. And a subsequent section of the same law provides, that if any free Negro shall travel without such pass, and shall be stopped, seized, or taken up, he shall pay all charges arising thereby. And this law was in full operation when the Constitution of the United States was adopted, and was not repealed till 1797. So that up to that time free Negroes and mulattos were associated with servants and slaves in the police regulations established by the laws of the State.

And again, in 1833, Connecticut passed another law, which made it penal to set up or establish any school in that State for the instruction of persons of the African race not inhabitants of the State, or to instruct or teach in any such school or institution, or board or harbor for that purpose, any such person, without the previous consent in writing of the civil authority of the town in which such school or institution might be.

And it appears by the case of *Crandall v. The State*, reported in 10 Conn. Rep., 340, that upon an information filed against Prudence Crandall for a violation of this law, one of the points raised in the defense was, that the law was a violation of the Constitution of the United States; and that the persons instructed, although of the African race, were citizens of other States, and therefore entitled to the rights and privileges of citizens in the State of Connecticut. But Chief Justice Dagget, before whom the case was tried, held, that persons of that description were not citizens of a State, within the meaning of the word citizen in the Constitution of the United States, and were not therefore entitled to the privileges and immunities of citizens in other States.

The case was carried up to the Supreme Court of Errors of the State, and the question fully argued there. But the case went off upon another point, and no opinion was expressed on this question.

We have made this particular examination into the legislative and judicial action of Connecticut, because, from the early hostility it displayed to the slave trade on the coast of Africa, we may expect to find the laws of that State as lenient and favorable to the subject race as those of any other State in the Union; and if we find that at the time the Constitution was adopted, they were not even there raised to the rank of citizens, but were still held and treated as property, and the laws relating to them passed with reference altogether to the interest and convenience of the white race, we shall hardly find them elevated to a higher rank anywhere else.

A brief notice of the laws of two other States, and we shall pass on to other considerations.

By the laws of New Hampshire, collected and finally passed in 1815, no one was permitted to be enrolled in the militia of the State, but free white citizens; and the same provision is found in a subsequent collection of the laws, made in 1855. Nothing could more strongly mark the entire repudiation of the African race. The alien is excluded, because, being born in a foreign country, he cannot be a member of the community until he is naturalized. But why are the African race, born in the State, not permitted to share in one of the highest duties of the citizen? The answer is obvious; he is not, by the institutions and laws of the State, numbered among its people. He forms no part of the sovereignty of the State, and is not therefore called on to uphold and defend it.

Again, in 1822, Rhode Island, in its revised code, passed a law forbidding persons who were authorized to join persons in marriage, from joining in marriage any white person with any Negro, Indian, or mulatto, under the penalty of two hundred dollars, and declaring all such marriages absolutely null and void; and the same law was again re-enacted in its revised code of 1844. So that, down to the last- mentioned period, the strongest mark of inferiority and degradation was fastened upon the American race in that State.

It would be impossible to enumerate and compress in the space usually allotted to an opinion of a court, the various laws, marking the condition of this race, which were passed from time to time after the Revolution, and before and since the adoption of the Constitution of the United States. In addition to those already referred to, it is sufficient to say, that Chancellor Kent, whose accuracy and research no one will question, states in the sixth edition of his Commentaries, (published in 1848, 2 vol., 258, note *b*,) that in no part of the country except Maine, did the African race, in point of fact, particulate equally with the whites in the exercise of civil and political rights.

The legislation of the States therefore shows, in a manner not to be mistaken, the inferior and subject condition of that race at the time the Constitution was adopted, and long afterwards, throughout the thirteen States by which that instrument was framed; and it is hardly consistent with the respect due to these States, to suppose that they regarded at that time, as fellow-citizens and members of the sovereignty, a class of beings whom they had thus stigmatized; whom, as we are bound, out of respect to the State sovereignties, to assume they had deemed it just and necessary thus to stigmatize, and upon whom they had impressed such deep and enduring marks of inferiority and degradation; or, that when they met in convention to form the Constitution, they looked upon them as a portion of their constituents, or designed to include them in the provisions so carefully inserted for the security and protection of the liberties and rights of their citizens. It cannot be supposed that they intended to secure to them rights, and privileges, and rank, in the new political body throughout the Union, which every one of them denied within the limits of its own dominion. More especially, it cannot be believed that the large slaveholding States regarded them as included in the word citizens, or would have consented to a Constitution which might compel them to receive them in that character from another State. For if they were so received, and entitled to the privileges and immunities of citizens, it would exempt them from the operation of the special laws and from the police regulations which they considered to be necessary for their own safety. It would give to persons of the Negro race, who were recognized as citizens in any one State of the Union, the right to enter every other State whenever they pleased, singly or in companies, without pass or passport, and without obstruction, to sojourn there as long as they pleased, to go where they pleased at every hour of the day or night without molestation, unless they committed some violation of law for which a white man would be punished; and it would give them the full liberty of speech in public and in private upon all subjects upon which its own citizens might speak; to hold public meetings upon political affairs, and to kept and carry arms wherever they went. And all of this would be done in the face of the subject race of the same color, both free and slaves, and inevitably producing discontent and insubordination among them, and endangering the peace and safety of the State.

It is impossible, it would seem, to believe that the great men of the slaveholding States, who took so large a share in framing the Constitution of the United States, and exercised so much influence in procuring its adoption, could have been so forgetful or regardless of their own safety and the safety of those who trusted and confided in them.

Besides, this want of foresight and care would have been utterly inconsistent with the caution displayed in providing for the admission of new members into this political family. For, when they gave to the citizens of each State the privileges and immunities of citizens in the several States, they at the same time took from the several States the power of naturalization, and confined that power exclusively to the Federal Government. No State was willing to permit another State to determine who could or should not be admitted as one of its citizens, and entitled to demand equal rights and privileges with their own people, within their own territories. The right of naturalization was therefore, with one accord, surrender by the States, and confided to the Federal Government. And this power granted to Congress to establish an uniform rule of *naturalization* is, by the well-understood meaning of the word, confined to persons born in a foreign country, under a foreign Government. It is not a power to raise to the rank of a citizen any one born in the United States, who, from birth or parentage, by the laws of the country, belongs to an inferior and subordinate class. And when we find the States guarding themselves from the indiscreet or improper admission by other States of emigrants from other countries, by giving the power exclusively to Congress, we cannot fail to see that they could never have left with the States a much more important power—that is, the power of transforming into citizens a numerous class of persons, who in that character would be much more dangerous to the peace and safety of a large portion of the Union, that the few foreigners one of the States might improperly naturalize. The Constitution upon its adoption obviously took from the States all power by any subsequent legislation to introduce as a citizen into the political family of the United States any one, no matter where he was born, or what might be his character or condition; and it gave to Congress the power to confer this character upon those only who were born outside of the dominions of the United States. And no law of a State, therefore, passed since the Constitution was adopted, can give any right of citizenship outside of its own territory.

A clause similar to the one in the Constitution, in relation to the rights and immunities of citizens of one State in the other States, was contained in the Articles of Confederation. But there is a difference of language, which is worthy of note. The provision in the Articles of Confederation was, "that the *free inhabitants* of each of the States, paupers, vagabonds, and fugitives from justice, excepted, should be entitled to all the privileges and immunities of free citizens in the several States."

It will be observed, that under this Confederation, each State had the right to decide for itself, and in its own tribunals, whom it would acknowledge as a free inhabitant of another State. The term *free inhabitant*, in the generality of its terms, would certainly include one of the African race who had been manumitted. But no example, we think, can be found of his admission to all the privileges of citizenship in any State of the Union after these Articles were formed, and while they continued in force. And, notwithstanding the generality of the words "free inhabitants," it is very clear that, according to their accepted meaning in that day, they did not include the African race, whether free or not: for the fifth section of the ninth article provides that Congress should have the power "to agree upon the number of land forces to be raised, and to make requisitions from each State for its quota in proportion to the number of *white* inhabitants in such State, which requisition should be binding."

Words could hardly have been used which more strongly mark the line of distinction between the citizen and the subject; the free and the subjugated races. The latter were not even counted when the inhabitants of a State were to be embodied in proportion to its numbers for the general defense. And it cannot for a moment be supposed, that a class of persons thus separated and rejected from those who formed the sovereignty of the States, were yet intended to be included under the words "free inhabitants," in the preceding article, to whom privileges and immunities were so carefully secured in every State.

But although this clause of the Articles of Confederation is the same in principle with that inserted in the Constitution, yet the comprehensive word *inhabitant*, which might be construed to include an emancipated slave, is omitted; and the privilege is confined to *citizens* of the State. And this alteration in words would hardly have been made, unless a different meaning was intended to be conveyed, or a possible doubt removed. The just and fair inference is, that as this privilege was about to be placed under the protection of the General Government, and the words expounded by its tribunals, and all power in relation to it taken from the State and its courts, it was deemed prudent to describe with precision and caution the persons to whom this high privilege was give—and the word *citizen* was on that account substituted for the words *free inhabitant*. The word citizen excluded, and no doubt intended to exclude, foreigners who had not become citizens of some one of the States when the Constitution was adopted; and also every description of persons who were not fully recognized as citizens in the several States. This, upon any fair construction of the instruments to which we have referred, was evidently the object and purpose of this change of words.

To all this mass of proof we have still to add, that Congress has repeatedly legislated upon the same construction of the Constitution that we have given. Three laws, two of which were passed almost immediately after the Government went into operation, will be abundantly sufficient to show this. The two first are particularly worthy of notice, because many of the men who assisted in framing the Constitution, and took an article part in procuring its adoption, were then in the halls of legislation, and certainly understood what they meant when they used the words "people of the United States" and "citizen" in that well-considered instrument.

The first of these acts is the naturalization law, which was passed at the second session of the first Congress, March 26, 1790, and confines the right of becoming citizens *to aliens being free white persons.*

Now, the Constitution does not limit the power the Congress in this respect to white persons. And they may, if they think proper, authorize the naturalization of any one, of any color, who was born under allegiance to another Government. But the language of the law above quoted, shows that citizenship at that time was perfectly understood to be confined to the white race; and that they alone constituted the sovereignty in the Government.

Congress might, as we before said, have authorized the naturalization of Indians, because they were aliens and foreigners. But, in their then untutored and savage state, no one would have thought of admitting them as citizens in a civilized community. And, moreover, the atrocities they had but recently committed, when they were the allies of Great Britain in the Revolutionary war, were yet fresh in the recollection of the people of the United States, and they were even then guarding themselves against the threatened renewal of Indian hostilities. No one supposed then that any Indian would ask for, or was capable of enjoying, the privileges of an American citizen, and the word white was not used with any particular reference to them.

Neither was it used with any reference to the African race imported into or born in this country; because Congress had no power to naturalize them, and therefore there was no necessity for using particular words to exclude them.

It would seem to have used merely because it followed out the line of division which the Constitution has drawn between the citizen race, who formed and held the Government, and the African race, which they held in subjection and slavery, and governed at their own pleasure.

Another of the early laws of which we have spoken, is the first militia law, which was passed in 1792, at the first session of the second Congress. The language of this law is equally plain and significant with the one just mentioned. It directs that every "free able-bodied white male citizen" shall be enrolled in the militia. The word *white* is evidently used to exclude the African race, and the word "citizen" to exclude unnaturalized foreigners; the latter forming no part of the sovereignty, owing it no allegiance, and therefore under no obligation to defend it. The African race, however, born in the country, did owe allegiance to the Government, whether they were slave or free; but it is repudiated, and rejected from the duties and obligations of citizenship in marked language.

The third act to which we have alluded is even still more decisive; it was passed as late as 1813, (2 Stat., 809,) and it provides: "That from and after the termination of the war in which the United States are now engaged with Great Britain, it shall not be lawful to employ, on board of any public or private vessels of the United States, any person or persons except citizens of the United States, *or* persons of color, natives of the United States."

Here the line of distinction is drawn in express words. Persons of color, in the judgment of Congress, were not included in the word citizens, and they are described as another and different class of persons, and authorized to be employed, if born in the United States.

And even as late as 1820, (chap. 104, sec. 8,) in the charter to the city of Washington, the corporation is authorized "to restrain and prohibit the nightly and other disorderly meetings of slaves, free Negroes, and mulattos," thus associating them together in its legislation; and after prescribing the punishment that may be inflicted on the slaves, proceeds in the following word: "And to punish such free Negroes and mulattos by penalties not exceeding twenty dollars for any one offense; and in case of the inability of any such free Negro or mulatto to pay any such penalty and cost thereon, to cause him or her to be confined to labor for any time not exceeding six calendar months." And in a subsequent part of the same section, the act authorizes the corporation "to prescribe the terms and conditions upon which free Negroes and mulattos may reside in the city."

This law, like the laws of the States, shows that this class of persons were governed by special legislation directed expressly to them and always connected with provisions for the government of slaves, and not with those for the government of free white citizens. And after such an uniform course of legislation as we have stated, by the colonies, by the States, and by Congress, running through a period of more than a century, it would seem that to call persons thus marked and stigmatized, "citizens" of the United States, "fellow-citizens," a constituent part of the sovereignty, would be an abuse of terms, and not calculated to exalt the character of an American citizen in the eyes of other nations.

The conduct of the Executive Department of the Government has been in perfect harmony upon this subject with this course of legislation. The question was brought officially before the late William Wirt, when he was the Attorney General of the United States, in 1821, and he decided that the words "citizens of the United States" were used in the acts of Congress in the same sense as in the Constitution; and that free persons of color were not citizens, within the meaning of the Constitution and laws; and this opinion has been confirmed by that of the late Attorney General, Caleb Cushing, in a recent case, and acted upon by the Secretary of State, who refused to grant passports to them as "citizens of the United States."

But it is said that a person may be a citizen, and entitled to that character, although he does not possess all the rights which may belong to other citizens; as, for example, the right to vote, or to hold particular offices; and that yet, when he goes into another State, he is entitled to be recognized there as a citizen, although the State may measure his rights by the rights which it allows to persons of a like character or class resident in the State, and refuse to him the full rights of citizenship.

This argument overlooks the language of the provision in the Constitution of which we are speaking.

Undoubtedly, a person may be a citizen, that is, a member of the community who form the sovereignty, although he exercises no share of the political power, and is incapacitated from holding particular offices. Women and minors, who form a part of the political family, cannot vote; and when a property qualification is required to vote or hold a particular office, those who have not the necessary qualification cannot vote or hold the office, yet they are citizens.

So, too, a person may be entitled to vote by the law of the State, who is not a citizen even of the State itself. And in some of the States of the Union foreigners not naturalized are allowed to vote. And the State may give the right to free Negroes and mulattos, but that does not make them citizens of the State, and still less of the United States. And the provision in the Constitution giving privileges and immunities in other States, does not apply to them.

Neither does it apply to a person who, being the citizen of a State, migrates to another State. For then he becomes subject to the laws of the State in which he lives, and he is no longer a citizen of the State from which he removed. And the State in which he resides may then, unquestionably, determine his *status* or condition, and place him among the class of persons who are not recognized as citizens, but belong to an inferior and subject race; and may deny him the privileges and immunities enjoyed by its citizens.

But so far as mere rights of person are concerned, the provision in question is confined to citizens of a State who are temporarily in another State without taking up their residence there. It gives them no political rights in the State, as to voting or holding office, or in any other respect. For a citizen of one State has no right to participate in the government of another. But if he ranks as a citizen in the State to which he belongs, within the meaning of the Constitution of the United States, then, whenever he goes into another State, the Constitution clothes him, as to the rights of person, with all the privileges and immunities which belong to citizens of the State. And if persons of the African race are citizens of a State, and of the United States, they would be entitled to all of these privileges and immunities in every State, and the State could not restrict them; for they would hold these privileges and immunities under the paramount authority of the Federal Government, and its courts would be bound to maintain and enforce them, the Constitution and laws of the State to the contrary notwithstanding. And if the States could limit or restrict them, or place the party in an inferior grade, this clause of the Constitution would be unmeaning, and could have no operation; and would give no rights to the citizen when in another State. He would have none but what the State itself chose to allow him. This is evidently not the construction or meaning of the clause in question. It guaranties rights to the citizen, and the State cannot withhold them. And these rights are of a character and would lead to consequences which make it absolutely certain that the African race were not included under the name of citizens of a State, and were not in the contemplation of the framers of the Constitution when these privileges and immunities were provided for the protection of the citizen in other States.

The case of *Legrand v. Darnall* (2 Peters, 664) has been referred to for the purpose of showing that this court has decided that the descendant of a slave may sue as a citizen in a court of the United States; but the case itself shows that the question did not arise and could not have arisen in the case.

It appears from the report, that Darnall was born in Maryland, and was the son of a white man by one of his slaves, and his father executed certain instruments to manumit him, and devised to him some landed property in the State. This property Darnall afterwards sold to Legrand, the appellant, who gave his notes for the purchase-money. But becoming afterwards apprehensive that the appellee had not been emancipated according to the laws of Maryland, he refused to pay the notes until he could be better satisfied as to Darnall's right to convey. Darnall, in the mean time, had taken up his residence in Pennsylvania, and brought suit on the notes, and recovered judgment in the Circuit Court for the district of Maryland.

The whole proceeding, as appears by the report, was an amicable one; Legrand being perfectly willing to pay the money, if he could obtain a title, and Darnall not wishing him to pay unless he could make him a good one. In point of fact, the whole proceeding was under the direction of the counsel who argued the case for the appellee, who was the mutual friend of the parties, and confided in by both of them, and whose only object was to have the rights of both parties established by judicial decision in the most speedy and least expensive manner.

Legrand, therefore, raised no objection to the jurisdiction of the court in the suit at law, because he was himself anxious to obtain the judgment of the court upon his life. Consequently, there was nothing in the record before the court to show that Darnall was of African descent, and the usual judgment and award of execution was entered. And Legrand thereupon filed his bill on the equity side of the Circuit Court, stating that Darnall was born a slave, and had not been legally emancipated, and could not therefore take the land devised to him, nor make Legrand a good title; and praying an injunction to restrain Darnall from proceeding to execution on the judgment, which was granted. Darnall answered, averring in his answer that he was a free man, and capable of conveying a good title. Testimony was taken on this point, and at the hearing the Circuit Court was of opinion that Darnall was a free man and his title good, and dissolved the injunction and dismissed the bill; and that decree was affirmed here, upon the appeal of Legrand.

Now, it is difficult to imagine how any question about the citizenship of Darnall, or his right to sue in that character, can be supposed to have arisen or been decided in that case. The fact that he was of African descent was first brought before the court upon the bill in equity. The suit at law had then passed into judgment and award of execution, and the Circuit Court, as a court of law, had no longer any authority over it. It was a valid and legal judgment, which the court that rendered it had not the power to reverse or set aside. And unless it had jurisdiction as a court of equity to restrain him from using its process as a court of law, Darnall, if he thought proper, would have been at liberty to proceed on his judgment, and compel the payment of the money, although the allegations in the bill were true, and he was incapable of making a title. No other court could have enjoined him, for certainly no State equity court could interfere in that way with the judgment of a Circuit of the United States.

But the Circuit Court as a court of equity certainly had equity jurisdiction over its own judgment as a court of law, without regard to the character of the parties; and had not only the right, but it was its duty—no matter who were the parties in the judgment—to prevent them from proceeding to enforce it by execution, if the court was satisfied that the money was not justly and equitably due. The ability of Darnall to convey did not depend upon his citizenship, but upon his title to freedom. And if he was free, he could hold and convey property, by the laws of Maryland, although he was not a citizen. But if he was by law still a slave, he could not. It was therefore the duty of the court, sitting as a court of equity in the latter case, to prevent him from using its process, as a court of common law, to compel the payment of the purchase-money, when it was evident that the purchaser must lose the hand. But if he was free, and could made a title, it was equally the duty of the court not to suffer Legrand to keep the land, and refuse the payment of the money, upon the ground that Darnall was incapable of suing or being sued as a citizen in a court of the United States. The character or citizenship of the parties had no connection with the question of jurisdiction, and the matter in dispute had no relation to the citizenship of Darnall. Nor is such a question alluded to in the opinion of the court.

Besides, we are by no means prepared to say that there are not many cases, civil as well as criminal, in which a Circuit Court of the United States may exercise jurisdiction, although one of the African race is a party; that broad question is not before the court. The question with which we are now dealing is, whether a person of the African race can be a citizen of the United States, and become thereby entitled to a special privilege, by virtue of his title to that character, and which, under the Constitution, no one but a citizen can claim. It is manifest that the case of Legrand and Darnall has no bearing on that question, and can have no application to the case now before the court.

This case, however, strikingly illustrates the consequences that would follow the construction of the Constitution which would give the power contended for to a State. If would in effect given it also to an individual. For if the father of young Darnall had manumitted him in his lifetime, and sent him to reside in a State which recognized him as a citizen, he might have visited and sojourned in Maryland when he pleased, and as long as he pleased, as a citizen of the United States; and the State officers and tribunals would be compelled, by the paramount authority of the Constitution, to receive him and treat him as one of its citizens, exempt from the laws and police of the State in relation to a person of that description and allow him to enjoy all the rights and privileges of citizenship, without respect to the laws of Maryland, although such laws were deemed by it absolutely essential to its own safety.

The only two provisions which point to them and include them, treat them as property, and make it the duty of the Government to protect it; no other power, in relation to this race, is to be found in the Constitution; and as it is a Government of special, delegated, powers, no authority beyond these two provisions can be constitutionally exercised. The Government of the United States had no right to interfere for any other purpose but that of protecting the rights of the owner, leaving it altogether with the several States to deal with this race, whether emancipated or not, as each State may think justice, humanity, and the interests and safety of society, require. The States evidently intended to reserve this power exclusively to themselves.

No one, we presume, supposes that any change in public opinion or feeling, in relation to this unfortunate race, in the civilized nations of Europe or in this country, should induce the court to give to the words of the Constitution a more liberal construction in their favor than they were intended to bear when the instrument was framed and adopted. Such an argument would be altogether inadmissible in any tribunal called on to interpret it. If any of its provisions are deemed unjust, there is a mode prescribed in the instrument itself by which it may be amended; but while it remains unaltered, it must be construed now as it was understood at the time of its adoption. It is not only the same in words, but the same in meaning, and delegates the same powers to the Government, and reserves and secures the same rights and privileges to the citizen; and as long as it continues to exist in its present form, it speaks not only in the same words, but with the same meaning and intend with which it spoke when it came from the hands of its framers, and was voted on and adopted by the people of the United States. Any other rule of construction would abrogate the judicial character of this court, and make it the mere reflex of the popular opinion or passion of the day. This court was not created by the Constitution for such purposes. Higher and graver trusts have been confided to it, and it must not falter in the path of duty.

What the construction was at that time, we think can hardly admit of doubt. We have the language of the Declaration of Independence and of the Articles of Confederation, in addition to the plain words of the Constitution itself; we have the legislation of the different States, before, about the time, and since, the Constitution was adopted; we have the legislation of Congress, from the time of its adoption to a recent period; and we have the constant and uniform action of the Executive Department, all concurring together, and leading to the same result. And if anything in relation to the construction of the Constitution can be regarded as settled, it is that which we now give to the word "citizen" and the word "people."

And upon a full and careful consideration of the subject, the court is of opinion, that, upon the facts stated in the plea in abatement, Dred Scott was not a citizen of Mis-

souri within the meaning of the Constitution of the United States, and not entitled as such to sue in its courts; and, consequently, that the Circuit Court had no jurisdiction of the case, and that the judgment on the plea in abatement is erroneous.

We are aware that doubts are entertained by some of the members of the court, whether the plea in abatement is legally before the court upon this writ of error; but if that plea is regarded as waived, or out of the case upon any other ground, yet the question as to the jurisdiction of the Circuit Court is presented on the face of the bill of exception itself, taken by the plaintiff at the trial; for he admits that he and his wife were born slaves, but endeavors to make out his title to freedom and citizenship by showing that they were taken by their owner to certain places, hereinafter mentioned, where slavery could not by law exist, and that they thereby became free, and upon their return to Missouri become citizens of that State.

Now, if the removal of which he speaks did not give them their freedom, then by his own admission he is still a slave; and whatever opinions may be entertained in favor of the citizenship of a free person of the African race, no one supposes that a slave is a citizen of the State or of the United States. If, therefore, the acts done by his owner did not make them free persons, he is still a slave, and certainly incapable of suing in the character of a citizen.

The principle of law is too well settled to be disputed, that a court can give no judgment for either party, where it has no jurisdiction; and if, upon the showing of Scott himself, it appeared that he was still a slave, the case ought to have been dismissed, and the judgment against him and in favor of the defendant for costs, is, like that on the plea in abatement, erroneous, and the suit ought to have been dismissed by the Circuit Court for want of jurisdiction in that court.

But, before we proceed to examine this part of the case, it may be proper to notice an objection taken to the judicial authority of this court to decide it; and it has been said, that as this court had decided against the jurisdiction of the Circuit Court on the plea in abatement, it has no right to examine any question presented by the exception; and that anything it may say upon that part of the case will be extra- judicial, and mere obiter dicta.

This is a manifest mistake; there can be no doubt as to the jurisdiction of this court to revise the judgment of a Circuit Court, and to reverse it for any error apparent on the record, whether it be the error of giving judgment in a case over which it had no jurisdiction, or any other material error; and this, too, whether there is a plea in abatement or not.

The objection appears to have arisen from confounding writs of error to a State court, with writs of error to a

Circuit Court of the United States. Undoubtedly, upon a writ of error to a State court, unless the record shows a case that gives jurisdiction, the case must be dismissed for want of jurisdiction in *this court*. And if it is dismissed on that ground, we have no right to examine and decide upon any question presented by the bill of exceptions, or any other part of the record. But writs of error to a State court, and to a Circuit Court of the United States, are regulated by different laws, and stand upon entirely different principles. And in a writ of error to a Circuit Court of the United States, the whole record is before this court for examination and decision; and if the sum in controversy is large enough to give jurisdiction, it is not only the right, but it is the judicial duty of the court, to examine the whole case as presented by the record; and if it appears upon its face that any material error or errors have been committed by the court below, it is the duty of this court to reverse the judgment, and remand the case. And certainly an error in passing a judgment upon the merits in favor of either party, in a case which it was not authorized to try, and over which it had no jurisdiction, is as grave an error as a court can commit.

The plea in abatement is not a plea to the jurisdiction of this court, but to the jurisdiction of the Circuit Court. And it appears by the record before us, that the Circuit Court committed an error, in deciding that it had jurisdiction, upon the facts in the case, admitted by the pleadings. It is the duty of the appellate tribunal to correct this error; but that could not be done by dismissing the case for want of jurisdiction here—for that would leave the erroneous judgment in full force, and the injured party without remedy. And the appellate court therefore exercises the power for which alone appellate courts are constituted, by reversing the judgment of the court below for this error. It exercises its proper and appropriate jurisdiction over the judgment and proceedings of the Circuit Court, as they appear upon the record brought up by the writ of error.

The correction of one error in the court below does not deprive the appellate court of the power of examining further into the record, and correcting any other material errors which may have been committed by the inferior court. There is certainly no rule of law—nor any practice—nor any decision of a court—which even questions this power in the appellate tribunal. On the contrary, it is the daily practice of this court, and of all appellate courts where they reverse the judgments of an inferior court for error, to correct by its opinions whatever errors may appear on the record material to the case; and they have always held it to be their duty to do so where the silence of the court might lead to misconstruction or future controversy, and the point has been relied on by either side, and argued before the court.

In the case before us, we have already decided that the Circuit Court erred in deciding that it had jurisdiction upon the facts admitted by the pleadings. And it appears that, in the further progress of the case, it acted upon the erroneous principle it had decided on the pleadings, and gave judgment for the defendant, where, upon the facts admitted in the exception, it had no jurisdiction.

We are at a loss to understand upon what principle of law, applicable to appellate jurisdiction, it can be supposed that this court has not judicial authority to correct the last-mentioned error, because they had before corrected the former; or by what process of reasoning it can be made out, that the error of an inferior court in actually pronouncing judgment for one of the parties, in a case in which it had no jurisdiction, cannot be looked into or corrected by this court, because we have decided a similar question presented in the pleadings. The last point is distinctly presented by the facts contained in the plaintiff's own bill of exceptions, which he himself brings here by this writ of error. It was the point which chiefly occupied the attention of the counsel on both sides in the argument—and the judgment which this court must render upon both errors is precisely the same. It must, in each of them, exercise jurisdiction over the judgment, and reverse it for the errors committed by the court below; and issue a mandate to the Circuit Court to conform its judgment to the opinion pronounced by this court, by dismissing the case for want of jurisdiction in the Circuit Court. This is the constant and invariable practice of this court, where it reverses a judgment for want of jurisdiction in the Circuit Court.

It can scarcely be necessary to pursue such a question further. The want of jurisdiction in the court below may appear on the record without any plea in abatement. This is familiarly the case where a court of chancery has exercised jurisdiction in a case where the plaintiff had a plain and adequate remedy at law, and it so appears by the transcript when brought here by appeal. So also where it appears that a court of admiralty has exercised jurisdiction in a case belonging exclusively to a court of common law. In these cases there is no plea in abatement. And for the same reason, and upon the same principles, where the defect of jurisdiction is patent on the record, this court is bound to reverse the judgment, although the defendant has not pleaded in abatement to the jurisdiction of the inferior court.

The cases of *Jackson v. Ashton* and of *Capron v. Van Noorden*, to which we have referred in a previous part of this opinion, are directly in point. In the last-mentioned case, Capron brought an action against Van Noorden in a Circuit Court of the United States, without showing, by the usual averments of citizenship, that the court had jurisdiction. There was no plea in abatement put in, and the parties went to trial upon the merits. The court gave judgment in favor of the defendant with costs. The plaintiff brought his writ of error, and this court reversed the judgment given in favor of the defendant, and remanded the case with directions to dismiss it, because it did not appear by the transcript that the Circuit Court had jurisdiction.

The case before us still more strongly imposes upon this court the duty of examining whether the court below has not committed an error, in taking jurisdiction and giving a judgment for costs in favor of the defendant; for in *Capron v. Van Noorden* the judgment was reversed, because it did *not appear* that the parties were citizens of different States. They might or might not be. But in this case it *does appear* that the plaintiff was born a slave; and if the facts upon which he relies have not made him free, then it appears affirmatively on the record that he is not a citizen, and consequently his suit against Sandford was not a suit between citizens of different States and the court had no authority to pass any judgment between the parties. The suit ought, in this view of it, to have been dismissed by the Circuit Court, and must be reversed.

It is true that the result either way, by dismissal or by a judgment for the defendant, makes very little, if any, difference in a pecuniary or personal point of view to either party. But the fact that the result would be very nearly the same to the parties in either form of judgment, would not justify this court in sanctioning an error in the judgment which is patent on the record, and which, if sanctioned, might be drawn into precedent and lead to serious mischief and injustice in some future suit.

We proceed, therefore, to inquire whether the facts relied on by the plaintiff entitled him to his freedom.

The case, as he himself states it, on the record brought here by his writ of error, is this:

The plaintiff was a negro slave, belonging to Dr. Emerson, who was a surgeon in the army of the United States. In the year 1834, he took the plaintiff from the State of Missouri to the military post at Rock Island, in the State of Illinois, and held him there as a slave until the month of April or May, 1836. At the time last mentioned, said Dr. Emerson removed the plaintiff from said military post at Rock Island to the military post at Fort Snelling, situate on the west bank of the Mississippi river, in the Territory known as Upper Louisiana, acquired by the United States of France, and situate north of the latitude of thirty-six degrees thirty minutes north, and north of the State of Missouri. Said Dr. Emerson held the plaintiff in slavery at said Fort Snelling, from said last-mentioned date until the year 1838.

In the year 1835, Harriet, who is named in the second count of the plaintiff's declaration, was the negro salve of Major Taliaferro, who belonged to the army of the United States. In that year, 1835, said Major Taliaferro took said Harriet to said Fort Snelling, a military post situated as hereinbefore stated, and kept her there as slave until the year 1836, and then sold and delivered her as a slave, at said Fort Snelling, unto the said Dr. Emerson hereinbefore named. Said Dr. Emerson held said Harriet in slavery at said Fort Snelling until the year 1838.

In the year 1836, the plaintiff and Harriet intermarried, at Fort Snelling, with the consent of Dr. Emerson, who then claimed to be their master and owner. Eliza and Lizzie, named in the third count of the plaintiff's declaration, are the fruit of that marriage. Eliza is about fourteen years old, and was born on board the steamboat Gipsey, north of the north line of the State of Missouri, and upon the river Mississippi. Lizzie is about seven years old, and was born in the State of Missouri, at the military post called Jefferson Barracks.

In the year 1838, said Dr. Emerson removed the plaintiff and said Harriet, and their said daughter Eliza, from said Fort Snelling to the State of Missouri, where they have ever since resided.

Before the commencement of this suit, said Dr. Emerson sold and conveyed the plaintiff, and Harriet, Eliza and Lizzie, to the defendant, as slaves, and the defendant has ever since claimed to hold them, and each of them, as slaves.

In considering this part of the controversy, two questions arise: 1. Was he, together with his family, free in Missouri by reason of the stay in the territory of the United States herein before mentioned? And 2. If they were not, is Scott himself free by reason of his removal to Rock Island, in the State of Illinois, as stated in the above admissions?

We proceed to examine the first question.

The act of Congress, upon which the plaintiff relies, declares that slavery and involuntary servitude, except as a punishment for crime, shall be forever prohibited in all that part of the territory ceded by France, under the name of Louisiana, which lies north of thirty-six degrees thirty minutes north latitude, and not included within the limits of Missouri. And the difficulty which meets us at the threshold of this part of the inquiry is, whether Congress was authorized to pass this law under any of the powers granted to it by the Constitution; for if the authority is not given by that instrument, it is the duty of this court to declare it void and inoperative, and incapable of conferring freedom upon any one who is held as a slave under the laws of any one of the States.

The counsel for the plaintiff has laid much stress upon that article in the Constitution which confers on Congress the power "to dispose of and make all needful rules and regulations respecting the territory or other property belonging to the United States": but, in the judgment of the court, that provision has no bearing on the present controversy, and the power there given, whatever it may be, is confined and was intended to be confined, to the territory which at that time belonged to, or was claimed by, the United States, and was within their boundaries as settled by the treaty with Great Britain, and can have no influence upon a territory afterwards acquired from a foreign Government. It was a special provision for a known and particular territory and to meet a present emergency, and nothing more.

A brief summary of the history of the times, as well as the careful and measured terms in which the article is framed, will show the correctness of this proposition.

It will be remembered that, from the commencement of the Revolutionary war, serious difficulties existed between the States, in relation to the disposition of large and unsettled territories which were included in the chartered limits of some of the States. And some of the other States, and more especially Maryland, which had no unsettled lands, insisted that as the unoccupied lands, if wrested from Great Britain, would owe their preservation to the common purse and the common sword, the money arising from them ought to be applied in just proportion among the several States to pay the expenses of the war, and ought not to be appropriated to the use of the State in whose chartered limits they might happen to lie, to the exclusion of the other States, by whose combined efforts and common expense the territory was defended and preserved against the claim of the British Government.

These difficulties cause much uneasiness during the war, while the issue was in some degree doubtful, and the future boundaries of the United States yet to be defined by treaty, if we achieved our independence.

The majority of the Congress of the Confederation obviously concurred in opinion with the State of Maryland, and desired to obtain from the States which claimed it a cession of this territory, in order that Congress might raise money on this security to carry on the war. This appears by the resolution passed on the 6th of September, 1780, strongly urging the States to cede these lands to the United States, both for the sake of peace and union among themselves, and to maintain the public credit; and this was followed by the resolution of October 10th, 1780, by which Congress pledged itself, that if the lands were ceded as recommended by the resolution above mentioned, they should be disposed of for the common benefit of the United States, and be settled and formed into distinct republican States, which should become members of the Federal Union, and have the same rights of sovereignty, and freedom, and independence, as other States.

But these difficulties became much more serious after peace took place, and the boundaries of the United States were established. Every State, at that time, felt severely the pressure of its was debt; but in Virginia, and some

other States, there were large territories of unsettled lands, the sale of which would enable them to discharge their obligations without much inconvenience; while other States, which had no such resource, saw before them many years of heavy and burdensome taxation; and the latter insisted, for the reasons before stated, that these unsettled lands should be treated as the common property of the States, and the proceeds applied to their common benefit.

The letters from the statesmen of that day will show how much this controversy occupied their thoughts, and the dangers that were apprehended from it. It was the disturbing element of the time, and fears were entertained that it might dissolve the Confederation by which the States were then united.

These fears and dangers were, however, at once removed, when the State of Virginia, in 1784, voluntarily ceded to the United States the immense tract of country lying northwest of the river Ohio, and which was within the acknowledged limits of the State. The only object of the State, in making this cession, was to put an end to the threatening and exciting controversy, and to enable the Congress of that time to dispose of the lands, and appropriate the proceeds as a common fund for the common benefit of the States. It was not ceded, because it was inconvenient to the State to hold and govern it, nor from any expectation that it could be better or more conveniently governed by the United States.

The example of Virginia was soon afterwards followed by other States, and, at the time of the adoption of the Constitution, all of the States, similarly situated, had ceded their unappropriated lands, except North Carolina and Georgia. The main object for which these cessions were desired and made was on account of their money value, and to put an end to a dangerous controversy, as to who was justly entitled to the proceeds when the lands should be sold. It is necessary to bring this part of the history of these cessions thus distinctly into view, because it will enable us the better to comprehend the phraseology of the article in the Constitution, so often referred to in the argument.

Undoubtedly the powers of sovereignty and the eminent domain were ceded with the land. This was essential, in order to make it effectual, and to accomplish its objects. But it must be remembered that, at that time, there was no Government of the United States in existence with enumerated and limited powers; what was then called the United States, were thirteen separate, sovereign, independent States, which had entered into a league or confederation for their mutual protection and advantage, and the Congress of the United States was composed of the representatives of these separate sovereignties, meeting together, as equals, to discuss and decide on certain measures which the States, by the Articles of Confederation, had agreed to submit to their decision. But this Confederation had none of the attributes of sovereignty in legislative, executive, or judicial power. It was little more than a congress of ambassadors, authorized to represent separate nations, in matters in which they had a common concern.

It was this Congress that accepted the cession from Virginia. They had no power to accept it under the Articles of Confederation. But they had an undoubted right, as independent sovereignties, to accept any cession of territory for their common benefit, which all of them assented to; and it is equally clear, that as their common property, and having no superior to control them, they had the right to exercise absolute dominion over it, subject only to the restrictions which Virginia had imposed in her act of cession. There was, as we have said, no Government of the United States then in existence with special enumerated and limited powers. The territory belonged to sovereignties, who, subject, to the limitations above mentioned, had a right to establish any form of government they pleased, by compact or treaty among themselves, and to regulate rights of person and rights of property in the territory, as they might deem proper. It was by a Congress, representing the authority of these several and separate sovereignties, and acting under their authority and command, (but not from any authority derived from the Articles of Confederation,) that the instrument usually called the ordinance of 1787 was adopted; regulating in much detail the principles and the laws by which the territory should be governed; and among other provisions, slavery is prohibited in it. We do not question the power of the States, by agreement among themselves, to pass this ordinance, nor its obligatory force in the territory, while this confederation or league of the States in their separate sovereign character continued to exist.

This was the state of things when the Constitution of the United States was formed. The territory ceded by Virginia belonged to the several confederated States as common property, and they had united in establishing in it a system of government and jurisprudence, in order to prepare it for admission as States, according to the terms of the cession. They were about to dissolve this federative Union, and to surrender a portion of their independent sovereignty to a new Government, which, for certain purposes, would make the people of the several States one people, and which was to be supreme and controlling within its sphere of action throughout the United States; but this Government was to be carefully limited in its powers, and to exercise no authority beyond those expressly granted by the Constitution, or necessarily to be implied from the language of the instrument, and the objects it was intended to accomplish; and as this league of States would, upon the adoption of the new Government, cease to have any power over the territory, and the ordinance they had

agreed upon be incapable of execution, and a mere nullity, if was obvious that some provision was necessary to give the new Government sufficient power to enable it to carry into effect the objects for which it was ceded, and the compacts and agreements which the States had made with each other in the exercise of their powers of sovereignty. It was necessary that the lands should be sold to pay the war debt; that a Government and system of jurisprudence should be maintained in it, to protect the citizens of the United States who should migrate to the territory, in their rights of person and of property. It was also necessary that the new Government, about to be adopted, should be authorized to maintain the claim of the United States to the unappropriated lands in North Carolina and Georgia, which had not been then called, but the cession of which was confidently anticipated upon some terms that would be arranged between the General Government and these two States. And, moreover, there were many articles of value besides this property in land, such as arms, military stores, munitions, and ships of war, which were the common property of the States, when acting in their independent characters as confederates, which neither the new Government nor any one else would have a right to take possession of, or control, without authority from them; and it was to place these things under guardianship and protection of the new Government, and to clothe it with the necessary powers, that the clause was inserted in the Constitution which gives Congress the power "to dispose of and make all needful rules and regulations respecting the territory or other property belonging to the United States." It was intended for a specific purpose, to provide for the things we have mentioned. It was to transfer to the new Government the property then held in common by the States, and to give to that Government power to apply it to the objects for which it had been destined by mutual agreement among the States before their league was dissolved. It applied only to the property which the States held in common at that time, and has no reference whatever to any territory or other property which the new sovereignty might afterwards itself acquire.

The language used in the clause, the arrangement and combination of the powers, and the somewhat unusual phraseology it uses, when it speaks of the political power to be exercised in the government of the territory, all indicate the design and meaning of the clause to be such as we have mentioned. It does not speak of *any* territory, nor of *Territories*, but uses language which, according to its legitimate meaning, points to a particular thing. The power is given in relation only to *the* territory of the United States—that is, to a territory then in existence, and then known or claimed as the territory of the United States. It begins its enumeration of powers by that of disposing, in other words, making sale of the lands, or raising money from them, which, as we have already said, was the main object of the cession, and which is accordingly the first thing provided for in the article. It then gives the power which was necessarily associated with the disposition and sale of the lands—that is, the power of making needful rules and regulations respecting the territory. And whatever construction may now be given to these words, every one, we think, must admit that they are not the words usually employed by statesman in giving supreme power of legislation. They are certainly very unlike the words used in the power granted to legislate over territory which the new Government might afterwards itself obtain by cession from a State, either for its seat of Government, or for forts, magazines, arsenals, dock yards, and other needful buildings.

And the same power of making needful rules respecting the territory is, in precisely the same language, applied to the *other* property belonging to the United States—associating the power over the territory in this respect with the power over movable or personal property—that is, the ships, arms, and munitions of war, which then belonged in common to the State sovereignties. And it will hardly be said, that this power, in relation to the last-mentioned objects, was deemed necessary to be thus specially given to the new Government, in order to authorize it to make needful rules and regulations respecting the ships it might itself build, or arms and munitions of war it might itself manufacture or provide for the public service.

No one, it is believed, would think a moment of deriving the power of Congress to make needful rules and regulations in relation to property of this kind from this clause of the Constitution. Nor can it, upon any fair construction, be applied to any property but that which the new Government was about to receive from the confederated States. And if this be true as to this property, it must be equally true and limited as to the territory, which is so carefully and precisely coupled with it—and like it referred to as property in the power granted. The concluding words of the clause appear to render this construction irresistible; for, after the provisions we have mentioned, it proceeds to say, "that nothing in the Constitution shall be so construed as to prejudice any claims of the United States, or of any particular State."

Now, as we have before said, all of the States, except North Carolina and Georgia, had made the cession before the Constitution was adopted, according to the resolution of Congress of October 10, 1780. The claims of other States, that the unappropriated lands in these two States should be applied to the common benefit, in like manner, was still insisted on, but refused by the States. And this member of the clause in question evidently applies to them, and can apply to nothing else. It was to exclude the conclusion that either party, by adopting the Constitution, would surrender what they deemed their rights. And when

the latter provision relates so obviously to the unappropriated lands not yet ceded by the States, and the first clause makes provision for those then actually ceded, it is impossible, by any just rule of construction, to make the first provision general, and extend to all territories, which the Federal Government might in any way afterwards acquire, when the latter is plainly and unequivocally confined to a particular territory; which was a part of the same controversy, and involved in the same dispute, and depended upon the same principles. The union of the two provisions in the same clause shows that they were kindred subjects; and that the whole clause is local, and relates only to lands, within the limits of the United States, which had been or then were claimed by a State; and that no other territory was in the mind of the framers of the Constitution, or intended to be embraced in it. Upon any other construction it would be impossible to account for the insertion of the last provision in the place where it is found, or to comprehend why, or for what object, it was associated with the previous provision.

This view of the subject is confirmed by the manner in which the present Government of the United States dealt with the subject as soon as it came into existence. It must be borne in mind that the same States that formed the Confederation also formed and adopted the new Government, to which so large a portion of their former sovereign powers were surrendered. It must also be borne in mind that all of these same States which had then ratified the new Constitution were represented in the Congress which passed the first law for the government of this territory; and many of the members of that legislative body had been deputies from the States under the Confederation—had united in adopting the ordinance of 1787, and assisted in forming the new Government under which they were then acting, and whose powers they were then exercising. And it is obvious from the law they passed to carry into effect the principles and provisions of the ordinance, that they regarded it as the act of the States done in the exercise of their legitimate powers at the time. The new Government took the territory as it found it, and in the condition in which it was transferred, and did not attempt to undo anything that had been done. And, among the earliest laws passed under the new Government, is one reviving the ordinance of 1787, which had become inoperative and a nullity upon the adoption of the Constitution. This law introduces no new form or principles for its government, but recites, in the preamble, that it is passed in order that this ordinance may continue to have full effect, and proceeds to make only those rules and regulations which were needful to adapt it to the new Government, into whose hands the power had fallen. It appears, therefore, that this Congress regarded the purposes to which the land in this Territory was to be applied, and the form of government and principles of jurisprudence which were to prevail there, while it remained in the Territorial state, as already determined on by the States when they had full power and right to make the decision; and that the new Government, having received it in this condition, ought to carry substantially into effect the plans and principles which had been previously adopted by the States, and which no doubt the States anticipated when they surrendered their power to the new Government. And if we regard this clause of the Constitution as pointing to this Territory, with a Territorial Government already established in it, which had been ceded to the States for the purposes hereinbefore mentioned—every word in it is perfectly appropriate and easily understood, and the provisions it contains are in perfect harmony with the objects for which it was ceded, and with the condition of its government as a Territory at the time. We can, then, easily account for the manner in which the first Congress legislated on the subject—and can also understand why this power over the territory was associated in the same clause with the other property of the United States, and subjected to the like power of making needful rules and regulations. But if the clause is construed in the expanded sense contended for, so as to embrace any territory acquired from a foreign nation by the present Government, and to give it in such territory a despotic and unlimited power over persons and property, such as the confederated States might exercise in their common property, it would be difficult to account for the phraseology used, when compared with other grants of power—and also for its association with the other provisions in the same clause.

The Constitution has always been remarkable for the felicity of its arrangement of different subjects, and the perspicuity and appropriateness of the language it uses. But if this clause is construed to extend to territory acquired by the present Government from a foreign nation, outside of the limits of any charter from the British Government to a colony, it would be difficult to say, why it was deemed necessary to give the Government the power to sell any vacant lands belonging to the sovereignty which might be found within it; and if this was necessary, why the grant of this power should precede the power to legislate over it and establish a Government there; and still more difficult to say, why it was deemed necessary so specially and particularly to grant the power to make needful rules and regulations in relation to any personal or movable property it might acquire there. For the words, *other property* necessarily, by every known rule of interpretation, must mean property of a different description from territory or land. And the difficulty would perhaps be insurmountable in endeavoring to account for the last member of the sentence, which provides that "nothing in this Constitution shall be so construed as to prejudice any claims of the United States or any particular State," or to say how any particular State could have claims in or to a territory ceded by a foreign Government, or to account for associating this provision with the preceding provisions of the clause, with which it would appear to have no connection.

The words "needful rules and regulations" would seem, also, to have been cautiously used for some definite object. They are not the words usually employed by statesmen, when they mean to give the powers of sovereignty, or to establish a Government, or to authorize its establishment. Thus, in the law to renew and keep alive the ordinance of 1787, and to reestablish the Government, the title of the law is: "An act to provide for the government of the territory northwest of the river Ohio." And in the Constitution, when granting the power to legislate over the territory that may be selected for the seat of Government independently of a State, it does not say Congress shall have power "to make all needful rules and regulations respecting the territory": but it declares that "Congress shall have power to exercise exclusive legislation in all cases whatsoever over such District (not exceeding ten miles square) as may, by cession of particular States and the acceptance of Congress, become the seat of the Government of the United States.

The words "rules and regulations" are usually employed in the Constitution in speaking of some particular specified power which it means to confer on the Government, and not, as we have seen, when granting general powers of legislation. As, for example, in the particular power to Congress "to make rules for the government and regulation of the land and naval forces, or the particular and specific power to regulate commerce": "to establish an uniform *rule* of naturalization": "to coin money and *regulate* the value thereof." And to construe the words of which we are speaking as a general and unlimited grant of sovereignty over territories which the Government might afterwards acquire, is to use them in a sense and for a purpose for which they were not used in any other part of the instrument. But if confined to a particular Territory, in which a Government and laws had already been established, but which would require some alterations to adapt it to the new Government, the words are peculiarly applicable and appropriate for that purpose.

The necessity of this special provision in relation to property and the rights or property held in common by the confederated States, is illustrated by the first clause of the sixth article. This clause provides that "all debts, contracts, and engagements entered into before the adoption of this Constitution, shall be as valid against the United States under this Government as under the Confederation." This provision, like the one under consideration, was indispensable if the new Constitution was adopted.

The new Government was not a mere change in a dynasty, or in a form of government, leaving the nation or sovereignty the same, and clothed with all the rights, and bound by all the obligations of the preceding one. But, when the present United States came into existence under the new Government, it was a new political body, a new nation, then for the first time taking its place in the family of nations. It took nothing by succession from the Confederation. It had no right, as its successor, to any property of rights of property which it had acquired, and was not liable for any of its obligations. It was evidently viewed in this light by the framers of the Constitution. And as the several States would cease to exist in their former confederated character upon the adoption of the Constitution, and could not, in that character, again assemble together, special provisions were indispensable to transfer to the new Government the property and rights which at that time they held in common; and at the same time to authorize it to lay taxes and appropriate money to pay the common debt which they had contracted; and this power could only be given to it by special provisions in the Constitution. The clause in relation to the territory and other property of the United States provided for the first, and the clause last quoted provided for the other. They have no connection with the general powers and rights of sovereignty delegated to the new Government, and can neither enlarge nor diminish them. They were inserted to meet a present emergency, and not to regulate its powers as a Government.

Indeed, a similar provision was deemed necessary, in relation to treaties made by the Confederation; and when in the clause next succeeding the one of which we have last spoken, it is declared that treaties shall be the supreme law of the land, care is taken to include, by express words, the treaties made by the confederated States. The language is: "and all treaties made, or which shall be made, under the authority of the United States, shall be the supreme law of the land."

Whether, therefore, we take the particular clause in question, by itself, or in connection with the other provisions of the Constitution, we think it clear, that it applies only to the particular territory of which we have spoken, and cannot, by any just rule of interpretation, be extended to territory which the new Government might afterwards obtain from a foreign nation. Consequently, the power which Congress may have lawfully exercised in this Territory, while it remained under a Territorial Government, and which may have been sanctioned by judicial decision, can furnish no justification and no argument to support a similar exercise of power over territory afterwards acquired by the Federal Government. We put aside, therefore, any argument, drawn from precedents, showing the extent of the power which the General Government exercised over slavery in this Territory, as altogether inapplicable to the case before us.

But the case of the *American and Ocean Insurance Companies v. Canter* (1 Pet., 511) has been quoted as establishing a different construction of this clause of the Constitution. There is, however, not the slightest conflict between the opinion now given and the one referred to; and it is only by taking a single sentence out of the latter and separating it from the context, that even an appearance of conflict can be shown. We need not comment on such a mode of expounding an opinion of the court. Indeed it most commonly misrepresents instead of expounding it. And this is fully exemplified in the case referred to, where, if one sentence it taken by itself, the opinion would appear to be in direct conflict with that now given; but the words which immediately follow that sentence show that the court did not mean to decide the point, but merely affirmed the power of Congress to established a Government in the Territory, leaving it an open question, whether that power was derived from this clause in the Constitution, or was to be necessarily inferred from a power to acquire territory by cession from a foreign Government. The opinion on this part of the case is short, and we give the whole of it to show how well the selection of a single sentence is calculated to mislead.

The passage referred to is in page 542, in which the court, in speaking of the power of Congress to establish a Territorial Government in Florida until it should become a State, uses the following language:

"In the mean time Florida continues to be a Territory of the United States, governed by that clause of the Constitution which empowers Congress to make all needful rules and regulations respecting the territory or other property of the United States. Perhaps the power of governing a Territory belonging to the United States, which has not, by becoming a State, acquired the means of self-government, may result, necessarily, from the facts that it is not within the jurisdiction of any particular State, and is within the power and jurisdiction of the United States. The right to govern may be the inevitable consequence of the right to acquire territory. *Whichever may be the source from which the power is derived, the possession of it is unquestionable.*"

It is thus clear, from the whole opinion on this point, that the court did not mean to decide whether the power was derived from the clause in the Constitution, or was the necessary consequence of the right to acquire. They do decide that the power in Congress is unquestionable, and in this we entirely concur, and nothing will be found in this opinion to the contrary. The power stands firmly on the latter alternative put by the court—that is, as *"the inevitable consequence of the right to acquire territory."*

And what still more clearly demonstrates that the court did not mean to decide the question, but leave it open for future consideration, is the fact that the case was decided in the Circuit Court by Mr. Justice Johnson, and his decision was affirmed by the Supreme Court. His opinion at the circuit is given in full in a note to the case, and in that opinion he states, in explicit terms, that the clause of the Constitution applies only to the territory then within the limits of the United States, and not to Florida, which had been acquired by cession from Spain. This part of his opinion will be found in the note in page 517 of the report. But he does not dissent from the opinion of the Supreme Court; thereby showing that, in his judgment, as well as that of the court, the case before them did not call for a decision on that particular point, and the court abstained from deciding it. And in part of its opinion subsequent to the passage we have quoted, where the court speak of the legislative power of Congress in Florida, they still speak with the same reserve. And in page 546, speaking of the power of Congress to authorize the Territorial Legislature to establish courts there, the court say: "They are legislative courts, created in virtue of the general right of sovereignty which exists in the Government, or in virtue of that clause which enables Congress to make all needful rules and regulations respecting the territory belonging to the United States."

It has been said that the construction given to this clause is new, and now for the first time brought forward. The case of which we are speaking, and which has been so much discussed, shows that the fact is otherwise. It shows the precisely the same question came before Mr. Justice Johnson, at his circuit, thirty years ago—was fully considered by him, and the same construction given to the clause in the Constitution which is now given by this court. And that upon an appeal from his decision the same question was brought before this court, but was not decided because a decision upon it was not required by the case before the court.

There is another sentence in the opinion which has been commented on, which even in a still more striking manner shows how one may mislead or be misled by taking out a single sentence from the opinion of a court, and leaving out of view what precedes and follows. It is in page 546, near the close of the opinion, in which the court say: "In legislating for them," (the territories of the United States,) "Congress exercises the combined powers of the General and of a State Government." And it is said, that as a State may unquestionably prohibit slavery within its territory, this sentence decides in effect that Congress may do the same in a Territory of the United States, exercising there the powers of a State, as well as the power of the General Government.

The examination of this passage in the case referred to, would be more appropriate when we come to consider in another part of this opinion what power Congress can constitutionally exercise in a Territory, over the rights of person or rights of property of a citizen. But, as it is in the same case with the passage we have before commented on, we dispose of it now, as it will save the court from the necessity of referring again to the case. And it will be seen upon reading the page in which this sentence is found, that it has no reference whatever to the power of Congress over rights of person or rights of property—but relates altogether to the power of establishing judicial tribunals to administer the laws constitutionally passed, and defining the jurisdiction they may exercise.

The law of Congress establishing a Territorial Government in Florida, provided that the Legislature of the Territory should have legislative powers over "all rightful objects of legislation; but no law should be valid which was inconsistent with the laws and Constitution of the United States."

Under the power thus conferred, the Legislature of Florida passed an act, erecting a tribunal at Key West to decide cases of salvage. And in the case of which we are speaking, the question arose whether the Territorial Legislature could be authorized by Congress to establish such a tribunal, with such powers; and one of the parties, among other objections, insisted that Congress could not under the Constitution authorize the Legislature of the Territory to establish such a tribunal with such powers, but that it must be established by Congress itself; and that a sale of cargo made under its order, to pay salvors, was void, as made without legal authority, and passed no property to the purchaser.

It is in disposing of this objection that the sentence relied on occurs, and the court begin that part of the opinion by stating with great precision the point which they are about to decide.

They say: "It has been contended that by the Constitution of the United States, the judicial power of the United States extends to all cases of admiralty and maritime jurisdiction; and that the whole of the judicial power must be vested 'in one Supreme Court, and in such inferior courts as Congress shall from time to time ordain and establish.' Hence it has been argued that Congress cannot vest admiralty jurisdiction in courts created by the Territorial Legislature."

And after thus clearly stating the point before them, and which they were about to decide, they proceed to show that these Territorial tribunals were not constitutional courts, but merely legislative, and that Congress might, therefore, delegate the power to the Territorial Government to establish the court in question; and they conclude that part of the opinion in the following words:

"Although admiralty jurisdiction can be exercised in the States in those courts only which are established in pursuance of the third article of the Constitution, the same limitation does not extend to the Territories. In legislating for them, Congress exercises the combined powers of the General and State Governments."

Thus it will be seen by these quotations from the opinion, that the court, after stating the question it was about to decide in a manner too plain to be misunderstood, proceeded to decide it, and announced, as the opinion of the tribunal, that in organizing the judicial department of the Government in a Territory of the United States, Congress does not act under, and is not restricted by, the third article in the Constitution, and is not bound, in a Territory, to ordain and establish courts in which the judges hold their offices during good behavior, but may exercise the discretionary power which a State exercises in establishing its judicial department, and regulating the jurisdiction of its courts, and may authorize the Territorial Government to establish, or may itself establish, courts in which the judges hold their offices for a term of years only; and may vest in them judicial power upon subjects confided to the judiciary of the United States. And in doing this, Congress undoubtedly exercises the combined power of the General and a State Government. It exercises the discretionary power of a State Government in authorizing the establishment of a court in which the judges hold their appointments for a term of years only, and not during good behavior; and it exercises the power of the General Government in investing that court with admiralty jurisdiction, over which the General Government had exclusive jurisdiction in the Territory.

No one, we presume, will question the correctness of that opinion; nor is there anything in conflict with it in the opinion now given. The point decided in the case cited has no relation to the question now before the court. That depended on the construction of the third article of the Constitution, in relation to the judiciary of the United States, and the power which Congress might exercise in a Territory in organizing the judicial department of the Government. The case before us depends upon other and different provisions of the Constitution, altogether separate and apart from the one above mentioned. The question as to what courts Congress may ordain or establish in a Territory to administer laws which the Constitution authorizes it to pass, and what laws it is or is not authorized by the Constitution to pass, are widely different—are regulated by different and separate articles of the Constitution, and stand upon different principles. And we are satisfied that no one who reads attentively the page in Peters's Reports to which we have referred, can suppose that the attention of the court was drawn for a moment to the question now before this court, or that it meant in that case to say that

Congress had a right to prohibit a citizen of the United States from taking any property which he lawfully held into a Territory of the United States.

This brings us to examine by what provision of the Constitution the present Federal Government, under its delegated and restricted powers, is authorized to acquire territory outside of the original limits of the United States, and what powers it may exercise therein over the person or property of a citizen of the United States, while it remains a Territory, and until it shall be admitted as one of the States of the Union.

There is certainly no power given by the Constitution to the Federal Government to establish or maintain colonies bordering on the United States or at a distance, to be ruled and governed at its own pleasure; nor to enlarge its territorial limits in any way, except by the admission of new States. That power is plainly given; and if a new State is admitted, it needs no further legislation by Congress, because the Constitution itself defines the relative rights and powers, and duties of the State, and the citizens of the State, and the Federal Government. But no power is given to acquire a Territory to be held and governed permanently in that character.

And indeed the power exercised by Congress to acquire territory and establish a Government there, according to its own unlimited discretion, was viewed with great jealousy by the leading statesmen of the day. And in the Federalist, (No. 38), written by Mr. Madison, he speaks of the acquisition of the Northwestern Territory by the confederated States, by the cession from Virginia, and the establishment of a Government there, as an exercise of power not warranted by the Articles of Confederation, and dangerous to the liberties of the people. And he urges the adoption of the Constitution as a security and safeguard against such an exercise of power.

We do not mean, however, to question the power of Congress in this respect. The power to expand the territory of the United States by the admission of new States is plainly given; and in the construction of this power by all the departments of the Government, it has been held to authorize the acquisition of territory, not fit for admission at the time, but to be admitted as soon as its population and situation would entitle it to admission. It is acquired to become a State, and not to be held as a colony and governed by Congress with absolute authority; and as the propriety of admitting a new State is committed to the sound discretion of Congress, the power to acquire territory for that purposes, to be held by the United States until it is in a suitable condition to become a State upon an equal footing with the other States, must rest upon the same discretion. It is a question for the political department of the Government, and not the judicial; and whatever the political department of the Government shall recognize as within the limits of the United States, the judicial department is also bound to recognize, and to administer in it the laws of the United States, so far as they apply, and to maintain in the Territory the authority and rights of the Government, and also the personal rights and rights of property of individual citizens, as secured by the Constitution. All we mean to say on this point is, that, as there is no express regulation in the Constitution defining the power which the General Government may exercise over the person or property of a citizen in a Territory thus acquired, the court must necessarily look to the provisions and principles of the Constitution, and its distribution of powers, for the rules and principles by which its decision must be governed.

Taking this rule to guide us, it may be safely assumed that citizens of the United States who migrate to a Territory belonging to the people of the United States, cannot be ruled as mere colonists, dependent upon the will of the General Government, and to be governed by any law it may think proper to impose. The principle upon which our Governments rest, and upon which alone they continue to exist, is the union of States, sovereign and independent within their own limits in their internal and domestic concerns, and bound together as one people by a General Government, possessing certain enumerated and restricted powers, delegated to it by the people of the several States, and exercising supreme authority within the scope of the powers granted to it, throughout the dominion of the United States. A power, therefore, in the General Government to obtain and hold colonies and dependent territories, over which they might legislate without restriction, would be inconsistent with its own existence in its present form. Whatever it acquires, it acquires for the benefit of the people of the several States who created it. It is their trustee acting for them, and charged with the duty of promoting the interests of the whole people of the Union in the exercise of the powers specifically granted.

At the time when the Territory in question was obtained by cession from France, it contained no population fit to be associated together and admitted as a State; and it therefore was absolutely necessary to hold possession of it, as a Territory belonging to the United States, until it was settled and inhabited by a civilized community capable of self-government, and in a condition to be admitted on equal terms with the other States as a member of the Union. But, as we have before said, it was acquired by the General Government, as the representative and trustee of the people of the United States, and it must therefore be held in that character for their common and equal benefit; for it was the people of the several States, acting through their agent and representative, the Federal Government, who in fact acquired the Territory in question, and the Government holds it for their common use until it shall be associated with the other States as a member of the Union.

But until that time arrives, it is undoubtedly necessary that some Government should be established, in order to organize society, and to protect the inhabitants in their persons and property; and as the people of the United States could act in this matter only through the Government which represented them, and through which they spoke and acted when the Territory was obtained, it was not only within the scope of its powers, but it was its duty to pass such laws and establish such a Government as would enable those by whose authority they acted to reap the advantages anticipated from its acquisition, and to gather there a population which would enable it to assume the position to which it was destined among the States of the Union. The power to acquire necessarily carries with it the power to preserve and apply to the purposes for which it was acquired. The form of government to be established necessarily rested in the discretion of Congress. It was their duty to establish the one that would be best suited for the protection and security of the citizens of the United States, and other inhabitants who might be authorized to take up their abode there, and that must always depend upon the existing condition of the Territory, as to the number and character of its inhabitants, and their situation in the Territory. In some cases a Government, consisting of persons appointed by the Federal Government, would best subserve the interests of the Territory, when the inhabitants were few and scattered, and new to one another. In other instances, it would be more advisable to commit the powers of self-government to the people who had settled in the Territory, as being the most competent to determine what was best for their own interests. But some form of civil authority would be absolutely necessary to organize and preserve civilized society, and prepare it to become a State; and what is the best form must always depend on condition of the Territory at the time, and the choice of the mode must depend upon the exercise of a discretionary power by Congress, acting within the scope of its constitutional authority, and not infringing upon the rights of person or rights or property of the citizen who might go there to reside, or for any other lawful purpose. It was acquired by the exercise of this discretion, and it must be held and governed in like manner, until it is fitted to be a State.

But the power of Congress over the person or property of a citizen can never be a mere discretionary power under our Constitution and form of Government. The powers of the Government and the rights and privileges of the citizen are regulated and plainly defined by the Constitution itself. And when the Territory becomes a part of the United States, the Federal Government enters into possession in the character impressed upon it by those who created it. It enters upon it with its powers over the citizen strictly defined, and limited by the Constitution, from which it derives its own existence, and by virtue of which alone it continues to exist and act as a Government and sovereignty. It has no power of any kind beyond it; and it cannot, when it enters a Territory of the United States, put off its character, and assume discretionary or despotic powers which the Constitution has denied to it. It cannot create for itself a new character separated from the citizens of the United States, and the duties it owes them under the provisions of the Constitution. The Territory being a part of the United States, the Government and the citizen both enter it under the authority of the Constitution, with their respective rights defined and marked out; and the Federal Government can exercise no power over his person or property, beyond what that instrument confers, nor lawfully deny any right which it has reserved.

A reference to a few of the provisions of the Constitution will illustrate this proposition.

For example, no one, we presume, will contend that Congress can make any law in a Territory respecting the establishment of religion, or the free exercise thereof, or abridging the freedom of speech or of the press, or the right of the people of the Territory peaceably to assemble, and to petition the Government for the redress of grievances.

Nor can Congress deny to the people the right to keep and bear arms, nor the right to trial by jury, nor compel any one to be a witness against himself in a criminal proceeding.

These powers, and others, in relation to rights of person, which it is not necessary here to enumerate, are, in express and positive terms, denied to the General Government; and the rights of private property have been guarded with equal care. Thus the rights of property are united with the rights of person, and placed on the same ground by the fifth amendment to the Constitution, which provides that no person shall be deprived of life, liberty, and property, without due process of law. And an act of Congress which deprives a citizen of the United States of his liberty or property, merely because he came himself or brought his property into a particular Territory of the United States, and who had committed no offense against the laws, could hardly be dignified with the name of due process of law.

So, too, it will hardly be contended that Congress could by law quarter a soldier in a house in a Territory without the consent of the owner, in time of peace; nor in time of war, but in a manner prescribed by law. Nor could they by law forfeit the property of a citizen in a Territory who was convicted of treason, for a longer period than the life of the person convicted; nor take private property for public use without just compensation.

The powers over person and property of which we speak are not only not granted to Congress, but are in express terms denied, and they are forbidden to exercise them. And this prohibition is not confined to the States, but the words are general, and extend to the whole territory over which the Constitution gives it power to legislate, including those portions of it remaining under Territorial Government, as well as that covered by States. It is a total absence of power everywhere within the dominion of the United States, and places the citizens of a Territory, so far as these rights are concerned, on the same footing with citizens of the States, and guards them as firmly and plainly against any inroads which the General Government might attempt, under the plea of implied or incidental powers. And if Congress itself cannot do this—if it is beyond the powers conferred on the Federal Government—it will be admitted, we presume, that it could not authorize a Territorial Government to exercise them. It could confer no power on any local Government, established by its authority, to violate the provisions of the Constitution.

It seems, however, to be supposed, that there is a difference between property in a slave and other property, and that different rules may be applied to it in expounding the Constitution of the United States. And the laws and usage's of nations, and the writings of eminent jurists upon the relation of master and slave and their mutual rights and duties, and the powers which Governments may exercise over it, have been dwelt upon in the argument.

But in considering the question before us, it must be borne in mind that there is no law of nations standing between the people of the United States and their Government, and interfering with their relation to each other. The powers of the Government and the rights of the citizen under t, are positive and practical regulations plainly written down. The people of the United States have delegated to it certain enumerated powers, and forbidden it to exercise others. It has no power over the person or property of a citizen but what the citizens of the United States have granted. And no laws or usage's of other nations, or reasoning of statesmen or jurists upon the relations of master and slave, can enlarge the powers of the Government, or take from the citizens the rights they have reserved. And if the Constitution recognizes the right of property of the master in a slave, and makes no distinction between that description of property and other property owned by a citizen, no tribunal, acting under the authority of the United States, whether it be legislative, executive, or judicial, has a right to draw such a distinction, or deny to it the benefit of the provisions and guarantees which have been provided for the protection of private property against the encroachments of the Government.

Now, as we have already said in an earlier part of this opinion, upon a different point, the right of property in a slave is distinctly and express affirmed in the Constitution. The right to traffic in it, like an ordinary article of merchandise and property, was guarantied to the citizens of the United States, in every State that might desire it, for twenty years. And the Government in express terms in pledged to protect it in all future time, if the slaves escapes from his owner. This is done in plain words—too plain to be misunderstood. And no word can be found in the Constitution which gives Congress a greater power over slave property, or which entitles property of that kind to less protection than property of any other description. The only power conferred is the power coupled with the duty of guarding and protecting the owner in his rights.

Upon these considerations, it is the opinion of the court that the act of Congress which prohibited a citizen from holding and owning property of this kind in the territory of the United States north of the line therein mentioned, is not warranted by the Constitution, and is therefore void; and that neither Dred Scott himself, nor any of his family, were made free by begin carried into this territory; even if they had been carried there by the owner, with the intention of becoming a permanent resident.

We have so far examined the case, as it stands under the Constitution of the United States, and the powers thereby delegated to the Federal Government.

But there is another point in the case which depends on State power and State law. And it is contended, on the part of the plaintiff, that he is made free by being taken to Rock Island, in the State of Illinois, independently of his residence in the territory of the United States; and being so made free, he was not again reduced to a state of slavery by being brought back to Missouri.

Our notice of this part of the case will be very brief; for the principle on which it depends was decided in this court, upon much consideration, in the case of *Strader et al. v. Graham*, reported in 10th Howard, 82. In that case, the slaves had been taken from Kentucky to Ohio, with the consent of the owner, and afterwards brought back to Kentucky. And this court held that their *status* or condition, as free or slave, depended upon the laws of Kentucky, when they were brought back into that State, and not of Ohio; and that this court had no jurisdiction to revise the judgment of a State court upon its own laws. This was the point directly before the court, and the decision that this court had not jurisdiction turned upon it, as will be seen by the report of the case.

So in this case. As Scott was a slave when taken into the State of Illinois by his owner, and was there held as such, and brought back in that character, his *status,* as free or slave, depended on the laws of Missouri, and not of Illinois.

It has, however, been urged in the argument, that by the laws of Missouri he was free on his return, and that this case, therefore, cannot be governed by the case of *Strader et al. v. Graham*, where it appeared, by the laws of Kentucky, that the plaintiffs continued to be slaves on their return from Ohio. But whatever doubts or opinions may, at one time, have been entertained upon this subject, we are satisfied, upon a careful examination of all the cases decided in the State courts of Missouri referred to, that it is now firmly settled by the decisions of the highest court in the State, that Scott and his family upon their return were not free, but were, by the laws of Missouri, the property of the defendant; and that the Circuit Court of the United States had no jurisdiction, when, by the laws of the State, the plaintiff was a slave, and not a citizen.

Moreover, the plaintiff, it appears, brought a similar action against the defendant in the State court of Missouri, claiming the freedom of himself and his family upon the same grounds and the same evidence upon which he relies in the case before the court. The case was carried before the Supreme Court of the State; was fully argued there; and that court decided that neither the plaintiff nor his family were entitled to freedom, and were still the slaves of the defendant; and reversed the judgment of the inferior State court, which had given a different decision. If the plaintiff supposed that this judgment of the Supreme Court of the State was erroneous, and that this court had jurisdiction to revise and reverse it, the only mode by which he could legally bring it before this court was by writ of error directed to the Supreme Court of the State, requiring it to transmit the record to this court. If this had been done, it is too plain for argument that the writ must have been dismissed for want of jurisdiction in this court. The case of *Strader and others. v. Graham* is directly in point; and, indeed, independent of any decision, the language of the 25th section of the act of 1789 is too clear and precise to admit of controversy.

But the plaintiff did not pursue the mode prescribed by law for bringing the judgment of a State court before this court for revision, but suffered the case to be remanded to the inferior State court, where it is still continued, and is, by agreement of parties, to await the judgment of this court on the point. All of this appears on the record before us, and by the printed report of the case.

And while the case is yet open and pending in the inferior State court, the plaintiff goes into the Circuit Court of the United States, upon the same case the same evidence, and against the same party, and proceeds to judgment, and then brings here the same case from the Circuit Court, which the law would not have permitted him to bring directly from the State court. And if this court takes jurisdiction in this form, the result, so far as the rights of the respective parties are concerned, is in every respect substantially the same as if it had in open violation of law entertained jurisdiction over the judgment of the State court upon a writ of error, and revised and reversed its judgment upon the ground that its opinion upon the question of law was erroneous. It would ill become this court to sanction such an attempt to evade the law, or to exercise an appellate power in this circuitous way, which it is forbidden to exercise in the direct and regular and invariable forms of judicial proceedings.

Upon the whole, therefore, it is the judgment of this court, that it appears by the record before us that the plaintiff in error is not a citizen of Missouri, in the sense in which that word is used in the Constitution; and that the Circuit Court of the United States, for that reason, had no jurisdiction in the case, and could give no judgment in it. Its judgment for the defendant must, consequently, be reversed, and a mandate issued, directing the suit to be dismissed for want of jurisdiction.

Source:

19 Howard (60 U.S.) 393.

The quotation in the introduction is by Walter Erlich, "Scott V. Sandford," in Kermit Hall, ed., *The Oxford Guide to United States Supreme Court Decisions.* New York: Oxford University Press, 1999, p. 278.

Lincoln-Douglas Debate Number 2, 1858

One of a historic series of debates on slavery and the Union between candidates Abraham Lincoln and Stephen Douglas during the 1858 campaign in Illinois for the U.S. Senate. These debates, among the most significant political discourses in American history, took on the explosive issue that would sunder the nation sectionally and bring civil war between North and South. The Democrat Douglas was seeking reelection to a third term against the Republican Lincoln's challenge. The tone of the campaign was set in mid-June by Lincoln in his "house divided" speech in Springfield, in which he warned that the nation must inevitably become either entirely slaveholding or entirely free. After weeks of attacking each other's positions on slavery, the rival candidates agreed to a series of seven debates in prairie towns throughout Illinois. The debates kicked off in Ottawa on August 21 and proceeded to Freeport on August 27, Jonesboro on September 15, Charleston on September 18, Galesburg on October 7, Quincy on October 13, and Alton on October 15. Lincoln, opposed on moral and constitutional grounds to slavery's extension to the territories, accused Douglas, who supported the doctrine of popular sovereignty (which held that residents of the territories should decide for themselves whether to permit slavery), of complicity in a conspiracy to expand slavery

everywhere. Popular sovereignty, Lincoln contended, contradicted the Supreme Court's landmark 1857 *Dred Scott* decision. Slavery was a moral wrong, he argued, because it denied blacks the right guaranteed to them in the Declaration of Independence to life, liberty, and the pursuit of happiness. At the same time Lincoln opposed the political and social equality of the races and assured southerners that he had no intention of interfering with slavery where it already existed. Lincoln accused Douglas of departing from the position of the founding fathers, who, Lincoln argued, had intended to restrict slavery's growth and thereby put it on a course to ultimate extinction. Douglas rejected both Lincoln's forecast of irrepressible sectional conflict and his interpretation of the founding fathers' intention. He observed that the founders were themselves slaveholders who had left the sovereign states free to do as they pleased on the slavery question. Douglas charged Lincoln and the so-called "Black Republican Party" with endorsing equality between the white and black races and with favoring black citizenship. Slavery, he supposed, would be restricted by economic, geographic, and demographic factors.

During the Freeport speech, excerpted below, Douglas responded to Lincoln's claim that popular sovereignty and *Dred Scott* were irreconcilable. Douglas contended that inhabitants could exclude slavery from a territory despite the Supreme Court's ruling by withholding local legislative protection. This became known as Douglas's "Freeport Doctrine."

Douglas won the election, but the debates helped earn Lincoln a national reputation, reinforced by his 1860 speech at Cooper Union in New York City, which helped make Lincoln better known in the East.

―――――――――――― ⌘ ――――――――――――

Freeport, Illinois
Mr. Lincoln's Speech.

Ladies and Gentlemen—On Saturday last, Judge Douglas and myself first met in public discussion. He spoke one hour, I an hour-and-a-half, and he replied for half an hour. The order is now reversed. I am to speak an hour, he an hour-and-a-half, and then I am to reply for half an hour. . . . In the course of that opening argument Judge Douglas proposed to me seven distinct interrogatories. . . . I now propose that I will answer any of the interrogatories . . . whether he answers mine or not; and that after I have done so, I shall propound mine to him.

I have supposed myself, since the organization of the Republican party at Bloomington, in May, 1856, bound as a party man by the platforms of the party, then and since. If in any interrogatories which I shall answer I go beyond the scope of what is within these platforms it will be perceived that no one is responsible but myself.

*   *   *

Question 1. "I desire to know whether Lincoln to-day stands, as he did in 1854, in favor of the unconditional repeal of the fugitive slave law?"

Answer. I do not now, nor ever did, stand in favor of the unconditional repeal of the fugitive slave law.

Q. 2. "I desire him to answer whether he stands pledged to-day, as he did in 1854, against the admission of any more slave States into the Union, even if the people want them?"

A. I do not now, nor ever did, stand pledged against the admission of any more slave States into the Union.

Q. 3. "I want to know whether he stands pledged against the admission of a new State into the Union with such a Constitution as the people of that State may see fit to make."

A. I do not stand pledged against the admission of a new State into the Union, with such a Constitution as the people of that State may see fit to make. [Cries of "good," "good."]

Q. 4. "I want to know whether he stands to-day pledged to the abolition of slavery in the District of Columbia?"

A. I do not stand to-day pledged to the abolition of slavery in the District of Columbia.

Q. 5. "I desire him to answer whether he stands pledged to the prohibition of the slave trade between the different States?"

A. I do not stand pledged to the prohibition of the slave trade between the different States.

Q. 6. "I desire to know whether he stands pledged to prohibit slavery in all the Territories of the United States, North as well as South of the Missouri Compromise line."

A. I am impliedly, if not expressly, pledged to a belief in the *right* and *duty* of Congress to prohibit slavery in all the United States Territories.

Q. 7. "I desire him to answer whether he is opposed to the acquisition of any new territory unless slavery is first prohibited therein."

A. I am not generally opposed to honest acquisition of territory; and, in any given case, I would or would not oppose such acquisition, accordingly as I might think such acquisition would or would not aggravate the slavery question among ourselves.

Now, my friends, it will be perceived upon an examination of these questions and answers, that so far I have only answered that I was not *pledged* to this, that or the other. The Judge has not framed his interrogatories to ask me anything more than this, and I have answered in strict accordance with the interrogatories, and have answered truly that I am not *pledged* at all upon any of the points to which I have answered. But I am not disposed to hang upon the exact form of his interrogatory. I am rather disposed to take up at least some of these questions, and state what I really think upon them.

As to the first one, in regard to the Fugitive Slave Law, I have never hesitated to say, and I do not now hesitate to say, that I think, under the Constitution of the United States, the people of the Southern States are entitled to a Congressional Fugitive Slave Law. Having said that, I have had nothing to say in regard to the existing Fugitive Slave Law further than that I think it should have been framed so as to be free from some of the objections that pertain to it, without lessening its efficiency. And inasmuch as we are not now in an agitation in regard to an alteration or modification of that law, I would not be the man to introduce it as a new subject of agitation upon the general question of slavery.

In regard to the other question of whether I am pledged to the admission of any more slave States into the Union, I state to you very frankly that I would be exceedingly sorry ever to be put in a position of having to pass upon that question. I should be exceedingly glad to know that there would never be another slave State admitted into the Union; [applause]; but I must add, that if slavery shall be kept out of the Territories during the territorial existence of any one given Territory, and then the people shall, having a fair chance and a clear field, when they come to adopt the Constitution, do such an extraordinary thing as to adopt a Slave Constitution, uninfluenced by the actual presence of the institution among them, I see no alternative, if we own the country, but to admit them into the Union.

The third interrogatory is answered by the answer to the second, it being, as I conceive, the same as the second.

The fourth one is in regard to the abolition of slavery in the District of Columbia. In relation to that, I have my mind very distinctly made up. I should be exceedingly glad to see slavery abolished in the District of Columbia. I believe that Congress possesses the constitutional power to abolish it. Yet as a member of Congress, I should not with my present views, be in favor of *endeavoring* to abolish slavery in the District of Columbia, unless it would be upon these conditions. *First,* that the abolition should be gradual. *Second,* that it should be on a vote of the majority of qualified voters in the District, and *third,* that compensation should be made to unwilling owners. With these three conditions, I confess I would be exceedingly glad to see Congress abolish slavery in the District of Columbia, and, in the language of Henry Clay, "sweep from our Capital that foul blot upon our nation."

In regard to the fifth interrogatory, I must say here, that as to the question of the abolition of the Slave Trade between the different States, I can truly answer, as I have, that I am *pledged* to nothing about it. It is a subject to which I have not given that mature consideration that would make me feel authorized to state a position so as to hold myself entirely bound by it. In other words, that question has never been prominently enough before me to induce me to investigate whether we really have the Constitutional power to do it. I could investigate it if I had sufficient time, to bring myself to a conclusion upon that subject, but I have not done so, and I say so frankly to you here, and to Judge Douglas. I must say, however, that if I should be of opinion that Congress does possess the Constitutional power to abolish the slave trade among the different States, I should still not be in favor of the exercise of that power unless upon some conservative principle as I conceive it, akin to what I have said in relation to the abolition of slavery in the District of Columbia.

My answer as to whether I desire that slavery should be prohibited in all the Territories of the United States is full and explicit within itself, and cannot be made clearer by any comments of mine. So I suppose in regard to the question whether I am opposed to the acquisition of any more territory unless slavery is first prohibited therein, my answer is such that I could add nothing by way of illustration, or making myself better understood, than the answer which I have placed in writing.

*　*　*

I now proceed to propound to the Judge the interrogatories. . . . [The four questions are answered in Douglas's reply.]

*　*　*

I have been in the habit of charging as a matter of belief on my part, that, in the introduction of the Nebraska bill [Kansas-Nebraska Act, 1854] into Congress, there was a conspiracy to make slavery perpetual and national. I have arranged from time to time the evidence which establishes and proves the truth of this charge. . . .

. . . I have called his attention to the fact that when he and some others began arguing that they were giving an increased degree of liberty to the people in the Territories over and above what they formerly had on the question of slavery. . . . A question was raised whether the law was enacted to give such unconditional liberty to the people and to test the sincerity of this mode of argument. Mr. Chase, of Ohio, introduced an amendment, in which he made the law—if the amendment were adopted—expressly declare that the people of the Territory should have the power to exclude slavery if they saw fit. I have asked attention also to the fact that Judge Douglas and those who acted with him, voted that amendment down, notwithstanding it expressed exactly the thing they said was the true intent and meaning of the law. I have called

attention to the fact that in subsequent times, a decision of the Supreme Court has been made in which it has been declared that a Territorial Legislature has no constitutional right to exclude slavery. And I have argued and said that for men who did intend that the people of the territory should have the right to exclude slavery absolutely and unconditionally, the voting down of Chase's amendment is wholly inexplicable. . . . They left room thereby for this Dred Scott decision, which goes very far to make slavery national throughout the United States.

. . . I ask him to give some attention to the evidence which I brought forward, that he himself had discovered a "fatal blow being struck" against the right of the people to exclude slavery from their limits. . . . He discovers a similar or identical provision in the Lecompton Constitution. Made by whom? The framers of that Constitution. Advocated by whom? By all the members of the party in the nation, who advocated the introduction of Kansas into the Union under the [proslavery] Lecompton Constitution.

*　*　*

Go on, Judge Douglas
Mr. Douglas' Speech:

Ladies and Gentlemen—
. . . I laid the foundation for those interrogatories by showing that they constituted the platform of the party whose nominee he is for the Senate. I did not presume that I had the right to catechize him as I saw proper, unless I showed that his party, or a majority of it, stood upon the platform and were in favor of the propositions upon which my questions were based. I desired simply to know, inasmuch as he had been nominated as the first, last, and only choice of his party, whether he concurred in the platform which that party had adopted for its government. . . . I will first respond to those which he has presented to me. Mark you, he has not presented interrogatories which have ever received the sanction of the party with which I am acting, and hence he has no other foundation for them than his own curiosity.

. . . In reference to Kansas; it is my opinion, that as she has population enough to constitute a slave State, she has people enough for a free State. I will not make Kansas an exceptional case to the other States of the Union. I hold it to be a sound rule of universal application to require a territory to contain the requisite population for a member of Congress, before it is admitted as a State into the Union. . . . Either Kansas must come in as a free State, with whatever population she may have, or the rule must be applied to all the other territories alike. I therefore answer at once, that it having been decided that Kansas has people enough for a slave State, I hold that she has enough for a free State. . . .

The next question propounded to me by Mr. Lincoln is, can the people of a territory in any lawful way against the wishes of any citizen of the United States; exclude slavery from their limits prior to the formation of a State Constitution? I answer emphatically, as Mr. Lincoln has heard me answer a hundred times from every stump in Illinois, that in my opinion the people of a territory can, by lawful means, exclude slavery from their limits prior to the formation of a State Constitution. . . . It matters not what way the Supreme Court may hereafter decide as to the abstract question whether slavery may or may not go into a territory under the constitution, the people have the lawful means to introduce it or exclude it as they please, for the reason that slavery cannot exist a day or an hour anywhere, unless it is supported by local police regulations. Those police regulations can only be established by the local legislature, and if the people are opposed to slavery they will elect representatives to that body who will by unfriendly legislation effectually prevent the introduction of it into their midst. If, on the contrary, they are for it, their legislation will favor its extension. Hence, no matter what the decision of the Supreme Court may be on that abstract question, still the right of the people to make a slave territory or a free territory is perfect and complete under the Nebraska bill. I hope Mr. Lincoln deems my answer satisfactory on that point.

[Re the Chase Amendment:] The language of that bill [Kansas-Nebraska Act] which I have quoted, gave the full power and the full authority over the subject of slavery, affirmatively and negatively, to introduce it or exclude it, so far as the Constitution of the United States would permit. What more could Mr. Chase give by his amendment? Nothing. He offered his amendment for the identical purpose for which Mr. Lincoln is using it, to enable demagogues in the country to try and deceive the people.

❖   ❖   ❖

The third question which Mr. Lincoln presented is, if the Supreme Court of the United States shall decide that a State of this Union cannot exclude slavery from its own limits will I submit to it? . . . Mr. Lincoln's object is to cast an imputation upon the Supreme Court. . . . He might as well ask me, suppose Mr. Lincoln should steal a horse would I sanction it; and it would be as genteel in me to ask him, in the event he stole a horse, what ought to be done with him. He casts an imputation upon the Supreme Court of the United States by supposing that they would violate the Constitution of the United States. I tell him that such a thing is not possible. I would be an act of moral treason that no man on the bench could ever descend to Mr. Lincoln himself would never in his partisan feelings so far forget what was right as to be guilty of such an act.

The fourth question of Mr. Lincoln is, are you in favor of acquiring additional territory in disregard as to how such acquisition may effect the Union on the slavery questions. This question is very ingeniously and cunningly put.

. . . I answer that whenever it becomes necessary, in our growth and progress to acquire more territory, that I am in favor of it, without reference to the question of slavery, and when we have acquired it, I will leave the people free to do as they please, either to make it slave or free territory, as they prefer. It is idle to tell me or you that we have territory enough. . . . With our natural increase, growing with a rapidity unknown in any other part of the globe, with the tide of emigration that is fleeing from despotism in the old world to seek a refuge in our own, there is a constant torrent pouring into this country that requires more land, more territory upon which to settle, and just as fast as our interests and our destiny require additional territory in the north, in the south, or on the islands of the ocean, I am for it, and when we acquire it will leave the people, according to the Nebraska bill, free to do as they please on the subject of slavery and every other question.

I trust now that Mr. Lincoln will deem himself answered of his four points. . . . You Black Republicans who say good, I have no doubt think that they are all good men. I have reason to recollect that some people in this country think that Fred. Douglass [former slave and prominent abolitionist] is a very good man. The last time I came here to make a speech, while talking from the stand to you, people of Freeport, as I am doing to-day, I saw a carriage and a magnificent one it was, drive up and take a position on the outside of the crowd; a beautiful young lady was sitting on the box seat, whilst Fred. Douglass and her mother reclined inside, and the owner of the carriage acted as driver. I saw this in your own town. All I have to say of it is this, that if you, Black Republicans, think that the negro ought to be on a social equality with your wives and daughters, and ride in a carriage with your wife, whilst you drive the team, you have a perfect right to do so. I am told that one of Fred. Douglass' kinsmen, another rich black Negro, is now traveling in this part of the State making speeches for his friend Lincoln as the champion of black men. All I have to say on that subject is that those of you who believe that the negro is your equal and ought to be on an equality with you socially, politically, and legally; have a right to entertain those opinions, and of course will vote for Mr. Lincoln.

I have a word to say on Mr. Lincoln's answer to the interrogatories contained in my speech at Ottawa, and which he has pretended to reply to here to-day. . . .

During the late discussions in this city, Lincoln made a speech, to which Judge Douglas replied. In Lincoln's speech he took the broad ground that, according to the Declaration of Independence, the whites and blacks are equal. From this he drew the conclusion, which he several times repeated, that the white man had no right to pass laws for the government of the black man without the nigger's consent. This speech of Lincoln's was heard and applauded by all the Abolitionists assembled in Springfield. . . . This platform was adopted in nearly every county that gave a Black Republican majority for the Legislature in that year, and . . . it was the creed of the Black Republican party at the time. . . . I will now read the resolutions adopted at the Rockford [Illinois] Convention on the 30th of August, 1854

Resolved, That the continued and increasing aggressions of slavery in our country are destructive of the best rights of a free people, and that such aggressions cannot be successfully resisted without the united political action of all good men.

Resolved, That the citizens of the United States hold in their hands peaceful, constitutional, and efficient remedy against the encroachments of the slave power, the ballot box, and, if that remedy is bodily and wisely applied, the principles of liberty and eternal justice will be established.

Resolved, That we accept this issue forced upon us by the slave power, and, in defense of freedom, will co-operate and be known as Republicans, pledged to the accomplishment of the following purposes:

To bring the Administration of the Government back to the control of first principles; to restore Kansas and Nebraska to the position of free Territories; to repeal and entirely abrogate the fugitive slave law; to restrict slavery to those States in which it exist; to prohibit the admission of any more slave States into the Union; to exclude slavery from all the territories over which the general government has exclusive jurisdiction, and to resist the acquisition of any more territories unless the introduction of slavery therein forever shall have been prohibited.

Resolved, That in furtherance of these principles we will use such constitutional and lawful means as shall seem best adapted to their accomplishment, and that we will support no man for office under the General or State Government who is not positively committed to the support of these principles and whose personal character and conduct is not a guaranty that he is reliable and shall abjure all party allegiance and ties. . . . Now, Mr. Lincoln complains; Mr. Lincoln charges that I did you and him injustice by saying that this was the platform of your party. . . .

❖　❖　❖

. . . The compromise measures of 1850 were . . . sanctioned by the National men of both parties. They constituted a common plank upon which both Whigs and Democrats stood. . . . Thus the old line Whigs and the old line Democrats stood pledged to the great principle of self-government, which guarantees to the people of each Territory the right to decide the slavery question for themselves. . . . As Mr. Lincoln would be very sorry to be placed in such an embarrassing position as to be obliged to vote on the admission of any more slave States, I propose, out of mere kindness, to relieve him from any such necessity.

❖　❖　❖

[In his "House Divided" speech] you find that Mr. Lincoln lays down the doctrine that this Union cannot endure divided as our Fathers made it, with free and slave States. He says they must all become one thing, or all the other; that they must be all free or all slave, or else the Union cannot continue to exist. It being his opinion that to admit any more slave States, to continue to divide the Union into free and slave States, will dissolve it. I want to know of Mr. Lincoln whether he will vote for the admission of another Slave state.

❖　❖　❖

If [President James] Buchanan stands, as I doubt not he will, by the recommendation contained in his message, that hereafter all State constitutions ought to be submitted to the people before the admission of the State into the Union, he will find me standing by him firmly, shoulder to shoulder, in carrying it out. I know Mr. Lincoln's object, he wants to divide the Democratic party, in order that he may defeat me and get to the Senate.

Mr. Douglas' time here expired, and he stopped on the moment.

Mr. Lincoln's Rejoinder

As Mr. Lincoln arose he was greeted with vociferous cheers. He said:

❖　❖　❖

. . . It is true that many of these resolutions are at variance with the positions I have here assumed. All I have to ask is that we talk reasonably and rationally about it. I happen to know, the Judge's opinion to the contrary notwithstanding, that I have never tried to conceal my opinions, nor tried to deceive any one in reference to them. . . . These meetings which the Judge has alluded to, and the resolutions he has read from were local and did not spread over the whole State. . . . I'll tell you what [Douglas] is afraid of. *He is afraid we'll all pull together.* This is what alarms him more than anything else. For my part, I do hope that all of us, entertaining a common sentiment in opposition to what appears to us a design to nationalize and perpetuate slavery, will waive minor differences on questions which either belong to the dead past or the distant future, and all pull together in this struggle. . . .

. . . If I were put to the test, and a Territory from which slavery had been excluded should present herself with a State Constitution sanctioning slavery—a most extraordinary thing and wholly unlikely ever to happen—I did not see how I could avoid voting for her admission. But he refuses to understand that I said so, and he wants this audience to understand that I did not say so. Yet it will be so reported in the printed speech that he cannot help seeing it. . . .

See also THE COMPROMISE OF 1850; KANSAS-NEBRASKA ACT, 1854; DRED SCOTT DECISION, 1857.

Source:
Abraham Lincoln, Speeches and Writings, 1832–58, pp. 537–580.

Ableman v. Booth; United States v. Booth, 1859

Case decided by the U.S. Supreme Court on March 7, 1859, on the broad issue of state and federal powers. In 1854 the Wisconsin Supreme Court freed an abolitionist editor, Sherman Booth, who had been convicted in federal court of aiding a runaway slave, in violation of the Fugitive Slave Law of 1850. The Supreme Court reversed the state court's decision. The majority opinion, written by Chief Justice Roger Taney, denied the right of the state judiciary to interfere in federal cases; it also upheld the constitutionality of the Fugitive Slave Law. The Wisconsin legislature responded by passing a resolution attempting to nullify the Supreme Court ruling.

———————————— ⌒⨯⌒ ————————————

STEPHEN V. R. ABLEMAN, PLAINTIFF IN ERROR, V. SHERMAN M. BOOTH; AND THE UNITED STATES, PLAINTIFF IN ERROR, V. SHERMAN M. BOOTH.

Mr. Chief Justice Taney delivered the opinion of the court.

The plaintiff in error in the first of these cases is the marshal of the United States for the district of Wisconsin, and the two cases have arisen out of the same transaction, and depend, to some extent, upon the same principles. On that account, they have been argued and considered together; and the following are the facts as they appear in the transcripts before us:

Sherman M. Booth was charged before Winfield Smith, a commissioner duly appointed by the District Court of the United States for the district of Wisconsin, with having, on the 11th day of March, 1854, aided and abetted, at Milwaukee, in the said district, the escape of a fugitive slave from the deputy marshal, who had him in custody under a warrant issued by the district judge of the United States for that district, under the act of Congress of September 18, 1850.

Upon the examination before the commissioner, he was satisfied that an offence had been committed as charged, and that there was probable cause to believe that Booth had been guilty of it; and thereupon held him to bail to appear and answer before the District Court of the United States for the district of Wisconsin, on the first Monday in July then next ensuing. But on the 26th of May his bail or surety in the recognisance delivered him to the marshal, in the presence of the commissioner, and requested the commissioner to recommit Booth to the custody of the marshal; and he having failed to recognise again for his appearance before the District Court, the commissioner committed him to the custody of the marshal, to be delivered to the keeper of the jail until he should be discharged by due course of law.

Booth made application on the next day, the 27th of May, to A. D. Smith, one of the justices of the Supreme Court of the State of Wisconsin, for a writ of *habeas corpus*, stating that he was restrained of his liberty by Stephen V. R. Ableman, marshal of the United States for that district, under the warrant of commitment hereinbefore mentioned; and alleging that his imprisonment was illegal, because the act of Congress of September 18, 1850, was unconstitutional and void; and also that the warrant was defective, and did not describe the offence created by that act, even if the act were valid.

Upon this application, the justice, on the same day, issued the writ of *habeas corpus*, directed to the marshal, requiring him forthwith to have the body of Booth before him, (the said justice,) together with the time and cause of his imprisonment. The marshal thereupon, on the day above mentioned, produced Booth, and made his return, stating that he was received into his custody as marshal on the day before, and held in custody by virtue of the warrant of the commissioner above mentioned, a copy of which he annexed to and returned with the writ.

To this return Booth demurred, as not sufficient in law to justify his detention. And upon the hearing the justice decided that his detention was illegal, and ordered the marshal to discharge him and set him at liberty, which was accordingly done.

Afterwards, on the 9th of June, in the same year, the marshal applied to the Supreme Court of the State for a *certiorari*, setting forth in his application the proceedings hereinbefore mentioned, and charging that the release of Booth by the justice was erroneous and unlawful, and praying that his proceedings might be brought before the Supreme Court of the State for revision.

The *certiorari* was allowed on the same day; and the writ was accordingly issued on the 12th of the same month, and returnable on the third Tuesday of the month; and on the 20th the return was made by the justice, stating the proceedings, as hereinbefore mentioned.

The case was argued before the Supreme Court of the State, and on the 19th of July if pronounced its judgment, affirming the decision of the associate justice discharging Booth from imprisonment, with costs against Ableman, the marshal.

Afterwards, on the 26th of October, the marshal sued out a writ of error, returnable to this court on the first Monday of December, 1854, in order to bring the judgment here for revision; and the defendant in error was regularly cited to appear on that day; and the record and proceedings were certified to this court by the clerk of the State court in the usual form, in obedience to the writ of error. And on the 4th of December, Booth, the defendant in error, filed a memorandum in writing in this court, stating that he had been cited to appear here in this case, and that he submitted it to the judgment of this court on the reasoning in the argument and opinions in the printed pamphlets therewith sent.

After the judgment was entered in the Supreme Court of Wisconsin, and before the writ of error was sued out, the State court entered on its record, that, in the final judgment it had rendered, the validity of the act of Congress of September 18, 1850, and of February 12, 1793, and the authority of the marshal to hold the defendant in his custody, under the process mentioned in his return to the writ of *habeas corpus,* were respectively drawn in question, and the decision of the court in the final judgment was against their validity, respectively.

This certificate was not necessary to give this court jurisdiction, because the proceedings upon their face show that these questions arose, and how they were decided; but it shows that at that time the Supreme Court of Wisconsin did not question their obligation to obey the writ of error, nor the authority of this court to re-examine their judgment in the cases specified. And the certificate is given for the purpose of placing distinctly on the record the points that were raised and decided in that court, in order that this court might have no difficulty in exercising its appellate power, and pronouncing its judgment upon all of them.

We come now to the second case. At the January term of the District Court of the United States for the district of Wisconsin, after Booth had been set at liberty, and after the transcript of the proceedings in the case above mentioned had been returned to and filed in this court, the grand jury found a bill of indictment against Booth for the offence with which he was charged before the commissioner, and from which the State court had discharged him. The indictment was found on the 4th of January, 1855. On the 9th a motion was made, by counsel on behalf of the accused, to quash the indictment, which was over-

ruled by the court; and he thereupon pleaded not guilty, upon which issue was joined. On the 10th a jury was called and appeared in court, when he challenged the array; but the challenge was overruled and the jury empanelled. The trial, it appears, continued from day to day, until the 13th, when the jury found him guilty in the manner and form in which he stood indicted in the fourth and fifth counts. On the 16th he moved for a new trial and in arrest of judgment, which motions were argued on the 20th, and on the 23d the court overruled the motions, and sentenced the prisoner to be imprisoned for one month, and to pay a fine of $1,000 and the costs of prosecution; and that he remain in custody until the sentence was complied with.

We have stated more particularly these proceedings, from a sense of justice to the District Court, as they show that every opportunity of making his defence was afforded him, and that his case was fully heard and considered.

On the 26th of January, three days after the sentence was passed, the prisoner by his counsel filed his petition in the Supreme Court of the State, and with his petition filed a copy of the proceedings in the District Court, and also affidavits from the foreman and one other member of the jury who tried him, stating that their verdict was, guilty on the fourth and fifth counts, and not guilty on the other three; and stated in his petition that his imprisonment was illegal, because the fugitive slave law was unconstitutional; that the District Court had no jurisdiction to try or punish him for the matter charged against him, and that the proceedings and sentence of that court were absolute nullities in law. Various other objections to the proceedings are alleged, which are unimportant in the questions now before the court, and need not, therefore, be particularly stated. On the next day, the 27th, the court directed two writs of *habeas corpus* to be issued—one to the marshal, and one to the sheriff of Milwaukee, to whose actual keeping the prisoner was committed by the marshal, by order of the District Court. The *habeas corpus* directed each of them to produce the body of the prisoner, and make known the cause of his imprisonment, immediately after the receipt of the writ.

On the 30th of January the marshal made his return, not acknowledging the jurisdiction, but stating the sentence of the District Court as his authority; that the prisoner was delivered to, and was then in the actual keeping of the sheriff of Milwaukee county, by order of the court, and he therefore had no control of the body of the prisoner; and if the sheriff had not received him, he should have so reported to the District Court, and should have conveyed him to some other place or prison, as the court should command.

On the same day the sheriff produced the body of Booth before the State court, and returned that he had been committed to his custody by the marshal, by virtue of a transcript, a true copy of which was annexed to his return, and which was the only process of authority by which he detained him.

This transcript was a full copy of the proceedings and sentence in the District Court of the United States, as hereinbefore stated. To this return the accused, by his counsel, filed a general demurrer.

The court ordered the hearing to be postponed until the 2d of February, and notice to be given to the district attorney of the United States. It was accordingly heard on that day, and on the next, (February 3d,) the court decided that the imprisonment was illegal, and ordered and adjudged that Booth be, and he was by the judgment, forever discharged from that imprisonment and restraint, and he was accordingly set at liberty.

On the 21st of April next following, the Attorney General of the United States presented a petition to the Chief Justice of the Supreme Court, stating briefly the facts in the case, and at the same time presenting an exemplification of the proceedings hereinbefore stated, duly certified by the clerk of the State court, and averring in his petition that the State court had no jurisdiction in the case, and praying that a writ of error might issue to bring its judgment before this court to correct the error. The writ of error was allowed and issued, and, according to the rules and practice of the court, was returnable on the first Monday of December, 1855, and a citation for the defendant in error to appear on that day was issued by the Chief Justice at the same time.

No return having been made to this writ, the Attorney General, on the 1st of February, 1856, filed affidavits, showing that the writ of error had been duly served on the clerk of the Supreme Court of Wisconsin, at his office, on the 30th of May, 1855, and the citation served on the defendant in error on the 28th of June, in the same year. And also the affidavit of the district attorney of the United States for the district of Wisconsin, setting forth that when he served the writ of error upon the clerk, as above mentioned, he was informed by the clerk, and has also been informed by one of the justices of the Supreme Court, which released Booth, *"that the court had directed the clerk to make no return to the writ of error, and to enter no order upon the journals or records of the court concerning the same."* And, upon these proofs, the Attorney General moved the court for an order upon the clerk to make return to the writ of error, on or before the first day of the next ensuing term of this court. The rule was accordingly laid, and on the 22d of July, 1856, the Attorney General filed with the clerk of this court the affidavit of the marshal of the district of Wisconsin, that he had served the rule on the clerk on the 7th of the month above mentioned; and no return having been made, the Attorney General, on the 27th of February, 1857, moved for leave to file the certi-

fied copy of the record of the Supreme Court of Wisconsin, which he had produced with his application for the writ of error, and to docket the case in this court, in conformity with a motion to that effect made at the last term. And the court thereupon, on the 6th of March, 1857, ordered the copy of the record filed by the Attorney General to be received and entered on the docket of this court, to have the same effect and legal operation as if returned by the clerk with the writ of error, and that the case stand for argument at the next ensuing term, without further notice to either party.

The case was accordingly docketed, but was not reached for argument in the regular order and practice of the court until the present term.

This detailed statement of the proceedings in the different courts has appeared to be necessary in order to form a just estimate of the action of the different tribunals in which it has been heard, and to account for the delay in the final decision of a case, which, from its character, would seem to have demanded prompt action. The first case, indeed, was reached for trial two terms ago. But as the two cases are different portions of the same prosecution for the same offense, they unavoidably, to some extent, involve the same principles of law, and it would hardly have been proper to hear and decide the first before the other was ready for hearing and decision. They have accordingly been argued together, by the Attorney General of the United States, at the present term. No counsel has in either case appeared for the defendant in error. But we have the pamphlet arguments filed and referred to by Booth in the first case, as hereinbefore mentioned, also the opinions and arguments of the Supreme Court of Wisconsin, and of the judges who compose it, in full, and are enabled, therefore, to see the grounds on which they rely to support their decisions.

It will be seen, from the foregoing statement of facts, that a judge of the Supreme Court of the State of Wisconsin in the first of these cases, claimed and exercised the right to supervise and annul the proceedings of a commissioner of the United States, and to discharge a prisoner, who had been committed by the commissioner for an office against the laws of this Government, and that this exercise of power by the judge was afterwards sanctioned and affirmed by the Supreme Court of the State.

In the second case, the State court has gone a step further, and claimed and exercised jurisdiction over the proceedings and judgment of a District Court of the United States, and upon a summary and collateral proceeding, by *habeas corpus,* has set aside and annulled its judgment, and discharged a prisoner who had been tried and found guilty of an offence against the laws of the United States, and sentenced to imprisonment by the District Court.

And it further appears that the State court have not only claimed and exercised this jurisdiction, but have also determined that their decision is final and conclusive upon all the courts of the United States, and ordered their clerk to disregard and refuse obedience to the writ of error issued by this court, pursuant to the act of Congress of 1789, to bring here for examination and revision the judgment of the State court.

These propositions are new in the jurisprudence of the United States, as well as of the States; and the supremacy of the State courts over the courts of the United States, in cases arising under the Constitution and laws of the United States, is now for the first time asserted and acted upon in the Supreme Court of a State.

The supremacy is not, indeed, set forth distinctly and broadly, in so many words, in the printed opinions of the judges. It is intermixed with elaborate discussions of different provisions in the fugitive slave law, and of the privileges and power of the writ of *habeas corpus*. But the paramount power of the State court lies at the foundation of these decision; for their commentaries upon the provisions of that law, and upon the privileges and power of the writ of *habeas corpus*, were out of place, and their judicial action upon them without authority of law, unless they had the power to revise and control the proceedings in the criminal case of which they were speaking; and their judgments, releasing the prisoner, and disregarding the writ of error from this court, can rest upon no other foundation.

If the criminal power exercised in this instance has been reserved to the States, no offence against the laws of the United States can be punished by their own courts, without the permission and according to the judgment of the courts of the State in which the party happens to be imprisoned; for, if the Supreme Court of Wisconsin possessed the power it has exercised in relation to offences against the act of Congress in question, it necessarily follows that they must have the same judicial authority in relation to any other law of the United States; and, consequently, their supervising and controlling power would embrace the whole criminal code of the United States, and extend to offences against our revenue laws, or any other law intended to guard the different departments of the General Government from fraud or violence. And it would embrace all crimes, from the highest to the lowest; including felonies, which are punished with death, as well as misdemeanors, which are punished by imprisonment. And, moreover, if the power is possessed by the Supreme Court of the State of Wisconsin, it must belong equally to every other State in the Union, when the prisoner is within its territorial limits; and it is very certain that the State courts would not always agree in opinion; and it would often happen, that an act which was admitted to be an offence, and justly punished, in one State, would be regarded as innocent, and indeed as praiseworthy, in another.

It would seem to be hardly to do more than state the result to which these decisions of the State courts must inevitably lead. It is, of itself, a sufficient and conclusive answer; for no one will suppose that a Government which has now lasted nearly seventy years, enforcing its laws by its own tribunals, and preserving the union of the States, could have lasted a single year, or fulfilled the high trusts committed to it, if offences its laws could not have been punished without the consent of the State in which the culprit was found.

The judges of the Supreme Court of Wisconsin do not distinctly state from what source they suppose they have derived this judicial power. There can be no such thing as judicial authority, unless it is conferred by a Government or sovereignty; and if the judges and courts of Wisconsin possess the jurisdiction they claim, they must derive it either from the United States or the State. It certainly has not been conferred on them by the United States; and it is equally clear it was not in the power of the State to confer it, even if it had attempted to do so; for no State can authorize one of its judges or courts to exercise judicial power, by *habeas corpus* or otherwise, within the jurisdiction of another and independent Government. And although the State of Wisconsin is sovereign within its territorial limits to a certain extent, yet that sovereignty is limited and restricted by the Constitution of the United States. And the powers of the General Government, and of the State, although both exist and are exercised within the same territorial limits, are yet separate and distinct sovereignties, acting separately and independently of each other, within their respective spheres. And the sphere of action appropriated to the United States is as far beyond the reach of the judicial process issued by a State judge or a State court, as if the line of division was traced by landmarks and monuments visible to the eye. And the State of Wisconsin had no more power to authorize these proceedings of its judges and courts, than it would have had if the prisoner had been confined in Michigan, or in any other State of the Union, for an offence against the laws of the State in which he was imprisoned.

It is, however, due to the State to say, that we do not find this claim of paramount jurisdiction in the State courts over the courts of the United States asserted or countenanced by the Constitution or laws of the State. We find it only in the decisions of the judges of the Supreme Court. Indeed, at the very time these decisions were made, there was a statute of the State which declares that a person brought up on a *habeas corpus* shall be remanded, if it appears that he is confined:

"1st. By virtue of process, by any court or judge of the United States, in a case where such court or judge has exclusive jurisdiction; or,

"2d. By virtue of the final judgment or decree of any competent court of civil or criminal jurisdiction." (Revised Statutes of the State of Wisconsin, 1849, ch. 124, page 629.)

Even, therefore, if these cases depended upon the laws of Wisconsin, it would be difficult to find in these provisions such a grant of judicial power as the Supreme Court claims to have derived from the State.

But, as we have already said, questions of this kind must always depend upon the Constitution and laws of the United States, and not of a State. The Constitution was not formed merely to guard the States against danger from foreign nations, but mainly to secure union and harmony at home; for if this object could be attained, there would be but little danger from abroad; and to accomplish this purpose, it was felt by the statesmen who framed the Constitution, and by the people who adopted it, that it was necessary that many of the rights of sovereignty which the States then possessed should be ceded to the General Government; and that, in the sphere of action assigned to it, it should be supreme, and strong enough to execute its own laws by its own tribunals, without interruption from a State or from State authorities. And it was evident that anything short of this would be inadequate to the main objects for which the Government was established; and that local interests, local passions or prejudices, incited and fostered by individuals for sinister purposes, would lead to acts of aggression and injustice by one State upon the rights of another, which would ultimately terminate in violence and force, unless there was a common arbiter between them, armed with power enough to protect and guard the rights of all, by appropriate laws, to be carried into execution peacefully by its judicial tribunals.

The language of the Constitution, by which this power is granted, is too plain to admit of doubt or to need comment. It declares that "this Constitution, and the laws of the United States which shall be passed in pursuance thereof, and all treaties made, or which shall be made, under the authority of the United States, shall be the supreme law of the land, and the judges in every State shall be bound thereby, anything in the Constitution or laws of any State to the contrary notwithstanding."

But the supremacy thus conferred on this Government could not peacefully be maintained, unless it was clothed with judicial power, equally paramount in authority to carry it into execution; for if left to the courts of justice of the several States, conflicting decisions would unavoidably take place, and the local tribunals could hardly be expected to be always free from the local influences of which we have spoken. And the Constitution and laws and treaties of the United States, and the powers granted to the Federal Government, would soon receive different interpretations in different States, and the Government of the United States would soon become one thing in one State and another thing in another. It was essential, therefore, to its very existence as a Government, that it should have the power of establishing courts of justice, altogether independent of State power, to carry into effect its own laws; and that a tribunal should be established in which all cases which might arise under the Constitution and laws and treaties of the United States, whether in a State court or a court of the United States, should be finally and conclusively decided. Without such a tribunal, it is obvious that there would be no uniformity of judicial decision; and that the supremacy, (which is but another name for independence,) so carefully provided in the clause of the Constitution above referred to, could not possibly be maintained peacefully, unless it was associated with this paramount judicial authority.

Accordingly, it was conferred on the General Government, in clear, precise, and comprehensive terms. It is declared that its judicial power shall (among other subjects enumerated) extend to all cases in law and equity arising under the Constitution and laws of the United States, and that in such cases, as well as the others there enumerated, this court shall have appellate jurisdiction both as to law and fact, with such exceptions and under such regulations as Congress shall make. The appellate power, it will be observed, is conferred on this court in all cases or suits in which such a question shall arise. It is not confined to suits in the inferior courts of the United States, but extends to all cases where such a question arises, whether it be in a judicial tribunal of a State or of the United States. And it is manifest that this ultimate appellate power in a tribunal created by the Constitution itself was deemed essential to secure the independence and supremacy of the General Government in the sphere of action assigned to it; to make the Constitution and laws of the United States uniform, and the same in every State; and to guard against evils which would inevitably arise from conflicting opinions between the courts of a State and of the United States, if there was no common arbiter authorized to decide between them.

The importance which the framers of the Constitution attached to such a tribunal, for the purpose of preserving internal tranquillity, is strikingly manifested by the clause which gives this court jurisdiction over the sovereign States which compose this Union, when a controversy arises between them. Instead of reserving the right to seek redress for injustice from another State by their sovereign powers, they have bound themselves to submit to the decision of this court, and to abide by its judgment. And it is not out of place to say, here, that experience has demonstrated that this power was not unwisely surrendered by the States; for in the time that has already elapsed since this Government came into existence, several irritating and angry controversies have taken place between adjoining States, in relation to their respective boundaries, and which have sometimes threatened to end in force and violence, but for the power vested in this court to hear them and decide between them.

The same purposes are clearly indicated by the different language employed when conferring supremacy upon the laws of the United States, and jurisdiction upon its courts. In the first case, it provides that "this Constitution, and the laws of the United States *which shall be made in pursuance thereof,* shall be the supreme law of the land, and obligatory upon the judges in every State." The words in italics show the precision and foresight which marks every clause in the instrument. The sovereignty to be created was to be limited in its powers of legislation, and if it passed a law not authorized by its enumerated powers, it was not to be regarded as the supreme law of the land, nor were the State judges bound to carry it into execution. And as the courts of a State, and the courts of the United States, might, and indeed certainly would, often differ as to the extent of the powers conferred by the General Government, it was manifest that serious controversies would arise between the authorities of the United States and of the States, which must be settled by force of arms, unless some tribunal was created to decide between them finally and without appeal.

The Constitution has accordingly provided, as far as human foresight could provide, against this danger. And in conferring judicial power upon the Federal Government, it declares that the jurisdiction of its courts shall extend to all cases arising under "this Constitution" and the laws of the United States—leaving out the words of restriction contained in the grant of legislative power which we have above noticed. The judicial power covers every legislative act of Congress, whether it be made within the limits of its delegated powers, or be an assumption of power beyond the grants in the Constitution.

This judicial power was justly regarded as indispensable, not merely to maintain the supremacy of the laws of the United States, but also to guard the States from any encroachment upon their reserved rights by the General Government. And as the Constitution is the fundamental and supreme law, if it appears that an act of Congress is not pursuant to and within the limits of the power assigned to the Federal Government, it is the duty of the courts of the United States to declare it unconstitutional and void. The grant of judicial power is not confined to the administration of laws passed in pursuance to the provisions of the Constitution, nor confined to the interpretation of such laws; but, by the very terms of the grant, the Constitution

is under their view when any act of Congress is brought before them, and it is their duty to declare the law void, and refuse to execute it, if it is not pursuant to the legislative powers conferred upon Congress. And as the final appellate power in all such questions is given to this court, controversies as to the respective powers of the United States and the States, instead of being determined by military and physical force, are heard, investigated, and finally settled, with the calmness and deliberation of judicial inquiry. And no one can fail to see, that if such an arbiter had not been provided, in our complicated system of government, internal tranquillity could not have been preserved; and if such controversies were left to arbitrament of physical force, our Government, State and National, would soon cease to be Governments of laws, and revolutions by force of arms would take the place of courts of justice and judicial decisions.

In organizing such a tribunal, it is evident that every precaution was taken, which human wisdom could devise, to fit it for the high duty with which it was intrusted. It was not left to Congress to create it by law; for the States could hardly be expected to confide in the impartiality of a tribunal created exclusively by the General Government, without any participation on their part. And as the performance of its duty would sometimes come in conflict with individual ambition or interests, and powerful political combinations, an act of Congress establishing such a tribunal might be repealed in order to establish another more subservient to the predominant political influences or excited passions of the day. This tribunal, therefore, was erected, and the powers of which we have spoken conferred upon it, not by the Federal Government, but by the people of the States, who formed and adopted that Government, and conferred upon it all the powers, legislative, executive, and judicial, which it now possesses. And in order to secure its independence, and enable it faithfully and firmly to perform its duty, it engrafted it upon the Constitution itself, and declared that this court should have appellate power in all cases arising under the Constitution and laws of the United States. So long, therefore, as this Constitution shall endure, this tribunal must exist with it, deciding in the peaceful forms of judicial proceeding the angry and irritating controversies between sovereignties, which in other countries have been determined by the arbitrament of force.

These principles of constitutional law are confirmed and illustrated by the clause which confers legislative power upon Congress. That power is specifically given in article 1, section 8, paragraph 18, in the following words:

"To make all laws which shall be necessary and proper to carry into execution the foregoing powers, and all other powers vested by this Constitution in the Government of the United States, or in any department or officer thereof."

Under this clause of the Constitution, it became the duty of Congress to pass such laws as were necessary and proper to carry into execution the powers vested in the judicial department. And in the performance of this duty, the First Congress, at its first session, passed the act of 1789, ch. 20, entitled *"An act to establish the judicial courts of the United States."* It will be remembered that many of the members of the Convention were also members of this Congress, and it cannot be supposed that they did not understand the meaning and intention of the great instrument which they had so anxiously and deliberately considered, clause by clause, and assisted to frame. And the law they passed to carry into execution the powers vested in the judicial department of the Government proves, past doubt, that their interpretation of the appellate powers conferred on this court was the same with that which we have now given; for by the 25th section of the act of 1789, Congress authorized writs of error to be issued from this court to a State court, whenever a right had been claimed under the Constitution or laws of the United States, and the decision of the State court was against it. And to make this appellate power effectual, and altogether independent of the action of State tribunals, this act further provides, that upon writs of error to a State court, instead of remanding the cause for a final decision in the State court, this court may at their discretion, if the cause shall have been once remanded before, proceed to a final decision of the same, and award execution.

These provisions in the act of 1789 tell us, in language not to be mistaken, the great importance which the patriots and statesmen of the First Congress attached to this appellate power, and the foresight and care with which they guarded its free and independent exercise against interference or obstruction by States or State tribunals.

In the case before the Supreme Court of Wisconsin, a right was claimed under the Constitution and laws of the United States, and the decision was against the right claimed; and it refuses obedience to the writ of error, and regards its own judgment as final. It has not only reversed and annulled the judgment of the District Court of the United States, but it has reversed and annulled the provisions of the Constitution itself, and the act of Congress of 1789, and made the superior and appellate tribunal the inferior and subordinate one.

We do not question the authority of State court, or judge, who is authorized by the laws of the State to issue the writ of *habeas corpus,* to issue it in any case where the party is imprisoned within its territorial limits, provided it does not appear, when the application is made, that the person imprisoned is in custody under the authority of the United States. The court or judge has a right to inquire, in this mode of proceeding, for what cause and by what authority the prisoner is confined within the territorial limits of the State sovereignty. And it is the duty of the marshal, or other person having the custody of the prisoner, to make known to the judge or court, by a proper return, the authority by which he holds him in custody. This right to inquire by process of *habeas corpus,* and the duty of the officer to make a return, grows, necessarily, out of the complex character of our Government, and the existence of two distinct and separate sovereignties within the same territorial space, each of them restricted in its powers, and each within its sphere of action, prescribed by the Constitution of the United States, independent of the other. But, after the return is made, and the State judge or court judicially apprized that the party is in custody under the authority of the United States, they can proceed no further. They then know that the prisoner is within the dominion and jurisdiction of another Government, and that neither the writ of *habeas corpus,* nor any other process issued under State authority, can pass over the line of division between the two sovereignties. He is then within the dominion and exclusive jurisdiction of the United States. If he has committed an offence against their laws, their tribunals alone can punish him. If he is wrongfully imprisoned, their judicial tribunals can release him and afford him redress. And although, as we have said, it is the duty of the marshal, or other person holding him, to make known, by a proper return, the authority under which he detains him, it is at the same time imperatively his duty to obey the process of the United States, to hold the prisoner in custody under it, and to refuse obedience to the mandate or process of any other Government. And consequently it is his duty not to take the prisoner, nor suffer him to be taken, before a State judge or court upon a *habeas corpus* issued under State authority. No State judge or court, after they are judicially informed that the party is imprisoned under the authority of the United States, has any right to interfere with him, or to require him to be brought before them. And if the authority of a State, in the form of judicial process or otherwise, should attempt to control the marshal or other authorized officer or agent of the United States, in any respect, in the custody of his prisoner, it would be his duty to resist it, and to call to his aid any force that might be necessary to maintain the authority of law against illegal interference. No judicial process, whatever form it may assume, can have any lawful authority outside of the limits of the jurisdiction of the court or judge by whom it is issued; and an attempt to enforce it beyond these boundaries is nothing less than lawless violence.

Nor is there anything in this supremacy of the General Government, or the jurisdiction of its judicial tribunals, to awaken the jealousy or offend the natural and just pride of State sovereignty. Neither this Government, nor the powers of which we are speaking, were forced upon the States.

The Constitution of the United States, with all the powers conferred by it on the General Government, and surrendered by the States, was the voluntary act of the people of the several States, deliberately done, for their own protection and safety against injustice from one another. And their anxiety to preserve it in full force, in all its powers, and to guard against resistance to or evasion of its authority, on the part of a State, is proved by the clause which requires that the members of the State Legislatures, and all executive and judicial officers of the several States, (as well as those of the General Government,) shall be bound, by oath or affirmation, to support this Constitution. This is the last and closing clause of the Constitution, and inserted when the whole frame of Government, with the powers hereinbefore specified, had been adopted by the Convention; and it was in that form, and with these powers, that the Constitution was submitted to the people of the several States, for their consideration and decision.

Now, it certainly can be no humiliation to the citizen of a republic to yield a ready obedience to the laws as administered by the constituted authorities. On the contrary, it is among his first and highest duties as a citizen, because free government cannot exist without it. Nor can it be inconsistent with the dignity of a sovereign State to observe faithfully, and in the spirit of sincerity and truth, the compact into which it voluntarily entered when it became a State of this Union. On the contrary, the highest honor of sovereignty is untarnished faith. And certainly no faith could be more deliberately and solemnly pledged than that which every State has plighted to the other States to support the Constitution as it is, in all its provisions, until they shall be altered in the manner which the Constitution itself prescribes. In the emphatic language of the pledge required, it is *to support this Constitution.* And no power is more clearly conferred by the Constitution and laws of the United States, than the power of this court to decide, ultimately and finally, all cases arising under such Constitution and laws; and for that purpose to bring here for revision, by writ of error, the judgment of a State court, where such questions have arisen, and the right claimed under them denied by the highest judicial tribunal in the State.

We are sensible that we have extended the examination of these decisions beyond the limits required by any intrinsic difficulty in the question. But the decisions in question were made by the supreme judicial tribunal of the State; and when a court so elevated in its position has pronounced a judgment which, if it could be maintained, would subvert the very foundations of this Government, is seemed to be the duty of this court, when exercising its appellate power, to show plainly the grave errors into which the State court has fallen, and the consequences to which they would inevitably lead.

But it can hardly be necessary to point out the errors which followed their mistaken view of the jurisdiction they might lawfully exercise; because, if there was any defect of power in the commissioner, or in his mode of proceeding, it was for the tribunals of the United States to revise and correct it, and not for a State court. And as regards the decision of the District Court, it had exclusive and final jurisdiction by the laws of the United States; and neither the regularity of its proceedings nor the validity of its sentence could be called in question in any other court, either of a State or the United States, by *habeas corpus* or any other process.

But although we think it unnecessary to discuss these questions, yet, as they have been decided by the State court, and are before us on the record, and we are not willing to be misunderstood, it is proper to say that, in the judgment of this court, the act of Congress commonly called the fugitive slave law is, in all of its provisions, fully authorized by the Constitution of the United States; that the commissioner had lawful authority to issue the warrant and commit the party, and that his proceedings were regular and conformable to law. We have already stated the opinion and judgment of the court as to the exclusive jurisdiction of the District Court, and the appellate powers which this court is authorized and required to exercise. And if any argument was needed to show the wisdom and necessity of this appellate power, the cases before us sufficiently prove it, and at the same time emphatically call for its exercise.

The judgment of the Supreme Court of Wisconsin must therefore be reserved in each of the cases now before the court.

Source:
21 Howard (62 U.S.) 506.

John Brown, Statement to the Court, 1859

Statement to the court delivered by John Brown on November 2, 1859. Convicted of treason for leading an armed raid against Harper's Ferry, Virginia, on October 16, Brown rejected the court's verdict. An abolitionist, Brown claimed that his only goal had been to free the slaves of the town. He denied the charges of treason and insurrection and rebuked slavery. Insisting that he felt no guilt for his actions, Brown told the court that "Now, if it is deemed necessary that I should forfeit my life for the furtherance of the ends of justice . . . mingle my blood . . . with the blood of millions in this slave country whose rights are disregarded by wicked, cruel, and unjust enactments—I submit; so let it be done."

Despite his pronouncements to the contrary, John Brown under 21st-century standards would be considered a terrorist no matter how noble his cause. And like other terrorists with a noble cause, he became a martyr for the abolitionists and a symbol of freedom for Union troops who marched to "John Brown's Body Lies a Mouldering in his Grave." Julia Ward Howe used the tune for her poem that then became the The Battle Hymn of the Republic.

Brown set himself up to be a martyr. During the fight to decide whether Kansas would become free or slave, Brown and his sons and sons-in-law, in what became known as the "Pottawatomi massacre," killed five men, four of whom were hacked to death. However, Brown became a hero to abolitionists, who raised money to help him start a rebellion in the South. Three years later, Brown convinced 13 whites and five blacks to join him in seizing the armory at Harper's Ferry, Virginia (now Harpers Ferry, West Virginia). He expected to be joined by local slaves who would rise up against their masters. However, the rebellion was unpublicized, and the slave uprising never occurred. Brown's men murdered the mayor and imprisoned a number of leading citizens. Brown and his men became trapped in the armory's enginehouse, where they continued to fight. Surrounded by the militia, they refused to surrender. It then took Colonel Robert E. Lee and his troops to break through and capture Brown. Only four of his men were alive and unwounded. Two of his sons had died at his side.

His trial began a week later. On October 31, 1859, the jury declared him guilty. He was hanged December 2, 1859. Although most newspapers and both the Republican and Democratic Parties condemned Brown's actions, his execution prompted huge mourning parades in the North.

I have, may it please the Court, a few words to say.

In the first place, I deny everything but what I have all along admitted—the design on my part to free the slaves. I intended certainly to have made a clean thing of that matter, as I did last winter, when I went into Missouri and there took slaves without the snapping of a gun on either side, moved them through the country, and finally left them in Canada. I designed to have done the same thing again, on a larger scale. That was all I intended. I never did intend murder, or treason, or the destruction of property, or to excite or incite slaves to rebellion, or to make insurrection.

I have another objection; and that is, it is unjust that I should suffer such a penalty. Had I interfered in the manner which I admit, and which I admit has been fairly proved (for I admire the truthfulness and candor of the greater portion of the witnesses who have testified in this case)—had I so interfered in behalf of the rich, the powerful, the intelligent, the so-called great, or in behalf of any of their friends,—either father, mother, brother, sister, wife, or children, or any of that class,—and suffered and sacrificed what I have in this interference, it would have been all right; and every man in this court would have deemed it an act worthy of reward rather than punishment.

This court acknowledges, as I suppose, the validity of the law of God. I see a book kissed here which I suppose to be the Bible, or at least the New Testament. That teaches me that all things whatsoever I would that men should do to me, I should do even so to them. It teaches me, further, to "remember them that are in bonds, as bound with them." I endeavored to act up to that instruction. I say, I am yet too young to understand that God is any respecter of persons. I believe that to have interfered as I have done—as I have always freely admitted I have done—in behalf of His despised poor, was not wrong, but right. Now, if it is deemed necessary that I should forfeit my life for the furtherance of the ends of justice, and mingle my blood further with the blood of my children and with the blood of millions in this slave country whose rights are disregarded by wicked, cruel, and unjust enactments—I submit; so let it be done!

Let me say one word further.

I feel entirely satisfied with the treatment I have received on my trial. Considering all the circumstances, it has been more generous than I expected. But I feel no consciousness of guilt. I have stated from the first what was my intention, and what was not. I never had any design against the life of any person, nor any disposition to commit treason, or excite slaves to rebel, or make any general insurrection. I never encouraged any man to do so, but always discouraged any idea of that kind.

Let me say, also, a word in regard to the statements made by some of those connected with me. I hear it has been stated by some of them that I have induced them to join me. But the contrary is true. I do not say this to injure them, but as regretting their weakness. There is not one of them but joined me of his own accord, and the greater part of them at their own expense. A number of them I never saw, and never had a word of conversation with, till the day they came to me; and that was for the purpose I have stated.

Now I have done.

Source:
Henry Steele Commager, ed. *Documents of American History.* New York: F.S. Crofts & Co., 1934.

Republican Party Platform, 1860

Political platform advanced by the Republicans at their national nominating convention held in Chicago in May 1860.

Under the specter of the slavery question and the threat of impending disunion it posed, the Republican Party nominated Abraham Lincoln of Illinois for president over New York's William H. Seward, whose reputation for antislavery radicalism was considered to be a major liability in the general election, where carrying the moderate lower Northern states was deemed crucial to a Republican victory. The platform was calculated to appeal to, and thus hold together, disparate regional and ideological constituencies. It rejected attempts to reinitiate the African slave trade and denied the authority of either Congress or a territorial legislature to make slavery legal in the territories. It warned Southern disunionists against "contemplated treason." Striking a moderate note, it denounced antislavery zealot John Brown's raid on Harper's Ferry. The platform reaffirmed the principles of the Declaration of Independence. It supported internal improvements, a homestead law, federal aid for a transcontinental railroad, and a protective tariff. It also steered the party away from nativism in immigration policy.

Three other parties vied for the presidency in 1860. Meeting in Charleston, South Carolina, in April, 1860, the Democratic Party split over its platform. Northerners designing the platform accepted the *Dred Scott* decision and condemned the personal liberty laws that states passed to circumvent the Fugitive Slave Act. However they objected to Southern insistence on advocating a "black code" for the territories. On April 30, the Northern position prevailed, causing most South Carolina, Georgia, Florida, Louisiana, and Arkansas delegates to leave. In so doing, they ensured a Republican victory. No one candidate garnered enough votes from the rump convention. It met again in Baltimore, where a second split occurred over seating the delegates who had walked out in Charleston. When those favoring the Southerners failed, they too walked out. The remaining Democrats nominated Stephen A. Douglas, and the seceding Democrats, later joined by the original seceders, named Vice President John C. Breckinridge as their candidate. Further complicating the election, former Whigs, Know-Nothings, and moderates from both sections came together as the Constitutional Union Party, with Senator John Bell of Tennessee for president and Edward Everett of Massachusetts for Vice President.

Lincoln, nominated by the Republicans on the third ballot, won all but one (New Jersey) of 18 free states and garnered a plurality of the popular vote and a majority of the electoral college.

Republican Platform

Resolved, That we, the delegated representatives of the Republican electors of the United States, in Convention assembled, in discharge of the duty we owe to our constituents and our country, unite in the following declarations:

1. That the history of the nation during the last four years, has fully established the propriety and necessity of the organization and perpetuation of the Republican party, and that the causes which called it into existence are permanent in their nature, and now, more than ever before, demand its peaceful and constitution triumph.

2. That the maintenance of the principles promulgated in the Declaration of Independence and embodied in the Federal Constitution. "That all men are created equal; that they are endowed by their Creator with certain inalienable rights; that among these are life, liberty and the pursuit of happiness; that no secure these rights, governments are instituted among men, deriving their just powers from the consent of the governed," is essential to the preservation of our Republican institutions; and that the Federal Constitution, the Rights of the States, and the Union of the States must and shall be preserved.

3. That to the Union of the States this nation owes its unprecedented increase in population, its surprising development of material resources, its rapid augmentation of wealth, its happiness at home and its honor abroad; and we hold in abhorrence all schemes for disunion, come from whatever source they may. And we congratulate the country that no Republican member of Congress has uttered or countenanced the threats of disunion so often made by Democratic members, without rebuke and with applause from their political associates; and we denounce those threats of disunion, in case of a popular overthrow of their ascendency as denying the vital principles of a free government, and as an avowal of contemplated treason, which it is imperative duty of an indignant people sternly to rebuke and forever silence.

4. That the maintenance inviolate of the rights of the states, and especially the right of each state to order and control its own domestic institutions according to its own judgment exclusively, is essential to that balance of powers on which the perfection and endurance of our political fabric depends; and we denounce the lawless invasion by armed force of the soil of any state or territory, no matter under what pretext, as among the gravest of crimes.

5. That the present Democratic Administration has far exceeded our worst apprehensions, in its measureless subserviency to the exactions of a sectional interest, as especially evinced in its desperate exertions to force the infamous Lecompton Constitution upon the protesting people of Kansas; in construing the personal relations between master and servant to involve an unqualified property in persons; in its attempted enforcement everywhere, on land and sea, through the intervention of Congress and of the Federal Courts of the extreme pretensions of a purely local interests; and in its general and unvarying abuse of the power intrusted to it by a confiding people.

6. That the people justly view with alarm the reckless extravagance which pervades every department of the Federal Government; that a return to rigid economy and accountability is indispensable to arrest the systematic plunder of the public treasury by favored partisans; while the recent startling developments of frauds and corruptions at the Federal metropolis, show that an entire change of administration is imperatively demanded.

7. That the new dogma that the Constitution, of its own force, carries slavery into any or all of the territories of the United States, is a dangerous political heresy, at variance with the explicit provisions of that instrument itself, with contemporaneous exposition, and with legislative and judicial precedent; is revolutionary in its tendency, and subversive of the peace and harmony of the country.

8. That the normal condition of all territory of the United States is that of freedom: That, as our Republican fathers, when they had abolished slavery in all our national territory, ordained that "no persons should be deprived of life, liberty or property without due process of law," it becomes our duty, by legislation, whenever such legislation is necessary, to maintain this provision of the Constitution against all attempts to violate it; and we deny the authority of Congress, of a territorial legislature, or of any individuals, to give legal existence to slavery in any territory of the United States.

9. That we brand the recent reopening of the African slave trade, under the cover of our national flag, aided by perversions of judicial power, as a crime against humanity and a burning shame to our country and age; and we call upon Congress to take prompt and efficient measures for the total and final suppression of that execrable traffic.

10. That in the vetoes, by their Federal Governors, of the acts of the legislatures of Kansas and Nebraska, prohibiting slavery in those territories, we find a practical illustration of the boasted Democratic principle of Non-Intervention and Popular Sovereignty, embodied in the Kansas-Nebraska Bill, and a demonstration of the deception and fraud involved therein.

11. That Kansas should, of right, be immediately admitted as a state under the Constitution recently formed and adopted by her people, and accepted by the House of Representatives.

12. That, while providing revenue for the support of the general government by duties upon imports, sound policy requires such an adjustment of these imports as to encourage the development of the industrial interests of the whole country; and we commend that policy of national exchanges, which secures to the workingmen liberal wages, to agriculture remunerative prices, to mechanics and manufacturers an adequate reward for their skill, labor, and enterprise, and to the nation commercial prosperity and independence.

13. That we protest against any sale or alienation to others of the public lands held by actual settlers, and against any view of the free-homestead policy which regards the settlers as paupers or suppliants for public bounty; and we demand the passage by Congress of the complete and satisfactory homestead measure which has already passed the House.

14. That the Republican party is opposed to any change in out naturalization laws or any state legislation by which the rights of citizens hitherto accorded to immigrants from foreign lands shall be abridged or impaired; and in favor of giving a full and efficient protection to the rights of all classes of citizens, whether native or naturalized, both at home and abroad.

15. That appropriations by Congress for river and harbor improvements of a national character, required for the accommodation and security of an existing commerce, are authorized by the Constitution, and justified by the obligation of Government to protect the lives and property of its citizens.

16. That a railroad to the Pacific Ocean is imperatively demanded by the interests of the whole country; that the federal government ought to render immediate and efficient aid in its construction; and that, as preliminary thereto, a daily overland mail should be promptly established.

17. Finally, having thus set forth our distinctive principles and views, we invite the co-operation of all citizens, however differing on the other questions, who substantially agree with us in their affirmance and support.

Source:

Arthur M. Schlesinger, *History of American Presidential Elections*, Vol. 2. Broomall, Penn.: Chelsea House Publishers, 1985, pp. 1,124–1,127.

South Carolina Ordinance of Secession, 1860

Resolution passed unanimously by a convention meeting at Charleston, South Carolina, on December 20, 1860, by which the state seceded from the Union in a prelude to the Civil War (1861–1865). The Charleston convention, its members chosen by popular vote, was called by the state legislature immediately after the election of Abraham Lincoln as president of the United States. In its "Declaration of Causes of Secession" of December 24, South Carolina affirmed state sovereignty and cited Northern opposition to slavery, the attainment of power by a sectional party, and the election of a president hostile to slavery. South Carolina, the first state to secede, was soon followed by the six other states of the Lower South.

The Secession Convention was called by the legislature to meet on December 17, and on December 20 the Secession Ordinance was adopted. The movement toward secession met with general approval throughout the state, although a group of unionists around Greenville had uncompromising objections.

At a Convention of the people of the State of South Carolina, begun and holden at Columbia on the seventeenth day of December, in the year of our Lord 1860, and thence continued by adjournment to Charleston and there, by divers adjournments, to the 20th day of December in the same year:

An ordinance to dissolve the union between the State of South Carolina and other states united with her under the compact entitled "The Constitution of the United States of America":

We, the people of the State of South Carolina in Convention assembled, do declare and ordain, and it is hereby declared and ordained, that the ordinance adopted by us in Convention on the twenty-third day of May, in the year of our Lord 1788, whereby the Constitution of the United States of America was ratified, and also all acts and parts of acts of the General Assembly of this State ratifying amendments of the said Constitution, are hereby repealed; and that the union now subsisting between South Carolina and the other States, under the name of the "United States of America" is hereby dissolved.

Done at Charleston the twentieth day of December, in the year of our Lord, 1860.

Source:

South Carolina Convention. *Ordinance of Secession.* Charleston, S.C.: Evans & Cogswell, 1860. (Courtesy University of South Carolina. South Caroliniana Library, Columbia, South Carolina.)

Abraham Lincoln, First Inaugural Address, 1861

Speech delivered by Abraham Lincoln on March 4, 1861, at his inauguration as the 16th president of the United States. By this date seven Southern states had seceded from the Union. Lincoln's address was firm but conciliatory toward the South. He pledged not to interfere with slavery in the states where it already existed, but he insisted that the Union was perpetual and secession unlawful. He stated that in defending the Union "there needs to be no bloodshed or violence; and there shall be none, unless it be forced upon the national authority." Lincoln closed: "We are not enemies, but friends. We must not be enemies. Though passion may have strained, it must not break, our bonds of affection." Six weeks later, on April 12, the Civil War began.

Fellow-Citizens of the United States:

In compliance with a custom as old as the Government itself, I appear before you to address you briefly and to take in your presence the oath prescribed by the Constitution of the United States to be taken by the President "before he enters on the execution of this office."

I do not consider it necessary at present for me to discuss those matters of administration about which there is no special anxiety or excitement.

Apprehension seems to exist among the people of the Southern States that by the accession of a Republican Administration their property and their peace and personal security are to be endangered. There has never been any reasonable cause for such apprehension. Indeed, the most ample evidence to the contrary has all the while existed and been open to their inspection. It is found in nearly all the published speeches of him who now addresses you. I do but quote from one of those speeches when I declare that—

I have no purpose, directly or indirectly, to interfere with the institution of slavery in the States where it exists. I believe I have no lawful right to do so, and I have no inclination to do so.

Those who nominated and elected me did so with full knowledge that I had made this and many similar declarations and had never recanted them; and more than this, they placed in the platform for my acceptance, and as a law to themselves and to me, the clear and emphatic resolution which I now read:

Resolved, That the maintenance inviolate of the rights of the States, and especially the right of each State to order and control its own domestic institutions according to its own judgment exclusively, is essential to that balance of power on which the perfection and endurance of our political fabric depend; and we denounce the lawless invasion by armed force of the soil of any State or Territory, no matter what pretext, as among the gravest of crimes.

I now reiterate these sentiments, and in doing so I only press upon the public attention the most conclusive evidence of which the case is susceptible that the property, peace, and security of no section are to be in any wise endangered by the now incoming Administration. I add, too, that all the protection which, consistently with the Constitution and the laws, can be given will be cheerfully given to all the States when lawfully demanded, for whatever cause—as cheerfully to one section as to another.

There is much controversy about the delivering up of fugitives from service or labor. The clause I now read is as plainly written in the Constitution as any other of its provisions:

No person held to service or labor in one State, under the laws thereof, escaping into another, shall in consequence of any law or regulation therein be discharged from such service or labor, but shall be delivered up on claim of the party to whom such service or labor may be due.

It is scarcely questioned that this provision was intended by those who made it for the reclaiming of what we call fugitive slaves; and the intention of the lawgiver is the law. All members of Congress swear their support to the whole Constitution—to this provision as much as to any other. To the proposition, then, that slaves whose cases come within the terms of this clause "shall be delivered up" their oaths are unanimous. Now, if they would make the effort in good temper, could they not with nearly equal unanimity frame and pass a law by means of which to keep good that unanimous oath?

There is some difference of opinion whether this clause should be enforced by national or by State authority, but surely that difference is not a very material one. If the slave is to be surrendered, it can be of but little consequence to him or to others by which authority it is done. And should anyone in any case be content that his oath shall go unkept on a merely unsubstantial controversy as to *how* it shall be kept?

Again: In any law upon this subject ought not all the safeguards of liberty known in civilized and humane jurisprudence to be introduced, so that a free man be not in any case surrendered as a slave? And might it not be well at the same time to provide by law for the enforcement of that clause in the Constitution which guarantees that "the citizens of each State shall be entitled to all privileges and immunities of citizens in the several States"?

I take the official oath to-day with no mental reservations and with no purpose to construe the Constitution or laws by any hypercritical rules; and while I do not choose now to specify particular acts of Congress as proper to be enforced, I do suggest that it will be much safer for all, both in official and private stations, to conform to and abide by all those acts which stand unrepealed than to violate any of them trusting to find impunity in having them held to be unconstitutional.

It is seventy-two years since the first inauguration of a President under our National Constitution. During that period fifteen different and greatly distinguished citizens have in succession administered the executive branch of the Government. They have conducted it through many perils, and generally with great success. Yet, with all this scope of precedent, I now enter upon the same task for the brief constitutional term of four years under great and peculiar difficulty. A disruption of the Federal Union, heretofore only menaced, is now formidably attempted.

I hold that in contemplation of universal law and of the Constitution the Union of these Sates is perpetual. Perpetuity is implied, if not expressed, in the fundamental law of all national governments. It is safe to assert that no government proper ever had a provision in its organic law for its own termination. Continue to execute all the express provisions of our National Constitution, and the Union will endure forever, it being impossible to destroy it except by some action not provided for in the instrument itself.

Again: If the United States be not a government proper, but an association of States in the nature of contract merely, can it, as a contract, be peaceably unmade by less than all the parties who made it? One party to a contract may violate it—break it, so to speak—but does it not require all to lawfully rescind it?

Descending from these general principles, we find the proposition that in legal contemplation the Union is perpetual confirmed by the history of the Union itself. The Union is much older than the Constitution. It was formed, in fact, by the Articles of Association in 1774. It was matured and continued by the Declaration of Independence in 1776. It was further matured, and the faith of all the then thirteen States expressly plighted and engaged that it should be perpetual, by the Articles of Confederation in 1778. And finally, in 1787, one of the declared objects for ordaining and establishing the Constitution was *"to form a more perfect Union."*

But if destruction of the Union by one or by a part only of the States be lawfully possible, the Union is *less* perfect than before the Constitution, having lost the vital element of perpetuity.

It follows from these views that no State upon its own mere motion can lawfully get out of the Union; that *resolves* and *ordinances* to that effect are legally void, and that acts of violence within any State or States against the authority of the United States are insurrectionary or revolutionary, according to circumstances.

I therefore consider that in view of the Constitution and the laws the Union is unbroken, and to the extent of my ability, I shall take care, as the Constitution itself expressly enjoins upon me, that the laws of the Union be faithfully executed in all the States. Doing this I deem to be only a simple duty on my part, and I shall perform it so far as practicable unless my rightful masters, the American people, shall withhold the requisite means or in some authoritative manner direct the contrary. I trust this will not be regarded as a menace, but only as the declared purpose of the Union that it *will* constitutionally defend and maintain itself.

In doing this there needs to be no bloodshed or violence, and there shall be none unless it be forced upon the national authority. The power confided to me will be used to hold, occupy, and possess the property and places belonging to the Government and to collect the duties and imposts; but beyond what may be necessary for these objects, there will be no invasion, no using of force against or among the people anywhere. Where hostility to the United States in any interior locality shall be so great and universal as to prevent competent resident citizens from holding the Federal offices, there will be no attempt to force obnoxious strangers among the people for that object. While the strict legal right may exist in the Government to enforce the exercise of these offices, the attempt to do so would be so irritating and so nearly impracticable withal that I deem it better to forego for the time the uses of such offices.

The mails, unless repelled, will continue to be furnished in all parts of the Union. So far as possible the people everywhere shall have that sense of perfect security which is most favorable to calm thought and reflection. The course here indicated will be followed unless current events and experience shall show a modification or change to be proper, and in every case and exigency my best discretion will be exercised, according to circumstances actually existing and with a view and a hope of a peaceful solution of the national troubles and the restoration of fraternal sympathies and affections.

That there are persons in one section or another who seek to destroy the Union at all events and are glad of any pretext to do it I will neither affirm nor deny; but if there be such, I need address no word to them. To those, however, who really love the Union may I not speak?

Before entering upon so grave a matter as the destruction of our national fabric, with all its benefits, its memories, and its hopes, would it not be wise to ascertain precisely why we do it? Will you hazard so desperate a step while there is any possibility that any portion of the ills you fly from have no real existence? Will you, while the certain ills you fly to are greater than all the real ones you fly from, will you risk the commission of so fearful a mistake?

All profess to be content in the Union if all constitutional rights can be maintained. Is it true, then, that any right plainly written in the Constitution has been denied? I think not. Happily, the human mind is so constituted that no party can reach to the audacity of doing this. Think, if you can, of a single instance in which a plainly written provision of the Constitution has ever been denied. If by the mere force of numbers a majority should deprive a minority of any clearly written constitutional right, might in a moral point of view justify revolution; certainly would if such right were a vital one. But such is not our case. All the vital rights of minorities and of individuals are so plainly assured to them by affirmations and negations, guaranties and prohibitions, in the Constitution that controversies

never arise concerning them. But no organic law can ever be framed with a provision specifically applicable to every question which may occur in practical administration. No foresight can anticipate nor any document of reasonable length contain express provisions for all possible questions. Shall fugitives from labor be surrendered by national or by State authority? The Constitution does not expressly say. *May* Congress prohibit slavery in the Territories? The Constitution does not expressly say. *Must* Congress protect slavery in the Territories? The Constitution does not expressly say.

From questions of this class spring all our constitutional controversies, and we divide upon them into majorities and minorities. If the minority will not acquiesce, the majority must, or the Government must cease. There is no other alternative, for continuing the Government is acquiescence on one side or the other. If a minority in such case will secede rather than acquiesce, they make a precedent which in turn will divide and ruin them, for a minority of their own will secede from them whenever a majority refuses to be controlled by such minority. For instance, why may not any portion of a new confederacy a year or two hence arbitrarily secede again, precisely as portions of the present Union now claim to secede from it? All who cherish disunion sentiments are now being educated to the exact temper of doing this.

Is there such perfect identity of interests among the States to compose a new union as to produce harmony only and prevent renewed secession?

Plainly the central idea of secession is the essence of anarchy. A majority held in restraint by constitutional checks and limitations, and always changing easily with deliberate changes of popular opinions and sentiments, is the only true sovereign of a free people. Whoever rejects it does of necessity fly to anarchy or to despotism. Unanimity is impossible. The rule of a minority, as a permanent arrangement, is wholly inadmissible; so that, rejecting the majority principle, anarchy or despotism in some form is all that is left.

I do not forget the position assumed by some that constitutional questions are to be decided by the Supreme Court, nor do I deny that such decisions must be binding in any case upon the parties to a suit as to the object of that suit, while they are also entitled to very high respect and consideration in all parallel cases by all other departments of the Government. And while it is obviously possible that such decision may be erroneous in any given case, still the evil effect following it, being limited to that particular case, with the chance that it may be overruled and never become a precedent for other cases, can better be borne that could the evils of a different practice. At the same time, the candid citizen must confess that if the policy of the Government upon vital questions affecting the whole people is to be irrevocably fixed by decisions of the Supreme Court, the instant they are made in ordinary litigation between parties in personal actions the people will have ceased to be their own rulers, having to that extent practically resigned their Government into the hands of that eminent tribunal. Nor is there in this view any assault upon the court or the judges. It is a duty from which they may not shrink to decide cases properly brought before them, and it is no fault of theirs if others seek to turn their decisions to political purposes.

One section of our country believes slavery is *right* and ought to be extended, while the other believes it is *wrong* and ought not to be extended. This is the only substantial dispute. The fugitive-slave clause of the Constitution and the law for the suppression of the foreign slave trade are each as well enforced, perhaps, as any law can ever be in a community where the moral sense of the people imperfectly supports the law itself. The great body of the people abide by the dry legal obligation in both cases, and a few break over in each. This, I think, can not be perfectly cured, and it would be worse in both cases *after* the separation of the sections than before. The foreign slave trade, now imperfectly suppressed, would be ultimately revived without restriction in one section, while fugitive slaves, now only partially surrendered, would not be surrendered at all by the other.

Physically speaking, we can not separate. We can not remove our respective sections from each other nor build an impassable wall between them. A husband and wife may be divorced and go out of the presence and beyond the reach of each other, but the different parts of our country can not do this. They can not but remain face to face, and intercourse, either amicable or hostile, must continue between them. Is it possible, then, to make that intercourse more advantageous or more satisfactory *after* separation than *before*? Can aliens make treaties easier than friends can make laws? Can treaties be more faithfully enforce between aliens than laws can among friends? Suppose you go to war, you can not fight always; and when, after much loss on both sides and no gain on either, you cease fighting, the identical old questions, as to terms of intercourse, are again upon you.

This country, with its institutions, belongs to the people who inhabit it. Whenever they shall grow weary of the existing Government, they can exercise their *constitutional* right of amending it or their *revolutionary* right to dismember or overthrow it. I can not be ignorant of the fact that many worthy and patriotic citizens are desirous of having the National Constitution amended. While I make no recommendation of amendments, I fully recognize the rightful authority of the people over the whole subject, to be exercised in either of the modes prescribed in the instrument itself; and I should, under existing circum-

stances, favor rather than oppose a fair opportunity being afforded the people to act upon it. I will venture to add that to me the convention mode seems preferable, in that it allows amendments to originate with the people themselves, instead of only permitting them to take or reject propositions originated by others, not especially chosen for the purpose, and which might not be precisely such as they would wish to either accept or refuse. I understand a proposed amendment to the Constitution—which amendment, however, I have not seen—has passed Congress, to the effect that the Federal Government shall never interfere with the domestic institutions of the States, including that of persons held to service. To avoid misconstruction of what I have said, I depart from my purpose not to speak of particular amendments so far as to say that, holding such a provision to now be implied constitutional law, I have no objection to its being made express and irrevocable.

The Chief Magistrate derives all his authority from the people, and they have referred none upon him to fix terms for the separation of the States. The people themselves can do this if also they choose, but the Executive as such has nothing to do with it. His duty is to administer the present Government as it came to his hands and to transmit it unimpaired by him to his successor.

Why should there not be a patient confidence in the ultimate justice of the people? Is there any better or equal hope in the world? In our present differences, is either party without faith of being in the right? If the Almighty Ruler of Nations, with His eternal truth and justice, be on your side of the North, or on yours of the South, that truth and that justice will surely prevail by the judgment of this great tribunal of the American people.

By the frame of the Government under which we live this same people have wisely given their public servants but little power for mischief, and have with equal wisdom provided for the return of that little to their own hands at very short intervals. While the people retain their virtue and vigilance no Administration by any extreme of wickedness or folly can very seriously injure the Government in the short space of four years.

My countrymen, one and all, think calmly and *well* upon this whole subject. Nothing valuable can be lost by taking time. If there be an object to *hurry* any of you in hot haste to a step which you would never take *deliberately*, that object will be frustrated by taking time; but no good object can be frustrated by it. Such of you as are now dissatisfied still have the old Constitution unimpaired, and, on the sensitive point, the laws of your own framing under it; while the new Administration will have no immediate power, if it would, to change either. If it were admitted that you who are dissatisfied hold the right side in the dispute, there still is no single good reason for precipitate action. Intelligence, patriotism, Christianity, and a firm reliance on Him who has never yet forsaken this favored land are still competent to adjust in the best way all our present difficulty.

In *your* hands, my dissatisfied fellow-countrymen, and not in *mine,* is the momentous issue of civil war. The Government will not assail *you.* You can have no conflict without being yourselves the aggressors. *You* have no oath registered in heaven to destroy the Government, while *I* shall have the most solemn one to "preserve, protect, and defend it."

I am loath to close. We are not enemies, but friends. We must not be enemies. Though passion may have strained it must not break our bonds of affection. The mystic chords of memory, stretching from every battlefield and patriot grave to every living heart and hearthstone all over this broad land, will yet swell the chorus of the Union, when again touched, as surely they will be, by the better angels of our nature.

See also JAMES BUCHANAN, FOURTH ANNUAL MESSAGE, 1861.

Source:
Landmark Documents in American History, Facts On File, Inc.

The Civil War Years

Civil War Anthems
Daniel Decatur Emmett, *Dixie*, 1859

Although written by Daniel Decatur Emmett, an Ohioan living in New York, *Dixie* was played at Jefferson Davis's inauguration and became the anthem for Confederate troops during the Civil War. It was originally used in minstrel shows, in which whites blackened their faces and sang in their conception of Negro dialect, as reproduced in the first version below.

The song appears to be the first recorded instance of using "Dixie" and "Dixieland" to refer to the South. No known authoritative explanation for the word exists, although several imaginative ones have been offered. The definition most often cited is that it referred to the land below the Mason-Dixon line.

───────────────────⟨✦⟩───────────────────

[Dialect version]

> I wish I was in de land ob cotton,
> Old times dar am not forgotten.
> Look away, look away,
> Look away, Dixie Land.
> I wish I was in Dixie! Hooray! Hooray!
> In Dixie's land, we'll took our stand,
> To lib an' die in Dixie!
> Away, away,
> Away down South in Dixie.

[Traditional version]

> O, I wish I was in the land of cotton
> Old times there are not forgotten
> Look away! Look away!
> Look away! Dixie Land.
>
> In Dixie Land where I was born in
> Early on one frosty mornin'
> Look away! Look away!
> Look away! Dixie Land.

Chorus:
> O, I wish I was in Dixie!
> Hooray! Hooray!
> In Dixie Land I'll take my stand
> To live and die in Dixie
> Away, away, Away down south in Dixie!

Source:
Dialect version: Representative Poetry Online. Available on-line. URL: http://eir.library.utoronto.ca/rpo/display/poem798.html. Accessed December 2003. Traditional version: Country Gold USA. Available on-line. URL: www.countrygoldusa.com/dixie.asp. Accessed December 2003.

Julia Ward Howe,
Battle Hymn of the Republic, 1862

Julia Ward Howe, the wife of a government official, initially wrote the words to this hymn in 1861after visiting a Union camp. The Union soldiers had made "John Brown's Body" set to the camp-meeting hymn "Oh brothers, will you meet us on Canaan's happy shore?" their marching song. But a friend of Howe's, the Rev. James Freeman Clarke, thought the tune should have more stirring lyrics. According to her 1899 memoirs, Howe wrote the song to meet Clarke's challenge. She published the poem, slightly changed from the original, in *The Atlantic Monthly,* for which she was paid $5. The magazine named it *Battle Hymn of the Republic.* Although many songs were associated with the Union army, this is known as its anthem.

Mine eyes have seen the glory of the coming of
  the Lord:
He is trampling out the vintage where the grapes
  of wrath are stored;
He hath loosed the fateful lightning of His terrible
  swift sword:
His truth is marching on.

I have seen Him in the watch-fires of a hundred
  circling camps,
They have builded Him an altar in the evening
  dews and damps;
I can read His righteous sentence by the dim and
  flaring lamps:
His day is marching on.

I have read a fiery gospel writ in burnished rows
  of steel:
"As ye deal with my contemners, so with you my
  grace shall deal;
Let the Hero, born of woman, crush the serpent
  with his heel,
Since God is marching on."

He has sounded forth the trumpet that shall never
  call retreat;
He is sifting out the hearts of men before His
  judgment-seat: Oh, be swift, my soul, to
  answer Him! be jubilant, my feet!
Our God is marching on.

In the beauty of the lilies Christ was born across
  the sea,
With a glory in his bosom that transfigures you
  and me:
As he died to make men holy, let us die to make
  men free,
While God is marching on.

Source:
Julia Ward Howe, "The Battle Hymn of the Republic"; *The Atlantic Monthly* 9, no. 52 (February 1862): p. 10; Available online. URL: www.theatlantic.com/issues/1862feb/batthym. htm.

Constitution of the Confederate States of America, 1861

Compact adopted at Montgomery, Alabama, on March 11, 1861, by the Confederate Congress, as the law of the Confederate States of America. Modeled on the U.S. Constitution, the document provided for a central government with three branches and a division of power between the central institution and state governments, while stressing the "sovereign and independent character" of each state. The president was elected for a single six-year term. The constitution protected the rights of slaveholders, especially in interstate traffic in slaves, and established slavery in the territories. The international slave trade, however, was banned. Protective tariffs were also forbidden.

We, the people of the Confederate States, each State acting in its sovereign and independent character, in order to form a permanent federal government, establish justice, insure domestic tranquillity, and secure the blessings of liberty to ourselves and our posterity—invoking the favor and guidance of Almighty God—do ordain and establish this Constitution for the Confederate States of America.

Art. I.
Sec. 1.—All legislative powers herein delegated shall be vested in a Congress of the Confederate States, which shall consist of a Senate and House of Representatives.

Sec. 2. (1) The House of Representatives shall be chosen every second year by the people of the several States; and the electors in each State shall be citizens of the Confederate States, and have the qualifications requisite for electors of the most numerous branch of the State Legislature; but no person of foreign birth, not a citizen of the Confederate States, shall be allowed to vote for any officer, civil or political, State or Federal.

(2) No person shall be a Representative who shall not have attained the age of twenty-five years, and be a citizen of the Confederate States, and who shall not, when elected, be an inhabitant of that State in which he shall be chosen.

(3) Representatives and direct taxes shall be apportioned among the several States which may be included within this Confederacy, according to their respective numbers, which shall be determined by adding to the whole number of free persons, including those bound to service for a term of years, and excluding Indians not taxed, three-fifths of all slaves. The actual enumeration shall be made within three years after the first meeting of the Congress of the Confederate States, and within every subsequent term

of ten years, in such manner as they shall by law direct. The number of Representatives shall not exceed one for every fifty thousand, but each State shall have at least one Representative; and until such enumeration shall be made, the State of South Carolina shall be entitled to choose six; the State of Georgia ten; the State of Alabama nine; the State of Florida two; the State of Mississippi seven; the State of Louisiana six; and the State of Texas six.

(4) When vacancies happen in the representation of any State, the Executive authority thereof shall issue writs of election to fill such vacancies.

(5) The House of Representatives shall choose their Speaker and other officers; and shall have the sole power of impeachment; except that any judicial or other federal officer resident and acting solely within the limits of any State, may be impeached by a vote of two-thirds of both branches of the Legislature thereof.

Sec. 3. (1) The Senate of the Confederate States shall be composed of two Senators from each State, chosen for six years by the Legislature thereof, at the regular session next immediately preceding the commencement of the term of service; and each Senator shall have one vote.

(2) Immediately after they shall be assembled, in consequence of the first election, they shall be divided as equally as may be into three classes. The seats of the Senators of the first class shall be vacated at the expiration of the second year; of the second class at the expiration of the fourth year; and of the third class at the expiration of the sixth year; so that one-third may be chosen every second year; and if vacancies happen by resignation or otherwise during the recess of the Legislature of any State, the Executive thereof may make temporary appointments until the next meeting of the Legislature, which shall then fill such vacancies.

(3) No person shall be a Senator, who shall not have attained the age of thirty years, and be a citizen of the Confederate States; and who shall not, when elected, be an inhabitant of the State for which he shall be chosen.

(4) The Vice-President of the Confederate States shall be President of the Senate, but shall have no vote, unless they be equally divided.

(5) The Senate shall choose their other officers, and also a President *pro tempore*, in the absence of the Vice-President, or when he shall exercise the office of President of the Confederate States.

(6) The Senate shall have sole power to try all impeachments. When sitting for that purpose they shall be on oath or affirmation. When the President of the Confederate States is tried, the Chief-Justice shall preside; and no person shall be convicted without the concurrence of two-thirds of the members present.

(7) Judgment in cases of impeachment shall not extend further than removal from office, and disqualification to hold and enjoy any office of honor, trust, or profit, under the Confederate States; but the party convicted shall, nevertheless, be liable to and subject to indictment, trial, judgment, and punishment according to law.

Sec. 4. (1) The times, places, and manner of holding elections for Senators and Representatives, shall be prescribed in each State by the Legislature thereof, subject to the provisions of this Constitution; but the Congress may, at any time, by law, make or alter such regulations, except as to the times and places of choosing Senators.

(2) The Congress shall assemble at least once in every year; and such meeting shall be on the first Monday in December, unless they shall, by law, appoint a different day.

Sec. 5. (1) Each House shall be the judge of the elections, returns, and qualifications of its own members, and a majority of each shall constitute a quorum to do business; but a smaller number may adjourn from day to day, and may be authorized to compel the attendance of absent members, in such manner and under such penalties as each House may provide.

(2) Each House may determine the rules of its proceedings, punish its members for disorderly behavior, and, with the concurrence of two-thirds of the whole number, expel a member.

(3) Each House shall keep a journal of its proceedings, and from time to time publish the same, excepting such part as may in its judgment require secrecy, and the ayes and nays of the members of either House, on any question, shall, at the desire of one-fifth of those present, be entered on the journal.

(4) Neither House, during the session of Congress, shall, without the consent of the other, adjourn for more than three days, nor to any other place than that in which the two Houses shall be sitting.

Sec. 6. (1) The Senators and Representatives shall receive a compensation for their services, to be ascertained by law, and paid out of the Treasury of the Confederate States. They shall, in all cases except treason and breach of the peace, be privileged from arrest during their attendance at the session of their respective Houses, and in going to and returning from the same; and for any speech or debate in either House, they shall not be questioned in any other place.

(2) No Senator or Representative shall, during the time for which he was elected, be appointed to any civil office under the authority of the Confederate States, which shall have been created, or the emoluments whereof shall have been increased during such time; and no person holding any office under the Confederate States shall be a member of either House during his continuance in office. But Congress may, by law, grant to the principal officer in

each of the Executive Departments a seat upon the floor of either House, with the privilege of discussing any measure appertaining to his department.

Sec. 7. (1) All bills for raising revenue shall originate in the House of Representatives; but the Senate may propose or concur with amendments as on other bills.

(2) Every bill which shall have passed both Houses shall, before it becomes a law, be presented to the President of the Confederate States; if he approve he shall sign it; but if not, he shall return it with his objections to that House in which it shall have originated, who shall enter the objections at large on their journal, and proceed to reconsider it. If, after such reconsideration, two-thirds of that House shall agree to pass the bill, it shall be sent, together with the objections, to the other House, by which it shall likewise be reconsidered, and if approved by two-thirds of that House, it shall become a law. But in all such cases, the votes of both Houses shall be determined by yeas and nays, and the names of the persons voting for and against the bill shall be entered on the journal of each House respectively. If any bill shall not be returned by the President within ten days (Sundays excepted) after it shall have been presented to him, the same shall be a law, in like manner as if he had signed it, unless the Congress, by their adjournment, prevent its return; in which case it shall not be a law. The president may approve any appropriation and disapprove any other appropriation in the same bill. In such case he shall, in signing the bill, designate the appropriations disapproved; and shall return a copy of such appropriations, with his objections, to the House in which the bill shall have originated; and the same proceedings shall then be had as in case of other bill disapproved by the President.

(3) Every order, resolution, or vote, to which the concurrence of both Houses may be necessary (except on questions of adjournment) shall be presented to the President of the Confederate States; and before the same shall take effect shall be approved by him; or being disapproved by him, may be repassed by two-thirds of both Houses, according to the rules and limitations prescribed in case of a bill.

Sec. 8.—The Congress shall have power—

(1) To lay and collect taxes, duties, imposts, and excises, for revenue necessary to pay the debts, provide for the common defence, and carry on the Government of the Confederate States; but no bounties shall be granted from the treasury; nor shall any duties or taxes on importations from foreign nations be laid to promote or foster any branch of industry; and all duties, imposts, and excises shall be uniform throughout the Confederate States.

(2) To borrow money on the credit of the Confederate States.

(3) To regulate commerce with foreign nations, and among the several States, and with the Indian tribes; but

neither this, nor any other clause contained in the Constitution shall be construed to delegate the power to Congress to appropriate money for any internal improvement intended to facilitate commerce; except for the purpose of furnishing lights, beacons, and buoys, and other aids to navigation upon the coasts, and the improvement of harbors, and the removing of obstructions in river navigation, in all which cases, such duties shall be laid on the navigation facilitated thereby, as may be necessary to pay the costs and expenses thereof.

(4) To establish uniform laws of naturalization, and uniform laws on the subject of bankruptcies throughout the Confederate States, but no law of Congress shall discharge any debt contracted before the passage of the same.

(5) To coin money, regulate the value thereof, and of foreign coin, and fix the standard of weights and measures.

(6) To provide for the punishment of counterfeiting the securities and current coin of the Confederate States.

(7) To establish post-offices and post-routes; but the expenses of the Post-office Department, after the first day of March, in the year of our Lord eighteen hundred and sixty-three, shall be paid out of its own revenues.

(8) To promote the progress of science and useful arts, by securing for limited times to authors and inventors the exclusive right to their respective writings and discoveries.

(9) To constitute tribunals inferior to the Supreme Court.

(10) To define and punish piracies and felonies committed on the high seas, and offences against the law of nations.

(11) To declare war, grant letters of marque and reprisal, and make rules concerning captures on land and water.

(12) To raise and support armies; but no appropriation of money to that use shall be for a longer term than two years.

(13) To provide and maintain a navy.

(14) To make rules for government and regulation of the land and naval forces.

(15) To provide for calling forth the militia to execute the laws of the Confederate States; suppress insurrections, and repel invasions.

(16) To provide for organizing, arming, and disciplining the militia, and for governing such part of them as may be employed in the service of the Confederate States; reserving to the States, respectively, the appointment of the officers, and the authority of training the militia according to the discipline prescribed by Congress.

(17) To exercise exclusive legislation, in all cases whatsoever, over such district (not exceeding ten miles square) as may, by cession of one or more States, and the acceptance of Congress, become the seat of the Government of the Confederate States; and to exercise a like authority

over all places purchased by the consent of the Legislature of the State in which the same shall be, for the erection of forts, magazines, arsenals, dock-yards, and other needful buildings, and

(18) To make all laws which shall be necessary and proper for carrying into execution the foregoing powers, and all other powers vested by this Constitution in the Government of the Confederate States, or in any department or officer thereof.

Sec. 9. (1) The importation of negroes of the African race, from any foreign country, other than the slaveholding States or Territories of the United States of America, is hereby forbidden; and Congress is required to pass such laws as shall effectually prevent the same.

(2) Congress shall also have power to prohibit the introduction of slaves from any State not a member of, or Territory not belonging to, this Confederacy.

(3) The privilege of the writ of *habeas corpus* shall not be suspended, unless when in cases of rebellion or invasion the public safety may require it.

(4) No bill of attainder, or *ex post facto* law, or law denying or impairing the right of property in negro slaves shall be passed.

(5) No capitation or other direct tax shall be laid unless in proportion to the census or enumeration hereinbefore directed to be taken.

(6) No tax or duty shall be laid on articles exported from any State, except by a vote of two-thirds of both Houses.

(7) No preference shall be given by any regulation of commerce or revenue to the ports of one State over those of another.

(8) No money shall be drawn from the treasury but in consequence of appropriations made by law; and a regular statement and account of the receipts and expenditures of all public money shall be published from time to time.

(9) Congress shall appropriate no money from the treasury except by a vote of two-thirds of both Houses, taken by yeas and nays, unless it be asked and estimated for by some one of the heads of departments, and submitted to Congress by the President; or for the purpose of paying its own expenses and contingencies; or for the payment of claims against the Confederate States, the justice of which shall have been judicially declared by a tribunal for the investigation of claims against the Government, which it is hereby made the duty of Congress to establish.

(10) All bills appropriating money shall specify in federal currency the exact amount of each appropriation and the purposes for which it is made; and Congress shall grant no extra compensation to any public contractor, officer, agent, or servant, after such contract shall have been made or such service rendered.

(11) No title of nobility shall be granted by the Confederate States; and no person holding any office of profit or trust under them shall, without the consent of the Congress, accept of any present, emoluments, office, or title of any kind whatever, from any king, prince, or foreign state.

(12) Congress shall make no law respecting an establishment of religion, or prohibiting the free exercise thereof; or abridging the freedom of speech or of the press; or the right of the people peaceably to assemble and petition the Government for a redress of grievances.

(13) A well-regulated militia being necessary to the security of a free State, the right of the people to keep and bear arms shall not be infringed.

(14) No soldier shall, in time of peace, be quartered in any house without the consent of the owner; nor in time of war, but in a manner prescribed by law.

(15) The right of the people to be secure in their persons, houses, papers, and against unreasonable searches and seizures, shall not be violated; and no warrant shall issue but upon probable cause, supported by oath or affirmation, and particularly describing the place to be searched, and the person or things to be seized.

(16) No person shall be held to answer for a capital or otherwise infamous crime, unless on a presentment or indictment of a grand jury, except in cases arising in the land or naval forces, or in the militia, when in actual service, in time of war, or public danger; nor shall any person be subject for the same offence to be twice put in jeopardy of life or limb; nor be compelled in any criminal case to be a witness against himself; nor be deprived of life, liberty, or property, without due process of law; nor shall any private property be taken for public use without just compensation.

(17) In all criminal prosecutions the accused shall enjoy the right to a speedy and public trial, by an impartial jury of the State and district wherein the crime shall have been committed, which district shall have been previously ascertained by law, and to be informed of the nature and cause of the accusation; to be confronted with the witnesses against him; to have compulsory process for obtaining witnesses in his favor; and to have the assistance of counsel for his defence.

(18) In suits at common law, where the value in controversy shall exceed twenty dollars, the right of trial by jury shall be preserved; and no fact so tried by a jury shall be otherwise reexamined in any court of the Confederacy, than according to the rules of the common law.

(19) Excessive bail shall not be required, nor excessive fines imposed, nor cruel or unusual punishment inflicted.

(20) Every law, or resolution having the force of law, shall relate to but one subject, and that shall be expressed in the title.

Sec. 10. (1) No State shall enter into any treaty, alliance, or confederation; grant letters of marque and reprisals; coin money; make any thing but gold and silver coin a tender in payment of debts; pass any bill of attainder, or *ex post facto* law, or law impairing the obligation of contracts; or grant any title of nobility.

(2) No State shall, without the consent of Congress, lay any imposts or duties on imports or exports, except what may be absolutely necessary for executing its inspection laws; and the net produce of all duties and imposts, laid by any State on imports or exports, shall be for the use of the Treasury of the Confederate States; and all such laws shall be subject to the revision and control of Congress.

(3) No State shall, without the consent of Congress, lay any duty of tonnage, except on sea-going vessels, for the improvement of its rivers and harbors navigated by the said vessels; but such duties shall not conflict with any treaties of the Confederate States with foreign nations; and any surplus of revenue, thus derived, shall, after making such improvement, be paid into the common treasury; nor shall any State keep troops or ships of war in time of peace, enter into any agreement or compact with another State, or with a foreign power, or engage in war, unless actually invaded, or in such imminent danger as will not admit of delay. But when any river divides or flows through two or more States, they may enter into compacts with each other to improve the navigation thereof.

Art. II.

Sec. 1. (1) The Executive power shall be vested in a President of the Confederate States of America. He and the Vice-President shall hold their offices for the term of six years; but the President shall not be reeligible. The President and Vice-President shall be elected as follows:

(2) Each State shall appoint, in such manner as the Legislature thereof may direct, a number of electors equal to the whole number of Senators and Representatives to which the State may be entitled in Congress; but no Senator or Representative, or person holding an office of trust or profit under the Confederate States, shall be appointed an elector.

(3) The electors shall meet in their respective States and vote by ballot for President and Vice-President, one of whom, at least, shall not be an inhabitant of the same State with themselves; they shall name in their ballots the person voted for as President, and in distinct ballots the person voted for as Vice-President, and they shall make distinct lists of all persons voted for as President, and of all persons voted for as Vice-President, and of the number of votes for each; which list they shall sign, and certify, and transmit, sealed, to the Government of the Confederate States, directed to the President of the Senate. The President of the Senate shall, in the presence of the Senate and House of Representatives, open all the certificates, and the votes shall then be counted; the person having the greatest number of votes for President shall be the President, if such number be a majority of the whole number of electors appointed; and if no person shall have such a majority, then, from the persons having the highest numbers, not exceeding three, on the list of those voted for as President, the House of Representatives shall choose immediately, by ballot, the President. But, in choosing the President, the votes shall be taken by States, the Representative from each State having one vote; a quorum for this purpose shall consist of a member or members from two-thirds of the States, and a majority of all the States shall be necessary to a choice. And if the House of Representatives shall not choose a President, whenever the right of choice shall devolve upon them, before the fourth day of March next following, then the Vice-President shall act as President, as in case of the death, or other constitutional disability of the President.

(4) The person having the greatest number of votes as Vice-President shall be the Vice-President, if such number be a majority of the whole number of electors appointed; and if no person have a majority, then from the two highest numbers on the list, the Senate shall choose the Vice-President; a quorum for the purpose shall consist of two-thirds of the whole number of Senators, and a majority of the whole number shall be necessary for a choice.

(5) But no person constitutionally ineligible to the office of President shall be eligible to that of Vice-President of the Confederate States.

(6) The Congress may determine the time of choosing the electors, and the day on which they shall give their votes; which day shall be the same throughout the Confederate States.

(7) No person except a natural born citizen of the Confederate States, or a citizen thereof, at the time of the adoption of this Constitution, or a citizen thereof born in the United States prior to the 20th December, 1860, shall be eligible to the office of President; neither shall any person be eligible to that office who shall not have attained the age of thirty-five years, and been fourteen years a resident within the limits of the Confederate States, as they may exist at the time of his election.

(8) In case of the removal of the President from office, or of his death, resignation, or inability to discharge the powers and duties of the said office, the same shall devolve on the Vice-President; and the Congress may, by law, provide for the case of the removal, death, resignation, or inability both of the President and the Vice-President, declaring what officer shall then act as President, and such

officer shall then act accordingly until the disability be removed or a President shall be elected.

(9) The President shall, at stated times, receive for his services a compensation, which shall neither be increased nor diminished during the period for which he shall have been elected; and he shall not receive within that period any other emolument from the Confederate States, or any of them.

(10) Before he enters on the execution of the duties of his office, he shall take the following oath or affirmation:

"I do solemnly swear (or affirm) that I will faithfully execute the office of President of the Confederate States, and will, to the best of my ability, preserve, protect, and defend the Constitution thereof."

Sec. 2. (1) The President shall be commander-in-chief of the army and navy of the Confederate States, and of the militia of the several States, when called into the actual service of the Confederate States; he may require the opinion, in writing, of the principal officer in each of the Executive Departments, upon any subject relating to the duties of their respective offices; and he shall have power to grant reprieves and pardons for offences against the Confederate States, except in cases of impeachment.

(2) He shall have power, by and with the advice and consent of the Senate, to make treaties, provided two-thirds of the Senators present concur; and he shall nominate, and, by and with the advice and consent of the Senate, shall appoint ambassadors, other public ministers, and consuls, Judges of the Supreme Court, and all other officers of the Confederate States, whose appointments are not herein otherwise provided for, and which shall be established by law; but the Congress may by law vest the appointment of such inferior officers, as they think proper, in the President alone, in the courts of law, or in the heads of departments.

(3) The principal officer in each of the Executive Departments, and all persons connected with the diplomatic service, may be removed from office at the pleasure of the President. All other civil officers of the Executive Department may be removed at any time by the President, or other appointing power, when their services are unnecessary, or for dishonesty, incapacity, inefficiency, misconduct, or neglect of duty; and when so removed, the removal shall be reported to the Senate, together with the reasons therefor.

(4) The President shall have power to fill all vacancies that may happen during the recess of the Senate, by granting commissions which shall expire at the end of the next session; but no person rejected by the Senate shall be reappointed to the same office during their ensuing recess.

Sec. 3. (1) The President shall, from time to time, give to the Congress information of the state of the Confeder-acy, and recommend to their consideration such measures as he shall judge necessary and expedient; he may, on extraordinary occasions, convene both Houses, or either of them; and, in case of disagreement between them, with respect to the time of adjournment he may adjourn them to such time as he shall think proper; he shall receive ambassadors and other public ministers; he shall take care that the laws be faithfully executed, and shall commission all the officers of the Confederate States.

Sec. 4. (1) The President and Vice-President, and all civil officers of the Confederate States, shall be removed from office on impeachment for, or conviction of, treason, bribery, or other high crimes and misdemeanors.

Art. III.

Sec. 1. (1) The judicial power of the Confederate States shall be vested in one Superior Court, and in such inferior courts as the Congress may from time to time ordain and establish. The judges, both of the Supreme and inferior courts, shall hold their offices during good behavior, and shall, at stated times, receive for their services a compensation, which shall not be diminished during their continuance in office.

Sec. 2. (1) The judicial power shall extend to all cases arising under the Constitution, the laws of the Confederate States, or treaties made or which shall be made under their authority; to all cases affecting ambassadors, other public ministers, and consuls; to all cases of admiralty or maritime jurisdiction; to controversies to which the Confederate States shall be a party; to controversies between two or more States; between a State and citizens of another State, where the State is plaintiff; between citizens claiming lands under grants of different States, and between a State or the citizens thereof, and foreign States, citizens, or subjects; but no State shall be sued by a citizen or subject of any foreign State.

(2) In all cases affecting ambassadors, other public ministers, and consuls, and those in which a State shall be a party, the Supreme Court shall have original jurisdiction. In all the other cases before mentioned, the Supreme Court shall have appellate jurisdiction, both as to law and fact, with such exceptions, and under such regulations as the Congress shall make.

(3) The trial of all crimes, except in cases of impeachment, shall be by jury, and such trial shall be held in the State where the said crimes shall have been committed; but when not committed within any State, the trial shall be at such place or places as the Congress may by law have directed.

Sec. 3. (1) Treason against the Confederate States shall consist only in levying war against them, or in adhering to their enemies, giving them aid and comfort. No person shall be convicted of treason unless on the testimony of two witnesses to the same overt act, or on confession in open court.

(2) The Congress shall have power to declare the punishment of treason, but no attainder of treason shall work corruption of blood, or forfeiture, except during the life of the person attainted.

Art. IV.

Sec. 1. (1) Full faith and credit shall be given in each State to the public acts, records, and judicial proceedings of every other State. And the Congress may, by general laws, prescribe the manner in which such acts, records, and proceedings shall be proved, and the effect thereof.

Sec. 2. (1) The citizens of each State shall be entitled to all the privileges and immunities of citizens of the several States, and shall have the right of transit and sojourn in any State of this Confederacy, with their slaves and other property; and the right of property in said slaves shall not be thereby impaired.

(2) A person charged in any State with treason, felony, or other crime against the laws of such State, who shall flee from justice, and be found in another State, shall, on demand of the executive authority of the State from which he fled, be delivered up to be removed to the State having jurisdiction of the crime.

(3) No slave or other person held to service or labor in any State or Territory of the Confederate States, under the laws thereof, escaping or unlawfully carried into another, shall, in consequence of any law or regulation therein, be discharged from such service or labor; but shall be delivered up on claim of the party to whom such slave belongs, or to whom such service or labor may be due.

Sec. 3. (1) Other States may be admitted into this Confederacy by a vote of two-thirds of the whole House of Representatives, and two-thirds of the Senate, the Senate voting by States; but no new State shall be formed or erected within the jurisdiction of any other State; nor any State be formed by the junction of two or more States, or parts of States, without the consent of the Legislatures of the States concerned as well as of the Congress.

(2) The Congress shall have power to dispose of and make all needful rules and regulations concerning the property of the Confederate States, including the lands thereof.

(3) The Confederate States may acquire new territory; and Congress shall have power to legislate and provide governments for the inhabitants of all territory belonging to the Confederate States, lying without the limits of the several States, and may permit them, at such times, and in such manner as it may by law provide, to form States to be admitted into the Confederacy. In all such territory, the institution of negro slavery, as it now exists in the Confederate States, shall be recognized and protected by Congress and by the territorial government; and the inhabitants of the several Confederate States and Territories shall have the right to take to such territory any slaves lawfully held by them in any of the States or Territories of the Confederate States.

(4) The Confederate States shall guarantee to every State that now is or hereafter may become a member of this Confederacy, a Republican form of Government, and shall protect each of them against invasion; and on application of the Legislature, (or of the Executive when the Legislature is not in session,) against domestic violence.

Art. V.

Sec. 1. (1) Upon the demand of any three States, legally assembled in their several Conventions, the Congress shall summon a Convention of all the States, to take into consideration such amendments to the Constitution as the said States shall concur in suggesting at the time when the said demand is made; and should any of the proposed amendments to the Constitution be agreed on by the said Convention—voting by States—and the same be ratified by the Legislatures of two-thirds of the several States, or by conventions in two-thirds thereof—as the one or the other mode of ratification may be proposed by the general convention—they shall thenceforward form a part of this Constitution. But no State shall, without its consent, be deprived of its equal representation in the Senate.

Art. VI.

1.—The Government established by this Constitution is the successor of the Provisional Government of the Confederate States of America, and all the laws passed by the latter shall continue in force until the same shall be repealed or modified; and all the officers appointed by the same shall remain in office until their successors are appointed and qualified, or the offices abolished.

2. All debts contracted and engagements entered into before the adoption of this Constitution, shall be as valid against the Confederate States under this Constitution as under the Provisional Government.

3. This Constitution, and the laws of the Confederate States, made in pursuance thereof, and all treaties made, or which shall be made, under the authority of the Confederate States, shall be the supreme law of the land; and the judges in every State shall be bound thereby, any thing in the Constitution or laws of any State to the contrary notwithstanding.

4. The Senators and Representatives before mentioned, and the members of the several State Legislatures,

and all executive and judicial offices, both of the Confederate States and of the several States, shall be bound, by oath or affirmation, to support this Constitution; but no religious test shall ever be required as a qualification to any office or public trust under the Confederate States.

5. The enumeration, in the Constitution, of certain rights, shall not be construed to deny or disparage others retained by the people of the several States.

6. The powers not delegated to the Confederate States by the Constitution, nor prohibited by it to the States, are reserved to the States, respectively, or to the people thereof.

Art. VII.

1.—The ratification of the conventions of five States shall be sufficient for the establishment of this Constitution between the States so ratifying the same.

2. When five States shall have ratified this Constitution in the manner before specified, the Congress, under the provisional Constitution, shall prescribe the time for holding the election of President and Vice-President, and for the meeting of the electoral college, and for counting the votes and inaugurating the President. They shall also prescribe the time for holding the first election of members of Congress under this Constitution, and the time for assembling the same. Until the assembling of such Congress, the Congress under the provisional Constitution shall continue to exercise the legislative powers granted them; not extending beyond the time limited by the Constitution of the Provisional Government.

Adopted unanimously by the Congress of the Confederate States of South Carolina, Georgia, Florida, Alabama, Mississippi, Louisiana, and Texas, sitting in convention at the capitol, in the city of Montgomery, Ala., on the eleventh day of March, in the year eighteen hundred and sixty-one.

Source:

Henry Steele Commager, ed. *Documents of American History.* New York: F.S. Crofts & Co., 1934.

T. J. "Stonewall" Jackson, First Battle of Manassas (Bull Run), 1861

A description of the first battle of the Civil War by the Confederate general Thomas J. Jackson. The Union had amassed 25,000 troops in Washington, D.C., and the population and press goaded President Lincoln, against General Winfield Scott's recommendation, into confronting the Confederates. They met near the stream Bull Run in Manassas, Virginia, some 20 miles outside the capital. Union general Irvin

McDowell's army was accompanied by the press, curiosity-seekers from the public, and members of Congress expecting to observe a great victory. Instead they witnessed the confusion of undisciplined troops on both sides wearing similar uniforms. The 22,000 Confederates under General P. G. T. Beauregard won the day with a reinforcement of an additional 9,000 troops and the stand of General Jackson that earned him the sobriquet "Stonewall." The defeated Union troops fled into Washington, but Beauregard, with his troops still disorganized, chose not to pursue them. After this battle, both sides knew that they were in for a long war.

HEADQUARTERS FIRST BRIGADE
Camp near Manassas, Va.
July 23, 1861

MAJOR: have the honor to submit the following report of the operations of my brigade on the 21st:

About 4 in the morning I received notice from Gen. Longstreet that he needed a re-enforcement of two regiments, which were accordingly ordered.

Subsequently I received an order from Gen. Beauregard to move to the support of Gen. Bonham, afterwards to support Gen. Cocke, and finally to take such position as would enable me to re-enforce either, as circumstances might require.

Whilst in the position last indicated I received a request from Gen. Cocke to guard the stone bridge, and immediately moved forward to effect the object in view.

Subsequently ascertaining that Gen. Bee, who was on the left of our line, was hard pressed, I marched to his assistance, notifying him at the same time that I was advancing to his support; but, before arriving within cannon range of the enemy, I met Gen. Bee's forces falling back. I continued to advance with the understanding that he would form in my rear. His battery, under its dauntless commander, Capt. Imboden, reversed and advanced with my brigade.

The first favorable position for meeting the enemy was at the next summit, where at 11.30 a.m., I posted Capt. Imboden's battery and two pieces of Capt. Stanard's, so as to play upon the advancing foe. The Fourth Regiment, commanded by Col. James F. Preston, and the Twenty-seventh Regiment, commanded by Lieut. Col. John F. Preston, and the Twenty-seventh Regiment, commanded by Lieut. Col. John Echols, were posted in rear of the batteries; the Fifth Regiment, commanded by Col. Kenton Harper, was posted on the right of the batteries; the Second Regiment, commanded by Col. James W. Allen, on the left, and the Thirty-third commanded by Col. A. C. Cummings, on his left. I also ordered forward the other two pieces of Capt. Stanard's and all those of Col. Pendleton's battery. They, as well as the battery under Lieut. Pelham, came into action on the same line as the others; and nobly did the artillery maintain for hours against the enemy's advancing thousands. Great praise is due to Col. Pendleton and the other officers and men.

Apprehensive lest my flanks should be turned, I sent an order to Cols. Stuart and Radford, of the cavalry, to secure them. Col. Stuart and that part of his command with him deserve great praise for the promptness with which they moved to my left and secured the flank by timely charging the enemy and driving him back.

Gen. Bee, with his rallied troops, soon marched to my support; and as re-enforcements continued to arrive Gen. Beauregard posted them so as to strengthen the flanks of my brigade. The enemy not being able to force our lines by a direct fire of artillery, inclined part of his batteries to the right, so as to obtain an oblique fire; but in doing so exposed his pieces to a more destructive fire from our artillery, and one of his batteries was thrown so near to Col. Cummings that it fell into his hands in consequence of his having made a gallant charge on it with his regiment; but owing to a destructive small-arm fire from the enemy he was forced to abandon it.

At 3.30 p.m. the advance of the enemy having reached a position which called for the use of the bayonet, I gave the command for the charge of the more than brave Fourth and Twenty-seventh, and, under commanders worth of such regiments, they, in the order in which they were posted, rushed forward obliquely to the left of our batteries, and through the blessing of God, who gave us the victory, pierced the enemy's center, and by co-operating with the victorious Fifth and other forces soon placed the field essentially in our possession.

About the time that Col. Preston passed our artillery the heroic Lieut.-Col. Lackland, of the Second Regiment, followed by the highly meritorious right of the Second, took possession of and endeavored to remove from the field the battery which Col. Cummings had previously been forced to abandon; but after removing one of the pieces some distance was also forced by the enemy's fire to abandon it.

The brigade, in connection with other troops, took seven field pieces in addition to the battery captured by Col. Cummings. The enemy, though repulsed in the center, succeeded in turning our flanks. But their batteries having been disabled by our fire, and also abandoned by reason of the infantry charges, the victory was soon completed by the fire of small-arms and occasional shots from a part of our artillery, which I posted on the next crest in rear.

By direction of Gen. Johnston I assumed the command of all the remaining artillery and infantry of the Army near the Lewis house, to act as circumstances might require. Part of this artillery fired on the retreating enemy. The colors of the First Michigan Regiment and an artillery flag were captured-the first by the Twenty-seventh Regiment and the other by the Fourth.

Lieut. Col. F. B. Jones, acting assistant adjutant-general; Lieut. T. G. Lee, aide-de-camp, and Lieut. A. A. Pendleton, brigade ordnance officer, and Capt. Thomas Marshall, volunteer aide, rendered valuable service. Cadets J. W. Thompson and N. W. Lee, also volunteer aides, merit special praise. Dr. Hunter H. McGuire has proved himself to be eminently qualified for his position–that of medical director of the brigade. Capt. Thomas L. Preston, though not of my command, rendered valuable service during the action.

It is with pain that I have to report as killed 11 officers, 14 non-commissioned officers, and 86 privates; wounded, 22 officers, 27 non-commissioned officers, and 319 privates; and missing, 1 officer and 4 privates.

I respectfully call attention to the accompanying reports of the commanders of the regiments and battery composing this brigade.

Your most obedient servant,
T.J. JACKSON,
Brig.-Gen., Provisional Army,
Confederate States

Source:

Valley of the Shadow: Two Communities in the American Civil War. Virginia Center for Digital History, University of Virginia. Available on-line. URL: http://valley.vcdh.Virginia.edu/OR/augustaor.html. Accessed December 2003.

Jefferson Davis, Message to the Congress of the Confederate States, 1861

Then provisional president Jefferson Davis delivered this message to the Confederate Congress in Richmond, Virginia, on November 18, 1861. Surveying the war, Davis extolled the Rebel victories and the spirit of the people. He discussed the building of financial and transportation infrastructures and asked for patience. Describing the Union army's tactics in scathing terms, Davis called Lincoln a "despot," and proclaimed that "the separation is final."

Davis was elected president under the Confederate constitution, and his formal inauguration took place February 22, 1862, in Montgomery, Alabama, the Confederacy's first capital. In his second inaugural address, he equated the South's struggle with the Patriots' heroic fight in the American Revolution for liberty and government by the people's consent. The

North's determination to violate the Southern states' sovereign rights by striking at slavery, he asserted, had virtually forced those states to withdraw from the Union and join the Confederacy to preserve their liberty. Davis charged the North with barbaric prosecution of the war, praised the Southern people for the great sacrifices they were enduring in service of the South's cause, and claimed that preservation of civil liberties in the South proved the Confederacy's sincerity of purpose.

The few weeks which have elapsed since your adjournment have brought us so near the close of the year that we are now able to sum up its general results. The retrospect is such as should fill the hearts of our people with gratitude to Providence for His kind interposition in their behalf. Abundant yields have rewarded the labor of the agriculturist, whilst the manufacturing industry of the Confederate States was never so prosperous as now. The necessities of the times have called into existence new branches of manufactures, and given a fresh impulse to the activity of those heretofore in operation. The means of the Confederate States for manufacturing the necessaries and comforts of life within themselves increase as the conflict continues, and we are gradually becoming independent of the rest of the world for the supply of such military stores and munitions as are indispensable for war. The operations of the army soon to the partially interrupted by the approaching winter have afforded a protection to the country, and shed a luster upon its arms through the trying vicissitudes of more than one arduous campaign, which entitle our brave volunteers to our praise and our gratitude.

From its commencement up to the present period, the war has been enlarging its proportions and expanding its boundaries, so as to include new fields. The conflict now extends from the shores of the Chesapeake to the confines of Missouri and Arizona; yet, sudden calls from the remotest points for military aid have been met with promptness enough not only to avert disaster in face of superior numbers, but, also, to roll back the tide of invasion from the border.

When the war commenced, the enemy were possessed of certain strategic points and strong places within the Confederate States. They greatly exceeded in numbers, in available resources, and in the supplies necessary for war. Military establishments had been long organized, and were complete; the navy, and for the most part, the army, once common to both, were in their possession. To meet all this, we had to create not only an army in the face of war itself, but also the military establishments necessary to equip and place it in the field. It ought indeed to be a subject of gratulation that the spirit of the volunteers and the patriotism of the people have enabled us, under Prov-

idence, to grapple successfully with these difficulties. A succession of glorious victories at Bethel, Bull Run, Manassas, Springfield, Lexington, Leesburg, and Belmont, has checked the wicked invasion which greed of gain and the unhallowed lust of power brought upon our soil, and has proved that numbers cease to avail when directed against a people fighting for the sacred right of Self-Government and the privileges of freemen. After more than seven months of war, the enemy have not only failed to extend their occupancy of our soil, but new States and Territories have been added to our Confederacy, while instead of their threatened march of unchecked conquest, they have been driven to assume the defensive; and upon a fair comparison between the two belligerents as to men, military means, and financial condition, the Confederate States are relatively much stronger now than when the struggle commenced.

Since your adjournment the people of Missouri have conducted the war in the face of almost unparalleled difficulties, with a spirit and success alike worthy of themselves and of the great cause in which they are struggling. Since that time Kentucky, too, has become the theater of active hostilities. The federal forces have not only refused to acknowledge her right to be neutral, and have insisted upon making her a party to the war, but have invaded her for the purpose of attacking the Confederate States. Outrages of the most despotic character have been perpetrated upon her people; some of her most eminent citizens have been seized and borne away to languish in foreign prisons without knowing who were their accusers, or the specific charges made against them, while others have been forced to abandon their homes, families, and property, and seek a refuge in distant lands.

Finding that the Confederate States were about to be invaded through Kentucky, and that her people after being deceived into a mistaken security, were unarmed, and in danger of being subjugated by the Federal forces, our armies were marched into that State to repel the enemy and prevent their occupation of certain strategic points which would have given them great advantages in the contest—a step which was justified, not only by the necessities of self-defense on the part of the Confederate States, but, also, by a desire to aid the people of Kentucky. It was never intended by the Confederate Government to conquer or coerce the people of that State; but, on the contrary, it was declared by our Generals that they would withdraw their troops if the Federal Government would do likewise. Proclamation was also made of the desire to respect the neutrality of Kentucky, and the intention to abide by the wishes of her people as soon as they were free to express their opinions. These declarations were approved by me, and I should regard it as one of the best effects of the march of our troops into Kentucky if it should end in giving to her people liberty of choice and a free opportunity to decide their own destiny according to their own will.

The army has been chiefly instrumental in prosecuting the great contest in which we are engaged; but the Navy has also been effective in full proportion to its means. The naval officers deprived to a great extent of an opportunity to make their professional skill available at sea have served with commendable zeal and gallantry on shore and upon inland waters, further detail of which will be found in the reports of the Secretaries of the Navy and War.

In the transportation of the mails many difficulties have arisen which will be found fully developed in the report of the Post Master General. The absorption of the ordinary means of transportation for the movement of troops and military supplies, the insufficiency of the rolling stock of rail-roads for the accumulation of business resulting both from military operations; and the obstruction of water communication by the presence of the enemy's fleet, the failure and even refusal of contractors to comply with the terms of their agreements, the difficulties inherent in inaugurating so vast and complicated a system as that which requires postal facilities for every town and village in a territory so extended as ours, have all combined to impede the best directed efforts of the Post Master General, whose zeal, industry and ability have been taxed to the utmost extent. Some of these difficulties can only be overcome by time and an improved condition of the country upon the restoration of peace, but others may be remedied by legislation, and your attention is invited to the recommendations contained in the report of the Head of that Department.

The condition of the Treasury will doubtless be a subject of anxious inquiry on your part. I am happy to say that the financial system already adopted has worked well so far, and promises good results for the future. To the extent that Treasury notes may be issued the Government is enabled to borrow money without interest and thus facilitate the conduct of the war. This extent is measured by the portion of the field of circulation which these notes can be made to occupy. The proportion of the field thus occupied depends again upon the amount of the debts for which they are receivable; and when dues not only to the Confederate and State Governments, but also to corporations and individuals, are payable in this medium, a large amount of it may be circulated at par. There is every reason to believe that the Confederate Treasury note is fast becoming such a medium. The provision that these notes shall be convertible into Confederate Stock bearing eight per cent interest at the pleasure of the holder ensures them against a depreciation below the value of that stock, and no considerable fall in that value need be feared so long as the interest shall be punctually paid. The punctual payment of this interest has been secured by the act passed

by you at the last session, imposing such a rate of taxation as must provide sufficient means for that purpose. For the successful prosecution of this war it is indispensable that the means of transporting troops and military supplies be furnished as far as possible in such manner as not to interrupt the commercial intercourse between our people, nor place a check on their productive energies. To this end the means of transportation from one section of our country to the other must be carefully guarded and improved. And this should be the object of anxious care on the part of State and Confederate Governments so far as they may have power over the subject.

We have already two main systems of through transportation from the North to the South,—one from Richmond along the seaboard; the other through Western Virginia to New Orleans Orleans. A third might be secured by completing a link of about forty miles between Danville in Virginia and Greensborough in North Carolina. The construction of this comparatively short line would give us a through route from North to South in the interior of the Confederate States, and give us access to a population and to military resources from which we are now in great measure debarred. We should increase greatly the safety and capacity of our means for transporting men and military supplies. If the construction of this road should in the judgment of Congress, as it is in mine, be indispensable for the most successful prosecution of the war, the action of the Government will not be restrained by the constitutional objection which would attach to a work for commercial purposes, and attention is invited to the practicability of securing its early completion by giving the needful aid to the company organized for its construction and administration.

If we husband our means and make a judicious use of our resources it would be difficult to fix a limit to the period during which we could conduct a war against the adversary whom we now encounter. The very efforts which he makes to isolate and invade us must exhaust his means whilst they serve to complete the circle and diversify the productions of our industrial system. The reconstruction which he seeks to effect by arms becomes daily more and more palpably impossible. Not only do the causes which induced us to separate still exist in full force, but they have been strengthened, and whatever doubt may have lingered in the minds of any have been completely dispelled by subsequent events. If instead of being a dissolution of a league, it were indeed a rebellion in which we are engaged, we might find ample vindication in the in the scenes which are now being enacted in the United States. Our people now look with contemptuous astonishment on those with whom they had been so recently associated. They shrink with aversion from the bare idea of renewing such a connection. When they see a President making war without the assent of Congress; when they behold judges threatened because they maintain the writ of habeas corpus so sacred to freemen; when they see justice and law trampled under the armed heel of military authority, and upright men and innocent women dragged to distant dungeons upon the mere edict of a despot; when they find all this tolerated and applauded by a people who had been in the full enjoyment of freedom but a few months ago—they believe that there must be some radical incompatibility between such a people and themselves. With such a people we may be content to live at peace, but the separation is final and for the independence we have asserted we will accept no alternative. The nature of the hostilities which they have waged against us must be characterized as barbarous wherever it is understood. They have bombarded undefended villages without giving notice to women and children to enable them to escape, and in one, instance selected the night as the period when they might surprise them most effectually whilst asleep and unsuspicious of danger. Arson and rapine, the destruction of private houses and property, and injuries of the most wanton character even upon non-combatants have marked their forays along our borders and upon our Territory. Although we ought to have been admonished by these things that they were disposed to make war upon us in the most cruel and relentless spirit, yet we were not prepared to see them fit out a large naval expedition with the confessed purpose not only to pillage, but to incite a servile insurrection in our midst.

If they convert their soldiers into incendiaries and robbers and involve us in a species of war which claims non-combatants, women and children as its victims, they must expect to be treated as outlaws and enemies of mankind. There are certain rights of humanity which are entitled to respect even in war, and he who refuses to regard them forfeits his claims, if captured, to be considered as a prisoner of war but must expect to be dealt with as an offender against all law human and divine. But not content with violating our rights under the law of nations at home, they have extended these injuries to us within other jurisdictions. The distinguished gentlemen whom, with your approval at the last session, I commissioned to represent the Confederacy at certain foreign courts, have been recently seized by the captain of a United States ship of War on board a British steamer on their voyage from the neutral Spanish port of Havana to England. The United States have thus claimed a general jurisdiction over the high seas, and entering a British ship sailing under its country's flag violated the rights of embassy, for the most part held sacred even amongst barbarians, by seizing our ministers whilst under the protection and within the dominions of a neutral nation. These gentlemen were as much under the jurisdiction of the British Government upon that ship and beneath its flag as if they had been on

its soil, and a claim on the part of the United States to seize them in the streets of London would have been as well founded as that to apprehend them where they were taken. Had they been malefactors and citizens even of the United States, they could not have been arrested on a British ship or on British soil unless under the express provisions of a treaty and according to the forms therein provided for the extradition of criminals.

But rights the most sacred seem to have lost all respect in their eyes. When Mr. Faulkner, a former minister of the United States to France commissioned before the secession of Virginia, his native State, returned in good faith to Washington to settle his accounts and fulfill all the obligations into which he had entered, he was perfidiously arrested and imprisoned in New York, where he now is. The unsuspecting confidence with which he reported to his Government was abused, and his desire to fulfill his trust to them was used to his injury.

In conducting this war we have sought no aid and proposed no alliances offensive and defensive abroad. We have asked for a recognized place in the great family of nations, but in doing so we have demanded nothing for which we did not offer a fair equivalent—The advantages of intercourse are mutual amongst Nations, and in seeking to establish diplomatic relations we were only endeavoring to place that intercourse under the regulation of public law. Perhaps we had the right if we had chosen to exercise it, to ask to know whether the principle that "blockades to be binding, must be effectual" so solemnly announced by the great Powers of Europe at Paris is to be generally enforced or applied only to particular parties.

When the Confederate States at your last session became a party to the declaration reaffirming this principle of international law which has been recognized so long by publicists and Governments, we certainly supposed that it was to be universally enforced. The customary law of nations is made up of their practice rather than their declarations; and if such declarations are only to be enforced in particular instances at the pleasure of those who make them, then the commerce of the world so far from being placed under the regulation of a general law, will become subject to the caprice of those who execute or suspend it at will—If such is to be the course of Nations in regard to this law, it is plain that it will thus become a rule for the weak and not for the strong.

Feeling that such views must be taken by the neutral nations of the Earth, I have caused the evidence to be collected which proves completely the utter inefficiency of the proclaimed blockade of our coast and shall direct it to be laid before such Governments as shall afford us the means of being heard—But although we should be benefited by the enforcement of this law so solemnly declared by the great Powers of Europe, we are not dependent on that enforcement for the successful prosecution of the war. As long as hostilities continue the Confederate States will exhibit a steadily increasing capacity to furnish their troops with food, clothing and arms. If they should be forced to forego many of the luxuries and some of the comforts of life, they will at least have the consolation of knowing that they are thus daily becoming more and more independent of the rest of the world. If in this process labor in the Confederate States should be gradually diverted from those great Southern Staples which have given life to so much of the commerce of mankind into other channels so as to make them rival producers instead of profitable customers, they will not be the only or even the chief losers by this change in the direction of their industry. Although it is true that the cotton supply from the Southern States could only be totally cut off by the subversion of our social system; yet it is plain that a long continuance of this blockade might by a diversion of labor and an investment of capital in other employments so diminish the supply as to bring ruin upon all those interests of foreign countries which are dependent on that Staple. For every laborer who is diverted from the culture of cotton in the South, perhaps four times as many elsewhere who have found subsistence in the various employments growing out of its use, will be forced also to change their occupation.

While the war which is waged to take from us the right of Self-Government can never attain that end, it remains to be seen how far it may work a revolution in the industrial system of the world, which may carry suffering to other lands as well as to our own. In the meantime we shall continue this struggle in humble dependence upon Providence from whose searching scrutiny we cannot conceal the secrets of our hearts, and to whose rule we confidently submit our destinies. For the rest we shall depend upon ourselves—Liberty is always won where there exists the unconquerable will to be free, and we have reason to know the strength that is given by a conscious sense, not only of the magnitude, but of the righteousness of our cause.

Source:

The Papers of Jefferson Davis. Vol. 7, 1861, pp. 412–421. The Museum of the Confederacy. Eleanor S. Brockenbrough Library. Richmond, Virginia.

U.S. Congress, District of Columbia Emancipation Act, 1862

An act of Congress, signed on April 16, 1862, that ended slavery in the District of Columbia. President Abraham Lincoln signed this bill nine months before he issued the Emancipation Proclamation. The act's passage ended decades of unrest in the district, the result of what antislavery advocates called "the national shame" of slavery in the nation's capital.

The District of Columbia Emancipation Act is the only example of compensated emancipation in the United States. It declared the immediate emancipation of all slaves within the confines of the district and provided up to $100 in aid to each slave choosing to emigrate to colonies outside of the United States. The act also provided slave owners loyal to the Union cause with up to $300 compensation for each of their slaves. Over the next nine months, the federal government paid nearly $1 million for the freedom of approximately 3,100 former slaves. Although the act's three-way approach of immediate emancipation, compensation, and colonization did not serve as a model for the future, the act's passage was an early signal of the death of slavery.

The same year, Lincoln requested, and Congress issued, a resolution providing compensation to states undertaking a program of gradual emancipation. When that program failed, Congress passed the U.S. Confiscation Act of 1862. This act, passed by Congress on July 17, 1862, provided for the seizure of property of disloyal slave owners and the emancipation of their slaves. The property of local, state, and Confederate civil and military officials was specifically noted as subject to confiscation. Like the U.S. Confiscation Act of 1861, the 1862 act treated slave emancipation as a punishment for insurrection and not as a moral goal in its own right. Signed by President Abraham Lincoln, the act was unenforceable until Union armies occupied the South. Because his proposal for gradual, compensated emancipation failed, in September 1862 the president issued his preliminary Emancipation Proclamation.

Be it enacted by the Senate and House of Representatives of the United States of America in Congress assembled, That all persons held to service or labor within the District of Columbia by reason of African descent are hereby discharged and freed of and from all claim to such service or labor; and from and after the passage of this act neither slavery nor involuntary servitude, except for crime, whereof the party shall be duly convicted, shall hereafter exist in said District.

Sec. 2. *And be it further enacted,* That all persons loyal to the United States, holding claims to service or labor against persons discharged therefrom by this act, may, within ninety days from the passage thereof, but not thereafter, present to the commissioners hereinafter mentioned their respective statements or petitions in writing, verified by oath or affirmation, setting forth the names, ages, and personal description of such persons, the manner in which said petitioners acquired such claim, and any facts touching the value thereof, and declaring his allegiance to the

Government of the United States, and that he has not borne arms against the United States during the present rebellion, nor in any way given aid or comfort thereto: *Provided,* That the oath of the party to the petition shall not be evidence of the facts therein stated.

Sec. 3. *And be it further enacted,* That the President of the United States, with the advice and consent of the Senate, shall appoint three commissioners, residents of the District of Columbia, any two of whom shall have power to act, who shall receive the petitions above mentioned, and who shall investigate and determine the validity and value of the claims therein presented, as aforesaid, and appraise and apportion, under the proviso hereto annexed, the value in money of the several claims by them found to be valid: *Provided, however,* That the entire sum so appraised and apportioned shall not exceed in the aggregate an amount equal to three hundred dollars for each person shown to have been so held by lawful claim: *And provided, further,* That no claim shall be allowed for any slave or slaves brought into said District after the passage of this act, nor for any slave claimed by any person who has borne arms against the Government of the United States in the present rebellion, or in any way given aid or comfort thereto, or which originates in or by virtue of any transfer heretofore made, or which shall hereafter be made by any person who has in any manner aided or sustained the rebellion against the Government of the United States.

Sec. 4. *And be it further enacted,* That said commissioners shall, within nine months from the passage of this act, make a full and final report of their proceedings, findings, and appraisement, and shall deliver the same to the Secretary of the Treasury, which report shall be deemed and taken to be conclusive in all respects, except as hereinafter provided; and the Secretary of the Treasury shall, with like exception, cause the amounts so apportioned to said claims to be paid from the Treasury of the United States to the parties found by said report to be entitled thereto as aforesaid, and the same shall be received in full and complete compensation: *Provided,* That in cases where petitions may be filed presenting conflicting claims, or setting up liens, said commissioners shall so specify in said report, and payment shall not be made according to the award of said commissioners until a period of sixty days shall have elapsed, during which time any petitioner claiming an interest in the particular amount may file a bill in equity in the Circuit Court of the District of Columbia, making all other claimants defendants thereto, setting forth the proceedings in such case before said commissioners and their actions therein, and praying that the party to whom payment has been awarded may be enjoined form receiving the same; and if said court shall grant such provisional order, a copy

thereof may, on motion of said complainant, be served upon the Secretary of the Treasury, who shall thereupon cause the said amount of money to be paid into said court, subject to its orders and final decree, which payment shall be in full and complete compensation, as in other cases.

Sec. 5. *And be it further enacted,* That said commissioners shall hold their sessions in the city of Washington, at such place and times as the President of the United States may direct, of which they shall give due and public notice. They shall have power to subpoena and compel the attendance of witnesses, and to receive testimony and enforce its production, as in civil cases before courts of justice, without the exclusion of any witness on account of color; and they may summon before them the persons making claim to service or labor, and examine them under oath; and they may also, for purposes of identification and appraisement, call before them the persons so claimed. Said commissioners shall appoint a clerk, who shall keep files and [a] complete record of all proceedings before them, who shall have power to administer oaths and affirmations in said proceedings, and who shall issue all lawful process by them ordered. The Marshal of the District of Columbia shall personally, or by deputy, attend upon the sessions of said commissioners, and shall execute the process issued by said clerk.

Sec. 6. *And be it further enacted,* That said commissioners shall receive in compensation for their services the sum of two thousand dollars each, to be paid upon the filing of their report; that said clerk shall receive for his services the sum of two hundred dollars per month; that said marshal shall receive such fees as are allowed by law for similar services performed by him in the Circuit Court of the District of Columbia; that the Secretary of the Treasury shall cause all other reasonable expenses of said commission to be audited and allowed, and that said compensation, fees, and expenses shall be paid from the Treasury of the United States.

Sec. 7. *And be it further enacted,* That for the purpose of carrying this act into effect there is hereby appropriated, out of any money in the Treasury not otherwise appropriated, a sum not exceeding one million of dollars.

Sec. 8. *And be it further enacted,* That any person or persons who shall kidnap, or in any manner transport or procure to be taken out of said District, any person or persons discharged and freed by the provisions of this act, or any free person or persons with intent to re-enslave or sell such person or person into slavery, or shall re-enslave any of said freed persons, the person of persons so offending shall be deemed guilty of a felony, and on conviction thereof in any court of competent jurisdiction in said District, shall be imprisoned in the penitentiary not less than five nor more that twenty years.

Sec. 9. *And be it further enacted,* That within twenty days, or within such further time as the commissioners herein provided for shall limit, after the passage of this act, a statement in writing or schedule shall be filed with the clerk of the Circuit court for the District of Columbia, by the several owners or claimants to the services of the persons made free or manumitted by this act, setting forth the names, ages, sex, and particular description of such persons, severally; and the said clerk shall receive and record, in a book by him to be provided and kept for that purpose, the said statements or schedules on receiving fifty cents each therefor, and no claim shall be allowed to any claimant or owner who shall neglect this requirement.

Sec. 10. *And be it further enacted,* That the said clerk and his successors in office shall, from time to time, on demand, and on receiving twenty-five cents therefor, prepare, sign, and deliver to each person made free or manumitted by this act, a certificate under the seal of said court, setting out the name, age, and description of such person, and stating that such person was duly manumitted and set free by this act.

Sec. 11. *And be it further enacted,* That the sum of one hundred thousand dollars, out of any money in the Treasury not otherwise appropriated, is hereby appropriated, to be expended under the direction of the President of the United States, to aid in the colonization and settlement of such free persons of African descent now residing in said District, including those to be liberated by this act, as may desire to emigrate to the Republics of Hayti or Liberia, or such other country beyond the limits of the United States as the President may determine: *Provided,* The expenditure for this purpose shall not exceed one hundred dollars for each emigrant.

Sec. 12. *And be it further enacted,* That all acts of Congress and all laws of the State of Maryland in force in said District, and all ordinances of the cities of Washington and Georgetown, inconsistent with the provisions of this act, are hereby repealed.

Approved, April 16, 1862.

Source:

National Archives and Records Administration. "An Act for the Release of certain Persons held to Service or Labor in the District of Columbia." Available on-line. URL: www.archives.gov/exhibit_hall/featured_documents/dc_emancipation_act/transcription.html. Accessed December 2003.

Homestead Act of 1862

First act passed by the U.S. Congress distributing public lands in the West to settlers. It was supposed to benefit laborers and tenant farmers. The Northern states had long desired such legislation, but the South had opposed the policy, fearing the effects of an influx of antislavery homesteaders in the West. It was only passed after the election of a Republican administration in 1860 and the secession of the Southern states. Consequently, it benefited Northern railroad and mining interests and halted the expansion of plantation farming by weakening sugar, cotton, and tobacco interests. The Homestead Act, enacted on May 20, 1862, provided 160 acres of unoccupied public land to any citizen (or intended citizen) who was willing to occupy and cultivate the land for five years and who was either head of a family or at least 21 years old. The land was free except for a small filing fee. By 1870 nearly 14 million acres had been homesteaded.

――――――――――――――― ⌒∞⌒ ―――――――――――――――

An Act

To secure Homesteads to actual Settlers on the Public Domain.

Be it enacted by the Senate and House of Representatives of the United States of America in Congress assembled, That any person who is the head of a family, or who has arrived at the age of twenty-one years, and is a citizen of the United States, or who shall have filed his declaration of intention to become such, as required by the naturalization laws of the United States, and who has never borne arms against the United States Government or given aid and comfort to its enemies, shall, from and after the first January, eighteen hundred and sixty-three, be entitled to enter one quarter section or a less quantity of unappropriated public lands, upon which said person may have filed a preemption claim, or which may, at the time the application is made, be subject to preemption at one dollar and twenty-five cents, or less, per acre; or eighty acres or less of such unappropriated lands, at two dollars and fifty cents per acre, to be located in a body, in conformity to the legal subdivisions of the public lands, and after the same shall have been surveyed: *Provided,* That any person owning and residing on land may, under the provisions of this act, enter other land lying contiguous to his or her said land, which shall not, with the land so already owned and occupied, exceed in the aggregate one hundred and sixty acres.

Sec. 2. *And be it further enacted,* That the person applying for the benefit of this act shall, upon application to the register of the land office in which he or she is about to make such entry, make affidavit before the said register or receiver that he or she is the head of a family, or is twenty-one years or more of age, or shall have performed service in the army or navy of the United States, and that he has never borne arms against the Government of the United States or given aid and comfort to its enemies, and that such application is made for his or her exclusive use and benefit, and that said entry is made for the purpose of actual settlement and cultivation, and not either directly or indirectly for the use or benefit of any other person or persons whomsoever; and upon filing the said affidavit with the register or receiver, and on payment of ten dollars, he or she shall thereupon be permitted to enter the quantity of land specified: *Provided, however,* That no certificate shall be given or patent issued therefor, until the expiration of five years from the date of such entry; and if, at the expiration of such time, or at any time within two years thereafter, the person making such entry; or, if he be dead, his widow; or in case of her death, his heirs or devisee; or in case of a widow making such entry, her heirs or devisee, in case of here death; shall prove by two credible witnesses that he, she, or they have resided upon or cultivated the same for the term of five years immediately succeeding the time of filing the affidavit aforesaid, and shall make affidavit that no part of said land has been alienated, and that he has borne true allegiance to the Government of the United States; then, in such case, he, she, or they, if at that time a citizen of the United States, shall be entitled to a patient, as in other cases provided for by law: *And provided, further,* That in case of the death of both father and mother, leaving an infant child, or children, under twenty-one years of age, the right and fee shall enure to the benefit of said infant child or children; and the executor, administrator, or guardian may, at any time within two years after the death of the surviving parent, and in accordance with the laws of the State in which such children for the time being have their domicil, sell said land for the benefit of said infants, but for no other purpose; and the purchaser shall acquire the absolute title by the purchase, and be entitled to a patent from the United States, on payment of the office fees and sum of money herein specified.

Sec. 3. *And be it further enacted* , That the register of the land office shall note all such applications on the tract books and plats of his office, and keep a register of all such entries, and make return thereof to the General Land Office, together with the proof upon which they have been founded.

Sec. 4. *And be it further enacted,* That no lands acquired under the provisions of this act shall in any event become liable to the satisfaction of any debt or debts contracted prior to the issuing of the patent therefor.

Sec. 5. *And be it further enacted,* That if, at any time after the filing of the affidavit, as required in the second section of this act, and before the expiration of the five years aforesaid, it shall be proven, after due notice to the settler, to the satisfaction of the register of the land office, that the person having filed such affidavit shall have actually changed his or her residence, or abandoned

the said land for more than six months at any time, then and in that event the land so entered shall revert to the government.

Sec. 6. *And be it further enacted,* That no individual shall be permitted to acquire title to more than one quarter section under the provisions of this act; and that the Commissioner of the General Land Office is hereby required to prepare and issue such rules and regulations, consistent with this act, as shall be necessary and proper to carry its provisions into effect; and that the registers and receivers of the several land offices shall be entitled to receive the same compensation for any lands entered under the provisions of this act that they are now entitled to receive when the same quantity of land is entered with money, one half to be paid by the person making the application at the time of so doing, and the other half on the issue of the certificate by the person to whom it may be issued; but this shall not be construed to enlarge the maximum of compensation now prescribed by law for any register or receiver; *Provided,* That nothing contained in this act shall be so construed as to impair or interfere in any manner whatever with existing preemption rights: *And provided, further,* That all persons who may have filed their applications for a preemption right prior to the passage of this act, shall be entitled to all privileges of this act: *Provided, further,* That no person who has served, or may hereafter serve, for a period of not less than fourteen days in the army or navy of the United States, either regular or volunteer, under the laws thereof, during the existence of an actual war, domestic or foreign, shall be deprived of the benefits of this act on account of not having attained the age of twenty-one years.

Sec. 7. *And be it further enacted,* That the fifth section of the act entitled "An act in addition to an act more effectually to provide for the punishment of certain crimes against the United States, and for other purposes," approved the third of March, in the year eighteen hundred and fifty-seven, shall extend to all oaths, affirmations, and affidavits, required or authorized by this act.

Sec. 8. *And be it further enacted,* That nothing in this act shall be so construed as to prevent any person who has availed him or herself of the benefits of the first section of this act, from paying the minimum price, or the price to which the same may have graduated, for the quantity of land so entered at any time before the expiration of the five years, and obtaining a patent thereto from the government, as in other cases provided by law, on making proof of settlement and cultivation as provided by existing laws granting preemption rights.

Source:
Statutes at Large, Vol. 12, pp. 392–393.

Morrill Act of 1862

Federal U.S. legislation passed on July 2, 1862, establishing land grant colleges through the sale of public lands. Sponsored by Vermont representative Justin S. Morrill, the bill gave to the states federal lands for the establishment of colleges offering programs in agriculture, mechanical sciences, and military science, as well as other scientific and classical subjects. Generally considered one of the most important pieces of educational legislation ever passed, the act spurred the development of state universities, made the federal government an important force in higher education, and helped democratize that education. Each state was granted 30,000 acres for each senator and representative in the U.S. Congress.

In 1887 Congress passed an act named for Missouri congressman William H. Hatch that provided federal funds for establishing experimental stations to conduct agricultural research. It granted $15,000 annually to each U.S. state "to aid in acquiring and diffusing among the people . . . useful and practical information on subjects connected with agriculture, and to promote scientific investigation and experiment respecting the principles and applications of agricultural science." The amount of the original subsidy was raised by later legislation.

An Act

Donating Public Lands to the several States and Territories which may provide Colleges for the Benefit of Agriculture and the Mechanic Arts.

Be it enacted by the Senate and House of Representatives of the United States of America in Congress assembled, That there be granted to the several States, for the purposes hereinafter mentioned, an amount of public land, to be apportioned to each State a quantity equal to thirty thousand acres for each senator and representative in Congress to which the States are respectively entitled by the apportionment under the census of eighteen hundred and sixty: *Provided,* That no mineral lands shall be selected or purchased under the provisions of this act.

Sec. 2. *And be it further enacted,* That the land aforesaid, after being surveyed, shall be apportioned to the several States in sections or subdivisions of sections, not less than one quarter of a section; and whenever there are public lands in a State subject to sale at private entry at one dollar and twenty-five cents per acre, the quantity to which said State shall be entitled shall be selected from such lands within the limits of such State, and the Secretary of the Interior is hereby directed to issue to each of the States in which there is not the quantity of public lands subject to sale at private entry at one dollar and twenty-five cents per acre, to which said State may be entitled under the provisions of this act, land scrip to the amount in acres for the deficiency of its distributive share: said scrip to be sold by said States and the proceeds thereof applied to the uses and purposes prescribed in this act, and for no other use or purpose whatsoever: *Provided,* That in no case shall any State to which land scrip may thus be issued be allowed to locate the same within the limits of any other State, or of any Territory of the United States, but their assignees may thus locate said land scrip upon any of the unappropriated lands of the United States subject to sale at private entry at one dollar and twenty-five cents, or less, per acre: *And provided, further,* That not more than one million acres shall be located by such assignees in any one of the States: *And provided, further,* That no such location shall be made before one year from the passage of this act.

Sec. 3. *And be it further enacted,* That all the expenses of management, superintendence, and taxes from date of selection of said lands, previous to their sales, and all expenses incurred in the management and disbursement of the moneys which may be received therefrom, shall be paid by the States to which they may belong, out of the treasury of said States, so that the entire proceeds of the sale of said lands shall be applied without any diminution whatever to the purposes hereinafter mentioned.

Sec. 4. *And be it further enacted,* That all moneys derived from the sale of the lands aforesaid by the States to which the lands are apportioned, and from the sales of land scrip hereinbefore provided for, shall be invested in stocks of the United States, or of the States, or some other safe stocks, yielding not less than five per centum upon the par value of said stocks; and that the moneys so invested shall constitute a perpetual fund, the capital of which shall remain forever undiminished, (except so far as may be provided in section fifth of this act,) and the interest, of which shall be inviolably appropriated, by each State which may take and claim the benefit of this act, to the endowment, support, and maintenance of at least one college where the leading object shall be, without excluding other scientific and classical studies, and including military tactics, to teach such branches of learning as are related to agriculture and the mechanic arts, in such manner as the legislatures of the States may respectively prescribe, in order to promote the liberal and practical education of the industrial classes in the several pursuits and professions in life.

Sec. 5. *And be it further enacted,* That the grant of land and land scrip hereby authorized shall be made on the following conditions, to which, as well as to the provisions hereinbefore contained, the previous assent of the several States shall be signified by legislative acts:

First. If any portion of the fund invested, as provided by the foregoing section, or any portion of the interest thereon, shall, by any action or contingency, be diminished or lost, it shall be replace by the State to which it belongs, so that the capital of the fund shall remain forever undiminished; and the annual interest shall be regularly applied without diminution to the purposes mentioned in the forth section of this act, except that a sum, not exceeding ten per centum upon the amount received by any State under the provisions of this act, may be expended for the purchase of lands for sites or experimental farms, whenever authorized by the respective legislatures of said States.

Second. No portion of said fund, nor the interest thereon, shall be applied, directly or indirectly, under any pretence whatever, to the purchase, erection, preservation, or repair of any building or buildings.

Third. Any State which may take and claim the benefit of the provisions of this act shall provide, within five years, at least not less than one college, as described in the fourth section of this act, or the grant to such State shall cease; and said State shall be bound to pay the United States the amount received of any lands previously sold, and that the title to purchasers under the State shall be valid.

Fourth. An annual report shall be made regarding the progress of each college, recording any improvements and experiments made, with their cost and results, and such other matters, including State industrial and economical statistics, as may be supposed useful; one copy of which shall be transmitted by mail free, by each, to all the other colleges which may be endowed under the provisions of this act, and also one copy to the Secretary of the Interior.

Fifth. When lands shall be selected from those which have been raised to double the minimum price, in consequence of railroad grants, they shall be computed to the States at the maximum price, and the number of acres proportionally diminished.

Sixth. No State while in a condition of rebellion or insurrection against the government of the United States shall be entitled to the benefit of this act.

Seventh. No State shall be entitled to the benefits of this act unless it shall express its acceptance thereof by its legislature within two years from the date of its approval by the President.

Sec. 6. *And be it further enacted,* That land scrip issued under the provisions of this act shall not be subject to location until after the first day of January, one thousand eight hundred and sixty-three.

Sec. 7. *And be it further enacted,* That the land officers shall receive the same fees for locating land scrip issued under the provisions of this act as is now allowed for the location of military bounty land warrants under existing laws; *Provided,* their maximum compensation shall not be thereby increased.

Sec. 8. *And be it further enacted,* That the Governors of the several States to which scrip shall be issued under this act shall be required to report annually to Congress all sales made of such scrip until the whole shall be disposed of, the amount received for the same, and what appropriation has been made of the proceeds.

Source:
Statutes at Large, Vol. 12, pp. 503–505.

Abraham Lincoln, Reply to Horace Greeley, 1862

Horace Greeley, founder and editor of the *New York Tribune,* addressed an open letter to President Abraham Lincoln, which he published in that newspaper on August 19, 1862. An ardent foe of slavery, Greeley exhorted Lincoln to commit himself to emancipation. He urged Lincoln to enforce strictly the provisions of the Confiscation Act of 1862 and to ignore the influence of proslavery "fossil politicians" from the border states. Greeley urged that the Union's efforts were suffering from mistaken deference to Rebel slavery. He opposed any concessions to or temporizing with armed traitors.

The president's reply, published August 22, 1862, in the *Tribune,* explained that his goal was neither to save nor to destroy slavery but to save the Union: "If I could save the Union without freeing *any* slave, I would do it; and if I could save it by freeing *all* the slaves, I would do it; and if I could do it by freeing some and leaving others alone, I would also do that." He noted that this statement represented his view of his official duty and did not alter his personal wish that "all men, everywhere, could be free."

Hon. Horace Greeley: Executive Mansion, Washington, August 22, 1862.

Dear Sir

I have just read yours of the 19th. addressed to myself through the New-York Tribune. If there be in it any statements, or assumptions of fact, which I may know to be erroneous, I do not, now and here, controvert them. If there be in it any inferences which I may believe to be falsely drawn, I do not now and here, argue against them. If there be perceptible in it an impatient and dictatorial tone, I waive it in deference to an old friend, whose heart I have always supposed to be right.

As to the policy I "seem to be pursuing" as you say, I have not meant to leave any one in doubt.

I would save the Union. I would save it the shortest way under the Constitution. The sooner the national authority can be restored; the nearer the Union will be "the Union as it was." If there be those who would not save the Union, unless they could at the same time *save* slavery, I do not agree with them. If there be those who would not save the Union unless they could at the same time *destroy* slavery, I do not agree with them. My paramount object in this struggle *is* to save the Union, and is *not* either to save or to destroy slavery. If I could save the Union without freeing *any* slave I would do it, and if I could save it by freeing *all* the slaves I would do it; and if I could save it by freeing some and leaving others alone I would also do that. What I do about slavery, and the colored race, I do because I believe it helps to save the Union; and what I forbear, I forbear because I do *not* believe it would help to save the Union. I shall do *less* whenever I shall believe what I am doing hurts the cause, and I shall do *more* whenever I shall believe doing more will help the cause. I shall try to correct errors when shown to be errors; and I shall adopt new views so fast as they shall appear to be true views.

I have here stated my purpose according to my view of *official* duty; and I intend no modification of my oft-expressed *personal* wish that all men every where could be free. Yours, A. Lincoln

Source:

Abraham Lincoln, *Abraham Lincoln, Speeches and Writings, 1859–65.* New York: Library of America, 1989, pp. 357–358.

Benjamin Franklin Butler, Order No. 28, 1862

Order issued by General Benjamin Franklin Butler, military governor of Union-occupied New Orleans, on May 15, 1862. Because of the hostility and insults directed toward Union troops by New Orleans residents, particularly women, Butler ordered that any female insulting or showing contempt for any U.S. officer or soldier should be treated as a prostitute. This order and other dictatorial actions raised a storm of public protest and earned Butler the title the "beast of New Orleans." He was removed from command of New Orleans on December 16, 1862.

─────────────── ⌒⊗⌒ ───────────────

GENERAL ORDERS, NO. 28.

Hdqrs. Department of the Gulf, *New Orleans, May, 15, 1862.*

As the officers and soldiers of the United States have been subject to repeated insults from the women (calling themselves ladies) of New Orleans in return for the most scrupulous non-interference and courtesy on our part, it is ordered that hereafter when any female shall by word, gesture, or movement insult or show contempt for any officer or soldier of the United States she shall be regarded and held liable to be treated as a woman of the town plying her avocation.

By command of Major-General Butler

Source:

The War of the Rebellion: A Compilation of the Official Records of the Union and Confederate Armies. Ser. 1, Vol. 15. Washington, D.C.: Government Printing Office, 1886. (Courtesy of Museum of the Confederacy, Richmond, Virginia.)

Abraham Lincoln, Emancipation Proclamation, 1863

Edict issued in preliminary form on September 22, 1862, and in final form on January 1, 1863, by President Abraham Lincoln, freeing all slaves in territories under Confederate control. It did not address the issue of slaves in states that had sided with the Union and thus did not apply to almost one-quarter of the nation's 4 million slaves. The proclamation enjoined the freed slaves to refrain from violence, except in self-defense, and opened the armed services to the former slaves. Lincoln, though personally opposed to slavery, had long resisted abolitionist urgings in order to avoid alienating border states. But by 1862 he concluded that emancipation was a military necessity. The final proclamation, which had no immediate effect in the Confederacy, mainly served to enhance the Union cause: The North was no longer fighting to preserve the old Union but to create a new one. The proclamation encouraged support for the Union in Europe, infuriated the South, and drew a mixed reaction in the North.

The Women's National Loyal League, an organization composed of Northern women, however, thanked President Lincoln for signing the Emancipation Proclamation and praised him for freeing millions of women "from the foulest bondage" and for protecting motherhood. Nevertheless, the following year a petition of more than 100,000 signatures was sent to Congress urging it to pass complete emancipation.

─────────────── ⌒⊗⌒ ───────────────

Whereas, on the twenty-second day of September, in the year of our Lord one thousand eight hundred and sixty-two, a proclamation was issued by the President of the United States, containing, among other things, the following, to wit:

"That on the first day of January, in the year of our Lord one thousand eight hundred and sixty-three, all persons held as slaves within any state, or designated part of a state, the people whereof shall then be in rebellion against the United States, shall be then, thenceforward, and forever free; and the Executive government of the United States, including the military and naval authority thereof, will recognize and maintain the freedom of such persons, and will do no act or acts to repress such persons, or any of them, in any efforts they may make for their actual freedom.

"That the Executive will, on the first day of January aforesaid, by proclamation, designate the states and parts of states, if any, in which the people thereof respectively shall then be in rebellion against the United States; and the fact that any state, or the people thereof, shall on that day be in good faith represented in the Congress of the United States by members chosen thereto at elections wherein a majority of the qualified voters of such state shall have participated, shall in the absence of strong countervailing testimony be deemed conclusive evidence that such state and the people thereof are not then in rebellion against the United States."

Now, therefore, I, Abraham Lincoln, President of the United States, by virtue of the power in me vested as commander-in-chief of the army and navy of the United States, in time of actual armed rebellion against the authority and government of the United States, and as a fit and necessary war measure for suppressing said rebellion, do, on this first day of January, in the year of our Lord one thousand eight hundred and sixty-three, and in accordance with my purpose so to do, publicly proclaim for the full period of 100 days from the day first above mentioned, order and designate as the states and parts of states wherein the people thereof, respectively, are this day in rebellion against the United States, the following, to wit:

Arkansas, Texas, Louisiana (except the parishes of St. Bernard, Plaquemines, Jefferson, St. John, St. Charles, St. James, Ascension, Assumption, Terre Bonne, Lafourche, St. Mary, St. Martin, and Orleans, including the city of New Orleans), Mississippi, Alabama, Florida, Georgia, South Carolina, North Carolina, and Virginia (except the forty-eight counties designated as West Virginia, and also the counties of Berkeley, Accomac, Northampton, Elizabeth City, York, Princess Ann, and Norfolk, including the cities of Norfolk and Portsmouth), and which excepted parts are for the present left precisely as if this proclamation were not issued.

And by virtue of the power and for the purpose aforesaid, I do order and declare that all persons held as slaves within said designated states and parts of states are, and henceforward shall be, free; and that the Executive government of the United States, including the military and naval authorities thereof, will recognize and maintain the freedom of said persons.

And I hereby enjoin upon the people so declared to be free to abstain from all violence, unless in necessary self-defense; and I recommend to them that, in all cases when allowed, they labor faithfully for reasonable wages.

And I further declare and make known that such persons of suitable condition will be received into the armed service of the United States to garrison forts, positions, stations, and other places, and to man vessels of all sorts in said service. And upon this act, sincerely believed to be an act of justice, warranted by the Constitution upon military necessity, I invoke the considerate judgment of mankind and the gracious favor of Almighty God.

Source:
John Scott, ed. *Living Documents in American History.* New York: Washington Square Press, 1964–68.

Habeas Corpus Act of 1863

Legislation enacted on March 3, 1863, that granted the president the power to suspend the privilege of habeas corpus. The habeas corpus writ states that no one can be imprisoned indefinitely without being charged in a court of law. President Abraham Lincoln had argued for the suspension of the writ because of the extenuating circumstances caused by the Civil War.

A similar power of indefinite detention was granted against alleged communists in early cold war regulations established by the Department of Justice and was claimed in 2002 by President George W. Bush regarding possible terrorists, although in neither case was there a declared war.

An Act
Relating to Habeas Corpus, and regulating Judicial Proceedings in Certain Cases.

Be it enacted by the Senate and House of Representatives of the United States of America in Congress assembled, That, during the present rebellion, the President of the United States, whenever, in his judgment, the public safety may require it, is authorized to suspend the privilege of the writ of habeas corpus in any case throughout the United States, or any part thereof. And whenever and wherever the said privilege shall be suspended, as aforesaid, no military or other officer shall be compelled, in answer to any writ of habeas corpus, to return the body of any person or persons detained by him by authority of the President; but upon the certificate, under oath, of the officer having charge of any one so detained that such person is detained by him as a prisoner under authority of the President, further proceedings under the writ of habeas corpus shall be suspended by the judge or court having issued the said writ, so long as said suspension by the President shall remain in force, and said rebellion continue.

Sec. 2. *And be it further enacted,* That the Secretary of State and the Secretary of War be, and they are hereby, directed, as soon as may be practicable, to furnish to the judges of the circuit and district courts of the United States and of the District of Columbia a list of the names of all persons, citizens of states in which the administration of the laws has continued unimpaired in the said Federal courts, who are now, or may hereafter be, held as prisoners of the United States, by order or authority of the President of the United States or either of said Secretaries, in any fort, arsenal, or other place, as state or political prisoners, or otherwise than as prisoners of war; the said list to contain the names of all those who reside in the respective jurisdictions of said judges, or who may be deemed by the said Secretaries, or either of them, to have violated any law of the United States in any of said jurisdictions, and also the date of each arrest; the Secretary of State to furnish a list of such persons as are imprisoned by the order or authority of the President, acting through the State Department, and the Secretary of War a list of such as are imprisoned by the order or authority of the President, acting through the Department of War. And in all cases where a grand jury, having attended any of said courts having jurisdiction in the premises, after the passage of this act, and after the furnishing of said list, as aforesaid has terminated its session without finding an indictment or presentment, or other proceeding against any such person, it shall be the duty of the judge of said court forthwith to make an order that any such prisoner desiring a discharge from said imprisonment be brought before him to be discharged; and every officer of the United States having custody of such prisoner is hereby directed immediately to obey and execute said judge's order; and in case he shall delay or refuse so to do, he shall be subject to indictment for a misdemeanor, and be punished by a fine of not less than five hundred dollars and imprisonment in the common jail for a period not less than six months, in the discretion of the court: *Provided however,* That no person shall be discharged by virtue of the provisions of this act until after he or she shall have taken an oath of allegiance to the Government of the United States, and to support the Constitution thereof; and that he or she will not hereafter in any way encourage or give aid and comfort to the present rebellion, or the supporters thereof: *And provided, also,* That the judge or court before whom such person may be brought, before discharging him or her from imprisonment, shall have power, on examination of the case, and, if the public safety shall require it, shall be required to cause him or her to enter into recognizance, with or without surety, in a sum to be fixed by said judge or court, to keep the peace and be of good behavior towards the United States and its citizens, and from time to time, and at such times as such judge or court may direct, appear before said judge or court to be further dealt with, according to law, as the circumstances may require. And it shall be the duty of the district attorney of the United States to attend such examination before the judge.

Sec. 3. *And be it further enacted,* That in case any of such prisoners shall be under indictment or presentment for any offence against the laws of the United States, and by existing laws bail or a recognizance may be taken for the appearance for trial of such person, it shall be the duty of said judge at once to discharge such person upon bail or recognizance for trial as aforesaid. And in case the said Secretaries of State and Was shall for any reason refuse or omit to furnish the said list of persons held as prisoners as aforesaid at the time of the passage of this act within twenty days thereafter, and of such persons as hereafter may be arrested within twenty days from the time of the arrest, any citizen may, after a grand jury shall have terminated its session without finding an indictment or presentment, as provided in the second section of this act, by a petition alleging the facts aforesaid touching any of the persons so as aforesaid imprisoned, supported by the oath of such petitioner or any other credible person, obtain and be entitled to have the said judge's order to discharge such prisoner on the same terms and conditions prescribed in the second section of this act: *Provided, however,* That the said judge shall be satisfied such allegations are true.

Sec. 4. *And be it further enacted,* That any order of the President, or under his authority, made at any time during the existence of the present rebellion, shall be a defence in all courts to any action or prosecution, civil or criminal, pending, or to be commenced, for any search, seizure, arrest, or imprisonment, made, done, or committed, or acts omitted to be done, under and by virtue of such order, or under color of any law of Congress, and such defence may be made by special plea, or under the general issue.

Sec. 5. *And be it further enacted,* That if any suit or prosecution, civil or criminal, has been or shall be commenced in any state court against any officer, civil or military, or against any other person, for any arrest of imprisonment made, or other trespasses or wrongs done or committed, or any act omitted to be done, at any time during the present rebellion, by virtue or under color of any authority derived from or exercised by or under the President of the United States, or any act of Congress, and the defendant shall, at the time of entering his appearance in such court, or if such appearance shall have been entered before the passage of this act, then at the next session of the court in which such suit or prosecution is pending, file a petition, stating the facts and verified by affidavit, for the removal of the cause for trial at the next circuit court of the United States, to be holden in the district where the suit is pending, and offer good and sufficient surety for his filing in such court, on the first day of its session, copies of such process and other proceedings against him, and also for his appearing in such court and entering special bail in the cause, if special bail was originally required therein. It shall then be the duty of the state court to accept the surety and proceed no further in the cause or prosecution, and the bail that shall have been originally taken shall be discharged. And such copies being filed as aforesaid in such court of the United States, the cause shall proceed therein in the same manner as if it had been brought in said court by original process, whatever may be the amount in dispute or the damages claimed, or whatever the citizenship of the parties, any former law to the contrary notwithstanding. And any attachment of the goods or estate of the defendant by the original process shall hold the goods or estate so attached to answer the final judgment in the same manner as by the laws of such state they would have been holden to answer final judgment had it been rendered in the court in which the suit or prosecution was commenced. And it shall be lawful in any such action or prosecution which may be now pending, or hereafter commenced, before any state court whatever, for any cause aforesaid, after final judgment, for either party to remove and transfer, by appeal, such case during the session or terms of said court at which the same shall have taken place, from such court to the next circuit court of the United States to be held in the district in which such appeal shall be taken, in manner aforesaid. And it shall be duty of the person taking such appeal to produce and file in the said circuit court attested copies of the process, proceedings, and judgment in such cause; and it shall also be competent for either party, within six months after the rendition of a judgment in any such cause, by writ of error or other process, to remove the same to the circuit court of the United States of that district in which such judgment shall have been rendered; and the said circuit court shall thereupon proceed to try and determine the facts and the law in such action, in the same manner as if the same had been there originally commenced, the judgment, in such case notwithstanding. And any bail which may have been taken, or property attached, shall be holden on the final judgment of the said circuit court in such action, in the same manner as if no such removal and transfer had been made, aforesaid. And the state court, from which any such action, civil or criminal, may be removed and transferred as aforesaid, upon the parties giving good and sufficient security for the prosecution thereof, shall allow the same to be removed and transferred, and proceed no further in the case: *Provided, however,* That if the party aforesaid shall fail duly to enter the removal and transfer, as aforesaid, in the circuit court of the United States, agreeably to this act, state court, by which judgment shall have been rendered, and from which the transfer and removal shall have been made, as aforesaid, shall be authorized, on motion for that purpose, to issue execution, and to carry into effect any such judgment, the same as if no such removal and transfer had been made. *And provided also,* That no such appeal or writ of error shall be allowed in any criminal action or prosecution where final judgment shall have been rendered in favor of the defendant or respondent by the state court. And if in any suit hereafter commenced the plaintiff is nonsuited or judgment pass against him, the defendant shall recover double costs.

Sec. 6. *And be it further enacted,* That any suit or prosecution described in this act, in which final judgment may be rendered in the circuit court, may be carried by writ of error to the supreme court, whatever may be the amount of said judgment.

Sec. 7. *And be it further enacted,* That no suit or prosecution, civil or criminal, shall be maintained for any arrest or imprisonment made, or other trespasses or wrongs done or committed, or act omitted to be done, at any time during the present rebellion, by virtue or under color of any authority derived from or exercised by or under the President of the United States, or by or under any act of Congress, unless the same shall have been commenced within two years next after such arrest, imprisonment, trespass, or wrong may have been done or committed or act may have been omitted to be done: *Provided,* That in no case shall the limitation herein provided commence to run until the passage of this act, so that no party shall, by virtue of this act, be debarred of his remedy by suit or prosecution until two years from and after the passage of this act.

Source:

Statutes at Large, Vol. 12, pp. 755–758.

Samuel Cormany, Battle of Gettysburg, 1863

These excerpts from Samuel Cormany's diary give his perspective on the climactic battle of Gettysburg, in which the Union was victorious. Very little is known about Samuel, a resident of Chambersburg, Pennsylvania, who enlisted in the Union army. He and his wife, Rachel, whose diary is also excerpted here, later moved to Missouri. Samuel's name appears on the Pennsylvania monument at Gettysburg.

The battle itself was a turning point in the war. General Robert E. Lee had moved his entire army into Pennsylvania. He was confronted by General George Gordon Meade. The Confederate troops held out for four days but were routed after George E. Pickett's charge resulted in defeat. The Union army had an opportunity to capture Lee's remaining troops when they were stopped by the flooded Potomac River, but Meade hesitated too long. The waters receded and Lee's army escaped.

———————————— ⌐∞⌐ ————————————

July 1, 1863 Wednesday. I had a fine chicken breakfast— and a feast of other good things. Took up march for Hanover. Very fine rich country–and such fine water–Settlers are Old Style People. Many Dunkerds [German Protestant sect]. We were given any amount to eat all along the way— The Rebs who had passed this way acted very meanly—All around—demanding setters to pay money to exempt horses from being taken and barns and houses from being burned—One old man said he paid $100 to exempt 2 horses—another paid $23 to save his horse–still another— $100 to save his barn. We found this hideous thing to be quite common–We struck Hanover at dark. Found N.C. R. R. badly torn up. During the day we heard heavy canonading–and later musketry firing—in the direction of Gettysburg. Rumor was, "Theres a Battle on at Gettysburg" and was not hard to believe—Some of our Cavalry had fought desperately here today, early—Charging into the enemy's rear and flanks—Killed some 30 rebs and hustled large forces on their way. So they had to abandon their dead and some of their wounded—We lay on arms in a field for the night—we were well fed, but awfully tired and sleepy—A shower of rain failed to awaken me—I was lying in a furrow, an old furrow. I partially awakened in the night feeling coolish on my lower side—but didn't fully awake. In the morning I discovered that water had run down the furrow—and I had "dam'd" it somewhat and so was pretty wet from below, while my poncho had kept me dry from the top—

July 2, 1863 Thursday. More or less Picket firing all night—We were aroused early, and inspection showed a lot of our horses too lame and used up for good action–So first, our good mounts were formed for moving out, and were soon off—with the Brigade and took Reb. Genl. Steward by surprise on the Deardorf Farm—on right and rear of the army line—where Steward was expected to at least annoy the rear of Genl Mead—But our boys charged him—and after severe fighting dealt him an inglorious defeat and later in the day came in and lay on arms in the rear of Meads right—While our mounted men were paying attention to Genl Steward, we fellows had our horses cared for and were marched down to the right of the main line—to occupy a gap and do Sharpshooting—at long range, with our Carbines—we soon attracted attention, and later an occasional shell fell conspicuously close—but far enough to the rear of us so we suffered no serious harm. Towards noon firing became more general and in almost all directions–and we were ordered to our horses—and joined our returned heroes, and lay in readiness for any emergency—The general battle increased in energy—and occasional fierceness—and by 2 P.M. the canonading was most terrific and continued til 5 P.M. and was interspersed with musketry—and Charge—yells and everything that goes to making up the indescribable battle of the best men on Earth, seemingly in the Fight to the Finish—At dark, our Cav Brig–2nd Brig 2" Div—was

moved to the left–many wounded came in—Taken as a whole from all one can see from one point—it seems as tho our men—The Union Army—is rather overpowered and worsted—Lay on arms to rest—Little chance to feed and eat.

July 4, 1863 Saturday. The great battle closed and quieted with the closing day—Some firing at various points—Our Regt layed on arms with Pickets out–on the ground where we had put in most of the day–Rather expecting attack momentarily—Rained furiously during the night—We had fed, eaten, and were standing "to horse" when about 6 ock NEWS CAME—"The Rebs are falling back!" and "Our Forces are following them" and our Regt went out towards Hunterstown reconnoitering. We found some confederates who had straggled, or were foraging, not knowing yet what had happened and was taking place—Of course, our Boys took them in–Making a little detour I captured two. Sergt. Major J. T. Richardson and Private Cox 9th Va Cav—disarming them and bringing them in—I guarded them—while the Regt gathered in some others—P.M. Captain Hughes came along and paroled them—and we were ordered to camp near Hanover—where we first lay on arriving near Gettysburg—Evening awfully muddy and disagreeable—I saw much of the destructiveness of the Johnies today—

See also RACHEL CORMANY, CIVIL WAR DIARY, 1863; ABRAHAM LINCOLN, GETTYSBURG ADDRESS, 1863.

Source:

Diary of Samuel Cormany, "Valley of the Shadow: Two Communities in the American Civil War," Virginia Center for Digital History, University of Virginia. Available on-line. URL: http://valley.vcdh.virginia.edu/personalpapers/collections/franklin/cormany.html. From James C. Mohr, editor, and Robert E. Winslow III, assistant editor. *The Cormany Diaries: A Northern Family in the Civil War.* Pittsburgh: University of Pittsburgh Press, 1982.

Rachel Cormany, Civil War Diary, 1863

Rachel Cormany, wife of Samuel, was born in Canada but moved to Chambersburg with her husband, Samuel, during the war. She began writing in her diary well before the war. Her diary entries for the war years vividly describe her life as a woman on the home front. Alone while her husband served in the Union army, Rachel often complained of depression and boredom. After the war, the Cormanys moved to Missouri to live on a farm. Chambersburg had been left undefended as Union troops moved toward Gettysburg and Confederate troops used it as a staging area.

Reproduced here are the same days as Samuel's diary, extended through his homecoming on July 6.

July 1, 1863 It is very muddy this morning of yesterdays rain—in fact I believe it has rained every day this week. I was out hunting [y]east & got some at last I have not a bit of bread left my [y]east got sour, so of course the [y]east I set last evening is sour & not fit to use. It is reported that Gen. Jenkins is wounded & a prisoner. Also that the rebel pickets were driven in this side of Greencastle—& that McClellan drove them to this side of Carlisle & that Milroy & Sigel are making a junction over by Strasburg—A darkey, Colonels waiter heard him say that he thought that Lee made a bad move this time—he (darkey) also said that that large wagon train was hid in the woods &c that they could not get out, that they are watching their chance to slip out—he said too that the officers were very uneasy— Every one can see by their actions that they do not feel quite as easy as they would like. They are chopping &c at a great rate over at the R.R. all morning. I judge they are breaking up the iron by the sound. Must now go & set my bread. Evening. Got good bread. Mrs. Fritz was here & told us of Emma Plough being sick from the fright & how the rebels have been carrying on out there. They robbed the country people of nearly everything they had and acted very insultingly.

July 2, 1863 At 3 A.M. I was wakened by the yells & howls of this dirty ragged lousy trash—they made as ugly as they could—all day they have been passing—part of the time on the double quick. At one time the report came that our men had come on them & that they were fighting—the excitement was high in town—but it was soon found out to be untrue—but the shock was so great that I got quite weak & immagined that I could already see My Samuel falling—I feel very uneasy about him–I cannot hear at all–They had quite a battle with Stuart—I almost fear to hear the result in who was killed & who wounded—still I want to know.

July 3, 1863 Started out with Cora & a little basket on the hunt for something to eat out of the garden. I am tired of bread & molasses—went to Mammy Royers & got some peas & new potatoes–Cora got as many raspberries as she could eat. Came home put Cora to sleep then went to Mrs McG's for milk. got a few cherries to eat also a few for Cora when I got back Daddy Byers was standing at the gate. he came to see how I was getting along & told me how the rebels acted—they robbed him of a good deal—they wanted the horse but he plead so hard for him that they agreed to leave him & while one wrote a paper of securety others plundered the house. I guess Samuels silk hat & all

that was in the box is gone. Took Ellies best shoes—took towels sheets &c &c— After they were gone others came & took the horse too yet—they did not care for his security. Other of their neighbors fared worse yet. He would not stay for dinner. After dinner Henry Rebok came—he walked part of the way had an old horse but feared to bring him in—they were robbed of their horses and cattle up there– many had their horses sent away—one of J. Cormanys horses was taken. Henry wanted me to go along home with him but I could not think of leaving now– Samuel might come this way & if I were out there I would not get to see him. He said he had started for me when they first heard of the rebels coming but when he came to Orrstown two were there already. There are no rebels in town today except the sick—& two or three squads passed through, in all not much over a hundred if that many. One squad asked the way to Getysburg & were sent towards Harisburg. they did not go very far until they asked again, when they were told the truth they came back very angry & wanted the man that sent them the wrong way but he was not to be found. Canonading was heard all day.

July 4, 1863 At daybreak the bells were rung—Then all was quiet until about 8 oclock when a flag was hoisted at the diamond. Soon after the band made its appearance & marched from square & played national airs—two rebels came riding along quite leisurely thinking I suppose to find their friends instead of that they were taken prisoners by the citizens—some 13 more footmen came and were taken prisoners. those were willing prisoners they had thrown their guns away before they reached this. The report has reached us that 6000 prisoners had been taken yesterday in Adams Co. near College Hill—also that Carlisle was shelled. It is getting very dark cloudy—I judge we will have a heavy rain. That Will Wampler does yell and cry like a panther. Evening We have had a powerful rain. Wild rumors of a dreadful fight are numerous.

July 5, 1863 I was roused out of sleep by Mr Early coming into Wampler & telling him something about wounded prisoners. so I got up took a bath dressed & went for a pitcher of water when I was told that 10, 4 or 6 horse wagons filled with wounded from the late battle were captured by citizens & brought to town–the wounded were put into the hospitals & the waggons & drivers were taken on toward Harisburg. Was also told that a great many more were out toward Greencastle—some went out to capture those but found that it was a train 20 miles long. P.M. A report has reached us that the whole rebel army is on the retreat—later that they are driven this way & are expected on soon–Have church S. School here today—seems like Sunday again Evening. At or after 4 P.M. I dressed myself & little girl and went to Mrs. Sulenbargers & while there we heard a fuss outside & when we got out lo our (Union of course) soldiers were coming in—she came along upstreet then to see them. They are of Milroys men. Just at dusk they went out the Greencastle road enroute to capture the waggon train which is trying to get over the river again. It is frightful how those poor wounded rebels are left to suffer. they are taken in large 4 horse waggons—wounds undressed—nothing to eat. Some are only about 4 miles from town & those that are here are as dirty and lousy as they well can be. The condition of those poor rebels all along from Getysburg to as far as they have come yet is reported dreadful. I am told they just beg the people along the road to help them—many have died by the way.

July 6, 1863 I was sitting reading, Pussy playing by my side when little Willie Wampler came running as fast as he could to tell me a soldier had come to see me & sure enough when I got to the door Mr Cormany just rode up. I was so very glad to see him that I scarcely knew how to act. He was very dirty & sweaty so he took a bath & changed clothes before he got himself dressed A. Holler & Barny Hampshire called—next Rev. Dixon & Dr Croft & others. Eve we went down into the parlor to hear some of the girls play—Mr. C was very much pleased with the music.

See also SAMUEL CORMANY, BATTLE OF GETTYSBURG, 1863.

Source:

Diary of Rachel Cormany, "Valley of the Shadow: Two Communities in the American Civil War," Virginia Center for Digital History, University of Virginia. Available on-line. URL: http://valley.vcdh.virginia.edu/personalpapers/collections/franklin/cormany.html. From James C. Mohr, editor, and Robert E. Winslow III, assistant editor, *The Cormany Diaries: A Northern Family in the Civil War*. Pittsburgh: University of Pittsburgh Press, 1982. The biographical information on Rachel Cormany is from "Valley of the Shadow."

Abraham Lincoln, "Gettysburg Address," 1863

Famous and eloquent speech delivered by President Abraham Lincoln on November 19, 1863. Five months after the pivotal Union victory at Gettysburg, President Lincoln traveled to the site of the battle for the dedication of a military cemetery. After a two-hour speech by scholar Edward Everett on the history of the battle, Lincoln delivered a 10-sentence address on Gettysburg's significance. His Gettysburg Address, which attracted little attention at the time, has come to be regarded as one of the greatest prose poems in the English language. The address expressed Lincoln's personal sorrow at the battlefield deaths, the purpose of the war, and his vision of American democracy that has been universally adopted as a "government of the people, by the people, for the people."

Four score and seven years ago our fathers brought forth on this continent, a new nation, conceived in Liberty, and dedicated to the proposition that all men are created equal.

Now we are engaged in a great civil war, testing whether that nation or any nation so conceived and so dedicated, can long endure. We are met on a great battlefield of that war. We have come to dedicate a portion of that field, as a final resting place for those who here gave their lives that that nation might live. It is altogether fitting and proper that we should do this.

But, in a larger sense, we can not dedicate—we can not consecrate—we can not hallow—this ground. The brave men, living and dead, who struggled here, have consecrated it, far above our poor power to add or detract. The world will little note, nor long remember what we say here, but it can never forget what they did here. It is for us the living, rather, to be dedicated here to the unfinished work which they who fought here have thus far so nobly advanced. It is rather for us to be here dedicated to the great task remaining before us—that from these honored dead we take increased devotion to that cause for they which gave the last full measure of devotion—that we here highly resolve that these dead shall not have died in vain—that this nation, under God, shall have a new birth of freedom—and that government of the people, by the people, for the people, shall not perish from the earth.

Source:

John Scott, ed. *Living Documents in American History*, New York: Washington Square Press, 1964–68.

National Bank Act, 1863

Federal legislation, enacted on February 25, 1863, and amended on June 3, 1864, that established a national banking system that lasted until the passage of the Federal Reserve Act of 1913. To provide a sounder currency than state banks then offered and to increase the sales of government bonds to finance the Civil War, the 1863 and 1864 acts organized federally chartered banks that were required to invest at least one-third of their capital in U.S. bonds. These banks could then issue national bank notes (paper money) at a value of 90 percent of their bond holdings. The acts regulated capital requirements, loans, and reserves, and provided for the supervision and examination of banks and the protection of note holders.

An Act

To provide a national Currency, secured by a Pledge of United States Stocks, and to provide for the Circulation and Redemption thereof.

Be it enacted by the Senate and House of Representatives of the United States of America in Congress assembled, That there shall be established in the Treasury Department a separate bureau, which shall be charged with the execution of this and all other laws that may be passed by Congress respecting the issue and regulation of a national currency secured by United States bonds. The chief officer of the said bureau shall be denominated the comptroller of the currency, and shall be under the general direction of the Secretary of the Treasury. He shall be appointed by the President, on the nomination of the Secretary of the Treasury, by and with the advice and consent of the Senate, and shall hold his office for the term of five years unless sooner removed by the President, by and with the advice and consent of the Senate; he shall receive an annual salary of five thousand dollars; he shall have a competent deputy, appointed by the Secretary, whose salary shall be two thousand five hundred dollars, and who shall possess the power and perform the duties attached by law to the office of comptroller during a vacancy in such office, and during his absence or inability; he shall employ, from time to time, the necessary clerks to discharge such duties as he shall direct, which clerks shall be appointed and classified by the Secretary of the Treasury in the manner now provided by law. Within fifteen days from the time of notice of his appointment, the comptroller shall take and subscribe the oath of office prescribed by the Constitution and laws of the United States; and he shall give to the United States a bond in the penalty of one hundred thousand dollars, with not less than two responsible freeholders as sureties, to be approved by the Secretary of the Treasury, conditioned for the faithful discharge of the duties of his office. The deputy comptroller so appointed shall also take the oath of office prescribed by the Constitution and laws of the United States, and shall give a like bond in the penalty of fifty thousand dollars. The comptroller and deputy comptroller shall not, either directly or indirectly, be interested in any association issuing national currency under the provisions of this act.

Sec. 2. *And be it further enacted,* That the comptroller of the currency, with the approval of the Secretary of the Treasury, shall devise a seal, with suitable inscriptions, for his office, a description of which, with a certificate of approval by the Secretary of the Treasury, shall be filed in the office of the Secretary of State with an impression thereof, which shall thereupon become the seal of office of the comptroller of the currency, and the same may be renewed when necessary. Every certificate, assignment, and conveyance executed by the comptroller, in pursuance of any authority conferred on him by law, and sealed with his seal of office, shall be received in evidence in all places and courts whatsoever; and all copies of papers in the office of the comptroller, certified by him and authenticated by the said seal, shall in all cases be evidence equally and in like manner as the original. An impression of such seal directly on the paper shall be as valid as if made on wax or wafer.

Sec. 3. *And be it further enacted,* That there shall be assigned to the comptroller of the currency by the Secretary of the Treasury suitable rooms in the treasury building for conducting the business of the currency bureau, in which shall be safe and secure fire-proof vaults, in which it shall be the duty of the comptroller to deposit and safely keep all the plates and other valuable things belonging to his department; and the comptroller shall from time to time furnish the necessary furniture, stationery, fuel, lights, and other proper conveniences for the transaction of the said business.

Sec. 4. *And be it further enacted,* That the term "United States bonds," as used in this act, shall be construed to mean all coupon and registered bonds now issued or that may hereafter be issued on the faith of the United States by the Secretary of the Treasury in pursuance of law.

Sec. 5. *And be it further enacted,* That associations for carrying on the business of banking may be formed by any number of persons, not less in any case than five.

Sec. 6. *And be it further enacted,* That persons uniting to form such an association shall, under their hands and seals, make a certificate which shall specify—

First. The name assumed by such association.

Second. The place where its operations of discount and deposit are to be carried on; designating the State, Territory, or district, and also the particular city, town, or village.

Third. The amount of its capital stock, and the number of shares into which the same shall be divided; which capital stock shall not be less than fifty thousand dollars; and in cities whose population is over ten thousand persons, the capital stock shall not be less than one hundred thousand dollars.

Fourth. The names and places of residence of the shareholders, and the number of shares held by each of them.

Fifth. The time when such association shall commence.

Sixth. A declaration that said certificate is made to enable such persons to avail themselves of the advantages of this act.

The said certificate shall be acknowledged before a judge of some court of record or a notary public, and the acknowledgment thereof certified under the seal of such court or notary, and shall be transmitted, together with a copy of the articles of association which shall have been adopted, to the comptroller of the currency, who shall record and carefully preserve the same in his office. Copies of such certificate, duly certified by the comptroller, and authenticated by his seal of office, shall be legal and sufficient evidence in all courts and places within the United States, or the jurisdiction of the Government thereof, of the existence of such association, and of every other matter or thing which could be proved by the production of the original certificate.

Sec. 7. *And be it further enacted,* That at least thirty per centum of the capital stock of such association shall be paid in at the time of the commencement of its banking business, and the remainder of the capital stock of such association shall be paid in instalments of at least ten per centum each on the whole amount to which the association shall be limited, as frequently as one instalment at the end of each succeeding two months from the time of the commencement of its banking operations, until the whole of the capital stock shall be paid in.

Sec. 8. *And be it further enacted,* That if any shareholder, or his assignee, shall fail to pay any instalment on the stock when the same is required, by the foregoing section to be paid, the directors of such association may sell the stock held by such delinquent shareholder, at public auction, having given three weeks' previous notice thereof in a newspaper published and of general circulation in the city where the association is located, if the same be located in a city, and if not so located, then in a newspaper printed, or of general circulation, in the county where the same is located, to any person who will pay the highest price therefor, and not less than the amount then due thereon, with the expenses of advertisement and sale; and the excess, if any, shall be paid to the delinquent shareholder. If no bidder can be found who will pay for such stock the amount due thereon to the association, and the costs of advertisement and sale, the amount previously paid shall be forfeited to the association, and such stock may subsequently be sold as the directors may order.

Sec. 9. *And be it further enacted,* That whenever a certificate shall have been transmitted to the comptroller of the currency, as provided in this act, and the association transmitting the same shall notify the comptroller that at least thirty per centum of its capital stock has been paid as aforesaid, and that such association has complied with all the provisions of this act required to be complied with before such association shall be authorized to commence the business of banking, and that such association is desirous of commencing such business, the comptroller shall immediately proceed, in such manner as he shall by general rules prescribe, to examine the condition of such association; to ascertain especially the amount of money paid in on account of its capital stock; the name and place of residence of each of the directors of such association, and the amount of the capital stock of which each is the bona fide owner, and generally whether such association has complied with all the requirements of this act to entitle it to engage in the business of banking; and shall cause to be made, and attested by the oaths of a majority of the directors and by the president or cashier of such association, a statement of all the facts necessary to enable the comptroller to determine whether such association is lawfully entitled to commence the business of banking under this act.

Sec. 10. *And be it further enacted,* That if, upon a careful examination of the facts so reported, and of any other facts which may come to the knowledge of the comptroller, whether by means of a special commission appointed by him for the purpose of inquiring into the condition of such association, or otherwise, it shall appear that such association is lawfully entitled to commence the business of banking, the comptroller shall give to such association a certificate under his hand and official seal, showing that such association has complied with all the provisions of this act required to be complied with before being entitled to commence the business of banking under it, and that such association is authorized to commence said business accordingly; and it shall be the duty of such association to cause said certificate to be published in some newspaper, published in the city or county where such association is located, for at least sixty days next after the issuing thereof: *Provided,* That if no newspaper is published in such city or county, such certificate shall be published as the comptroller of the currency shall direct.

Sec. 11. *And be it further enacted,* That every association formed pursuant to the provisions of this act may make and use a common seal, and shall have succession by the name designated in its articles of association and for the period limited therein, not, however, exceeding twenty years from the passage of this act; by such name may make contracts, sue and be sued, complain and defend in any court of law or equity as fully as natural persons, and may make by-laws, approved by the comptroller of the currency, not inconsistent with the laws of the United States or the provisions of this act, for the election of directors, the management of its property, the regulation of its affairs, and for the transfer of its stock; and shall have power to carry on the business of banking by obtaining and issuing circulating notes in accordance with the provisions of this act; by discounting bills, notes, and other evidences of debt; by receiving deposits; by buying and selling gold and silver bullion, foreign coins, and bills of exchange; by loaning money on real and personal security, in the manner specified in their articles of association, for the purposes authorized by this act, and by exercising such incidental powers as shall be necessary to carry on such business; to choose one of their number as president of such association, and to appoint a cashier and such other officers and agents as their business may require; and to remove such president, cashier, officers, and agents at pleasure, and appoint others in their place; and their usual business shall be transacted in banking offices located at the places specified respectively in its certificate of association, and not elsewhere.

Sec. 12. *And be it further enacted,* That the shares of associations formed under this act shall be deemed personal property, and shall be transferable on the books of the association in such manner as may be prescribed in the by-laws or articles of association; and every person becoming a shareholder by such transfer shall, in proportion to his shares, succeed to all the rights and liabilities of the prior holder of such shares; and no change shall be made in the articles of association by which the rights, remedies, or security of the existing creditors of the association shall be impaired. For all debts, contracted by such association for circulation, deposits, or otherwise, each shareholder shall be liable to the amount, at their par value, of the shares held by him in addition to the amount invested in such shares.

Sec. 13. *And be it further enacted,* That it shall be lawful for any association formed under this act, by its articles of association, to provide for an increase of its capital from time to time as may be deemed expedient, subject to the limitations of this act; but no such increase shall be valid until the increased capital shall be paid in, and notice thereof shall have been transmitted to the comptroller of the currency, and his certificate obtained, specifying the amount of such increase of capital stock, and that the same has been duly paid to such association.

Sec. 14. *And be it further enacted,* That it shall be lawful for any such association to purchase, hold, and convey real estate as follows:

First. Such as shall be necessary for its immediate accommodation in the transaction of its business.

Second. Such as shall be mortgaged to it in good faith by way of security for loans made by such association, or for moneys due thereto.

Third. Such as shall be conveyed to it in satisfaction of debts previously contracted in the course of its dealings.

Fourth. Such as it shall purchase at sales under judgments, decrees, or mortgages held by such association.

Such association shall not purchase or hold real estate in any other case or for any other purpose than as specified in this section.

Sec. 15. *And be it further enacted,* That every association, after having complied with the provisions of this act preliminary to the commencement of banking business under its provisions, shall transfer and deliver to the treasurer of the United States any United States bonds bearing interest to an amount not less than one third of the capital stock paid in; which bonds shall be deposited with the treasurer of the United States, and by him safely kept in his office until the same shall be otherwise disposed of, in pursuance of the provisions of this act.

Sec. 16. *And be it further enacted,* That upon the making of any such transfer and delivery, the association making the same shall be entitled to receive from the comptroller of the currency circulating notes of different denominations, in blank, registered and countersigned as hereinafter provided, equal in amount to ninety per centum of the current market value of the United States bonds so transferred and delivered, but not exceeding the par value thereof, if bearing interest at the rate of six per centum, or of equivalent United States bonds bearing a less rate of interest; and at no time shall the total amount of such notes, issued to any such association, exceed the amount at such time actually paid in of its capital stock.

Sec. 17. *And be it further enacted,* That the entire amount of circulating notes to be issued under this act shall not exceed three hundred millions of dollars. One hundred and fifty millions of which sum shall be apportioned to associations in the States, in the District of Columbia, and in the Territories, according to representative population, and the remainder shall be apportioned by the Secretary of the Treasury among associations formed in the several States, in the District of Columbia, and in the Territories, having due regard to the existing banking capital, resources, and business, of such States, District, and Territories.

Sec. 18. *And be it further enacted,* That, in order to furnish suitable notes for circulation, the comptroller of the currency is hereby authorized and required, under the direction of the Secretary of the Treasury, to cause plates to be engraved in the best manner to guard against counterfeiting and fraudulent alterations, and to have printed therefrom, and numbered, such quantity of circulating notes, in blank, of the denominations of five dollars, ten dollars, twenty dollars, fifty dollars, one hundred dollars, five hundred dollars, and one thousand dollars, as may be required to supply, under this act, the associations entitled to receive the same; which notes shall express upon their face that they are secured by United States bonds, deposited with the treasurer of the United States, and issued under the provisions of this act, which statement shall be attested by the written or engraved signatures of the treasurer and register, and by the imprint of the seal of the treasury; and shall also express upon their face the promise of the association receiving the same, to pay on demand, attested by the signatures of the president, or vice-president, and cashier; and the said notes shall bear such devices and such other statements, and shall be in such form, as the Secretary of the Treasury shall, by regulation, direct.

Sec. 19. *And be it further enacted,* That the plates and special dies to be procured by the comptroller of the currency for the printing of such circulating notes shall remain under his control and direction, and the expenses necessarily incurred in executing the provisions of this act respecting the procuring of such notes, shall be audited and paid as contingent expenses of the Treasury Department; and for the purpose of reimbursing the same, and all other expenses incurred under this act, and in lieu of all taxes upon the circulation authorized by this act, or upon the bonds deposited for the security of the same, such association organized under this act shall semi-annually, on the first days of January and July, after its organization, pay to the comptroller of the currency, in lawful money of the United States, one per centum on the amount of circulating notes received by such association, and in default thereof, the treasurer of the United States is hereby authorized to reserve and retain one per centum on the amount of said bonds so deposited, at each semi-annual payment of interest thereon; and all sums so reserved and retained shall be paid into the treasury under the direction of the Secretary, and every bank, banking association, or corporation, not organized under the provisions of this act, issuing notes calculated or intended to circulate as money, shall, on the first day of July next, and regularly on the first days of January and July thereafter, make and deliver to the comptroller of the currency a true and accurate return of the gross amount of notes issued by it, whether in circulation, or in its vaults, or on deposit elsewhere, and in default of any such return, the bank, banking association, or corporation so failing to make return, shall pay to the United States a penalty of two per centum upon its entire capital stock, to be recovered, for the use of the United States, in any court of competent jurisdiction.

Sec. 20. *And be it further enacted,* That after any such association shall have caused its promise to pay such notes on demand to be signed by the president or vice-president and cashier thereof, in such manner as to make them obligatory promissory notes, payable on demand, at its place of business, such association is hereby authorized to issue and circulate the same as money; and the same shall be received at par in all parts of the United States in payment of taxes, excises, public lands, and all other dues to the United States, except for duties on imports, and also for all salaries and other debts and demands owing by the United States to individuals, corporations, and associations within the United States, except interest on public debt; and no such association shall issue post notes, or any other notes to circulate as money, than such as are authorized by the foregoing provisions of this act.

Sec. 21. *And be it further enacted,* That all transfers of United States bonds which shall be made by any association as security for circulating notes under the provisions of this act, shall be made to the treasurer of the United States, with a memorandum written or printed on the certificate of such bonds, and signed by the cashier, or some other officer of the association making the deposit, stating that it is held in trust for the association on whose behalf such transfer is made, and as security for the redemption and payment of the circulating notes delivered to such association; and no transfer of any such bonds by the treasurer shall be deemed valid, or of binding force and effect, unless sanctioned by the order or request of the comptroller of the currency upon the treasurer It shall be the duty of the comptroller of the currency to keep in his office a book in which shall be entered the name of every association from whose account such transfer of bonds is made by the treasurer, and the name of the party to whom such transfer is made, unless such transfer is made in blank, in which case the fact shall be stated in said book, and in either case the par value of the bonds so transferred shall be entered therein; and it shall be the duty of the comptroller, immediately upon countersigning and entering the same, to advise by mail the association from whose account such transfer was made, the kind of bonds and the amount thereof so transferred.

Sec. 22. *And be it further enacted,* That it shall be the duty of the comptroller of the currency to countersign and enter in the book, in the manner aforesaid, every transfer or assignment of any bonds held by the treasurer presented for his signature; and the comptroller shall have at all times during office hours access to the books of the treasurer, for the purpose of ascertaining the correctness of the transfer or assignment presented to him to countersign; and the treasurer shall have the like access to the book above mentioned, kept by the comptroller, during office hours to ascertain the correctness of the entries in the same.

Sec. 23. *And be it further enacted,* That it shall be the duty of either the president or cashier of every banking association having stocks deposited in the office of the treasurer of the United States, once or more in each fiscal year, and at such time or times during the ordinary business hours as said officer or officers may select, to examine and compare the bonds so pledged with the books of said Department, and, if found correct, to execute to the said treasurer a certificate setting forth the different kinds and the amounts thereof, and that the same are in the possession and custody of the treasurer at the date of such certificate. Such examination may be made by an agent of such association, duly appointed in writing for that purpose, whose certificate before mentioned shall be of like force and validity as if executed by such president or cashier.

Sec. 24. *And be it further enacted,* That every association issuing circulating notes under the provisions of this act, shall make a quarterly report to the comptroller of the currency commencing on the first day of the quarter of the year next succeeding the organization of such association, and continuing on the first days of each succeeding quarter in every year thereafter, which report shall be verified by the oath or affirmation of the president and cashier, and all wilful false swearing in respect to such report shall be perjury, and subject to the punishment prescribed by law for such offence. The report hereby required shall be in the form prescribed by the comptroller, and shall contain a true statement of the condition of the association making such report, before the transaction of any business on the morning of the day specified, next preceding the date of such report, in respect to the following items and particulars, to wit: Loans and discounts, overdrafts due from banks, amount due from the directors of the association, real estate, specie, cash items, stocks, bonds, and promissory notes, bills of solvent banks, bills of suspended banks, loss and expense account, capital, circulation, profits, amount due to banks, amount due to individuals and corporations other than banks, amount due the treasurer of the United States, amount due to depositors on demand, amount due, not included under either of the above heads. And it shall be the duty of the comptroller to publish full abstracts of such reports together in two newspapers to be designated by him for that purpose, one in the city of Washington and the other in the city of New York, exhibiting the items of capital, circulation, and deposits, specie and cash items, public securities and private securities; and the separate report of each association shall be published in a newspaper published in the place where such association is established, or, if there be no newspaper at such place, then in a newspaper published at the capital of the State, at the expense of the association making such report. In addition to the quarterly reports required by this section, every association located and doing business in the cities of Boston, Providence, New York, Philadelphia, Baltimore, Cincinnati, Chicago, St. Louis, and New Orleans, shall publish, or cause to be published, on the morning of the first Tuesday in each month, in a newspaper printed in the city in which the association making such report is located, to be designated by the comptroller of the currency, a statement, under the oath of the president or cashier, showing the condition of the association making such statement, on the morning of the day next preceding the date of such statement, in respect to the following items and particulars, to wit: average amount of loans and discounts, specie, deposits, and circulation.

Sec. 25. *And be it further enacted,* That if any such association shall, at any time fail to redeem, in the lawful money of the United States, any of its circulating notes, when payment thereof shall be lawfully demanded, during the usual hours of business, at the office of such association, the holder may cause the same to be protested, in one package, by a notary public, unless the president or cashier of the association shall offer to waive demand and notice of the protest, and shall, in pursuance of such offer, make, sign, and deliver to the party making such demand an admission in writing, stating the time of the demand, the amount demanded, and the fact of the non-payment thereof; and such notary public, on making such protest, or upon receiving such admission, shall forthwith forward such admission or notice of protest to the comptroller of the currency; and after such default it shall not be lawful for the association suffering the same to pay out any of its notes, discount any notes or bills, or otherwise prosecute the business of banking, except to receive and safely keep money belonging to it, and to deliver special deposits: *Provided however,* That if satisfactory proof be produced to such notary public that the payment of any such notes is restrained by order of any court of competent jurisdiction, such notary public shall not protest the same; and when the holder of such notes shall cause more than one note or package to be protested on the same day, he shall not receive pay for more than one protest.

Sec. 26. *And be it further enacted,* That on receiving notice that any such association has failed to redeem any of its circulating notes, as specified in the next preceding section, the comptroller of the currency, with the concurrence of the Secretary of the Treasury, may appoint a special agent, (of whose appointment immediate notice shall be given to such association,) who shall immediately proceed to ascertain whether such association has refused to pay its circulating notes, in the lawful money of the United States, when demanded as aforesaid, and report to the comptroller the facts so ascertained; and if, from such protest or the reports so made, the comptroller shall be satisfied that such association has refused to pay its circulating notes as aforesaid, and is in default, he shall, within thirty days after he shall have received notice of such failure, declare the United States bonds and securities pledged by such association forfeited to the United States, and the same shall thereupon be forfeited accordingly; and thereupon the comptroller shall immediately give notice, in such manner as the Secretary of the Treasury shall, by general rules or otherwise, direct, to the holders of the circulating notes of such association to present them for payment at the treasury of the United States; and the same shall be paid as presented, whereupon said comptroller may, in his discretion, cancel an equal amount of the bonds pledged by such association, equal at current market rates, not exceeding par, to the notes paid; and it shall be lawful for the Secretary of the Treasury, from time to time, to make such regulations respecting the disposition to be made of such circulating notes after presentation thereof for payment as aforesaid, and respecting the perpetuation of the evidence of the payment thereof, as may seem to him proper; but all such notes, on being paid, shall be cancelled; and for any deficiency in the proceeds of the bonds pledged by such association, when disposed of as hereinafter specified, to reimburse to the United States the amount so expended in paying the circulating notes of such association, the United States shall have a first and paramount lien upon all the assets of such association, and such deficiency shall be made good out of such assets in preference to any and all other claims whatsoever, except the necessary costs and expense of administering the same.

Sec. 27. *And be it further enacted,* That whenever the comptroller shall become satisfied, as in the last preceding section specified, that any such association has refused to pay its circulating notes as therein mentioned, he may, instead of cancelling the United States bonds pledged by such association, as provided in the next preceding section, cause so much of them as may be necessary to redeem the outstanding circulating notes of such association to be sold at public auction in the city of New York, after giving thirty days' notice of such sale to such association.

Sec. 28. *And be it further enacted,* That the comptroller of the currency may, if he shall be of opinion that the interests of the United States will be best promoted thereby, sell at private sale any of the stock so transferred to him by such association, and receive therefor either money or the circulating notes of such failing association: *Provided,* That no such bonds shall be sold by private sale for less than the par, nor less than the market value thereof at the time of sale. *And provided further,* That no sales of any such stock, either public or private, shall be complete until the transfer thereof shall have been made with the formalities prescribed in this act.

Sec. 29. *And be it further enacted,* That on becoming satisfied, as specified in this act, that any such association has refused to pay its circulating notes as therein mentioned, and is in default, the comptroller of the currency may forthwith appoint a receiver, and require of him such bond and security as he shall deem proper, who, under the direction of the comptroller, shall take possession of the books, records, and assets of every description of such association, collect all debts, dues, and claims belonging to such association, and, upon the order of a court of record of competent jurisdiction, may sell or compound all bad or doubtful debts, and, on a like order, sell all the real and personal property of such association, on such terms as the court shall direct; and such receiver shall pay over all moneys so made to the treasurer of the United States, and also

make report to the comptroller of the currency of all his acts and proceedings. The comptroller shall thereupon cause notice to be given, by advertisement in such newspapers as he may direct, for three consecutive months, calling on all persons who may have claims against such association to present the same, and to make legal proof thereof; and from time to time the comptroller, after full provision shall have been first made for refunding to the United States any such deficiency in redeeming the notes of such association as is mentioned in this act, shall make a ratable dividend of the moneys so paid over to him by such receiver on all such claims as may have been so proved or adjudicated in a court of competent jurisdiction, and from time to time, as the proceeds of the assets of such association shall be paid over to him, he shall make further dividends, as aforesaid, on all claims previously proved or adjudicated; and the remainder of such proceeds, if any, shall be paid over to the shareholders of such association, or their legal representatives, in proportion to the stock by them respectively held: *Provided, however,* That if any such association, against which proceedings have been so instituted on account of any alleged refusal to redeem its circulating notes as aforesaid, shall deny having failed to do so, such association may at any time within ten days after such association shall have been notified of the appointment of an agent, as provided in this act, apply to the nearest circuit, or district, or territorial court of the United States, to enjoin further proceeding in the premises; and such court, after citing the comptroller of the currency to show cause why further proceedings should not be enjoined, and after the decision of the court or finding of a jury that such association has not refused to redeem its circulating notes, when legally presented, in the lawful money of the United States, shall make an order enjoining the comptroller, and any receiver acting under his direction, from all further proceedings on account of such alleged refusal.

Sec. 30. *And be it further enacted,* That the bonds transferred to the treasurer of the United States, as hereinbefore provided, by any banking association for the security of its circulating notes, shall be held exclusively for that purpose, until such notes shall be redeemed, except as provided in this act; but the comptroller of the currency may give to any such banking association powers of attorney to receive and appropriate to its own use the interest on the bonds which shall have been so transferred to the treasurer by it; but such powers shall become inoperative whenever such banking association shall fail to redeem its circulating notes as aforesaid; and said comptroller may direct the return of any of said bonds to the banking association which transferred the same, upon the surrender to him and the cancellation of a proportionate amount of such circulating notes: *Provided,* That ninety per centum of the current market value of the remaining bonds which shall have been transferred by the banking association offering to surrender such circulating notes shall be equal to the amount of all the circulating notes retained by such banking association: *And provided, further,* That there shall have been no failure by such association to redeem its circulating notes, and that there shall have been no other violation by such association of any of the provisions of this act for the security of the creditors of such association; nor shall the treasurer be required to surrender such bonds in fractional sums of less than one thousand dollars; and if, at any time after said bonds shall be deposited with the treasurer of the United States, as aforesaid, the market or cash value shall be reduced, the comptroller of the currency is hereby authorized to demand and receive the amount of such depreciation in other United States bonds at cash value, or in money, from the association receiving said bills, to be deposited with the treasurer of the United States, as long as such depreciation continues.

Sec. 31. *And be it further enacted,* That whenever the price of any of the bonds pledged as aforesaid for the redemption of the circulating notes of any such banking association shall be, at the stock exchange in the city of New York, for four consecutive weeks, at a rate less than that at which they shall have been estimated when so pledged, and such depreciation shall not have been made good by a deposit of other bonds or money, it shall be the duty of the comptroller of the currency to notify the treasurer of the United States of such fact, and the payment of interest upon such depreciated bonds shall be suspended, and such interest shall be retained by said treasurer until the same, when added to the current market value of the bonds so pledged, to be ascertained as before provided, shall be equal to the amount for which such bonds were pledged: *Provided,* That it shall be the duty of the comptroller of the currency, at the expiration of every period of three months, to cause the whole of the sums so retained, and then remaining in the treasury of the United States, to be invested in United States bonds, in the name of the comptroller of the currency, in trust for the respective associations by which the bonds on which such interest shall have accrued shall have been pledged; and whenever the price of such depreciated bonds at the stock exchange in New York shall rise to the price at which they were pledged, and so remain for four consecutive weeks, such investment shall be assigned to such association, and all accruing interest on such pledged bonds shall thereafter be paid to such association on demand thereof.

Sec. 32. *And be it further enacted,* That it shall be the duty of the comptroller of the currency to receive worn-out or mutilated circulating notes issued by any such banking association, and to deliver in place thereof to such association other blank circulating notes to an equal amount; and such worn-out or mutilated notes, after a memorandum shall have been entered in the proper books, in accordance with such regulations as may be established by the comptroller, as well as all circulating notes which shall have been paid or surrendered to be cancelled, shall be burned to ashes in presence of three persons, one to be appointed by the Secretary of the Treasury, one by the comptroller of the currency, and one by the treasurer of the United States, under such regulations as the Secretary of the Treasury may prescribe; and in case such notes shall have been delivered to the comptroller by an officer or agent of such association, then in the presence, also, of such officer or agent; and a certificate of such burning, signed by the parties so appointed, shall be made in the books of the comptroller, and a duplicate thereof given to such officer or agent.

Sec. 33. *And be it further enacted,* That it shall be unlawful for any officer acting under the provisions of this act to countersign or deliver to any such association, or to any other company or person, any circulating notes contemplated by this act, except as hereinbefore provided, and in accordance with the true intent and meaning of this act; and any officer who shall violate the provisions of this section shall be deemed guilty of a high misdemeanor, and on conviction thereof shall be punished by fine not exceeding double the amount so countersigned and delivered, and imprisonment not exceeding fifteen years, at the discretion of the court in which he shall be tried.

Sec 34. *And be it further enacted,* That all fees for protesting the notes issued by any such banking association shall be paid by the person procuring the protest to be made, and such banking association shall be liable therefor; but no part of the stock pledged by such banking association, as aforesaid, shall be applied to the payment of such fees; and all expenses of any preliminary or other examinations into the condition of any association shall be paid by such association; and all expenses of any receivership shall be paid out of the assets of such association before distribution of the proceeds thereof.

Sec. 35. *And be it further enacted,* That the stockholders, collectively, of any such association shall at no time be liable to such association, either as principal debtors or sureties, or both, to an amount greater than three fifths of the capital stock actually paid in and remaining undiminished by losses or otherwise; nor shall the directors be so liable, except to such amount and in such manner as shall be prescribed by the by-laws of such association, adopted by its stockholders to regulate such liabilities.

Sec. 36. *And be it further enacted,* That the capital stock of any association formed under this act shall be divided into shares of one hundred dollars each, and shall be assignable on the books of the association in such manner as its by-laws shall prescribe; but no shareholder in any association under this act shall have power to sell or transfer any share held in his own right so long as he shall be liable, either as principal, debtor, surety, or otherwise, to the association for any debt which shall have become due and remain unpaid, nor in any case shall such shareholder be entitled to receive any dividend, interest, or profit on such shares so long as such liabilities shall continue, but all such dividends, interests, and profits shall be retained by the association, and applied to the discharge of such liabilities; and no stock shall be transferred without the consent of a majority of the directors while the holder thereof is thus indebted to the association.

Sec. 37. *And be it further enacted,* That no banking association shall take, as security for any loan or discount, a lien upon any part of its capital stock; but the same security, both in kind and amount, shall be required of shareholders as of other persons; and no such banking association shall be the purchaser or holder of any portion of its capital stock, or of the capital stock of any other incorporated company, unless such purchase shall be necessary to prevent loss upon a debt previously contracted in good faith, on security which, at the time, was deemed adequate to insure the payment of such debt, independent of any lien upon such stock; or in case of forfeiture of stock for the non-payment of installments due thereon, and stock so purchased or acquired, shall in no case be held by such association so purchasing for a longer period of time than six months, if the same can, within that time, be sold for what the stock cost.

Sec. 38. *And be it further enacted,* That in all elections of directors, and in deciding all questions at meetings of shareholders, each shareholder shall be entitled to one vote on each share of stock held by him; shareholders may vote by proxies duly authorized in writing; but no officer, clerk, teller, or book-keeper of such association shall act as proxy; and no stockholder whose liability is past due and unpaid shall be allowed to vote.

Sec. 39. *And be it further enacted,* That the affairs of every such association shall be managed by not less than five nor more than nine directors, one of whom shall be president of the association; every director shall, during his whole term of service, be a citizen of the United States and a resident of the state in which such association is located. At least three fourths of the directors shall have resided in the state in which such association is located one year next preceding their election as directors; and each director shall own in his own right, at least one per centum of the capital stock of such association not exceeding two hundred thousand dollars, and the half of one per centum of its capital if over two hundred thousand dollars. Each director shall take an oath that he will, so far as the duty devolves on him, diligently and honestly administer the

affairs of such association, and will not knowingly violate, or willingly permit to be violated, any of the provisions of this act, and that he is the bona fide owner, in his own right, of the shares of stock standing in his name on the books of the association, and that the same is not hypothecated, or in any way pledged, as security for any loan obtained or debt owing to the association of which he is a director, which oath, subscribed by himself, and certified by the officer before whom it is taken, shall be immediately transmitted to the comptroller of the currency, and by him filed and preserved in his office.

Sec. 40. *And be it further enacted,* That the directors of any such association first elected shall hold their places until their successors shall be elected and qualified. All subsequent elections shall be held annually, on such day in the month of January as the stockholders of said association may prescribe; and the directors so elected shall hold their places for one year, and until their successors are elected and qualified. But any director removing from the state, or ceasing to be the owner of the requisite amount of stock, shall thereby vacate his place. Any vacancy in the board shall be filled by appointment by the remaining directors. The director so appointed shall hold his place until the next annual election; and if, from any cause, an election of directors shall not be made at the time appointed, the association shall not for that cause be dissolved, but an election may be held on any subsequent day, thirty days' notice thereof having been given in a newspaper printed, or of general circulation, in the city, town, or county in which the association is located, and if no newspaper is published in such city, town, or county such notice shall be published in a newspaper in the county adjoining.

Sec. 41. *And be it further enacted,* That every such association shall at all times have on hand, in lawful money of the United States, an amount equal to at least twenty-five per centum of the aggregate amount of its outstanding notes of circulation and its deposits; and whenever the amount of its outstanding notes of circulation and its deposits shall exceed the above-named proportion for the space of twelve days, or whenever such lawful money of the United States shall at any time fall below the amount of twenty-five per centum of its circulation and deposits, such association shall not increase its liabilities by making any new loans or discounts otherwise than by discounting or purchasing bills of exchange, payable at sight, nor make any dividend of its profits, until the required proportion between the aggregate amount of its outstanding notes of circulation and its deposits and lawful money of the United States shall be restored: *Provided, however,* That clearing-house certificates, representing specie or lawful money specially deposited for the purpose of any clearing-house association, shall be deemed to be lawful money in the possession of any association belonging to such clearing-house holding and owning such certificates, and considered to be a part of the lawful money which such association is required to have, under the foregoing provisions of this section: *Provided, further,* That any balance due to any association organized under this act in other places from any association in the cities of Boston, Providence, New York, Philadelphia, Baltimore, Cincinnati, Chicago, St. Louis, or New Orleans, in good credit, subject to be drawn for at sight, and available to redeem their circulating notes and deposits, may be deemed to be a part of the lawful money which such association in other places than the cities of Boston, Providence, New York, Philadelphia, Baltimore, Cincinnati, Chicago, St. Louis, and New Orleans, are required to have by the foregoing provisions of this section, to the extent of three fifths of the said amount of twenty-five per centum required. And it shall be competent for the comptroller of the currency to notify any such association whose lawful money reserve, as aforesaid, shall fall below said proportion of twenty-five per centum, to make good such reserve; and if such association shall fail for thirty days thereafter so to make good its reserve of lawful money of the United States, the comptroller may, with the concurrence of the Secretary of the Treasury, appoint a receiver to wind up the business of such association, as provided in this act.

Sec. 42. *And be it further enacted,* That no association shall at any time be indebted, or in any way liable, to an amount exceeding the amount of its capital stock at such time actually paid in, and remaining undiminished by losses or otherwise, except on the following accounts, that is to say:

First. On account of its notes of circulation.

Second. On account of moneys deposited with, or collected by, such association.

Third. On account of bills of exchange or drafts drawn against money actually on deposit to the credit of such association, or due thereto.

Fourth. On account of liabilities to its stockholders, for money paid in on capital stock, and dividends thereon, and reserved profits.

Sec. 43. *And be it further enacted,* That no association shall, either directly or indirectly, pledge or hypothecate any of its notes or circulation, for the purpose of procuring money to be paid in on its capital stock, or to be used in its banking operations, or otherwise.

Sec. 44. *And be it further enacted,* That no association, or any member thereof, shall, during the time it shall continue its banking operations, withdraw, or permit to be withdrawn, either in form of dividends, loans to stockholders for a longer time than six months or in any other manner, any portion of its capital; and if losses shall at any time

have been sustained by any such association equal to or exceeding its undivided profits then on hand, no dividend shall be made; and no dividend shall ever be made by any association, while it shall continue its banking operations, to an amount greater than its net profits then on hand, deducting therefrom its losses and bad debts; and all debts due to any association, on which interest is past due and unpaid for a period of six months, unless the same shall be well secured, and shall be in process of collection, shall be considered bad debts within the meaning of this act.

Sec. 45. *And be it further enacted,* That the directors of every association shall semi-annually in the months of May and November, declare a dividend of so much of the profits of such association as they shall judge expedient; and on each dividend day, the cashier shall make and verify by his oath, a full, clear, and accurate statement of the condition of the association, as it shall be on that day after declaring the dividend; which statement shall contain—

First. The amount of the capital stock actually paid in and then remaining, as the capital stock of such association.

Secondly. The amount of the circulating notes of such association then in circulation.

Thirdly. The greatest amount in circulation at any time since the making of the last previous statement, as shall have been exhibited by the weekly statements of the cashier, specifying the times when the same occurred.

Fourthly. The amount of balances and debts of every kind due to other banks and banking associations.

Fifthly. The amount due to depositors.

Sixthly. The total amount of debts and liabilities of every description, and the greatest amount since the making of the last previous statement, specifying the time when the same accrued.

Seventhly. The total amount of dividend declared on the day of making the statement.

Eighthly. The amount of lawful money of the United States belonging to the association, and in its possession at the time of making the statement.

Ninthly. The amount subject to be drawn at sight, in lawful money of the United States, then remaining on deposit with any associations, banks or bankers; specifying the amounts so on deposit in the cities of Boston, Providence, New York, Philadelphia, Baltimore, Cincinnati, Chicago, St. Louis, and New Orleans.

Tenthly. The amount then on hand of bills or notes, issued by other banks and banking associations.

Eleventhly. The amount of balances due from other banks, bankers, and banking associations, excluding deposits subject to be drawn at sight as aforesaid.

Twelfthly. The amount on hand of bills, bonds, stocks, notes, and other evidences of debts, discounted or purchased by the association, specifying particularly the amount of suspended debt, the amount considered bad, the amount considered doubtful, and the amount in suit or judgment.

Thirteenthly. The value of the real and personal property held for the convenience of the association, specifying the amount of each.

Fourteenthly. The amount of real estate taken in payment of debts due to the association.

Fifteenthly. The amount of the undivided profits of the association.

Sixteenthly. The total amount of the liability to the association by the directors thereof collectively, specifying the gross amount of such liabilities as principal debtors, and the gross amount of indorsers or sureties.

The statement thus made shall forthwith be transmitted to the comptroller of the currency.

Sec. 46. *And be it further enacted,* That every association may take, reserve, receive, and charge on any loan, or discount made, or upon any note, bill of exchange, or other evidence of debt, such rate of interest or discount as is for the time the established rate of interest for delay in the payment of money, in the absence of contract between the parties, by the laws of the several States in which the associations are respectively located, and no more: *Provided, however,* That interest may be reserved or taken, in advance, at the time of making the loan or discount, according to the usual rules of banking; and the knowingly taking, reserving, or charging of a rate of interest greater than that allowed by this section shall be held and adjudged a forfeiture of the debt or demand on which the same is taken, reserved, or charged; but the purchase, discount, or sale of a bill of exchange, drawn on actually existing values, and payable at another place than the place of such purchase, discount, or sale, at the current discount or premium, shall not be considered as taking, reserving, or charging interest.

Sec. 47. *And be it further enacted,* That the total liabilities of any person, or of any company or firm, (including in the liabilities of a company or firm the liabilities of the several members thereof,) to any association, including liabilities as acceptor or bona fide bills of exchange, payable out of the state where the association is located, shall at no time exceed one third; exclusive of liabilities as acceptor, one fifth; and exclusive of liabilities on such bills of exchange, one tenth part of the amount of the capital stock of such association actually paid in.

Sec. 48. *And be it further enacted,* That no association shall, at any time, pay out on loans or discounts, or in purchasing drafts or bills of exchange, or in payment of deposits, nor shall it in any other mode put in circulation the notes of any bank or banking association, which notes shall not, at any such time, be receivable, at par, on deposit, and in payment of debts by the association so pay-

ing out or circulating such notes; nor shall it knowingly pay out or put in circulation any notes issued by any bank or banking association which at the time of such paying out or putting in circulation is not redeeming its circulating notes in lawful money of the United States.

Sec. 49. *And be it further enacted,* That all transfer of the notes, bonds, bills of exchange, and other evidences of debt owing to any association, or of deposits to its credit; all assignments of mortgages, sureties on real estate, or of judgments or decrees in its favor; all deposits of money, bullion, or other valuable thing for its use, or for the use of any of its shareholders or creditors; and all payments of money to either, made after the commission of an act of insolvency, or in contemplation thereof, with a view to prevent the application of its assets in the manner prescribed by this act, or with a view to the preference of one creditor to another, except in payment of its circulating notes, shall be utterly null and void.

Sec. 50. *And be it further enacted,* That if the directors of any association shall knowingly violate, or knowingly permit any of the officers, agents, or servants of the association to violate any of the provisions of this act, all the rights, privileges, and franchises of the association derived from this act shall be thereby forfeited; such violation shall, however, be determined and adjudged by a proper circuit, district, or territorial court of the United States, before the association shall be declared dissolved; and in cases of such violation, every director who participated in or assented to the same shall be held liable in his personal and individual capacity for all damages which the association, its shareholders, or any other person, shall have sustained in consequence of such violation.

Sec. 51. *And be it further enacted,* That the comptroller of the currency, with the approbation of the Secretary of the Treasury, as often as shall be deemed necessary or proper, shall appoint a suitable person or persons to make an examination of the affairs of every banking association, which person shall not be a director or other officer in any association whose affairs he shall be appointed to examine, and who shall have power to make a thorough examination into all the affairs of the association, and, in doing so, to examine any of the officers and agents thereof on oath, and shall make a full and detailed report of the condition of the association to the comptroller; and the association shall not be subject to any other visitorial powers than such as are authorized by this act, except such as are vested in the several courts of law and chancery. And every person appointed to make such examination shall receive for his services at the rate of five dollars for each day by him employed in such examination, and two dollars for every twenty-five miles he shall necessarily travel in the performance of his duty, which shall be paid by the association by him examined.

Sec. 52. *And be it further enacted,* That every president, director, cashier, teller, clerk, or agent of any association, who shall embezzle, abstract, or wilfully misapply any of the moneys, funds, or credits of the association, or shall, without authority from the directors, issue or put in circulation any of the notes of the association, or shall, without such authority, issue or put forth any certificate of deposit, draw any order or bill of exchange, make any acceptance, assign any note, bond, draft, bill of exchange, mortgage, judgment, or decree, or shall make any false entry in any book, report, or statement of the association, with intent, in either case, to injure or defraud any other company, body politic, or corporate, or any individual person, or to deceive any officer or agent appointed to examine the affairs of any such association, shall be deemed guilty of a misdemeanor, and upon conviction thereof shall be punished by imprisonment not less than five nor more than ten years.

Sec. 53. *And be it further enacted,* That the president and cashier of every such association shall cause to be kept at all times a full and correct list of the names and residences of all the shareholders in the association in the office where its business is transacted; and such list shall be subject to the inspection of all the shareholders and creditors of the association during business hours of each day in which business may be legally transacted; and a copy of such list, verified by the oath of such president or cashier, shall, at the beginning of every year, be transmitted to the comptroller of the currency, commencing on the first day of the first quarter after the organization of the association.

Sec. 54. *And be it further enacted,* That the Secretary of the Treasury is hereby authorized, whenever, in his judgment, the public interests will be promoted thereby, to employ and of such associations doing business under this act as depositaries of the public moneys, except receipts from customs.

Sec. 55. *And be it further enacted,* That all suits and proceedings arising out of the provisions of this act, in which the United States or its officers or agents shall be parties, shall be conducted by the district attorneys of the several districts, under the direction and supervision of the solicitor of the treasury.

Sec. 56. *And be it further enacted,* That every person who shall mutilate, cut, deface, disfigure, or perforate with holes, or shall unite or cement together, or do any other thing to any bank bill, draft, note, or other evidence of debt issued by any such association, or shall cause or procure the same to be done, with intent to render such bank bill, draft, note, or other evidence of debt, unfit to be reissued by said association, shall upon conviction forfeit fifty dollars to the association who shall be injured thereby, to be recovered by action in any court having jurisdiction.

Sec. 57. *And be it further enacted,* That if any person shall falsely make, forge, or counterfeit, or cause or procure to be made, forged, or counterfeited, or willingly aid or assist in falsely making, forging, or counterfeiting, any note in imitation of, or purporting to be in imitation of, the circulating notes issued under the provisions of this act, or shall pass, utter, or publish, or attempt to pass, utter, or publish any false, forged, or counterfeited note, purporting to be issued by any association doing a banking business under the provisions of this act, knowing the same to be falsely made, forged, or counterfeited, or shall falsely alter, or cause or procure to be falsely altered, or willingly aid or assist in falsely altering, any such circulating notes, issued as aforesaid, or shall pass, utter or publish, or attempt to pass, utter or publish as true, any falsely altered or spurious circulating note, issued or purporting to have been issued as aforesaid, knowing the same to be falsely altered or spurious, every such person shall be deemed and adjudged guilty of felony, and being thereof convicted by due course of law, shall be sentenced to be imprisoned and kept at hard labor for a period not less than five years nor more than fifteen years, and to be fined in a sum not exceeding one thousand dollars.

Sec. 58. *And be it further enacted,* That if any person shall make or engrave, or cause or procure to be made or engraved, or shall have in his custody or possession any engraved plate or block after the similitude of any plate from which any circulating notes issued as aforesaid shall have been printed, with intent to use such plate or block, or cause or suffer the same to be used, in forging or counterfeiting any of the notes issued as aforesaid, or shall have in his custody or possession any blank note or notes engraved and printed after the similitude of any notes issued as aforesaid, with intent to use such blanks, or cause or suffer the same to be used, in forging or counterfeiting any of the notes issued as aforesaid, or shall have in his custody or possession any paper adapted to the making of such notes, and similar to the paper upon which any such notes shall have been issued, with intent to use such paper, or cause or suffer the same to be used, in forging or counterfeiting any of the notes issued as aforesaid, every such person, being thereof convicted by due course of law, shall be sentenced to be imprisoned and kept to hard labor for a term not less than five nor more than fifteen years, and fined in a sum not exceeding one thousand dollars.

Sec. 59. *And be it further enacted,* That suits, actions, and proceedings, by and against any association under this act may be had in any circuit, district, or territorial court of the United States held within the district in which such association may be established.

Sec. 60. *And be it further enacted,* That is shall be the duty of the comptroller of the currency to report annually to Congress, at the commencement of its session—

First. A summary of the state and condition of every association from whom reports have been received the preceding year, at the several dates to which such reports refer, with an abstract of the whole amount of banking capital returned by them, of the whole amount of their debts and liabilities, the amount of circulating notes outstanding, and the total amount of means and resources, specifying the amount of specie held by them at the times of their several returns, and such other information in relation to said associations as, in his judgment, may be useful.

Second. A statement of the associations whose business has been closed during the year, with the amount of their circulation redeemed, and the amount outstanding.

Third. To suggest any amendment to the laws relative to banking by which the system may be improved, and the security of the bill-holders and depositors may be increased.

Fourth. To report the names and compensation of the clerks employed by him, and the whole amount of the expenses of the banking department during the year; and such report shall be made by or before the first day of December in each year, and the usual number of copies for the use of the Senate and House, and one thousand copies for the use of the Department, shall be printed by the public printer and in readiness for distribution on the first meeting of congress.

Sec. 61. *And be it further enacted*, That any banking association or corporation lawfully in existence as a bank of circulation on the first day of January, Anno Domini eighteen hundred, and sixty-three, organized in any state, either under a special act of incorporation or a general banking law, may, at any time within—years after the passage of this act become an association under the provisions of this act; that in such case the certificate of association provided for by this act shall be signed by the directors of such banking association or corporation, and in addition to the specifications required by this act, shall specify that such directors are authorized by the owners of two thirds of the capital stock of such banking association or corporation, to make such certificate of association, and such certificate of association shall thereafter have the same effect, and the same proceedings shall be had thereon, as is provided for as to other associations organized under this act. And such association or corporation thereafter shall have the same powers and privileges, and shall be subject to the same duties, responsibilities, and rules, in all respects, as is [are] prescribed in this act for other associations organized under it, and shall be held and regarded as an association under this act.

Sec. 62. *And be it further enacted*, That any bank or banking association, authorized by any State law to engage in the business of banking, and duly organized under such State law at the time of the passage of this act, and which shall be the holder and owner of United States bonds to the amount of fifty per centum of its capital stock, may transfer and deliver to the treasurer of the United States such bonds, or any part thereof, in the manner provided by this act; and upon making such transfer and delivery, such bank or banking association shall be entitled to receive from the comptroller of the currency, circulating notes, as herein provided, equal in amount to eighty per centum of the amount of the bonds so transferred and delivered.

Sec. 63. *And be it further enacted*, That upon the failure of any such State bank or banking association, to redeem any of its circulating notes issued under the provisions of the preceding section, the comptroller of the currency shall, when satisfied that such default has been made, and within thirty days after notice of such default, proceed to declare the bonds transferred and delivered to the treasurer, forfeited to the United States, and the same shall thereupon be forfeited accordingly. And thereupon the circulating notes which have been issued by such bank or banking association shall be redeemed and paid at the treasury of the United States, in the same manner as other circulating notes issued under the provisions of this act are redeemed and paid.

Sec. 64. *And be it further enacted*, That the bonds forfeited, as provided in the last preceding section, may be cancelled to an amount equal to the circulating notes redeemed and paid, or such bonds may be sold, under the direction of the Secretary of the Treasury, and after retaining out of the proceeds a sum sufficient to pay the whole amount of circulating notes, for the redemption of which such bonds are held, the surplus, if any remains, shall be paid to the bank, or banking association from which such bonds were received.

Sec. 65. *And be it further enacted*, That Congress reserves the right, at any time, to amend, alter, or repeal this act.

Source:
*Statutes at Large,*Vol. 12, pp. 665–682.

Charles Sumner, Speech on the Presentation of the First Installment of the Emancipation Petition of the Woman's National Loyal League, 1864

Text of a speech given by Senator Charles Sumner on February 9, 1864, to the United States Senate. In this speech, Sumner presents a petition signed by 100,000 American citizens asking Congress to pass an act to emancipate slaves. The total number of signatures are broken down by state and sex. The petition had been circulated by the Women's National Loyal League, an organization founded by Susan B. Anthony and Elizabeth Cady Stanton in 1863 to fight slavery and work for African-American rights.

Sumner opens his speech by pointing out the sheer size of the petition, presented in rolls, with each roll representing the signatures gathered in each state. He reads the text of the petition, noting that it is signed by both women and men. Declaring that it asks "nothing less than universal emancipation," he notes that no grounds for this plea are given, because "the prayer speaks for itself." Sumner condemns slavery as the cause of the Civil War and observes that Congress is the governmental entity with the power to remedy the threat that slavery poses to the nation. He concludes by noting the logic of the petitioners' appeal to Congress, to whom "belongs the prerogative of the Roman Dictator to see that the Republic receives no detriment."

Soon after Sumner's speech, on April 9, 1864, the Senate passed the Thirteenth Amendment and abolished slavery by a vote of 38 to 6. Although it took two attempts to pass the House of Representatives, the amendment was ratified in 1865.

In the Senate of the United States . . .

Mr. Sumner—Mr. President: I offer a petition which is now lying on the desk before me. It is too bulky for me to take up. I need not add that it is too bulky for any of the pages of this body to carry.

This petition marks a stage of public opinion in the history of slavery, and also in the suppression of the rebellion. As it is short I will read it:

"To the Senate and House of Representatives of the United States:

"The undersigned, women of the United States above the age of eighteen years, earnestly pray that your honorable body will pass at the earliest practicable day an act emancipating all persons of African descent held to involuntary service or labor in the United States."

There is also a duplicate of this petition signed by "men above the age of eighteen years."

It will be perceived that the petition is in rolls. Each roll represents a State. For instance, here is New York with a list of seventeen thousand seven hundred and six names; Illinois with fifteen thousand three hundred and eighty; and Massachusetts with eleven thousand six hundred and forty-one. These several petitions are consolidated into one petition, being another illustration of the motto on our coin—*E pluribus unum.*

This petition is signed by one hundred thousand men and women, who unite in this unparalleled number to support its prayer. They are from all parts of the country and from every condition of life. They are from the sea-board, fanned by the free airs of the ocean, and from the Mississippi and the prairies of the West, fanned by the free airs which fertilize that extensive region. They are from the families of the educated and uneducated, rich and poor, of every profession, business, and calling in life, representing every sentiment, thought, hope, passion, activity, intelligence which inspires, strengthens, and adorns our social system. Here they are, a mighty army, one hundred thousand strong, without arms or banners; the advance-guard of a yet larger army.

But though memorable for their numbers, these petitioners are more memorable still for the prayer in which they unite. They ask nothing less than universal emancipation; and this they ask directly at the hands of Congress. No reason is assigned. The prayer speaks for itself. It is simple, positive. So far as it proceeds from the women of the country, it is naturally a petition, and not an argument. But I need not remind the Senate that there is no reason so strong as the reason of the heart. Do not all great thoughts come from the heart?

It is not for me, on presenting this petition, to assign reasons which the army of petitioners has forborne to assign. But I may not improperly add that, naturally and obviously, they all feel in their hearts, what reason and knowledge confirm: not only that slavery *as a unit*, one and indivisible, is the guilty origin of the rebellion, but that its influence everywhere, even outside the rebel States, has been hostile to the Union, always impairing loyalty, and sometimes openly menacing the national government. It requires no difficult logic to conclude that such a monster, wherever it shows its head, is a *national enemy*, to be pursued and destroyed as such, or at least a nuisance to the national cause to be abated as such. The petitioners know well that Congress is the depository of those supreme powers by which the rebellion, alike in its root and in its distant offshoots, may be surely crushed, and by which unity and peace may be permanently secured. They know well that the action of Congress may be with the co-operation of the slave-masters, or even without the co-operation, under the overruling law of military necessity, or the commanding precept of the Constitution "to guarantee to every State a Republican form of government." Above all, they know well that to save the country from peril, especially to save the national life, there is no power, in the ample arsenal of self-defense, which Congress may not grasp; for to Congress, under the Constitution, belongs the prerogative of the Roman Dictator to see that the Republic receives no detriment. Therefore to Congress these petitioners now appeal. I ask the reference of the petition to the Select Committee on Slavery and Freedmen.

*State.	Men.	Women.	Total.
New York	6,519	11,187	17,706
Illinois	6,382	8,998	15,380
Massachusetts	4,248	7,392	11,641
Pennsylvania	2,259	6,366	8,625
Ohio	3,676	4,654	8,330
Michigan	1,741	4,441	6,182
Iowa	2,025	4,014	6,039
Maine	1,225	4,362	5,587
Wisconsin	1,639	2,391	4,030
Indiana	1,075	2,591	3,666
New Hampshire	393	2,261	2,654
New Jersey	824	1,709	2,533
Rhode Island	827	1,451	2,278
Vermont	375	1,183	1,558
Connecticut	393	1,162	1,555
Minnesota	396	1,094	1,490
West Virginia	82	100	182
Maryland	115	50	165
Kansas	84	74	158
Delaware	67	70	137
Nebraska	13	20	33
Kentucky	21		21
Louisiana (New Orleans)		14	14
Citizens of the U.S. living in New Brunswick	19	17	36
	34,399	65,601	100,000

See also RECONSTRUCTION AMENDMENTS, 1865, 1868, 1870.

Source:

Elizabeth Frost and Kathryn Cullen-DuPont, *Women's Suffrage in America: An Eyewitness History.* New York: Facts On File, Inc., 1992.

Nancy Emerson, Civil War Diary of a Southern Woman, 1864

Born in 1807 in Massachusetts, Nancy Emerson lived with her brother Luther Emerson and his family in Augusta County, Virginia. Luther, a minister at Shemeriah Presbyterian Church in Augusta County, Virginia, was relatively prosperous. A strong supporter of the Confederacy, Nancy Emerson believed that the Civil War was divine punishment against Northern abolitionists. The excerpts below describe a Union raid of the Emerson's town on June 9 and 10, 1864. The bracketed words were placed in the narrative by the diary's editor.

⁓⊷⊶⊷⊷⊶⊷⊷⊶⊷⊶⊷⊷⊶⊷⊶⊷⊶⊷

July 9, [1864]

❖   ❖   ❖

But I commenced with the intention of telling a story about some Yankee raiders. We have often had alarms about their coming but have been preserved by a kind Providence until this season. Not long since, they favored us with two visits which will not soon be forgotten in these parts. The first day, they came in from the West, across the mountain. A party of 40 or 50 perhaps, came riding up, dismounted & rushed in. "Have you got any whiskey" said they, "got any flour? got any bacon?". . . "Come on boys," says one, "we'll find it all." With that, they pushed rudely by Sister C. who was terribly alarmed, & had been from the first news of their coming, & spread them selves nearly all over the house. Finding their way to a fine barrel of flour which a neighbor had given us, they proceeded to fill their sacks & pillow cases, scattering a large percent on the floor, till it was nearly exhausted. The last one told us, on our remonstrating, to hide the rest.

Some went upstairs, opened every trunk & drawer & tossed things upside down or on the floor, even my nice bonnets, pretending to be looking for arms. They stole's gold sleeve buttons & pin (a present to him) his best shirt, a good coat, & pair of shoes. The shoes, it being nearly impossible to get shoes these days, he afterwards persuaded the fellow to *sell* him back for an Ohio ten dollar note, as good as gold to him. He could with a much better appetite doubtless have knocked him down, but there was no choice in the matter.

We did not say anything to provoke them, but did not disguise our sentiments. They went peeping under the beds, looking for rebels as they said. told them there were no rebels here (meaning rebel soldiers) spoke & said We are all rebels. spoke & said "Yes, I am a rebel." The Yankee looked [up] from her drawer, which he [was] searching just then, & said "That's right." Then said, "I am a rebel too & I *glory* in it." When Sister C. remonstrated with them about taking the shoes, asking them why they injured innocent persons who had taken no part in the war, one of them replied, "You need not tell me that, I know all the people along here have sons in the army." She then pointed to B & said "That is my only son." Then said, "I have no brothers in the army, I wish from my heart I had." He then said, "Now Sis, I don't wish you had brothers in the army. I wouldn't like to kill one of your brothers. I got some corn here." (pointing to his plunder) An officer rode up after the rest had gone having the appearance of a gentleman, & asked civilly if he could get some flour. Sister C. telling [him] how they had stripped us of nearly every thing they could find, said he could go & see what they had left, & help himself. He said no, he never had searched a house & never would, & it was a shame they should [do so.]

That night they camped [away] a mile or two from us, extending along the road two or three miles, & got a fine supper from the farms around them. Sister C. was afraid to undress, but lay down quite exhausted two or three hours in the night. kept watch the first part of the night, & the last. E soon called to him, "I hear footsteps." He went out & saw some coming up the road with a torch. Thinking they might be coming to burn the house, he came to our door, saying we had better have something ready to throw around us if we should be called out for any reason [taking care not to alarm us]. But our fears were groundless. They started off in the night for Staunton where there were several thousand of them. Our visitors belonged to's [command]

July 13, [1864] They told us that men were a great deal worse than they, & that was true, but they were bad enough & worse at some other places than with us. At one of our neighbors, they took every thing they had to eat, all the pillow cases & sheets but what were on the beds, & the towels & some of the ladies stockings. One of them made up a bundle of ladies clothing to take, but his comrade shamed him out of it. They then poured out their molasses, scattered their preserves & sugar & other things about the floor, & mixed them all together & destroyed things generally.

The ladies there are very amiable & genteel in their [appearance] which makes it the more strange. Their visitors as well as ours however had taken a drop too much. This gentleman had kept some things for sale of late, had a quantity of tobacco & some other things on hand, all which they took to the amount of several thousand dollars.

At another neighbors, they took all of their meat (some 30 pieces of bacon) & nearly everything else they had to eat, all their horses (4) & persuaded off their two negro men. One of these was afterwards seen by one of our men crying to come back, but was watched so closely that he could not escape. No wonder he cried. He has been twice on the brink of the grave with pneumonia, & was nursed by his mistress as tenderly as if he had been a brother, & she was always kind to him, his master also. He will not find such treatment anywhere.

The Yankees (I give them this appellation be cause every body else does) took off all the negro men & boys they could, as well as all the horses, told the women they would take *them* next time they came. Many sent their horses to the woods. Some of these were found & cap-

tured. People here do their farming with horses instead of oxen, & it is an immense loss to have them & the servants swept off to such an extent, just as harvest is about to begin too. Many sent off their servants in one direction & another, some of whom were overtaken & captured & others escaped.

The lady before mentioned has told me since that no tongue can tell her feelings the day the Yankees were there. In the first place, they fired on her little son & another boy several times, as they sat on the fence watching their approach, & afterwards pretended that they took them for confederate soldiers from their being dressed in gray. Then her husband & oldest son were hid in the bushes in the garden. & she was in momentary fear of their being discovered & fired upon. The men & boys always kept out of the way, as they were sometimes taken off, & did not know what treat ment they might receive, & thus the women were left to shift for themselves as best they could. Another of our neighbors was fired upon several times until he either dropped or lay down, it was not known which. They said it was because he ran, but he was passing between their pickets & ours, who were firing at each other, & was obliged to run. We heard of the circumstance, & were very uneasy, but he providentially escaped injury. They always fire upon those who run from them.

July 15, 1864 Those who left their houses fared worse than others, at least their houses did. The wife of a worthy miller living near us, became so much alarmed that went with her little children to a neighbors'. They stripped her house completely, destroying everything, left nothing but a straw bed & one sheet. It was a hard case, for it was with difficulty that Mr. H. with his large family, could get along before. Another lady who was alone, was so much frightened by a drunken soldier who came in, that she left the house. The Yankees destroyed every thing there too.

We were better off than most in having Cousin S with us. We feared they would take him, but they only inquired if he was a soldier, & when told that he was a teacher, did not molest him. He had a large school (upwards of 40) & had refused many more applications. It was nearly out at that time, & was closed abruptly because parents liked to stay at home & keep their children with them. He was the chief man in hiding our things. I know not wha[t] we should have done without him. Some hid their things & had them discovered but we were more fortunate . (Some were betrayed by their servants) Some hid nothing, thinking they would not be disturbed but found themselves woefully mistaken. Others thought they might be worse dealt [with] if they hid anything.

A lady near Staunton a little time since had two Yankee officers come to take tea with her. She was strong "secesh," but she got them a good sup per . It was served up in very plain dishes. They perceived that she was wealthy, & inquired if she had not hid her plate &c. She told them she had. They asked <u>where</u>. She told them in the ash heap. They said "That is not a good place. It is the first place searched." They then very kindly & politely showed her a good place (in their opinion) She followed their advice & saved her things. In another instance, some Yankee officers politely showed a lady where to hide her [illeg.] silver &c. The soldiers came & searched in vain. Just as they were going away, a little black chap who had followed them around says to them in a tone of triumph, "Ah you did not find Missis things hid inside the ____" They went & found & took them.

Source:

The American Civil War. The Diary of Nancy Emerson: An American Civil War Woman. Available on-line. URL: www. geocities.com/Athens/Colum/1122/CVWRDRY2.htm. Accessed December 2003.

Wade-Davis Bill, 1864

Severe reconstruction plan passed by Congress on July 2, 1864, that provided for the governmental reorganization of a seceded state only after a majority of white male citizens had taken an oath of allegiance to the Union and after a constitution acceptable to the president and Congress had been adopted. The bill was sponsored by Senator Benjamin F. Wade of Ohio and Representative Henry W. Davis of Maryland and was supported by other Radical Republicans, who believed that reconstruction was a congressional function. When Lincoln refused to sign the bill, killing it by pocket veto on July 4, 1864, its sponsors issued the Wade-Davis Manifesto, attacking the president's "studied outrage" and defiance of congressional authority. The manifesto, possibly the harshest criticism of Lincoln coming from fellow Republicans, appeared in the *New York Tribune* on August 5, 1864.

An Act

To guarantee to certain States whose governments have been usurped or overthrown a republican form of government.

Be it enacted by the Senate and House of Representatives of the United States of America in Congress assembled, That in the States declared in rebellion against the United States the President shall, by and with the advice and consent of the Senate, appoint for each a provisional governor, whose pay and emoluments shall not exceed that of a brigadier-general of volunteers, who shall be charged with the civil administration of such State until a State government therein shall be recognized as hereinafter provided.

Sec. 2. *And be it further enacted,* That so soon as the military resistance to the United States shall have been suppressed in any such State and the people thereof shall have sufficiently returned to their obedience to the Constitution and the laws of the United States the provisional governor shall direct the marshal of the United States, as speedily as may be, to name a sufficient number of deputies, and to enroll all white male citizens of the United States resident in the State in their respective counties, and to request each one to take the oath to support the Constitution of the United States, and in his enrollment to designate those who take and those who refuse to take that oath, which rolls shall be forthwith returned to the provisional governor; and if the persons taking that oath shall amount to a majority of the persons enrolled in the State, he shall, by proclamation, invite the loyal people of the State to elect delegates to a convention charged to declare the will of the people of the State relative to the reestablishment of a State government, subject to and in conformity with the Constitution of the United States.

Sec. 3. *And be it further enacted,* That the convention shall consist of as many members as both houses of the last constitutional State legislature, apportioned by the provisional governor among the counties, parishes, or districts of the State, in proportion to the white population returned as electors by the marshal in compliance with the provisions of this act. The provisional governor shall, by proclamation, declare the number of delegates to be elected by each county, parish, or election district; name a day of election not less than thirty days thereafter; designate the places of voting in each county, parish, or district, conforming as nearly as may be convenient to the places used in the State elections next preceding the rebellion; appoint one or more commissioners to hold the election at each place of voting, and provide an adequate force to keep the peace during the election.

Sec. 4. *And be it further enacted,* That the delegates shall be elected by the loyal white male citizens of the United States of the age of 21 years, and resident at the time in the county, parish, or district in which they shall offer to vote, and enrolled as aforesaid, or absent in the military service of the United States, and who shall take and subscribe the oath of allegiance to the United States in the form contained in the act of Congress of July 2, 1862; and all such citizens of the United States who are in the military service of the United States shall vote at the headquarters of their respective commands, under such regulations as may be prescribed by the provisional governor for the taking and return of their votes; but no person who has held or exercised any office, civil or military, State or Confederate, under the rebel usurpation, or who has voluntarily borne arms against the United States, shall vote or be eligible to be elected as delegate at such election.

Sec. 5. *And be it further enacted,* That the said commissioners, or either of them, shall hold the election in conformity with this act, and, so far as may be consistent therewith, shall proceed in the manner used in the State prior to the rebellion. The oath of allegiance shall be taken and subscribed on the poll book by every voter in the form above prescribed, but every person known by or proved to the commissioners to have held or exercised any office, civil or military, State or Confederate, under the rebel usurpation, or to have voluntarily borne arms against the United States, shall be excluded though he offer to take the oath; and in case any person who shall have borne arms against the United States shall offer to vote, he shall be deemed to have borne arms voluntarily unless he shall prove the contrary by the testimony of a qualified voter. The poll book, showing the name and oath of each voter, shall be returned to the provisional governor by the commissioners of election, or the one acting, and the provisional governor shall canvass such returns and declare the person having the highest number of votes elected.

Sec. 6. *And be it further enacted,* That the provisional governor shall, by proclamation, convene the delegates elected as aforesaid at the capital of the State on a day not more than three months after the election, giving at least thirty days' notice of such day. In case the said capital shall in his judgment be unfit, he shall in his proclamation appoint another place. He shall preside over the deliberations of the convention and administer to each delegate, before taking his seat in the convention, the oath of allegiance to the United States in the form above prescribed.

Sec. 7. *And be it further enacted,* That the convention shall declare on behalf of the people of the State their submission to the Constitution and laws of the United States, and shall adopt the following provisions, hereby prescribed by the United States in the execution of the constitutional duty to guarantee a republican form of government to every State, and incorporate them in the constitution of the State; that is to say:

First. No person who has held or exercised any office, civil or military (except offices merely ministerial and military offices below the grade of colonel), State or Confederate, under the usurping power, shall vote for or be a member of the legislature or governor.

Second. Involuntary servitude is forever prohibited, and the freedom of all persons is guaranteed in said State.

Third. No debt, State or Confederate, created by or under the sanction of the usurping power shall be recognized or paid by the State.

Sec. 8. *And be it further enacted,* That when the convention shall have adopted those provisions it shall proceed to reestablish a republican form of government and ordain a constitution containing those provisions, which, when adopted, the convention shall by ordinance provide for submitting to the people of the State entitled to vote under this law, at an election to be held in the manner prescribed by the act for the election of delegates, but at a time and place named by the convention, at which election the said electors, and none others, shall vote directly for or against such constitution and form of State government. And the returns of said election shall be made to the provisional governor, who shall canvass the same in the presence of the electors, and if a majority of the votes cast shall be for the constitution and form of government, he shall certify the same, with a copy thereof, to the President of the United States, who, after obtaining the assent of Congress, shall, by proclamation, recognize the government so established, and none other, as the constitutional government of the State; and from the date of such recognition, and not before, Senators and Representatives and electors for President and Vice-President may be elected in such State, according to the laws of the State and of the United States.

Sec. 9. *And be it further enacted,* That if the convention shall refuse to reestablish the State government on the conditions aforesaid the provisional governor shall declare it dissolved; but it shall be the duty of the President, whenever he shall have reason to believe that a sufficient number of the people of the State entitled to vote under this act, in number not less than a majority of those enrolled as aforesaid, are willing to reestablish a State government on the conditions aforesaid, to direct the provisional governor to order another election of delegates to a convention for the purpose and in the manner prescribed in this act, and to proceed in all respects as hereinbefore provided, either to dissolve the convention or to certify the State government reestablished by it to the President.

Sec. 10. *And be it further enacted,* That until the United States shall have recognized a republican form of State government the provisional governor in each of said States shall see that this act and the laws of the United States and the laws of the State in force when the State government was overthrown by the rebellion are faithfully executed within the State; but no law or usage whereby any person was heretofore held in involuntary servitude shall be recognized or enforced by any court or officer in such State; and the laws for the trial and punishment to white persons shall extend to all persons, and jurors shall have the qualifications of voters under this law for delegates to the convention. The President shall appoint such officer provided for by the laws of the State when its government was overthrown as he may find necessary to the civil administration of the State, all which officers shall be entitled to receive the fees and emoluments provided by the State laws for such officers.

Sec. 11. *And be it further enacted,* That until the recognition of a State government as aforesaid the provisional governor shall, under such regulations as he may prescribe, cause to be assessed, levied, and collected, for the year 1864 and every year thereafter, the taxes provided by the laws of such State to be levied during the fiscal year preceding the overthrow of the State government thereof, in the manner prescribed by the laws of the State, as nearly as may be; and the officers appointed as aforesaid are vested with all powers of levying and collecting such taxes, by distress or sale, as were vested in any officers or tribunal of the State government aforesaid for those purposes. The proceeds of such taxes shall be accounted for to the provisional governor and be by him applied to the expenses of the administration of the laws in such State, subject to the direction of the President, and the surplus shall be deposited in the Treasury of the United States to the credit of such State, to be paid to the State upon an appropriation therefor to be made when a republican form of government shall be recognized therein by the United States.

Sec. 12. *And be it further enacted,* That all persons held to involuntary servitude or labor in the States aforesaid are hereby emancipated and discharged therefrom, and they and their posterity shall be forever free. And if any such persons or their posterity shall be restrained of liberty under pretense of any claim to such service or labor, the courts of the United States shall, on *habeas corpus,* discharge them.

Sec. 13. *And be it further enacted,* That if any person declared free by this act, or any law of the United States or any proclamation of the President, be restrained of liberty with intent to be held in or reduced to involuntary servitude or labor, the person convicted before a court of competent jurisdiction of such act shall be punished by fine of not less than $1,500 and be imprisoned not less than five nor more than twenty years.

Sec. 14. *And be it further enacted,* That every person who shall hereafter hold or exercise any office, civil or military (except offices merely ministerial and military offices below the grade of colonel), in the rebel service, State or Confederate, is hereby declared not to be a citizen of the United States.

Source:

James D. Richardson, ed. *A Compilation of the Messages and Papers of the Presidents, 1789–1897.* Washington, D.C.: Government Printing Office, 1899, pp. 223–226.

U.S. Army, Treatment of Black POWs, 1864

"The issues of emancipation and military service were intertwined from the onset of the Civil War. News from Fort Sumter set off a rush by free black men to enlist in U.S. military units. They were turned away, however, because a Federal law dating from 1792 barred Negroes from bearing arms for the U.S. Army (although they had served in the American Revolution and in the War of 1812). In Boston disappointed would-be volunteers met and passed a resolution requesting that the government modify its laws to permit their enlistment.

. . . By mid-1862, however, the escalating number of former slaves (contrabands), the declining number of white volunteers, and the increasingly pressing personnel needs of the Union Army pushed the Government into reconsidering the ban.

". . . After the Union Army turned back Lee's first invasion of the North at Antietam, MD, and the Emancipation Proclamation was subsequently announced, black recruitment was pursued in earnest. Volunteers from South Carolina, Tennessee, and Massachusetts filled the first authorized black regiments. Recruitment was slow until black leaders such as Frederick Douglass encouraged black men to become soldiers to ensure eventual full citizenship. . . . Volunteers began to respond, and in May 1863 the Government established the Bureau of Colored Troops to manage the burgeoning numbers of black soldiers.

"By the end of the Civil War, roughly 179,000 black men (10% of the Union Army) served as soldiers in the U.S. Army and another 19,000 served in the Navy. [Blacks also served in the Confederate forces although rarely in a combat capacity.] Nearly 40,000 black soldiers died over the course of the war—30,000 of infection or disease. Black soldiers served in artillery and infantry and performed all noncombat support functions that sustain an army, as well. Black carpenters, chaplains, cooks, guards, laborers, nurses, scouts, spies, steamboat pilots, surgeons, and teamsters also contributed to the war cause. There were nearly 80 black commissioned officers. Black women, who could not formally join the Army, nonetheless served as nurses, spies, and scouts, the most famous being Harriet Tubman, of Underground Railroad fame, who scouted for the 2d South Carolina Volunteers."

African Americans were placed in segregated units usually commanded by white officers and black noncommissioned officers. "Black soldiers were discriminated against in other ways as well. Initially paid $10 per month, from which $3 was automatically deducted for clothing, resulting in a net pay of $7. In contrast, white soldiers received $13 per month, from which no clothing allowance was drawn." In June 1864 Congress granted equal pay to the U.S. Colored Troops and made the action retroactive. Black soldiers received the same rations and supplies. In addition, they received comparable medical care.

"The black troops, however, faced greater peril than white troops when captured by the Confederate army. In 1863 the Confederate Congress threatened to punish severely officers of black troops and to enslave black soldiers. As a result, President Lincoln issued General Order 233, threatening reprisal on Confederate prisoners of war (POWs) for any mistreatment of black troops." The document reproduced here echoes that order. It concerns Private Wilson Wood of the 6th U.S. Colored Heavy Artillery who was captured July 22, 1864, by Confederate forces and held in a prison camp. The letter from the commanding officer, William P. Hardeman, alerting Union forces to Wood's capture reinforced Confederate policies toward African American prisoners.

Although black units were not used extensively in combat, African-American soldiers served with distinction in a number of battles including Milliken's Bend, Louisiana; Port Hudson, Louisiana; Petersburg, Virginia; and Nashville, Tennessee. The July 1863 assault on Fort Wagner, South Carolina, in which the 54th Regiment of Massachusetts Volunteers lost two-thirds of their officers and half of their troops provided the story for the movie *Glory*. By war's end, 16 black soldiers had been awarded the Medal of Honor for their valor.

Head-Quarters United States Forces, Natchez, Miss.
July 31st 1864
Lieut. Col. L. A. McCaleb
Com'dg Vidalia-La

Sir:

I have through you this day the communication of Col. Wm. P. Hardeman, Com'dg rebel forces at Trinity, La., in reply to your inquiry concerning the treatment of Private Wilson of your command, captured by the enemy on the 22nd instant.

Please advise him in reply that when the Government of the United States made negroes soldiers it assumed towards them the same obligations as were due to any other who might wear its uniform and bear its flag.

The honest, patriotic negro, who though of an oppressed race, and lowly condition, with few memories of past blessings to inspire him, gives his service and offers his life in defense of good government is in the judgment of his God and humanity, more than the peer of the man who, while enjoying the protection of that Government and crowned with its benefactions, would destroy it.

As the matter is understood by me, the Government will, for every black soldier reduced to slavery, put a rebel soldier in like condition and will, for every violation of the usages of war respecting these men, exact ample retaliation.

Respectfully,
Yours, &c.
(signed) J. M. Brayman
Brig. Gen. Com'g.

See also CONFEDERATE CONGRESS, ACT TO INCREASE THE MILITARY FORCE OF THE CONFEDERATE STATES, 1865.

Source:
NARA: U.S. National Archives and Records Administration. Digital Classroom: "The Fight for Equal Rights: Black soldiers in the Civil War." Available on-line. URL: www.archives.gov/digital_classroom/lessons/blacks_in_civil_war/blacks_in_civil_war.html. The introduction to this document also comes from the NARA website.

Confederate Congress, Act to Increase the Military Force of the Confederate States, 1865

Also known as the Negro Soldier Act, this act superceded the Confederate Conscription Act, passed February 17, 1864. It authorized slaves and free blacks to serve as armed soldiers in the Confederate army, and to receive the same benefits and treatment as "other troops in the same branch of the service." The act also authorized President Jefferson Davis to draft a total of 300,000 slaves into the Confederate army by calling on the Confederate states to enlist up to 25 percent of their male slave populations. The act was not an order of emancipation; it declared that slaves will remain slaves at the discretion of their owners.

At the onset of the Civil War, a small number of free black volunteers were employed as armed soldiers, but as the Confederate army became more organized, they were relegated to duties such as digging canals, trenches, and graves. In February of 1864, President Jefferson Davis issued the Confederate Conscription Act, drafting all free blacks, and up to 20,000 slaves, for employment by the Confederate army. Slaves were put to work digging trenches and canals, and building batteries and fortifications. Others acted as ambulance drivers, hospital workers, cooks, horse drivers, lumberjacks, foragers, servants, and gravediggers. According to the act, slave owners were to be compensated for their slaves' work and, in the event of a slave's death, reimbursed for the net worth of that worker. Following later consignment orders, it is estimated that the Confederate army eventually obtained the employment of more than 500,000 slaves

When the fighting grew intense, some Confederates suggested converting the slaves into soldiers, but far more worried that armed slaves would revolt. The opinion of Major General Howell Cobb explains why most Confederates were reluctant to arm the slave population: "I think the proposition to make soldiers of our slaves is the most pernicious idea that has been suggested since the war began . . . The moment you resort to negro [sic] soldiers your white soldiers will be lost to you. The day you make soldiers of them is the beginning of the end of the revolution. If slaves will make good soldiers our whole theory of slavery is wrong."

Only in the last year of the war did Confederate leaders begin to seriously consider using slaves as soldiers. Confederate forces were losing the war—they had suffered major defeats at the battles of Gettysburg, Vicksburg, and Nashville. In addition to their military losses, the army's lack of supplies and failing morale made desertion a serious problem. Desperate to replenish its army, the Confederate Congress passed the act authorizing the arming of slaves. Less than one month later, on April 9, 1865, the Civil War came to an end.

Whereas, the efficiency of the Army is greatly diminished by the withdrawal from the ranks of able-bodied soldiers to act as teamsters, and in various other capacities in which free negroes and slaves might be advantageously employed: Therefore,

The Congress of the Confederate States of America do enact, That all male free negroes and other free persons of color, not including those who are free under the treaty of Paris of eighteen hundred and three, or under the treaty with Spain of eighteen hundred and nineteen, resident in the Confederate States, between the ages of eighteen and fifty years, shall be held liable to perform such duties with the army, or in connection with the military defenses of the country, in the way of work upon fortifications or in Government works for the production or preparation of material of war, or in military hospitals, as the Secretary of War or the commanding general of the Trans-Mississippi Department may, from time to time, prescribe, and while engaged in the performance of such duties shall receive rations and clothing and compensation at the rate of eleven dollars a month. . . .

SEC. 2. That the Secretary of War is hereby authorized to employ for duties similar to those indicated in the preceding section of this act, as many male negro slaves, not to exceed twenty thousand, as in his judgment, the wants of the service may require, furnishing them, while so employed, with proper rations and clothing, under rules

and regulations to be established by him, and paying to the owners of said slaves such wages as may be agreed upon with said owners for their use and service, and in the event of the loss of any slaves while so employed, by the act of the enemy, or by escape to the enemy, or by death inflicted by the enemy, or by disease contracted while in any service required of said slaves, then the owners of the same shall be entitled to receive the full value of such slaves. . . .

SEC. 3. That when the Secretary of War shall be unable to procure the service of slaves in any military department in sufficient numbers for the necessities of the Department, upon the terms and conditions set forth in the preceding section, then he is hereby authorized to impress the services of as many male slaves, not to exceed twenty thousand, as may be required, from time to time, to discharge the duties indicated in the first section of this act . . . Provided, That if the owner have but one male slave between the age of eighteen and fifty, he shall not be impressed against the will of said owner: Provided further, That free negroes shall be first impressed, and if there should be a deficiency, it shall be supplied by the impressment of slaves according to the foregoing provisions: Provided further, That in making the impressment, not more than one of every five male slaves between the ages of eighteen and forty-five shall be taken from any owner. . . .

Source:
Dorothy Schneider and Carl J. Schneider. *An Eyewitness History: Slavery in America From Colonial Times to the Civil War.* New York: Facts On File, Inc., 2000.

Abraham Lincoln, Second Inaugural Address, 1865

Speech delivered on March 4, 1865, by Abraham Lincoln at his second presidential inauguration, outlining a philosophy of reconstruction as the U.S. Civil War (1861–65) drew to a close. The president appealed to the nation for a spirit of forgiveness, for a peace without hatred. In his famous and eloquent closing, Lincoln said, "With malice toward none, with charity for all . . . let us strive on to finish the work we are in, to bind up the nation's wounds . . . to do all which may achieve and cherish a just and lasting peace among ourselves and with all nations." Although Lincoln saw the end of the Civil War, he did not live to implement his plans for reconstruction.

Fellow-Countrymen:

At this second appearing to take the oath of the Presidential office there is less occasion for an extended address than there was at the first. Then a statement somewhat in detail of a course to be pursued seemed fitting and proper. Now, at the expiration of four years, during which public declarations have been constantly called forth on every point and phase of the great contest which still absorbs the attention and engrosses the energies of the nation, little that is new could be presented. The progress of our arms, upon which all else chiefly depends, is as well known to the public as to myself, and it is, I trust, reasonably satisfactory and encouraging to all. With high hope for the future, no prediction in regard to it is ventured.

On the occasion corresponding to this four years ago all thoughts were anxiously directed to an impending civil war. All dreaded it, all sought to avert it. While the inaugural address was being delivered from this place, devoted altogether to *saving* the Union without war, insurgent agents were in the city seeking to *destroy* it without war—seeking to dissolve the Union and divide effects by negotiation. Both parties depreciated war, but one of them would *make* war rather than let the nation survive, and the other would *accept* war rather than let it perish, and the war came.

One-eighth of the whole population were colored slaves, not distributed generally over the Union, but localized in the southern part of it. These slaves constituted a peculiar and powerful interest. All knew that this interest was somehow the cause of the war. To strengthen, perpetuate, and extend this interest was the object for which the insurgents would rend the Union even by war, while the Government claimed no right to do more than to restrict the territorial enlargement of it. Neither party expected for the war the magnitude or the duration which it has already attained. Neither anticipated that the *cause* of the conflict might cease with or even before the conflict itself should cease. Each looked for an easier triumph, and a result less fundamental and astounding. Both read the same Bible and pray to the same God, and each invokes His aid against the other. It may seem strange that any men should dare to ask a just God's assistance in wringing their bread from the sweat of other men's faces, but let us judge not, that we be not judged. The prayers of both could not be answered. That of neither has been answered fully. The Almighty has His own purposes. "Woe unto the world because of offenses; for it must needs be that offenses come, but woe to that man by whom the offense cometh." If we shall suppose that American slavery is one of those offenses which, in the providence of God, must needs come, but which, having continued through His appointed time, He now wills to remove, and that He gives to both North and South this terrible war as the woe due to those by whom the offense came, shall we discern therein any departure from those divine attributes which the believers in a living God always ascribe to Him? Fondly do we hope,

fervently do we pray, that this mighty scourge of war may speedily pass away. Yet, if God wills that it continue until all the wealth piled by the bondsman's two hundred and fifty years of unrequited toil shall be sunk, and until every drop of blood drawn with the lash shall be paid by another drawn with the sword, as was said three thousand years ago, so still it must be said "the judgments of the Lord are true and righteous altogether."

With malice toward none, with charity for all, with firmness in the right as God gives us to see the right, let us strive on to finish the work we are in, to bind up nation's wounds, to care for him who shall have borne the battle and for his widow and his orphan, to do all which may achieve and cherish a just and lasting peace among ourselves and with all nations.

Source:
Landmark Documents in American History, Facts On File, Inc.

Surrender Terms at Appomattox Court House, 1865

Terms governing surrender in the Civil War of the Confederacy's Army of Northern Virginia. Victorious Union general Ulysses S. Grant presented the terms to surrendering Confederate general Robert E. Lee on April 9, 1865, at Appomattox Court House, Virginia. They arranged for the immediate disposition of Confederate arms and property, permitting officers to retain their sidearms and horses. Lee's officers were required to pledge themselves and the men under their command not to take up arms against the U.S. government pending the war's conclusion. All of Lee's soldiers were to be allowed to return to their homes undisturbed by federal authority, provided that they abided by their pledge against insurrection. Lee composed a letter accepting Grant's terms. The surrender of the Army of Northern Virginia, the bulwark of the Confederate military effort, spelled the effective end of the Civil War.

―――――――――――⧫―――――――――――

Appomattox C. H., Va. Apr. 9th, 1865.
Gen. R. E. Lee, "Comd. C.S.A.

Gen.

In accordance with the substance of my letter to you of the 8th instant I propose to receive the surrender of the Army of N. Va. on the following terms, to-wit:

Rolls of all the officers and men to be made in duplicate, one copy to be given to an officer designated by me, the other to be retained by such officer or officers as you may designate. The officers to give their individual paroles not to take up arms against the Government of the United States until properly exchanged and each company or regimental commander sign a like parole for the men of their command.

The arms, artillery and public property to be parked and stacked and turned over to the officer appointed by me to receive them.

This will not embrace the side arms of the officers, nor their private horses or baggage. This done each officer and man will be allowed to return to their homes not to be disturbed by United States authority so long as they observe their paroles and the laws in force where they may reside.

Very respectfully, U. S. Grant, Lt Gl.

Source:
Eleanor S. Brockenbrough Library. The Museum of the Confederacy. Richmond, Virginia.

Jefferson Davis, Last Message to the People of the Confederacy, 1865

President Jefferson Davis's final message to the Confederate people, delivered on April 4, 1865, under the specter of the Confederacy's imminent defeat in the Civil War. The besieged Confederate government abandoned Richmond, its capital, for Danville, Virginia, on April 2. The next day the Union army occupied Richmond. On April 4, Davis, defiantly determined to continue the war despite the South's collapsing military and political situation, appealed to the Confederate people to summon the resolve, in the face of dispiriting reverses, to continue fighting. To buoy Southern morale, he suggested Richmond's fall actually benefited the Confederacy strategically, contending that General Robert E. Lee's Army of Northern Virginia, freed of responsibility for protecting the capital, would enjoy greater mobility. He implored his countrymen to show fortitude under adversity, lest the North conclude that its occupation of Richmond signaled the South's submission.

───────── ⚜ ─────────

Danville, Virginia, April 4, 1865.

To the People of the Confederate States of America.

The General in Chief of our Army has found it necessary to make such movements of the troops as to uncover the capital and thus involve the withdrawal of the Government from the city of Richmond.

It would be unwise, even were it possible, to conceal the great moral as well as material injury to our cause that must result from the occupation of Richmond by the enemy. It is equally unwise and unworthy of us, as patriots engaged in a most sacred cause, to allow our energies to falter, our spirits to grow faint, or our efforts to become relaxed under reverses, however calamitous. While it has been to us a source of national pride that for four years of unequaled warfare we have been able, in close proximity to the center of the enemy's power, to maintain the seat of our chosen Government free from the pollution of his presence; while the memories of the heroic dead who have freely given their lives to its defense must ever remain enshrined in our hearts; while the preservation of the capital, which is usually regarded as the evidence to mankind of separate national existence, was an object very dear to us, it is also true, and should not be forgotten, that the loss which we have suffered is not without compensation. For many months the largest and finest army of the Confederacy, under the command of a leader whose presence inspires equal confidence in the troops and the people, has been greatly trammeled by the necessity of keeping constant watch over the approaches to the capital, and has thus been forced to forego more than one opportunity for promising enterprise. The hopes and confidence of the enemy have been constantly excited by the belief that their possession of Richmond would be the signal for our submission to their rule, and relieve them from the burden of war, as their failing resources admonish them it must be abandoned if not speedily brought to a successful close. It is for us, my countrymen, to show by our bearing under reverses how wretched has been the self-deception of those who have believed us less able to endure misfortune with fortitude than to encounter danger with courage. We have now entered upon a new phase of a struggle the memory of which is to endure for all ages and to shed an increasing luster upon our country.

Relieved from the necessity of guarding cities and particular points, important but not vital to our defense, with an army free to move from point to point and strike in detail the detachments and garrisons of the enemy, operating on the interior of our own country, where supplies are more accessible, and where the foe will be far removed from his own base and cut off from all succor in case of reverse, nothing is now needed to render our triumph certain but the exhibition of our own unquenchable resolve. Let us but will it, and we are free; and who, in the light of the past, dare doubt your purpose in the future?

Animated by the confidence in your spirit and fortitude, which never yet has failed me, I announce to you, fellow-countrymen, that it is my purpose to maintain your cause with my whole heart and soul; that I will never consent to abandon to the enemy one foot of the soil of any one of the States of the Confederacy; that Virginia, noble State, whose ancient renown has been eclipsed by her still more glorious recent history, whose bosom has been bared to receive the main shock of this war, whose sons and daughters have exhibited heroism so sublime as to render her illustrious in all times to come—that Virginia, with the help of her people, and by the blessing of Providence, shall be held and defended, and no peace ever be made with the infamous invaders of her homes by the sacrifice of any of her rights or territory. If by stress of numbers we should ever be compelled to a temporary withdrawal from her limits, or those of any other border State, again and again will we return, until the baffled and exhausted enemy shall abandon in despair his endless and impossible task of making slaves of a people resolved to be free.

Let us not, then, despond, my countrymen; but, relying on the never-failing mercies and protecting care of our God, let us meet the foe with fresh defiance, with unconquered and unconquerable hearts.

Jeff'n Davis.

Source:

James D. Richardson, ed. *Messages and Papers of Jefferson Davis and the Confederacy: Including Diplomatic Correspondence, 1861–1865.* New York: Chelsea House, 2001.

Abraham Lincoln, Victory Speech from the White House, 1865

Speech delivered by President Abraham Lincoln at the White House on April 11, 1865. Lincoln celebrated the end of the Civil War and credited General Ulysses Grant and the Union forces with the victory. He turned quickly to the issue of Reconstruction and the plan already taking effect in Louisiana. Lincoln defended the plan, asking the rhetorical question: "Can Louisiana be brought into proper practical relation with the Union sooner by sustaining or by discarding her new state government?"

It followed, the presidential plan of Reconstruction issued by Abraham Lincoln on December 8, 1863, which offered to pardon most Rebels who were willing to take an oath of loyalty to the U.S. Constitution and to abide by federal laws and proclamations concerning slaves. At that time, Lincoln proposed that new state governments could be formed when a number equal to 10 percent of the state's voting population in 1860 took the prescribed oath. The program assumed that Reconstruction was a presidential, not congressional, function. Even as the war continued, Radical Republicans found the proposal too moderate; Congress instead passed the Wade-Davis Bill.

─────────── ∽⟨∾⟩∾ ───────────

We meet this evening, not in sorrow, but in gladness of heart. The evacuation of Petersburg and Richmond, and the surrender of the principal insurgent army, give hope of a righteous and speedy peace whose joyous expression can not be restrained. In the midst of this, however, He, from Whom all blessings flow, must not be forgotten. A call for a national thanksgiving is being prepared, and will be duly promulgated. Nor must those whose harder part gives us the cause of rejoicing, be overlooked. Their honors must not be parcelled out with others. I myself, was near the front, and had the high pleasure of transmitting much of the good news to you; but no part of the honor, for plan or execution, is mine. To Gen. Grant, his skillful officers, and brave men, all belongs. The gallant Navy stood ready, but was not in reach to take active part.

By these recent successes the re-inauguration of the national authority—reconstruction—which has had a large share of thought from the first, is pressed much more closely upon our attention. It is fraught with great difficulty. Unlike the case of a war between independent nations, there is no authorized organ for us to treat with. No one man has authority to give up the rebellion for any other man. We simply must begin with, and mould from, disorganized and discordant elements. Nor is it a small additional embarrassment that we, the loyal people, differ among ourselves as to the mode, manner, and means of reconstruction.

As a general rule, I abstain from reading the reports of attacks upon myself, wishing not to be provoked by that to which I can not properly offer an answer. In spite of this precaution, however, it comes to my knowledge that I am much censured for some supposed agency in setting up, and seeking to sustain, the new State Government of Louisiana. In this I have done just so much as, and no more than, the public knows. In the Annual Message of Dec. 1863 and accompanying Proclamation, I presented *a* plan of reconstruction (as the phrase goes) which, I promised, if adopted by any State, should be acceptable to, and sustained by, the Executive government of the nation. I distinctly stated that this was not the only plan which might possibly be acceptable; and I also distinctly protested that the Executive claimed no right to say when, or whether members should be admitted to seats in Congress from such States. This plan was, in advance, submitted to the then Cabinet, and distinctly approved by every member of it. One of them suggested that I should then, and in that connection, apply the Emancipation Proclamation to the theretofore excepted parts of Virginia and Louisiana; that I should drop the suggestion about apprenticeship for freed-people, and that I should omit the protest against my own power, in regard to the admission of members to Congress; but even he approved every part and parcel of the plan which has since been employed or touched by the action of Louisiana. The new constitution of Louisiana, declaring emancipation for the whole State, practically applies the Proclamation to the part previously excepted. It does not adopt apprenticeship for freed-people; and it is silent, as it could not well be otherwise, about the admission of members to Congress. So that, as it applies to Louisiana, every member of the Cabinet fully approved the plan. The Message went to Congress, and I received many commendations of the plan, written and verbal; and not a single objection to it, from any professed emancipationist, came to my knowledge, until after the news reached Washington that the people of Louisiana had begun to move in accordance with it. From about July 1862, I has corresponded with different persons, supposed to be interested, seeking a reconstruction of a State government for Louisiana. When the Message of 1863, with the plan before mentioned, reached New-Orleans, Gen. Banks wrote me that he was confident the people, with his military co-operation, would reconstruct, substantially on that plan. I wrote him, and some of them to try it; they tried it, and the result is known. Such only has been my agency in getting up the Louisiana government. As to sustaining it, my promise is out, as before stated. But, as bad promises are better broken than kept, I shall treat this as a bad promise, and break it, whenever I shall be convinced that keeping it is adverse to the public interest. But I have not yet been so convinced.

I have been shown a letter on this subject, supposed to be an able one, in which the writer expresses regret that my mind has not seemed to be definitely fixed on the question whether the seceded States, so called, are in the Union or out of it. It would perhaps, add astonishment to his regret, were he to learn that since I have found professed Union men endeavoring to make that question, I have *purposely* forborne any public expression upon it. As appears to me that question has not been, nor yet is, a practically material one, and that any discussion of it, while it thus remains practically immaterial, could have no effect other than the mischievous one of dividing our friends. As yet, whatever it may hereafter become, that question is bad, as the basis of a controversy, and good for nothing at all—a merely pernicious abstraction.

We all agree that the seceded States, so called, are out of their proper practical relation with the Union; and that the sole object of the government, civil and military, in regard to those States is to again get them into that proper practical relation. I believe it is not only possible, but in fact, easier, to do this, without deciding, or even considering, whether these states have even been out of the Union, than with it. Finding themselves safely at home, it would be utterly immaterial whether they had ever been abroad. Let us all join in doing the acts necessary to restoring the proper practical relations between these states and the Union; and each forever after, innocently indulge his own opinion whether, in doing the acts, he brought the States from without, into the Union, or only gave them proper assistance, they never having been out of it.

The amount of constituency, so to speak, on which the new Louisiana government rests, would be more satisfactory to all, if it contained fifty, thirty, or even twenty thousand, instead of only about twelve thousand, as it does. It is also unsatisfactory to some that the elective franchise is not given to the colored man. I would myself prefer that it were now conferred on the very intelligent, and on those who serve our cause as soldiers. Still the question is not whether the Louisiana government, as it stands, is quite all that is desirable. The question is "Will it be wiser to take it as it is, and help to improve it; or to reject, and disperse it?" "Can Louisiana be brought into proper practical relation with the Union *sooner* by *sustaining*, or by *discarding* her new State Government?"

Some twelve thousand voters in the heretofore slave-state of Louisiana have sworn allegiance to the Union, assumed to be the rightful political power of the State, held elections, organized a State government, adopted a free-state constitution, giving the benefit of public schools equally to black and white, and empowering the Legislature to confer the elective franchise upon the colored man. Their Legislature has already voted to ratify the constitutional amendment recently passed by Congress, abolishing slavery throughout the nation. These twelve thousand persons are thus fully committed to the Union, and to perpetual freedom in the state—committed to the very things, and nearly all the things the nation wants—and they ask the nations recognition, and it's assistance to make good their committal. Now, if we reject, and spurn them, we do our utmost to disorganize and disperse them. We in effect say to the white men "You are worthless, or worse—we will neither help you, nor be helped by you." To the blacks we say "This cup of liberty which these, your old masters, hold to your lips, we will dash from you, and leave you to the chances of gathering the spilled and scattered contents in some vague and undefined when, where, and how." If this course, discouraging and paralyzing both white and black, has any tendency to bring Louisiana into proper practical relations with the Union, I have, so far, been unable to perceive it. If, on the contrary, we recognize, and sustain the new government of Louisiana the converse of all this is made true. We encourage the hearts, and nerve the arms of the twelve thousand to adhere to their work, and argue for it, and proselyte for it, and fight for it, and feed it, and grow it, and ripen it to a complete success. The colored man too, in seeing all united for him, is inspired with vigilance, and energy, and daring, to the same end. Grant that he desires the elective franchise, will he not attain it sooner by saving the already advanced steps toward it, than by running backward over them? Concede that the new government of Louisiana is only to what it should be as the egg is to the fowl, we shall sooner have the fowl by hatching the egg than by smashing it? Again, if we reject Louisiana, we also reject one vote in favor of the proposed amendment to the national constitution. To meet this proposition, it has been argued that no more than three fourths of those States which have not attempted secession are necessary to validly ratify the amendment. I do not commit myself against this, further than to say that such a ratification would be questionable, and sure to be persistently questioned; while a ratification by three fourths of all the States would be unquestioned and unquestionable.

I repeat the question. "Can Louisiana be brought into proper practical relation with the Union *sooner* by *sustaining* or by *discarding* her new State Government?"

What has been said of Louisiana will apply generally to other States. And yet so great peculiarities pertain to each state; and such important and sudden changes occur in the same state; and, withal, so new and unprecedented is the whole case, that no exclusive, and inflexible plan can safely be prescribed as to details and colaterals. Such exclusive, and inflexible plan, would surely become a new entanglement. Important principles may, and must, be inflexible.

In the present "*situation*" as the phrase goes, it may be my duty to make some new announcement to the people of the South. I am considering, and shall not fail to act, when satisfied that action will be proper.

See also WADE-DAVIS BILL, 1864.

Source:

Abraham Lincoln, *Abraham Lincoln: Speeches and Writings, 1859–65,* New York: Library of America, 1989, pp. 697–701.

Reconstruction

Reconstruction Amendments, 1865, 1868, 1870

The purpose of these amendments to the U.S. Constitution was to take a step toward the ideal that all men are created equal. The Thirteenth Amendment abolished slavery, the Fourteenth Amendment defined citizenship, and the Fifteenth Amendment extended the federal vote to all American males over 21. However, interpretation of those amendments at times limited them and at times extended their reach.

Congress adopted the Thirteenth Amendment as the Civil War was drawing to a close in early 1865; it was ratified by a sufficient number of states in 1865. Lincoln's Emancipation Proclamation in 1863 did not actually free any slaves because it applied only to parts of the Confederacy not under Union control. This article represented the first major reform amendment as opposed to one correcting a technical defect that aimed at state matters. It not only freed the slaves; it established federal protection against peonage (involuntary servitude for such reasons as debt or threat of exposure for illegal aliens). By holding that the Confederate states had never left the Union, Congress required 27 states to ratify the Amend-

ment. Two slaveholding border states, Maryland and Delaware, had remained in the Union and refused to ratify. However, eight Reconstruction governments among the 11 former Confederate states also ratified the amendment, and it went into effect December 18, 1865. A short time later, Congress refused to recognize these provisional governments. However, their ratification was allowed to stand. Although slavery itself was outlawed, Southern governments instituted black codes that in effect could re-enslave African Americans. In 1867, Congress sought to overcome the black codes with the Peonage Act, which declared that holding any person to service or labor under the peonage system is unlawful and forever prohibited. It defined peonage as the "voluntary or involuntary service or labor of any persons . . . in liquidation of any debt or obligation."

The Fourteenth Amendment to the Constitution, adopted in 1868, overcame the Dred Scott decision by clarifying that former slaves were citizens of both the United States and the individual states. By adopting it, Congress intended to make sure that federal civil rights laws would be constitutional. In addition, the amendment required the states to extend due process of law and equal protection of the laws to all persons.

This amendment epitomized a shift in authority from the states to the national government. Nevertheless, beginning with the Slaughterhouse Cases in 1873, the Supreme Court rejected until well into the 20th century the notion that this amendment made the Bill of Rights apply to the states as well as to the federal government. The decade following saw a further shift in the use of this amendment: to protect private property from state regulation. In the mid-20th century, the amendment was used to invalidate racial segregation and discrimination against women. However, the Rehnquist Court has once again elevated state power, and the debate over the "real" meaning of the Fourteenth Amendment continues into the 21st century.

This amendment also provided for apportionment of members of the U.S. House of Representative on the basis of the total population—without regard for race—within a state, wiping out the constitutional clause establishing that five slaves would count as three persons in apportioning representatives. The second part of the Fourteenth Amendment, reducing representation to states that denied the vote to adult male citizens, was never applied. Sections three and four referred to re-enfranchising former Confederates and the public debt—affirming Union debts while invalidating Confederate claims, including those for emancipated slaves.

The Fourteenth Amendment also barred more than 150,000 Rebels from holding civil or military office unless Congress, by a vote, removed their disabilities. Congress proceeded to pass individual amnesty acts, especially for those willing to join the Radical Republicans, but public demand grew for broader action, and general amnesty became an issue in the presidential campaign of 1872. Congress passed a general amnesty on May 22, 1872, re-enfranchising most supporters of the Confederacy. Only some 500 to 750 Confederate officials were excepted from the 1872 act, and all disabilities were removed by 1898.

However, the Fourteenth Amendment did not guarantee suffrage for African Americans. When it became clear in 1869 that another amendment was required, the issue of including women was raised. The argument prevailed that it was more important for black males to vote than to tie one controversial franchise to another, and women were excluded. Until the passage of the Twenty-fourth Amendment in 1964 and the Voting Rights Act of 1965, Southern whites continued to deny blacks the vote through various means, including poll taxes, literacy and property tests, or residence and registration "requirements." Previously, the Supreme Court outlawed some tactics like the "grandfather clause," which exempted from various requirements anyone whose ancestor had the right to vote before 1867 (declared unconstitutional in 1915), and white primaries (declared unconstitutional in 1944).

Thirteenth Amendment to the U.S. Constitution, 1865

AMENDMENT 13
SLAVERY ABOLISHED (1865)

Section 1. Neither slavery nor involuntary servitude, except as a punishment for crime whereof the party shall have been duly convicted, shall exist within the United States, or any place subject to their jurisdiction.

Section 2. Congress shall have power to enforce this article by appropriate legislation.

Fourteenth Amendment to the U.S. Constitution, 1868

AMENDMENT 14
RIGHTS OF CITIZENS (1868)

Section 1. Citizenship Defined All persons born or naturalized in the United States. and subject to the jurisdiction thereof, are citizens of the United States and of the state wherein they reside. No state shall make or enforce any law which shall abridge the privileges or immunities of citizens of the United States; nor shall any state deprive any person of life, liberty, or property, without due process of law; nor deny to any person within its jurisdiction the equal protection of the laws.

Section 2. Apportioning Representatives Representatives shall be apportioned among the several states according to their respective numbers, counting the whole number of persons in each state [excluding Indians not taxed]. But when the right to vote at any election for the choice of electors for President and Vice President of the United States, Representatives in Congress, the executive and judicial officer of a state, or the members of the legislature thereof, is denied to any of the [male] inhabitants of such state, [being twenty-one years of age] and citizens of the United States, or in any way abridged, except for participation in rebellion, or other crime, the basis of representation therein shall be reduced in the proportion which the number of such [male] citizens shall bear to the whole number of male citizens [twenty-one years of age] in such state.

Section 3. Disability for Insurrection No person shall be a Senator or Representative in Congress, or elector of President and Vice President, or hold any office, civil or military, under the United States, or under any state, who, having previously taken an oath, as a member of Congress, or as an officer of the United States, or as a member of any state legislature, or as an executive or judicial officer of any state, to support the Constitution of the United States, shall have engaged in insurrection or rebellion against the same, or given aid or comfort to the enemies thereof. But Congress may by vote of two thirds of each house, remove such disability.

Section 4. Public Debt The validity of the public debt of the United States, authorized by law, including debts incurred for payment of pensions and bounties for services in suppressing insurrection or rebellion, shall not be questioned. But neither the United States nor any state shall assume or pay any debt or obligation incurred in aid of insurrection or rebellion against the United States [or any claim for the loss or emancipation of any slave]; but all such debts, obligations and claims shall be held illegal and void.

Section 5. Enforcement The Congress shall have power to enforce, by appropriate legislation, the provisions of this article.

Fifteenth Amendment to the U.S. Constitution, 1870

AMENDMENT 15
RIGHT OF SUFFRAGE (1870)

Section 1. The right of citizens of the United States to vote shall not be denied or abridged by the United States or by any state on account of race, color, or previous condition of servitude.

Section 2. The Congress shall have power to enforce this article by appropriate legislation.

Source:

Lewis Paul Todd and Merle Curti, eds. *Triumph of the American Nation.* Orlando, Fla.: Harcourt Brace Jovanovich, 1986.

Freedmen's Bureau Act of 1865

Legislation enacted by the U.S. Congress on March 3, 1865, to establish a "bureau of refugees, freedmen and abandoned lands" to aid some 4 million destitute, newly freed slaves. In 1866 Congress, overriding the veto of President Andrew Johnson, who thought the bureau was unconstitutional and unnecessary, extended its life and scope. Organized under the War Department and headed by General O. O. Howard, the bureau provided relief for the needy—both black and white—assigned homesteads on public lands, supervised labor contracts to protect illiterate former slaves, established hospitals and schools, and protected civil rights for freedmen. By the time the bureau ceased operations in 1872, most of its duties had been abolished or adopted by other agencies.

An Act
To establish a Bureau for the Relief of Freedman and Refugees.

Be it enacted by the Senate and House of Representatives of the United States of America in Congress assembled, That there is here by established in the War Department, to continue during the present war of rebellion, and for one year thereafter, a bureau of refugees, freedmen, and abandoned lands, to which shall be committed, as hereinafter provided, the supervision and management of all abandoned lands, and the control of all subjects relating to refugees and freedmen from rebel states, or from any district of country within the territory embraced in the operations of the army, under such rules and regulations as may be prescribed by the head of the bureau and approved by the President. The said bureau shall be under the management and control of a commissioner to be appointed by the President, by and with the advice and consent of the Senate, whose compensation shall be three thousand dollars per annum, and such number of clerks as may be assigned to him by the Secretary of War, no exceeding one chief clerk, two of the fourth class, two of the third class, and five of the first class. And the Commissioner and all persons appointed under this act, shall, before entering upon their duties, take the oath of office prescribed in an act entitled "An act to prescribe an oath of office, and for other purposes," approved July second, eighteen hundred and sixty-two, and the commissioner and the chief clerk shall, before entering upon their duties, give bonds to the treasurer of the United States, the former in the sum of fifty thousand dollars, and the latter in the sum of ten thousand dollars, conditioned for the faithful discharge of their duties respectively, with securities to be approved as sufficient by the Attorney-General, which bonds shall be filed in the office of the first comptroller of the treasury, to be by him put in suit for the benefit of any injured party upon any breach of the conditions thereof.

Sec. 2. And be it further enacted, That the Secretary of War may direct such issues of provisions, clothing, and fuel, as he may deem needful for the immediate and temporary shelter and supply of destitute and suffering refugees and freedmen and their wives and children, under such rules and regulations as he may direct.

Sec. 3. And be it further enacted, That the President may, by and with the advice and consent of the Senate, appoint an assistant commissioner for each of the states declared to be in insurrection, not exceeding ten in number, who shall, under the direction of the commissioner, aid in the execution of the provisions of this act; and he shall give a bond to the Treasurer of the United States, in the sum of twenty thousand dollars, in the form and manner prescribed in the first section of this act. Each of said commissioners shall receive an annual salary of two thousand five hundred dollars in full compensation for all his services. And any military officer may be detailed and assigned to duty under this act without increase of pay or allowances. The commissioner shall, before the commencement of each regular session of congress, make full report of his proceedings with exhibits of the state of his accounts to the President, who shall communicate the same to congress, and shall also make special reports whenever required to do so by the President or either house of congress; and the assistant commissioners shall make quarterly reports of their proceedings to the commissioner, and also such other special reports as from time to time may be required.

Sec. 4. *And be it further enacted,* That the commissioner, under the direction of the President, shall have authority to set apart, for the use of loyal refugees and freedmen, such tracts of land within the insurrectionary states as shall have been abandoned, or to which the United States shall have acquired title by confiscation or sale, or otherwise, and to every male citizen, whether refugee or freedman, as aforesaid, there shall be assigned not more than forty acres of such land, and the person to whom it was so assigned shall be protected in the use and enjoyment of the land for the term of three years at an annual rent not exceeding six per centum upon the value of such land, as it was appraised by the state authorities in the year eighteen hundred and sixty, for the purpose of taxation, and in case no such appraisal can be found, then the rental shall be based upon the estimated value of the land in said year, to be ascertained in such manner as the commissioner may by regulation prescribe. At the end of said term, or at any time during said term, the occupants of any parcels so assigned may purchase the land and receive such title thereto as the United States can convey, upon paying therefor the value of the land, as ascertained and fixed for the purpose of determining the annual rent aforesaid.

Sec. 5. *And be it further enacted,* That all acts and parts of acts inconsistent with the provisions of this act, are hereby repealed.

Source:
Statutes at Large, Vol. 13, pp. 507–509.

Three Views on Reconstruction, 1865, 1866

The historic 39th Congress convened in December 1865 to confront the issue of reuniting the divided nation following the Civil War. President Andrew Johnson favored a lenient policy aimed at hasty restoration of the South to the Union, arguing that a Draconian approach would postpone national healing by perpetuating enmities and envenoming the defeated Confederate states. The Radical Republicans, led by

Pennsylvania representative Thaddeus Stevens, bitterly opposed Johnson's conciliatory plan. They asserted a clear congressional prerogative to determine the method of reconstruction. On December 18, 1865, Stevens gave a speech before the U.S. House of Representatives urging a harsh policy of Reconstruction toward the defeated Confederacy. In his speech Stevens advocated treating the Southern states as conquered provinces. He disparaged the constitutional theory that the Confederate states, though insurrectionist, had never technically left the Union. To deny the North's right to treat the traitorous states as conquered belligerents, he contended, was mockery. He urged a policy of military rule in the South, advocated enfranchising emancipated blacks, demanded severe punishment of Confederate leaders, and asserted Congress's supremacy in deciding how the South should be restored to the Union.

Union Republican Henry Raymond of New York followed with a speech before the U.S. House of Representatives on December 21, 1865, advocating a moderate Reconstruction policy toward the defeated Confederacy. Raymond, who entered national politics from his editorship of the *New York Times,* delivered the moderates' response to congressional Radical Republicans. He endorsed President Andrew Johnson's lenient plan for national restoration following the Civil War and rejected Stevens's "conquered province" theory on grounds that the Confederate states had never actually separated from the Union because the Constitution granted no legal right of secession. In an emotional plea for national healing and reconciliation, Raymond appealed for an end to the hatreds engendered by the war, urging reunion on the basis of a common commitment to freedom and prosperity in the United States.

On January 6, 1866, Republican representative Samuel Shellabarger delivered a speech to the House of Representatives outlining the moderate Republicans' position for readmitting Southern states to the Union. The plan cut a middle road between the proposals of the Radical Republicans and President Andrew Johnson. Shellabarger agreed with the Radicals that the South had disavowed their rights under the U.S. Constitution, as they had repudiated the document by rebelling against the Union. While demanding that only Congress could allow readmission to the Union, he did not call on Johnson to dissolve his reorganization plan. Shellabarger did insist, however, that the new constitutions of the Southern states must include "irreversible guarantees for the rights of freedmen."

These speeches were interrupted at times by questions and challenges. These have not been excerpted. The full text of these speeches including the remarks of others is in *Landmark Documents in American History,* www.facts onfile.com.

Thaddeus Stevens, Speech on Reconstruction, 1865

Fellow Citizens: In compliance with your request I have come to give my views of the present condition of the rebel States; of the proper mode of reorganizing the Government, and the future prospects of the Republic. During the whole progress of the war . . . I knew that the loyal North would conquer the rebel despots who sought to destroy freedom. But since that traitorous confederation has been subdued, and we have entered upon the work of "reconstruction" or "restoration," I cannot deny that my heart has become sad at the gloomy prospects before us.

Four years of bloody and expensive war waged against the United States by eleven States, under a government called the "Confederate States of America" to which they acknowledged allegiance, have overthrown all governments within those States, which could be acknowledged as legitimate by the Union. The armies of the Confederate States having been conquered and subdued, and their territories possessed by the United States, it becomes necessary to establish governments therein, which shall be republican in "form and principles, and form a more perfect union" with the parent government. It is desirable that such a course should be pursued as to exclude from those governments every vestige of human bondage and render the same forever impossible in this nation, and to take care that no principles of self-destruction shall be incorporated therein. . . . We hold it to be the duty of the Government to inflict condign punishment on the rebel belligerents, and so weaken their hands that they can never again endanger the Union; and so reform their municipal institutions as to make them republican in spirit as well as in name.

We especially insist that the property of the chief rebels should be seized and appropriated to the payment of the national debt, caused by the unjust and wicked war which they instigated. . . .

How can such punishments be inflicted and such forfeitures produced without doing violence to established principles?

Two positions have been suggested.

1st To treat those States as never having been out of the Union, because the Constitution forbids secession, and, therefore, a fact forbidden by law could not exist.

2nd To accept the position in which they placed themselves as severed from the Union; an independent government *de facto,* and an alien enemy to be dealt with according to the laws of war.

✧　　✧　　✧

. . .That Government raised large armies, and by its formidable power, compelled the nations of the civilized world as well as our Government, to acknowledge them as an independent belligerent, entitled by the law of nations to be considered as engaged in a public war, and not merely in an insurrection. It is idle to deny that we treated them as a belligerent entitled to all the rights and subject to all the liabilities of an alien enemy. We blockaded their ports, which is an undoubted belligerent right; the extent of coast blockaded, marked the acknowledged extent of their territory—the territory criminally acquired but *de facto* theirs. We acknowledged their sea-rovers as privateers and not as pirates, by ordering their captive crews to be treated as prisoners of war. . . . The Confederate States were for four years what they claimed to be—an alien enemy in all their rights and liabilities. To say that they were states under the protection of that Constitution which they were rending, and within the Union which they were assaulting with bloody defeats, simply because they became belligerents through crime, is making theory overrule fact to an absurd degree. . . . The United States, if not obliged so to do, has a right to treat them as an alien enemy now conquered, and subject to all the liabilities of a vanquished foe.

. . . Let us inquire which position is best for the United States. . . .

In reconstruction, therefore, no reform can be effected in the Southern States if they have never left the Union. But reformation *must* be effected; the foundation of their institutions, both political, municipal, and social *must* be broken up and *relaid,* or all our blood and treasure have been spent in vain. This can only be done by treating and holding them as a conquered people. Then all things which we can desire to do follow with logical and legitimate authority. . . .

I do not touch on the question of Negro suffrage. If in the Union, the States have long ago regulated that, and for the Central Government to interfere with it would be mischievous impertinence. If they are to be admitted as new States they must form their own Constitutions; and no enabling act could dictate its terms. . . . Whether those who have fought our battles shall all be allowed to vote, or only those of a paler hue, I leave to be discussed in the future when Congress can take legitimate cognizance of it.

✧　　✧　　✧

. . . We propose to confiscate all the estate of every rebel belligerent whose estate was worth $10,000, or whose land exceeded two hundred acres in quantity. Policy if not justice would require that the poor, the ignorant, and the coerced should be forgiven. They followed the example and teachings of their wealthy and intelligent neighbors.. The rebellion would never have originated with them. Fortunately those who would thus escape form a large majority of the people, though possessing but a small portion of the wealth. The proportion of those exempt compared with the punished would be I believe about nine-tenths.

There are about six millions of freemen in the South. The number of acres of land is 465,000,000. Of this those who own above two hundred acres each, number about 70,000 persons, holding in the aggregate (together with the States) about 394,000,000 acres, leaving for all the others below 200 each about 71,000,000 of acres. By thus forfeiting the estates of the leading rebels, the Government would have 394,000,000 of acres beside their town property, and yet nine-tenths of the people would remain untouched. Divide this land into convenient farms. Give if you please forty acres to each adult male freedman. Suppose there are one million of them. That would require 40,000,000 of acres, which deducted from 394,000,000 leaves three hundred and fifty-four millions of acres for sale. Divide it into suitable farms and sell it to the highest bidders. I think it, including town property, would average at least ten dollars per acre. That would produce $3,540,000,000—Three billions, five hundred and forty millions of dollars.

Let that be applied as follows to wit: 1. Invest $300,000,000 in six percent government bonds, and add the interest semi-annually to the pensions of those who have become entitled by this villainous war. 2. Appropriate $200,000,000 to pay the damages done to loyal men North and South by the rebellion. 3. Pay the residue being $3,040,000,000 towards the payment of the National debt.

❖ ❖ ❖

The only argument of the Restorationists is, that the States could not and did not go out of the Union because the Constitution forbids it. By the same reasoning you could prove that no crime ever existed. No man ever committed murder for the law forbids it. He is a shallow reasoner who could make theory overrule fact!

❖ ❖ ❖

I assert that upon that theory not a Slave has been liberated; not a Slave law has been abrogated; but on the "Restoration" the whole Slave code is in legal force. Slavery was protected by our Constitution in every State in the Union where it existed. While they remained under that protection no power in the Federal Government could abolish Slavery. . . . The laws of war enabled us to declare every bondman free, so long as we held them in military possession. And the conqueror, through Congress, may declare them forever emancipated. But if the States are "States in the Union," then when war ceases they resume their positions with all their privileges untouched. . . .

The President says to the rebel States "before you can participate in the government you must abolish Slavery and reform your election laws." *That* is the command of a Conqueror. *That* is Reconstruction not Restoration— Reconstruction too by assuming the powers of Congress. This theory will lead to melancholy results. Nor can the constitutional amendment abolishing Slavery ever be ratified by three-fourths of the States, if *they* are States to be counted. Bogus Conventions of those States may vote for it. But no Convention honestly and fairly elected will ever do it. The frauds will not permanently avail. The cause of Liberty must rest on a firmer basis. Counterfeit governments like the Virginia, Louisiana, Tennessee, Mississippi, and Arkansas pretenses, will be disregarded by the sober sense of the people, by future law, and by the courts. "Restoration" is replanting the seeds of rebellion, which within the next quarter of a century will germinate and produce the same bloody strife which has just ended.

. . . This plan would, no doubt, work a radical reorganization in southern institutions, habits, and manners. It is intended to revolutionize their principles and feelings. This may startle feeble minds and shake weak nerves. So do all great improvements in the political and moral world. It requires a heavy impetus to drive forward a sluggish people. When it was first proposed to free the slaves, and arm the blacks, did not half the nation tremble? The prim conservatives, the snobs, and the male waiting-maids in Congress were in hysterics.

The whole fabric of southern society *must* be changed, and never can it be done if this opportunity is lost. Without this, this Government can never be, as it never has been, a true republic. . . .

If the South is ever to be a safe republic let her lands be cultivated by the toil of the owners or the free labor of intelligent citizens. This must be done even though it drive her nobility into exile. If they go, all the better.

❖ ❖ ❖

Let us forget all parties, and build on the broad platform of "reconstructing" the Government out of the conquered territory, converted into new and free States, and admitted into the Union by the sovereign power of Congress, with another plank—"The Property of the Rebels shall Pay Our National Debt, *and indemnify freedmen and loyal sufferers*" and that under no circumstances will we suffer the National debt to be repudiated, or the interest scaled below the contract rates; or permit any part of the rebel debt to be assumed by the nation.

Let all who approve of these principles rally with us. Let all others go with Copperheads and rebels. Those will be the opposing parties. Young men, this duty devolves on you. Would to God, if only for that, that I were still in the prime of life, that I might aid you to fight through this last and greatest battle of freedom.

Henry J. Raymond, Speech on Reconstruction, 1865

* * *

. . . I am glad to assume and to believe that there is not a member of this House, nor a man in this country, who does not wish, from the bottom of his heart, to see the day speedily come when we shall have this nation—the great American Republic—again united, more harmonious in its action than it has ever been, and forever one and indivisible. We in this Congress are to devise the means to restore its union and its harmony, to perfect its institutions, and to make it in all its parts and in all its action, through all time to come, too strong, too wise, and too free ever to invite or ever to permit the hand of rebellion again to be raised against it.

* * *

I cannot believe that these States have ever been out of the Union, or that they are now out of the Union. I cannot believe that they ever have been, or are now, in any sense a separate Power. If they were, sir, how and when did they become so? . . . by what specific act, and at what precise time, any one of these States took itself out of the American Union. Was it by the ordinance of secession? I think we all agree that an ordinance of secession passed by any State of this Union is simply a nullity, because it encounters in its practical operation the Constitution of the United States, which is the supreme law of the land. It could have no legal, actual force or validity. It could not operate to effect any actual change in the relations of the State adopting it to the national Government, still less to accomplish the removal of that State from the sovereign jurisdiction of the Constitution of the United States.

Well, sir, did the resolutions of these States, the declarations of their officials, the speeches of members of their Legislatures, or the utterances of their press accomplish the result? Certainly not. They could not possibly work any change whatever in the relations of these States to the General Government. All their ordinances and all their resolutions were simply declarations of a purpose to secede. . . . After declaring that intention, they proceeded to carry it into effect. How? By war. By sustaining their purpose by arms against the force which the United States brought to bear against it. Did they sustain it? Were their arms victorious? If they were, then their secession was an accomplished fact. If not, it was nothing more than an abortive attempt—a purpose unfulfilled. This, then, is simply a question of fact, and we all know what the fact is.

They did not succeed. They failed to maintain their ground by force of arms—in other words, they failed to secede.

. . . I think I need not argue any further the position that the rebel States have never for one moment, by any ordinances of secession, or by any successful war, carried themselves beyond the rightful jurisdiction of the Constitution of the United States. They have interrupted for a time the practical enforcement and exercise of that jurisdiction; they rendered it impossible for a time for this Government to enforce obedience to its laws; but there has never been an hour when this Government, or this Congress, or this House, or the gentleman from Pennsylvania [Thaddeus Stevens] himself, ever conceded that those States were beyond the jurisdiction of the Constitution and laws of the United States.

. . . What the States did was to endeavor to interpose their State authority between the individuals in rebellion and the Government of the United States, which assumed, and which would carry out the assumption, to declare those individuals traitors for their acts. The individuals in the States who were in rebellion, it seems to me, were the only parties who under the Constitution and laws of the United States could incur the penalties of treason. I know of no law, I know of nothing in the Constitution of the United States, I know of nothing in any recognized or established code of international law, which can punish a State as a State for any act it may perform. It is certain that our Constitution assumes nothing of the kind. It does not deal with States, except in one or two instances, such as elections of members of Congress, and the election of electors of President and Vice President.

Indeed, the main feature which distinguishes the Union under the Constitution from the old Confederation is this, that whereas the old Confederation did deal with States directly, making requisitions upon them for supplies and relying upon them for the execution of its laws, the Constitution of the United States, in order to form a more perfect Union, made its laws binding on the individual citizens of the several States, whether living in one State or in another. . . .

. . . Let me next cite some of the consequences which, it seems to me, must follow the acceptance of his position. If, as he asserts, we have been waging war with an independent Power, with a separate nation, I cannot see how we can talk of treason in connection with our recent conflict. . . .

* * *

. . . If that confederacy was an independent Power, a separate nation, it had the right to contract debts; and we, having overthrown and conquered that independent Power, according to the theory of the gentleman from Pennsylvania, would become the successors, the inheritors, of its debts and assets, and we must pay them.

*   *   *

Now, if according to the view I have presented, we are to deal with those States as States within the Union, the next question that recurs is, *how* are we to deal with them? . . .I think we have a full and perfect right to require certain conditions, in the nature of guarantees for the future, and that right rests, primarily and technically, on the surrender we may and must require at their hands. . . . In a political sense a surrender implies more than the transfer of the arms used on the field of battle. It implies, in the case of civil war, a surrender of the principles and doctrines, of all the weapons and agencies, by which the war has been carried on. The military surrender was made on the field of battle, to our generals as the agents and representatives of the Commander-in-Chief of the armies of the United States. . . .

*   *   *

Why do we seek in this and all similar cases a surrender of the principles for which they fought? It is that they may never again be made the basis of controversy and rebellion against the Government of the United States.

Now, what are those principles which should be thus surrendered? The principle of State sovereignty is one of them. It was the cornerstone of the rebellion—at once its animating spirit, and its fundamental basis. . . . Now there is another thing to be surrendered by the defeated rebellion, and that is the obligation to pay the rebel war debt.

*   *   *

There is another thing which we have the right to require; and that is the prohibition of slavery. We have the right to require them to do this, not only in their State constitutions, but in the Constitution of the United States. And we have required it, and it has been conceded. They have also conceded that Congress may make such laws as may be requisite to carry that prohibition into effect, which includes such legislation as may be required to secure for them protection of their civil and personal rights—their "right to life, liberty, and the pursuit of happiness." This I am sure the gentleman will concede to be a substantial guarantee—one placed beyond the power of any State to recall or repeal.

These things the President of the United States has deemed it his right as Commander-in-Chief of the armies of the United States, to demand at the hands of the States which have been defeated in their attempt to separate themselves from the Union, as the condition of relaxing the bonds of military authority over them and restoring to them again the control of their local State affairs. He made these the conditions upon which they would be allowed, so far as his rightful authority extended, to resume the practical exercise of their functions as members of the Union, which had been suspended by their rebellion. . . . I am here to act with those who seek to complete the restoration of the Union, as I have acted with those through the last four years who have sought to maintain its integrity and prevent its destruction. I shall say no word and do no act and give no vote to recognize its division, or to postpone or disturb its rapidly-approaching harmony and peace. . . .

. . . I would exact of them all needed and all just guarantees for their future loyalty to the Constitution and laws of the United States. I would exact from them, or impose upon them through the constitutional legislation of Congress, and by enlarging and extending, if necessary, the scope and powers of the Freedmen's Bureau, proper care and protection for the helpless and friendless freedmen, so lately their slaves. I would exercise a rigid scrutiny into the character and loyalty of the men whom they may send to Congress, before I allowed them to participate in the high prerogative of legislating for the nation. But I would seek to allay rather than stimulate the animosities and hatred, however just they may be, to which the war has given rise. But for our own sake as well as for theirs I would not visit upon them a policy of confiscation which has been discarded in the policy and practical conduct of every civilized nation on the face of the globe.

I believe it important for us as well as for them that we should cultivate friendly relations with them, that we should seek the promotion of their interests as part and parcel of our own. We have been their enemies in war, in peace let us show ourselves their friends. Now that slavery has been destroyed—that prolific source of all our alienations, all our hatreds, and all our disasters—there is nothing longer to make us foes. They have the same interests, the same hopes, the same aspirations that we have. They are one with us; we must share their sufferings and they will share our advancing prosperity. They have been punished as no community was ever punished before for the treason they have committed. I trust, sir, the day will come ere long when all traces of this great conflict will be effaced, except those which mark the blessings that follow in its train.

I hope and believe we shall soon see the day when the people of the southern States will show us, by evidences that we cannot mistake, that they have returned, in all sincerity and good faith, to their allegiance to the Union; that they intend to join henceforth with us in promoting its prosperity, in defending the banner of its glory, and in fighting the battles of democratic freedom, not only here, but wherever the issue may be forced upon our acceptance. I rejoice with heartfelt satisfaction that we have in these seats of power—in the executive department and in these halls of Congress—men who will cooperate for the attainment of these great and beneficent ends. I trust they will act with wisdom; I know they will act from no other motives than those of patriotism and love of their fellowmen.

Samuel Shellabarger, Speech on Reconstruction, 1866

I shall inquire whether the Constitution deals with States. I shall discuss the question whether an organized rebellion against a Government is an organized "State" in that Government; whether that which cannot *become* a "State" until all its officers have sworn to support the Constitution, *remains* a State after they have all sworn to overthrow that Constitution; and if I find it does continue to be a State after that, then I shall strive to ascertain whether it will so continue to be a government, a State, after, by means of universal treason, it has ceased to have any constitution, laws, Legislature, courts, or citizens in it.

What is before this Congress—by far the most momentous constitutional question ever here considered—I at once condense and affirm in a single sentence.

It is under our Constitution possible to, and the late rebellion did in fact, so overthrow and usurp in the insurrectionary States the loyal State governments as that, during such usurpation, such States and their people ceased to have any of the rights or powers of government as States of this Union; and this loss of the rights and powers of government was such that the United States may and ought to assume and exercise local powers of the lost State governments, and may control the readmission of such States to their powers of government in this Union, subject to and in accordance with the obligation to "guaranty to each State a republican form of government."

❖   ❖   ❖

What, then, is required to constitute a State by the law of nations?

We answer:

1. "A fixed abode and definite territory belonging to the people who occupy it." (Wheaton 33.)

2. "A society of men united together for the purpose of promoting their mutual safety and advantage by their combined strength." (*Ibid.* 32.)

3. "The legal idea of a State, necessarily implies that of habitual obedience of its members to those in whom the superiority is vested." (*Ibid.* 33.)

This third necessary element of a State is the only important one in this discussion. . . .

❖   ❖   ❖

I might add to these all the writers on public law for centuries, in confirmation of what is self-evident without proof, that there can be no State where the people do not habitually obey the laws. For four hundred years the unanimous conscience and common sense of the civilized world has refused to recognize the existence of a people who were habitually disobedient to their own laws, or the law of nations. Such a people is blotted out.

Now, surely, if habitual obedience to law "was necessary to the legal idea of a State," even under the vague and general precepts of the international code, it will not be insisted that habitual, persistent, and universal disobedience will be tolerated by the well-defined, express, and rigorous provisions of the American Constitution in the citizens of one of its States.

❖   ❖   ❖

Surely, Mr. Chairman, it is not too much to say that even under the settled precepts of public law those eleven districts, called "confederate States," ceased to be States. . . .

❖   ❖   ❖

. . . That which is required . . . in order to constitute a State of our Union, is—1. Its citizens must owe, acknowledge, and render supreme and habitual allegiance and obedience to the Constitution, laws, and treaties of the United States in all Federal matters, these being the supreme laws to the States and their citizens. (Constitution, article VI.)

2. All "the members of the State Legislatures, and its executive and judicial officers, shall be bound by oath or affirmation to support the Constitution" of the United States. (Constitution, article VI.)

3. That the United States shall have so "admitted it into this Union" (Constitution, article V, section 3) as to have assumed "to guaranty to it a republican form of government, and to protect it against invasion, and," on application, "against domestic violence."

4. And by such recognition and "admission into this Union" to have secured to it, as a body-politic, or "State," certain rights of participation in the control of the Federal Government; which rights I shall name hereafter. (See also 1 Bishop on Criminal Law, sections 128 to 137, inclusive.)

No one who can read the Constitution will deny that each State in this Union must have every one of these properties before it can *commence* to exist in the Union, because the Constitution so declares. Now the question I consider is, whether if shall *continue* to be a State, in the sense that it holds the powers and rights of a State, after it has lost every property which it must have before it could *commence* to exist in the Union.

❖   ❖   ❖

The Constitution. It deals with States, in the way of imposing restraints and obligations upon them as States, in the following matters: regulating commerce among the States; requiring Representatives, also United States Senators, to reside in their respective States; prohibiting States from entering into any treaty, alliance, or confederation, coining money, emitting bills of credit [etc.].

❖   ❖   ❖

My object, Mr. Chairman, in reciting these fifty or more supremely important provisions of the Constitution, in every one of which it is evident, both by the nature and express terms of the provisions themselves, and by the innumerable adjudications of the courts, that the Constitution "deals with" the States, as such, was not the frivolous one of showing that there were more than "one or two" of these. My purpose was the higher one of showing how baseless that argument was which was based upon the assertion that the Constitution did not deal with States but individuals only. . . .

❖   ❖   ❖

. . . The most solemn and deliberate action of your Government in all its departments, and recently all its actions, proceeds upon the assumption that these rebel States had lost all the rights of States.

❖   ❖   ❖

The President has assumed that the rebel States ceased to be States in the sense I am considering. . . .

❖   ❖   ❖

. . . The third or judicial branch of the Government is, by solemn and unanimous judgments, twice repeated, committed, in principle, to the same exact conclusions.

❖   ❖   ❖

I ask when and by what specific act does "tumult" become "war" in law? I answer, in the language of Chief Justice Marshall, when it, in fact, assumes "warlike array and strength." What in a civil war is the specific act and time which changes, in law, an "insurrectionary party" into a "belligerent"? I answer, in the language of the Supreme Court, when in fact "the regular course of justice is interrupted by revolt, rebellion, or insurrection, so that the courts of justice cannot be kept open." When, in law, does a revolt become civil war? I answer, in the language of Wheaton, when "the insurrection becomes, in fact, so strong as no longer to obey the sovereign, and to be able by war to make head against him." When, in law, and by what specific act, did the entire population of Virginia, including the loyal men, cease to be "friends," and become

"enemies of the United States"? I answer, when, in fact, they became "belligerents."

❖   ❖   ❖

These rebel States,

1. Acted *as States* in organizing the rebellion.

2. That *all* their citizens, innocent and guilty, were thereby made *"enemies* of the United States."

3. That though they became "enemies" *that* did not make them "foreign" States so as that when we take them back we must pay their debts.

4. That, as the court decides that the United States may exercise over these people *both* "belligerent" and "sovereign" rights, therefore we may, as sovereign, try [Confederate President Jefferson] Davis for treason, although we did treat and hold these States as an "enemy's" country.

5. As these States became "enemies" territory, and all persons residing within it became "enemies of the United States," they cannot at the same time have been a people having any political rights to govern in this Union, unless indeed this Union can be governed by a body of people, every one of whom are held by its law to be the "public enemies of the United States."

❖   ❖   ❖

Now, Mr. Chairman, if the combined forces of the Constitution and the Public Law, the obvious dictates of reason, justice, and common sense, and these enforced by the approval of repeated and unanimous judgments of the Supreme Court can settle for our own Government any principle of its law, then it is established that organized rebellions are not "States," and that these eleven distinct political treasons, which they organized into one, and called it "the confederate States," had *no* powers or rights as States of this Union, nor had the people thereof.

RESTORATION OF THE STATES

If these States lost their powers and rights as States, by what authority and means are they restored? It is accomplished by mere cessation of war and the determination of the rebel inhabitants to resume the powers of State; or is this Government entitled to take jurisdiction over the time and manner of their return?

I hold that the latter is the obvious truth.

❖   ❖   ❖

. . . Let this noble utterance—"*Irreversible guarantees for the rights" of American citizens of every race and condition* —be written with pen of iron and point of diamond in your constitution. Let it thus be made "irreversible" indeed, by the action of the State, in the only way it can be made irreversible; and then, to establish this and every other guarantee of the Constitution upon the only sure foundation of a free republic—the equality of the people and of the States—make, by the same organic law, every elector in the Union absolutely equal in his right of representation in that renovated Union, and I am content.

Let the revolted States base their republican State governments upon a general and sincere loyalty of the people and come to us under the guarantees of this renewed Union, and we hail their coming and the hour that brings them.

If you ask again, "Suppose such general loyalty should never reappear, shall they be dependencies forever?"

Sir, convince me that the case is supposable, then with deepest sorrow I answer—FOREVER!

Source:

John Scott, ed., *Living Documents in American History*, New York: Washington Square Press, 1964–68, pp. 19–33; 36–63; 66–87.

Black Codes, 1865–1890

The black codes were statutes passed by the former Confederate states between 1865 and 1908 regulating the status of some 4 million newly freed black slaves. Though the codes differed from state to state, all were intended to control and suppress freedom, ensure a supply of cheap labor, and continue white supremacy. While African Americans were granted rights to marry, to own personal property, and to sue other blacks in court, they were denied the rights to testify against whites in court, to vote, or to serve on juries. Employment, freedom of speech and movement, and ownership of real estate were restricted. In an attempt to override these codes, Congress passed the Civil Rights Act of 1866 and the Fourteenth Amendment (1868). Between the end of Reconstruction and the beginning of the Civil Rights movement (from 1877 through the 1950s), state statutes were passed that enforced racial segregation. These laws, called Jim Crow laws after a minstrel show character, were enacted primarily in the South and border states. They were designed to deny blacks the civil rights they had gained during Reconstruction by forcing segregation between blacks and whites in public transportation, schools, restaurants, hospitals, factories, housing, and other public institutions. Supreme Court rulings in the Civil Rights Cases of 1883 and *Plessy v. Ferguson* (1896) upheld Jim Crow laws. It was not until *Brown* v. *Board of Education of Topeka* in 1954 that the Court overturned constitutional protection for racial segregation.

Black Codes, 1865

I. An Act

To confer Civil Rights on freedmen, and for other purposes.

(1) Be it enacted by the Legislature of the State of Mississippi, That all freedmen, free Negroes and mulattoes may sue and be sued, implead and be impleaded, in all the courts of law and equity of this State, and may acquire personal property and *choses,* in action, by descent or purchase, and may dispose of the same, in the same manner, and to the same extent that white persons may: Provided that the provisions of this section shall not be so construed as to allow any Negro, freedman, free Negro, or mulatto, to rent or lease any lands or tenements, except in incorporated towns or cities in which places the corporate authorities shall control the same.

(2) Be it further enacted, That all freedmen, free Negroes and mulattoes may intermarry with each other, in the same manner and under the same regulations that are provided by law for white persons: Provided, that the clerk of probate shall keep separate records of the same.

(3) Be it further enacted, That all freedmen, free Negroes and mulattoes who do now and have heretofore lived and cohabited together as husband and wife shall be taken and held in law as legally married, and the issue shall be taken and held as legitimate for all purposes. That it shall not be lawful for any freedman, free Negro, or mulatto to intermarry with any white person; nor for any white person to intermarry with any freedman, free Negro, or mulatto; and any person who shall so intermarry shall be deemed guilty of felony, and on conviction thereof, shall be confined in the State Penitentiary for life; and those shall be deemed freedmen, free Negroes, and mulattoes who are of pure Negro blood, and those descended from a Negro to the third generation inclusive, though one ancestor of each generation may have been a white person.

(4) Be it further enacted, That in addition to cases in which freedmen, free Negroes, and mulattoes are now by law competent witnesses, freedmen, free Negroes, or mulattoes shall be competent in civil cases when a party or parties to the suit, either plaintiff or plaintiffs, defendant or defendants, also in cases where freedmen, free Negroes, and mulattoes is or are either plaintiff or plaintiffs, defendant or defendants, and a white person or white persons is or are the opposing party or parties, plaintiff or plaintiffs, defendant or defendants. They shall also be competent witnesses in all criminal prosecutions where the crime charged is alleged to have been committed by a white person upon or against the person or property of a freedman, free Negro, or mulatto: Provided that in all cases said witnesses shall be examined in open court on the

stand, except however, they may be examined before the grand jury, and shall in all cases be subject to the rules and tests of common law as to competence and credibility.

(5) Be it further enacted, That every freedman, free Negro, and mulatto, shall, on the second Monday of January, one thousand and eight hundred and sixty-six, and annually thereafter, have a lawful home or employment, and shall have written evidence thereof, as follows, to wit: if living in an incorporated city, town or village, a license from the mayor thereof; and if living outside of any incorporated city, town or village, from the member of the board of police of his beat, authorizing him or her to do irregular and job work, or a written contract, as provided in section sixth of this act, which licenses may be revoked for cause, at any time, by the authority granting the same.

(6) Be it further enacted, That all contracts for labor made with freedmen, free Negroes, and mulattoes, for a longer period than one month shall be in writing or duplicate, attested and read to said freedman, free Negro, or mulatto, by a beat, city, or county officer, or two disinterested white persons of the county in which the labor is to be performed, of which each party shall have one; and said contracts shall be taken and held as entire contracts, and if the laborer shall quit the service of the employer, before expiration of his term of service, without good cause, he shall forfeit his wages for that year, up to the time of quitting.

(7) Be it further enacted, That every civil officer shall, and every person may arrest and carry back to his or her legal employer any freedman, free Negro, or mulatto, who shall have quit the service of his or her employer before the expiration of his or her term of service without good cause, and said officer and person shall be entitled to receive for arresting and carrying back every deserting employee aforesaid, the sum of five dollars, and ten cents per mile from the place of arrest to the place of delivery, and the same shall be paid by the employer, and held as a set-off for so much against the wages of said deserting employee: Provided that said arrested party after being so returned may appeal to a justice of the peace or member of the board of police of the county, who on notice to the alleged employer, shall try summarily whether said appellant is legally employed by the alleged employer and has good cause to quit said employer; either party shall have the right of appeal to the county court, pending which the alleged deserter shall be remanded to the alleged employer, or otherwise disposed of, as shall be right and just, and the decision of the county court shall be final.

(8) Be it further enacted, That upon affidavit made by the employer of any freedman, free Negro, or mulatto, or other credible person, before any justice of the peace or member of the board of police, that any freedman, free Negro, or mulatto, legally employed by said employer, has illegally deserted said employment, such justice of the peace or member of the board of police, shall issue his warrant or warrants, returnable before himself, or other such officer, directed to any sheriff, constable or special deputy, commanding him to arrest said deserter and return him or her to said employer, and the like proceedings shall be had as provided in the preceding section; and it shall be lawful for any officer to whom such warrant shall be directed, to execute said warrant in any county of this State, and that said warrant may be transmitted without endorsement to any like officer of another county, to be executed and returned as aforesaid, and the said employer shall pay the cost of said warrants and arrest and return, which shall be set off for so much against the wage of said deserter.

(9) Be it further enacted, That if any person shall persuade or attempt to persuade, entice, or cause any freedman, free Negro, or mulatto, to desert from the legal employment of any person, before the expiration of his or her term of service, or shall knowingly employ any such deserting freedman, free Negro, or mulatto, or shall knowingly give or sell to any such deserting freedman, free Negro, or mulatto, any food, raiment, or other thing, he or she shall be guilty of a misdemeanor, and upon conviction, shall be fined not less than twenty-five dollars and not more than two hundred dollars and the costs, and if said fines and costs shall not be immediately paid, the court shall sentence said convict to not exceeding two months imprisonment in the county jail, and he or she shall moreover be liable to the party injured in damages: Provided, if any person shall, or shall attempt to persuade, entice, or cause any freedman, free Negro, or mulatto, to desert from any legal employment of any person, with the view to employ said freedman, free Negro, or mulatto, without the limits of this State, such person, on conviction, shall be fined not less than fifty dollars and not more than five hundred dollars and costs, and if said fines and costs shall not be immediately paid, the court shall sentence said convict to not exceeding six months imprisonment in the county jail.

(10) Be it further enacted, That it shall be lawful for any freedman, free Negro, or mulatto, to charge any white person, freedman, free Negro, or mulatto, by affidavit, with any criminal offence against his or her person or property, and upon such affidavit the proper process shall be issued and executed as if said affidavit was made by a white person, and it shall be lawful for any freedman, free Negro, or mulatto, in any action, suit, or controversy pending, or about to be instituted, in any court of law or equity of this State, to make all needful and lawful affidavits, as

shall be necessary for the institution, prosecution or defense of such suit or controversy.

(11) Be it further enacted, That the penal laws of this State, in all cases not otherwise specially provided for, shall apply and extend to all freedmen, free Negroes, and mulattoes.

(12) Be it further enacted, That this act take effect and be in force from and after its passage.

II. An Act

To regulate the relation of master and apprentice, as relates to freedmen, free negroes, and mulattoes.

(1) Be it enacted by the Legislature of the State of Mississippi, That it shall be the duty of all sheriffs, justices of the peace, and other civil officers of the several counties in this State, to report to the probate courts of their respective counties, semi-annually, at the January and July terms of said courts, all freedmen, free Negroes, and mulattoes, under the age of eighteen, within their respective counties, beats, or districts, who are orphans, or whose parent or parents have not the means, or who refuse to provide for and support said minors, and thereupon it shall be the duty of said probate court, to order the clerk of said court to apprentice said minors to some competent and suitable person, on such terms as the court may direct, inviting a particular care to the interest of said minor: Provided, that the former owner of said minors shall have the preference, when in the opinion of the court, he or she shall be a suitable person for that purpose.

(2) Be it further enacted, That the said court shall be fully satisfied that the person or persons to whom said minor shall be apprenticed, shall be a suitable person to have the charge and care of said minor, and fully to protect the interest of said minor. The said court shall require of the said master or mistress to execute bond and security, payable to the State of Mississippi, conditioned that he or she shall furnish said minor with sufficient food and clothing, to treat said minor humanely, to furnish medical attention in case of sickness; teach or cause to be taught him or her to read and write, if under fifteen years old, and will conform to any law that may be hereafter passed for the regulation of the duties and relation of master and apprentice: Provided, that said apprentice shall be bound by indenture, in cases of males until they are twenty-one years old, and in case of females until they are eighteen years old.

(3) Be it further enacted, That in the management and control of said apprentices, said master or mistress shall have power to inflict such moderate corporeal chastisement as a father or guardian is allowed to inflict on his or her child or ward at common law: Provided, that in no case shall cruel or inhuman punishment be inflicted.

(4) Be it further enacted, That if any apprentice shall leave the employment of his or her master or mistress, without his or her consent, said master or mistress may pursue and recapture said apprentice, and bring him or her before any justice of the peace of the county, whose duty shall be to remand said apprentice to the service of his or her master or mistress; and in the event of a refusal on the part of said apprentice to return, then said justice shall commit said apprentice to the jail of said county on failure to give bond, until the next term of the county court; and it shall be the duty of said court, at the first term thereafter, to investigate said case, and if the court shall be of opinion that said apprentice left the employment of his or her master or mistress without good cause, to order him or her to be punished, as provided for the punishment of hired freedmen, as may be from time to time provided by law, for desertion, until he or she shall agree to return to his or her master or mistress: Provided, that the court may grant continuances, as in other cases; and provided, further, that if the court shall believe that said apprentice had good cause to quit his said master or mistress, the court shall discharge said apprentice from said indenture, and also enter a judgment against the master or mistress, for not more than one hundred dollars, for the use and benefit of said apprentice, to be collected on execution, as in other cases.

(5) Be it further enacted, That if any person entice away any apprentice from his or her master or mistress, or shall knowingly employ an apprentice, or furnish him or her food or clothing, without the written consent of his or her master or mistress, or shall sell or give said apprentice ardent spirits, without such consent, said person so offending shall be deemed guilty of a high misdemeanor, and shall, on conviction thereof before the county court, be punished as provided for the punishment of persons enticing from their employer hired freedmen, free Negroes, or mulattoes.

(6) Be it further enacted, that it shall be the duty of all civil officers of their respective counties to report any minors within their respective counties, to said probate court, who are subject to be apprenticed under the provisions of this act, from time to time, as the facts may come to their knowledge, and it shall be the duty of said court, from time to time, as said minors shall be reported to them or otherwise come to their knowledge, to apprentice said minors as hereinbefore provided.

(7) Be it further enacted, That in case the master or mistress of any apprentice shall desire, he or she shall have the privilege to summon his or her said apprentice, to the probate court, and thereupon, with the approval of the court, he or she shall be released from all liability as master of said apprentice, and his bond shall be cancelled, and it shall be the duty of the court forthwith to re-apprentice

said minor: and in the event any master of an apprentice shall die before the close of the term of service of said apprentice, it shall be the duty of the court to give the preference in re-apprenticing said minor to the widow, or other member of said master's family: Provided, that said widow, or other member of said family shall be a suitable person for that purpose.

(8) Be it further enacted, That in case any master or mistress of any apprentice, bound to him or her under this act, shall be about to remove, or shall have removed to any other State of the United States by the laws of which such apprentice may be an inhabitant thereof, the probate court of the proper county may authorize the removal of such apprentice to such State, upon the said master or mistress entering into bond, with security, in a penalty to be fixed by the judge, conditioned that said master or mistress will, upon such removal, comply with the laws of such State in such cases: Provided, that said master shall be cited to attend the court at which such order is proposed to be made, and shall have a right to resist the same by next friend, or otherwise.

(9) Be it further enacted, That it shall be lawful for any freedman, free Negro, or mulatto, having a minor child or children, to apprentice the said minor child or children as provided for by this act.

(10) Be it further enacted, That in all cases where the age of the freedman, free Negro, or mulatto, cannot be ascertained by record testimony, the judge of the county court shall fix the age.

(11) Be it further enacted, That this act take effect and be in force from after its passage.

III. An Act

To amend the vagrant laws of the State

(1) Be it enacted by the Legislature of the State of Mississippi, That all rogues and vagabonds, idle and dissipated persons, beggars, jugglers, or persons practicing unlawful games or plays, runaways, common drunkards, common night-walkers, pilferers, lewd, wanton, or lascivious persons in speech or behavior, common railers and brawlers, persons who neglect their calling or employment, misspend what they earn, or do not provide for the support of themselves or their families or dependents, and all other idle and disorderly persons, including all who neglect all lawful business, or habitually misspend their time by frequenting houses of ill-fame, gaming-houses, or tippling shops, shall be deemed and considered vagrants under the provisions of this act, and on conviction thereof shall be fined not exceeding one hundred dollars, with all accruing costs, and be imprisoned at the discretion of the court not exceeding ten days.

(2) Be it further enacted, That all freedmen, free Negroes, and mulattoes in this State, over the age of eighteen years, found on the second Monday of January, 1866, or thereafter, with no lawful employment or business, or found unlawfully assembling themselves together either in the day or night time, and all white persons so assembling with freedmen, free Negroes, or mulattoes, or usually associating with freedmen, free Negroes, or mulattoes on terms of equality, or living in adultery or fornication with a freedwoman, free Negro, or mulatto, shall be deemed vagrants, and on conviction thereof, shall be fined not exceeding, in the case of a freedman, free Negro, or mulatto, fifty dollars, and a white man two hundred dollars, and imprisoned at the discretion of the court, the free Negro not exceeding ten days, and the white man not exceeding six months.

(3) Be it further enacted, That all justices of the peace, mayors and aldermen, of incorporated towns and cities of the several counties in this State, shall have jurisdiction to try all questions of vagrancy, in their respective towns, counties and cities, and it is hereby made their duty, whenever they shall ascertain that any person or persons, in their respective towns, counties and cities, are violating any of the provisions of this act, to have said party or parties arrested and brought before them, and immediately investigate said charge, and on conviction, punish said party or parties as provided for herein. And it is hereby made the duty of all sheriffs, constables, town constables, city marshals and all like officers, to report to some officer having jurisdiction, all violations of any of the provisions of this act; and it shall be the duty of the county courts to inquire if any officers have neglected any of the duties required by this act, and in case any officer shall fail or neglect any duty herein, it shall be the duty of the county court to fine said officer upon conviction, not exceeding one hundred dollars, to be paid into the county treasury for county purposes.

(4) Be it further enacted, That keepers of gaming houses, houses of prostitution, all prostitutes public or private, and all persons who derive their chief support in employments that militate against good morals or against law, shall be deemed and held to be vagrants.

(5) Be it further enacted, That all fines and forfeitures collected under the provisions of this act shall be paid into the county treasury for general county purposes, and in case any freedman, free Negro, or mulatto shall fail for five days after the imposition of any fine or forfeiture upon him or her for violation of any of the provisions of this act, to pay the same, that it shall be, and is hereby made the duty of the sheriff of the proper county, to hire out said freedman, free Negro, or mulatto, to any person who will, for the shortest period of service, pay said fine or forfeiture and all costs: Provided, a preference shall be given to the employer, if there be one, in which case the employer shall be entitled to deduct and retain the amount so paid from the wages of such freedman, free Negro, or mulatto, then

due or to become due; and in case such freedman, free Negro, or mulatto cannot be hired out he or she may be dealt with as a pauper.

(6) Be it further enacted, That the same duties and liabilities existing among white persons of this State shall attach to freedmen, free Negroes, and mulattoes, to support their indigent families, and all colored paupers; and that in order to secure a support for such indigent freedmen, free Negroes, and mulattoes, it shall be lawful, and it is hereby made the duty of the boards of county police of each county in this State, to levy a poll or capitation tax on each and every freedman, free Negro, or mulatto, between the ages of eighteen and sixty years, not to exceed the sum of one dollar annually, to each person so taxed, which tax, when collected, shall be paid into the county treasurer's hands, and constitute a fund to be called the Freedman's Pauper Fund, which shall be applied by the commissioners of the poor for the maintenance of the poor of the freedmen, free Negroes, and mulattoes of this State, under such regulations as may be established by the boards of county police, in the respective counties of this State.

(7) Be it further enacted, That if any freedman, free Negro, or mulatto shall fail, or refuse to pay any tax levied according to the provisions of the sixth section of this act, it shall be *prima facie* evidence of vagrancy, and it shall be the duty of the sheriff to arrest such freedman, free Negro, or mulatto, or such person refusing or neglecting to pay such tax, and proceed at once to hire, for the shortest time, such delinquent tax payer to any one who will pay the said tax, with accruing costs, giving preference to the employer, if there be one.

(8) Be it further enacted, That any person feeling himself or herself aggrieved by the judgment of any justice of the peace, mayor, or alderman, in cases arising under this act, may, within five days, appeal to the next term of the county court of the proper county, upon giving bond and security in a sum not less than twenty-five, nor more than one hundred and fifty dollars, conditioned to appear and prosecute said appeal, and abide by the judgment of the county court, and said appeal shall be tried *deb novo* in the county court, and the decision of said court shall be final.

IV. An Act
In Relation to Railroads and for other purposes

[. . .] (6) Be it further enacted, That it shall be unlawful for any officer, station agent, conductor, or employee on any railroad in this State, to allow any freedman, Negro, or mulatto, to ride in any first-class passenger cars, set apart, or used by and for white persons; and any person offending against the provision of this section, shall be deemed guilty of a misdemeanor; and on conviction thereof, before the circuit court of the county in which said

offence was committed, shall be fined not less than fifty dollars, nor more than five hundred dollars; and shall be imprisoned in the county jail, until such fine and costs of prosecution are paid. Provided, that this section, of this act, shall not apply, in the case of Negroes or mulattoes, travelling with their mistresses, in the capacity of nurses.

V. An Act
To punish certain offences therein named and for other purposes.

(1) Be it enacted by the Legislature of the State of Mississippi, That no freedman, free Negro, or mulatto, not in the military service of the United States Government, and not licensed so to do by the board of police of his or her county, shall keep or carry fire-arms of any kind, or any ammunition, dirk, or bowie knife, and on conviction thereof, in the county court, shall be punished by fine, not exceeding ten dollars, and pay the costs of such proceedings, and all such arms or ammunition shall be forfeited to the informer, and it shall be the duty of every civil and military officer to arrest any freedman, free Negro, or mulatto found with any such arms or ammunition, and cause him or her to be committed for trial in default of bail.

(2) Be it further enacted, That any freedman, free Negro, or mulatto, committing riots, routes, affrays, trespasses, malicious mischief, cruel treatment to animals, seditious speeches, insulting gestures, language, or acts, or assaults on any person, disturbance of the peace, exercising the function of a minister of the Gospel, without a license from some regularly organized church, vending spirituous or intoxicating liquors, or committing any other misdemeanor, the punishment of which is not specifically provided for by law, shall, upon conviction thereof, in the county court, be fined, not less than ten dollars, and may be imprisoned, at the discretion of the court, not exceeding thirty days.

(3) Be it further enacted, That if any white person shall sell, lend, or give to any freedman, free Negro, or mulatto, any fire-arms, dirk, or bowie-knife, or ammunition, or any spirituous or intoxicating liquors, such person or persons so offending, upon conviction thereof, in the county court of his or her county, shall be fined, not exceeding fifty dollars, and may be imprisoned, at the discretion of the court, not exceeding thirty days: Provided, that any master, mistress, or employer of any freedman, free Negro, or mulatto, may give to any freedman, free Negro, or mulatto, apprenticed to or employed by such master, mistress, or employer, spirituous or intoxicating liquors, but not in sufficient quantities to produce intoxication.

(4) Be it further enacted, That all the penal and criminal laws now in force in this State, defining offences and prescribing the mode of punishment for crimes and misdemeanors committed by slaves, free Negroes, or mulat-

toes, be, and the same are, hereby reenacted, and declared to be in full force and effect, against freedmen, free Negroes, and mulattoes, except so far as the mode and manner of trial and punishment have been changed or altered by law.

(5) Be it further enacted, That if any freedman, free Negro, or mulatto, convicted of any of the misdemeanors provided against in this act, shall fail or refuse, for the space of five days after conviction, to pay the fine and costs imposed, such person shall be hired out by the sheriff or other officer, at public outcry, to any white person who will pay said fine and all costs, and take such convict for the shortest time.

(6) Be it further enacted, That this act shall be in force and take effect from and after its passage.

Amendments to the Constitution Articles XIII, XIV, AND XV

ARTICLE XIII

[DECLARED IN FORCE, DECEMBER 18, 1865]

Section 1. Neither slavery nor involuntary servitude, except as a punishment for crime whereof the party shall have been duly convicted, shall exist within the United States, or any place subject to their jurisdiction.

Section 2. Congress shall have power to enforce this article by appropriate legislation.

ARTICLE XIV

[DECLARED IN FORCE, JULY 23, 1868.]

Section 1. All persons born or naturalized in the United States, and subject to the jurisdiction thereof, are citizens of the United States and of the state wherein they reside. No state shall make or enforce any law which shall abridge the privileges or immunities of citizens of the United States; nor shall any state deprive any person of life, liberty, or property without due process of law; nor deny to any person within its jurisdiction the equal protection of the laws.

Section 2. Representatives shall be apportioned among the several states according to their respective numbers, counting the whole number of persons in each state, excluding Indians not taxed. But when the right to vote at any election for the choice of electors for President and Vice-President of the United States, representatives in Congress, the executive and judicial officers of a state, or the members of the legislature thereof, is denied to any of the male inhabitants of such state, being twenty-one years of age, and citizens of the United States, or in any way abridged, except for participation in rebellion or other crime, the basis of representation therein shall be reduced in the proportion which the number of such male citizens shall bear to the whole number of male citizens twenty-one years of age in such state.

Section 3. No person shall be a Senator or Representative in Congress, or elector of President and Vice-President, or hold any office, civil or military, under the United States, or under any state, who, having previously taken an oath, as a member of Congress, or as an officer of the United States, or as a member of any state legislature, or as an executive or judicial officer of any state, to support the Constitution of the United States, shall have engaged in insurrection or rebellion against the same, or given aid and comfort to the enemies thereof. But Congress may, by a vote of two-thirds of each House, remove such disability.

Section 4. The validity of the public debt of the United States, authorized by law, including debts incurred for payment of pensions and bounties for services in suppressing insurrection or rebellion, shall not be questioned. But neither the United States nor any state shall assume or pay any debt or obligation incurred in aid of insurrection or rebellion against the United States, or any claim for the loss or emancipation of any slave; but all such debts, obligations, and claims shall be held illegal and void.

Section 5. The Congress shall have power to enforce, by appropriate legislation, the provisions of this article.

ARTICLE XV

[DECLARED IN FORCE, MARCH 30, 1870.]

Section 1. The right of the citizens of the United States to vote shall not be denied or abridged by the United States or by any state, on account of race, color, or previous condition of servitude.

Section 2. The Congress shall have power to enforce this article by appropriate legislation.

Source:

John A. Scott, ed., *Living Documents in American History*. Vol 1. New York: Washington Square Press, 1964–1968, pp. 597–609.

Black Codes (Louisiana), 1865

An Act

Relative to apprenticas and indentured servants.

Section 1. Be it enacted by the Senate and House of Representatives of the State of Louisiana, in General Assembly convened, That it shall be the duty of Sheriffs, Justices of the Peace and other civil officers of this State, to report to the Clerks of the District Courts of their respective Parishes, and in the Parish of Orleans (left bank) to the Mayor of the City of New Orleans, and on the right bank to tee President of the Police Jury, on the first Monday of each month, for each and every year, all persons under the age of eighteen years, if females, and twenty-one, if males, who are orphans, or whose parent, parents, or tutor, have not the means, or who refuse to provide for and maintain said minors; and, thereupon, it shall be the duty of the Clerks of the District Courts, Mayor and President of the Police Jury aforesaid, to examine whether the party or parties, so reported from time to time, come within the purview and meaning of this Act, and if so, to apprentice said minor or minors, in manner and form as prescribed by the Civil Code of the State of Louisiana; provided, that orphans coming under the provisions of this Act shall be authorized to select said employers when they have arrived at the age of puberty, unless they shall have been previously apprenticed; provided, that nay indenture of apprentice or indented servant, made before a Justice of the Peace and two disinterested witnesses, and the original deposited with and recorded by the Recorder of Mortgages for the Parish, in a book provided for that purpose, shall be valid and binding on the parties, and when made by the clerk, shall be also deposited with the Recorder of Mortgages, and all expenses for passing said acts of indenture shall be paid by the employer.

Sec. 2. Be it further enacted, &c., That persons who have attained the age of majority, whether in this State or any other State of the United States, or in a foreign country, may bind themselves to services to be performed in this country, for the term of five years, on such terms as they may stipulate, as domestic servants and to work on farms, plantations or in manufacturing establishments, which contracts shall be valid and binding on the parties to the same.

Sec. 3. Be it further enacted, &c., That in all cases, when the age of the minor cannot be ascertained by record testimony, the Clerks of the District Courts, Mayor and President of the Police Jury, or Justices of the Peace aforesaid, shall fix the age, according to the best evidence before them.

Sec. 4. Be it further enacted, &c., That all laws or parts of laws conflicting with the provisions of this Act, be, and the same are hereby repealed, and that this Act take effect from and after its passage.

Source:

Acts Passed by the General Assembly of Louisiana, 1865, pp. 28–30.

Mississippi Code of 1890, Sections 1276, 3562

Section 1276

The same, not providing separate cars, etc.—If any persons or corporation operating a railroad shall fail to provide two or more passenger-cars for each passenger-train, or to divide the passenger-cars by a partition, to secure separate accommodations for the white and colored races, as provided by law, or if any railroad passenger conductor shall fail to assign each passenger to the car or the compartment of the car used for the race to which the passenger belongs, he or it shall be guilty of a misdemeanor, and, on conviction, shall be fined not less than twenty dollars nor more than five hundred dollars.

Section 3562

Equal but separate accommodations for the races.—Every railroad carrying passengers in this state shall provide equal but separate accommodations for the white and colored races by providing two or more passenger-cars for each passenger-train, or by dividing the passenger-cars by a partition to secure separate accommodations; and the conductor of such passenger-train shall have power, and is required, to assign each passenger to the car, or the compartment of a car, used for the race to which such passenger belongs; and should any passenger refuse to occupy the car to which he or she is assigned by the conductor, the conductor shall have power to refuse to carry such passenger on the train, and for such refusal neither he nor the railroad company shall be liable for damages in any court.

Source:

Annotated Code of the Public Statute Laws of the State of Mississippi. Mississippi Legislature, 1890, pp. 371–797.

Louisiana Act 64 of 1902

An Act

To promote the comfort of passengers on street railways, requiring all street railways in this State to provide equal but separate accommodations for the white and colored races, by providing separate cars or compartments so as to secure separate accommodations; defining the duties of the officers of such street railways; directing them to assign passengers to the cars or compartments set aside for the use of the races to which such passengers belong; authorizing them to refuse to carry on their cars such passengers as may refuse to occupy the car or compartment to which he or she is assigned; to exonerate such street railway companies from any or all blame and damages that might proceed or result from such a refusal; to prescribe penalties for all violations of this act; to put this act into effect ninety (90) days after its promulgation; and to repeal all laws or parts of laws contrary to or inconsistent with the provisions of this act.

Section 1. Be it enacted by the General Assembly of the State of Louisiana, That all street railway companies carrying passengers in their cars in this State shall provide equal but separate accommodations for the white and colored races by providing two or more cars or by dividing their cars by wooden or wire screen partitions so as to secure separate accommodations for the white and colored races, no person or persons shall be permitted to occupy seats in cars or compartments other than the ones assigned to them on account of the race they belong to.

Sec. 2. Be it further enacted, etc., That the officers of such street cars shall have power and are hereby required to assign each passenger to the car or compartment used for the race to which such passenger belongs; any passenger insisting upon going into a car or compartment to which by race he or she does not belong shall be liable to a fine of twenty-five dollars ($25.00), or in lieu thereof be imprisoned for a period of not more than thirty (30) days in the parish prison, and any officer of any street railway insisting on assigning a passenger to a car or compartment other than the one set aside for the race to which said passenger belongs, shall be liable to a fine of twenty-five dollars ($25.00), or in lieu thereof, to imprisonment for a period of not more than thirty (30) days in the parish prison; and should any passenger refuse to occupy the car or compartment to which he or she is assigned by the officer of such street railway, said officer shall have the power to refuse to carry such passenger on his car or cars, and for such refusal neither he nor the street railway company which he represents shall be liable for damages in any of the courts of this State.

Sec. 3. Be it further enacted, etc., That all officers and directors of street railway companies that shall refuse or neglect to comply with the provisions and requirements of this act shall be deemed guilty of misdemeanor, and shall upon conviction before any court of competent jurisdiction be fined not less than one hundred ($100.00) dollars, or be imprisoned in the parish jail not less than sixty (60) days and not more than six (6) months; and any conductor or other employee of such street car having charge of the same, who shall refuse or neglect to carry out the provisions of this act shall, on conviction be fined not less than twenty-five ($25.00) dollars, or be imprisoned in the parish jail for not less than ten (10) days, nor more than thirty (30) days for each and every offense. All street railway corporations carrying passengers in this State shall keep this law posted up in a conspicuous place in each and every car and at their transfer stations; provided that nothing in this act shall be construed as applying to nurses attending children of the other race.

Sec. 4. Be it further enacted, etc., That all laws or parts of laws contrary to or inconsistent with the provisions of this act, be and the same are hereby repealed and that this act shall take effect and be in full force ninety (90) days after its promulgation.

Source:

Acts Passed by the General Assembly of the State of Louisiana, 1902, pp. 89–90.

Louisiana Act 87 of 1908

An Act

To make concubinage between a person of the Caucasian race and a person of the negro race a felony, fixing the punishment therefor and defining what shall constitute concubinage.

Section 1. Be it enacted by the General Assembly of the State of Louisiana. That concubinage between a person of the Caucasian or white race and a person of the negro or black race is hereby made a felony, and whoever shall be convicted thereof in any court of competent jurisdiction shall for each offense be sentenced to imprisonment at the discretion of the court for a term of not less than one month nor more than one year with or without hard labor.

Section 2. Be it further enacted, etc., That the living together or cohabitation of persons of the Caucasian and of the negro races shall be proof of the violation of the provision of Section 1 of this Act. For the purpose of this Act concubinage is hereby defined to be the unlawful co-habitation of person of the Caucasian and of the negro races whether open or secret.

Section 3. Be it further enacted, etc., That it shall be the duty of the judges of the several district courts of this State to specially charge the grand juries upon this Act.

Section 4. Be it further enacted, etc., That all laws and parts of laws in conflict with the provisions of this Act be and the same are hereby repealed.

Louisiana Act 176 of 1908

An Act

To regulate and license the business of conducting a barroom, cabaret, coffee house, cafe, beer saloon, liquor exchange, drinking saloon, grog shop, beer house, beer garden or other place where alcoholic or spirituous, vinous and malt liquors or intoxicating beverages, bitters or medicinal preparations of any kind are sold, directly or indirectly, in quantities of less than five gallons, and to provide penalties for violations of this Act; to limit the effect and operation of this Act to cities, towns, villages and parishes of the State of Louisiana where the sale of liquor is permitted; to prevent this act from affecting, modifying, amending or repealing any local option laws; or from interfering with or preventing the exercise of local option on the liquor traffic; to prevent this Act from affecting, modifying, amending or repealing any existing special or local Act or Acts prohibiting or restricting the sale of liquor from or within any locality or localities in this State . . .

Section 5. Be it further enacted, etc., That hereafter no license as a retail liquor dealer or as a retail malt and vinous liquor dealer shall be issued to any woman; and no woman or girl, or minor, shall serve in any barroom, cabaret, coffee house, cafe, beer saloon, liquor exchange, drinking saloon, grog shop, beer house or beer garden.

Section 6. Be it further enacted, etc., That hereafter it shall be unlawful for any person, firm, or corporation, conducting a barroom, cabaret, coffee house, cafe, beer saloon, liquor exchange, drinking saloon, grog house, beer house, beer garden, or other place where spirituous, vinous or malt liquors or intoxicating beverages are sold, in this State, to sell or permit to be sold or to give or permit to be given, any intoxicating liquors to women, or girls, or minors, or to set apart in such places any apartment where intoxicating liquors are sold to girls or women, or minors, or to permit girls or women, or minors, to enter or drink in any such apartment; provided that nothing in the foregoing part of this section shall apply to hotels, boarding houses or restaurants where malt, vinous or other liquors are sold in connection with the service of meals or supplied to requests.

That hereafter it shall be unlawful for any person, firm or corporation conducting a barroom, cabaret, coffee house, cafe, beer saloon, liquor exchange, drinking saloon, grog shop, beer house, beer garden, or other place where spirituous, vinous or malt liquors or intoxicating beverages are sold, to permit in the same building the sale for consumption on the premises of intoxicating liquors to whites and negroes.

Any person violating any of the provisions of this section shall be deemed guilty of a misdemeanor and upon conviction therefore, be fined in a sum not less than $50 nor more than $500, or by imprisonment in the parish jail or parish prison for not more than two (2) years, or by both such fine and imprisonment . . .

Section 15. Be it further enacted, etc., That subject tot he limitation s contained in Section 14 of this Act, all laws and parts of laws contrary to or inconsistent with this Act be and the same are hereby repealed.

Section 16. Be it further enacted, etc., That this Act shall take effect from and after December 31, 1908.

Source:

Acts Passed by the General Assembly of Louisiana, 1908, pp. 105–106.

Civil Rights Act of 1866

First federal U.S. legislation enacted to ensure equal rights for blacks. Passed by Congress on March 13, 1866, it was vetoed by President Andrew Johnson, who charged that it was an unwarranted invasion of states' rights; Congress overrode the veto on April 9. The act, designed to overcome the restrictive Black Codes, conferred citizenship upon black people and conferred the same rights and responsibilities on all persons born in the United States, except Native Americans. Because there was some doubt about the constitutionality of the act, Congress incorporated most of its provisions into the Fourteenth Amendment.

These acts, as later encoded first as U.S.C. 51 and U.S.C. 52 and now U.S.C. 141 and U.S.C. 142 have been the principal means for the federal government to combat violence directed against those attempting to exercise their civil rights, especially voting. Because Supreme Court decisions severely restricted federal civil rights jurisdiction (and Southern white juries rarely convicted perpetrators), even violent Klan terrorism was difficult to prosecute until 1966, after the Supreme Court clarified 141 and 142 in *U.S. v Price* (re: the murders of civil rights workers Goodwin, Schwerner, and Chaney) and *U.S. v Guest* (re: the murder of Colonel Lemuel Penn).

An Act

To protect all Persons in the United States in their Civil Rights, and furnish the Means of their Vindication.

Be it enacted by the Senate and House of Representatives of the United States of America in Congress assembled, That all persons born in the United States and not subject to any foreign power, excluding Indians not taxed, are hereby declared to be citizens of the United States; and such citizens, of every race and color, without regard to any previous condition of slavery or involuntary servitude, except as a punishment for crime whereof the party shall have been duly convicted, shall have the same right, in every State and Territory in the United States, to make and enforce contracts, to sue, be parties, and give evidence, to inherit, purchase, lease, sell, hold, and convey real and personal property, and to full and equal benefit of all laws and proceedings for the security of person and property, as is enjoyed by white citizens, and shall be subject to like punishment, pains, and penalties, and to none other, any law, statute, ordinance, regulation, or custom, to the contrary notwithstanding.

Sec. 2. *And be it further enacted,* That any person who, under color of any law, statute, ordinance, regulation, or custom, shall subject, or cause to be subjected, any inhabitant of any State or Territory to the deprivation of any right secured or protected by this act, or to different punishment, pains, or penalties on account of such person having at any time been held in a condition of slavery or involuntary servitude, except as a punishment for crime whereof the party shall have been duly convicted, or by reason of his color or race, than is prescribed for the punishment of white persons, shall be deemed guilty of a misdemeanor, and, on conviction, shall be punished by fine not exceeding one thousand dollars, or imprisonment not exceeding one year, or both, in the discretion of the court.

Sec. 3. *And be it further enacted,* That the district courts of the United States, within their respective districts, shall have, exclusively of the courts of the several States, cognizance of all crimes and offences committed against the provisions of this act, and also, concurrently with the circuit courts of the United States, of all causes, civil and criminal, affecting persons who are denied or cannot enforce in the courts or judicial tribunals of the State or locality where they may be any of the rights secured to them by the first section of this act; and if any suit or prosecution, civil or criminal, has been or shall be commenced in any State court, against any such person, for any cause whatsoever, or against any officer, civil or military, or other person, for any arrest or imprisonment, trespasses, or wrongs done or committed by virtue or under color of authority derived from this act or the act establishing a Bureau for the relief of Freedmen and Refugees, and all acts amendatory thereof, or for refusing to do any act upon the ground that it would be inconsistent with this act, such defendant shall have the right to remove such cause for trial to the proper district or circuit court in the manner prescribed by the "Act relating to habeas corpus and regulating judicial proceedings in certain cases," approved March three, eighteen hundred and sixty-three, and all acts amendatory thereof. The jurisdiction in civil and criminal matters hereby conferred on the district and circuit courts of the United States shall be exercised and enforced in conformity with the laws of the United States, so far as such laws are suitable to carry the same into effect; but in all cases where such laws are not adapted to the object, or are deficient in the provisions necessary to furnish suitable remedies and punish offences against law, the common law, as modified and changed by the constitution and statutes of the State wherein the court having jurisdiction of the cause, civil or criminal, is held, so far as the same is not inconsistent with the Constitution and laws of the United States, shall be extended to and govern said courts in the trial and disposition of such cause, and, if of a criminal nature, in the infliction of punishment on the party found guilty.

Sec. 4. *And be it further enacted,* That the district attorneys, marshals, and deputy marshals of the United States, the commissioners appointed by the circuit and territorial courts of the United States, with powers of arresting, imprisoning, or bailing offenders against the laws of the United States, the officers and agents of the Freedmen's Bureau, and every other officer who may be specially empowered by the President of the United States, shall be, and they are hereby, specially authorized and required, at the expense of the United States, to institute proceedings against all and every person who shall violate the provisions of this act, and cause him or them to be arrested and imprisoned, or bailed, as the case may be, for trial before such court of the United States or territorial court as by this act has cognizance of the offence. And with a view to affording reasonable protection to all persons in their constitutional rights of equality before the law, without distinction of race or color, or previous condition of slavery or involuntary servitude, except as a punishment for crime, whereof the party shall have been duly convicted, and to the prompt discharge of the duties of this act, it shall be the duty of the circuit courts of the United States and the superior courts of the Territories of the United States, from time to time, to increase the number of commissioners, so as to afford a speedy and convenient means for the arrest and examination of persons charged with a violation of this act; and such commissioners are hereby authorized and required to exercise and discharge all the powers and duties conferred on them by this act, and the same duties with regard to offences created by this act, as they are authorized by law to exercise with regard to other offences against the laws of the United States.

Sec. 5. *And be it further enacted,* That it shall be the duty of all marshals and deputy marshals to obey and execute all warrants and precepts issued under the provisions of this act, when to them directed; and should any marshal or deputy marshal refuse to receive such warrant or other process when tendered, or to use all proper means diligently to execute the same, he shall, on conviction thereof, be fined in the sum of one thousand dollars, to the use of the person upon whom the accused is alleged to have committed the offence. And the better to enable the said commissioners to execute their duties faithfully and efficiently, in conformity with the Constitution of the United States and the requirements of this act, they are hereby authorized and empowered, within their counties respectively, to appoint in writing, under their hands, any one or more suitable persons, from time to time, to execute all such warrants and other process as may be issued by them in the lawful performance of their respective duties; and the persons so appointed to execute any warrant or process as aforesaid shall have authority to summon and call to their aid the bystanders or posse comitatus of the proper county, or such portion of the land or naval forces of the United States, or of the militia, as may be necessary to the performance of the duty with which they are charged, and to insure a faithful observance of the clause of the Constitution which prohibits slavery, in conformity with the provisions of this act; and said warrants shall run and be executed by said officers anywhere in the State or Territory within which they are issued.

Sec. 6. *And be it further enacted,* That any person who shall knowingly and willfully obstruct, hinder, or prevent any officer, or other person charged with the execution of any warrant or process issued under the provisions of this act, or any person or persons lawfully assisting him or them, from arresting any person for whose apprehension such warrant or process may have been issued, or shall rescue or attempt to rescue such person from the custody of the officer, other person or persons, or those lawfully assisting as aforesaid, when so arrested pursuant to the authority herein given and declared, or shall aid, abet, or assist any person so arrested as aforesaid, directly or indirectly, to escape from the custody of the officer or other person legally authorized as aforesaid, or shall harbor or conceal any person for whose arrest a warrant or process shall have been issued as aforesaid, so as to prevent his discovery and arrest after notice or knowledge of the fact that a warrant has been issued for the apprehension of such person, shall, for either of said offences, be subject to a fine not exceeding one thousand dollars, and imprisonment not exceeding six months, by indictment and conviction before the district court of the United States for the district in which said offence may have been committed, or before the proper court of criminal jurisdiction, if committed within any one of the organized Territories of the United States.

Sec. 7. *And be it further enacted,* That the district attorneys, the marshals, their deputies, and the clerks of the said district and territorial courts shall be paid for their services the like fees as may be allowed to them for similar services in other cases; and in all cases where the proceedings are before a commissioner, he shall be entitled to a fee of ten dollars in full for his services in each case, inclusive of all services incident to such arrest and examination. The person or persons authorized to execute the process to be issued by such commissioners for the arrest of offenders against the provisions of this act shall be entitled to a fee of five dollars for each person he or they may arrest and take before any such commissioner as aforesaid, with such other fees as may be deemed reasonable by such commissioner for such other additional services as may be necessarily performed by him or them, such as attending at the examination, keeping the prisoner in custody, and providing him with food and lodging during his detention, and until the final determination of such commissioner, and in general for performing such other duties as may be required in the premises; such fees to be made up in conformity with the fees usually charged by the officers of the courts of justice within the proper district or county, as near as may be practicable, and paid out of the Treasury of the United States on the certificate of the judge of the district within which the arrest is made, and to be recoverable from the defendant as part of the judgment in case of conviction.

Sec. 8. *And be it further enacted,* That whenever the President of the United States shall have reason to believe that offences have been or are likely to be committed against the provisions of this act within any judicial district, it shall be lawful for him, in his discretion, to direct the judge, marshal, and district attorney of such district to attend at such place within the district, and for such time as he may designate, for the purpose of the more speedy arrest and trial of persons charged with a violation of this act; and it shall be the duty of every judge or other officer, when any such requisition shall be received by him, to attend at the place and for the time therein designated.

Sec. 9. *And be it further enacted,* That it shall be lawful for the President of the United States, or such person as he may empower for that purpose, to employ such part of the land or naval forces of the United States, or of the militia, as shall be necessary to prevent the violation and enforce the due execution of this act.

Sec. 10. *And be it further enacted,* That upon all questions of law arising in any cause under the provisions of this act a final appeal may be taken to the Supreme Court of the United States.

Source:
Statutes at Large, Vol. 14, pp. 27–30.

Tenure of Office Act of 1867

Legislation passed by Congress on March 2, 1867, over the veto of President Andrew Johnson, that required the Senate's approval before the president could remove from office anyone appointed by, and with the advice and consent of, the Senate. This included members of the president's own cabinet. Violation of the law was a high misdemeanor. In 1868, when Johnson defied the act and tried to fire Secretary of War Edwin M. Stanton, he was impeached in the House of Representatives; the Senate failed by one vote to convict him. The act was never again enforced and was repealed in 1887. The Supreme Court ruled it unconstitutional retroactively in 1926.

An Act
Regulating the Tenure of Certain Civil Offices.

Be it enacted by the Senate and House of Representatives of the United States of America in Congress assembled, That every person holding any civil office to which he has been appointed by and with the advice and consent of the Senate, and every person who shall hereafter be appointed to any such office, and shall become duly qualified to act therein, is, and shall be entitled to hold such office until a successor shall have been in like manner appointed and duly qualified, except as herein otherwise provided: *Provided,* That the Secretaries of State, of the Treasury, of War, of the Navy, and of the Interior, the Postmaster-General, and the Attorney-General, shall hold their offices respectively for and during the term of the President by whom they may have been appointed and for one month thereafter, subject to removal by and with the advice and consent of the Senate.

Sec. 2. *And be it further enacted,* That when any officer appointed as aforesaid, excepting judges of the United States courts, shall, during a recess of the Senate, be shown, by evidence satisfactory to the President, to be guilty of misconduct in office, or crime, or for any reason shall become incapable or legally disqualified to perform its duties, in such case, and in no other, the President may suspend such officer and designate some suitable person to perform temporarily the duties of such office until the next meeting of the Senate, and until the case shall be acted upon by the Senate, and such person so designated shall take the oaths and give the bonds required by law to be taken and given by the person duly appointed to fill such office; and in such case it shall be the duty of the President, within twenty days after the first day of such next meeting of the Senate, to report to the Senate such suspension, with the evidence and reasons for his action in the case, and the name of the person so designated to perform the duties of such office. And if the Senate shall concur in such suspension and advise and consent to the removal of such officer, they shall so certify to the President, who may thereupon remove such officer, and, by and with the advice and consent of the Senate, appoint another person to such office. But if the Senate shall refuse to concur in such suspension, such officer so suspended shall forthwith resume the functions of his office, and the powers of the person so performing its duties in his stead shall cease, and the official salary and emoluments of such officer shall, during such suspension, belong to the person so performing the duties thereof, and not to the officer so suspended: *Provided, however,* That the President, in case he shall become satisfied that such suspension was made on insufficient grounds, shall be authorized, at any time before reporting such suspension to the Senate as above provided, to revoke such suspension and reinstate such officer in the performance of the duties of his office.

Sec. 3. *And be it further enacted,* That the President shall have power to fill all vacancies which may happen during the recess of the Senate, by reason of death or resignation, by granting commissions which shall expire at the end of their next session thereafter. And if no appointment, by and with the advice and consent of the Senate, shall be made to such office so vacant or temporarily filled as aforesaid during such next session of the Senate, such office shall remain in abeyance, without any salary, fees, or emoluments attached thereto, until the same shall be filled by appointment thereto, by and with the advice and consent of the Senate; and during such time all the powers and duties belonging to such office shall be exercised by such other officer as may by law exercise such powers and duties in case of a vacancy in such office.

Sec. 4. *And be it further enacted,* That nothing in this act contained shall be construed to extend the term of any office the duration of which is limited by law.

Sec. 5. *And be it further enacted,* That if any person shall, contrary to the provisions of this act, accept any appointment to or employment in any office, or shall hold or exercise or attempt to hold or exercise, any such office or employment, he shall be deemed, and is hereby declared to be, guilty of a high misdemeanor, and, upon trial and conviction thereof, he shall be punished therefor by a fine not exceeding ten thousand dollars, or by imprisonment not exceeding five years, or both said punishments, in the discretion of the court.

Sec. 6. *And be it further enacted,* That every removal, appointment, or employment, made, had, or exercised, contrary to the provisions of this act, and the making, signing, sealing, countersigning, or issuing of any commission or letter of authority for or in respect to any such appointment or employment, shall be deemed, and are hereby declared to be, high misdemeanors, and, upon trial and conviction thereof, every person guilty thereof shall be punished by a fine not exceeding ten thousand dollars, or by imprisonment not exceeding five years, or both said punishments, in the discretion of the court: *Provided,* That the President shall have power to make out and deliver, after the adjournment of the Senate, commissions for all officers whose appointment shall have been advised and consented to by the Senate.

Sec. 7. *And be it further enacted,* That it shall be the duty of the Secretary of the Senate, at the close of each session thereof, to deliver to the Secretary of the Treasury, and to each of his assistants, and to each of the auditors, and to each of the comptrollers in the treasury, and to the treasurer, and to the register of the treasury, a full and complete list, duly certified, of all the persons who shall have been nominated to and rejected by the Senate during such session, and a like list of all the offices to which nominations shall have been made and not confirmed and filled at such session.

Sec. 8. *And be it further enacted,* That whenever the President shall, without the advice and consent of the Senate, designate, authorize, or employ any person to perform the duties of any office, he shall forthwith notify the Secretary of the Treasury thereof; and it shall be the duty of the Secretary of the Treasury thereupon to communicate such notice to all the proper accounting and disbursing officers of his department.

Sec. 9. *And be it further enacted,* That no money shall be paid or received from the treasury, or paid or received from or retained out of any public moneys or funds of the United States, whether in the treasury or not, to or by or for the benefit of any person appointed to or authorized to act in or holding or exercising the duties or functions of any office contrary to the provisions of this act; nor shall any claim, account, voucher, order, certificate, warrant, or other instrument providing for or relating to such payment, receipt, or retention, be presented, passed, allowed, approved, certified, or paid by any officer of the United States, or by any person exercising the functions or performing the duties of any office or place of trust under the United States, for or in respect to such office, or the exercising or performing the functions or duties thereof; and every person who shall violate any of the provisions of this section shall be deemed guilty of a high misdemeanor, and, upon trial and conviction thereof, shall be punished therefor by a fine not exceeding ten thousand dollars, or by imprisonment not exceeding ten years, or both said punishments, in the discretion of the court.

See also COVODE RESOLUTION (ARTICLES OF IMPEACHMENT OF ANDREW JOHNSON), 1868.

Source:
Statutes at Large, Vol. 14, pp. 430–432.

Reconstruction Acts, 1867–1868

Series of four related acts that provided for the military occupation of the former Confederacy. They were passed between March 1867 and March 1868 over the vetoes of President Andrew Johnson. Under the first act, the former Confederate states (except for Tennessee, which had already been readmitted to the Union) were divided into five military districts under military commanders with broad civil powers, including appointing and removing state officials. The act also required ratification of the Fourteenth Amendment before a state could be readmitted to the Union. Many Southern officials balked and refused to register voters, so Congress passed the Second Reconstruction Act, which put the military commanders in charge of enrolling voters. Johnson tried to reduce the power of the military commanders, and in response Congress passed the third act, which granted the commanders authority in all matters pertaining to voting. Elections were finally held to ratify the new state constitutions, but many white registered voters abstained in protest. Congress then passed the final act, which held that a state constitution could be ratified even if only a minority of voters participated in the election. Between 1868 and 1870 all of the Southern states were readmitted.

Reconstruction Act (1867)

An Act

To provide for the more efficient Government of the Rebel States.

Whereas no legal State governments or adequate protection for life or property now exists in the rebel States of Virginia, North Carolina, South Carolina, Georgia, Mississippi, Alabama, Louisiana, Florida, Texas, and Arkansas; and whereas it is necessary that peace and good order should be enforced in said States until loyal and republican State governments can be legally established: Therefore,

Be it enacted by the Senate and House of Representatives of the United States of America in Congress assembled, That said rebel States shall be divided into military districts and made subject to the military authority of the United States as hereinafter prescribed, and for that purpose Virginia shall constitute the first district; North Carolina and South Carolina the second district; Georgia, Alabama, and Florida the third district; Mississippi and Arkansas the fourth district; and Louisiana and Texas the fifth district.

Sec. 2. *And be it further enacted,* That it shall be the duty of the President to assign to the command of each of said districts an officer of the army, not below the rank of brigadier-general, and to detail a sufficient military force to enable such officer to perform his duties and enforce his authority within the district to which he is assigned.

Sec. 3. *And be it further enacted,* That it shall be the duty of each officer assigned as aforesaid, to protect all persons in their rights of person and property, to suppress insurrection, disorder, and violence, and to punish, or cause to be punished, all disturbers of the public peace and criminals; and to this end he may allow local civil tribunals to take jurisdiction of and to try offenders, or, when in his judgment it may be necessary for the trial of offenders, he shall have power to organize military commissions or tribunals for that purpose, and all interference under color of State authority with the exercise of military authority under this act, shall be null and void.

Sec. 4. *And be it further enacted,* That all persons put under military arrest by virtue of this act shall be tried without unnecessary delay, and no cruel or unusual punishment shall be inflicted, and no sentence of any military commission or tribunal hereby authorized, affecting the life or liberty of any person, shall be executed until it is approved by the officer in command of the district, and the laws and regulations for the government of the army shall not be affected by this act, except in so far as they conflict with its provisions: *Provided,* That no sentence of death under the provisions of this act shall be carried into effect without the approval of the President.

Sec. 5. *And be it further enacted,* That when the people of any one of said rebel States shall have formed a constitution of government in conformity with the Constitution of the United States in all respects, framed by a convention of delegates elected by the male citizens of said State, twenty-one years old and upward, of whatever race, color, or previous condition, who have been resident in said State for one year previous to the day of such election, except such as may be disfranchised for participation in the rebellion or for felony at common law, and when such constitution shall provide that the elective franchise shall be enjoyed by all such persons as have the qualifications herein stated for electors of delegates, and when such constitution shall be ratified by a majority of the persons voting on the question of ratification who are qualified as electors for delegates, and when such constitution shall have been submitted to Congress for examination and approval, and Congress shall have approved the same, and when said State, by a vote of its legislature elected under said constitution, shall have adopted the amendment to the Constitution of the United States, proposed by the Thirty-ninth Congress, and known as article fourteen, and when said article shall have become a part of the Constitution of the United States, said State shall be declared entitled to representation in Congress, and senators and representatives shall be admitted therefrom on their taking the oath prescribed by law, and then and thereafter the preceding sections of this act shall be inoperative in said State: *Provided,* That no person excluded from the privilege of holding office by said proposed amendment to the Constitution of the United States, shall be eligible to election as a member of the convention to frame a constitution for any of said rebel States, nor shall any such person vote for members of such convention.

Sec. 6. *And be it further enacted,* That, until the people of said rebel States shall be by law admitted to representation in the Congress of the United States, any civil governments which may exist therein shall be deemed provisional only, and in all respects subject to the paramount authority of the United States at any time to abolish, modify, control, or supersede the same; and in all elections to any office under such provisional governments all persons shall be entitled to vote, and none others, who are entitled to vote, under the provisions of the fifth section of this act; and no person shall be eligible to any office under any such provisional governments who would be disqualified from holding office under the provisions of the third *article* of said constitutional amendment.

Reconstruction Act of 1867 (Supplement I)

An Act

Supplementary to an Act entitled "An Act to provide for the more efficient Government of the Rebel States," passed March second, eighteen hundred and sixty-seven, and to facilitate Restoration.

Be it enacted by the Senate and House of Representatives of the United States of America in Congress assembled, That before the first day of September, eighteen hundred and sixty-seven, the commanding general in each district defined by an act entitled "An act to provide for the more efficient government of the rebel States," passed March second, eighteen hundred and sixty-seven, shall cause a registration to be made of the male citizens of the United States, twenty-one years of age and upwards, resident in each county or parish in the State or States included in his district, which registration shall include only those persons who are qualified to vote for delegates by the act aforesaid, and who shall have taken and subscribed the following oath or affirmation: "I, _____, do solemnly swear (or affirm), in the presence of Almighty God, that I am a citizen of the State of ____; that I have resided in said State of ____ months next preceding this day, and now reside in the county of ____, or the parish of ____, in said State (as the case may be); that I am twenty-one years old; that I have not been disfranchised for participation in any rebellion or civil war against the United States, nor for felony committed against the laws of any State or of the United States; that I have never been a member of any State legislature, nor held any executive or judicial office in any State and afterwards engaged in insurrection or rebellion against the United States, or given aid or comfort to the enemies thereof; that I have never taken an oath as a member of Congress of the United States, or as an officer of the United States, or as a member of any State legislature, or as an executive or judicial officer of any State, to support the Constitution of the United States, and afterwards engaged in insurrection or rebellion against the United States, or given aid or comfort to the enemies thereof; that I will faithfully support the Constitution and obey the laws of the United States, and will, to the best of my ability, encourage others so to do, so help me God"; which oath or affirmation may be administered by any registering officer.

Sec. 2. *And be it further enacted,* That after the completion of the registration hereby provided for in any State, at such time and places therein as the commanding general shall appoint and direct, of which at least thirty days' public shall be given, an election shall be held of delegates to a convention for the purpose of establishing a constitution and civil government for such State loyal to the Union, said convention in each State, except Virginia, to consist of the same number of members as the most numerous branch of the State legislature of such State in the year eighteen hundred and sixty, to be apportioned among the several district, counties, or parishes of such State by the commanding general, giving to each representation in the ratio of voters registered as aforesaid as nearly as may be. The convention in Virginia shall consist of the same number of members as represented the territory now constituting Virginia in the most numerous branch of the legislature of said State in the year eighteen hundred and sixty, to be apportioned as aforesaid.

Sec. 3. *And be it further enacted,* That at said election the registered voters of each State shall vote for or against a convention to form a constitution therefor under this act. Those voting in favor of such a convention shall have written or printed on the ballots by which they vote for delegates, as aforesaid, the words "For a convention," and those voting against such a convention shall have written or printed on such ballots the words "Against a convention." The persons appointed to superintend said election, and to make return of the voters given thereat, as herein provided, shall count and make return of the votes given for and against a convention; and the commanding general to whom the same shall have been returned shall ascertain and declare the total vote in each State for and against a convention. If a majority of the votes given on that question shall be for a convention, then such convention shall be held as hereinafter provided; but if a majority of said votes shall be against a convention, then no such convention shall be held under this act: *Provided,* That such convention shall not be held unless a majority of all such registered voters shall have voted on the question of holding such convention.

Sec. 4. *And be if further enacted,* That the commanding general of each district shall appoint as many boards of registration as may be necessary, consisting of three loyal officers or persons, to make and complete the registration, superintend the election, and make the return to him of the votes, list of voters, and of the persons elected as delegates by a plurality of the votes cast at said election; and upon receiving said returns he shall open the same, ascertain the persons elected as delegates, according to the returns of the officers who conducted said election, and make proclamation thereof; and if a majority of the votes given on that question shall be for a convention, the commanding general, within sixty days from the date of election, shall notify the delegates to assemble in convention, at a time and place to be mentioned in the notification, and said convention, when organized, shall proceed to frame a constitution and civil government according to the provisions of this act, and the act to which it is supplementary; and when the same shall have been so framed, said constitution shall be submitted by the convention for ratification to the persons registered under the provisions of this act at an election to be conducted by the officers or persons appointed or to be appointed by the commanding general, as hereinbefore provided, and to be held after the expiration of thirty days from the date of notice thereof, to be given by said convention; and the returns thereof shall be made to the commanding general of the district.

Sec. 5. *And be it further enacted,* That if, according to said returns, the constitution shall be ratified by a majority of the votes of the registered electors qualified as herein specified, cast at said election, at least one half of all the registered voters voting upon the question of such ratification, the president of the convention shall transmit a copy of the same, duly certified, to the President of the United States, who shall forthwith transmit the same to Congress, if then in session, and if not in session, then immediately upon its next assembling; and if it shall moreover appear to Congress that the election was one at which all the registered and qualified electors in the State had an opportunity to vote freely and without restraint, fear, or the influence of fraud, and if the Congress shall be satisfied that such constitution meets the approval of a majority of all the qualified electors in the State, and if the said constitution shall be declared by Congress to be in conformity with the provisions of the act to which this is supplementary, and the other provisions of said act shall have been complied with, and the said constitution shall be approved by Congress, the State shall be declared entitled to representation, and senators and representatives shall be admitted therefrom as therein provided.

Sec. 6. *And be it further enacted,* That all elections in the States mentioned in the said "Act to provide for the more efficient government of the rebel States," shall, during the operation of said act, be by ballot; and all officers making the said registration of voters and conducting said elections shall, before entering upon the discharge of their duties, take and subscribe the oath prescribed by the act approved July second, eighteen hundred and sixty-two, entitled "An act to prescribe an oath of office": *Provided,* That if any person shall knowingly and falsely take and subscribe any oath in this act prescribed, such person so offending and being thereof duly convicted shall be subject to the pains, penalties, and disabilities which by law are provided for the punishment of the crime of wilful and corrupt perjury.

Sec. 7. *And be it further enacted,* That all expenses incurred by the several commanding generals, or by virtue of any orders issued, or appointments made, by them, under or by virtue of this act, shall be paid out of any moneys in the treasury not otherwise appropriated.

Sec. 8. *And be it further enacted,* That the convention for each State shall prescribe the fees, salary, and compensation to be paid to all delegates and other officers and agents herein authorized or necessary to carry into effect the purposes of this act not herein otherwise provided for, and shall provide for the levy and collection of such taxes on the property in such State as may be necessary to pay the same.

Sec. 9. *And be it further enacted,* That the word "article," in the sixth section of the act to which this is supplementary, shall be construed to mean "section."

Reconstruction Act of 1867 (Supplement II)

An Act

Supplementary to an Act entitled "An Act to provide for the more efficient Government of the Rebel States," passed on the second day of March, eighteen hundred and sixty-seven, and the Act supplementary thereto, passed on the twenty-third day of March, eighteen hundred and sixty-seven.

Be it enacted by the Senate and House of Representatives of the United States of America in Congress assembled, That it is hereby declared to have been the true intent and meaning of the act of the second day of March, one thousand eight hundred and sixty-seven, entitled "An act to provide for the more efficient government of the rebel States," and of the act supplementary thereto, passed on the twenty-third day of March, in the year one thousand eight hundred and sixty-seven, that the governments then existing in the rebel States of Virginia, North Carolina, South Carolina, Georgia, Mississippi, Alabama, Louisiana, Florida, Texas, and Arkansas were not legal State governments; and that thereafter said governments, if continued, were to be continued subject in all respects to the military commanders of the respective districts, and to the paramount authority of Congress.

Sec. 2. *And be it further enacted,* That the commander of any district named in said act shall have power, subject to the disapproval of the General of the army of the United States, and to have effect till disapproved, whenever in the opinion of such commander the proper administration of said act shall require it, to suspend or remove from office, or from the performance of official duties and the exercise of official powers, any officer or person holding or exercising, or professing to hold or exercise, any civil or military office or duty in such district under any power, election, appointment or authority derived from, or granted by, or claimed under, any so-called State or the government thereof, or any municipal or other division thereof, and upon such suspension or removal such commander, subject to the disapproval of the General as aforesaid, shall have power to provide from time to time for the performance of the said duties of such officer or person so suspended or removed, by the detail of some competent officer or soldier of the army, or by the appointment of some other person, to perform the same, and to fill vacancies occasioned by death, resignation, or otherwise.

Sec. 3. *And be it further enacted,* That the General of the army of the United States shall be invested with all the powers of suspension, removal, appointment, and detail granted in the preceding section to district commanders.

Sec. 4. *And be it further enacted,* That the acts of the officers of the army already done in removing in said districts persons exercising the functions of civil officers, and appointing others in their stead, are hereby confirmed: *Provided,* That any person heretofore or hereafter appointed by any district commander to exercise the functions of any civil office, may be removed either by the military officer in command of the district, or by the General of the army. And it shall be the duty of such commander to remove from office as aforesaid all persons who are disloyal to the government of the United States, or who use their official influence in any manner to hinder, delay, prevent, or obstruct the due and proper administration of this act and the acts to which it is supplementary.

Sec. 5. *And be it further enacted,* That the boards of registration provided for in the act entitled "An act supplementary to an act entitled 'An act to provide for the more efficient government of the rebel States,' passed March two, eighteen hundred and sixty-seven, and to facilitate restoration," passed March twenty-three, eighteen hundred and sixty-seven, shall have power, and it shall be their duty before allowing the registration of any person, to ascertain, upon such facts or information as they can obtain, whether such person is entitled to be registered under said act, and the oath required by said act shall not be conclusive on such question, and no person shall be registered unless such board shall decide that he is entitled thereto; and such board shall also have power to examine, under oath, (to be administered by any member of such board,) any one touching the qualification of any person claiming registration; but in every case of refusal by the board to register an applicant, and in every case of striking his name from the list as hereinafter provided, the board shall make a note or memorandum, which shall be returned with the registration list to the commanding general of the district, setting forth the grounds of such refusal or such striking from the list: *Provided,* That no person shall be disqualified as member of any board of registration by reason of race or color.

Sec. 6. *And be it further enacted,* That the true intent and meaning of the oath prescribed in said supplementary act is, (among other things,) that no person who has been a member of the legislature of any State, or who has held any executive or judicial office in any State, whether he has taken an oath to support the Constitution of the United States or not, and whether he was holding such office at the commencement of the rebellion, or had held it before, and who has afterwards engaged in insurrection or rebellion against the United States, or given aid or comfort to the enemies thereof, is entitled to be registered or to vote; and the words "executive or judicial office in any State" in said oath mentioned shall be construed to include all civil offices created by law for the administration of any general law of State, or for the administration of justice.

Sec. 7. *And be it further enacted*, That the time for completing the original registration provided for in said act may, in the discretion of the commander of any district be extended to the first day of October, eighteen hundred and sixty-seven; and the boards of registration shall have power, and it shall be their duty, commencing fourteen days prior to any election under said act, and upon reasonable public notice of the time and place thereof, to revise, for a period of five days, the registration lists, and upon being satisfied that any person not entitled thereto has been registered, to strike the name of such person from the list, and such person shall not be allowed to vote. And such board shall also, during the same period, add to such registry the names of all persons who at that time possess the qualifications required by said act who have not been already registered; and no person shall, at any time, be entitled to the registered or to vote by reason of any executive pardon or amnesty for any act or thing which, without such pardon or amnesty, would disqualify him from registration or voting.

Sec. 8. *And be it further enacted*, That section four of said last-named act shall be construed to authorize the commanding general named therein, whenever he shall deem it needful, to remove any member of a board of registration and to appoint another in his stead, and to fill any vacancy in such board.

Sec. 9. *And be it further enacted*, That all members of said boards of registration and all persons hereafter elected or appointed to office in said military districts, under any so-called State or municipal authority, or by detail or appointment of the district commanders, shall be required to take and to subscribe the oath of office prescribed by law for officers or the United States.

Sec. 10. *And be it further enacted*, That no district commander or member of the board of registration, or any of the officers or appointees acting under them, shall be bound in his action by any opinion of any civil officer of the United States.

Sec. 11. *And be it further enacted*, That all the provisions of this act and of the acts to which this is supplementary shall be construed liberally, to the end that all the intents thereof may be fully and perfectly carried out.

Reconstruction Act of 1868

An Act

To amend the Act passed March twenty-third, eighteen hundred and sixty-seven, entitled "An Act supplementary to 'An Act to provide for the more efficient Government of the rebel States,' passed March second, eighteen hundred and sixty-seven, and to facilitate their Restoration."

Be it enacted by the Senate and House of Representatives of the United States of America in Congress assembled, That hereafter any election authorized by the act passed March twenty-three, eighteen hundred and sixty-seven, entitled "An act supplementary to 'An act to provide for the more efficient government of the rebel States,' passed March *two*, [second,] eighteen hundred and sixty-seven, and to facilitate their restoration," shall be decided by a majority of the votes actually cast; and at the election in which the question of the adoption or rejection of any constitution is submitted, any person duly registered in the State may vote in the election district where he offers to vote when he has resided therein for ten days next preceding such election, upon presentation of his certificate of registration, his affidavit, or other satisfactory evidence, under such regulations as the district commanders may prescribe.

Sec. 2. *And be it further enacted*, That the constitutional convention of any of the States mentioned in the acts to which this is amendatory may provide that at the time of voting upon the ratification of the constitution the registered voters may vote also for members of the House of Representatives of the United States, and for all elective officers provided for by the said constitution; and the same election officers who shall make the return of the votes cast on the ratification or rejection of the constitution, shall enumerate and certify the votes cast for members of Congress.

Source:

Statutes at Large, Vol. 14, pp. 428–430; Vol. 15, pp. 14–16, p. 41.

Mississippi v. Johnson, 1867

Suit filed on April 5, 1867, by the state of Mississippi asking the U.S. Supreme Court to prohibit President Andrew Johnson from enforcing the Reconstruction Acts of 1867 passed by the Radical Republican Congress. Though Johnson had opposed the acts as unconstitutional, and Congress had passed them over his veto, he nonetheless ordered the U.S. attorney general to fight the Mississippi suit. The Court unanimously denied the petition for lack of jurisdiction, stating that purely executive or purely legislative acts were not subject to judicial restraint.

———————————— ⚬⊗⚬ ————————————

The Chief Justice delivered the opinion of the court.

A motion was made, some days since, in behalf of the State of Mississippi, for leave to file a bill in the name of the State, praying this court perpetually to enjoin and restrain Andrew Johnson, President of the United States, and E. O. C. Ord, general commanding in the District of

Mississippi and Arkansas, from executing, or in any manner carrying out, certain acts of Congress therein named.

The acts referred to are those of March 2d and March 23d, 1867, commonly known as the Reconstruction Acts.

The Attorney-General objected to the leave asked for, upon the ground that no bill which makes a President a defendant, and seeks an injunction against him to restrain the performance of his duties as President, should be allowed to be filed in this court.

This point has been fully argued, and we will now dispose of it.

We shall limit our inquiry to the question presented by the objection, without expressing any opinion on the broader issues discussed in argument, whether, in any case, the President of the United States may be required, by the process of this court, to perform a purely ministerial act under a positive law, or may be held amenable, in any case, otherwise than by impeachment for crime.

The single point which requires consideration is this: Can the President be restrained by injunction from carrying into effect an act of Congress alleged to be unconstitutional?

It is assumed by the counsel for the State of Mississippi, that the President, in the execution of the Reconstruction Acts, is required to perform a mere ministerial duty. In this assumption there is, we think, a confounding of the terms ministerial and executive, which are by no means equivalent in import.

A ministerial duty, the performance of which may, in proper cases, be required of the head of a department, by judicial process, is one in respect to which nothing is left to discretion. It is a simple, definite duty, arising under conditions admitted or proved to exist, and imposed by law.

The case of *Marbury v. Madison, Secretary of State,* furnishes an illustration. A citizen had been nominated, confirmed, and appointed a justice of the peace for the District of Columbia, and his commission had been made out, signed, and sealed. Nothing remained to be done except delivery, and the duty of delivery was imposed by law on the Secretary of State. It was held that the performance of this duty might be enforced by *mandamus* issuing from a court having jurisdiction.

So, in this case of *Kendall, Postmaster-General, v. Stockton & Stokes,* an act of Congress had directed the Postmaster-General to credit Stockton & Stokes with such sums as the Solicitor of the Treasury should find due to them; and that officer refused to credit them with certain sums, so found due. It was held that the crediting of this money was a mere ministerial duty, the performance of which might be judicially enforced.

In each of these cases nothing was left to discretion. There was no room for the exercise of judgment. The law required the performance of a single specific act; and that performance, it was held, might be required by *mandamus.*

Very difficult is the duty of the President in the exercise of the power to see that the laws are faithfully executed, and among these law the acts named in the bill. By the first of these acts he is required to assign generals to command in the several military districts, and to detail sufficient military force to enable such officers to discharge their duties under the law. By the supplementary act, other duties are imposed on the several commanding generals, and these duties must necessarily be performed under the supervision of the President as commander-in-chief. The duty thus imposed on the President is in no just sense ministerial. It is purely executive and political.

An attempt on the part of the judicial department of the government to enforce the performance of such duties by the President might be justly characterized, in the language of Chief Justice Marshal, as "an absurd and excessive extravagance."

It is true that in the instance before us the interposition of the court is not sought to enforce action by the Executive under constitutional legislation, but to restrain such action under legislation alleged to be unconstitutional. But we are unable to perceive that this circumstance takes the case out of the general principles which forbid judicial interference with the exercise of Executive discretion.

It was admitted in the argument that the application now made to us is without a precedent; and this is of much weight against it.

Had it been supposed at the bar that this court would, in any case, interpose, by injunction, to prevent the execution of an unconstitutional act of Congress, it can hardly be doubted that applications with that object would have been heretofore addressed to it.

Occasions have not been wanting.

The constitutionality of the act for the annexation of Texas was vehemently denied. It made important and permanent changes in the relative importance of States and sections, and was by many supposed to be pregnant with disastrous results to large interests in particular States. But no one seems to have thought of an application for an injunction against the execution of the act by the President.

And yet it is difficult to perceive upon what principle the application now before us can be allowed and similar applications in that and other cases have been denied.

The fact that no such application was ever before made in any case indicates the general judgment of the profession that no such application should be entertained.

It will hardly be contended that Congress can interpose, in any case, to restrain the enactment of an unconstitutional law; and yet how can the right to judicial interposition to prevent such an enactment, when the purpose is evident and the execution of that purpose certain, be distinguished, in principle, from the right to such interposition against the execution of such a law by the President?

The Congress is the legislative department of the government; the President is the executive department. Neither can be restrained in its action by the judicial department; though the acts of both, when performed, are, in proper cases, subject to its cognizance.

The impropriety of such interference will be clearly seen upon consideration of its possible consequences.

Suppose the bill filed and the injunction prayed for allowed. If the President refuse obedience, it is needless to observe that the court is without power to enforce its process. If, on the other hand, the President complies with the order of the court and refuses to execute the acts of Congress, is it no clear that a collision may occur between the executive and legislative departments of the government? May not the House of Representatives impeach the President for such refusal? And in that case could this court interfere, in behalf of the President, thus endangered by compliance with its mandate, and restrain by injunction the Senate of the United States from sitting as a court of impeachment? Would the strange spectacle be offered to the public world of an attempt by this court to arrest proceedings in that court?

These questions answer themselves.

It is true that a State may file an original bill in this court. And it may be true, in some cases, that such a bill may be filed against the United States. But we are fully satisfied that this court has no jurisdiction of a bill to enjoin the President in the performance of his official duties; and that no such bill ought to be received by us.

It has been suggested that the bill contains a prayer that, if the relief sought cannot be had against Andrew Johnson, as President, it may be granted against Andrew Johnson as a citizen of Tennessee. But it is plain that relief as against the execution of an act of Congress by Andrew Johnson, is relief against its execution by the President. A bill praying an injunction against the execution of an act of Congress by the incumbent of the presidential office cannot be received, whether it describes him a President or as a citizen of a State.

Source:
U.S. Reports, Vol. 71, p. 475.

Covode Resolution (Articles of Impeachment of Andrew Johnson), 1868

Resolution passed by the U.S. House of Representatives on February 24, 1868, impeaching President Andrew Johnson for "high crimes and misdemeanors." The resolution cited 11 charges, including alleged violations of the Tenure of Office Act and the Command of the Army Act (which largely deprived the president of command of the army by requiring that he issue all military orders through the general of the army, Ulysses S. Grant). The resolution also claimed that Johnson had attempted to bring disgrace and ridicule upon Congress. The Senate failed by one vote to achieve the two-thirds majority necessary to convict the president.

———————— ⌇ ————————

In the House of Representatives, United States.

Articles Exhibited by the House of Representatives of the United States, in the Name of Themselves and All the People of the United States, Against Andrew Johnson, President of the United States, in Maintenance and Support of Their Impeachment Against Him for High Crimes and Misdemeanors in Office.

Article I. The said Andrew Johnson, President of the United States, on the 21st day of February, A.D. 1868, at Washington, in the District of Columbia, unmindful of the high duties of his office, of his oath of office, and of the requirement of the Constitution that he should take care that the laws be faithfully executed, did unlawfully and in violation of the Constitution and laws of the United States issue an order in writing for the removal of Edwin M. Stanton from the office of Secretary for the Department of War, said Edwin M. Stanton having been theretofore duly appointed and commissioned, by and with the advice and consent of the Senate of the United States, as such Secretary; and said Andrew Johnson, President of the United States, on the 12th day of August, A.D. 1867, and during the recess of said Senate, having suspended by his order Edwin M. Stanton from said office, and within twenty days after the first day of the next meeting of said Senate—that is to say, on the 12th day of December, in the year last aforesaid—having reported to said Senate such suspension, with the evidence and reasons for his action in the case and the name of the person designated to perform the duties of such office temporarily until the next meeting of the Senate; and said Senate thereafterwards, on the 13th day of January, A.D. 1868, having duly considered the evidence and reasons reported by said Andrew Johnson for said suspension, and having refused to concur in said suspension, whereby and by force of the provisions of an act entitled "An act regulating the tenure of certain civil offices," passed March 2, 1867, said Edwin M. Stanton did forthwith resume the functions of his office, whereof the said Andrew Johnson had then and there due notice; and said Edwin M. Stanton, by reason of the premises, on said 21st day of February, being lawfully entitled to hold said office of Secretary for the Department of War; which said order for the removal of said Edwin M. Stanton is in substance as follows; that is to say:

Executive Mansion,
Washington, D.C., February 21, 1868.
Hon. Edwin M. Stanton,
Washington, D.C.

Sir: By virtue of the power and authority vested in me as President by the Constitution and laws of the United States, you are hereby removed from office as Secretary for the Department of War, and your functions as such will terminate upon the receipt of this communication.

You will transfer to Brevet Major-General Lorenzo Thomas, Adjutant-General of the Army, who has this day been authorized and empowered to act as Secretary of War ad interim, all records, books, papers, and other public property now in your custody and charge.

Respectfully, yours,
Andrew Johnson.

which order was unlawfully issued with intent then and there to violate the act entitled "An act regulating the tenure of certain civil offices," passed March 2, 1867, and with the further intent, contrary to the provisions of said act, in violation thereof, and contrary to the provisions of the Constitution of the United States, and without the advice and consent of the Senate of the United States, the said Senate then and there being in session, to remove said Edwin M. Stanton from the office of Secretary for the Department of War, the said Edwin M. Stanton being then and there Secretary for the Department of War, and being then and there in the due and lawful execution and discharge of the duties of said office; whereby said Andrew Johnson, President of the United States, did then and there commit and was guilty of a high misdemeanor in office.

Art. II. That on said 21st day of February, A.D. 1868, at Washington, in the District of Columbia, said Andrew Johnson, President of the United States, unmindful of the high duties of his office, of his oath of office, and in violation of the Constitution of the United States, and contrary to the provisions of an act entitled "An act regulating the tenure of certain civil offices," passed March 2, 1867, without the advice and consent of the Senate of the United States, said Senate then and there being in session, and without authority of law, did, with intent to violate the Constitution of the United States and the act aforesaid, issue and deliver to one Lorenzo Thomas a letter of authority in substance as follows; that is to say:

Executive Mansion,
Washington, D.C., February 21, 1868.
Brevet Major-General Lorenzo Thomas,
Adjutant-General United States Army, Washington, D.C.

Sir: The Hon. Edwin M. Stanton having been this day removed from office as Secretary for the Department of War, you are hereby authorized and empowered to act as Secretary of War ad interim, and will immediately enter upon the discharge of the duties pertaining to that office.

Mr. Stanton has been instructed to transfer to you all the records, books, papers, and other public property now in his custody and charge.

Respectfully, yours,
Andrew Johnson.

then and there being no vacancy in said office of Secretary for the Department of War; whereby said Andrew Johnson, President of the United States, did then and there commit and was guilty of a high misdemeanor in office.

Art. III. That said Andrew Johnson, President of the United States, on the 21st day of February, A.D. 1868, at Washington, in the District of Columbia, did commit and was guilty of a high misdemeanor in office in this, that without authority of law, while the Senate of the United States was then and there in session, he did appoint one Lorenzo Thomas to be Secretary for the Department of War ad interim, without the advice and consent of the Senate, and with intent to violate the Constitution of the United States, no vacancy having happened in said office of Secretary for the Department of War during the recess of the Senate, and no vacancy existing in said office at the time, and which said appointment, so made by said Andrew Johnson, of said Lorenzo Thomas, is in substance as follows: that is to say:

Executive Mansion,
Washington, D.C., February 21, 1868.
Brevet Major-General Lorenzo Thomas,
Adjutant-General United States Army, Washington, D.C.

Sir: The Hon. Edwin M. Stanton having been this day removed from office as Secretary for the Department of War, you are hereby authorized and empowered to act as Secretary of War ad interim, and will immediately enter upon the discharge of the duties pertaining to that office.

Mr. Stanton has been instructed to transfer to you all the records, books, papers, and other public property now in his custody and charge.

Respectfully, yours,
Andrew Johnson.

Art. IV. That said Andrew Johnson, president of the United States, unmindful of the high duties of his office and his oath of office, in violation of the Constitution and laws of the United States, on the 21st day of February, A.D. 1868, at Washington, in the District of Columbia, did unlawfully conspire with one Lorenzo Thomas, and with other persons to the House of Representatives unknown, with intent, by intimidation and threats, unlawfully to hinder and prevent Edwin M. Stanton, then and there the Secretary for the Department of War, duly appointed under the laws of the United States, from holding said office of Secretary for the Department of War, contrary to and in violation of the Constitution of the United States and of the provisions of an act entitled "An act to define and punish certain conspiracies," approved July 31, 1861; whereby said Andrew Johnson, President of the United States, did then and there commit and was guilty of a high crime in office.

Art. V. That said Andrew Johnson, President of the United States, unmindful of the high duties of his office and of his oath of office, on the 21st day of February, A.D. 1868, and on divers other days and times in said year before the 2d day of March, A.D. 1868, at Washington, in the District of Columbia, did unlawfully conspire with one Lorenzo Thomas, and with other persons to the House of Representatives unknown, to prevent and hinder the execution of an act entitled "An act regulating the tenure of certain civil offices," passed March 2, 1867, and in pursuance of said conspiracy did unlawfully attempt to prevent Edwin M. Stanton, then and there being Secretary for the Department of War, duly appointed and commissioned under the laws of the United States, from holding said office; whereby the said Andrew Johnson, President of the United States, did then and there commit and was guilty of a high misdemeanor in office.

Art. VI. That said Andrew Johnson, President of the United States, unmindful of the high duties of his office and of his oath of office, on the 21st day of February, A.D. 1868, at Washington, in the District of Columbia, did unlawfully conspire with one Lorenzo Thomas by force to seize, take, and possess the property of the United States in the Department of War, and then and there in the custody and charge of Edwin M. Stanton, Secretary for said Department, contrary to the provisions of an act entitled "An act to define and punish certain conspiracies," approved July 31, 1861, and with intent to violate and disregard an act entitled "An act regulating the tenure of certain civil offices," passed March 2, 1867; whereby said Andrew Johnson, President of the United States, did then and there commit a high crime in office.

Art. VII. That said Andrew Johnson, President of the United States, unmindful of the high duties of his office and of his oath of office, on the 21st day of February, A.D. 1868, at Washington, in the District of Columbia, did unlawfully conspire with one Lorenzo Thomas with intent unlawfully to seize, take, and possess the property of the United States in the Department of War, in the custody and charge of Edwin M. Stanton, Secretary for said Department, with intent to violate and disregard the act entitled "An act regulating the tenure of certain civil offices," passed March 2, 1867; whereby said Andrew Johnson, President of the United States, did then and there commit a high misdemeanor in office.

Art. VIII. That said Andrew Johnson, President of the United States, unmindful of the high duties of his office and of his oath of office, with intent unlawfully to control the disbursement of the moneys appropriated for the military service and for the Department of War, on the 21st day of February, A.D. 1868, at Washington, in the District of Columbia, did unlawfully, and contrary to the provisions of an act entitled "An act regulating the tenure of certain civil offices," passed March 2, 1867, and in violation of the Constitution of the United States, and without the advice and consent of the Senate of the United States, and while the Senate was then and there is session, there being no vacancy in the office of Secretary for the Department of War, and with intent to violate and disregard the act aforesaid, then and there issue and deliver to one Lorenzo Thomas a letter of authority, in writing, in substance as follows; that is to say:

Executive Mansion,
Washington, D.C., February 21, 1868.
Brevet Major-General Lorenzo Thomas,
Adjutant-General United States Army, Washington, D.C.

Sir: The Hon. Edwin M. Stanton having been this day removed from office as Secretary for the Department of War, you are hereby authorized and empowered to act as Secretary of War ad interim, and will immediately enter upon the discharge of the duties pertaining to that office.

Mr. Stanton has been instructed to transfer to you all the records, books, papers, and other public property now in his custody and charge.

Respectfully, yours,
Andrew Johnson.

whereby said Andrew Johnson, President of the United States, did then and there commit and was guilty of a high misdemeanor in office.

Art. IX. That said Andrew Johnson, President of the United States, on the 22d day of February, A.D. 1868, at Washington, in the District of Columbia, in disregard of the Constitution and the laws of the United States duly enacted, as Commander in Chief of the Army of the United States, did bring before himself then and there William H. Emory, a major-general by brevet in the Army of the United States, actually in command of the Department of Washington and the military forces thereof, and did then and there, as such Commander in Chief, declare to and instruct said Emory that part of a law of the United States, passed March 2, 1867, entitled "An act making appropriations for the support of the Army for the year ending June 30, 1868, and for other purposes," especially the second section hereof, which provides, among other things, that "all orders and instructions relating to military operations issued by the president or Secretary of War shall be issued through the General of the Army, and in case of his inability through the next in rank," was unconstitutional and in contravention of the commission of said Emory, and which said provision of law had been theretofore duly and legally promulgated by general order for the government and direction of the Army of the United States, as the said Andrew Johnson then and there well knew, with intent thereby to induce said Emory, in his official capacity as commander of the Department of Washington, to violate the provisions of said act and to take and receive, act upon, and obey such orders as he, the said Andrew Johnson, might make and give, and which should not be issued through the General of the Army of the United States, according to the provisions of said act, and with the further intent thereby to enable him, the said Andrew Johnson, to prevent the execution of the act entitled "An act regulating the tenure of certain civil offices," passed March 2, 1867, and to unlawfully prevent Edwin M. Stanton, then being Secretary for the Department of War, from holding said office and discharging the duties thereof; whereby said Andrew Johnson, President of the United States, did then and there commit and was guilty of a high misdemeanor in office.

And the House of Representatives, by protestation, saving to themselves liberty of exhibiting at any time hereafter any further articles or other accusation or impeachment against the said Andrew Johnson, President of the United States, and also of replying to his answers which he shall make unto the articles herein preferred against him, and of offering proof to the same, and every part thereof, and to all and every other article, accusation, or impeachment which shall be exhibited by them, as the case shall require, do demand that the said Andrew Johnson may be put to answer the high crimes and misdemeanors in office herein charged against him, and that such proceedings, examinations, trials, and judgments may be thereupon had and given as may be agreeable to law and justice.

See also TENURE OF OFFICE ACT OF 1867.

Source:

James D. Richardson, ed. *A Compilation of the Messages and Papers of the Presidents, 1789–1897*. Washington, D.C.: Government Printing Office, 1899.

Texas v. White, 1869

U.S. Supreme Court decision in 1869 that upheld the indissolubility of the Union and the authority of Congress to reconstruct the states. The governor of Texas sued to prevent payment on U.S. bonds that the secessionist Texas government had disposed of to pay for Confederate supplies. He contended that the secessionist state government had been illegal and therefore its disposition of bonds had been illegal. The Court agreed, ruling that secession had been invalid and that the Union was perpetual and indissoluble. While not ruling on the validity of specific Reconstruction acts, the Court stated that Congress had the duty to guarantee republican governments in the states. That part of the Court's opinion on the indissolubility of the Union is excerpted.

⸺⸺⸺⸺⸺⸺⸺⸺⸺⸺⸺⸺⸺⸺

The Chief Justice delivered the opinion of the court.

This is an original suit in this court, in which the State of Texas, claiming certain bonds of the United States as her property, asks an injunction to restrain the defendants from receiving payment from the National government, and to compel the surrender of the bonds to the State.

It appears from the bill, answers, and proofs, that the United States, by act of September 9, 1850, offered to the State of Texas, in compensation for her claims connected with the settlement of her boundary, $10,000,000 in five per cent bonds, each for the sum of $1000; and that this offer was accepted by Texas. One-half of these bonds were retained for certain purposes in the National treasury, and the other half were delivered to the State. The bonds thus delivered were dated January 1, 1851, and were all made payable to the State of Texas, or bearer, and redeemable after the 31st day of December, 1864. They were received in behalf of the State by the comptroller of public accounts, under authority of an act of the legislature, which, besides giving that authority, provided that no bond should be available in the hands of any holder until after indorsement by the governor of the State.

After the breaking out of the rebellion, the insurgent legislature of Texas, on the 11th of January, 1862, repealed the act requiring the indorsement of the governor, and on the same day provided for the organization of a military board, composed of the governor, comptroller, and treasurer; and authorized a majority of that board to provide for the defence of the State by means of any bonds in the treasury, upon any account, to the extent of $1,000,000. The defence contemplated by the act was to be made against the United States by war. Under this authority the military board entered into an agreement with George W. White and John Chiles, two of the defendants, for the sale to them of one hundred and thirty-five of these bonds, then in the treasury of the State, and seventy-six more, then deposited with Droege & Co., in England; in payment for which they engaged to deliver to the board a large quantity of cotton cards and medicines. This agreement was made on the 12th of January, 1865. On the 12th of March, 1865, White and Chiles received from the military board one hundred and thirty-five of these bonds, none of which were indorsed by any governor of Texas. Afterward, in the course of the years 1865 and 1866, some of the same bonds came into the possession of others of the defendants, by purchase, or as security for advances of money.

Such is a brief outline of the case. It will be necessary hereafter to refer more in detail to some particular circumstances of it.

The first inquiries to which our attention was directed by counsel, arose upon the allegations of the answer of Chiles, (1) that no sufficient authority is shown for the prosecution of the suit in the name and on the behalf of the State of Texas; and (2) that the State, having severed her relations with a majority of the States of the Union, and having by her ordinance of secession attempted to throw off her allegiance to the Constitution and government of the United States, has so far changed her status as to be disabled from prosecuting suits in the National courts.

The first of these allegations is disproved by the evidence. A letter of authority, the authenticity of which is not disputed, has been produced, in which J. W. Throckmorton, elected governor under the constitution adopted in 1866, and proceeding under an act of the State legislature relating to these bonds, expressly ratifies and confirms the action of the solicitors who filed the bill, and empowers them to prosecute this suit; and it is further proved by the affidavit of Mr. Paschal, counsel for the complainant, that he was duly appointed by Andrew J. Hamilton, while provisional governor of Texas, to represent the State of Texas in reference to the bonds in controversy, and that his appointment has been renewed by E.M. Pease, the actual governor. If Texas was a State of the Union at the time of these acts, and these persons, or either of them, were competent to represent the State, this proof leaves no doubt upon the question of authority.

The other allegation presents a question of jurisdiction. It is not to be questioned that this court has original jurisdiction of suits by States against citizens of other States, or that the States entitled to invoke this jurisdiction must be States of the Union. But, it is equally clear that no such jurisdiction has been conferred upon this court of suits by any other political communities than such States.

If, therefore, it is true that the State of Texas was not at the time of filing this bill, or is not now, one of the United States, we have no jurisdiction of this suit, and it is our duty to dismiss it.

We are very sensible of the magnitude and importance of this question, of the interest it excites, and of the difficulty, not to say impossibility, of so disposing of it as to satisfy the conflicting judgments of men equally enlightened, equally upright, and equally patriotic. But we meet it in the case, and we must determine it in the exercise of our best judgment, under the guidance of the Constitution alone.

Some not unimportant aid, however, in ascertaining the true sense of the Constitution, may be derived from considering what is the correct idea of a State, apart from any union or confederation with other States. The poverty of language often compels the employment of terms in quite different significations; and of this hardly any example more signal is to be found than in the use of the word we are now considering. It would serve no useful purpose to attempt an enumeration of all the various senses in which it is used. A few only need be noticed.

It describes sometimes a people or community of individuals united more or less closely in political relations, inhabiting temporarily or permanently the same country; often it denotes only the country or territorial region, inhabited by such a community; not unfrequently it is applied to the government under which the people live; at other times it represents the combined idea of people, territory, and government.

It is not difficult to see that in all these senses the primary conception is that of a people or community. The people, in whatever territory dwelling, either temporarily or permanently, and whether organized under a regular government, or united by looser and less definite relations, constitute the state.

This is undoubtedly the fundamental idea upon which the republican institutions of our own country are established. It was stated very clearly by an eminent judge, in one of the earliest cases adjudicated by this court, and we are not aware of anything, in any subsequent decision, of a different tenor.

In the Constitution the term state most frequently expresses the combined idea just noticed, of people, territory, and government. A state, in the ordinary sense of the Constitution, is a political community of free citizens, occupying a territory of defined boundaries, and organized under a government sanctioned and limited by a written constitution, and established by the consent of the governed. It is the union of such states, under a common constitution, which forms the distinct and greater political unit, which that Constitution designates as the United States, and makes of the people and states which compose it one people and one country.

The use of the word in this sense hardly requires further remark. In the clauses which impose prohibitions upon the States in respect to the making of treaties, emitting of bills of credit, and laying duties of tonnage, and which guarantee to the States representation in the House of Representatives and in the Senate, are found some instances of this use in the Constitution. Others will occur to every mind.

But it is also used in its geographical sense, as in the clauses which require that a representative in Congress shall be an inhabitant of the State in which he shall be chosen, and that the trial of crimes shall be held within the State where committed.

And there are instances in which the principal sense of the word seems to be that primary one to which we have adverted, of a people or political community, as distinguished from a government.

In this latter sense the word seems to be used in the clause which provides that the United States shall guarantee to every State in the Union a republican form of government, and shall protect each of them against invasion.

In this clause a plain distinction is made between a State and the government of a State.

Having thus ascertained the senses in which the word state is employed in the Constitution, we will proceed to consider the proper application of what has been said.

The Republic of Texas was admitted into the Union, as a State, on the 27th of December, 1845. By this act the new State, and the people of the new State, were invested with all the rights, and became subject to all the responsibilities and duties of the original States under the Constitution.

From the date of admission, until 1861, the State was represented in the Congress of the United States by her senators and representatives, and her relations as a member of the Union remained unimpaired. In that year, acting upon the theory that the rights of a State under the Constitution might be renounced, and her obligations thrown off at pleasure, Texas undertook to sever the bond thus formed, and to break up her constitutional relations with the United States.

On the 1st of February, a convention, called without authority, but subsequently sanctioned by the legislature regularly elected, adopted an ordinance to dissolve the union between the State of Texas and the other States under the Constitution of the United States, whereby Texas was declared to be "a separate and sovereign State," and "her people and citizens" to be "absolved from all allegiance to the United States, or the government thereof."

It was ordered by a vote of the convention and by an act of the legislature, that this ordinance should be submitted to the people, for approval or disapproval, on the 23d of February, 1861.

Without awaiting, however, the decision thus invoked, the convention, on the 4th of February, adopted a resolution designating seven delegates to represent the State in the convention of seceding States at Montgomery, "in order," as the resolution declared, "that the wishes and interests of the people of Texas may be consulted in reference to the constitution and provisional government that may be established by said convention."

Before the passage of this resolution the convention had appointed a committee of public safety, and adopted an ordinance giving authority to that committee to take measures for obtaining possession of the property of the United States in Texas, and for removing the National troops from her limits. The members of the committee, and all officers and agents appointed or employed by it, were sworn to secrecy and to allegiance to the State. Commissioners were to once appointed, with instructions to repair to the headquarters of General Twiggs, then representing the United States in command of the department, and to make the demands necessary for the accomplishment of the purposes of the committee. A military force was organized in support of these demands, and an arrangement was effected with the commanding general, by which the United States troops were engaged to leave the State, and the forts and all the public property, not necessary to the removal of the troops, were surrendered to the commissioners.

These transactions took place between the 2d and the 18th of February, and it was under these circumstances that the vote upon the ratification or rejection of the ordinance of secession was taken on the 23d of February. It was ratified by a majority of the voters of the State.

The convention, which had adjourned before the vote was taken, reassembled on the 2d of March, and instructed the delegates already sent to the Congress of the seceding States, to apply for admission into the confederation, and to give the adhesion of Texas to its provisional constitution.

It proceeded, also, to make the changes in the State constitution which this adhesion made necessary. The words "United States," were stricken out wherever they occurred, and the words "Confederate States" substituted; and the members of the legislature, and all officers of the State, were required by the new constitution to take an oath of fidelity to the constitution and laws of the new confederacy.

Before, indeed, these changes in the constitution had been completed, the officers of the State had been required to appear before the committee and take an oath of allegiance to the Confederate States.

The governor and secretary of state, refusing to comply, were summarily ejected from office.

The members of the legislature, which had also adjourned and reassembled on the 18th of March, were more compliant. They took the oath, and proceeded on the 8th of April to provide by law for the choice of electors of president and vice-president of the Confederate States.

The representatives of the State in the Congress of the United States were withdrawn, and as soon as the seceded States become organized under a constitution, Texas sent senators and representatives to the Confederate Congress.

In all respects, so far as the object could be accomplished by ordinances of the convention, by acts of the legislature, and by votes of the citizens, the relations of Texas to the Union were broken up, and new relations to a new government were established for them.

The position thus assumed could only be maintained by arms, and Texas accordingly took part, with the other Confederate States, in the war of the rebellion, which these events made inevitable. During the whole of that war there was no governor, or judge, or any other State officer in Texas, who recognized the National authority. Nor was any officer of the United States permitted to exercise any authority whatever under the National government within the limits of the State, except under the immediate protection of the National military forces.

Did Texas, in consequence of these acts, cease to be a State? Or, if not, did the State cease to be a member of the Union?

It is needless to discuss, at length, the question, whether the right of a State to withdraw from the Union for any cause, regarded by herself as sufficient, is consistent with the Constitution of the United States.

The Union of the States never was a purely artificial and arbitrary relation. It began among the Colonies, and grew out of common origin, mutual sympathies, kindred principles, similar interests, and geographical relations. It was confirmed and strengthened by the necessities of war, and received definite form, and character, and sanction from the Articles of Confederation. By these the Union was solemnly declared to "be perpetual." And when these Articles were found to be inadequate to the exigencies of the country, the Constitution was ordained "to form a more perfect Union." It is difficult to convey the idea of indissoluble unity more clearly than by these words. What can be indissoluble if a perpetual Union, made more perfect, is not?

But the perpetuity and indissolubility of the Union, by no means implies the loss of distinct and individual existence, or of the right of self-government by the States. Under the Articles of Confederation each State retained its sovereignty, freedom, and independence, and every power, jurisdiction, and right not expressly delegated to the United States. Under the Constitution, though the powers of the States were much restricted, still, all powers no delegated to the United States, nor prohibited to the States, are reserved to the States respectively, or to the people. And we have already had occasion to remark at his term, that "the people of each State compose a State, having its own government, and endowed with all the func-

tions essential to separate and independent existence," and that "without the States in union, there could be no such political body as the United States." Not only, therefore, can there be no loss of separate and independent autonomy to the States, through their union under the Constitution, but it may be not unreasonably said that the preservation of the States, and the maintenance of their governments, are as much within the design and care of the Constitution as the preservation of the Union and the maintenance of the National government. The Constitution, in all its provisions, looks to an indestructible Union, composed of indestructible States.

When, therefore, Texas became one of the United States, she entered into an indissoluble relation. All the obligations of perpetual union, and all the guaranties of republican government in the Union, attached at once to the State. The act which consummated her admission into the Union was something more than a compact; it was the incorporation of a new member into the political body. And it was final. The union between Texas and the other States was as complete, as perpetual, and as indissoluble as the union between the original States. There was no place for reconsideration, or revocation, except through revolution, or through consent of the States.

Considered therefore as transactions under the Constitution, the ordinance of secession, adopted by the convention and ratified by a majority of the citizens of Texas, and all the acts of her legislature intended to give effect to that ordinance, were absolutely null. They were utterly without operation in law. The obligations of the States, as a member of the Union, and of every citizen of the State, as a citizen of the United States, remained perfect and unimpaired. It certainly follows that the State did not cease to be a State, nor her citizens to be citizens of the Union. If this were otherwise, the State must have become foreign, and her citizens foreigners. The war must have ceased to be a war for the suppression or rebellion, and must have become a war for conquest and subjugation.

Our conclusion therefore is, that Texas continued to be a State, and a State of the Union, notwithstanding the transactions to which we have referred. And this conclusion, in our judgment, is not in conflict with any act or declaration of any department of the National government, but entirely in accordance with the whole series of such acts and declarations since the first outbreak of the rebellion.

But in order to the exercise, by a State, of the right to sue in this court, there needs to be a State government, competent to represent the State in its relations with the National government, so far at least as the institution and prosecution of a suit is concerned.

And it is by no means a logical conclusion, from the premises which we have endeavored to establish, that the governmental relations of Texas to the Union remained unaltered. Obligations often remain unimpaired, while relations are greatly changed. The obligations of allegiance to the State, and of obedience to her laws, subject to the Constitution of the United States, are binding upon all citizens, whether faithful or unfaithful to them; but the relations which subsist while these obligations are performed, are essentially different from those which arise when they are disregarded and set at nought. And the same must necessarily be true of the obligations and relations of States and citizens to the Union. No one has been bold enough to contend that, while Texas was controlled by a government hostile to the United States, and in affiliation with a hostile confederation, waging war upon the United States, senators chosen by her legislature, or representatives elected by her citizens, were entitled to seats in Congress; or that any suit, instituted in her name, could be entertained in this court. All admit that, during this condition of civil war, the rights of the State as a member, and of her people as citizens of the Union, were suspended. The government and the citizens of the State, refusing to recognize their constitutional obligations, assumed the character of enemies, and incurred the consequences of rebellion.

These new relations imposed new duties upon the United States. The first was that of suppressing the rebellion. The next was that of re-establishing the broken relations of the State with the Union. The first of these duties having been performed, the next necessarily engaged the attention of the National government.

The authority for the performance of the first had been found in the power to suppress insurrection and carry on war; for the performance of the second, authority was derived from the obligation of the United States to guarantee to every State in the Union a republican form of government. The latter, indeed, in the case of a rebellion which involves the government of a State, and for the time excludes the National authority from its limits, seems to be a necessary complement to the former.

Of this, the case of Texas furnishes a striking illustration. When the war closed there was no government in the State except that which had been organized for the purpose of waging war against the United States. That government immediately disappeared. The chief functionaries left the State. Many of the subordinate officials followed their example. Legal responsibilities were annulled or greatly impaired. It was inevitable that great confusion should prevail. If order was maintained, it was where the good sense and virtue of the citizens gave support to local acting magistrates, or supplied more directly the needful restraints.

A great social change increased the difficulty of the situation. Slaves, in the insurgent States, with certain local exceptions, had been declared free by the Proclamation of Emancipation; and whatever questions might be made as to the effect of that act, under the Constitution, it was clear, from the beginning, that its practical operation, in connection with legislative acts of like tendency, must be complete enfranchisement. Wherever the National forces obtained control, the slaves became freemen. Support to the acts of Congress and the proclamation of the President, concerning slaves, was made a condition of amnesty by President Lincoln, in December, 1863, and by President Johnson in May, 1865. And emancipation was confirmed, rather than ordained, in the insurgent States, by the amendment to the Constitution prohibiting slavery throughout the Union, which was proposed by Congress in February, 1865, and ratified, before the close of the following autumn, by the requisite three-fourths of the States.

The new freemen necessarily became part of the people, and the people still constituted the State; for States, like individuals, retain their identity, though changed to some extent in their constituent elements. And it was the State, thus constituted, which was now entitled to the benefit of the constitutional guaranty.

There being then no government in Texas in constitutional relations with the Union, it became the duty of the United States to provide for the restoration of such a government. But the restoration of the government which existed before the rebellion, without a new election of officers, was obviously impossible; and before any such election could be properly held, it was necessary that the old constitution should receive such amendments as would conform its provisions to the new conditions created by emancipation, and afford adequate security to the people of the State.

In the exercise of the power conferred by the guaranty clause, as in the exercise of every other constitutional power, a discretion in the choice of means is necessarily allowed. It is essential only that the means must be necessary and proper for carrying into execution the power conferred, through the restoration of the State to its constitutional relations, under a republican form of government, and that no acts be done, and no authority exerted, which is either prohibited or unsanctioned by the Constitution.

It is not important to review, at length, the measures which have been taken, under this power, by the executive and legislative departments of the National government. It is proper, however, to observe that almost immediately after the cessation of organized hostilities, and while the war yet smouldered in Texas, the President of the United States issued his proclamation appointing a provisional governor for the State, and providing for the assembling of a convention, with a view to the re-establishment of a republican government, under an amended constitution, and to the restoration of the State to her proper constitutional relations. A convention was accordingly assembled, the constitution amended, elections held, and a State government, acknowledging its obligations to the Union, established.

Whether the action then taken was, in all respects, warranted by the Constitution, it is not now necessary to determine. The power exercised by the President was supposed, doubtless, to be derived from his constitutional functions, as commander-in-chief; and, so long as the war continued, it cannot be denied that he might institute temporary government within insurgent districts, occupied by the National forces, or take measures, in any State, for the restoration of State government faithful to the Union, employing, however, in such efforts, only such means and agents as were authorized by constitutional laws.

But, the power to carry into effect the clause of guaranty is primarily a legislative power, and resides in Congress. "Under the fourth article of the Constitution, it rests with Congress to decide what government is the established one in a State. For, as the United States guarantee to each State a republican government, Congress must necessarily decide what government is established in the State, before it can determine whether it is republican or not."

This is the language of the late Chief Justice, speaking for this court, in a case from Rhode Island, arising from the organization of opposing governments in that State. And, we think that the principle sanctioned by it may be applied, with even more propriety, to the case of a State deprived of all rightful government, by revolutionary violence; though necessarily limited to cases where the rightful government is thus subverted, or in imminent danger of being overthrown by an opposing government, set up by force within the State.

The action of the President must, therefore, be considered as provisional, and, in that light, it seems to have been regarded by Congress. It was taken after the term of the 38th Congress had expired. The 39th Congress, which assembled in December, 1865, followed by the 40th Congress, which met in March, 1867, proceeded, after long deliberation, to adopt various measures for reorganization and restoration. These measures were embodied in proposed amendments to the Constitution, and in the acts known as the Reconstruction Acts, which have been so far carried into effect, that a majority of the States which were engaged in the rebellion have been restored to their constitutional relations, under forms of government, adjudged to be republican by Congress, through the admission of their "Senators and Representatives into the councils of the Union."

Nothing in the case before us requires the court to pronounce judgment upon the constitutionality of any particular provision of these acts.

But, it is important to observe that these acts themselves show that the governments, which had been established and had been in actual operation under executive direction, were recognized by Congress as provisional, as existing, and as capable of continuance.

By the act of March 2, 1867, the first of the series, these governments were, indeed, pronounced illegal and were subjected to military control, and were declared to be provisional only; and by the supplementary act of July 19, 1867, the third of the series, it was further declared that it was the true intent and meaning of the act of March 2, that the governments then existing were not legal State governments, and if continued, were to be continued subject to the military commanders of the respective districts and to the paramount authority of Congress. We do not inquire here into the constitutionality of this legislation so far as it relates to military authority, or to the paramount authority of Congress. It suffices to say, that the terms of the acts necessarily imply recognition of actually existing governments; and that in point of fact, the governments thus recognized, in some imported respects, still exist.

What has thus been said generally describes, with sufficient accuracy, the situation of Texas. A provisional governor of the State was appointed by the President in 1865; in 1866 a governor was elected by the people under the constitution of that year; at a subsequent date a governor was appointed by the commander of the district. Each of the three exercised executive functions and actually represented the State in the executive department.

In the case before us each has given his sanction to the prosecution of the suit, and we find no difficulty, without investigating the legal title of either to the executive office, in holding that the sanction thus given sufficiently warranted the action of the solicitor and counsel in behalf of the State. The necessary conclusion is that the suit was instituted and is prosecuted by competent authority.

The question of jurisdiction being thus disposed of, we proceed to the consideration of the merits as presented by the pleadings and the evidence.

And the first question to be answered is, whether or not the title of the State to the bonds in controversy was divested by the contract of the military board with White and Chiles?

That the bonds were the property of the State of Texas on the 11th of January, 1862, when the act prohibiting alienation without the indorsement of the governor, was repealed, admits of no question, and is not denied. They came into her possession and ownership through public acts of the general government and of the State, which gave notice to all the world of the transaction consummated by them. And, we think it clear that, if a State, by a public act of her legislature, imposes restrictions upon the alienation of her property, that every person who takes a transfer of such property must be held affected by notice of them. Alienation, in disregard of such restrictions, can convey no title to the alienee.

In this case, however, it is said that the restriction imposed by the act of 1851 was repealed by the act of 1862. And this is true if the act of 1862 can be regarded as valid. But, was it valid?

The legislature of Texas, at the time of the repeal, constituted one of the departments of a State government, established in hostility to the Constitution of the United States. It cannot be regarded, therefore, in the courts of the United States, as a lawful legislature, or its acts as lawful acts. And, yet, it is an historical fact that the government of Texas, then in full control of the State, was its only actual government; and certainly if Texas had been a separate State, and not one of the United States, the new government, having displaced the regular authority, and having established itself in the customary seats of power, and in the exercise of the ordinary functions of administration, would have constituted, in the strictest sense of the words, a *de facto* government, and its acts, during the period of its existence as such, would be effectual, and, in almost all respects, valid. And, to some extent, this is true of the actual government of Texas, though unlawful and revolutionary, as to the United States.

It is not necessary to attempt any exact definitions, within which the acts of such a State government must be treated as valid, or invalid. It may be said, perhaps with sufficient accuracy, that acts necessary to peace and good order among citizens, such for example, as acts sanctioning and protecting marriage and the domestic relations, governing the course of descents, regulating the conveyance and transfer of property, real and personal, and providing remedies for injuries to person and estate, and other similar acts, which would be valid if emanating from a lawful government, must be regarded in general as valid when proceeding from an actual, though unlawful government; and that acts in furtherance or support of rebellion against the United States, or intended to defeat the just rights of citizens, and other acts of like nature, must, in general, be regarded as invalid and void.

What, then, tried by these general tests, was the character of the contract of the military board with White and Chiles?

That board, as we have seen, was organized, not for the defence of the State against a foreign invasion, or for its protection against domestic violence, within the meaning of these words as used in the National Constitution, but for the purpose, under the name of defence, of levying war against the United States. This purpose was, undoubtedly, unlawful, for the acts which it contemplated are, within the express definition of the Constitution, treasonable.

It is true that the military board was subsequently reorganized. It consisted, thereafter, of the governor and two other members, appointed and removable by him; and was, therefore, entirely subordinate to executive control. Its general object remained without change, but its powers were "extended to the control of all public works and supplies, and to the aid of producing within the State, by the importation of articles necessary and proper for such aid."

And it was insisted in argument on behalf of some of the defendants, that the contract with White and Chiles, being for the purchase of cotton-cards and medicines, was not a contract in aid of the rebellion, but for obtaining goods capable of a use entirely legitimate and innocent, and, therefore, that payment for those goods by the transfer of any property of the State was not unlawful. We cannot adopt this view. Without entering, at this time, upon the inquiry whether any contract made by such a board can be sustained, we are obliged to say that the enlarged powers of the board appear to us to have been conferred in furtherance of its main purpose, of war against the United States, and that the contract, under consideration, even if made in the execution of those enlarged powers, was still a contract in aid of the rebellion, and, therefore, void. And we cannot shut our eyes to the evidence which proves that the act of repeal was intended to aid rebellion by facilitating the transfer of these bonds. It was supposed, doubtless, that negotiation of them would be less difficult if they bore upon their face no direct evidence of having come from the possession of any insurgent State government. We can give no effect, therefore, to this repealing act.

It follows that the title of the State was not divested by the act of the insurgent government in entering into this contract.

But it was insisted further, in behalf of those defendants who claim certain of these bonds by purchase, or as collateral security, that however unlawful may have been the means by which White and Chiles obtained possession of the bonds, they are innocent holders, without notice, and entitled to protection as such under the rules which apply to securities which pass by delivery. These rules were fully discussed in *Murray v. Lardner*. We held in that case that the purchaser of coupon bonds, before due, without notice and in good faith, is unaffected by want of title in the seller, and that the burden of proof in respect to notice and want of good faith, is on the claimant of the bonds as against the purchaser. We are entirely satisfied with this doctrine.

Does the State, then, show affirmatively notice to these defendants of want of title to the bonds in White and Chiles?

It would be difficult to give a negative answer to this question if there were no other proof than the legislative acts of Texas. But there is other evidence which might fairly be held to be sufficient proof of notice, if the rule to which we have adverted could be properly applied to this case.

But these rules have never been applied to matured obligations. Purchasers of notes or bonds past due take nothing but the actual right and title of the vendors.

The bonds in question were dated January 1, 1851, and were redeemable after the 31st of December, 1864. In strictness, it is true they were not payable on the day when they became redeemable; but the known usage of the United States to pay all bonds as soon as the right of payment accrues, except where a distinction between redeemability and payability is made by law, and shown on the face of the bonds, requires the application of the rule respecting overdue obligations to bonds of the United States which have become redeemable, and in respect to which no such distinction has been made.

Now, all the bonds in controversy had become redeemable before the date of the contract with White and Chiles; and all bonds of the same issue which have the indorsement of a governor of Texas made before the date of the secession ordinance—and there were no others indorsed by any governors—had been paid in coin on presentation at the Treasury Department; while, on the contrary, applications for the payment of bonds, without the required indorsement, and of coupons detached from such bonds, made to that department, had been denied.

As a necessary consequence, the negotiation of these bonds became difficult. They sold much below the rates they would have commanded had the title to them been unquestioned. They were bought in fact, and under the circumstances could only have been bought, upon speculation. The purchasers took the risk of a bad title, hoping, doubtless, that through the action of the National government, or of the government of Texas, it might be converted into a good one.

And it is true that the first provisional governor of Texas encouraged the expectation that these bonds would be ultimately paid to the holders. But he was not authorized to make any engagement in behalf of the State, and in fact made none. It is true, also, that the Treasury Department, influenced perhaps by these representations, departed to some extent from its original rule, and paid bonds held by some of the defendants without the required indorsement. But it is clear that this change in the action of the department could not affect the rights of Texas as a State of the Union, having a government acknowledging her obligations to the National Constitution.

It is impossible, upon this evidence, to hold the defendants protected by absence of notice of the want of title in White and Chiles. As these persons acquired no right to payment of these bonds as against the State, purchasers could acquire none through them.

On the whole case, therefore, our conclusion is that the State of Texas is entitled to the relief sought by her bill, and a decree must be made accordingly.

Mr. Justice Grier, dissenting.

I regret that I am compelled to dissent from the opinion of the majority of the court on all the points raised and decided in this case.

The first question in order is the jurisdiction of the court to entertain this bill in behalf of the State of Texas.

The original jurisdiction of this court can be invoked only by one of the United States. The Territories have no such right conferred on them by the Constitution, nor have the Indian tribes who are under the protection of the military authorities of the government.

Is Texas one of these United States? Or was she such at the time this bill was filed, or since?

This is to be decided as *a political fact,* not as a *legal fiction.* This court is bound to know and notice the public history of the nation.

If I regard the truth of history for the last eight years, I cannot discover the State of Texas as one of the United States. I do not think it necessary to notice any of the very astute arguments which have been advanced by the learned counsel in this case, to find the definition of a State, when we have the subject treated in a clear and common sense manner by Chief Justice Marshall, in the case of *Hepburn & Dundass* v. *Ellxey.* As the case is short, I hope to be excused for a full report of it, as stated and decided by the court. He says:

"The question is, whether the plaintiffs, as residents of the District of Columbia, can maintain an action in the Circuit Court of the United States for the District of Virginia. This depends on the act of Congress describing the jurisdiction of the court. The act gives jurisdiction to the Circuit Courts in cases between a citizen of the State in which the suit is brought, and a citizen of another State. To support the jurisdiction in this case, it must appear that Columbia is a State. On the part of the plaintiff, it has been urged that Columbia is a distinct political society, and is, therefore, a 'State' according to the definition of writers on general law. This is true; but as the act of Congress obviously uses the word 'State' in reference to that term as used in the Constitution, it becomes necessary to inquire whether Columbia is a State in the sense of that instrument. The result of that examination is a conviction that the members of the American Confederacy *only* are the States contemplated in the Constitution. The House of Representatives is to be composed of members chosen by the people of the several States, and each State shall have at least one representative. 'The Senate of the United

States shall be composed of two senators from each State.' Each State shall appoint, for the election of the executive, a number of electors equal to its whole number of senators and representatives. These clauses show that the word 'State' is used in the Constitution as designating a member of the Union, and excludes from the term the signification attached to it by writers on the law of nations."

Now we have here a clear and well-defined test by which we may arrive at a conclusion with regard to the questions of fact now to be decided.

Is Texas a State, now represented by members chosen by the people of that State and received on the floor of Congress? Has she two senators to represent her as a State in the Senate of the United States? Has her voice been heard in the late election of President? Is she not now held and governed as a conquered province by military force? The act of Congress of March 2d, 1867, declares Texas to be a "rebel State," and provides for its government until a legal and republican State government could be legally established. It constituted Louisiana and Texas the fifth military district, and made it subject, not to the civil authority, but to the "military authorities of the United States."

It is true that no organized rebellion now exists there, and the courts of the United States now exercise jurisdiction over the people of that province. But this is no test of the State's being in the Union; Dacotah is no State, and yet the courts of the United States administer justice there as they do in Texas. The Indian tribes, who are governed by military force, cannot claim to be States of the Union. Wherein does the condition of Texas differ from theirs?

Now, by assuming or admitting *as a fact* the present *status* of Texas as a State not in the Union *politically*, I beg leave to protest against any charge of inconsistently as to judicial opinions heretofore expressed as a member of this court, or silently assented to. I do not consider myself bound to express any opinion judicially as to the constitutional right of Texas to exercise the rights and privileges of a State of this Union, or the power of Congress to govern her as a conquered province, to subject her to military domination, and keep her in pupilage. I can only submit to *the fact* as decided by the political position of the government; and I am not disposed to join in any essay to prove Texas to be a State of the Union, when Congress have decided that she is not. It is a question of fact, I repeat, and of fact only. *Politically,* Texas is not *a State in this Union.* Whether rightfully out of it or not is a question not before the court.

But conceding now the fact to be as judicially assumed by my brethren, the next question is, whether she has a right to repudiate her contracts? Before proceeding to answer this question, we must notice a fact in this case that was forgotten in the argument. I mean that the United States are no party to this suit, and refusing to pay the bonds because the money paid would be used to advance the interests of the rebellion. It is a matter of utter insignificance to the government of the United States to whom she makes the payment of these bonds. They are payable to the bearer. The government is not bound to inquire into the *bona fides* of the holder, nor whether the State of Taxes has parted with the bonds wisely or foolishly. And although by the Reconstruction Acts she is required to repudiate all debts contracted for the purposes of the rebellion, this does not annul all acts of the State government during the rebellion, or contracts for other purposes, nor authorize the State to repudiate them.

Now, whether we assume the State of Texas to be judicially in the Union (though actually out of it) or not, it will not alter the case. The contest now is between the State of Texas and her own citizens. She seeks to annual a contract with the respondents, based on the allegation that there was no authority in Texas competent to enter into an agreement during the rebellion. Having relied upon one fiction, namely, that she *is* a State in the Union, she now relies upon a second one, which she wishes this court to adopt, that she was not a State at all during the five years that she was in rebellion. She now sets up upon the plea of *insanity,* and asks the court to treat all her acts made during the disease as void.

We have had some very astute logic to prove that judicially she was not a State at all, although governed by her own legislature and executive as "a distinct political body."

The ordinance of secession was adopted by the convention on the 18th of February, 1861; submitted to a vote of the people, and ratified by an overwhelming majority. I admit that this was a very ill-advised measure. Still it was the sovereign act of a sovereign State, and the verdict on the trial of this question, "by battle," as to her right to secede, has been against her. But that verdict did not settle any question not involved in the case. It did not settle the question of her right to plead insanity and set aside all her contracts, made during the pending of the trial, with her own citizens, for food, clothing, or medicines. The same "organized political body," exercising the sovereign power of the State, which required the indorsement of these bonds by the governor, also passed the laws authorizing the disposal of them without such indorsement. She cannot, like the chameleon, assume the color of the object to which she adheres, and ask this court to involve itself in the contradictory positions, that she is a State in the Union and was never out of it, and yet not a State at all for four years, during which she acted and claims to be "an organized political body," exercising all the powers and functions of an independent sovereign State. Whether a State *de facto* or *de jure,* she is estopped from denying her identity in disputes with her own citizens. If they have not fulfilled their contract, she can have her legal remedy for the breach of it in her own courts.

But the case of Hardenberg differs from that of the other defendants. He purchased the bonds in open market, *bona fide,* and for a full consideration. Now, it is to be observed that these bonds are payable to bearer, and that this court is appealed to as a court of equity. The argument to justify a decree in favor of the commonwealth of Texas as against Hardenberg, is simply this: these bonds, though payable to bearer, are redeemable fourteen years from date. The government has exercised her privilege of paying the interest for a term without redeeming the principal, which gives an additional value to the bonds. *Ergo,* the bonds are dishonored. *Ergo,* the former owner has a right to resume the possession of them, and reclaim them from a *bona fide* owner by a decree of a court of equity.

This is the legal argument, when put in the form of a logical sorites, by which Texas invokes our aid to assist her in the perpetration of this great wrong.

A court of chancery is said to be a court of conscience; and however astute may be the argument introduced to *defend* this decree, I can only say that neither my reason nor my conscience can give assent to it.

Mr. Justice Swayne:

I concur with my brother Grier as to the incapacity of the State of Texas, in her present condition, to maintain an original suit in this court. The question, in my judgment, is one in relation to which this court is bound by the action of the legislative department of the government.

Upon the merits of the case, I agree with the majority of my brethren.

I am authorized to say that my brother Miller unites with me in these views.

The Decree.

The decree overruled the objection interposed by way of plea, in the answer of defendants to the authority of the solicitors of the complainant to institute this suit, and to the right of Texas, as one of the States of the National Union, to bring a bill in this court.

It declared the contract of 12th January, 1865, between the Military Board and White and Chiles void, and enjoined White and Chiles from asserting any claim under it, and decreed that the complainant was entitled to receive the bonds and coupons mentioned in the contract, as having been transferred or sold to White and Chiles, which, at the several times of service of process, in this suit, were in the possession, or under the control of the defendants respectively, and any proceeds thereof which had come into such possession or control, with notice of the equity of the complainant.

It enjoined White, Chiles, Hardenberg, Birch, Murray, Jr., and other defendants, from setting up any claim to any of the bonds and coupons attached, described in the first article of said contract, and that the complainant was entitled to restitution of such of the bonds and coupons and proceeds as had come into the possession or control of the defendants respectively.

And the court, proceeding to determine for which and how many bonds the defendants respectively were accountable to make restitution of, or make good the proceeds of, decreed that Birch and Murray were so accountable for eight, numbered in a way stated in the decree, with coupons attached; and one Stewart (a defendant mentioned in the note at page 702), accountable for four others, of which the numbers were given, with coupons; decreed that Birch and Murray, as also Stewart, should deliver to the complainant the bonds for which they were thus made accountable, with the coupons, and execute all necessary transfers and instruments, and that payment of those bonds, or any of them, by the Secretary of the Treasury, to the complainant, should be an acquittance of Birch and Murray, and of Stewart, to that extent, and that for such payment this decree should be sufficient warrant to the secretary.

And, it appearing—the decree went on to say—upon the pleadings and proofs, that before the filing of the bill, Birch and Murray had received and collected from the United States the full amount of four other bonds, numbered, &c., and that Hardenberg, before the commencement of the suit, had deposited thirty-four bonds, numbered, &c., in the Treasury Department for redemption, of which bonds he claimed to have received payment from the Secretary of the Treasury before the service of process upon him in this suit, in respect to which payment and the effect thereof the counsel for the said Birch and Murray, and for the said Hardenberg respectively, desired to be heard, it was ordered that time for such hearing should be given to the said parties.

Both the complainant and the defendants had liberty to apply for further directions in respect to the execution of the decree.

Source:

U.S Reports, Vol. 74, p. 700.

Force Acts of 1870–1871

Series of three laws passed in 1870–1871, by the Radical Republicans who controlled Congress, to protect the constitutional rights granted to blacks by the Fourteenth and Fifteenth Amendments. The first act imposed severe penalties on anyone preventing qualified citizens (black men) from voting. The second act provided for federally appointed election supervisors. The third act, aimed particularly at the Ku Klux Klan and other terrorist organizations, empowered the president to suspend the writ of habeas corpus in lawless areas. These statutes resulted in martial law in nine South Carolina counties, thousands of indictments, and hundreds of convictions. The Supreme Court later declared various sections of the acts unconstitutional, and most of their provisions were repealed in 1894.

Force Act of May 31, 1870

To enforce the Right of Citizens of the United States to vote in the several States of this Union, and for other Purposes.

Be it enacted by the Senate and House of Representatives of the United States of America in Congress assembled, That all citizens of the United States who are or shall be otherwise qualified by law to vote at any election by the people in any State, Territory, district, county, city, parish, township, school district, municipality, or other territorial subdivision, shall be entitled and allowed to vote at all such elections, without distinction of race, color, or previous condition of servitude; any constitution, law, custom, usage, or regulation of any State or Territory, or by or under its authority, to the contrary notwithstanding.

Sec. 2. *And be it further enacted,* That if by or under the authority of the constitution or laws of any State, or the laws of any Territory, any act is or shall be required to be done as a prerequisite or qualification for voting, and by such constitution or laws persons or officers are or shall be charged with the performance of duties in furnishing to citizens an opportunity to perform such prerequisite, or to become qualified to vote, it shall be the duty of every such person and officer to give to all citizens of the United States the same and equal opportunity to perform such prerequisite, and to become qualified to vote without distinction of race, color, or previous condition of servitude; and if any such person or officer shall refuse or knowingly omit to give full effect to this section, he shall, for every such offence, forfeit and pay the sum of five hundred dollars to the person aggrieved thereby, to be recovered by an action on the case, with full costs, and such allowance for counsel fees as the court shall deem just, and shall also, for every such offence, be deemed guilty of a misdemeanor, and shall, on conviction thereof, be fined not less than five hundred dollars, or be imprisoned not less than one month and not more than one year, or both, at the discretion of the court.

Sec. 3. *And be it further enacted,* That whenever, by or under the authority of the constitution or laws of any State, or the laws of any Territory, any act is or shall be required to [be] done by any citizen as a prerequisite to qualify or entitle him to vote, the offer of any such citizen to perform the act required to be done as aforesaid shall, if it fail to be carried into execution by reason of the wrongful act or omission aforesaid of the person or officer charged with the duty of receiving or permitting such performance or offer to perform, or acting thereon, be deemed and held as a performance in law of such act; and the person so offering and failing as aforesaid, and being otherwise qualified, shall be entitled to vote in the same manner and to the same extent if he had in fact performed such act; and any judge, inspector, or other officer of election whose duty it is or shall be to receive, count, certify, register, report, or give effect to the vote of any such citizen who shall wrongfully refuse or omit to receive, count, certify, register, report, or give effect to the vote of such citizen upon the presentation by him of his affidavit stating such offer and the time and place thereof, and the name of the officer or person whose duty it was to act thereon, and that he was wrongfully prevented by such person or officer from performing such act, shall for every such offence forfeit and pay the sum of five hundred dollars to the person aggrieved thereby, to be recovered by an action on the case, with full costs, and such allowance for counsel fees as the court shall deem just, and shall also for every such offence be guilty of a misdemeanor, and shall, on conviction thereof, be fined not less than five hundred dollars, or be imprisoned not less than one month and not more than one year, or both, at the discretion of the court.

Sec. 4. *And be it further enacted,* That if any person, by force, bribery, threats, intimidation, or other unlawful means, shall hinder, delay, prevent, or obstruct, or shall combine and confederate with others to hinder, delay, prevent, or obstruct, any citizen from doing any act required to be done to qualify him to vote or from voting at any election as aforesaid, such person shall for every such offence forfeit and pay the sum of five hundred dollars to the person aggrieved thereby, to be recovered by an action on the case, with full costs, and such allowance for counsel fees as the court shall deem just, and shall also for every such offence be guilty of a misdemeanor, and shall, on conviction thereof, be fined not less than five hundred dollars, or be imprisoned not less than one month and not more than one year, or both, at the discretion of the court.

Sec. 5. *And be it further enacted,* That if any person shall prevent, hinder, control, or intimidate, or shall attempt to prevent, hinder, control, or intimidate, any person from exercising or in exercising the right of suffrage, to whom the right of suffrage is secured or guaranteed by the fifteenth amendment to the Constitution of the United States, by means of bribery, threats, or threats of depriving such person of employment or occupation, or of ejecting such person from rented house, lands, or other property, or by threats of refusing to renew leases or contracts for labor, or by threats of violence to himself or family, such person so offending shall be deemed guilty of a misdemeanor, and shall, on conviction thereof, be fined not less than five hundred dollars, or be imprisoned not less than one month and not more than one year, or both, at the discretion of the court.

Sec. 6. *And be it further enacted,* That if two or more persons shall band or conspire together, or go in disguise upon the public highway, or upon the premises of another, with intent to violate any provision of this act, or to injure, oppress, threaten, or intimidate any citizen with intent to prevent or hinder his free exercise and enjoyment of any right or privilege granted or secured to him by the Constitution or laws of the United States, or because of his having exercised the same, such persons shall be held guilty of felony, and, on conviction thereof, shall be fined or imprisoned, or both, at the discretion of the court—the fine not to exceed five thousand dollars, and the imprisonment not to exceed ten years—and shall, moreover, be thereafter ineligible to, and disabled from holding, any office or place of honor, profit, or trust created by the Constitution or laws of the United States.

Sec. 7. *And be it further enacted,* That if in the act of violating any provision in either of the two preceding sections, any other felony, crime, or misdeameanor shall be committed, the offender, or conviction of such violation of said sections, shall be punished for the same with such punishments as are attached to the said felonies, crimes, and misdemeanors by the laws of the State in which the offence may be committed.

Sec. 8. *And be it further enacted,* That the district courts of the United States, within their respective districts, shall have, exclusively of the courts of the several States, cognizance of all crimes and offences committed against the provisions of this act, and also, concurrently with the circuit courts of the United States, of all causes, civil and criminal, arising under this act, except as herein otherwise provided, and the jurisdiction hereby conferred shall be exercised in conformity with the laws and practice governing United States courts, and all crimes and offences committed against the provisions of this act may be prosecuted by the indictment of a grand jury, or, in cases of crimes and offences not infamous, the prosecution may be either by indictment or information filed by the district attorney in a court having jurisdiction.

Sec. 9. *And be it further enacted,* That the district attorneys, marshals, and deputy marshals of the United States, the commissioners appointed by the circuit and territorial courts of the United States, with powers of arresting, imprisoning, or bailing offenders against the laws of the United States, and every other officer who may be spe-cially empowered by the President of the United States, shall be, and they are hereby, specially authorized and required, at the expense of the United States, to institute proceedings against all and every person who shall violate the provisions of this act, and cause him or them to be arrested and imprisoned, or bailed, as the case may be, for trial before such court of the United States or territorial court as has cognizance of the offense. And with a view of afford reasonable protection to all persons in their constitutional right to vote without distinction of race, color, or previous condition of servitude, and to the prompt discharge of the duties of this act, it shall be the duty of the circuit courts of the United States, and the superior courts of the Territories of the United States, from time to time, to increase the number of commissioners, so as to afford a speedy and convenient means for the arrest and examination of persons charged with a violation of this act; and such commissioners are hereby authorized and required to exercise and discharge all the powers and duties conferred on them by this act, and the same duties with regard to offences created by this act as they are authorized by law to exercise with regard to other offences against the laws of the United States.

Sec. 10. *And be it further enacted,* That it shall be the duty of all marshals and deputy marshals to obey and execute all warrants and precepts issued under the provisions of this act, when to them directed; and should any marshal or deputy marshal refuse to receive such warrant or other process when tendered, or to use all proper means diligently to execute the same, he shall, on conviction thereof, be fined in the sum of one thousand dollars, to the use of the person deprived of the rights conferred by this act. And the better to enable the said commissioners to execute their duties faithfully and efficiently, in conformity with the Constitution of the United States and the requirements of this act, they are hereby authorized and empowered, within their districts respectively, to appoint, in writing, under their hands, any one or more suitable persons, from time to time, to execute all such warrants and other process as may be issued by them in the lawful performance of their respective duties, and the persons so appointed to execute any warrant or process as aforesaid shall have authority to summon and call to their aid the bystanders or posse comitatus of the proper county, or such portion of the land or naval forces of the United States, or of the militia, as may be necessary to the performance of the duty with which they are charged, and to insure a faithful observance of the fifteenth amendment to the Constitution of the United States; and such warrants shall run and be executed by said officers anywhere in the State of Territory within which they are issued.

Sec. 11. *And be it further enacted,* That any person who shall knowingly and wilfully obstruct, hinder, or prevent any officer or other person charged with the execution of any warrant or process issued under the provisions of this act, or any person or persons lawfully assisting him or them from arresting any person for whose apprehension such warrant or process may have been issued, or shall rescue or attempt to rescue such person from the custody of the officer or other person or persons, or those lawfully assisting as aforesaid, when so arrested pursuant to the authority herein given and declared, or shall aid, abet, or assist any person so arrested as aforesaid, directly or indirectly, to escape from the custody of the officer or other person legally authorized as aforesaid, or shall harbor or conceal any person for whose arrest a warrant or process shall have been issued as aforesaid, so as to prevent his discovery and arrest after notice or knowledge of the fact that a warrant has been issued for the apprehension of such person, shall, for either of said offences, be subject to a fine not exceeding one thousand dollars, or imprisonment not exceeding six months, or both, at the discretion of the court, on conviction before the district or circuit court of the United States for the district or circuit in which said offence may have been committed, or before the proper court of criminal jurisdiction, if committed within any one of the organized Territories of the United States.

Sec. 12. *And be it further enacted,* That the commissioners, district attorneys, the marshals, their deputies, and the clerks of the said district, circuit, and territorial courts shall be paid for their services the like fees as may be allowed to them for similar services in other cases. The person or persons authorized to execute the process to be issued by such commissioners for the arrest of offenders against the provisions of this act shall be entitled to the usual fees allowed to the marshal for an arrest for each person he or they may arrest and take before any such commissioner as aforesaid, with such other fees as may be deemed reasonable by such commissioner for such other additional services as may be necessarily performed by him or them, such as attending at the examination, keeping the prisoner in custody, and providing him with food and lodging during his detention and until the final determination of such commissioner, and in general for performing such other duties as may be required in the premises; such fees to be made up in conformity with the fees usually charged by the officers of the courts of justice within the proper district or county as near as may be practicable, and paid out of the treasury of the United States on the certificate of the judge of the district within which the arrest is made, and to be recoverable from the defendant as part of the judgment in case of conviction.

Sec. 13. *And be it further enacted,* That is shall be lawful for the President of the United States to employ such part of the land or naval forces of the United States, or of the militia, as shall be necessary to aid in the execution of judicial process issued under this act.

Sec. 14. *And be it further enacted,* That whenever any person shall hold office, except as a member of Congress or of some State legislature, contrary to the provisions of the third section of the fourteenth article of amendment of the Constitution of the United States, it shall be the duty of the district attorney of the United States for the district in which such person shall hold office, as aforesaid, to proceed against such person, by writ of quo warranto, returnable to the circuit or district court of the United States in such district, and to prosecute the same to the removal of such person from office; and any writ of quo warranto so brought, as aforesaid, shall take precedence of all other cases on the docket of the court to which it is made returnable, and shall not be continued unless for cause proved to the satisfaction of the court.

Sec. 15. *And be it further enacted,* That any person who shall hereafter knowingly accept or hold any office under the United States, or any State to which he is ineligible under the third section of the fourteenth article of amendment of the Constitution of the United States, or who shall attempt to hold or exercise the duties of any such office, shall be deemed guilty of a misdemeanor against the United States, and, upon conviction thereof before the circuit or district court of the United States, shall be imprisoned not more than one year, or fined not exceeding one thousand dollars, or both, at the discretion of the court.

Sec. 16. *And be it further enacted,* That all persons within the jurisdiction of the United States shall have the same right in every State and Territory in the United States to make and enforce contracts, to sue, be parties, give evidence, and to the full and equal benefit of all laws and proceedings for the security of person and property as is enjoyed by white citizens, and shall be subject to like punishment, pains, penalties, taxes, licenses, and exactions of every kind, and none other, any law, statute, ordinance, regulation, or custom to the contrary notwithstanding. No tax or charge shall be imposed or enforced by any State upon any person immigrating thereto from a foreign country which is not equally imposed and enforced upon every person immigrating to such State from any other foreign country; and any law of any State in conflict with this provision is hereby declared null and void.

Sec. 17. *And be it further enacted,* That any person who, under color of any law, statute, ordinance, regulation, or custom, shall subject, or cause to be subjected, any inhabitant of any State or Territory to the deprivation of any right secured or protected by the last preceding section of this act, or to different punishment, pains, or penalties on account of such person being an alien, or by reason of his color or race, than is prescribed for the punishment of citizens, shall be deemed guilty of a misdemeanor, and, on conviction, shall be punished by fine not exceeding one thousand dollars, or imprisonment not exceeding one year, or both, in the discretion of the court.

Sec. 18. *And be it further enacted,* That the act to protect all persons in the United States in their civil rights, and furnish the means of their vindication, passed April nine, eighteen hundred and sixty-six, is hereby re-enacted; and sections sixteen and seventeen hereof shall be enforced according to the provisions of said act.

Sec. 19. *And be it further enacted,* That if at any election for representative or delegate in the Congress of the United States any person shall knowingly personate and vote, or attempt to vote, in the name of any other person, whether living, dead, or fictitious; or vote more than once at the same election for any candidate for the same office; or vote at a place where he may not be lawfully entitled to vote; or vote without having a lawful right to vote; or do any unlawful act to secure a right or an opportunity to vote for himself or any other person; or by force, threat, menace, intimidation, bribery, reward, or offer, or promise thereof, or otherwise unlawfully prevent any qualified voter of any State of the United States of America, or of any Territory thereof, from freely exercising the right of suffrage, or by any such means induce any voter to refuse to exercise such right; or compel or induce by any such means, or otherwise, any officer of an election in any such State or Territory to receive a vote from a person not legally qualified or entitled to vote; or interfere in any manner with any officer of said elections in the discharge of his duties; or by any of such means, or other unlawful means, induce any officer of an election, or officer whose duty it is to ascertain, announce, or declare the result of any such election, or give or make any certificate, document, or evidence in relation thereto, to violate or refuse to comply with his duty, or any law regulating the same; or knowingly and willfully receive the vote of any person not entitled to vote, or refuse to receive the vote of any person entitled to vote; or aid, counsel, procure, or advise any such voter, person, or officer to do any act hereby made a crime, or to omit to do any duty the omission of which is hereby made a crime, or attempt to do so, every such person shall be deemed guilty of a crime, and shall for such crime be liable to prosecution in any court of the United States of competent jurisdiction, and, on conviction thereof, shall be punished by a fine not exceeding five hundred dollars, or by imprisonment for a term not exceeding three years, or both, in the discretion of the court, and shall pay the costs of prosecution.

Sec. 20. *And be it further enacted,* That if, at any registration of voters for an election for representative or delegate in the Congress of the United States, any person shall knowingly personate and register, or attempt to register, in the name of any other person, whether living, dead, or fictitious, or fraudulently register, or fraudulently attempt to register, not having a lawful right so to do; or do any unlawful act to secure registration for himself or any other person; or by force, threat, menace, intimidation, bribery, reward, or offer, or promise thereof, or other unlawful means, prevent or hinder any person having a lawful right to register from duly exercising such right; or compel or induce, by any of such means, or other unlawful means, any officer of registration to admit to registration any person not legally entitled thereto, or interfere in any manner with any officer of registration in the discharge of his duties, or by any such means, or other unlawful means, induce any officer of registration to violate or refuse to comply with his duty, or any law regulating the same; or knowingly and wilfully receive the vote of any person not entitled to vote, or refuse to receive the vote of any person entitled to vote, or aid, counsel, procure, or advice any such voter, person, or officer to do any act hereby made a crime, or to omit any act, the omission of which is hereby made a crime, every such person shall be deemed guilty of a crime, and shall be liable to prosecution and punishment therefor, as provided in section nineteen of this act for persons guilty of any of the crimes therein specified: *Provided,* That every registration made under the laws of any State or Territory, for any State or other election at which such representative or delegate in Congress shall be chosen, shall be deemed to be a registration within the meaning of this act, notwithstanding the same shall also be made for the purposes of any State territorial, or municipal election.

Sec. 21. *And be it further enacted,* That whenever, by the laws of any State or Territory, the name of any candidate or person to be voted for as representative or delegate in Congress shall be required to be printed, written, or contained in any ticket or ballot with other candidates or persons to be voted for at the same election for State, territorial, municipal, or local officers, it shall be sufficient prima facie evidence, either for the purpose of indicting or convicting any person charged with voting, or attempting or offering to vote, unlawfully under the provisions of the preceding sections, or for committing either of the offenses thereby created, to prove that the person so charged or indicted, voted, or attempted or offered to vote, such ballot or ticket, or committed either of the offenses named in the preceding sections of this act with reference to such ballot. And the proof and establishment of such facts shall be taken, held, and deemed to be presumptive evidence that such person voted, or attempted or offered to vote, for such representative or delegate, as the case may be, or that such offense was committed with reference to the election of such representative or delegate, and shall be sufficient to warrant his conviction, unless it shall be shown that any such ballot, when cast, or attempted or offered to be cast, by him, did not contain the name of any candidate for the office of representative or delegate in the Congress of the United States, or that such offense was not committed with reference to the election of such representative or delegate.

Sec. 22. *And be it further enacted,* That any officer of any election at which any representative or delegate in the Congress of the United States shall be voted for, whether such officer of election be appointed or created by or under any law or authority of the United States, or by or under any State, territorial, district, or municipal law or authority, who shall neglect or refuse to perform any duty in regard to such election required of him by any law of the United States, or of any State or Territory thereof, or violate any duty so imposed, or knowingly do any act thereby unauthorized, with intent to affect any such election, or the result thereof; or fraudulently make any false certificate of the result of such election in regard to such representative or delegate; or withhold, conceal, or destroy any certificate of record so required by law respecting, concerning, or pertaining to the election of any such representative or delegate; or neglect or refuse to make and return the same as so required by law; or aid, counsel, procure, or advise any voter, person, or officer to do any act by this or any of the preceding sections made a crime; or to omit to do any duty the omission of which is by this or any of said sections made a crime, or attempt to do so, shall be deemed guilty of a crime and shall be liable to prosecution and punishment therefor, as provided in the nineteenth section of this act for persons guilty of any of the crimes therein specified.

Sec. 23. *And be it further enacted,* That whenever any person shall be defeated or deprived of his election to any office, except elector of President or Vice-President, representative or delegate in Congress, or member of a State legislature, by reason of the denial to any citizen or citizens who shall offer to vote, of the right to vote, on account of race, color, or previous condition of servitude, his right to hold and enjoy such office, and the emoluments thereof, shall not be impaired by such denial; and such person may bring any appropriate suit or proceeding to recover possession of such office, and in cases where it shall appear that the sole question touching the title to such office arises out of the denial of the right to vote to citizens who so offered to vote, on account of race, color, or previous condition of servitude, such suit or proceeding may be instituted in the circuit or district court of the United States of the circuit or district in which such person resides. And said circuit or district court shall have, concurrently with the State courts, jurisdiction thereof so far as to determine the rights of the parties to such office by reason of the denial of the right guaranteed by the fif-

teenth article of amendment to the Constitution of the United States, and secured by this act.

Force Act of February 28, 1870

To amend an Act approved May thirty-one, eighteen hundred and seventy, entitled "An Act to enforce the Rights of Citizens of the United States to vote in the several States of this Union, and for other Purposes."

Be it enacted by the Senate and House of Representatives of the United States of America in Congress assembled, That section twenty of the "Act to enforce the rights of citizens of the United States to vote in the several States of this Union, and for other purposes," approved May thirty-one, eighteen hundred and seventy, shall be, and hereby is, amended so as to read as follows:—

"Sec. 20. *And be it further enacted,* That if, [at] any registration of voters for an election for representative or delegate in the Congress of the United States, any person shall knowingly personate and register, or attempt to register, in the name of any other person, whether living, dead, or fictitious, or fraudulently register, or fraudulently attempt to register, not having a lawful right so to do; or do any unlawful act to secure registration for himself or any other person; or by force, threat, menace, intimidation, bribery, reward, or offer, or promise thereof, or other unlawful means, prevent or hinder any person having a lawful right to register from duly exercising such right; or compel or induce, by any of such means, or other unlawful means, any officer of registration to admit to registration any person not legally entitled thereto, or interfere in any manner with any officer of registration in the discharge of his duties, or by any such means, or other unlawful means, induce any officer of registration to violate or refuse to comply with his duty or any law regulating the same; or if any such officer shall knowingly and wilfully register as a voter any person not entitled to be registered, or refuse to so register any person entitled to be registered; or if any such officer or other person whose duty it is to perform any duty in relation to such registration or election, or to ascertain, announce, or declare the result thereof, or give or make any certificate, document, or evidence in relation thereto, shall knowingly neglect or refuse to perform any duty required by law, or violate any duty imposed by law, or do any act unauthorized by law relating to or affecting such registration or election, or the result thereof, or any certificate, document, or evidence in relation thereto, or if any person shall aid, counsel, procure, or advice any such voter, person, or officer to do any act hereby made a crime, or to omit any act the omission of which is hereby made a crime, every such person shall be deemed guilty of a crime, and shall be liable to prosecution and punishment therefor as provided in section nineteen of said act of May thirty-one, eighteen hundred and seventy, for persons guilty of any of the crimes therein specified: *Provided,* That every registration made under the laws of any State or Territory for any State or other election at which such representative or delegate in Congress shall be chosen, shall be deemed to be a registration within the meaning of this act, notwithstanding the same shall also be made for the purposes of any State, territorial, or municipal election."

Sec. 2. *And be it further enacted,* That whenever in any city or town having upward of twenty thousand inhabitants, there shall be two citizens thereof who, prior to any registration of voters for an election for representative or delegate in the Congress of the United States, or prior to any election at which a representative to delegate in Congress is to be voted for, shall make known, in writing, to the judge of the circuit court of the United States for the circuit wherein such city or town shall be, their desire to have said registration, or said election, or both, guarded and scrutinized, it shall be the duty of the said judge of the circuit court, within not less than ten days prior to said registration, if one there be, or, if no registration be required, within not less than ten days prior to said election, to open the said circuit court at the most convenient point in said circuit. And the said court, when so opened by said judge, shall proceed to appoint and commission, from day to day and from time to time, and under the hand of the said circuit judge, and under the seal of said court, for each election district or voting precinct in each and every such city or town as shall, in the manner herein prescribed, have applied therefor, and to revoke, change, or renew said appointment from time to time, two citizens, residents of said city or town, who shall be of different political parties, and able to read and write the English language, and who shall be known and designated as supervisors of election. And the said circuit court, when opened by the said circuit judge as required herein, shall therefrom and thereafter, and up to and including the day following the day of election, be always open for the transaction of business under this act, and the powers and jurisdiction hereby granted and conferred shall be exercised as well in vacation as in term time; and a judge sitting at chambers shall have the same powers and jurisdiction, including the power of keeping order and of punishing any contempt of his authority, as when sitting in court.

Sec. 3. *And be it further enacted,* That whenever, from sickness, injury, or otherwise, the judge of the circuit court of the United States in any judicial circuit shall be unable to perform and discharge the duties by this act imposed, it shall be his duty, and he is hereby required, to select and to direct and assign to the performance thereof, in his place and stead, such one of the judges of the district courts of the United States within his circuit as he shall deem best; and upon such selection and assignment being made, it shall be lawful for, and shall be the duty of, the district judge so designated to perform and discharge, in the place and stead of the said circuit judge, all the duties, powers, and obligations imposed and conferred upon the said circuit judge by the provisions of this act.

Sec. 4. *And be it further enacted,* That it shall be the duty of the supervisors of election, appointed under this act, and they and each of them are hereby authorized and required, to attend at all times and places fixed for the registration of voters, who, being registered, would be entitled to vote for a representative or delegate in Congress, and to challenge any person offering to register; to attend at all times and places when the names of registered voters may be marked for challenge, and to cause such names of registered as they shall deem proper to be so marked; to make, when required, the lists, or either of them, provided for in section thirteen of this act, and verify the same; and upon any occasion, and at any time when in attendance under the provisions of this act, to personally inspect and scrutinize such registry, and for purposes of identification to affix their or his signature to each and every page of the original list, and of each and every copy of any such list of registered voters, at such times, upon each day when any name may or shall be received, entered, or registered, and in such manner as will, in their or his judgment, detect and expose the improper or wrongful removal therefrom, or addition thereto, in any way, of any name or names.

Sec. 5. *And be it further enacted,* That it shall also be the duty of the said supervisors of election, and they, and each of them, are hereby authorized and required, to attend at all times and places for holding elections of representatives or delegates in Congress, and for counting the votes cast at said elections; to challenge any vote offered by any person whose legal qualifications the supervisors, or either of them, shall doubt; to be and remain where the ballot-boxes are kept at all times after the polls are open until each and every vote cast at said time and place shall be counted, the canvass of all votes polled be wholly completed, and the proper and requisite certificates or returns made, whether said certificates or returns be required under any law of the United States, or any States, territorial, or municipal law, and to personally inspect and scrutinize, from time to time, and at all times, on the day of election, the manner in which the voting is done, and the way and method in which the poll-books, registry-lists, and tallies or check-books, whether the same are required by any law of the United States, or any State, territorial, or municipal law, are kept; and to the end that each candidate for the office of representative or delegate in Congress shall obtain the benefit of every vote for him cast, the said supervisors of election are, and each of them is, hereby required, in their or his respective election districts or voting precincts, to personally scrutinize, count, and canvass each and every ballot in their or his election district or voting precinct cast, whatever may be the indorsement on said ballot, or in whatever box it may have been placed or be found; to make and forward to the officer who, in accordance with the provisions of section thirteen of this act, shall have been designated as the chief supervisor of the judicial district in which the city or town wherein they or he shall serve shall be, such certificates and returns of all such ballots as said officer may direct and require, and to attach to the registry list, and any and all copies thereof, and to any certificate, statement, or return, whether the same, or any part or portion thereof, be required by any law of the United States, or of any State, territorial, or municipal law, any statement touching the truth or accuracy of the registry, or the truth or fairness of the election and canvass, which the said supervisors of election, or either of them, may desire to make or attach, or which should properly and honestly be made or attached, in order that the facts may become known, any law of any State or Territory to the contrary notwithstanding.

Sec. 6. *And be it further enacted,* That the better to enable the said supervisors of election to discharge their duties, they are, and each of them is, hereby authorized and directed, in their or his respective election districts or voting precincts, on the day or days of registration, on the day or days when registered voters may be marked to be challenged, and on the day or days of election, to take, occupy, and remain in such position or positions, from time to time, whether before or behind the ballot- boxes, as will, in their judgment, best enable them or him to see each person offering himself for registration or offering to vote, and as will best conduce to their or his scrutinizing the manner in which the registration or voting is being conducted; and at the closing of the polls for the reception of votes, they are, and each of them is, hereby required to place themselves or himself in such position in relation to the ballot-boxes for the purpose of engaging in the work of canvassing the ballots in said boxes contained as will enable them or him to fully perform the duties in respect to such canvass provided in this act, and shall there remain until every duty in respect to such canvass, certificates, returns, and statements shall have been wholly completed, any law of any State or Territory to the contrary notwithstanding.

Sec. 7. *And be it further enacted,* That if any election district or voting precinct in any city, town, or village, for which there shall have been appointed supervisors of election for any election at which a representative or delegate in Congress shall be voted for, the said supervisors of election, or either of them, shall not be allowed to exercise and discharge, fully and freely, and without bribery, solicitation, interference, hindrance, molestation, violence, or threats thereof, on the part of or from any person or persons, each and every of the duties, obligations, and powers conferred upon them by this act and the act hereby amended, it shall be the duty of the supervisors of election, and each of them, to make prompt report, under oath, within ten days after the day of election, to the officer who, in accordance with the provisions of section thirteen of this act, shall have been designated as the chief supervisor of the judicial district in which the city or town wherein they or he served shall be, of the manner and means by which they were, or he was, not so allowed to fully and freely exercise and discharge the duties and obligations required and imposed by this act. And upon receiving any such report, it shall be the duty of the said chief supervisor, acting both in such capacity and officially as a commissioner of the circuit court, to forthwith examine into all the facts thereof; to subpoena and compel the attendance before him of any witnesses; administer oaths and take testimony in respect to the charges made; and prior to the assembling of the Congress for which any such representative or delegate was voted for, to have filed with the clerk of the House of Representatives of the Congress of the United States all the evidence by him taken, all information by him obtained, and all reports to him made.

Sec. 8. *And be it further enacted,* That whenever an election at which representatives or delegates in Congress are to be chosen shall be held in any city or town of twenty thousand inhabitants or upward, the marshal of the United States for the district in which said city or town is situated shall have power, and it shall be his duty, on the application, in writing, of at least two citizens residing in any such city or town, to appoint special deputy marshals, whose duty it shall be, when required as provided in this act, to aid and assist the supervisors of election in the verification of any list of persons made under the provisions of this act, who may have registered, or voted, or either; to attend in each election district or voting precinct at the times and places fixed for the registration of voters, and at all times and places when and where said registration may by law be scrutinized, and the names of registered voters be marked for challenge; and also to attend, at all times for holding such elections, the polls of the election in such district or precinct. And the marshal and his general deputies, and such special deputies, shall have power, and it shall be the duty of such special deputies, to keep the peace, and support and protect the supervisors of elections in the discharge of their duties, preserve order at such places of registration and at such polls, prevent fraudulent registration and fraudulent voting thereat, or fraudulent conduct on the part of any officer of election, and immediately, either at said place of registration or polling-place, or elsewhere, and either before or after registering or voting, to arrest and take into custody, with or without process, any person who shall commit, or attempt or offer to commit, any of the acts or offences prohibited by this act, or the act hereby amended, or who shall commit any offence against the laws of the United States: *Provided,* That no person shall be arrested without process for any offence not committed in the presence of the marshal or his general or special deputies, or either of them, or of the supervisors of election, or either of them, and, for the purposes of arrest or the preservation of the peace, the supervisors of election, and each of them, shall, in the absence of the marshal's deputies, or if required to assist said deputies, have the same duties and powers as deputy marshals: *And provided further,* That no person shall, on the day or days of any such election, be arrested without process for any offence committed on the day or days of registration.

Sec. 9. *And be it further enacted,* That whenever any arrest is made under any provision of this act, the person so arrested shall forthwith be brought before a commissioner, judge, or court of the United States for examination of the offences alleged against him; and such commissioner, judge, or court shall proceed in respect thereto as authorized by law in case of crimes against the United States.

Sec. 10. *And be it further enacted,* That whoever, with or without any authority, power, or process, or pretended authority, power, or process, of any State, territorial, or municipal authority, shall obstruct, hinder, assault, or by bribery, solicitation, or otherwise, interfere with or prevent the supervisors of election, or either of them, or the marshal or his general or special deputies, or either of them, in the performance of any duty required of them, or either of them, or which he or they, or either of them, may be authorized to perform by any law of the United States, whether in the execution of process or otherwise, or shall by any of the means before mentioned hinder or prevent the free attendance and presence at such places of registration or at such polls of election, or full and free access and egress to and from any such place of registration or poll of election, or in going to and from any such place of registration or poll of election, or to and from any room where any such registration or election or canvass of votes, or of making any returns or certificates thereof, may be had, or shall molest, interfere with, remove, or eject from any such place of registration or poll of election, or of canvassing votes cast thereat, or of making returns or certificates thereof, any supervisor of election, the marshal, or his general or special deputies, or either of them, or shall threaten, or attempt, or offer so to do, or shall refuse or neglect to aid and assists any supervisor of election, or the marshal or his general or special deputies, or either of them, in the performance of his or their duties when required by him or them, or either of them, to give such aid and assistance, he shall be guilty of a misdemeanor, and liable to instant arrest without process, and on conviction

thereof shall be punished by imprisonment not more than two years, or by fine not more than three thousand dollars, or by both such fine and imprisonment, and shall pay the costs of the prosecution. Whoever shall, during the progress of any verification of any list of the persons who may have registered or voted, and which shall be had or made under any of the provisions of this act, refuse to answer, or refrain from answering, or answering shall knowingly give false information in respect to any inquiry lawfully made, such person shall be liable to arrest and imprisonment as for a misdemeanor, and on conviction thereof shall be punished by imprisonment not to exceed thirty days, or by fine not to exceed one hundred dollars, or by both such fine and imprisonment, and shall pay the costs of the prosecution.

Sec. 11. *And be it further enacted,* That whoever shall be appointed a supervisor of election or a special deputy marshal under the provisions of this act, and shall take the oath of office as such supervisor of election or such special deputy marshal, who shall thereafter neglect or refuse, without good and lawful excuse, to perform and discharge fully the duties, obligations, and requirements of such office until the expiration of the term for which he was appointed, shall not only be subject to removal from office with loss of all pay or emoluments, but shall be guilty of a misdemeanor, and on conviction shall be punished by imprisonment for not less than six months nor more than one year, or by fine not less than two hundred dollars and not exceeding five hundred dollars, or by both fine and imprisonment, and shall pay the costs of prosecution.

Sec. 12. *And be it further enacted,* That the marshal, or his general deputies, or such special deputies as shall be thereto specially empowered by him, in writing, and under his hand and seal, whenever he or his said general deputies or his special deputies, or either or any of them, shall be forcibly resisted in executing their duties under this act, or the act hereby amended, or shall, by violence, threats, or menaces, be prevented from executing such duties, or from arresting any person or persons who shall commit any offence for which said marshal or his general or his special deputies are authorized to make such arrest, are, and each of them is hereby, empowered to summon and call to his or their aid the bystanders or posse comitatus of his district.

Sec. 13. *And be it further enacted,* That it shall be the duty of each of the circuit courts of the United States in and for each judicial circuit, upon the recommendation in writing of the judge thereof, to name and appoint, on or before the first day of May, in the year eighteen hundred and seventy-one, and thereafter as vacancies may from any cause arise, from among the circuit court commissioners in and for each judicial district in each of said judicial circuits, one of such officers, who shall be known for the duties required of him under this act as the chief supervisor of elections of the judicial district in and for which he shall be a commissioner, and shall, so long as faithful and capable, discharge the duties in this act imposed, and whose duty it shall be to prepare and furnish all necessary books, forms, blanks, and instructions for the use and direction of the supervisors of election in the several cities and towns in their respective districts; to receive the applications of all parties for appointment to such positions; and upon the opening, as contemplated in this act, of the circuit court for the judicial circuit in which the commissioner so designated shall act, to present such applications to the judge thereof, and furnish information to said judge in respect to the appointment by the said court of such supervisors of election; to require of the supervisors of election, where necessary, lists of the persons who may register and vote, or either, in their respective election districts or voting precincts, and to cause the names of those upon any such list whose right to register or vote shall be honestly doubted to be verified by proper inquiry and examination at the respective places by them assigned as their residences; and to receive, preserve, and file all oaths of office of said supervisors of election, and of all special deputy marshals appointed under the provisions of this act, and all certificates, returns, reports, and records of every kind and nature contemplated or made requisite under and by the provisions of this act, save where otherwise herein specially directed. And it is hereby made the duty of all United States marshals and commissioners who shall in any judicial district perform any duties under the provisions of this act, or the act hereby amended, relating to, concerning, or affecting the election of representatives or delegates in the Congress of the United States, to, from time to time, and with all due diligence, forward to the chief supervisor in and for their judicial district all complaints, examinations, and records pertaining thereto, and all oaths of office by them administered to any supervisor of election or special deputy marshal, in order that the same may be properly preserved and filed.

Sec. 14. *And be it further enacted,* That there shall be allowed and paid to each chief supervisor, for his services as such officer, the following compensation, apart from and in excess of all fees allowed by law for the performance of any duty as circuit court commissioner: For filing and caring for every return, report, record, document, or other paper required to be filed by him under any of the provisions of this act, ten cents; for affixing a seal to any paper, record, report, or instrument, twenty cents; for entering and indexing the records of his office, fifteen cents per folio; and for arranging and transmitting to Congress, as provided for in section seven of this act, any report, statement, record, return, or examination, for each folio, fifteen cents; and for any copy thereof, or of any paper on file, a

like sum. And there shall be allowed and paid to each and every supervisor of election, and each and every special deputy marshal who shall be appointed and shall perform his duty under the provisions of this act, compensation at the rate of five dollars per day for each and every day he shall have actually been on duty, not exceeding ten days. And the fees of the said chief supervisors shall be paid at the treasury of the United States, such accounts to be made out, verified, examined, and certified as in the case of accounts of commissioners, save that the examination or certificate required may be made by either the circuit or district judge.

Sec. 15. *And be it further enacted,* That the jurisdiction of the circuit court of the United States shall extend to all cases in law or equity arising under the provisions of this act or the act hereby amended; and if any person shall receive any injury to his person or property for or on account of any act by him done under any of the provisions of this act or the act hereby amended, he shall be entitled to maintain suit for damages therefor in the circuit court of the United States in the district wherein the party doing the injury may reside or shall be found.

Sec. 16. *And be it further enacted,* That in any case where suit or prosecution, civil or criminal, shall be commenced in a court of any State against any officer of the United States, or other person, for or on account of any act done under the provisions of this act, or under color thereof, or for or on account of any right, authority, or title set up or claimed by such officer or other person under any of said provisions, it shall be lawful for the defendant in such suit or prosecution, at any time before trial, upon a petition to the circuit court of the United States in and for the district in which the defendant shall have been served with process, setting forth the nature of said suit or prosecution, and verifying the said petition by affidavit, together with a certificate signed by an attorney or counsellor at law of some court of record of the State in which such suit shall have been commenced, or of the United States, setting forth that as counsel for the petition[er] he has examined the proceedings against him, and has carefully inquired into all the matters set forth in the petition, and that he believes the same to be true, which petition, affidavit, and certificate shall be presented to the said circuit court, if in session, and, if not, to the clerk thereof at his office, and shall be filed in said office, and the cause shall thereupon be entered on the docket of said court, and shall be thereafter proceeded in as a cause originally commenced in that court; and it shall be the duty of the clerk of said court, if the suit was commenced in the court below by summons, to issue a writ of certiorari to the State court, requiring said court to send to the said circuit court the record and proceedings in said cause; or if it was commenced by capias, he shall issue a writ of habeas corpus cum causa, a duplicate of which said writ shall be delivered to the clerk of the State court, or left at his office by the marshal of the district, or his deputy, or some person duly authorized thereto; and thereupon it shall be the duty of the said State court to stay all further proceedings in such cause, and the said suit or prosecution, upon delivery of such process, or leaving the same as aforesaid, shall be deemed and taken to be moved to the said circuit court, and any further proceedings, trial, or judgment therein in the State court shall be wholly null and void; and any person, whether an attorney or officer of any State court, or otherwise, who shall thereafter take any steps, or in any manner proceed in the State court in any action so removed, shall be guilty of a misdemeanor, and liable to trial and punishment in the court to which the action shall have been removed, and upon conviction thereof shall be punished by imprisonment for not less than six months nor more than one year, or by fine not less than five hundred nor more than one thousand dollars, or by both such fine and imprisonment, and shall in addition thereto be amenable to the said court to which said action shall have been removed as for a contempt; and if the defendant in any such suit be in actual custody on mesne process therein, it shall be the duty of the marshal, by virtue of the writ of habeas corpus cum causa, to take the body of the defendant into his custody, to be dealt with in the said cause according to the rules of law and the order of the circuit court, or of any judge thereof in vacation. And all attachments made and all bail or other security given upon such suit or prosecution shall be and continue in like force and effect as if the same suit or prosecution had proceeded to final judgment and execution in the State court. And if upon the removal of any such suit or prosecution it shall be made to appear to the said circuit court that no copy of the record and proceedings therein in the State court can be obtained, it shall be lawful for said circuit court to allow and require the plaintiff to proceed de novo, and to file a declaration of his cause of action, and the parties may thereupon, proceed as in actions originally brought in said circuit court; and on failure of so proceeding judgment of non prosequitur may be rendered against the plaintiff, with costs for the defendant.

Sec. 17. *And be it further enacted,* That in any case in which any party is or may be by law entitled to copies of the record and proceedings in any suit or prosecution in any State court, to be used in any court of the United States, if the clerk of said State court shall, upon demand and the payment or tender of the legal fees, refuse or neglect to deliver to such party certified copies of such record and proceedings, the court of the United States in which such record and proceedings may be needed, on proof by affidavit that the clerk of such State court has

refused or neglected to deliver copies thereof on demand as aforesaid, may direct and allow such record to be supplied by affidavit or otherwise, as the circumstances of the case may require and allow; and thereupon such proceeding, trial, and judgment may be had in the said court of the United States, and all such processes awarded, as if certified copies of such records and proceedings had been regularly before the said court; and hereafter in all civil actions in the courts of the United States either party thereto may notice the same for trial.

Sec. 18. *And be it further enacted,* That sections five and six of the act of the Congress of the United States approved July fourteen, eighteen hundred and seventy, and entitled "An act to amend the naturalization laws, and to punish crimes against the same," be, and the same are hereby, repealed; but this repeal shall not affect any proceeding or prosecution now pending for any offence under the said sections, or either of them, or any question which may arise therein respecting the appointment of the persons in said sections, or either of them, provided for, or the powers, duties, or obligations of such persons.

Sec. 19. *And be it further enacted,* That all votes for representatives in Congress shall hereafter be by written or printed ballot, any law of any State to the contrary notwithstanding; and all votes received or recorded contrary to the provisions of this section shall be of none effect.

Force Act of April 20, 1870

To enforce the Provisions of the Fourteenth Amendment to the Constitution of the United States, and for other Purposes.

Be it enacted by the Senate and House of Representatives of the United States of America in Congress assembled, That any person who, under color of any law, statute, ordinance, regulation, custom, or usage of any State, shall subject, or cause to be subjected, any person within the jurisdiction of the United States to the deprivation of any rights, privileges, or immunities secured by the Constitution of the United States, shall, any such law, statute, ordinance, regulation, custom, or usage of the State to the contrary notwithstanding, be liable to the party injured in any action at law, suit in equity, or other proper proceeding for redress; such proceeding to be prosecuted in the several district or circuit courts of the United States, with and subject to the same rights of appeal, review upon error, and other remedies, provided in like cases in such courts, under the provisions of the act of the ninth of April, eighteen hundred and sixty-six, entitled "An act to protect all persons in the United States in their civil rights, and to furnish the means of their vindication"; and the other remedial laws of the United States which are in their nature applicable in such cases.

Sec. 2. That if two or more persons within any State or Territory of the United States shall conspire together to overthrow, or to put down, or to destroy by force the government of the United States, or to levy war against the United States, or to oppose by force the authority of the government of the United States, or by force, intimidation, or threat to prevent, hinder, or delay the execution of any law of the United States, or by force of seize, take, or possess any property of the United States contrary to the authority thereof, or by force, intimidation, or threat to prevent any person from accepting or holding any office or trust or place of confidence under the United States, or from discharging the duties thereof, or by force, intimidation, or threat to induce any office of the United States to leave any State, district, or place where his duties as such officer might lawfully be performed, or to injure him in his person or property on account of his lawful discharge of the duties of his office, or to injure his person while engaged in the lawful discharge of the duties of his office, or to injure his property so as to molest, interrupt, hinder, or impede him in the discharge of his official duty, or by force, intimidation, or threat to deter any party or witness in any court of the United States from attending such court, or from testifying in any matter pending in such court fully, freely, and truthfully, or to injure any such party or witness in his person or property on account of his having so attended or testified, or by force, intimidation, or threat to influence the verdict, presentment, or indictment, of any juror or grand juror in any court of the United States, or to injure such juror in his person or property on account of any verdict, presentment, or indictment lawfully assented to by him, or on account of his being or having been such juror, or shall conspire together, or go in disguise upon the public highway or upon the premises of another for the purpose, either directly or indirectly, of depriving any person or any class of persons of the equal protection of the laws, or of equal privileges of immunities under the laws, or for the purpose of preventing or hindering the constituted authorities of any State from giving or securing to all persons within such State the equal protection of the laws, or shall conspire together for the purpose of in any manner impeding, hindering, obstructing, or defeating the due course of justice in any State of Territory, with intent to deny to any citizen of the United States the due and equal protection of the laws, or to injure any person in his person or his property for lawfully enforcing the right of any person or class of persons to the equal protection of the laws, or by force, intimidation, or threat to prevent any citizen of the United States lawfully entitled to vote from giving his support or advocacy in a lawful manner towards or in favor of the election of any lawfully qualified person as an elector of President or Vice-President of the United States, or as a member of the Congress of the United States, or to injure any such citizen in his person or property on account of such support or advocacy, each and every person so offending shall be deemed guilty of a high crime, and, upon conviction thereof in any district or circuit court of the United States or district or supreme court of any Territory of the United States having jurisdiction of similar offenses, shall be punished by a fine not less than five hundred nor more than five thousand dollars, or by imprisonment, with or without hard labor, as the court may determine, for a period of not less than six months nor more than six years, as the court may determine, or by both such tine and imprisonment as the court shall determine. And if any one or more persons engaged in any such conspiracy shall do, or cause to be done, any act in furtherance of the object of such conspiracy, whereby any person shall be injured in his person or property, or deprived of having and exercising any right or privilege of a citizen of the United States, the person so injured or deprived of such rights and privileges may have and maintain an action for the recovery of damages occasioned by such injury of deprivation of rights and privileges against any one or more of the persons engaged in such conspiracy, such action to be prosecuted in the proper district or circuit court of the United States, with and subject to the same rights of appeal, review upon error, and other remedies provided in like cases in such courts under the provisions of the act of April ninth, eighteen hundred and sixty-six, entitled "An act to protect all persons in the United States in their civil rights, and to furnish the means of their vindication."

Sec. 3. That in all cases where insurrection, domestic violence, unlawful combinations, or conspiracies in any State shall so obstruct or hinder the execution of the laws thereof, and of the United States, as to deprive any portion or class of the people of such State of any of the rights, privileges, or immunities, or protection, named in the Constitution and secured by this act, and the constituted authorities of such State shall either be unable to protect, or shall, from any cause, fail in or refuse protection of the people in such rights, such facts shall be deemed a denial by such State of the equal protection of the laws to which they are entitled under the Constitution of the United States; and in all such cases, or whenever any such insurrection, violence, unlawful combination, or conspiracy shall oppose or obstruct the laws of the United States or the due execution thereof, or impede or obstruct the due course of justice under the same, it shall be lawful: for the President, and it shall be his duty to take such measures, by the employment of the militia or the land and naval forces of the United States, or of either, or by other means, as he may deem necessary for the suppression of such insurrection, domestic violence, or combinations; and any person who shall be arrested under the provisions of this and the preceding section shall be delivered to the marshal of the proper district, to be dealt with according to law.

Sec. 4. That whenever in any State or part of a State the unlawful combinations named in the preceding section of this act shall be organized and armed, and so numerous and powerful as to be able, by violence, to either overthrow or set at defiance the constituted authorities of such State, and of the United States within such State, or when the constituted authorities are in complicity with, or shall connive at the unlawful purposes of, such powerful and armed combinations; and whenever, by reason of either or all of the causes aforesaid, the conviction of such offenders and the preservation of the public safety shall become in such district impracticable, in every such case such combinations shall be deemed a rebellion against the government of the United States, and during the continuance of such rebellion, and within the limits of the district which shall be so under the sway thereof, such limits to be prescribed by proclamation, it shall be lawful for the President of the United States, when in his judgment the public safety shall require it, to suspend the privileges of the writ of habeas corpus, to the end that such rebellion may be overthrown: *Provided,* That all the provisions of the second section of an act entitled "An act relating to habeas corpus, and regulating judicial proceedings in certain cases," approved March third, eighteen hundred and sixty-three, which relate to the discharge of prisoners other than prisoners of war, and to the penalty for refusing to obey the order of the court, shall be in full force so far as the same are applicable to the provisions of this section: *Provided further,* That the President shall first have made proclamation, as now provided by law, commanding such insurgents to disperse: *And provided also,* That the provisions of this section shall not be in force after the end of the next regular session of Congress.

Sec. 5. That no person shall be a grand or petit juror in any court of the United States upon any inquiry, hearing, or trial of any suit, proceeding, or prosecution based upon or arising under the provisions of this act who shall, in the judgment of the court, be in complicity with any such combination or conspiracy; and every such juror shall, before entering upon any such inquiry, hearing, or trial, take and subscribe an oath in open court that he has never, directly or indirectly, counselled, advised, or voluntarily aided any such combination or conspiracy; and each and every person who shall take this oath, and shall therein swear falsely, shall be guilty of perjury, and shall be subject to the pains and penalties declared against that crime, and the first section of the act entitled "An act defining additional causes of challenge and prescribing an additional oath for grand and petit jurors in the United States courts," approved June seventeenth, eighteen hundred and sixty-two, be, and the the same is hereby, repealed.

Sec. 6. That any person or persons, having knowledge that any of the wrongs conspired to be done and mentioned in the second section of this act are about to be committed, and having power to prevent or aid in preventing the same, shall neglect or refuse so to do, and such wrongful act shall be committed, such person or persons shall be liable to the person injured, or his legal representatives, for all damages caused by any such wrongful act which such first-named person or persons by reasonable diligence could have prevented; and such damages may be recovered in an action on the case in the proper circuit court of the United States, and any number of persons guilty of such wrongful neglect or refusal may be joined as defendants in such action: *Provided,* That such action shall be commenced within one year after such cause of action shall have accrued; and if the death of any person shall be caused by any such wrongful act and neglect, the legal representatives of such deceased person shall have such action therefor, and may recover not exceeding five thousand dollars damages therein, for the benefit of the widow of such deceased person, if any there be, or if there be no widow, for the benefit of the next of kin of such deceased person.

Sec. 7. That nothing herein contained shall be construed to supersede or repeal any former act or law except so far as the same may be repugnant thereto; and any offences heretofore committed against the tenor of any former act shall be prosecuted, and any proceeding already commenced for the prosecution thereof shall be continued and completed, the same as if this act had not been passed, except so far as the provisions of this act may go to sustain and validate such proceedings.

Source:
Statutes at Large, Vol. 16, pp. 140–146, 433–440, 13–15.

The Slaughterhouse Cases, 1873

Two related cases dealing with the right of state governments to create monopolies in private industry. In 1869 the Louisiana legislature enacted a law that authorized the operation of only one private slaughterhouse in the city of New Orleans. Since this state-sanctioned monopoly obviously deprived many of the city's butchers of employment, they filed suit in federal court for relief. Associate Justice Bradley heard this case on circuit. Interpreting the "privileges and immunities" clause of the Fourteenth Amendment as protecting the right of every American citizen to pursue his chosen profession, he ruled that the state law violated the spirit of that amendment. The case was subsequently appealed to the Supreme Court, and the side of the butchers was argued by former associate justice Campbell, who had resigned from the Court at the start of the Civil War. On April 14, 1873, the Court held by a vote of 5 to

4, with Chief Justice Chase and Bradley, Field, and Swayne, associate justices, dissenting, that the Louisiana legislature was not acting unconstitutionally in its enforcement of the slaughterhouse monopoly. Associate Justice Miller, speaking for the majority, held that the civil rights of U.S. citizens protected by the Fourteenth Amendment did not include the right to engage in a particular business. Furthermore, Miller held that a particular profession could not be considered to be "property," which would be protected by the "due process" of that amendment. This was the first judicial test of the Fourteenth Amendment, and it severely limited the extent to which the federal government could utilize it to overrule state laws.

———————————— ⌀ ————————————

THE BUTCHERS' BENEVOLENT ASSOCIATION OF NEW ORLEANS V. THE CRESCENT CITY LIVESTOCK LANDING AND SLAUGHTER-HOUSE COMPANY.

PAUL ESTEBEN, L. RUCH, J. P. ROUEDE, W. MAYLIE, S., FIRMBERG, B. BEAUBAY, WILLIAM FAGAN, J. D. BRODERICK, N. SEIBEL, M. LANNES, J. GITZINGER, J. P. AYCOCK, D. VERGES, THE LIVE-STOCK DEALERS' AND BUTCHERS' ASSOCIATION OF NEW ORLEANS, AND CHARLES CAVAROC V. THE STATE OF LOUISIANA, EX REL. S. BELDEN, ATTORNEY-GENERAL.

THE BUTCHERS' BENEVOLENT ASSOCIATION OF NEW ORLEANS V. THE CRESCENT CITY LIVESTOCK LANDING AND SLAUGHTER-HOUSE COMPANY.

Mr. Justice Miller, now, April 14th, 1873, delivered the opinion of the court.

These cases are brought here by writs of error to the Supreme Court of the State of Louisiana. They arise out of the efforts of the butchers of New Orleans to resist the Crescent City Live-Stock Landing and Slaughter-House Company in the exercise of certain powers conferred by the charter which created it, and which was granted by the legislature of that State.

The cases named on a preceding page, with others which have been brought here and dismissed by agreement, were all decided by the Supreme Court of Louisiana in favor of the Slaughter-House Company, as we shall hereafter call it for the sake of brevity, and these writs were brought to reverse those decisions.

The records were filed in this court in 1870, and were argued before it at length on a motion made by plaintiffs in error for an order in the nature of an injunction or supersedes, pending the action of the court on the merits. The opinion on that motion is reported in 10 Wallace, 273.

On account of the importance of the questions involved in these cases they were, by permission of the

court, taken up out of their order on the docket and argued in January 1872. At that hearing one of the justices was absent, and it was found, on consultation, that there was a diversity of views among those who were present. Impressed with the gravity of the questions raised in the argument, the court under these circumstances ordered that the cases be placed on the calendar and reargued before a full bench. This argument was had early in February last.

Preliminary to the consideration of those questions is a motion by the defendant to dismiss the cases, on the ground that the contest between the parties has been adjusted by an agreement made since the records came into this court, and that part of that agreement is that these writs should be dismissed. This motion was heard with the argument on the merits, and was much pressed by counsel. It is supported by affidavits and by copies of the written agreement relied on. It is sufficient to say of these that we do not find in them satisfactory evidence that the agreement is binding upon all the parties to the record who are named as plaintiffs in the several writs of error, and that there are parties now before the court, in each of the three cases, the names of which appear on a preceding page, who have not consented to their dismissal, and who are not bound by the action of those who have so consented. They have a right to be heard, and the motion to dismiss cannot prevail.

The records show that the plaintiffs in error relied upon, and asserted throughout the entire course of the litigation in the State courts, that the grant of privileges in the charter of defendant, which they were contesting, was a violation of the most important provisions of the thirteenth and fourteenth articles of amendment of the Constitution of the United States. The jurisdiction and the duty of this court to review the judgment of the State court on those questions is clear and is imperative.

The statute thus assailed as unconstitutional was passed March 8th, 1869, and is entitled "An act to protect the health of the city of New Orleans, to locate the stock-landings and slaughter-houses, and to incorporate the Crescent City Live-Stock Landing and Slaughter-House Company."

The first section forbids the landing or slaughtering of animals whose flesh is intended for food, within the city of New Orleans and other parishes and boundaries named and defined, or the keeping or establishing any slaughter-houses or *abattoirs* within those limits except by the corporation thereby created, which is also limited to certain places afterwards mentioned. Suitable penalties are enacted for violations of this prohibition.

The second section designates the corporators, gives the name of the corporation, and confers on it the usual corporate powers.

The third and fourth sections authorize the company to establish and erect within certain territorial limits, therein defined, one or more stock-yards, stock-landings, and slaughter-houses, and imposes upon it the duty of erecting, on or before the first day of June, 1869, one grand slaughter-house of sufficient capacity for slaughtering five hundred animals per day.

It declares that the company, after it shall have prepared all the necessary buildings, yards, and other conveniences for that purpose, shall have the sole and exclusive privilege of conducting and carrying on the live-stock landing and slaughter-house business within the limits and privilege granted by the act, and that all such animals shall be landed at the stock-landings and slaughtered at the slaughter-houses of the company, and nowhere else. Penalties are enacted for infractions of this provision, and prices fixed for the maximum charges of the company for each steamboat and for each animal landed.

Section five orders the closing up of all other stock-landings and slaughter-houses after the first day of June, in the parishes of Orleans, Jefferson, and St. Bernard, and makes it the duty of the company to permit any person to slaughter animals in their slaughter-houses under a heavy penalty for each refusal. Another section fixes a limit to the charges to be made by the company for each animal so slaughtered in their building, and another provides for an inspection of all animals intended to be so slaughtered, by an officer appointed by the governor of the State for that purpose.

These are the principal features of the statute, and are all that have any bearing upon the questions to be decided by us.

This statute is denounced not only as creating a monopoly and conferring odious and exclusive privileges upon a small number of persons at the expense of the great body of the community of New Orleans, but it is asserted that it deprives a large and meritorious class of citizen—the whole of the butchers of the city—of the right to exercise their trade, the business to which they have been trained and on which they depend for the support of themselves and their families; and that the unrestricted exercise of the business of butchering is necessary to the daily subsistence of the population of the city.

But a critical examination of the act hardly justifies these assertions.

It is true that it grants, for a period of twenty-five years, exclusive privileges. And whether those privileges are at the expense of the community in the sense of a curtailment of any of their fundamental rights, or even in the sense of doing them an injury, is a question open to considerations to be hereafter stated. But it is not true that it deprives the butchers of the right to exercise their trade, or imposes upon them any restriction incompatible with its successful pursuit, or furnishing the people of the city with the necessary daily supply of animal food.

The act divides itself into two main grants of privilege,—the one in reference to stock-landings and stock-yards, and the other to slaughter-houses. That the landing of livestock in large droves, from steamboats on the bank of the river, and from railroad trains, should, for the safety and comfort of the people and the care of animals, be limited to proper places, and those not numerous, it needs no argument to prove. Nor can it be injurious to the general community that while the duty of making ample preparation for this is imposed upon a few men, or a corporation, they should, to enable them to do it successfully, have the exclusive right of providing such landing-places, and receiving a fair compensation for the service.

It is, however, the slaughter-house privilege, which is mainly relied on to justify the charges of gross injustice to the public, and invasion of private right.

It is not, and cannot be successfully controverted; that it is both the right and the duty of the legislative body—the supreme power of the State or municipality—to prescribe and determine the localities where the business of slaughtering for a great city may be conducted. To do this effectively it is indispensable that all persons who slaughter animals for food shall do it in those places *and nowhere else*.

The statute under consideration defines these localities and forbids slaughtering in any other. It does not, as has been asserted, prevent the butcher from doing his own slaughtering. On the contrary, the Slaughter-House Company is required, under a heavy penalty, to permit any person who wishes to do so, to slaughter in their houses; and they are bound to make ample provision for the convenience of all the slaughtering for the entire city. The butcher then is still permitted to slaughter, to prepare, and to sell his own meats; but he is required to slaughter at a specified place and to pay a reasonable compensation for the use of the accommodations furnished him at that place.

The wisdom of the monopoly granted by the legislature may be open to question, but it is difficult to see a justification for the assertion that the butchers are deprived of the right to labor in their occupation, or the people of their daily service in preparing food, or how this statute, with the duties and guards imposed upon the company, can be said to destroy the business of the butcher, or seriously interfere with its pursuit.

The power here exercised by the legislature of Louisiana is, in its essential nature, one which has been, up to the present period in the constitutional history of this country, always conceded to belong to the States, however it may *now* be questioned in some of its details.

"Unwholesome trades, slaughter-houses, operations offensive to the senses, the deposit of powder, the application of steam power to propel cars, the building with combustible materials, and the burial of the dead, may all," says Chancellor Kent, "be interdicted by law, in the midst of dense masses of population, on the general and rational principle, that every person ought so to use his property as not to injure his neighbors; and that private interests must be made subservient to the general interests of the community." This is called the police power; and it is declared by Chief Justice Shaw that it is much easier to perceive and realize the existence and sources of it than to mark its boundaries, or prescribe limits to its exercise.

This power is, and must be from its very nature, incapable of any very exact definition or limitation. Upon it depends the security of social order, the life and health of the citizen, the comfort of an existence in a thickly populated community, the enjoyment of private and social life, and the beneficial use of property. "It extends," says another eminent judge, "to the protection of the lives, limbs, health, comfort, and quiet of all persons, and the protection of all property within the State; . . . and persons and property are subjected to all kinds of restraints and burdens in order to secure the general comfort, health, and prosperity of the State. Of the perfect right of the legislature to do this no question ever was, or, upon acknowledged general principles, ever can be made, so far as natural persons are concerned."

The regulation of the place and manner of conducting the slaughtering of animals, and the business of butchering within a city, and the inspection of the animals to be killed for meat, and of the meat afterwards, are among the most necessary and frequent exercises of this power. It is not, therefore, needed that we should seek for a comprehensive definition, but rather look for the proper source of its exercise.

In *Gibbons v. Ogden,* Chief Justice Marshall, speaking of inspection laws passed by the States, says: "They form a portion of that immense mass of legislation which controls everything within the territory of a State not surrendered to the General Government—all which can be most advantageously administered by the States themselves. Inspection laws, quarantine laws, health laws of every description, as well as laws for regulating the internal commerce of a State, and those which respect turnpike roads, ferries, &c., are component parts. No direct general power over these objects is granted to Congress; and consequently they remain subject to State legislation."

The exclusive authority of State legislation over this subject is strikingly illustrated in the case of the *City of New York v. Miln.* In that case the defendant was prosecuted for failing to comply with a statute of New York which required of every master of a vessel arriving from a foreign port, in that of New York City, to report the names of all his passengers, with certain particulars of their age, occupation, last place of settlement, and place of their birth. It was argued that this act was an invasion of the exclusive right of Congress to regulate commerce. And it cannot be denied that such a statute operated at least indirectly upon the commercial intercourse between the citizens of the United States and of foreign countries. But notwithstanding this it was held to be an exercise of the police power properly within the control of the State, and unaffected by the clause of the Constitution which conferred on Congress the right to regulate commerce.

To the same purpose are the recent cases of the *The License Tax,* and *United States v. De Witt.* In the latter case an act of Congress which undertook as a part of the internal revenue laws to make it a misdemeanor to mix for sale naphtha and illuminating oils, or to sell oil of petroleum inflammable at less than a prescribed temperature, was held to be void, because as a police regulation the power to make such a law belonged to the States, and did not belong to Congress.

It cannot be denied that the statute under consideration is aptly framed to remove from the more densely populated part of the city, the noxious slaughter-houses, and large and offensive collections of animals necessarily incident to the slaughtering business of a large city, and to locate them where the convenience, health, and comfort of the people require they shall be located. And it must be conceded that the means adopted by the act for this purpose are appropriate, are stringent, and effectual. But it is said that in creating a corporation for this purpose, and conferring upon it exclusive privileges—privileges which it is said constitute a monopoly—the legislature has exceeded its power. If this statute had imposed on the city of New Orleans precisely the same duties, accompanied by the same privileges, which it has on the corporation which it created, it is believed that no question would have been raised as to its constitutionality. In that case the effect on the butchers in pursuit of their occupation and on the public would have been the same as it is now. Why cannot the legislature confer the same powers on another corporation, created for a lawful and useful public object, that it can on the municipal corporation already existing? That wherever a legislature has the right to accomplish a certain result, and that result is best attained by means of a corporation, it has the right to create such a corporation, and to endow it with the powers necessary to effect the desired and lawful purpose, seems hardly to admit of debate. The proposition is ably discussed and affirmed in the case of *McCulloch v. The State of Maryland,* in relation to the power of Congress to organize the Bank of the United States to aid in the fiscal operations of the government.

It can readily be seen that the interested vigilance of the corporation created by the Louisiana legislature will be more efficient in enforcing the limitation prescribed for the stock-landing and slaughtering business for the good of the city than the ordinary efforts of the officers of the law.

Unless, therefore, it can be maintained that the exclusive privilege granted by this charter to the corporation, is beyond the power of the legislature of Louisiana, there can be no just exception to the validity of the statute. And in this respect we are not able to see that these privileges are especially odious or objectionable. The duty imposed as a consideration for the privilege is well defined, and its enforcement well guarded. The prices or charges to be made by the company are limited by the statute, and we are not advised that they are on the whole exorbitant or unjust.

The proposition is, therefore, reduced to these terms: Can any exclusive privileges be granted to any of its citizens, or to a corporation, by the legislature of a State?

The eminent and learned counsel who has twice argued the negative of this question, has displayed a research into the history of monopolies in England, and the European continent, only equaled by the eloquence with which they are denounced.

But it is to be observed, that all such references are to monopolies established by the monarch in derogation of the rights of his subjects, or arise out of transactions in which the people were unrepresented, and their interests uncared for. The great *Case of Monopolies,* reported by Coke, and so fully stated in the brief, was undoubtedly a consent of the commons against the monarch. The decision is based upon the ground that it was against common law, and the argument was aimed at the unlawful assumption of power by the crown; for whoever doubted the authority of Parliament to change or modify the common law? The discussion in the House of Commons cited from Macaulay clearly establishes that the contest was between the crown, and the people represented in Parliament.

But we think it may be safely affirmed, that the Parliament of Great Britain, representing the people in their legislative functions, and the legislative bodies of this country, have from time immemorial to the present day, continued to grant to persons and corporations exclusive privileges—privileges denied to other citizens—privileges which come within any just definition of the word monopoly, as much as those now under consideration; and that the power to do this has never been questioned or denied. Nor can it be truthfully denied, that some of the most useful and beneficial enterprises set on foot for the general good, have been made successful by means of

these exclusive rights, and could only have been conducted to success in that way.

It may, therefore, be considered as established, that the authority of the legislature of Louisiana to pass the present statute is ample, unless some restraint in the exercise of that power be found in thee constitution of that State or in the amendments to the Constitution of the United States, adopted since the date of the decisions we have already cited.

If any such restraint is supposed to exist in the constitution of the State, the Supreme Court of Louisiana having necessarily passed on that question, it would not be open to review in this court.

The plaintiffs in error accepting this issue, allege that the statute is a violation of the Constitution of the United States in these several particulars:

That it creates an involuntary servitude forbidden by the thirteenth article of amendment;

That it abridges the privileges and immunities of citizens of the United States;

That it denies to the plaintiffs the equal protection of the laws; and

That it deprives them of their property without due process of law; contrary to the provisions of the first section of the fourteenth article of amendment.

This court is thus called upon for the first time to give construction to these articles.

We do not conceal from ourselves the great responsibility which this duty devolves upon us. No questions so far-reaching and pervading in their consequences, so profoundly interesting to the people of this country, and so important in their bearing upon the relations of the United States, and of the several States to each other and to the citizens of the States and of the United States, have been before this court during the official life of any of its present members. We have given every opportunity for a full hearing at the bar; we have discussed it freely and compared views among ourselves; we have taken ample time for careful deliberation, and we now propose to announce the judgments which we have formed in the construction of those articles, so far as we have found them necessary to the decision of the cases before us, and beyond that we have neither the inclination nor the right to go.

Twelve articles of amendment were added to the Federal Constitution soon after the original organization of the government under it in 1789. Of these all but the last were adopted so soon afterwards as to justify the statement that they were practically contemporaneous with the adoption of the original; and the twelfth, adopted in eighteen hundred and three, was so nearly so as to have become, like all the others, historical and of another age. But within the last eight years three other articles of amendment of vast importance have been added by the voice of the people to that now venerable instrument.

The most cursory glance at these articles discloses a unity of purpose, when taken in connection with the history of the times, which cannot fail to have an important bearing on any question of doubt concerning their true meaning. Nor can such doubts, when any reasonably exist, be safely and rationally solved without a reference to that history; for in it is found the occasion and the necessity for recurring again to the great source of power in this country, the people of the States, for additional guarantees of human rights; additional powers to the Federal government; additional restraints upon those of the States. Fortunately that history is fresh within the memory of us all, and its leading features, as they bear upon the matter before us, free from doubt.

The institution of African slavery, as it existed in about half the States of the Union, and the contests pervading the public mind for many years, between those who desired its curtailment and ultimate extinction and those who desired additional safeguards for its security and perpetuation, culminated in the effort, on the part of most of the States in which slavery existed, to separate from the Federal government, and to resist its authority. This constituted the war of the rebellion, and whatever auxiliary causes may have contributed to bring about this war, undoubtedly the overshadowing and efficient cause was African slavery.

In that struggle slavery, as a legalized social relation, perished. It perished as a necessity of the bitterness and force of the conflict. When the armies of freedom found themselves upon the soil of slavery they could do nothing less than free the poor victims whose enforced servitude was the foundation of the quarrel. And when hard pressed in the contest these men (for they proved themselves men in that terrible crisis) offered their services and were accepted by thousands to aid in suppressing the unlawful rebellion, slavery was at an end wherever the Federal government succeeded in that purpose. The proclamation of President Lincoln expressed an accomplished fact as to a large portion of the insurrectionary districts, when he declared slavery abolished in them all. But the war being over, those who had succeed in re-establishing the authority of the Federal government were not content to permit this great act of emancipation to rest on the actual results of the contest or proclamation of the Executive, both of which might have been questioned in after times, and they determined to place this main and most valuable result in the Constitution of the restored Union as one of its fundamental articles. Hence the thirteenth article of amendment of that instrument. Its two short sections seem hardly to admit of construction, so vigorous is their expression and so appropriate to the purpose we have indicated.

"1. Neither slavery nor involuntary servitude, except as a punishment for crime, whereof the party shall have been duly convicted, shall exist within the United States or any place subject to their jurisdiction.

"2. Congress shall have power to enforce this article by appropriate legislation."

To withdraw the mind from the contemplation of this grand yet simple declaration of the personal freedom of all the human race within the jurisdiction of this government—a declaration designed to establish the freedom of four millions of slaves—and with a microscopic search endeavor to find in it a reference to servitude's, which may have been attached to property in certain localities, requires an effort, to say the least of it.

That a personal servitude was meant is proved by the use of the word "involuntary," which can only apply to human beings. The exception of servitude as a punishment for crime gives an idea of the class of servitude that is meant. The word servitude is of larger meaning than slavery, as the latter is popularly understood in this country, and the obvious purpose was to forbid all shades and conditions of African slavery. It was very well understood that in the form of apprenticeship for long terms, as it had been practiced in the West India Islands, on the abolition of slavery by the English government, or by reducing the slaves to the condition of serfs attached to the plantation, the purpose of the article might have been evaded, if only the word slavery had been used. The case of the apprentice slave, held under a law of Maryland, liberated by Chief Justice Chase, on a writ of habeas corpus under this article, illustrates this course of observation. And it is all that we deem necessary to say on the application of that article to the statute of Louisiana, now under consideration.

The process of restoring to their proper relations with the Federal government and with the other States those which had sided with the rebellion, undertaken under the proclamation of President Johnson in 1865, and before the assembling of Congress, developed the fact that, notwithstanding the formal recognition by those States of the abolition of slavery, the condition of the slave race would, without further protection of the Federal government, be almost as bad as it was before. Among the first acts of legislation adopted by several of the States, in the legislative bodies which claimed to be in their normal relations with the Federal government, were laws which imposed upon the colored race onerous disabilities and burdens, and curtailed their rights in the pursuit of life, liberty, and property to such an extent that their freedom was of little value, while they had lost the protection which they had received from their former owners from motives both of interest and humanity.

They were in some States forbidden to appear in the towns in any other character than menial servants. They were required to reside on and cultivate the soil without the right to purchase or own it. They were excluded from many occupations of gain, and were not permitted to give testimony in the courts in any case where a white man was a party. It was said that their lives were at the mercy of bad men, either because the laws for their protection were insufficient or were not enforced.

These circumstances, whatever of falsehood or misconception may have been mingled with their presentation, forced upon the statesmen who had conducted the Federal government in safety through the crisis of the rebellion, and who supposed that by the thirteenth article of amendment they had secured the result of their labors, the conviction that something more was necessary in the way of constitutional protection to the unfortunate race who had suffered so much. They accordingly passed through Congress the proposition for the fourteenth amendment, and they declined to treat as restored to their full participation in the government of the Union the States which had been in insurrection, until they ratified that article by a formal vote of their legislative bodies.

Before we proceed to examine more critically the provisions of this amendment, on which the plaintiffs in error rely, let us complete and dismiss the history of the recent amendments, as that history relates to the general purpose which pervades them all. A few years' experience satisfied the thoughtful men who had been the authors of the other two amendments that, notwithstanding the restraints of those articles on the States, and the laws passed under the additional powers granted to Congress, these were inadequate for the protection of life, liberty, and property, without which freedom to the slave was no boon. They were in all those States denied the right of suffrage. The laws were administered by the white man alone. It was urged that a race of men distinctively marked as was the Negro, living in the midst of another and dominant race, could never be fully secured in their person and their property without the right of suffrage.

Hence the fifteenth amendment, which declares that "the right of a citizen of the United States to vote shall not be denied or abridged by any State on account of race, color, or previous condition of servitude." The Negro having, by the fourteenth amendment, been declared to be a citizen of the United States, is thus made a voter in every State of the Union.

We repeat, then, in the light of this recapitulation of events, almost too recent to be called history, but which are familiar to us all; and on the most casual examination of the language of these amendments, no one can fail to be impressed with the one pervading purpose found in them all, lying at the foundation of each, and without which none of them would have been even suggested; we mean the freedom of the slave race, the security and firm estab-

lishment of that freedom, and the protection of the newly-made freeman and citizen from the oppressions of those who had formerly exercised unlimited dominion over him. It is true that only the fifteenth amendment, in terms, mentions the Negro by speaking of his color and his slavery. But it is just as true that each of the other articles was addressed to the grievances of that race, and designed to remedy them as the fifteenth.

We do not say that no one else but the Negro can share in this protection. Both the language and spirit of these articles are to have their fair and just weight in any question of construction. Undoubtedly while Negro slavery alone was in the mind of the Congress which proposed the thirteenth article, it forbids any other kind of slavery, now or hereafter. If Mexican peonage or the Chinese coolie labor system shall develop slavery of the Mexican or Chinese race within our territory, this amendment may safely be trusted to make it void. And so if other rights are assailed by the States which properly and necessarily fall within the protection of these articles, that protection will apply, though the party interested may not be of African descent. But what we do say, and what we wish to be understood is, that in any fair and just construction of any section or phrase of these amendments, it is necessary to look to the purpose which we have said was the pervading spirit of them all, the evil which they were designed to remedy, and the process of continued addition to the Constitution, until that purpose was supposed to be accomplished, as far as constitutional law can accomplish it.

The first section of the fourteenth article, to which our attention is more specially invited, opens with a definition of citizenship—not only citizenship of the United States, but citizenship of the States. No such definition was previously found in the Constitution, nor had any attempt been made to define it by act of Congress. It had been the occasion of much discussion in the courts, by the executive departments, and in the public journals. It had been said by eminent judges that no man was a citizen of the United States, except as he was a citizen of one of the States composing the Union. Those, therefore, who had been born and resided always in the District of Columbia or in the Territories, though within the United States, were not citizens. Whether this proposition was sound or not had never been judicially decided. But it had been held by this court, in the celebrated Dred Scott case, only a few years before the outbreak of the civil war, that a man of African descent, whether a slave or not, was not and could not be a citizen of a State or of the United States. This decision, while it met the condemnation of some of the ablest statesmen and constitutional lawyers of the country, had never been overruled; and if it was to be accepted as a constitutional limitation of the right of citizenship, then all the Negro race who had recently been made freemen, were still, not only not citizens, but were incapable of becoming so by anything short of an amendment to the Constitution.

To remove this difficulty primarily, and to establish a clear and comprehensive definition of citizenship which should declare what should constitute citizenship of the United States, and also citizenship of a State, the first clause of the first section was framed.

"All persons born or naturalized in the United States, and subject to the jurisdiction thereof, are citizens of the United States and of the State wherein they reside."

The first observation we have to make on this clause is, that it puts at rest both the questions which we stated to have been the subject of differences of opinion. It declares that persons may be citizens of the United States without regard to their citizenship of a particular State, and it overturns the Dred Scott decision by making *all persons* born within the United States and subject to its jurisdiction citizens of the United States. That its main purpose was to establish the citizenship of the Negro can admit of no doubt. The phrase, "subject to its jurisdiction" was intended to exclude from its operation children of ministers, consuls, and citizens or subjects of foreign States born within the United States.

The next observation is more important in view of the arguments of counsel in the present case. It is, that the distinction between citizenship of the United States and citizenship of a State is clearly recognized and established. Not only may a man be a citizen of the United States without being a citizen of a State, but an important element is necessary to convert the former into the latter. He must reside within the State to make him a citizen of it, but it is only necessary that he should be born or naturalized in the United States to be a citizen of the Union.

It is quite clear, that there is a citizenship of the United States, and a citizenship of a State, which are distinct from each other, and which depend upon different characteristics or circumstances in the individual.

We think this distinction and its explicit recognition in this amendment of great weight in this argument, because the next paragraph of this same section, which is the one mainly relied on by the plaintiffs in error, speaks only of privileges and immunities of citizens of the United States, and does no speak of those of citizens of the several States. The argument, however, in favor of the plaintiffs rests wholly on the assumption that the citizenship is the same, and the privileges and immunities guaranteed by the clause are the same.

The language is, "No State shall make or enforce any law which shall abridge the privileges or immunities of citizens of *the United States.*" It is a little remarkable, if this clause was intended as a protection to the citizen of a State against the legislative power of his own State, that word citizen of the State should be left out when it is so carefully

used, and used in contradistinction to citizens of the United States, in the very sentence which precedes it. It is too clear for argument that the change in phraseology was adopted understandingly and with a purpose.

Of the privileges and immunities of the citizen of the United States, and of the privileges and immunities of the citizen of the State, and what they respectively are, we will presently consider; but we wish to state here that it is only the former which are placed by this clause under the protection of the Federal Constitution, and that the latter, whatever they may be; are not intended to have any additional protection by this paragraph of the amendment.

If, then, there is a difference between the privileges and immunities belonging to a citizen of the United States as such, and those belonging to the citizen of the State as such the latter must rest for their security and protection where they have heretofore rested; for they are not embraced by this paragraph of the amendment.

The first occurrence of the words "privileges and immunities" in our constitutional history, is to be found in the fourth of the articles of the old Confederation.

It declares "that the better to secure and perpetuate mutual friendship and intercourse among the people of the different States in this Union, the free inhabitants of each of these States, paupers, vagabonds, and fugitives from justice excepted, shall be entitled to all the privileges and immunities of free citizens in the several States; and the people of each State shall have free ingress and regress to and from any other State, and shall enjoy therein all the privileges of trade and commerce, subject to the same duties, impositions, and restrictions as the inhabitants thereof respectively.

In the Constitution of the United States, which superseded the Articles of Confederation, the corresponding provision is found in section two of the fourth article, in the following words: "The citizens of each State shall be entitled to all the privileges and immunities of citizens of the several States."

There can be but little question that the purpose of both these provisions is the same, and that the privileges and immunities intended are the same in each. In the article of the Confederation we have some of these specifically mentioned, and enough perhaps to give some general idea of the class of civil rights meant by the phrase.

Fortunately we are not without judicial construction of this clause of the Constitution. The first and the leading case on the subject is that of *Corfield v. Coryell*, decided by Mr. Justice Washington in the Circuit Court for the District of Pennsylvania in 1823.

"The inquiry," he says, "is, what are the privileges and immunities of citizens of the several States? We feel no hesitation in confining these expressions to those privileges and immunities which are *fundamental;* which belong of right to the citizens of all free governments, and which have at all times been enjoyed by citizens of the several States which compose this Union, from the time of their becoming free, independent, and sovereign. What these fundamental principles are, it would be more tedious than difficult to enumerate. They may all, however, be comprehended under the following general heads: protection by the government, with the right to acquire and possess property of every kind, and to pursue and obtain happiness and safety, subject, nevertheless, to such restraints as the government may prescribe for the general good of the whole."

This definition of the privileges and immunities of citizens of the States is adopted in the main by this court in the recent case of *Ward v. The State of Maryland,* while it declines to undertake an authoritative definition beyond what was necessary to that decision. The description, when taken to include others not named, but which are of the same general character, embraces nearly every civil right for the establishment and protection of which organized government is instituted. They are, in the language of Judge Washington, those rights which are fundamental. Throughout his opinion, they are spoken of as rights belonging to the individual as a citizen of a State. They are so spoken of in the constitutional provision which he was construing. And they have always been held to be the class of rights which the State governments were created to establish and secure.

In the case of *Paul v. Virginia,* the court, in expounding this clause of the Constitution, says that "the privileges and immunities secured to citizens of each State in the several States, by the provision in question, are those privileges and immunities which are common to the citizens in the latter States under their constitution and laws by virtue of their being citizens."

The constitutional provision there alluded to did not create those rights, which it called privileges and immunities of citizens of the States. It threw around them in that clause no security for the citizen of the States in which they were claimed or exercised. Nor did it profess to control the power of the State governments over the rights of its own citizens.

Its sole purpose was to declare to the several States, that whatever those rights, as you grant or establish them to your own citizens, or as you limit or qualify, or impose restrictions on their exercise, the same, neither more nor less, shall be the measure of the rights of citizens of other States within your jurisdiction.

It would be the vainest show of learning to attempt to prove by citations of authority, that up to the adoption of the recent amendments, no claim or pretense was set up that those rights depended on the Federal government for their existence or protection, beyond the very few express

limitations which the Federal Constitution imposed upon the States—such, for instance, as the prohibition against ex post facto laws, bills of attainder, and laws impairing the obligation of contracts. But with the exception of these and a few other restrictions, the entire domain of the privileges and immunities of citizens of the States, as above defined, lay within the constitutional and legislative power of the States, and without that of the Federal government. Was it the purpose of the fourteenth amendment, by the simple declaration that no State should make or enforce any law which shall abridge the privileges and immunities of *citizens of the United States,* to transfer the security and protection of all the civil rights which we have mentioned, from the States to the Federal government? And where it is declared that Congress shall have the power to enforce that article, was it intended to bring within the power of Congress the entire domain of civil rights heretofore belonging exclusively to the States?

All this and more must follow, if the proposition of the plaintiffs in error be sound. For not only are these rights subject to the control of Congress whenever in its discretion any of them are supposed to be abridged by State legislation, but that body may also pass laws in advance, limiting and restricting the exercise of legislative power by the States, in their most ordinary and usual functions, as in its judgment it may think proper on all such subjects. And still further, such a construction followed by the reversal of the judgments of the Supreme Court of Louisiana in these cases, would constitute this court a perpetual censor upon all legislation of the States, on the civil rights of their own citizens, with authority to nullify such as it did not approve as consistent with those rights, as they existed at the time of the adoption of this amendment. The argument we admit is not always the most conclusive which is drawn from the consequences urged against the adoption of a particular construction of an instrument. But when, as in the case before us, these consequences are so serious, so far reaching and pervading, so great a departure from the structure and spirit of our institutions; when the effect is to fetter and degrade the State governments by subjecting them to the control of Congress, in the exercise of powers heretofore universally conceded to them of the most ordinary and fundamental character; when in fact it radically changes the whole theory of the relations of the State and Federal governments to each other and of both these governments to the people; the argument has a force that is irresistible, in the absence of language which expresses such a purpose too clearly to admit of doubt.

We are convinced that no such results were intended by the Congress which proposed these amendments, nor by the legislatures of the States which ratified them.

Having shown that the privileges and immunities relied on in the argument are those which belong to citizens of the States as such, and that they are left to the State governments for security and protection, and not by this article placed under the special care of the Federal government, we may hold ourselves excused from defining the privileges and immunities of citizens of the United States which no State can abridge, until some case involving those privileges may make it necessary to do so.

But lest it should be said that no such privileges and immunities are to be found if those we have been considering are excluded, we venture to suggest some which own their existence to the Federal government, its National character, its Constitution, or its laws.

One of these is well described in the case of *Crandall v. Nevada.* It is said to be the right of the citizen of this great country, protected by implied guarantees of its Constitution, "to come to the seat of government to assert any claim he may have upon that government, to transact any business he may have with it, to seek its protection, to share its offices, to engage in administering its functions. He has the right of free access to its seaports, through which all operations of foreign commerce are conducted, to the subtreasuries, land offices, and courts of justice in the several States." And quoting from the language of Chief Justice Taney in another case, it is said "that *for all the great purposes for which the Federal government* was established, we are one people, with one common country, *we are all citizens of the United States*", and it is, as such citizens, that their rights are supported in this court in *Crandall v. Nevada.*

Another privilege of a citizen of the United States is to demand the care and protection of the Federal government over his life, liberty, and property when on the high seas or within the jurisdiction of a foreign government. Of this there can be no doubt, nor that the right depends upon his character as a citizen of the United States. The right to peaceably assemble and petition for redress of grievances, the privilege of the writ of *habeas corpus,* are rights of the citizen guaranteed by the Federal Constitution. The right to use the navigable waters of the United States, however they may penetrate the territory of the several States, all rights secured to our citizens by treaties with foreign nations, are dependent upon citizenship of the United States, and not citizenship of a State. One of these privileges is conferred by the very article under consideration. It is that a citizen of the United States can, of his own volition, become a citizen of any State of the Union by a *bona fide* residence therein, with the same rights as other citizens of that State. To these may be added the rights secured by the thirteenth and fifteenth articles of amendment, and by the other clause of the fourteenth, next to be considered.

But it is useless to pursue this branch of the inquiry, since we are of opinion that the rights claimed by these plaintiffs in error, if they have any existence, are not privileges and immunities of citizens of the United States within the meaning of the clause of the fourteenth amendment under consideration.

"All persons born or naturalized in the United States, and subject to the jurisdiction thereof, are citizens of the United States and of the State wherein they reside. No State shall make or enforce any law which shall abridge the privileges or immunities of citizens of the United States; nor shall any State deprive any person of life, liberty, or property without due process of law, nor deny to any person within its jurisdiction the equal protection of its laws."

The argument has not been much pressed in these cases that the defendant's charter deprives the plaintiffs of their property without due process of law, or that it denies to them the equal protection of the law. The first of these paragraphs has been in the Constitution since the adoption of the fifth amendment, as a restraint upon the Federal power. It is also to be found in some form of expression in the constitutions of nearly all the States, as a restraint upon the power of the States. This law then, has practically been the same as it now is during the existence of the government, except so far as the present amendment may place the restraining power over the States in this matter in the hands of the Federal government.

We are not without judicial interpretation, therefore, both State and National, of the meaning of this clause. And it is sufficient to say that under no construction of that provision that we have ever seen, or any that we deem admissible, can the restraint imposed by the State of Louisiana upon the exercise of their trade by the butchers of New Orleans be held to be a deprivation of property within the meaning of that provision.

"Nor shall any State deny to any person within its jurisdiction the equal protection of the laws."

In the light of the history of these amendments, and the pervading purpose of them, which we have already discussed, it is not difficult to give a meaning to this clause. The existence of laws in the States where the newly emancipated negroes resided, which discriminated with gross injustice and hardship against them as a class, was the evil to be remedied by this clause, and by it such laws are forbidden.

If, however, the States did not conform their laws to its requirements, then by the fifth section of the article of amendment Congress was authorized to enforce it by suitable legislation. We doubt very much whether any action of a State not directed by way of discrimination against the Negroes as a class, or on account of their race, will ever be held to come within the purview of this provision. It is so clearly a provision for that race and that emergency, that a strong case would be necessary for its application to any other. But as it is a State that is to be dealt with, and not alone the validity of its laws, we may safely leave that matter until Congress shall have exercised its power, or some case of State oppression, by denial of equal justice in its courts, shall have claimed a decision at our hands. We find to such case in the one before us, and do not deem it necessary to go over the argument again, as it may have relation to this particular clause of the amendment.

In the early history of the organization of the government, its statesmen seem to have divided on the line which should separate the powers of the National government from those of the State governments, and though this line has never been very well defined in public opinion, such a division has continued from that day to this.

The adoption of the first eleven amendments to the Constitution so soon after the original instrument was accepted, shows a prevailing sense of danger at that time from the Federal power. And it cannot be denied that such a jealousy continued to exist with many patriotic men until the breaking out of the late civil war. It was then discovered that the true danger to the perpetuity of the Union was in the capacity of the State organizations to combine and concentrate all the powers of the State, and of contiguous States, for a determine resistance to the General Government.

Unquestionably this has given great force to the argument, and added largely to the number of those who believe in the necessity of a strong National government.

But, however pervading this sentiment, and however it may have contributed to the adoption of the amendments we have been considering, we do not see in those amendments any purpose to destroy the main features of the general system. Under the pressure of all the excited feeling growing out of the war, our statesmen have still believed that the existence of the States with powers for domestic and local government, including the regulation of civil rights—the rights of person and of property—was essential to the perfect working of our complex form of government, though they have thought proper to impose additional limitations on the States, and to confer additional power on that of the Nation.

But whatever fluctuations may be seen in the history of public opinion on this subject during the period of our national existence, we think it will be found that this court, so far as its functions required, has always held with a steady and an even hand the balance between State and Federal power, and we trust that such may continue to be the history of its relation to that subject so long as it shall have duties to perform which demand of it a construction of the Constitution, or of any of its parts.

Source:

16 Wallace (83 U.S.) 36.

Rutherford B. Hayes, Inaugural Address, 1877

Speech delivered by Rutherford B. Hayes on March 5, 1877, at his inauguration as the 19th president of the United States. His elevation to the presidency marked the end of Reconstruction. Hayes took office under a cloud, having been outpolled in the popular vote (and probably in the electoral count as well) by Samuel J. Tilden. Only a hard-fought congressional compromise, in which pro-Hayes forces agreed to end federal rule over the states undergoing Reconstruction, salvaged the presidency for Hayes. In his inaugural speech, Hayes backed a return to "self-government" in the South, provided that the Southern states agreed to guard "the interests of both races carefully and equally" and to acknowledge the authority of federal law. He added that the federal government had a moral obligation to safeguard the rights of emancipated former slaves. Hayes also advocated "liberal and permanent" federal funding of free schools across the country on the grounds that "Universal suffrage should rest upon universal education." In response to the rampant corruption that had plagued the administration of his predecessor, Ulysses S. Grant, Hayes called for reform of the civil service system, declaring, "He serves his party best who serves the country best."

―――――――――――― ∽∞∾ ――――――――――――

Fellow-Citizens:

We have assembled to repeat the public ceremonial, begun by Washington, observed by all my predecessors, and now a time-honored custom, which marks the commencement of a new term of the Presidential office. Called to the duties of this great trust, I proceed, in compliance with usage, to announce some of the leading principles, on the subjects that now chiefly engage the public attention, by which it is my desire to be guided in the discharge of those duties. I shall not undertake to lay down irrevocably principles or measures of administration, but rather to speak of the motives which should animate us, and to suggest certain important ends to be attained in accordance with our institutions and essential to the welfare of our country.

At the outset of the discussions which preceded the recent Presidential election it seemed to me fitting that I should fully make known my sentiments in regard to several of the important questions which then appeared to demand the consideration of the country. Following the example, and in part adopting the language, of one of my predecessors, I wish now, when every motive for misrepresentation has passed away, to repeat what was said before the election, trusting that my countrymen will candidly weigh and understand it, and that they will feel assured that the sentiments declared in accepting the nomination for the Presidency will be the standard of my conduct in the path before me, charged, as I now am, with the grave and difficult task of carrying them out in the practical administration of the Government so far as depends, under the Constitution and laws on the Chief Executive of the nation.

The permanent pacification of the country upon such principles and by such measures as will secure the complete protection of all its citizens in the free enjoyment of all their constitutional rights is now the one subject in our public affairs which all thoughtful and patriotic citizens regard as of supreme importance.

Many of the calamitous efforts of the tremendous revolution which has passed over the Southern States still remain. The immeasurable benefits which will surely follow, sooner or later, the hearty and generous acceptance of the legitimate results of that revolution have not yet been realized. Difficult and embarrassing questions meet us at the threshold of this subject. The people of those States are still impoverished, and the inestimable blessing of wise, honest, and peaceful local self-government is not fully enjoyed. Whatever difference of opinion may exist as to the cause of this condition of things, the fact is clear that in the progress of events the time has come when such government is the imperative necessity required by all the varied interests, public and private, of those States. But it must not be forgotten that only a local government which recognizes and maintains inviolate the rights of all is a true self-government.

With respect to the two distinct races whose peculiar relations to each other have brought upon us the deplorable complications and perplexities which exist in those States, it must be a government which guards the interests of both races carefully and equally. It must be a government which submits loyally and heartily to the Constitution and the laws—the laws of the nation and the laws of the States themselves—accepting and obeying faithfully the whole Constitution as it is.

Resting upon this sure and substantial foundation, the superstructure of beneficent local governments can be built up, and not otherwise. In furtherance of such obedience to the letter and the spirit of the Constitution, and in behalf of all that its attainment implies, all so-called party interests lose their apparent importance, and party lines may well be permitted to fade into insignificance. The question we have to consider for the immediate welfare of those States of the Union is the question of government or no government; of social order and all the peaceful industries and the happiness that belongs to it, or a return to barbarism. It is a question in which every citizen of the nation is deeply interested, and with respect to which we ought not to be, in a partisan sense, either Republicans or Democrats, but fellow-citizens and fellow-men, to whom the interests of a common country and a common humanity are dear.

The sweeping revolution of the entire labor system of a large portion of our country and the advance of 4,000,000 people from a condition of servitude to that of citizenship, upon an equal footing with their former masters, could not occur without presenting problems of the gravest moment, to be dealt with by the emancipated race, by their former masters, and by the General Government, the author of the act of emancipation. That it was a wise, just, and providential act, fraught with good for all concerned, is not generally conceded throughout the country. That a moral obligation rests upon the National Government to employ its constitutional power and influence to establish the rights of the people it has emancipated, and to protect them in the enjoyment of those rights when they are infringed or assailed, is also generally admitted.

The evils which afflict the Southern States can only be removed or remedied by the united and harmonious efforts of both races, actuated by motives of mutual sympathy and regard; and while in duty bound and fully determined to protect the rights of all by every constitutional means at the disposal of my Administration, I am sincerely anxious to use every legitimate influence in favor of honest and efficient local *self*-government as the true resource of those States for the promotion of the contentment and prosperity of their citizens. In the effort I shall make to accomplish this purpose I ask the cordial cooperation of all who cherish an interest in the welfare of the country, trusting that party ties and the prejudice of race will be freely surrendered in behalf of the great purpose to be accomplished. In the important work of restoring the South it is not the political situation alone that merits attention. The material development of that section of the country has been arrested by the social and political revolution through which it has passed, and now needs and deserves the considerate care of the National Government within the just limits prescribed by the Constitution and wise public economy.

But at the basis of all prosperity, for that as well as for every other part of the country, lies the improvement of the intellectual and moral condition of the people. Universal suffrage should rest upon universal education. To this end, liberal and permanent provision should be made for the support of free schools by the State governments, and, if need be, supplemented by legitimate aid from national authority.

Let me assure my countrymen of the Southern States that it is my earnest desire to regard and promote their truest interest—the interests of the white and of the colored people both and equally—and to put forth my best efforts in behalf of a civil policy which will forever wipe out in our political affairs the color line and the distinction between North and South, to the end that we may have not merely a united North or a united South, but a united country.

I ask the attention of the public to the paramount necessity of reform in our civil service—a reform not merely as to certain abuses and practices of so-called official patronage which have come to have the sanction of usage in the several Departments of our Government, but a change in the system of appointment itself; a reform that shall be thorough, radical, and complete; a return to the principles and practices of the founders of the Government. They neither expected nor desired from public officers any partisan service. They meant that public officers should owe their whole service to the Government and to the people. They meant that the officer should be secure in his tenure as long as his personal character remained untarnished and the performance of his duties satisfactory. They held that appointments to office were not to be made nor expected merely as rewards for partisan services, nor merely on the nomination of members of Congress, as being entitled in any respect to the control of such appointments.

The fact that both the great political parties of the country, in declaring their principles prior to the election, gave a prominent place to the subject of reform of our civil service, recognizing and strongly urging its necessity, in terms almost identical in their specific import with those I have here employed, must be accepted as a conclusive argument in behalf of these measures. It must be regarded as the expression of the united voice and will of the whole country upon this subject, and both political parties are virtually pledged to give it their unreserved support.

The President of the United States of necessity owes his election to office to the suffrage and zealous labors of a political party, the members of which cherish with ardor and regard as of essential importance the principles of their party organization; but he should strive to be always mindful of the fact that he serves his party best who serves the country best.

In furtherance of the reform we seek, and in other important respects a change of great importance, I recommend an amendment to the Constitution prescribing a term of six years for the Presidential office and forbidding a reelection.

With respect to the financial condition of the country, I shall not attempt an extended history of the embarrassment and prostration which we have suffered during the past three years. The depression in all our varied commercial and manufacturing interests throughout the country, which began in September, 1873, still continues. It is very gratifying, however, to be able to say that there are indications all around us of a coming change to prosperous times.

Upon the currency question, intimately connected, as it is, with this topic, I may be permitted to repeat here the statement made in my letter of acceptance, that in my judgment the feeling of uncertainty inseparable from an irredeemable paper currency, with its fluctuation of values, is one of the greatest obstacles to a return to prosperous times. The only safe paper currency is one which rests upon a coin basis and is at all times and promptly convertible into coin.

I adhere to the views heretofore expressed by me in favor of Congressional legislation in behalf of an early resumption of specie payments, and I am satisfied not only that this is wise, but that the interests, as well as the public sentiment, of the country imperatively demand it.

Passing from these remarks upon the condition of our own country to consider our relations with other lands, we are reminded by the international complications abroad, threatening the peace of Europe, that our traditional rule of noninterference in the affairs of foreign nations has proved of great value in past times and ought to be strictly observed.

The policy inaugurated by my honored predecessor, President Grant, of submitting to arbitration grave questions in dispute between ourselves and foreign powers points to a new, and incomparably the best, instrumentality for the preservation of peace, and will, as I believe, become a beneficent example of the course to be pursued in similar emergencies by other nations.

If, unhappily, questions of difference should at any time during the period of my Administration arise between the United States and any foreign government, it will certainly be my disposition and my hope to aid in their settlement in the same peaceful and honorable way, thus securing to our country the great blessings of peace and mutual good offices with all the nations of the world.

Fellow-citizens, we have reached the close of a political contest marked by the excitement which usually attends the contests between great political parties whose members espouse and advocate with earnest faith their respective creeds. The circumstances were, perhaps, in no respect extraordinary save in the closeness and the consequent uncertainty of the result.

For the first time in the history of the country it has been deemed best, in view of the peculiar circumstances of the case, that the objections and questions in dispute with reference to the counting of the electoral votes should be referred to the decision of a tribunal appointed for this purpose.

That tribunal—established by law for this sole purpose; its members, all of them, men of long-established reputation for integrity and intelligence, and, with the exception of those who are also members of the supreme judiciary, chosen equally from both political parties; its deliberations enlightened by the research and the arguments of able counsel—was entitled to the fullest confidence of the American people. Its decisions have been patiently waited for, and accepted as legally conclusive by the general judgment of the public. For the present, opinion will widely vary as to the wisdom of the several conclusions announced by that tribunal. This is to be anticipated in every instance where matters of dispute are made the subject of arbitration under the forms of law. Human judgment is never unerring, and is rarely regarded as otherwise than wrong by the unsuccessful party in the contest.

The fact that two great political parties have in this way settled a dispute in regard to which good men differ as to the facts and the law no less than as to the proper course to be pursued in solving the question in controversy is an occasion for general rejoicing.

Upon one point there is entire unanimity in public sentiment—that conflicting claims to the Presidency must be amicably and peaceably adjusted, and that when so adjusted the general acquiescence of the nation ought surely to follow.

It has been reserved for a government of the people, where the right of suffrage is universal, to give to the world the first example in history of a great nation, in the midst of the struggle of opposing parties for power, hushing its party tumults to yield the issue of the contest to adjustment according to the forms of law.

Looking for the guidance of that Divine Hand by which the destinies of nations and individuals are shaped, I call upon you, Senators, Representatives, judges, fellow-citizens, here and everywhere, to unite with me in an earnest effort to secure to our country the blessings, not only of material prosperity, but of justice, peace, and union—a union depending not upon the constraint of force, but upon the loving devotion of a free people; "and that all things may be so ordered and settled upon the best and surest foundations that peace and happiness, truth and justice, religion and piety, may be established among us for all generations."

Source:

Inaugural Addresses of the Presidents of the United States: From George washington to George W. Bush. Washington, D.C.: Government.Printing Office, 1989.

Women's Rights

Frances Willard, "Women's Lesser Duties," 1863

Speech on the duties and responsibilities of the mid-19th-century woman, given by suffragist, teacher, and temperance leader Frances Willard on March 24, 1863, to the Browning Association of Pittsburgh Female College. Willard firmly believed that a woman's duties were much different from a man's. She stressed that, as well as being pure, charming, and moral, women should be learned in the arts and domestic duties. Willard later became the president of the Evanston College for Ladies, and she became dean of women when the college merged with Northwestern University.

───────── ⌇ ─────────

Ladies of the Browning Association: Concerning the vocation of woman a great deal has been said. Her moral susceptibility, her purity of influence, have been acknowledged since civilization's morning; her abounding charity,

our own day and the exigencies of our national cause abundantly demonstrate. But of her work, aesthetically considered—of the duty that she owes to be skilled in the arts that enrich social intercourse, true to her character in the minor matters of life—less has been said. Be this our theme.

It is a principle acted upon, if not acknowledged, that process and result stand to each other in the same relation as light and darkness, sound and silence, do. For e find that processes are occult, inferior—while results are superior and luminous. An oak stands before you. What strength is in the gnarled trunk and brawny arms! What symmetry in the proportions; and

Not a prince in all the proud old world beyond the deep E'er wore his crown so loftily as he Wears that green coronal of leaves with which God's hand hath graced him.

But where are the dewy evenings, the genial showers, the yellow sun-beams, that nurtured the acorn into the tree? They are past and forgotten. Where will you find the spongioles that absorbed the nourishment? They are buried out of sight. No sound tells you of the ascending sap—the life-blood of the tree; all this pertains to process, and is hidden—result only stands before you, complete and wonderful. So is it always. The great earth, bearing her freight of bud and blossom, works silently for their growth and maintenance. The scaffolding is taken down when the obelisk is finished. A heathen imagination even, presents us with the image of Minerva leaping *full-armed* from the brain of Jove.

In the social world this principle is potent in its action. The question is not. How did you achieve it? but, What have you achieved? That inexorable *What* meets us at the threshold of the mansion—at the door of the salon. It is a peculiarity of Republican governments. At Windsor it is, Who are you? Who was your father? At Washington, Have you value? What have *you* done? True, as there are drones in every hive, so in all societies we shall find persons who are there by tolerance only. We hear them called "wall flowers," stupid old dears," and other unflattering names. Yet the *fact* remains, that to be admitted into really good society, one must have innate value—must have some return to make for the benefits which he receives. Into the social sunshine we bring results, processes being left to the obscurity of private life. Men grow good and great otherwhere than in society; they ponder and discover in secret places; their hard-earned spoils they lay down at the feet of the banquet's Queen, and she puts laurel wreaths upon their brows. For society is "made up of every creature's best." As the phrase has it, every one is "on his good behavior" there. So that it should seem philosophically advisable to go much into the world, that acting habitually, as well as we know how, it shall grow to be "second nature" to us after a while.

"Think of me at my best," says David Copperfield's erring friend to the gentle "Trotwood." His words are ours, said by look and tone and bearing, to every one with whom we have to do. "Think of me at my best; I will try to make your thinking only just to my acting, if you will be thus generous with me." Society cultivates the spirit of tolerance. We learn there to recognize the rights of others, to seek their happiness. In the best circles the "Golden" is also the fashionable rule, but with this difference, that in society no thought is had of the intention, the outward act alone being regarded—the retribution following instantly, no one daring to deviate from it who would win and maintain a reputation for gentility. You shall not offend my tastes; you are forbidden to put me to inconvenience, is the well understood though always *implied* "Bill of Rights," here.

To worry others—to damage them in person or estate, is to lose caste in society. Witness the discomfiture of the blundering beau who upsets his saucer of ice-cream upon his fair companion's dress, though he would fain conduct himself with Chesterfieldian elegance. His good intention cannot save him. He is marked, the chagrined man of the evening. For blunderers are not to be tolerated; they are a disfigurement—an excrescence upon the face of society. Only the graceful, the self-possessed and agreeable are in demand as members of the social commonwealth. Smiles and hand-shakings are the "small change" of its currency; good looks, good dress, good talk, its "checks" and "notes of hand," honored at sight. If one is beautiful, witty or wise, he throws this, his own peculiar gift into the general stock, receiving again that which is so sweet to every heart—the praises of his peers. There is much talk about a noble contempt for the world's opinion—but everybody's secret heart must tell him that it is a false philosophy which would lead him to be careless of a verdict so authoritative as that which society has in her power to pronounce. And what is a temperate love of praise, but a just anxiety that the verdict shall be in favor, not in disapproval of us? The enjoyment of a pleasant reputation among our companions is one of the truest delights of life.

We come, then, into society. What are the offerings that we must bring? Fortunately for us, there is choice. One need not be an Admirable Crichton in order to gain a recognition. Let each come, bringing that one preeminent gift with which his Creator has endowed him. To some, that gift is beauty; and these are always welcome. Whoever brings a lovely face or graceful form to the social assemblage, confers upon each beholder a benefit which he will be loyal enough to acknowledge in his heart, for, as one of our deepest thinkers has said: "Every man's mission is order. He is here to make what was disorderly and chaotic into a thing ruled and regular. Disorder is dissolution, death." And we may ask: What is beauty of figure or of face but an agreement in something outside of us with conceptions of fitness and order that dwell within? Beauty is food to the eye, as music is to the ear. Our souls have been called "sweet bells jangled," but still they are "*sweet* bells." We have that within us which feels worshipful before beauty in whatever form it comes, but most when we discern it in the human face—prophetic as it is of that One ineffable Countenance which we shall one day behold. Bring on your good looks, then, and an admiring world shall thank you.

But, though we cannot stipulate (as some over-nice critics have endeavored to do,) that you shall not be conscious of your charms—knowing that your mirrors are before us in this matter—yet, let us beg, for your sakes as well as for ours who are pleased by the sight of you, Keep your own counsel on this most interesting subject, and never let a mincing air, affected tone, or a vain toss of the regal head, betray your knowledge of your dowry. You have often been told that a modest little flower, the violet, has a lesson for such as you. Do not let the advice to heed its teachings be lost upon you because you have heard it so often. As a parabola pleases the eye more than a perpendicular, so gracefulness is grateful to the aesthetic sense to often outraged by awkward angularity. It is a duty that we owe, to be as graceful as we can. We have all seen bows so awkward, attitudes and movements so full of clumsiness, that something of a moral turpitude has seemed to attach to them. Who knows that there shall not come an age when to outrage the taste—to agonize the delicate perception—to impose discord upon the sensitive ear, shall be in some way punishable as a grave offense? One of the gifts, then, which society gladly receives, is an individual of fine appearance, or grace of manner. "But I cannot bring either of those," is the plaintive cry from scores of aspiring maidens.

Well, it has been often, yet not *too* often said, that there is another kind of beauty which the soul seeks—a higher kind, because more spiritual, hence more lasting than the first, speaking of which a writer has said (describing one of the persons he met on a promenade down Broadway): "There comes the ever welcome ugly face of a beautiful soul!" All true culture at the last amounts to this. Plato's prayer we are still offering, in this Christian land, "O make me beautiful within!" or, paraphrased by Milton:

What in me is dark illume;

What is low, raise and support.

To grow pure and good is in the power of all. That is the greatest gift. But the subject is a wide one, and is made familiar to us by every sermon to which we listen, by every prayer we hear.

To be of highest value in society, a lady should have some accomplishments—should be able, in some way, to be a felt force in the entertainments of the hour. Can you sing a song for us? Can you render poetry into music by a fantasie of Thalberg, a sonata or a symphony by Beethoven? Can you give us a pathetic ballad or a humorous roundelay to the accompaniment of your harp or guitar? If so, you are welcome, says Society, and we need you hardly less than you need us. But, better than all, can you talk? Are you quick at retort—fluent, fond of badinage? Have you good descriptive powers? Are you kindly and generous in your estimates of persons and their acts? Is your language choice and free from provincial and inelegant words and phrases? Are you well read? If so, you are a prize indeed. These questions must be all affirmatively answered before one is a candidate for society's highest awards. For, though music is charming, though beauty and grace are as rich in attractions as they are rare in actualization, it remains true that conversational powers rank highest in the scale of social gifts.

It is the duty of all to do their best, even should they carry their industry so far as to prepare bon-mots beforehand, like Sheridan, or make memoranda of things suitable to be said, upon their thumb nails, like one less famous than the great wit. But all cannot talk well, though many make a feint of doing so, poising themselves over a subject like a humming-bird over a flower; dallying with ideas, playing hide- and-seek with them, the hiding being for the most part done by the ideas. But not so, your real Talker, endowed for the purpose. He can take a subject, like a flower, up by the *roots,* to look into its philosophy; or he can merely descant upon its beauties, as he would call attention to the coloring of a corolla, its size and outline— or, if botanically inclined, its species, habits and uses; or he can be so transcendental as give you what might be termed the perfume of the subject, as he would direct your attention to the aroma of the flower. So that, as it seems, he can give to society "small talk," if the relations in which he is placed demand it (his "relations," for example, to a pouting, wordless beauty of "sweet sixteen"); or he can be descriptive, didactic, historic, polemic—what you will.

It is related to the credit of Socrates, that he said on one occasion, as his apology for leaving a social circle: "That which I know would not be suited to the occasion; and what would be suited to the occasion, of that I am ignorant." But surely these words detract from his reputation as a conversationalist, and do not add to his fame as a philosopher. Versatility may be named as the first qualification of a good talker. Practice is requisite—tact—with generosity enough to be a good listener also. Some persons wait impatiently for their *vis-a-vis* to put in a few words, and then make their next sentence tangent to his, touching it at the point of departure only. To be a good listener is not only one of the minor duties of morality, but is a *sine qua non* in polite life. Monopoly of words is intolerable. Here, then, in powers of conservation we have the highest gift that one can exercise for the benefit of the circle in which he moves. It can dispense with accessories, if need be. The nimble, eloquent, versatile tongue alone is requisite. There is no formula of invitation to the exercise of this gift, as, "May I have the honor of conducting you to the talker's chair?" "Won't you talk? Please do! Give us that imitation of Dr. Johnson, with variations; that monologue a la Coleridge. That's in your best style, I have heard." Or, "Please favor us with your new bon mot, that original conceit which is considered so amusing-" No, all is simple and direct. The machinery is not cumbrous, it can be brought into action at a moment's warning. Grammatical propriety has suggested the use of the pronoun in the third person, masculine gender, while this gift has been treated of; but its feminine correlative was all along intended. For with her quickness, her fineness of taste and delicacy of perception, woman has it in her power to be unrivaled as a conversationalist; and in Madame Roland, whose eloquence, never heard beyond her own salon, helped to kindle a revolution—Madame De Stael, whose powers were feared by even Napoleon the Great—and Margaret Fuller Ossoli, the best conversationalist of our own age and country, we have a few among the many names that might be cited to prove that woman has done much already in this department.

Another most desirable accomplishment, akin to that last mentioned, is the ability to write a good letter—one that shall be racy, genial, varied in contents—passing readily from grave to gay, from lively to severe; though of this last quality it is possible to have too much. Gray and Charles Lamb furnish us with models of epistolary style, as faultless as our literature can boast, unless we name Lady Mary Wortley Montague or Hannah More, who, in some valuable remarks upon the subject under consideration, mentions as one cardinal virtue of a letter, that it be written as one would talk; that it furnish a fair index to the mind of the writer at the time of the writing, and that it be not too long. The vivacious Gail Hamilton, in a recent number of the *"Atlantic,"* gives some hints on letter-writing to the soldiers, that are most timely. At the mention of the soldiers, our thoughts revert to the peculiar courtesies that, as American women, we owe to them. We feel deep regret, often, that we can do so little for our country, now that her need for help is sorest. Yet not at small cost have mothers, sisters and wives, stilled the cry of nature in their breasts, and sent forth to the battle-field those who were dearest to them, to encounter danger and privation, or death itself perhaps, and in its most hideous forms. Not from weak hearts come utterances like these, though the burden of them has been often on woman's lips during the last two years:

O friend! by few is glory's wreath attained, But death or soon or late awaiteth all;

To fight in Freedom's cause is something gained, And nothing lost, to fall.

Under the heroism that they evince, lies the heartache of a nation. By a thousand lonely hearth- stones, tonight, the kneeling figure seen in the flickering fire-light tells how well the soldier is remembered. And it is fitting that we should be mindful of the heroes to whom we owe the comfort and security, which this hour and this occasion may index to our minds. Can "fourteen dollars a month, with rations," pay the hundreds of thousands who are at this very moment making with their own brave breasts a wall between us and our foes, compared with which rampart and bastion are as vacancy itself? For cannon balls may batter down the strongest fortifications, but only through millions of loyal hearts can the enemy attack the homes and altars of the North. To the courage that faces death on the field when he comes with sickle keen, and reaps down rank after rank in his pitiless march; to the heroism that shrinks not, when he steals in like a ghost, and watches with hollow eyes the lonely couch, forsaken, save

by him; to the generosity that lays life, youth, ambition, on the altar, we give but little in giving all we have—our prayers, our tears, our sympathies and toil. While the numerous Soldiers' Aid Societies all over the North attest the willing industry of the "loved ones at home"—while the store-houses of that noble organization, the Sanitary Commission, are supplied by offerings continually pouring in from town and country—while in no prayer is the soldier's name forgotten—yet may it not be true, that of the "small, sweet courtesies of life" we owe to him, we have not thought enough? We would "gather up the fragments, that nothing be lost." Is it not doubtful, then, whether we manifest enough real, personal interest in the soldiers whom we meet—who are at home on furlough, or from temporal disability—whom we see in church and drawing-room, in car and omnibus—whom we do not see, as those in the field, who were our friends at home, but who never hear from us personally, now that they have joined the army?

A soldier who had been for eighteen months in the army of the Potomac without once leaving camp, except for the march or the battle-field, brought home the report, a few days since, that in his regiment the soldiers received very few letters or messages from their friends. "A man's heart is tender when he is far from what is dearest to him, and his life is in constant peril," said the young soldier, while his eyes grew luminous. Take an incident in point. A soldier from your own State had not heard from home in months, but at first had generously apologized for his friends' neglect by saying, "Our folks were never in the habit of writing letters much, and then they don't realize how lonesome a fellow gets when he's away from what he likes best." But as weeks passed, and no tidings came, he grew moody and discontented, and at last became reckless, saying, in soldier's phrase: "Well, I don't care; I can stand it if they can." At last he ceased to inquire for letters; bad habits grew upon him. A secret mission was at this time intrusted to a favorite officer, and a certain number of men were to volunteer to go with him on a dangerous expedition. A flag, which was torn and discolored by several battles, in which it had always waved over victorious troops, was brought out, and the men who were willing to volunteer were told to gather around it. Nearly all the friends of the discontented soldier—those of his company—had offered themselves. His special friend and comrade had done so, urging him to go also. "No," he said; "he was getting tired, and wasn't going to fight, unless he was obliged to. Since nobody seemed to care about his life, he guessed he'd look after it a little himself." Soon after, a letter was handed to him, superscribed in a graceful, lady's hand. The soldier's eye kindled—he tore it open, but before he had read a page, he snatched his gun, and rushed toward the group of volunteers, singing.

Yes, we'll rally round the flag, boys, rally once again, in ringing tones, and thrusting the paper into his friend's hand, he said, "See there, Harry! what my sister says! 'We know you'll never flinch; and proudly remember, when others boast of the heroism of their friends, that our brother is a soldier, too.'"

It is observed that after letters come from home, the soldier is more thoughtful, oaths are less often on his lips, cards are laid aside—the reason often being assigned: "My mother wrote me that she knew I would be true to her and to the teaching of my home. I was growing forgetful, but her letter has reminded me."

To write often to the soldiers is as much a duty, we maintain, as to send delicacies for the hospital or books for their idle hours. I know a sweet, Christian girl, whose correspondence with the army is large enough to occupy a good deal of her time, and whose sisterly letters to her soldier friends are more highly prized by them than any other of their possessions. Aside from the racy gossip of home news—the friendly messages—the words of kind solicitude, and the quiet utterances of Christian faith, the very delicacy of the letter—the fineness of its execution—the dainty sheets of paper and corresponding envelope—the faint perfume, perhaps, discernible about it—have all a charm that will refine and elevate the soldier, and which may prove to him a shield against the temptations of his wild, abnormal life.

In the songs we sing, the soldier can not be too often named. The "Evening Song to the Virgin," "Meet me by moon-light," and "Comin thro' the Rye," make pleasant music; but for our day, the "Battle Hymn of the Republic," "Rally round the Flag" and the "Picket Guard," come nearer to men's hearts. I have in memory a scene that may be but an example of what many of you have witnessed. A group of graceful girls standing round a piano, singing, to the accompaniment played by the oldest sister, a touching song—an outgrowth of the crisis of our times. Their brothers—with the lover of one of them—were soldiers in the army of the Cumberland. Remembering this, it was doubly affecting to listen to the clear tones of the air, with the mournful alto running through them, in the chorus beginning:

Brave boys are they; Gone at their country's call; And yet, and yet we cannot forget That many brave boys must fall.

We have read of the power of their sublime "Marseillaise" over the French soldiery. At the time of the Revolution, it was terribly shown. The principle seen there in its grander development we may trace to advantage in the life of every day. For the fires of patriotism reach white heat when music lends to glowing words her potency.

Let us think, then, of the many little things which, along with the great, we may do to show that our hearts are with those who are fighting battles, winning victories for us. "Why did you shake hands with young Dufrees at the church door, after service?" asked a fastidious friend. "Because he is a soldier," returned Arabella, with the proper emphasis. The recognition more cordially given to our soldier friends than to others—the acknowledgment in frank, ingenuous manner of our great debt—the interest freely expressed for their comfort—the enthusiastic praise of their courage in trying emergencies—all these are inexpressibly grateful to a soldier's heart, and will not be misinterpreted or misapplied. "We are proud of all our army," said a beautiful girl to a young lieutenant, who had distinguished himself in a recent engagement; "but we glory in the—Regiment, Pennsylvania Volunteers. They never fail. And then, we know so many members of that regiment; they went from our own town, and we watch their career with great interest." His comrades and himself deserved her praise. So the young soldier knew; but he answered modestly, while his eyes were bright with gratitude, "If our friends at home speak thus concerning us, we will deserve their praise in future—not to speak of the past."

Recently, on a train from the east, the passengers were leaving a car, upon arriving in this city. Lying across the tops of several seats was a soldier's cot, and upon it a white-faced boy—somebody's darling—going home to die. His look told that. The passengers all gazed at him with attention, some with sympathy, some with curiosity in their eyes. Last of all, came a lady of noble face and mien. She stopped a moment, her eyes filled with tears. "God bless you! dear boy," she said, "for helping us!" The youth's face flushed with pleasure. "Thank, you," he said; "I did not think my life too much to give, since the country needed me."

It is in our power to speak many words which shall drop like balm into hearts bruised and bleeding. Through thoughtlessness, let not one remain unsaid. Mourners are multiplying among us—the sable garments of the bereaved we may see on every hand. The end is not yet. We are passing on into the cloud. The eye of God alone can pierce its darkness. Let us weep for the "unreturning brave." Let us keep our kindliest words for those who fight our battles; remembering how graceful will be our sympathy to them, for it has been truly said:

O soldier! to thine early grave Thy love and valor bearing, The bravest are the tenderest, The loving are the daring.

Source:
James Andrews and David Zarefsky, eds. *American Voices: Significant Speeches in American History, 1640–1945*, Reading, Mass.: Longman, 1989, pp. 236-233.

John Todd, *Woman's Rights*, 1867

Pamphlet written in 1867 by the Reverend John Todd to demonstrate why women cannot be independent of men. Todd argues that although women have strong minds, they simply lack the physical stamina to compete with men in any field, from the sciences to literature to the arts, including playing the piano, an instrument that men have "invented, manufactured, and bought, and brought home" expressly for the woman.

He develops his argument by looking at contemporary issues regarding women's rights, such as dress, voting, wages, and education. Todd believes that a woman's place is in the home, where she has the power to shape a man's character. In his belief, a woman who votes, or earns wages, or does anything outside of the sphere of the household is trying "to be a man"; a woman who attempts such things ruins society and transgresses God's design.

These arguments are not so different from those offered in the 1970s when women again asserted their rights. It was not until the 1970s, for example, that women began attending medical and law school and holding office in significant numbers. Interestingly, the notion of equal wages or comparable wages raised by Todd still resonates in the 21st century.

The complete pamphlet is in *Landmark Documents in American History*, www.factsonfile.com.

Introduction

The tendency of our generation to break up old associations, and to be emancipated from the beliefs of our fathers, is so strong that many would rather feel relieved to have you convince them that they sprang from a race of apes and gorillas. This is among the male sex. Among the other sex, there is a wide-spread uneasiness,—a discontentment with woman's lot, impatient of its burdens, rebellious against its sufferings, an undefined hope of emancipation from the ordinary lot of humanity by some great revolution, so that her condition will be entirely changed! This feeling crops out in publicly ridiculing marriage, dwelling on its evils, raving about the tyranny of men, crying for the "emancipation of woman," getting up Women's Conventions, and propagating theories, weak, foolish, and criminal. The demand is that we shall acknowledge our abominable cruelty exercised towards woman since her first creation;—that she shall be allowed hereafter to be in all respects equal to man,—shall be educated as he is, enter the same pursuits that he does, receive the same wages,-occupy the same posts and professions,—wield the same influence, and, in a word, be independent of man,—far more independent of him than he ever was or can be of woman. This undefined feeling is not confined to the strong-minded women, who clamor and disgust their sex and ours in demanding "women's rights." . . . It is to this class of the sisterhood I am wishing to address myself at this time. Will you allow me then to come and sit down by your side, making no claim to superiority, but sincerely wishing to aid you in coming to most important conclusions?

WOMAN'S RIGHTS. EQUALITY OF THE SEXES. On this question I shall waste no words. Nobody pretends that the sexes are equal in weight, in height, or in bodily strength. The bodies of the two sexes seem to have been planned for different ends. As to the *mind*, I have no difficulty in admitting that the mind of woman is equal to ours,-nay, if you please, superior. It is quicker, more flexible, more elastic. I certainly have never seen boys learn languages or mathematics, up to a certain point, as fast or as easy as some girls. Woman's intuitions also are far better than ours. She reads character quicker, comes to conclusions quicker, and if I must make a decision on the moment, I had much rather have the woman's decision than man's. She has intuitions given her for her own protection which we have not. She has a delicacy of taste to which we can lay no claim. "Why, then," my lady reader will say, "*why can't we be independent of man?*" for this is the gist of the whole subject. I reply, you can't, for two reasons; first, God never designed you should, and secondly, your own deep instincts are in the way. God never designed that woman should occupy the same sphere as man, because he has given her *a physical organization* so refined and delicate that it can never bear the strain which comes upon the rougher, coarser nature of man. He has hedged her in by laws which no desires or efforts can alter. We, sons of dust, move slower; we creep, where you bound to the head of the stairs at a single leap. And now bear with me, and keep good-natured, while I show you, what you, dear ladies, cannot do, and God don't ask you to do.

1. You cannot invent. . . . I suppose this power was denied you, lest it should take you out of your most important sphere . . .

2. You cannot compete with men in a long course of mental labor. Your delicate organization never has and never can bear the study by which you can become Newtons, La Places, or Bowditches in mathematics or astronomy. . . . So of painting and sculpture. . . .

But, you will perhaps say, "we have never had a fair chance-a fair fight in the field. We have been held down by prejudice, and tyranny, and public opinion against us, and all that." Suppose it be so, fair one, there is *one* field you have had to yourself, and nobody has lifted against you one finger. I mean that, for the last half century, we, cruel men, have invented, manufactured, and bought, and brought home, the *piano*, and you have had it all to yourselves. What is the result? It is, that the master performers, and teachers, and musicians, are men. . . . In none of these departments can woman compete with man. Not because her immortal mind is inferior,—far from it,—but because her bodily organization cannot endure the pressure of continued and long labor as we can. . . . In none of these departments can woman compete with man. Not because her immortal mind is inferior,—far from it,—but because her bodily organization cannot endure the pressure of continued and long labor as we can. . . .

Woman's Sphere

The design of God in creating woman was to complete man-a one-sided being without her. Together they make a complete, perfect unit. She has a mission-no higher one could be given her-to be the mother, and *the former of all character of the human race.* For the first, most important earthly period of life, the race is committed to her, for about twelve years, almost entirely. The human family is what she makes them. She is the queen of the home, its centre, its light and glory. The home, the home is the fountain of all that is good on earth. If she desires a higher, loftier, nobler trust than this, I know not where she can find it. Mother, wife, daughter, sister, are the tenderest, most endearing words in language. Our mothers train us, and we owe everything to them. Our wives perfect all that is good in us, and no man is ashamed to say he is indebted to his wife for his happiness, his influence, and his character, if there is anything noble about him. Woman is the highest, holiest, most precious gift to man. Her mission and throne is the family, and if anything is withheld that would make her more efficient, useful, or happy in that sphere, she is wronged, and has not her "rights."

What Her "Rights" Are

If woman steps out of her sphere, and demands to be and to do what men do, to enter political life, to enter the professions, to wrestle with us for office and employments and gains, she must understand that she will have to take the low prices as well as the high places of life. She will not be allowed to be a man and be treated with the tenderness due to women. If she goes to Congress, she must also go to the heavy drudgery of earth.

I claim then for her, that it is her "right" to be treated with the utmost love, respect, honor, and consideration in her sphere. I claim that it is her "right" to have every possible aid and advantage to fulfill her mission. I claim that she has a "right" to be let alone there, and not be teased, or flattered, or wheedled out for her place, and made to believe what can never be.

She has a "right" then to be exempted from certain things which men must endure. It is her privilege and her right. She ought to be exempted from the hard drudgery of earth. She ought not to be made a sailor, to hang on the yard-arms,—to chase and kill and try up whales,—to be a surgeon, to pull teeth, cut off legs, or cut out tumors,-to go into the mines, and dig ore and coal,—to burn over the smelting-furnace. She ought not to be compelled to be a barber, a boot-black, to carry hods of brick and mortar up the ladder,—to be a soap boiler, to groom horses, dig canals, [Etc.] Has she not a *natural* right to enter any and all employments as well as men? Suppose we allow it, and admit that she has a *natural* right to wear jack-boots and spurs, horse-pistols and a sword, and be a complete soldier, and a "natural" right to sing bass and beat a bass-drum, and that *men* have a "natural" right to wear petticoats, dress with low necks, short sleeves, wear pink slippers with paper soles,—but, would it be wise to do so? Dear sisters, you *can't* be good wives, mothers, and crowns of your families, and go into these things—can you?

Dress

Some have tried to become semi-men by putting on the Bloomer dress. Let me tell you in a word why it can never be done. It is the: woman, robed and folded in her long dress, is beautiful. She walks gracefully. . . . If she attempts to *run*, the charm is gone. . . . So long as she is thus clothed, there is just enough of mystery about woman to challenge admiration, and almost reverence.

Take off the robes, and put on pants and show the limbs, and grace and mystery are all gone. And yet, to be like a man, you must doff your own dress and put on ours. In doing it, you lose more than I can tell. No! Ladies want or respect, and admiration, and reverence too much ever to lay aside their appropriate dress. Their very instincts make them safe here.

Voting

A great hue and cry is set up about the right of women to vote, and the cruelty of denying them this right. Plainly this is merely a civil and not a natural right. Minors, foreigners, and idiots are denied it. The property of the world, for the most part is, and ever has been, and must be, earned by men. It is useful only to support and educate families-our own, or those of others. It would seem best, then, for those who, at any hazard or labor, earn the property, to select the rulers, and have this responsibility. . . . Moreover, there is something so unseemly in having woman wading in the dirty waters of politics, draggling and wrangling around the ballot-boxes, *e.g.,* mingling with the mobs and rowdies in New York city, that I wonder she ever thinks of it. But "she is a widow, and has property, and pays taxes,-why not vote?" Being a widow, or fatherless, is a misfortune. But the husband or father earned the property, and voted as long as he lived. It may be a misfortune that the property does not now vote, but not so great a misfortune to the world as to have the sex go out of their sphere and enter into political life. Indeed, it is allowed that voting is only the stepping-stone to civil office. But it is stepping out of her sphere, and the moment you do that, you put a few of the sex into office, but depress and degrade at least a thousand where you elevate one. If a few go up, the many go down.

Wages

There is great complaint made because justice is not done in compensating labor. . . . But bear in mind that God has put the labor and the duty on men to support the families-wives and children. The man is recreant and guilty if he does not do that; and to do it, and bear the responsibility, he must receive wages accordingly. Is it then so very unjust that women, who has no such responsibility, does not receive so high wages? You blame employers, and demand that they give females more—a vain demand so long as there are thousands ready to underbid them and do the work cheaper. The demand will pay in proportion to the supply, and no legislation or human power can alter this, Woman can't endure such heavy toil; she can't toil as many hours year after year; she expects to continue the employment but a short time; and the result is, she has to take for her labor the market price for that commodity. But there is a wonderful reason for this great supply, at our day, to which I will allude.

❋   ❋   ❋

Woman's Education

I lately took up a religious paper, in which no less than *six* "Female Colleges" were advertised and puffed. And we are getting our legislatures to charter new "Female Colleges," and we are boasting how we are about to introduce all the studies and the curriculum of the colleges for men, and we are to put our daughters through them, and educate just as we do men. The thing can never be done. For forty years I have been connected with female seminaries, and have carefully watched their training and results. I say deliberately, that the female has mind enough, talent enough, to go through a complete college course, but her physical organization, as a general thing, will never admit of it. I think the great danger of our day is forcing the intellect of woman beyond what her physical organization will possibly bear. . . . We Americans belong to the Over-do family. We want to fish the brook dry if we fish at all. We mount hobbies easily because we are "spry"; and now that we have taken woman in hand, we are in danger of education [educating?] her into the grave; taking her out of her own beautiful, honored sphere, and making her an hermaphrodite, instead of what God made her to be.

The root of great error of our day is, that *woman is to be made independent and self-supporting*—precisely what she never can be, because God never designed she should be. Her support, her dignity, her beauty, her honor, and happiness lie in her dependence as wife, mother, and daughter. Any other theory is rebellion against God's law of the sexes, against marriage, which it assails in its fundamental principles, and against the family organization, the holiest thing that is left from Eden.

O woman! your worst enemy if he who scouts at marriage; who tries to flatter you with honeyed words about your rights, while he sneers in his own circle, boasting that "it is cheaper to buy milk than to keep a cow"; who could cruelly lift you out of your sphere, and try to reverse the very laws of God; who tries to make you believe that you will find independence, wealth, and renown in man's sphere, when your only safety and happiness is in patiently, lovingly, and faithfully performing the duties and enacting the relations of your own sphere.

Women of my country! beloved and honored in your own sphere, can't see that man, rough, stern, cold, almost nerveless, was made to be the *head* of human society; and woman, patient, quick, sensitive, loving, and gentle, is the *heart* of the world? where she may rule and move the world to an extent second to no human power, and where she becomes a blessing greater than we can ever acknowledge, because it is greater than we can measure!

❋   ❋   ❋

Source:
Library of Congress. Rare Book and Special Collections Division. National American Woman Suffrage Association Collection.

Proceedings of the First Anniversary of the American Equal Rights Association, 1867

Transcript of a phonograph recording by H. M. Parkhurst of the proceedings of the first annual meeting of the American Equal Rights Association, held in New York City on at the Church of the Puritans, May 9 and 10, 1867. The association was formed to work toward gaining the vote for African Americans and women. The transcript includes speeches delivered by prominent suffrage activists; the organization's constitution (placed first here, although it follows the sessions in the transcript); resolutions; letters of support (not reproduced here); and a list of finances (not reproduced here). The association resolved to support only activity that would lead to the emancipation of every adult citizen. Much of the discussion, including that which is reproduced here, concerned whether the group should refuse to promote the franchise for black men until all women were also included. Black men received the vote through the Fifteenth Amendment. Eventually, some of the leaders in the fight for women's suffrage used as an argument the fact that "unqualified" or "inferior" black men could vote while white women could not.

The same year that the Association was founded, Elizabeth Cady Stanton ran for a seat in Congress from the Eighth Congressional District in New York. The letter indicates that Stanton's candidacy was meant to highlight the absurdity of refusing women the vote. She stated that she was a candidate because, although women were prohibited from voting, they were technically eligible to hold elective office.

The entire transcript of the association meeting and appended documents is in the on-line Landmark Documents in American History, www.factsonfile.com.

―――――――――― ⌒⌬⌐ ――――――――――

Constitution of the American Equal Rights Association

Preamble

Whereas, By the war, society is once more resolved into its original elements, and in the reconstruction of our government we again stand face to face with the broad question of natural rights, all associations based on special claims for special classes are too narrow and partial for the hour; Therefore, from the baptism of this second revolution-purified and exalted through suffering-seeing with a holier vision that the peace, prosperity and perpetuity of the Republic rest on **Equal Rights to all** we, to-day, assembled in our Eleventh National Woman's Rights Convention, bury the Woman in the Citizen, and our organization in that of the **American Equal Rights Association**.

❖   ❖   ❖

Done in the City of New York on the tenth day of May, in the year 1866.

[Announcement of Meeting:]

The object of this Association is to "secure Equal Rights to all American citizens, especially the Right of Suffrage, irrespective of race, color or sex." American Democracy has interpreted the Declaration of Independence in the interest of slavery, restricting suffrage and citizenship to a *white male minority*. The black man is still denied the crowning right of citizenship, even in the nominally free States, though the fires of civil war have melted the chains of chattelism, and a hundred battle-fields attest his courage and patriotism. Half our population are disfranchised on the ground of sex; and though compelled to obey the law and taxed to support the government, they have no voice in the legislation of the country. This Association, then, has a mission to perform, the magnitude and impor-

tance of which cannot be over-estimated. The recent war has unsettled all our governmental foundations. Let us see that in their restoration, all these unjust proscriptions are avoided. Let Democracy be defined anew, as *the government of the people*, AND THE WHOLE PEOPLE. Let the gathering, then, at this anniversary be, in numbers and character, worthy, in some degree, the demands of the hour. The black man, even the black soldier, is yet but half emancipated, nor will he be, until full suffrage and citizenship, *are secured to him in the Federal Constitution*. Still more deplorable is the condition of the black woman; and legally, that of the white woman is no better!

❖   ❖   ❖

[May 9, 10 a.m.] **SECRETARY'S REPORT**

Susan B. Anthony said: It is my duty to present to you at this time a written Report of all that has been done by this Equal Rights Association during the past year; but those of us who have been active in this movement, have been so occupied in doing the work, that no one has found time to chronicle the progress of events. With but half a dozen live men and women, to canvass the State of New York, to besiege the Legislature and the delegates to the Constitutional Convention with tracts and petitions, to write letters and send documents to every State Legislature that has moved on this question, to urge Congress to its highest duty in the reconstruction, by both public and private appeals, has been a work that has taxed every energy and dollar at our command.

Money being the vital power of all movements-the Wood and water of the engine-and, as our work through the past winter has been limited only by the want of it, there is no difficulty in reporting on finance. The receipts of our Association, during the year, have amounted to $4,096 78; the expenditures, for lectures and conventions, for printing and circulating tracts and documents, to $4,714 11—leaving us in debt $617 33.

The Secretary then rapidly rehearsed the signs of progress. She spoke of the discussion in the United States Senate on the Suffrage bill, through three entire days, resulting in a vote in a nine Senators in favor of extending suffrage to the women as well as black men of the District of Columbia; of the section of the Legislatures of Kansas and Wisconsin to strike the words "white male" from their Constitutions; of the discussions and minority votes in the Legislatures of Maine, Massachusetts, New York, Ohio and Missouri; of the addresses Elizabeth Cady Stanton and Lucy Stone before the Judiciary Committees of the New York and New Jersey Legislatures. . . . In Kansas they are planning mass conventions, to be held throughout the State through September and October; and they urge us to send out at least a dozen able men and women, with a hundred thousand tracts, to help them educate the people into the grand idea of universal suffrage, that they may carry the State at the November election. . . . Two of our agents, Lucy Stone and Henry B. Blackwell, are already in Kansas, speaking in all her towns and cities-in churches, school-houses, barns and the open air; travelling night and day. . . .

The **President** (Mrs. **Mott**) said: . . . My age and feeble health have precluded my engaging actively engaged in the cause, other than in a very limited way. . . . Being a native of the island of Nantucket, where women were thought something of, and had some connection with the business arrangements of life, as well as with their domestic homes, I grew up so thoroughly imbued with woman's rights that it was the most important question of my life from a very early day. I hail this more public movement for its advocacy, and have been glad that I had strength enough to co-operate to some extent. . . .

Address of Elizabeth Cady Stanton

In considering the question of suffrage, there are two starting points: one, that this right is a gift of society, in which certain men, having inherited this privilege from some abstract body and abstract place, have now the right to secure it for themselves and their privileged order to the end of time. This principle leads logically to governing races, classes, families; and, in direct antagonism to our idea of self-government, takes us back to monarchies despotisms, to a experiment that has been tried over and over again, 6,000 years, and uniformly failed. . . . Ignoring this point of view as untenable and anti-republican, and taking the opposite, that suffrage is a natural right—as necessary to man under government, for the protection of person and property, as are air and motion to life—we hold talisman by which to show the right of all classes to the ballot, to remove every obstacle, to answer every objection, to point out the tyranny of every qualification to the free exercise of this sacred right. To discuss the question of suffrage for women and negroes, as women and negroes, and not as citizens of a republic, implies that there are some reasons for demanding this right for these classes that do not apply to "white males."

. . . As in the war, freedom was the key-note of victory, so now is universal suffrage the key-note of reconstruction.

❊   ❊   ❊

When woman understands the momentous interests that depend on the ballot, she will make it her first duty to educate every American boy and girl into the idea that to vote is the most sacred act of citizenship-a religious duty not to be discharged thoughtlessly, selfishly or corruptly; but conscientiously, remembering that, in a republican government, to every citizen is entrusted the interests of the nation. . . .

❊   ❊   ❊

Never, until woman is an independent, self-sustaining force in society, can she take her true, exalted position as the mother, the educator of the race. Never, as a dependent on his wish, his will, his bounty to be sheltered, fed and clothed, will man recognize in woman an equal moral power in the universe of mind. The same principle that governed plantation life, governs the home. The master could quote law and gospel for his authority over the slave, so can the husband still.

❊   ❊   ❊

. . . For this stage of civilization, I would draw a line half way between our poets . . . and place woman neither at man's feet nor above his head, but on an even platform by his side.

Susan B. Anthony, in behalf of the Executive Committee, reported the following resolutions for consideration:

❊   ❊   ❊

Resolved, That the present claim for "manhood suffrage," masked with the words "equal," "impartial," "universal," is a cruel abandonment of the slave women of the South, a fraud on the tax-paying women of the North, and an insult to the civilization of the nineteenth century.

Resolved, That the proposal to reconstruct our government on the basis of manhood suffrage, which emanated from the Republican party and has received the recent sanction of the American Anti-Slavery Society, is but a continuation of the old system of class and caste legislation, always cruel and proscriptive in itself, and ending in all ages in national degradation and revolution.

❊   ❊   ❊

Mr. C. C. Burleigh:

❊   ❊   ❊

It is said also, that if you allow women to vote, the logic of your argument will go further and require that women shall be voted for, and they may chance to receive votes enough for election; and they may even go to the State Legislature or to Congress. Suppose such a thing should happen, would a city which is represented in the Congress of the United States by John Morrissey and Fernando Wood, have reason to blush if by some singular good fortune she should chance to be represented by Elizabeth Cady Stanton? (Applause.) Would the Halls of Congress suffer any loss of dignity, or any loss of efficiency, even if John Morrissey's place should the vacated to make room for Mrs. Stanton, or if some Pennsylvania Democrat should be allowed to remain at home while Lucretia Mott occupied his chair? (Applause.) . . .

Somebody says that "the child is father to the man." You know who govern the children. Who governed you when you were children? Is it not as safe that woman should govern in the halls of national legislation as in the family and in the school? You will find in hundreds of schools, governed a few years ago by men, only women for teachers to-day. I remember that in a building which contained some three hundred pupils, the last man employed as a teacher, was an assistant teacher under the supervision of a woman as principal; a woman who has vindicated her right to the place by her admirable administration, and her admirable adaption to the business of teaching, so that she has become, as it were, a fixture in that schoolhouse. And that is only one case among many. And if woman excels in government in those spheres in which she has had an opportunity to prove her ability, it is at least safe to try the experiment further.

❋   ❋   ❋

We have heard the argument over and over again that women should leave to man the counting-house, the work-bench, and all the duties supposed peculiarly to appertain to masculine humanity, and should attend to "household" matters. If, then, suffrage is a household matter, why should not woman attend to it, in her feminine capacity, as peculiarly within her domestic province, and relieve man from the interruption of his appropriate duties?

❋   ❋   ❋

I think it is quite possible, from the education the people have had so long, that in the first instance those who go to the polls will be the two extremes, the best women and the worst, and that the great body of the intermediate class will stay away, partly because not thoroughly and clearly convinced of their right and duty, and still more because they have not yet summoned up courage enough to face the terrible sneer which our friend has told us is more fearful than the ballot. Possibly we should see at the polls, at first, those who are with us on the platform of this Association, on the one hand, and on the other extreme, the vilest who can be brought up to serve the purposes of any demagogue unscrupulous enough to use them. I do not by any means admit that this is certain. I have my doubts about it. But suppose it to be so; what will be the consequence? If the better element were not sufficient to neutralize the worst at once, in which case no evil would result, the middle class of women would have the duty pressed right home upon them to give their influence and their votes to counteract the evil tendency of the action of the more degraded and ignorant of their own sex; just a we see in great emergencies, inn critical periods in political affairs, multitudes of men are drawn to the polls from the exigency of the time, who ordinarily do not go. . . .

❋   ❋   ❋

Stephen S. Foster. —Will you give us the evidence that the statement that the women of this country do not want the ballot is not true? I should be glad to believe that; but in may experience the worst opposition to the progress of Woman's Right has come from woman herself. . . . I wish it were not so. I hope I am mistaken. . . .

Rev. **S. J May**. —I should like to have that question settled, so far as the women present are concerned. Will as many of you as *will vote* when the right is awarded to you, please to manifest it by rising.

Nearly the whole of the ladies present immediately arose. Indeed, the reporter, from the platform, could not see a single lady who retained to seat.

❋   ❋   ❋

Evening Session:

❋   ❋   ❋

Mrs. Ernestine Rose:

❋   ❋   ❋

I have sometimes been asked, even by sensible men, "If woman had the elective franchise, would she got to the polls to mix with rude men?" Well, would I go to the church to mix with rude men? And should not the ballot-box be as respectable, and as respected, and as sacred as the church? Aye, infinitely more so, because it is of greater importance. Men can pray in secret, but must vote in public. (Applause.) Hence the ballot, of the two, ought to be the most respected; and it would be if women were once there; but it never will be until they are there. . . .

May 10, Morning Session:

❋   ❋   ❋

George T. Downing wished to know whether he had rightly understood that Mrs. Stanton and Mrs. Mott were opposed to the enfranchisement of the colored man, unless the ballot should also be accorded to woman at the same time.

Mrs. **Stanton** said:

All history proves that despotisms, whether of one man or millions, cannot stand, and there is no use of wasting centuries of men and means in trying that experiment again. Hence I have no faith or interest in any reconstruction on that old basis. To say that politicians always do one thing at a time is no reason why philosophers should not enunciate the broad principles that underlie that one thing and a dozen others. We do not take the right step for this hour in demanding suffrage for any class; as a matter of principle I claim it for all.

But in a narrow view of the question as a matter of feeling between classes, when Mr. Downing puts the question to me, are you willing to have the colored man enfranchised before the woman, I say, no; I would not trust him with all my rights; degraded, oppressed himself, he would be more despotic with the governing power than even our Saxon rulers are. I desire that we go into the kingdom together, for individual and national safety demand that not another man be enfranchised without the woman by his side.

❖   ❖   ❖

Mrs. **Stanton** said she demanded the ballot for all. She asked for reconstruction on the basis of self-government; but if we are to have further class legislation, she thought the wisest order of enfranchisement was to take the educated classes first. If women are still to be represented by men, then I say let only the highest type of manhood stand at the helm of State. But if all men are to vote, black and white, lettered and unlettered, washed and unwashed, the safety of the nation as well as the interests of woman that we outweigh this incoming tide of ignorance, poverty and vice, with the virtue, wealth and education of the women of the country.

With the black man you have no new force in government—it is manhood still; but with the enfranchisement of woman, you have a new and essential element of life and power. . . .

❖   ❖   ❖

Abby Kelley Foster:

. . . Were the negro and woman in the same civil, social and political status to-day, I should respond eye, with all my heart, to this sentiment. What are the facts? . . . He is treated as a slave to-day in the several districts of the South. Without wages, without family rights, whipped and beaten by thousands, given up to the most horrible outrages, without that protection which his value as property formerly gave him. Again, he is liable, without farther guarantees, to be plunged into peonage, serfdom or even into chattel slavery. Have we any true sense of justice, are we not dead to the sentiment of humanity if we shall wish to postpone his security against present woes and future enslavement till woman shall obtain political rights?

❖   ❖   ❖

Sojourner Truth was called for and said: I am glad to see that men are getting their rights, but I want women to get theirs, and while the water is stirring I will step into the pool. Now that there is a great stir about colored men's getting their rights is the time for women to step in and have theirs. I am sometimes told that "Women ain't fit to vote. Why, don't you know that a woman had seven devils in her: and do you suppose a woman is fit to rule the nation?" Seven devils ain't no account; a man had a legion in him. (Great laughter.) The devils didn't know where to go; and so they asked that they might go into the swine. They thought that was as good a place as they came out from. (Renewed laughter.) They didn't ask to go into sheep-no, into the hog; that was the selfishest beast; and man is so selfish that he has got women's rights and his own too, and yet he won't give women their rights. He keeps them all to himself. If a woman did have seven devils, see how lovely she was when they were cast out, how much she loved Jesus, how she followed him. When the devils were gone out of the man, he wanted to follow Jesus, too, but Jesus told him to go home, and didn't seem to want to have him round. And when the men went to look for Jesus at the sepulchre they didn't stop long enough to find out whether he was there or not; but Mary stood there and waited, and said to him, thinking it was the gardener, "Tell me where they have laid him and I will carry him away." See what a spirit there is. Just so let women be true to this object, and the truth will reign triumphant.

❖   ❖   ❖

Mr. E. H. Heywood [Boston]: . . . It was said that the women on this platform were coquetting with the Democrats [who oppose Negro suffrage]. Why shouldn't they? The Democrats take the true position. He had heard a Democrat say, "Talk of negro suffrage, and then refuse women the right to vote. All I have to say is, when the negroes of Connecticut go to the polls, my wife and daughter will go, too."

Evening session:

❖   ❖   ❖

Miss **Anthony** announced that they would have another opportunity to hear Sojourner Truth, and, for the information of those who did not know, she would say that Sojourner was for forty years a slave in this State. She is not a product of the barbarism of South Carolina, but of the barbarism of New York, and one of her fingers was chopped off by her cruel master in a moment of anger.

❖   ❖   ❖

Source:

"Proceedings of the First Anniversary of the American Equal Rights Association." Library of Congress, Rare Book and Special Collections Division, National American Woman Suffrage Association Collection.

Constitutions of Two Major Feminist Organizations, 1869

The 19th-century movement in the United States for woman suffrage split between radical activists, who agitated for a federal constitutional amendment granting women the franchise, and moderates, who sought remedy through the state legislatures. The division emerged after the Civil War over the issue of black suffrage and the proposed Fifteenth Amendment to the Constitution, which would grant the vote to black males. The radicals, led by suffragists Susan B. Anthony and Elizabeth Cady Stanton, opposed the amendment for failure to extend the franchise to women. The moderates, represented by social reformers Lucy Stone and Julia Ward Howe, backed the amendment as proposed, arguing that women should not demand federal action until black suffrage had been won.

In 1869 the rival factions organized into the separate National Woman Suffrage Association (NWSA), founded by Anthony and Stanton, and the American Woman Suffrage Association (AWSA), founded by Stone and Howe. AWSA adopted its constitution in November 1869 at its founding convention in Cleveland, Ohio. This organization planned to achieve woman suffrage through state-level initiatives. NWSA on the other hand, expected to secure votes for women by campaigning on a national level.

Constitution of the American Woman Suffrage Association (AWSA), 1869
November 24-25, 1869

The undersigned, friends of woman suffrage, assembled in delegate Convention in Cleveland, Ohio, November 24th and 25th, 1869, in response to a call widely signed and after a public notice duly given, believing that a truly representative National organization is needed for the orderly and efficient prosecution of the suffrage movement in America, which shall embody the deliberate action of State and local organizations, and shall carry with it their united weight, do hereby form the American Woman Suffrage Association.

ARTICLE I.
Name: This Association shall be known as the American Woman Suffrage Association.

ARTICLE II.
Object: Its object shall be to concentrate the efforts of all the advocates of woman suffrage in the United States for National purposes only, viz:

Sec. 1. To form auxiliary State Associations in every State where none such now exist, and to co-operate with those already existing, which shall declare themselves auxiliary before the first day of March next, the authority of the auxiliary Societies being recognized in their respective localities, and their plan being promoted by every means in our power.

Sec. 2. To hold an annual meeting of delegates for the transaction of business and the election of officers for the ensuing year; also, one or more national conventions for the advocacy of woman suffrage.

Sec. 3. To publish tracts, documents, and other matter for the supply of State and local societies and individuals at actual cost.

Sec. 4. To prepare and circulate petitions to State Legislatures, to Congress, or to constitutional conventions in behalf of the legal and political equality of woman; to employ lecturers and agents, and to take any measures the Executive Committee may think fit, to forward the objects of the Association.

ARTICLE III.—ORGANIZATION.
Sec. 1. The officers of this Association shall be a President, eight Vice-Presidents at Large, Chairman of the Executive Committee, Foreign Corresponding Secretary, two Recording Secretaries, and a Treasurer, all of whom shall be *ex-officio* members of the Executive Committee from each State and Territory, and from the District of Columbia, as hereinafter provided.

Sec. 2. Every President of an auxiliary State society shall be *ex-officio* a vice- president of this Association.

Sec. 3. Every chairman of the Executive Committee of an auxiliary State society shall be *ex- officio* a member of the Executive Committee of this Association.

Sec. 4. In cases where no auxiliary State society exists, a suitable person may be selected by the annual meeting, by the Executive Committee, as Vice-President or member of the Executive Committee, to serve only until the organization of said State Association.

Sec. 5. The Executive Committee may fill all vacancies that may occur prior to the next annual meeting.

Sec. 6. All officers shall be elected annually at any annual meeting of delegates, on the basis of the Congressional representation of the respective States and Territories, except as above provided.

Sec. 7. No distinction on account of sex shall ever be made in the membership or in the selection of officers of this Society; but the general principle shall be that one half of the officers shall, as nearly as convenient, be men, and one half women.

Sec. 8. No money shall be paid by the Treasurer except under such restrictions as the Executive Committee may provide.

Sec. 9. Five members of the Executive Committee, when convened by the Chairman, after fifteen days written notice previously mailed to each of its members, shall constitute a quorum. But no action thus taken shall be final, until such proceedings shall have been ratified in writing by at least fifteen members of the Committee.

Sec. 10. The Chairman shall convene a meeting whenever requested to do so by five members of the Executive Committee.

ARTICLE IV.

This Association shall have a branch office in every State in connection with the office of the auxiliary State Society therein and shall have a central office at such place as the Executive Committee may determine.

ARTICLE V.

This Constitution may be amended at any annual meeting, by a vote of three-fifths of the delegates present therein.

ARTICLE VI.

Any person may become a member of the American Woman Suffrage Association by signing the Constitution and paying the sum of $1 annually, or life members by paying the sum of $10, which membership shall entitle the individual to attend the business meetings of delegates and participate in their deliberations.

ARTICLE VII.

Honorary members may be appointed by the annual meeting or by the Executive Committee, in consideration of services rendered.

National Woman Suffrage Association (NWSA), NWSA Constitution, 1869

Constitution—

Article 1. This organization shall be called the National Woman Suffrage Association.

Article 2. Its object shall be to secure the Ballot to the women of the nation on equal terms with men.

Article 3. Any citizen of the United States favoring this object, shall, by the payment of the sum of one dollar annually into the treasury, be considered a member of the Association, and no other shall be entitled to vote in its deliberations.

Article 4. The officers of the Association shall be a President, a Vice-President from each of the States and Territories, Corresponding and Recording Secretaries, Treasurer, an Executive Committee of not less than five nor more than nine members, located in New York City, and an Advisory Counsel of one person from each State and Territory, who shall be members of the National Executive Committee. The officers shall be chosen at each annual meeting of the Association.

Article 5. Any Woman's Suffrage Association may become auxiliary to the National Association by its officers becoming members of the Parent Association and sending an annual contribution of not less than twenty-five dollars.

Source:

Elizabeth Frost and Kathryn Cullen-DuPont. *Women's Suffrage in America: An Eyewitness History.* New York: Facts On File, Inc., 1992.

SUGGESTED READING

The Causes of the Civil War
Paul Finkelman, *And His Soul Goes Marching On: Responses to John Brown and the Harpers Ferry Raid.* Charlottesville: University of Virginia Press, 1995.

Eric Foner, *Free Soil, Free Labor, Free Men, 1955.* Reprint, New York, Oxford University Press, 1970.

Thomas M. Gossett, *Uncle Tom's Cabin and American Culture.* Dallas, Tex.: Southern University Methodist Press, 1985.

Kenneth S. Greenberg, *Masters and Statesmen: The Political Culture of American Slavery.* Baltimore: Johns Hopkins University Press, 1985.

Bruce Levine, *Half Slave, Half Free: The Roots of the Civil War,* New York: Noonday Press, 1992.

Stephen B. Oates, *To Purge This Land with Blood: A Biography of John Brown.* New York: HarperCollins, 1970.

William McFeeley, ed. *Frederick Douglass.* New York: W.W. Norton, 1991.

David M. Potter, *The Impending Crisis, 1848–1861.* New York: HarperCollins, 1976.

Richard H. Sewell, *A House Divided: Sectionalism and Civil War, 1848–1860.* Baltimore: Johns Hopkins University Press, 1988.

Kenneth M. Stampp, *America in 1857: A Nation on the Brink.* New York: Oxford University Press, 1990.

The Civil War Years
Jean H. Baker, *Mary Todd Lincoln: A Biography* New York: W.W. Norton, 1987.

Bruce Catton, Noah Andre Trudeau, James M. McPherson, eds., *The America Heritage New History of The Civil War.* New York: Viking Press, 2001.

David J. Eicher, James M. McPherson, *The Longest Night: A Military History of the Civil War.* New York: Simon & Schuster, 2001.

Drew Gilpin Faust, *The Creation of Confederate Nationalism.* Baton Rouge: Louisiana University State Press, 1988.

———, *Mothers of Invention: Women of the Slaveholding South in the American Civil War.* Chapel Hill, N.C.: University of North Carolina Press, 1996.

Barbara Fields, *Slavery and Freedom on the Middle Ground.* New Haven, Conn.: Yale University Press, 1985.

Eric Foner, *Politics and Ideology in the Age of the Civil War.* New York: Oxford University Press, 1980.

Joseph Glattner, *Forged in Battle: The Civil War Alliance of Black Soldiers and White Officers.* New York: Free Press, 1990.

Herman Hattaway and Archer Jones, *How the North Won.* Champaign: University of Illinois Press, 1983.

Elizabeth D. Leonard, *Yankee Women: Gender Battles in the Civil War.* New York: W.W. Norton, 1994.

James M. McPherson, *Battle Cry of Freedom: the Civil War Era.* New York, Balantine, 1988.

Steven F. Miller, Marc Favreau, Ira Berlin, eds. *Remembering Slavery: African Americans Talk about Their Personal Experiences of Slavery and Emancipation.* New York: The New Press, 2000.

Stephen B. Oates, *With Malice Toward None: The Life of Abraham Lincoln.* New York: HarperCollins, 1977.

Michael Perman, *The Road to Redemption: Southern Politics, 1869–1879.* Chapel Hill.: University of North Carolina Press, 1984.

Lawrence Powell, *New Masters: Northern Planters During the Civil War and Reconstruction.* New York: Fordham University Press, 1980.

James Roark, *Masters Without Slaves: Southern Planters in the Civil War and Reconstruction.* New York: W.W. Norton, 1977.

Reconstruction

Michael Les Benedict, *The Impeachment and Trial of Andrew Johnson.* New York: W.W. Norton, 1973.

Richard N. Current, *Those Terrible Carpetbaggers.* New York: Oxford University Press, 1988.

Eric Foner, *Reconstruction: America's Unfinished Revolution, 1863-1877.* New York: HarperCollins, 1988.

Thomas Holt, *Black over White: Negro Political Leadership in South Carolina During Reconstruction.* Champaign: University of Illinois Press, 1977.

Leon Litwack, *Been in the Storm So Long.* New York: Random House, 1979.

Peyton McCrary, *Abraham Lincoln and Reconstruction.* Princeton, N.J.: Princeton University Press, 1978.

James McPherson, *Ordeal by Fire: The Civil War and Reconstruction.* New York: McGraw Hill—Higher Education, 1981, 2000.

Otto H. Olson, *Reconstruction and Redemption in the South.* Baton Rouge: Louisiana State University Press, 1980.

Lawrence Powell, *New Masters: Northern Planters During the Civil War and Reconstruction.* New York: Fordham University Press, 1980.

Howard O. Rabinowitz, *Southern Black Leaders of the Reconstruction Era.* Champaign: University of Illinois Press, 1982.

James Roark, *Masters Without Slaves: Southern Planters in the Civil War and Reconstruction.* New York: W.W. Norton, 1977.

Women's Rights

Andrea Moore Kerr, *Lucy Stone: Speaking out for Equality.* Piscataway, N.J.: Rutgers University Press, 1992.

Mary Gabriel, *Notorious Victoria: The Life of Victoria Woodhull, Uncensored.* Chapel Hill, N.C.: Algonquin Books of Chapel Hill, 1997.

Geoffrey C. Ward, Ken Burns, Ellen Carol Dubois, Ann D. Gordon, Martha Saxton, *Not for Ourselves Alone: The Story of Elizabeth Cady Stanton and Susan B. Anthony.* New York: Knopf, 1999.

ERA 6

The Development of the Industrial United States (CA. 1870–1900)

The post-Reconstruction period in U.S. history sets the stage for the 20th century–its technological successes, scientific endeavors, and political democratization. But it also holds the roots of the next century's biggest problems: racism, increased immigration, imperialism, industrialization, and urbanization. Although the Industrial Age had its roots in the early 19th century, this period has also been termed "the Gilded Age," a phrase coined by Mark Twain, because of the great wealth (and tasteless opulence) spawned by industrial development, mechanized agriculture, and the rise of corporations. The huge disparities between rich and poor influenced developments politically, with small farmers and with labor. Many of their ideas, promoted by the Populist Party and the Knights of Labor, would come to fruition with the Progressive Era early in the next century.

Among the technological achievements of this period were the telephone and the electric light. Electricity also aided mass transportation with the trolley car. Railroads became the major means of moving goods from one area of the country to the other, vastly speeding the process. At the same time, cities developed along rail hubs. Farmers and manufacturers found themselves at the mercy of the rails. As their operations grew, farmers also became dependent on machinery, which tied them to the merchants who sold it and the bankers who lent them the money to buy it. Labor, too, was able to succeed in reforming wages and working conditions. Lending its weight to big business, the U.S. Supreme Court interpreted the Fourteenth Amendment, originally written to ensure African Americans citizenship, to free corporations (legally "persons") from most restraints Congress or state legislatures tried to impose on them.

The post-Reconstruction courts also institutionalized racism. The Supreme Court made healing the divided country paramount. Many of their decisions promoting that healing were at the expense of people of color. The persistence and legalization of segregation can be traced to this era. By putting state and local governments in charge of "the Negro problem," the Court also in effect abrogated the political and economic rights of Southern and border state African Americans, and put the lives of black dissenters at risk.

Asians, brought over to the United States to build railroads and handle risky and low-paying jobs, were also marginalized by post-Reconstruction policies. Although not subject to the same laws that discriminated against

Asians and blacks, immigrants from southern and eastern Europe found that they, too, would be unprotected by American laws and often kept in poverty by discrimination. Recent immigrants who stayed in the cities often lived in tenements and slums and worked in appalling conditions in sweatshops. As early as 1866, the New York City council reported on slum conditions in its immigrant ghettos. Those who escaped the cities helped feed the growth of the West. They built railroads, opened small businesses, and turned the prairie into farmland. Populating the West, however, had ecological effects that were not appreciated until the next century. Wherever they landed, immigrants wanting to achieve the American dream; they attended public schools and studied English at the same time that their cultures began to change the dominant Protestant American culture.

Mechanization of farming hurt small farmers, but American agribusiness made the United States the world's major producer of food, a position it has never relinquished. Yet as western agriculture and mining developed, Native Americans were pushed off valuable land and were forced onto unproductive reservations. The final Indian wars take place in this era. Innovations in capitalism like trusts and cartels also spurred industrial advances, along with the stunning wealth it brought its leaders and financiers. Without an income tax to disturb their riches and protected by sympathetic assemblies and courts, railroad, banking, oil, and other barons built palaces as summer homes, patronized the arts, and financed libraries.

Grass-roots movements sprang up to try to counteract the dominance of big business and "robber barons." The Knights of Labor represented an attempt to create an all-encompassing union. The more conservative American Federation of Labor limited its membership to skilled workers and its goals to working conditions and wages. It persisted. Yet labor suffered as it had throughout the 19th century and would for most of the future. The American dream was too powerful: Every person in the United States by birth or immigration had the opportunity to attain economic success, and capitalism was the best way to keep that opportunity alive.

Farmers also banded together. They produced the Populist Party from their attempts to gain independence from bankers and "middlemen" who gave them little for their produce but charged high prices for farm machinery. Populism spread to other sectors through efforts to democratize the economy by making silver a monetary standard.

In 1890, the U.S. census declared that the frontier had closed. The United States began looking to extend its influence outside its borders. When the battleship *Maine* blew up in Havana Harbor, the nation had its excuse. The Spanish-American War of 1898 really marks the beginning of the 20th century for U.S. foreign affairs. Its success against Spain brought Cuba and the Philippines under American jurisdiction, making the United States an imperial power. Despite American flirtation with isolation between World Wars I and II, it has maintained its world-power status ever since.

The Rise of Corporations, Heavy Industry, and Mechanized Farming

Russell Conwell, "Acres of Diamonds," 1876–1925

Inspirational speech given by American Baptist minister Russell H. Conwell more than 6,000 times between 1876 and 1925. Heard first by Conwell's Civil War regiment, the speech quickly gained fame because of its dominant theme: "It is your duty to be rich." Everyone, he said, has the "opportunity to be rich"—to have "acres of diamonds"—because "you must look around and see what people need and then invest yourself, or your money, in that which they need most." Conwell believed that the rich are rich because God made them so, and his lecture was used as a rationalization of the robber-baron mentality of the Gilded Age in America. Conwell founded Temple University in 1884 for the explicit purpose of training poor boys to rise in status through education. However, the mentality defined by Conwell describes the American dream that has undercut every socialist reform movement from the Jacksonian Era to the present.

(excerpt)

The title of this lecture originated away back in 1869. When going down the Tigris River, we hired a guide from Bagdad to show us down to the Arabian Gulf. That guide whom we employed resembled the barbers we find in America. That is, he resembled the barbers in certain mental characteristics. He thought it was not only his duty to guide us down the river, but also to entertain us with stories; curious and weird, ancient and modern, strange and familiar; many of them I have forgotten, and I am glad I have. But there was one which I recall tonight. The guide grew irritable over my lack of appreciation, and a he led my camel by the halter he introduced his story by saying: "This is a tale I reserve for my *particular friends.*" So I then gave him my close attention. He told me that there once lived near the shore of the River Indus, toward which we were then traveling, an ancient Persian by the name of Al Hafed. He said that Al Hafed owned a large farm, with orchards, grain fields and gardens; that he had money at interest, had a beautiful wife and lovely children, and was a wealthy and contented man. Contented because he was wealthy, and wealthy because he was contented.

One day there visited this old Persian farmer one of those ancient Buddhist priests, one of the wise men of the East, who sat down by Al Hafed's fireside and told the old farmer how this world was made. He told him that this world was once a great bank of fog, and that the Almighty thrust His finger into this bank of fog, and began slowly to move his finger around, and then increased the speed of his finger until he whirled this bank of fog into a solid ball of fire; and as it went rolling through the universe, burning its way through other banks of fog, it condensed the moisture, until it fell in floods of rain upon the heated surface of the world, and cooled the outward crust; then the internal fires, bursting the cooling crust, threw up the mountains, and the hills, and the valleys of this wonderful world of ours.

"And" said the old priest, "if this internal melted mass burst forth and cooled very quickly it became granite, if it cooled more slowly, it became copper; if it cooled less quickly, silver; less quickly, gold; and after gold, diamonds were made." Said the old priest, "A diamond is a congealed drop of sunlight." That statement is literally true.

And the old priest said another very curious thing. He said that a diamond was the last and the highest of God's mineral creations, as a woman is the last and highest of God's animal creations. That is the reason, I suppose, why the two have such a liking for each other.

The old priest told Al Hafed if he had a diamond the size of his thumb, he could purchase a dozen farms like his. "And," said the priest, "if you had a handful of diamonds, you could purchase the county, and if you had a mine of diamonds you could purchase kingdoms, and place your children upon thrones, through the influence of your great wealth."

Al Hafed heard all about the diamonds that night, and went to bed a poor man. He wanted a whole mine of diamonds. Early in the morning he sought the priest and awoke him. Well, I know, by experience, that a priest is very cross when awakened early in the morning.

Al Hafed said: "Will you tell me where I can find diamonds?"

The priest said: "Diamonds? What do you want of diamonds?"

Said Al Hafed: "I want to be immensely rich."

"Well," said the priest, "if you want diamonds, all you have to do is to go and find them, and then you will have them."

"But," said Al Hafed, "I don't know where to go."

"If you will find a river that runs over white sands, between high mountains, in those white sands you will always find diamonds," answered the priest.

"But," asked Al Hafed, "do you believe there is such a river?"

"Plenty of them; all you have to do is just go where they are."

"Well," said Al Hafed, "I will go."

So he sold his farm; collected his money that was at interest; left his family in charge of a neighbor, and away he went in search of diamonds.

He began his search, very properly to my mind, at the Mountains of the Moon. Afterwards he came around into Palestine, and then wandered on into Europe. At last, when his money was all gone and he was in rags, poverty and wretchedness, he stood on the shore at Barcelona, in Spain, when a great tidal wave swept through the pillars of Hercules; and the poor, starving, afflicted stranger could not resist the awful temptation to cast himself into that incoming tide; and he sank beneath its foaming crest, never to rise in this life again.

When the old guide had told me that story, he stopped the camel I was riding upon and went back to arrange the baggage on another camel, and I had an opportunity to muse over his story. And I asked myself this question: "Why did this old guide reserve this story for his *particular friends?*" But when he came back and took up the camel's halter once more, I found that was the first story I ever heard wherein the hero was killed in the first chapter. For he went on into the second chapter, just as though there had been no break.

Said he: "The man who purchased Al Hafed's farm, led his camel out into the garden to drink, and as the animal put his nose into the shallow waters of the garden brook, Al Hafed's successor noticed a curious flash of light from the white sands of the stream. Reaching in he pulled out a black stone containing a strange eye of light. He took it into the house as a curious pebble and, putting it on the mantel that covered the central fire, went his way and forgot all about it.

"But not long after that that some old priest came to visit Al Hafed's successor. The moment he opened the door he noticed the flash of light. He rushed to the mantel and said:

"'Here is a diamond! Here is a diamond! Has Al Hafed returned?'

"'Oh no, Al Hafed has not returned and we have not heard from him since he went away, and that is not a diamond. It is nothing but a stone we found out in our garden.'

"'But,' said the priest, 'I know a diamond when I see it. I tell you that is a diamond.'

"Then together they rushed out into the garden. They stirred up the white sands with their fingers, and there came up other more beautiful, more valuable gems than the first.

"Thus," said the guide—and friends, it is historically true—"was discovered the diamond minds of Golconda, the most valuable diamond mines in the history of the ancient world."

Well, when the guide had added the second chapter to his story, he then took off his Turkish red cap, and swung it in the air to call my special attention to the moral; those Arab guides always have morals to their stores, though the stories are not always moral.

He said to me: "Had Al Hafed remained at home, and dug in his own cellar, or underneath his own wheat field, instead of wretchedness, starvation, poverty and death in a strange land, he would have had *acres of diamonds.*"

Acres of diamonds! For every acre of that old farm, yes, every shovelful, afterwards revealed the gems which since have decorated the crowns of monarchs.

When the guide had added the moral to this story, I saw why he reserved if for his *particular friends.* But I didn't tell him that I could see it. It was that mean, old Arab's way of going around a thing, like a lawyer, and saying indirectly what he didn't dare say directly; that in his private opinion "there was a certain young man traveling down the Tigris River, who might better be at home, in America."

I told him his story reminded me of one. You all know it. I told him that a man in California, in 1847, owned a ranch there. He heard that they had discovered gold in Southern California, though they had not. And he sold his farm to Colonel Sutter, who put a mill on the little stream below the house. One day his little girl gathered some of the sand in her hands from the raceway, and brought it into the house. And while she was sifting it through her fingers, a visitor there noticed the first shining scales of real gold that were ever discovered in California. Acres and acres of

gold. I was introduced, a few years ago, while in California, to the one-third owner of the farm, and he was then receiving one hundred and twenty dollars in gold for every fifteen minutes of his life, sleeping or waking. You and I would enjoy an income like that, now that we have no income tax.

Professor Agassiz, the great geologist of Harvard University, that magnificent scholar, told us, at the Summer School of Mineralogy, that there once lived in Pennsylvania a man who owned a farm—and he did with his farm just what I should do if I had a farm in Pennsylvania. He sold it. But, before he sold it, he decided to secure employment, collecting coal oil. He wrote to his cousin in Canada that he would like to go into that business. His cousin wrote back to him: "I cannot engage you, because you don't understand the oil business." "Then," said he, "I will understand it," and with commendable zeal, he set himself at the study of the whole theory of the coal-oil subject. He began away back at the second day of God's creation. He found that there was once another sun that shone on this world, and that then there were immense forests of vegetation. He found that the other sun was put out, and that this world after a time fell into the wake of the present sun. It was then locked in blocks of ice. Then there rose mighty icebergs that human imagination cannot grasp, and as those mountains of ice did ride those stormy seas, they beat down this original vegetation, they planed down the hills, toppled over the mountains, and everywhere buried this original vegetation which has since been turned by chemical action to the primitive beds of coal, and in connection with which only is found coal oil in paying quantities.

So he found out where oil originated. He studied it until he knew what it looked like, what is smelled like, how to refine it, and where to sell it.

"Now," said he to his cousin in a letter, "I know all about the oil business, from the second day of God's creation to the present time."

His cousin replied to him to "come on." So he his farm in Pennsylvania for $833—even money, no cents.

After he had gone from the farm, the farmer who had purchased his place, went out to arrange for watering the cattle; and he found that the previous owner had already arranged for that matter. There was a stream running down the hillside back of the barn; and across that stream from bank to bank, the previous owner had put in a plank edgewise at a slight angle, for the purpose of throwing over to one side of the brook a dreadful looking scum through which the cattle would not put their noses, although they would drink on this side below the plank. Thus that man, who had gone to Canada, and who had studied all about the oil business, had been himself damming back for twenty-three years a flood of coal oil, which the state geologist said in 1870 was worth to our state a hundred millions of dollars. A hundred millions! The city of Titusville stands bodily on that farm now. And yet, though he knew all about the theory, he sold the farm for $833—again I say "no *sense.*"

I need another illustration. I find it in Massachusetts. The young man went down to Yale College and studied mines and mining, and became such an adept at mineralogy, that during his senior year in the Sheffield School, they paid him as a tutor fifteen dollars a week for the spare time in which he taught. When he graduated they raised his pay to forty-five dollars a week and offered him a professorship. As soon as they did that he went home to his mother! If they had raised his salary to fifteen dollars and sixty cents, then he would have stayed. But when they made it forty-five dollars a week he said: "I won't work for forty-five dollars a week! The idea of a man with a brain like mine, working for forty-five dollars a week! Let us go out to California and stake out gold and silver and copper claims, and be rich!"

Said his mother: "Now Charley, it is just as well to be happy as it is to be rich."

"Yes," said he, "It is just as well to be rich and happy too."

They were both right about it. And as he was the only son, and she was a widow, of course he had his way. They always do. So they sold out in Massachusetts and went, not to California, but to Wisconsin, and there he entered the employ of the Superior Copper Mining Company, at fifteen dollars a week again. But with the proviso that he should have an interest in any mines he should discover for the company. I don't believe he ever discovered a mine there. Still I have often felt when I mentioned this fact in Northern Wisconsin, that he might be in the audience and feel mad at the way I speak about it. Still here is the fact, and it seems unfortunate to be in the way of a good illustration. But I don't believe he ever found any other mine. Yet I don't know anything about that end of the line. I know that he had scarcely gone for Massachusetts, before the farmer who had purchased his farm was bringing a large basket of potatoes in through the gateway. You know in Massachusetts our farms are almost entirely stone wall. Hence the basket hugged very close in the gate, and he dragged it on one side and then on the other. And as he was pulling that basket through the gateway, the farmer noticed in the upper and outer corner of that stone wall next to the gate, a block of native silver eight inches square. And this professor of mines and mining and mineralogy, who would not work for forty-five dollars a week, because he knew so much about the subject, when he sold that homestead, sat on that very stone to make the bargain. He was born on that very farm, and they told me that he had gone by that piece of silver and rubbed it with his

sleeve, until it reflected his countenance and seemed to say to him, "Here, take me! Here is a hundred thousand dollar right down here in the rocks just for the taking." But he wouldn't take it. This was near Newburyport, Massachusetts. He wouldn't believe in silver at home. He said: "There is no silver in Newburyport. It is all away off,—well, I don't know where,"—and he didn't. But somewhere else. And he was a professor of mineralogy. I don't know of anything I would better enjoy in taking the whole time, than telling of the blunders like this which I have heard that "professors" have made.

I say that I would enjoy it. But after all there is another side of the question. For the more I think about it, the more I would like to know what he is doing in Wisconsin tonight. I don't believe he has found any mines, but I can tell you what I do believe is the case. I think he sits out there by his fireside tonight, and his friends are gathered around him and he is saying to them something like this:

"Do you know that man Conwell who lives in Philadelphia?"

"Oh, yes, I have heard of him."

"Well you know that man Jones who live in—"

"Yes, I have also heard of him," say they.

Then he begins to shake his sides with laughter, and he says:

"They have both done the same thing I did precisely!" And that spoils the whole joke.

Because you and I have done it. Yet nearly every person here will say: "Oh no, I never had any acres of diamonds or any gold mines or any silver mines."

But I say to you that you did have silver mines, and gold mines, and acres of diamonds, and you have them now.

Now let me speak with the greatest care lest my eccentricity of manner should mislead my listeners, and make you think I am here to entertain more than to help. I want to hold your attention on this oppressive night, with sufficient interest to leave my lesson with you.

You had an opportunity to be rich; and to some of you it has been a hardship to purchase a ticket for this lecture. Yet you have no right to be poor. It is all wrong. You have no right to be poor. It is your duty to be rich.

Source:

James Andrews and David Zarefsky, eds., *American Voices: Significant Speeches in American History, 1640–1945*. Reading, Mass.: Longman, 1989.

Munn v. Illinois, 1877

The most important of several decisions of the U.S. Supreme Court involving agricultural issues, called the Granger Cases.

Issued on March 1, 1877, it concerned the validity of an Illinois law regulating maximum grain storage charges. In 1872 the Chicago storage company of Munn and Cott was found guilty of violating that law. The company appealed the decision, claiming that fixing maximum rates violated the Fourteenth Amendment by confiscating private property without due process of law. The Supreme Court ruled that because the warehouses were "affected with a public interest," their rates were subject to public regulation. The principle thus established led to further public regulation of private businesses serving the public interest. But by the end of the 1870s, the granger movement had lost its influence.

On October 25, 1886, in *Wabash, St. Louis and Pacific Railroad Company v. Illinois* (118 U.S. 557), concerning the legality of an Illinois statute prohibiting long- and short-haul clauses in transportation contracts, the U.S. Supreme Court weakened the ruling in *Munn v. Illinois*. It denied the state on the grounds that it interfered with interstate commerce, a ruling that helped lead to the passage of the Interstate Commerce Act.

(excerpt)

Mr. Chief Justice Waite delivered the opinion of the court.

The question to be determined in this case is whether the general assembly of Illinois can, under the limitations upon the legislative power of the States imposed by the Constitution of the United States, fix by law the maximum of charges for the storage of grain in warehouses at Chicago and other places in the State having not less than one hundred thousand inhabitants, "in which grain is stored in bulk, and in which the grain of different owners is mixed together, or in which grain is stored in such a manner that the identity of different lots or parcels cannot be accurately preserved."

It is claimed that such a law is repugnant—

1. To that part of sect. 8, art. 1, of the Constitution of the United States which confers upon Congress the power "to regulate commerce with foreign nations and among the several States";

2. To that part of sect. 9 of the same article which provides that "no preference shall be given by any regulation of commerce or revenue to the ports of one State over those of another"; and

3. To that part of amendment 14 which ordains that no State shall "deprive any person of life, liberty, or property, without due process of law, nor deny to any person within its jurisdiction the equal protection of the laws."

We will consider the last of these objections first.

Every statute is presumed to be constitutional. The courts ought not to declare one to be unconstitutional, unless it is clearly so. If there is doubt, the expressed will of the legislature should be sustained.

The Constitution contains no definition of the word "deprive," as used in the Fourteenth Amendment. To determine its signification, therefore, it is necessary to ascertain the effect which usage has given it, when employed in the same or a like connection.

While this provision of the amendment is new in the Constitution of the United States, as a limitation upon the powers of the States, it is old as a principle of civilized government. It is found in Magna Charta, and, in substance if not in form, in nearly or quite all the constitutions that have been from time to time adopted by the several States of the Union. By the Fifth Amendment, it was introduced into the Constitution of the United States as a limitation upon the powers of the national government, and by the Fourteenth, as a guaranty against any encroachment upon an acknowledged right of citizenship by the legislatures of the States.

When the people of the United Colonies separated from Great Britain, they changed the form, but not the substance, of their government. They retained for the purposes of government all the powers of the British Parliament, and through their State constitutions, or other forms of social compact, undertook to give practical effect to such as they deemed necessary for the common good and the security of life and property. All the powers which they retained they committed to their respective States, unless in express terms or by implication reserved to themselves. Subsequently, when it was found necessary to establish a national government for national purposes, a part of the powers of the States and of the people of the States was granted to the United States and the people of the United States. This grant operated as a further limitation upon the powers of the States, so that now the governments of the States possess all the powers of the Parliament of England, except such as have been delegated to the United States or reserved by the people. The reservations by the people are shown in the prohibitions of the constitutions.

When one becomes a member of society, he necessarily parts with some rights or privileges which, as an individual not affected by his relations to others, he might retain. "A body politic," as aptly defined in the preamble of the Constitution of Massachusetts, "is a social compact by which the whole people covenants with each citizen, and each citizen with the whole people, that all shall be governed by certain laws for the common good." This does not confer power upon the whole people to control rights which are purely and exclusively private, *Thorpe v. R. & B. Railroad Co.*, 27 Vt. 143; but it does authorize the establishment of laws requiring each citizen to so conduct himself, and so use his own property, as not unnecessarily to injure another. This is the very essence of government, and has found expression in the maxim *sic utere tuo ut alienum non loedas*. From this source come the police powers, which, as was said by Mr. Chief Justice Taney in the *License Cases*, 5 How. 583, "are nothing more or less than the powers of government inherent in every sovereignty . . . that is to say, . . . the power to govern men and things." Under these powers the government regulates the conduct of its citizens one towards another, and the manner in which each shall use his own property, when such regulation becomes necessary for the public good. In their exercise it has been customary in England from time immemorial, and in this country from its first colonization, to regulate ferries, common carriers, hackmen, bakers, millers, wharfingers, innkeepers, &c., and is so doing to fix a maximum of charge to be made for services rendered, accommodations furnished, and articles sold. To this day, statutes are to be found in many of the States upon some or all these subjects; and we think it has never yet been successfully contended that such legislation came within any of the constitutional prohibitions against interference with private property. With the Fifth Amendment in force, Congress, in 1820, conferred power upon the city of Washington "to regulate . . . the rates of wharfage at private wharves, . . . the sweeping of chimneys, and to fix the rates of fees therefor, . . . and the weight and quality of bread," 3-Stat. 587, sect. 7; and, in 1848, "to make all necessary regulations respecting hackney carriages and the rates of fare of the same, and the rates of hauling by cartmen, wagoners, carmen, and draymen, and the rates of commission of auctioneers," 9 id. 224, sect. 2.

From this it is apparent that, down to the time of the adoption of the Fourteenth Amendment, it was not supposed that statutes regulating the use, or even the price of the use, of private property necessarily deprived an owner of his property without due process of law. Under some circumstances they may, but not under all. The amendment does not change the law in this particular; it simply prevents the States from doing that which will operate as such a deprivation . . .

Source:
Supreme Court Reporter, Vol. 4, pp. 113–154.

Interstate Commerce Act, 1887

Federal law that established the Interstate Commerce Commission (ICC), the first federal administrative agency. The act, introduced by Illinois senator Shelby M. Cullom and enacted on February 4, 1887, came as the result of public outcry over railroad abuses. The act applied only to railroads traveling through two or more states and provided that all railroad charges be "reasonable and just." It prohibited pooling arrangements, rebates, drawbacks, and other discriminatory rates, and it made the practice of charging more for a short haul than a long haul illegal. The ICC, charged with regulating railroad management, had the power to subpoena witnesses and documents and to require annual reports. The commission was strengthened by later legislation.

Be it enacted by the Senate and House of Representatives of the United States of America in Congress assembled, That the provisions of this act shall apply to any common carrier or carriers engaged in the transportation of passengers or property wholly by railroad, or partly by railroad and partly by water when both are used, under a common control, management, or arrangement, for a continuous carriage or shipment, from one State or Territory of the United States, or the District of Columbia, to any other State or Territory of the United States, or the District of Columbia, or from any place in the United States to an adjacent foreign country, or from any place in the United States through a foreign country to any other place in the United States, and also to the transportation in like manner of property shipped from any place in the United States to a foreign country and carried from such place to a port of trans-shipment, or shipped from a foreign country to any place in the United States and carried to such place from a port of entry either in the United States or an adjacent foreign country: Provided, however, That the provisions of this act shall not apply to the transportation of passengers or property, or to the receiving, delivering, storage, or handling of property, wholly within one State, and not shipped to or from a foreign country from or to any State or Territory as aforesaid.

The term "railroad" as used in this act shall include all bridges and ferries used or operated in connection with any railroad, and also all the road in use by any corporation operating a railroad, whether owned or operated under a contract, agreement, or lease; and the term "transportation" shall include all instrumentalities of shipment or carriage.

All charges made for any service rendered or to be rendered in the transportation of passengers or property as aforesaid, or in connection therewith, or for the receiving, delivering, storage, or handling of such property, shall be reasonable and just; and every unjust and unreasonable charge for such service is prohibited and declared to be unlawful.

Sec. 2. That if any common carrier subject to the provisions of this act shall, directly or indirectly, by any special rate, rebate, drawback, or other device, charge, demand, collect, or receive from any person or persons a greater or less compensation for any service rendered, or to be rendered, in the transportation of passengers or property, subject to the provisions of this act, than it charges, demands, collects, or receives from any other person or persons for doing for him or them a like and contemporaneous service in the transportation of a like kind of traffic under substantially similar circumstances and conditions, such common carrier shall be deemed guilty of unjust discrimination, which is hereby prohibited and declared to be unlawful.

Sec. 3. That it shall be unlawful for any common carrier subject to the provisions of this act to make or give any undue or unreasonable preference or advantage to any particular person, company, firm, corporation, or locality, or any particular description of traffic, in any respect whatsoever, or to subject any particular person, company, firm, corporation, or locality, or any particular description of traffic, to any undue or unreasonable prejudice or disadvantage in any respect whatsoever.

Every common carrier subject to the provisions of this act shall according to their respective powers, afford all reasonable, proper, and equal facilities for the interchange of traffic between their respective lines, and for the receiving, forwarding, and delivering of passengers and property to and from their several lines and those connection therewith, and shall not discriminate in their rates and charges between such connecting lines; but this shall not be construed as requiring any such common carrier to give the use of its tracks or terminal facilities to another carrier engaged in like business.

Sec. 4. That it shall be unlawful for any common carrier subject to the provisions of this act to charge or receive any greater compensation in the aggregate for the transportation of passengers or of like kind of property, under substantially similar circumstances and conditions, for a shorter than for a longer distance over the same line, in the same direction, the shorter being included within the longer distance; but this shall not be construed as authorizing any common carrier within the terms of this act to charge and receive as great compensation for a shorter as for a longer distance: Provided, however, That upon application to the Commission appointed under the provisions of this act, such common carrier may, in special cases, after investigation by the Commission, be authorized to charge less for longer than for shorter distances for the transportation of passengers or property; and the Commission may from time to time prescribe the extent to which such designated common carrier may be relieved from the operation of this section of this act.

Sec. 5. That it shall be unlawful for any common carrier subject to the provisions of this act to enter into any contract, agreement, or combination with any other common carrier or carriers for the pooling of freights of differ-

ent and competing railroads, or to divide between them the aggregate or net proceeds of the earnings of such railroads, or any portion thereof; and in any case of an agreement for the pooling of freights as aforesaid, each day of its continuance shall be deemed a separate offense.

Sec. 6. That every common carrier subject to the provisions of this act shall print and keep for public inspection schedules showing the rates and fares and charges for the transportation of passengers and property which any such common carrier has established and which are in force at the time upon its railroad, as defined by the first section of this act. The schedules printed as aforesaid by any such common carrier shall plainly state the places upon its railroad between which property and passengers will be carried, and shall contain the classification of freight in force upon such railroad, and shall also state separately the terminal charges and any rules or regulations which in any wise change, affect, or determine any part or the aggregate of such aforesaid rates and fares and charges. Such schedules shall be plainly printed in large type, of at least the size of ordinary pica, and copies for the use of the public shall be kept in every depot or station upon any such railroad, in such places and in such form that they can be conveniently inspected.

* * *

Every common carrier subject to the provisions of this act shall file with the Commission hereinafter provided for copies of its schedules of rates, fares, and charges which have been established and published in compliance with the requirements of this section, and shall promptly notify said Commission of all changes made in the same. Every such common carrier shall also file with said Commission copies of all contracts, agreements, or arrangements with other common carriers in relation to any traffic affected by the provisions of this act to which it may be a party. And in cases where passengers and freight pass over continuous lines or routes operated by more than one common carrier, and the several common carriers operating such lines or routes establish joint tariffs of rates or fares or charges for such continuous lines or routes, copies of such joint tariffs shall also, in like manner, be filed with said Commission. Such joint rates, fares, and charges on such continuous lines so filed as aforesaid shall be made public by such common carriers when directed by said Commission. . . .

If any such common carrier shall neglect or refuse to file or publish its schedules or tariffs of rates, fares, and charges as provided in this section, or any part of the same, such common carrier shall, in addition to other penalties herein prescribed, be subject to a writ of mandamus. . .and failure to comply with its requirements shall be punishable as and for a contempt; and the said Commissioners, as complainants, may also apply, in any such circuit of the

United States, for a writ of injunction against such common carrier, to restrain such common carrier from receiving or transporting property among the several States and Territories of the United States. . . .

Sec. 7. That it shall be unlawful for any common carrier subject to the provisions of this act to enter into any combination, contract, or agreement, expressed or implied, to prevent, by change of time schedule, carriage in different cars, or by other means or devices, the carriage of freights from being continuous from the place of shipment to the place of destination; and no break of bulk, stoppage, or interruption made by such common carrier shall prevent the carriage of freights from being and being treated as one continuous carriage from the place of shipment to the place of destination, unless such break, stoppage, or interruption was made in good faith for some necessary purpose, and without any intent to avoid or unnecessarily interrupt such continuous carriage or to evade any of the provisions of this act.

Sec. 8. That in case any common carrier subject to the provisions of this act shall do, cause to be done, or permit to be done any act, matter, or thing in this act prohibited or declared to be unlawful, or shall omit to do any act, matter, or thing in this act required to be done, such common carrier shall be liable to the person or persons injured thereby for the full amount of damages sustained in consequence of any such violation of the provisions of this act, together with a reasonable counsel or attorney's fee, to be fixed by the court in every case of recovery, which attorney's fee shall be taxed and collected as part of the costs in the case.

Sec. 10. That any common carrier subject to the provisions of this act, or, whenever such common carrier is a corporation, any director or officer thereof, or any receiver, trustee, lessee, agent, or person acting for or employed by such corporation, who, alone or with any other corporation, company, person, or party, shall willfully do or cause to be done, or shall willingly suffer or permit to be done, any act, matter, or thing in this act prohibited or declared to be unlawful . . . shall be deemed guilty of a misdemeanor, and shall . . . be subject to a fine of not to exceed five thousand dollars for each offense.

Sec. 11. That a Commission is hereby created and established to be known as the Inter-State Commerce Commission, which shall be composed of five Commissioners, who shall be appointed by the President, by and with the advice and consent of the Senate. . . . Any Commissioner may be removed by the President for inefficiency, neglect of duty, or malfeasance in office. Not more than three of the Commissioners shall be appointed from the same political party. No person in the employ of or holding any official relation to any common carrier subject to the provisions of this act, or owning stock or bonds thereof, or who is in any manner pecuniarily interested therein, shall enter upon the duties of or hold such office. Said Commissioners shall not engage in any other business, vocation, or employment. No vacancy in the Commission shall impair the right of the remaining Commissioners to exercise all the powers of the Commission.

Sec. 12. That the Commission hereby created shall have authority to inquire into the management of the business of all common carriers subject to the provisions of this act . . . and shall have the right to obtain from such common carriers full and complete information necessary to enable the Commission to perform the duties and carry out the objects for which it was created; and for the purposes of this act the Commission shall have power to require the attendance and testimony of witnesses and the production of all books, papers, tariffs, contracts, agreements, and documents relating to any matter under investigation, and to that end may invoke the aid of any court of the United States in requiring the attendance and testimony of witnesses and the production of books, papers, and documents under the provisions of this section.

Sec. 13. That any person, firm, corporation, or association, or any mercantile, agricultural, or manufacturing society, or any body politic or municipal organization complaining of anything done or omitted to be done by any common carrier subject to the provisions of this act in contravention of the provisions thereof, may apply to said Commission by petition. . . .

Said Commission shall in like manner investigate any complaint forwarded by the railroad commissioner or railroad commission of any State or Territory . . . and may institute any inquiry on its own motion in the same manner and to the same effect as though complaint had been made.

✸ ✸ ✸

Sec. 16. That whenever any common carrier, as defined in and subject to the provisions of this act, shall violate or refuse or neglect to obey any lawful order or requirement of the Commission in this act named, it shall be the duty of the Commission, and lawful for any company or person interested in such order or requirement, to apply, in a summary way, by petition . . . and the said court shall have power to hear and determine the matter. . . .

✸ ✸ ✸

Sec. 20. That the Commission is hereby authorized to require annual reports from all common carriers subject to the provisions of this act. . . .

Sec. 21. That the Commission shall, on or before the first day of December in each year, make a report to the Secretary of the Interior, which shall be by him transmitted to Congress. . . . This report shall contain such information and data collected by the Commission as may be considered of value in the determination of questions connected with the regulation of commerce, together with such recommendations as to additional legislation relating thereto as the Commission may deem necessary.

Sec. 22. That nothing in this act shall apply to the carriage, storage, or handling of property free or at reduced rates for the United States, State, or municipal governments, or for charitable purposes, or to or from fairs and expositions for exhibition thereat, or the issuance of mileage, excursion, or commutation passenger tickets; nothing in this act shall be construed to prohibit any common carrier from giving reduced rates to ministers of religion; nothing in this act shall be construed to prevent railroads from giving free carriage to their own officers and employees, or to prevent the principal officers of any railroad company or companies from exchanging passes or tickets with other railroad companies for their officers and employees; and nothing in this act contained shall in any way abridge or alter the remedies now existing at common law or by statute, but the provisions of this act are in addition to such remedies: Provided, That no pending litigation shall in any way be affected by this act.

❖ ❖ ❖

Approved, February 4, 1887.

Source:
Statutes at Large, Vol. 25, pp. 379–387.

Andrew Carnegie, "Wealth," 1889

Essay, sometimes called "The Gospel of Wealth," written by American industrialist and philanthropist Andrew Carnegie and published in the *North American Review* in June 1889; he defended laissez-faire capitalism and also argued that rich men must use their surplus wealth to benefit the community. After claiming that competition and inequality of wealth are the inevitable costs of material development, Carnegie enunciated the duties of the rich man: to live modestly, to provide moderately for his dependents, and to administer all surplus revenues as trust funds, which he must administer to advance the general welfare of the community. The millionaire should be the "trustee for the poor." Carnegie followed this philosophy in his own life, donating some $350 million to various social, educational, and cultural causes, especially public libraries, many of which are still in regular use.

⸺⸺⸺⸺⸺ ⸙ ⸺⸺⸺⸺⸺

The problem of our age is the proper administration of wealth, so that the ties of brotherhood may still bind together the rich and poor in harmonious relationship. The conditions of human life have not only been changed, but revolutionized, within the past few hundred years. In former days there was little difference between the dwelling, dress, food, and environment of the chief and those of his retainers. The Indians are to-day where civilized man then was. When visiting the Sioux, I was led to the wigwam of the chief. It was just like the others in external appearance, and even within the difference was trifling between it and those of the poorest of his braves. The contrast between the palace of the millionaire and the cottage of the laborer with us to-day measures the change which has come with civilization.

This change, however, is not to be deplored, but welcomed as highly beneficial. It is well, nay, essential for the progress of the race, that the houses of some should be homes for all that is highest and best in literature and the arts, and for all the refinements of civilization, rather than that none should be so. Much better this great irregularity than universal squalor. Without wealth there can be no Maecenas. The "good old times" were not good old times. Neither master nor servant was as well situated then as to-day. A relapse to old conditions would be disastrous to both—not the least so to him who serves—and would sweep away civilization with it. But whether the change be for good or ill, it is upon us, beyond our power to alter, and therefore to be accepted and made the best of. It is a waste of time to criticize the inevitable.

It is easy to see how the change has come. One illustration will serve for almost every phase of the cause. In the manufacture of products we have the whole story. It applies to all combinations of human industry, as stimulated and enlarged by the inventions of this scientific age. Formerly articles were manufactured at the domestic hearth or in small shops which formed part of the household. The master and his apprentices worked side by side, the latter living with the master, and therefore subject to the same conditions. When these apprentices rose to be masters, there was little or no change in their mode of life, and they, in turn, educated in the same routine succeeding apprentices. There was, substantially, social equality, and even political equality, for those engaged in industrial pursuits had then little or no political voice in the State.

But the inevitable result of such a mode of manufacture was crude articles at high prices. To-day the world obtains commodities of excellent quality at prices which even the generation preceding this would have deemed incredible. In the commercial world similar causes have produced similar results, and the race is benefited thereby. The poor enjoy what the rich could not before afford. What were the luxuries have become the necessaries of life. The laborer has now more comforts than the farmer had a few generations ago. The farmer has more luxuries than the landlord had, and is more richly clad and better housed. The landlord has books and pictures rarer, and appointments more artistic, than the King could then obtain.

The price we pay for this salutary change is, no doubt, great. We assemble thousands of operatives in the factory, in the mine, and in the counting-house, of whom the employer can know little or nothing, and to whom the employer is little better than a myth. All intercourse between them is at an end. Rigid Castes are formed, and, as usual, mutual ignorance breeds mutual distrust. Each Caste is without sympathy for the other, and ready to credit anything disparaging in regard to it. Under the law of competition, the employer of thousands is forced into the strictest economies, among which the rates paid to labor figure prominently, and often there is friction between the employer and the employed, between capital and labor, between rich and poor. Human society loses homogeneity.

The price which society pays for the law of competition, like the price it pays for cheap comforts and luxuries, is also great; but the advantages of this law are also greater still, for it is to this law that we owe our wonderful material development, which brings improved conditions in its train. But, whether the law is benign or not, we must say of it, as we say of the change in the conditions of men to which we have referred: It is here, we cannot evade it; no substitutes for it have been found; and while the law may be sometimes hard for the individual, it is best for the race, because it insures the survival of the fittest in every department. We accept and welcome, therefore, as conditions to which we must accommodate ourselves, great inequality of environment, the concentration of business, industrial and commercial, in the hands of a few, and the law of competition between these, as being not only beneficial, but essential for the future progress of the race. Having accepted these, it follows that there must be great scope for the exercise of special ability in the merchant and in the manufacturer who has to conduct affairs upon a great scale. That this talent for organization and management is rare among men is proved by the fact that it invariably secures for its possessor enormous rewards, no matter where or under what laws or conditions. The experienced in affairs always rate the Man whose services can be obtained as a partner as not only the first consideration, but such as to render the question of his capital scarcely worth considering, for such men soon create capital; while, without the special talent required, capital soon takes wings. Such men become interested in forms or corporations using millions; and estimating only simple interest to be made upon the capital invested, it is inevitable that their income must exceed their expenditures, and that they

must accumulate wealth. Nor is there any middle ground which such men can occupy, because the great manufacturing or commercial concern which does not earn at least interest upon its capital soon becomes bankrupt. It must either go forward or fall behind: to stand still is impossible. It is a condition essential for its successful operation that it should be thus far profitable, and even that, in addition to interest on capital, it should make profit. It is a law, as certain as any of the others named, that men possessed of this peculiar talent for affairs, under the free play of economic forces, must, of necessity, soon be in receipt of more revenue than can be judiciously expended upon themselves; and this law is as beneficial for the race as the others.

Objections to the foundations upon which society is based are not in order, because the condition of the race is better with these than it has been with any others which have been tried. Of the effect of any new substitutes proposed we cannot be sure. The Socialist or Anarchist who seeks to overturn present conditions is to be regarded as attacking the foundation upon which civilization itself rests, for civilization took its start from the day that the capable, industrious workman said to his incompetent and lazy fellow, "If thou dost not sow, thou shalt not reap," and thus ended primitive Communism by separating the drones from the bees. One who studies this subject will soon be brought face to face with the conclusion that upon the sacredness of property civilization itself depends—the right of the laborer to his hundred dollars in the savings bank, and equally the legal right of the millionaire to his millions. To those who propose to substitute Communism for this intense Individualism the answer, therefore, is: The race has tried that. All progress from that barbarous day to the present time has resulted from its displacement. Not evil, but good, has come to the race from the accumulation of wealth by those who have the ability and energy that produce it.

But even if we admit for a moment that it might be better for the race to discard its present foundation, Individualism, that it is a nobler ideal that man should labor, not for himself alone, but in and for a brotherhood of his fellows, and share with them all in common, realizing Swedenborg's idea of Heaven, where, as he says, the angels derive their happiness, not from laboring for self, but for each other—even admit all this, and a sufficient answer is, This is not evolution, but revolution. It necessitates the changing of human nature itself—a work of aeons, even if it were good to change it, which we cannot know. It is not practicable in our day or in our age. Even if desirable theoretically, it belongs to another and long-succeeding sociological stratum. Our duty is with what is practicable now; with the next step possible in our day and generation. It is criminal to waste our energies in endeavoring to uproot, when all we can profitably or possibly accomplish is to bend the universal tree of humanity a little in the direction most favorable to the production of good fruit under existing circumstances. We might as well urge the destruction of the highest existing type of man because he failed to reach our ideal as to favor the destruction of Individualism, Private Property, the Law of Accumulation of Wealth, and the Law of Competition; for these are the highest results of human experience, the soil in which society so far has produced the best fruit. Unequally or unjustly, perhaps, as these laws sometimes operate, and imperfect as they appear to the Idealist, they are, nevertheless, like the highest type of man, the best and most valuable of all that humanity has yet accomplished.

We start, then, with a condition of affairs under which the best interests of the race are promoted, but which inevitably gives wealth to the few. Thus far, accepting conditions as they exist, the situation can be surveyed and pronounced good. The question then arises—and, if the foregoing be correct, it is the only question with which we have to deal—What is the proper mode of administering wealth after the laws upon which civilization is founded have thrown it into the hands of the few? And it is of this great question that I believe I offer the true solution. It will be understood that *fortunes* are here spoken of, not moderate sums saved by many years of effort, the returns from which are required for the comfortable maintenance and education of families. This is not *wealth,* but only *competence,* which it should be the aim of all to acquire.

There are but three modes in which surplus wealth can be disposed of. It can be left to the families of the decedents; or it can be bequeathed for public purposes; or, finally, it can be administered during their lives by its possessors. Under the first and second modes most of the wealth of the world that has reached the few has hitherto been applied. Let us in turn consider each of these modes. The first is the most injudicious. In monarchical countries, the estates and the greatest portion of the wealth are left to the first son, that the vanity of the parent may be gratified by the thought that his name and title are to descend to succeeding generations unimpaired. The condition of this class in Europe to-day teaches the futility of such hopes or ambitions. The successors have become impoverished through their follies or from the fall in the value of land. Even in Great Britain the strict law of entail has been found inadequate to maintain the status of an hereditary class. Its soil is rapidly passing into the hands of the stranger. Under republican institutions the division of property among the children is much fairer, but the question which forces itself upon thoughtful men in all lands is: Why should men leave great fortunes to their children? If this is done from affection, is it not misguided affection? Observation teaches that, generally speaking, it is not well

for the children that they should be so burdened. Neither is it well for the state. Beyond providing for the wife and daughters moderate sources of income, and very moderate allowances indeed, if any, for the sons, men may well hesitate, for it is no longer questionable that great sums bequeathed oftener work more for the injury than for the good of the recipients. Wise men will soon conclude that, for the best interests of the members of their families and of the state, such bequests are an improper use of their means.

It is not suggested that men who have failed to educate their sons to earn a livelihood shall cast them adrift in poverty. If any man has seen fit to rear his sons with a view to their living idle lives, or, what is highly commendable, has instilled in them the sentiment that they are in a position to labor for public ends without reference to pecuniary considerations, then, of course, the duty of the parent is to see that such are provided for *in moderation.* There are instances of millionaires' sons unspoiled by wealth, who, being rich, still perform great services in the community. Such are the very salt of the earth, as valuable as, unfortunately, they are rare; still it is not the exception, but the rule, that men must regard; and, looking at the usual result of enormous sums conferred upon legatees, the thoughtful man must shortly say, "I would as soon leave to my son a curse as the almighty dollar," and admit to himself that it is not the welfare of the children, but family pride, which inspires these enormous legacies.

As to the second mode, that of leaving wealth at death for public uses, it may be said that this is only a means for the disposal of wealth, provided a man is content to wait until he is dead before it becomes of much good in the world. Knowledge of the results of legacies bequeathed is not calculated to inspire the brightest hopes of much posthumous good being accomplished. The cases are not few in which the real object sought by the testator is not attained, nor are they few in which his real wishes are thwarted. In many cases the bequests are so used as to become only monuments of his folly. It is well to remember that it requires the exercise of not less ability than that which acquired the wealth to use it so as to be really beneficial to the community. Besides this, it may fairly be said that no man is to be extolled for doing what he cannot help doing, nor is he to be thanked by the community to which he only leaves wealth at death. Men who leave vast sums in this way may fairly be thought men who would not have left it at all, had they been able to take it with them. The memories of such cannot be held in grateful remembrance, for there is no grace in their gifts. It is not to be wondered at that such bequests seem so generally to lack the blessing.

The growing disposition to tax more and more heavily large estates left at death is a cheering indication of the growth of a salutary change in public opinion. The State of Pennsylvania now takes—subject to some exceptions—one-tenth of the property left by its citizens. The budget presented in the British Parliament the other day proposes to increase the death-duties; and, most significant of all, the new tax is to be a graduated one. Of all forms of taxation, this seems the wisest. Men who continue hoarding great sums all their lives, the proper use of which for public ends would work good to the community, should be made to feel that the community, in the form of the state, cannot thus be deprived of its proper share. By taxing estates heavily at death the state marks its condemnation of the selfish millionaire's unworthy life.

It is desirable that nations should go much further in this direction. Indeed, it is difficult to set bounds to the share of a rich man's estate which should go at his death to the public through the agency of the state, and by all means such taxes should be graduated, beginning at nothing upon moderate sums to dependents, and increasing rapidly as the amounts swell, until of the millionaire's hoard, as of Shylock's, at least:

"... The other half Comes to the privy coffer of the state."

This policy would work powerfully to induce the rich man to attend to the administration of wealth during his life, which is the end that society should always have in view, as being that by far most fruitful for the people. Nor need it be feared that this policy would sap the root of enterprise and render men less anxious to accumulate, for to the class whose ambition it is to leave great fortunes and be talked about after their death, it will attract even more attention, and, indeed, be a somewhat nobler ambition to have enormous sums paid over to the state from their fortunes.

There remains, then, only one mode of using great fortunes; but in this we have the true antidote for the temporary unequal distribution of wealth, the reconciliation of the rich and the poor—a reign of harmony—another ideal, differing, indeed, from that of the Communist in requiring only the further evolution of existing conditions, not the total overthrow of our civilization. It is founded upon the present most intense individualism, and the race is prepared to put it in practice by degrees whenever it pleases. Under its sway we shall have an ideal state, in which the surplus wealth of the few will become, in the best sense, the property of the many, because administered for the common good; and this wealth, passing through the hands of the few, can be made a much more potent force for the elevation of our race than if it had been distributed in small sums to the people themselves. Even the poorest can be made to see this, and to agree that great sums gathered by some of their fellow-citizens and spent for public purposes, from which the masses reap the principal benefit, are more valuable to them than if scattered among them through the course of many years in trifling amounts.

If we consider what results flow from the Cooper Institute, for instance, to the best portion of the race in New York not possessed of means, and compare these with those which would have arisen for the good of the masses from an equal sum distributed by Mr. Cooper in his lifetime in the form of wages, which is the highest form of distribution, being for work done and not for charity, we can form some estimate of the possibilities for the improvement of the race which lie embedded in the present law of the accumulation of wealth. Much of this sum, if distributed in small quantities among the people, would have been wasted in the indulgence of appetite, some of it in excess; and it may be doubted whether even the part put to the best use, that of adding to the comforts of the home, would have yielded results for the race, as a race, at all comparable to those which are flowing and are to flow from the Cooper Institute from generation to generation. Let the advocate of violent or radical change ponder well this thought.

We might even go so far as to take another instance, that of Mr. Tilden's bequest of five millions of dollars for a free library in the city of New York; but in referring to this one cannot help saying involuntarily, How much better if Mr. Tilden had devoted the last years of his own life to the proper administration of this immense sum; in which case neither legal contest nor any other cause of delay could have interfered with his aims. But let us assume that Mr. Tilden's millions finally become the means of giving to this city a noble public library, where the treasures of the world contained in books will be open to all forever, without money and without price. Considering the good of that part of the race which congregates in and around Manhattan Island, would its permanent benefit have been better promoted had these millions been allowed to circulate in small sums through the hands of the masses? Even the most strenuous advocate of Communism must entertain a doubt upon this subject. Most of those who think will probably entertain no doubt whatever.

Poor and restricted are our opportunities in this life; narrow our horizon; our best work most imperfect; but rich men should be thankful for one inestimable boon. They have it in their power during their lives to busy themselves in organizing benefactions from which the masses of their fellows will derive lasting advantage, and thus dignify their own lives. The highest life is probably to be reached, not by such imitation of the life of Christ as Count Tolstoi gives us, but, while animated by Christ's spirit, by recognizing the changed conditions of this age, and adopting modes of expressing this spirit suitable to the changed conditions under which we live; still laboring for the good of our fellows, which was the essence of his life and teaching, but laboring in a different manner.

This, then, is held to be the duty of the man of Wealth: First, to set an example of modest, unostentatious living, shunning display or extravagance; to provide moderately for the legitimate wants of those dependent upon him; and after doing so to consider all surplus revenues which come to him simply as trust funds, which he is called upon to administer, and strictly bound as a matter of duty to administer in the manner which, in his judgment, is best calculated to produce the most beneficial results for the community—the man of wealth thus becoming the mere agent and trustee for his poorer brethren, bringing to their service his superior wisdom, experience, and ability to administer, doing for them better than they would or could do for themselves.

We are met here with the difficulty of determining what are moderate sums to leave to members of the family; what is modest, unostentatious living; what is the test of extravagance. There must be different standards for different conditions. The answer is that it is as impossible to name exact amounts or actions as it is to define good manners, good taste, or the rules of propriety; but, nevertheless, these are verities, well known although undefinable. Public sentiment is quick to know and to feel what offends these. So in the case of wealth. The rule in regard to good taste in the dress of men or women applies here. Whatever makes one conspicuous offends the canon. If any family be chiefly known for display, for extravagance in home, table, equipage, for enormous sums ostentatiously spent in any form upon itself—if these be its chief distinctions, we have no difficulty in estimating its nature or culture. So likewise in regard to the use or abuse of its surplus wealth, or to generous, free-handed cooperation in good public uses, or to unabated efforts to accumulate and hoard to the last, whether they administer or bequeath. The verdict rests with the best and most enlightened public sentiment. The community will surely judge, and its judgments will not often be wrong.

The best uses to which surplus wealth can be put have already been indicated. Those who would administer wisely must, indeed, be wise, for one of the serious obstacles to the improvement of our race is indiscriminate charity. It were better for mankind that the millions of the rich were thrown into the sea than so spent as to encourage the slothful, the drunken, the unworthy. Of every thousand dollars spent in so called charity to-day, it is probable that $950 is unwisely spent; so spent, indeed, as to produce the very evils which it proposes to mitigate or cure. A well-known writer of philosophic books admitted the other day that he had given a quarter of a dollar to a man who approached him as he was coming to visit the house of his

friend. He knew nothing of the habits of this beggar, knew not the use that would be made of this money, although he had every reason to suspect that it would be spent improperly. This man professed to be a disciple of Herbert Spencer; yet the quarter-dollar given that night will probably work more injury than all the money which its thoughtless donor will ever be able to give in true charity will do good. He only gratified his own feelings, saved himself from annoyance—and this was probably one of the most selfish and very worst actions of his life, for in all respects he is most worthy.

In bestowing charity, the main consideration should be to help those who will help themselves; to provide part of the means by which those who desire to improve may do so; to give those who desire to rise the aids by which they may rise; to assist, but rarely or never to do all. Neither the individual nor the race is improved by alms-giving. Those worthy of assistance, except in rare cases, seldom require assistance; the really valuable men of the race never do, except in cases of accident or sudden change. Every one has, of course, cases of individuals brought to his own knowledge where temporary assistance can do genuine good, and these he will not overlook. But the amount which can be wisely given by the individual for individuals is necessarily limited by his lack of knowledge of the circumstances connected with each. He is the only true reformer who is as careful and as anxious not to aid the unworthy as he is to aid the worthy, and, perhaps, even more so, for in alms-giving more injury is probably done by rewarding vice than by relieving virtue.

The rich man is thus almost restricted to following the examples of Peter Cooper, Enoch Pratt of Baltimore, Mr. Pratt of Brooklyn, Senator Stanford, and others, who know that the best means of benefiting the community is to place within its reach the ladders upon which the aspiring can rise—parks, and means of recreation, by which men are helped in body and mind; works of art, certain to give pleasure and improve the public taste, and public institutions of various kinds, which will improve the general condition of the people—in this manner returning their surplus wealth to the mass of their fellows in the forms best calculated to do them lasting good.

Thus is the problem of Rich and Poor to be solved. The laws of accumulation will be left free; the laws of distribution free. Individualism will continue, but the millionaire will be but a trustee for the poor; intrusted for a season with a great part of the increased wealth of the community, but administering it for the community far better than it could or would have done for itself. The best minds will thus have reached a stage in the development of the race in which it is clearly seen that there is no mode of disposing of surplus wealth creditable to thoughtful and earnest men into whose hands it flows save by using it year by year for the general good. This day already dawns. But a little while, and although, without incurring the pity of their fellows, men may die sharers in great business enterprises from which their capital cannot be or has not been withdrawn, and is left chiefly at death for public uses; yet the man who dies leaving behind him millions of available wealth, which was his to administer during life, will pass away "unwept, unhonored, and unsung," no matter to what uses he leaves the dross which he cannot take with him. Of such as these the public verdict will then be: "The man who dies thus rich dies disgraced."

Such, in my opinion, is the true Gospel concerning Wealth, obedience to which is destined some day to solve the problem of the Rich and the Poor, and to bring "Peace on earth, among men Good-Will."

Source:

John Scott, ed., *Living Documents in American History*, New York: Washington Square Press, 1964–68.

Wilson-Gorman Tariff Act, 1894

Federal legislation passed on August 27, 1894. It succeeded the protectionist McKinley Tariff introduced by Republican congressman William McKinley and passed by Congress in 1890. With the fostering of American industry as its goal, the McKinley act established the highest tariff for dutiable imports in U.S. history up to that point, with rates averaging 49 percent; it effectively barred some foreign-made goods from the United States. In the interest of American farmers, tariffs were raised on wheat, corn, potatoes, and eggs. When prices rose faster than wages as a result of the tariff, the Republicans lost popular support and were defeated in the next elections.

Representative W. L. Wilson first drafted what became the 1894 tariff that lowered protective duties on manufactured goods. Although the original bill placed basic raw materials—wool, iron ore, lumber, and sugar—on the free list, the Senate, led by A. P. Gorman, amended the bill drastically, removing many raw materials from the free list and making the average protective tariff rate 40 percent. President Grover Cleveland denounced the bill for its protectionism but allowed it to become law without his signature. To make up for lost revenue, the act taxed certain luxuries and incomes over $4,000. The Supreme Court in *Pollock v. Farmers' Loan and Trust Company* (157 U.S. 429) found the tax unconstitutional the following year. This finding led in 1919 to the Sixteenth Amendment, permitting a federal income tax.

The excerpts here give examples of goods that have tariffs, those exempt, and some sections concerning the income tax.

An Act

To reduce taxation, to provide revenue or the Government, and for other purposes.

Be it enacted by the Senate and House of Representatives of the United States of America in Congress assembled, That on and after the first day of August, eighteen hundred and ninety-four, unless otherwise specially provided for in this Act, there shall be levied, collected, and paid upon all articles imported from foreign countries or withdrawn for consumption, and mentioned in the schedules herein contained, the rates of duty which are, by the schedules and paragraphs, respectively prescribed, namely:

Schedule A—Chemicals, Oils, and Paints.

❖　❖　❖

Coal-tar preparations—

❖　❖　❖

16. Coloring for brandy, wine, beer, or other liquors, fifty per centum ad valorem.

❖　❖　❖

Oils.—

❖　❖　❖

35. Opium, aqueous extract of, for medicinal uses, and tincture of, as laudanum, and all other liquid preparations of opium, not specially provided for in this Act, twenty per centum ad valorem.

36. Opium containing less than nine per centum of morphia, and opium prepared for smoking, six dollars per pound; but opium prepared for smoking and other preparations of opium deposited in bonded warehouse shall not be removed therefrom without payment of duties, and such duties shall not be refunded.

Paints, colors, and varnishes.—

❖　❖　❖

40. Black, made from bone, ivory, or vegetable, under whatever name known, including bone black and lampblack, dry or ground in oil or water, twenty per centum ad valorem.

❖　❖　❖

Lead Products.—

❖　❖　❖

Soda.—

64. Bicarbonate of soda or supercarbonate of soda or saleratus, one-half cent per pound.

❉   ❉   ❉

Schedule B.—Earths, Earthenware, and Glassware.

❉   ❉   ❉

Schedule C.—Metals and Manufactures of.
    Iron and Steel.

❉   ❉   ❉

Manufactures of Iron and Steel.

❉   ❉   ❉

Cutlery:

❉   ❉   ❉

Firearms:

❉   ❉   ❉

Miscellaneous Metals and Manufactures of.

❉   ❉   ❉

Gold and Silver:

❉   ❉   ❉

Lead:

❉   ❉   ❉

Watches:

❉   ❉   ❉

Zinc or Spelter:

❉   ❉   ❉

Schedule D.—Wood and Manufactures of.

❉   ❉   ❉

Schedule E.—Sugar.

❉   ❉   ❉

183. Sugar candy and all confectionery, made wholly or in part of sugar, and on sugars after being refined, when tinctured, colored, or in any way adulterated, thirty-five per centum ad valorem; glucose, or grape sugar, fifteen per centum ad valorem; saccharine, twenty-five per centum ad valorem.
    Schedule F.—Tobacco . . .

❉   ❉   ❉

188. Cigars, cigarettes, and cheroots of all kinds, four dollars per pound and twenty-five per centum ad valorem; and paper cigars and cigarettes, including wrappers, shall be subject to the same duties as are herein imposed upon cigars.
    Schedule G.—Agricultural Products and Provisions.
    Animals Live:
189. All live animals, not specially provided for in this Act, twenty per centum ad valorem.
    Breadstuffs and Farinaceous Substances:

❉   ❉   ❉

Dairy Products:

❉   ❉   ❉

Farm and Field Products:

❉   ❉   ❉

Fish

❉   ❉   ❉

Nuts.—

❉   ❉   ❉

224. Cocoanuts in the shell, and other nuts shelled or unshelled, not specially provided for in this Act, twenty per centum ad valorem.
    Meat Products:
224 1/2. Fresh beef, mutton, and pork, twenty per centum ad valorem.

❉   ❉   ❉

Miscellaneous Products:
235. Spices, ground or powdered, not specially provided for in this Act, three cents per pound; capsicum or red pepper, two and one-half cents per pound, unground; sage, one cent per pound.

❉   ❉   ❉

Schedule H.—Spirits, Wines, and other Beverages.
    Spirits:
237. Brandy and other spirits manufactured or distilled from grain or other materials, and not specially provided for in this Act, one dollar and eighty cents per proof gallon.

❉   ❉   ❉

Wines:

❉   ❉   ❉

248. Ginger ale or ginger beer, twenty per centum ad valorem, but no separate or additional duty shall be assessed on the bottles.
249. All imitations of natural mineral waters, and all artificial mineral waters, twenty per centum ad valorem.
    Schedule I.—Cotton Manufactures.

❊   ❊   ❊

251. Spool thread of cotton, containing on each spool not exceeding one hundred yards of thread, five and one-half . . .

Schedule J.—Flax, Hemp, and Jute, and Manufactures of.
    Schedule K—Wool and Manufactures of Wool.

❊   ❊   ❊

Schedule L.—Silks and Silk Goods.
    Schedule M.—Pulp, Papers, and Books.
    Pulp and Paper:

❊   ❊   ❊

Explosive Substances:

❊   ❊   ❊

331. Gun wads of all descriptions, ten per centum ad valorem.

332. Hair, human, if clean or drawn but not manufactured, twenty per centum ad valorem.

❊   ❊   ❊

Jewelry and Precious Stones:

❊   ❊   ❊

Leather, and manufactures of:

❊   ❊   ❊

Free List
    Sec. 2. On and after the first day of August, eighteen hundred and ninety-four, unless otherwise provided for in this Act, the following articles, when imported, shall be exempt from duty: [An alphabetical list follows.]
    363. Acids used for medicinal, chemical, or manufacturing purposes, not especially provided for in this Act.

❊   ❊   ❊

690. Zaffer. [impure cobalt oxide]
    Sec. 3. That there shall be levied, collected, and paid on the importation of all raw or unmanufactured articles, not enumerated or provided for in this Act, a duty of ten per centum ad valorem; and on all articles manufactured, in whole or in part, not provided for in this Act, a duty of twenty per centum ad valorem.
    Sec. 4. That each and every imported article, not enumerated in this Act, which is similar, either in material, quality, texture, or the use to which it may be applied, to any article enumerated in this Act as chargeable with duty shall pay the same rate of duty which is levied on the enumerated article which it most resembles in any of the particulars before mentioned. . . .

❊   ❊   ❊

A careful account shall be kept by the collector of all merchandise delivered by him to any bonded manufacturing warehouse, and a sworn monthly return, verified by the customs officers in charge, shall be made by the manufacturers containing a detailed statement of all imported merchandise used by him in the manufacture of exported articles.

❊   ❊   ❊

Sec. 10. That all persons are prohibited from importing into the United States from any foreign country any obscene book, pamphlet, paper, writing, advertisement, circular, print, picture, drawing, or other representation, figure, or image on or of paper or other material, or any cast, instrument, or other article of an immoral nature, or any drug or medicine, or any article whatever for the prevention of conception or for causing unlawful abortion, or any lottery ticket or any advertisement of any lottery. No such articles, whether imported separately or contained in packages with other goods entitled to entry, shall be admitted to entry; and all such articles shall be proceeded against, seized, and forfeited by due course of law. All such prohibited articles and the package in which they are contained in the course of importation shall be detained by the officer of customs, and proceedings taken against the same as hereinafter prescribed, unless it appears to the satisfaction of the collector of customs that the obscene articles contained in the package were inclosed therein without the knowledge or consent of the importer, owner, agent, or consignee: Provided, That the drugs hereinbefore mentioned, when imported in bulk and not put up for any of the purposes hereinbefore specified, are excepted from the operation of this section.
    Sec. 11. That whoever, being an officer, agent, or employee of the Government of the United States, shall knowingly aid or abet any person engaged in any violation of any of the provisions of law prohibiting importing, advertising, dealing in, exhibiting, or sending or receiving by mail obscene or indecent publications or representations, or means for preventing conception or procuring abortion, or other articles of indecent or immoral use or tendency, shall be deemed guilty of a misdemeanor, and shall for every offense be punishable by a fine of not more than five thousand dollars, or by imprisonment at hard labor for not more than ten years, or both.

❊   ❊   ❊

Sec. 29. That it shall be the duty of all persons of lawful age having an income of more than three thousand five hundred dollars for the taxable year, computed on the basis herein prescribed, to make and render a list or return, on or before the day provided by law, in such form and manner as may be directed by the Commissioner of Internal Revenue, with the approval of the Secretary of the Treasury, to the collector or a deputy collector of the district in which they reside, of the amount of their income, gains, and profits, as aforesaid; and all guardians and trustees, executors, administrators, agents, receivers, and all persons or corporations acting in any fiduciary capacity, shall make and render a list or return, as aforesaid, to the collector or a deputy collector of the district in which such person or corporation acting in a fiduciary capacity resides or does business, of the amount of income, gains, and profits of any minor or person for whom they act, but persons having less than three thousand five hundred dollars income are not required to make such report; and the collector or deputy collector, shall require every list or return to be verified by the oath or affirmation of the party rendering it, and may increase the amount of any list or return if he has reason to believe that the same is understated; and in case any such person having a taxable income shall neglect or refuse to make and render such list and return, or shall render a willfully false or fraudulent list or return, it shall be the duty of the collector or deputy collector, to make such list, according to the best information he can obtain, by the examination of such person, or any other evidence, and to add fifty per centum as a penalty to the amount of the tax due on such list in all cases of willful neglect or refusal to make and render a list or return; and in all cases of a willfully false or fraudulent list or return having been rendered to add one hundred per centum as a penalty to the amount of tax ascertained to be due, the tax and the additions thereto as a penalty to be assessed and collected in the manner provided for in other cases of willful neglect or refusal to render a list or return, or of rendering a false or fraudulent return: Provided, That any person, or corporation in his, her, or its own behalf, or as such fiduciary, shall be permitted to declare, under oath or affirmation, the form and manner of which shall be prescribed by the Commissioner of Internal Revenue, with the approval of the Secretary of the Treasury, that he, or she, or his or her, or its ward or beneficiary, was not possessed of an income of four thousand dollars, liable to be assessed according to the provisions of this Act; or may declare that he, she, or it, or his, her, or its ward or beneficiary has been assessed and has paid an income tax elsewhere in the same year, under authority of the United States, upon all his, her, or its income, gains, or profits, and upon all the income, gains, or profits for which he, she, or it is liable as such fiduciary, as prescribed by law; and if the collector or deputy collector shall be satisfied of the truth of the declaration, such

person or corporation shall thereupon be exempt from income tax in the said district for that year; or if the list or return of any person or corporation, company, or association shall have been increased by the collector or deputy collector, such person or corporation, company, or association may be permitted to prove the amount of income liable to be assessed; but such proof shall not be considered as conclusive of the facts, and no deductions claimed in such cases shall be made or allowed until approved by the collector or deputy collector. . . .

* * *

Sec. 32. That there shall be assessed, levied, and collected, except as herein otherwise provided, a tax of two per centum annually on the net profits or income above actual operating and business expenses, including expenses for materials purchased for manufacture or bought for resale, losses, and interest on bonded and other indebtedness of all banks, banking institutions, trust companies, saving institutions, fire, marine, life, and other insurance companies, railroad, canal, turnpike, canal navigation, slack water, telephone, telegraph, express, electric light, gas, water, street railway companies, and all other corporations, companies, or associations doing business for profit in the United States, no matter how created and organized, but not including partnerships.

* * *

The net profits or income of all corporations, companies, or associations shall include the amounts paid to shareholders, or carried to the account of any fund, or used for construction, enlargement of plant, or any other expenditure or investment paid from the net annual profits made or acquired by said corporations, companies, or associations.

* * *

That nothing herein contained shall apply to States, counties, or municipalities; nor to corporations, companies, or associations organized and conducted solely for charitable, religious, or educational purposes. . . .

Nor to any insurance company or association which conducts all its business solely upon the mutual plan, and only for the benefit of its policy holders or members, and having no capital stock and no stock or shareholders, and holding all its property in trust and in reserve for its policy holders or members; nor to that part of the business of any insurance company having a capital stock and stock and shareholders, which is conducted on the mutual plan, separate from its stock plan of insurance, and solely for the benefit of the policy holders and members insured on said mutual plan, and holding all the property belonging to and derived from said mutual part of its business in trust and reserve for the benefit of its policy holders and members insured on said mutual plan.

That all State, county, municipal, and town taxes paid by corporations, companies, or associations, shall be included in the operating and business expenses of such corporations, companies, or associations.

Sec. 33. That there shall be levied, collected, and paid on all salaries of officers, or payments for services to persons in the civil, military, naval, or other employment or service of the United States, including Senators and Representatives and Delegates in Congress, when exceeding the rate of four thousand dollars per annum, a tax of two per centum on the excess above the said four thousand dollars

❖   ❖   ❖

[The next sections concern stamp taxes on playing cards, tobacco, and liquor.]

❖   ❖   ❖

Sec. 73. That every combination, conspiracy, trust, agreement, or contract is hereby declared to be contrary to public policy, illegal, and void, when the same is made by or between two or more persons or corporations either or whom is engaged in importing any article from any foreign country into the United States, and when such combination, conspiracy, trust, agreement, or contract is intended to operate in restraint of lawful trade, or free competition in lawful trade or commerce, or to increase the market price in any part of the United States of any article or articles imported or intended to be imported into the United States, or of any manufacture into which such imported article enters or is intended to enter. Every person who is or shall hereafter be engaged in the importation of goods or any commodity from any foreign country in violation of this Section of this Act, or who shall combine or conspire with another to violate the same, is guilty of a misdemeanor, and, on conviction thereof in any court of the United States, such person shall be fined in a sum not less than one hundred dollars and not exceeding five thousand dollars, and shall be further punished by imprisonment, in the discretion of the court, for a term not less than three months nor exceeding twelve months.

❖   ❖   ❖

Received by the President, August 15, 1894.

Source:
Statutes at Large, Vol. 28, pp. 509–570.

United States v. E. C. Knight Company (156 U.S. 1), 1895

Also known as the Sugar Trust Case, this was the first U.S. Supreme Court interpretation of the Sherman Antitrust Act, issued on January 21, 1895, and a serious setback to its enforcement. E. C. Knight, a holding company that controlled the American Sugar Refining Company, had purchased competing sugar refineries, securing a near monopoly on the manufacture of refined sugar in the United States. The government charged that the purchases were a combination in restraint of trade. In its 8-to-1 decision against the government, the Supreme Court ruled that the Sherman Antitrust Act applied only to interstate commerce, narrowly defined, not to intrastate manufacturing, even of articles made for export to another state. On December 4, 1899, the U.S. Supreme Court, based on the Sherman Antitrust Act, enjoined six producers of cast-iron pipe from maintaining an agreement to eliminate competition among themselves. In its unanimous decision in *Addyston Pipe and Steel Company v. United States* (175 U.S. 211), the Court ruled that the companies, in establishing a market-allocation scheme, had conspired to interfere with the flow of interstate commerce, to limit competition, and to fix prices. That decision strengthened the effectiveness of the Sherman Antitrust Act.

———————— ⌒∞⌒ ————————

Mr. Chief Justice Fuller . . . delivered the opinion of the court.

By the purchase of the stock of the four Philadelphia refineries with shares of its own stock the American Sugar Refining Company acquired nearly complete control of the manufacture of refined sugar within the United States. The bill charged that the contracts under which these purchases were made constituted combinations in restraint of trade, and that in entering into them the defendants combined and conspired to restrain the trade and commerce in refined sugar among the several states and with foreign nations, contrary to the act of congress of July 2, 1890.

The relief sought was the cancellation of the agreements under which the stock was transferred, the redelivery of the stock to the parties respectively, and an injunction against the further performance of the agreements and further violations of the act. As usual, there was a prayer for general relief, but only such relief could be afforded under that prayer as would be agreeable to the case made by the bill and consistent with that specifically prayed. And as to the injunction asked, that relief was ancillary to and in aid of the primary equity, or ground of suit, and, if that failed, would fall with it. That ground here was the existence of contracts to monopolize interstate or international trade or commerce, and to restrain such trade or commerce which, by the provisions of the act, could be rescinded, or operations thereunder arrested.

In commenting upon the statute (21 Jac. 1. c. 3), at the commencement of chapter 85 of the third institute, entitled "Against Monopolists. Propounders, and Projectors," Lord Coke, in language often quoted, said:

* * *

"A monopoly is an institution, or allowance by the king by his grant, commission, or otherwise to any person or persons, bodies politique, or corporate, of or for the sole buying, selling, making, working, or using of anything, whereby any person or persons, bodies politique, or corporate, are sought to be restrained of any freedom or liberty that they had before, or hindred in their lawfull trade. . . ."

Counsel contend that this definition, as explained by the derivation of the word, may be applied to all cases in which "one person sells alone the whole of any kind of marketable thing, so that only he can continue to sell it, fixing the price at his own pleasure," whether by virtue of legislative grant or agreement; that the monopolization referred to in the act of congress is not confined to the common-law sense of the terms as implying an exclusive control, by authority, of one branch of industry without legal right of any other person to interfere therewith by competition or otherwise, but that it . . . covers controlling the market by contracts securing the advantage of selling alone or exclusively all, or some considerable portion, of a particular kind of merchandise or commodity to the detriment of the public; and that such contracts amount to that restraint of trade or commerce declared to be illegal. But the monopoly and restraint denounced by the act are the monopoly and restraint of interstate and international trade or commerce, while the conclusion to be assumed on this record is that the result of the transaction complained of was the creation of a monopoly in the manufacture of a necessary of life.

In the view which we take of the case, we need not discuss whether, because the tentacles which drew the outlying refineries into the dominant corporation were separately put out, therefore there was no combination to monopolize; or because, according to political economists, aggregations of capital may reduce prices, therefore the objection to concentration of power is relieved; or, because others were theoretically left free to go into the business of refining sugar, and the original stockholders of the Philadelphia refineries, after becoming stockholders of the American Company, might go into competition with themselves, or, parting with that stock, might set up again for themselves, therefore no objectionable restraint was imposed.

The fundamental question is whether, conceding that the existence of a monopoly in manufacture is established by the evidence, that monopoly can be directly suppressed under the act of congress in the mode attempted by this bill.

It cannot be denied that the power of a state to protect the lives, health, and property of its citizens, and to preserve good order and the public morals, "the power to govern men and things within the limits of its dominion," is a power originally and always belonging to the states, not surrendered by them to the general government, nor directly restrained by the constitution of the United States, and essentially exclusive. The relief of the citizens of each state from the burden of monopoly and the evils resulting from the restraint of trade among such citizens was left with the states to deal with, and this court has recognized their possession of that power even to the extent of holding that an employment or business carried on by private individuals, when it becomes a matter of such public interest and importance as to create a common charge or burden upon the citizen—in other words, when it becomes a practical monopoly, to which the citizen is compelled to resort, and by means of which a tribute can be exacted from the community—is subject to regulation by state legislative power. On the other hand, the power of congress to regulate commerce among the several states is also exclusive. The constitution does not provide that interstate commerce shall be free, but, by the grant of this exclusive power to regulate it, it was left free, except as congress might impose restraints. Therefore it has been determined that the failure of congress to exercise this exclusive power in any case is an expression of its will that the subject shall be free from restrictions or impositions upon it by the several states, and if a law passed by a state in the exercise of its acknowledged powers comes into conflict with that will, the congress and the state cannot occupy the position of equal opposing sovereignties, because the constitution declares its supremacy, and that of the laws passed in pursuance thereof; and that which is not supreme must yield to that which is supreme. "Commerce undoubtedly is traffic," said Chief Justice Marshall, "but it is something more; it is intercourse. It describes the commercial intercourse between nations and parts of nations in all its branches, and is regulated by prescribing rules for carrying on that intercourse." That which belongs to commerce is within the jurisdiction of the United States, but that which does not belong to commerce is within the jurisdiction of the police power of the state. . . .

The argument is that the power to control the manufacture of refined sugar is a monopoly over a necessary of life, to the enjoyment of which by a large part of the population of the United States interstate commerce is indispensable, and that, therefore, the general government, in the exercise of the power to regulate commerce, may repress such monopoly directly, and set aside the instruments which have created it. . . . The power to regulate commerce is the power to prescribe the rule by which commerce shall be governed, and is a power independent of the power to suppress monopoly. But it may operate in repression of monopoly whenever that comes within the rules by which commerce is governed, or whenever the transaction is itself a monopoly of commerce.

It is vital that the independence of the commercial power and of the police power, and the delimitation between them, however sometimes perplexing, should always be recognized and observed, for, while the one furnishes the strongest bond of union, the other is essential to the preservation of the autonomy of the states as required by our dual form of government; and acknowledged evils, however grave and urgent they may appear to be, had better be borne, than the risk be run, in the effort to suppress them, of more serious consequences by resort to expedients of even doubtful constitutionality.

It will be perceived how far-reaching the proposition is that the power of dealing with a monopoly directly may be exercised by the general government whenever interstate or international commerce may be ultimately affected. The regulation of commerce applies to the subjects of commerce, and not to matters of internal police. Contracts to buy, sell, or exchange goods to be transported among the several states, the transportation and its instrumentalities, and articles bought, sold, or exchanged for the purposes of such transit among the states, or put in the way of transit, may be regulated; but this is because they form part of interstate trade or commerce. The fact that an article is manufactured for export to another state does not of itself make it an article of interstate commerce, and the intent of the manufacturer does not determine the time when the article or product passes from the control of the state and belongs to commerce. . . .

❧   ❧   ❧

Contracts, combinations, or conspiracies to control domestic enterprise in manufacture, agriculture, mining, production in all its forms, or to raise or lower prices or wages, might unquestionably tend to restrain external as well as domestic trade, but the restraint would be an indirect result, however inevitable, and whatever its extent, and such result would not necessarily determine the object of the contract, combination, or conspiracy.

. . . Slight reflection will show that, if the national power extends to all contracts and combinations in manufacture, agriculture, mining, and other productive industries, whose ultimate result may affect external commerce, comparatively little of business operations and affairs would be left for state control.

It was in the light of well-settled principles that the act of July 2, 1890, was framed. Congress did not attempt thereby to assert the power to deal with monopoly directly as such; or to limit and restrict the rights of corporations created by the states or the citizens of the states in the acquisition, control, or disposition of property; or to regulate or prescribe the price or prices at which such property or the products thereof should be sold; or to make criminal the acts of persons in the acquisition and control of property which the states of their residence or creation sanctioned or permitted. Aside from the provisions applicable where congress might exercise municipal power, what the law struck at was combinations, contracts, and conspiracies to monopolize trade and commerce among the several states or with foreign nations; but the contracts and acts of the defendants related exclusively to the acquisition of the Philadelphia refineries and the business of sugar refining in Pennsylvania, and bore no direct relation to commerce between the states or with foreign nations. The object was manifestly private gain in the manufacture of the commodity, but not through the control of interstate or foreign commerce. It is true that the bill alleged that the products of these refineries were sold and distributed among the several states, and that all the companies were engaged in trade or commerce with the several states and with foreign nations; but this was no more than to say that trade and commerce served manufacture to fulfill its function. Sugar was refined for sale, and sales were probably made at Philadelphia for consumption, and undoubtedly for resale by the first purchasers throughout Pennsylvania and other states, and refined sugar was also forwarded by the companies to other states for sale. Nevertheless it does not follow that an attempt to monopolize, or the actual monopoly of, the manufacture was an attempt, whether executory or consummated, to monopolize commerce, even though, in order to dispose of the product, the instrumentality of commerce was necessarily invoked. There was nothing in the proofs to indicate any intention to put a restraint upon trade or commerce, and the fact, as we have seen, that trade or commerce might be indirectly affected, was not enough to entitle complainants to a decree. The subject-matter of the sale was shares of manufacturing stock, and the relief sought was the surrender of property which had already passed, and the suppression of the alleged monopoly in manufacture by the restoration of the status quo before the transfers; yet the act of congress only authorized the circuit courts to proceed by way of preventing and restraining violations of the act in respect of contracts, combinations, or conspiracies in restraint of interstate or international trade or commerce.

The circuit court declined, upon the pleadings and proofs, to grant the relief prayed, and dismissed the bill, and we are of opinion that the circuit court of appears did not err in affirming that decree.

Decree affirmed.

Source:
Supreme Court Reporter, Vol. 15, p. 249-266.

Growth of the West and Federal Indian Policy

Treaties of Medicine Lodge, 1867

Agreements of October 1867 concluded at Medicine Lodge Creek, Kansas, between the U.S. government and a confederacy of Kiowa, Cheyenne, Comanche, Arapaho, and Apache that ended long-standing hostilities over the encroachments of white settlers and displaced eastern tribes into the southwestern Indian Territory. Under the terms of the first treaty, the Kiowa and Comanche agreed to relinquish their claims to lands in the Texas Panhandle; they and the other Native American participants also agreed to move to new reservations in Oklahoma. The continued resistance of some Kiowa culminated in the Red River Indian conflict of 1874–75, which ended when U.S. troops defeated the Native American forces.

First Treaty of Medicine Lodge, 1867
ANDREW JOHNSON,
President of the United States of America,

To All and Singular to Whom These Presents Shall Come, Greeting:

Whereas a treaty was made and concluded at the Council Camp, on Medicine Lodge Creek, seventy miles south of Fort Larned, in the State of Kansas, on the twenty-first day of October, in the year of our Lord one thousand eight hundred sixty-seven, by and between N.G. Taylor, Brevet Major-General William S. Harney, Brevet Major-General C. C. Augur, Brevet Major-General Alfred H. Terry, John B. Sanborn, Samuel F. Tappan, and J. B. Henderson, commissioners, on the part of the United States, and Satanka, (Sitting Bear,) Sa-Tan-Ta, (White Bear,) Parry-Wah-Say-Men, (Ten Bears,) Tep-Pe-Navon, (Painted Lips,) Mah-Vip-Pah, (Wolf's Sleeve,) Kon-Zhon-Ta-Co, (Poor Bear,) and other chiefs and headmen of the Kiowa, Comanche, and Apache tribes of Indians, on the

part of said Indians, and duly authorized thereto by them, which treaty is in the words and figures following, to wit—

Articles of a treaty concluded at the Council Camp on Medicine Lodge Creek, seventy miles south of Forth Larned, in the State of Kansas, on the twenty-first day of October, eighteen hundred and sixty-seven, by and between the United States of America, represented by its commissioners duly appointed thereto, to wit: Nathaniel G. Taylor, William S. Harney, C. C. Augur, Alfred S. [H.] Terry, John B. Sanborn, Samuel F. Tappan, and J. B. Henderson, of the one part, and the Kiowa, Comanche, and Apache Indians, represented by their chiefs and headmen duly authorized and empowered to act for the body of the people of said tribes (the names of said chiefs and headmen being hereto subscribed) of the other part, witness.—

Whereas, on the twenty-first day of October, eighteen hundred and sixty-seven, a treaty of peace was made and entered into at the Council Camp, on Medicine Lodge Creek, seventy miles south of Fort Larned, in the State of Kansas, by and between the United States of America, by its commissioners Nathaniel G. Taylor, William S. Harney, C. C. Augur, Alfred H. Terry, John B. Sanborn, Samuel F. Tappan, and J. B. Henderson, of the one part, and the Kiowa and Comanche tribes of Indians, of the Upper Arkansas, by and through their chiefs and headmen whose names are subscribed thereto, of the other part, reference being had to said treaty; and whereas, since the making and signing of said treaty, at a council held at said camp on this day, the chiefs and headmen of the Apache nation or tribe of Indians express to the commissioners on the part of the United States, as aforesaid, a wish to be confederated with the said Kiowa and Comanche tribes, and to be placed, in every respect, upon an equal footing with said tribes; and whereas, at a council held at the same place and on the same day, with the chiefs and headmen of the said Kiowa and Comanche tribes, they consent to the confederation of said Apache tribe, as desired by it, upon the terms and conditions hereinafter set forth in this supplementary treaty: Now, therefore, it is hereby stipulated and agreed by and between the aforesaid commissioners, on the part of the United States, and the chiefs and headmen of the Kiowa and Comanche tribes, and, also, the chiefs and headmen of the said Apache tribe, as follows, to wit.—

Article I. The said Apache tribe of Indians agree to confederate and become incorporated with the said Kiowa and Comanche Indians, and to accept as their permanent home the reservation described in the aforesaid treaty with said Kiowa and Comanche tribes, concluded as aforesaid at this place, and they pledge themselves to make no permanent settlement at any place, nor on any lands, outside of said reservation.

Article II. The Kiowa and Comanche tribes, on their part, agree that all the benefits and advantages arising from the employment of physicians, teachers, carpenters, millers, engineers, farmers, and blacksmiths, agreed to be furnished under the provisions of their said treaty, together with all the advantages to be derived from the construction of agency buildings, warehouses, mills, and other structures, and also from the establishment of schools upon their said reservation, shall be jointly and equally shared and enjoyed by the said Apache Indians, as though they had been originally a part of said tribes; and they further agree that all other benefits arising from said treaty shall be jointly and equally shared as aforesaid.

Article III. The United States, on its part, agrees that clothing and other articles named in Article X. of said original treaty, together with all money or other annuities agreed to be furnished under any of the provisions of said treaty, to the Kiowas and Comanches, shall be shared equally by the Apaches. In all cases where specific articles of clothing are agreed to be furnished to the Kiowas and Comanches, similar articles shall be furnished to the Apaches, and a separate census of the Apaches shall be annually taken and returned by the agent, as provided for the other tribes. And the United States further agrees, in consideration of the incorporation of the said Apaches, to increase the annual appropriation of money, as provided for in Article X. of said treaty, from twenty-five thousand to thirty thousand dollars; and the latter amount shall be annually appropriated, for the period therein named, for the use and benefit of said three tribes, confederated as herein declared; and the clothing and other annuities, which may from time to time be furnished to the Apaches, shall be based upon the census of the three tribes, annually to be taken by the agent, and shall be separately marked, forwarded, and delivered to them at the agency house, to be built under the provisions of said original treaty.

Article IV. In consideration of the advantages conferred by this supplementary treaty upon the Apache tribe of Indians, they agree to observe and faithfully comply with all the stipulations and agreements entered into by the Kiowas and Comanches in said original treaty. They agree, in the same manner, to keep the peace toward the whites and all other persons under the jurisdiction of the United States, and to do and perform all other things enjoined upon said tribes by the provisions of said treaty; and they hereby give up and forever relinquish to the United States all rights, privileges, and grants now vested in them, or intended to be transferred to them, by the treaty between the United States and the Cheyenne and Arapahoe tribes of Indians, concluded at the camp on the Little Arkansas river, in the State of Kansas, on the fourteenth day of October, one thousand eight hundred and sixty-five, and also by the supplementary treaty, concluded at the same place on the seventeenth day of the same month, between the United States, of the one part, and the Cheyenne, Arapahoe, and Apache tribes, of the other part.

In testimony of all which, the said parties have hereunto set their hands and seals at the place and on the day hereinbefore stated.

Second Treaty of Medicine Lodge, 1867

ANDREW JOHNSON,
President of the United States of America,

To All and Singular to Whom These Presents Shall Come, Greeting:

Whereas a treaty was made and concluded at the Council Camp, on Medicine Lodge creek, seventy miles south of Fort Larned, in the State of Kansas, on the twenty-eighth day of October, in the year of our Lord one thousand eight hundred and sixty-seven, by and between N. G. Taylor, Brevet Major-General William S. Harney, Brevet Major-General C. C. Augur, Brevet Major-General Alfred H. Terry, John B. Sanborn, Samuel F. Tappan, and J. B. Henderson, commissioners, on the part of the United States, and O-to-ah-nac-co (Bull-Bear), Moke-tav-a-to (Black Kettle), Little Raven, Yellow Bear, and other chiefs and headmen of the Cheyenne and Arapahoe tribes of Indians, on the part of said Indians, and duly authorized thereto by them, which treaty is in the words and figures following, to wit.—

Articles of a treaty and agreement made and entered into at the Council Camp on Medicine Lodge creek, seventy miles south of Fort Larned, in the State of Kansas, on the twenty-eighth day of October, eighteen hundred and sixty-seven, by and between the United States of America, represented by its commissioners duly appointed thereto, to wit: Nathaniel G. Taylor, William S. Harney, C. C. Augur, Alfred H. Terry, John B. Sanborn, Samuel F. Tappan and John B. Henderson, of the one part, and the

Cheyenne and Arapahoe tribes of Indians, represented by their chiefs and headmen duly authorized and empowered to act for the body of the people of said tribes—the names of said chiefs and headmen being hereto subscribed—of the other part, witness:—

Article I. From this day forward all war between the parties to this agreement shall forever cease. The Government of the United States desires peace, and its honor is here pledged to keep it. The Indians desire peace, and they now pledge their honor to maintain it.

If bad men among the whites, or among other people subject to the authority of the United States, shall commit any wrong upon the person or property of the Indians, the United States will, upon proof made to the agent and forwarded to the Commissioner of Indian Affairs at Washington City, proceed at once to cause the offender to be arrested and punished according to the laws of the United States, and also reimburse the injured person for the loss sustained.

If bad men among the Indians shall commit a wrong or depredation upon the person or property of any one, white, black, or Indian, subject to the authority of the United States and at peace therewith, the tribes herein named solemnly agree that they will, on proof made to their agent, and notice by him, deliver up the wrongdoer to the United States, to be tried and punished according to its laws; and in case they wilfully refuse so to do, the person injured shall be reimbursed for his loss from the annuities or other moneys due or to become due to them under this or other treaties made with the United States. And the President, on advising with the Commissioner of Indian Affairs, shall prescribe such rules and regulations for ascertaining damages, under the provisions of this article, as in his judgment may be proper. But no such damages shall be adjusted and paid until thoroughly examined and passed upon by the Commissioner of Indian Affairs and the Secretary of the Interior; and no one sustaining loss, while violating, or because of his violating, the provisions of this treaty or the laws of the United States, shall be reimbursed therefor.

Article II. The United States agrees that the following district of country, to wit: commencing at the point where the Arkansas river crosses the 37th parallel of north latitude, thence west, on said parallel—the said line being the southern boundary of the State of Kansas—to the Cimarone river (sometimes called the Red Fork of the Arkansas river), thence down said Cimarone river, in the middle of the main channel thereof, to the Arkansas river; thence up the Arkansas river, in the middle of the main channel thereof, to the place of beginning, shall be and the same is hereby set apart for the absolute and undisturbed use and occupation of the Indians herein named, and for such other friendly tribes or individual Indians, as from time to time they may be willing, with the consent of the United States, to admit among them; and the United States now solemnly agrees that no persons except those herein authorized so to do, and except such officers, agents and employees of the Government as may be authorized to enter upon Indian reservations in discharge of duties enjoined by law, shall ever be permitted to pass over, settle upon, or reside in the territory described in this article, or in such territory as may be added to this reservation for the use of said Indians.

Article III. If it should appear from actual survey or other examination of said tract of land, that it contains less than one hundred and sixty acres of tillable land for each person, who at the time may be authorized to reside on it, under the provisions of this treaty, and a very considerable number of such persons shall be disposed to commence cultivating the soil as farmers, the United States agrees to set apart for the use of said Indians as herein provided, such additional quantity of arable land adjoining to said reservation, or as near the same as it can be obtained, as may be required to provide the necessary amount.

Article IV. The United States agrees at its own proper expense to construct at some place near the centre of said reservation, where timber and water may be convenient, the following buildings, to wit: a warehouse or store-room for the use of the agent in storing goods belonging to the Indians, to cost not exceeding fifteen hundred dollars; an agency building for the residence of the agent, to cost not exceeding three thousand dollars; a residence for the physician, to cost not more than three thousand dollars; and five other buildings, for a carpenter, farmer, blacksmith, miller, and engineer, each to cost not exceeding two thousand dollars; also a school-house or mission building, so soon as a sufficient number of children can be induced by the agent to attend school, which shall not cost exceeding five thousand dollars. The United States agrees, further, to cause to be erected on said reservation, near the other buildings herein authorized, a good steam circular saw mill, with a grist mill and shingle machine attached; the same to cost not exceeding eight thousand dollars.

Article V. The United States agrees that the agents for said Indians in the future shall make his home at the agency building; that he shall reside among them, and keep an office open at all times for the purpose of prompt and diligent inquiry into such matters of complaint by and against the Indians as may be presented for investigation, under the provisions of their treaty stipulations, as also for the faithful discharge of other duties enjoined on him by law. In all cases of depredation on person or property, he shall cause the evidence to be taken in writing and forwarded, together with his finding, to the Commissioner of

Indian Affairs, whose decision, subject to the revision of the Secretary of the Interior, shall be binding on the parties to this treaty.

Article VI. If any individual, belonging to said tribes of Indians, or legally incorporated with them, being the head of a family, shall desire to commence farming, he shall have the privilege to select, in the presence and with the assistance of the agent then in charge, a tract of land within said reservation not exceeding three hundred and twenty acres in extent, which tract when so selected, certified, and recorded in the land-book as herein directed, shall cease to be held in common, but the same may be occupied and held in the exclusive possession of the person selecting it, and of his family, so long as he or they may continue to cultivate it. Any person over eighteen years of age, not being the head of a family, may in like manner select and cause to be certified to him, or her, for purposes of cultivation, a quantity of land not exceeding eighty acres in extent, and thereupon be entitled to the exclusive possession of the same as above directed.

For each tract of land so selected, a certificate containing a description thereof, and the name of the person selecting it, with a certificate endorsed thereon, that the same has been recorded, shall be delivered to the party entitled to it by the agent, after the same shall have been recorded by him in a book to be kept in his office, subject to inspection, which said book shall be known as the "Cheyenne and Arapahoe Land Book." The President may at any time order a survey of the reservation, and, when so surveyed, Congress shall provide for protecting the rights of settlers in their improvements, and may fix the character of the title held by each.

The United States may pass such laws on the subject of alienation and descent of property, and on all subjects connected with the government of the Indians on said reservations, and the internal police thereof as may be thought proper.

Article VII. In order to insure the civilization of the tribes entering into this treaty, the necessity of education is admitted, especially by such of them as are or may be settled on said agricultural reservation, and they therefore pledge themselves to compel their children, male and female, between the ages of six and sixteen years, to attend school; and it is hereby made the duty of the agent for said Indians to see that this stipulation is strictly complied with; and the United States agrees that for every thirty children between said ages, who can be induced or compelled to attend school, a house shall be provided, and a teacher competent to teach the elementary branches of an English education shall be furnished, who will reside among said Indians, and faithfully discharge his or her duties as a teacher. The provisions of this article to continue for not less than twenty years.

Article VIII. When the head of a family or lodge shall have selected lands and received his certificate as above directed, and the agent shall be satisfied that he intends in good faith to commence cultivating the soil for a living, he shall be entitled to receive seeds and agricultural implements for the first year, not exceeding in value one hundred dollars; and for each succeeding year he shall continue to farm for a period of three years more, he shall be entitled to receive seeds and implements as aforesaid, not exceeding in value twenty-five dollars.

And it is further stipulated that such persons as commence farming shall receive instruction from the farmer herein provided for; and whenever more than on hundred persons shall enter upon the cultivation of the soil, a second blacksmith shall be provided, with such iron, steel, and other material as may be needed.

Article IX. At any time after ten years from the making of this treaty the United States shall have the privilege of withdrawing the physician, farmer, blacksmith, carpenter, engineer, and miller, herein provided for, but in case of such withdrawal, an additional sum, thereafter, of ten thousand dollars per annum shall be devoted to the education of said Indians, and the Commissioner of Indian Affairs shall upon careful inquiry into their condition make such rules and regulations for the expenditure of said sum as will best promote the educational and moral improvement of said tribes.

Article X. In lieu of all sums of money or other annuities provided to be paid to the Indians herein named, under the treaty of October fourteenth, eighteen hundred and sixty-five, made at the mouth of the Little Arkansas, and under all treaties made previous thereto, the United States agrees to deliver at the agency house on the reservation herein named, on the fifteenth day of October, of each year, for thirty years, the following articles, to wit.—

For each male person over fourteen years of age, a suit of good, substantial woolen clothing, consisting of coat, pantaloons, flannel shirt, hat, and a pair of home-made socks.

For each female over twelve years of age, a flannel skirt, or the goods necessary to make it, a pair of woolen hose, twelve yards of calico and twelve yards of cotton domestics.

For the boys and girls under the ages named, such flannel and cotton goods as may be needed to make each a suit as aforesaid, together with a pair of woolen hose for each.

And in order that the Commissioner of Indian Affairs may be able to estimate properly for the articles herein named, it shall be the duty of the agent each year to forward to him a full and exact census of the Indians on which the estimate from year to year can be based.

And, in addition to the clothing herein named, the sum of twenty thousand dollars shall be annually appropriated for a period of thirty years, to be used by the Secretary of the Interior in the purchase of such articles as, from time to time, the condition and necessities of the Indians may indicate to be proper. And if at any time, within the thirty years, it shall appear that the amount of money needed for clothing, under this article, can be appropriated to better uses for the tribe herein named, Congress may, by law, change the appropriation to other purposes; but, in no event, shall the amount of this appropriation be withdrawn or discontinued for the period named. And the President shall, annually, detail an officer of the army to be present, and attest the delivery of all the goods herein named to the Indians, and he shall inspect and report on the quantity and quality of the goods and the manner of their delivery.

Article XI. In consideration of the advantages and benefits conferred by this treaty, and the many pledges of friendship by the United States, the tribes who are parties to this agreement hereby stipulate that they will relinquish all right to occupy permanently the territory outside of their reservation as herein defined, but they yet reserve the right to hunt on any lands south of the Arkansas so long as the buffalo may range thereon in such numbers as to justify the chase; and no white settlements shall be permitted on any part of the lands contained in the old reservation as defined by the treaty made between the United States and the Cheyenne, Arapahoe, and Apache tribes of Indians, at the mouth of the Little Arkansas, under date of October fourteenth, eighteen hundred and sixty-five, within three years from this date, and they, the said tribes, further expressly agree.—

1st. That they will withdraw all opposition to the construction of the railroad now being built on the Smoky Hill river, whether it be built to Colorado or New Mexico.

2d. That they will permit the peaceable construction of any railroad not passing over their reservation as herein defined.

3d. That they will not attack any persons at home or travelling, nor molest or disturb any wagon trains, coaches, mules, or cattle belonging to the people of the United States or to persons friendly therewith.

4th. They will never capture or carry off from the settlements white women or children.

5th. They will never kill or scalp white men, nor attempt to do them harm.

6th. They withdraw all pretence of opposition to the construction of the railroad now being built along the Platte river, and westward to the Pacific Ocean; and they will not in future object to the construction of railroads, wagon roads, mail stations, or other works of utility or necessity, which may be ordered or permitted by the laws of the United States. But should such roads or other works be constructed on the lands of their reservation, the government will pay the tribe whatever amount of damage may be assessed by three disinterested commissioners to be appointed by the President for that purpose, one of said commissioners to be a chief or headman of the tribe.

7th. They agree to withdraw all opposition to the military posts or roads now established, or that may be established, not in violation of treaties heretofore made or hereafter to be made with any of the Indian tribes.

Article XII. No treaty for the cession of any portion or part of the reservation herein described, which may be held in common, shall be of any validity or force as against the said Indians unless executed and signed by at least three fourths of all the adult male Indians occupying or interested in the same; and no cession by the tribe shall be understood or construed in such manner as to deprive without his consent any individual member of the tribe of his rights to any tract of land selected by him as provided in Article VI. of this treaty.

Article XIII. The United States hereby agree to furnish annually to the Indians the physician, teachers, carpenter, miller, engineer, farmer, and blacksmiths, as herein contemplated, and that such appropriations shall be made from time to time, on the estimates of the Secretary of the Interior, as will be sufficient to employ such persons.

Article XIV. It is agreed that the sum of five hundred dollars, annually, for three years from date, shall be expended in presents to the ten persons of said tribe who, in the judgment of the agent, may grow the most valuable crops for the respective year.

Article XV. The tribes herein named agree that when the agency-house and other buildings, shall be constructed on the reservation named, they will regard and make said reservation their permanent home, and they will make no permanent settlement elsewhere, but they shall have the right, subject to the conditions and modifications of this treaty, to hunt on the lands south of the Arkansas river, formerly called theirs, in the same manner as agreed on by the treaty of the "Little Arkansas," concluded the fourteenth day of October, eighteen hundred and sixty-five.

In testimony of which, we have hereunto set our hands and seals, on the day and year aforesaid.

Source:
Statutes at Large, Vol. 15, pp. 589–599.

Treaty of Fort Laramie, 1868

Agreement whereby the United States government agreed to halt its efforts to build a road to Bozeman, Montana, across Sioux hunting grounds in the Big Horn Mountains and guaranteed the Sioux exclusive possession of the land in South Dakota west of the Missouri River. The treaty ended a series of uprisings that had begun after the Treaties of Fort Laramie of 1851. After the discovery of gold in the Black Hills in the 1870s, the second treaty was largely ignored as thousands of prospectors invaded the Sioux Reservation.

——————————————— ⌘ ———————————————

ANDREW JOHNSON,
President of the United States of America,

To All and Singular to Whom These Presents Shall Come, Greeting:

Whereas a treaty was made and concluded at Fort Laramie, in the Territory of Dakota [now in the Territory of Wyoming], on the twenty-ninth day of April, and afterwards, in the year of our Lord one thousand eight hundred and sixty-eight, by and between Nathaniel G. Taylor, William T. Sherman, William S. Harney, John B. Sanborn, S. F. Tappan, C. C. Augur, and Alfred H. Terry, commissioners, on the part of the United States, and Ma-za-pon-kaska, Tah-shun-ka-co-qui-pah, Heh-won-ge-chat, Mah-to-non-pah, Little Chief, Makh-pi-ah-lu-tah, Cocam-i-ya-ya, Con-te-pe-ta, Ma-wa-tau-ni-hav-ska, He-na-pin-wa-ni-ca, Wah-pah-shaw, and other chiefs and headmen of different tribes of Sioux Indians, on the part of said Indians, and duly authorized, thereto by them, which treaty is in the words and figures following, to wit:

Articles of a treaty made and concluded by and between Lieutenant-General William T. Sherman, General William S. Harney, General Alfred H. Terry, General C. C. Augur, J. B. Henderson, Nathaniel G. Taylor, John B. Sanborn, and Samuel F. Tappan, duly appointed commissioners on the part of the United States, and the different bands of the Sioux Nation of Indians, by their chiefs and headmen, whose names are hereto subscribed, they being duly authorized to act in the premises.

Article I. From this day forward all war between the parties to this agreement shall forever cease. The government of the United States desires peace, and its honor is hereby pledged to keep it. The Indians desire peace, and they now pledge their honor to maintain it.

If bad men among the whites, or among other people subject to the authority of the United States, shall commit any wrong upon the person or property of the Indians, the United States will, upon proof made to the agent and forwarded to the Commissioner of Indian Affairs at Washington city, proceed at once to cause the offender to be arrested and punished according to the laws of the United States, and also reimburse the injured person for the loss sustained.

If bad men among the Indians shall commit a wrong or depredation upon the person or property of any one,

white, black, or Indian, subject to the authority of the United States, and at peace therewith, the Indians herein named solemnly agree that they will, upon proof made to their agent and notice by him, deliver up the wrong-doer to the United States, to be tried and punished according to its laws; and in case they wilfully refuse so to do, the person injured shall be reimbursed for his loss from the annuities or other moneys due or to become due to them under this or other treaties made with the United States. And the President, on advising with the Commissioner of Indian Affairs, shall prescribed such rules and regulations for ascertaining damages under the provisions of this article as in his judgment may be proper. But no one sustaining loss while violating the provisions of this treaty or the laws of the United States shall be reimbursed therefor.

Article II. The United States agrees that the following district of country, to wit, viz: commencing on the east bank of the Missouri river where the forty-sixth parallel of north latitude crosses the same, thence along low-water mark down said east bank to a point opposite where the northern line of the State of Nebraska strikes the river, thence west across said river, and along the northern line of Nebraska to the one hundred and fourth degree of longitude west from Greenwich, thence north on said meridian to a point where the forty-sixth parallel of north latitude intercepts the same, thence due east along said parallel to the place of beginning; and in addition thereto, all existing reservations on the east bank of said river shall be, and the same is, set apart for the absolute and undisturbed use and occupation of the Indians herein named, and for such other friendly tribes or individual Indians as from time to time they may be willing, with the consent of the United States, to admit amongst them; and the United States now solemnly agrees that no persons except those herein designated and authorized so to do, and except such officers, agents, and employee's of the government as may be authorized to enter upon Indian reservations in discharge of duties enjoined by law, shall ever be permitted to pass over, settle upon, or reside in the territory described in this article, or in such territory as may be added to this reservation for the use of said Indians, and henceforth they will and do hereby relinquish all claims or rights in and to any portion of the United States or Territories, except such as is embraced within the limits aforesaid, and except as hereinafter provided.

Article III. If it should appear from actual survey or other satisfactory examination of said tract of land that it contains less than one hundred and sixty acres of tillable land for each person who, at the time, may be authorized to reside on it under the provisions of this treaty, and a very considerable number of such persons shall be disposed to commence cultivating the soil as farmers, the United States agrees to set apart, for the use of said Indians, as herein provided, such additional quantity of arable land, adjoining to said reservation, or as near to the same as it can be obtained, as may be required to provide the necessary amount.

Article IV. The United States agrees, at its own proper expense, to construct at some place on the Missouri river, near the centre of said reservation, where timber and water may be convenient, the following buildings, to wit: a warehouse, a storeroom for the use of the agent in storing good belonging to the Indians, to cost not less than twenty-five hundred dollars; an agency building for the residence of the agent, to cost not exceeding three thousand dollars; a residence for the physician, to cost not more than three thousand dollars; and five other buildings, for a carpenter, farmer, blacksmith, miller, and engineer, each to cost not exceeding two thousand dollars; also a school-house or mission building, as soon as a sufficient number of children can be induced by the agent to attend school, which shall not cost exceeding five thousand dollars.

The United States agrees further to cause to be erected on said reservation, near the other buildings herein authorized, a good steam circular saw-mill, with a grist-mill and shingle machine attached to the same, to cost not exceeding eight thousand dollars.

Article V. The United States agrees that the agent for said Indians shall in the future make his home at the agency building; that he shall reside among them, and keep an office open at all times for the purpose of prompt and diligent inquiry into such matters of complaint by and against the Indians as may be presented for investigation under the provisions of their treaty stipulations, as also for the faithful discharge of other duties enjoined on him by law. In all cases of depredation on person or property he shall cause the evidence to be taken in writing and forwarded, together with his findings, to the Commissioner of Indian Affairs, whose decision, subject to the revision of the Secretary of the Interior, shall be binding on the parties to this treaty.

Article VI. If any individual belonging to said tribes of Indians, or legally incorporated with them, being the head of a family, shall desire to commence farming, he shall have the privilege to select, in the presence and with the assistance of the agent then in charge, a tract of land within said reservation, not exceeding three hundred and twenty acres in extent, which tract when so selected, certified, and recorded in the "land book," as herein directed, shall cease to be held in common, but the same may be occupied and held in the exclusive possession of the person selecting it, and of his family, so long as he or they may continue to cultivate it.

Any person over eighteen years of age, not being the head of a family, may in like manner select and cause to be certified to him or her, for purposes of cultivation, a quantity of land not exceeding eighty acres in extent, and thereupon be entitled to the exclusive possession of the same as above directed.

For each tract of land so selected a certificate, containing a description thereof and the name of the person selecting it, with a certificate endorsed thereon that the same has been recorded, shall be delivered to the party entitled to it, by the agent, after the same shall have been recorded by him in a book to be kept in his office, subject to inspection, which said book shall be known as the "Sioux Land Book."

The President may, at any time, order a survey of the reservation, and, when so surveyed, Congress shall provide for protecting the rights of said settlers in their improvements, and may fix the character of the title held by each. The United States may pass such laws on the subject of alienation and descent of property between the Indians and their descendants as may be thought proper. And it is further stipulated that any male Indians over eighteen years of age, of any band or tribe that is or shall hereafter become a party to this treaty, who now is or who shall hereafter become a resident or occupant of any reservation or territory not included in the tract of country designated and described in this treaty for the permanent home of the Indians, which is not mineral land, nor reserved by the United States for special purposes other than Indian occupation, and who shall have made improvements thereon of the value of two hundred dollars or more, and continuously occupied the same as a homestead for the term of three years, shall be entitled to receive from the United States a patent for one hundred and sixty acres of land including his said improvements, the same to be in the form of the legal subdivisions of the surveys of the public lands. Upon application in writing, sustained by the proof of two disinterested witnesses, made to the register of the local land office when the land sought to be entered is within a land district, and when the tract sought to be entered is not in any land districts, then upon said application and proof being made to the commissioner of the general land office, and the right of such Indian or Indians to enter such tract or tracts of land shall accrue and be perfect from the date of his first improvements thereon, and shall continue as long as he continues his residence and improvements, and no longer. And any Indian or Indians receiving a patent for land under the foregoing provisions, shall thereby and from thenceforth become and be a citizen of the United States, and be entitled to all the privileges and immunities of such citizens, and shall, at the same time, retain all his rights to benefits accruing to Indians under this treaty.

Article VII. In order to insure the civilization of the Indians entering into this treaty, the necessity of education is admitted, especially of such of them as are or may be settled on said agricultural reservations, and they therefore pledge themselves to compel their children, male and female; between the ages of six and sixteen years, to attend school; and it is hereby made the duty of the agent for said Indians to see that this stipulation is strictly complied with; and the United States agrees that for every thirty children between said ages who can be induced or compelled to attend school, a house shall be provided and a teacher competent to teach the elementary branches of an English education shall be furnished, who will reside among said Indians, and faithfully discharge his or her duties as a teacher. The provisions of this article to continue for not less than twenty years.

Article VIII. When the head of a family or lodge shall have selected lands and received his certificate as above directed, and the agent shall be satisfied that he intends in good faith to commence cultivating the soil for a living, he shall be entitled to receive seeds and agricultural implements for the first year, not exceeding in value one hundred dollars, and for each succeeding year he shall continue to farm, for a period of three years more, he shall be entitled to receive seeds and implements as aforesaid, not exceeding in value twenty-five dollars.

And it is further stipulated that such persons as commence farming shall receive instruction from the farmer herein provided for, and whenever more than one hundred persons shall enter upon the cultivation of the soil, a second blacksmith shall be provided, with such iron, steel, and other material as may be needed.

Article IX. At any time after ten years from the making of this treaty, the United States shall have the privilege of withdrawing the physician, farmer, blacksmith, carpenter, engineer, and miller herein provided for, but in case of such withdrawal, an additional sum thereafter of ten thousand dollars per annum shall be devoted to the education of said Indians, and the Commissioner of Indian Affairs shall, upon careful inquiry into their condition, make such rules regulations for the expenditure of said sum as will best promote the educational and moral improvement of said tribes.

Article X. In lieu of all sums of money or other annuities provided to be paid to the Indians herein named, under any treaty or treaties heretofore made, the United States agrees to deliver at the agency house on the reservation herein named, on [or before] the first day of August of each year, for thirty years, the following articles, to wit:

For each male person over fourteen years of age, a suit of good substantial woollen clothing, consisting of coat, pantaloons, flannel shirt, hat, and a pair of home-made socks.

For each female over twelve years of age, a flannel skirt, or the goods necessary to make it, a pair of woollen hose, twelve yards of calico, and twelve yards of cotton domestics.

For the boys and girls under the ages named, such flannel and cotton goods as may be needed to make each a suit as aforesaid, together with a pair of woollen hose for each.

And in order that the Commissioner of Indian Affairs may be able to estimate properly for the articles herein named, it shall be the duty of the agent each year to forward to him a full and exact census of the Indians, on which the estimate from year to year can be based.

And in addition to the clothing herein named, the sum of ten dollars for each person entitled to the beneficial effects of this treaty shall be annually appropriated for a period of thirty years, while such persons roam and hunt, and twenty dollars for each person who engages in farming, to be used by the Secretary of the Interior in the purchase of such articles as from time to time the condition and necessities of the Indians may indicate to the proper. And if within the thirty years, at any time, it shall appear that the amount of money needed for clothing under this article can be appropriated to better uses for the Indians named herein, Congress may, by law, change the appropriation to other purposes; but in no event shall the amount of this appropriation be withdrawn or discontinued for the period named. And the President shall annually detail an officer of the army to be present and attest the delivery of all the goods herein named to the Indians, and he shall inspect and report on the quantity and quality of the goods and the manner of their delivery. And it is hereby expressly stipulated that each Indian over the age of four years, who shall have removed to and settled permanently upon said reservation and complied with the stipulations of this treaty, shall be entitled to receive from the United States, for the period of four years after he shall have settled upon said reservation, one pound of meat and one pound of flour per day, provided the Indians cannot furnish their own subsistence at an earlier date. And it is further stipulated that the United States will furnish and deliver to each lodge of Indians or family of persons legally incorporated with them, who shall remove to the reservation herein described and commence farming, one good American cow, and one good well-broken pair of American oxen within sixty days after such lodge or family shall have so settled upon said reservation.

Article XI. In consideration of the advantages and benefits conferred by this treaty and the many pledges of friendship by the United States, the tribes who are parties to this agreement hereby stipulate that they will relinquish all right to occupy permanently the territory outside their reservation as herein defined, but yet reserve the right to hunt on any lands north of North Platte, and on the Republican Fork of the Smoky Hill river, so long as the buffalo may range thereon in such numbers as to justify the chase. And they, the said Indians, further expressly agree:

1st. That they will withdraw all opposition to the construction of the railroads now being built on the plains.

2d. That they will permit the peaceful construction of any railroad not passing over their reservation as herein defined.

3d. That they will not attack any persons at home, or travelling, nor molest or disturb any wagon trains, coaches, mules, or cattle belonging to the people of the United States, or to persons friendly therewith.

4th. They will never capture, or carry off from the settlements, white women or children.

5th. They will never kill or scalp white men, nor attempt to do them harm.

6th. They withdraw all pretence of opposition to the construction of the railroad now being built along the Platte river and westward to the Pacific ocean, and they will not in future object to the construction of railroads, wagon roads, mail stations, or other works of utility or necessity, which may be ordered or permitted by the law of the United States. But should such roads or other works be constructed on the lands of their reservation, the government will pay the tribe whatever amount of damage may be assessed by three disinterested commissioners to be appointed by the President for that purpose, one of said commissioners to be a chief or headman of the tribe.

7th. They agree to withdraw all opposition to the military posts or roads now established south of the North Platte river, or that may be established, not in violation of treaties heretofore made or hereafter to be made with any of the Indian tribes.

Article XII. No treaty for the cession of any portion or part of the reservation herein described which may be held in common shall be of any validity or force as against the said Indians, unless executed and signed by at least three fourths of all the adult male Indians, occupying or interested in the same; and no cession by the tribe shall be understood or construed in such manner as to deprive, without his consent, any individual member of the tribe of his rights to any tract of land selected by him, as provided in Article VI. of this treaty.

Article XIII. The United States hereby agrees to finish annually to the Indian the physician, teachers, carpenter, miller, engineer, farmer, and blacksmiths, as herein contemplated, and that such appropriations shall be made from time to time, on the estimates of the Secretary of the Interior, as will be sufficient to employ such persons.

Article XIV. It is agreed that the sum of five hundred dollars annually, for three years from date, shall be expended in presents to the ten persons of said tribe who in the judgment of the agent may grow the most valuable crops for the respective year.

Article XV. The Indians herein named agree that when the agency house and other buildings shall be constructed on the reservation named, they will regard said reservation their permanent home, and they will make no permanent settlement elsewhere; but they shall have the right, subject to the conditions and modifications of this treaty, to hunt, as stipulated in Article XI. hereof.

Article XVI. The United States hereby agrees and stipulates that the country north of the North Platte river and east of the summits of the Big Horn mountains shall be held and considered to be unceded Indian territory, and also stipulates and agrees that no white person or persons shall be permitted to settle upon or occupy any portion of the same; or without the consent of the Indians, first had and obtained, to pass through the same; and it is further agreed by the United States, that within ninety days after the conclusion of peace with all the bands of the Sioux nation, the military posts now established in the territory in this article named shall be abandoned, and that the road leading to them and by them to the settlements in the Territory of Montana shall be closed.

Article XVII. It is hereby expressly understood and agreed by and between the respective parties to this treaty that the execution of this treaty and its ratification by the United States Senate shall have the effect, and shall be construed as abrogating and annulling all treaties and agreements heretofore entered into between the respective parties hereto, so far as such treaties and agreements obligate the United States to furnish and provide money, clothing, or other articles of property to such Indians and bands of Indians as become parties to this treaty, but no further.

In testimony of all which, we, the said commissioners, and we, the chiefs and headmen of the Brule band of the Sioux nation, have hereunto set our hands and seals at Fort Laramie, Dakota Territory, this twenty-ninth day of April, in the year one thousand eight hundred and sixty-eight.

Source:
Landmark Documents in American History, Facts On File, Inc.

Yellowstone National Park Act, 1872

Federal law enacted on March 1, 1872, that established Yellowstone as the world's first national park. In the 19th century, to spur westward expansion, federal land policy had been dedicated to transferring public lands to private ownership through various laws. By the late 1800s, with the western frontier rapidly diminishing, a gradual shift toward maintaining permanent federal control over some public lands was underway, prompted in part by concern for conserving areas of great natural beauty and historical significance for the enjoyment of future generations of Americans. One of the earliest legislative steps in this direction was the Yellowstone National Park Act, which set aside lands encompassing parts of present-day Wyoming, Montana, and Idaho as Yellowstone National Park. Yellowstone became the flagship of the National Park System, which Congress created in 1916.

An Act

To set apart a certain Tract of Land lying near the Headwaters of the Yellowstone River as a public Park.

Be it enacted by the Senate and House of Representatives of the United States of America in Congress assembled, That the tract of land in the Territories of Montana and Wyoming, lying near the head-waters of the Yellowstone river, and described as follows, to wit, commencing at the junction of Gardiner's river with the Yellowstone river, and running east to the meridian passing ten miles to the eastward of the most eastern point of Yellowstone lake; thence south along said meridian to the parallel of latitude passing ten miles south of the most southern point of Yellowstone lake; thence west along said parallel to the meridian passing fifteen miles west of the most western point of Madison lake; thence north along said meridian to the latitude of the junction of the Yellowstone and Gardiner's rivers; thence east to the place of beginning, is hereby reserved and withdrawn from settlement, occupancy, or sale under the laws of the United States, and dedicated and set apart as a public park or pleasuring-ground for the benefit and enjoyment of the people; and all persons who shall locate or settle upon or occupy the same, or any part thereof, except as hereinafter provided, shall be considered trespassers and removed therefrom.

Sec. 2. That said public park shall be under the exclusive control of the Secretary of the Interior, whose duty it shall be, as soon as practicable, to make and publish such rules and regulations as he may deem necessary or proper for the care and management of the same. Such regulations shall provide for the preservation, from injury or spoliation, of all timber, mineral deposits, natural curiosities, or wonders within said park, and their retention in their natural condition. The secretary may in his discretion, grant leases for building purposes for terms not exceeding ten years, of small parcels of ground, at such places in said park as shall require the erection of buildings for the accommodation of visitors; all of the proceeds of said leases, and all other revenues that may be derived from any source connected with said park, to be expended under his direction in the management of the same, and the construction of roads and bridle-paths therein. He shall provide against the wanton destruction of the fish and game found within said park, and against their capture or destruction for the purposes of merchandise or profit. He shall also cause all persons trespassing upon the same after the passage of this act to be removed therefrom, and generally shall be authorized to take all such measures as shall be necessary or proper to fully carry out the objects and purposes of this act.

Source:
Statutes at Large, Vol. 18, pp. 32–33.

Medal of Honor Recipients, Seminole-Negro Indian Scouts, 1875

Thirty to 50 Seminole-Negro Indian Scouts served during the Plains Indians Wars, and the highest honor of valor during war, the Medal of Honor, was awarded four of them. These men of exclusively African-American or mixed African-American and Seminole ancestry, had moved to Mexico to avoid slavery. To lure them back to the United States, the government promised to grant them land, pay their transportation costs, and provide provisions for their families. In the end, the government denied there was any proof that these soldiers had served, and they did not get either the land or pensions promised for their service. Yet, according to one commentator they served under, Lt. John L. Bullis, a Quaker who commanded United States Colored Troops in the Civil War, "They were probably the best desert fighters and trackers in the history of the United States Army."

Pvt. Adam Paine, September 20, 1874. The Staked Plains, Texas. Sept. 26–27, 1874. Inducted: Fort Duncan, Texas. Born: Florida. Issued: Oct 13, 1875.

Citation: Rendered invaluable service to Col. R. S. Mackenzie, 4th U.S. Cavalry., during this engagement.

Pvt. Pompey Factor, April 25,1875. Eagle's Nest Crossing, Pecos River, Texas. Issued March 15, 1875. Citation: With 3 other men, he participated in a charge against 25 hostiles while on a scouting patrol

Pvt. Isaac Payne, April 25, 1875. Eagle's Nest Crossing, Pecos River, Texas. April 25, 1875. Born: Mexico. Issued: May 25, 1875. Citation: With 3 other men, he participated in a charge against 25 hostiles while on a scouting patrol.

Sgt. John Ward, April 25,1875. Eagle's Nest Crossing, Pecos River, Texas. April 25, 1875. Entered service at. Fort Duncan, Tex. Born: Arkansas. Issued: May 28, 1875.

Citation. With 3 other men, he participated in a charge against 25 hostiles while on a scouting patrol.

Source:
"Seminole-Negro Scouts." Buffalosoldier.net. Available on-line. URL: www.buffalosoldier.net/SeminoleNegroIndian Scouts.htm. Accessed November 2003.

Desert Land Act of 1877

Legislation passed by Congress March 3, 1877, allowing settlers to acquire large tracts of federally owned dry land on condition that they irrigate the property. The act permitted settlers to purchase up to 640 acres, with a down payment of 25 cents per acre, and a payment of an additional dollar per acre after three years if the tract had been irrigated. Thousands of homesteaders attempted to establish small farms, but few succeeded in obtaining enough water to grow crops. Instead, the act benefited cattle barons, who collected vast holdings by registering lands in the names of their cowhands. By 1890, 3.5 million acres had been distributed.

An Act
To provide for the sale of desert lands in certain States and Territories

Be it enacted by the Senate and House of Representatives of the United States of America in Congress assembled, That it shall be lawful for any citizen of the United States, or any person of requisite age "who may be entitled to become a citizen, and who has filed his declaration to become such" and upon payment of twenty five cents per acre—to file a declaration under oath with the register and the receiver of the land district in which any desert land is situated, that he intends to reclaim a tract of desert land not exceeding one section, by conducting water upon the same, within the period of three years thereafter, *Provided however* that the right to the use of water by the person so conducting the same, on or to any tract of desert land of six hundred and forty acres shall depend upon bona fide prior appropriation: and such right shall not exceed the amount of water actually appropriated, and necessarily used for the purpose of irrigation and reclamation: and all surplus water over and above such actual appropriation and use, together with the water of all, lakes, rivers and other sources of water supply upon the public lands and not navigable, shall remain and be held free for the appropriation and use of the public for irrigation, mining and manufacturing purposes subject to existing rights. Said declaration shall describe particularly said section of land if surveyed, and, if unsurveyed, shall describe the same as nearly as possible

without a survey. At any time within the period of three years after filing said declaration, upon making satisfactory proof to the register and receiver of the reclamation of said tract of land in the manner aforesaid, and upon the payment to the receiver of the additional sum of one dollar per acre for a tract of land not exceeding six hundred and forty acres to any one person, a patent for the same shall be issued to him. *Provided,* that no person shall be permitted to enter more than one tract of land and not to exceed six hundred and forty acres which shall be in compact form.

Section 2. That all lands exclusive of timber lands and mineral lands which will not, without irrigation, produce some agricultural crop, shall be deemed desert lands, within the meaning of this act, which fact shall be ascertained by proof of two or more credible witnesses under oath, whose affidavits shall be filed in the land office in which said tract of land may be situated—

Section 3. That this act shall only apply to and take effect in the States of California, Oregon and Nevada, and the Territories of Washington, Idaho, Montana, Utah, Wyoming Arizona, New Mexico and Dakota, and the determination of what may be considered desert land shall be subject to the decision and regulation of the Commissioner of the General Land Office.

Source:
Statutes at Large, Vol. 20, p. 377.

Chief Joseph, "I Will Fight No More Forever," 1877

Anguished valedictory of Nez Percé chief Joseph upon his tribe's surrender in October 1877 to the U.S. military, marking the end of the Nez Percé War. Chief Joseph directed Nez Percé resistance to the U.S. effort—begun in 1875—to force the tribe off its Oregon lands and resettle it on the Lapwai reservation in Idaho. Under his leadership, the Nez Percé evaded the pursuing U.S. Army during an extraordinary 1,500-mile retreat from Oregon to Montana. Exhausted and hungry, Joseph and his followers, numbering some 430, submitted to U.S. troops near the Canadian border in early October 1877. Upon surrender, Joseph gave his speech, in which he declared himself weary of fighting, lamented the Nez Percé dead, and described the pitiable condition of his people following their arduous trek. In closing, he said, "my heart is sick and sad. From where the sun now stands, I will fight no more forever."

Tell General Howard I know his heart. What he told me before, I have in my heart, I am tired of fighting. Our Chiefs are killed. Looking Glass is dead. Toohoolhoolzote is dead. The old men are all dead. It is the young men who say yes and no. He who led on the young men is dead. It is cold and we have no blankets. The little children are freezing to death. My people, some of them, have run away to the hills and have no blankets, no food; no one knows where they are—perhaps freezing to death. I want to have time to look for my children among the dead. Hear me, my chiefs. I am tired; my heart is sick and sad. From where the sun now stands I will fight no more forever.

Source:

Nez Perce Tribe, Department of Natural Resources, Lapwai, ID.

Dawes Severalty Act, 1887

Federal U.S. legislation enacted on February 8, 1887, that provided for the dissolution of the Indian tribes as legal entities and the distribution of tribal lands among individual members. In an attempt to remove any remaining authority from the Native peoples, the act granted citizenship to Indians who renounced tribal allegiance and "adopted the habits of civilized life." It allotted to heads of families 160 acres of reservation land and to adult single people 80 acres; the land was initially awarded in trust, with full title to be transferred after 25 years. Many Native Americans, unprepared for homesteading and farming, lost their lands—and in many cases their lives—to whites, who would stop at nothing to wrestle these newly allotted lands from them.

In 1906 Congress passed the Burke Act, amending the Dawes Severalty Act, in an effort to protect Native American landholdings. Like the earlier law, the Burke Act granted to Native Americans who renounced their tribal allegiance full title to the homestead after a 25-year probationary period; but, unlike the Dawes Severalty Act, it granted citizenship only after the probationary period ended. Indian agents could, however, grant citizenship earlier to Native Americans they deemed trustworthy. The act also prohibited the sale of liquor to Native Americans who were not citizens. Many American Indians considered the act patronizing, and it was amended in 1924, when all Native Americans were made citizens.

───────── ⸎ ─────────

An Act

To provide for the allotment of lands in severalty to Indians on the various reservations, and to extend the protection of the laws of the United States and the Territories over the Indians, and for other purposes.

Be it enacted by the Senate and House of Representatives of the United States of America in Congress assembled, That in all cases where any tribe or band of Indians has been, or shall hereafter be, located upon any reserva-

tion created for their use, either by treaty stipulation or by virtue of an act of Congress or executive order setting apart the same for their use, the President of the United States be, and he hereby is, authorized, whenever in his opinion any reservation or any part thereof of such Indians is advantageous for agricultural and grazing purposes, to cause said reservation, or any part thereof, to be surveyed, or resurveyed if necessary, and to allot the lands in said reservation in severalty to any Indian located thereon in quantities as follows:

To each head of a family, one-quarter of a section;

To each single person over eighteen years of age, one-eighth of a section;

To each orphan child under eighteen years of age, one-eighth of a section; and

To each other single person under eighteen years now living, or who may be born prior to the date of the order of the President directing an allotment of the lands embraced in any reservation, one-sixteenth of a section: *Provided,* That in case there is not sufficient land in any of said reservations to allot lands to each individual of the classes above named in quantities as above provided, the lands embraced in such reservation or reservations shall be allotted to each individual of each of said classes pro rata in accordance with the provisions of this act: *And provided further,* That where the treaty or act of Congress setting apart such reservation provides for the allotment of lands in severalty in quantities in excess of those herein provided, the President, in making allotments upon such reservation, shall allot the lands to each individual Indian belonging thereon in quantity as specified in such treaty or act: *And provided further,* That when the lands allotted are only valuable for grazing purposes, an additional allotment of such grazing lands, in quantities as above provided, shall be made to each individual.

Sec. 2. That all allotments set apart under the provisions of this act shall be selected by the Indians, heads of families selecting for their minor children, and the agents shall select for each orphan child, and in such manner as to embrace the improvements of the Indians making the selection. Where the improvements of two or more Indians have been made on the same legal subdivision of land, unless they shall otherwise agree, a provisional line may be run dividing said lands between them, and the amount to which each is entitled shall be equalized in the assignment of the remainder of the land to which they are entitled under this act: *Provided,* That if any one entitled to an allotment shall fail to make a selection within four years after the President shall direct that allotments may be made on a particular reservation, the Secretary of the Interior may direct the agent of such tribe or band, if such there be, and if there be no agent, then a special agent appointed for that purpose, to make a selection for such Indian, which election shall be allotted as in cases where selections are made by the Indians, and patents shall issue in like manner.

Sec. 3. That the allotments provided for in this act shall be made by special agents appointed by the President for such purpose, and the agents in charge of the respective reservations on which the allotments are directed to be made, under such rules and regulations as the Secretary of the Interior may from time to time prescribe, and shall be certified by such agents to the Commissioner of Indian Affairs, in duplicate, one copy to be retained in the Indian Office and the order to be transmitted to the Secretary of the Interior for his action, and to be deposited in the General Land Office.

Sec. 4. That where any Indian not residing upon a reservation, or for whose tribe no reservation has been provided by treaty, act of Congress, or executive order, shall make settlement upon any surveyed or unsurveyed lands of the United States not otherwise appropriated, he or she shall be entitled, upon application to the local land-office for the district in which the lands are located, to have the same allotted to him or her, and to his or her children, in quantities and manner as provided in this act for Indians residing upon reservations; and when such settlement is made upon unsurveyed lands, the grant to such Indians shall be adjusted upon the survey of the lands so as to conform thereto; and patents shall be issued to them for such lands in the manner and with the restrictions as herein provided. And the fees to which the officers of such local land-office would have been entitled had such lands been entered under the general laws for the disposition of the public lands shall be paid to them, from any moneys in the Treasury of the United States not otherwise appropriated, upon a statement of an account in their behalf for such fees by the Commissioner of the General Land Office, and a certification of such account to the Secretary of the Treasury by the Secretary of the Interior.

Sec. 5. That upon the approval of the allotments provided for in this act by the Secretary of the Interior; he shall cause patents to issue therefor in the name of the allottees, which patents shall be of the legal effect, and declare that the United States does and will hold the land thus allotted, for the period of twenty-five years, in trust for the sole use and benefit of the Indian to whom such allotment shall have been made, or, in case of his decease, of his heirs according to the laws of the State or Territory where such land is located, and that at the expiration of said period the United States will convey the same by patent to said Indian, or his heirs as aforesaid, in fee, discharged of said trust and free of all charge or incumbrance whatsoever: *Provided,* That the President of the United States may in any case in his discretion extend the period. And if any conveyance shall be made of the lands set apart and allotted as herein provided, or any contract made touching the same, before the expiration of the time above mentioned, such conveyance or contract shall be absolutely null and void: *Provided,* That the law of descent and partition in force in the State or Territory where such lands are situate shall apply thereto after patents therefor have been executed and delivered, except as herein otherwise provided; and the laws of the State of Kansas regulating the descent and partition of real estate shall, so far as practicable, apply to all lands in the Indian Territory which may be allotted in severalty under the provisions of this act: *And provided further,* That at any time after lands have been allotted to all the Indians of any tribe as herein provided, or sooner if in the opinion of the President it shall be for the best interests of said tribe, it shall be lawful for the Secretary of the Interior to negotiate with such Indian tribe for the purchase and release by said tribe, in conformity with the treaty or statute under which such reservation is held, of such portions of its reservation not allotted as such tribe shall, from time to time, consent to sell, on such terms and conditions as shall be considered just and equitable between the United States and said tribe of Indians, which purchase shall not be complete until ratified by Congress, and the form and manner of executing such release shall also be prescribed by Congress: *Provided however,* That all lands adapted to agriculture, with or without irrigation so sold or released to the United States by any Indian tribe shall be held by the United States for the sole purpose of securing homes to actual settlers and shall be disposed of by the United States to actual and bona fide settlers only in tracts not exceeding one hundred and sixty acres to any one person, on such terms as Congress shall prescribe, subject to grants which Congress may make in aid of education: *And provided further,* That no patents shall issue therefor except to the person so taking the same as and for a homestead, or his heirs, and after the expiration of five years occupancy thereof as such homestead; and any conveyance of said lands so taken as a homestead, or any contract touching the same, or lien thereon, created prior to the date of such patent, shall be null and void. And the sums agreed to be paid by the United States as purchase money for any portion of any such reservation shall be held in the Treasury of the United States for the sole use of the tribe or tribes of Indians; to whom such reservations belonged; and the same, with interest thereon at three per cent per annum, shall be at all times subject to appropriation by Congress for the education and civilization of such tribe or tribes of Indians or the members thereof. The patents aforesaid shall be recorded in the General Land Office, and afterward delivered, free of charge, to the allottee entitled thereto. And if any religious society or other organization is now occupying any of the public lands to which this act is applicable, for religious or educational work among the Indians, the Secretary of the Interior is hereby authorized to confirm such occupation to such society or organization, in quantity not exceeding one hundred and sixty acres in any one tract, so long as the same shall be so occupied, on such terms as he shall deem just; but nothing herein contained shall change or alter any claim of such society for religious or educational purposes heretofore granted by law. And hereafter in the employment of Indian police, or any other employees in the public service among any of the Indian tribes or bands affected by this act, and where Indians can perform the duties required, those Indians who have availed themselves of the provisions of this act and become citizens of the United States shall be preferred.

Sec. 6. That upon the completion of said allotments and the patenting of the lands to said allottees, each and every member of the respective bands or tribes of Indians to whom allotments have been made shall have the benefit of and be subject to the laws, both civil and criminal, of the State or Territory in which they may reside; and no Territory shall pass or enforce any law denying any such Indian within its jurisdiction the equal protection of the law. And every Indian born within the territorial limits of the United States to whom allotments shall have been made under the provisions of this act, or under any law or treaty, and every Indian born within the territorial limits of the United States who has voluntarily taken up, within said limits, his residence separate and apart from any tribe of Indians therein, and has adopted the habits of civilized life, is hereby declared to be a citizen of the United States, and is entitled to all the rights, privileges, and immunities of such citizens, whether said Indian has been or not, by birth or otherwise, a member of any tribe of Indians within the territorial limits of the United States without in any manner impairing or otherwise affecting the right of any such Indian to tribal or other property.

Sec. 7. That in cases where the use of water for irrigation is necessary to render the lands within any Indian reservation available for agricultural purposes, the Secretary of the Interior be, and he is hereby, authorized to prescribe such rules and regulations as he may deem necessary to secure a just and equal distribution thereof among the Indians residing upon any such reservations; and no other appropriation or grant of water by any riparian proprietor shall be authorized or permitted to the damage of any other riparian proprietor.

Sec. 8. That the provision of this act shall not extend to the territory occupied by the Cherokees, Creeks, Choctaws, Chickasawas, Seminoles, and Osage, Miamies and Peorias, and Sacs and Foxes, in the Indian Territory,

nor to any of the reservations of the Seneca Nation of New York Indians in the State of New York, nor to that strip of territory in the State of Nebraska adjoining the Sioux Nation on the south added by executive order.

Sec. 9. That for the purpose of making the surveys and resurveys mentioned in section two of this act, there be, and hereby is, appropriated, out of any moneys in the Treasury not otherwise appropriated, the sum of one hundred thousand dollars, to be repaid proportionately out of the proceeds of the sales of such land as may be acquired from the Indians under the provisions of this act.

Sec. 10. That nothing in this act contained shall be so construed as to affect the right and power of Congress to grant the right of way through any lands granted to an Indian, or a tribe of Indians, for railroads or other highways, or telegraph lines, for the public use, or to condemn such lands to public uses, upon making just compensation.

Sec. 11. That nothing in this act shall be so construed as to prevent the removal of the Southern Ute Indians from their present reservation in Southwestern Colorado to a new reservation by and with the consent of a majority of the adult male members of said tribe.

Source:
United States Statutes at Large, Vol. 25, pp. 388–391.

Forest Reserve Act, 1891

Federal legislation passed March 3, 1891, that codified many public land laws.

Previously, in the Timber Culture Act, enacted March 3, 1873, Congress authorized any person who kept 40 acres of timber land in good condition to acquire title to 160 additional acres of timber land. Congress made 10 million acres of federal lands in the Great Plains available for private forestation in hopes of reducing erosion, retaining rainfall, and improving the climate. In 1878 the minimum tree-growing requirement was reduced from 40 to 10 acres. The act resulted in little permanent tree growth on the arid land, but it did cause widespread land speculation. Because cattlemen and speculators abused the act at the expense of the settlers, it was repealed in 1891 by the Forest Reserve Act.

This act authorized the president to reserve certain public lands from the public domain and reversed the policy of transferring public lands to private ownership. Though the act failed to specify the purpose of these reserves and to provide for their administration (the Forest Management Act of 1897 did both), President Benjamin Harrison used the authority to reserve 22 million acres, thus beginning the national forest system. The act was amended in 1907 to forbid the creation or enlargement of national forests in six western states without congressional action.

An Act

To repeal timber-culture laws, and for other purposes.

Be it enacted by the Senate and House of Representatives of the United States of America in Congress assembled,. That an act entitled "An act to amend an act entitled 'An act to encourage the growth of timber on the Western prairies,'" approved June four-teenth, eighteen hundred and seventy eight, and all laws supplementary thereto or amendatory thereof, be, and the same are hereby, repealed: *Provided,* That this repeal shall not affect any valid rights heretofore accrued or accruing under said laws, but all bona fide claims lawfully initiated before the passage of this act may be perfected upon due compliance with law, in the same manner, upon the same terms and conditions, and subject to the same limitations, forfeitures, and contests as if this act had not been passed: *And provided further,* That the following words of the last clause of section two of said act, namely, "That not less than twenty-seven hundred trees were planted on each acre," are hereby repealed: *And provided further,* That in computing the period of cultivation the time shall run from the date of the entry, if the necessary acts of cultivation were performed within the proper time: *And provided further,* That the preparation of the land and the planting of trees shall be construed as acts of cultivation, and the time authorized to be so employed and actually employed shall be computed as a part of the eight years of cultivation required by statute: *Provided,* That any person who has made entry of any public lands of the United States under the timber-culture laws, and who has for a period of four years in good faith complied with the provisions of said laws and who is an actual bona fide resident of the State or Territory in which said land is located shall be entitled to make final proof thereto, and acquire title to the same, by the payment of one dollar and twenty five cents per acre for such tract, under such rules and regulations as shall be prescribed by the Secretary of the Interior, and registers and receivers shall be allowed the same fees and compensation for final proofs in timber-culture entries as is now allowed by law in homestead entries: *And provided further,* That no land acquired under the provisions of this act shall in any event become liable to the satisfaction of any debt or debts contracted prior to the issuing of the final certificate therefor.

Sec. 2. That an act to provide for the sale of desert lands in certain States and Territories, approved March third, eighteen hundred and seventy-seven, is hereby amended by adding thereto the following sections:

Sec. 4. That at the time of filing the declaration herein before required the party shall also file a map of said land, which shall exhibit a plan showing the mode of contemplated irrigation, and which plan shall be sufficient to thoroughly irrigate and reclaim said land, and prepare it to raise ordinary agricultural crops, and shall also show the source of the water to be used for irrigation and reclamation. Persons entering or proposing to enter separate sections, or fractional parts of sections, of desert lands may associate together in the construction of canals and ditches for irrigating and reclaiming all of said tracts, and may file a joint map or maps showing their plan of internal improvements.

Sec. 5. That no land shall be patented to any person under this act unless he or his assignors shall have expended in the necessary irrigation, reclamation, and cultivation thereof, by means of main canals and branch ditches, and in permanent improvements upon the land, and in the purchase of water rights for the irrigation of the same, at least three dollars per acre of whole tract reclaimed and patented in the manner following: Within one year after making entry for such tract of desert land as aforesaid the party so entering shall expend not less than one dollar per acre for the purposes aforesaid: and he shall in like manner expend the sum of one dollar per acre during the second and also during the third year thereafter, until the full sum of three dollars per acre is so expended. Said party shall file during each year with the register proof, by the affidavits of two or more credible witnesses, that the full sum of one dollar per acre has been expended in such necessary improvements during such year, and the manner in which expended, and at the expiration of the third year a map or plan showing the character and extent of such improvements. If any party who has made such application shall fail during any year to file the testimony aforesaid the lands shall revert to the United States, and the twenty-five cents advanced payment shall be forfeited to the United States, and the entry shall be cancelled. Nothing herein contained shall prevent a claimant from making his final entry and receiving his patent at an earlier date than hereinbefore prescribed, provided that he then makes the required proof of reclamation to the aggregate extent of three dollars per acre: *Provided,* That proof be further required of the cultivation of one-eighth of the land.

Sec. 6. That this act shall not affect any valid rights heretofore accrued under said act of March third, eighteen hundred and seventy-seven, but all bona-fide claims heretofore lawfully initiated may be perfected, upon due compliance with the provisions of said act, in the same manner, upon the same terms and conditions, and subject to the same limitations, forfeitures, and contests as if this act had not been passed; or said claims, at the option of the claimant, may be perfected and patented under the provisions of said act, as amended by this act, so far as applicable; and all acts and parts of acts in conflict with this act are hereby repealed.

Sec. 7. That at any time after filing the declaration, and within the period of four years thereafter, upon making satisfactory proof to the register and the receiver of the reclamation and cultivation of said land to the extent and cost and in the manner aforesaid, and substantially in accordance with the plans herein provided for, and that he or she is a citizen of the United States, and upon payment to the receiver of the additional sum of one dollar per acre for said land, a patent shall issue therefor to the applicant or his assigns; but no person or association of persons shall hold by assignment or otherwise prior to the issue of patent, more than three hundred and twenty acres of such arid or desert lands but this section shall not apply to entries made or initiated prior to the approval of this act. *Provided, however,* That additional proofs may be required at any time within the period prescribed by law, and that the claims or entries made under this or any preceding act shall be subject to contest, as provided by the law, relating to homestead cases, for illegal inception, abandonment, or failure to comply with the requirements of law, and upon satisfactory proof thereof shall be canceled, and the lands, and moneys paid therefor, shall be forfeited to the United States.

Sec. 8. That the provisions of the act to which this is an amendment, and the amendments thereto, shall apply to and be in force in the State of Colorado, as well as the States named in the original act; and no person shall be entitled to make entry of desert land except he be a resident citizen of the State or Territory in which the land sought to be entered is located.

Sec. 3. That section twenty-two hundred and eighty-eight of the Revised Statutes be amended so as to read as follows:

Sec. 2288. Any bona fide settler under the pre-emption, homestead, or other settlement law shall have the right to transfer, by warranty against his own acts, any portion of his claim for church, cemetery, or school purposes, or for the right of way of railroads, canals, reservoirs, or ditches for irrigation or drainage across it; and the transfer for such public purposes shall in no way vitiate the right to complete and perfect the title to his claim."

Sec. 4. That chapter four of title thirty-two, excepting sections twenty-two hundred and seventy-five, twenty-two hundred and seventy-six, twenty-two hundred and eighty-six, of the Revised Statutes of the United States, and all other laws allowing pre-emption of the public lands of the United States, are hereby repealed, but all bona fide claims lawfully initiated before the passage of this act, under any of said provisions of law so repealed, may be perfected upon due compliance with law, in the same manner, upon the same terms and conditions, and subject to

the same limitations, forfeitures, and contests, as if this act had not been passed.

Sec. 5. That sections twenty two hundred and eighty-nine and twenty-two hundred and ninety, in said chapter numbered five of the Revised Statutes, be, and the same are hereby, amended, so that they shall read as follows:

Sec. 2289. Every person who is the head of a family, or who has arrived at the age of twenty-one years, and is a citizen of the United States, or who has filed his declaration of intention to become such, as required by the naturalization laws, shall be entitled to enter one-quarter section, or a less quantity, of unappropriated public lands, to be located in a body in conformity to the legal subdivisions of the public lands; but no person who is the proprietor of more than one hundred and sixty acres of land in any State or Territory, shall acquire any right under the homestead law. And every person owning and residing on land may, under the provisions of this section, enter other land lying contiguous to his land, which shall not, with the land so already owned and occupied, exceed in the aggregate one hundred and sixty acres.

Sec. 2290. That any person applying to enter land under the preceding section shall first make and subscribe before the proper officer and file in the proper land office an affidavit that he or she is the head of a family, or is over twenty-one years of age, and that such application is honestly and in good faith made for the purpose of actual settlement and cultivation, and not for the benefit of any other person, persons or corporation, and that he or she will faithfully and honestly endeavor to comply with all the requirements of law as to settlement, residence, and cultivation necessary to acquire title to the land applied for; that he or she is not acting as agent of any person, corporation, or syndicate in making such entry, nor in collusion with any person, corporation, or syndicate to give them the benefit of the land entered, or any part thereof, or the timber thereon; that he or she does not apply to enter the same for the purpose of speculation, but in good faith to obtain a home for himself, or herself, and that he or she has not directly or indirectly made, and will not make, any agreement or contract in any way or manner, with any person or persons, corporation or syndicate whatsoever, by which the title which he or she might acquire from the Government of the United States should inure, in whole or in part, to the benefit of any person, except himself, or herself, and upon filing such affidavit with the register or receiver on payment of five dollars when the entry is of not more than eighty acres, and on payment of ten dollars when the entry is for more than eighty acres, he or she shall thereupon be permitted to enter the amount of land specified."

Sec. 6. That section twenty-three hundred and one of the Revised Statutes be amended so as to read as follows:

"Sec. 2301. Nothing in this chapter shall be so construed as to prevent any person who shall hereafter avail himself of the benefits of section twenty-two hundred and eighty nine from paying the minimum price for the quantity of land so entered at any time after the expiration of fourteen calendar months from the date of such entry, and obtaining a patent therefor, upon making proof of settlement and of residence and cultivation for such period of fourteen months," and the provision of this section shall apply to lands on the ceded portion of the Sioux Reservation by act approved March second, eighteen hundred and eighty-nine, in South Dakota, but shall not relieve said settlers from any payments now required by law.

Sec. 7. That whenever it shall appear to the Commissioner of the General Land Office that a clerical error has been committed in the entry of any of the public lands such entry may be suspended, upon proper notification to the claimant, through the local land office, until the error has been corrected; and all entries made under the preemption, homestead, desert-land, or timber-culture laws, in which final proof and payment may have been made and certificates issued, and to which there are no adverse claims originating prior to final entry and which have been sold or incumbered prior to the first day of March, eighteen hundred and eighty-eight, and after final entry, to bona-fide purchasers, or incumbrancers, for a valuable consideration, shall unless upon an investigation by a Government Agent, fraud on the part of the purchaser has been found, be confirmed and patented upon presentation of satisfactory proof to the Land Department of such sale or incumbrance: *Provided,* That after the lapse of two years from the date of the issuance of the receiver's receipt upon the final entry of any tract of land under the homestead, timber-culture, desert-land, or pre-emption laws, or under this act, and when there shall be no pending contest or protest against the validity of such entry, the entryman shall be entitled to a patent conveying the land by him entered, and the same shall be issued to him; but this proviso shall not be construed to require the delay of two years from the date of said entry before the issuing of a patent therefor.

Sec. 8. That suits by the United States to vacate and annual any patent heretofore issued shall only be brought within five years from the passage of this act, and suits to vacate and annual patents hereafter issued shall only be brought within six years after the date of the issuance of such patents. And in the States of Colorado, Montana, Idaho, North Dakota and South Dakota, Wyoming, and in the District of Alaska and the gold and silver regions of Nevada, and the Territory of Utah, in any criminal prosecution or civil action by the United States for a trespass on such public timber lands or to recover timber or lumber cut thereon, it shall be a defense if the defendant shall show that the said timber was so cut or removed from the timber lands for use in such State or Territory by a resident thereof for agricultural, mining, manufacturing, or domestic purposes, and has not been transported out of the same; but nothing herein contained shall apply to operate to enlarge the rights of any railway company to cut timber on the public domain: *Provided,* That the Secretary of the Interior may make suitable rules and regulations to carry out the provisions of this section.

Sec. 9. That hereafter no public lands of the United States, except abandoned military or other reservations, isolated and disconnected fractional tracts authorized to be sold by section twenty-four hundred and fifty-five of the Revised Statutes, and mineral and other lands the sale of which at public auction has been authorized by acts of Congress of a special nature having local application, shall be sold at public sale.

Sec. 10. That nothing in this act shall change, repeal, or modify any agreements or treaties made with any Indian tribes for the disposal of their lands, or of land ceded to the United States to be disposed of for the benefit of such tribes, and the proceeds thereof to be placed in the Treasury of the United States; and the disposition of such lands shall continue in accordance with the provisions of such treaties or agreements, except as provided in section 5 of this act.

Sec. 11. That until otherwise ordered by Congress lands in Alaska may be entered for town-site purposes, for the several use and benefit of the occupants of such town sites, by such trustee or trustees as may be named by the Secretary of the Interior for that purpose, such entries to be made under the provisions of section twenty-three hundred and eighty-seven of the Revised Statutes as near as may be; and when such entries shall have been made the Secretary of the Interior shall provide by regulation for the proper execution of the trust in favor of the inhabitants of the town site, including the survey of the land into lots, according to the spirit and intent of said section twenty-three hundred and eighty-seven of the Revised Statutes, whereby the same results would be reached as though the entry had been made by a county judge and the disposal of the lots in such town site and the proceeds of the sale thereof had been prescribed by the legislative authority of a State or Territory: *Provided,* That no more than six hundred and forty acres shall be embraced in one townsite entry.

Sec. 12. That any citizen of the United States twenty-one years of age, and any association of such citizens, and any corporation incorporated under the laws of the United States, or of any State or Territory of the United States now authorized by law to hold lands in the Territories now or hereafter in possession of and occupying public lands in Alaska for the purpose of trade or manufactures, may purchase not exceeding one hundred and sixty acres to be taken as near as practicable in a square form, of such land at two dollars and fifty cents per acre: *Provided,* That in case more than one person, association or corporation shall claim the same tract of land the person, association or corporation having the prior claim by reason of possession and continued occupation shall be entitled to purchase the same; but the entry of no person, association, or corporation shall include improvements made by or in possession of another prior to the passage of this act.

Sec. 13. That it shall be the duty of any person, association, or corporation entitled to purchase land under this act to make an application to the United States marshal, ex officio surveyor-general of Alaska, for an estimate of the cost of making a survey of the lands occupied by such person, association, or corporation, and the cost of the clerical work necessary to be done in the office of the said United States marshal, ex officio surveyor-general; and on the receipt of such estimate from the United States marshal, ex officio surveyor general, the said person, association, or corporation shall deposit the amount in a United States depository, as is required by section numbered twenty-four hundred and one, Revised Statutes, relating to deposits for surveys.

That on the receipt by the United States marshal, ex-officio surveyor-general, of the said certificates of deposit, he shall employ a competent person to make such survey, under such rules and regulations as may be adopted by the Secretary of the Interior, who shall make his return of his field notes and maps to the office of the said United States marshal, ex-officio surveyor-general; and the said United States marshal, ex officio surveyor-general, shall cause the said field notes and plats of such survey to be examined, and, if correct, approve the same, and shall transmit certified copies of such maps and plats to the office of the Commissioner of the General Land Office.

That when the said field notes and plats of said survey shall have been approved by the said Commissioner of the General Land Office, he shall notify such person, association, or corporation, who shall then, within six months after such notice, pay to the said United States marshal, ex officio surveyor-general, for such land, and patent shall issue for the same.

Sec. 14. That none of the provisions of the last two preceding sections of this act shall be so construed as to warrant the sale of any lands belonging to the United States which shall contain coal or the precious metals, or any town site, or which shall be occupied by the United States for public purposes, or which shall be reserved for such purposes, or to which the natives of Alaska have prior rights by virtue of actual occupation, or which shall be selected by the United States Commissioner of Fish and Fisheries on the island of Kadiak and Afognak for the purpose of establishing fish-culture stations. And all tracts of land not exceeding six hundred and forty acres in any one tract now occupied as missionary stations in said district of Alaska are hereby excepted from the operation of the last three proceeding sections of this act. No portion of the islands of the Pribylov Group or the Seal Islands of Alaska shall be subject to sale under this act; and the United States reserves, and there shall be reserved in all patents issued under the provisions of the last two preceding sections the right of the United States to regulate the taking of salmon and to do all things necessary to protect and prevent the destruction of salmon in all the waters of the lands granted frequented by salmon.

Sec. 15. That until otherwise provided by law the body of lands known as Annette Islands, situated in Alexander Archipelago in Southeastern Alaska, on the north side of Dixon's entrance, be, and the same is hereby, set apart as a reservation for the use of the Metlakahtla Indians, and those people known as Metlakahtlans who have recently emigrated from British Columbia to Alaska, and such other Alaskan natives as may join them, to be held and used by them in common, under such rules and regulations, and subject to such restrictions, as may prescribed from time to time by the Secretary of the Interior.

Sec. 16. That town-site entries may be made by incorporated towns and cities on the mineral lands of the United States, but no title shall be acquired by such towns or cities to any vein of gold, silver, cinnabar, copper, or lead, or to any valid mining claim or possession held under existing law. When mineral veins are possessed within the limits of an incorporated town or city, and such possession is recognized by local authority or by the laws of the United States, the title to town lots shall be subject to such recognized possession and the necessary use thereof and when entry has been made or patent issued for such town sites to such incorporated town or city, the possessor of such mineral vein may enter and receive patent for such mineral vein, and the surface ground appertaining thereto: *Provided,* That no entry shall be made by such mineral-vein claimant for surface ground where the owner or occupier of the surface ground shall have had possession of the same before the inception of the title of the mineral-vein applicant.

Sec. 17. That reservoir sites located or selected and to be located and selected under the provisions of "An act making appropriations for sundry civil expenses of the Government for the fiscal year ending June thirtieth, eighteen hundred and eighty-nine, and for other purposes," and amendments thereto, shall be restricted to and shall contain only so much land as is actually necessary for the construction and maintenance of reservoirs; excluding so far as practicable lands occupied by actual settlers at the date of the location of said reservoirs and that the provision of "An Act making appropriations for sundry civil expenses of the Government for the fiscal year ending June thirtieth, eighteen hundred and ninety-one, and for other purposes," which reads as follows, viz: "No person who shall after the passage of this act enter upon any of the public lands with a view to occupation, entry, or settlement under any of the land laws shall be permitted to acquire title to more than three hundred and twenty acres in the aggregate under all said laws," shall be construed to include in the maximum amount of lands the title to which is permitted to be acquired by one person only agricultural lands and not to include lands entered or sought to be entered under mineral land laws.

Sec. 18. That the right of way through the public lands and reservations of the United States is hereby granted to any canal or ditch company formed for the purpose of irrigation and duly organized under the laws of any State or Territory, which shall have filed, or may hereafter file, with the Secretary of the Interior a copy of its articles of incorporation, and due proofs of its organization under the same, to the extent of the ground occupied by the water of the reservoir and of the canal and its laterals, and fifty feet on each side of the marginal limits thereof; also the right to take, from the public lands adjacent to the line of the canal or ditch, material, earth, and stone necessary for the construction of such canal or ditch: *Provided,* That no such right of way shall be so located as to interfere with the proper occupation by the Government of any such reservation, and all maps of location shall be subject to the approval of the Department of the Government having jurisdiction of such reservation, and the privilege herein granted shall not be construed to interfere with the control of water for irrigation and other purposes under authority of the respective States or Territories.

Sec. 19. That any canal or ditch company desiring to secure the benefits of this act shall, within twelve months after the location of ten miles of its canal, if the same be upon surveyed lands, and if upon unsurveyed lands, within twelve months after the survey thereof by the United States, file with the register of the land office for the district where such land is located a map of its canal or ditch and reservoir; and upon the approval thereof by the Secretary of the Interior the same shall be noted upon the plats in said office, and thereafter all such lands over which such rights of way shall pass shall be disposed of subject to such right of way. Whenever any person or corporation, in the construction of any canal, ditch, or reservoir, injures or damages the possession of any settler on the public domain, the party committing such injury or damage shall be liable to the party injured for such injury or damage.

Sec. 20. That the provisions of this act shall apply to all canals, ditches, or reservoirs, heretofore or hereafter constructed, whether constructed by corporations, individuals, or association of individuals, on the filing of the certificates and maps herein provided for. If such ditch, canal, or reservoir, has been or shall be constructed by an individual or association of individuals, it shall be sufficient for such individual or association of individuals to file with the Secretary of the Interior, and with the register of the land office where said land is located, a map of the line of such canal, ditch, or reservoir, as in case of a corporation, with the name of the individual owner or owners thereof, together with the articles of association, if any there be. Plats heretofore filed shall have the benefits of this act from the date of their filing, as though filed under it: *Provided,* That if any section of said canal, or ditch, shall not be completed within five years after the location of said section, the rights herein granted shall be forfeited as to any uncompleted section of said canal, ditch, or reservoir, to the extent that the same is not completed at the date of the forfeiture.

Sec. 21. That nothing in this act shall authorize such canal or ditch company to occupy such right of way except for the purpose of said canal or ditch, and then only so far as may be necessary for the construction, maintenance, and care of said canal or ditch.

Sec. 22. That the section of land reserved for the benefit of the Dakota Central Railroad Company on the west bank of the Missouri River, at the mouth of Bad River, as provided by section sixteen of "An act to divide a portion of the reservation of the Sioux Nation of Indians in Dakota into separate reservations and to secure the relinquishment of the Indian title to the remainder and for other purposes," approved March second, eighteen hundred and eighty-nine, shall be subject to entry under the town-site law only.

Sec. 23. That in all cases where second entries of land on the Osage Indian trust and diminished reserve lands in Kansas, to which at the time there were no adverse claims, have been made and the law complied with as to residence and improvement, said entries be, and the same are hereby, confirmed, and in all cases where persons were actual settlers and residing upon their claims upon said Osage Indian trust and diminished reserve lands in the State of Kansas on the ninth day of May, eighteen hundred and seventy two, and who have made subsequent preemption entries either upon public or upon said Osage Indian trust and diminished reserve lands, upon which there were no legal prior adverse claims at the time, and the law complied with as to settlement, said subsequent entries be, and the same are hereby, confirmed.

Sec. 24. That the President of the United States may, from time to time, set apart and reserve, in any State or Territory having public land bearing forests, in any part of the public lands wholly or in part covered with timber or undergrowth, whether of commercial value or not, as public reservations, and the President shall, by public proclamation, declare the establishment of such reservations and the limits thereof.

Source:
Statutes at Large, Vol. 27, 561, pp. 1,095–1,103.

Frederick Jackson Turner, "The Significance of the Frontier in American History," 1893

In 1890, the U.S. Census declared that a frontier no longer existed. Upon learning this, Turner developed his eponymous "Thesis": Existence of the frontier turned those raised in a European culture into Americans, and "American democracy is fundamentally the outcome of the experience of the American people in dealing with the West," which led to the creation of a distinct American character. His work influenced several generations of historians.

———————————————— ⌘ ————————————————

Up to our own day American history has been in a large degree the history of the colonization of the Great West. The existence of an area of free land, continuous recession, and the advance of American settlements westward, explain American development. Behind institutions, behind constitutional forms and modifications lie the vital forces that call these organs into life and shape them to meet changing conditions. The peculiarity of American institutions is, the fact that they have been compelled to adapt themselves to the changes of an expanding people-to the changes involved in crossing a continent, this winning a wilderness, and in developing at each area of this progress out of the primitive economic and political conditions of the frontier into the complexity of city life. . . . Thus American development has exhibited not merely advance along a single line, but a return to primitive conditions on a continually advancing frontier line, and a new development for that area. American social development has been continually beginning over again on the frontier. This perennial rebirth, this fluidity of American life, this expansion westward with its new opportunities, its continuous touch with the simplicity of primitive society, furnish the forces dominating American character. The true point of view in the history of this nation is not the Atlantic coast, it is the West. . . .

The frontier is the line of most rapid and effective Americanization. The wilderness masters the colonist. It finds him a European in dress, industries, tools, modes of travel, and thought. It takes him from the railroad car and puts him in the birch canoe. It strips off the garments of civilization and arrays him in the hunting shirt and the moccasin. It puts him in the log cabin of the Cherokee and Iroquois and runs and Indian palisade around him. Before long he has gone to planting Indian corn and plowing with a sharp stick; he shouts the war cry and takes the scalp in orthodox Indian fashion. In short, at the frontier the environment is at first too strong for the man. He must accept the conditions which it furnishes, or perish, and so he fits himself into the Indian clearings and follows the Indian trails. Little by little he transforms the wilderness but the outcome is not the old Europe, not simply the development of Germanic germs, any more than the first phenomenon was a case of reversion to the Germanic mark. The fact is, that here is a new product that is American. At first, the frontier was the Atlantic coast. It was the frontier of Europe in a very real sense. Moving westward, the frontier became more and more American. As successive terminal moraines result from successive glaciations, so each frontier leaves its traces behind it, and when it becomes a settled area the region still partakes of the frontier characteristics. Thus the advance of the frontier has meant a steady movement away from the influence of Europe, a steady growth of independence on American lines. And to study this advance, the men who grew up under these conditions, and the political, economic, and social results of its, is to study the really American part of our history. . . .

Since the days when the fleet of Columbus sailed into the waters of the New World, America has been another name for opportunity, and the people of the United States have taken their tone form the incessant expansion which has not only been open but has been forced upon them. He would be a rash prophet who should assert that the expansive character has now entirely ceased. Movement has been its dominant fact, and unless this training has no effect upon a people, the American energy will continually demand a wider field for its exercise. But never again will such gifts of free land offer themselves. For a moment, at the frontier, the bonds of custom are broken and unrestraint is triumphant. There is not tabula rasa. The stubborn American environment is there with its imperious summons to accept its conditions; the inherited ways of doing things are also there; and yet, in spite of environment, and in spite of custom, each frontier did indeed furnish a new field of opportunity, a gate of escape from the bondage of the past; and freshness and confidence, and scorn of older society, impatience of its restrains and its ideas, and indifference to its lessons, have accompanied the frontier. What the Mediterranean Sea was to the Greeks, breaking the bond of custom, offering new experiences, calling out new institutions and activities, that, and more, the ever retreating frontier has been to the United States directly, and to the nations of Europe more remotely. And now, four centuries from the discovery of America, at the end of a hundred years of life under the Constitution, the frontier has gone, and with its going has closed the first period in American history.

Source:
Frederick Jackson Turner, *The Frontier in American History.* New York: Henry Holt and Company, 1921.

Carey Desert Land Grant Act, 1894

Federal U.S. legislation, passed on August 18, 1894, that made federally owned arid lands available to settlers for agricultural purposes. The act authorized the president to turn over to each of the public-land states (those created out of the public domain) up to 1 million acres of public desert land to sell to settlers for irrigation, reclamation, cultivation, and occupancy. The states could charge no more than 50 cents per acre (though additional fees could be levied for water rights), and tract size could range up to 160 acres. At least 20 acres of the tract had to be cultivated or the land would revert to public domain. But large-scale irrigation was prohibitively expensive until the Newlands Reclamation Act authorized federal funds for irrigation.

An Act

To amend sections twenty-four hundred and one and twenty-four hundred and three of the Revised Statutes.

Be it enacted by the Senate and House of Representatives of the United States of America in Congress assembled, That section twenty-four hundred and one of the Revised Statutes of the United States is hereby amended so as to read as follows:

"Sec. 2401. When the settlers in any township not mineral or reserved by the Government, or persons and associations lawfully possessed of coal lands and otherwise qualified to make entry thereof, or when the owners or grantees of public lands of the United States, under any law thereof, desire a survey made of the same under the authority of the surveyor-general and shall file an application therefor in writing, and shall deposit in a proper United States depository to the credit of the United States a sum sufficient to pay for such survey, together with all expenditures incident thereto, without cost or claim for indemnity on the United States, it shall be lawful for the surveyor-general, under such instructions as may be given him by the Commissioner of the General Land Office, and in accordance with law, to survey such township or such public lands owned by said grantees of the Government, and make return therefor to the general and proper local land office: *Provided,* That no application shall be granted unless the township so proposed to be surveyed is within the range of the regular progress of the public surveys embraced by existing standard lines or bases for township and subdivisional surveys."

Sec 2. That section twenty-four hundred and three of the Revised Statutes of the United States as heretofore amended is hereby amended so as to read as follows:

"Sec. 2403. Where settlers or owners or grantees of public lands make deposits in accordance with the provisions of section twenty-four hundred and one, as hereby amended, certificates shall be issued for such deposits which may be used by settlers in part payment for the lands settled upon by them, the survey of which is paid for out of such deposits, or said certificates may be assigned by indorsement and may be received by the Government in payment for any public lands of the United States in the States where the surveys were made, entered or to be entered under the laws thereof."

Sec. 3. That all laws and parts of laws inconsistent with this Act be, and the same are hereby, repealed.

Source:
Statutes at Large, Vol. 28, p. 423.

Cultural Diversity and National Unity

Charles Darwin, Introduction to *On the Origin of Species,* 1859

Charles Darwin's *On the Origin of Species* (1859) sets forth the theory that evolution is governed by a process called natural selection. According to Darwin, natural selection is the process by which genetic mutations and recombinations occur in such a way that only the individual most suited, or most "fit" to a particular environment, survives. Darwin had spent five years in South America as a naturalist on the HMS *Beagle.* In his introduction, he states how this experience shaped his ideas about how and why variation occurs in a species. Darwin outlines the 14 chapters of his book, beginning with a study of domesticated plants and animals. The early chapters set the foundation for his discussion of natural selection in chapter 4. The remaining chapters elaborate on the theory in more detail, treating such topics as instinct and hybridism.

Darwin's theories did not enter the dominant American culture until the end of the 19th century, when a philosophy called Social Darwinism took hold. Popularized by Yale professor William Graham Sumner, his brand emphasized "survival of the fittest," in which the best and most efficient businesses would drive out those that were a drag on the economy. Under this philosophy, government regulation only impeded the process. As oil magnate John D. Rockefeller wrote in a metaphor for his own practices, "The American beauty rose can be produced in the splendor and fragrance which bring cheer to its beholder only by sacrificing the early buds which grow up about it. . . . It is merely the working out of a law of Nature and of God."

———————————— ⌇ ————————————

WHEN on board H.M.S. *Beagle*, as naturalist, I was much struck with certain facts in the distribution of the inhabitants of South America, and in the geological relations of the present to the past inhabitants of that continent. These facts seemed to me to throw some light on the origin of species — that mystery of mysteries, as it has been called by one of our greatest philosophers. On my return home, it occurred to me, in 1837, that something might perhaps be made out on this question by patiently accumulating and reflecting on all sorts of facts which could possibly have any bearing on it. After five years' work I allowed myself to speculate on the subject, and drew up some short notes; these I enlarged in 1844 into a sketch of the conclusions, which then seemed to me probable: from that period to the present day I have steadily pursued the same object. I hope that I may be excused for entering on these personal details, as I give them to show that I have not been hasty in coming to a decision.

My work is now nearly finished; but as it will take me two or three more years to complete it, and as my health is far from strong, I have been urged to publish this Abstract. I have more especially been induced to do this, as Mr Wallace, who is now studying the natural history of the Malay archipelago, has arrived at almost exactly the same general conclusions that I have on the origin of species. Last year he sent to me a memoir on this subject, with a request that I would forward it to Sir Charles Lyell, who sent it to the Linnean Society, and it is published in the third volume of the journal of that Society. Sir C. Lyell and Dr Hooker, who both knew of my work—the latter having read my sketch of 1844—honoured me by thinking it advisable to publish, with Mr Wallace's excellent memoir, some brief extracts from my manuscripts.

This Abstract, which I now publish, must necessarily be imperfect. I cannot here give references and authorities for my several statements; and I must trust to the reader reposing some confidence in my accuracy. No doubt errors will have crept in, though I hope I have always been cautious in trusting to good authorities alone. I can here give only the general conclusions at which I have arrived, with a few facts in illustration, but which, I hope, in most cases will suffice. No one can feel more sensible than I do of the necessity of hereafter publishing in detail all the facts, with references, on which my conclusions have been grounded; and I hope in a future work to do this. For I am well aware that scarcely a single point is discussed in this volume on which facts cannot be adduced, often apparently leading to conclusions directly opposite to those at which I have arrived. A fair result can be obtained only by fully stating and balancing the facts and arguments on both sides of each question; and this cannot possibly be here done.

I much regret that want of space prevents my having the satisfaction of acknowledging the generous assistance which I have received from very many naturalists, some of them personally unknown to me. I cannot, however, let this opportunity pass without expressing my deep obligations to Dr Hooker, who for the last fifteen years has aided me in every possible way by his large stores of knowledge and his excellent judgement.

In considering the Origin of Species, it is quite conceivable that a naturalist, reflecting on the mutual affinities of organic beings, on their embryological relations, their geographical distribution, geological succession, and other such facts, might come to the conclusion that each species had not been independently created, but had descended, like varieties, from other species. Nevertheless, such a conclusion, even if well founded, would be unsatisfactory, until it could be shown how the innumerable species inhabiting this world have been modified so as to acquire that perfection of structure and co-adaptation which most justly excites our admiration. Naturalists continually refer to external conditions, such as climate, food, &c., as the only possible cause of variation. In one very limited sense, as we shall hereafter see, this may be true; but it is preposterous to attribute to mere external conditions, the structure, for instance, of the woodpecker, with its feet, tail, beak, and tongue, so admirably adapted to catch insects under the bark of trees. In the case of the misseltoe, which draws its nourishment from certain trees, which has seeds that must be transported by certain birds, and which has flowers with separate sexes absolutely requiring the agency of certain insects to bring pollen from one flower to the other, it is equally preposterous to account for the structure of this parasite, with its relations to several distinct organic beings, by the effects of external conditions, or of habit, or of the volition of the plant itself.

The author of the 'Vestiges of Creation' would, I presume, say that, after a certain unknown number of generations, some bird had given birth to a woodpecker, and some plant to the misseltoe, and that these had been produced perfect as we now see them; but this assumption seems to me to be no explanation, for it leaves the case of the coadaptations of organic beings to each other and to their physical conditions of life, untouched and unexplained.

It is, therefore, of the highest importance to gain a clear insight into the means of modification and coadaptation. At the commencement of my observations it seemed to me probable that a careful study of domesticated animals and of cultivated plants would offer the best chance of making out this obscure problem. Nor have I been disappointed; in this and in all other perplexing cases I have invariably found that our knowledge, imperfect though it be, of variation under domestication, afforded the best and safest clue. I may venture to express my conviction of the high value of such studies, although they have been very commonly neglected by naturalists.

From these considerations, I shall devote the first chapter of this Abstract to Variation under Domestication. We shall thus see that a large amount of hereditary modification is at least possible, and, what is equally or more important, we shall see how great is the power of man in accumulating by his Selection successive slight variations. I will then pass on to the variability of species in a state of nature; but I shall, unfortunately, be compelled to treat this subject far too briefly, as it can be treated properly only by giving long catalogues of facts. We shall, however, be enabled to discuss what circumstances are most favourable to variation. In the next chapter the Struggle for Existence amongst all organic beings throughout the world, which inevitably follows from their high geometrical powers of increase, will be treated of. This is the doctrine of Malthus, applied to the whole animal and vegetable kingdoms. As many more individuals of each species are born than can possibly survive; and as, consequently, there is a frequently recurring struggle for existence, it follows that any being, if it vary however slightly in any manner profitable to itself, under the complex and sometimes varying conditions of life, will have a better chance of surviving, and thus be naturally selected. From the strong principle of inheritance, any selected variety will tend to propagate its new and modified form.

This fundamental subject of Natural Selection will be treated at some length in the fourth chapter; and we shall then see how Natural Selection almost inevitably causes much Extinction of the less improved forms of life and induces what I have called Divergence of Character. In the next chapter I shall discuss the complex and little known laws of variation and of correlation of growth. In the four succeeding chapters, the most apparent and gravest difficulties on the theory will be given: namely, first, the difficulties of transitions, or understanding how a simple being or a simple organ can be changed and perfected into a highly developed being or elaborately constructed organ; secondly the subject of Instinct, or the mental powers of animals, thirdly, Hybridism, or the infertility of species and the fertility of varieties when intercrossed; and fourthly, the imperfection of the Geological Record. In the next chapter I shall consider the geological succession of organic beings throughout time; in the eleventh and twelfth, their geographical distribution throughout space; in the thirteenth, their classification or mutual affinities, both when mature and in an embryonic condition. In the last chapter I shall give a brief recapitulation of the whole work, and a few concluding remarks.

No one ought to feel surprise at much remaining as yet unexplained in regard to the origin of species and varieties, if he makes due allowance for our profound ignorance in regard to the mutual relations of all the beings which live around us. Who can explain why one species ranges widely and is very numerous, and why another allied species has a narrow range and is rare? Yet these relations are of the highest importance, for they determine the present welfare, and, as I believe, the future success and modification of every inhabitant of this world. Still less do we know of the mutual relations of the innumerable inhabitants of the world during the many past geological epochs in its history. Although much remains obscure, and will long remain obscure, I can entertain no doubt, after the most deliberate study and dispassionate judgement of which I am capable, that the view which most naturalists entertain, and which I formerly entertained—namely, that each species has been independently created—is erroneous. I am fully convinced that species are not immutable; but that those belonging to what are called the same genera are lineal descendants of some other and generally extinct species, in the same manner as the acknowledged varieties of any one species are the descendants of that species. Furthermore, I am convinced that Natural Selection has been the main but not exclusive means of modification.

Source:
Landmark Documents in American History, Facts On File, Inc.

Civil Rights Act, 1875

Federal act designed to prohibit social discrimination against blacks, passed by Congress on March 1, 1875. The act guaranteed to all citizens—regardless of race, color, or previous condition of servitude—equal rights in public places, such as inns, theaters, restaurants, and public conveyances. Denial of these rights was punishable by payment to the aggrieved person and fine or imprisonment. Many whites refused to obey the act, and in 1883 the Supreme Court struck down the law as unconstitutional on the grounds that Congress did not have the authority to legislate the social customs of any state. The 1875 act was the last federal civil rights legislation until the Civil Rights Act of 1957.

An Act

To protect all citizens in their civil and legal rights.

Whereas, it is essential to just government we recognize the equality of all men before the law, and hold that it is the duty of government in its dealings with the people to mete out equal and exact justice to all, of whatever nativity, race, color, or persuasion, religious or political; and it being the appropriate object of legislation to enact great fundamental principles into law: Therefore,

Be it enacted by the Senate and House of Representatives of the United States of America in Congress assembled, That all persons within the jurisdiction of the United States shall be entitled to the full and equal enjoyment of the accommodations, advantages, facilities, and privileges of inns, public conveyances on land or water, theaters, and other places of public amusement; subject only to the conditions and limitations established by law, and applicable alike to citizens of every race and color, regardless of any previous condition of servitude.

Sec. 2. That any person who shall violate the foregoing section by denying to any citizen, except for reasons by law applicable to citizens of every race and color, and regardless of any previous condition of servitude, the full enjoyment of any of the accommodations, advantages, facilities, or privileges in said section enumerated, or by aiding or inciting such denial, shall, for every such offense, forfeit and pay the sum of five hundred dollars to the person aggrieved thereby, to be recovered in an action of debt, with full costs; and shall also, for every such offense, be deemed guilty of a misdemeanor, and, upon conviction thereof, shall be fined not less than five hundred nor more than one thousand dollars, or shall be imprisoned not less than thirty days nor more than one year: *Provided,* That all persons may elect to sue for the penalty aforesaid or to proceed under their rights at common law and by State statutes; and having so elected to proceed in the one mode or the other, their right to proceed in the other jurisdiction shall be barred. But this proviso shall not apply to criminal proceedings, either under this act or the criminal law of any State: *And provided further,* That a judgment for the penalty in favor of the party aggrieved, or a judgment upon an indictment, shall be a bar to either prosecution respectively.

Sec. 3. That the district and circuit courts of the United States shall have, exclusively of the courts of the several States, cognizance of all crimes and offenses against, and violations of, the provisions of this act; and actions for the penalty given by the preceding section may be prosecuted in the territorial, district, or circuit courts of the United States wherever the defendant may be found, without regard to the other party; and the district attorneys, marshals, and deputy marshals of the United States, and commissioners appointed by the circuit and territorial courts of the United States, with powers of arresting and imprisoning or bailing offenders against the laws of the United States, are hereby specially authorized and required to institute proceedings against every person who shall violate the provisions of this act, and cause him to be arrested and imprisoned or bailed, as the case may be, for trial before such court of the United States, or territorial court, as by law has cognizance of the offense, except in respect of the right of action accruing to the person aggrieved; and such district attorneys shall cause such proceedings to be prosecuted to their termination as in other cases: *Provided,* That nothing contained in this section shall be construed to deny or defeat any right of civil action accruing to any person, whether by reason of this act or otherwise; and any district attorney who shall willfully fail to institute and prosecute the proceedings herein required, shall, for every such offense, forfeit and pay the sum of five hundred dollars to the person aggrieved thereby, to be recovered by an action of debt, with full costs, and shall, on conviction thereof, be deemed guilty of a misdemeanor, and be fined not less than one thousand nor more than five thousand dollars: *And provided further,* That a judgment for the penalty in favor or the party aggrieved against any such district attorney, or a judgment upon an indictment against any such district attorney, shall be a bar to either prosecution respectively.

Sec. 4. That no citizen possessing all other qualifications which are or may be prescribed by law shall be disqualified for service as grand or petit juror in any court of the United States, or of any State, on account of race, color, or previous condition of servitude; and any officer or other person charged with any duty in the selection or summoning of jurors who shall exclude or fail to summon any citizen for the cause aforesaid shall, on conviction thereof, be deemed guilty of a misdemeanor, and be fined not more than five thousand dollars.

Sec. 5. That all cases arising under the provisions of this act in the courts of the United States shall be reviewable by the Supreme Court of the United States, without regard to the sum in controversy, under the same provisions and regulations as are now provided by law for the review of other causes in said court.

Source:
Statutes at Large, Vol. 19, pp. 333–337.

Chinese Exclusion Act of 1882

Legislation passed by the U.S. Congress suspending the immigration of Chinese laborers to the United States for 10 years. Although the Burlingame Treaty of 1868 had permitted immigration, by the 1870s the large influx of Chinese laborers, especially to California, was producing increasing resentment among competing white laborers, including the Knights of Labor. In 1879 Congress passed a bill prohibiting further Chinese immigration, but it was vetoed by President Rutherford B. Hayes. The following year a new treaty with China gave the United States the right to limit or suspend the entry of Chinese labor but not to prohibit it absolutely. The 1882 suspension of immigration was renewed for another decade in 1892. The 1902 act, more restrictive than previous measures, extended the law to the Philippines and Hawaii and prevented Chinese migration from these islands to the mainland. Its prohibitions remained in effect until 1943, when immigration was permitted under a strict quota system.

In 1907 the United States and Japan concluded what is known as "The Gentlemen's Agreement" to limit Japanese immigration. It was first affirmed in a Japanese diplomatic note on February 24, 1907, and later confirmed in another Japanese note on February 18, 1908.

───────── ⌘ ─────────

An Act

To execute certain treaty stipulations relating to Chinese.

Whereas, in the opinion of the Government of the United States the coming of Chinese laborers to this country endangers the good order of certain localities within the territory thereof: Therefore,

Be it enacted by the Senate and House of Representatives of the United States of America in Congress assembled, That from and after the expiration of ninety days next after the passage of this act, and until the expiration of ten years next after the passage of this act, the coming of Chinese laborers to the United States be, and the same is hereby, suspended; and during such suspension it shall not be lawful for any Chinese laborer to come, or, having so come after the expiration of said ninety days, to remain within the United States.

Sec. 2. That the master of any vessel who shall knowingly bring within the United States on such vessel, and land or permit to be landed, any Chinese laborer, from any foreign port or place, shall be deemed guilty of a misdemeanor, and on conviction thereof shall be punished by a fine of not more than five hundred dollars for each and every such Chinese laborer so brought, and may be also imprisoned for a term not exceeding one year.

Sec. 3. That the two foregoing sections shall not apply to Chinese laborers who were in the United States on the seventeenth day of November, eighteen hundred and eighty, or who shall have come into the same before the expiration of ninety days next after the passage of this act, and who shall produce to such master before going on board such vessel, and shall produce to the collector of the port in the United States at which such vessel shall arrive, the evidence hereinafter in this act required of his being one of the laborers in this section mentioned; nor shall the two foregoing sections apply to the case of any master whose vessel, being bound to a port not within the United States, shall come within the jurisdiction of the United States by reason of being in distress or in stress of weather, or touching at any port of the United States on its voyage to any foreign port or place: *Provided,* That all Chinese laborers brought on such vessel shall depart with the vessel on leaving port.

Sec. 4. That for the purpose of properly identifying Chinese laborers who were in the United States on the seventeenth day of November, eighteen hundred and eighty, or who shall have come into the same before the expiration of ninety days next after the passage of this act, and in order to furnish them with the proper evidence of their right to go from and come to the United States of their free will and accord, as provided by the treaty between the United States and China dated November seventeenth, eighteen hundred and eighty, the collector of customs of the district from which any such Chinese laborer shall depart from the United States shall, in person or by deputy, go on board each vessel having on board any such Chinese laborer and cleared or about to sail from his district for a foreign port, and on such vessel make a list of all such Chinese laborers, which shall be entered in registry-books to be kept for that purpose, in which shall be stated the name, age, occupation, last place of residence, physical marks or peculiarities, and all facts necessary for the identification of each of such Chinese laborers, which books shall be safely kept in the custom-house; and every such Chinese laborer so departing from the United States shall be entitled to, and shall receive, free of any charge or cost upon application therefor, from the collector or his deputy, at the time such list is taken, a certificate, signed by the collector or his deputy and attested by his seal of office, in such form as the Secretary of the Treasury shall prescribe, which certificate shall contain a statement of the name, age, occupation, last place of residence, personal description, and facts of identification of the Chinese laborer to whom the certificate is issued, corresponding with the said list and registry in all particulars. In case any Chinese laborer after having received such certificate shall leave such vessel before her departure he shall deliver his certificate to the master of the vessel, and if such Chinese laborer shall fail to return to such vessel before her departure from port the certificate shall be delivered by the master to the collector of customs for cancellation. The certificate herein provided for shall entitle the Chinese laborer to whom the same is issued to return to and re-enter the United States upon producing and delivering the same to the collector of customs of the district at which such Chinese laborer shall seek to re-enter; and upon delivery of such certificate by such Chinese laborer to the collector of customs at the time of re-entry in the United States, said collector shall cause the same to be filed in the custom-house and duly canceled.

Sec. 5. That any Chinese laborer mentioned in section four of this act being in the United States, and desiring to depart from the United States by land, shall have the right to demand and receive, free of charge or cost, a certificate of identification similar to that provided for in section four of this act to be issued to such Chinese laborers as may desire to leave the United States by water; and it is hereby made the duty of the collector of customs of the district next adjoining the foreign country to which said Chinese laborer desires to go to issue such certificate, free of charge or cost, upon application by such Chinese laborer, and to enter the same upon registry-books to be kept by him for the purpose, as provided for in section four of this act.

Sec. 6. That in order to the faithful execution of articles one and two of the treaty in this act before mentioned, every Chinese person other than a laborer who may be entitled by said treaty and this act to come within the United States, and who shall be about to come to the United States, shall be identified as so entitled by the Chinese Government in each case, such identity to be evidenced by a certificate issued under the authority of said government, which certificate shall be in the English language or (if not in the English language) accompanied by a translation into English, stating such right to come, and which certificate shall state the name, title, or official rank, if any, the age, height, and all physical peculiarities, former and present occupation or profession, and place of residence in China of the person to whom the certificate is issued and that such person is entitled conformably to the treaty in this act mentioned to come within the United States. Such certificate shall be prima-facie evidence of the fact set forth therein, and shall be produced to the collector of customs, or his deputy, of the port in the district in the United States at which the person named therein shall arrive.

Sec. 7. That any person who shall knowingly and falsely alter or substitute any name for the name written in such certificate or forge any such certificate, or knowingly utter any forged or fraudulent certificate, or falsely personate any person named in any such certificate, shall be deemed guilty of a misdemeanor; and upon conviction thereof shall be fined in a sum not exceeding one thousand dollars, and imprisoned in a penitentiary for a term of not more than five years.

Sec. 8. That the master of any vessel arriving in the United States from any foreign port or place shall, at the same time he delivers a manifest of the cargo, and if there be no cargo, then at the time of making a report of the entry of the vessel pursuant to law, in addition to the other matter required to be reported, and before landing, or permitting to land, any Chinese passengers, deliver and report to the collector of customs of the district in which such vessels shall have arrived a separate list of all Chinese passengers taken on board his vessel at any foreign port or place, and all such passengers on board the vessel at that time. Such list shall show the names of such passengers (and if accredited officers of the Chinese Government traveling on the business of that government, or their servants, with a note of such facts), and the names and other particulars, as shown by their respective certificates; and such list shall be sworn to by the master in the manner required by law in relation to the manifest of the cargo. Any willful refusal or neglect of any such master to comply with the provisions of this section shall incur the same penalties and forfeiture as are provided for a refusal or neglect to report and deliver a manifest of the cargo.

Sec. 9. That before any Chinese passengers are landed from any such vessel, the collector, or his deputy, shall proceed to examine such passengers, comparing the certificates with the list and with the passengers; and no passenger shall be allowed to land in the United States from such vessel in violation of law.

Sec. 10. That every vessel whose master shall knowingly violate any of the provisions of this act shall be deemed forfeited to the United States, and shall be liable to seizure and condemnation in any district of the United States into which such vessel may enter or in which she may be found.

Sec. 11. That any person who shall knowingly bring into or cause to be brought into the United States by land, or who shall knowingly aid or abet the same, or aid or abet the landing in the United States from any vessel of any Chinese person not lawfully entitled to enter the United States, shall be deemed guilty of a misdemeanor, and shall, on conviction thereof, be fined in a sum not exceeding one thousand dollars, and imprisoned for a term not exceeding one year.

Sec. 12. That no Chinese person shall be permitted to enter the United States by land without producing to the proper officer of customs the certificate in this act required of Chinese persons seeking to land from a vessel.

And any Chinese person found unlawfully within the United States shall be caused to be removed therefrom to the country from whence he came, by direction of the President of the United States, and at the cost of the United States, after being brought before some justice, judge, or commissioner of a court of the United States and found to be one not lawfully entitled to be or remain in the United States.

Sec. 13. That this act shall not apply to diplomatic and other officers of the Chinese Government traveling upon the business of that government, whose credentials shall be taken as equivalent to the certificate in this act mentioned, and shall exempt them and their body and household servants from the provisions of this act as to other Chinese persons.

Sec. 14. That hereafter no State court of the United States shall admit Chinese to citizenship; and all laws in conflict with this act are hereby repealed.

Sec. 15. That the words "Chinese laborers," wherever used in this act, shall be construed to mean both skilled and unskilled laborers and Chinese employed in mining.

Source:
United States Statutes at Large, Vol. 22, pp. 58–61.

Jacob A. Riis, *How the Other Half Lives*, 1890

Jacob Riis, a Danish-born journalist, published his scathing description of New York City tenement life in 1890, awakening public opinion to the slum conditions that nurtured disease and crime. *How the Other Half Lives* was the first of a number of influential works by Riis and others bringing the living and working conditions of urban dwellers, especially immigrant women and children, to the attention of civic reformers and health and social workers on the eve of the Progressive Era. After reading his book, Theodore Roosevelt, then a civil service commissioner, left his card with Riis, on which he wrote "I have read your book and I have come to help." Today readers are put off by Riis's undisguised anti-Semitism, but the book remains as one of the most influential of the late 19th century.

———— ⌒⊗⌒ ————

Introduction

LONG ago it was said that "one half of the world does not know how the other half lives." That was true then. It did not know because it did not care. The half that was on top cared little for the struggles, and less for the fate of those who were underneath, so long as it was able to hold them there and keep its own seat. There came a time when the discomfort and crowding below were so great, and the consequent upheavals so violent, that it was no longer an easy thing to do, and then the upper half fell to inquiring what was the matter. Information on the subject has been accumulating rapidly since, and the whole world has had its hands full answering for its old ignorance.   1 In New York, the youngest of the world's great cities, that time came later than elsewhere, because the crowding had not been so great. There were those who believed that it would never come; but their hopes were vain. Greed and reckless selfishness wrought like results here as in the cities of older lands. "When the great riot occurred in 1863," so reads the testimony of the Secretary of the Prison Association of New York before a legislative committee appointed to investigate causes of the increase of crime in the State twenty-five years ago, "every hiding-place and nursery of crime discovered itself by immediate and active participation in the operations of the mob. Those very places and domiciles, and all that are like them, are to-day nurseries of crime, and of the vices and disorderly courses which lead to crime. By far the largest part—eighty per cent. at least—of crimes against property and against the person are perpetrated by individuals who have either lost connection with home life, or never had any, or whose homes had ceased to be sufficiently separate, decent, and desirable to afford what are regarded as ordinary wholesome influences of home and family. . . . The younger criminals seem to come almost exclusively from the worst tenement house districts, that is, when traced back to the very places where they had their homes in the city here." Of one thing New York made sure at that early stage of the inquiry: the boundary line of the Other Half lies through the tenements.   2 It is ten years and over, now, since that line divided New York's population evenly. To-day three-fourths of its people live in the tenements, and the nineteenth century drift of the population to the cities is sending ever-increasing multitudes to crowd them. The fifteen thousand tenant houses that were the despair of the sanitarian in the past generation have swelled into thirty-seven thousand, and more than twelve hundred thousand persons call them home. The one way out he saw—rapid transit to the suburbs—has brought no relief. We know now that there is no way out; that the "system" that was the evil offspring of public neglect and private greed has come to stay, a storm-centre forever of our civilization. Nothing is left but to make the best of a bad bargain.   3 What the tenements are and how they grew to what they are, we shall see hereafter. The story is dark enough, drawn from the plain public records, to send a chill to any heart. If it shall appear that the sufferings and the sins of the "other half," and the evil they breed, are but as a just punishment upon the community that gave it no other choice, it will be because that is the truth. The boundary line lies there because, while the forces for good on one side vastly outweigh the bad—it were not well otherwise—in the tenements all the influences make for evil; because they are the hot-beds of the epidemics that carry death to rich and poor alike; the nurseries of pauperism and crime that fill our jails and police courts; that throw off a scum of forty thousand human wrecks to the island asylums and workhouses year by year; that turned out in the last eight years a round half million beggars to prey upon our charities; that maintain a standing army of ten thousand tramps with all that that implies; because, above all, they touch the family life with deadly moral contagion. This is their worst crime, inseparable from the system. That we have to own it the child of our own wrong does not excuse it, even though it gives it claim upon our utmost patience and tenderest charity.   4 What are you going to do about it? is the question of to-day. It was asked once of our city in taunting defiance by a band of political cutthroats, the legitimate outgrowth of life on the tenement-house level. 1 Law and order found the answer then and prevailed. With our enormously swelling population held in this galling bondage, will that answer always be given? It will depend on how fully the situation that prompted the challenge is grasped. Forty per cent. of the distress among the poor, said a recent official report, is due to drunkenness. But the first legislative committee ever appointed to probe this sore went deeper down and uncovered its roots. The "conclusion forced itself upon it that certain conditions and associations of human life and habitation are the prolific parents of corresponding habits and morals," and it recommended "the prevention of drunkenness by providing for every man a clean and comfortable home." Years after, a sanitary inquiry brought to light the fact that "more than one-half of the tenements with two-thirds of their population were held by owners who made the keeping of them a business, generally a speculation. The owner was seeking a certain percentage on his outlay, and that percentage very rarely fell below fifteen per cent., and frequently exceeded thirty. 2 ... The complaint was universal among the tenants that they were entirely uncared for, and that the only answer to their requests to have the place put in order by repairs and necessary improvements was that they must pay their rent or leave. The agent's instructions were simple but emphatic: 'Collect the rent in advance, or, failing, eject the occupants.' Upon such a stock grew this upas-tree. Small wonder the fruit is bitter. The remedy that shall be an effective answer to the coming appeal for justice must proceed from the public conscience. Neither legislation nor charity can cover the ground. The greed of capital that wrought the evil must itself undo it, as far as it can now be undone. Homes must be built for the working masses by those who employ their labor; but tenements must cease to be "good property" in the old, heartless

sense. "Philanthropy and five per cent." is the penance exacted.   5 If this is true from a purely economic point of view, what then of the outlook from the Christian standpoint? Not long ago a great meeting was held in this city, of all denominations of religious faith, to discuss the question how to lay hold of these teeming masses in the tenements with Christian influences, to which they are now too often strangers. Might not the conference have found in the warning of one Brooklyn builder, who has invested his capital on this plan and made it pay more than a money interest, a hint worth heeding: "How shall the love of God be understood by those who have been nurtured in sight only of the greed of man?"

Note 1. The Tweed band of municipal robbers.
Note 2. Forty per cent. was declared by witnesses before a Senate Committee to be a fair average interest on tenement property. Instances were given of its being one hundred per cent. and over.

Source:
Jacob Riis, *How the Other Half Lives.* New York: Charles Scribner's Sons, 1890.

Frances E. Willard, "The Do Everything Policy," 1893

Address by Frances Willard, the president of the National Women's Christian Temperance Union (WCTU), delivered to the Second Biennial Convention of the World's Woman's Christian Temperance Union, and the Twentieth Annual Convention of the National Woman's Christian Temperance Union at the World's Columbian Exposition in Chicago in October 1893. According to WCTU's "Do Everything Policy," a woman will do everything possible "to antagonize the alcohol habit and the liquor traffic." Her speech also suggests that the temperance movement is dependent upon the suffrage movement. Willard believed that the vote for women needed to be secured before any legislation that would prohibit the consumption of alcohol could be enacted.

In the second half of her speech, Willard notes that in general, support for woman suffrage has increased. She concludes with a list of achievements made by women over the course of the past year, such as the growth of the number of women in religious office and other professional fields.

───────── ⌁⊗⌁ ─────────

Beloved Comrades of the White Ribbon Army:
    WHEN we began the delicate, difficult, and dangerous operation of dissecting out the alcohol nerve from the body politic, we did not realize the intricacy of the under-

taking nor the distances that must be traversed by the scalpel of investigation and research. In about seventy days from now, twenty years will have elapsed since the call of battle sounded its bugle note among the homes and hearts of Hillsboro, Ohio. We have all been refreshing our knowledge of those days by reading the "Crusade Sketches" of its heroic leader, **Mrs. Eliza J. Thompson**, "the mother of us all," and we know that but one thought, sentiment and purpose animated those saintly "Praying Bands" whose name will never die out from human history. "Brothers, we beg you not to drink and not to sell!" This was the one wailing note of these moral Paganinis, playing on one string. It caught the universal ear and set the key of that mighty orchestra, organised with so much toil and hardship, in which the tender and exalted strain of the Crusade violin still soars aloft, but upborne now by the clanging cornets of science, the deep trombones of legislation, and the thunderous drums of politics and parties. The "Do Everything Policy" was not of our choosing, but is an evolution as inevitable as any traced by the naturalist or described by the historian. Woman's genius for details, and her patient steadfastness in following the enemies of those she loves "through every lane of life," have led her to antagonise the alcohol habit and the liquor traffic *just where they are*, wherever that may be. If she does this, since they are *everywhere*, her policy will be *"Do Everything."*

A one-sided movement makes one-sided advocates. Virtues, like hounds, hunt in packs. Total abstinence is not the crucial virtue in life that excuses financial crookedness, defamation of character, or habits of impurity. The fact that one's father was, and one's self is, a bright and shining light in the total abstinence galaxy, does not give one a vantage ground for high-handed behaviour toward those who have not been trained to the special virtue that forms the central idea of the Temperance Movement. We have known persons who, because they had "never touched a drop of liquor," set themselves up as if they belonged to a royal line, but whose tongues were as biting as alcohol itself, and whose narrowness had no competitor save a straight line. An all-round movement can only be carried forward by all-round advocates; a scientific age requires the study of every subject in its correlations. It was once supposed that light, heat, and electricity were wholly separate entities; it is now believed and practically proved that they are but different modes of motion. Standing in the valley we look up and think we see an isolated mountain; climbing to its top we see that it is but one member of a range of mountains many of them of well-nigh equal altitude.

Some bright women who have opposed the "Do-Everything Policy" used as their favourite illustration a flowing river, and expatiated on the ruin that would follow if that river (which represents their do-one-thing policy) were diverted into many channels, but it should be remembered that the most useful of all rivers is the Nile, and that the agricultural economy of Egypt consists in the effort to spread its waters upon as many fields as possible. It is not for the river's sake that it flows through the country but for the sake of the fertility it can bring upon adjoining fields, and this is pre-eminently true of the Temperance Reform.

Joseph Cook, that devoted friend of every good cause has wisely said: "If England were at war with Russia, and the latter were to have several allies, it would obviously be necessary for England to attack the allies as well as the principal enemy. Not to do this would be foolishness, and might be suicide. In the conflict with the liquor traffic, the policy of the W.C.T.U. is to attack not only the chief foe, but also its notorious and open allies. This is the course dictated not only by common sense, but by absolute necessity. If the home is to be protected, not only must the dram-shop be made an outlaw, but its allies, the gambling hells, the houses of unreportable infamy, the ignorance of the general population as to alcoholics and other narcotics, the timidity of trade, the venality of portions of the press, and especially the subserviency of political parties to the liquor traffic, must be assailed as confederates of the chief enemy of the home. . . . It is certain that the broad and progressive policy of the W.C.T.U. in the United States makes the whiskey rings and time-serving politicians greatly dread its influence. They honour the Union by frequent and bitter attacks. It is a recognised power in international affairs. If its policy were made narrow and non-partisan, its influence would immensely wane in practical matters of great importance.

"The department of Scientific Temperance Instruction, conducted by the W.C.T.U., and led by **Mrs. Mary H. Hunt,** of Boston, has now made such instruction mandatory in thirty-six States of the Republic. This is a very large and substantial triumph of the broad and progressive policy. Instead of the National W.C.T.U. having lost the confidence of the churches by its broad policy, I believe, after much travel and years of observation, that it never had more of that confidence than at the present hour. At a recent Congressional Hearing, in Washington, I heard a distinguished Presbyterian Professor of Theology, **Rev. Dr. Herrick Johnson,** of Chicago, call the W.C.T.U. the most powerful, the most beneficent, and the most successful organization ever formed by women. Similar testimony abounds in all the most enlightened circles of the land."

Let us not be disconcerted, but stand bravely by that blessed trinity of movements, Prohibition, Woman's Liberation and Labour's uplift.

Everything is not in the Temperance Reform, but the Temperance Reform should be in everything.

There is no better motto for the "Do-Everything-Policy," than this which we are saying by our deeds: "Make a chain, for the land is full of bloody crimes and the city of violence."

If we can remember this simple rule, it will do much to unravel the mystery of the much controverted "Do-Everything-Policy," viz: *that every question of practical philanthropy or reform has its temperance aspect, and with that we are to deal.*

Methods that were once the only ones available may become, with the passage of years, less useful because less available. In earlier times the manly art of hunting was most helpful to civilization, because before fields could be cleared and tilled, they had to be free from the danger of wild beasts, and no method of obtaining food was more important than the chase; but when the forests have been cleared away and the pastoral condition of life has supervened, nay, more, when the highest civilization peoples the hills and valleys, it certainly evinces a lack of imagination to present such a spectacle as do the hunters who in England to-day place a poor stag in a van, convey him on four wheels to a wood, let him out through a door, and set trained dogs upon him, while they follow with guns and halloos, and call it "sport"! The same absurdity has been illustrated by **Baron Hirsch,** who recently imported 6,000 caged partridges to his country place, let them loose in the groves, and set himself and friends peppering away at them. Surely such conduct is the reverse of manly, and must bring what was once a noble occupation into contempt. But, in a different way, we illustrate the same principle, when we forget that

"New occasions teach new duties, Time makes ancient good uncouth."

We are too apt to think that what makes for us makes for the truth, and what makes for the truth must be true. Such a circle of reasoning leaves us, so far as logic goes, in the attitude said to have been assumed by the coffin of Mohammed-suspended between earth and heaven. A reformer is very apt to fall into this line of argumentation, a tendency which is perhaps most likely to be corrected by studying the correlated movements of other groups of men and women equally excellent, and by allying to the reform of which he is an advocate as many others germaine to it as may be practicable, always asking this question as the touchstone of the natural selection he would make "What is the Temperance aspect of this cognate reform and what its aspect toward the liquor traffic?"

The Temperance cause started out well night alone, but mighty forces have joined us in the long march. We are now in the midst of the Waterloo battle, and in the providence of God the Temperance army will not have to fight that out all by itself. For Science has come up with its glittering contingent, political economy deploys its legions, the woman question brings an Amazonian army upon the field, and the stout ranks of labor stretch away far as the eye can reach. As in the old Waterloo against Napoleon, so now against the Napoleon of the liquor traffic, no force is adequate except the *allied* forces.

The Quenchless Woman Question.

Perhaps the novel is the barometer of women's rise. Professor Swing, in his famous lecture on the novel, set forth his favourite theory that it is the apotheosis of woman, a creature far too bright and good to be cribbed, cabinned and confined within the conventional limits of the sphere that man's selfishness had circumscribed for her, and hence she expanded into the wider circle of the novel, where she played the public part denied her in real life; for she was made and meant to be a thing of beauty and a joy for ever, not to her home alone, but to the great world; and this is so true that in the less-developed ages, when man's self-restraint did not permit her to be a figure on the stage, young men and beautiful were attired in women's garb to act her part. When she became the central figure of the novel, it grew to be the most fascinating of all books, hence the most widely-read, in all the wilderness of literature. But this was only a figure of things to come, and predicted her admission to all the world contains. It was a sort of dress rehearsal for her part on the stage of life, wide as the planet and high as human need and sympathy. It is to be regretted that the woman, who in these regnant days of scientific Christianity and Christian science is not only "the coming woman," but has already come, should be a character so individual that the old-line novelists cannot adapt their concept or their style to her bright, new lineaments; but we, as women, should be devoutly thankful that the novelist of the future has some forerunners, in our own country, **Mrs. Elizabeth Stuart Phelps Ward,** and in England **George Meredith**, who, as one of our ablest woman journalists has said, "shows that it is possible for women to despise inconstancy and weakness, and not to cling to unworthiness in men with that blind doting love ascribed to them; that the rigid demand of a higher moral standard for women than for men frequently has its origin in the desire of brute force for absolute possession; that the faults and the virtues of women are the faults and virtues of the race; that a woman in her best estate is not an angel, nor in her worst worse than a bad man."

I wish we did not so much use the expression "emancipated woman." Its associations and history are not to our advantage. It would be far better to combine our efforts to make the term "awakened woman" current coin in the world's great exchange of speech.

Of all the fallacies ever concocted, none is more idiotic than the one indicated in the saying, "A woman's strength consists in her weakness." One might as well say that a man's purity consisted in his vileness, or that his sobriety consisted in his drunkenness! When was ever strength discounted, except by those who would have women kept in a condition of perpetual tutelage, or ignorance glorified except by those who desire her as a parasite? Nothing proves more conclusively the wretched nonsense of the conservative position on the "Woman Question" than that so noble an expression as "strong minded" should have become a synonym of reproach. It is the off-set of "weak minded," and to be weak minded is the greatest calamity that can fall upon a human being. Let us have done with this nomenclature, and the shallow wit that gives it currency, and let us insist first, last, and always that gentleness is never so attractive as when joined with strength, purity never so invincible as when leagued with intelligence, beauty never so charming as when it is seen to be the embellishment of reason and the concomitant of character. What we need to sound in the ears of girlhood is *to be brave*, and in the ears of boyhood *to be gentle*. There are not two sets of virtues; and there is but one greatness of character; it is that of him (or her) who combines the noblest traits of man and woman in nature, words, and deeds.

One of our leading literary men in America, recently put forth the theory that the reason that the male bird sings is because he is a male, and the reason why no woman has been a great poet-which premise we will not for a moment grant him-is that she is a female. He does, however, except Sappho, explaining her by this remarkable sentence: "There may have been at some time a chance female mocking bird which sang the dropping song, if one ever did this she performed a masculine act, a function of the male nature." But perhaps the male bird would not let the female sing, any more than priests in the high church to-day will permit that women shall chant the services. At least nobody can prove the contrary, and our argument stands on the same foundations as that of our brother who thinks that all art is an irradiation of masculinity. It seems unreasonable that the female thrush, as our logician states, "has just as perfect a singing box as the male, not a valve, not a muscle, intrinsic or extrinsic, not a line of contour in the whole windpipe, from the glottis down to the lowest bronchial extremities, yet the female thrush never sings a real song." But the fact that she has a throat made for singing proves that she is capable of song. The Creator has provided for it, and it is altogether probable that the male thrush, like the "male man," has preferred that she should "be in quietness."

But the time is past when any woman of sense rings the changes on the old phrase, "Our enemy, man." Nothing is more apparent than that the movement for our equal participation in all phases of the great world-life is as warmly, and perhaps more strenuously advocated by an army of progressive men than by any other class.

A London grand jury has recently declared that it finds nearly 20% of the prisoners with whose cases it has to deal, have been committed for assaults on women and girls, and the suggestion is made that some severer punishment than fines and imprisonment should be inflicted. Flogging is suggested, but doubtless a time will come when an effectual and reasonable, even if severe remedy will be ordained, namely, one that will in the nature of the case render impossible a recurrence of the crime.

It is said that Norway has a law by which the man must stand side by side with the woman as equally responsible for making away with their child. When such a law becomes general, infanticide will practically cease.

Words go a long way, phrases make epochs, and it is no small indication of progress that in the course of the hearing of a petition for divorce before **Sir Francis Jeune** in London within a few months past, it was agreed between the husband and wife that they should live apart, the husband receiving an allowance of 30s. a week so long as "he remained chaste." The judge said it was the first time he had seen such an expression in relation to the man in a contract of legal separation. We are glad to believe it will not be the last.

Social Purity.

When a man would rob a woman of her virtue or a woman is about to sell herself in the most degraded bargain that the mind can contemplate, what does he give her, and what does she take? Strong Drink.

Mrs. Josephine Butler says that in the early days of **Queen Victoria** the British Government wished to introduce a Contagious Diseases Act, but could not make up its mind to ask the virgin queen to sign such a bill. England has carried the Bible, alcoholic drink, and legalized harlotry to every country she has conquered. This has been the work of man: if woman were added to the Government she surely could do no worse, and in simple self-defence would be likely to do a great deal better. It is significant that the conception of legalized vice was, so far as we know, hatched in the brain of **Napoleon Bonaparte** that arch-despiser of women.

The cause of Social Purity has grown in the year past like "the stone cut out of the mountain." The history of the reform has not a parallel to the heroic undertaking of those brave, true-hearted women, **Mrs. Elizabeth Wheeler Andrew** and **Dr. Kate Bushnell**, whom I am proud to have had as my fellow-townswomen for twenty years or more. Their three months in India, during which under the most difficult conditions they followed the subtle intricacies of officialism in its illegal and covert relation to legalized vice, even as the hound follows the hare, have written their names high on the white arch of our roll of honour. But the secular press in both countries has overlooked the fact that they were sent out by the general officers of the World's W.C.T.U., and made their investigations in India by the special request of **Mrs. Josephine Butler**, World's W.C.T.U. superintendent of Social Purity work.

There are three sets of slaves that we women are working to emancipate. They are, white slaves, that is degraded women; wage slaves, that is the working classes; and whiskey slaves, that is the product furnished by brewers and distillers.

Dr. Mary Wood Allen has vindicated the choice that I suggested and you confirmed in making her our National Superintendent of Social Purity Work last year: she has invested a year of work memorable in the annals of our Society, and unique in that she has traversed several of the Southern States to which the message of the department had not before been carried save by the printed page.

The generous gifts of **Charles N. Crittenton, Esq.**, of California, have enabled us to found five Florence Crittenton Homes (named for the little daughter he loved and lost), in as many leading cities this year. Our Chicago "Anchorage" is one of these, and **Mr. Crittenton** is coming to England, where, under the auspices of the B.W.T.A., he will soon found another in London.

Woman's Ballot.

He who knows what ought to be knows what will be, and we know that the home vote ought to be let loose on the saloon; as our English leader has said, "She who is life-giver ought to be law-giver." The Michigan Liquor Dealers Association have decided to do their utmost to destroy the law that arms women in that State with the municipal ballot and declares that "when the Legislature granted this power to women (with an educational restriction) it struck a blow directly at the Liquor Dealers interests and rights."

"The eye of the law" is a correct phrase, for up to date the law has but one eye, it needs two, and women must furnish the other.

Local control of the Liquor Traffic by all the people (as **Abraham Lincoln** said, "by no means excluding women") is believed in England to be the best practicable measure that can be sought, and our forces there, much as they are divided on other lines, have united upon this. There is a tendency among temperance workers everywhere to the opinion that as a wise general first recruits and drills his troops, then marches them on to the enemy, it would be wiser in the Temperance forces to unite their efforts to secure the ballot for women before they further expend their energies in seeking the submission of constitutional amendments to be voted down by men. I have never made any secret of the opinion that if our forces could but have seen this as the wiser way, it would have been to our advantage, and I have heard Professor **Dickie**-that trusted leader of the Prohibition party-make the same

declaration; but it has been our view that the loyal thing to do was to march with the army and abide the decision of the majority as to methods of work, trusting that time, with its logic of events and its argument of defeat, would lead us all, sooner or later, to the right path, the true method of attack, and unite us in its application to the pulverization of the rum power.

Progress of Women in 1892–93.

If we think the cause of woman is not progressing as rapidly as it should for the interest of men and women, we must look back and see from what degradation she has escaped; for example, take this account from the *London Times*, July 18th, 1797, less than a hundred years ago. It reads as follows:

"On Friday a butcher exposed his wife for sale in Smithfield Market with a strap about her waist which tied her to a railing. A drover was the purchaser at three guineas and a crown." But **Petruchio** is still at large, that famous creation of **Shakespeare,** who said of his wife,

> "She is my goods, my chattels,
> She is my house, my household furniture,
> My field, my barn, my anything."

At the inauguration of the World's Columbian Exposition, in Machinery Hall, with an audience of one hundred and twenty-five thousand persons present, women shared in the speaking-a woman architect received the prize for designing the Woman's Building, and women participated equally with men throughout the exercises which were presided over by the Vice-President of the United States.

Women were represented as officers and speakers in the World's Columbian Congress of Religions, at which noted representatives of the ten great Religions were participants.

At the World's Catholic Congress (Columbian Exposition), women were not only on the platform, but on the programme—for the first time in the history of that great hierarchy.

The province of Nova Scotia has this year made the greatest advance that has been noted along ecclesiastical lines. **Miss M. Dauphinie** was elected as a lay delegate to the Methodist Annual Conference. There was no controversy concerning her admission; it was a ruling of the chair. The **Rev. Dr. Moore**, President of the Conference, should receive the thanks of all awakened women for having taken a position so honourable to himself and to us. Best of all, the *Wesleyan Methodist Journal* of the maritime province of Canada, says: "The ruling of the chair was received with great enthusiasm, and the report of the committee adopted."

The New Church (Swedenborgian) has authorised women to preach.

At our last National Convention, thirty-five women on a single Sunday occupied pulpits as preachers in Denver, Colorado. At the Autumn Conference of the National B.W.T.A. in Cardiff (Wales), nineteen pulpits were occupied by women.

An agitation is beginning among the Jews for the equal representation of women as voters and office holders in the congregation, and an influential Jewish journal declares this to be right, and claims that there is no valid obstacle in the way of its being carried into effect.

In two or more of the United States the Episcopal Church has voted to strike the word "male" from the constitutional provisions for the election of vestrymen and wardens.

The title of D.D. has been conferred upon a woman minister.

"The Foresters" is a benefit Society in England having a very large membership and great influence. At its recent annual meeting, a resolution was carried forbidding the women (who are now beginning to form auxiliary branches,) to hold their meetings in liquor shops, although the men have always done so, and do still. But it may be reasonably predicted that since the men so clearly perceive the demoralization likely to result from having their "women folks" meet in such an environment, they will in time cease to do so themselves, and we have every confidence that the women will help them to attain the higher standard by which they are now "unequally yoked."

Women are employed at railway switches and crossings in Italy because they do not get intoxicated.

Finland has 50,000 women who are total abstainers, in a population of two million persons.

The Queen Regent of Holland was the patron and official president of the recent International Temperance Congress at The Hague. She however delegated her duties to a man!

The National Republican League at its Convention in Louisville, Kentucky, May 11th, recommended to the favourable consideration of the Republican Clubs of the United States, the question of granting the women of the State and nation the right to vote at all elections on the same terms and conditions as the male citizens.

Kansas and Colorado have submitted amendments to their constitutions giving women the full ballot.

One of the best phases of the Temperance question in England just now is, that when the Direct Veto is obtained—and it seems quite sure to be given to the people before the year 1894 is out—it will be backed up by the municipal ballot for women, and thus local option will have a far better chance to win than it has ever known in the Republic.

The Legislature of Michigan has given to all women the municipal ballot.

New Zealand stands at the head of the list this year, having given the ballot to women, married and single, on all questions that affect the Government.

In Connecticut, the women vote this fall on school matters.

The American Federation of Labour, representing 700,000 working men, has declared for Woman's Suffrage.

The Farmers Alliance in most of the States adopts resolutions favourable to the ballot for women.

For the first time, a woman has been heard officially in Austria. A socialistic leader of Vienna, **Fraulein Dworzak**, was invited by the Minister of Commerce to speak as an expert before the Austrian Board of Trade, on the position of the working women of that country. She spoke for three hours, and described all the horrors of the working women's status.

The participation of women from almost all the leading European countries in the International Socialist Congress at Zurich, and the fact that a woman presided over one of the public sessions is a significant item in our progress for this year.

When Bryn Mawr College opened for instruction in the fall of 1885 there were 44 students, now there are over 200, and many are refused admission for lack of room. This is typical of the growth in all the leading women's colleges.

The first congress of lady-lawyers ever held, met at the Columbian Exposition, on August 3rd. There are 110 ladies in America who have been called to the Bar, and eight have earned the right to practise before the Supreme Court of the United States after having for three years pleaded at the Bar of the state or territory without any flaw in their public or private career.

Twenty-five years ago women writers were excluded from the **Charles Dickens** banquet in New York City by the Press Club. These women were individually indignant, and there the matter would have ended had they not had the wit to organize themselves into what has become the greatest, as it was the first notable literary society of women in the New World. Recently, this Society (the famous "Sorosis") has celebrated its "quarter-centennial," and the record of its successful work for the development and enfranchisement of women is known to all thoughtful minds throughout the world.

Nearly all the northern States have lady pharmacists. Illinois has over one hundred.

There are 30,000 women cyclists in America. France has 10,000; 9,000 of them living in Paris. There was recently in that city a cycling wedding party who went to church and thence to breakfast on their safeties. A French lady has established a record for herself by riding 17 1/2 miles in one hour.

Perhaps the most remarkable programme for the future relations of women to public affairs is the manifesto issued by the Women's Rights Party in Paris in connection with the recent elections. They declare that the existing state should be replaced by what they call the Mother State, which, by its foresight and solicitude would insure certainty of work to all able-bodied men, assistance to children and to the aged, the sick, and the deformed. They declare that

"The State, thoroughly informed with regard to the requirements of production in every industry, should, in accordance with this knowledge, enlist workers, and should provide for their being classed in society according to their talents, just as she classes them in the army according to their stature. The Mother State would suppress the liberty to die of hunger.

"There should be really universal suffrage—that is to say, exercised by both men and women.

"The revision of the Constitution by an assembly composed of both men and women.

"Free access, without distinction of sex, to all public employment and offices.

"The lightening of the burden on women, who have charge of and responsibility for human lives, the grant to every mother, married or not married, of an indemnity to be called the maternal indemnity.

"Obligatory military service for men, obligatory humanitarian service for women; the defence of the territory entrusted to men, the Philanthropies confided to women."

Source:
Library of Congress. Rare Book and Special Collections Division. National American Woman Suffrage Association Collection.

Booker T. Washington, "Atlanta Compromise Speech," 1895

Controversial speech delivered by African-American educator Booker T. Washington in Atlanta, Georgia, on September 18, 1895, that accepted a socially subordinated position for African Americans in the South. While calling for economic opportunity for his people, Washington stated that blacks should accept that they must climb up from the bottom of the economic ladder. He urged Southern whites to encourage and educate African-American laborers while maintaining social separation: "In all things that are purely social we can be as separate as the fingers, yet one as the hand in all things essential to mutual progress." He also called agitation for social equality "the extremist folly." Blacks, he argued, must earn and prepare for social "privileges." The speech gained national acclaim from whites, but some black leaders—most notably W. E .B. DuBois—denounced Washington's position.

Mr. President and Gentlemen of the Board of Directors and Citizens:

One-third of the population of the South is of the Negro race. No enterprise seeking the material, civil, or moral welfare of this section can disregard this element of our population and reach the highest success. I but convey to you, Mr. President and Directors, the sentiment of the masses of my race when I say that in no way have the value and manhood of the American Negro been more fittingly and generously recognized than by the managers of this magnificent Exposition at every stage of its progress. It is a recognition that will do more to cement the friendship of the two races than any occurrence since the dawn of our freedom.

Not only this, but the opportunity here afforded will awaken among us a new era of industrial progress. Ignorant and inexperienced, it is not strange that in the first years of our new life we began at the top instead of at the bottom; that a seat in Congress or the state legislature was more sought than real estate or industrial skill; that the political convention of stump speaking had more attractions than starting a dairy farm or truck garden.

A ship lost at sea for many days suddenly sighted a friendly vessel. From the mast of the unfortunate vessel was seen a signal, "Water, water; we die of thirst!" The answer from the friendly vessel at once came back, "Cast down your bucket where you are." A second time the signal, "Water, water; send us water!" ran up from the distressed vessel, and was answered, "Cast down your bucket where you are." And a third and fourth signal for water was answered, "Cast down your bucket where you are." The captain of the distressed vessel, at least heeding the injunction, cast down his bucket, and it came up full of fresh, sparkling water from the mouth of the Amazon River. To those of my race who depend on bettering their condition in a foreign land or who underestimate the importance of cultivating friendly relations with the southern white man, who is their next-door neighbour, I would say: "Cast down your bucket where you are"—cast it down in making friends in every manly way of the people of all races by whom we are surrounded.

Cast it down in agriculture, mechanics, in commerce, in domestic service, and in the professions. And in this connection it is well to bear in mind that whatever other sins the South may be called to bear, when it comes to business, pure and simple, it is in the South that the Negro is given a man's chance in the commercial world, and in nothing is this Exposition more eloquent than in emphasizing this chance. Our greatest danger is that in the great leap from slavery to freedom we may overlook the fact that the masses of us are to live by the productions of our hands, and fail to keep in mind that we shall prosper in proportion as we learn to dignify and glorify common labour and put brains and skill into the common occupations of life; shall prosper in proportion as we learn to draw the line between the superficial and the substantial, the ornamental gewgaws of life and the useful. No race can prosper till it learns that there is as much dignity in tilling a field as in writing a poem. It is at the bottom of life we must begin, and not at the top. Nor should we permit our grievances to overshadow our opportunities.

To those of the white race who look to the incoming of those of foreign birth and strange tongue and habits for the prosperity of the South, were I permitted I would repeat what I say to my own race, "Cast down your bucket where you are." Cast it down among the eight millions of Negroes whose habits you know, whose fidelity and love you have tested in days when to have proved treacherous meant the ruin of your firesides. Cast down your bucket among these people who have, without strikes and labor wars, tilled your fields, cleared your forests, builded your railroads and cities, and brought forth treasures from the bowels of the earth, and helped make possible this magnificent representation of the progress of the South. Casting down your bucket among my people, helping and encouraging them as you are doing on these grounds, and to education of head, hand, and heart, you will find that they will buy your surplus land, make blossom the waste places in your fields, and run your factories.

While doing this, you can be sure in the future, as in the past, that you and your families will be surrounded by the most patient, faithful, law-abiding, and unresentful people that the world has seen. As we have proved our loyalty to you in the past, in nursing your children, watching by the sickbed of your mothers and fathers, and often following them with tear-dimmed eyes to their graves, so in the future, in our humble way, we shall stand by you with a devotion that no foreigner can approach, ready to lay down our lives, if need be, in defence of yours, interlacing our industrial, commercial, civil, and religious life with yours in a way that shall make the interests of both races one. In all things that are purely social we can be as separate as the fingers, yet one as the hand in all things essential to mutual progress.

There is no defence or security for any of us except in the highest intelligence and development of all. If anywhere there are efforts tending to curtail the fullest growth of the Negro, let these efforts be turned into stimulating, encouraging, and making him the most useful and intelligent citizen. Effort or means so invested will pay a thousand percent interest. These efforts will be twice blessed—"blessing him that gives and him that takes."

There is no escape through law of man or God from the inevitable:

The laws of changeless justice bind Oppressor with oppressed; And close as sin and suffering joined We march to fate abreast.

Nearly sixteen millions of hands will aid you in pulling the load upward, or they will pull against you the load downward. We shall constitute one-third and more of the ignorance and crime of the South, or one-third of its intelligence and progress; we shall contribute one-third to the business and industrial prosperity of the South, or we shall prove a veritable body of death, stagnating, depressing, retarding every effort to advance the body politic.

Gentlemen of the Exposition, as we present to you our humble effort at an exhibition of our progress, you must not expect overmuch. Starting thirty years ago with ownership here and there in a few quilts and pumpkins and chickens (gathered from miscellaneous sources), remember the path that has led from these to the inventions and production of agricultural implements, buggies, steam-engines, newspapers, books, statuary, carving, paintings, the management of drugstores and banks, has not been trodden without contact with thorns and thistles. While we take pride in what we exhibit as a result of our independent efforts, we do not for a moment forget that our part in this exhibition would fall far short of your expectations but for the constant help that has come to our educational life, not only from the southern States, but especially from northern philanthropists, who have made their gifts a constant stream of blessing and encouragement.

The wisest among my race understand that the agitation of questions of social equality is the extremest folly, and that progress in the enjoyment of all the privileges that will come to us must be the result of severe and constant struggle rather than of artificial forcing. No race that has anything to contribute to the markets of the world is long in any degree ostracized. It is important and right that all privileges of the law be ours, but it is vastly more important that we be prepared for the exercises of these privileges. The opportunity to earn a dollar in a factory just now is worth infinitely more than the opportunity to spend a dollar in an opera-house.

In conclusion, may I repeat that nothing in thirty years has given us more hope and encouragement, and drawn us so near to you of the white race, as this opportunity offered by the Exposition; here bending, as it were, over the altar that represents the results of the struggles of your race and mine, both starting practically empty-handed three decades ago, I pledge that in your effort to work out the great and intricate problem which God has laid at the doors of the South, you shall have at all times the patient, sympathetic help of my race. Only let this be constantly in mind, that, while from representations in these buildings of the product of field, of forest, of mine, of factory, letters, and art, much good will come, yet far above and beyond material benefits will be that higher good, that, let us pray God, will come, in a blotting out of sectional differences and racial animosities and suspicions, and in a determination to administer absolute justice, even in the remotest corner; in a willing obedience among all classes to the mandates of law and a spirit that will tolerate nothing but the highest equity in the enforcement of law. This, then, coupled with our material prosperity, will bring into our beloved South a new heaven and a new earth.

Source:

John Scott, ed. *Living Documents in American History.* New York: Washington Square Press, 1964–68.

National Association of Colored Women (NACW), Resolutions, 1895

Resolutions presented by the National Association of Colored Women (NACW) upon its formation in 1896. The NACW, an amalgamation of several black women's groups, was established in response to the increasing social welfare needs of the African-American community. Aligning itself with white women's reform movements, the organization taught child-rearing methods, raised money for the poor, and promoted education. These resolutions establish "Lifting as We Climb" as the NACW's motto and also address a variety of concerns: condemning lynchings and segregation, thanking various political benefactors including Theodore Roosevelt, and endorsing the Women's Christian Temperance Union, an organization that favored the prohibition of alcoholic beverages.

───────────── ⸎ ─────────────

The National Association of Colored Women's Clubs in the fourth convention assembled, with gratitude acknowledge the Divine guidance of the Supreme Ruler of the Universe and thank Him for the preservation of our President, executive officers and other members.

We pledge renewed efforts and loyalty along all lines in this, our national organization, continuing to stand for adherence to our motto "Lifting as We Climb," for we believe that in it lies the future hope of the race.

In view of the fact of the numerous lynchings and the many victims burned at the stake, extending even to women, which have occurred in nearly every section of our country;

Be it Resolved, That we, the representatives of Negro womanhood, do heartily deplore and condemn this barbarous taking of human life, and that we appeal to the sentiment of a Christian world to check and eradicate this growing evil; and be it further

Resolved, That we do all in our power to bring criminals to justice, and that we appeal to all legislative bodies and courts of justice to see that all persons are protected in their rights as citizens.

Whereas, Our people throughout the South are discriminated against by railroads, being compelled to ride in offensive and inadequate cars, after paying first-class fares; and,

Whereas, Some of the Southern cities have introduced separate street cars,

Be it Resolved, That this body condemn such action, and that in all such states and towns the club women unite in trying to induce our people to refrain from patronizing street cars and running excursions from town to town, thus encouraging the railroads to continue their unjust discrimination.

Be it Resolved, That a vote of thanks be extended to Theodore Roosevelt, President of the United States, for his fearless and manly stand in defense of the Negro race, in declaring that he would not shut the door of hope and opportunity in the face of any one, on account of race, color or previous condition.

Be it Resolved, That we commend the action of the National Republican Convention in the adoption of that part of its platform which asserts that any state disfranchising its voters shall be limited in its Congressional representation.

Be it Resolved, That the women of our Association prepare themselves by the study of civil government and kindred subjects for the problems of city, state and national life, that they may be able to perform intelligently the duties that have come to some and will come to others in the natural progress of the women's suffrage question.

Be it Resolved, That the Colored Women's Clubs endorse the W.C.T.U., and urge that we emphasize more fully the work among the young people, and do all in their power to create a sentiment against the practice of taking them to places of amusement where intoxicants are sold, and further that we do all in our power to prevent the diffusion of improper and pernicious literature that saps the vitality of the moral life of our young people.

Believing that the mother is the rock upon which the home is built, therefore, be it

Resolved, That we pledge ourselves to hold and encourage mothers' meetings whenever practicable, in order to instruct mothers in all that pertains to home building and child-life.

Source:

African-American History and Culture. CD-ROM. Facts On File, 1999.

Plessy v. Ferguson, 1896

U.S. Supreme Court decision of May 18, 1896, upholding the doctrine of "separate but equal facilities for blacks and whites, thus legitimizing Jim Crow laws. Homer Plessy, a light-skinned "mulatto," challenged the constitutionality of an 1890 Louisiana statute requiring railroads to provide "equal but separate accommodations" for the two races. Ruling 8–1 against Plessy, the Supreme Court declared that the Fourteenth Amendment guaranteed legal equality, not social equality; that the statute was reasonable; and that separate facilities were not a "badge of inferiority" for blacks. This segregationist doctrine was overturned in *Brown v. Board of Education of Topeka* in 1954.

———————————— ⁓⊰⊱⁓ ————————————

Civil Rights—Negroes—Separate Traveling Accommodations.

1. An act requiring white and colored persons to be furnished with separate accommodations on railway trains does not violate Const. Amend. 13, abolishing slavery and involuntary servitude. 11 South. 948, affirmed.

2. A state statute requiring railway companies to provide separate accommodations for white and colored persons, and making a passenger insisting on occupying a coach or compartment other than the one set apart for his race liable to fine or imprisonment, does not violate Const. Amend. 14, by abridging the privileges or immunities of United States citizens, or depriving persons of liberty or property without due process by law, or by denying them the equal protection of the laws. 11 South. 948, affirmed.

Mr. Justice Harlan dissenting.

In Error to the Supreme Court of the State of Louisiana.

This was a petition for writs of prohibition and certiorari originally filed in the supreme court of the state by Plessy, the plaintiff in error, against the Hon. John H. Ferguson, judge of the criminal district court for the parish of Orleans, and setting forth, in substance, the following facts:

That petitioner was a citizen of the United States and a resident of the state of Louisiana, of mixed descent, in the proportion of seven-eighths Caucasian and one-eighth African blood; that the mixture of colored blood was not discernible in him, and that he was entitled to every recognition, right, privilege, and immunity secured to the citizens of the United States of the white race by its constitution and laws; that on June 7, 1892, he engaged and paid for a first-class passage on the East Louisiana Railway, from New Orleans to Covington, in the same state, and thereupon entered a passenger train, and took possession of a vacant seat in a coach where passengers of the white race were accommodated; that such railroad company was incorporated by the laws of Louisiana as a common carrier, and was not authorized to distinguish between citizens according to their race, but, notwithstanding this, petitioner was required by the conductor, under penalty of ejection from said train and imprisonment, to vacate said coach, and occupy another seat, in a coach assigned by said company for persons not of the white race, and for no other reason than that petitioner was of the colored race; that, upon petitioner's refusal to comply with such order, he was, with the aid of a police officer, forcibly ejected from said coach, and hurried off to, and imprisonment in, the parish jail of New Orleans, and there held to answer a charge made by such officer to the effect that he was guilty of having criminally violated an act of the general assembly of the state, approved July 10, 1890, in such case made and provided.

The petitioner was subsequently brought before the recorder of the city for preliminary examination, and committed for trial to the criminal district court for the parish of Orleans, where an information was filed against him in the matter above set forth, for a violation of the above act, which act the petitioner affirmed to be null and void, because in conflict with the constitution of the United States; that petitioner interposed a plea to such information, based upon the unconstitutionality of the act of the general assembly, to which the district attorney, on behalf of the state, filed a demurrer; that, upon issue being joined upon such demurrer and plea, the court sustained the demurrer, overruled the plea, and ordered petitioner to plead over to the facts set forth in the information, and that, unless the judge of the said court be enjoined by a writ of prohibition from further proceeding in such case, the court will proceed to fine and sentence petitioner to imprisonment, and thus deprive him of his constitutional rights set forth in his said plea, notwithstanding the unconstitutionality of the act under which he has being prosecuted; that no appeal lay from such sentence, and petitioner was without relief or remedy except by writs of prohibition and certiorari. Copies of the information and other proceedings in the criminal district court were annexed to the petition as an exhibit.

Upon the filing of this petition, an order was issued upon the respondent to show cause why a writ or prohibition should not issue, and be made perpetual, and a further order that the record of the proceedings had in the criminal cause be certified and transmitted to the supreme court.

To this order the respondent made answer, transmitting a certified copy of the proceedings, asserting the constitutionality of the law, and averring that, instead of pleading or admitting that he belonged to the colored race, the said Plessy declined and refused, either by pleading or otherwise, to admit that he was in any sense or in any proportion a colored man.

The case coming on for hearing before the supreme court, that court was of opinion that the law under which the prosecution was had was constitutional and denied the relief prayed for by the petitioner (Ex parte Plessy, 45 La. Ann. 80, 11 South. 948); whereupon petitioner prayed for a writ of error from this court, which was allowed by the chief justice of the supreme court of Louisiana.

A. W. Tourgee and S. F. Phillips, for plaintiff in error. Alex. Porter Morse, for defendant in error.

Mr. Justice Brown, after stating the facts in the foregoing language, delivered the opinion of the court.

This case turns upon the constitutionality of an act of the general assembly of the state of Louisiana, passed in 1890, providing for separate railway carriages for the white and colored races. Acts 1890, No. 111, p. 152.

The first section of the statute enacts "that all railway companies carrying passengers in their coaches in this state, shall provide equal but separate accommodations for the white, and colored races, by providing two or more passenger coaches for each passenger train, or by dividing the passenger coaches by a partition so as to secure separate accommodations: provided, that this section shall not be construed to apply to street railroads. No person or persons shall be permitted to occupy seats in coaches, other than the ones assigned to them, on account of the race they belong to."

By the second section it was enacted "that the officers of such passenger trains shall have power and are hereby required to assign each passenger to the coach or compartment used for the race to which such passenger belongs; any passenger insisting on going into a coach or compartment to which by race he does not belong, shall be liable to a fine of twenty-five dollars, or in lieu thereof to imprisonment for a period of no more than twenty days in the parish prison, and any officer of any railroad insisting on assigning a passenger to a coach or compartment other than the one set aside for the race to which said passenger belongs, shall be liable to a fine of twenty-five dollars, or in lieu thereof to imprisonment for a period of not more than twenty days in the parish prison; and should any passenger refuse to occupy the coach or compartment to which he or she is assigned by the officer of such railway, said officer shall have power to refuse to carry such passenger on his train, and for such refusal neither he nor the railway company which he represents shall be liable for damages in any of the courts of this state."

The third section provides penalties for the refusal or neglect of the officers, directors, conductors, and employees or railway companies to comply with the act, with a proviso that "nothing in this act shall be construed as applying to nurses attending children of the other race." The fourth section is immaterial.

The information filed in the criminal district court changed, in substance, that Plessy, being a passenger between two stations within the state of Louisiana, was assigned by officers of the company to the coach used for the race to which he belonged, but he instilled up-on going into a coach used by the race to which he did not belong. Neither in the information nor plea was the particular race or color averred.

The petition for the writ of prohibition averred that petitioner was seven-eighths Caucasian and one-eighth African blood; that the mixture of colored blood was not discernible in him; and that he was entitled to every right, privilege, and immunity secured to citizens of the United States of the white race; and that, upon such theory, he took possession of a vacant seat in a coach where passengers of the white race were accommodated, and was ordered by the conductor to vacate said coach, and take a seat in another, assigned to persons of the colored race, and, having refused to comply with such demand, he was forcibly ejected, with the aid of a police officer, and imprisoned in the parish jail to answer a charge of having violated the above act.

The constitutionality of this act is attacked upon the ground that it conflicts both with the thirteenth amendment of the constitution, abolishing slavery, and the fourteenth amendment, which prohibits certain restrictive legislation on the part of the states.

1. That it does not conflict with the thirteenth amendment, which abolished slavery and involuntary servitude, except as a punishment for crime, is too clear for argument. Slavery implies involuntary servitude,—a state of bondage; the ownership of mankind as a chattel, or, at least, the control of the labor and services of one man for the benefit of another, and the absence of legal right to the disposal of his own person, property, and services. This amendment was said in the Slaughter-House Cases, 16 Wall. 36, to have been intended primarily to abolish slavery, as it had been previously known in this country, and that it equally forbade Mexican peonage or the Chinese coolie trade, when they amounted to slavery or involuntary servitude, and that the use of the word "servitude" was intended to prohibit the use of all forms of involuntary slavery, of whatever class or name. It was intimated, however, in that case, that this amendment was regarded by the statesmen of that day as insufficient to protect the colored race from certain laws which had been enacted in the Southern states, imposing upon the colored race onerous disabilities and burdens, and curtailing their rights in the pursuit of life, liberty, and property to such an extent that their freedom was of little value; and that the fourteenth amendment was devised to meet this exigency.

So, too, in the Civil Rights Cases, 109 U.S. 3, 3 Sup. Ct. 18, it was said that the act of a mere individual, the owner of an inn, a public conveyance or place or amuse-ment, refusing accommodations to colored people, cannot be in justly regarded as imposing any badge of slavery or servitude upon the applicant, but only as involving an ordi-nary civil injury, properly cognizable by the laws of the state, and presumably subject to redress by those laws until the contrary appears. "It would be running the slavery question into the ground," said Mr. Justice Bradley, "to make it apply to every act of discrimination which a person may see fit to make as to the guests he will entertain, or as to the people he will take into his coach or cab or car, or admit to his concert or theater, or deal with in other mat-ters of intercourse or business."

A statute which implies merely a legal distinction between the white and colored races—a distinction which is founded in the color of the two races, and which must always exist so long as white men are distinguished from the other race by color—has no tendency to destroy the legal equality of the two races, or re-establish a state of involuntary servitude. Indeed, we do not understand that the thirteenth amendment is strenuously relied upon by the plaintiff in error in this connection.

2. By the fourteenth amendment, all persons born or naturalized in the United States, and subject to the juris-diction thereof, are made citizens of the United States and of the state wherein they reside; and the states are forbid-den from making or enforcing any law which shall abridge the privileges or immunities of citizens of the United States, or shall deprive any person of life, liberty, or prop-erty without due process of law, or deny to any person within their jurisdiction the equal protection of the laws.

The proper construction of this amendment was first called to the attention of this court in the Slaughter-House Cases, 16 Wall. 36, which involved, however, not a ques-tion of race, but one of exclusive privileges. The case did not call for any expression of opinion as to the exact rights it was intended to secure to the colored race, but it was said generally that its main purpose was to establish the cit-izenship of the negro, to give definitions or citizenship of the United States and of the states, and to protect from the hostile legislation of the states the privileges and immuni-ties of citizens of the United States, as distinguished from those of citizens of the states.

The object of the amendment was undoubtedly to enforce the absolute equality of the two races before the law, but, in the nature of things, it could not have been intended to abolish distinctions based upon color, or to enforce social, as distinguished from political, equality, or a commingling of the two races upon terms unsatisfactory to either. Laws permitting, and even requiring, their sepa-ration, in places where they are liable to be brought into contact, do not necessarily imply the inferiority of either race to the other, and have been generally, if not univer-sally, recognized as within the competency of the state leg-islatures in the exercise of their police power. The most common instance of this is connected with the establish-ment of separate schools for white and colored children, which have been held to be a valid exercise of the legisla-tive power even by courts of states where the political rights of the colored race have been longest and most earnestly enforced.

One of the earliest of these cases is that of *Roberts v. City of Boston*, 5 Cush. 198, in which the supreme judicial court of Massachusetts held that the general school com-mittee of Boston had power to make provision for the instruction of colored children in separate schools estab-lished exclusively for them, and to prohibit their atten-dance upon the other schools. "The great principle," said Chief Justice Shaw, "advanced by the learned and eloquent advocate for the plaintiff [Mr. Charles Sumner], is that, by the constitution and laws of Massachusetts, all persons, without distinction of age or sex, birth or color, origin or condition, are equal before the law. ° ° ° But, when this great principle comes to be applied to the actual and vari-ous conditions of persons in society, it will not warrant the assertion that men and women are legally clothed with the same civil and political powers, and that children and adults are legally to have the same functions and be sub-ject to the same treatment; but only that the rights of all, as they are settled and regulated by law, are equally enti-tled to the paternal consideration and protection of the law for their maintenance and security." It was held that the powers of the committee extended to the establishment of separate schools for children of different ages, sexes and colors, and that they might also establish special schools for poor and neglected children, who have become too old to attend the primary school, and yet have not acquired the rudiments of learning, to enable them to enter the ordi-nary schools. Similar laws have been enacted by congress under its general power of legislation over the District of Columbia (sections 281–283, 310, 319, Rev. St. D. C.), as well as by the legislatures of many of the states, and have been generally, if not uniformly, sustained by the courts. *State v. McCann*, 21 Ohio St. 210; *Lehew v. Brummell* (Mo. Sup.) 15 S. W. 765; Ward v. Flood, 48 Cal. 36; *Berton-neau v. Directors of City Schools*, 3 Woods, 177, Fed. Cas. No. 1,361; *People v. Gallagher*, 93 N. Y. 438; *Cory v. Carter*, 48 Ind. 337; *Dawson v. Lee*, 83 Ky. 49.

Laws forbidding the intermarriage of the two races may be said in a technical sense to interfere with the free-dom of contract, and yet have been universally recognized as within the police power of the state. State v. Gibson, 36 Ind. 389.

The distinction between laws interfering with the political equality of the negro and those requiring the sep-aration of the two races in schools, theaters, and railway carriages has been frequently drawn by this court. Thus, in *Strauder v. West Virginia,* 100 U. S. 303, it was held that a law of West Virginia limiting to white male persons 21 years of age, and citizens of the state, the right to sit upon juries, was a discrimination which implied a legal inferiority in civil society, which lessened the security of the right of the colored race, and was a step towards reducing them to a condition of servility. Indeed, the right of a colored man that, in the selection of jurors to pass upon his life, liberty, and property, there shall be no exclusion of his race, and no discrimination against them because of color, has been asserted in a number of cases. *Virginia v. Rives,* 100 U. S. 313; *Neal v. Delaware,* 103 U. S. 370; *Bush v. Com,* 107 U. S. 110, 1 Sup. Ct. 625; *Gibson v. Mississippi,* 162 U. S. 565, 16 Sup. Ct. 904. So, where the laws of a particular locality or the charter of a particular railway corporation has provided that no person shall be excluded from the cars on account of color, we have held that this meant that persons of color should travel in the same car as white ones, and that the enactment was not satisfied by the company providing cars assigned exclusively to people of color, though they were as good as those which they assigned exclusively to white persons. *Railroad Co. v. Brown,* 17 Wall. 445.

Upon the other hand, where a statute of Louisiana required those engaged in the transportation of passengers among the states to give to all persons traveling within that state, upon vessels employed in that business, equal rights and privileges in all parts of the vessel, without distinction on account of race or color, and subjected to an action for damages the owner of such a vessel who excluded colored passengers on account of their color from the cabin set aside by him for the use of whites, it was held to be, so far as it applied to interstate commerce, unconstitutional and void. *Hall v. De Cuir,* 95 U. S. 485. The court in this case, however, expressly disclaimed that it had anything whatever to do with the statute as a regulation of internal commerce, or affecting anything else than commerce among the states.

In the Civil Rights Cases, 109 U. S. 3, 3 Sup. Ct. 18, it was held that an act of congress entitling all persons within the jurisdiction of the United States to the full and equal enjoyment of the accommodations, advantages, facilities, and privileges of inns, public conveyances, on land or water, theaters, and other places of public amusement, and made applicable to citizens of every race and color, regardless of any previous condition of servitude, was unconstitutional and void, upon the ground that the fourteenth amendment was prohibitory upon the states only, and the legislation authorized to be adopted by congress for enforcing it was not direct legislation on matters respecting which the states were prohibited from making or enforcing certain laws, or doing certain acts, but was cor-

rective legislation, such as might be necessary or proper for counteracting and redressing the effect of such laws or acts. In delivering the opinion of the court, Mr. Justice Bradley observed that the fourteenth amendment "does not invest congress with power to legislate upon subjects that are within the domain the state legislation, but to provide modes of relief against state legislation or state action of the kind referred to. It does not authorize congress to create a code of municipal law for the regulation of private rights, but to provide modes of redress against the operation of state laws, and the action of state officers, executive or judicial, when these are subversive of the fundamental rights specified in the amendment. Positive rights and privileges are undoubtedly secured by the fourteenth amendment; but they are secured by way of prohibition against state laws and state proceedings affecting those rights and privileges, and by power given to congress to legislate for the purpose of carrying such prohibition into effect; and such legislation must necessarily be predicated upon such supposed state laws or state proceedings, and be directed to the correction of their operation and effect."

Much nearer, and, indeed, almost directly in point, is the case of the *Louisville, N. O. & T. Ry. Co. v. State,* 133 U. S. 587, 10 Sup. Ct. 348, wherein the railway company was indicted for a violation of a statute of Mississippi, enacting that all railroads carrying passengers should provide equal, but separate, accommodations for the white and colored races, by providing two or more passenger cars for each passenger train, or by dividing the passenger cars by a partition, so as to secure separate accommodations. The case was presented in a different aspect from the one under consideration, inasmuch as it was an indictment against the railway company for failing to provide the separate accommodations, but the question considered was the constitutionality of the law. In that case, the supreme court of Mississippi (66 Miss. 662, 6 South. 203) had held that the statute applied solely to commerce within the state, and, that being the construction of the state statute by its highest court, was accepted as conclusive. "If it be a matter," said the court (page 591, 133 U.S., and page 348, 10 Sup. Ct.), "respecting commerce wholly within a state, and not interfering with commerce between the states, then, obviously, there is no violation of the commerce clause of the federal constitution. ° ° ° No question arises under this section as to the power of the state to separate in different compartments interstate passengers, or affect, in any manner, the privileges and rights of such passengers. All that we can consider is whether the state has the power to require that railroad trains within her limits shall have separate accommodations for the two races. That affecting only commerce within the state is no invasion of the power given to congress by the commerce clause."

A like course of reasoning applies to the case under consideration, since the supreme court of Louisiana, in the case of *State v. Judge,* 44 La. Ann. 770, 11 South. 74, held that the statute in question did not apply to interstate passengers, but was confined in its application to passengers traveling exclusively within the borders of the state. The case was decided largely upon the authority of *Louisville, N. O. & T. Ry. Co. v. State,* 66 Miss. 662, 6 South. 203, and affirmed by this court in 133 U. S. 587, 10 Sup. Ct. 348. In the present case no question of interference with interstate commerce can possibly arise, since the East Louisiana Railway appears to have been purely a local line, with both its termini within the state of Louisiana. Similar statutes for the separation of the two races upon public conveyances were held to be constitutional in *Railroad v. Miles,* 55 Pa. St. 209; *Day v. Owen,* 5 Mich. 520; *Railway Co. v. Williams,* 55 Ill. 185; *Railroad Co. v. Wells,* 85 Tenn. 613; 4 S. W. 5; *Railroad Co. v. Benson,* 85 Tenn. 627, 4 S. W. 5; *The Sue,* 22 Fed. 843; *Logwood v. Railroad Co.,* 23 Fed. 318; *McGuinn v. Forbes,* 37 Fed. 639; *People v. King* (N. Y. App.) 18 N. E. 245; *Houck v. Railway Co.,* 38 Fed. 226; *Heard v. Railroad Co.,* 3 Inter St. Commerce Com. R. 111, 1 Inter St. Commerce Com. R. 428.

While we think the enforced separation of the races, as applied to the internal commerce of the state, neither abridges the privileges or immunities of the colored man, deprives him of his property without due process of law, nor denies him the equal protection of the laws, within the meaning of the fourteenth amendment, we are not prepared to say that the conductor, in assigning passengers to the coaches according to their race, does not act at his peril, or that the provision of the second section of the act that denies to the passenger compensation in damages for a refusal to receive him into the coach in which he properly belongs is a valid exercise of the legislative power. Indeed, we understand it to be conceded by the state's attorney that such part of the act as exempts from liability the railway company and its officers is unconstitutional. The power to assign to a particular coach obviously implies the power to determine to which race the passenger belongs, as well as the power to determine who, under the laws of the particular state, is to be deemed a white, and who a colored, person. This question, though indicated in the brief of the plaintiff in error, does not properly arise upon the record in this case, since the only issue made is as to the unconstitutionality of the act, so far as it requires the railway to provide separate accommodations, and the conductor to assign passengers according to their race.

It is claimed by the plaintiff in error that, in any mixed community, the reputation of belonging to the dominant race, in this instance the white race, is "property," in the same sense that a right of action or of inheritance is property. Conceding this to be so, for the purposes of this case,

we are unable to see how this statute deprives him of, or in any way affects his right to, such property. If he be a white man, and assigned to a colored coach, he may have his action for damages against the company for being deprived of his so-called "property." Upon the other hand, if he be a colored man, and be so assigned, he has been deprived of no property, since he is not lawfully entitled to the reputation of being a white man.

In this connection, it is also suggested by the learned counsel for the plaintiff in error that the same argument that will justify the state legislature in requiring railways to provide separate accommodations for the two races will also authorize them to require separate cars to be provided for people whose hair is of a certain color, or who are aliens, or who belong to certain nationalities, or to enact laws requiring colored people to walk upon one side of the street, and white people upon the other, or requiring white men's houses to be painted white, and colored men's black, or their vehicles or business signs to be of different colors, upon the theory that one side of the street is as good as the other, or that a house or vehicle of one color is as good as one of another color. The reply to all this is that every exercise of the police power must be reasonable, and extend only to such laws as are enacted in good faith for the promotion of the public good, and not for the annoyance or oppression of a particular class. Thus, in *Yick Wo v. Hopkins,* 118 U. S. 356, 6 Sup. Ct. 1064, it was held by this court that a municipal ordinance of the city of San Francisco, to regulate the carrying on of public laundries within the limits of the municipality, violated the provisions of the constitution of the United States, if it conferred, upon the municipal authorities arbitrary power, at their own will, and without regard to discretion, in the legal sense of the term, to give or withhold consent as to persons or places, without regard to the competency of the persons applying or the propriety of the places selected for the carrying on of the business. It was held to be a covert attempt on the part of the municipality to make an arbitrary and unjust discrimination against the Chinese race. While this was the case of a municipal ordinance, a like principle has been held to apply to acts of a state legislature passed in the exercise of the police power. *Railroad Co. v. Husen,* 95 U. S. 465; *Louisville & N. R. Co. v. Kentucky,* 161 U. S. 677, 16 Sup. Ct. 714, and cases cited on page 700, 161 U. S., and page 714, 16 Sup. Ct.; *Daggett v. Hudson,* 43 Ohio St. 548, 3 N. E. 538; *Capen v. Foster,* 12 Pick. 485; State v. Baker, 38 Wis. 71; *Monroe v. Collins,* 17 Ohio St. 665; *Hulseman v. Rems,* 41 Pa. St. 396; *Osman v. Riley,* 15 Cal. 48.

So far, then, as a conflict with the fourteenth amendment is concerned, the case reduces itself to the question whether the statute of Louisiana is a reasonable regulation, and with respect to this there must necessarily be a large discretion on the part of the legislature. In determining the question of reasonableness, it is at liberty to act with reference to the established usages, customs, and traditions of the people, and with a view to the promotion of their comfort, and the preservation of the public peace and good order. Gauged by this standard, we cannot say that a law which authorizes or even requires the separation of the two races in public conveyances is unreasonable, or more obnoxious to the fourteenth amendment than the acts of congress requiring separate schools for colored children in the District of Columbia, the constitutionality of which does not seem to have been questioned, or the corresponding acts of state legislatures.

We consider the underlying fallacy of the plaintiff's argument to consist in the assumption that the enforced separation of the two races stamps the colored race with a badge of inferiority. If this be so, it is not by reason of anything found in the act, but solely because the colored race chooses to put that construction upon it. The argument necessarily assumes that if, as has been more than once the case, and is not unlikely to be so again, the colored race should become the dominant power in the state legislature, and should enact a law in precisely similar terms, it would thereby relegate the white race to an inferior position. We imagine that the white race, at least, would not acquiesce in this assumption. The argument also assumes that social prejudices may be overcome by legislation, and that equal rights cannot be secured to the negro except by an enforced commingling of the two races. We cannot accept this proposition. If the two races are to meet upon terms of social equality, it must be the result of natural affinities, a mutual appreciation of each other's merits, and a voluntary consent of individuals. As was said by the court of appeals of New York in *People v. Gallagher,* 93 N. Y. 438, 448: "This end can neither be accomplished nor promoted by laws which conflict with the general sentiment of the community upon whom they are designed to operate. When the government, therefore, has secured to each of its citizens equal rights before the law, and equal opportunities for improvement and progress, it has accomplished the end for which it was organized, and performed all of the functions respecting social advantages with which it is endowed." Legislation is powerless to eradicate racial instincts, or to abolish distinctions based upon physical differences, and the attempt to do so can only result in accentuating the difficulties of the present situation. If the civil and political rights of both races be equal, one cannot be inferior to the other civilly or politically. If one race be inferior to the other socially, the constitution of the United States cannot put them upon the same plane.

It is true that the question of the proportion of colored blood necessary to constitute a colored person, as distinguished from a white person, is one upon which there is a difference of opinion in the different states; some holding

that any visible admixture of black blood stamps the person as belonging to the colored race (*State v. Chavers,* 5 Jones [N. C.] 1); others, that it depends upon the preponderance of blood (*Gray v. State,* 4 Ohio, 354; *Monroe v. Collins,* 17 Ohio St. 665); and still others, that the predominance of white blood must only be in the proportion of three-fourths (*People v. Dean,* 14 Mich. 406; *Jones v. Com.,* 80 Va. 544). But these are questions to be determined under the laws of each state, and are not properly put in issue in this case. Under the allegations of his petition, it may undoubtedly become a question of importance whether, under the laws of Louisiana, the petitioner belongs to the white or colored race.

The judgment of the court below is therefore affirmed.

Mr. Justice Brewer did not hear the argument or participate in the decision of this case.

Mr. Justice Harlan dissenting.

By the Louisiana statute the validity of which is here involved, all railway companies (other than street-railroad companies) carrying passengers in that state are required to have separate but equal accommodations for white and colored persons, "by providing two or more passenger coaches for each passenger train, or by dividing the passenger coaches by a partition so as to secure separate accommodations." Under this statute, no colored person is permitted to occupy a seat in a coach assigned to white persons; nor any white person to occupy a seat in a coach assigned to colored persons. The managers of the railroad are not allowed to exercise any discretion in the premises, but are required to assign each passenger to some coach or compartment set apart for the exclusive use of his race. If a passenger insists upon going into a coach or compartment not set apart for persons of his race, he is subject to be fined, or to be imprisoned in the parish jail. Penalties are prescribed for the refusal or neglect of the officers, directors, conductors, and employes or railroad companies to comply with the provisions of the act.

Only "nurses attending children of the other race" are excepted from the operation of the statute. No exception is made of colored attendants traveling with adults. A white man is not permitted to have his colored servant with him in the same coach, even if his condition of health requires the constant personal assistance of such servant. If a colored maid insists upon riding in the same coach with a white woman whom she has been employed to serve, and who may need her personal attention while traveling, she is subject to be fined or imprisoned for such an exhibition of zeal in the discharge of duty.

While there may be in Louisiana persons of different races who are not citizens of the United States, the words in the act "white and colored races" necessarily include all citizens of the United States of both races residing in that state. So that we have before us a state enactment that compels, under penalties, the separation of the two races in railroad passenger coaches, and makes it a crime for a citizen of either race to enter a coach that has been assigned to citizens of the other race.

Thus, the state regulates the use of a public highway by citizens of the United States solely upon the basis of race.

However apparent the injustice of such legislation may be, we have only to consider whether it is consistent with the constitution of the United States.

That a railroad is a public highway, and that the corporation which owns or operates it is in the exercise of public functions, is not, at this day, to be disputed. Mr. Justice Nelson, speaking for this court in *New Jersey Steam Nav. Co. v. Merchants' Bank,* 6 How. 344, 382, said that a common carrier was in the exercise "of a sort of public office, and has public duties to perform, from which he should not be permitted to exonerate himself without the assent of the parties concerned." Mr. Justice Strong, delivering the judgment of this court in *Olcott v. Supervisors,* 16 Wall. 678, 694, said: "That railroads, though constructed by private corporations, and owned by them, are public highways, has been doctrine of nearly all the courts ever since such conveniences for passage and transportation have had any existence. Very early the question arose whether a state's right of eminent domain could be exercised by a private corporation created for the purpose of constructing a railroad. Clearly, it could not, unless taking land for such a purpose by such an agency is taking land for public use. The right of eminent domain nowhere justifies taking property for a private use. Yet it is a doctrine universally accepted that a state legislature may authorize a private corporation to take land for the construction of such a road, making compensation to the owner. What else does this doctrine mean if not that building a railroad, though it be built by a private corporation, is an act done for a public use?" So, in Township of *Pine Grove v. Talcott,* 19 Wall. 666, 676: "Though the corporation [a railroad company] was private, its work was public, as much as so as if it were to be constructed by the state." So, in Inhabitants of *Worcester v. Western R. Corp.,* 4 Metc. (Mass) 564: "The establishment of that great thoroughfare is regarded as a public work, established by public authority, intended for the public use and benefit, the use of which is secured to the whole community, and constitutes, therefore, like a canal, turnpike, or highway, a public easement." "It is true that the real and personal property, necessary to the establishment and management of the railroad, is vested in the corporation; but it is in trust for the public."

In respect of civil rights, common to all citizens, the constitution of the United States does not, I think, permit any public authority to know the race of those entitled to be protected in the enjoyment of such rights. Every true man has pride of race, and under appropriate circumstances, when the rights of others, his equals before the law, are not to be affected, it is his privilege to express such pride and to take such action based upon it as to him seems proper. But I deny that any legislative body or judicial tribunal may have regard to the race of citizens when the civil rights of those citizens are involved. Indeed, such legislation as that here in question is inconsistent not only with that equality of rights which pertains to citizenship, national and state, but with the personal liberty enjoyed by every one within the United States.

The thirteenth amendment does not permit the withholding or the deprivation of any right necessarily inhering in freedom. It not only struck down the institution of slavery as previously existing in the United States, but it prevents the imposition of any burdens or disabilities that constitute badges of slavery or servitude. It decreed universal civil freedom in this country. This court has so adjudged. But, that amendment having been found inadequate to the protection of the rights of those who had been in slavery, it was followed by the fourteenth amendment, which added greatly to the dignity and glory of American citizenship, and to the security of personal liberty, by declaring that "all persons born or naturalized in the United States, and subject to the jurisdiction thereof, are citizens of the United States and of the state wherein they reside," and that "no state shall make or enforce any law which shall abridge the privileges or immunities of citizens of the United States; nor shall any state deprive any person of life, liberty or property without due process of law, nor deny to any person within its jurisdiction the equal protection of the laws." These two amendments, if enforced according to their true intent and meaning, will protect all the civil rights that pertain to freedom and citizenship. Finally, and to the end that no citizen should be denied, on account of his race, the privilege of participating in the political control of his country, it was declared by the fifteenth amendment that "the right of citizens of the United States to vote shall not be denied or abridged by the United States or by any state on account of race, color or previous condition of servitude."

These notable addition to the fundamental law were welcomed by the friends of liberty throughout the world. They removed the race line from our governmental systems. They had, as this court has said, a common purpose, namely, to secure "to a race recently emancipated, a race that through many generations have been held in slavery, all the civil rights that the superior race enjoy." They declared, in legal effect, this court has further said, "that the law in the states shall be the same for the black as for the white; that all persons, whether colored or white; shall stand equal before the laws of the states; and in regard to the colored race, for whose protection the amendment was primarily designed, that no discrimination shall be made against them by law because of their color." We also said: "The words of the amendment, it is true, are prohibitory, but they contain a necessary implication of a positive immunity or right, most valuable to the colored race—the right to exemption from unfriendly legislation against them distinctively as colored; exemption from legal discriminations, implying inferiority in civil society, lessening the security of their enjoyment of the rights which others enjoy; and discriminations which are steps towards reducing them to the condition of a subject race." It was, consequently, adjudged that a state law that excluded citizens of the colored race from juries, because of their race, however well qualified in other respects to discharge the duties of jurymen, was repugnant to the fourteenth amendment. *Strauder v. West Virginia,* 100 U.S. 303, 306, 307; *Virginia v. Rives,* Id. 313; *Ex parte Virginia,* Id. 339; *Neal v. Delaware,* 103 U.S. 370, 386; *Bush v. Com.,* 107 U.S. 110, 116, 1 Sup. Ct. 625. At the present term, referring to the previous adjudications, this court declared that "underlying all of those decisions is the principle that the constitution of the United States, in its present form, forbids, so far as civil and political rights are concerned, discrimination by the general government or the states against any citizen because of his race. All citizens are equal before the law." *Gibson v. State,* 162 U.S. 565, 16 Sup. Ct. 904.

The decisions referred to show the scope of the recent amendments of the constitution. They also show that it is not within the power of a state to prohibit colored citizens, because of their race, from participating as jurors in the administration of justice.

It was said in argument that the statute of Louisiana does not discriminate against either race, but prescribes a rule applicable alike to white and colored citizens. But this argument does not meet the difficulty. Every one knows that the statute in question had its origin in the purpose, not so much to exclude white persons from railroad cars occupied by blacks, as to exclude colored people from coaches occupied by or assigned to white persons. Railroad corporations of Louisiana did not make discrimination among whites in the matter of accommodation for travelers. The thing to accomplish was, under the guise of giving equal accommodation for whites and blacks, to compel the latter to keep to themselves while traveling in railroad passenger coaches. No one would be so wanting in candor as to assert the contrary. The fundamental objection, therefore, to the statute, is that it interferes with the personal freedom of citizens. "Personal liberty," it has been well said, "consists in the power of locomotion, of changing situation, or removing one's person to whatsoever places one's own inclination may direct, without imprisonment or restraint, unless by due course of law." 1 Bl. Comm. 134. If

a white man and a black man choose to occupy the same public conveyance on a public highway, it is their right to do so; and no government, proceeding alone on grounds of race, can prevent it without infringing the personal liberty of each.

It is one thing for railroad carriers to furnish, or to be required by law to furnish, equal accommodations for all whom they are under a legal duty to carry. It is quite another thing for government to forbid citizens of the white and black races from traveling in the same public conveyance, and to punish officers of railroad companies for permitting persons of the two races to occupy the same passenger coach. If a state can prescribe, as a rule of civil conduct, that whites and blacks shall not travel as passengers in the same railroad coach, why may it not so regulate the use of the streets of its cities and towns as to compel white citizens to keep on one side of a street, and black citizens to keep on the other? Why may it not, upon like grounds, punish whites and blacks who ride together in street cars or in open vehicles on a public road or street? Why may it not require sheriffs to assign whites to one side of a court room, and blacks to the other? And why may it not also prohibit the commingling of the two races in the galleries of legislative halls or in public assemblages convened for the consideration of the political questions of the day? Further, if this statute of Louisiana is consistent with the personal liberty of citizens, why may not the state require the separation in railroad coaches of native and naturalized citizens of the United States, or of Protestants and Roman Catholics?

The answer given at the argument to these questions was that regulations of the kind they suggest would be unreasonable, and could not, therefore, stand before the law. Is it meant that the determination of questions of legislative power depends upon the inquiry whether the statute whose validity is questioned is, in the judgment of the courts, a reasonable one, taking all the circumstances into consideration? A statute may be unreasonable merely because a sound public policy forbade its enactment. But I do not understand that the courts have anything to do with the policy or expediency of legislation. A statute may be valid, and yet, upon grounds of public policy, may well be characterized as unreasonable. Mr. Sedgwick correctly states the rule when he says that, the legislative intention being clearly ascertained, "the courts have no other duty to perform than to execute the legislative will, without any regard to their views as to the wisdom or justice of the particular enactment." Sedg. St. & Const. Law, 324. There is a dangerous tendency in these latter days to enlarge the functions of the courts, by means of judicial interference with the will of the people as expressed by the legislature. Our institutions have the distinguishing characteristic that the three departments of government are co-ordinate and separate. Each must keep within the limits defined by the constitution. And the courts best discharge their duty by executing the will of the lawmaking power, constitutionally expressed, leaving the results of legislation to be dealt with by the people through their representatives. Statutes must always have a reasonable construction. Sometimes they are to be construed strictly, sometimes literally, in order to carry out the legislative will. But, however construed, the intent of the legislature is to be respected if the particular statute in question is valid, although the courts, looking at the public interests, may conceive the statute to be both unreasonable and impolitic. If the power exists to enact a statute, that ends the matter so far as the courts are concerned. The adjudged cases in which statutes have been held to be void, because unreasonable, are those in which the means employed by the legislature were not at all germane to the end to which the legislature was competent.

The white race deems itself to be the dominant race in the country. And so it is, in prestige, in achievements, in education, in wealth, and in power. So, I doubt not, it will continue to be for all time, if it remains true to its great heritage, and holds fast to the principles of constitutional liberty. But in view of the constitution, in the eye of the law, there is in this country no superior, dominant, ruling class of citizens. There is no caste here. Our constitution is color-blind, and neither knows nor tolerates classes among citizens. In respect of civil rights, all citizens are equal before the law. The humblest is the peer of the most powerful. The law regards man as man, and takes no account of his surroundings or of his color when his civil rights as guarantied by the supreme law of the land are involved. It is therefore to be regretted that this high tribunal, the final expositor of the fundamental law of the land, has reached the conclusion that it is competent for a state to regulate the enjoyment by citizens of their civil rights solely upon the basis of race.

In my opinion, the judgment this day rendered will, in time, prove to be quite as pernicious as the decision made by this tribunal in the Dred Scott Case.

It was adjudged in that case that the descendants of Africans who were imported into this country, and sold as slaves, were not included nor intended to be included under the word "citizens" in the constitution, and could not claim any of the rights and privileges which that instrument provided for and secured to citizens of the United States; that, at the time of the adoption of the constitution, they were "considered as a subordinate and inferior class of beings, who had been subjugated by the dominant race, and, whether emancipated or not, yet remained subject to their authority, and had no rights or privileges but such as those who held the power and the government might choose to grant them." 17 How. 393, 404. The recent amendments of the constitution, it was supposed, had eradicated these principles from our institutions. But it seems that we have yet, in some of the states, a dominant race—a superior class of citizens—which assumes to regulate the enjoyment of civil rights, common to all citizens, upon the basis of race. The present decision, it may well be apprehended, will not only stimulate aggressions, more or less brutal and irritating, upon the admitted rights of colored citizens, but will encourage the belief that it is possible, by means of state enactments, to defeat the beneficent purposes which the people of the United States had in view when they adopted the recent amendments of the constitution, by one of which the blacks of this country were made citizens of the United States and of the states in which they respectively reside, and whose privileges and immunities, as citizens, the states are forbidden to abridge. Sixty millions of whites are in no danger from the presence here of eight millions of blacks. The destinies of the two races, in this country, are indissolubly linked together, and the interests of both require that the common government of all shall not permit the seeds of race hate to be planted under the sanction of law. What can more certainly arouse race hate, what more certainly create and perpetuate a feeling of distrust between these races, than state enactments which, in fact, proceed on the ground that colored citizens are so inferior and degraded that they cannot be allowed to sit in public coaches occupied by white citizens? That, as all will admit, is the real meaning of such legislation as was enacted in Louisiana.

The sure guaranty of the peace and security of each race is the clear, distinct, unconditional recognition by our governments, national and state, of every right that inheres in civil freedom, and of the equality before the law of all citizens of the United States, without regard to race. State enactments regulating the enjoyment of civil rights upon the basis of race, and cunningly devised to defeat legitimate results of the war, under the pretense of recognizing equality of rights, can have no other result than to render permanent peace impossible, and to keep alive a conflict of races, the continuance of which must do harm to all concerned. This question is not met by the suggestion that social equality cannot exist between the white and black races in this country. That argument, if it can be properly regarded as one, is scarcely worthy of consideration; for social equality no more exists between two races when traveling in a passenger coach or a public highway than when members of the same races sit by each other in a street car or in the jury box, or stand or sit with each other in a political assembly, or when they use in common the streets of a city or town, or when they are in the same room for the purpose of having their names placed on the registry of voters, or when they approach the ballot box in order to exercise the high privilege of voting.

There is a race so different from our own that we do not permit those belonging to it to become citizens of the United States. Persons belonging to it are, with few exceptions, absolutely excluded from our country. I allude to the Chinese race. But, by the statute in question, a Chinaman can ride in the same passenger coach with white citizens of the United States, while citizens of the black race in Louisiana, many of whom, perhaps, risked their lives for the preservation of the Union, who are entitled, by law, to participate in the political control of the state and nation, who are not excluded, by law or by reason of their race, from public stations of any kind, and who have all the legal rights that belong to white citizens, are yet declared to be criminals, liable to imprisonment, if they ride in a public coach occupied by citizens of the white race. It is scarcely just to say that a colored citizen should not object to occupying a public coach assigned to his own race. He does not object, nor, perhaps, would he object to separate coaches for his race if his rights under the law were recognized. But he does object, and he ought never to cease objecting, that citizens of the white and black races can be adjudged criminals because they sit, or claim the right to sit, in the same public coach on a public highway.

The arbitrary separation of citizens, on the basis of race, while they are on a public highway, is a badge of servitude wholly inconsistent with the civil freedom and the equality before the law established by the constitution. It cannot be justified upon any legal grounds.

If evils will result from the commingling of the two races upon public highways established for the benefit of all, they will be infinitely less than those that will surely come from state legislation regulating the enjoyment of civil rights upon the basis of race. We boast of the freedom enjoyed by our people above all other peoples. But it is difficult to reconcile that boast with a state of the law which, practically, puts the brand of servitude and degradation upon a large class of our fellow citizens—our equals before the law. The thin disguise of "equal" accommodations for passengers in railroad coaches will not mislead any one, nor atone for the wrong this day done.

The result of the whole matter is that while this court has frequently adjudged, and at the present term has recognized the doctrine, that a state cannot, consistently with the constitution of the United States, prevent white and black citizens, having the required qualifications for jury service, from sitting in the same jury box, it is now solemnly held that a state may prohibit white and black citizens from sitting in the same passenger coach on a public highway, or may require that they be separated by a "partition" when in the same passenger coach. May it not now be reasonably expected that astute men of the dominant race, who affect to be disturbed at the possibility that the integrity of the white race may be corrupted, or that its supremacy will be imperiled, by contact on public highways with black people, will endeavor to procure statutes requiring white and black jurors to be separated in the jury box by a "partition," and that, upon retiring from the court room to consult as to their verdict, such partition, if it be a movable one, shall be taken to their consultation room, and set up in such way as to prevent black jurors from coming too close to their brother jurors of the white race. If the "partition" used in the court room happens to be stationary, provision could be made for screens with openings through which jurors of the two races could confer as to their verdict without coming into personal contact with each other. I cannot see but that, according to the principles this day announced, such state legislation, although conceived in hostility to, and enacted for the purpose of humiliating, citizens of the United States of a particular race, would be held to be consistent with the constitution.

I do not deem it necessary to review the decisions of state courts to which reference was made in argument. Some, and the most important, of them, are wholly inapplicable, because rendered prior to the adoption of the last amendments of the constitution, when colored people had very few rights which the dominant race felt obliged to respect. Others were made at a time when public opinion, in many localities, was dominated by the institution of slavery; when it would not have been safe to do justice to the black man; and when, so far as the rights of blacks were concerned, race prejudice was, practically, the supreme law of the land. Those decisions cannot be guides in the era introduced by the recent amendments of the supreme law, which established universal civil freedom, gave citizenship to all born or naturalized in the United States, and residing here, obliterated the race line from our systems of governments, national and state, and placed our free institutions upon the broad and sure foundation of the equality of all men before the law.

I am of opinion that the statute of Louisiana is inconsistent with the personal liberty of citizens, white and black, in that state, and hostile to both the spirit and letter of the constitution of the United States. If laws of like character should be enacted in the several states of the Union, the effect would be in the highest degree mischievous. Slavery, as an institution tolerated by law, would, it is true, have disappeared from our country; but there would remain a power in the states, by sinister legislation, to interfere with the full enjoyment of the blessings of freedom, to regulate civil rights, common to all citizens, upon the basis of race, and to place in a condition of legal inferiority a large body of American citizens, now constituting a part of the political community, called the "People of the United States," for whom, and by whom through representatives, our government is administered.

Such a system is inconsistent with the guaranty given by the constitution to each state of a republican form of government, and may be stricken down by congressional action, or by the courts in the discharge of their solemn duty to maintain the supreme law of the land, anything in the constitution or laws of any state to the contrary notwithstanding.

For the reason stated, I am constrained to withhold my assent from the opinion and judgment of the majority.

Source:
Supreme Court Reporter, Vol. 16, pp. 1,138–1,148.

Theodore Roosevelt, "Strenuous Life," 1899

Celebrated speech given by New York governor Theodore Roosevelt to the Hamilton Club of Chicago on April 10, 1899. He firmly asserted that "the strenuous life, the life of toil and effort" was exemplary, that idleness did not befit those desiring to do serious work, and that self respect and success in life meant endeavoring "not to shirk difficulties but to overcome them." Roosevelt said that these principles also applied to the United States, which cannot be timid and shrink from responsibilities at home and abroad and from "a legacy of duty" left to the American people after the Spanish-American War (1898). Hawaii, Cuba, Puerto Rico, and the Philippines presented new, difficult problems, which America could solve through upholding the "qualities of courage, of honesty, and of good judgment." Roosevelt became U.S. president in 1901.

In speaking to you, men of the greatest city of the West, men of the State which gave to the country Lincoln and Grant, men who preeminently and distinctly embody all that is most American in the American character, I wish to preach, not the doctrine of ignoble ease, but the doctrine of the strenuous life, the life of toil and effort, of labor and strife; to preach that highest form of success which comes, not to the man who desires mere easy peace, but to the man who does not shrink from danger, from hardship, or from bitter toil, and who out of these wins the splendid ultimate triumph.

A life of slothful ease, a life of that peace which springs merely from lack either of desire or of power to strive after great things, is as little worthy of a nation as of an individual. I ask only that what every self-respecting American demands from himself and from his sons shall be demanded of the American nation as a whole. Who among you would teach you boys that ease, that peace, is to be the first consideration in their eyes—to be the ultimate goal after which they strive? You men of Chicago have made this city great, you men of Illinois have done your share, and more than your share, in making America great, because you neither preach nor practice such a doctrine. You work yourselves, and you bring up your sons to work. If you are rich and are worth your salt, you will teach your sons that though they may have leisure, it is not to be spent in idleness; for wisely used leisure merely means that those who possess it, being free from the necessity of working for their livelihood, are all the more bound to carry on some kind of non-remunerative work in science, in letters, in art, in exploration, in historical research—work of the type we most need in this country, the successful carrying out of which reflects most honor upon the nation. We do not admire the man of timid peace. We admire the man who embodies victorious effort; the man who never wrongs his neighbor, who is prompt to help a friend, but who has those virile qualities necessary to win in the stern strife of actual life. It is hard to fail, but it is worse never to have tried to succeed. In this life we get nothing save by effort. Freedom from effort in the present merely means that there has been stored up effort in the past. A man can be freed from the necessity of work only by the fact that he or his fathers before him have worked to good purpose. If the freedom thus purchased is used aright, and the man still does actual work, though of a different kind, whether as a writer or a general, whether in the field of politics or in the field of exploration and adventure, he shows he deserves his good fortune. But if he treats this period of freedom from the need of actual labor as a period, not of preparation, but of mere enjoyment, even though perhaps not of vicious enjoyment, he shows that he is simply a cumberer of the earth's surface, and he surely unfits himself to hold his own with his fellows if the need to do so should again arise. A mere life of ease is not in the end a very satisfactory life, and, above all, it is a life which ultimately unfits those who follow it for serious work in the world.

In the last analysis a healthy state can exist only when the men and women who make it up lead clean, vigorous, healthy lives; when the children are so trained that they shall endeavor, not to shirk difficulties, but to overcome them; not to seek ease, but to know how to wrest triumph from toil and risk. The man must be glad to do a man's work, to dare and endure and to labor; to keep himself, and to keep those dependent upon him. The woman must be the housewife, the helpmeet of the homemaker, the wise and fearless mother of many healthy children. In one of Daudet's powerful and melancholy books he speaks of "the fear of maternity, the haunting terror of the young wife of the present day." When such words can be truthfully written of a nation, that nation is rotten to the heart's core. When men fear work or fear righteous war, when women fear motherhood, they tremble on the brink of doom; and well it is that they should vanish from the earth, where they are fit subjects for the scorn of all men and women who are themselves strong and brave and high-minded.

As it is with the individual, so it is with the nation. It is a base untruth to say that happy is the nation that has no history. Thrice happy is the nation that has a glorious history. Far better it is to dare mighty things, to win glorious triumphs, even though checkered by failure, than to take rank with those poor spirits who neither enjoy much nor suffer much, because they live in the gray twilight that knows not victory nor defeat. If in 1861 the men who loved the Union had believed that peace was the end of all things, and war and strife the worst of all things, and had acted up to their belief, we would have saved hundreds of thousands of lives, we would have saved hundreds of millions of dollars. Moreover, besides saving all the blood and treasure we then lavished, we would have prevented the heartbreak of many women, the dissolution of many homes, and we would have spared the country those months of gloom and shame when it seemed as if our armies marched only to defeat. We could have avoided all this suffering simply by shrinking from strife. And if we had thus avoided it, we would have shown that we were weaklings, and that we were unfit to stand among the great nations of the earth. Thank God for the iron in the blood of our fathers, the men who upheld the wisdom of Lincoln, and bore sword or rifle in the armies of Grant! Let us, the children of the men who proved themselves equal to the mighty days, let us, the children of the men who carried the great Civil War to a triumphant conclusion, praise the God of our fathers that the ignoble counsels of peace were rejected; that the suffering and loss, the blackness of sorrow and despair, were unflinchingly faced, and the years of strife endured; for in the end the slave was freed, the Union restored, and the mighty American republic placed once more as a helmeted queen among nations.

We of this generation do not have to face a task such as that our fathers faced, but we have our tasks, and woe to us if we fail to perform them! We cannot, if we would, play the part of China, and be content to rot by inches in ignoble ease within our borders, taking no interest in what goes on beyond them, sunk in a scrambling commercialism; heedless of the higher life, the life of aspiration, of toil and risk, busying ourselves only with the wants of our bodies for the day, until suddenly we should find, beyond a shadow of question, what China has already found, that in this world the nation that has trained itself to a career of unwarlike and isolated ease is bound, in the end, to go down before other nations which have not lost the manly and adventurous qualities. If we are to be a really great people, we must strive in good faith to play a great part in the world. We cannot avoid meeting great issues. All that

we can determine for ourselves is whether we shall meet them well or ill. In 1898 we could not help being brought face to face with the problem of war with Spain. All we could decide was whether we should shrink like cowards from the contest, or enter into it as beseemed a brave and high-spirited people; and, once in, whether failure or success should crown our banners. So it is now. We cannot avoid the responsibilities that confront us in Hawaii, Cuba, Porto Rico, and the Philippines. All we can decide is whether we shall meet them in a way that will redound to the national credit, or whether we shall make of our dealings with these new problems a dark and shameful page in our history. To refuse to deal with them at all merely amounts to dealing with them badly. We have a given problem to solve. If we undertake the solution, there is, of course, always danger that we may not solve it aright; but to refuse to undertake the solution simply renders it certain that we cannot possibly solve it aright. The timid man, the lazy man, the man who distrusts his country, the over-civilized man, who has lost the great fighting, masterful virtues, the ignorant man, and the man of dull mind, whose soul is incapable of feeling the mighty lift that thrills "stern men with empires in their brains"—all these, of course, shrink from seeing the nation undertake its new duties; shrink from seeing us build a navy and an army adequate to our needs; shrink from seeing us do our share of the world's work, by bringing order out of chaos in the great, fair tropic islands from which the valor of our soldiers and sailors has driven the Spanish flag. These are the men who fear the strenuous life, who fear the only national life which is really worth leading. They believe in that cloistered life which saps the hardy virtues in a nation, as it saps them in the individual; or else they are wedded to that base spirit of gain and greed which recognizes in commercialism the be-all and end-all of national life, instead of realizing that, though an indispensable element, it is, after all, but one of the many elements that go to make up true national greatness. No country can long endure if its foundations are not laid deep in the material prosperity which comes from thrift, from business energy and enterprise, from hard, unsparing effort in the fields of industrial activity; but neither was any nation ever yet truly great if it relied upon material prosperity alone. All honor must be paid to the architects of our material prosperity, to the great captains of industry who have built our factories and our rail-roads, to the strong men who toil for wealth with brain or hand; for great is the debt of the nation to these and their kind. But our debt is yet greater to the men whose highest type is to be found in a statesman like Lincoln, a soldier like Grant. They showed by their lives that they recognized the law of work, the law of strife; they toiled to win a competence for themselves and those dependent upon them; but they recognized that there were yet other and even loftier duties—duties to the nation and duties to the race.

We cannot sit huddled within our own borders and avow ourselves merely an assemblage of well-to-do hucksters who care nothing for what happens beyond. Such a policy would defeat even its own end; for as the nations grow to have ever wider and wider interests, and are brought into closer and closer contact, if we are to hold our own in the struggle for naval and commercial supremacy, we must build up our power without our own borders. We must build the isthmian canal, and we must grasp the points of vantage which will enable us to have our say in deciding the destiny of the oceans of the East and the West.

So much for the commercial side. From the standpoint of international honor the argument is even stronger. The guns that thundered off Manila and Santiago left us echoes of glory, but they also left us a legacy of duty. If we drove out a medieval tyranny only to make room for savage anarchy, we had better not have begun the task at all. It is worse than idle to say that we have no duty to perform, and can leave to their fates the islands we have conquered. Such a course would be the course of infamy. It would be followed at once by utter chaos in the wretched islands themselves. Some stronger, manlier power would have to step in and do the work, and we would have shown ourselves weaklings, unable to carry to successful completion the labors that great and high-spirited nations are eager to undertake.

The work must be done; we cannot escape our responsibility; and if we are worth our salt, we shall be glad of the chance to do the work—glad of the chance to show ourselves equal to one of the great tasks set modern civilization. But let us not deceive ourselves as to the importance of the task. Let us not be misled by vainglory into underestimating the strain it will put on our powers. Above all, let us, as we value our own self-respect, face the responsibilities with proper seriousness, courage, and high resolve. We must demand the highest order of integrity and ability in our public men who are to grapple with these new problems. We must hold to a rigid accountability those public servants who show unfaithfulness to the interests of the nation or inability to rise to the high level of the new demands upon our strength and our resources.

Of course we must remember not to judge any public servant by any one act, and especially should we beware of attacking the men who are merely the occasions and not the causes of disaster. Let me illustrate what I mean by the army and the navy. If twenty years ago we had gone to war, we should have found the navy as absolutely unprepared as the army. At that time our ships could not have encountered with success the fleets of Spain any more than nowadays we can put untrained soldiers, no matter how brave, who are armed with archaic black-powder weapons,

against well-drilled regulars armed with the highest type of modern repeating rifle. But in the early eighties the attention of the nation became directed to our naval needs. Congress most wisely made a series of appropriations to build up a new navy, and under a succession of able and patriotic secretaries, of both political parties, the navy was gradually built up, until its material became equal to its splendid personnel, with the result that in the summer of 1898 it leaped to its proper place as one of the most brilliant and formidable fighting navies in the entire world. We rightly pay all honor to the men controlling the navy at the time it won these great deeds, honor to Secretary Long and Admiral Dewey, to the captains who handled the ships in action, to the daring lieutenants who braved death in the smaller craft, and to the heads of bureaus at Washington who saw that the ships were so commanded, so armed, so equipped, so well engined, as to insure the best results. But let us also keep ever in mind that all of this would not have availed if it had not been for the wisdom of the men who during the preceding fifteen years had built up the navy. Keep in mind the secretaries of the navy during those years; keep in mind the senators and congressmen who by their votes gave the money necessary to build and to armor the ships, to construct the great guns, and to train the crews; remember also those who actually did build the ships, the armor, and the guns; and remember the admirals and captains who handled battle-ship, cruiser, and torpedo-boat on the high seas, alone and in squadrons, developing the seamanship, the gunnery, and the power of acting together, which their successors utilized so gloriously at Manila and off Santiago. And, gentlemen, remember the converse, too. Remember that justice has two sides. Be just to those who built up the navy, and, for the sake of the future of the country, keep in mind those who opposed its building up. Read the "Congressional Record." Find out the senators and congressmen who opposed the grants for building the new ships; who opposed the purchase of armor, without which the ships were worthless; who opposed any adequate maintenance for the Navy Department, and strove to cut down the number of men necessary to man our fleets. The men who did these things were one and all working to bring disaster on the country. They have no share in the glory of Manila, in the honor of Santiago. They have no cause to feel proud of the valor of our sea-captains, of the renown of our flag. Their motives may or may not have been good, but their acts were heavily fraught with evil. They did ill for the national honor, and we won in spite of their sinister opposition.

Now, apply all this to our public men of to-day. Our army has never been built up as it should be built up. I shall not discuss with an audience like this the puerile suggestion that a nation of seventy millions of freemen is in danger of losing its liberties from the existence of an army of one hundred thousand men, three fourths of whom will be employed in certain foreign islands, in certain coast fortresses, and on Island reservations. No man of good sense and stout heart can take such a proposition seriously. If we are such weaklings as the proposition implies, then we are unworthy of freedom in any event. To no body of men in the United States is the country so much indebted as to the splendid officers and enlisted men of the regular army and navy. There is no body from which the country has less to fear, and none of which it should be prouder, none which it should be more anxious to upbuild.

Our army needs complete reorganization—not merely enlarging—and the reorganization can only come as the result of legislation. A proper general staff should be established, and the positions of ordinance, commissary, and quartermaster officers should be filled by detail from the line. Above all, the army must be given the chance to exercise in large bodies. Never again should we see, as we saw in the Spanish war, major-generals in command of divisions who had never before commanded three companies together in the field. Yet, incredible to relate, Congress has shown a queer inability to learn some of the lessons of the war. There were large bodies of men in both branches who opposed the declaration of war, who opposed the ratification of peace, who opposed the upbuilding of the army, and who even opposed the purchase of armor at a reasonable price for the battle-ships and cruisers, thereby putting an absolute stop to the building of any new fighting-ships for the navy. If, during the years to come, any disaster should befall our arms, afloat or ashore, and thereby any shame come to the United States, remember that the blame will lie upon the men whose names appear upon the roll-calls of Congress on the wrong side of these great questions. On them will lie the burden of any loss of our soldiers and sailors, of any dishonor to the flag; and upon you and the people of this country will lie the blame if you do not repudiate, in no unmistakable way, what these men have done. The blame will not rest upon the untrained commander of untried troops, upon the civil officers of a department the organization of which has been left utterly inadequate, or upon the admiral with an insufficient number of ships; but upon the public men who have so lamentably failed in forethought as to refuse to remedy these evils long in advance, and upon the nation that stands behind those public men.

So, at the present hour, no small share of the responsibility for the blood shed in the Philippines, the blood of our brothers, and the blood of their wild and ignorant foes, lies at the thresholds of those who so long delayed the adoption of the treaty of peace, and of those who by their worse than foolish words deliberately invited a savage people to plunge into a war fraught with sure disaster for them—a war, too, in which our own brave men who follow the flag must pay with their blood for the silly, mock humanitarianism of the prattlers who sit at home in peace.

The army and the navy are the sword and the shield which this nation must carry if she is to do her duty among the nations of the earth—if she is not to stand merely as the China of the western hemisphere. Our proper conduct toward the tropic islands we have wrested from Spain is merely the form which our duty has taken at the moment. Of course we are bound to handle the affairs of our own household well. We must see that there is civic honesty, civic cleanliness, civic good sense in our home administration of city, State, and nation. We must strive for honesty in office, for honesty toward the creditors of the nation and of the individual; for the widest freedom of individual initiative where possible, and for the wisest control of individual initiative where it is hostile to the welfare of the many. But because we set our own household in order we are not thereby excused from playing our part in the great affairs of the world. A man's first duty is to his own home, but he is not thereby excused from doing his duty to the State; for if he fails in this second duty it is under the penalty of ceasing to be a freeman. In the same way, while a nation's first duty is within its own borders, it is not thereby absolved from facing its duties in the world as a whole; and if it refuses to do so, it merely forfeits its right to struggle for a place among the peoples that shape the destiny of mankind.

In the West Indies and the Philippines alike we are confronted by most difficult problems. It is cowardly to shrink from solving them in the proper way; for solved they must be, if not by us, then by some stronger and more manful race. If we are too weak, too selfish, or too foolish to solve them, some bolder and abler people must undertake the solution. Personally, I am far too firm a believer in the greatness of my country and the power of my countrymen to admit for one moment that we shall ever be driven to the ignoble alternative.

The problems are different for the different islands. Porto Rico is not large enough to stand alone. We must govern it wisely and well, primarily in the interest of its own people. Cuba is, in my judgment, entitled ultimately to settle for itself whether it shall be an independent state or an integral portion of the mightiest of republics. But until order and stable liberty are secured, we must remain in the island to insure them, and infinite tact, judgment, moderation, and courage must be shown by our military and civil representatives in keeping the island pacified, in relentlessly stamping out brigandage, in protecting all alike, and yet in showing proper recognition to the men who have fought for Cuban liberty. The Philippines offer a yet graver problem. Their population includes half-caste and native Christians, warlike Moslems, and wild pagans.

Many of their people are utterly unfit for self-government, and show no signs of becoming fit. Others may in time become fit but at present can only take part in self-government under a wise supervision, at once firm and beneficent. We have driven Spanish tyranny from the islands. If we now let it be replaced by savage anarchy, our work has been for harm and not for good. I have scant patience with those who fear to undertake the task of governing the Philippines, and who openly avow that they do fear to undertake it, or that they shrink from it because of the expense and trouble; but I have even scanter patience with those who make a pretense of humanitarianism to hide and cover their timidity, and who can about "liberty" and the "consent of the governed," in order to excuse themselves for their unwillingness to play the part of men. Their doctrines, if carried out, would make it incumbent upon us to leave the Apaches of Arizona to work out their own salvation, and to decline to interfere in a single Indian reservation. Their doctrines condemn your forefathers and mine for ever having settled in these United States.

England's rule in India and Egypt has been of great benefit to England, for it has trained up generations of men accustomed to look at the larger and loftier side of public life. It has been of even greater benefit to India and Egypt. And finally, and most of all, it has advanced the cause of civilization. So, if we do our duty aright in the Philippines, we will add to that national renown which is the highest and finest part of national life, will greatly benefit the people of the Philippine Islands, and, above all, we will play our part well in the great work of uplifting mankind. But to do this work, keep ever in mind that we must show in a very high degree the qualities of courage, of honesty, and of good judgment. Resistant must be stamped out. The first and all-important work to be done is to establish the supremacy of our flag. We must put down armed resistance before we can accomplish anything else, and there should be no parleying, no faltering, in dealing with our foe. As for those in our own country who encourage the foe, we can afford contemptuously to disregard them; but it must be remembered that their utterances are not saved from being treasonable merely by the fact that they are despicable.

When once we have put down armed resistance, when once our rule is acknowledged, then an even more difficult task will begin, for then we must see to it that the islands are administered with absolute honesty and with good judgment. If we let the public service of the islands be turned into the prey of the spoils politician, we shall have begun to tread the path which Spain trod to her own destruction. We must send out there only good and able men, chosen for their fitness, and not because of their partizan service, and these men must not only administer impartial justice to the natives and serve their own government with honesty and fidelity, but must show the utmost tact and firmness, remembering that, with such people as those with whom we are to deal, weakness is the greatest of crimes, and that next to weakness comes lack of consideration for their principles and prejudices.

I preach to you, then, my countrymen, that our country calls not for the life of ease but for the life of strenuous endeavor. The twentieth century looms before us big with the fate of many nations. If we stand idly by, if we seek merely swollen, slothful ease and ignoble peace, if we shrink from the hard contests where men must win at hazard of their lives and at the risk of all they hold dear, then the bolder and stronger peoples will pass us by, and will win for themselves the domination of the world. Let us therefore boldly face the life of strife, resolute to do our duty well and manfully; resolute to uphold righteousness by deed and by word; resolute to be both honest and brave, to serve high ideals, yet to use practical methods. Above all, let us shrink from no strife, moral or physical, within or without the nation, provided we are certain that the strife is justified, for it is only through strife, through hard and dangerous endeavor, that we shall ultimately win the goal of true national greatness.

Source:

Theodore Roosevelt, *The Strenuous Life: Essays and Addresses.* New York: The Century Co., 1900, pp. 381–388.

Mary Antin, *The Promised Land*, 1912

Mary Antin was born in 1881 into a relatively prosperous family in the Jewish ghetto of the Russian Pale. In earlier chapters she describes the anti-Semitism suffered by Russian Jews. "In Russian cities, and even more in the country districts, where Jewish families lived scattered, by special permission of the police, who were always changing their minds about letting them stay, the Gentiles made the Passover a time of horror for the Jews. Somebody would start up that lie about murdering Christian children, and the stupid peasants would get mad about it, and fill themselves with vodka, and set out to kill the Jews. They attacked them with knives and clubs and scythes and axes, killed them or tortured them, and burned their houses. This was called a 'pogrom.' People who saw such things never smiled any more, no matter how long they lived; and sometimes their hair turned white in a day, and some people became insane on the spot." Her families' status changed when both her parents suffered illnesses. Her father emigrated to the Boston, Massachusetts, area when Mary was ten, and the rest of the family, now impoverished, followed three years later.

Unlike Riis, who viewed urban tenements from a reformer's perspective, Antin found American life so much better than what she left behind. "Happening when it did, the emigration became of the most vital importance to me personally. All the processes of uprooting, transportation, replanting, acclimatization, and development took place in my own soul. I felt the pang, the fear, the wonder, and the joy of it. I can never forget, for I bear the scars." In the Introduction she recounts a common immigrant experience where parents find themselves at sea in an alien culture and language: "When I discovered my own friends, and ran home with them to convert my parents to a belief in their excellence, did I not begin to make my father and mother, as truly as they had ever made me? Did I not become the parent and they the children, in those relations of teacher and learner?"

This excerpt from chapter XIX tells of Antin's experience using a public library. Like the public schools, the library became a major democratizing and educational institution for immigrants.

Chapter XIX. A Kingdom in the Slums

Truly my education was not entirely in the hands of persons who had licenses to teach. My sister's fat baby taught me things about the origin and ultimate destiny of dimples that were not in any of my school-books. Mr. Casey, of the second floor, who was drunk whenever his wife was sober, gave me an insight into the psychology of the beer mug that would have added to the mental furniture of my most scholarly teacher. The bold-faced girls who passed the evening on the corner, in promiscuous flirtation with the cock-eyed youths of the neighborhood, unconsciously revealed to me the eternal secrets of adolescence. My neighbor of the third floor, who sat on the curb-stone with the scabby baby in her bedraggled lap, had things to say about the fine ladies who came in carriages to inspect the public bathhouse across the street that ought to be repeated in the lecture halls of every school of philanthropy. Instruction poured into my brain at such a rate that I could not digest it all at the time; but in later years, when my destiny had led me far from Dover Street, the emphatic moral of those lessons became clear. The memory of my experience on Dover street became the strength of my convictions, the illumined index of my purpose, the aureola of my happiness. And if I paid for those lessons with days of privation and dread, with nights of tormenting anxiety, I count the price cheap. Who would not go to a little trouble to find out what life is made of? Life in the slums spins busily as a schoolboy's top, and one who has heard its humming never forgets. I look forward to telling, when I get to be a master of language, what I read in the crooked cobblestones when I revisited Dover Street the other day.

Dover Street was never really my residence–at least, not the whole of it. It happened to be the nook where my

bed was made, but I inhabited the City of Boston. In the pearl-misty morning, in the ruby-red evening, I was empress of all I surveyed from the roof of the tenement house. I could point in any direction and name a friend who would welcome me there. Off towards the northwest, in the direction of Harvard Bridge, which some day I should cross on my way to Radcliffe College, was one of my favorite palaces, whither I resorted every day after school.

A low, wide-spreading building with a dignified granite front it was, flanked on all sides by noble old churches, museums, and school-houses, harmoniously disposed around a spacious triangle, called Copley Square. Two thoroughfares that came straight from the green suburbs swept by my palace, one on either side, converged at the apex of the triangle, and pointed off, past the Public Garden, across the historic Common, to the domed State House sitting on a height.

It was my habit to go very slowly up the low, broad steps to the palace entrance, pleasing my eyes with the majestic lines of the building, and lingering to read again the carved inscriptions: *Public Library—Built by the People—Free to All.*

Did I not say it was my palace? Mine, because I was a citizen; mine, though I was born an alien; mine, though I lived on Dover Street. My palace—*mine!*

I loved to lean against a pillar in the entrance hall, watching the people go in and out. Groups of children hushed their chatter at the entrance, and skipped, whispering and giggling in their fists, up the grand stairway, patting the great stone lions at the top, with an eye on the aged policemen down below. Spectacled scholars came slowly down the stairs, loaded with books, heedless of the lofty arches that echoed their steps. Visitors from out of town lingered long in the entrance hall, studying the inscriptions and symbols on the marble floor. And I loved to stand in the midst of all this, and remind myself that I was there, that I had a right to be there, that I was at home there. All these eager children, all these fine-browed women, all these scholars going home to write learned books. I and they had this glorious thing in common, this noble treasure house of learning. It was wonderful to say, *This is mine;* it was thrilling to say, *This is ours.*

I visited every part of the building that was open to the public. I spent rapt hours studying the Abbey pictures. I repeated to myself lines from Tennyson's poem before the glowing scenes of the Holy Grail. Before the "Prophets" in the gallery above I was mute, but echoes of the Hebrew Psalms I had long forgotten throbbed somewhere in the depths of my consciousness. The Chavannes series around the main staircase I did not enjoy for years. I thought the pictures looked faded, and their symbolism somehow failed to move me at first.

Bates Hall was the place where I spent my longest hours in the library. I chose a seat far at one end, so that looking up from my books I would get the full effect of the vast reading-room. I felt the grand spaces under the soaring arches as a personal attribute of my being.

The courtyard was my sky-roofed chamber of dreams. Slowly strolling past the endless pillars of the colonnade, the fountain murmured in my ear of all the beautiful things in all the beautiful world. I imagined that I was a Greek of the classic days, treading on sandalled feet through the glistening marble porticoes of Athens. I expected to see, if I looked over my shoulder, a bearded philosopher in a drooping mantle, surrounded by beautiful youths with wreathed locks. Everything I read in school, in Latin or Greek, everything in my history books, was real to me here, in this courtyard set about with stately columns.

Here is where I liked to remind myself of Polotzk, the better to bring out the wonder of my life. That I who was born in the prison of the Pale should roam at will in the land of freedom was a marvel that it did me good to realize. That I who was brought up to my teens almost without a book should be set down in the midst of all the books that ever were written was a miracle as great as any on record. That an outcast should become a privileged citizen, that a beggar should dwell in a palace— this was a romance more thrilling than poet ever sung. Surely I was rocked in an enchanted cradle.

Source:

Mary Antin, *The Promised Land*, Boston & New York: Houghton Mifflin Company, 1912.

The Rise of the American Labor Movement

Knights of Labor Constitution, 1878

Constitution drawn up in 1878 by the Noble Order of the Knights of Labor, an outgrowth of a secret society of garment cutters organized in Philadelphia in 1869. The Knights, composed of men and women, whites and blacks, skilled and unskilled workers, advocated industrial democracy. The preamble to the constitution stated that a united effort was necessary to protect workers from the "aggression of aggregated wealth." The constitution called for the establishment of cooperatives, weekly pay, equal justice for workers and capitalists, prohibition of child labor, arbitration instead of strikes, an eight-hour day, and equal pay for both sexes for equal work. The Knights flourished until 1886, when labor unrest and violence, especially the Haymarket affair, led to its decline.

⸺⸻⸺

The alarming development and aggressiveness of the power of great capitalists and corporations under the present industrial system will inevitably lead to the pauperization and hopeless degradation of the toiling masses. It is imperative, if we desire to enjoy the full blessings of life,

the unjust accumulation and this power for evil of aggregated wealth shall be prevented. This mush-desired object can be accomplished only by the united efforts of those who obey the divine injunction: "In the sweat of thy face shalt thou eat bread." Therefore we have formed the Order of the Knights of Labor for the purpose of organizing, educating and directing the power of the industrial masses.

It is not a political party, it is more, for in it are crystallized sentiments and measures for the benefit of the whole people; but it should be borne in mind, when exercising the right of suffrage, that most of the objects herein set forth can only be obtained through legislation, and that it is the duty, regardless of party, of all to assist in nominating and supporting with their votes such candidates as will support these measures. No one shall, however, be compelled to vote with the majority.

Calling upon all who believe in securing "the greatest good to the greatest number" to join and assist us, we declare to the world that our aims are:

I. To make industrial and moral worth, not wealth, the true standard of individual and national greatness.

II. To secure to the workers the full enjoyment of, the wealth they create; sufficient leisure in which to develop their intellectual, moral and social faculties; all of the benefits, recreations and pleasures of association; in a word, to enable them to share in the gains and honor of advancing civilization.

In order to secure these results, we demand at the hands of the law-making power of Municipality, State and Nation:

III. The establishment of the Referendum in the making of all laws.

IV. The establishment of Bureaus of labor Statistics, that we may arrive at a correct knowledge of the educational, moral and financial condition of the laboring masses, and the establishment of free State Labor Bureaus.

V. The land, including all the natural sources of wealth, is the heritage of all the people, and should not be subject to speculative traffic. Occupancy and use should be the only title to the possession of land. The taxes upon land should be levied upon its full value for use, exclusive of improvements, and should be sufficient to take for the community all unearned increment.

VI. The abrogation of all laws that do not bear equally upon capitalists and laborers, and the removal of unjust technicalities, delays and discriminations in the administration of justice.

VII. The adoption of measures providing for the health and safety of those engaged in mining, manufacturing and building industries, and for indemnification to those engaged therein for injuries received through lack of necessary safeguards.

VIII. The recognition, by incorporation, of orders and other associations organized by the workers to improve their condition and to protect their rights.

IX. The enactment of laws to compel corporations to pay their employes weekly, in lawful money, for the labor of the proceeding week, and giving mechanics and laborers a first lien upon the product of their labor to the extent of their full wages.

X. The abolition of the contract system on National, State and Municipal works.

XI. The enactment of laws providing for arbitration between employers and employed, and to enforce the decision of the arbitrators.

XII. The prohibition by law of the employment of children under fifteen years of age; the compulsory attendance at school for at least ten months in the year of all children between the ages of seven and fifteen years; and the furnishing at the expense of the State of free text books.

XIII. That a graduated tax on incomes and inheritances be levied.

XIV. To prohibit the hiring out of convict labor.

XV. The establishment of a national monetary system in which a circulating medium in necessary quantity shall issue directly to the people without the intervention of banks; that all the national issue shall be full legal tender in payment of all debts, public and private; and that the government shall not guarantee or recognize any private banks or create any banking corporations.

XVI. That interest-bearing bonds, bills of credit or notes shall never be issued by the government; but that, when need arises, the emergency shall be met by issue of legal-tender, non-interest-bearing money.

XVII. That the importation of foreign labor under contract be prohibited.

XVIII. That, in connection with the post office, the government shall provide facilities for deposits of savings of the people in small sums.

XIX. That the government shall obtain possession, under the right of eminent domain, of all telegraphs, telephones and railroads; and that hereafter no charter or license be issued to any corporation for construction or operation of any means of transporting intelligence, passengers or freight.

And while making the foregoing demands upon the State and National Governments, we will endeavor to associate our own labors:

XX. To establish co-operative institutions, such as will tend to supersede the wage system, by the introduction of a co-operative industrial system.

XXI. To secure for both sexes equal rights.

XXII. To gain some of the benefits of labor-saving machinery by a gradual reduction of the hours of labor to eight per day.

XXIII. To persuade employers to agree to arbitrate all differences which may arise between them and their employes, in order that the bonds of sympathy between them may be strengthened and that strikes may be rendered unnecessary.

Constitution of the General Assembly of the Knights of Labor.

Article I
Name, Jurisdiction and Membership.

Section 1. This body shall be known as the General Assembly of the Knights of Labor, and shall be composed of Representatives selected according to the constitution. The General Assembly has full and final jurisdiction, and is the highest tribunal of the Order of the Knights of Labor. It alone possesses the power and authority to make, amend or repeal the fundamental and general laws and regulations of the Order, and to finally decide all controversies arising in the Order. It shall issue, or cause to be issued, charters to State, National Trade, District and Local Assemblies, traveling and transfer cards, and all supplies requiring uniformity. It shall prohibit the sale of intoxicants at entertainments given by the Assemblies of this Order. It may also tax the members of the Order for its maintenance.

Sec. 2. To facilitate the work of the Order there may be established State, National Trade, District and Local Assemblies under such regulations as may be hereinafter provided. These several subdivisions of the Order shall subject to the absolute control of the General Assembly.

Sec. 3. In each of the States and Territories of the United States of America, as soon as ten or more Local Assemblies are founded therein, there may be established a State or (as the case may be) Territorial Assembly. In foreign countries an Assembly similar in power and purpose may be established in each Province or other subdivision into which said country may be divided. Said Assembly shall be known by the name of the State, Territory, Province or other division in which it is located. All reference hereinafter made, and all laws, rules or regulations of the Order applying to a State Assembly, shall be construed as in like manner applying to a Territorial, Province, etc., Assembly. The jurisdiction of a State Assembly shall include all of the territory of the State not assigned to a Mixed District Assembly existing at the time said State Assembly is organized, together with such territory as may be surrendered by any such District Assembly.

Sec. 4. District Assemblies may be instituted within the limits of a State Assembly with such jurisdiction as said State Assembly may define.

Sec. 5. Local Assemblies may be founded within the limits of a District Assembly with such jurisdiction as said District Assembly may define. Local Assemblies may be attached to a State, National Trade, District or to the General Assembly. Local Assemblies shall have the right to transfer from the higher body to which they are attached to another higher body for reasons satisfactory to the General Executive Board. This decision, to be lawful, must be arrived at by two-thirds the members present at a meeting of the Local specially called for the purpose, after the Local has met all lawful demands of the higher body from which it may desire to detach itself. Notice of action taken, with receipts for all indebtedness to superior body the Local Assembly desires to withdraw from up to date of quarter preceding application for transfer, must at once be forwarded by the Local to the General Secretary-Treasurer, and a similar notice and copy to the higher body to which the Local desires to attach itself. A Trade Assembly belonging to a National Trade Assembly may also join a State of Mixed District Assembly in the locality in which it is situated and under such regulations as said District Assembly may enact, provided that the delegates of such Local Assembly shall have no vote in electing representatives of the State or of the District Assembly to the General Assembly and its membership shall be credited to the National Trade Assembly as a basis of representation.

Source:
Department of Archives and Manuscripts, The Catholic University of America, Washington, D.C.

The Haymarket "Massacre," 1886

On May 4, 1886, anarchists sympathetic to the labor cause held a rally in Chicago's Haymarket Square to protest police violence against striking workers. Although many anarchists were nonviolent, their literature, such as "To Tramps," encouraged terrorism, and a number engaged in arson and assassinations. The media usually depicted anarchists throwing bombs. When the police arrived to disperse the meeting, a bomb was thrown into their ranks, killing one officer. Amid firing, allegedly from both sides, some 60 people were wounded. Police began rounding up known anarchists, but the bomber was never found. Eight men were eventually indicted, tried, and convicted of murder.

At the trial, the prosecution argued that even if the defendants did not set off the explosion themselves, their speech and opinions encouraged violence in others and they were therefore indirectly responsible. In turn, the defense argued that the defendants did not plan or execute the bombing, and that many of the prosecution's witnesses had been bribed or coerced into providing false testimony. The jury took only three hours to deliberate. Seven defendants received the death sentence, and one received 15 years' hard labor. Over the next six years, four were executed, including the husband of Lucy Parsons, author of "To Tramps," and one committed suicide. According to one historian, "Haymarket broke the force of direct labor resistance to the new industrial order for nearly a decade."

In 1893, the new governor of Illinois, John Altgeld, pardoned the three remaining prisoners. In his pardon statement, the governor declares that the jury was "a packed jury selected to convict," that the defendants were not proven guilty of the crime they were indicted for, and that the trial judge, Judge Joseph Gary, "was so prejudiced against the defendants, or else so determined to win the applause of a certain class in the community, that he could not and did not grant a fair trial." The pardon was extremely unpopular and Altgeld was not reelected.

For the complete police report which contains several accounts, and for the complete 63-page pardon, see *Landmark Documents in American History*, www.factsonfile. com

Lucy Parson, "To Tramps," 1884

TO TRAMPS
The Unemployed, the Disinherited, and Miserable.

A word to the 35,000 now tramping the streets of this great city, with hands in pockets, gazing listlessly about you at the evidences of wealth and pleasure of which you own no part, not sufficient even to purchase yourself a bit of food with which to appease the pangs of hunger now knawing at your vitals. It is with you and the hundreds of thousands of others similarly situated in this great land of plenty, that I wish to have a word.

Have you not worked hard all your life, since you were old enough for your labor to be of use in the production of wealth? Have you not toiled so long, hard and laboriously in producing wealth? And in all those years of drudgery do you not know you have produced thousand upon thousands of dollars' worth of wealth, which you did not then, do not now, and unless you ACT, never will, own any part in? Do you not know that when you were harnessed to a machine and that machine harnessed to steam, and thus you toiled your 10, 12 and 16 hours in the 24, that during this time in all those years you received only enough of your labor product to furnish yourself the bare, coarse necessaries of life, and that when you wished to purchase anything for yourself and family it always had to be of the cheapest quality? If you wanted to go anywhere you had to wait until Sunday, so little did you receive for your unremitting toil that you dare not stop for a moment, as it were? And do you not know that with all your squeezing, pinching and economizing you never were enabled to keep but a few days ahead of the wolves of want? And that at last when the caprice of your employer saw fit to create an artificial famine by limiting production, that the fires in the furnace were extinguished, the iron horse to which you had been harnessed was stilled; the factory door locked up, you turned upon the highway a tramp, with hunger in your stomach and rags upon your back?

Yet your employer told you that it was overproduction which made him close up. Who cared for the bitter tears and heart-pangs of your loving wife and helpless children, when you bid them a loving "God bless you" and turned upon the tramper's road to seek employment elsewhere? I say, who cared for those heartaches and pains? You were only a tramp now, to be execrated and denounced as a "worthless tramp and a vagrant" by that very class who had been engaged all those years in robbing you and yours. Then can you not see that the "good boss" or the "bad boss" cuts no figure whatever? that you are the common prey of both, and that their mission is simply robbery? Can you not see that it is the INDUSTRIAL SYSTEM and not the "boss" which must be changed?

Now, when all these bright summer and autumn days are going by and you have no employment, and consequently can save up nothing, and when the winter's blast sweeps down from the north and all the earth is wrapped in a shroud of ice, hearken not to the voice of the hypocrite who will tell you that it was ordained of God that "the poor ye have always"; or to the arrogant robber who will say to you that you "drank up all your wages last summer when you had work, and that is the reason why you have nothing now, and the workhouse or the workyard is too good for you; that you ought to be shot." And shoot you they will if you present your petitions in too emphatic a manner. So hearken not to them, but list! Next winter when the cold blasts are creeping through the rents in your seeding garments, when the frost is biting your feet through the holes in your word-out shoes, and when all wretchedness seems to have centered in and upon you, whose misery has marked you for her own and life has become a burden and existence a mockery, when you have walked the streets by day and slept upon hard boards by night, and at last determine by your own hand to take your life—for you would rather go out into utter nothingness than to longer endure an existence which has become such a burden—so, perchance, you determine to dash yourself into the cold embrace of the lake than longer suffer thus. But halt, before you commit this last tragic act in the drama of your simple existence. Stop! Is there nothing you can do to insure those whom you are about to orphan, against a like fate? The waves will only dash over you in mockery of your rash act; but stroll you down the avenues of the rich and look through the magnificent plate windows into their voluptuous homes, and here you will discover the *very identical robbers* who have despoiled you and yours. Then let your tragedy be enacted *here!* Awaken them from their wanton sports at your expense! Send forth your petition and let them read it by the red glare of destruction. Thus when you cast "one long, lingering look behind" you can be assured that you have spoken to these robbers in the only language which they have ever been able to understand, for they have never yet deigned to notice any petition from their slaves that they were not *compelled* to read by the red glare bursting from the cannon's mouths, or that was not handed to them upon the point of the sword. You need no organization when you make up your mind to present this kind of petition. In fact, an organization would be a detriment to you; but each of you hungry tramps who read these lines, avail yourselves of those little methods of warfare which Science has placed in the hands of the poor man, and you will become a power in this or any other land.

Learn the use of explosives!

Dedicated to the tramps by
Lucy E. Parsons

John Bonfield, Police Report, 1886

DEPARTMENT OF POLICE
INSPECTOR AND SECRETARY'S OFFICE
CHICAGO, ILLS,
. . . . 1886
Frdrk. Ebersold, Esqr, General Superintendent of Police

Sir:

On Tuesday, May 4th, the attention of our department was called to a circular headed, "Revenge," and also to the fact that an Anarchist meeting was to be held that evening . . . on the square known in years gone by, as the haymarket, but owing to reasons known only to the prime movers of the meeting it was changed to about 90 feet north . . . near the intersection of an alley, to better serve their purposes.

On the afternoon of the day above mentioned, his Honor, the Mayor, ordered that the Department of Police keep watch of the meeting, and if any of the speakers should advise their hearers to acts of violence, it would be our duty as conservators of the peace, to go to the place of meeting in sufficient force and order them to peaceably disperse, the order to be as directed by law {See Revised Statutes of Illinois, Chapter 38, Section 253}. To carry out the instructions of the Mayor, Captain Ward of the 3rd precinct was ordered to call all his available men to DesPlaines Street Station. Capt. Ward's command consisted of one hundred men. . . . In addition . . . there was present 26 men from the Central Detail and 50 men from the 4th Precinct. The entire force present consisting of one Captain, seven Lieutenants and one hundred and seventy-six men.

At the suggestion of the Mayor, and with your permission I went to DesPlaines Street Station and took command of the entire force assembled at that point. By your orders detectives were sent out to mingle with the crowd and were ordered to pay strict attention to the speakers, and if any thing of an incendiary nature was advised, the officers were to report to me at the DesPlaines Street Station.

About 9 o'clock, P.M., I was informed that the meeting had moved to a point about 350 feet from DesPlaines Street Station. At different times, between 8:00 and 9:30 o'clock, P.M., officers in plain clothes reported the progress of the meeting and stated that nothing of a very inflammatory nature was said until a man named Fielden or Fielding took the stand. He advised his hearers, "To throttle the law," "It would be as well for them to die fighting as to starve to death." He further advised them "To exterminate the capitalists and to do it that night." Wanting to be clearly within the law, and wishing to leave no room for doubt as to the propriety of our actions, I did not act on the first reports, but sent the officers back to make

further observations. A few minutes after 10 o'clock, P.M., the officers returned and reported that the crowd were getting excited and the speaker growing more incendiary in his language. I then felt to hesitate any longer would be criminal on my part, and then gave the order to fall in and our force formed on Waldo Place.

[The report included a diagram showing where the different companies were placed.]

. . . We marched north on DesPlaines Street, {Captain Ward and myself in front of the first division,} until within a few feet of the truck upon which the speakers were standing and around which a large crowd had congregated. The command, halt, was given, and Captain Ward stepping forward to within about three feet of the truck, said, "I command you, in the name of the People of the State to immediately and peaceably disperse," and turning to the crowd of persons on the right and left, said, "I command you and you to assist." Fielden or Fielding turned and got off the truck and as he reached the sidewalk, said in rather a loud voice, "We are peaceable." Almost instantly, I heard a hissing sound behind me followed by a tremendous explosion. The explosion was immediately followed by a volley of pistol shots from the sidewalks and street in front of us.

The explosion was caused by a dynamite bomb which was thrown into our ranks from the east sidewalk, and fell in the second division and near the dividing line between the companies of Lieuts. Stanton and Bowler. For an instant the entire command of the above named officers, with many of the first and third divisions was thrown to the ground. Alas many never to rise again. The men recovered, instantly, and returned the fire of the mob. Lieuts. Steele and Quinn charged the mob on the street, while the company of Lieut. Hubbard with the few uninjured members of the second division swept both sidewalks with a hot and telling fire, and in a few minutes the Anarchists were flying in every direction. I then gave the order to cease firing, fearing that some of our men, in the darkness might fire into each other.

I then ordered the patrol wagons to called, made details to take care of the dead and wounded, placed guards around the station and called for physicians to attend to our wounded men.

The reports of Captain Ward and the Lieutenants engaged which are attached and form a part of this report will give all details as to the killed and wounded. It is surprising to many that our men stood and did not get demoralized under such trying circumstances.

It has been asserted that regular troops have become panic stricken from less cause. I see no way to account for it except this: The soldier acts as part of a machine, rarely, if ever, when on duty is he allowed to act as an individual or to use his personal judgement. A police officers training teaches him to be self-reliant. Day after day and night after night he goes on duty alone, and when in conflict with the thief and the burglar, he has to depend upon his own individual exertions. The soldier being part of a machine it follows that when a part of it gives out, the rest is useless until the injury is repaired. The policeman being a machine in himself, rarely, if ever gives up until he is laid on the ground and unable to rise again.

In conclusion, I beg leave to report, that the conduct of the men and officers, with few exceptions, was admirable. As a military man said to me the next day, "Worthy the heroes of a hundred battles." Of one officer, I beg leave to make special mention. Immediately after the explosion I looked behind me and saw the greater portion of the second division on the ground. I gave the order to the men to close up, and in an instant, Sergeant John E. Fitzpatrick was at my side and repeated the order. To show our appreciation of the Sergeants gallant conduct, I would respectfully recommend to his Honor, the Mayor, and yourself, the promotion of the Sergeant to a Lieutenancy as soon as a vacancy occurs. I am satisfied that the department does not contain a braver or a better officer.

Respectfully Submitted,
John Bonfield Insp & Secty Department of Police

John Altgeld, Reasons for Pardoning Fielden, Neebe and Schwab, 1893

STATEMENT OF THE CASE On the night of May 4, 1886, a public meeting was held on Haymarket Square in Chicago; there were from 800 to 1,000 people present, nearly all being laboring men. There had been trouble, growing out of the effort to introduce an eight-hour day, resulting in some collisions with the police, in one of which several laboring people were killed, and this meeting was called as a protest against alleged police brutality. The meeting was orderly and was attended by the mayor, who remained until the crowd began to disperse and then went away. As soon as Capt. John Bonfield, of the police department, learned that the mayor had gone, he took a detachment of police and hurried to the meeting for the purpose of dispersing the few that remained, and as the police approached the place of meeting a bomb was thrown by some unknown person, which exploded and wounded many and killed several policemen, among the latter being one Mathias Degan. A number of people were arrested and after a time August Spies, Albert R. Parsons, Louis Lingg, Michael Schwab, Samuel Fielden, George Engle, Adolph Fischer and Oscar Neebe were indicted for the murder of Mathias Degan. The prosecution could not discover who had thrown the bomb and could not bring the really guilty man to justice, and, as some of the men indicted were not at the Haymarket meeting and had nothing to do with it, the prosecution was forced to proceed on the theory that the men indicted were guilty of murder because it was claimed they had at various times in the past uttered and printed incendiary and seditious language, practically advising the killing of policemen, of Pinkerton men and others acting in that capacity, and that they were therefore responsible for the murder of Mathias Degan. The public was greatly excited and after a prolonged trial all of the defendants were found guilty. . . . The several thousand merchants, bankers, judges, lawyers and other prominent citizens of Chicago who have by petition, by letter and in other ways urged executive clemency, mostly base their appeal on the ground that, assuming the prisoners to be guilty, they have been punished enough, but a number of them who have examined the case more carefully . . . and are more familiar with the record. . . assert,

1. FIRST—That the jury which tried the case was a packed jury selected to convict. SECOND—That according to the law as laid down by the supreme court, both prior to and again since the trial of this case, the jurors, according to their own answers, were not competent jurors and the trial was therefore not a legal trial. THIRD—That the defendants were not proven to be guilty of the crime charged in the indictment. FOURTH—That as to the defendant Neebe, the state's attorney had declared at the close of the evidence that there was no case against him, and yet he has been kept in prison all these years. Upon the question of having been punished enough I will simply say that if the defendants had a fair trial, and nothing has developed since to show that they are not guilty of the crime charged in the indictment, then there ought to be no executive interference, for no punishment under our laws could then be too severe. . . . The soil of America is not adapted for the growth of anarchy. While our institutions are not free from injustice, they are still the best that have yet been devised, and therefore must be maintained.

❖   ❖   ❖

[The judge concluded that the defendants did not have a fair trial.]

I am convinced that it is clearly my duty to act in this case . . . and I, therefore, grant an absolute pardon to Samuel Fielden, Oscar Neebe and Michael Schwab this 26th day of June, 1893.

JOHN P. ALTGELD,
Governor of Illinois.

Source:
Chicago Historical Society, Haymarket Affair Digital Collection.

Constitution of the American Federation of Labor, 1886

From the Report of the Sixth Annual Session of the Federation of Organized Trades and Labor Unions of the United States and Canada, this is the charter of organization for the American Federation of Labor (AFL), the association of trade unions formed in December 1886 at a national labor convention in Columbus, Ohio. Delegates of the Federation of Organized Trades and Labor Unions and other labor groups, representing virtually the whole American trade union movement, assembled at Columbus in hopes of organizing all skilled craft unions under a single aegis. They founded the AFL as a permanent federation of trade unions and elected Samuel Gompers its first president, a post he held every year except one until 1924. The constitution spelled out the AFL's structure and principles. It pledged strict recognition of each trade's autonomy and established the national or international union as the new federation's basic organizational unit. A membership tax was to be levied to raise money to assist striking workers and fund AFL legislative initiatives. The executive council, responsible for administering affairs at the national level, was charged with settling jurisdictional disputes, lobbying for legislation, investigating strikes and lockouts, and influencing public opinion.

Preamble

Whereas, A struggle is going on in all the nations of the civilized world, between the oppressors and the oppressed of all countries, a struggle between the capitalist and the laborer, which grows in intensity from year to year, and will work disastrous results to the toiling millions, if they are not combined for mutual protection and benefit.

It therefore behooves the representatives of the Trades and Labor Unions of America, in Convention, assembled, to adopt such measures and disseminate such principles among the mechanics and laborers of our country as will permanently unite them, to secure the recognition of the rights to which they are justly entitled.

We therefore declare ourselves in favor of the formation of a thorough Federation, embracing every Trade and Labor Organization in America.

Constitution.
Article I.—Name.

Section 1. This association shall be known as "The American Federation of Labor," and shall consist of such Trades and Labor Unions as shall conform to its rules and regulations.

Article II.—Objects.

Section 1. The objects of this Federation shall be the encouragement and formation of local Trades and Labor Unions, and the closer Federation of such societies through the organization of Central Trades and Labor Unions in every city, and the further combination of such bodies into state, territorial, or provincial organizations, to secure legislation in the interests of the working masses.

Sec. 2. The establishment of National and International Trades Unions, based upon a strict recognition of the autonomy of each trade, and the promotion and advancement of such bodies.

Sec. 3. An American Federation of all National and International Trades Unions, to aid and assist each other; and, furthermore, to secure National Legislation in the interests of the working people, and influence public opinion, by peaceful and legal methods, in favor of Organized Labor.

Sec. 4. To aid and encourage the labor press of America.

Article III.—Convention.

Section 1. The convention of the Federation shall be held annually, on the second Tuesday of December, at such place as the delegates have selected at the preceding Convention.

Article IV.—Representation.

Section 1. The basis of representation in the convention shall be: From National or International Unions, for less than four thousand members, one delegate; four thousand or more, two delegates; eight thousand or more, three delegates; sixteen thousand or more, four delegates; thirty-two thousand or more, five delegates; and so on; and from each Local or District Trades Union, not connected with, or having a National or International head, affiliated with this Federation, one delegate.

Sec. 2. No organization which has seceded from any Local, National or International or organization, shall be allowed a representation or recognition in this Federation.

Article V.—Officers.

Section 1. The officers of the Federation shall consist of a President, two Vice-Presidents, a Secretary, and a Treasurer, to be elected by the Convention.

Sec. 2. At the opening of the Convention the President shall take the chair and call the Convention to order, and preside until his successor is elected.

Sec. 3. The following Committee, consisting of three members each, shall be appointed by the President: 1st, Credentials; 2d, Rules and Order of Business; 3d, Resolutions; 4th, Finance; 5th, Report of Executive Council.

Sec. 4. Should a vacancy in any office occur between the annual meetings of the Convention, such vacancies shall be filled by the President of the Federation, by and with consent of the Executive Council. When a vacancy occurs in the office of President, the Vice-Presidents shall succeed in their respective order.

Sec. 5. The President and Secretary shall be members of the succeeding Convention in case they are not delegates, but without vote.

Article VI.—Executive Council.

Section 1. The Officers shall be an Executive Council with power to watch legislative measures directly affecting the interests of working people, and to initiate, whenever necessary, such legislative action as the Convention may direct.

Sec. 2. The Executive Council shall use every possible means to organize new National or International Trades Unions, and to organize local Trades Unions and connect them with the Federation, until such time as there are a sufficient number to form a National or International Union, when it shall be the duty of the President of the Federation to see that such organization is formed.

Sec. 3. While we recognize the right of each trade to manage its own affairs, it shall be the duty of the Executive Council to secure the unification of all labor organizations, so far as to assist each other in any justifiable boycott, and with voluntary financial help in the event of a strike or lock-out, when duly approved by the Executive Council.

Sec. 4. When a strike has been approved by the Executive Council, the particulars of the difficulty, even if it be a lock-out, shall be explained in a circular issued by the President of the Federation to the unions affiliated therewith. It shall then be the duty of all affiliated societies to urge their Local Unions and members to make liberal financial donations in aid of the working people involved.

Article VII.—Revenue.

Section 1. The revenue of the Federation shall be derived from International, National, District and Local organizations, which shall pay into the treasury of the Federation a per capita tax of one-half cent per month for each member in good standing, the same to be payable monthly to the Treasurer of the Federation.

Sec. 2. Delegates shall not be entitled to a seat in this Federation, unless the per capita tax of their organization is paid in full.

Sec. 3. Any organization, affiliated with this Federation, not paying its per capita tax on or before the 15th of each month, shall be notified of the fact by the President of the Federation, and if at the end of three months it is still in arrears, it shall be suspended from membership in the Federation, and can only be reinstated by vote of the Convention.

Sec. 4. Each society affiliated with this Federation, shall make a monthly report of its standing and progress to the President of the Federation.

Sec. 5. It shall be the duty of the President to attend to all correspondence, publish a monthly journal, and travel, with consent of the Executive Council, wherever required in the interest of the Federation. His salary shall be $1,000 per year, payable monthly, with mileage and expenses.

Sec. 6. Whenever the revenue of the Federation shall warrant such action, the Executive Council shall authorize the sending out of Trades Union speakers, from place to place, in the interests of the Federation.

Sec. 7. The funds of the Federation shall be banked monthly by three Trustees, who shall be selected by the Executive Council. The said Trustees shall be residents of the same city with the Treasurer. No money shall be paid out only in conformity with the rules laid down by the Executive Council.

Sec. 8. It shall be the duty of the Secretary to attend to such business as may be decided by the Executive Council.

Sec. 9. The accounts of the year shall be closed fourteen days prior to the assembling of the Convention, and a balance sheet, duly certified, shall be presented to the same.

Sec. 10. The remuneration for the loss of time by the executive council shall be at the rate of $3.000 per diem; traveling and incidental expenses to be also defrayed.

Article VIII.—Miscellaneous.

Section 1. In all questions not covered by this Constitution, the Executive Council shall have power to make rules to govern the same, and shall report accordingly to the Federation.

Sec. 2. Charters for the Federation shall be granted by the President of the Federation, by and with the consent of the Executive Council, to all National and International, and Local bodies affiliated with this Federation.

Sec. 3. Any seven wage workers of good character, an favorable to Trades Unions, and not members of any body affiliated with this Federation, who will subscribe to this Constitution, shall have the power to form a local body, to be known as a "Federal Labor Union," and they shall hold regular meetings for the purpose of strengthening and advancing the Trades Union movement, and shall have the power to make their own rules in conformity with this Constitution, and shall be granted a local charter by the President of this Federation, provided the request for a charter be endorsed by the nearest Local or National Trades Union officials connected with this Federation.

Sec. 4. The charter fee for affiliated bodies shall be $5.00, payable to the Treasurer of the Federation.

Sec. 5. Where there are one or more Local Unions in any city, belonging to a National or International Union, affiliated with this Federation, it shall be their duty to organize a Trades Assembly or Central Labor Union, or join such body, if already in existence.

Article IX.—Amendments.

Section 1. This Constitution can be amended or altered only at a regular session of the Convention, and to do so, it shall require a two-thirds vote of the delegates, and must be ratified within six weeks thereafter, by a majority vote of the members of the societies composing this Federation.

Sec. 2. This Constitution shall go into effect March 1st, 1887.

Source:

Official Archives of the American Federation of Labor and Congress of Individual Organizations, Silver Spring, Md.

Sherman Antitrust Act, 1890

First federal U.S. legislation to regulate trusts, enacted on July 2, 1890. Introduced by Republican senator John Sherman, it declared illegal "every contract, combination in the form of trust or otherwise, or conspiracy, in restraint of trade or commerce among the several States, or with foreign nations." The legislation, based on Congress's constitutional power to regulate interstate commerce, grew out of public dissatisfaction with the abuses of business trusts and corporations controlling various commodities. While at first, Supreme Court decisions condemned labor rather than business practices, the act was used successfully in President Theodore Roosevelt's "trust-busting" campaigns and in later actions. The law was strengthened and clarified by the Clayton Antitrust Act of 1914.

An Act
To protect trade and commerce against unlawful restraints and monopolies.

Be it enacted by the Senate and House of Representatives of the United States of America in Congress assembled,

Sec. 1. Every contract, combination in the form of trust or otherwise, or conspiracy, in restraint of trade or commerce among the several States, or with foreign nations, is hereby declared to be illegal. Every person who shall make any such contract or engage in any such combination or conspiracy, shall be deemed guilty of a misdemeanor, and, on conviction thereof, shall be punished by fine not exceeding five thousand dollars, or by imprisonment not exceeding one year, or by both said punishments, in the discretion of the court.

Sec. 2. Every person who shall monopolize, or attempt to monopolize, or combine or conspire with any other person or persons, to monopolize any part of the trade or commerce among the several States, or with foreign nations, shall be deemed guilty of a misdemeanor, and, on conviction thereof, shall be punished by fine not exceeding five thousand dollars, or by imprisonment not exceeding one year, or by both said punishments, in the discretion of the court.

Sec. 3. Every contract, combination in form of trust or otherwise, or conspiracy, in restraint of trade or commerce in any Territory of the United States or of the District of Columbia, or in restraint of trade or commerce between any such Territory and another, or between any such Territory or Territories and any State or States or the District of Columbia, or with foreign nations, or between the District of Columbia and any State or States or foreign nations, is hereby declared illegal. Every person who shall make any such contract or engage in any such combination or conspiracy, shall be deemed guilty of a misdemeanor, and, on conviction thereof, shall be punished by fine not exceeding five thousand dollars, or by imprisonment not exceeding one year, or by both said punishments, in the discretion of the court.

Sec. 4. The several circuit courts of the United States are hereby invested with jurisdiction to prevent and restrain violations of this act; and it shall be the duty of the several district attorneys of the United States, in their respective districts, under the direction of the Attorney-General, to institute proceedings in equity to prevent and restrain such violations. Such proceedings may be by way of petition setting forth the case and praying that such violation shall be enjoined or otherwise prohibited. When the parties complained of shall have been duly notified of such petition the court shall proceed, as soon as may be, to the hearing and determination of the case; and pending such petition and before final decree, the court may at any time make such temporary restraining order or prohibition as shall be deemed just in the premises.

Sec. 5. Whenever it shall appear to the court before which any proceeding under section four of this act may be pending, that the ends of justice require that other parties should be brought before the court, the court may cause them to be summoned, whether they reside in the district in which the court is held or not; and subpoenas to that end may be served in any district by the marshal thereof.

Sec. 6. Any property owned under any contract or by any combination, or pursuant to any conspiracy (and being the subject thereof) mentioned in section one of this act, and being in the course of transportation from one State to another, or to a foreign country, shall be forfeited to the United States, and may be seized and condemned by like proceedings as those provided by law for the forfeiture, seizure, and condemnation of property imported into the United States contrary to law.

Sec. 7. Any person who shall be injured in his business or property by any other person or corporation by reason of anything forbidden or declared to be unlawful by this act, may sue therefor in any circuit court of the United States in the district in which the defendant resides or is found, without respect to the amount in controversy, and shall recover three fold the damages by him sustained, and the costs of suit, including a reasonable attorney's fee.

Sec. 8. That the word "person," or "persons," wherever used in this act shall be deemed to include corporations and associations existing under or authorized by the laws of either the United States, the laws of any of the Territories, the laws of any State, or the laws of any foreign country.

Source:
Statutes at Large, Vol. 26, pp. 209–210.

In re Debs, 1895

(*In re*, a Latin term meaning "in the matter of," is used to indicate cases that lack formally adversarial parties and refers to whatever is the subject of the litigation.) U.S. Supreme Court decision of May 27, 1895, concerning the case of *United States v. Debs et al*. Eugene V. Debs, a socialist and major labor leader, organized railroad workers into the American Railway Union. Those who worked for the Pullman Company, which manufactured sleeping cars, lived in a "model town" near Chicago. During the panic of 1893, Pullman cut wages but left rents alone. In 1894, workers struck and many engaged in violence. Using the rationale that the striking workers were preventing the mail from going through, U.S. Attorney General Richard Olney, who previously represented railroads, sent federal troops to crush the strike. Debs was imprisoned for violating an injunction against interfering with the railroads. He asked for the Supreme Court for a writ of habeas corpus. The writ was denied, not on the grounds of the Sherman Antitrust Act (the basis for the injunction), but on the broader grounds that the federal government's constitutional authority over interstate commerce and the transportation of the mails justified the issuance of such injunctions to prevent forcible obstructions.

Mr. Justice Brewer, after stating the facts in the foregoing language, delivered the opinion of the court.

The case presented by the bill is this: The United States, finding that the interstate transportation of persons and property, as well as the carriage of the mails, is forcibly obstructed, and that a combination and conspiracy exists to subject the control of such transportation to the will of the conspirators, applied to one of their courts, sitting as a court of equity, for an injunction to restrain such obstruction and prevent carrying into effect such conspiracy. Two questions of importance are presented: First. Are the relations of the general government to interstate commerce and the transportation of the mails such as authorize a direct interference to prevent a forcible obstruction thereof? Second. If authority exists, as authority in governmental affairs implies both power and duty, has a court of equity jurisdiction to issue an injunction in aid of the performance of such duty?

1. What are the relations of the general government to interstate commerce and the transportation of the mails? They are those of direct supervision, control, and management. While, under the dual system which prevails with us, the powers of government are distributed between the state and the nation, and while the latter is properly styled a government of enumerated powers, yet within the limits of such enumeration it has all the attributes of sovereignty, and, in the exercise of those enumerated powers, acts directly upon the citizen, and not through the intermediate agency of the state.

"The government of the Union, then, is, emphatically and truly, a government of the people. In form and in substance it emanates from them. Its powers are granted by them, and are to be exercised directly on them, and for their benefit."

"No trace is to be found in the constitution of an intention to create a dependence of the government of the Union on those of the states, for the execution of the great powers assigned to it. Its means are adequate to its ends, and on those means alone was it expected to rely for the accomplishment of its ends. To impose on it the necessity of resorting to means which it cannot control, which another government may furnish or withhold, would render its course precarious, the result of its measures uncertain, and create a dependence on other governments, which might disappoint its most important designs, and is incompatible with the language of the constitution." Chief Justice Marshall in *McCulloch v. State of Maryland*, 4 Wheat. 316, 405, 424.

"Both the states and the United States existed before the constitution. The people, through that instrument, established a more perfect union by substituting a national government, acting, with ample power, directly upon the citizens, instead of the confederate government, which acted with powers, greatly restricted, only upon the states." Chief Justice Chase in *Lane Co. v. Oregon*, 7 Wall. 71, 76.

"We hold it to be an incontrovertible principle that the government of the United States may, by means of physical force, exercised through its official agents, execute on every foot of American soil the powers and functions that belong to it. This necessarily involves the power to command obedience to its laws, and hence the power to keep the peace to that extent."

"This power to enforce its laws and to execute its functions in all places does not derogate from the power of the state to execute its laws at the same time and in the same places. The one does not exclude the other, except where both cannot be executed at the same time. In that case the words of the constitution itself show which is to yield. "This constitution, and all laws which shall be made in pursuance thereof, ° ° ° shall be the supreme law of the land.'" Mr. Justice Bradley in Ex parte Siebold, 100 U.S. 371, 395.

See, also, *The Exchange v. McFaddon,* 7 Cranch, 116, 136; *Cohens v. Virginia,* 6 Wheat. 264, 413; Legal Tender Cases, 12 Wall. 457, 555; *Tennessee v. Davis,* 100 U.S. 257; The Chinese Exclusion Case, 130 U.S. 581, 9 Sup. Ct. 623; In re Neagle, 135 U.S. 1, 10 Sup. Ct. 658; *Logan v. U.S.,* 144 U.S. 263, 12 Sup. Ct. 617; *Fong Yue Ting v. U.S.,* 149 U.S. 698, 13 Sup. Ct. 1016; In re Quarles, 158 U.S. 532, 15 Sup. Ct. 959.

Among the powers expressly given to the national government are the control of interstate commerce and the creation and management of a post-office system for the nation. Article 1, Section 8, of the constitution provides that "the congress shall have power: ° ° ° Third, to regulate commerce with foreign nations and among the several states, and with the Indian tribes. ° ° ° Seventh, to establish post offices and post roads."

Congress has exercised the power granted in respect to interstate commerce in a variety of legislative acts. Passing by all that legislation in respect to commerce by water, and considering only that which bears upon railroad interstate transportation (for this is the specific matter involved in this case), these acts may be noticed: First. That of June 15, 1866 (14 Stat. 66), carried into the Revised Statutes as section 5258, which provides:

"Whereas the constitution of the United States confers upon congress, in express terms, the power to regulate commerce among the several states, to establish post roads, and to raise and support armies: Therefore, be it enacted by the senate and house of representatives of the United States of America in congress assembled, that every railroad company in the United States whose road is operated by steam, its successors and assigns, be, and is hereby, authorized to carry upon and over its road, boats, bridges, and ferries all passengers, troops, government supplies, mails, freight, and property on their way from any state to another state, and to receive compensation therefor, and to connect with roads of other states so as to form continuous lines for the transportation of the same to the place of destination."

Second. That of March 3, 1873 (17 Stat. 584; Rev. St. Sections 4386–4389), which regulates the transportation of live stock over interstate railroads. Third. That of May 29, 1884 (chapter 60, Section 6, 23 Stat. 32), prohibiting interstate transportation by railroads of live stock affected with any contagious or infectious disease. Fourth. That of February 4, 1887 (24 Stat. 379), with its amendments of March 2, 1889 (25 Stat. 855), and February 10, 1891 (26 Stat. 743), known as the "Interstate Commerce Act," by which a commission was created with large powers of regulation and control of interstate commerce by railroads, and the sixteenth section of which act gives to the courts of the United States power to enforce the orders of the commission. Fifth. That of October 1, 1888 (25 Stat. 501), providing for arbitration between railroad interstate companies and their employes. And, sixth, the act of March 2, 1893 (27 Stat. 531), requiring the use of automatic couplers on interstate trains, and empowering the interstate commerce commission to enforce its provisions. . . .

. . . Constitutional provisions do not change, but their operation extends to new matters, as the modes of business and the habits of life of the people vary with each succeeding generation. The law of the common carrier is the same to-day as when transportation on land was by coach and wagon, and on water by canal boat and sailing vessel; yet in its actual operation it touches and regulates transportation by modes then unknown—the railroad train and the steamship. Just so is it with the grant to the national government of power over interstate commerce. The constitution has not changed. The power is the same. But it operates to-day upon modes of interstate commerce unknown to the fathers, and it will operate with equal force upon any new modes of such commerce which the future may develop.

It is said that seldom have the courts assumed jurisdiction to restrain by injunction in suits brought by the government, either state or national, obstructions to highways either artificial or natural. This is undoubtedly true, but the reason is that the necessity for such interference has only been occasional. Ordinarily, the local authorities have taken full control over the matter, and by indictment for misdemeanor, or in some kindred way, have secured the removal of the obstruction and the cessation of the nuisance. As said in *Attorney General v. Brown,* 24 N. J. Eq. 89, 91: "The jurisdiction of courts of equity to redress the grievance of public nuisances by injunction is undoubted and clearly established; but it is well settled that, as a general rule, equity will not interfere where the object sought can be as well attained in the ordinary tribunals. *Attorney General v. New Jersey R. & T. Co.,* 3 N. J. Eq. 136; *Water Com'rs of Jersey City v. City of Hudson,* 13 N. J. Eq. 426; *Attorney General v. Heishon,* 18 N. J. Eq. 410; *Railroad Co. v. Prudden,* 20 N. J. Eq. 532; High, Inj. Section 521. And, because the remedy by indictment is so efficacious, courts of equity entertain jurisdiction in such cases with great reluctance, whether their intervention is invoked at the instance of the attorney general, or of a private individual who suffers some injury therefrom distinct from that of the public, and they will only do so where there appears to be a necessity for their interference. *Rowe v. Granite Bridge*, 21 Pick. 347; *Railroad Co. v. Prudden*, supra. The jurisdiction of the court of chancery with regard to public nuisances is founded on the irreparable damage to individuals, or the great public injury which is likely to ensue. 3 Daniell, Ch. Prac. 1740." Indeed, it may be affirmed that in no well-considered case has the power of a court of equity to interfere by injunction in cases of public nuisance been denied, the only denial ever being that of a necessity for the exercise of that jurisdiction under the circumstances of the particular case. Story, Eq. Jur. Sections 921, 923, 924; Pom. Eq. Jur. Section 1349; High, Inj. Sections 745, 1554; 2 Daniell, Ch. Pl. & Prac. (4th Ed.) p. 1636.

That the bill filed in this case alleged special facts calling for the exercise of all the powers of the court is not open to question. The picture drawn in it of the vast interests involved, not merely of the city of Chicago and the state of Illinois, but of all the states, and the general confusions into which the interstate commerce of the country was thrown; the forcible interference with that commerce; the attempted exercise by individuals of powers belonging only to government, and the threatened continuance of such invasions of public right, presented a condition of affairs which called for the fullest exercise of all the powers of the courts. If ever there was a special exigency, one which demanded that the courts should do all that courts can do, it was disclosed by this bill, and we need not turn to the public history of the day, which only reaffirms with clearest emphasis all its allegations.

The difference between a public nuisance and a private nuisance is that the one affects the people at large and the other simply the individual. The quality of the wrongs is the same, and the jurisdiction of the courts over them rests upon the same principles and goes to the same extent. Of course, circumstances may exist in one case, which do not in another, to induce the court to interfere or to refuse to interfere by injunction; but the jurisdiction—the power to interfere—exists in all cases of nuisance. True, many more suits are brought by individuals than by the public to enjoin nuisances, but there are two reasons for this: First, the instances are more numerous of private than of public nuisances; and, second, often that which is in fact a public nuisance is restrained at the suit of a private individual, whose right to relief arises because of a special injury resulting therefrom.

Again, it is objected that it is outside of the jurisdiction of a court of equity to enjoin the commission of crimes. This, as a general proposition, is unquestioned. A chancel-

lor has no criminal jurisdiction. Something more than the threatened commission of an offense against the laws of the land is necessary to call into exercise the injunctive powers of the court. There must be some interferences, actual or threatened, with property or rights of a pecuniary nature; but when such interferences appear the jurisdiction of a court of equity arises, and is not destroyed by the fact that they are accompanied by or are themselves violations of the criminal law. Thus, in *Cranford v. Tyrrell*, 128 N. Y. 341, 28 N. E. 514, an injunction to restrain the defendant from keeping a house of ill fame was sustained; the court saying, on page 344, 128 N.Y., and page 514, 28 N.E.: "That the perpetrator of the nuisance is amenable to the provisions and penalties of the criminal law is not an answer to an action against him by a primary person to recover for injury sustained, and for an injunction against the continued use of his premises in such a manner." And in *Port of Mobile v. Louisville & N.R. Co.*, 84 Ala. 115, 126, 4 South, 106, is a similar declaration in these words: "The mere fact that an act is criminal does not divest the jurisdiction of equity to prevent it by injunction, if it be also a violation of property rights, and the party aggrieved has no other adequate remedy for the prevention of the irreparable injury which will result from the failure or inability of a court of law to redress such rights."

The law is full of instances in which the same act may give rise to a civil action and a criminal prosecution. An assault with intent to kill may be punished criminally, under an indictment therefor, or will support a civil action for damages; and the same is true of all other offenses which cause injury to person or property. In such cases the jurisdiction of the civil court is invoked, not to enforce the criminal law and punish the wrongdoer, but to compensate the injured party for the damages which he or his property has suffered; and it is no defense to the civil action that the same act by the defendant exposes him also to indictment and punishment in a court of criminal jurisdiction. So here the acts of the defendants may or may not have been violations of the criminal law. If they were, that matter is for inquiry in other proceedings. The complaint made against them in this is of disobedience to an order of a civil court, made for the protection of property and the security of rights. If any criminal prosecution be brought against them for the criminal offenses alleged in the bill of complaint, of derailing and wrecking engines and trains, assaulting and disabling employes of the railroad companies, it will be no defense to such prosecution that they disobeyed the orders of injunction served upon them, and have been punished for such disobedience.

Nor is there in this any invasion of the constitutional right of trial by jury. We fully agree with counsel that "it matters not what form the attempt to deny constitutional right may take; it is vain and ineffectual, and must be so declared by the courts." And we reaffirm the declaration made for the court by Mr. Justice Bradley in *Boyd v. U.S.*, 116 U.S. 616, 635, 6 Sup. Ct. 524, that "it is the duty of courts to be watchful for the constitutional rights of the citizen, and against any stealthy encroachments thereon. Their motto should be obsta principiis." But the power of a court to make an order carries with it the equal power to punish for a disobedience of that order, and the inquiry as to the question of disobedience has been from time immemorial, the special function of the court. And this is no technical rule. In order that a court may compel obedience to its orders, it must have the right to inquire whether there has been any disobedience thereof. To submit the question of disobedience to another tribunal, be it a jury or another court, would operate to deprive the proceeding of half its efficiency. In the Case of Yates, 4 Johns. 317, 369, Chancellor Kent, then chief justice of the supreme court of the state of New York, said: "In the Case of Earl of Shaftsbury, 2 State Tr. 615, 1 Mod. 144, who was imprisoned by the house of lords for 'high contempts committed against it,' and brought into the king's bench, the court held that they had no authority to judge of the contempt, and remanded the prisoner. The court in that case seem to have laid down a principle from which they never have departed, and which is essential to the due administration of justice. This principle that every court, at least of the superior kind, in which great confidence is placed, must be the sole judge, in the last resort, of contempts arising therein, is more explicitly defined and more emphatically enforced in the two subsequent cases of *The Queen v. Paty* [2 Ld. Raym 1105], and of *The King v. Grosby* [3 Wils. 188]." And again, on page 371: "Mr. Justice Blackstone pursued the same train of observation, and declared that all courts, by which he meant to include the two houses of parliament and the courts of Westminster Hall, could have no control in matters of contempt; that the sole adjudication of contempts, and the punishments thereof belonged exclusively, and without interfering, to each respective court." In *Watson v. Williams*, 36 Miss. 331, 341, it was said: "The power to fine and imprison for contempt, from the earliest history of jurisprudence, has been regarded as a necessary incident and attribute of a court, without which it could no more exist than without a judge. It is a power inherent in all courts of record, and coexisting with them by the wise provisions of the common law. A court without the power effectually to protect itself against the assaults of the lawless, or to enforce its orders, judgments, or decrees against the recusant parties before it, would be a disgrace to the legislation, and a stigma upon the age which invented it." In Cartwright's Case, 114 Mass. 230, 238, we find this language: "The summary power to commit and punish for contempts tending to obstruct or degrade the administration of justice is inherent in courts

of chancery and other superior courts, as essential to the execution of their powers and to the maintenance of their authority, and is part of the law of the land, within the meaning of Magna Charta and of the twelfth article of our Declaration of Rights." See, also, *U.S. v. Hudson*, 7 Cranch, 32; *Anderson v. Dunn*, 6 Wheat. 204; Ex parte Robinson, 19 Wall. 505; *Mugler v. Kansas*, 123 U.S. 623-672, 8 Sup. Ct. 273; Ex parte Terry, 128 U.S. 289, 9 Sup. Ct. 77; *Eilenbecker v. Plymouth Co.*, 134 U.S. 31-36, 10 Sup. Ct. 424, in which Mr. Justice Miller observed: "If it has ever been understood that proceedings according to the common law for contempt of court have been subject to the right of trial by jury, we have been unable to find any instance of it." *Commission v. Brimson*, 154 U.S. 447-488, 14 Sup. Ct. 1125. In this last case it was said: "Surely it cannot be supposed that the question of contempt of the authority of a court of the United States, committed by a disobedience of its orders, is triable, of right, by a jury."

In brief, a court enforcing obedience to its orders by proceedings for contempt is not executing the criminal laws of the land, but only securing to suitors the rights which it has adjudged them entitled to.

Further, it is said by counsel in their brief:

"No case can be cited where such a bill in behalf of the sovereign has been entertained against riot and mob violence, though occurring on the highway. It is not such fitful and temporary obstruction that constitutes a nuisance. The strong hand of executive power is required to deal with such lawless demonstrations.

"The courts should stand aloof from them and not invade executive prerogative, nor, even at the behest or request of the executive, travel out of the beaten path of well-settled judicial authority. A mob cannot be suppressed by injunction; nor can its leaders be tried, convicted, and sentenced in equity.

"It is too great a strain upon the judicial branch of the government to impose this essentially executive and military power upon courts of chancery."

We do not perceive that this argument questions the jurisdiction of the court, but only the expediency of the action of the government in applying for its process. It surely cannot be seriously contended that the court has jurisdiction to enjoin the obstruction of a highway by one person, but that its jurisdiction ceases when the obstruction is by a hundred persons. It may be true, as suggested, that in the excitement of passion a mob will pay little heed to processes issued from the courts, and it may be, as said by counsel in argument, that it would savor somewhat of the puerile and ridiculous to have read a writ of injunction to Lee's army during the late Civil war. It is doubtless true that inter arma leges silent, and in the throes of rebellion or revolution the processes of civil courts are of little avail, for the power of the courts rests on the general support of the people, and their recognition of the fact that peaceful remedies are the true resort for the correction of wrongs. But does not counsel's argument imply too much? Is it to be assumed that these defendants were conducting a rebellion or inaugurating a revolution, and that they and their associates were thus placing themselves beyond the reach of the civil process of the courts? We find in the opinion of the circuit court a quotation from the testimony given by one of the defendants before the United States strike commission, which is sufficient answer to this suggestion:

"As soon as the employes found that we were arrested, and taken from the scene of action, they became demoralized, and that ended the strike. It was not the soldiers that ended the strike. It was not the old brotherhoods that ended the strike. It was simply the United States courts that ended the strike. Our men were in a position that never would have been shaken, under any circumstances, if we had been permitted to remain upon the field, among them. Once we were taken from the scene of action, and restrained from sending telegrams or issuing orders or answering questions, then the minions of the corporations would be put to work. ° ° ° Our headquarters were temporarily demoralized and abandoned, and we could not answer any messages. The men went back to work, and the ranks were broken, and the strike was broken up, ° ° ° not by the army, and not by any other power, but simply and solely by the action of the United States courts in restraining us from discharging our duties as officers and representatives of our employers."

Whatever any single individual may have thought or planned, the great body of those who were engaged in these transactions contemplated neither rebellion nor revolution, and when in the due order of legal proceedings the question of right and wrong was submitted to the courts, and by them decided, they unhesitatingly yielded to their decisions. The outcome, by the very testimony of the defendants, attests the wisdom of the course pursued by the government, and that it was well not to oppose force simply by force, but to invoke the jurisdiction and judgment of those tribunals to whom by the constitution and in accordance with the settled conviction of all citizens is committed the determination of questions of right and wrong between individuals, masses, and states.

It must be borne in mind that this bill was not simply to enjoin a mob and meb violence. It was not a bill to command a keeping of the peace; much less was its purport to restrain the defendants from abandoning whatever employment they were engaged in. The right of any laborer, or any number of laborers, to quit work was not challenged. The scope and purpose of the bill was only to restrain forcible obstructions of the highways along which interstate commerce travels and the mails are carried. And

the facts set forth at length are only those facts which tended to show that the defendants were engaged in such obstructions.

A most earnest and eloquent appeal was made to us in eulogy of the heroic spirit of those who threw up their employment, and gave up their means of earning a livelihood, not in defense of their own rights, but in sympathy for and to assist others whom they believed to be wronged. We yield to none in our admiration of any act of heroism or self-sacrifice, but we may be permitted to add that it is a lesson which cannot be learned too soon or too thoroughly that under this government of and by the people the means of redress of all wrongs are through the courts and at the ballot box, and that no wrong, real or fancied, carries with it legal warrant to invite as a means of redress the co-operation of a mob, with its accompanying acts of violence.

We have given to this case the most careful and anxious attention, for we realize that it touches closely questions of supreme importance to the people of this country. Summing up our conclusions, we hold that the government of the United States is one having jurisdiction over every foot of soil within its territory, and acting directly upon each citizen; that, while it is a government of enumerated powers, it has within the limits of those powers all the attributes of sovereignty; that to it is committed power over interstate commerce and the transmission of the mail; that the powers thus conferred upon the national government are not dormant, but have been assumed and put into practical exercise by the legislation of congress; that in the exercise of those powers it is competent for the nation to remove all obstructions upon highways, natural or artificial, to the passage of interstate commerce or the carrying of the mail; that, while it may be competent for the government (through the executive branch and in the use of the entire executive power of the nation) to forcibly remove all such obstructions, it is equally within its competency to appeal to the civil courts for an inquiry and determination as to the existence and character of any alleged obstructions, and if such are found to exist, or threaten to occur, to invoke the powers of those courts to remove or restrain such obstructions; that the jurisdiction of courts to interfere in such matters by injunction is one recognized from ancient times and by indubitable authority; that such jurisdiction is not ousted by the fact that the obstructions are accompanied by or consist of acts in themselves violations of the criminal law; that the proceeding by injunction is of a civil character, and may be enforced by proceedings in contempt; that such proceedings are not in execution of the criminal laws of the land; that the penalty for a violation of injunction is no substitute for and no defense to a prosecution for any criminal offenses committed in the course of such violation; that the complaint filed in this case clearly showed an existing obstruction of artificial highways for the passage of interstate commerce and the transmission of the mail,—an obstruction not only temporarily existing, but threatening to continue; that under such complaint the circuit court had power to issue its process of injunction; that, it having been issued and served on these defendants, the circuit court had authority to inquire whether its orders had been disobeyed, and, when it found that they had been, then to proceed under section 725, Rev. St., which grants power "to punish, by fine or imprisonment, . . . disobedience, . . . by any party . . . or other person, to any lawful writ, process, order, rule, decree, or command," and enter the order of punishment complained of; and, finally, that the circuit court having full jurisdiction in the premises, its finding of the fact of disobedience is not open to review on habeas corpus in this or any other court.

The petition for a writ of habeas corpus is denied.

Source:
Supreme Court Reporter, Vol. 15, pp. 900–912.

Holden v. Hardy, 1898

U.S. Supreme Court decision of February 28, 1898, upholding a Utah statute regulating the hours of labor for men who worked in underground mines and in the smelting, reduction, and refining of ores or metals. The law was challenged as a violation of the Fourteenth Amendment, a denial of due process and equal protection for both employer and employee. The Supreme Court ruled, however, that the state had the right, under its police power, to protect the health of citizens involved in dangerous occupations. It also argued that the state may interfere in a contract when the two parties have unequal bargaining power. The ruling served as a precedent for later state regulation of labor conditions.

───────────── ⌘ ─────────────

Mr. Justice Brown, after stating the facts in the foregoing language, delivered the opinion of the court.

This case involves the constitutionality of an act of the legislature of Utah entitled "An act regulating the hours of employment in underground mines and in smelters and ore reduction works." The following are the material provisions:

"Section 1. The period of employment of workingmen in all underground mines or workings shall be eight hours per day, except in cases of emergency where life or property is in imminent danger.

"Sec. 2. The period of employment of workingmen in smelters and all other institutions for the reduction or refining of ores or metals shall be eight hours per day,

except in cases of emergency where life or property is in imminent danger.

"Sec. 3. Any person, body corporate, agent, manager, or employer, who shall violate any of the provisions of sections one and two of this act, shall be guilty of a misdemeanor."

The supreme court of Utah was of opinion that, if authority in the legislature were needed for the enactment of the statute in question, it was found in that part of article 16 of the constitution of the state which declared that "the legislature shall pass laws to provide for the health and safety of employees in factories, smelters and mines." As the article deals exclusively with the rights of labor, it is here reproduced in full, as exhibiting the authority under which the legislature acted, and as throwing light upon its intention in enacting the statute in question (Laws 1896, p. 219):

"Section 1. The rights of labor shall have just protection through laws calculated to promote the industrial welfare of the state.

"Sec. 2. The legislature shall provide by law for a board of labor, conciliation and arbitration which shall fairly represent the interests of both capital and labor. The board shall perform duties and receive compensation as prescribed by law.

"Sec. 3. The legislature shall prohibit:

"(1) The employment of women, or of children under the age of fourteen years, in underground mines.

"(2) The contracting of convict labor.

"(3) The labor of convicts outside prison grounds, except on public works under the direct control of the state.

"(4) The political and commercial control of employees.

"Sec. 4. The exchange of blacklists by railroad companies, or other corporations, associations or persons is prohibited.

"Sec. 5. The right of action to recover damages for injuries resulting in death shall never be abrogated, and the amount recoverable shall not be subject to any statutory limitation.

"Sec. 6. Eight hours shall constitute a day's work on all works or undertakings carried on or aided by the state, county or municipal governments; and the legislature shall pass laws to provide for the health and safety of employees in factories, smelters and mines.

"Sec. 7. The legislature, by appropriate legislation, shall provide for the enforcement of the provisions of this article."

The validity of the statute in question is, however, challenged upon the ground of an alleged violation of the fourteenth amendment to the constitution of the United States, in that it abridges the privileges or immunities of citizens of the United States, deprives both the employer and the laborer of his property without due process of law, and denies to them the equal protection of the laws. As the three questions of abridging their immunities, depriving them of their property, and denying them the protection of the laws, are so connected that the authorities upon each are, to a greater or less extent, pertinent to the others, they may properly be considered together.

Prior to the adoption of the fourteenth amendment, there was a similar provision against deprivation of life, liberty, or property without due process of law incorporated in the fifth amendment; but as the first eight amendments to the constitution were obligatory only upon congress, the decisions of this court under this amendment have but a partial application to the fourteenth amendment, which operates only upon the action of the several states. The fourteenth amendment which was finally adopted July 28, 1868, largely expanded the power of the federal courts and congress, and for the first time authorized the former to declare invalid all laws and judicial decisions of the states abridging the rights of citizens, or denying them the benefit of due process of law.

This amendment was first called to the attention of this court in 1872, in an attack upon the constitutionality of a law of the state of Louisiana, passed in 1869, vesting in a slaughter-house company therein named the sole and exclusive privilege of conducting and carrying on a live-stock landing and slaughter-house business within certain limits specified in the act, and requiring all animals intended for sale and slaughter to be landed at their wharves or landing places. Slaughter-House Cases, 16 Wall. 36. While the court in that case recognized the fact that the primary object of this amendment was to secure to the colored race, then recently emancipated, the full enjoyment of their freedom, the further fact that it was not restricted to that purpose was admitted both in the prevailing and dissenting opinions, and the validity of the act was sustained as a proper police regulation for the health and comfort of the people. A majority of the cases which have since arisen have turned, not upon a denial to the colored race of rights therein secured to them, but upon alleged discriminations in matters entirely outside of the political relations of the parties aggrieved.

These cases may be divided, generally, into two classes: First, where a state legislature or a state court is alleged to have unjustly discriminated in favor of or against a particular individual or class of individuals, as distinguished from the rest of the community, or denied them the benefit of due process of law; second, where the legislature has changed its general system of jurisprudence by abolishing what had been previously considered necessary to the proper administration of justice, or the protection of the individual.

Among those of the first class, which, for the sake of brevity, may be termed "unjust discriminations," are those wherein the colored race was alleged to have been denied the right of representation upon juries (*Strauder v. West Virginia,* 100 U.S. 303; *Virginia v. Rives,* Id. 313; *Ex parte Virginia,* Id. 339; *Neal v. Delaware,* 103 U.S. 370; *Bush v. Kentucky,* 107 U.S. 110, 1 Sup. Ct. 625; *Gibson v. Mississippi,* 162, U.S. 565, 16 Sup. Ct. 904), as well as those wherein the state was charged with oppressing and unduly discriminating against persons of the Chinese race (*Barbier v. Connolly,* 113 U.S. 27, 5 Sup. Ct. 357; *Soon Hing v. Crowley,* 113 U.S. 703, 5 Sup. Ct. 730; *Yick Wo v. Hopkins,* 118 U.S. 356, 6 Sup. Ct. 1064; and *Chy Lung v. Freeman,* 92 U.S. 275), and those wherein it was sought, under this amendment, to enforce the right of women to suffrage, and to admission to the learned professions (*Minor v. Happersett,* 21 Wall. 162; *Bradwell v. State,* 16 Wall. 130).

To this class is also referable all those cases wherein the state courts were alleged to have denied to particular individuals the benefit of due process of law secured to them by the statutes of the state (In re Converse, 137 U.S. 624, 11 Sup. Ct. 191; *Arrowsmith v. Harmoning,* 118 U.S. 194, 6 Sup. Ct. 1023), as well as that other large class, to be more specifically mentioned hereafter, wherein the state legislature was charged with having transcended its proper police power in assuming to legislate for the health or morals of the community.

Cases arising under the second class, wherein a state has chosen to change its methods of trial to meet a popular demand for simpler and more expeditious forms of administering justice, are much less numerous, though of even greater importance, than the others. A reference to a few of these cases may not be inappropriate in this connection. Thus, in *Walker v. Sauvinet,* 92 U.S. 90, which was an action brought by a colored man against the keeper of a coffee house in New Orleans for refusing him refreshments, in violation of the constitution of the state securing to the colored race equal rights and privileges in such cases, a statute of the state provided that such cases should be tried by jury, if either party demanded it, but, if the jury failed to agree, the case should be submitted to the judge, who should decide the same. It was held that a trial by jury was not a privilege or immunity of citizenship which the states were forbidden to abridge, but the requirement of due process of law was met if the trial was had according to the settled course of judicial proceedings. "Due process of law," said Chief Justice Waite, "is process due according to the law of the land. This process in the states is regulated by the law of the state." This law was held not to be in conflict with the constitution of the United States.

Similar rulings with regard to the necessity of a jury or of a judicial trial in special proceedings were made in *Kennard v. Louisiana,* 92 U.S. 480; *McMillan v. Anderson,* 95

U.S. 37; *Davidson v. New Orleans,* 96 U.S. 97; *Walston v. Nevin,* 128 U.S. 578, 9 Sup. Ct. 192; Ex parte Wall, 107 U.S. 265, 2 Sup. Ct. 569.

In *Hurtado v. California,* 110 U.S. 516, 4 Sup. Ct. 111, 292, it was held that due process of law did not necessarily require an indictment by a grand jury in a prosecution by a state for murder. The constitution of California authorized prosecutions for felonies by information, after examination and commitment by a magistrate, without an indictment by a grand jury, in the discretion of the legislature. It was held that conviction upon such an information, followed by sentence of death, was not illegal, under the fourteenth amendment.

In *Hayes v. Missouri,* 120 U.S. 68, 7 Sup. Ct. 350, it was held that a statute of a state which provided that, in capital cases, in cities having a population of over 100,000 inhabitants, the state shall be allowed 15 peremptory challenges to jurors, while elsewhere in the state it was allowed only 8 peremptory challenges, did not deny to a person tried for murder, in a city containing over 100,000 inhabitants, the equal protection of the laws enjoined by the fourteenth amendment, and that there was no error in refusing to limit the state's peremptory challenges to 8.

In *Railway Co. v. Mackey,* 127 U.S. 205, 8 Sup. Ct. 1161, it was said that a statute in Kansas abolishing the fellow-servant doctrine, as applied to railway accidents, did not deny to railroads the equal protection of the laws, and was not in conflict with the fourteenth amendment. The same ruling was made with reference to statutes requiring railways to erect and maintain fences and cattle guards, and make them liable in double the amount of damages claimed, for the want of them.

In *Hallinger v. Davis,* 146 U.S. 314, 13 Sup. Ct. 105, it was held that a state statute conferring upon an accused person the right to waive a trial by jury, and to elect to be tried by the court, and conferring power upon the court to try the accused in such case, was not a violation of the due-process clause of the fourteenth amendment.

So, In re Kemmler, 136 U.S. 436, 10 Sup. Ct. 930, it was held that the law providing for capital punishment by electricity was not repugnant to this amendment. And in *Duncan v. Missouri,* 152 U.S. 377, 14 Sup. Ct. 570, it was said that the prescribing of different modes of procedure, and the abolition of courts, and the creation of new ones, leaving untouched all the substantial protections with which the existing law surrounds persons accused of crime, are not considered within the constitutional inhibition. See, also, Medley, Petitioner, 134 U.S. 160, 10 Sup. Ct. 384, and *Holden v. Minnesota,* 137 U.S. 484, 11 Sup. Ct. 143.

An examination of both these classes of cases under the fourteenth amendment will demonstrate that, in passing upon the validity of state legislation under that amendment, this court has not failed to recognize the fact that the law is, to a certain extent, a progressive science; that, in some of the states, methods of procedure which, at the time the constitution was adopted, were deemed essential to the protection and safety of the people, or to the liberty of the citizen, have been found to be no longer necessary; that restrictions which had formerly been laid upon the conduct of individuals, or of classes of individuals, had proved detrimental to their interests, while, upon the other hand, certain other classes of persons (particularly those engaged in dangerous or unhealthful employments) have been found to be in need of additional protection. Even before the adoption of the constitution, much had been done towards mitigating the severity of the common law, particularly in the administration of its criminal branch. The number of capital crimes in this country, at least, had been largely decreased. Trial by ordeal and by battle had never existed here, and had fallen into disuse in England. The earlier practice of the common law, which denied the benefit of witnesses to a person accused of felony, had been abolished by statute, though, so far as it deprived him of the assistance of counsel and compulsory process for the attendance of his witnesses, it had not been changed in England. But, to the credit of her American colonies, let it be said that so oppressive a doctrine had never obtained a foothold there.

The present century has originated legal reforms of no less importance. The whole fabric of special pleading, once thought to be necessary to the elimination of the real issue between the parties, has crumbled to pieces. The ancient tenures of real estate have been largely swept away, and land is now transferred almost as easily and cheaply as personal property. Married women have been emancipated from the control of their husbands, and placed upon a practical equality with them, with respect to the acquisition, possession, and transmission of property. Imprisonment for debt has been abolished. Exemptions from execution have been largely added to, and in most of the states homesteads are rendered incapable of seizure and sale upon forced process. Witnesses are no longer incompetent by reason of interest, even though they be parties to the litigation. Indictments have been simplified, and an indictment for the most serious of crimes is now the simplest of all. In several of the states, grand juries, formerly the only safeguard against a malicious prosecution, have been largely abolished; and in others the rule of unanimity, so far as applied to civil cases, has given way to verdicts rendered by a three-fourths majority. This case does not call for an expression of opinion as to the wisdom of these changes, or their validity under the fourteenth amendment, although the substitution of prosecution by information in lieu of indictment was recognized as valid in *Hurtado v. California,* 110 U.S. 516, 4 Sup. Ct. 111, 292. They are mentioned only for the purpose of calling attention to the probability that other changes of no less importance may be made in the future, and that, while the cardinal principles of justice are immutable, the methods by which justice is administered are subject to constant fluctuation, and that the constitution of the United States, which is necessarily and to a large extent inflexible, and exceedingly difficult of amendment, should not be so construed as to deprive the states of the power to so amend their laws as to make them conform to the wishes of the citizens, as they may deem best for the public welfare, without bringing them into conflict with the supreme law of the land.

Of course, it is impossible to forecast the character or extent of these changes; but in view of the fact that, from the day Magna Charta was signed to the present moment, amendments to the structure of the law have been made with increasing frequency, it is impossible to suppose that they will not continue, and the law be forced to adapt itself to new conditions of society, and particularly to the new relations between employers and employes, as they arise.

Similar views have been heretofore expressed by this court. Thus, in the case of *Missouri v. Lewis,* 101 U.S. 22, 31, it was said by Mr. Justice Bradley: "We might go still further, and say, with undoubted truth, that there is nothing in the constitution to prevent any state from adopting any system of laws or judicature it sees fit for all or any part of its territory. If the state of New York, for example, should see fit to adopt the civil law and its method of procedure for New York City and the surrounding counties, and the common law and its methods of procedure for the rest of the state, there is nothing in the constitution of the United States to prevent its doing so. This would not, of itself, within the meaning of the fourteenth amendment, be a denial to any person of the equal protection of the laws. . . . The fourteenth amendment does not profess to secure to all persons in the United States the benefit of the same laws and the same remedies. Great diversities in these respects may exist in two states separated only by an imaginary line. On one side of this line there may be a right of trial by jury, and on the other no such right. Each state prescribes its own modes of judicial proceeding. If diversities of laws and judicial proceedings may exist in the several states without violating the equality clause in the fourteenth amendment, there is no solid reason why there may not be such diversities in different parts of the same state."

The same subject was also elaborately discussed by Mr. Justice Matthews in delivering the opinion of this court in *Hurtado v. California,* 110 U.S. 516, 530, 4 Sup. Ct. 118: "This flexibility and capacity for growth is the peculiar boast and excellence of the common law. . . . The constitution of the United States was ordained, it is true, by descendants of Englishmen, who inherited the traditions of English law and history; but it was made for an undefined and expanding future, and for a people gath-

ered and to be gathered from many nations, and of many tongues. And, while we take just pride in the principles and institutions of common law, we are not to forget that, in lands where other systems of jurisprudence prevail, the ideas and processes of civil justice are also not unknown. Due process of law, in spite of the absolutism of continental governments, is not alien to that code which survived the Roman Empire as the foundation of modern civilization in Europe, and which has given us that fundamental maxim of distributive justice—'Suum cuique tribuere.' There is nothing in Magna Charta, rightly construed as a broad charter of public right and law, which ought to exclude the best ideas of all systems and of every age; and, as it was the characteristic principle of the common law to draw its inspiration from every fountain of justice, we are not to assume that the sources of its supply have been exhausted. On the contrary, we should expect that the new and various experiences of our own situation and system will mold and shape it into new, and not less useful, forms." We have seen no reason to doubt the soundness of these views. In the future growth of the nation, as heretofore, it is not impossible that congress may see fit to annex territories whose jurisprudence is that of the civil law. One of the considerations moving to such annexation might be the very fact that the territory so annexed should enter the Union with its traditions, laws, and systems of administration unchanged. It would be a narrow construction of the constitution to require them to abandon these, or to substitute for a system which represented the growth of generations of inhabitants a jurisprudence with which they had had no previous acquaintance or sympathy.

We do not wish, however, to be understood as holding that this power is unlimited. While the people of each state may doubtless adopt such systems of laws as best conform to their own traditions and customs, the people of the entire country have laid down in the constitution of the United States certain fundamental principles, to which each member of the Union is bound to accede as a condition of its admission as a state. Thus, the United States are bound to guaranty to each state a republican form of government, and the tenth section of the first article contains certain other specified limitations upon the power of the several states, the object of which was to secure to congress paramount authority with respect to matters of universal concern. In addition, the fourteenth amendment contains a sweeping provision forbidding the states from abridging the privileges and immunities of citizens of the United States, and denying them the benefit of due process or equal protection of the laws.

This court has never attempted to define with precision the words "due process of law," nor is it necessary to do so in this case. It is sufficient to say that there are certain immutable principles of justice, which inhere in the very idea of free government, which no member of the Union may disregard, as that no man shall be condemned in his person or property without due notice, and an opportunity of being heard in his defense. What shall constitute due process of law was perhaps as well stated by Mr. Justice Curtis in *Murray's Lessees v. Land Co.,* 18 How. 272, 276, as anywhere. He said: "The constitution contains no description of those processes which it was intended to allow or forbid. It does not even declare what principles are to be applied to ascertain whether it be due process. It is manifest that it was not left to the legislative power to enact any process which might be devised. The article is a restraint on the legislative as well as on the executive and judicial powers of the government, and cannot be so construed as to leave congress free to make any process 'due process of law' by its mere will. To what principles, then, are we to resort to ascertain whether this process enacted by congress is due process? To this the answer must be twofold: We must examine the constitution itself, to see whether this process be in conflict with any of its provisions. If not found to be so, we must look to those settled usages and modes of proceeding existing in the common and statute law of England, before the emigration of our ancestors, and which are shown not to have been unsuited to their civil and political condition, by having been acted on by them after the settlement of this country."

It was said by Mr. Justice Miller, in delivering the opinion of this court in *Davidson v. New Orleans,* 96 U.S. 97, that the words "law of the land," as used in Magna Charta, implied a conformity with the "ancient and customary laws of the English people," and that it was wiser to ascertain their intent and application by the "gradual process of judicial inclusion and exclusion as the cases presented for decision shall require, with the reasoning on which such decisions may be founded." Recognizing the difficulty in defining with exactness the phrase "due process of law," it is certain that these words imply a conformity with natural and inherent principles of justice, and forbid that one man's property, or right to property, shall be taken for the benefit of another, or for the benefit of the state, without compensation, and that no one shall be condemned in his person or property without an opportunity of being heard in his own defense.

As the possession of property, of which a person cannot be deprived, doubtless implies that such property may be acquired, it is safe to say that a state law which undertakes to deprive any class of persons of the general power to acquire property would also be obnoxious to the same provision. Indeed, we may go a step further, and say that as property can only be legally acquired, as between living persons, by contract, a general prohibition against entering into contracts with respect to property, or having as their object the acquisition of property, would be equally invalid.

The latest utterance of this court upon this subject is contained in the case of *Allgeyer v. Louisiana,* 165 U.S. 578, 591, 17 Sup. Ct. 427, in which it was held that an act of Louisiana which prohibited individuals within the state from making contracts of insurance with corporations doing business in New York was a violation of the fourteenth amendment. In delivering the opinion of the court, Mr. Justice Peckham remarked: "In the privilege of pursuing an ordinary calling or trade, and of acquiring, holding, and selling property, must be embraced the right to make all proper contracts in relation thereto; and, although it may be conceded that this right to contract in relation to persons or property, or to do business within the jurisdiction of the state, may be regulated, and sometimes prohibited, when the contracts or business conflict with the policy of the state as contained in its statutes, yet the power does not and cannot extend to prohibiting a citizen from making contracts of the nature involved in this case, outside of the limits and jurisdiction of the state, and which are also to be performed outside of such jurisdiction."

This right of contract, however, is itself subject to certain limitations which the state may lawfully impose in the exercise of its police powers. While this power is inherent in all governments, it has doubtless been greatly expanded in its application during the past century, owing to an enormous increase in the number of occupations which are dangerous or so far detrimental to the health of employes as to demand special precautions for their well-being and protection, or the safety of adjacent property. While this court has held (notably in the cases of *Davidson v. New Orleans,* 96 U.S. 97, and *Yick Wo v. Hopkins,* 118 U.S. 356, 6 Sup. Ct. 1064) that the police power cannot be put forward as an excuse for oppressive and unjust legislation, it may be lawfully resorted to for the purpose of preserving the public health, safety, or morals, or the abatement of public nuisances, and a large discretion "is necessarily vested in the legislature, to determine, not only what the interests of the public require, but what measures are necessary for the protection of such interests." *Lawton v. Steele,* 152 U.S. 133, 136, 14 Sup. Ct. 499.

The extent and limitations upon this power are admirably stated by Chief Justice Shaw in the following extract from his opinion in *Massachusetts v. Alger,* 7 Cush. 84.

"We think it a settled policy, growing out of the nature of well-ordered civil society, that every holder of property, however absolute and unqualified his title, holds it under the implied liability that its use may be so regulated that it shall not be injurious to the equal enjoyment of others having an equal right to the enjoyment of their property, nor injurious to the rights of the community. All property in this commonwealth, as well in the interior as that bordering on the tide waters, is derived directly or indirectly from the government, and held subject to those general regulations which are necessary to the common good and general welfare. Rights of property, like all other social and conventional rights, are subject to such reasonable limitation in their enjoyment as will prevent them from being injurious, and to such reasonable restraints and regulations by law as the legislature, under the government and controlling power vested in them by the constitution, may think necessary and expedient."

This power, legitimately exercised, can neither be limited by contract nor bartered away by legislation.

While this power is necessarily inherent in every form of government, it was, prior to the adoption of the constitution, but sparingly used in this country. As we were then almost purely an agricultural people, the occasion for any special protection of a particular class did not exist. Certain profitable employments, such as lotteries and the sale of intoxicating liquors, which were then considered to be legitimate, have since fallen under the ban of public opinion, and are now either altogether prohibited, or made subject to stringent police regulations. The power to do this has been repeatedly affirmed by this court. *Stone v. Mississippi*, 101 U.S. 814; *Douglas v. Kentucky*, 168 U.S. 488, 18 Sup. Ct. 199; *Giozza v. Tiernan*, 148 U.S. 657, 13 Sup. Ct. 721; *Kidd v. Pearson*, 128 U.S. 1, 9 Sup. Ct. 6; *Crowley v. Christensen*, 137 U.S. 86, 11 Sup. Ct. 13.

While the business of mining coal and manufacturing iron began in Pennsylvania as early as 1716, and in Virginia, North Carolina, and Massachusetts even earlier than this, both mining and manufacturing were carried on in such a limited way, and by such primitive methods, that no special laws were considered necessary, prior to the adoption of the constitution, for the protection of the operatives; but, in the vast proportions which these industries have since assumed, it has been found that they can no longer be carried on, with due regard to the safety and health of those engaged in them, without special protection against the dangers necessarily incident to these employments. In consequence of this, laws have been enacted in most of the states designed to meet these exigencies, and to secure the safety of persons peculiarly exposed to these dangers. Within this general category are ordinances providing for fire escapes for hotels, theaters, factories, and other large buildings; a municipal inspection of boilers; and appliances designed to secure passengers upon railways and steamboats against the dangers necessarily incident to these methods of transportation. In states where manufacturing is carried on to a large extent, provision is made for the protection of dangerous machinery against accidental contact; for the cleanliness and ventilation of working rooms; for the guarding of well holes, stairways, elevator shafts; and for the employment of sanitary appliances. In others, where mining is the principal industry, special provision is made for the shoring up of dangerous walls; for ventilation shafts, boreholes, escapement shafts, means of signaling the surface; for the supply of fresh air, and the elimination, as far as possible, of dangerous gases; for safe means of hoisting and lowering cages; for a limitation upon the number of persons permitted to enter a cage; that cages shall be covered; and that there shall be fences and gates around the top of shafts, besides other similar precautions. Sand. & H. Dig. Ark. p. 1149; Rev. St. Cal. Sections 5045–5062; Supp. Mills' Ann. St. Colo. c. 85; Gen. St. Conn. 1888, Sections 2645–2647, 2263–2272; Rev. St. Ill. 1889, p. 980; Thornt. Ind. St. 1897, c. 98, p. 1652; 2 Gen. St. Kan. 1897, pp. 813–824; Ky. St. (Barbour & Carroll) c. 88. p. 951; Supp. Pub. St. Mass. 1889–95, pp. 582, 746, 1163; How. Ann. St. Mich. Section 9209b et seq.; 3 Gen. St. N.J. p. 1900 et seq.; 2 Rev. St. (Code & Gen. Laws N.Y.) p. 2069; Supp. Bright. Purd. Dig. Pa. p. 2241 et seq.

These statutes have been repeatedly enforced by the courts of the several states; their validity assumed; and, so far as we are informed, they have been uniformly held to be constitutional.

In *Daniels v. Hilgard*, 77 Ill. 640, it was held that the legislature had power, under the constitution, to establish reasonable police regulations for the operating of mines and collieries, and that an act providing for the health and safety of persons employed in coal mines, which required the owner or agent of every coal mine or colliery employing 10 men or more to make or cause to be made an accurate map or plan of the workings of such coal mine or colliery, was not unconstitutional, and that the question whether certain requirements are a part of a system of police regulations adopted to aid in the protection of life and health was properly one of legislative determination, and that a court should not lightly interfere with such determination, unless the legislature had manifestly transcended its province. See, also, *Coal Co. v. Taylor*, 81 Ill. 590.

In *Pennsylvania v. Bonnell*, 8 Phila. 534, a law providing for the ventilation of coal mines, for speaking tubes, and the protection of cages, was held to be constitutional, and subject to strict enforcement. *Pennsylvania v. Conyngham*, 66 Pa. St. 99; *Durant v. Coal Co.*, 97 Mo. 62.

But, if it be within the power of a legislature to adopt such means for the protection of the lives of its citizens, it is difficult to see why precautions may not also be adopted for the protection of their health and morals. It is as much for the interest of the state that the public health should be preserved as that life should be made secure. With this end in view, quarantine laws have been enacted in most, if not all, of the states; insane asylums, public hospitals, and institutions for the care and education of the blind established; and special measures taken for the exclusion of infected cattle, rags, and decayed fruit. In other states laws have been enacted limiting the hours during which women and children shall be employed in factories; and while their constitutionality, at least as applied to women, has been doubted in some of the states, they have been generally upheld. Thus, in the case of *Com. v. Hamilton Mfg. Co.*, 120 Mass. 383, it was held that a statute prohibiting the employment of all persons under the age of 18, and of all women laboring in any manufacturing establishment more than 60 hours per week, violates no contract of the commonwealth implied in the granting of a charter to a manufacturing company, nor any right reserved under the constitution to any individual citizen, and may be maintained as a health or police regulation.

Upon the principles above stated, we think the act in question may be sustained as a valid exercise of the police power of the state. The enactment does not profess to limit the hours of all workmen, but merely those who are employed in underground mines, or in the smelting, reduction, or refining of ores or metals. These employments, when too long pursued, the legislature had judged to be detrimental to the health of the employes; and, so long as there are reasonable grounds for believing that this is so, its decision upon this subject cannot be reviewed by the federal courts.

While the general experience of mankind may justify us in believing that men may engage in ordinary employments more than eight hours per day without injury to their health, it does not follow that labor for the same length of time is innocuous when carried on beneath the surface of the earth, where the operative is deprived of fresh air and sunlight, and is frequently subjected to foul atmosphere and a very high temperature, or to the influence of noxious gases generated by the processes of refining or smelting.

We concur in the following observations of the supreme court of Utah in this connection:

"The conditions with respect to health of laborers in underground mines doubtless differ from those in which they labor in smelters and other reduction works on the surface. Unquestionably, the atmosphere and other conditions in mines and reduction works differ. Poisonous gases, dust, and impalpable substances arise and float in the air in stamp mills, smelters, and other works in which ores containing metals, combined with arsenic or other poisonous elements or agencies, are treated, reduced, and refined, and there can be no doubt that prolonged effort, day after day, subject to such conditions and agencies, will produce morbid, noxious, and often deadly effects in the human system. Some organisms and systems will resist and endure such conditions and effects longer than others. It may be said that labor in such conditions must be performed. Granting that, the period of labor each day should be of a reasonable length. Twelve hours per day would be less injurious than fourteen, ten than twelve, and eight than

ten. The legislature has named eight. Such a period was deemed reasonable. . . . The law in question is confined to the protection of that class of people engaged in labor in underground mines, and in smelters and other works wherein ores are reduced and refined. This law applies only to the classes subjected by their employment to the peculiar conditions and effects attending underground mining and work in smelters, and other works for the reduction and refining of ores. Therefore it is not necessary to discuss or decide whether the legislature can fix the hours of labor in other employments. Though reasonable doubts may exist as to the power of the legislature to pass a law, or as to whether the law is calculated or adapted to promote the health, safety, or comfort of the people, or to secure good order or promote the general welfare, we must resolve them in favor of the right of that department of government." 46 Pac. 1105.

The legislature has also recognized the fact, which the experience of legislators in many states has corroborated, that the proprietors of these establishments and their operatives do not stand upon an equality, and that their interests are, to a certain extent, conflicting. The former naturally desire to obtain as much labor as possible from their employes, while the latter are often induced by the fear of discharge to conform to regulations which their judgment, fairly exercised, would pronounce to be detrimental to their health or strength. In other words, the proprietors lay down the rules, and the laborers are practically constrained to obey them. In such cases self-interest is often an unsafe guide, and the legislature may properly interpose its authority.

It may not be improper to suggest in this connection that although the prosecution in this case was against the employer of labor, who apparently, under the statute, is the only one liable, his defense is not so much that his right to contract has been infringed upon, but that the act works a peculiar hardship to his employes, whose right to labor as long as they please is alleged to be thereby violated. The argument would certainly come with better grace and greater cogency from the latter class. But the fact that both parties are of full age, and competent to contract, does not necessarily deprive the state of the power to interfere, where the parties do not stand upon an equality, or where the public health demands that one party to the contract shall be protected against himself. "The state still retains an interest in his welfare, however reckless he may be. The whole is no greater than the sum of all the parts, and when the individual health, safety, and welfare are sacrificed or neglected, the state must suffer."

We have no disposition to criticise the many authorities which hold that state statutes restricting the hours of labor are unconstitutional. Indeed, we are not called upon to express an opinion upon this subject. It is sufficient to say of them that they have no application to cases where the legislature had adjudged that a limitation is necessary for the preservation of the health of employes, and there are reasonable grounds for believing that such determination is supported by the facts. The question in each case is whether the legislature has adopted the statute in exercise of a reasonable discretion, or whether its action be a mere excuse for an unjust discrimination, or the oppression or spoliation of a particular class. The distinction between these two different classes of enactments cannot be better stated than by a comparison of the views of this court found in the opinions in *Barbier v. Connolly*, 113 U.S. 27,

5 Sup. Ct. 357, and *Soon Hing v. Crowley*, 113 U.S. 703, 5 Sup. Ct. 730, with those later expressed in *Yick Wo v. Hopkins*, 118 U.S. 356, 6 Supp. Ct. 1064.

We are of opinion that the act in question was a valid exercise of the police power of the state, and the judgments of the supreme court of Utah are therefore affirmed.

Mr. Justice Brewer and Mr. Justice Peckham dissented.

Source:

Supreme Court Reporter, Vol. 18, pp. 383–390.

Politics, Economy, and Society

Victoria C. Woodhull, Memorial, 1870; Reply from the House of Representatives, Report #22, 1871

Controversial women's-rights activist Victoria C. Woodhull presented this memorial to the Judiciary Committee of the United States House of Representatives on December 19, 1870. A memorial, as defined here, is a written statement presented to a governing body.

Woodhull was a proponent of the idea that since women were citizens of the United States, the U.S. Constitution already provided them with the right to vote. Here she pointed out that "the several states and territories," following election laws adopted prior to the passage of the Fifteenth Amendment, continued to refuse women this right. These old laws, she stated, directly conflicted with the Fifteenth Amendment, which prohibited states from denying citizens the vote. Woodhull requested that Congress pass a law reinforcing women's constitutional right, so that the states would no longer be able to deny women the vote.

In December 1865, Susan B. Anthony and Elizabeth Cady Stanton had petitioned both houses of Congress requesting an amendment to the Constitution prohibiting the states from disfranchising women. They based their argument on the discrepancy between the wording of the Constitution, which states that women are "free people" counted and taxed as citizens, and the political reality that refused women a voice in choosing their representatives and shaping their govern-

ment. They then noted that, upon the ratification of the Thirteenth Amendment to eliminate slavery, women remained the only disfranchised class. By this exclusion, they stated, Congress failed, "'to guarantee to every State in the Union a Republican form of government.'" This petition, of course, failed.

The majority of the House Judiciary Committee replied to Woodhull's memorial. Written by John Bingham, one of the framers of the Fourteenth Amendment, the committee's response argued that the Fourteenth Amendment did not confer rights and privileges on citizens that they would not have had prior to the passage of the amendment, but only ensured that those rights and privileges would be extended to all people regardless of race. The committee supported its rejection of Woodhull's argument that the Fifteenth Amendment recognized the right to vote for all citizens by citing *Bank of the United States v. Primrose*. In this case, the Supreme Court ruled that political rights conferred upon citizens of one state did not necessarily apply to citizens of other states, nor could citizens of one state necessarily exercise their rights in another state. While the committee recognized that states had the right to grant women suffrage, they stated that they also had the right to deny suffrage because of sex. The committee conceded the possibility that, as Woodhull claimed, the Constitution did grant women the right to vote; they decided, however, that if this were so, it was a matter to be undertaken by the courts, not Congress. The report closes with a resolution not to grant Woodhull's petition.

Victoria Woodhull, Memorial, 1870

To the Honorable the Senate and House of Representatives of the United States in Congress assembled, respectfully showeth:

That she was born in the State of Ohio, and is above the age of twenty-one years; that she has resided in the State of New York during the past three years; that she is still a resident thereof, and that she is a citizen of the United States, as declared by the XIV. Article of the Amendments to the Constitution of the United States.

That since the adoption of the XV. Article of the Amendments to the Constitution, neither the State of New York nor any other State, nor any Territory, has passed any law to abridge the right of any citizen of the United States to vote, as established by said article, neither on account of sex or otherwise. That, nevertheless, the right to vote is denied to women citizens of the United States by the operation of Election Laws in the several States and Territories, which laws were enacted prior to the adoption of the said XV. Article, and which are inconsistent with the Constitution as amended, and, therefore, are void and of no effect; but which, being still enforced by the said States and Territories, render the Constitution inoperative as regards the right of women citizens to vote:

And whereas, Article VI., Section 2, declares "That this Constitution and the laws of the United States which shall be made in pursuance thereof, and all treaties made, or which shall be made, under the authority of the United States, shall be the supreme law of the land; and all judges in every State shall be bound thereby, anything in the Constitution and laws of any State to the contrary, notwithstanding."

And whereas, no distinction between citizens is made in the Constitution of the United States on account of sex; but the XV. Article of Amendments to it provides that "No State shall make or enforce any law which shall abridge the privileges and immunities of citizens of the United States, nor deny to any person within its jurisdiction the equal protection of the laws."

And whereas, Congress has power to make laws which shall be necessary and proper for carrying into execution all powers vested by the Constitution in the Government of the United States; and to make or alter all regulations in relation to holding elections for senators or representatives, and especially to enforce, by appropriate legislation, the provisions of the said XIV. Article:

And whereas, the continuance of the enforcement of said local election laws, denying and abridging the right of citizens to vote on account of sex, is a grievance to your memorialist and to various other persons, citizens of the United States,

Therefore, your memorialist would most respectfully petition your honorable bodies to make such laws as in the wisdom of Congress shall be necessary and proper for carrying into execution the right vested by the Constitution in the citizens of the United States to vote, without regard to sex.

And your memorialist will ever pray.

House of Representatives, Committee of the Judiciary, Report #22, 1871

The Memorialist asks the enactment of a law by Congress which shall secure to citizens of the United States in the several States the right to vote "without regard to sex." Since the adoption of the XIV. Amendment of the Constitution, there is no longer any reason to doubt that all persons, born or naturalized in the United States, and subject to the jurisdiction thereof, are citizens of the United States and of the State wherein they reside, for that is the express declaration of the amendment.

The clause of the XIV. Amendment, "No State shall make or enforce any law which shall abridge the privileges or immunities of citizens of the United States," does not, in the opinion of the Committee, refer to privileges and immunities of citizens of the United States other than those privileges and immunities embraced in the original text of the Constitution, article IV., section 2. The XIV. Amendment, it is believed, did not add to the privileges or immunities before mentioned, but was deemed necessary for their enforcement, as an express limitation upon the powers of the States. It has been judicially determined that the first eight articles of amendment of the Constitution were not limitations on the power of the States, and it was apprehended that the same might be held of the provision of section 2, article iv.

To remedy this defect of the Constitution, the express limitations upon the States contained in the first section of the XIV. Amendment, together with the grant of power in Congress to enforce them by legislation, were incorporated in the Constitution. The words "citizens of the United States," and "citizens of the States," as employed in the XIV. Amendment, did not change or modify the relations of citizens of the State and Nation as they existed under the original Constitution.

Attorney-General Bates gave the opinion that the Constitution uses the word "citizen," only to express the political quality of the individual in his relation to the Nation; to declare that he is a member of the body politic, and bound to it by the reciprocal obligation of allegiance on the one side and protection on the other. The phrase "a citizen of the United States," without addition or qualification, means neither more nor less than a member of the Nation. (Opinion of Attorney-General Bates on citizenship.)

The Supreme Court of the United States has ruled that, according to the express words and clear meaning of the section 2, article iv. of the Constitution, no privileges are secured by it except those which belong to citizenship. (*Connor et al. vs. Elliott et al.*, 18 Howard, 593). In *Corfield vs. Coryell*, 4 Washington Circuit Court Reports, 380, the Court say:

> The inquiry is, what are the privileges and immunities of citizens in the several States? We feel no hesitation in confining these expressions to those privileges and immunities which are in their nature fundamental; which belong of right to the citizens of all free governments; and which have at all times been enjoyed by the citizens of the several States which compose this Union, from the time of their becoming free, independent, and sovereign. What these fundamental principles are would, perhaps, be more tedious than difficult to enumerate. They may, however, be all comprehended under the following general heads: Protection by the Government; the enjoyment of life and liberty, with the right to acquire and possess property of every kind, and to pursue and obtain happiness and safety, subject, nevertheless, to such restraints as the Government may justly prescribe for the general good of the whole; the right of a citizen of one State to pass through or to reside in any other State, for the purpose of trade, agriculture, professional pursuits, or otherwise; to claim the benefit of the writ of *habeas corpus;* to institute and maintain actions of any kind in the courts of the State; to take, hold, and dispose of property, either real or personal; and an exemption from higher taxes or impositions than are paid by the other citizens of the State, may be mentioned as some of the particular privileges and immunities of citizens which are clearly embraced by the general description of privileges deemed to be fundamental; to which may be added the elective franchise, as regulated and established by the laws or Constitution of the State in which it is to be exercised . . . But we can not accede to the proposition which was insisted on by the counsel, that under this provision of the Constitution, sec. 2, art. 4, the citizens of the several States are permitted to participate in all the rights which belong exclusively to the citizens of any other particular State.

The learned Justice Story declared that the intention of the clause—"the citizens of each State shall be entitled to all the privileges and immunities of citizens in the several States"—was to confer on the citizens of each State a general citizenship, and communicated all the privileges and immunities which a citizen of the same State would be entitled to under the circumstances. (*Story on the Constitution*, vol. 2, p. 605.)

In the case of the *Bank of the United States vs. Primrose,* in the Supreme Court of the United States, Mr. Webster said:

> That this article in the Constitution (art. 4, sec. 2) does not confer on the citizens of each State political rights in every other State, is admitted. A citizen of Pennsylvania can not go into Virginia and vote at any election in that State, though when he has acquired a residence in Virginia, and is otherwise qualified, as required by the Constitution (of Virginia), he becomes, without formal adoption as a citizen of Virginia, a citizen of that State politically. (Webster's Works, vol. 6, p. 112.)

It must be obvious that Mr. Webster was of opinion that the privileges and immunities of citizens, guaranteed to them in the several States, did not include the privilege of the elective franchise otherwise than as secured by the State Constitution. For, after making the statement above quoted, that a citizen of Pennsylvania can not go into Virginia and vote, Mr. Webster adds, "but for the purposes of trade, commerce, buying and selling, it is evidently not in the power of any State to impose any hindrance or embarrassment, etc., upon citizens of other States, or to place them, going there, upon a different footing from her own citizens." (Ib.) The proposition is clear that no citizen of the United States can rightfully vote in any State of this Union who has not the qualifications required by the Constitution of the State in which the right is claimed to be exercised, except as to such conditions in the constitutions of such States as deny the right to vote to citizens resident therein "on account of race, color, or previous condition of servitude."

The adoption of the XV. Amendment to the Constitution imposing these three limitations upon the power to the several States, was by necessary implication, a declaration that the States had the power to regulate by a uniform rule the conditions upon which the elective franchise should be exercised by citizens of the United States resident therein. The limitations specified in the XV. Amendment exclude the conclusion that a State of this Union, having a government republican in form, may not prescribe conditions upon which alone citizens may vote other than those prohibited. It can hardly be said that a State law which excludes from voting women citizens, minor citizens, and non-resident citizens of the United States, on account of sex, minority, or domicil, is a denial of the right to vote on account of race, color, or previous condition of servitude.

It may be further added that the 2d section of the XIV. Amendment, by the provision that "when the right to vote at any election for the choice of electors of President and Vice-President of the United States, Representatives in Congress, or executive and judicial officers of the State, or the members of the Legislature thereof, is denied to any of the male inhabitants of such State, being twenty-one years of age, a citizen of the United States, or in any way abridged, except for participation in rebellion or other crime, the basis of representation therein shall be reduced in the proportion which the number of such male citizens shall bear to the whole number of male citizens twenty-one years of age in such State," implies that the several States may restrict the elective franchise as to other than male citizens. In disposing of this question effect must be given, if possible, to every provision of the Constitution. Article 1, section 2, of the Constitution provides:

> That the House of Representatives shall be composed of members chosen every second year by the people of the several States, and the electors in each State shall have the qualifications requisite for electors of the most numerous branch of the State Legislature.

This provision has always been construed to vest in the several States the exclusive right to prescribe the qualifications of electors for the most numerous branch of the State Legislature, and therefore for Members of Congress. And this interpretation is supported by section 4, article 1, of the Constitution, which provides:

> That the time, places, and manner of holding elections for Senators and Representatives shall be prescribed in each State by the Legislature thereof but the Congress may at any time by law make or alter such regulations except as to the place of choosing Senators.

Now it is submitted, if it had been intended that Congress should prescribe the qualifications of electors, that the grant would have read: The Congress may at any time by law make or alter such regulations, and also prescribe the qualifications of electors, etc. The power, on the contrary, is limited exclusively to the time, place, and manner, and does not extend to the qualification of the electors. This power to prescribe the qualification of electors in the several States has always been exercised, and is, to-day, by the several States of the Union; and we apprehend, until the Constitution shall be changed, will continue to be so exercised, subject only to express limitations imposed by the Constitution upon the several States, before noticed. We are of opinion, therefore, that it is not competent for the Congress of the United States to establish by law the right to vote without regard to sex in the several States of this Union, without the consent of the people of such States, and against their constitutions and laws; and that

such legislation would be, in our judgment, a violation of the Constitution of the United States, and of the rights reserved to the States respectively by the Constitution. It is undoubtedly the right of the people of the several States so to reform their constitutions and laws as to secure the equal exercise of the right of suffrage at all elections held therein under the Constitution of the United States, to all citizens, without regard to sex; and as public opinion creates constitutions and governments in the several States, it is not to be doubted that whenever, in any State, the people are of opinion that such a reform is advisable, it will be made.

If however, as is claimed in the memorial referred to, the right to vote "is vested by the Constitution in the citizens of the United States without regard to sex," that right can be established in the courts without further legislation.

The suggestion is made that Congress, by a mere declaratory act, shall say that the construction claimed in the memorial is the true construction of the Constitution, or in other words, that by the Constitution of the United States the right to vote is vested in citizens of the United States "without regard to sex," anything in the constitution and laws of any State to the contrary notwithstanding. In the opinion of the Committee, such declaratory act is not authorized by the Constitution nor within the legislative power of Congress. We therefore recommend the adoption of the following resolution:

Resolved, That the prayer of the petitioner be not granted, that the memorial be laid on the table, and that the Committee on the Judiciary be discharged from the further consideration of the subject.

See also SUSAN B. ANTHONY, PETITION TO CONGRESS REQUESTING WOMEN'S SUFFRAGE, 1865; FRANCIS MINOR, RESOLUTIONS, 1869; SUFFRAGE CONFERRED BY THE FOURTEENTH AMENDMENT.

Source:

Elizabeth Frost and Kathryn Cullen-DuPont. *Women's Suffrage in America: An Eyewitness History.* New York: Facts On File, Inc., 1992.

Victoria C. Woodhull, Address to the Judiciary Committee of the House of Representatives, 1871

This document is the text of Victoria C. Woodhull's January 11, 1871, address to the House Judiciary Committee. Woodhull spoke before the committee at the invitation of one of its members, Benjamin Butler, a Massachusetts Republican who supported labor reform and woman suffrage. Her argument relied on the premise that women were, in fact, already granted suffrage in the Constitution. They should, therefore, attempt to exercise that right and challenge denial in the courts.

Woodhull argued that a person's sex had nothing to do with the right to vote. Men, she said, did not have the right to deny the vote to women any more than women had the right to deny the vote to men. Furthermore, since women paid taxes and owned property, denying them the vote was the equivalent of "taxation without representation." Woodhull implored Congress to annul the state laws that prohibited women from voting, stating her belief that the Constitution gave Congress the power to do so. Finally, she anticipated the argument that the power to decide this question lay with the Supreme Court; she noted that this would entail costly and pointless litigation, all of which could be avoided if Congress declared that the Constitution extended suffrage to women.

Woodhull also believed that marriage laws were proof that Americans had achieved religious, but not political, freedom because they restricted a woman's rights as an individual. She delivered a speech outlining her ideas on "free love" or "social freedom" before 3,000 people at Steinway Hall in New York City on November 20, 1871. According to her philosophy, a couple should only marry for love, and if that love failed, the marriage would be invalidated. For these reasons, she advocated the repeal of all marriage laws. She makes clear that her doctrine of "Free Love" did not give license for "sexual debauchery" but instead granted a woman the freedom to follow her heart without the restriction of contemporary social codes.

───────────── ⚬✖⚬ ─────────────

Having most respectfully memorialized Congress for the passage of such laws as in its wisdom shall seem necessary and proper to carry into effect the rights vested by the Constitution of the United States in the citizens to vote, without regard to sex, I beg leave to submit to your honorable body the following in favor of my prayer in said memorial which has been referred to your Committee.

The public law of the world is founded upon the conceded fact that sovereignty can not be forfeited or renounced. The sovereign power of this country is perpetually in the politically organized people of the United States, and can neither be relinquished nor abandoned by any portion of them. The people in this republic who confer sovereignty are its citizens: in a monarchy the people are the subjects of sovereignty. All citizens of a republic by rightful act or implication confer sovereign power. All people of a monarchy are subjects who exist under its supreme shield and enjoy its immunities. The subject of a monarch takes municipal immunities from the sovereign as a gracious favor; but the woman citizen of this country has the inalienable "sovereign" right of self-government in her own proper person. Those who look upon woman's status by the dim light of the common law, which unfolded itself under the feudal and military institutions that establish

right upon physical power, can not find any analogy in the status of the woman citizen of this country, where the broad sunshine of our Constitution has enfranchised all.

As sovereignty can not be forfeited, relinquished, or abandoned, those from whom it flows—the citizens—are equal in conferring the power, and should be equal in the enjoyment of its benefits and in the exercise of its rights and privileges. One portion of citizens have no power to deprive another portion of rights and privileges such as are possessed and exercised by themselves. The male citizen has no more right to deprive the female citizen of the free, public, political, expression of opinion than the female citizen has to deprive the male citizen thereof.

The sovereign will of the people is expressed in our written Constitution, which is the supreme law of the land. The Constitution makes no distinction of sex. The Constitution defines a woman born or naturalized in the United States, and subject to the jurisdiction thereof, to be a citizen. It recognizes the right of citizens to vote. It declares that the right of citizens of the United States to vote shall not be denied or abridged by the United States or by any State on account of "race, color, or previous condition of servitude."

Women, white and black, belong to races, although to different races. A race of people comprises all the people, male and female. The right to vote can not be denied on account of race. All people included in the term race have the right to vote, unless otherwise prohibited. Women of all races are white, black, or some intermediate color. Color comprises all people, of all races and both sexes. The right to vote can not be denied on account of color. All people included in the term color have the right to vote unless otherwise prohibited.

With the right to vote sex has nothing to do. Race and color include all people of both sexes. All people of both sexes have the right to vote, unless prohibited by special limited terms less comprehensive than race or color. No such limiting terms exist in the Constitution. Women, white and black, have from time immemorial groaned under what is properly termed in the Constitution "previous condition of servitude." Women are the equals of men before the law, and are equal in all their rights as citizens. Women are debarred from voting in some parts of the United States, although they are allowed to exercise that right elsewhere. Women were formerly permitted to vote in places where they are now debarred therefrom. The naturalization laws of the United States expressly provide for the naturalization of women. But the right to vote has only lately been definitely declared by the Constitution to be inalienable, under three distinct conditions—in all of which woman is clearly embraced.

The citizen who is taxed should also have a voice in the subject matter of taxation. "No taxation without representation" is a right which was fundamentally established at the very birth of our country's independence; and by what ethics does any free government impose taxes on women without giving them a voice upon the subject or a participation in the public declaration as to how and by whom these taxes shall be applied for common public use? Women are free to own and to control property, separate and free from males, and they are held responsible in their own proper persons, in every particular, as well as men, in and out of court. Women have the same inalienable right to life, liberty, and the pursuit of happiness that men have. Why have they not this right politically, as well as men?

Women constitute a majority of the people of this country—they hold vast portions of the nation's wealth and pay a proportionate share of the taxes. They are intrusted with the most vital responsibilities of society; they bear, rear, and educate men; they train and mould their characters; they inspire the noblest impulses in men; they often hold the accumulated fortunes of a man's life for the safety of the family and as guardians of the infants, and yet they are debarred from uttering any opinion by public vote, as to the management by public servants of these interests; they are the secret counselors, the best advisers, the most devoted aids in the most trying periods of men's lives, and yet men shrink from trusting them in the common questions of ordinary politics. Men trust women in the market, in the shop, on the highway and railroad, and in all other public places and assemblies, but when they propose to carry a slip of paper with a name upon it to the polls, they fear them. Nevertheless, as citizens, women have the right to vote; they are part and parcel of that great element in which the sovereign power of the land had birth; and it is by usurpation only that men debar them from this right. The American nation, in its march onward and upward, can not publicly choke the intellectual and political activity of half its citizens by narrow statutes. The will of the entire people is the true basis of republican government, and a free expression of that will by the public vote of all citizens, without distinctions of race, color, occupation, or sex, is the only means by which that will can be ascertained. As the world has advanced into civilization and culture; as mind has risen in its dominion over matter; as the principle of justice and moral right has gained sway, and merely physical organized power has yielded thereto; as the might of right has supplanted the right of might, so have the rights of women become more fully recognized, and that recognition is the result of the development of the minds of men, which through the ages she has polished, and thereby heightened the lustre of civilization.

It was reserved for our great country to recognize by constitutional enactment that political equality of all citizens which religion, affection, and common sense should have long since accorded; it was reserved for America to sweep away the mist of prejudice and ignorance, and that chivalric condescension of a darker age, for in the language of Holy Writ, "The night is far spent, the day is at hand, let us therefore cast off the work of darkness and let us put on the armor of light. Let us walk honestly as in the day." It may be argued against the proposition that there still remains upon the statute books of some States the word "male" to an exclusion; but as the Constitution, in its paramount character, can only be read by the light of the established principle, *ita lex Scripta est,* and as a subject of sex is not mentioned, and the Constitution is not limited either in terms or by necessary implication in the general rights of citizens to vote, this right can not be limited on account of anything in the spirit of inferior or previous enactments upon a subject which is not mentioned in the supreme law. A different construction would destroy a vested right in a portion of the citizens, and this no legislature has a right to do without compensation, and nothing can compensate a citizen for the loss of his or her suffrage—its value is equal to the value of life. Neither can it be presumed that women are to be kept from the polls as a mere police regulation: it is to be hoped, at least, that police regulations in their case need not be very active. The effect of the amendments to the Constitution must be to annul the power over this subject in the States, whether past, present, or future, which is contrary to the amendments. The amendments would even arrest the action of the Supreme Court in cases pending before it prior to their adoption, and operate as an absolute prohibition to the exercise of any other jurisdiction than merely to dismiss the suit. 8 Dall., 382: 6 Wheaton, 405; 9 ib., 868; 3d Circ. Pa., 1832.

And if the restrictions contained in the Constitution as to color, race or servitude, were designed to limit the State governments in reference to their own citizens, and were intended to operate also as restrictions on the federal power, and to prevent interference with the rights of the State and its citizens, how, then, can the State restrict citizens of the United States in the exercise of rights not mentioned in any restrictive clause in reference to actions on the part of those citizens having reference solely to the necessary functions of the General Government, such as the election of representatives and senators to Congress, whose election the Constitution expressly gives Congress the power to regulate? S. C., 1847: *Fox vs. Ohio,* 5 Howard, 410.

Your memorialist complains of the existence of State laws, and prays Congress, by appropriate legislation, to declare them, as they are, annulled, and to give vitality to the Constitution under its power to make and alter the regulations of the States contravening the same.

It may be urged in opposition that the courts have power, and should declare upon this subject. The Supreme

Court has the power, and it would be its duty to declare the law: but the court will not do so unless a determination of such point as shall arise make it necessary to the determination of a controversy, and hence a case must be presented in which there can be no rational doubt. All this would subject the aggrieved parties to much dilatory, expensive and needless litigation, which your memorialist prays your honorable body to dispense with by appropriate legislation, as there can be no purpose in special arguments *"ad inconvenienti,"* enlarging or contracting the import of the language of the Constitution.

Therefore, Believing firmly in the right of citizens to freely approach those in whose hands their destiny is placed under the Providence of God, your memorialist has frankly, but humbly, appealed to you, and prays that the wisdom of Congress may be moved to action in this matter for the benefit and the increased happiness of our beloved country.

Source:

Elizabeth Frost and Kathryn Cullen-DuPont. *Women's Suffrage in America: An Eyewitness History.* New York: Facts On File, Inc., 1992.

Specie Resumption Act of 1875

Federal legislation passed on January 14, 1875, providing for a return to specie payment. It called for the reduction of the amount of greenbacks (legal tender notes not backed by gold) in circulation, from $382 million to $300 million. The act represented a victory for the supporters of "hard money" over those who favored the continued use of the greenbacks that had been introduced during the Civil War. The act directed the secretary of the treasury to redeem legal tender notes presented on and after January 1, 1879, with coin currency. The act reassured Americans that paper money was backed by gold, and they soon accepted the use of the more convenient greenbacks.

In 1884, the Supreme Court in *Julliard v. Greenman* (110 U.S. 421), also known as the Legal Tender Cases, upheld the power of Congress to make U.S. notes legal tender in peacetime as well as wartime. The ruling supported the constitutionality of an 1878 act providing that Civil War legal tender notes should not be concealed or retired but should be reissued and kept in circulation. The Court argued that the power of Congress to make notes legal tender did not rest solely on its war power but derived from Congress's authority to provide a uniform national currency.

───────────⟨∞⟩───────────

An Act

To provide for the resumption of specie payments.

*Be it enacted by the Senate and House of Representatives of the United States of American in Congress assem-*bled, That the Secretary of the Treasury is hereby authorized and required, as rapidly as practicable, to cause to be coined at the mints of the United States, silver coins of the denominations of ten, twenty-five, and fifty cents, of standard value, and to issue them in redemption of an equal number and amount of fractional currency of similar denominations, or, at his discretion, he may issue such silver coins through the mints, the subtreasuries, public depositories, and post-offices of the United States; and, upon such issue, he is hereby authorized and required to redeem an equal amount of such fractional currency, until the whole amount of such fractional currency outstanding shall be redeemed.

Sec. 2. That so much of section three thousand five hundred and twenty-four of the Revised Statutes of the United States as provides for a charge of one-fifth of one per centum for converting standard gold bullion into coin is hereby repealed, and hereafter no charge shall be made for that service.

Sec. 3. That section five thousand one hundred and seventy-seven of the Revised Statutes of the United States, limiting the aggregate amount of circulating-notes of national banking-associations, be, and is hereby, repealed; and each existing banking-association may increase its circulating-notes in accordance with existing law without respect to said aggregate limit; and new banking-associations may be organized in accordance with existing law without respect to said aggregate limit; and the provisions of law for the withdrawal and redistribution of national-bank currency among the several States and Territories are hereby repealed. And whenever, and so often, as circulating notes shall be issued to any such banking-association, so increasing its capital or circulating-notes, or so newly organized as aforesaid, it shall be the duty of the Secretary of the Treasury to redeem the legal-tender United States notes in excess only of three hundred million of dollars, to the amount of eighty per centum of the sum of national-bank notes so issued to any such banking-association as aforesaid, and to continue such redemption as such circulating-notes are issued until there shall be outstanding the sum of three hundred million dollars of such legal-tender United States notes, and no more. And on and after the first day of January, anno Domini eighteen hundred and seventy-nine, the Secretary of the Treasury shall redeem, in coin, the United States legal-tender notes then outstanding on their presentation for redemption, at the office of the assistant treasurer of the United States in the city of New York, in sums of not less than fifty dollars. And to enable the Secretary of the Treasury to prepare and provide for the redemption in this act authorized or required, he is authorized to used any surplus revenues, from time to time, in the Treasury not otherwise appropriated, and to issue, sell, and dispose of, at not less than par, in coin, either of the descriptions of bonds of the United States described in the act of Congress approved July fourteenth, eighteen hundred and seventy, entitled, "An act to authorize the refunding of the national debt," with like qualities, privileges, and exemptions, to the extent necessary to carry this act into full effect, and to use the proceeds thereof for the purposes aforesaid. And all provisions of law inconsistent with the provisions of this act are hereby repealed.

Source:
Statutes at Large, Vol. 19, p. 296.

Minor v. Happersett, 1875

An 1875 Supreme Court decision that found women were not entitled to the right of suffrage under the United States Constitution as amended by the Fourteenth Amendment.

Although the language of the Fourteenth Amendment was opposed by many 19th-century women's rights leaders, Francis Minor, a lawyer and husband of Virginia Minor, president of the Woman Suffrage Association of Missouri, argued that Section 1 of the amendment represented an advance for women.

Women refused to give up the idea that they were entitled to suffrage under the Constitution. In 1871 and 1872 they tried to vote in various states. About 150 women succeeded, Susan B. Anthony among them. (She was arrested, tried, and convicted.) Women who were turned away in 1871 brought suit unsuccessfully, including Ellen Rand Van Valkenburg of Santa Cruz, California; Carrie S. Burnham of Philadelphia; and Catherine V. Waite of Illinois. Virginia Minor was one of the women turned away from the polls in 1872. She and her husband (since married women were not allowed to bring legal action on their own) sued St. Louis registrar Reese Happersett. The case ultimately reached the Supreme Court.

In their December 1872 lower-court petition, Virginia Minor, Francis Minor, and two other attorneys, John M. Krum and John B. Henderson, argued that Virginia Minor's constitutional rights had been abridged and specifically cited Article I, Section 9 ("Which declares that no Bill of Attainder shall be passed"); Article I, Section 10 (prohibiting the states from passing bills of attainder and outlawing "any title of nobility"—a status that "male citizens" appeared to have been granted); Article IV, Section 2 ("The citizens of each State shall be entitled to all privileges and immunities of citizens in the several States"); Article IV, Section 4 ("The United States shall guarantee to every State a republican form of government"); and the Fifth Amendment's guarantee that "No person shall be . . . deprived of life, liberty, or property without due process of law." It also cited the Ninth Amendment (granting all rights not expressly the province of the government to the people, from which the right

to privacy is derived). (This amendment would be used with greater success in two landmark 20th-century cases, *Griswold v. Connecticut* [1965] and *Roe v. Wade* [1973].) Last, they cited Section 1 of the Fourteenth Amendment.

The plaintiffs' argument and brief, presented to the Supreme Court in 1874, claimed, in addition, that "There can be no half-way citizenship. Woman, as a citizen of the United States, is entitled to all the benefits of that position, and liable to all its obligations, or to none." Among other Supreme Court decisions, it cited *Dred Scott v. Sandford,* the notorious 1857 response to the question of whether "the class of persons who had been imported as slaves, [or] their descendants . . . *free or not,*" were or ever could be citizens. Roger Taney, chief justice of the United States, found that they could not (a decision that was later invalidated by the adoption of the Fourteenth Amendment), but he also made clear that such citizenship would confer rights no state could refuse to recognize.

The Minors' attorneys pointed out that Section 1 of the Fourteenth Amendment granted citizenship to women as well as to African American males. They argued that the members of both groups, by the standards set in *Dred Scott,* were now in possession of a citizen's "privileges and immunities." And they cited the Supreme Court's 1873 *Slaughter-House* decision as evidence that the court considered suffrage a right of citizenship.

Therefore, they claimed, Missouri's state constitution, which abridged its female citizens' right of suffrage, was in violation of the United States Constitution.

In its unanimous decision, the Supreme Court found otherwise. Morrison R. Waite, chief justice of the United States, declared in his opinion that women born or naturalized in the United States were indeed—and had been even before the adoption of the Fourteenth Amendment—citizens. However, he also declared that the right of suffrage was not one of the privileges and immunities of citizenship and that states could therefore continue to disfranchise their female citizens.

The Supreme Court did not apply any provision of the Fourteenth Amendment to women until 1971, almost 100 years after the amendment's adoption.

———————————— ⌒✖⌒ ————————————

(NOTE: Where it is feasible, a syllabus [headnote] is released, as was done in connection with this case, at the time the opinion is issued. The syllabus constitutes no part of the opinion of the Court, which is given under the relevant heading.)

No. 182
SUPREME COURT OF THE UNITED STATES
88 U.S. 162
February 9, 1875
March 29, 1875
ERROR TO THE SUPREME COURT of MISSOURI

Syllabus

ERROR to the Supreme Court of Missouri; the case being thus:

The fourteenth amendment to the Constitution of the United States, in its first section, thus ordains;[n1]

"All persons born or naturalized in the United States, and subject to the jurisdiction thereof, are citizens of the United States, and of the State wherein they reside. No State shall make or enforce any law, which shall abridge the privileges or immunities of citizens of the United States. Nor shall any State deprive any person of life, liberty, or property, without due process of law; nor deny to any person within its jurisdiction, the equal protection of the laws."

And the constitution of the State of Missouri thus ordains:

"Every male citizen of the United States shall be entitled to vote."

Under a statute of the State all persons wishing to vote at any election, must previously have been registered in the manner pointed out by the statute, this being a condition precedent to the exercise of the elective franchise.

In this state of things, on the 15th of October, 1872 (one of the days fixed by law for the registration of voters), Mrs. Virginia Minor, a native born, free, white citizen of the United States, and of the State of Missouri, over the age of twenty-one years, wishing to vote for electors for President and Vice-President of the United States, and for a representative in Congress, and for other officers, at the general election held in November, 1872, applied to one Happersett, the registrar of voters, to register her as a lawful voter, which he refused to do, assigning for cause that she was not a "male citizen of the United States," but a woman. She thereupon sued him in one of the inferior State courts of Missouri, for wilfully refusing to place her name upon the list of registered voters, by which refusal she was deprived of her right to vote.

The registrar demurred, and the court in which the suit was brought sustained the demurrer, and gave judgment in his favor; a judgment which the Supreme Court affirmed. Mrs. Minor now brought the case here on error.

1. The word "citizen" is often used to convey the idea of membership in a nation.

2. In that sense, women, of born of citizen parents within the jurisdiction of the United States, have always been considered citizens of the United States, as much so before the adoption of the fourteenth amendment to the Constitution as since.

3. The right of suffrage was not necessarily one of the privileges or immunities of citizenship before the adoption of the fourteenth amendment, and that amendment does not add to these privileges and immunities. It simply furnishes additional guaranty for the protection of such as the citizen already had.

4. At the time of the adoption of that amendment, suffrage was not coextensive with the citizenship of the States; nor was it at the time of the adoption of the Constitution.

5. Neither the Constitution nor the fourteenth amendment made all citizens voters.

6. A provision in a State constitution which confines the right of voting to "male citizens of the United States," is no violation of the Federal Constitution. In such a State women have no right to vote.

Opinions

WAITE, C.J., Opinion of the Court

The CHIEF JUSTICE delivered the opinion of the court.

The question is presented in this case, whether, since the adoption of the fourteenth amendment, a woman, who is a citizen of the United States and of the State of Missouri, is a voter in that State, notwithstanding the provision of the constitution and laws of the State, which confine the right of suffrage to men alone. We might, perhaps, decide the case upon other grounds, but this question is fairly made. From the opinion we find that it was the only one decided in the court below, and it is the only one which has been argued here. The case was undoubtedly brought to this court for the sole purpose of having that question decided by us, and in view of the evident propriety there is of having it settled, so far as it can be by such a decision, we have concluded to waive all other considerations and proceed at once to its determination.

It is contended that the provisions of the constitution and laws of the State of Missouri which confine the right of suffrage and registration therefor to men, are in violation of the Constitution of the United States, and therefore void. The argument is, that as a woman, born or naturalized in the United States and subject to the jurisdiction thereof, is a citizen of the United States and of the State in which she resides, she has the right of suffrage as one of the privileges and immunities of her citizenship, which the State cannot by its laws or constitution abridge.

There is no doubt that women may be citizens. They are persons, and by the fourteenth amendment "all persons born or naturalized in the United States and subject to the jurisdiction thereof" are expressly declared to be "citizens of the United States and of the State wherein they reside." But, in our opinion, it did not need this amendment to give them that position. Before its adoption the Constitution of the United States did not in terms prescribe who should be citizens of the United States or of the several States, yet there were necessarily such citizens without such provision. There cannot be a nation without a people. The very idea of a political community, such as a nation is, implies an association of persons for the promotion of their general welfare. Each one of the persons associated becomes a member of the nation formed by the association. He owes it allegiance and is entitled to its protection. Allegiance and protection are, in this connection, reciprocal obligations. The one is a compensation for the other; allegiance for protection and protection for allegiance.

For convenience it has been found necessary to give a name to this membership. The object is to designate by a title the person and the relation he bears to the nation. For this purpose the words "subject," "inhabitant," and "citizen" have been used, and the choice between them is sometimes made to depend upon the form of the government. Citizen is now more commonly employed, however, and as it has been considered better suited to the description of one living under a republican government, it was adopted by nearly all of the States upon their separation from Great Britain, and was afterwards adopted in the Articles of Confederation and in the Constitution of the United States. When used in this sense it is understood as conveying the idea of membership of a nation, and nothing more.

To determine, then, who were citizens of the United States before the adoption of the amendment it is necessary to ascertain what persons originally associated themselves together to form the nation, and what were afterwards admitted to membership.

Looking at the Constitution itself we find that it was ordained and established by "the people of the United States," and then going further back, we find that these were the people of the several States that had before dissolved the political bands which connected them with Great Britain, and assumed a separate and equal station among the powers of the earth, and that had by Articles of Confederation and Perpetual Union, in which they took the name of "the United States of America," entered into a firm league of friendship with each other for their common defence, the security of their liberties and their mutual and general welfare, binding themselves to assist each other against all force offered to or attack made upon them, or any of them, on account of religion, sovereignty, trade, or any other pretence whatever.

Whoever, then, was one of the people of either of these States when the Constitution of the United States was adopted, became ipso facto a citizen—a member of the nation created by its adoption. He was one of the persons associating together to form the nation, and was, consequently, one of its original citizens. As to this there has never been a doubt. Disputes have arisen as to whether or not certain persons or certain classes of persons were part of the people at the time, but never as to their citizenship if they were.

Additions might always be made to the citizenship of the United States in two ways: first, by birth, and second, by naturalization. This is apparent from the Constitution itself, for it provides that "no person except a natural-born citizen, or a citizen of the United States at the time of the adoption of the Constitution, shall be eligible to the office of President," and that Congress shall have power "to establish a uniform rule of naturalization." Thus new citizens may be born or they may be created by naturalization.

The Constitution does not, in words, say who shall be natural-born citizens. Resort must be had elsewhere to ascertain that. At common-law, with the nomenclature of which the framers of the Constitution were familiar, it was never doubted that all children born in a country of parents who were its citizens became themselves, upon their birth, citizens also. These were natives, or natural-born citizens, as distinguished from aliens or foreigners. Some authorities go further and include as citizens children born within the jurisdiction without reference to the citizenship of their parents. As to this class there have been doubts, but never as to the first. For the purposes of this case it is not necessary to solve these doubts. It is sufficient for everything we have now to consider that all children born of citizen parents within the jurisdiction are themselves citizens. The words "all children" are certainly as comprehensive, when used in this connection, as "all persons," and if females are included in the last they must be in the first. That they are included in the last is not denied. In fact the whole argument of the plaintiffs proceeds upon that idea.

Under the power to adopt a uniform system of naturalization Congress, as early as 1790, provided "that any alien, being a free white person," might be admitted as a citizen of the United States, and that the children of such persons so naturalized, dwelling within the United States, being under twenty-one years of age at the time of such naturalization, should also be considered citizens of the United States, and that the children of citizens of the United States that might be born beyond the sea, or out of the limits of the United States, should be considered as natural-born citizens. These provisions thus enacted have, in substance, been retained in all the naturalization laws adopted since. In 1855, however, the last provision was somewhat extended, and all persons theretofore born or thereafter to be born out of the limits of the jurisdiction of the United States, whose fathers were, or should be at the time of their birth, citizens of the United States, were declared to be citizens also.

As early as 1804 it was enacted by Congress that when any alien who had declared his intention to become a citizen in the manner provided by law died before he was actually naturalized, his widow and children should be considered as citizens of the United States, and entitled to all rights and privileges as such upon taking the necessary oath; and in 1855 it was further provided that any woman who might lawfully be naturalized under the existing laws, married, or who should be married to a citizen of the United States, should be deemed and taken to be a citizen.

From this it is apparent that from the commencement of the legislation upon this subject alien women and alien minors could be made citizens by naturalization, and we think it will not be contended that this would have been done if it had not been supposed that native women and native minors were already citizens by birth.

But if more is necessary to show that women have always been considered as citizens the same as men, abundant proof is to be found in the legislative and judicial history of the country. Thus, by the Constitution, the judicial power of the United States is made to extend to controversies between citizens of different States. Under this it has been uniformly held that the citizenship necessary to give the courts of the United States jurisdiction of a cause must be affirmatively shown on the record. Its existence as a fact may be put in issue and tried. If found not to exist the case must be dismissed. Notwithstanding this the records of the courts are full of cases in which the jurisdiction depends upon the citizenship of women, and not one can be found, we think, in which objection was made on that account. Certainly none can be found in which it has been held that women could not sue or be sued in the courts of the United States. Again, at the time of the adoption of the Constitution, in many of the States (and in some probably now) aliens could not inherit or transmit inheritance. There are a multitude of cases to be found in which the question has been presented whether a woman was or was not an alien, and as such capable or incapable of inheritance, but in no one has it been insisted that she was not a citizen because she was a woman. On the contrary, her right to citizenship has been in all cases assumed. The only question has been whether, in the particular case under consideration, she had availed herself of the right.

In the legislative department of the government similar proof will be found. Thus, in the pre-emption laws, a widow, "being a citizen of the United States," is allowed to make settlement on the public lands and purchase upon the terms specified, and women, "being citizens of the United States," are permitted to avail themselves of the benefit of the homestead law.

Other proof of like character might be found, but certainly more cannot be necessary to establish the fact that sex has never been made one of the elements of citizenship in the United States. In this respect men have never had an advantage over women. The same laws precisely apply to both. The fourteenth amendment did not affect the citizenship of women any more than it did of men. In this particular, therefore, the rights of Mrs. Minor do not depend upon the amendment. She has always been a citizen from her birth, and entitled to all the privileges and immunities of citizenship. The amendment prohibited the State, of which she is a citizen, from abridging any of her privileges and immunities as a citizen of the United States; but it did not confer citizenship on her. That she had before its adoption.

If the right of suffrage is one of the necessary privileges of a citizen of the United States, then the constitution and laws of Missouri confining it to men are in violation of the Constitution of the United States, as amended, and consequently void. The direct question is, therefore, presented whether all citizens are necessarily voters.

The Constitution does not define the privileges and immunities of citizens. For that definition we must look elsewhere. In this case we need not determine what they are, but only whether suffrage is necessarily one of them.

It certainly is nowhere made so in express terms. The United States has no voters in the States of its own creation. The elective officers of the United States are all elected directly or indirectly by State voters. The members of the House of Representatives are to be chosen by the people of the States, and the electors in each State must have the qualifications requisite for electors of the most numerous branch of the State legislature. Senators are to be chosen by the legislatures of the States, and necessarily the members of the legislature required to make the choice are elected by the voters of the State. Each State must appoint in such manner, as the legislature thereof may direct, the electors to elect the President and Vice-President. The times, places, and manner of holding elections for Senators and Representatives are to be prescribed in each State by the legislature thereof; but Congress may at any time, by law, make or alter such regulations, except as to the place of choosing Senators. It is not necessary to inquire whether this power of supervision thus given to Congress is sufficient to authorize any interference with the State laws prescribing the qualifications of voters, for no such interference has ever been attempted. The power of the State in this particular is certainly supreme until Congress acts.

The amendment did not add to the privileges and immunities of a citizen. It simply furnished an additional guaranty for the protection of such as he already had. No new voters were necessarily made by it. Indirectly it may have had that effect, because it may have increased the number of citizens entitled to suffrage under the constitution and laws of the States, but it operates for this purpose, if at all, through the States and the State laws, and not directly upon the citizen.

It is clear, therefore, we think, that the Constitution has not added the right of suffrage to the privileges and immunities of citizenship as they existed at the time it was adopted. This makes it proper to inquire whether suffrage was coextensive with the citizenship of the States at the time of its adoption. If it was, then it may with force be argued that suffrage was one of the rights which belonged to citizenship, and in the enjoyment of which every citizen must be protected. But if it was not, the contrary may with propriety be assumed.

When the Federal Constitution was adopted, all the States, with the exception of Rhode Island and Connecticut, had constitutions of their own. These two continued to act under their charters from the Crown. Upon an examination of those constitutions we find that in no State were all citizens permitted to vote. Each State determined for itself who should have that power. Thus, in New Hampshire, "every male inhabitant of each town and parish with town privileges, and places unincorporated in the State, of twenty-one years of age and upwards, excepting paupers and persons excused from paying taxes at their own request," were its voters; in Massachusetts "every male inhabitant of twenty-one years of age and upwards, having a freehold estate within the commonwealth of the annual income of three pounds, or any estate of the value of sixty pounds"; in Rhode Island "such as are admitted free of the company and society" of the colony; in Connecticut such persons as had "maturity in years, quiet and peaceable behavior, a civil conversation, and forty shillings freehold or forty pounds personal estate," if so certified by the selectmen; in New York "every male inhabitant of full age who shall have personally resided within one of the counties of the State for six months immediately preceding the day of election . . . if during the time aforesaid he shall have been a freeholder, possessing a freehold of the value of twenty pounds within the county, or have rented a tenement therein of the yearly value of forty shillings, and been rated and actually paid taxes to the State"; in New Jersey "all inhabitants . . . of full age who are worth fifty pounds, proclamation-money, clear estate in the same, and have resided in the county in which they claim a vote for twelve months immediately preceding the election"; in Pennsylvania "every freeman of the age of twenty-one years, having resided in the State two years next before the election, and within that time paid a State or county tax which shall have been assessed at least six months before the election"; in Delaware and Virginia "as exercised by law at present"; in Maryland "all freemen above twenty-one years of age having a freehold of fifty acres of land in the county in which they offer to vote and residing therein, and all freemen having property in the State above the value of thirty pounds current money, and having resided in the county in which they offer to vote one whole year next preceding the election"; in North Carolina, for senators, "all freemen of the age of twenty-one years who have been inhabitants of any one county within the State twelve months immediately preceding the day of election, and

possessed of a freehold within the same county of fifty acres of land for six months next before and at the day of election," and for members of the house of commons "all freemen of the age of twenty-one years who have been inhabitants in any one county within the State twelve months immediately preceding the day of any election, and shall have paid public taxes"; in South Carolina "every free white man of the age of twenty-one years, being a citizen of the State and having resided therein two years previous to the day of election, and who hath a freehold of fifty acres of land, or a town lot of which he hath been legally seized and possessed at least six months before such election, or (not having such freehold or town lot), hath been a resident within the election district in which he offers to give his vote six months before said election, and hath paid a tax the preceding year of three shillings sterling towards the support of the government"; and in Georgia such "citizens and inhabitants of the State as shall have attained to the age of twenty-one years, and shall have paid tax for the year next preceding the election, and shall have resided six months within the county."

In this condition of the law in respect to suffrage in the several States it cannot for a moment be doubted that if it had been intended to make all citizens of the United States voters, the framers of the Constitution would not have left it to implication. So important a change in the condition of citizenship as it actually existed, if intended, would have been expressly declared.

But if further proof is necessary to show that no such change was intended, it can easily be found both in and out of the Constitution. By Article 4, section 2, it is provided that "the citizens of each State shall be entitled to all the privileges and immunities of citizens in the several States." If suffrage is necessarily a part of citizenship, then the citizens of each State must be entitled to vote in the several States precisely as their citizens are. This is more than asserting that they may change their residence and become citizens of the State and thus be voters. It goes to the extent of insisting that while retaining their original citizenship they may vote in any State. This, we think, has never been claimed. And again, by the very terms of the amendment we have been considering (the fourteenth), "Representatives shall be apportioned among the several States according to their respective numbers, counting the whole number of persons in each State, excluding Indians not taxed. But when the right to vote at any election for the choice of electors for President and Vice-President of the United States, representatives in Congress, the executive and judicial officers of a State, or the members of the legislature thereof, is denied to any of the male inhabitants of such State, being twenty-one years of age and citizens of the United States, or in any way abridged, except for participation in the rebellion, or other crimes, the basis of representation therein shall be reduced in the proportion which the number of such male citizens shall bear to the whole number of male citizens twenty-one years of age in such State." Why this, if it was not in the power of the legislature to deny the right of suffrage to some male inhabitants? And if suffrage was necessarily one of the absolute rights of citizenship, why confine the operation of the limitation to male inhabitants? Women and children are, as we have seen, "persons." They are counted in the enumeration upon which the apportionment is to be made, but if they were necessarily voters because of their citizenship unless clearly excluded, why inflict the penalty for the exclusion of males alone? Clearly, no such form of words would have been selected to express the idea here indicated if suffrage was the absolute right of all citizens.

And still again, after the adoption of the fourteenth amendment, it was deemed necessary to adopt a fifteenth, as follows: "The right of citizens of the United States to vote shall not be denied or abridged by the United States, or by any State, on account of race, color, or previous condition of servitude." The fourteenth amendment had already provided that no State should make or enforce any law which should abridge the privileges or immunities of citizens of the United States. If suffrage was one of these privileges or immunities, why amend the Constitution to prevent its being denied on account of race, &c.? Nothing is more evident than that the greater must include the less, and if all were already protected why go through with the form of amending the Constitution to protect a part?

It is true that the United States guarantees to every State a republican form of government. It is also true that no State can pass a bill of attainder, and that no person can be deprived of life, liberty, or property without due process of law. All these several provisions of the Constitution must be construed in connection with the other parts of the instrument, and in the light of the surrounding circumstances.

The guaranty is of a republican form of government. No particular government is designated as republican, neither is the exact form to be guaranteed, in any manner especially designated. Here, as in other parts of the instrument, we are compelled to resort elsewhere to ascertain what was intended.

The guaranty necessarily implies a duty on the part of the States themselves to provide such a government. All the States had governments when the Constitution was adopted. In all the people participated to some extent, through their representatives elected in the manner specially provided. These governments the Constitution did not change. They were accepted precisely as they were, and it is, therefore, to be presumed that they were such as

it was the duty of the States to provide. Thus we have unmistakable evidence of what was republican in form, within the meaning of that term as employed in the Constitution.

As has been seen, all the citizens of the States were not invested with the right of suffrage. In all, save perhaps New Jersey, this right was only bestowed upon men and not upon all of them. Under these circumstances it is certainly now too late to contend that a government is not republican, within the meaning of this guaranty in the Constitution, because women are not made voters.

The same may be said of the other provisions just quoted. Women were excluded from suffrage in nearly all the States by the express provision of their constitutions and laws. If that had been equivalent to a bill of attainder, certainly its abrogation would not have been left to implication. Nothing less than express language would have been employed to effect so radical a change. So also of the amendment which declares that no person shall be deprived of life, liberty, or property without due process of law, adopted as it was as early as 1791. If suffrage was intended to be included within its obligations, language better adapted to express that intent would most certainly have been employed. The right of suffrage, when granted, will be protected. He who has it can only be deprived of it by due process of law, but in order to claim protection he must first show that he has the right.

But we have already sufficiently considered the proof found upon the inside of the Constitution. That upon the outside is equally effective.

The Constitution was submitted to the States for adoption in 1787, and was ratified by nine States in 1788, and finally by the thirteen original States in 1790. Vermont was the first new State admitted to the Union, and it came in under a constitution which conferred the right of suffrage only upon men of the full age of twenty-one years, having resided in the State for the space of one whole year next before the election, and who were of quiet and peaceable behavior. This was in 1791. The next year, 1792, Kentucky followed with a constitution confining the right of suffrage to free male citizens of the age of twenty-one years who had resided in the State two years or in the county in which they offered to vote one year next before the election. Then followed Tennessee, in 1796, with voters of freemen of the age of twenty-one years and upwards, possessing a freehold in the county wherein they may vote, and being inhabitants of the State or freemen being inhabitants of any one county in the State six months immediately preceding the day of election. But we need not particularize further. No new State has ever been admitted to the Union which has conferred the right of suffrage upon women, and this has never been considered a valid objection to her admission. On the contrary, as is claimed in the argument, the right of suffrage was withdrawn from women as early as 1807 in the State of New Jersey, without any attempt to obtain the interference of the United States to prevent it. Since then the governments of the insurgent States have been reorganized under a requirement that before their representatives could be admitted to seats in Congress they must have adopted new constitutions, republican in form. In no one of these constitutions was suffrage conferred upon women, and yet the States have all been restored to their original position as States in the Union.

Besides this, citizenship has not in all cases been made a condition precedent to the enjoyment of the right of suffrage. Thus, in Missouri, persons of foreign birth, who have declared their intention to become citizens of the United States, may under certain circumstances vote. The same provision is to be found in the constitutions of Alabama, Arkansas, Florida, Georgia, Indiana, Kansas, Minnesota, and Texas.

Certainly, if the courts can consider any question settled, this is one. For nearly ninety years the people have acted upon the idea that the Constitution, when it conferred citizenship, did not necessarily confer the right of suffrage. If uniform practice long continued can settle the construction of so important an instrument as the Constitution of the United States confessedly is, most certainly it has been done here. Our province is to decide what the law is, not to declare what it should be.

We have given this case the careful consideration its importance demands. If the law is wrong, it ought to be changed; but the power for that is not with us. The arguments addressed to us bearing upon such a view of the subject may perhaps be sufficient to induce those having the power, to make the alteration, but they ought not to be permitted to influence our judgment in determining the present rights of the parties now litigating before us. No argument as to woman's need of suffrage can be considered. We can only act upon her rights as they exist. It is not for us to look at the hardship of withholding. Our duty is at an end if we find it is within the power of a State to withhold.

Being unanimously of the opinion that the Constitution of the United States does not confer the right of suffrage upon any one, and that the constitutions and laws of the several States which commit that important trust to men alone are not necessarily void, we AFFIRM THE JUDGMENT.

Source:

Cornell Law School, The Legal Information Institute. Supreme Court Collection. Available on-line. URL: supct.law.cornell. edu/supct/. Accessed November 2003.

Bland-Allison Act, 1878

Legislation coauthored by Representatives Richard P. Bland of Missouri and William B. Allison of Iowa and passed by the U.S. Congress on February 28, 1878, to provide for freer coinage of silver. The Coinage Act of 1873 had eliminated the silver dollar from U.S. currency. Coming at a time when silver supplies were increasing as a result of new discoveries in the West, the act was dubbed the "crime of '73" by silver interests. The subsequent free-silver movement was supported especially by western farmers and silver miners, who demanded a return to bimetallism. The Bland-Allison Act was an attempt to compromise between the call for free, unlimited silver coinage and the demands of eastern financiers for a gold standard. The act required the Treasury Department to purchase between $2 million and $4 million worth of silver each month for coinage. It was passed over the veto of President Rutherford B. Hayes and remained in effect until replaced by the Sherman Silver Purchase Act of 1890.

———————————————⎯⎯⎯⎯⎯⎯⎯⎯⎯

An Act

To authorize the coinage of the standard silver dollar, and to restore its legal-tender character.

Be it enacted by the Senate and House of Representatives of the United States of America in Congress assembled, That there shall be coined, at the several mints of the United States, silver dollars of the weight of four hundred and twelve and a half grains Troy of standard silver, as provided in the act of January eighteenth, eighteen hundred thirty-seven, on which shall be the devices and superscriptions provided by said act; which coins together with all silver dollars heretofore coined by the United States, of like weight and fineness, shall be a legal tender, at their nominal value, for all debts and dues public and private, except where otherwise expressly stipulated in the contract. And the Secretary of the Treasury is authorized and directed to purchase, from time to time, silver bullion, at the market price thereto, not less than two million dollars worth per month, nor more than four million dollars worth per month, and cause the same to be coined monthly, as fast as so purchased, into such dollars; and a sum sufficient to carry out the foregoing provision of this act is hereby appropriated out of any money in the Treasury not otherwise appropriated. And any gain or seigniorage arising from this coinage shall be accounted for and paid into the Treasury, as provided under existing laws relative to the subsidiary coinage: *Provided,* That the amount of money at any one time invested in such silver bullion, exclusive of such resulting coin, shall not exceed five million dollars: *And provided further,* That nothing in this act shall be construed to authorize the payment in silver of certificates of deposit issued under the provisions of section two hundred and fifty-four of the Revised Statutes.

Sec. 2. That immediately after the passage of this act, the President shall invite the governments of the countries composing the Latin Union, so-called, and of such other European nations as he may deem advisable, to join the United States in a conference to adopt a common ratio between gold and silver, for the purpose of establishing, internationally, the use of bi-metallic money, and securing fixity of relative value between those metals; such conference to be held at such place, in Europe or in the United States, at such time within six months, as may be mutually agreed upon by the executives of the governments joining in the same, whenever the governments so invited, or any three of them, shall have signified their willingness to unite in the same.

The President shall, by and with the advice and consent of the Senate, appoint three commissioners, who shall attend such conference on behalf of the United States, and shall report the doings thereof to the President, who shall transmit the same to Congress.

Said commissioners shall each receive the sum of two thousand five hundred dollars and their reasonable expenses, to be approved by the Secretary of State; and the amount necessary to pay such compensation and expenses is hereby appropriated out of any money in the Treasury not otherwise appropriated.

Sec. 3. That any holder of the coin authorized by this act may deposit the same with the Treasurer or any assistant treasurer of the United States, in sums not less than ten dollars, and receive therefor certificates of not less than ten dollars each, corresponding with the denominations of the United States notes. The coin deposited for or representing the certificates shall be retained in the Treasury for the payment of the same on demand. Said certificates shall be receivable for customs, taxes, and all public dues, and, when so received, may be reissued.

Sec. 4. All acts and parts of acts inconsistent with the provisions of this act are hereby repealed.

Sam. J. Randall *Speaker of the House of Representatives.* W. A. Wheeler *Vice-President of the United States and President of the Senate* in the House of Representatives U.S. *February 28, 1878.*

The President of the United States having returned to the House of Representatives, in which it originated the bill, entitled "An act to authorize the coinage of the standard silver dollar, and to restore its legal-tender character," with his objections thereto; the House of Representatives proceeded in pursuance of the Constitution to reconsider the same; and

Resolved, That the said bill pass, two thirds of the House of Representatives agreeing to pass the same.

Attest:
Geo. M Adams *Clerk* By Green Adams *Chief Clerk*

In the Senate of the United States *February 28,* 1878.

The Senate having proceeded, in pursuance of the Constitution, to reconsider the bill entitled "An act to authorize the coinage of the standard silver dollar, and to restore its legal-tender character," returned to the House of Representatives by the President of the United States, with his objections, and sent by the House of Representatives to the Senate with the message of the President returning the bill;

Resolved, That the bill do pass, two-thirds of the Senate agreeing to pass the same.

See also SHERMAN SILVER PURCHASE ACT, 1890.

Source:
Statutes at Large, Vol. 20, pp. 25–26.

U.S. House of Representatives, Committee on Privileges and Elections, Negative Report Regarding Proposed Amendment, 1878

Report of the Committee on Privileges and Elections produced in 1878 opposing the proposed constitutional amendment granting women equal voting rights with men. The proposed amendment was introduced to the Senate and the House of Representatives by California Senator Aaron A. Sargent, who had been persuaded to do so by Elizabeth Cady Stanton.

The document provides a series of reasons why the committee opposed a constitutional amendment requiring the states to adopt woman suffrage. Ironically, the committee's primary reason, that women were politically inexperienced and dependent upon men, was the very issue women's rights activists were striving to overcome. Secondly, citing as evidence the relatively low number of signatures on petitions (30,000) circulated by woman-suffrage organizations, the committee concluded that women themselves did not want the vote. The committee noted that most states had enacted legislation favorable to women and currently might grant suffrage if they so chose. Therefore, even if the required three-fourths of the states should ratify a constitutional amendment, the committee was reluctant to impose suffrage on the one-fourth that opposed it.

The text of the amendment, which stated very simply that "the right of citizens of the United States to vote shall not be denied or abridged by the United States or by any state on account of sex," was drafted by Susan B. Anthony. It would be introduced, its wording unchanged, to every session of Congress for the next 32 years, until its adoption as the Nineteenth Amendment in 1920.

───────────── ∞ ─────────────

The Committee on Privileges and Elections, to whom was referred the Resolution (S.Res.12) proposing an Amendment to the Constitution of the United States, and certain Petitions for and Remonstrances against the same, make the following Report:

This proposed amendment forbids the United States, or any State to deny or abridge the right to vote on account of sex. If adopted, it will make several millions of female voters, totally inexperienced in political affairs, quite generally dependent upon the other sex, all incapable of performing military duty and without the power to enforce the laws which their numerical strength may enable them to make, and comparatively very few of whom wish to assume the irksome and responsible political duties which this measure thrusts upon them. An experiment so novel, a change so great, should only be made slowly and in response to a general public demand, of the existence of which there is no evidence before your committee.

Petitions from various parts of the country, containing by estimate about 30,000 names, have been presented to congress asking for this legislation. They were procured through the efforts of woman suffrage societies, thoroughly organized, with active and zealous managers. The ease with which signatures may be procured to any petition is well known. The small number of petitioners, when compared with that of the intelligent women in the country, is striking evidence that there exists among them no general desire to take up the heavy burden of governing, which so many men seek to evade. It would be unjust, unwise and impolitic to impose that burden on the great mass of women throughout the country who do not wish for it, to gratify the comparatively few who do.

It has been strongly urged that without the right of suffrage, women are, and will be, subjected to great oppression and injustice.

But every one who has examined the subject at all knows that, without female suffrage, legislation for years has improved and is still improving the condition of woman. The disabilities imposed upon her by the common law have, one by one, been swept away, until in most of the States she has the full right to her property and all, or nearly all, the rights which can be granted without impairing or destroying the marriage relation. These changes have been wrought by the spirit of the age, and are not, generally at least, the result of any agitation by women in their own behalf.

Nor can women justly complain of any partiality in the administration of justice. They have the sympathy of judges and particularly of juries to an extent which would warrant loud complaint on the part of their adversaries of the sterner sex. Their appeals to legislatures against injustice are never unheeded, and there is no doubt that when any considerable part of the women of any State really wish for the right to vote, it will be granted without the intervention of congress.

Any State may grant the right of suffrage to women. Some of them have done so to a limited extent, and perhaps with good results. It is evident that in some States public opinion is much more strongly in favor of it than it is in others. Your committee regard it as unwise and inexpedient to enable three-fourths in number of the States, through an amendment to the national constitution, to force woman suffrage upon the other fourth in which the public opinion of both sexes may be strongly adverse to such a change.

For these reasons, your committee report back said resolution with a recommendation that it be indefinitely postponed.

See also JOINT RESOLUTION PROPOSING AN AMENDMENT TO THE CONSTITUTION OF THE UNITED STATES, 1878; SUSAN B. ANTHONY, SPEECH ON BEHALF OF THE WOMAN SUFFRAGE AMENDMENT, 1884; ISABELLA BEECHER HOOKER, "THE CONSTITUTIONAL RIGHTS OF THE WOMEN OF THE UNITED STATES," 1888.

Source:

Elizabeth Frost and Kathryn Cullen-DuPont. *Women's Suffrage in America: An Eyewitness History.* New York: Facts On File, Inc., 1992.

Reynolds v. United States, 1879

A unanimous U.S. Supreme Court handed down in May, 1879 concerning the constitutional separation of church and state. The case raised the question of whether a U.S. statute prohibiting polygamy could be applied to a Mormon, whose religion encouraged a man to marry more than one wife. The Court, in deciding whether "religious belief can be accepted as a justification of an overt act made criminal by the law of the land," unanimously upheld the statute. The Court ruled that Congress had the authority to enact such a law and that the statute must be applied to everyone, without regard to religious convictions; to excuse from compliance some individuals would be to punish others for not subscribing to the same beliefs. In his decision, Chief Justice Morrison R. Waite declared that religious practices contrary to the public interest could be outlawed. Waite used the phrase, borrowed from

Thomas Jefferson, "a wall of separation [existed] between church and state." This metaphor has haunted religious clause decisions ever since.

———————————⚬⚭⚬———————————

Mr. Chief Justice Waite delivered the opinion of the court.

The assignments of error, when grouped, present the following questions:—

1. Was the indictment bad because found by a grand jury of less than sixteen persons?

2. Were the challenges of certain petit jurors by the accused improperly overruled?

3. Were the challenges of certain other jurors by the government improperly sustained?

4. Was the testimony of Amelia Jane Schofield, given at a former trial for the same offence, but under another indictment, improperly admitted in evidence?

5. Should the accused have been acquitted if he married the second time, because he believed it to be his religious duty?

6. Did the court err in that part of the charge which directed the attention of the jury to the consequences of polygamy?

These questions will be considered in their order.

1. As to the grand jury.

The indictment was found in the District Court of the third judicial district of the Territory. The act of Congress "in relation to courts and judicial officers in the Territory of Utah," approved June 23, 1874 (18 Stat. 253), while regulating the qualifications of jurors in the Territory, and prescribing the mode of preparing the lists from which grand and petit jurors are to be drawn, as well as the manner of drawing, makes no provision in respect to the number of persons of which a grand jury shall consist. Sect. 808, Revised Statutes, requires that a grand jury impanelled before any district or circuit court of the United States shall consist of not less than sixteen nor more than twenty-three persons, while a statute of the Territory limits the number in the district court of the Territory to fifteen. Comp. Laws Utah, 1876, 357. The grand jury which found this indictment consisted of only fifteen persons, and the question to be determined is, whether the section of the Revised Statutes referred to or the statute of the Territory governs the case.

By sect. 1910 of the Revised Statutes the district courts of the Territory have the same jurisdiction in all cases arising under the Constitution and laws of the United States as is vested in the circuit and district courts of the United States; but this does not make them circuit and district courts of the United States. We have often so decided. *American Insurance Co. v. Canter*, 1 Pet. 511; *Benner et al. v. Porter*, 9 How. 235; *Clinton v. Englebrecht*, 13 Wall. 434. They are courts of the Territories, invested for some pur-

poses with the powers of the courts of the United States. Writs of error and appeals lie from them to the Supreme Court of the Territory, and from that court as a territorial court to this in some cases.

Sect. 808 was not designed to regulate the impanelling of grand juries in all courts where offenders against the laws of the United States could be tried, but only in the circuit and district courts. This leaves the territorial courts free to act in obedience to the requirements of the territorial laws in force for the time being. *Clinton v. Englebrecht, supra; Hornbuckle v. Toombs*, 18 Wall. 648. As Congress may at any time assume control of the matter, there is but little danger to be anticipated from improvident territorial legislation in this particular. We are therefore of the opinion that the court below no more erred in sustaining this indictment than it did at a former term, at the instance of this same plaintiff in error, in adjudging another bad which was found against him for the same offence by a grand jury composed of twenty-three persons. 1 Utah, 226.

2. As to the challenges by the accused.

By the Constitution of the United States (Amend. VI.), the accused was entitled to a trial by an impartial jury. A juror to be impartial must, to use the language of Lord Coke, "be indifferent as he stands unsworn." Co. Litt. 155 *b*. Lord Coke also says that a principal cause of challenge is "so called because, if it be found true, it standeth sufficient of itself, without leaving any thing to the conscience or discretion of the triers" (id. 156 *b*); or, as stated in Bacon's Abridgment, "it is grounded on such a manifest presumption of partiality, that, if found to be true, it unquestionably sets aside the . . . juror." Bac. Abr., tit. Juries, E.1. "If the truth of the matter alleged is admitted, the law pronounces the judgment; but if denied, it must be made out by proof to the satisfaction of the court or the triers." Id.E. 12. To make out the existence of the fact, the juror who is challenged may be examined on his *voire dire*, and asked any questions that do not tend to his infamy or disgrace.

All of the challenges by the accused were for principal cause. It is good ground for such a challenge that a juror has formed an opinion as to the issue to be tried. The courts are not agreed as to the knowledge upon which the opinion must rest in order to render the juror incompetent, or whether the opinion must be accompanied by malice or ill-will; but all unite in holding that it must be founded on some evidence, and be more than a mere impression. Some say it must be positive (Gabbet, Criminal Law, 391); others, that it must be decided and substantial (*Armistead's Case*, 11 Leigh (Va.), 659; *Wormley's Case*, 10 Gratt. (Va.) 658; *Neely v. The People*, 13 Ill. 685); others, fixed (*State v. Benton*, 2 Dev. & B. (N.C.) L. 196); and, still others, deliberate and settled (*Staup v. Common-*

wealth, 74 Pa.St. 458; *Curley v. Commonwealth,* 84 id. 151). All concede, however, that, if hypothetical only, the partiality is not so manifest as to necessarily set the juror aside. Mr. Chief Justice Marshall, in *Burr's Trial* (1 Burr's Trial, 416), states the rule to be that "light impressions, which may fairly be presumed to yield to the testimony that may be offered, which may leave the mind open to a fair consideration of the testimony, constitute no sufficient objection to a juror; but that those strong and deep impressions which close the mind against the testimony that may be offered in opposition to them, which will combat that testimony and resist its force, do constitute a sufficient objection to him." The theory of the law is that a juror who has formed an opinion cannot be impartial. Every opinion which he may entertain need not necessarily have that effect. In these days of newspaper enterprise and universal education, every case of public interest is almost, as a matter of necessity, brought to the attention of all the intelligent people in the vicinity, and scarcely any one can be found among those best fitted for jurors who has not read or heard of it, and who has not some impression or some opinion in respect to its merits. It is clear, therefore, that upon the trial of the issue of fact raised by a challenge for such cause the court will practically be called upon to determine whether the nature and strength of the opinion formed are such as in law necessarily to raise the presumption of partiality. The question thus presented is one of mixed law and fact, and to be tried, as far as the facts are concerned, like any other issue of that character, upon the evidence. The finding of the trial court upon that issue ought not to be set aside by a reviewing court, unless the error is manifest. No less stringent rules should be applied by the reviewing court in such a case than those which govern in the consideration of motions for new trial because the verdict is against the evidence. It must be made clearly to appear that upon the evidence the court ought to have found the juror had formed such an opinion that he could not in law be deemed impartial. The case must be one in which it is manifest the law left nothing to the "conscience or discretion" of the court.

The challenge in this case most relied upon in the argument here is that of Charles Read. He was sworn on his *voire dire;* and his evidence, taken as a whole, shows that he "believed" he had formed an opinion which he had never expressed, but which he did not think would influence his verdict on hearing the testimony. We cannot think this is such a manifestation of partiality as to leave nothing to the "conscience or discretion" of the triers. The reading of the evidence leaves the impression that the juror had some hypothetical opinion about the case, but it falls far short of raising a manifest presumption of partiality. In considering such questions in a reviewing court, we ought not to be unmindful of the fact we have so often observed

in our experience, that jurors not unfrequently seek to excuse themselves on the ground of having formed an opinion, when, on examination, it turns out that no real disqualification exists. In such cases the manner of the juror while testifying is oftentimes more indicative of the real character of his opinion than his words. That is seen below, but cannot always be spread upon the record. Care should, therefore, be taken in the reviewing court not to reverse the ruling below upon such a question of fact, except in a clear case. The affirmative of the issue is upon the challenger. Unless he shows the actual existence of such an opinion in the mind of the juror as will raise the presumption of partiality, the juror need not necessarily be set aside, and it will not be error in the court to refuse to do so. Such a case, in our opinion, was not made out upon the challenge of Read. The fact that he had not expressed his opinion is important only as tending to show that he had not formed one which disqualified him. If a positive and decided opinion had been formed, he would have been incompetent even though it had not been expressed. Under these circumstances, it is unnecessary to consider the case of Ransohoff, for it was confessedly not as strong as that of Read.

3. As to the challenges by the government.

The questions raised upon these assignments of error are not whether the district attorney should have been permitted to interrogate the jurors while under examination upon their *voire dire* as to the fact of their living in polygamy. No objection was made below to the questions, but only to the ruling of the court upon the challenges after the testimony taken in answer to the questions was in. From the testimony it is apparent that all the jurors to whom the challenges related were or had been living in polygamy. It needs no argument to show that such a jury could not have gone into the box entirely free from bias and prejudice, and that if the challenge was not good for principal cause, it was for favor. A judgment will not be reversed simply because a challenge good for favor was sustained in form for cause. As the jurors were incompetent and properly excluded, it matters not here upon what form of challenge they were set aside. In one case the challenge was for favor. In the courts of the United States all challenges are tried by the court without the aid of triers (Rev. Stat. sect. 819), and we are not advised that the practice in the territorial courts of Utah is different.

4. As to the admission of evidence to prove what was sworn to by Amelia Jane Schofield on a former trial of the accused for the same offence but under a different indictment.

The Constitution gives the accused the right to a trial at which he should be confronted with the witnesses against him; but if a witness is absent by his own wrongful procurement, he cannot complain if competent evidence is admitted to supply the place of that which he has kept away. The Constitution does not guarantee an accused person against the legitimate consequences of his own wrongful acts. It grants him the privilege of being confronted with the witnesses against him; but if he voluntarily keeps the witnesses away, he cannot insist on his privilege. If, therefore, when absent by his procurement, their evidence is supplied in some lawful way, he is in no condition to assert that his constitutional rights have been violated.

In *Lord Morley's Case* (6 State Trials, 770), as long ago as the year 1666, it was resolved in the House of Lords "that in case oath should be made that any witness, who had been examined by the coroner and was then absent, was detained by the means or procurement of the prisoner, and the opinion of the judges asked whether such examination might be read, we should answer, that if their lordships were satisfied by the evidence they had heard that the witness was detained by means or procurement of the prisoner, then the examination might be read; but whether he was detained by means or procurement of the prisoner was matter of fact, of which we were not the judges, but their lordships." This resolution was followed in *Harrison's Case* (12 id. 851), and seems to have been recognized as the law in England ever since. In *Regina v. Scaife* (17 Ad. & El. n. s. 242), all the judges agreed that if the prisoner had resorted to a contrivance to keep a witness out of the way, the deposition of the witness, taken before a magistrate and in the presence of the prisoner, might be read. Other cases to the same effect are to be found, and in this country the ruling has been in the same way. *Drayton v. Wells*, 1 Nott & M. (S. C.) 409; *Williams v. The State*, 19 Ga. 403. So that now, in the leading text-books, it is laid down that if a witness is kept away by the adverse party, his testimony, taken on a former trial between the same parties upon the same issues, may be given in evidence. 1 Greenl. Evid., sect. 163; 1 Taylor, Evid., sect. 446. Mr. Wharton (1 Whart. Evid., sect. 178) seemingly limits the rule somewhat, and confines it to cases where the witness has been corruptly kept away by the party against whom he is to be called, but in reality his statement is the same as that of the others; for in all it is implied that the witness must have been wrongfully kept away. The rule has its foundation in the maxim that no one shall be permitted to take advantage of his own wrong; and, consequently, if there has not been, in legal contemplation, a wrong committed, the way has not been opened for the introduction of the testimony. We are content with this long-established usage, which, so far as we have been able to discover, has rarely been departed from. It is the outgrowth of a maxim based on the principles of common honesty, and, if properly administered, can harm no one.

Such being the rule, the question becomes practically one of fact, to be settled as a preliminary to the admission of secondary evidence. In this respect it is like the preliminary question of the proof of loss of a written instrument, before secondary evidence of the contents of the instrument can be admitted. In *Lord Morley's Case (supra)*, it would seem to have been considered a question for the trial court alone, and not subject to review on error or appeal; but without deeming it necessary to this case to go so far as that, we have no hesitation in saying that the finding of the court below is, at least, to have the effect of a verdict of a jury upon a question of fact, and should not be disturbed unless the error is manifest.

The testimony shows that the absent witness was the alleged second wife of the accused; that she had testified on a former trial for the same offence under another indictment; that she had no home, except with the accused; that at some time before the trial a subpoena had been issued for her, but by mistake she was named as Mary Jane Schobold; that an officer who knew the witness personally went to the house of the accused to serve the subpoena, and on his arrival inquired for her, either by the name of Mary Jane Schofield or Mrs. Reynolds; that he was told by the accused she was not at home; that he then said, "Will you tell me where she is?" that the reply was "No; that will be for you to find out;" that the officer then remarked she was making him considerable trouble, and that she would get into trouble herself; and the accused replied, "Oh, no; she won't, till the subpoena is served upon her," and then, after some further conversation, that "She does not appear in this case."

It being discovered after the trial commenced that a wrong name had been inserted in the subpoena, a new subpoena was issued with the right name, at nine o'clock in the evening. With this the officer went again to the house, and there found a person known as the first wife of the accused. He was told by her that the witness was not there, and had not been for three weeks. He went again the next morning, and not finding her, or being able to ascertain where she was by inquiring in the neighborhood, made return of that fact to the court. At ten o'clock that morning the case was again called; and the foregoing facts being made to appear, the court ruled that evidence of what the witness had sworn to at the former trial was admissible.

In this we see no error. The accused was himself personally present in court when the showing was made, and had full opportunity to account for the absence of the witness, if he would, or to deny under oath that he had kept her away. Clearly, enough had been proven to cast the burden upon him of showing that he had not been instrumental in concealing or keeping the witness away. Having the means of making the necessary explanation, and having every inducement to do so if he would, the presumption is that he considered it better to rely upon the weakness of the case made against him than to attempt to develop the strength of his own. Upon the testimony as it stood, it is clear to our minds that the judgment should not be reversed because secondary evidence was admitted.

This brings us to the consideration of what the former testimony was, and the evidence by which it was proven to the jury.

It was testimony given on a former trial of the same person for the same offence, but under another indictment. It was substantially testimony given at another time in the same cause. The accused was present at the time the testimony was given, and had full opportunity of cross-examination. This brings the case clearly within the well-established rules. The cases are fully cited in 1 Whart. Evid., sect. 177.

The objection to the reading by Mr. Patterson of what was sworn to on the former trial does not seem to have been because the paper from which he read was not a true record of the evidence as given, but because the foundation for admitting the secondary evidence had not been laid. This objection, as has already been seen, was not well taken.

5. As to the defence of religious belief or duty.

On the trial, the plaintiff in error, the accused, proved that at the time of his alleged second marriage he was, and for many years before had been, a member of the Church of Jesus Christ of Latter- Day Saints, commonly called the Mormon Church, and a believer in its doctrines; that it was an accepted doctrine of that church "that it was the duty of male members of said church, circumstances permitting, to practice polygamy; . . . that this duty was enjoined by different book which the members of said church believed to be of divine origin, and among others the Holy Bible, and also that the members of the church believed that the practice of polygamy was directly enjoined upon the male members thereof by the Almighty God, in a revelation to Joseph Smith, the founder and prophet of said church; that the failing or refusing to practice polygamy by such male members of said church, when circumstances would admit, would be punished, and that the penalty for such failure and refusal would be damnation in the life to come." He also proved "that he had received permission from the recognized authorities in said church to enter into polygamous marriage; . . . that Daniel H. Wells, one having authority in said church to perform the marriage ceremony, married the said defendant on or about the time the crime is alleged to have been committed, to some woman by the name of Schofield, and that such marriage ceremony was performed under and pursuant to the doctrines of said church."

Upon this proof he asked the court to instruct the jury that if they found from the evidence that he "was married

as charged—if he was married—in pursuance of and in conformity with what he believed at the time to be a religious duty, that the verdict must be 'not guilty.'" This request was refused, and the court did charge "that there must have been a criminal intent, but that if the defendant, under the influence of a religious belief that it was right —under an inspiration, if you please, that it was right— deliberately married a second time, having a first wife living, the want of consciousness of evil intent—the want of understanding on his part that he was committing a crime —did not excuse him; but the law inexorably in such case implies the criminal intent."

Upon this charge and refusal to charge the question is raised, whether religious belief can be accepted as a justification of an overt act made criminal by the law of the land. The inquiry is not as to the power of Congress to prescribe criminal laws for the Territories, but as to the guilt of one who knowingly violates a law which has been properly enacted, if he entertains a religious belief that the law is wrong.

Congress cannot pass a law for the government of the Territories which shall prohibit the free exercise of religion. The first amendment to the Constitution expressly forbids such legislation. Religious freedom is guaranteed everywhere throughout the United States, so far as congressional interference is concerned. The question to be determined is, whether the law now under consideration comes within this prohibition.

The word "religion" is not defined in the Constitution. We must go elsewhere, therefore, to ascertain its meaning, and nowhere more appropriately, we think, than to the history of the times in the midst of which the provision was adopted. The precise point of the inquiry is, what is the religious freedom which has been guaranteed.

Before the adoption of the Constitution, attempts were made in some of the colonies and States to legislate not only in respect to the establishment of religion, but in respect to its doctrines and precepts as well. The people were taxed, against their will, for the support of religion, and sometimes for the support of particular sects to whose tenets they could not and did not subscribe. Punishments were prescribed for a failure to attend upon public worship, and sometimes for entertaining heretical opinions. The controversy upon this general subject was animated in many of the States, but seemed at last to culminate in Virginia. In 1784, the House of Delegates of that State having under consideration "a bill establishing provision for teachers' of the Christian religion," postponed it until the next session, and directed that the bill should be published and distributed, and that the people be requested "to signify their opinion respecting the adoption of such a bill at the next session of assembly."

This brought out a determined opposition. Amongst others, Mr. Madison prepared a "Memorial and Remonstrance," which was widely circulated and signed, and in which he demonstrated "that religion, or the duty we owe the Creator," was not within the cognizance of civil government. Semple's Virginia Baptists, Appendix. At the next session the proposed bill was not only defeated, but another, "for establishing religious freedom," drafted by Mr. Jefferson, was passed. 1 Jeff. Works, 45; 2 Howison, Hist. of Va. 298. In the preamble of this act (12 Hening's Stat. 84) religious freedom is defined; and after a recital "that to suffer the civil magistrate to intrude his powers into the field of opinion, and to restrain the profession or propagation of principles on supposition of their ill tendency, is a dangerous fallacy which at once destroys all religious liberty," it is declared "that it is time enough for the rightful purposes of civil government for its officers to interfere when principles break out into overt acts against peace and good order." In these two sentences is found the true distinction between what properly belongs to the church and what to the State.

In a little more than a year after the passage of this statute the convention met which prepared the Constitution of the United States." Of this convention Mr. Jefferson was not a member, he being then absent as minister to France. As soon as he saw the draft of the Constitution proposed for adoption, he, in a letter to a friend, expressed his disappointment at the absence of an express declaration insuring the freedom of religion (2 Jeff. Works, 355), but was willing to accept it as it was, trusting that the good sense and honest intentions of the people would bring about the necessary alterations. 1 Jeff. Works, 79. Five of the States, while adopting the Constitution, proposed amendments. Three—New Hampshire, New York, and Virginia—included in one form or another a declaration of religious freedom in the changes they desired to have made, as did also North Carolina, where the convention at first declined to ratify the Constitution until the proposed amendments were acted upon. Accordingly, at the first session of the first Congress the amendment now under consideration was proposed with others by Mr. Madison. It met the views of the advocates of religious freedom, and was adopted. Mr. Jefferson afterwards, in reply to an address to him by a committee of the Danbury Baptist Association (8 id. 113), took occasion to say: "Believing with you that religion is a matter which lies solely between man and his God; that he owes account to none other than his faith or his worship; that the legislative powers of the government reach actions only, and not opinions,—I contemplate with sovereign reverence that act of the whole American people which declared that their legislature should 'make no law respecting an establishment of religion or prohibiting the free exercise thereof,' thus building a wall of separation between church and State. Adhering to this expression of the supreme will of the nation in behalf of the rights of conscience, I shall see with sincere satisfaction the progress of those sentiments which tend to restore man to all his natural rights, convinced he has no natural right in opposition to his social duties." Coming as this does from an acknowledged leader of the advocates of the measure, it may be accepted almost as an authoritative declaration of the scope and effect of the amendment thus secured. Congress was deprived of all legislative power over mere opinion, but was left free to reach actions which were in violation of social duties or subversive of good order.

Polygamy has always been odious among the northern and western nations of Europe, and, until the establishment of the Mormon Church, was almost exclusively a feature of the life of Asiatic and of African people. At common law, the second marriage was always void (2 Kent, Com. 79), and from the earliest history of England polygamy has been treated as an offence against society. After the establishment of the ecclesiastical courts, and until the time of James I., it was punished through the instrumentality of those tribunals, not merely because ecclesiastical rights had been violated, but because upon the separation of the ecclesiastical courts from the civil the ecclesiastical were supposed to be the most appropriate for the trial of matrimonial causes and offences against the rights of marriage, just as they were for testamentary causes and the settlement of the estates of deceased persons.

By the statute of 1 James I. (c. 11), the offence, if committed in England or Wales, was made punishable in the civil courts, and the penalty was death. As this statute was limited in its operation to England and Wales, it was at a very early period re-enacted, generally with some modifications, in all the colonies. In connection with the case we are now considering, it is a significant fact that on the 8th of December, 1788, after the passage of the act establishing religious freedom, and after the convention of Virginia had recommended as an amendment to the Constitution of the United States the declaration in a bill of rights that "all men have an equal, natural, and unalienable right to the free exercise of religion, according to the dictates of conscience," the legislature of that State substantially enacted the statute of James I., death penalty included, because, as recited in the preamble, "it hath been doubted whether bigamy or poligamy be punishable by the laws of this Commonwealth." 12 Hening's Stat. 691. From that day to this we think it may safely be said there never has been a time in any State of the Union when polygamy has not been an offence against society, cognizable by the civil courts and punishable with more or less severity. In the face of all this evidence, it is impossible to believe that the constitutional guaranty of religious freedom was intended to prohibit legislation in respect to this most important feature of social life. Marriage, while from its very nature a sacred obligation, is nevertheless, in most civilized nations, a civil contract, and usually regulated by law. Upon it society may be said to be built, and out of its fruits spring social relations and social obligations and duties, with which government is necessarily required to deal. In fact, according as monogamous or polygamous marriages are allowed, do we find the principles on which the government of the people, to a greater or less extent, rests. Professor Lieber says, polygamy leads to the patriarchal principle, and which, when applied to large communities, fetters the people in stationary despotism, while that principle cannot long exist in connection with monogamy. Chancellor Kent observes that this remark is equally striking and profound. 2 Kent, Com. 81, note (*e*). An exceptional colony of polygamists under an exceptional leadership may sometimes exist for a time without appearing to disturb the social condition of the people who surround it; but there cannot be a doubt that, unless restricted by some form of constitution, it is within the legitimate scope of the power of every civil government to determine whether polygamy or monogamy shall be the law of social life under its dominion.

In our opinion, the statute immediately under consideration is within the legislative power of Congress. It is constitutional and valid as prescribing a rule of action for all those residing in the Territories, and in places over which the United States have exclusive control. This being so, the only question which remains is, whether those who make polygamy a part of their religion are excepted from the operation of the statute. If they are, then those who do not make polygamy a part of their religious belief may be found guilty and punished, while those who do, must be acquitted and go free. This would be introducing a new element into criminal law. Laws are made for the government of actions, and while they cannot interfere with mere religious belief and opinions, they may with practices. Suppose one believed that human sacrifices were a necessary part of religious worship, would it be seriously contended that the civil government under which he lived could not interfere to prevent a sacrifice? Or if a wife religiously believed it was her duty to burn herself upon the funeral pile of her dead husband, would it be beyond the power of the civil government to prevent her carrying her belief into practice?

So here, as a law of the organization of society under the exclusive dominion of the United States, it is provided that plural marriages shall not be allowed. Can a man excuse his practices to the contrary because of his religious belief? To permit this would be to make the professed doctrines of religious belief superior to the law of the land, and in effect to permit every citizen to become a law unto him-

self. Government could exist only in name under such circumstances.

A criminal intent is generally an element of crime, but every man is presumed to intend the necessary and legitimate consequences of what he knowingly does. Here the accused knew he had been once married, and that his first wife was living. He also knew that his second marriage was forbidden by law. When, therefore, he married the second time, he is presumed to have intended to break the law. And the breaking of the law is the crime. Every act necessary to constitute the crime was knowingly done, and the crime was therefore knowingly committed. Ignorance of a fact may sometimes be taken as evidence of a want of criminal intent, but not ignorance of the law. The only defence of the accused in this case in his belief that the law ought not to have been enacted. It matters not that his belief was a part of his professed religion: it was still belief, and belief only.

In *Regina v. Wagstaff* (10 Cox Crim. Cases, 531), the parents of a sick child, who omitted to call in medical attendance because of their religious belief that what they did for its cure would be effective, were held not to be guilty of man-slaughter, while it was said the contrary would have been the result if the child had actually been starved to death by the parents, under the notion that it was their religious duty to abstain from giving it food. But when the offence consists of a positive act which is knowingly done, it would be dangerous to hold that the offender might escape punishment because he religiously believed the law which he had broken ought never to have been made. No case, we believe, can be found that has gone so far.

6. As to that part of the charge which directed the attention of the jury to the consequences of polygamy.

The passage complained of is as follows: "I think it not improper, in the discharge of your duties in this case, that you should consider what are to be the consequences to the innocent victims of this delusion. As this contest goes on, they multiply, and there are pure-minded women and there are innocent children,—innocent in a sense even beyond the degree of the innocence of childhood itself. These are to be the sufferers; and as jurors fail to do their duty, and as these cases come up in the Territory of Utah, just so do these victims multiply and spread themselves over the land."

While every appeal by the court to the passions or the prejudices of a jury should be promptly rebuked, and while it is the imperative duty of a reviewing court to take care that wrong is not done in this way, we see no just cause for complaint in this case. Congress, in 1862 (12 Stat. 501), saw fit to make bigamy a crime in the Territories. This was done because of the evil consequences that were supposed to flow from plural marriages. All the court did was to call the attention of the jury to the peculiar character of the crime for which the accused was on trial, and to remind them of the duty they had to perform. There was no appeal to the passions, no instigation of prejudice. Upon the showing made by the accused himself, he was guilty of a violation of the law under which he had been indicted: and the effort of the court seems to have been not to withdraw the minds of the jury from the issue to be tried, but to bring them to it; not to make them partial, but to keep them impartial.

Upon a careful consideration of the whole case, we are satisfied that no error was committed by the court below.

Judgment affirmed.

Mr. Justice Field. I concur with the majority of the court on the several points decided except one,—that which relates to the admission of the testimony of Amelia Jane Schofield given on a former trial upon a different indictment. I do not think that a sufficient foundation was laid for its introduction. The authorities cited by the Chief Justice to sustain its admissibility seem to me to establish conclusively the exact reverse.

Source:

U.S. Reports, Vol. 98, pp. 145–168.

Pendleton Act, 1883

Legislation passed on January 16, 1883, establishing the U.S. Civil Service Commission and thus ending a long political battle over patronage vs. merit for federal jobs. The act was passed after the 1881 assassination of President James A. Garfield by a disgruntled office-seeker dramatized the need for reform. It established the merit system for federal employment, replacing the spoils system whereby jobs were granted to party loyalists without regard to their competence. Sponsored by Senator George H. Pendleton of Ohio, the legislation provided for a bipartisan three-person commission to administer competitive examinations for civil service appointments. Although the act originally affected only a small percentage of federal employees, it has been broadened considerably over the years.

───────────── ❧ ─────────────

An Act

To regulate and improve the civil service of the United States.

Be it enacted by the Senate and House of Representatives of the United States of America in Congress assembled, That the President is authorized to appoint, by and with the advice and consent of the Senate, three persons, not more than two of whom shall be adherents of the same party, as Civil Service Commissioners, and said three commissioners shall constitute the United States Civil Service Commission. Said commissioners shall hold no other official place under the United States.

The President may remove any commissioner; and any vacancy in the position of commissioner shall be so filled by the President, by and with the advice and consent of the Senate, as to conform to said conditions for the first selection of commissioners.

The commissioners shall each receive a salary of three thousand five hundred dollars a year. And each of said commissioners shall be paid his necessary traveling expenses incurred in the discharge of his duty as a commissioner.

Sec. 2. That it shall be the duty of said commissioners:

First. To aid the President, as he may request, in preparing suitable rules for carrying this act into effect, and when said rules shall have been promulgated it shall be the duty of all officers of the United States in the departments and offices to which any such rules may relate to aid, in all proper ways, in carrying said rules, and any modifications thereof, into effect.

Second. And, among other things, said rules shall provide and declare, as nearly as the conditions of good administration will warrant, as follows:

First, for open, competitive examinations for testing the fitness of applicants for the public service now classified or to be classified hereunder. Such examinations shall be practical in their character, and so far as may be shall relate to those matters which will fairly test the relative capacity and fitness of the persons examined to discharge the duties of the service into which they seek to be appointed.

Second, that all the offices, places, and employments so arranged or to be arranged in classes shall be filled by selections according to grade from among those graded highest as the results of such competitive examinations.

Third, appointments to the public service aforesaid in the departments at Washington shall be apportioned among the several States and Territories and the District of Columbia upon the basis of population as ascertained at the last preceding census. Every application for an examination shall contain, among other things, a statement, under oath, setting forth his or her actual bona fide residence at the time of making the application, as well as how long he or she has been a resident of such place.

Fourth, that there shall be a period of probation before any absolute appointment or employment aforesaid.

Fifth, that no person in the public service is for that reason under any obligations to contribute to any political fund, or to render any political service, and that he will not be removed or otherwise prejudiced for refusing to do so.

Sixth, that no person in said service has any right to use his official authority or influence to coerce the political action of any person or body.

Seventh, there shall be non-competitive examinations in all proper cases before the commission, when competent persons do not compete, after notice has been given of the existence of the vacancy, under such rules as may be prescribed by the commissioners as to the manner of giving notice.

Eighth, that notice shall be given in writing by the appointing power to said commission of the persons selected for appointment or employment from among those who have been examined, of the place of residence of such persons, of the rejection of any such persons after probation, of transfers, resignations, and removals, and of the date thereof, and a record of the same shall be kept by said commission. And any necessary exceptions from said eight fundamental provisions of the rules shall be set forth in connection with such rules, and the reasons therefor shall be stated in the annual reports of the commission.

Third. Said commission shall, subject to the rules that may be made by the President, make regulations for, and have control of, such examinations, and, through its members or the examiners, it shall supervise and preserve the records of the same; and said commission shall keep minutes of its own proceedings.

Fourth, Said commission may make investigations concerning the facts, and may report upon all matters touching the enforcement and effects of said rules and regulations, and concerning the action of any examiner or board of examiners hereinafter provided for, and its own subordinates, and those in the public service, in respect to the execution of this act.

Fifth. Said commission shall make an annual report to the President for transmission to Congress, showing its own action, the rules and regulations and the exceptions thereto in force, the practical effects thereof, and any suggestions it may approve for the more effectual accomplishment of the purposes of this act.

Sec. 3. That said commission is authorized to employ a chief examiner, a part of whose duty it shall be, under its direction, to act with the examining boards, so far as practicable, whether at Washington or elsewhere, and to secure accuracy, uniformity, and justice in all their proceedings, which shall be at all times open to him. The chief examiner shall be entitled to receive a salary at the rate of three thousand dollars a year, and he shall be paid his necessary traveling expenses incurred in the discharge of his duty. The commission shall have a secretary, to be appointed by the President, who shall receive a salary of one thousand six hundred dollars per annum. It may, when necessary, employ a stenographer, and a messenger, who shall be paid, when employed, the former at the rate of one thousand six hundred dollars a year, and the latter at the rate of six hundred dollars a year. The commission shall, at Washington, and in one or more places in each State and Terri-

tory where examinations are to take place, designate and select a suitable number of persons, not less than three, in the official service of the United States, residing in said State or Territory, after consulting the head of the department or office in which such persons serve, to be members of boards of examiners, and may at any time substitute any other person in said service living in such State or Territory in the place of any one so selected. Such boards of examiners shall be so located as to make it reasonably convenient and inexpensive for applicants to attend before them; and where there are persons to be examined in any State or Territory, examinations shall be held therein at least twice in each year. It shall be the duty of the collector, postmaster, and other officers of the United States, at any place outside of the District of Columbia where examinations are directed by the President or by said board to be held, to allow the reasonable use of the public buildings for holding such examinations, and in all proper ways to facilitate the same.

Sec. 4. That it shall be the duty of the Secretary of the Interior to cause suitable and convenient rooms and accommodations to be assigned or provided, and to be furnished, heated, and lighted, at the city of Washington, for carrying on the work of said commission and said examinations, and to cause the necessary stationery and other articles to be supplied, and the necessary printing to be done for said commission.

Sec. 5. That any said commissioner, examiner, copyist, or messenger, or any person in the public service who shall willfully and corruptly, by himself or in co-operation with one or more other persons, defeat, deceive, or obstruct any person in respect of his or her right of examination according to any such rules or regulations, or who shall willfully, corruptly, and falsely mark, grade, estimate, or report upon the examination or proper standing of any person examined hereunder, or aid in so doing, or who shall willfully and corruptly make any false representations concerning the same or concerning the person examined, or who shall willfully and corruptly furnish to any person any special or secret information for the purpose of either improving or injuring the prospects or chances of any person so examined, or to be examined, being appointed, employed, or promoted, shall for each such offense be deemed guilty of a misdemeanor, and upon conviction thereof, shall be punished by a fine of not less than one hundred dollars, nor more than one thousand dollars, or by imprisonment not less than ten days, nor more than one year, or by both such fine and imprisonment.

Sec. 6. That within sixty days after the passage of this act it shall be the duty of the Secretary of the Treasury, in as near conformity as may be to the classification of certain clerks now existing under the one hundred and sixty-third section of the Revised Statutes, to arrange in classes the several clerks and persons employed by the collector, naval officer, surveyor, and appraisers, or either of them, or being in the public service, at their respective offices in each customs district where the whole number of said clerks and persons shall be all together as many as fifty. And thereafter, from time to time, on the direction of the President, said Secretary shall make the like classification or arrangement of clerks and persons so employed, in connection with any said office or offices, in any other customs district. And, upon like request, and for the purposes of this act, said Secretary shall arrange in one or more of said classes, or of existing classes, any other clerks, agents, or persons employed under his department in any said district not now classified; and every such arrangement and classification upon being made shall be reported to the President.

Second. Within said sixty days it shall be the duty of the Postmaster, to separately arrange in classes the several clerks and persons employed, or in the public service, at each post-office, or under any postmaster of the United States, where the whole number of said clerks and persons shall together amount to as many as fifty. And thereafter, from time to time, on the direction of the President, it shall be the duty of the Postmaster-General to arrange in like classes the clerks and persons so employed in the postal service in connection with any other post office; and every such arrangement and classification upon being made shall be reported to the President.

Third. That from time to time said Secretary, the Postmaster-General, and each of the heads of departments mentioned in the one hundred and fifty-eighth section of the Revised Statutes, and each head of an office, shall, on the direction of the President, and for facilitating the execution of this act, respectively revise any then existing classification or arrangement of those in their respective departments and offices, and shall, for the purposes of the examination herein provided for, include in one or more of such classes, so far as practicable, subordinate places, clerks, and officers in the public service pertaining to their respective departments not before classified for examination.

Sec. 7. That after the expiration of six months from the passage of this act no officer or clerk shall be appointed, and no person shall be employed to enter or be promoted in either of the said classes now existing, or that may be arranged hereunder pursuant to said rules, until he has passed an examination, or is shown to be specially exempted from such examination in conformity herewith. But nothing herein contained shall be construed to take from those honorably discharged from the military or naval service any preference conferred by the seventeen hundred and fifty-four section of the Revised Statutes, nor to take from the President any authority not inconsistent with this act conferred by the seventeen hundred and fifty-third section of said statutes; nor shall any officer not in the executive branch of the government, or any person merely employed as a laborer or workman, be required to be classified hereunder; nor, unless by direction of the Senate, shall any person who has been nominated for confirmation by the Senate be required to be classified or to pass an examination.

Sec. 8. That no person habitually using intoxicating beverages to excess shall be appointed to, or retained in, any office, appointment, or employment to which the provisions of this act are applicable.

Sec. 9. That whenever there are already two or more members of a family in the public service in the grades covered by this act, no other member of such family shall be eligible to appointment to any of said grades.

Sec. 10. That no recommendation of any person who shall apply for office or place under the provisions of this act which may be given by any Senator or member of the House of Representatives, except as to the character or residence of the applicant, shall be received or considered by any person concerned in making any examination or appointment under this act.

Sec. 11. That no Senator, or Representative, or Territorial Delegate of the Congress, or Senator, Representative, or Delegate elect, or any officer or employee of either of said houses, and no executive, judicial, military, or naval officer of the United States, and no clerk or employee of any department, branch or bureau of the executive, judicial, or military or naval service of the United States, shall, directly or indirectly, solicit or receive, or be in any manner concerned in soliciting or receiving, any assessment, subscription, or contribution for any political purpose whatever, from any officer, clerk, or employee of the United States, or any department, branch, or bureau thereof, or from any person receiving any salary of compensation from moneys derived from the Treasury of the United States.

Sec. 12. That no person shall, in any room or building occupied in the discharge of official duties by any officer or employee of the United States mentioned in this act, or in any navy-yard, fort, or arsenal, solicit in any manner whatever, or receive any contribution of money or any other thing of value for any political purpose whatever.

Sec. 13. No officer or employee of the United States mentioned in this act shall discharge, or promote, or degrade, or in manner change the official rank or compensation of any other officer or employee, or promise or threaten so to do, for giving or withholding or neglecting to make any contribution of money or other valuable thing for any political purpose.

Sec. 14. That no officer, clerk, or other person in the service of the United States shall, directly or indirectly, give or hand over to any other officer, clerk, or person in the service of the United States, or to any Senator or Member of the House of Representatives, or Territorial Delegate, any money or other valuable thing on account of or to be applied to the promotion of any political object whatever.

Sec. 15. That any person who shall be guilty of violating any provision of the four foregoing sections shall be deemed guilty of a misdemeanor, and shall, on conviction thereof, be punished by a fine not exceeding five thousand dollars, or by imprisonment for a term not exceeding three years, or by such fine and imprisonment both, in the discretion of the court.

Source:
Statutes at Large, Vol. 23, pp. 403–407.

Electoral Count Act, 1887

Federal legislation passed in 1887 that was designed to prevent a disputed national election. The act provided that each state is the final judge over its own electoral returns and that Congress must accept returns certified by the authorized state tribunal in accordance with the state's own laws. Congress may intervene only if the state itself is unable to decide or has made an irregular decision. In such cases the two houses of Congress shall decide concurrently. The act resulted from the 1876 presidential election dispute between Samuel J. Tilden and Rutherford B. Hayes. It was also relevant for the election of 2000, when the presidency hung on the Florida vote count.

An Act
To fix the day for the meeting of the electors of President and Vice-President, and to provide for and regulate the counting of the votes for President and Vice-President, and the decision of questions arising thereon.

Be it enacted by the Senate and House of Representatives of the United States of America in Congress assembled, That the electors of each State shall meet and give their votes on the second Monday in January next following their appointment, at such place in each State as the legislature of such State shall direct.

Sec. 2. That if any State shall have provided, by laws enacted prior to the day fixed for the appointment of the electors, for its final determination of any controversy or contest concerning the appointment of all or any of the electors of such State, by judicial or other methods or procedures, and such determination shall have been made at least six days before the time fixed for the meeting of the electors, such determination made pursuant to such law so

existing on said day, and made at least six days prior to the said time of meeting of the electors, shall be conclusive, and shall govern in the counting of the electoral votes as provided in the Constitution, and as hereinafter regulated, so far as the ascertainment of the electors appointed by such State is concerned.

Sec. 3. That it shall be the duty of the executive of each State, as soon as practicable after the conclusion of the appointment of electors in such State, by the final ascertainment under and in pursuance of the laws of such State providing for such ascertainment, to communicate, under the seal of the State, to the Secretary of State of the United States, a certificate of such ascertainment of the electors appointed, setting forth the names of such electors and the canvass or other ascertainment under the laws of such State of the number of votes given or cast for each person for whose appointment any and all votes have been given or cast; and it shall also thereupon be the duty of the executive of each State to deliver to the electors of such State, on or before the day on which they are required by the preceding section to meet the same certificate, in triplicate, under the seal of the State; and such certificate shall be inclosed and transmitted by the electors at the same time and in the same manner as is provided by law for transmitting by such electors to the seat of Government the lists of all persons voted for as President and of all persons voted for as Vice-President; and section one hundred and thirty-six of the Revised Statutes is hereby repealed; and if there shall have been any final determination in a State of a controversy or contest as provided for in section two of this act, it shall be the duty of the executive of such State, as soon as practicable after such determination, to communicate, under the seal of the State, to the Secretary of State of the United States, a certificate of such determination, in form and manner as the same shall have been made; and the Secretary of State of the United States, as soon as practicable after the receipt at the State Department of each of the certificates hereinbefore directed to be transmitted to the Secretary of State, shall publish, in such public newspaper as he shall designate, such certificates in full; and at the first meeting of Congress thereafter he shall transmit to the two Houses of Congress copies in full of each and every such certificate so received theretofore at the State Department.

Sec. 4. That Congress shall be in session on the second Wednesday in February succeeding every meeting of the electors. The Senate and House of Representatives shall meet in the Hall of the House of Representatives at the hour of one o'clock in the afternoon on that day, and the President of the Senate shall be their presiding officer. Two tellers shall be previously appointed on the part of the Senate and two on the part of the House of Representatives, to whom shall be handed, as they are opened by the

President of the Senate, all the certificates and papers purporting to be certificates of the electoral votes, which certificates and papers shall be opened, presented, and acted upon in the alphabetical order of the States, beginning with the letter A; and said tellers, having then read the same in the presence and hearing of the two Houses, shall make a list of the votes as they shall appear from the said certificates; and the votes having been ascertained and counted in the manner and according to the rules in this act provided, the result of the same shall be delivered to the President of the Senate, who shall thereupon announce the state of the vote, which announcement shall be deemed a sufficient declaration of the persons, if any, elected President and Vice-President of the United States, and, together with a list of the votes, be entered on the Journals of the two Houses. Upon such reading of any such certificate or paper, the President of the Senate shall call for objections, if any. Every objection shall be made in writing, and shall state clearly and concisely, and without argument, the ground thereof, and shall be signed by at least one Senator and one Member of the House of Representatives before the same shall be received. When all objections so made to any vote or paper from a State shall have been received and read, the Senate shall thereupon withdraw, and such objections shall be submitted to the Senate for its decision; and the Speaker of the House of Representatives shall, in like manner, submit such objections to the House of Representatives for its decision; and no electoral vote or votes from any State which shall have been regularly given by electors whose appointment has been lawfully certified to according to section three of this act from which but one return has been received shall be rejected, but the two Houses concurrently may reject the vote or votes when they agree that such vote or votes have not been so regularly given by electors whose appointment has been so certified. If more than one return or paper purporting to be a return from a State shall have been received by the President of the Senate, those votes, and those only, shall be counted which shall have been regularly given by the electors who are shown by the determination mentioned in section two of this act to have been appointed, if the determination in said section provided for shall have been made, or by such successors or substitutes, in case of a vacancy in the board of electors so ascertained, as have been appointed to fill such vacancy in the mode provided by the laws of the State; but in case there shall arise the question which of two or more of such State authorities determining what electors have been appointed, as mentioned in section two of this act, is the lawful tribunal of such State, the votes regularly given of those electors, and those only, of such State shall be counted whose title as electors the two Houses, acting separately, shall concurrently decide is supported by the deci-

sion of such State so authorized by its laws; and in such case of more than one return or paper purporting to be a return from a State, if there shall have been no such determination of the question in the State aforesaid, then those votes, and those only, shall be counted which the two Houses shall concurrently decide were cast by lawful electors appointed in accordance with the laws of the State, unless the two Houses, acting separately, shall concurrently decide such votes not to be the lawful votes of the legally appointed electors of such State. But if the two Houses shall disagree in respect of the counting of such votes, then, and in that case, the votes of the electors whose appointment shall have been certified by the Executive of the State, under the seal thereof, shall be counted. When the two Houses have voted, they shall immediately again meet, and the presiding officer shall then announce the decision of the questions submitted. No votes or papers from any other State shall be acted upon until the objections previously made to the votes or papers from any State shall have been finally disposed of.

Sec. 5. That while the two Houses shall be in meeting as provided in this act the President of the Senate shall have power to preserve order; and no debate shall be allowed and no question shall be put by the presiding officer except to either House on a motion to withdraw.

Sec. 6. That when the two Houses separate to decide upon an objection that may have been made to the counting of any electoral vote or votes from any State, or other question arising in the matter, each Senator and Representative may speak to such objection or question five minutes, and not more than once; but after such debate shall have lasted two hours it shall be the duty of the presiding officer of each House to put the main question without further debate.

Sec. 7. That at such joint meeting of the two Houses seats shall be provided as follows: For the President of the Senate, the Speaker's chair; for the Speaker, immediately upon his left; the Senators, in the body of the Hall upon the right of the presiding officer; for the Representatives, in the body of the Hall not provided for the Senators; for the tellers, Secretary of the Senate, and Clerk of the House of Representatives, at the Clerk's desk; for the other officers of the two Houses, in front of the Clerk's desk and upon each side of the Speaker's platform. Such joint meeting shall not be dissolved until the count of electoral votes shall be completed and the result declared; and no recess shall be taken unless a question shall have arisen in regard to counting any such votes, or otherwise under this act, in which case it shall be competent for either House, acting separately, in the manner hereinbefore provided, to direct a recess of such House not beyond the next calendar day, Sunday excepted, at the hour of ten o'clock in the forenoon. But if the counting of the electoral votes and the declaration of the result shall not have been completed before the fifth calendar day next after such first meeting of the two Houses, no further or other recess shall be taken by either House.

Source:
Statutes at Large, Vol. 25, pp. 373–375.

Sherman Silver Purchase Act, 1890

Federal legislation enacted on July 14, 1890, requiring the federal government to purchase 4.5 million ounces of silver per month at the prevailing market price. It also required the U.S. Treasury to issue, in payment, legal tender notes redeemable in gold or silver coin. The bill was a compromise between free-silver advocates and gold supporters; both groups had been dissatisfied with the Bland-Allison Act. The act, named for Republican senator John Sherman, failed to raise the price of silver and seriously weakened the federal gold reserve by increasing the circulation of redeemable paper currency. In 1893 President Grover Cleveland called a special session of Congress to repeal the act.

─────────── ❦ ───────────

An Act
Directing the purchase of silver bullion and the issue of Treasury notes thereon, and for other purposes.

Be it enacted by the Senate and House of Representatives of the United States of America in Congress assembled, That the Secretary of the Treasury is hereby directed to purchase, from time to time, silver bullion to the aggregate amount of four million five hundred thousand ounces, or so much thereof as may be offered in each month, at the market price thereof, not exceeding one dollar for three hundred and seventy-one and twenty-five hundredths grains of pure silver, and to issue in payment for such purchases of silver bullion Treasury notes of the United States to be prepared by the Secretary of the Treasury, in such form and of such denominations, not less than one dollar nor more than one thousand dollars, as he may prescribe, and a sum sufficient to carry into effect the provisions of this act is hereby appropriated out of any money in the Treasury not otherwise appropriated.

Sec. 2. That the Treasury notes issued in accordance with the provisions of this act shall be redeemable on demand, in coin, at the Treasury of the United States, or at the office of any assistant treasurer of the United States, and when so redeemed may be reissued; but no greater or less amount of such notes shall be outstanding at any time than the cost of the silver bullion and the standard silver dollars coined therefrom, then held in the

Treasury purchased by such notes; and such Treasury notes shall be a legal tender in payment of all debts, public and private, except where otherwise expressly stipulated in the contract, and shall be receivable for customs, taxes, and all public dues, and when so received may be reissued; and such notes, when held by any national banking association, may be counted as a part of its lawful reserve. That upon demand of the holder of any of the Treasury notes herein provided for the Secretary of the Treasury shall, under such regulations as he may prescribe, redeem such notes in gold or silver coin, at his discretion, it being the established policy of the United States to maintain the two metals on a parity with each other upon the present legal ratio, or such ratio as may be provided by law.

Sec. 3. That the Secretary of the Treasury shall each month coin two million ounces of the silver bullion purchased under the provisions of this act into standard silver dollars until the first day of July eighteen hundred and ninety-one, and after that time he shall coin of the silver bullion purchased under the provisions of this act as much as may be necessary to provide for the redemption of the Treasury notes herein provided for, and any gain or seigniorage arising from such coinage shall be accounted for and paid into the Treasury.

Sec. 4. That the silver bullion purchased under the provisions of this act shall be subject to the requirements of existing law and the regulations of the mint service governing the methods of determining the amount of pure silver contained, and the amount of charges or deductions, if any, to be made.

Sec. 5. That so much of the act of February twenty-eighth, eighteen hundred and seventy-eight, entitled "An act to authorize the coinage of the standard silver dollar and to re tore its legal-tender character," as requires the monthly purchase and coinage of the same into silver dollars of not less than two million dollars, nor more than four million dollars' worth of silver bullion, is hereby repealed.

Sec. 6. That upon the passage of this act the balances standing with the Treasurer of the United States to the respective credits of national banks for deposits made to redeem the circulating notes of such banks, and all deposits thereafter received for like purpose, shall be covered into the Treasury as a miscellaneous receipt, and the Treasury of the United States shall redeem from the general cash in the Treasury the circulating notes of said banks which may come into his possession subject to redemption; and upon the certificate of the Comptroller of the Currency that such notes have been received by him and that they have been destroyed and that no new notes will be issued in their place, reimbursement of their amount shall be made to the Treasurer, under such regulations as the Secretary of the Treasury may prescribe, from an appropriation hereby, created, to be known as 'National bank notes: Redemption account, but the provisions of this act shall not apply to the deposits received under section three of the act of June twentieth, eighteen hundred and seventy-four, requiring every National bank to keep in lawful money with the Treasurer of the United States a sum equal to five percentum of its circulation, to be held and used for the redemption of its circulating notes; and the balance remaining of the deposits so covered shall, at the close of each month, be reported on the monthly public debt statement as debt of the United States bearing no interest.

Sec. 7. That this act shall take effect thirty days from and after its passage.

Source:
Statutes at Large, Vol. 26, pp. 289–290.

"Pitchfork" Ben Tillman, "Shell Manifesto," 1890

American address written by Benjamin Tillman, a Democrat and leader of the agrarian movement in South Carolina; published over the signature of G. W. Shell, president of the Farmers' Association of South Carolina, during Tillman's successful campaign for the governorship in 1890. The document combined disdain for the "aristocratic coterie" governing the state and elements of agrarian reform with a call for the preservation of white supremacy. The manifesto demanded greater economy and efficiency in government, cheaper and more practical education for farmers and mechanics, and protection of agricultural interests from greedy phosphate miners and fertilizer companies. Tillman went on to perfect race-baiting as a political technique and to become one of the leading racists in congress.

───────────⟨∞⟩───────────

To the Democracy of South Carolina: For four years the Democratic party in the State has been deeply agitated, and efforts have been made at the primaries and conventions to secure retrenchment and reform, and a recognition of the needs and rights of the masses. The first Farmers' Convention met in April, 1886. Another in November of the same year perfected a permanent organization under the name of the "Farmers' Association of South Carolina." This association, representing the reform element in the party, has held two annual sessions since, and at each of these four conventions, largely attended by representative farmers from nearly all the counties, the demands of the people for greater economy in the Government, greater efficiency in its officials, and a fuller recognition of the necessity for cheaper and mere practical education have been pressed upon the attention of our Legislators.

In each of the two last Democratic State Conventions the "Farmers' Movement" has had a large following, and we only failed of controlling the Convention of 1888 by a small vote-less than twenty-five—and that, too, in the face of the active opposition of nearly every trained politician in the State. We claim that we have always had a majority of the people on our side, and have only failed by reason of the superior political tactics of our opponents and our lack of organization. In proof of this we point to Abbeville and Chester, the only counties except Charleston which had not already appointed delegates to the State Convention before the campaign meetings two years ago, at which Governor Richardson spoke. Both of those counties, after hearing the Governor defend his policy and that of his faction, repudiated defend him and it, and he received only two votes from them.

The executive committee of the Farmers Association did not deem it worth while to hold any convention last November, but we have watched closely every move of the enemies of economy—the enemies of agricultural education, the enemies of true Jefferson in Democracy—and we think the time has come to show the people what it is they need and how to accomplish their desires. We will draw up the indictment against those who have been and are still governing our State, because it is at once the cause and justification of the course we intend to pursue.

South Carolina has never had a real Republican government. Since the days of the "Lords Proprietors" it has been an aristocracy under the forms of Democracy, and whenever a champion of the people has attempted to show them their rights and advocate those rights as aristocratic oligarchy has bought him with an office, or falling in that turned loose the floodgates of misrepresentation and slander in order to destroy his influence.

The peculiar situation now existing in the State, requiring the united efforts of every true white man to preserve white supremacy and our very civilization even, has intensified and tended to make permanent the conditions which existed before the war. Fear of a division among us and consequent return of negro rule has kept the people quiet, and they have submitted to many grievances imposed by the ruling faction because they dreaded to risk such a division.

The "Farmers' Movement" has been hampered and retarded in this work by this condition of the public mind, but we have shown our realty to race by submitting to the edicts of the party, and we intend, as heretofore, to make our fight inside the party lines, fooling assured that truth and justice must finally prevail. The results of the agitation thus far are altogether encouraging. Inch by inch and step by step true Democracy the rule of the people—has won its way. We have carried all the outposts. Only two strongholds remain to be taken, and with the issues fairly made up and plainly put the people we have no fear of the result. The House of Representatives has been carried twice, and at last held after a desperate struggle.

The advocates of reform and economy are no longer sneered at as "Three for a quarter statesmen." They pass measures of economy which four years ago would have excited only decision, and with the Farmers' Movement to strengthen their backbone have withstood the cajo'ery, threats and impotent rage of the old "ring losses." The Senate is now the main reliance of the enemies of retrenchment and reform, who oppose giving the people their rights. The Senate is the stronghold of "existing institutions," and the main dependence of those who are antagonistic to all progress. As we captured the House we can capture the Senate; but we must control the Democratic State Convention before we can hope to make economy popular in Columbia, or be assured of no more pocket vetoes.

The General Assembly is largely influenced by the idea and policy of the State officers, and we must elect those before we can say the Farmers' Movement has accomplished its mission. It is true that we have wrenched from the aristocratic coterie who were educated at and sought to monopolize everything for the South Carolina College, the right to control the land scrip and Hatch fund and a part of the privilege tax on fertilizers for one year, and we have $10,000 with which to commence building a separate agricultural college, where the sons of poor farmers can get a practical education at small expense.

But we dare not relax our efforts or rely upon the loud professions of our opponents as to their willingness now to build and equip this agricultural school. Senator McMaster, a trustee of the South Carolina College, gave voice to the sentiments and wishes which are prevalent at the University and Military Academy when he "hoped to see the infernal Clemeon College sink out of sight next year." They all want to sink the "internal" Agricultural College out of sight, and if its friends do not rally once more to its support it will either be destroyed or starved, so that it cannot do the great work it is expected to accomplish.

All the cry about "existing institutions" which must remain inviolate shows that the ring—the South Carolina University, Citadel, Agricultural Bureau, Columbia Club, Greenfield building ring—intend in the future, as in the past, to get all they can, and keep all they get. These pets of the aristocracy and its nurseries are only hoping that the people will again sink into their accustomed apathy. The mechanical department of the University was given an increased appropriation, and there is no thought of transferring it to Fort Hill, although the land scrip fund, which

is sent there, was expressly donated for the purpose of mechanical as well as agricultural education, and so with experiment stations. The Hatch fund is given to the Clemeon College, but the stations are left at Columbia and Spartanburg, under the control of the South Carolina College.

Is it not plain that these people intend to yield obedience to the law only when they are made to do it? The Farmers' Association demands that the land scrip and Hatch funds and the fertilizer tax shall be consolidated and used for the building and maintenance of a first class industrial school, with experiment stations attached, for farmers and mechanics. We hold that the experimental work, the educational work and the inspection and analysis of fertilizers can all be more efficiently and economically carried on under one board, mostly at one place, and much of it by the same corps of men and who teach.

We have never and do not now want any increase of taxes to accomplish those ends. But our opponents having seized the opportunity afforded by our agitation to double the income of the South Carolina College and call it a university, and in addition, obtained the Hatch fund of $15,000, donated for experiment stations, cry out: "Take your Clemson College. We will give you $98,000 or $198,000, if you want it raised by taxation, but you don't touch existing institutions." They have built with our bricks but say we must not take them, but that we can build if we make others. Was there ever such impudence?

They seized first the land scrip fund. Then they misappropriated the Hatch fund: they increased the taxes $65,000 a year to equip and maintain the different departments of the grand University: they voted $60,000 in one jump without even a division to rebuild, repair and equip the Citadel Academy, and then say to taxpaying farmers. "Leave our existing institutions" alone. Let the agricultural bureau with its board—who are our chosen sons every man of them belonging to or aspiring to belong to our aristocratic ring—let this bureau waste $30,000 a year more. Leave our experiment stations at Darlington, Columbia and Spartanburg alone. We expect to control votes with them and they must not be touched.

Put your hands in your pockets and pay for your Clemson College if you will have it, and we will vote the taxes. An analysis of the vote in the House and Senate which defeated the consolidations of all our agricultural work shows that the board and department of agriculture are sustained by the fertilizer manufacturers, the phosphate miners and the University and Citadel. If a farmer voted for its continuance it is because he felt that the South Carolina University would lose something by abolition. The support of the fertilizer companies is easy to understand. This bureau has been their best friend. Year after year we have been told by Commissioner Butter, that the guanos inspected were below the guarantees, but nobody has been punished, in fact there is no adequate punishment for selling fraudulent guanos in this State.

The bill prepared by the committee of the Farmers' Association for the reorganization or the board of agriculture would have secured our farmers against swindling fertilizer dealers, but it was amended to death by the lawyers in the Senate, who are attorneys for the phosphate miners and fertilizer companies, and the men who were elected on the board over the nominees of the Farmers' Convention were chosen not because they are more loyal to the agricultural interests, or better fitted for the position, but because they are friends of the University and belong or are subservient to our aristocracy—"so called"—and the phosphate miners are too well satisfied with the system of collecting the state royalty to permit a change if they can help it.

How wonderfully perfect or defective this system is, is shown by the fact that during ten years under the same officials not a single indictment has been brought against any one for attempting to swindle the State out of its dues. No wonder Charleston is in love with the agricultural bureau, and cannot bear to see that "existing institution" disturbed.

The recent proposal to sell the State's interest in the phosphate beds is fortunate, because thereby the attention of taxpayers is attracted to this most important matter. The Farmers' Association proposed in 1880 to increase the royalty as a means of lowering taxes, and we believe this can be safely done to the extent of $100,000.

A legislative committee was appointed to "investigate" and report on the subject. This was only done to give time—waiting ten months until the market had been manipulated, etc. This committee proceeded to show how well it had been chosen "not to do it." There was no honest effort made to get at the real facts as to the profits of the business and its ability to stand an increase of royalty, and after it had been "wined and dined" and brought into a suitable frame of mind that committee came to Columbia and actually proposed to give the six largest companies a monopoly for a less annual rental than the State was then receiving. Only one Senator, to whom all honor is due, dissented from this outrageous proposal. What was the result?

Of course the General Assembly did not act favorably upon it, but all thought of an increase of royalty was also abandoned, and this was what the corporation attorneys who were there in the interest of their clients and not of their constituents had been working for. "The goose that lays the golden egg" was not killed—"existing institutions" were not disturbed. Phosphate rock, which had been manipulated down to $3.40 per ton, advanced in two months after the Legislature adjourned to $6, and has

since ruled between $5.50 and $7.50 per ton. The golden eggs are still being laid, but not in the State's neat—whether some of them have not gone into pockets which they ought not to an open question.

Now we want to warn the people that the charter of the Coosaw Company obtained by bribery, it is said, of a Radical Legislature—expires in 1891. This company, which has grown fabulously rich, claims to have a perpetual contract, with exclusive right to mine in Coosaw River and pay only one dollar a ten for the privilege. The next Legislature must act on this question, and the next Attorney General may have to test those claims in Court. The whole question of phosphate management, or mismanagement, must be settled. Can the taxpayers afford to allow any but true men to go to the Senate, or elect a corporations lawyer as Attorney General? Shall the politicians choose him, or shall we, casting about among the many honorable, patriotic lawyers of the State, make the selection ourselves?

The Legislature which has just adjourned has other sins to answer for, or rather the Senate must be held responsible. The people demanded that the railroad commissioners should have something to do besides draw their salaries and spend them. We want protection against the greed of the gigantic corporations owned at the North, which regard South Carolina as a lemon to be squeezed and care nothing for the welfare of our towns, our State, our people.

The railroad laws of 18—made the commission a power to defend the people against imposition. The same Legislature which enacted it, having been Bamboozled or debauched, at the very next session left it only as a sinecure with fat salaries and no power. We have just seen the same disgraceful farce repeated. This law was vastly improved at the session of 1888, but after a year which has shown the weakness and unfitness of the press it incumbents, for they have done very little, the Senate peremptorily refused to make any changes.

The railroad commissioners now in office have been "tamed," so to speak, by the railroads, and men who have not been so long under their wing might have done something in the interest of the people; but that same Senate which has again and again thwarted the people, which refuses to reduce salaries, which fought the Clemson College and yielded at last to necessity only, which is the strong-hold of aristocracy with its non-progressive, impracticable ideas, which, in a word, is dominated by Charleston's a rich politicians—that Senate resolved to maintain this "existing institution," too, status quo.

Of all the taxes we pay, the pensions to Confederate veterans are submitted to most willingly, and we regret that we cannot increase the pittance they receive. But the continuance of men in office as political pensioners, after their ability or willingness to serve the people is gone—when the interests and even rights of the people are thereby sacrificed, this pandering to sentiment, this favoritism—is a crime, nothing more and nothing less. Rotation in office is a cardinal Democratic principle, and the neglect to practice it is the cause of many of the ills we suffer.

We cannot elaborate the other counts in this indictment. We can only point briefly to the mismanagement of the Penitentiary, which is a burden on the taxpayers, even while engaged in no public works which might benefit the State. To this wrong committed against the people of many counties (strongholds of Democracy) by the failure to reapportion representation according to population, whereby Charleston has five votes in the House and ten votes in the State Convention, which choose our State officers, to which it is not entitled.

To the zeal and extravagance of this aristocratic oligarchy, whose sins we are pointing out, in promising higher education for every class except farmers, while it neglects the free schools which are the only chance for an education to thousands of poor children, whose fathers bore the brunt in the struggle for our redemption in 1876. To the continued recurrence of horrible lynchings—which we can but attribute to bad laws and their inefficient administration. To the impotence of justice to punish criminals who have money. To the failure to call a constitutional convention that we may have an organic law framed by South Carolinians for South Carolinians, and suited to our wants, thereby lessening the burdens of taxation and giving us better government.

Fellow Democrats, do not all these things cry out for a change? Is it not opportune, when there is no national election, for the common people who redeemed the State from Radical rule to take charge of it? Can we afford to leave it longer in the hands of those who, wedded to ante-bellum ideas, but possessing little of ante-bellum patriotism and honor, are running it in the interest of a few families and for the benefit of a selfish ring of politicians? As real Democrats and white men, those who here renew our pledge to make the fight inside the Democratic party and abide the result, we call upon every true Carolinian, of all classes and callings, to help us purify and reform the Democratic party and give us a government of the people, by the people and for the people.

If we control the State Democratic Convention, a Legislature in sympathy will naturally follow; failing to do this, we risk losing all we have gained, and have no hope of any change for the better. The logic of events and pass experience show that we must nominate candidates and put them in the field early, so that the masses will understand what they must do to bring about the change we so

desire. Such course will cause an active canvas, wide discussion of the issues presented, and the people thus learning the truth can show whether, they are in favor of the Farmers" Movement or not, by electing or rejecting our nominees.

We therefore issue this call for a Convention of those Democrats who sympathize with our views and purposes, as herein set forth, to meet in Columbia, in the House of Representatives, on Thursday, the 27th day of March proximo, at 12 o'clock M, to nominate a ticket for every State office, from Governor down, to be put in the field for ratification or rejection by the next Democratic State Convention, and we pledge ourselves to abide the remit, whether that is for or against us.

Each county will sent as many delegates as it sends to the State Convention, and we suggest that a mass meeting or convention be called in each county to elect delegates on salesday in March.

By order of the executive committee of the Farmers' Association of South Carolina.

Source:

Benjamin R. Tillman. *The Coming Campaign: A Contest Proposed Within the Democratic Party.* Columbia, S.C.: 1961. (Courtesy of University of South Carolina. South Caroliniana Library, Columbia, South Carolina.)

Ocala Platform, 1890

Set of demands adopted by the National Farmers' Alliance and Industrial Union, meeting at Ocala, Florida, in December 1890. The platform demanded the abolition of national banks, the establishment of subtreasuries to provide low interest loans, an increase in circulating money, the prohibition of futures dealings on agricultural and mechanical production, free and unlimited coinage of silver, a graduated income tax, elimination of tax on the necessities of life, government control and supervision of public communication and transportation, and the direct election of U.S. senators. The meeting, drawing agrarian leaders from across the United States, represented a landmark in the formation of a national farmers' movement.

───────── ∞ ─────────

1. a. We demand the abolition of national banks.

b. We demand that the government shall establish sub-treasuries or depositories in the several states, which shall loan money direct to the people at a low rate of interest, not to exceed two per cent per annum, on non-perishable farm products, and also upon real estate, with proper limitations upon the quantity of land and amount of money.

c. We demand that the amount of the circulating medium be speedily increased to not less than $50 per capita.

2. We demand that Congress shall pass such laws as will effectually prevent the dealing in futures of all agricultural and mechanical productions; providing a stringent system of procedure in trials that will secure the prompt conviction, and imposing such penalties as shall secure the most perfect compliance with the law.

3. We condemn the silver ill recently passed by Congress, and demand in lieu thereof the free and unlimited coinage of silver.

4. We demand the passage of laws prohibiting alien ownership of land, and that Congress take prompt action to devise some plan to obtain all lands now owned by aliens and foreign syndicates; and that all lands now held by railroads and other corporations in excess of such as is actually used and needed by them be reclaimed by the government and held for actual settlers only.

5. Believing in the doctrine of equal rights to all and special privileges to none, we demand—

a. That our national legislation shall be so framed in the future as not to build up one industry at the expense of another.

b. We further demand a removal of the existing heavy tariff tax from the necessities of life, that the poor of our land must have.

c. We further demand a just and equitable system of graduated tax on incomes.

d. We believe that the money of the county should be kept as much as possible in the hands of the people, and hence we demand that all national and state revenues shall be limited to the necessary expenses of the government economically and honestly administered.

6. We demand the most rigid, honest and just state and national government control and supervision of the means of public communication and transportation, and if this control and supervision does not remove 0the abuse now existing, we demand the government ownership of such means of communication and transportation.

7. We demand that the Congress of the United States submit an amendment to the Constitution providing for the election of United States Senators by direct vote of the people of each state.

Source:

John D. Hicks, *The Populist Revolt: A History of the Farmers' Alliance and the People's Party*, Lincoln: University of Nebraska Press, 1966, pp. 430–431.

Elizabeth Cady Stanton, "The Solitude of Self," 1892

Valedictory statement of feminism delivered by radical social reformer and suffragist Elizabeth Cady Stanton on January 18, 1892, upon resigning the presidency of the National Woman Suffrage Association (NWSA). In the speech, Stanton expounded the feminist philosophy by which women, she suggested, must approach their lives to secure the safety and happiness to which individual sovereignty entitled them. Solitude of self, she asserted, was fundamental to the human experience, regardless of gender. The solitude at the heart of the human condition made imperative the development of self-reliance, independence, and self-responsibility. Because life placed the same material and psychological demands on men and women, Stanton argued, the genders should enjoy the same individual rights and be guaranteed the same opportunity to become independent, resourceful beings equipped to deal with the tragedies and triumphs of life.

Mr. Chairman and gentlemen of the committee: We have been speaking before Committees of the Judiciary for the last twenty years, and we have gone over all the arguments in favor of a sixteenth amendment which are familiar to all you gentlemen; therefore, it will not be necessary that I should repeat them.

The point I wish plainly to bring before you on this occasion is the individuality of each human soul; our Protestant idea, the right of individual conscience and judgment—our republican idea, individual citizenship. In discussing the rights of woman, we are to consider, first, what belongs to her as an individual, in a world of her own, the arbiter of her own destiny, an imaginary Robinson Crusoe with her woman Friday on a solitary island. Her rights under such circumstances are to use all her faculties for her own safety and happiness.

Secondly, if we consider her as a citizen, as a member of a great nation, she must have the same rights as all other members, according to the fundamental principles of our Government.

Thirdly, viewed as a woman, an equal factor in civilization, her rights and duties are still the same—individual happiness and development.

Fourthly, it is only the incidental relations of life, such as mother, wife, sister, daughter, that may involve some special duties and training. In the usual discussion in regard to woman's sphere, such men as Herbert Spencer, Frederic Harrison, and Grant Allen uniformly subordinate her rights and duties as an individual, as a citizen, as a woman, to the necessities of these incidental relations, some of which a large class of women may never assume. In discussing the sphere of man we do not decide his rights as an individual, as a citizen, as a man by his duties as a father, a husband, a brother, or a son, relations some of which he may never fill. Moreover, he would be better fitted for these very relations, and whatever special work he might choose to do to earn his bread, by the complete development of all his faculties as an individual.

Just so with woman. The education that will fit her to discharge the duties in the largest sphere of human usefulness, will best fit her for whatever special work she may be compelled to do.

The isolation of every human soul and the necessity of self-dependence must give each individual the right to choose his own surroundings. The strongest reason for giving woman all the opportunities for higher education, for the full development of her faculties, forces of mind and body; for giving her the most enlarged freedom of thought and action; a complete emancipation from all forms of bondage, of custom, dependence, superstition; from all the crippling influences of fear, is the solitude and personal responsibility of her own individual life. The strongest reason why we ask for woman a voice in the government under which she lives; in the religion she is asked to believe; equality in social life, where she is the chief factor; a place in the trades and professions, where she may earn her bread, is because of her birthright to self-sovereignty; because, as an individual, she must rely on herself. No matter how much women prefer to lean, to be protected and supported, nor how much men desire to have them do so, they must make the voyage of life alone, and for safety in an emergency they must know something of the laws of navigation. To guide our own craft, we must be captain, pilot, engineer; with chart and compass stand at the wheel; watch the wind and waves and know when to take in the sail, and read the signs in the firmament over all. It matters not whether the solitary voyager is man or woman.

Nature having endowed them equally, leaves them to their own skill and judgment in the hour of danger, and, if not equal to the occasion, alike they perish.

To appreciate the importance of fitting every human soul for independent action, think for a moment of the immeasurable solitude of self. We come into the world alone, unlike all who have gone before us; we leave it alone under circumstances peculiar to ourselves. No mortal ever has been, nor mortal ever will be like the soul just launched on the sea of life. There can never again be just such environments as make up the infancy, youth and manhood of this one. Nature never repeats herself, and the possibilities of one human soul will never be found in another. No one has ever found two blades of grass alike, and no one will ever find two human beings alike. Seeing, then, what must be the infinite diversity in human charac-

ter, we can in a measure appreciate the loss to a nation when any large class of the people is uneducated and unrepresented in the government. We ask for the complete development of every individual, first, for his own benefit and happiness. In fitting out an army we give each soldier his own knapsack, arms, powder, his blanket, cup, knife, fork and spoon. We provide alike for all their individual necessities, then each man bears his own burden.

Again we ask complete individual development for the general good; for the consensus of the competent on the whole round of human interests; on all questions of national life, and here each man must bear his share of the general burden. It is sad to see how soon friendless children are left to bear their own burdens before they can analyze their feelings; before they can even tell their joys and sorrows, they are thrown on their own resources. The great lesson that nature seems to teach us at all ages is self-dependence, self-protection, self-support. What a touching instance of a child's solitude, of that hunger of the heart for love and recognition, in the case of the little girl who helped to dress a Christmas tree for the children of the family in which she served. On finding there was no present for herself, she slipped away in the darkness and spent the night in an open field sitting on a stone, and when found in the morning, was weeping as if her heart would break. No mortal will ever know the thoughts that passed through the mind of that friendless child in the long hours of that cold night, with only the silent stars to keep her company. The mention of her case in the daily papers moved many generous hearts to send her presents; but in the hours of her keenest suffering, she was thrown wholly on herself for consolation.

In youth our most bitter disappointments, our brightest hopes and ambitions are know only to ourselves; even our friendship and love we never fully share with another; there is something of every passion, in every situation we conceal. Even so in our triumphs and our defeats. The successful candidate for the Presidency and his opponent each have a solitude peculiarly his own, and good form forbids either to speak of his pleasure or regret. The solitude of the king on his throne and the prisoner in his cell differs in character and degree, but it is solitude nevertheless.

We ask no sympathy from others in the anxiety and agony of a broken friendship or shattered love. When death sunders our nearest ties, alone we sit in the shadow of our affliction. Alike mid the greatest triumphs and darkest tragedies of life we walk alone. On the divine heights of human attainments, eulogized and worshipped as a hero or saint, we stand alone. In ignorance, poverty, and vice, as a pauper or criminal, alone we starve or steal; alone we suffer the sneers and rebuffs of our fellows; alone we are hunted and hounded through dark courts and alleys, in byways and highways; alone we stand before the judgment seat; alone in the prison cell we lament our crimes and misfortunes; alone we expiate them on the gallows. In hours like these we realize the awful solitude of individual life, its pains, its penalties, its responsibilities; hours in which the youngest and most helpless are thrown on their own resources for guidance and consolation. Seeing them that life must ever be a march and a battle, that each soldier must be equipped for his own protection, it is the height of cruelty to rob the individual of a single natural right.

To throw obstacles in the way of a complete education is like putting out the eyes; to deny the rights of property, like cutting off the hands. To deny political equality is to rob the ostracised of all self- respect; of credit in the market place; of recompense in the world of work; of a voice among those who make and administer the law; a choice in the jury before whom they are tried, and in the judge who decides their punishment. Shakespeare's play of Titus and Andronicus contains a terrible satire on woman's position in the nineteenth century—"Rude men" (the play tell us) "seized the king's daughter, cut out her tongue, cut off her hands, and then bade her go call for water and wash her hands." What a picture of woman's position. Robbed of her natural rights, handicapped by law and custom at every turn, yet compelled to fight her own battles, and in the emergencies of life to fall back on herself for protections.

The girl of sixteen, thrown on the world to support herself, to make her own place in society, to resist the temptations that surround her and maintain a spotless integrity, must do all this by native force or superior education. She does not acquire this power by being trained to trust others and distrust herself. If she wearies of the struggle, finding it hard work to swim upstream, and allows herself to drift with the current, she will find plenty of company, but not one to share her misery in the hour of her deepest humiliation. If she tries to retrieve her position, to conceal the past, her life is hedged about with fears lest willing hands should tear the veil from what she fain would hide. Young and friendless, *she* knows the bitter solitude of self.

How the little courtesies of life on the surface of society, deemed so important from man towards woman, fade into utter insignificance in view of the deeper tragedies in which she must play her part alone, where no human aid is possible.

The young wife and mother, at the head of some establishment with a kind husband to shield her from the adverse winds of life, with wealth, fortune and position, has a certain harbor of safety, secure against the ordinary ills of life. But to manage a household, have a desirable influence in society, keep her friends and the affections of her husband, train her children and servants well, she must

have rare common sense, wisdom, diplomacy, and a knowledge of human nature. To do all this she needs the cardinal virtues and the strong points of character that the most successful statesman possesses.

An uneducated woman, trained to dependence, with no resources in herself must make a failure of any position in life. But society says women do not need a knowledge of the world, the liberal training that experience in public life must give, all the advantages of collegiate education; but when for the lack of all these, the woman's happiness is wrecked, alone she bears her humiliation. The solitude of the weak and the ignorant is indeed pitiable; in the wild chase for the prizes of life they are ground the powder.

In age, when the pleasures of youth are passed, children grown up, married and gone, the hurry and bustle of life in a measure over, when the hands are weary of active service, when the old arm chair and the fireside are the chosen resorts, then men and women alike must fall back on their own resources. If they cannot find companionship in books, if they have no interest in the vital questions of the hour, no interest in watching the consummation of reforms, with which they might have been identified, they soon pass into their dotage. The more fully the faculties of the mind are developed and kept in use, the longer the period of vigor and active interest in all around us continues. If from a lifelong participation in public affairs a woman feels responsible for the laws regulating our system of education, the discipline of our jails and prisons, the sanitary condition of out private homes, public buildings, the thoroughfares, an interest in commerce, finance, our foreign relations, in any or all of these questions, her solitude will at least be respectable, and she will not be driven to gossip or scandal for entertainment.

The chief reason for opening to every soul the doors to the whole round of human duties and pleasures, is the individual development thus attained, the resources thus provided under all circumstances to mitigate the solitude that at times must come to everyone. I once asked Prince Krapotkin, the Russian nihilist, how he endured his long years in prison, deprived of books, pen, ink, and paper. "Ah," he said, "I thought out many questions in which I had a deep interest. In the pursuit of an idea I took no note of time. When tired of solving knotty problems, I recited all the beautiful passages in prose or verse I had ever learned. I became acquainted with myself and my own resources. I had a world of my own, a vast empire, that no Russian jail or Czar could invade." Such is the value of liberal thought and broad culture when shut off from all human companionship, bringing comfort and sunshine within even the four walls of a prison cell.

As women ofttimes share a similar fate, should they not have all the consolation that the most liberal education can give? Their suffering in the prisons of St. Petersburg, in the long, weary marches to Siberia, and in the mines, working side by side with men, surely call for all the self-support that the most exalted sentiments of heroism can give. When suddenly roused at midnight, with the startling cry of "fire! fire!" to find the house over their heads in flames, do women wait for men to point the way to safety? And are the men, equally bewildered and half suffocated with smoke, in a position to more than try to save themselves? At such times the most timid women have shown a courage and heroism in saving their husbands and children that has surprised everybody. Inasmuch, then, as woman shares equally the joys and sorrows of time and eternity, is it not the height of presumption in man to propose to represent her at the ballot box and the throne of grace, to do her voting in the state, her praying in the church, and to assume the position of high priest at the family altar?

Nothing strengthens the judgment and quickens the conscience like individual responsibility. Nothing adds such dignity to character as the recognition of one's self-sovereignty; the right to an equal place, everywhere conceded; a place earned by personal merit, not an artificial attainment, by inheritance, wealth, family, and position. Seeing, then, that the responsibilities of life rest equally on man and woman, that their destiny is the same, they need the same preparation for time and eternity. The talk of sheltering woman from the fierce storms of life is the sheerest mockery, for they beat on her from every point of the compass, just as they do on man, and with more fatal results, for he has been trained to protect himself, to resist, to conquer. Such are the facts in human experience, the responsibilities of individual sovereignty. Rich and poor, intelligent and ignorant, wise and foolish, virtuous and vicious, man and woman, it is ever the same, each soul must depend wholly on itself.

Whatever the theories may be of woman's dependence on man, in the supreme moments of her life he cannot bear her burdens. Alone she goes to the gates of death of give life to every man that is born into the world. No one can share her fears, no one can mitigate her pangs; and if her sorrow is greater than she can bear, alone she passes beyond the gates into the vast unknown. From the mountain tops of Judea, long ago, a heavenly voice bade his disciples, "Bear ye one another's burdens," but humanity has not yet risen to that point of self-sacrifice, and if ever so willing, how few the burdens are that one soul can bear for another. In the highways of Palestine; in prayer and fasting on the solitary mountain top; in the Garden of Gethsemane; before the judgment seat of Pilate; betrayed by one of this trusted disciples at his last supper; in his agonies on the cross, even Jesus of Nazareth, in these last sad days on earth, felt the awful solitude of self. Deserted by man, in agony he cries, "My God! My God! why hast Thou forsaken me?" And so it ever must be in the conflicting scenes of life, in the long, weary march, each one walks alone. We may have many friends, love, kindness, sympathy and charity to smooth our pathway in everyday life, but in the tragedies and triumphs of human experience each mortal stands alone.

But when all artificial trammels are removed, and women are recognized as individuals, responsible for their own environments, thoroughly educated for all positions in life they may be called to fill; with all the resources in themselves that liberal thought and broad culture can give; guided by their own conscience and judgment; trained to self-protection by a healthy development of the muscular system and skill in the use of weapons of defense, and stimulated to self-support by a knowledge of the business world and the pleasure that pecuniary independence must ever give; when women are trained in this way they will, in a measure, be fitted for those hours of solitude that come alike to all, whether prepared or otherwise. As in our extremity we must depend on ourselves, the dictates of wisdom point to complete individual development.

In talking of education how shallow the argument that each class must be educated for the special work it proposes to do, and all those faculties not needed in this special walk must lie dormant and utterly wither for want of use, when, perhaps, these will be the very faculties needed in life's greatest emergencies. Some say, "Where is the use of drilling girls in the languages, the sciences, in law, medicine, theology? As wives, mothers, housekeepers, cooks, they need a different curriculum from boys who are to fill all positions." The chief cooks in our great hotels and ocean steamers are men. In our large cities men run the bakeries, they make our bread, cake and pies, they manage the laundries, they are now considered our best milliners and dressmakers. Because some men fill these departments of usefulness, shall we regulate the curriculum in Harvard and Yale to their present necessities? If not, why this talk in our best colleges of a curriculum for girls are crowding into the trades and professions, teachers in all our public schools, rapidly filling many lucrative and honorable positions in life?

They are showing, too, their calmness and courage in the most trying hours of human experience. You have probably all read in the daily papers of the terrible storm in the Bay of Biscay when a tidal wave made such havoc on the shore, wrecking vessels, unroofing houses, and carrying destruction everywhere. Among other buildings the woman's prison was demolished. Those who escaped saw men struggling to reach the shore. They promptly by clasping hands made a chain of themselves and pushed out into the sea, again and again, at the risk of their lives until they had brought six men to shore, carried them to a shelter, and did all in their power for their comfort and protection.

What special school of training could have prepared these women for this sublime moment in their lives? In times like this humanity rises above all college curriculums and recognizes Nature as the greatest of all teachers in the hour of danger and death. Women are already the equals of men in the whole realm of thought, in art, science, literature, and government. With telescopic vision they explore the starry firmament and bring back the history of the planetary world. With chart and compass they pilot ships across the mighty deep, and with skillful finger send electric messages around the globe. In galleries of art the beauties of nature and the virtues of humanity are immortalized by them on canvas, and by their inspired touch dull blocks of marble are transformed into angels of light.

In music they speak again the language of Mendelssohn, Beethoven, Chopin, Schumann, and are worthy interpreters of their great thoughts. The poetry and novels of the century are theirs, and they have touched the keynote of reform in religion, politics, and social life. They fill the editor's and professor's chair, and plead at the bar of justice, walk the wards of the hospital, and speak from the pulpit and the platform; such is the type of womanhood that an enlightened public sentiment welcomes to-day, and such the triumph of the facts of life over the false theories of the past.

Is it, then, consistent to hold the developed woman of this day within the same narrow political limits as the dame with the spinning wheel and knitting needle occupied in the past? No! no! Machinery has taken the labors of woman as well as man on its tireless shoulders; the loom and the spinning wheel are but dreams of the past; the pen, the brush, the easel, the chisel, have taken their places, while the hopes and ambitions of women are essentially changed.

We see reason sufficient in the outer conditions of human beings for individual liberty and development, but then we consider the self-dependence of every human soul we see the need of courage, judgment, and the exercise of every faculty of mind and body, strengthened and developed by use, in woman as well as man.

Whatever may be said of man's protecting power in ordinary conditions, mid all the terrible disasters by land and sea, in the supreme moments of danger, alone, woman must ever meet the horrors of the situation, the Angel of Death even makes no royal pathway for her. Man's love and sympathy enter only into the sunshine of our lives. In that solemn solitude of self, that links us with the immeasurable and the eternal, each soul lives alone forever. A recent writer says:

I remember once, in crossing the Atlantic, to have gone upon the deck of the ship at midnight, when a dense black cloud enveloped the sky, and the great deep was roaring madly under the lashes of demoniac winds. My feeling was not of danger or fear (which is a base surrender of the immortal soul), but of utter desolation and loneliness; a little speck of life shut in by a tremendous darkness. Again I remember to have climbed the slopes of the Swiss Alps, up beyond the point where vegetation ceases, and the stunted confiners no longer struggle against the unfeeling blasts. Around me lay a huge confusion of rocks, out of which the gigantic ice peaks shot into the measureless blue of the heavens, and again my only feeling was the awful solitude.

And yet, there is a solitude, which each and every one of us has always carried with him, more inaccessible than the ice-cold mountains, more profound than the midnight sea; the solitude of self. Our inner being, which we call ourself, no eye nor touch of man or angel has ever pierced. It is more hidden than the caves of the gnome; the sacred adytum of the oracle; the hidden chamber of eleusinian mystery, for to it only omniscience is permitted to enter.

Such is individual life. Who, I ask you, can take, dare take, on himself the rights, the duties, the responsibilities of another human soul?

Source:

James Andrews and David Zarefsky, eds., *American Voices: Significant Speeches in American History, 1640–1945.* Reading, Mass.: Longman, 1989.

Thomas Watson, "Negro Question in the South," 1892

Address, delivered in 1892 by Southern populist leader and agrarian firebrand Thomas E. Watson, urging a political union across racial lines of the South's poor white and black farmers to win redress of their common economic troubles. Poor farmers of both races in the Jim Crow South were casualties of collapsing farm prices, deteriorating land, and crippling debt. Agrarian reactionaries such as Watson blamed Northern commercial and banking interests for the cycle of poverty in which the Southern farmer found himself trapped. Rising farmer unrest coalesced into a powerful populist agrarian political movement by 1890. In "The Negro Question in the South," Watson, who was elected in 1892 to the U.S. House of Representatives from Georgia on the Farmers' Alliance ticket, addressed the race issue directly. He called on the rural South's poor whites and blacks to shed their historic antagonisms and prejudices and join forces in order to fight their shared economic plight. Their material condition and interest, he argued, was identical; only by uniting politically, he ventured, could white and black farmers hope to secure the political changes necessary to relieve their shared miseries.

In 1896, the Populist Party, which adopted the Democratic candidate William Jennings Bryan for president, made

Watson their vice presidential nominee. Bryan lost and the Populist Party never regained the status it had in the early 1890s.

The Negro Question in the South has been for nearly thirty years a source of danger, discord, and bloodshed. It is an ever-present irritant and menace. Several millions of slaves were told that they were the prime cause of the Civil War; that their emancipation was the result of the triumph of the North over the South; that the ballot was placed in their hands as a weapon of defence against their former masters; that the war-won political equality of the black man with the white, must be asserted promptly and aggressively, under the leadership of adventurers who had swooped down upon the conquered section in the wake of the Union armies.

No one, who wishes to be fair, can fail to see that, in such a condition of things, strife between the freedman and his former owner was inevitable. In the clashing of interests and of feelings, bitterness was born. The black man was kept in a continual fever of suspicion that we meant to put him back into slavery. In the assertion of his recently acquired privileges, he was led to believe that the best proof of his being on the right side of any issue was that his old master was on the other. When this was the case, he felt easy in his mind. But if, by any chance, he found that he was voting the same ticket with his former owner, he at once became reflective and suspicious. In the irritable temper of the times, a whispered warning from a northern "carpet-bagger," having no jurisdiction in rhyme or reason, outweighed with him a carload of sound argument and earnest expostulation from the man whom he had known all his life; who had hunted with him through every swamp and wooded upland for miles around; who had wrestled and run foot-races with him in the "Negro quarters" on many a Saturday afternoon; who had fished with him at every "hole" in the creek; and who had played a thousand games of "marble" with him under the cool shade of the giant oaks which, in those days, sheltered a home they had both loved.

In brief, the end of the war brought changed relations and changed feelings. Heated antagonisms produced mutual distrust and dislike—ready, at any accident of unusual provocation on either side, to break out into passionate and bloody conflict.

Quick to take advantage of this deplorable situation, the politicians have based the fortunes of the old parties upon it. Northern leaders have felt that at the cry of "southern outrage" they could not only "fire the northern heart," but also win a unanimous vote from the colored people. Southern politicians have felt that at the cry of "Negro domination" they could drive into solid phalanx every white man in all the southern States.

Both the old parties have done this thing until they have constructed as perfect a "slot machine" as the world ever saw. Drop the old, worn nickel of the "party slogan" into the slot, and the machine does the rest. You might beseech a southern white tenant to listen to you upon questions of finance, taxation, and transportation; you might demonstrate with mathematical precision that herein lay his way out of poverty into comfort; you might have him "almost persuaded" to the truth, but if the merchant who furnished his farm supplies (at tremendous usury) or the town politician (who never spoke to him exception at election times) came along and cried "Negro rule!" the entire fabric of reason and common sense which you had patiently constructed would fall, and the poor tenant would joyously hug the chains of an actual wretchedness rather than do any experimenting on a question of mere sentiment.

Thus the northern Democrats have ruled the South with a rod of iron for twenty years. We have had to acquiesce when the time-honored principles we loved were sent to the rear and new doctrines and policies we despised were engrafted on our platform. All this we have had to do to obtain the assistance of northern Democrats to prevent what was called "Negro supremacy." In other words, the Negro has been as valuable a portion of the stock in trade of a Democrat as he was of a Republican. Let the South ask relief from Wall Street; let it plead for equal and just laws on finance; let it beg for mercy against crushing taxation, and northern Democracy, with all the coldness, cruelty, and subtlety of Mephistopheles, would hint "Negro rule!" and the white farmer and laborer of the South had to choke down his grievance and march under Tammany's orders.

Reverse the statement, and we have the method by which the black man was managed by the Republicans.

Reminded constantly that the North had emancipated him; that the North had given him the ballot; that the North had upheld him in his citizenship; that the South was his enemy, and meant to deprive him of his suffrage and put him "back into slavery," it is no wonder he has played as nicely into the hands of the Republicans as his former owner has played into the hands of the northern Democrats.

Now consider: here were two distinct races dwelling together, with political equality established between them by law. They lived in the same section; won their livelihood by the same pursuits; cultivated adjoining fields on the same terms; enjoyed together the bounties of a generous climate; suffered together the rigors of cruelly unjust laws; spoke the same language; bought and sold in the same markets; classified themselves into churches under the same denominational teachings; neither race antagonizing the other in any branch of industry; each absolutely dependent on the other in all the avenues of labor and employment; and yet, instead of being allies, as every dictate of reason and prudence and self-interest and justice said they should be, they were kept apart, in dangerous hostility, that the sordid aims of partisan politics might be served!

So completely has this scheme succeeded that the southern black man almost instinctively supports any measure the southern white man condemns, while the latter almost universally antagonizes any proposition suggested by a northern Republican. We have, then, a solid South as opposed to a solid North; and in the South itself, a solid black vote against the solid white.

That such a condition is most ominous to both sections and both races, is apparent to all.

If we were dealing with a few tribes of red men or a few sporadic Chinese, the question would be easily disposed of. The Anglo-Saxon would probably do just as he pleased, whether right or wrong, and the weaker man would go under.

But the Negroes number 8,000,000. They are interwoven with our business, political, and labor systems. They assimilate with our customs, our religion, our civilization. They meet us at every turn—in the fields, the shops, the mines. They are a part of our system, and they are here to stay.

Those writers who tediously wade through census reports to prove that the Negro is disappearing, are the most absurd mortals extant. The Negro is not disappearing. A southern man who looks about him and who sees how rapidly the colored people increase, how cheaply they can live, and how readily they learn, has no patience whatever with those statistical lunatics who figure out the final disappearance of the Negro one hundred years hence. The truth is, that the "black belts" in the South are getting blacker. The race is mixing less than it ever did. Mulattoes are less common (in proportion) than during the times of slavery. Miscegenation is further off (thank God) than ever. Neither the blacks nor the whites have any relish for it. Both have a pride of race which is commendable, and which, properly directed, will lead to the best results for both. The home of the colored man is chiefly with us in the South, and there he will remain. It is there he is founding churches, opening schools, maintaining newspapers, entering the professions, serving on juries, deciding doubtful elections, drilling as a volunteer soldier, and piling up a cotton crop which amazes the world.

II

This preliminary statement is made at length that the gravity of the situation may be seen. Such a problem never confronted any people before.

Never before did two distinct races, dwell together under such conditions.

And the problem is, can these two races, distinct in color, distinct in social life, and distinct as political powers, dwell together in peace and prosperity?

Upon a question so difficult and delicate no man should dogmatize—nor dodge. The issue is here; grows more urgent every day, and must be met.

It is safe to say that the present status of hostility between the races can only be sustained at the most imminent risk to both. It is leading by logical necessity to results which the imagination shrinks from contemplating. And the horrors of such a future can only be averted by honest attempts at a solution of the question which will be just to both races and beneficial to both.

Having given this subject much anxious thought, my opinion is that the future happiness of the two races will never be assured until the political motives which drive them asunder, into two distinct and hostile factions, can be removed. There must be a new policy inaugurated, whose purpose is to allay the passions and prejudices of race conflict, and which makes its appeal to the sober sense and honest judgment of the citizen regardless of his color.

To the success of this policy two things are indispensable—a common necessity acting upon both races, and a common benefit assured to both—without injury or humiliation to either.

Then, again, outsiders must let us alone. We must work out our own salvation. In no other way can it be done. Suggestions of Federal interference with our elections postpone the settlement and render our task the more difficult. Like all free people, we love home rule, and resent foreign compulsion of any sort. The northern leader who really desires to see a better state of things in the South, puts his finger on the hands of the clock and forces them backward every time he intermeddles with the question. This is the literal truth; and the sooner it is well understood, the sooner we can accomplish our purpose.

What is that purpose? To outline a policy which compels the support of a great body of both races, from those motives which imperiously control human action, and which will thus obliterate forever the sharp and unreasoning political divisions of to-day.

The white people of the South will never support the Republican party. This much is certain. The black people of the South will never support the Democratic party. This is equally certain.

Hence, at the beginning, we are met by the necessity of new political alliances. As long as the whites remain solidly Democratic, the blacks will remain solidly Republican.

As long as there was no choice, except as between the Democrats and the Republicans, the situation of the two races was bound to be one of antagonism. The Republican party represented everything which was hateful to the whites; the Democratic party, everything which was hateful to the blacks.

Therefore a new party was absolutely necessary. It has come, and it is doing its work with marvelous rapidity.

Why does a southern Democrat leave his party and come to ours?

Because his industrial condition is pitiably bad; because he struggles against a system of laws which have almost filled him with despair; because he is told that he is without clothing because he produces too much cotton, and without food because corn is too plentiful; because he sees everybody growing rich off the products of labor except the laborer; because the millionaires who manage the Democratic party have contemptuously ignored his plea for a redress of grievances and have nothing to say to him beyond the cheerful advice to "work harder and live closer."

Why has this man joined the PEOPLE'S PARTY? Because the same grievances have been presented to the Republicans by the farmer of the West, and the millionaires who control that party have replied to the petition with the soothing counsel that the Republican farmer of the West should "work more and talk less."

Therefore, if he were confined to a choice between the two old parties, the question would merely be (on these issues) whether the pot were larger than the kettle—the color of both being precisely the same.

III

The key to the new political movement called the People's party has been that the Democratic farmer was as ready to leave the Democratic ranks as the Republican farmer was to leave the Republican ranks. In exact proportion as the West received the assurance that the South was ready for a new party, it has moved. In exact proportion to the proof we could bring that the West had broken Republican ties, the South has moved. *Without* a decided break in both sections, neither would move. *With* that decided break, both moved.

The very same principle governs the race question in the South. The two races can never act together permanently, harmoniously, beneficially, till each race demonstrates to the other a readiness to leave old party affiliations and to form new ones, based upon the profound conviction that, in acting together, both races are seeking new laws which will benefit both. On no other basis under heaven can the "Negro Question" be solved.

IV

Now, suppose that the colored man were educated upon these questions just as the whites have been; suppose he were shown that his poverty and distress came from the same sources as ours; suppose we should convince him that our platform principles assure him an escape from the ills he now suffers, and guarantee him the fair measure of prosperity his labor entitles him to receive—would he not act just as the white Democrat who joined us did? Would he not abandon a party which ignores him as a farmer and laborer; which offers him no benefits of an equal and just financial system; which promises him no relief from oppressive taxation; which assures him of no legislation which will enable him to obtain a fair price of his produce?

Granting to him the same selfishness common to us all; granting him the intelligence to know what is best for him and the desire to attain it, why would he not act from that motive just as the white farmer has done?

That he would do so, is as certain as any future event can be made. Gratitude may fail; so may sympathy and friendship and generosity and patriotism; but in the long run, self-interest *always* controls. Let it once appear plainly that it is to the interest of a colored man to vote with the white man, and he will do it. Let it plainly appear that it is to the interest of the white man that the vote of the Negro should supplement his own, and the question of having that ballot freely cast and fairly counted, becomes vital to the *white man*. He will see that it is done.

Now let us illustrate: Suppose two tenants on my farm; one of them white, the other black. They cultivate their crops under precisely the same conditions. Their labors, discouragements, burdens, grievances, are the same.

The white tenant is driven by cruel necessity to examine into the causes of his continued destitution. He reaches certain conclusions which are not complimentary to either of the old parties. He leaves the Democracy in angry disgust. He joins the People's party. Why? Simply because its platform recognizes that he is badly treated and proposes to fight his battle. Necessity drives him from the old party, and hope leads him into the new. In plain English, he joins the organization whose declaration of principles is in accord with his conception of what he needs and justly deserves.

Now go back to the colored tenant. His surroundings being the same and his interests the same, why is it impossible for him to reach the same conclusions? Why is it unnatural for him to go into the new party at the same time and with the same motives?

Cannot these two men act together in peace when the ballot of the one is a vital benefit to the other? Will not political friendship be born of the necessity and the hope which is common to both? Will not race bitterness disappear before this common suffering and this mutual desire to escape it? Will not each of these citizens feel more kindly for the other when the vote of each defends the home of both? If the white man becomes convinced that the Democratic party has played upon his prejudices, and has used his quiescence to the benefit of interests adverse to his own, will he not despise the leaders who seek to perpetuate the system?

V

The People's party will settle the race question. First, by enacting the Australian ballot system. Second, by offering to white and black a rallying point which is free from the odium of former discords and strifes. Third, by presenting a platform immensely beneficial to both races and injurious to neither. Fourth, by making it to the *interest* of both races to act together for the success of the platform. Fifth, by making it to the *interest* of the colored man to have the same patriotic zeal for the welfare of the South that the whites possess.

Now to illustrate. Take two planks of the People's party platform: that pledging a free ballot under the Australian system and that which demands a distribution of currency to the people upon pledges of land, cotton, etc.

The guaranty as to the vote will suit the black man better than the Republican platform, because the latter contemplates Federal interference, which will lead to collisions and bloodshed. The Democratic platform contains no comfort to the Negro, because, while it denounces the Republican programme, as usual, it promises nothing which can be specified. It is a generality which does not even possess the virtue of being "glittering."

The People's party, however, not only condemns Federal interference with elections, but also distinctly commits itself to the method by which every citizen shall have his constitutional right to the free exercise of his electoral choice. We pledge ourselves to isolate the voter from all coercive influences and give him the free and fair exercise of his franchise under state laws.

Now couple this with the financial plank which promises equality in the distribution of the national currency, at low rates of interest.

The white tenant lives adjoining the colored tenant. Their houses are almost equally destitute of comforts. Their living is confined to bare necessities. They are equally burdened with heavy taxes. They pay the same high rent for gullied and impoverished land.

They pay the same enormous prices for farm supplies. Christmas finds them both without any satisfactory return for a year's toil. Dull and heavy and unhappy, they both start the plows again when "New Year's" passes.

Now the People's party says to these two men, "You are kept apart that you may be separately fleeced of your earnings. You are made to hate each other because upon that hatred is rested the keystone of the arch of financial despotism which enslaves you both. You are deceived and blinded that you may not see how this race antagonism perpetuates a monetary system which beggars both."

This is so obviously true it is no wonder both these unhappy laborers stop to listen. No wonder they begin to realize that no change of law can benefit the white tenant which does not benefit the black one likewise; that no system which now does injustice to one of them can fail to injure both. Their every material interest is identical. The moment this becomes a conviction, mere selfishness, the mere desire to better their conditions, escape onerous taxes, avoid usurious charges, lighten their rents, or change their precarious tenements into smiling, happy homes, will drive these two men together, just as their mutually inflamed prejudices now drive them apart.

Suppose these two men now to have become fully imbued with the idea that their material welfare depends upon the reforms we demand. Then they act together to secure them. Every white reformer finds it to the vital interest of his home, his family, his fortune, to see to it that the vote of the colored reformer is freely cast and fairly counted.

Then what? Every colored voter will be thereafter a subject of industrial education and political teaching.

Concede that in the final event, a colored man will vote where his material interests dictate that he should vote; concede that in the South the accident of color can make no possible difference in the interests of farmers, croppers, and laborers; concede that under full and fair discussion the people can be depended upon to ascertain where their interests lie—and we reach the conclusion that the southern race question can be solved by the People's party on the simple proposition that each race will be led by self-interest to support that which benefits it, when so presented that neither is hindered by the bitter party antagonisms of the past.

Let the colored laborer realize that our platform gives him a better guaranty for political independence; for a fair return for his work; a better chance to buy a home and keep it; a better chance to educate his children and see them profitably employed; a better chance to have public life freed from race collisions; a better chance for every citizen to be considered as a *citizen* regardless of color in the making and enforcing of laws—let all this be fully realized, and the race question at the South will have settled itself through the evolution of a political movement in which both whites and blacks recognize their surest way out of wretchedness into comfort and independence.

The illustration could be made quite as clearly from other planks in the People's party platform. On questions of land, transportation, and finance, especially, the welfare of the two races so clearly depends upon that which benefits either, that intelligent discussion would necessarily lead to just conclusions.

Why should the colored man always be taught that the white man of his neighborhood hates him, while a northern man, who taxes every rag on his back, loves him? Why should not my tenant come to regard me as his friend rather than the manufacturer who plunders us both? Why should we perpetuate a policy which drives the black man into the arms of the northern politician?

Why should we always allow northern and eastern Democrats to enslave us forever by threats of the Force Bill?

Let us draw the supposed teeth of this fabled dragon by founding our new policy upon justice—upon the simple but profound truth that, if the voice of passion can be hushed, the self-interest of both races will drive them to act in concert. There never was a day during the last twenty years when the South could not have flung the money power into the dust by patiently teaching the Negro that we could not be wretched under any system which would not afflict him likewise; that we could not prosper under any law which would not also bring its blessings to him.

To the emasculated individual who cries "Negro supremacy!" there is little to be said. His cowardice shows him to be a degeneration from the race which has never yet feared any other race. Existing under such conditions as they now do in this country, there is no earthly chance for Negro domination, unless we are ready to admit that the colored man is our superior in will power, courage, and intellect.

Not being prepared to make any such admission in favor of any race the sun ever shone on, I have no words which can portray my contempt for the white men, Anglo-Saxons, who can knock their knees together, and through their chattering teeth and pale lips admit that they are afraid the Negroes will "dominate us."

The question of social equality does not enter into the calculation at all. That is a thing each citizen decides for himself. No statute ever yet drew the latch of the humblest home—or ever will. Each citizen regulates his own visiting list—and always will.

The conclusion, then, seems to me to be this: the crushing burdens which now oppress both races in the South will cause each to make an effort to cast them off. They will see a similarity of cause and a similarity of remedy. They will recognize that each should help the other in the work of repealing bad laws and enacting good ones. They will become political allies, and neither can injure the other without weakening both. It will be to the interest of both that each should have justice. And on these broad lines of mutual interest, mutual forbearance, and mutual support the present will be made the stepping-stone to future peace and prosperity.

Source:

John Scott, ed. *Living Documents in American History.* New York: Washington Square Press, 1964–68.

William Jennings Bryan, "Cross of Gold" Speech, 1896

Attack upon America's gold standard delivered by William Jennings Bryan on July 8, 1896, at the Democratic National Convention in Chicago. In this dramatic speech, the former congressman from Nebraska called for the free and unlimited coinage of silver to relieve the economic distress of farmers and industrial workers, attacking his opponents for their hard-money views: "You shall not press down upon the brow of labor this crown of thorns, you shall not crucify mankind upon a cross of gold." The speech helped gain Bryan the Democratic nomination for the presidency. He lost the election to Republican William McKinley.

———————————— ⌒∞⌒ ————————————

Mr. Chairman and Gentlemen of the Convention—I would be presumptuous, indeed, to present myself against the distinguished gentlemen to whom you have listened if this was a mere measuring of abilities; but this is not a contest between persons. The humblest citizen in all the land, when clad in the armor of a righteous cause, is stronger than all the hosts of error. I come to speak to you in defense of a cause as holy as the cause of liberty—the cause of humanity.

When this debate is concluded a motion will be made to lay upon the table the resolution offered in commendation of the administration and also the resolution offered in condemnation of the administration. We object to bringing this question down to the level of persons. The individual is but an atom; he is born, he acts, he dies; but principles are eternal; and this has been a contest over a principle.

Principles, Not Men.

Never before in the history of this country has there been witnessed such a contest as that through which we have just passed. Never before in the history of American politics has a great issue been fought out, as this issue has been, by the voters of a great party. On the fourth of March, 1895, a few democrats, most of them members of congress, issued an address to the democrats of the nation, asserting that the money question was the paramount issue of the hour; declaring that a majority of the democratic party had the right to control the action of the party on this paramount issue; and concluding with the request that the believers in the free coinage of silver in the democratic party should organize, take charge of, and control the policy of the democratic party. Three months later, at Memphis, an organization was perfected, and the silver democrats went forth openly and courageously proclaiming their belief, and declaring that, if successful, they would crystallize into a platform the declaration which they had made. Then began the conflict. With a zeal approaching the zeal which inspired the crusaders who followed Peter the Hermit, our silver democrats went forth from victory unto victory until they are now assembled, not to discuss, not to debate, but to enter up the judgment already rendered by the plain people of this country. In this contest brother has been arrayed against brother, father against son. The warmest ties of love, acquaintance and association have been disregarded; old leaders have been cast aside when they have refused to give expression to the sentiments of those whom they would lead, and new leaders have sprung up to give direction to this cause of truth. Thus has the contest been waged, and we have assembled here under a binding and solemn instructions as were ever imposed upon representatives of the people.

We do not come as individuals. As individuals we might have been glad to compliment the gentleman from New York (Senator Hill), but we know that the people for whom we speak would never be willing to put him in a position where he could thwart the will of the democratic party. I say it was not a question of persons; it was a question of principle, and it is not with gladness, my friends, that we find ourselves brought into conflict with those who are now arrayed on the other side.

The gentleman who preceded me (ex-Governor Russell) spoke of the state of Massachusetts; let me assure him that not one present in all this convention entertains the least hostility to the people of the state of Massachusetts, but we stand here representing people who are the equals before the law of the greatest citizens in the state of Massachusetts. When you (turning to the gold delegates) come before us and tell us that we are about to disturb your business interests, we reply that you have disturbed our business interests by your course.

The Real Business Men.
We say to you that you have made the definition of a business man too limited in its application. The man who is employed for wages is as much a business man as his employer; the attorney in a country town is as much a business man as the corporation counsel in a great metropolis; the merchant at the cross- roads store is as much a business man as the merchant of New York; the farmer who goes forth in the morning and toils all day—who begins in the spring and toils all summer—and who by the application of brain and muscle to the natural resources of the country creates wealth, is as much a business man as

the man who goes upon the board of trade and bets upon the price of grain; the miners who go down a thousand feet into the earth, or climb two thousand feet upon the cliffs, and bring forth from their hiding places the precious metals to be poured into the channels of trade are as much business men as the few financial magnates who, in a back room, corner the money of the world. We come to speak for this broader class of business men.

Ah, my friends, we say not one word against those who live upon the Atlantic coast, but the hardly pioneers who have braved all the dangers of the wilderness, who have made the desert to blossom as the rose—the pioneers away out there (pointing to the West), who rear their children near to Nature's heart, where they can mingle their voices with the voices of the birds—out there where they have erected school houses for the education of their young, churches where they praise their Creator, and cemeteries where rest the ashes of their dead—these people, we say, are as deserving of the consideration of our party as any people in this country. It is for these that we speak. We do not come as aggressors. Our war is not a war of conquest; we are fighting in the defense of our homes, our families, and posterity. We have petitioned, and our petitions have been scorned; we have entreated, and our entreaties have been disregarded; we have begged, and they have mocked when our calamity came. We beg no longer; we entreat no more; we petition no more. We defy them.

The gentleman from Wisconsin has said that he fears a Robespierre. My friends, in this land of the free you need not fear that a tyrant will spring up from among the people. What we need is an Andrew Jackson to stand, as Jackson stood, against the encroachments of organized wealth.

Must Meet New Conditions.
They tell us that this platform was made to catch votes. We reply to them that changing conditions make new issues; that the principles upon which democracy rests are as everlasting as the hills, but that they must be applied to new conditions as they arise. Conditions have arisen, and we are here to meet those conditions. They tell us that the income tax ought not to be brought in here; that it is a new idea. They criticise us for our criticism of the Supreme Court of the United States. My friends, we have not criticised; we have simply called attention to what you already know. If you want criticisms, read the dissenting opinions of the court. There you will find criticisms. They say that we passed an unconstitutional law; we deny it. The income tax law was not unconstitutional when it was passed; it was not unconstitutional when it went before the supreme court for the first time; it did not become unconstitutional until

one of the judges changed his mind, and we cannot be expected to know when a judge will change his mind. The income tax is just. It simply intends to put the burdens of government justly upon the backs of the people. I am in favor of an income tax. When I find a man who is not willing to bear his share of the burdens of the government which protects him, I find a man who is unworthy to enjoy the blessings of a government like ours.

Against a National Bank Currency.

They say that we are opposing national bank currency; it is true. If you will read what Thomas Benton said, you will find he said that, in searching history, he could find but one parallel to Andrew Jackson; that was Cicero who destroyed the conspiracy of Cataline and saved Rome. Benton said that Cicero only did for Rome what Jackson did for us when he destroyed the bank conspiracy and saved America. We say in our platform that we believe that the right to coin and issue money is a function of government. We believe it. We believe that it is a part of sovereignty, and can no more with safety be delegated to private individuals than we could afford to delegate to private individuals the power to make penal statutes or levy taxes. Mr. Jefferson, who was once regarded as good democratic authority, seems to have differed in opinion from the gentleman who has addressed us on the part of the minority. Those who are opposed to this proposition tell us that the issue of paper money is function of the bank, and that the government ought to go out of the banking business. I stand with Jefferson rather than with them, and tell them, as he did, that the issue of money is a function of government, and that the banks ought to go out of the governing business.

They complain about the plank which declares against life tenure in office. They have tried to strain it to mean that which it does not mean. What we oppose by that plank is the life tenure which is being built up in Washington, and which excludes from participation in official benefits the humbler members of society.

The Minority Amendments.

Let me call your attention to two or three important things. The gentleman from New York says that he will propose an amendment to the platform providing that the proposed change in our monetary system shall not affect contracts already made. Let me remind you that there is not intention of affecting those contracts which according to present laws are made payable in gold, but if he means to say that we cannot change our monetary system without protecting those who have loaned money before the change was made, I desire to ask him where, in law or morals, he can find justification for not protecting the

debtors when the act of 1873 was passed, if he now insists that we must protect the creditors.

He says he will also propose an amendment which will provide for the suspension of free coinage if we fail to maintain the parity within a year. We reply that when we advocate a policy which we believe will be successful, we are not compelled to raise a doubt as to our own sincerity by suggesting what we shall do if we fail. I ask him, if he would apply his logic to us, why he does not apply it to himself. He says he wants this country to try to secure an international agreement. Why does he not tell us what he is going to do if he fails to secure an international agreement? There is more reason for him to do that than there is for us to provide against the failure to maintain the parity. Our opponents have tried for twenty years to secure an international agreement, and those are waiting for it most patiently who do not want it at all.

The Paramount Issue.

And now, my friends, let me come to the paramount issue. If they ask us why it is that we say more on the money question than we say upon the tariff question, I reply that, if protection has slain its thousands, the gold standard has slain its tens of thousands. If they ask us why we do not embody in our platform all the things that we believe in, we reply that when we have restored the money of the constitution all other necessary reforms will be possible; but that until this is done there is no other reform that can be accomplished.

Why is it that within three months such a change has come over the country? Three months ago, when it was confidently asserted that those who believe in the gold standard would frame our platform and nominate our candidates, even the advocates of the gold standard did not think that we could elect a president. And they had good reason for their doubt, because there is scarcely a state here to-day asking for the gold standard which is not in the absolute control of the republican party. But note the change Mr. McKinley was nominated at St. Louis upon a platform which declared for the maintenance of the gold standard until it can be changed into bimetallism by international agreement. Mr. McKinley was the most popular man among the republicans, and three months ago everybody in the republican party prophesied his election. How is to-day? Why, the man who was once pleased to think that he looked like Napoleon—than man shudders to-day when he remembers that he was nominated on the anniversary of the battle of Waterloo. Not only that, but, as the listens, he can hear with ever-increasing distinctness the sound of the waves as they beat upon the lonely shores of St. Helena.

Why this change? Ah, my friends, is not the reason for the change evident to any one who will look at the matter? No private character, however pure, no personal popularity, however great, can protect from the avenging wrath of an indignant people a man who will declare that he is in favor of fastening the gold standard upon this country or who is willing to surrender the right of self government and place the legislative control of our affairs in the hands of foreign potentates and powers.

Confident of Success.

We go forth confident that we shall win. Why? Because upon the paramount issue of this campaign there is not a spot of ground upon which the enemy will dare to challenge battle. If they tell us that the gold standard is a good thing, we shall point to their platform and tell them that their platform pledges the party to get rid of the gold standard and substitute bimetallism. If the gold standard is a good thing, why try to get rid of it? I call your attention to the fact that some of the very people who are in this convention to-day and who tell us that we ought to declare in favor of international bimetallism—thereby declaring that the gold standard is wrong and that the principle of bimetallism is better—these very people four months ago were open and avowed advocates of the gold standard, and were then telling us that we could not legislate two metals together, even with the aid of all the world. If the gold standard is a good thing, we ought to declare in favor of its retention and not in favor of abandoning it; and if the gold standard is a bad thing why should we wait until other nations are willing to help us to let go? Here is the line of battle, and we care not upon which issue they force the fight; we are prepared to meet them on either issue or on both. If they tell us that the gold standard is the standard of civilization, we reply to them that this, the most enlightened of all the nations of the earth, has never declared for a gold standard and that both the great parties this year are declaring against it. If the gold standard is the standard of civilization why, my friends, should we not have it? If they come to meet us on that issue we can present the history of our nation. More than that; we can tell them that they will search the pages of history in vain to find a single instance where the common people of any land have ever declared themselves in favor of the gold standard. They can find where the holders of fixed investments have declared for a gold standard, but not where the masses have.

Carlisle Defines the Issue.

Mr. Carlisle said in 1878 that this was a struggle between "the idle holders of idle capital" and "the struggling masses, who produce the wealth and pay the taxes of the country," and, my friends, the question we are to decide is: Upon which side will the Democratic party fight: upon the side of the "idle holders of idle capital" or upon the side of "the struggling masses"? That is the question which the party must answer first, and then it must be answered by each individual hereafter. The sympathies of the Democratic party, as shown by the platform, are on the side of the struggling masses who have ever been the foundation of the Democratic party. There are two ideas of government. There are those who believe that, if you will only legislate to make the well- to-do prosperous, their prosperity will leak through on those below. The Democratic idea, however, has been that if you legislate to make the masses prosperous, their prosperity will find its way up through every class which rests upon them.

You come to us and tell us that the great cities are in favor of the gold standard; we reply that the great cities rest upon our broad and fertile prairies. Burn down your cities and leave our farms and your cities will spring up again as if by magic; but destroy our farms and the grass will grow in the streets of every city in the country.

A New Declaration of Independence.

My friends, we declare that this nation is able to legislate for its own people on every question, without waiting for the aid or consent of any other nation on earth; and upon that issue we expect to carry every state in the Union. I shall not slander the inhabitants of the fair state of Massachusetts nor the inhabitants of the state of New York by saying that, when they are confronted with the proposition, they will declare that this nation is not able to attend to its own business. It is the issue of 1776 over again. Our ancestors, when but three millions in number, had the courage to declare their political independence of every other nation; shall we, their descendants, when we have grown to seventy millions, declare that we are less independent than our forefathers? No, my friends, that will never be the verdict of our people. Therefore, we care not upon what lines the battle is fought. If they say bimetallism is good, but that we cannot have it until other nations help us, we reply that, instead of having a gold standard because England has, we will restore bimetallism, and then let England have bimetallism because the United States has it. If they dare to come out in the open field and defend the gold standard as a good thing, we will fight them to the uttermost. Having behind us the producing masses of this nation and the world, supported by the commercial interests, the laboring interests, and the toilers everywhere, we will answer their demand for a gold standard by saying to them: "You shall not press down upon the brow of labor this crown of thorns; you shall not crucify mankind upon a cross of gold."

Source:
Library of Congress, Manuscript Division, Bryan Papers, Container 49.

William Allen White, "What's the Matter with Kansas?", 1896

Scathing editorial attack on the Populist Party written by editor and publisher William Allen White, appearing first in his *Emporia Gazette* on August 3, 1896. Using sarcasm and picturesque language, White argued that Populists were driving people and money out of Kansas. Deriding one of the party's candidates as "an old jay," another as a "shabby, wild-eyed, rattle-brained fanatic," he mocked their competence and excoriated the Populist proposals as financially inane. The editorial was widely reprinted and was distributed by the opposing Republican Party, making White famous nationwide.

Today the Kansas Department of Agriculture sent out a statement which indicates that Kansas has gained less than two thousand people in the past year. There are about two hundred and twenty-five thousand families in this state, and there were ten thousand babies born in Kansas, and yet so many people have left the state that the natural increase is cut down to less than two thousand net.

This has been going on for eight years.

If there had been a high brick wall around the state eight years ago, and not a soul had been admitted or permitted to leave, Kansas would be a half million souls better off than she is today. And yet the nation has increased in population. In five years ten million people have been added to the national population, yet instead of gaining a share of this—say, half a million—Kansas has apparently been a plague spot and, in the very garden of the world, has lost population by ten thousands every year.

Not only has she lost population, but she has lost money. Every moneyed man in the state who could get out without loss has gone. Every month in every community sees someone who has a little money pack up and leave the state. This has been going on for eight years. Money has been drained out all the time. In towns where ten years ago there were three or four or half a dozen money-lending concerns, stimulating industry by furnishing capital, there is now none, or one or two that are looking after the interests and principal already outstanding.

No one brings any money into Kansas any more. What community knows over one or two men who have moved in with more than $5,000 in the past three years? And what community cannot count half a score of men in that time who have left, taking all the money they could scrape together?

Yet the nation has grown rich; other states have increased in population and wealth—other neighboring states. Missouri has gained over two million, while Kansas has been losing half a million. Nebraska has gained in wealth and population while Kansas has gone downhill. Colorado has gained every way, while Kansas has lost every way since 1888.

What's the matter with Kansas?

There is no substantial city in the state. Every big town save one has lost in population. Yet Kansas City, Omaha, Lincoln, St. Louis, Denver, Colorado Springs, Sedalia, the cities of the Dakotas, St. Paul and Minneapolis and Des Moines—all cities and towns in the West—have steadily grown.

Take up the government blue book and you will see that Kansas is virtually off the map. Two or three little scrubby consular places in yellow-fever-stricken communities that do not aggregate ten thousand dollars a year is all the recognition that Kansas has. Nebraska draws about one hundred thousand dollars; little old North Dakota draws about fifty thousand dollars; Oklahoma doubles Kansas; Missouri leaves her a thousand miles behind; Colorado is almost seven times greater than Kansas—the whole west is ahead of Kansas.

Take it by any standard you please, Kansas is not in it.

Go east and you hear them laugh at Kansas; go west and they sneer at her; go south and they "cuss" her; go north and they have forgotten her. Go into any crowd of intelligent people gathered anywhere on the globe, and you will find the Kansas man on the defensive. The newspaper columns and magazines once devoted to praise of her, to boastful facts and startling figures concerning her resources, are now filled with cartoons, jibes and Pefferian speeches. Kansas just naturally isn't in it. She has traded places with Arkansas and Timbuctoo.

What's the matter with Kansas?

We all know; yet here we are at it again. We have an old mossback Jacksonian who snorts and howls because there is a bathtub in the State House; we are running that old jay for Governor. We have another shabby, wild-eyed, rattle-brained fanatic who has said openly in a dozen speeches that "the rights of the user are paramount to the rights of the owner"; we are running him for Chief Justice, so that capital will come tumbling over itself to get into the state. We have raked the old ash heap of failure in the state and found an old human hoop skirt who has failed as a businessman, who has failed as an editor, who has failed as a preacher, and we are going to run him for Congressman-at-Large. He will help the looks of the Kansas delegation at Washington. Then we have discovered a kid without a law practice and have decided to run him for Attorney General. Then, for fear some hint that the state had become respectable might percolate through the civilized portions of the nation, we have decided to send three or four harpies out lecturing, telling the people that Kansas is raising hell and letting the corn go to weed.

Oh, this is a state to be proud of! We are a people who can hold up our heads! What we need is not more money, but less capital, fewer white shirts and brains, fewer men with business judgment, and more of those fellows who boast that they are "just ordinary clodhoppers, but they know more in a minute about finance than John Sherman"; we need more men who are "posted," who can bellow about the crime of '73, who hate prosperity, and who think, because a man believes in national honor, he is a tool of Wall Street. We have had a few of them—some hundred fifty thousand—but we need more.

We need several thousand gibbering idiots to scream about the "Great Red Dragon" of Lombard Street. We don't need population, we don't need wealth, we don't need well-dressed men on the streets, we don't need cities on the fertile prairies; you bet we don't! What we are after is the money power. Because we have become poorer and ornerier and meaner than a spavined, distempered mule, we, the people of Kansas, propose to kick; we don't care to build up, we wish to tear down.

"There are two ideas of government," said our noble Bryan at Chicago. "There are those who believe that if you legislate to make the well-to-do prosperous, this prosperity will leak through on those below. The Democratic idea has been that if you legislate to make the masses prosperous their prosperity will find its way up and through every class and rest upon them."

That's the stuff! Give the prosperous man the dickens! Legislate the thriftless man into ease, whack the stuffing out of the creditors and tell the debtors who borrowed the money five years ago when money "per capita" was greater than it is now, that the contraction of currency gives him a right to repudiate.

Whoop it up for the ragged trousers; put the lazy, greasy fizzle, who can't pay his debts, on the altar, and bow down and worship him. Let the state ideal be high. What we need is not the respect of our fellow men, but the chance to get something for nothing.

Oh, yes, Kansas is a great state. Here are people fleeing from it by the score every day, capital going out of the state by the hundreds of dollars; and every industry but farming paralyzed, and that crippled, because its products have to go across the ocean before they can find a laboring man at work who can afford to buy them. Let's don't stop this year. Let's drive all the decent, self- respecting men out of the state. Let's keep the old clodhoppers who know it all. Let's encourage the man who is "posted." He can talk, and what we need is not mill hands to eat our meat, nor factory hands to eat our wheat, nor cities to oppress the farmer by consuming his butter and eggs and chickens and produce. What Kansas needs is men who can talk, who have large leisure to argue the currency question while their wives wait at home for that nickel's worth of bluing.

What's the matter with Kansas?

Nothing under the shining sun. She is losing her wealth, population and standing. She has got her statesmen, and the money power is afraid of her. Kansas is all right. She has started in to raise hell, as Mrs. Lease advised, and she seems to have an over-production. But that doesn't matter. Kansas never did believe in diversified crops. Kansas is all right. There is absolutely nothing wrong with Kansas. "Every prospect pleases and only man is vile."

I remember even cross these years that I slammed the editorial above on the copy spike with a passionate satisfaction that I had answered those farmer hooligans. I was happy and turned to something else for the afternoon. Before I left I had read the proof on it, which meant that I probably revised it two or three or four times, as I always do even now when I have for the paper an editorial that I am proud of. And so, late that afternoon I gathered up my proofs, a book or two that had come, the magazines of the week, and took the train for Colorado to lay my treasures before the feet of my lady love, fancying myself a romantic figure. And so there at the little red-stone depot at Manitou, where she came running down the platform to meet me, and I hurried with all my treasures for her, the book of our pride, the papers and magazines which would bring us together so happily, a journey ended in lover's meeting.

Source:

The Autobiography of William Allen White. New York: Macmillan, 1946.

Gold Standard Act, 1900

Federal legislation enacted March 14, 1900, that placed the United States on the gold standard, after years of controversy over bimetallism and the coinage of silver. The act declared that the dollar, consisting of 25.8 grains of gold, 0.9 fine, would be the standard unit of value, and that all forms of money issued or coined by the United States should be maintained at a parity of value with this standard. The act established a gold reserve of $150 million for the redemption of legal tender notes.

An Act

To define and fix the standard of value, to maintain the parity of all forms of money issued or coined by the United States, to refund the public debt, and for other purposes.

Be it enacted by the Senate and House of Representative of the United States of America in Congress assembled, That the dollar consisting of twenty-five and eight-tenths grains of gold nine-tenths fine, as established by section thirty-five hundred and eleven of the Revised Statutes of the United States, shall be the standard unit of value, and all forms of money issued or coined by the United States shall be maintained at a parity of value with this standard, and it shall be the duty of the Secretary of the Treasury to maintain such parity.

Sec. 2. That United States notes, and Treasury notes issued under the Act of July fourteenth, eighteen hundred and ninety, when presented to the Treasury for redemption, shall be redeemed in gold coin of the standard fixed in the first section of this Act, and in order to secure the prompt and certain redemption of such notes as herein provided it shall be the duty of the Secretary of the Treasury to set apart in the Treasury a reserve fund of one hundred and fifty million dollars in gold coin and bullion, which fund shall be used for such redemption purposes only, and whenever and as often as any of said notes shall be redeemed from said fund it shall be the duty of the Secretary of the Treasury to use said notes so redeemed to restore and maintain such reserve fund in the manner following, to wit: First, by exchanging the notes so redeemed for any gold coin in the general fund of the Treasury; second, by accepting deposits of gold coin at the Treasury or at any subtreasury in exchange for the United States notes so redeemed; third, by procuring gold coin by the use of said notes, in accordance with the provisions of section thirty-seven hundred of the Revised Statutes of the United States. If the Secretary of the Treasury is unable to restore and maintain the gold coin in the reserve fund by the foregoing methods, and the amount of such gold coin and bullion in said fund shall at any time fall below one hundred million dollars, then it shall be his duty to restore the same to the maximum sum of one hundred and fifty million dollars by borrowing money on the credit of the United States, and for the debt thus incurred to issue and sell coupon or registered bonds of the United States, in such form as he may prescribe, in denominations of fifty dollars or any multiple thereof, bearing interest at the rate of not exceeding three per centum per annum, payable quarterly, such bonds to be payable at the pleasure of the United States after one year from the date of their issue, and to be payable, principal and interest, in gold coin of the present

standard value, and to be exempt from the payment of all taxes or duties of the United States, as well as from taxation in any form by or under State, municipal, or local authority; and the gold coin received from the sale of said bonds shall first be covered into the general fund of the Treasury and then exchanged, in the manner hereinbefore provided, for an equal amount of the notes redeemed and held for exchange, and the Secretary of the Treasury may, in his discretion, use said notes in exchange for gold, or to purchase or redeem any bonds of the United States, or for any other lawful purpose the public interests may require, except that they shall not be used to meet deficiencies in the current revenues. That United States notes when redeemed in accordance with the provisions of this section shall be reissued, but shall be held in the reserve fund until exchanged for gold, as herein provided; and the gold coin and bullion in the reserve fund, together with the redeemed notes held for use as provided in this section, shall at no time exceed the maximum sum of one hundred and fifty million dollars.

Sec. 3. That nothing contained in this Act shall be construed to affect the legal-tender quality as now provided by law of the silver dollar, or of any other money coined or issued by the United States.

Sec. 4. That there be established in the Treasury Department, as a part of the office of the Treasurer of the United States, divisions to be designated and known as the division of issue and the division of redemption, to which shall be assigned, respectively, under such regulations as the Secretary of the Treasury may approve, all records and accounts relating to the issue and redemption of United States notes, gold certificates, silver certificates, and currency certificates. There shall be transferred from the accounts of the general fund of the Treasury of the United States, and taken up on the books of said divisions, respectively, accounts relating to the reserve fund for the redemption of United States notes and Treasury notes, the gold coin held against outstanding gold certificates, the United States notes held against outstanding currency certificates, and the silver dollars held against outstanding silver certificates, and each of the funds represented by these accounts shall be used for the redemption of the notes and certificates for which they are respectively pledged, and shall be used for no other purpose, the same being held as trust funds.

Sec. 5. That it shall be the duty of the Secretary of the Treasury, as fast as standard silver dollars are coined under the provisions of the Acts of July fourteenth, eighteen hundred and ninety, and June thirteenth, eighteen hundred and ninety-eight, from bullion purchased under the Act of July fourteenth, eighteen hundred and ninety, to retire and cancel an equal amount of Treasury notes whenever received into the Treasury, either by exchange in accordance with the provisions of this Act or in the ordinary course of business, and upon the cancellation of Treasury notes silver certificates shall be issued against the silver dollars so coined.

Sec. 6. That the Secretary of the Treasury is hereby authorized and directed to receive deposits of gold coin with the Treasurer or any assistant treasurer of the United States in sums of not less than twenty dollars, and to issue gold certificates therefor in denominations of not less than twenty dollars, and the coin so deposited shall be retained in the Treasury and held for the payment of such certificates on demand, and used for no other purpose. Such certificates shall be receivable for customs, taxes, and all public dues, and when so received may be reissued, and when held by any national banking association may be counted as a part of its lawful reserve: *Provided*, That whenever and so long as the gold coin held in the reserve fund in the Treasury for the redemption of United States notes and Treasury notes shall fall and remain below one hundred million dollars the authority to issue certificates as herein provided shall be suspended: *And provided further*, That whenever and so long as the aggregate amount of United States notes and silver certificates in the general fund of the Treasury shall exceed sixty million dollars the Secretary of the Treasury may, in his discretion, suspend the issue of the certificates herein provided for: *And provided further*, That of the amount of such outstanding certificates one-fourth at least shall be in denominations of fifty dollars or less: *And provided further*, That the Secretary of the Treasury may, in his discretion, issue such certificates in denominations of ten thousand dollars, payable to order. And section fifty-one hundred and ninety-three of the Revised Statutes of the United States is hereby repealed.

Sec. 7. That hereafter silver certificates shall be issued only of denominations of ten dollars and under, except that not exceeding in the aggregate ten per centum of the total volume of said certificates, in the discretion of the Secretary of the Treasury, may be issued in denominations of twenty dollars, fifty dollars, and one hundred dollars; and silver certificates of higher denominations than ten dollars, except as herein provided, shall, whenever received at the Treasury or redeemed, be retired and canceled, and certificates of denominations of ten dollars or less shall be substituted therefor, and after such substitution, in whole or in part, a like volume of United States notes of less denomination than ten dollars shall from time to time be retired and canceled, and notes of denominations of ten dollars and upward shall be reissued in substitution therefor, with like qualities and restrictions as those retired and canceled.

Sec. 8. That the Secretary of the Treasury is hereby authorized to use, at his discretion, any silver bullion in the Treasury of the United States purchased under the Act of July fourteenth, eighteen hundred and ninety, for coinage into such denominations of subsidiary silver coin as may be necessary to meet the public requirements for such coin: *Provided* , That the amount of subsidiary silver coin outstanding shall not at any time exceed in the aggregate one hundred millions of dollars. Whenever any silver bullion purchased under the Act of July fourteenth, eighteen hundred and ninety, shall be used in the coinage of subsidiary silver coin, an amount of Treasury notes issued under said Act equal to the cost of the bullion contained in such coin shall be canceled and not reissued.

Sec. 9. That the Secretary of the Treasury is hereby authorized and directed to cause all worn and uncurrent subsidiary silver coin of the United States now in the Treasury, and hereafter received, to be recoined, and to reimburse the Treasury of the United States for the difference between the nominal or face value of such coin and the amount the same will produce in new coin from any moneys in the Treasury not otherwise appropriated.

Sec. 10. That section fifty-one hundred and thirty-eight of the Revised Statutes is hereby amended so as to read as follows:

"Section 5138. No association shall be organized with a less capital than one hundred thousand dollars, except that banks with a capital of not less than fifty thousand dollars may, with the approval of the Secretary of the Treasury, be organized in any place the population of which does not exceed six thousand inhabitants, and except that banks with a capital of not less than twenty-five thousand dollars may, with the sanction of the Secretary of the Treasury, be organized in any place the population of which does not exceed three thousand inhabitants. No association shall be organized in a city the population of which exceeds fifty thousand persons with a capital of less than two hundred thousand dollars."

Sec. 11. That the Secretary of the Treasury is hereby authorized to receive at the Treasury any of the outstanding bonds of the United States bearing interest at five per centum per annum, payable February first, nineteen hundred and four, and any bonds of the United States bearing interest at four per centum per annum, payable July first, nineteen hundred and seven, and any bonds of the United States bearing interest at three per centum per annum, payable August first, nineteen hundred and eight, and to issue in exchange therefor an equal amount of coupon or registered bonds of the United States in such form as he may prescribe, in denominations of fifty dollars or any multiple thereof, bearing interest at the rate of two per centum per annum, payable quarterly, such bonds to be payable at the pleasure of the United States after thirty years from the date of their issue, and said bonds to be payable, principal and interest, in gold coin of the present standard value, and to be exempt from the payment of all taxes or duties of the United States, as well as from taxation in any form by or under State, municipal, or local authority: *Provided,* That such outstanding bonds may be received in exchange at a valuation not greater than their present worth to yield an income of two and one-quarter per centum per annum; and in consideration of the reduction of interest effected, the Secretary of the Treasury is authorized to pay to the holders of the outstanding bonds surrendered for exchange, out of any money in the Treasury not otherwise appropriated, a sum not greater than the difference between their present worth, computed as aforesaid, and their par value, and the payments to be made hereunder shall be held to be payments on account of the sinking fund created by section thirty-six hundred and ninety-four of the Revised Statutes: *And provided further,* That the two per centum bonds to be issued under the provisions of this Act shall be issued at not less than par, and they shall be numbered consecutively in the order of their issue, and when payment is made the last numbers issued shall be first paid, and this order shall be followed until all the bonds are paid, and whenever any of the outstanding bonds are called for payment interest thereon shall cease three months after such call; and there is hereby appropriated out of any money in the Treasury not otherwise appropriated, to effect the exchanges of bonds provided for in this Act, a sum not exceeding one-fifteenth of one per centum of the face value of said bonds, to pay the expense of preparing and issuing the same and other expenses incident thereto.

Sec. 12. That upon the deposit with the Treasurer of the United States, by any national banking association, of any bonds of the United States in the manner provided by existing law, such association shall be entitled to receive from the Comptroller of the Currency circulating notes in blank, registered and countersigned as provided by law, equal in amount to the par value of the bonds so deposited; and any national banking association now having bonds on deposit for the security of circulating notes, and upon which an amount of circulating notes has been issued less than the par value of the bonds, shall be entitled, upon due application to the Comptroller of the Currency, to receive additional circulating notes in blank to an amount which will increase the circulating notes held by such association to the par value of the bonds deposited, such additional notes to be held and treated in the same way as circulating notes of national banking associations heretofore issued, and subject to all the provisions of law affecting such notes: *Provided,* That nothing herein contained shall be con-

strued to modify or repeal the provisions of section fifty-one hundred and sixty-seven of the Revised Statutes of the United States, authorizing the Comptroller of the Currency to require additional deposits of bonds or of lawful money in case the market value of the bonds held to secure the circulating notes shall fall below the par value of the circulating notes outstanding for which such bonds may be deposited as security: *And provided further,* That the circulating notes furnished to national banking associations under the provisions of this Act shall be of the denominations prescribed by law, except that no national banking association shall, after the passage of this Act, be entitled to receive from the Comptroller of the Currency, or to issue or reissue or place in circulation, more than one-third in amount of its circulating notes of the denomination of five dollars: *And provided further,* That the total amount of such notes issued to any such association may equal at any time but shall not exceed the amount of such time of its capital stock actually paid in: *And provided further,* That under regulations to be prescribed by the Secretary of the Treasury any national banking association may substitute the two per centum bonds issued under the provisions of this Act for any of the bonds deposited with the Treasurer to secure circulation or to secure deposits of public money; and so much of an Act entitled "An Act to enable national banking associations to extend their corporate existence, and for other purposes," approved July twelfth, eighteen hundred and eighty-two, as prohibits any national bank which makes any deposit of lawful money in order to withdraw its circulating notes from receiving any increase of its circulation for the period of six months from the time it made such deposit of lawful money for the purpose aforesaid, is hereby repealed, and all other Acts or parts of Acts inconsistent with the provisions of this section are hereby repealed.

Sec. 13. That every national banking association having on deposit, as provided by law, bonds of the United States bearing interest at the rate of two per centum annum, issued under the provisions of this Act, to secure its circulating notes, shall pay to the Treasurer of the United States, in the months of January and July, a tax of one-fourth of one per centum each half year upon the average amount of such of its notes in circulation as are based upon the deposit of said two per centum bonds; and such taxes shall be in lieu of existing taxes on its notes in circulation imposed by section fifty-two hundred and fourteen of the Revised Statutes.

Sec. 14. That the provisions of this Act are not intended to preclude the accomplishment of international bimetallism whenever conditions shall make it expedient and practicable to secure the same by concurrent action of the leading commercial nations of the world and at a ratio which shall insure permanence of relative value between gold and silver.

Source:
Statutes at Large, Vol. 31, pp. 45–50.

The Development of an Expansionist Foreign Policy

Alaska Purchase Treaty, 1867

Treaty concluded on March 30, 1867, by which the United States purchased Alaska from Russia for $7.2 million. The treaty was negotiated by Baron Edouard de Stoeckl, Russian minister to the United States, and U.S. secretary of state William Seward. The Russians considered Alaska a financial liability, which they were reluctant to administer and defend. Seward, an expansionist, was the prime promoter of the purchase, which was for many years considered foolish, hence the names "Seward's Folly" and "Seward's Icebox" for the territory. There were rumors that Senate ratification (April 9) was accomplished through Russian bribery of key senators.

On February 29, 1892, the United States and Great Britain signed the Bering Sea Treaty to resolve a dispute over pelagic (deep sea) sealing rights. With the purchase of Alaska in 1867, the United States had acquired the Pribilof Islands, the site of seal breeding grounds. To prevent other nations, especially Canada, from overhunting the herds at sea, the United States in 1890 declared dominion over the Bering Sea, calling it a *mare clausum* (closed sea). The Anglo-American arbitration treaty of 1892 referred the matter to an international tribunal, which ruled in 1893 against the U.S. claim to exclusive rights in the Bering Sea but did prohibit pelagic sealing around the Pribilof Islands at specified times each year.

The United States of America and His Majesty the Emperor of all the Russias, being desirous of strengthening, if possible, the good understanding which exists between them, have, for that purpose, appointed as their Plenipotentiaries: the President of the United States, William H. Seward, Secretary of State; and His Majesty the Emperor of all the Russias, the Privy Counsellor Edward de Stoeckl, his Envoy Extraordinary and Minister Plenipotentiary to the United States.

And the said Plenipotentiaries, having exchanged their full powers, which were found to be in due form, have agreed upon and signed the following articles:

Article I

His Majesty the Emperor of all the Russias agrees to cede to the United States, by this convention, immediately upon the exchange of the ratifications thereof, all the territory and dominion now possessed by his said Majesty on the continent of America and in the adjacent islands, the same being contained within the geographical limits herein set forth, to wit: The eastern limit is the line of demarcation between the Russian and the British possessions in North America, as established by the convention between Russia and Great Britain, of February 28–16, 1825, and described in Articles III and IV of said convention, in the following terms:

"Commencing from the southernmost point of the island called Prince of Wales Island, which point lies in the parallel of 54 degrees 40 minutes north latitude, and between the 131st and the 133d degree of west longitude, (meridian of Greenwich,) the said line shall ascend to the north along the channel called Portland channel, as far as the point of the continent where it strikes the 56th degree of north latitude; from this last mentioned point, the line of demarcation shall follow the summit of the mountains situated parallel to the coast as far as the point of intersection of the 141st degree of west longitude, (of the same meridian;) and finally, from the said point of intersection, the said meridian line of the 141st degree, in its prolongation as far as the Frozen ocean.

"IV. With reference to the line of demarcation laid down in the preceding article, it is understood—

"1st. That the island called Prince of Wales Island shall belong wholly to Russia" (now, by this cession, to the United States).

"2d. That whenever the summit of the mountains which extend in a direction parallel to the coast from the

56th degree of north latitude to the point of intersection of the 141st degree of west longitude shall prove to be at the distance of more than ten marine leagues from the ocean, the limit between the British possessions and the line of coast which is to belong to Russia as above mentioned (that is to say, the limit to the possessions ceded by this convention) shall be formed by a line parallel to the winding of the coast, and which shall never exceed the distance of ten marine leagues therefrom."

The western limit within which the territories and dominion conveyed, are contained, passes through a point in Behring's straits on the parallel of sixty-five degrees thirty minutes north latitude, at its intersection by the meridian which passes midway between the islands of Krusenstern, or Ignalook, and the island of Ratmanoff, or Noonarbook, and proceeds due north, without limitation, into the same Frozen ocean. The same western limit, beginning at the same initial point, proceeds thence in a course nearly southwest, through Behring's straits and Behring's sea, so as to pass midway between the northwest point of the island of St. Lawrence and the southeast point of Cape Choukotski, to the meridian of one hundred and seventy-two west longitude; thence, from the intersection of that meridian, in a southwesterly direction, so as to pass midway between the island of Attou and the Copper island of the Kormandorski couplet or group in the North Pacific ocean, to the meridian of one hundred and ninety-three degrees west longitude, so as to include in the territory conveyed the whole of the Aleutian islands east of that meridian.

Article II

In the cession of territory and dominion made by the preceding article, are included the right of property in all public lots and squares, vacant lands, and all public buildings, fortifications, barracks, and other edifices which are not private individual property. It is, however, understood and agreed, that the churches which have been built in the ceded territory by the Russian government, shall remain the property of such members of the Greek Oriental Church resident in the territory, as may choose to worship therein. Any government archives, papers, and documents relative to the territory and dominion aforesaid, which may be now existing there, will be left in the possession of the agent of the United States; but an authenticated copy of such of them as may be required, will be, at all times, given by the United States to the Russian government, or to such Russian officers or subjects, as they may apply for.

Article III

The inhabitants of the ceded territory, according to their choice, reserving their natural allegiance, may return to Russia within three years; but if they should prefer to remain in the ceded territory, they, with the exception of uncivilized native tribes, shall be admitted to the enjoyment of all the rights, advantages and immunities of citizens of the United States, and shall be maintained and protected in the free enjoyment of their liberty, property and religion. The uncivilized tribes will be subject to such laws and regulations as the United States may, from time to time, adopt in regard to aboriginal tribes of that country.

Article IV

His Majesty the Emperor of all the Russias shall appoint, with convenient despatch, an agent or agents for the purpose of formally delivering to a similar agent or agents appointed on behalf of the United States, the territory, dominion, property, dependencies and appurtenances which are ceded as above, and for doing any other act which may be necessary in regard thereto. But the cession, with the right of immediate possession, is nevertheless to be deemed complete and absolute on the exchange of ratifications, without waiting for such formal delivery.

Article V

Immediately after the exchange of the ratifications of this convention, any fortifications or military posts which may be in the ceded territory, shall be delivered to the agent of the United States, and any Russian troops which may be in the territory shall be withdrawn as soon as may be reasonably and conveniently practicable.

Article VI

In consideration of the cession aforesaid, the United States agree to pay at the treasury in Washington, within ten months after the exchange of the ratifications of this convention, to the diplomatic representative or other agent of his Majesty the Emperor of all the Russias, duly authorized to receive the same, seven million two hundred thousand dollars in gold. The cession of territory and dominion herein made is hereby declared to be free and unencumbered by any reservations, privileges, franchises, grants, or possessions, by any associated companies, whether corporate or incorporate, Russian or any other, or by any parties, except merely private individual property holders; and the cession hereby made, conveys all the rights, franchises, and privileges now belonging to Russia in the said territory or dominion, and appurtenances thereto.

Article VII

When this Convention shall have been duly ratified by the President of the United States, by and with the advice and consent of the Senate, on the one part, and on the other by his Majesty the Emperor of all the Russias, the ratifications shall be exchanged at Washington within three months from the date hereof, or sooner, if possible.

In faith whereof, the respective plenipotentiaries have signed this convention, and thereto affixed the seals of their arms.

Done at Washington, the thirtieth day of March in the year of our Lord one thousand eight hundred and sixty-seven.

Source:

Charles I. Bevans, *Treaties and Other Agreements of the United States of America, 1776–1949.* Washington, D.C.: Government Printing Office, 1968–76.

Burlingame Treaty, 1868

Treaty between the United States and China, negotiated by "envoy extraordinary" of the emperor of China, Anson Burlingame, and signed July 28, 1868; recognized China's basic sovereign rights in international law. The treaty, a supplement to the U.S.-Chinese Treaty of 1858, acknowledged Chinese territorial jurisdiction within China; guaranteed that the U.S. would not intervene in China's domestic affairs; confirmed the Chinese government's discretion in granting trade privileges in China; and provided for free Chinese immigration to the United States. It gave citizens of the two countries mutual most-favored-nation privileges within each other's borders. These privileges entitle the country holding them to the same economic advantages as "the most favored nation." Anti-Chinese agitation led to revision of the treaty in 1880, allowing the United States to limit entry of Chinese laborers.

───────── ∽∞ゎ ─────────

ADDITIONAL ARTICLES TO THE TREATY BE-TWEEN THE UNITED STATES OF AMERICA AND THE TA-TSING EMPIRE OF THE 18TH OF JUNE, 1858

Whereas since the conclusion of the treaty between the United of America and the Ta-Tsing Empire (China) of the 18th of June, 1858, circumstances have arisen showing the necessity of additional articles thereto, the President of the United States and the august sovereign of the Ta-Tsing Empire have named for their plenipotentiaries, to wit: the President of the United States of America, William H. Seward, Secretary of State, and his Majesty the Emperor of China, Anson Burlingame, accredited as his Envoy Extraordinary and Minister Plenipotentiary, and Chih-Kang and Sun Chia-Ku, of the second Chinese rank, associated high envoys and ministers of his said Majesty, and the said plenipotentiaries, after having exchanged their full powers, found to be in due and proper form, have agreed upon the following articles:

Article I

His Majesty the Emperor of China, being of the opinion that, in making concessions to the citizens or subjects of foreign Powers of the privilege of residing on certain tracts of land, or resorting to certain waters of that empire purposes of trade, he has by no means relinquished his right of eminent domain or dominion over the said land and waters, hereby agrees that no such concession or grant shall be construed to give to any Power or party which may be at war with or hostile to the United States the right to attack the citizens of the United States or their property within the said lands or waters; and the United States, for themselves, hereby agree to abstain from offensively attacking the citizens or subjects of any Power or party or their property with which they may be at war on any such tract of land or waters of the said empire; but nothing in this article shall be construed to prevent the United States from resisting an attack by any hostile Power or party upon their citizens or their property. It is further agreed that if any right or interest in any tract of land in China has been or shall hereafter be granted by the Government of China to the United States or their citizens for purposes of trade or commerce, that grant shall in no event be construed to divest the Chinese authorities of their right of jurisdiction over persons and property within said tract of land, except so far as that right may have been expressly relinquished by treaty.

Article II

The United States of America and his Majesty the Emperor of China, believing that the safety and prosperity of commerce will thereby best be promoted, agree that any privilege or immunity in respect to trade or navigation within the Chinese dominions which may not have been stipulated for by treaty, shall be subject to the discretion of the Chinese Government and may be regulated by it accordingly, but not in a manner or spirit incompatible with the treaty stipulations of the parties.

Article III

The Emperor of China shall have the right to appoint consuls at ports of the United States, who shall enjoy the same privileges and immunities as those which are enjoyed by public law and treaty in the United States by the consuls of Great Britain and Russia, or either of them.

Article IV

The twenty-ninth article of the treaty of the 18th of June, 1858, having stipulated for the exemption of Christian citizens of the United States and Chinese converts from persecution in China on account of their faith, it is further agreed that citizens of the United States in China of every religious persuasion and Chinese subjects in the United

States shall enjoy entire liberty of conscience and shall be exempt from all disability or persecution on account of their religious faith or worship in their country. Cemeteries for sepulture of the dead of whatever nativity or nationality shall be held in respect and free from disturbance or profanation.

Article V

The United States of America and the Emperor of China cordially recognize the inherent and inalienable right of man to change his home and allegiance, and also the mutual advantage of the free migration and emigration of their citizens and subjects respectively from the one country to the other, for purposes of curiosity, of trade, or as permanent residents. The high contracting parties, therefore, join in reprobating any other than an entirely voluntary emigration for these purposes. They consequently agree to pass laws making it a penal offence for a citizen of the United States or Chinese subjects to take Chinese subjects either to the United States or to any other foreign country, or for a Chinese subject or citizen of the United States to take citizens of the United States to China or to any other foreign country, without their free and voluntary consent respectively.

Article VI

Citizens of the United States visiting or residing in China shall enjoy the same privileges, immunities or exemptions in respect to travel or residence as may there be enjoyed by the citizens or subjects of the most favored nation, and, reciprocally, Chinese subjects visiting or residing in the United States, shall enjoy the same privileges, immunities and exemptions in respect to travel or residence as may there be enjoyed by the citizens or subjects of the most favored nation. But nothing herein contained shall be held to confer naturalization upon citizens of the United States in China, nor upon the subjects of China in the United States.

Article VII

Citizens of the United States shall enjoy all the privileges of the public educational institutions under the control of the government of China, and reciprocally, Chinese subjects shall enjoy all the privileges of the public educational institutions under the control of the government of the United States, which are enjoyed in the respective countries by the citizens or subjects of the most favored nation. The citizens of the United States may freely establish and maintain schools within the Empire of China at those places where foreigners are by treaty permitted to reside, and, reciprocally, Chinese subjects may enjoy the same privileges and immunities in the United States.

Article VIII

The United States, always disclaiming and discouraging all practices of unnecessary dictation and intervention by one nation in the affairs or domestic administration of another, do hereby freely disclaim and disavow any intention or right to intervene in the domestic administration of China in regard to the construction of railroads, telegraphs or other material internal improvements. On the other hand, his Majesty, the Emperor of China, reserves to himself the right to decide the time and manner and circumstances of introducing such improvements within his dominions. With this mutual understanding it is agreed by the contracting parties that if at any time hereafter his imperial Majesty shall determine to construct or cause to be constructed works of the character mentioned within the empire, and shall make application to the United States or any other Western Power for facilities to carry out that policy, the United States will, in that case, designate and authorize suitable engineers to be employed by the Chinese Government, and will recommend to other nations an equal compliance with such application, the Chinese Government in that case protecting such engineers in their persons and property, and paying them a reasonable compensation for their service.

In faith whereof the respective Plenipotentiaries have signed this treaty and thereto affixed the seals of their arms.

Done at Washington the twenty-eight day of July, in the year of our Lord one thousand eight hundred and sixty-eight.

Source:

Charles I. Bevans, *Treaties and Other Agreements of the United States of America, 1776–1949.* Washington, D.C.: Government Printing Office, 1968–76.

Olney-Pauncefote Treaty, 1896

British-American arbitration agreement, drafted by U.S. secretary of state Richard Olney and the British ambassador to the United States, Sir Julian Pauncefote, in 1896. The agreement (signed on January 11, 1897, in Washington, D.C.) made financial and most other nonterritorial disputes entirely arbitrable. It made territorial disputes and certain important principles arbitrable but subject to an appeal to a six-member court; if more than one member of the court dissented, the decision was not binding. Although the British Parliament ratified the treaty, the U.S. Senate failed to do so. The U.S. Senate continues into the 21st century to avoid endorsing treaties that subject the United States to international tribunals.

By the President of the United States of America.
A PROCLAMATION.

Whereas, a Convention between the Governments of the United States of America and Great Britain, providing for the settlement of claims presented by Great Britain against the United States in virtue of the Convention of February 29, 1892, between the same High Contracting Parties, was concluded and signed by their respective Plenipotentiaries at the City of Washington, on the eighth day of February, 1896, which Convention, being in the English language, and as amended by the Senate of the United States, is word for word as follows:

Whereas by a Treaty between the United States of America and Her Majesty the Queen of the United Kingdom of Great Britain and Ireland, signed at Washington on February 29, 1892, the questions which had arisen between their respective Governments concerning the jurisdictional rights of the United States in the waters of Behring Sea, and concerning also the preservation of the fur-seal in, or habitually resorting to, the said Sea, and the rights of the citizens and subjects of either country as regards the taking of fur-seal in, or habitually resorting to, the said waters, were submitted to a Tribunal of Arbitration as therein constituted;

And whereas the High Contracting Parties having found themselves unable to agree upon a reference which should include the question of the liability of each for the injuries alleged to have been sustained by the other, or by its citizens, in connection with the claims presented and urged by it, did, by Article VIII of the said Treaty, agree that either party might submit to the Arbitrators any questions of fact involved in said claims and ask for a finding thereon, the question of the liability of either Government on the facts found to be the subject of further negotiations;

And whereas the Agent of Great Britain did, in accordance with the provisions of said Article VIII, submit to the Tribunal or Arbitration certain findings of fact which were agreed to as proved by the Agent of the United States, and the Arbitrators did unanimously find the facts so set forth to be true, as appears by the Award of the Tribunal rendered on the 15th day of August, 1893;

And whereas in view of the said findings of fact and of the decision of the Tribunal of Arbitration concerning the jurisdictional rights of the United States in Behring Sea and the right of protection or property of the United States in the fur-seals frequenting the islands of the United States in Behring Sea, the Government of the United States is desirous that in so far as its liability is not already fixed and determined by the findings of fact and the decision of said Tribunal of Arbitration, the question of such liability should be definitely and fully settled and determined, and compensation made, for any injuries for which, in the con-

templation of the Treaty aforesaid, and the award and findings of the Tribunal of Arbitration compensation may be due to great Britain from the United States;

And whereas it is claimed by Great Britain, though not admitted by the United States, that prior to the said award certain other claims against the United States accrued in favor of Great Britain on account of seizures of or interference with the following named British sealing vessels,— to wit, the "Wanderer," the "Winnifred," the "Henrietta" and the "Oscar and Hattie," and it is for the mutual interest and convenience of both the High Contracting Parties that the liability of the United States, if any, and the amount of compensation to be paid, if any, in respect of such claims and each of them should also be determined under the provisions of this Convention—all claims by Great Britain under Article V of the Modus Vivendi of April 18, 1892 for the abstention from fishing of British sealers during the pendency of said arbitration having been definitely waived before the Tribunal of Arbitration:

The United States of America and Her Majesty the Queen of the United Kingdom of Great Britain and Ireland, to the end of concluding a Convention for that purpose, have appointed as their respective Plenipotentiaries:

The President of the United States, the Honorable Richard Olney, Secretary of State; and Her Majesty the Queen of the United Kingdom of Great Britain and Ireland, the Right Honorable Sir Julian Pauncefote, G.C.B., G.C.M.G., Her Majesty's Ambassador Extraordinary and Plenipotentiary to the United States;

Who, after having communicated to each other their respective full powers, which were found in due and proper form, have agreed to and concluded the following Articles:

Article I

The high Contracting Parties agree that all claims on account of injuries sustained by persons in whose behalf Great Britain is entitled to claim compensation from the United States and arising by virtue of the Treaty aforesaid, the award and the findings of the said Tribunal of Arbitration, as also the additional claims specified in the 5th paragraph of the preamble hereto, shall be referred to two Commissioners, one of whom shall be appointed by the President of the United States, and the other by Her Britannic Majesty, and each of whom shall be learned in the law. Appended to this Convention is a list of the claims intended to be referred.

Article II

The two Commissioners shall meet at Victoria, in the Province of British Columbia, Canada, as soon as practicable after the exchange of the ratifications of this Convention, and, after taking an oath that they will fairly and impartially investigate the claims referred to them and render a just decision thereon, they shall proceed jointly to the discharge of their duties.

The Commission shall also sit at San Francisco, California, as well as Victoria, provided either Commissioner shall so request if he shall be of opinion that the interests of justice shall so require, for reasons to be recorded on the minutes.

Article III

The said Commissioner shall determine the liability of the United States, if any, in respect of each claim and assess the amount of compensation, if any, to be paid on account thereof—so far as they shall be able to agree thereon—and their decision shall be accepted by the two Governments as final.

They shall be authorized to hear and examine, on oath or affirmation, which each of said Commissioners is hereby empowered to administer or receive, every question of fact not found by the Tribunal of Arbitration, and to receive all suitable authentic testimony concerning the same; and the Government of the United States shall have the right to raise the question of its liability before the Commissioners in any case where it shall be proved that the vessel was wholly or in part the actual property of a citizen of the United States.

The said Commission, when sitting at San Francisco or Victoria, shall have and exercise all such powers for the procurement or enforcement of testimony as may hereafter be provided by appropriate legislation.

Article IV

The Commissioners may appoint a Secretary and a clerk or clerks to assist them in the transaction of the business of the Commission.

Article V

In the cases, if any, in which the Commissioners shall fail to agree, they shall transmit to each Government a joint report stating in detail the points on which they differ, and the grounds on which their opinions have been formed; and any such difference shall be referred for final adjustment to an Umpire to be appointed by the two Governments jointly, or, in case of disagreement, to be nominated by the President of the Swiss Confederation at the request of the two Governments.

Article VI

In case of the death, or incapacity to serve, from sickness or any other cause, of either of the two Commissioners, or of the Umpire, if any, his place shall be filled in the manner herein provided for the original appointment.

Article VII

Each Government shall provide for the remuneration of the Commissioner appointed by it.

The remuneration of the Umpire, if one should be appointed, and all contingent and incidental expenses of the Commission, or of the Umpire, shall be defrayed by the two Governments in equal moieties.

Article VIII

The amount awarded to Great Britain under this Convention on account of any claimant shall be paid by the Government of the United States to the Government of Her Britannic Majesty within six months after the amount thereof shall have been finally ascertained.

Article IX

The present Convention shall be duly ratified by the President of the United States of America, by and with the advice and consent of the Senate thereof, and by Her Britannic Majesty; and the ratifications shall be exchanged either at Washington or at London within six months from the date hereof, or earlier, if possible.

In faith whereof, we, the respective Plenipotentiaries, have signed this Convention and have hereunto affixed our seals.

Done in duplicate at Washington, the eighth day of February, 1896.

Richard Olney [seal] Julian Pauncefote [seal]

And Whereas the said Convention has been duly ratified on both parts, and the ratifications of the two Governments were exchanged in the City of London on the third day of June, one thousand eight hundred and ninety-six;

Now, Therefore, be it known that I, Grover Cleveland, President of the United States of America, have caused the said Convention to be made public, as amended, to the end that the same and every article and clause thereof may be observed and fulfilled with good faith by the United States and the citizens thereof.

In Testimony whereof, I have hereunto set my hand and caused the seal of the United States to be affixed.

Done at the City of Washington this 11th day of June, in the year of our Lord one thousand eight hundred and ninety-six and of the Independence of the United States the one hundred and twentieth . . .

Source:

Charles I. Bevans, *Treaties and Other Agreements of the United States of America, 1776–1949*. Washington, D.C.: Government Printing Office, 1968–76.

Hawaiian Treaty, 1897, 1898

Treaty annexing the Hawaiian Islands to the United States. In 1893 American settlers had engineered the overthrow of the Hawaiian monarchy and installed a provisional government, which negotiated a treaty of annexation. U.S. president Grover Cleveland withdrew this treaty from the Senate on grounds that the provisional government was illegitimate and without popular support. Pressure for annexation continued, and a second treaty was concluded in 1897. While it was pending in the Senate, the Spanish-American War (1898) broke out. To secure U.S. use of Hawaiian harbors for naval bases, the treaty was adopted by a joint resolution of Congress on July 7, 1898, avoiding the need for a two-thirds vote in the Senate for ratification.

--------- ⌖ ---------

Joint Resolution
To provide for annexing the Hawaiian Islands to the United States.

Whereas the Government of the Republic of Hawaii having, in due form, signified its consent, in the manner provided by its constitution, to cede absolutely and without reserve to the United States of America all rights of sovereignty of whatsoever kind in and over the Hawaiian Islands and their dependencies, and also to cede and transfer to the United States the absolute fee and ownership of all public, Government, or Crown lands, public buildings or edifices, ports, harbors, military equipment, and all other public property of every kind and description belonging to the Government of the Hawaiian Islands, together with every right and appurtenance thereunto appertaining: Therefore, *Resolved by the Senate and House of Representatives of the United States of America in Congress assembled,* That said cession is accepted, ratified, and confirmed, and that the said Hawaiian Islands and their dependencies be, and they are hereby, annexed as a part of the territory of the United States and are subject to the sovereign dominion thereof, and that all and singular the property and rights hereinbefore mentioned are vested in the United States of America.

The existing laws of the United States relative to public lands shall not apply to such lands in the Hawaiian Islands; but the Congress of the United States shall enact special laws for their management and disposition: *Provided,* That all revenue from all proceeds of the same, except as regards such part thereof as may be used or occupied for the civil, military, or naval purposes of the United States, or may be assigned for the use of the local government, shall be used solely for the benefit of the inhabitants of the Hawaiian Islands for educational and other public purposes.

Until Congress shall provide for the government of such islands all the civil, judicial, and military powers exercised by the officers of the existing government in said islands shall be vested in such person or persons and shall be exercised in such manner as the President of the United States shall direct; and the President shall have power to remove said officers and fill the vacancies so occasioned.

The existing treaties of the Hawaiian Islands with foreign nations shall forthwith cease and determine, being replaced by such treaties as may exists, or as may be hereafter concluded, between the United States and such foreign nations. The municipal legislation of the Hawaiian Islands, not enacted for the fulfillment of the treaties so extinguished, and not inconsistent with this joint resolution nor contrary to the Constitution of the United States nor to any existing treaty of the United States, shall remain in force until the Congress of the United States shall otherwise determine.

Until legislation shall be enacted extending the United States customs laws and regulations to the Hawaiian Islands the existing customs relations of the Hawaiian Islands with the United States and other countries shall remain unchanged.

The public debt of the Republic of Hawaii, lawfully existing at the date of the passage of this joint resolution, including the amounts due to depositors in the Hawaiian Postal Savings Bank, is hereby assumed by the Government of the United States; but the liability of the United States in this regard shall in no case exceed four million dollars. So long, however, as the existing Government and the present commercial relations of the Hawaiian Islands are continued as hereinbefore provided said Government shall continue to pay the interest on said debt.

There shall be no further immigration of Chinese into the Hawaiian Islands, except upon such conditions as are now or may hereafter be allowed by the laws of the United States; and no Chinese, by reason of anything herein contained, shall be allowed to enter the United States from the Hawaiian Islands.

The President shall appoint five commissioners, at least two of whom shall be residents of the Hawaiian Islands, who shall, as soon as reasonably practicable, recommend to Congress such legislation concerning the Hawaiian Islands as they deem necessary or proper.

Sec. 2. That the commissioners hereinbefore provided for shall be appointed by the President, by and with the advice and consent of the Senate.

Sec. 3. That the sum of one hundred thousand dollars, or so much thereof as may be necessary, is hereby appropriated, out of any money in the Treasury not otherwise appropriated, and to be immediately available, to be expended at the discretion of the President of the United

States of America, for the purpose of carrying this joint resolution into effect.

Source:
Statutes at Large, Vol. 30, pp. 750–751.

William McKinley, War Message, 1898

Message from President William McKinley to Congress on April 11, 1898, requesting the "forcible intervention of the United States" to end the Cuban rebellion against Spain. Two incidents particularly influenced McKinley's decision. In December 1897, Enrique de Lôme, Spanish minister to the United States, wrote to a Cuban friend calling President William McKinley "weak and a bidder for the admiration of the crowd." Cuban revolutionaries released the document to a U.S. newspaper owned and published by William Randolph Hearst, who favored a war with Spain. Although de Lôme resigned immediately, the desire for war grew.

Second, after the destruction of the U.S. battleship *Maine* in Havana Harbor on February 15, 1898, American sentiment for war against Spain increased. McKinley, rejecting Spain's offer of major concessions, justified intervention as a means to end the bloodshed in Cuba, to protect American commercial interests on the island, and to protect the safety and property of American citizens. On April 19 Congress authorized the president to initiate military intervention, and on April 25 the United States declared war on Spain.

To the Congress of the United States:

Obedient to that precept of the Constitution which commands the President to give from time to time to the Congress information of the state of the Union and to recommend to their consideration such measures as he shall judge necessary and expedient, it becomes my duty to now address your body with regard to the grave crisis that has arisen in the relations of the United States to Spain by reason of the warfare that for more than three years has raged in the neighboring island of Cuba.

I do so because of the intimate connection of the Cuban question with the state of our own Union and the grave relation the course which it is now incumbent upon the nation to adopt must needs bear to the traditional policy of our Government if it is to accord with the precepts laid down by the founders of the Republic and religiously observed by succeeding Administrations to the present day.

The present revolution is but the successor of other similar insurrections which have occurred in Cuba against the dominion of Spain, extending over a period of nearly half a century, each of which during its progress has subjected the United States to great effort and expense in enforcing its neutrality laws, caused enormous losses to American trade and commerce, caused irritation, annoyance, and disturbance among our citizens, and, by the exercise of cruel, barbarous, and uncivilized practices of warfare, shocked the sensibilities and offended the humane sympathies of our people.

Since the present revolution begin, in February, 1895, this country has been the fertile domain at our threshold ravaged by fire and sword in the course of a struggle unequaled in the history of the island and rarely paralleled as to the numbers of the combatants and the bitterness of the contest by any revolution of modern times where a dependent people striving to be free have been opposed by the power of the sovereign state.

Our people have beheld a once prosperous community reduced to comparative want, its lucrative commerce virtually paralyzed, its exceptional productiveness diminished, its fields laid waste, its mills in ruins, and its people perishing by tens of thousands from hunger and destitution. We have found ourselves constrained, in the observance of that strict neutrality which our laws enjoin and which the law of nations commands, to police our own waters and watch our own seaports in prevention of any unlawful act in aid of the Cubans.

Our trade has suffered, the capital invested by our citizens in Cuba has been largely lost, and the temper and forbearance of our people have been so sorely tried as to beget a perilous unrest among our own citizens, which has inevitably found its expression from time to time in the National Legislature, so that issues wholly external to our own body politic engross attention and stand in the way of that close devotion to domestic advancement that becomes a self-contained commonwealth whose primal maxim has been the avoidance of all foreign entanglements. All this must needs awaken, and has, indeed, aroused, the utmost concern on the part of this Government, as well during my predecessor's term as in my own.

In April, 1896, the evils from which our country suffered through the Cuban war became so onerous that my predecessor made an effort to bring about a peace through the mediation of this Government in any way that might tend to an honorable adjustment of the contest between Spain and her revolted colony, on the basis of some effective scheme of self-government for Cuba under the flag and sovereignty of Spain. It failed through the refusal of the Spanish government then in power to consider any form or mediation or, indeed, any plan of settlement which did not begin with the actual submission of the insurgents to the mother country, and then only on such terms as Spain herself might see fit to grant. The war continued unabated. The resistance of the insurgents was in no wise diminished.

The efforts of Spain were increased both by the dispatch of fresh levies to Cuba and by the addition to the horrors of the strife of a new and inhuman phase happily unprecedented in the modern history of civilized Christian peoples. The policy of devastation and concentration, inaugurated by the Captain-General's *bando* of October 21, 1896, in the Province of Pinar del Rio was thence extended to embrace all of the island to which the power of the Spanish arms was able to reach by occupation or by military operations. The peasantry, including all dwelling in the open agricultural interior, were driven into the garrison towns or isolated places held by the troops.

The raising and movement of provisions of all kinds were interdicted. The fields were laid waste, dwellings unroofed and fired, mills destroyed, and, in short, everything that could desolate the land and render it unfit for human habitation or support was commanded by one or the other of the contending parties and executed by all the powers at their disposal.

By the time the present Administration took office, a year ago, reconcentration (so called) had been made effective over the better part of the four central and western provinces—Santa Clara, Matanzas, Havana, and Pinar del Rio.

The agricultural population to the estimated number of 300,000 or more was herded within the towns and their immediate vicinage, deprived of the means of support, rendered destitute of shelter, left poorly clad, and exposed to the most unsanitary conditions. As the scarcity of food increased with the devastation of the depopulated areas of production, destitution and want became misery and starvation. Month by month the death rate increased in an alarming ratio. By March, 1897, according to conservative estimates from official Spanish sources, the mortality among the reconcentrados from starvation and the diseases thereto incident exceeded 50 per cent of their total number.

No practical relief was accorded to the destitute. The overburdened towns, already suffering from the general dearth, could give no aid. So called "zones of cultivation" established within the immediate areas of effective military control about the cities and fortified camps proved illusory as a remedy for the suffering. The unfortunates, being for the most part women and children, with aged and helpless men, enfeebled by disease and hunger, could not have tilled the soil without tools, seed, or shelter for their own support or for the supply of the cities. Reconcentration, adopted avowedly as a war measure in order to cut off the resources of the insurgents, worked its predestined result. As I said in my message of last December, it was not civilized warfare; it was extermination. The only

peace it could beget was that of the wilderness and the grave.

Meanwhile the military situation in the island had undergone a noticeable change. The extraordinary activity that characterized the second year of the war, when the insurgents invaded even the thitherto unharmed fields of Pinar del Rio and carried havoc and destruction up to the walls of the city of Havana itself, had relapsed into a dogged struggle in the central and eastern provinces. The Spanish arms regained a measure of control in Pinar del Rio and parts of Havana, but, under the existing conditions of the rural country, without immediate improvement of their productive situation. Even thus partially restricted, the revolutionists held their own, and their conquest and submission, put forward by Spain as the essential and sole basis of peace, seemed as far distant as at the outset.

In this state of affairs my Administration found itself confronted with the grave problem of its duty. My message of last December reviewed the situation and narrated the steps taken with a view to relieving its acuteness and opening the way to some form of honorable settlement. The assassination of the prime minister, Canovas, led to a change of government in Spain. The former administration, pledged to subjugation without concession, gave place to that of a more liberal party, committed long in advance to a policy of reform involving the wider principle of home rule for Cuba and Puerto Rico.

The overtures of this Government made through its new envoy, General Woodford, and looking to an immediate and effective amelioration of the condition of the island, although not accepted to the extent of admitted mediation in any shape, were met by assurances that home rule in an advanced phase would be forthwith offered to Cuba, without waiting for the war to end, and that more humane methods should thenceforth prevail in the conduct of hostilities. Coincidentally with these declarations the new government of Spain continued and completed the policy, already begun by its predecessor, of testifying friendly regard for this nation by releasing American citizens held under one charge or another connected with the insurrection, so that by the end of November not a single person entitled in any way to our national protection remained in a Spanish prison.

While these negotiations were in progress the increasing destitution of the unfortunate reconcentrados and the alarming mortality among them claimed earnest attention. The success which had attended the limited measure of relief extended to the suffering American citizens among them by the judicious expenditure through the consular agencies of the money appropriated expressly for their succor by the joint resolution approved May 24, 1897, prompted the humane extension of a similar scheme of aid to the great body of sufferers. A suggestion to this end was acquiesced in by the Spanish authorities.

On the 24th of December last I caused to be issued an appeal to the American people inviting contributions in money or in kind for the succor of the starving sufferers in Cuba, following this on the 8th of January by a similar public announcement of the formation of a central Cuban relief committee, with headquarters in New York City, composed of three. members representing the American National Red Cross and the religious and business elements of the community.

The efforts of that committee have been untiring and have accomplished much. Arrangements for free transportation to Cuba have greatly aided the charitable work. The president of the American Red Cross and representatives of other contributory organizations have generously visited Cuba and cooperated with the consul-general and the local authorities to make effective distribution of the relief collected through the efforts of the central committee. Nearly $200,000 in money and supplies has already reached the sufferers, and more is forthcoming. The supplies are admitted duty free, and transportation to the interior has been arranged, so that the relief, at first necessarily confined to Havana and the larger cities, is now extended through most, if not all, of the towns where suffering exists.

Thousands of lives have already been saved. The necessity for a change in the condition of the reconcentrados is recognized by the Spanish Government. Within a few days past the orders of General Weyler have been revoked. The reconcentrados, it is said, are to be permitted to return to their homes and aided to resume the self-supporting pursuits of peace. Public works have been ordered to give them employment and a sum of $600,000 has been appropriated for their relief.

The war in Cuba is of such a nature that, short of subjugation or extermination, a final military victory for either side seems impracticable. The alternative lies in the physical exhaustion of the one or the other party, or perhaps of both—a condition which in effect ended the ten years' war by the truce of Zanjon. The prospect of such a protraction and conclusion of the present strife is a contingency hardly to be contemplated with equanimity by the civilized world, and least of all by the United States, affected and injured as we are, deeply and intimately, by its very existence.

Realizing this, it appeared to be my duty, in a spirit of true friendliness, no less to Spain than to the Cubans, who have so much to lose by the prolongation of the struggle, to seek to bring about an immediate termination of the war. To this end I submitted on the 27th ultimo, as a result of much representation and correspondence, through the United States minister at Madrid, propositions to the Spanish Government looking to an armistice until October 1 for the negotiation of peace with the good offices of the President.

In addition I asked the immediate revocation of the order of reconcentration, so as to permit the people to return to their farms and the needy to be relieved with provisions and supplies from the United States, cooperating with the Spanish authorities, so as to afford full relief.

The reply of the Spanish cabinet was received on the night of the 31st ultimo. It offered, as the means to bring about peace in Cuba, to confide the preparation thereof to the insular parliament, inasmuch as the concurrence of that body would be necessary to reach a final result, it being, however, understood that the powers reserved by the constitution to the central Government are not lessened or diminished. As the Cuban parliament does not meet until the 4th of May next, the Spanish Government would not object for its part to accept at once a suspension of hostilities if asked for by the insurgents from the general in chief, to whom it would pertain in such case to determine the duration and conditions of the armistice.

The propositions submitted by General Woodford and the reply of the Spanish Government were both in the form of brief memoranda, the texts of which are before me and are substantially in the language above given. The function of the Cuban parliament in the matter of "preparing" peace and the manner of its doing so are not expressed in the Spanish memorandum, but from General Woodford's explanatory reports of preliminary discussions preceding the final conference it is understood that the Spanish Government stands ready to give the insular congress full powers to settle the terms of peace with the insurgents, whether by direct negotiation or indirectly by means of legislation does not appear.

With this last overture in the direction of immediate peace, and its disappointing reception by Spain, the Executive is brought to the end of his effort.

In my annual message of December last I said:

Of the untried measures there remain only: Recognition of the insurgents as belligerents; recognition of the independence of Cuba; neutral intervention to end the war by imposing a rational compromise between the contestants, and intervention in favor of one or the other party. I speak not of forcible annexation, for that can not be thought of. That, by our code of morality, would be criminal aggression.

Thereupon I reviewed these alternatives in the light of President Grant's measured words, uttered in 1875, when, after seven years of sanguinary, destructive, and cruel hostilities in Cuba, he reached the conclusion that the recognition of the independence of Cuba was impracticable and indefensible and that the recognition of belligerence was not warranted by the facts according to the tests of public law. I commented especially upon the latter aspect of the question, pointing out the inconveniences and positive dangers of a recognition of belligerence, which, while adding to the already onerous burdens of neutrality within our own jurisdiction, could not in any way extend our influence or effective offices in the territory of hostilities.

Nothing has since occurred to change my view in this regard, and I recognize as fully now as then that the issuance of a proclamation of neutrality, by which process the so-called recognition of belligerents is published, could of itself and unattended by other action accomplish nothing toward the one end for which we labor—the instant pacification of Cuba and the cessation of the misery that afflicts the island.

Turning to the question of recognizing at this time the independence of the present insurgent government in Cuba, we find safe precedents in our history from an early day. They are well summed up in President Jackson's message to Congress, December 21, 1836, on the subject of the recognition of the independence of Texas. He said:

In all the contest that have arisen out of the revolutions of France, out of the disputes relating to the crowns of Portugal and Spain, out of the revolutionary movements of those Kingdoms, out of the separation of the American possessions of both from the European Governments, and out of the numerous and constantly occurring struggles for dominion in Spanish America, so wisely consistent with out just principles has been the action of our Government that we have under the most critical circumstances avoided all censure and encountered no other evil than that produced by a transient estrangement of good will in those against whom we have been by force of evidence compelled to decide.

It has thus been made known to the world that the uniform policy and practice of the United States is to avoid all interference in disputes which merely relate to the internal government of other nations, and eventually to recognize the authority of the prevailing party, without reference to our particular interests and views or to the merits of the original controversy.

But on this as on every trying occasion safety is to be found in a rigid adherence to principle.

In the contest between Spain and her revolted colonies we stood aloof and waited, not only until the ability of the new States to protect themselves was fully established, but until the danger of their being again subjugated had entirely passed away. Then, and not till then, were they recognized. Such was our course in regard to Mexico herself.

It is true that, with regard to Texas, the civil authority of Mexico has been expelled, its invading army defeated, the chief of the Republic himself captured, and all present power to control the newly organized Government of Texas annihilated within its confines. But,on the other hand, there is, in appearance at least, an immense dispar-

ity of physical force on the side of Mexico. The Mexican Republic under another Executive is rallying its forces under a new leader and menacing a fresh invasion to recover its lost dominion.

Upon the issue of this threatened invasion the independence of Texas may be considered as suspended, and were there nothing peculiar in the relative situation of the United States and Texas our acknowledgment of its independence at such a crisis could scarcely be regarded as consistent with that prudent reserve with which we have heretofore held ourselves bound to treat all similar questions.

Thereupon Andrew Jackson proceeded to consider the risk that there might be imputed to the United States motives of selfish interest in view of the former claim on our part to the territory of Texas and of the avowed purpose of the Texans in seeking recognition of independence as an incident to the incorporation of Texas in the Union, concluding thus:

Prudence, therefore, seems to dictate that we should still stand aloof and maintain our present attitude, if not until Mexico itself or one of the great foreign powers shall recognize the independence of the new Government, at least until the lapse of time or the course of events shall have proved beyond cavil or dispute the ability of the people of that country to maintain their separate sovereignty and to uphold the Government constituted by them. Neither of the contending parties can justly complain of this course. By pursuing it we are but carrying out the long-established policy of our Government—a policy which has secured to us respect and influence abroad and inspired confidence at home.

These are the words of the resolute and patriotic Jackson. They are evidence that the United States, in addition to the test imposed by public law as the condition of the recognition of independence by a neutral state (to wit, that the revolted state shall "constitute in fact a body politic, having a government in substance as well as in name, possessed of the elements of stability," and forming *de facto*, "if left to itself, a state among the nations, reasonably capable of discharging the duties of a state"), has imposed for its own governance in dealing with cases like these the further condition that recognition of independent statehood is not due to a revolted dependency until the danger of its being again subjugated by the parent state has entirely passed away.

This extreme test was, in fact, applied in the case of Texas. The Congress to whom President Jackson referred the question as one "probably leading to war," and therefore a proper subject for "a previous understanding with that body by whom war can alone be declared and by whom all the provisions for sustaining its perils must be furnished," left the matter of the recognition of Texas to the discretion of the Executive, providing merely for the sending of a diplomatic agent when the President should be satisfied that the Republic of Texas had become "an independent state." It was so recognized by President Van Buren, who commissioned a charge d'affaires March 7, 1837, after Mexico had abandoned an attempt to reconquer the Texan territory, and when there was at the time no *bona fide* contest going on between the insurgent province and its former sovereign.

I said in my message of December last:

It is to be seriously considered whether the Cuban insurrection possesses beyond dispute the attributes of statehood, which alone can demand the recognition of belligerency in its favor.

The same requirement must certainly be no less seriously considered when the graver issue of recognizing independence is in question, for no less positive test can be applied to the greater act than to the lesser, while, on the other hand, the influences and consequences of the struggle upon the internal policy of the recognizing state, which form important factors when the recognition of belligerency is concerned, are secondary, if not rightly eliminable, factors when the real question is whether the community claiming recognition is or is not independent beyond per-adventure.

Nor from the standpoint of expediency do I think it would be wise or prudent for this Government to recognize at the present time the independence of the so-called Cuban Republic. Such recognition is not necessary in order to enable the United States to intervene and pacify the island. To commit this country now to the recognition of any particular government in Cuba might subject us to embarrassing conditions of international obligation toward the organization so recognized. In case of intervention our conduct would be subject to the approval or disapproval of such government. We would be required to submit to its direction and to assume to it the mere relation of a friendly ally.

When it shall appear hereafter that there is within the island a government capable of performing the duties and discharging the functions of a separate nation, and having as a matter of fact the proper forms and attributes of nationality, such government can be promptly and readily recognized and the relations and interests of the United States with such nation adjusted.

There remain the alternative forms of intervention to end the war, either as an impartial neutral, by imposing a rational compromise between the contestants, or as the active ally of the one party or the other.

As to the first, it is not to be forgotten that during the last few months the relation of the United States has virtually been one of friendly intervention in many ways, each not of itself conclusive, but all tending to the exertion of a potential influence toward an ultimate pacific result, just

and honorable to all interests concerned. The spirit of all our acts hitherto has been an earnest, unselfish desire for peace and prosperity in Cuba, untarnished by differences between us and Spain and unstained by the blood of American citizens.

The forcible intervention of the United States as a neutral to stop the war, according to the large dictates of humanity and following many historical precedents where neighboring states have interfered to check the hopeless sacrifices of life by internecine conflicts beyond their borders, is justifiable on rational grounds. It involves, however, hostile constraint upon both the parties to the contest, as well to enforce a truce as to guide the eventual settlement.

The grounds for such intervention may be briefly summarized as follows:

First. In the cause of humanity and to put an end to the barbarities, bloodshed, starvation, and horrible miseries now existing there, and which the parties to the conflict are either unable or unwilling to stop or mitigate. It is no answer to say this is all in another country, belonging to another nation, and is therefore none of our business. It is specially our duty, for it is right at our door.

Second. We owe it to our citizens in Cuba to afford them that protection and indemnity for life and property which no government there can or will afford, and to that end to terminate the conditions that deprive them of legal protection.

Third. The right to intervene may be justified by the very serious injury to the commerce, trade, and business of our people and by the wanton destruction of property and devastation of the island.

Fourth, and which is of the utmost importance. The present condition of affairs in Cuba is a constant menace to our peace and entails upon this Government an enormous expense. With such a conflict waged for years in an island so near us and with which our people have such trade and business relations; when the lives and liberty of our citizens are in constant danger and their property destroyed and themselves ruined; where our trading vessels are liable to seizure and are seized at our very door by war ships of a foreign nation; the expeditions of filibustering that we are powerless to prevent altogether, and the irritating questions and entanglements thus arising—all these and others that I need not mention, with the resulting strained relations, are a constant menace to our peace and compel us to keep on a semi war footing with a nation with which we are at peace.

These elements of danger and disorder already pointed out have been strikingly illustrated by a tragic event which has deeply and justly moved the American people. I have already transmitted to Congress the report of the naval court of inquiry on the destruction of the battle ship *Maine* in the harbor of Havana during the night of the 15th of February. The destruction of that noble vessel has filled the national heart with inexpressible horror. Two hundred and fifty-eight brave sailors and marines and two officers of our Navy, reposing in the fancied security of a friendly harbor, have been hurled to death, grief and want brought to their homes and sorrow to the nation.

The naval court of inquiry, which, it is needless to say, commands the unqualified confidence of the Government, was unanimous in its conclusion that the destruction of the *Maine* was caused by an exterior explosion—that of a submarine mine. It did not assume to place the responsibility. That remains to be fixed.

In any event, the destruction of the *Maine*, by whatever exterior cause, is a patent and impressive proof of a state of things in Cuba that is intolerable. That condition is thus shown to be such that the Spanish Government can not assure safety and security to a vessel of the American Navy in the harbor of Havana on a mission of peace, and rightfully there.

Further referring in this connection to recent diplomatic correspondence, a dispatch from our minister to Spain of the 26th ultimo contained the statement that the Spanish minister for foreign affairs assured him positively that Spain will do all that the highest honor and justice require in the matter of the *Maine*. The reply above referred to, of the 31st ultimo, also contained an expression of the readiness of Spain to submit to an arbitration all the differences which can arise in this matter, which is subsequently explained by the note of the Spanish minister at Washington of the 10th instant, as follows:

As to the question of fact which springs from the diversity of views between the reports of the American and Spanish boards, Spain proposes that the facts be ascertained by an impartial investigation by experts, whose decision Spain accepts in advance.

To this I have made no reply.

President Grant, in 1875, after discussing the phases of the contest as it then appeared and its hopeless and apparent indefinite prolongation, said:

In such event I am of opinion that other nations will be compelled to assume the responsibility which devolves upon them, and to seriously consider the only remaining measures possible—mediation and intervention. Owing, perhaps, to the large expanse of water separating the island from the peninsula,

* * *

. . . the contending parties appear to have within themselves no depository of common confidence to suggest wisdom when passion and excitement have their sway and to assume the part of peacemaker. In this view in the earlier days of the contest the good offices of the United

States as a mediator were tendered in good faith, without any selfish purpose, in the interest of humanity and in sincere friendship for both parties, but were at the time declined by Spain, with the declaration, nevertheless, that at a future time they would be indispensable. No intimation has been received that in the opinion of Spain that time has been reached. And yet the strife continues, with all its dread horrors and all its injuries to the interests of the United States and of other nations. Each party seems quite capable of working great injury and damage to the other, as well as to all the relations and interests dependent on the existence of peace in the island; but they seem incapable of reaching any adjustment, and both have thus far failed of achieving any success whereby one party shall possess and control the island to the exclusion of the other. Under these circumstances the agency of others, either by mediation or by intervention, seems to be the only alternative which must, sooner or later, be invoked for the termination of the strife.

In the last annual message of my immediate predecessor, during the pending struggle, it was said:

When the inability of Spain to deal successfully with the insurrection has become manifest and it is demonstrated that her sovereignty is extinct in Cuba for all purposes of its rightful existence, and when a hopeless struggle for its reestablishment has degenerated into a strife which means nothing more than the useless sacrifice of human life and the utter destruction of the very subject-matter of the conflict, a situation will be presented in which our obligations to the sovereignty of Spain will be superseded by higher obligations, which we can hardly hesitate to recognize and discharge.

In my annual message to Congress December last, speaking to this question, I said:

The near future will demonstrate whether the indispensable condition of a righteous peace, just alike to the Cubans and to Spain, as well as equitable to all our interests so intimately involved in the welfare of Cuba, is likely to be attained. If not, the exigency of further and other action by the United States will remain to be taken. When that time comes, that action will be determined in the line of indisputable right and duty. It will be faced, without misgiving or hesitancy, in the light of the obligation this Government owes to itself, to the people who have confided to it the protection of their interests and honor, and to humanity.

Sure of the right, keeping free from all offense ourselves, actuated only by upright and patriotic considerations, moved neither by passion nor selfishness, the Government will continue its watchful care over the rights and property of American citizens and will abate none of its efforts to bring about by peaceful agencies a peace which shall be honorable and enduring. If it shall hereafter appear to be a duty imposed by our obligations to ourselves, to civilization, and humanity to intervene with force, it shall be without fault on our part and only because the necessity for such action will be so clear as to command the support and approval of the civilized world.

The long trial has proved that the object for which Spain has waged the war can not be attained. The fire of insurrection may flame or may smolder with varying seasons, but it has not been and it is plain that it can not be extinguished by present methods. The only hope of relief and repose from a condition which can no longer be endured is the enforced pacification of Cuba. In the name of humanity, in the name of civilization, in behalf of endangered American interests which give us the right and the duty to speak and to act, the war in Cuba must stop.

In view of these facts and of these considerations I ask the Congress to authorize and empower the President to take measures to secure a full and final termination of hostilities between the Government of Spain and the people of Cuba, and to secure in the island the establishment of a stable government, capable of maintaining order and observing its international obligations, insuring peace and tranquillity and the security of its citizens as well as our own, and to use the military and naval forces of the United States as may be necessary for these purposes.

And in the interest of humanity and to aid in preserving the lives of the starving people of the island I recommend that the distribution of food and supplies be continued and that an appropriation be made out of the public Treasury to supplement the charity of our citizens.

The issue is now with the Congress. It is a solemn responsibility. I have exhausted every effort to relieve the intolerable condition of affairs which is at our doors. Prepared to execute every obligation imposed upon me by the Constitution and the law, I await your action.

Yesterday, and since the preparation of the foregoing message, official information was received by me that the latest decree of the Queen Regent of Spain directs General Blanco, in order to prepare and facilitate peace, to proclaim a suspension of hostilities, the duration and details of which have not yet been communicated to me.

This fact, with every other pertinent consideration, will, I am sure, have your just and careful attention in the solemn deliberations upon which you are about to enter. If this measure attains a successful result, then our aspirations as a Christian, peace-loving people will be realized. If it fails, it will be only another justification for our contemplated action.

Source:

James D. Richardson, ed. *A Compilation of the Messages and Papers of the Presidents, 1789–1897.* Vol. 10. Washington, D.C.: Government Printing Office, 1899, pp. 139–150.

Treaty of Paris, 1898

Treaty signed on December 10, 1898, ending the Spanish-American War (1898). According to the treaty terms, Spain would abandon its claim to Cuba (which remained a U.S. protectorate until 1934) and cede Puerto Rico and Guam to the United States (both of which remain U.S. territories). In the Philippines, Spain—already besieged by an ascendant Filipino national insurgency—would capitulate to the American forces that had arrived in Manila Bay, turning the archipelago over to the United States for $20 million. The treaty sparked a controversy in the Senate and in American culture at large over U.S. imperialism. Treaty supporters, including President William McKinley, hoped to "help" the people of the Philippines, establish a market there for U.S. goods, and establish a base for Far East trade. Opponents decried U.S. control of distant people as a violation of self-determination. The Senate ratified the treaty by a narrow margin on February 6, 1899. Actually establishing American sovereignty in the Philippines would eventually require the U.S. Army to occupy the islands and fight a brutal and protracted guerrilla war against its erstwhile Filipino allies, finally quashing the indigenous republic in 1901 at a cost in dollars and lives that far exceeded the Spanish-American War itself. The Philippines were granted their independence through the Tydings-McDuffie Act of March 24, 1934, which became effective July 4, 1946.

The United States of America and Her Majesty the Queen Regent of Spain, in the name of her August Son Don Alfonso XIII, desiring to end the state of war now existing between the two countries, have for that purpose appointed as Plenipotentiaries:

The President of the United States, William R. Day, Cushman K. Davis, William P. Frye, George Gray, and Whitelaw Reid, citizens of the United States;

and Her Majesty the Queen Regent of Spain, Don Eugenio Montero Rios, President of the Senate, Don Buenaventura de Abarzuza, Senator of the Kingdom and ex-Minister of the Crown, Don Jose de Garnica, Deputy to the Cortes and Associate Justice of the Supreme Court, Don Wenceslao Ramirez de Villa-Urrutia, Envoy Extraordinary and Minister Plenipotentiary at Brussels, and Don Rafael Cerero, General of Division;

Who, having assembled in Paris, and having exchanged their full powers, which were found to be in due and proper form, have, after discussion of the matters before them, agreed upon the following articles:

Article I

Spain relinquishes all claim of sovereignty over and title to Cuba.

And as the island is, upon its evacuation by Spain, to be occupied by the United States, the United States will, so long as such occupation shall last, assume and discharge the obligations that may under international law result from the fact of its occupation, for the protection of life and property.

Article II

Spain cedes to the United States the island of Porto Rico and other islands now under Spanish sovereignty in the West Indies, and the island of Guam in the Marianas or Ladrones.

Article III

Spain cedes to the United States the archipelago known as the Philippine Islands, and comprehending the islands lying within the following line:

A line running from west to east along or near the twentieth parallel of north latitude, and through the middle of the navigable channel of Bachi, from the one hundred and eighteenth (118th) to the one hundred and twenty seventh (127th) degree meridian of longitude east of Greenwich, thence along the one hundred and twenty seventh (127th) degree meridian of longitude east of Greenwich to the parallel of four degrees and forty five minutes (4 degree 45') north latitude, thence along the parallel of four degrees and forty five minutes (4 degree 45') north latitude to its intersection with the meridian of longitude one hundred and nineteen degrees and thirty-five minutes (119 degree 35') east of Greenwich, thence along the meridian of longitude one hundred and nineteen degrees and thirty-five minutes (119 degree 35') east of Greenwich to the parallel of latitude seven degrees and forty minutes (7 degree 40') north, thence along the parallel of latitude seven degrees and forty minutes (7 degree 40') north to its intersection with the one hundred and sixteenth (116th) degree meridian of longitude east of Greenwich, thence by a direct line to the intersection of the tenth (10th) degree parallel of north latitude with the one hundred and eighteenth (118th) degree meridian of longitude east of Greenwich, and thence along the one hundred and eighteenth (118th) degree meridian of longitude east of Greenwich, to the point of beginning.

The United States will pay to Spain the sum of twenty million dollars ($20,000,000) within three months after the exchange of the ratifications of the present treaty.

Article IV

The United States will, for the term of ten years from the date of the exchange of the ratifications of the present treaty, admit Spanish ships and merchandise to the ports of the Philippine Islands on the same terms as ships and merchandise of the United States.

Article V

The United States will, upon the signature of the present treaty, send back to Spain, at its own cost, the Spanish soldiers taken as prisoners of war on the capture of Manila by the American forces. The arms of the soldiers in question shall be restored to them.

Spain will, upon the exchange of the ratifications of the present treaty, proceed to evacuate the Philippines, as well as the island of Guam, on terms similar to those agreed upon by the Commissioners appointed to arrange for the evacuation of Porto Rico and other islands in the West Indies, under the Protocol of August 12, 1898, which is to continue in force until its provisions are completely executed.

The time within which the evacuation of the Philippine Islands and Guam shall be completed shall be fixed by the two Governments. Stands of colors, uncaptured war vessels, small arms, guns of all calibres, with their carriages and accessories, powder, ammunition, livestock, and materials and supplies of all kinds, belonging to the land and naval forces of Spain in the Philippines and Guam, remain the property of Spain. Pieces of heavy ordnance, exclusive of field artillery, in the fortifications and coast defences, shall remain in their emplacements for the term of six months, to be reckoned from the exchange of ratifications of the treaty; and the United States may, in the mean time, purchase such material from Spain, if a satisfactory agreement between the two Governments on the subject shall be reached.

Article VI

Spain will, upon the signature of the present treaty, release all prisoners of war, and all persons detained or imprisoned for political offences, in connection with the insurrections in Cuba and the Philippines and the war with the United States.

Reciprocally, the United States will release all persons made prisoners of war by the American forces, and will undertake to obtain the release of all Spanish prisoners in the hands of the insurgents in Cuba and the Philippines.

The Government of the United States will at its own cost return to Spain and the Government of Spain will at its own cost return to the United States, Cuba, Porto Rico, and the Philippines, according to the situation of their respective homes, prisoners released or caused to be released by them, respectively, under this article.

Article VII

The United States and Spain mutually relinquish all claims for indemnity, national and individual of every kind, of either Government, or of its citizens or subjects, against the other Government, that may have arisen since the beginning of the late insurrection in Cuba and prior to the exchange of ratifications of the present treaty, including all claims for indemnity for the cost of the war.

The United States will adjudicate and settle the claims of its citizens against Spain relinquished in this article.

Article VIII

In conformity with the provisions of Articles I, II, and III of this treaty, Spain relinquishes in Cuba, and cedes in Porto Rico and other islands in the West Indies, in the island of Guam, and in the Philippine Archipelago, all the buildings, wharves, barracks, forts, structures, public highways and other immovable property which, in conformity with law, belong to the public domain, and as such belong to the Crown of Spain.

And it is hereby declared that the relinquishment or cession, as the case may be, to which the preceding paragraph refers, cannot in any respect impair the property or rights which by law belong to the peaceful possession of property of all kinds, of provinces, municipalities, public or private establishments, ecclesiastical or civic bodies, or any other associations having legal capacity to acquire and possess property in the aforesaid territories renounced or ceded, or of private individuals, of whatsoever nationality such individuals may be.

The aforesaid relinquishment or cession, as the case may be, includes all documents exclusively referring to the sovereignty relinquished or ceded that may exist in the archives of the Peninsula. Where any document in such archives only in part relates to said sovereignty, a copy of such part will be furnished whenever it shall be requested. Like rules shall be reciprocally observed in favor of Spain in respect of documents in the archives of the islands above referred to.

In the aforesaid relinquishment or cession, as the case may be, are also included such rights as the Crown of Spain and its authorities possess in respect of the official archives and records, executive as well as judicial, in the islands above referred to, which relate to said islands or the rights and property of their inhabitants. Such archives and records shall be carefully preserved, and private persons shall without distinction have the right to require, in accordance with law, authenticated copies of the contracts, wills and other instruments forming part of notarial protocols or files, or which may be contained in the executive or judicial archives, be the latter in Spain or in the islands aforesaid.

Article IX

Spanish subjects, natives of the Peninsula, residing in the territory over which Spain by the present treaty relin-

quishes or cedes her sovereignty, may remain in such territory or may remove therefrom, retaining in either event all their rights of property, including the right to sell or dispose of such property or of its proceeds; and they shall also have the right to carry on their industry, commerce and professions, being subject in respect thereof to such laws as are applicable to other foreigners. In case they remain in the territory they may preserve their allegiance to the Crown of Spain by making, before a court of record, within a year from the date of the exchange of ratifications of this treaty, a declaration of their decision to preserve such allegiance; in default of which declaration they shall be held to have renounced it and to have adopted the nationality of the territory in which they may reside.

The civil rights and political status of the native inhabitants of the territories hereby ceded to the United States shall be determined by the Congress.

Article X

The inhabitants of the territories over which Spain relinquishes or cedes her sovereignty shall be secured in the free exercise of their religion.

Article XI

The Spaniards residing in the territories over which Spain by this treaty cedes or relinquishes her sovereignty shall be subject in matters civil as well as criminal to the jurisdiction of the courts of the country wherein they reside, pursuant to the ordinary laws governing the same; and they shall have the right to appear before such courts, and to pursue the same course as citizens of the country to which the courts belong.

Article XII

Judicial proceedings pending at the time of the exchange of ratifications of this treaty in the territories over which Spain relinquishes or cedes her sovereignty shall be determined according to the following rules:

1. Judgments rendered either in civil suits between private individuals, or in criminal matters, before the date mentioned, and with respect to which there is no recourse or right of review under the Spanish law, shall be deemed to be final, and shall be executed in due form by competent authority in the territory within which such judgments should be carried out.

2. Civil suits between private individuals which may on the date mentioned be undetermined shall be prosecuted to judgment before the court in which they may then be pending or in the court that may be substituted therefor.

3. Criminal actions pending on the date mentioned before the Supreme Court of Spain against citizens of the

territory which by this treaty ceases to be Spanish shall continue under its jurisdiction until final judgment; but, such judgment having been rendered, the execution thereof shall be committed to the competent authority of the place in which the case arose.

Article XIII

The rights of property secured by copyrights and patents acquired by Spaniards in the Island of Cuba, and in Porto Rico, the Philippines and other ceded territories, at the time of the exchange of the ratifications of this treaty, shall continue to be respected. Spanish scientific, literary and artistic works, not subversive of public order in the territories in question, shall continue to be admitted free of duty into such territories, for the period of ten years, to be reckoned from the date of the exchange of the ratifications of this treaty.

Article XIV

Spain shall have the power to establish consular officers in the ports and places of the territories, the sovereignty over which has been either relinquished or ceded by the present treaty.

Article XV

The Government of each country will, for the term of ten years, accord to the merchant vessels of the other country the same treatment in respect of all port charges, including entrance and clearance dues, light dues, and tonnage duties, as it accords to its own merchant vessels, not engaged in the coastwise trade.

This article may at any time be terminated on six months' notice given by either Government to the other.

Article XVI

It is understood that any obligations assumed in this treaty by the United States with respect to Cuba are limited to the time of its occupancy thereof; but it will upon the termination of such occupancy, advise any Government established in the island to assume the same obligations.

Article XVII

The present treaty shall be ratified by the President of the United States, by and with the advice and consent of the Senate thereof, and by Her Majesty the Queen Regent of Spain; and the ratifications shall be exchanged at Washington within six months from the date hereof, or earlier if possible.

In faith whereof, we, the respective Plenipotentiaries, have signed this treaty and have hereunto affixed our seals.

Done in duplicate at Paris, the tenth day of December, in the year of Our Lord one thousand eight hundred and ninety eight.

See also THE JONES ACT, 1916; THE JONES ACT, 1917; TYDINGS-McDUFFIE ACT, 1934.

Source:

Charles I. Bevans, *Treaties and Other Agreements of the United States of America, 1776–1949.* Washington, D.C.: Government Printing Office, 1968–76.

Platform of American Anti-Imperialist League, 1899

Set of principles condemning U.S. colonialism in the Philippines, issued on October 18, 1899, by a coalition of local and regional anti-imperialist organizations meeting in Chicago. The platform declared that U.S. efforts to control the Philippines after that nation had declared its independence from Spain constituted "criminal aggression" and violated the fundamental principles of American government. The league condemned the use of American military force to suppress the Filipino rebellion against U.S. control, calling the slaughter of Filipinos a "needless horror" in an unjust war, and urged Congress to cease the war immediately. Although the league attracted many influential supporters, the rebellion collapsed and the Philippines remained a U.S. possession until 1946.

───────── ❧ ─────────

We hold that the policy known as imperialism is hostile to liberty and tends toward militarism, an evil from which it has been our glory to be free. We regret that it has become necessary in the land of Washington and Lincoln to reaffirm that all men, of whatever race or color, are entitled to life, liberty, and the pursuit of happiness. We maintain that governments derive their just powers from the consent of the governed. We insist that the subjugation of any people is "criminal aggression" and open disloyalty to the distinctive principles of our government.

We earnestly condemn the policy of the present national administration in the Philippines. It seeks to extinguish the spirit of 1776 in those islands. We deplore the sacrifice of our soldiers and sailors, whose bravery deserves admiration even in an unjust war. We denounce the slaughter of the Filipinos as a needless horror. We protest against the extension of American sovereignty by Spanish methods.

We demand the immediate cessation of the war against liberty, begun by Spain and continued by us. We urge that Congress be promptly convened to announce to the Filipinos our purpose to concede to them the independence for which they have so long fought and which of right is theirs.

The United States have always protested against the doctrine of international law which permits the subjugation of the weak by the strong. A self-governing state cannot accept sovereignty over an unwilling people. The United States cannot act upon the ancient heresy that might makes right.

Imperialists assume that with the destruction of self-government in the Philippines by American hands, all opposition here will cease. This is a grievous error. Much as we abhor the war of "criminal aggression" in the Philippines, greatly as we regret that the blood of the Filipinos is on American hands, we more deeply resent the betrayal of American institutions at home. The real firing line is not in the suburbs of Manila. The foe is of our own household. The attempt of 1861 was to divide the country. That of 1899 is to destroy its fundamental principles and noblest ideals.

Whether the ruthless slaughter of the Filipinos shall end next month or next year is but an incident in a contest that must go on until the Declaration of Independence and the Constitution of the United States are rescued from the hands of their betrayers. Those who dispute about standards of value while the foundation of the republic is undermined will be listened to as little as those who would wrangle about the small economies of the household while the house is on fire. The training of a great people for a century, the aspiration for liberty of a vast immigration are forces that will hurl aside those who in the delirium of conquest seek to destroy the character of our institutions.

We deny that the obligation of all citizens to support their government in times of grave national peril applies to the present situation. If an administration may with impunity ignore the issues upon which it was chosen, deliberately create a condition of war anywhere on the face of the globe, debauch the civil service for spoils to promote the adventure, organize a truth-suppressing censorship, and demand of all citizens a suspension of judgment and their unanimous support while it chooses to continue the fighting, representative government itself is imperiled.

We propose to contribute to the defeat of any person or party that stands for the forcible subjugation of any people. We shall oppose for reelection all who in the White House or in Congress betray American liberty in pursuit of un-American ends. We still hope that both of our great political parties will support and defend the Declaration of Independence in the closing campaign of the century.

We hold with Abraham Lincoln, that "no man is good enough to govern another man without that other's consent. When the white man governs himself, that is self-government, but when he governs himself and also governs another man, that is more than self-government—that is despotism." "Our reliance is in the love of liberty which God has planted in us. Our defense is in the spirit which prizes liberty as the heritage of all men in all lands. Those who deny freedom to others deserve it not for themselves, and under a just God, cannot long retain it."

We cordially invite the cooperation of all men and women who remain loyal to the Declaration of Independence and the Constitution of the United States.

Source:

John Scott, ed. *Living Documents in American History*. New York: Washington Square Press, 1964–68.

Circular Letter (also known as The Open Door Policy), 1899

Letter of September 6, 1899, written by U.S. secretary of state John Hay, that announced the Open Door policy toward China, an attempt to protect American commercial interests at a time when European nations were establishing spheres of influence in China. Hay's letter instructed U.S. embassies in Germany, Russia, Great Britain, France, Italy, and Japan to seek assurances that those powers would respect the trading rights of other nations within their spheres of influence; that the Chinese treaty tariff would apply to all spheres of influence and would be collected by the Chinese government; and that discriminatory tariffs and fees would not be applied to any nation. Although the various nations gave evasive replies, on March 20, 1900, Hay announced the acceptance of the Open Door policy as "final and definitive."

Mr. Hay to Mr. White.
Department of State, Washington, September 6, 1899.

Sir: At the time when the Government of the United States was informed by that of Germany that it had leased from His Majesty the Emperor of China the port of Kiao-chao and the adjacent territory in the province of Shantung, assurances were given to the ambassador of the United States at Berlin by the Imperial German minister for foreign affairs that the rights and privileges insured by treaties with China to citizens of the United States would not thereby suffer or be in anywise impaired within the area over which Germany had thus obtained control.

More recently, however, the British Government recognized by a formal agreement with Germany the exclusive right of the latter country to enjoy in said leased area an the contiguous "sphere of influence or interest" certain privileges, more especially those relating to railroads and mining enterprises; but, as the exact nature and extent of the rights thus recognized have not been clearly defined, it is possible that serious conflicts of interest may at any time arise, not only between British and German subjects within said area, but that the interests of our citizens may also be jeopardized thereby.

Earnestly desirous to remove any cause of irritation and to insure at the same time to the commerce of all nations in China the undoubted benefits which should accrue from a formal recognition by the various powers claiming "spheres of interest" that they shall enjoy perfect equality of treatment for their commerce and navigation within such "spheres," the Government of the United States would be pleased to see His German Majesty's Government give formal assurances and lend its cooperation in securing like assurances from the other interested powers that each within its respective spheres of whatever influence—

First. Will in no way interfere with any treaty port or any vested interest within any so-called "sphere of interest" or leased territory it may have in China.

Second. That the Chinese treaty tariff of the time being shall apply to all merchandise landed or shipped to all such ports as are within said "sphere of interest" (unless they be "free ports"), no matter to what nationality it may belong, and that duties so leviable shall be collected by the Chinese Government.

Third. That it will levy no higher harbor dues on vessels of another nationality frequenting any port in such "sphere" than shall be levied on vessels of its own nationality, and no higher railroad charges over lines built, controlled, or operated within its "sphere" on merchandise belonging to citizens or subjects of other nationalities transported through such "sphere" than shall be levied on similar merchandise belonging to its own nationals transported over equal distances.

The liberal policy pursued by His Imperial German Majesty in declaring Kiao-chao a free port and in aiding the Chinese Government in the establishment there of a custom-house are so clearly in line with the proposition which this Government is anxious to see recognized that it entertains the strongest hope that Germany will give its acceptance and hearty support.

The recent ukase of His Majesty the Emperor of Russia declaring the port of Ta-lien-wan open during the whole of the lease under which it is held from China, to the merchant ships of all nations, coupled with the categorical assurances made to this Government by His Imperial Majesty's representative at this capital at the time, and since repeated to me by the present Russian ambassador, seem to insure the support of the Emperor to the proposed measure. Our ambassador at the Court of St. Petersburg has, in consequence, been instructed to submit it to the Russian Government and to request their early consideration of it.

A copy of my instruction on the subject to Mr. Tower is herewith enclosed for your confidential information.

The commercial interests of Great Britain and Japan will be so clearly served by the desired declaration of intentions, and the views of the Governments of these countries as to the desirability of the adoption of measures insuring the benefits of equality of treatment of all foreign trade throughout China are so similar to those entertained by the United States, that their acceptance of the propositions herein outlined and their cooperation in advocating their adoption by the other powers can be confidently expected. I inclose herewith copy of the instruction which I have sent to Mr. Choate on the subject.

In view of the present favorable conditions, you are instructed to submit the above considerations to His Imperial German Majesty's minister for foreign affairs, and to request his early consideration of the subject.

Copy of this instruction is sent to our ambassadors at London and at St. Petersburg for their information.

I have, etc.,

John Hay.

Source:

Treaties, Conventions, International Acts, Protocols and Agreement Between the United States of America and Other Powers, 1776–1909. Vol 1, Part 1. Westport, Conn.: Greenwood Publishing Group, 1970, pp. 246–247.

Foraker Act, 1900

Law sponsored by Senator Joseph B. Foraker of Ohio and enacted on April 12, 1900, to provide for a civil government in Puerto Rico. After two years of military government following the cession of Puerto Rico to the United States by the 1898 Treaty of Paris, which ended the Spanish-American War (1898), the act established a presidential-type government in which the governor, his cabinet, and the judges of the Supreme Court were all to be appointed by the U.S. president. The will of the people of Puerto Rico was represented only in a 35-member House of Delegates. The act benefited the U.S. economically, because the island was incorporated within the U.S. tariff system, and the free movement of goods between Puerto Rico and the mainland was established; however, the Foraker Act pleased almost no one in Puerto Rico, since the island now possessed less autonomy than it had under monarchical Spain.

***

An Act

Temporarily to provide revenues and a civil government for Porto Rico, and for other purposes.

Be it enacted by the Senate and House of Representatives of the United States of America in Congress assembled, That the provisions of this Act shall apply to the island of Porto Rico and to the adjacent islands and waters of the islands lying east of the seventy-fourth meridian of longitude west of Greenwich, which were ceded to the United States by the Government of Spain by treaty entered into on the tenth day of December, eighteen hundred and ninety-eight; and the name Porto Rico, as used in this Act, shall be held to include not only the island of that name, but all the adjacent islands as aforesaid.

Sec. 2. That on and after the passage of this Act the same, tariffs, customs, and duties shall be levied, collected, and paid upon all articles imported into Porto Rico from ports other than those of the United States which are required by law to be collected upon articles imported into the United States from foreign countries: *Provided,* That on all coffee in the bean or ground imported into Porto Rico there shall be levied and collected a duty of five cents per pound, any law or part of law to the contrary notwithstanding: *And provided further,* That all Spanish scientific, literary, and artistic works, not subversive of public order in Porto Rico, shall be admitted free of duty into Porto Rico for a period of ten years, reckoning from the eleventh day of April, eighteen hundred and ninety-nine, as provided in said treaty of peace between the United States and Spain: *And provided further,* That all books and pamphlets printed in the English language shall be admitted into Porto Rico free of duty when imported from the United States.

Sec. 3. That on and after the passage of this Act all merchandise coming into the United States from Porto Rico and coming into Porto Rico from the United States shall be entered at the several ports of entry upon payment of fifteen per centum of the duties which are required to be levied, collected, and paid upon like articles of merchandise imported from foreign countries; and in addition thereto upon articles of merchandise of Porto Rican manufacture coming into the United States and withdrawn for consumption or sale upon payment of a tax equal to the internal-revenue tax imposed in the United States upon the like articles of merchandise of domestic manufacture; such tax to be paid by internal-revenue stamp or stamps to be purchased and provided by the Commissioner of Internal Revenue and to be procured from the collector of internal revenue at or most convenient to the port of entry of said merchandise in the United States, and to be affixed under such regulations as the Commissioner of Internal Revenue, with the approval of the Secretary of the Treasury, shall prescribe; and on all articles of merchandise of United States manufacture coming into Porto Rico in addition to the duty above provided upon payment of a tax equal in rate and amount to

the internal-revenue tax imposed in Porto Rico upon the like articles of Porto Rican manufacture: *Provided,* That on and after the date when this Act shall take effect, all merchandise and articles, except coffee, not dutiable under the tariff laws of the United States, and all merchandise and articles entered in Porto Rico free of duty under orders heretofore made by the Secretary of War, shall be admitted into the several ports thereof, when imported from the United States, free of duty, all laws or parts of laws to the contrary notwithstanding; and whenever the legislative assembly of Porto Rico shall have enacted and put into operation a system of local taxation to meet the necessities of the government of Porto Rico, by this Act established, and shall by resolution duly passed so notify the President, he shall make proclamation thereof, and thereupon all tariff duties on merchandise and articles going into Porto Rico from the United States or coming into the United States from Porto Rico shall cease, and from and after such date all such merchandise and articles shall be entered at the several ports of entry free of duty; and in no event shall any duties be collected after the first day of March, nineteen hundred and two, on merchandise and articles going into Porto Rico from the United States or coming into the United States from Porto Rico.

Sec. 4. That the duties and taxes collected in Porto Rico in pursuance of this Act, less the cost of collecting the same, and the gross amount of all collections of duties and taxes in the United States upon articles of merchandise coming from Porto Rico, shall not be covered into the general fund of the Treasury, but shall be held as a separate fund, and shall be placed at the disposal of the President to be used for the government and benefit of Porto Rico until the government of Porto Rico herein provided for shall have been organized, when all moneys therefore collected under the provisions hereof, then unexpended, shall be transferred to the local treasury of Porto Rico, and the Secretary of the Treasury shall designate the several ports and subports of entry in Porto Rico and shall make such rules and regulations and appoint such agents as may be necessary to collect the duties and taxes authorized to be levied, collected, and paid in Porto Rico by the provisions of this Act, and he shall fix the compensation and provide for the payment thereof of all such officers, agents, and assistants as he may find it necessary to employ to carry out the provisions hereof: *Provided, however,* That as soon as a civil government for Porto Rico shall have been organized in accordance with the provisions of this Act and notice thereof shall have been given to the President he shall make proclamation thereof, and thereafter all collections of duties and taxes in Porto Rico under the provisions of this Act shall be paid into the treasury of Porto Rico, to be expended as required by law for the government and benefit thereof instead of being paid into the Treasury of the United States.

Sec. 5. That on and after the day when this Act shall go into effect all goods, wares, and merchandise previously imported from Porto Rico, for which no entry has been made, and all goods, wares, and merchandise previously entered without payment of duty and under bond for warehousing, transportation, or any other purpose, for which no permit of delivery to the importer or his agent has been issued, shall be subjected to the duties imposed by this Act, and to no other duty, upon the entry or the withdrawal thereof: *Provided,* That when duties are based upon the weight of merchandise deposited in any public or private bonded warehouse said duties shall be levied and collected upon the weight of such merchandise at the time of its entry.

General Provisions.

Sec. 6. That the capital of Porto Rico shall be at the city of San Juan and the seat of government shall be maintained there.

Sec. 7. That all inhabitants continuing to reside therein who were Spanish subjects on the eleventh day of April, eighteen hundred and ninety-nine, and then resided in Porto Rico, and their children born subsequent thereto, shall be deemed and held to be citizens of Porto Rico, and as such entitled to the protection of the United States, except such as shall have elected to preserve their allegiance to the Crown of Spain on or before the eleventh day of April, nineteen hundred, in accordance with the provisions of the treaty of peace between the United States and Spain entered into on the eleventh day of April, eighteen hundred and ninety-nine; and they, together with such citizens of the United States as may reside in Porto Rico, shall constitute a body politic under the name of The People of Porto Rico, with governmental powers as hereinafter conferred, and with power to sue and be sued as such.

Sec. 8. That the laws and ordinances of Porto Rico now in force shall continue in full force and effect, except as altered, amended, or modified hereinafter, or as altered or modified by military orders and decrees in force when this Act shall take effect, and so far as the same are not inconsistent or in conflict with the statutory laws of the United States not locally inapplicable, or the provisions hereof, until altered, amended, or repealed by the legislative authority hereinafter provided for Porto Rico or by Act of Congress of the United States: *Provided,* That so much of the law which was in force at the time of cession, April eleventh, eighteen hundred and ninety-nine, forbidding the marriage of priests, ministers, or followers of any faith because of vows they may have taken, being paragraph four, article eighty-three, chapter three, civil code, and which was continued by the order of the secretary of jus-

tice of Porto Rico, dated March seventeenth, eighteen hundred and ninety-nine, and promulgated by Major-General Guy V. Henry, United States Volunteers, is hereby repealed and annulled, and all persons lawfully married in Porto Rico shall have all the rights and remedies conferred by law upon parties to either civil or religious marriages: *And provided further,* That paragraph one, article one hundred and five, section four, divorce, civil code, and paragraph two, section nineteen, of the order of the minister of justice of Porto Rico, dated March seventeenth, eighteen hundred and ninety-nine, and promulgated by Major- General Guy V. Henry, United States Volunteers, be, and the same hereby are, so amended as to read: "Adultery on the part of either the husband or the wife."

Sec. 9. That the Commissioner of Navigation shall make such regulations, subject to the approval of the Secretary of the Treasury, as he may deem expedient for the nationalization of all vessels owned by the inhabitants of Porto Rico on the eleventh day of April, eighteen hundred and ninety-nine, and which continued to be so owned up to the date of such nationalization, and for the admission of the same to all the benefits of the coasting trade of the United States; and the coasting trade between Porto Rico and the United States shall be regulated in accordance with the provisions of law applicable to such trade between any two great coasting districts of the United States.

Sec. 10. That quarantine stations shall be established at such places in Porto Rico as the Supervising Surgeon-General of the Marine-Hospital Service of the United States shall direct, and the quarantine regulations relating to the importation of diseases from other countries shall be under the control of the Government of the United States.

Sec. 11. That for the purpose of retiring the Porto Rican coins now in circulation in Porto Rico and substituting therefor the coins of the United States, the Secretary of the Treasury is hereby authorized to redeem, on presentation in Porto Rico, and the silver coins of Porto Rico known as the peso and all other silver and copper Porto Rican coins now in circulation in Porto Rico, not including any such coins that may be imported into Porto Rico after the first day of February, nineteen hundred, at the present established rate of sixty cents in the coins of the United States for one peso of Porto Rican coin, and for all minor or subsidiary coins the same rate of exchange shall be applied. The Porto Rican coins so purchased or redeemed shall be recoined at the expense of the United States, under the direction of the Secretary of the Treasury, into such coins of the United States now authorized by law as he may direct, and from and after three months after the date when this Act shall take effect no coins shall be a legal tender, in payment of debts thereafter contracted, for any amount in Porto Rico, except those of the United States; and whatever sum may be required to carry out the provisions hereof, and to pay all expenses that may be incurred in connection therewith, is hereby appropriated, and the Secretary of the Treasury is hereby authorized to establish such regulations and employ such agencies as may be necessary to accomplish the purposes hereof: *Provided, however,* That all debts owing on the date when this Act shall take effect shall be payable in the coins of Porto Rico now in circulation, or in the coins of the United States at the rate of exchange above named.

Sec. 12. That all expenses that may be incurred on account of the government of Porto Rico for salaries of officials and the conduct of their offices and departments, and all expenses and obligations contracted for the internal improvement or development of the island, not, however, including defenses, barracks, harbors, light-houses, buoys, and other works undertaken by the United States, shall be paid by the treasurer of Porto Rico out of the revenues in his custody.

Sec. 13. That all property which may have been acquired in Porto Rico by the United States under the cession of Spain in said treaty of peace in any public bridges, road houses, water powers, highways, unnavigable streams, and the beds thereof, subterranean waters, mines, or minerals under the surface of private lands, and all property which at the time of the cession belonged, under the laws of Spain then in force, to the various harbor-works boards of Porto Rico, and all the harbor shores, docks, slips, and reclaimed lands, but not including harbor areas or navigable waters, is hereby placed under the control of the government established by this Act to be administered for the benefit of the people of Porto Rico; and the legislative assembly hereby created shall have authority, subject to the limitations imposed upon all its acts, to legislate with respect to all such matters as it may deem advisable.

Sec. 14. That the statutory laws of the United States not locally inapplicable, except as hereinbefore or hereinafter otherwise provided, shall have the same force and effect in Porto Rico as in the United States, except the internal-revenue laws, which, in view of the provisions of section three, shall not have force and effect in Porto Rico.

Sec. 15. That the legislative authority hereinafter provided shall have power by due enactment to amend, alter, modify, or repeal any law or ordinance, civil or criminal, continued in force by this Act, as it may from time to time see fit.

Sec. 16. That all judicial process shall run in the name of "United States of America, ss: the President of the United States," and all criminal or penal prosecutions in the local courts shall be conducted in the name and by the authority of "The people of Porto Rico"; and all officials authorized by this Act shall before entering upon the duties of their respective offices take an oath to support the Constitution of the United States and the laws of Porto Rico.

The Governor.

Sec. 17. That the official title of the chief executive officer shall be "The Governor of Porto Rico." He shall be appointed by the President, by and with the advice and consent of the Senate; he shall hold his office for a term of four years and until his successor is chosen and qualified unless sooner removed by the President; he shall reside in Porto Rico during his official incumbency, and shall maintain his office at the seat of government; he may grant pardons and reprieves, and remit fines and forfeitures for offenses against the laws of Porto Rico, and respites for offenses against the laws of the United States, until the decision of the President can be ascertained; he shall commission all officers that he may be authorized to appoint, and may veto any legislation enacted, as hereinafter provided; he shall be the commander in chief of the militia, and shall at all times faithfully execute the laws, and he shall in that behalf have all the powers of governors of the Territories of the United States that are not locally inapplicable; and he shall annually, and at such other times as he may be required, make official report of the transactions of the government in Porto Rico, through the Secretary of State, to the President of the United States: *Provided,* That the President may, in his discretion, delegate and assign to him such executive duties and functions as may in pursuance with law be so delegated and assigned.

The Executive Council.

Sec. 18. That there shall be appointed by the President, by and with the advice and consent of the Senate, for the period of four years, unless sooner removed by the President, a secretary, an attorney- general, a treasurer, an auditor, a commissioner of the interior, and a commissioner of education, each of whom shall reside in Porto Rico during his official incumbency and have the powers and duties hereinafter provided for them, respectively, and who, together with five other persons of good repute, to be also appointed by the President for a like term of four years, by and with the advice and consent of the Senate, shall constitute an executive council, at least five of whom shall be native inhabitants of Porto Rico, and, in addition to the legislative duties hereinafter imposed upon them as a body, shall exercise such powers and perform such duties as are hereinafter provided for them, respectively, and who shall have power to employ all necessary deputies and assistants for the proper discharge of their duties as such officials and as such executive council.

Sec. 19. That the secretary shall record and preserve minutes of the proceedings of the executive council and the laws enacted by the legislative assembly and all acts and proceedings of the governor, and shall promulgate all proclamations and orders of the governor and all laws enacted by the legislative assembly. He shall, within sixty days after the end of each session of the legislative assembly, transmit to the President, the President of the Senate, the Speaker of the House of Representatives, and the Secretary of State of the United States one copy each of the laws and journals of such session.

Sec. 20. That in case of the death, removal, resignation, or disability of the governor, or his temporary absence from Porto Rico, the secretary shall exercise all the powers and perform all the duties of the governor during such vacancy, disability, or absence.

Sec. 21. That the attorney-general shall have all the powers and discharge all the duties provided by law for an attorney of a Territory of the United States is so far as the same are not locally inapplicable, and he shall perform such other duties as may be prescribed by law, and make such reports, through the governor, to the Attorney-General of the United States as he may require, which shall annually be transmitted to Congress.

Sec. 22. That the treasurer shall give bond, approved as to form by the attorney-general of Porto Rico, in such sum as the executive council may require, not less, however, than the sum of one hundred thousand dollars, with surety approved by the governor, and he shall collect and be the custodian of the public funds, and shall disburse the same when appropriated by law, on warrants signed by the auditor and countersigned by the governor, and shall perform such other duties as may be prescribed by law, and make, through the governor, such reports to the Secretary of the Treasury of the United States as he may require, which shall annually be transmitted to Congress.

Sec. 23. That the auditor shall keep full and accurate accounts, showing the receipts and disbursements, and perform such other duties as may be prescribed by law, and make, through the governor, such reports to the Secretary of the Treasury of the United States as he may require, which shall annually be transmitted to Congress.

Sec. 24. That the commissioner of the interior shall superintend all works of a public nature, and shall have charge of all public buildings, grounds, and lands, except those belonging to the United States, and shall execute such requirements as may be imposed by law with respect thereto, and shall perform such other duties as may be prescribed by law, and make such reports through the governor to the Secretary of the Interior of the United States as he may require, which shall annually be transmitted to Congress.

Sec. 25. That the commissioner of education shall superintend public instruction throughout Porto Rico, and all disbursements on account thereof must be approved by him; and he shall perform such other duties as may be pre-

scribed by law, and make such reports through the governor as may be required by the Commissioner of Education of the United States, which shall annually be transmitted to Congress.

Sec. 26. That the other five members of the executive council, to be appointed as hereinbefore provided, shall attend all meetings of the executive council and participate in all business of every character that may be transacted by it; and they shall receive as compensation for their services such annual salaries as may be provided by the legislative assembly.

House of Delegates.

Sec. 27. That all local legislative powers hereby granted shall be vested in a legislative assembly which shall consist of two houses; one the executive council, as hereinbefore constituted, and the other a house of delegates, to consist of thirty-five members elected biennially by the qualified voters as hereinafter provided; and the two houses thus constituted shall be designated "The legislative assembly Porto Rico."

Sec. 28. That for the purposes of such elections Porto Rico shall be divided by the executive council into seven districts, composed of contiguous territory and as nearly equal as may be in population, and each district shall be entitled to five members of the house of delegates.

Election of Delegates.

Sec. 29. That the first election for delegates shall be held on such date and under such regulations as to ballots and voting as the executive council may prescribe; and at such elections the voters of each legislative district shall choose five delegates to represent them in the house of delegates from the date of their election and qualification until two years from and after the first day of January next ensuing; of all which thirty days' notice shall be given by publication in the Official Gazette, or by printed notices distributed and posted throughout the district, or by both, as the executive council may prescribe. At such elections all citizens of Porto Rico shall be allowed to vote who have been bona fide residents for one year and who possess the other qualifications of voters under the laws and military orders in force on the first day of March, nineteen hundred, subject to such modifications and additional qualifications and such regulations and restrictions as to registration as may be prescribed by the executive council. The house of delegates so chosen shall convene at the capital and organize by the election of a speaker, a clerk, a sergeant-at-arms, and such other officers and assistants as it may require, at such time as may be designated by the executive council; but it shall not continue in session longer than sixty days in any one year, unless called by the governor to meet in extraordinary session. The enacting clause of the laws shall be, "Be it enacted by the legislative assembly of Porto Rico"; and each member of the house of delegates shall be paid for his services at the rate of five dollars per day for each day's attendance while the house is in session, and mileage at the rate of ten cents per mile for each mile necessarily traveled each way to and from each session of the legislative assembly.

All future elections of delegates shall be governed by the provisions hereof, so far as they are applicable, until the legislative assembly shall otherwise provide.

Sec. 30. That the house of delegates shall be the sole judge of the elections, returns, and qualifications of its members, and shall have and exercise all the powers with respect to the conduct of its proceedings that usually appertain to parliamentary legislative bodies. No person shall be eligible to membership in the house of delegates who is not twenty-five years of age and able to read and write either the Spanish or the English language, or who is not possessed in his own right of taxable property, real or personal, situated in Porto Rico.

Sec. 31. That all bills may originate in either house, but no bill shall become a law unless it be passed in each house by a majority vote of all the members belonging to such house and be approved by the governor within ten days thereafter. If, when a bill that has been passed is presented to the governor for signature, he approves the same, he shall sign it, or if not he shall return it, with his objections, to that house in which it originated, which house shall enter his objections at large on its journal, and proceed to reconsider the bill. If, after such reconsideration, two-thirds of that house shall agree to pass the bill, it shall be sent, together with the objections, to the other house, by which it shall likewise be considered, and if approved by two-thirds of that house it shall become a law. But in all such cases the votes of both houses shall be determined by yeas and nays, and the names of the persons voting for and against the bill shall be entered upon the journal of each house, respectively. If any bill shall not be returned by the governor within ten days (Sundays excepted) after it shall have been presented to him, the same shall be a law in like manner as if he had signed it, unless the legislative assembly by adjournment prevent its return, in which case it shall not be a law: *Provided, however,* That all laws enacted by the legislative assembly shall be reported to the Congress of the United States, which hereby reserves the power and authority, if deemed advisable, to annul the same.

Sec. 32. That the legislative authority herein provided shall extend to all matters of a legislative character not locally inapplicable, including power to create, consolidate, and reorganize the municipalities, so far as may be necessary, and to provide and repeal laws and ordinances therefor; and also power to alter, amend, modify, and repeal any and all laws and ordinances of every character now in force in Porto Rico, or any municipality or district thereof, not inconsistent with the provisions hereof: *Provided, however,* That all grants of franchises, rights, and privileges or concessions of a public or quasi-public nature shall be made by the executive council, with the approval of the governor, and all franchises granted in Porto Rico shall be reported to Congress, which hereby reserves the power to annul or modify the same.

The Judiciary.
Sec. 33. That the judicial power shall be vested in the courts and tribunals of Porto Rico as already established and now in operation, including municipal courts, under and by virtue of General Orders, Numbered One hundred and eighteen, as promulgated by Brigadier-General Davis, United States Volunteers, August sixteenth, eighteen hundred and ninety-nine, and including also the police courts established by General Orders, Numbered One hundred and ninety-five, promulgated November twenty-ninth, eighteen hundred and ninety-nine, by Brigadier-General Davis, United States Volunteers, and the laws and ordinances of Porto Rico and the municipalities thereof in force, so far as the same are not in conflict herewith, all which courts and tribunals are hereby continued. The jurisdiction of said courts and the form of procedure in them, and the various officials and attaches thereof, respectively, shall be the same as defined and prescribed in and by said laws and ordinances, and said General Orders, Numbered One hundred and eighteen and One hundred and ninety-five, until otherwise provided by law: *Provided, however,* That the chief justice and associate justices of the supreme court and the marshal thereof shall be appointed by the President, by and with the advice and consent of the Senate, and the judges of the district courts shall be appointed by the governor, by and with the advice and consent of the executive council, and all other officials and attaches of all the other courts shall be chosen as may be directed by the legislative assembly, which shall have authority to legislate from time to time as it may see fit with respect to said courts, and any others they may deem it advisable to establish, their organization, the number of judges and officials and attaches for each, their jurisdiction, their procedure, and all other matters affecting them.

Sec. 34. That Porto Rico shall constitute a judicial district to be called "the district of Porto Rico." The President, by and with the advice and consent of the Senate, shall appoint a district judge, a district attorney, and a marshal for said district, each for a term of four years, unless sooner removed by the President. The district court for said district shall be called the district court of the United States for Porto Rico and shall have power to appoint all necessary officials and assistants, including clerk, an interpreter, and such commissioners as may be necessary, who shall have like power and duties as are exercised and performed by commissioners of the circuit courts of the United States, and shall have, in addition to the ordinary jurisdiction of district courts of the United States, jurisdiction of all cases cognizant in the circuit courts of the United States, and shall proceed therein in the same manner as a circuit court. The laws of the United States relating to appeals, writs of error and certiorari, removal of causes, and other matters and proceedings as between the courts of the United States and the courts of the several States shall govern in such matters and proceedings as between the district court of the United States and the courts of Porto Rico. Regular terms of said court shall be held at San Juan, commencing on the second Monday in April and October of each year, and also at Ponce on the second Monday in January of each year, and special terms may be held at Mayaguez at such other stated times as said judge may deem expedient. All pleadings and proceedings in said court shall be conducted in the English language.

The United States district court hereby established shall be the successor to the United States provisional court established by General Orders, Numbered Eighty-eight, promulgated by Brigadier- General Davis, United States Volunteers, and shall take possession of all records of that court, and take jurisdiction of all cases and proceedings pending therein, and said United States provisional court is hereby discontinued.

Sec. 35. That writs of error and appeals from the final decisions of the supreme court of Porto Rico and the district court of the United States shall be allowed and may be taken to the Supreme Court of the United States in the same manner and under the same regulations and in the same cases as from the supreme courts of the Territories of the United States; and such writs of error and appeal shall be allowed in all cases where the Constitution of the United States, or a treaty thereof, or an Act of Congress is brought in question and the right claimed thereunder is denied; and the supreme and district courts of Porto Rico and the respective judges thereof may grant writs of habeas corpus in all cases in which the same are grantable by the judges of the district and circuit courts of the United States. All such proceedings in the Supreme Court of the United States shall be conducted in the English language.

Sec. 36. That the salaries of all officials of Porto Rico not appointed by the President, including deputies, assistants, and other help, shall be such, and be so paid out of the revenues of Porto Rico, as the executive council shall from time to time determine: *Provided, however,* That the salary of no officer shall be either increased or diminished during his term of office. The salaries of all officers and all expenses of the offices of the various officials of Porto Rico, appointed as herein provided by the President, including deputies, assistants, and other help, shall also be paid out of the revenues of Porto Rico on the warrant of the auditor, countersigned by the governor.

The annual salaries of the officials appointed by the President, and so to be paid, shall be as follows:

The governor, eight thousand dollars; in addition thereto he shall be entitled to the occupancy of the buildings heretofore used by the chief executive of Porto Rico, with the furniture and effects therein, free of rental.

The secretary, four thousand dollars.

The attorney-general, four thousand dollars.

The treasurer, five thousand dollars.

The auditor, four thousand dollars.

The commissioner of the interior, four thousand dollars.

The commissioner of education, three thousand dollars.

The chief justice of the supreme court, five thousand dollars.

The associate justices of the supreme court (each), four thousand five hundred dollars.

The marshal of the supreme court, three thousand dollars.

The United States district judge, five thousand dollars.

The United States district attorney, four thousand dollars.

The United States district marshal, three thousand five hundred dollars.

Sec. 37. That the provisions of the foregoing section shall not apply to the municipal officials. Their salaries and the compensation of their deputies, assistants, and other help, as well as all other expenses incurred by the municipalities, shall be paid out of the municipal revenues in such manner as the legislative assembly shall provide.

Sec. 38. That no export duties shall be levied or collected on exports from Porto Rico; but taxes and assessments on property, and license fees for franchises, privileges, and concessions may be imposed for the purposes of the insular and municipal governments, respectively, as may be provided and defined by act of the legislative assembly; and where necessary to anticipate taxes and revenues, bonds and other obligations may be issued by Porto Rico or any municipal government therein as may be provided by law to provide for expenditures authorized by law, and to protect the public credit, and to reimburse the United States for any moneys which have been or may be expended out of the emergency fund of the War Department for the relief of the industrial conditions of Porto Rico caused by the hurricane of August eighth, eighteen hundred and ninety-nine: *Provided, however,* That no public indebtedness of Porto Rico or of any municipality thereof shall be authorized or allowed in excess of seven per centum of the aggregate tax valuation of its property.

Sec. 39. That the qualified voters of Porto Rico shall, on the first Tuesday after the first Monday of November, anno Domini nineteen hundred, and every two years thereafter, choose a resident commissioner to the United States, who shall be entitled to official recognition as such by all Departments, upon presentation to the Department of State of a certificate of election of the governor of Porto Rico, and who shall be entitled to a salary, payable monthly by the United States, at the rate of five thousand dollars per annum: *Provided,* That no person shall be eligible to such election who is not a bona fide citizen of Porto Rico, who is not thirty years of age, and who does not read and write the English language.

Sec. 40. That a commission, to consist of three members, at least one of whom shall be a native citizen of Porto Rico, shall be appointed by the President, by and with the advice and consent of the Senate, to compile and revise the laws of Porto Rico; also the various codes of procedure and systems of municipal government now in force, and to frame and report such legislation as may be necessary to make a simple, harmonious, and economical government, establish justice and secure its prompt and efficient administration, inaugurate a general system of education and public instruction, provide buildings and funds therefor, equalize and simplify taxation and all the methods of raising revenue, and, make all other provisions that may be necessary to secure and extend the benefits of a republican form of government to all the inhabitants of Porto Rico; and all the expenses of such commissioners, including all necessary clerks and other assistants that they may employ, and a salary to each member of the commission at the rate of five thousand dollars per annum, shall be allowed and paid out of the treasury of Porto Rico as a part of the expenses of the government of Porto Rico. And said commission shall make full and final report, in both the English and Spanish languages, of all its revisions, compilations, and recommendations, with explanatory notes as to the changes and the reasons therefor, to the Congress on or before one year after the passage of this Act.

Sec. 41. That this Act shall take effect and be in force from and after the first day of May, nineteen hundred.

Source:
Statutes at Large, Vol. 31, pp. 77–86.

William Jennings Bryan, Imperialism Speech, 1900

Speech deploring U.S. imperialism delivered on August 8, 1900, at the Democratic National Convention in Indianapolis, Indiana, by party presidential nominee William Jennings Bryan. Bryan, an outspoken critic of the Republican McKinley administration's imperialist policy in the Spanish-American War, made the 1900 election a referendum on American imperialism. In his acceptance speech, he outlined his constitutional and moral objections to McKinley's annexation of the Spanish colonies Puerto Rico and the Philippines. The extension of U.S. sovereignty over foreign territories, Bryan asserted, not only smacked of colonialism, but it was legally specious, contradicted America's heritage of democratic self-rule, and eroded the nation's moral authority at home and abroad. McKinley won reelection by a wide margin over Bryan.

———————————— ⌘ ————————————

Mr. Chairman and Members of the Notification Committee: I shall, at an early day, and in a more formal manner, accept the nomination which you tender, and shall at that time discuss the various questions covered by the Democratic platform. It may not be out of place, however, to submit a few observations at this time upon the general character of the contest before us and upon the question which is declared to be of paramount importance in this campaign.

When I say that the contest of 1900 is a contest between Democracy on the one hand and plutocracy on the other I do not mean to say that all our opponents have deliberately chosen to give to organized wealth a predominating influence in the affairs of the Government, but I do assert that on the important issues of the day the Republican party is dominated by those influences which constantly tend to substitute the worship of mammon for the protection of the rights of man.

In 1859 Lincoln said that the Republican party believed in the man and the dollar, but that in case of conflict it believed in the man before the dollar. This is the proper relation which should exist between the two. Man, the handiwork of God, comes first; money, the handiwork of man, is of inferior importance. Man is the master, money the servant, but upon all important questions today Republican legislation tends to make money the master and man the servant.

The maxim of Jefferson, "Equal rights to all and special privileges to none," and the doctrine of Lincoln, that this should be a government "of the people, by the people and for the people," are being disregarded and instrumentalities of government are being used to advance the interest of those who are in a position to secure favors from the Government.

The Democratic party is not making war upon the honest acquisition of wealth; it has no desire to discourage industry, economy and thrift. On the contrary, it gives to every citizen the greatest possible stimulus to honest toil when it promises him protection in the enjoyment of the proceeds of his labor. Property rights are most secure when human rights are most respected. Democracy strives for a civilization in which every member of society will share according to his merits.

No one has a right to expect from society more than a fair compensation for the services which he renders to society, if he secures more it is at the expense of some one else. It is no injustice to him to prevent his doing injustice to another. To him who would, either through class legislation or in the absence of necessary legislation, trespass upon the rights of another the Democratic party says, "Thou shalt not."

Against us are arrayed a comparatively small but politically and financially powerful number who really profit by Republican policies; but with them are associated a large number who, because of their attachment to their party name, are giving their support to doctrines antagonistic to the former teachings of their own party.

Republicans who used to advocate bimetalism now try to convince themselves that the gold standard is good; Republicans who were formerly attached to the greenback are now seeking an excuse for giving national banks control of the Nation's paper money; Republicans who used to boast that the Republicans party was paying off the national debt are now looking for reasons to support a perpetual and increasing debt; Republicans who formerly abhorred a trust now beguile themselves with the delusion that there are good trusts and bad trusts, while, in their minds, the line between the two is becoming more and more obscure; Republicans who, in time past, congratulated the country upon the small expense of our standing army, are now making light of the objections which are urged against a large increase in the permanent military establishment; Republicans who gloried in our independence when the Nation was less powerful now look with favor upon a foreign alliance; Republicans who three years ago condemned "forcible annexation" as immoral and even criminal are now sure that it is both immoral and criminal to oppose forcible annexation. That partizanship has already blinded many to present dangers is certain; how large a portion of the Republican party can be drawn over to the new policies remains to be seen.

For a time Republican leaders were inclined to deny to opponents the right to criticize the Philippine policy of the administration, but upon investigation they found that both Lincoln and Clay asserted and exercised the right to critize a President during the progress of the Mexican war.

Instead of meeting the issue boldly and submitting a clear and positive plan for dealing with the Philippine question, the Republican convention adopted a platform the larger part of which was devoted to boasting and self-congratulation.

In attempting to press economic questions upon the country to the exclusion of those which involve the very structure of our government, the Republican leaders give new evidence of their abandonment of the earlier ideals of the party and of their complete subserviency to pecuniary considerations.

But they shall not be permitted to evade the stupendous and far-reaching issue which they have deliberately brought into the arena of politics. When the President, supported by a practically unanimous vote of the House and Senate, entered upon a war with Spain for the purpose of aiding the struggling patriots of Cuba, the country, without regard to party, applauded.

Altho the Democrats realized that the administration would necessarily gain a political advantage from the conduct of a war which in the very nature of the case must soon end in a complete victory, they vied with the Republicans in the support which they gave to the President. When the war was over and the Republican leaders began to suggest the propriety of a colonial policy opposition at once manifested itself.

When the President finally laid before the Senate a treaty which recognized the independence of Cuba, but provided for the cession of the Philippine Islands to the United States, the menace of imperialism became so apparent that many preferred to reject the treaty and risk the ills that might follow rather than take the chance of correcting the errors of the treaty by the independent action of this country.

I was among the number of those who believed it better to ratify the treaty and end the war, release the volunteers, remove the excuse for war expenditures and then give the Filipinos the independence which might be forced from Spain by a new treaty.

In view of the criticism which my action aroused in some quarters, I take this occasion to restate the reasons given at that time. I thought it safer to trust the American people to give independence to the Filipinos than to trust the accomplishment of that purpose to diplomacy with an unfriendly nation.

Lincoln embodied an argument in the question when he asked, "Can aliens make treaties easier than friends can make laws?" I believe that we are now in a better position to wage a successful contest against imperialism than we would have been had the treaty been rejected. With the treaty ratified a clean-cut issue is presented between a government by consent and a government by force, and imperialists must bear the responsibility for all that happens until the question is settled.

If the treaty had been rejected the opponents of imperialism would have been held responsible for any international complications which might have arisen before the ratification of another treaty. But whatever difference of opinion may have existed as to the best method of opposing a colonial policy, there never was any difference as to the great importance of the question and there is no difference now as to the course to be pursued.

The title of Spain being extinguished we were at liberty to deal with the Filipinos according to American principles. The Bacon resolution, introduced a month before hostilities broke out at Manila, promised independence to the Filipinos on the same terms that it was promised to the Cubans. I supported this resolution and believe that its adoption prior to the breaking out of hostilities would have prevented bloodshed, and that its adoption at any subsequent time would have ended hostilities.

If the treaty had been rejected considerable time would have necessarily elapsed before a new treaty could have been agreed upon and ratified, and during that time the question would have been agitating the public mind. If the Bacon resolution had been adopted by the Senate and carried out by the President, either at the time of the ratification of the treaty or at any time afterwards, it would have taken the question of imperialism out of politics, and left the American people free to deal with their domestic problems. But the resolution was defeated by the vote of the Republican Vice-President, and from that time to this a Republican Congress has refused to take any action whatever in the matter.

When hostilities broke out at Manila Republican speakers and Republican editors at once sought to lay the blame upon those who had delayed the ratification of the treaty, and, during the progress of the war, the same Republicans have accused the opponents of imperialism of giving encouragement of the Filipinos. This is a cowardly evasion of responsibility.

If it is right for the United States to hold the Philippine Islands permanently and imitate European empires in the government of colonies, the Republican party ought to state its position and defend it, but it must expect the subject races to protest against such a policy and to resist to the extent of their ability.

The Filipinos do not need any encouragement from Americans now living. Our whole history has been an encouragement, not only to the Filipinos, but to all who are denied a voice in their own government. If the Republicans are prepared to censure all who have used language calculated to make the Filipinos hate foreign domination, let them condemn the speech of Patrick Henry. When he uttered that passionate appeal, "Give me liberty or give me death," he exprest a sentiment which still echoes in the hearts of men.

Let them censure Jefferson; of all the statesmen of history none have used words so offensive to those who would hold their fellows in political bondage. Let them censure Washington, who declared that the colonists must choose between liberty and slavery. Or, if the statute of limitations has run against the sins of Henry and Jefferson and Washington, let them censure Lincoln, whose Gettysburg speech will be quoted in defense of popular government when the present advocates of force and conquest are forgotten.

Some one has said that a truth once spoken can never be recalled. It goes on and on, and on one can set a limit to its ever-widening influence. But if it were possible to obliterate every word written or spoken in defense of the principles set forth in the Declaration of Independence, a war of conquest would still leave its legacy of perpetual hatred, for it was God himself who placed in every human heart the love of liberty. He never made a race of people so low in the scale of civilization or intelligence that it would welcome a foreign master.

Those who would have this Nation enter upon a career of empire must consider, not only the effect of imperialism on the Filipinos, but they must also calculate its effects upon our own nation. We cannot repudiate the principle of self-government in the Philippines without weakening that principle here.

Lincoln said that the safety of this Nation was not in its fleets, its armies, or its forts, but in the spirit which prizes liberty as the heritage of all men, in all lands, everywhere, and he warned his countrymen that they could not destroy this spirit without planting the seeds of despotism at their own doors.

Even now we are beginning to see the paralyzing influence of imperialism. Heretofore this Nation has been prompt to express its sympathy with those who were fighting for civil liberty. While our sphere of activity has been limited to the Western Hemisphere, our sympathies have not been bounded by the seas. We have felt it due to ourselves and to the world, as well as to those who were struggling for the right to govern themselves, to proclaim the interest which our people have, from the date of their own independence, felt in every contest between human rights and arbitrary power.

Three-quarters of a century ago, when our nation was small, the struggles of Greece aroused our people, and Webster and Clay gave eloquent expression to the universal desire for Grecian independence. In 1898 all parties manifested a lively interest in the success of the Cubans, but now when a war is in progress in South Africa, which must result in the extension of the monarchical idea, or in the triumph of a republic, the advocates of imperialism in this country dare not say a word in behalf of the Boers.

Sympathy for the Boers does not arise from any unfriendliness towards England; the American people are not unfriendly toward the people of any nation. This sympathy is due to the fact that, as stated in our platform, we believe in the principles of self-government and reject, as did our forefathers, the claims of monarchy. If this nation surrenders its belief in the universal application of the principles set forth in the Declaration of Independence, it will lose the prestige and influence which it has enjoyed among the nations as an exponent of popular government.

Our opponents, conscious of the weakness of their cause, seek to confuse imperialism with expansion, and have even dared to claim Jefferson as a supporter of their policy. Jefferson spoke so freely and used language with such precision that no one can be ignorant of his views. On one occasion he declared: "If there be one principle more deeply rooted than any other in the mind of every American, it is that we should have nothing to do with conquest." And again he said: "Conquest is not in our principles; it is inconsistent with our government."

The forcible annexation of territory to be governed by arbitrary power differs as much from the acquisition of territory to be built up into States as a monarchy differs from a democracy. The Democratic party does not oppose expansion when expansion enlarges the area of the Republic and incorporates land which can be settled by American citizens, or adds to our population people who are willing to become citizens and are capable of discharging their duties as such.

The acquisition of the Louisiana territory, Florida, Texas and other tracts which have been secured from time to time enlarged the Republic and the Constitution followed the flag into the new territory. It is now proposed to seize upon distant territory already more densely populated than our own country and to force upon the people a government for which there is no warrant in our Constitution or our laws.

Even the argument that this earth belongs to those who desire to cultivate it and who have the physical power to acquire it cannot be invoked to justify the appropriation of the Philippine Islands by the United States. If the islands were uninhabited American citizens would not be willing to go there and till the soil. The white race will not live so near the equator. Other nations have tried to colonize in the same latitude. The Netherlands have controlled Java for three hundred years and yet today there are less than sixty thousand people of European birth scattered among the twenty-five million natives.

After a century and a half of English domination in India, less than one-twentieth of one per cent. of the people of India are of English birth, and it requires an army of seventy thousand British soldiers to take care of the tax collectors. Spain had asserted title to the Philippine Islands for three centuries and yet when our fleet entered Manila bay there were less than ten thousand Spaniards residing in the Philippines.

A colonial policy means that we shall send to the Philippine Islands a few traders, a few taskmasters and a few office-holders and an army large enough to support the authority of a small fraction of the people while they rule the natives.

If we have an imperial policy we must have a great standing army as its natural and necessary complement. The spirit which will justify the forcible annexation of the Philippine Islands will justify the seizure of other islands and the domination of other people, and with wars of conquest we can expect a certain, if not rapid, growth of our military establishment.

That a large permanent increase in our regular army is intended by Republican leaders is not a matter of conjecture, but a matter of fact. In his message of December 5, 1898, the President asked for authority to increase the standing army to 100,000. In 1896 the army contained about 25,000. Within two years the President asked for four times that many, and a Republican House of Representatives complied with the request after the Spanish treaty had been signed, and when no country was at war with the United States.

If such an army is demanded when an imperial policy is contemplated, but not openly avowed, what may be expected if the people encourage the Republican party by indorsing its policy at the polls?

A large standing army is not only a pecuniary burden to the people and, if accompanied by compulsory service, a constant source of irritation, but it is ever a menace to a republican form of government.

The army is the personification of force and militarism will inevitably change the ideals of the people and turn the thoughts of our young men from the arts of peace to the science of war. The government which relies for its defense upon its citizens is more likely to be just than one which has at call a large body of professional soldiers.

A small standing army and a well-equipped and well-disciplined State militia are sufficient at ordinary times, and in an emergency the nation should in the future as in the past place its dependence upon the volunteers who come from all occupations at their country's call and return to productive labor when their services are no longer required—men who fight when the country needs fighters and work when the country needs workers.

The Republican platform assumes that the Philippine Islands will be retained under American sovereignty, and we have a right to demand of the Republican leaders a discussion of the future status of the Filipino. Is he to be a citizen or a subject? Are we to bring into the body politic eight or ten million Asiatics, so different from us in race and history that amalgamation is impossible? Are they to share with us in making the laws and shaping the destiny of this nation? No Republican of prominence has been bold enough to advocate such a proposition.

The McEnery resolution, adopted by the Senate immediately after the ratification of the treaty, expressly negatives this idea. The Democratic platform describes the situation when it says that the Filipinos cannot be citizens without endangering our civilization. Who will dispute it? And what is the alternative? If the Filipino is not to be a citizen, shall we make him a subject? On that question the Democratic platform speaks with equal emphasis. It declares that the Filipino cannot be a subject without endangering our form of government. A republic can have no subjects. A subject is possible only in a government resting upon force; he is unknown in a government deriving its just powers from the consent of the governed.

The Republican platform says that "the largest measure of self-government consistent with their welfare and our duties shall be secured to them (the Filipinos) by law." This is a strange doctrine for a government which owes its very existence to the men who offered their lives as a protest against government without consent and taxation without representation.

In what respect does the position of the Republican party differ from the position taken by the English government in 1776? Did not the English government promise a good government to the colonists? What king ever promised a bad government to his people? Did not the English government promise that the colonists should have the largest measure of self-government consistent with their welfare and English duties? Did not the Spanish government promise to give to the Cubans the largest measure of self-government consistent with their welfare and Spanish duties? The whole difference between a monarchy and a republic may be summed up in one sentence. In a monarchy the king gives to the people what he believes to be a good government; in a republic the people secure for themselves what they believe to be a good government.

The Republican party has accepted the European idea and planted itself upon the ground taken by George III., and by every ruler who distrusts the capacity of the people for self-government or denies them a voice in their own affairs.

The Republican platform promises that some measure of self-government is to be given the Filipinos by law; but even this pledge is not fulfilled. Nearly sixteen months elapsed after the ratification of the treaty before the adjournment of Congress last June and yet no law was passed dealing with the Philippine situation. The will of the President has been the only law in the Philippine Islands wherever the American authority extends.

Why does the Republican party hesitate to legislate upon the Philippine question? Because a law would disclose the radical departure from history and precedent contemplated by those who control the Republican party.

The storm of protest which greeted the Porto Rican bill was an indication of what may be expected when the American people are brought face to face with legislation upon this subject.

If the Porto Ricans, who welcomed annexation, are to be denied the guarantees of our Constitution, what is to be the lot of the Filipinos, who resisted our authority? If secret influences could compel a disregard of our plain duty toward friendly people, living near our shores, what treatment will those same influences provide for unfriendly people 7,000 miles away? If, in this country where the people have a right to vote, Republican leaders dare not take the side of the people against the great monopolies which have grown up within the last few years, how can they be trusted to protect the Filipinos from the corporations which are waiting to exploit the islands?

Is the sunlight of full citizenship to be enjoyed by the people of the United States, and the twilight of semi-citizenship endured by the people of Porto Rico, while the thick darkness of perpetual vassalage covers the Philippines? The Porto Rico tariff law asserts the doctrine that the operation of the Constitution is confined to the forty-five States.

The Democratic party disputes this doctrine and denounces it as repugnant to both the letter and spirit of our organic law. There is no place in our system of government for the deposit of arbitrary and irresponsible power. That the leaders of a great party should claim for any President or Congress the right to treat millions of people as mere "possessions" and deal with them unrestrained by the Constitution or the bill of rights shows how far we have already departed from the ancient landmarks and indicates what may be expected if this nation deliberately enters upon a career of empire.

The territorial form of government is temporary and preparatory, and the chief security a citizen of a territory has is found in the fact that he enjoys the same constitutional guarantees and is subject to the same general laws as the citizen of a State. Take away this security and his rights will be violated and his interests sacrificed at the demand of those who have political influence. This is the evil of the colonial system, no matter by what nation it is applied.

What is our title of the Philippine Islands? Do we hold them by treaty or by conquest? Did we buy them or did we take them? Did we purchase the people? If not, how did we secure title to them? Were they thrown in with the land? Will the Republicans say that inanimate earth has value but that when that earth is molded by the divine hand and stamped with the likeness of the Creator it becomes a fixture and passes with the soil? If governments derive their just powers from the consent of the governed, it is impossible to secure title to people, either by force or by purchase.

We could extinguish Spain's title by treaty, but if we hold title we must hold it by some method consistent with our ideas of government. When we made allies of the Filipinos and armed them to fight against Spain, we disputed Spain's title. If we buy Spain's title we are not innocent purchasers.

There can be no doubt that we accepted and utilized the services of the Filipinos, and that when we did so we had full knowledge that they were fighting for their own independence, and I submit that history furnishes no example of turpitude baser than ours if we now substitute our yoke for the Spanish yoke.

Let us consider briefly the reasons which have been given in support of an imperialistic policy. Some say that it is our duty to hold the Philippine Islands. But duty is not an argument; it is a conclusion. To ascertain what our duty is, in any emergency, we must apply well-settled and generally accepted principles. It is our duty to a void stealing, no matter whether the thing to be stolen is of great or little value. It is our duty to avoid killing a human being, no matter where the human being lives or to what race or class he belongs.

Every one recognizes the obligation imposed upon individuals to observe both the human and the moral law, but as some deny the application of those laws to nations, it may not be out of place to quote the opinions of others. Jefferson, than whom there is no higher political authority, said:

I know of but one code of morality for men, whether acting singly or collectively.

Franklin, whose learning, wisdom and virtue are a part of the priceless legacy bequeathed to us from the revolutionary days, exprest the same idea in even stronger language when he said:

Justice is strictly due between neighbor nations as between neighbor citizens. A highwayman is as much a robber when he plunders in a gang as when single; and the nation that makes an unjust war is only a great gang.

Many may dare to do in crowds that they would not dare to do as individuals, but the moral character of an act is not determined by the number of those who join it. Force can defend a right, but force has never yet created a right. If it was true, as declared in the resolutions of intervention, that the Cubans "are and of right ought to be free and independent" (language taken from the Declaration of Independence), it is equally true that the Filipinos "are and of right ought to be free and independent."

The right of the Cubans to freedom was not based upon their proximity to the United States, nor upon the language which they spoke, nor yet upon the race or races to which they belonged. Congress by a practically unanimous vote declared that the principles enunciated at Philadelphia in 1776 were still alive and applicable to the Cubans. Who will draw a line between the natural rights of the Cubans and the Filipinos? Who will say that the former has a right to liberty and that the latter has no rights which we are bound to respect? And, if the Filipinos "are and of right ought to be free and independent," what right have we to force our government upon them without their consent? Before our duty can be ascertained their rights must be determined, and when their rights are once determined it is as much our duty to respect those rights as it was the duty of Spain to respect the rights of the people of Cuba or the duty of England to respect the rights of the American colonists. Rights never conflict; duties never clash. Can it be our duty to usurp political rights which belong to others? Can it be our duty to kill those who, following the example of our forefathers, love liberty well enough to fight for it?

Some poet has described the terror which overcame a soldier who in the midst of the battle discovered that he had slain his brother. It is written "All yet are brethren." Let us hope for the coming of the day when human life—which when once destroyed cannot be restored—will be so sacred that it will never be taken except when necessary to punish a crime already committed, or to prevent a crime about to be committed.

It is said that we have assumed before the world obligations which make it necessary for us to permanently maintain a government in the Philippine Islands. I reply first, that the highest obligation of this nation is to be true to itself. No obligation to any particular nations, or to all the nations combined, can require the abandonment of our theory of government, and the substitution of doctrines against which our whole national life has been a protest. And, second, that our obligation to the Filipinos, who inhabit the islands, is greater than any obligation which we can owe to foreigners who have a temporary residence in the Philippines or desire to trade there.

It is argued by some that the Filipinos are incapable of self-government and that, therefore, we owe it to the world to take control of them. Admiral Dewey, in an official report to the Navy Department, declared the Filipinos more capable of self-government than the Cubans and said that he based his opinion upon a knowledge of both races. But I will not rest the case upon the relative advancement of the Filipinos, Henry Clay, in defending the right of the people of South America to self-government, said:

It is the doctrine of thrones that man is too ignorant to govern himself. Their partizans assert his incapacity in reference to all nations; if they cannot command universal assent to the proposition, it is then demanded to particular nations; and our pride and our presumption too often make converts of us. I contend that it is to arraign the disposition of Providence himself to suppose that he has created beings incapable of governing themselves, and to be trampled on by kings. Self-government is the natural government of man.

Clay was right. There are degrees of proficiency in the art of self-government, but it is a reflection upon the Creator to say that he denied to any people the capacity for self-government. Once admit that some people are capable of self-government and that others are not and that the capable people have a right to seize upon and govern the incapable, and you make force—brute force—the only foundation of government and invite the reign of a despot. I am not willing to believe that an all-wise and an all-loving God created the Filipinos and then left them thousands of years helpless until the islands attracted the attention of European nations.

Republicans ask, "Shall we haul down the flag that floats over our dead in the Philippines?" The same question might have been asked, when the American flag floated over Chapultepec and waved over the dead who fell there; but the tourist who visits the city of Mexico finds there a national cemetery owned by the United States and cared for by an American citizen.

Our flag still floats over our dead, but when the treaty with Mexico was signed American authority withdrew to the Rio Grande, and I venture the opinion that during the last fifty years the people of Mexico have made more progress under the stimulus of independence and self-government than they would have made under a carpet-bag government held in place by bayonets. The United States and Mexico, friendly republics, are each stronger and happier than they would have been had the former been cursed and the latter crushed by an imperialistic policy disguised as "benevolent assimilation."

"Can we not govern colonies?" we are asked. The question is not what we can do, but what we ought to do. This nation can do whether it desires to do, but it must accept responsibility for what it does. If the Constitution stands in the way, the people can amend the Constitution. I repeat, the nation can do whatever it desires to do, but it cannot avoid the natural and legitimate results of its own conduct.

The young man upon reaching his majority can do what he pleases. He can disregard the teachings of his parents; he can trample upon all that he has been taught to consider sacred; he can disobey the laws of the State, the laws of society and the laws of God. He can stamp failure upon his life and make his very existence a curse to his fellow men, and he can bring his father and mother in sorrow to the grave; but he cannot annul the sentence, "The wages of sin is death."

And so with the nation. It is of age and it can do what is pleases; it can spurn the traditions of the past; it can repudiate the principles upon which the nation rests; it can employ force instead of reason; it can substitute might of right; it can conquer weaker people; it can exploit their lands, appropriate their property and kill their people; but it cannot repeal the moral law or escape the punishment decreed for the violation of human rights.

Would we tread in the paths of tyranny, Nor reckon the tyrant's cost? Who taketh another's liberty His freedom is also cost. Would we win as the strong have ever won, Make ready to pay the debt, For the God who reigned over Babylon Is the God who is reigning yet.

Some argue that American rule in the Philippine Islands will result in the better education of the Filipinos. Be not deceived. If we expect to maintain a colonial policy, we shall not find it to our advantage to educate the people. The educated Filipinos are now in revolt against us, and the most ignorant ones have made the least resistance to our domination. If we are to govern them without their consent and give them no voice in determining the taxes which they must pay, we dare not educate them, lest they learn to read the Declaration of Independence and Constitution of the United States and mock us for our inconsistency.

The principal arguments, however, advanced by those who enter upon a defense of imperialism are:

First—That we must improve the present opportunity to become a world power and enter into international politics.

Second—That our commercial interests in the Philippine Islands and in the Orient make it necessary for us to hold the islands permanently.

Third—That the spread of the Christian religion will be facilitated by a colonial policy.

Fourth—That there is no honorable retreat from the position which the nation has taken.

The first argument is addrest to the nation's pride and the second to the nation's pocket-book. The third is intended of the church member and the fourth for the partizan.

It is sufficient answer to the first argument to say that for more than a century this nation has been a world power. For ten decades it has been the most potent influence in the world. Not only has it been a world power, but it has done more to shape the politics of the human race than all the other nations of the world combined. Because our Declaration of Independence was promulgated others have been promulgated. Because the patriots of 1776 fought for liberty others have fought for it. Because our Constitution was adopted other constitutions have been adopted.

The growth of the principle of self-government, planted on American soil, has been the overshadowing political fact of the nineteenth century. It has made this nation conspicuous among the nations and given it a place in history such as no other nation has ever enjoyed. Nothing has been able to check the onward march of this idea. I am not willing that this nation shall cast aside the omnipotent weapon of truth to seize again the weapons of physical welfare. I would not exchange the glory of this Republic for the glory of all the empires that have risen and fallen since time began.

The permanent chairman of the last Republican National Convention presented the pecuniary argument in all its baldness when he said:

We make no hypocritical pretense of being interested in the Philippines solely on account of others. While we regard the welfare of those people as a sacred trust, we regard the welfare of the American people first. We see our duty to ourselves as well as to others. We believe in trade expansion. By every legitimate means within the province of government and constitution we mean to stimulate and expansion of our trade and open new markets.

This is the commercial argument. It is based upon the theory that war can be rightly waged for pecuniary advantage, and that it is profitable to purchase trade by force and violence. Franklin denied both of these propositions. When Lord Howe asserted that the acts of Parliament which brought on the revolution were necessary to prevent American trade from passing into foreign channels, Franklin replied:

To me it seems that neither the obtaining nor retaining of any trade, howsoever valuable, is an object for which men may justly spill each other's blood; that the true and sure means of extending and securing commerce are the goodness and cheapness of commodities, and that the profits of no trade can ever be equal to the expense of compelling it and holding it by fleets and armies. I consider this war against us, therefore, as both unjust and unwise.

I place the philosophy of Franklin against the sordid doctrine of those who would put a price upon the head of an American soldier and justify a war of conquest upon the ground that it will pay. The Democratic party is in favor of the expansion of trade. It would extend our trade by every legitimate and peaceful means; but it is not willing to make merchandise of human blood.

But a war of conquest is as unwise as it is unrighteous. A harbor and coaling station in the Philippines would answer every trade and military necessity and such a concession could have been secured at any time without difficulty.

It is not necessary to own people in order to trade with them. We carry on trade today with every part of the world, and our commerce has expanded more rapidly than the commerce of any European empire. We do not own Japan or China, but we trade with their people. We have not absorbed the republics of Central and South America, but we trade with them. It has not been necessary to have

any political connection with Canada or the nations of Europe in order to trade with them. Trade cannot be permanently profitable unless it is voluntary.

When trade is secured by force, the cost of securing it and retaining it must be taken out of the profits, and the profits are never large enough to cover the expense. Such a system would never be defended but for the fact that the expense is borne by all the people, while the profits are enjoyed by a few.

Imperialism would be profitable to the army contractors; it would be profitable to the ship owners, who would carry live soldiers to the Philippines and bring dead soldiers back; it would be profitable to those who would seize upon the franchises, and it would be profitable to the officials whose salaries would be fixt here and paid over there; but to the farmer, to the laboring man and to the vast majority of those engaged in other occupations it would bring expenditure without return and risk without reward.

Farmers and laboring men have, as a rule, small incomes and under systems which place the tax upon consumption pay much more than their fair share of the expenses of government. Thus the very people who receive least benefit from imperialism will be injured most by the military burdens which accompany it.

In addition the evils which he and the farmer share in common, the laboring man will be the first to suffer if oriental subjects seek work in the United States; the first to suffer if American capital leaves our shores to employ oriental labor in the Philippines to supply the trade of China and Japan; the first to suffer from the violence which the military spirit arouses and the first to suffer when the methods of imperialism are applied to our own Government.

It is not strange, therefore, that the labor organizations have been quick to note the approach of these dangers and prompt to protest against both militarism and imperialism.

The pecuniary argument, tho more effective with certain classes, is not likely to be used so often or presented with so much enthusiasm as the religious argument. If what has been termed the "gunpowder gospel" were urged against the Filipinos only it would be a sufficient answer to say that a majority of the Filipinos are now members of one branch of the Christian church; but the principle involved is one of much wider application and challenges serious consideration.

The religious argument varies in positiveness from a passive belief that Providence delivered the Filipinos into our hands, for their good and our glory, to the exultation of the minister who said that we ought to "thrash the natives (Filipinos) until they understand who we are," and that "every bullet sent, every cannon shot and every flag waved means righteousness."

We cannot approve of this doctrine in one place unless we are willing to apply it everywhere. If there is poison in the blood of the hand it will ultimately reach the heart. It is equally true that forcible Christianity, if planted under the American flag in the far-away Orient, will sooner or later be transplanted upon American soil.

If true Christianity consists in carrying out in our daily lives the teachings of Christ, who will say that we are commanded to civilize with dynamite and proselyte with the sword? He who would declare the divine will must prove his authority either by Holy Writ or by evidence of a special dispensation.

Imperialism finds no warrant in the Bible. The command, "Go ye into all the world and preach the gospel to every creature," has no Gatling gun attachment. When Jesus visited a village of Samaria and the people refused to receive him, some of the disciples suggested that fire should be called down from heaven to avenge the insult; but the Master rebuked them and said: "Ye know not what manner of spirit ye are of; for the Son of Man is not come to destroy men's lives, but to save them." Suppose he had said: "We will thrash them until they understand who we are," how different would have been the history of Christianity! Compare, if you will, the swaggering, bullying, brutal doctrine of imperialism with the golden rule and the commandment, "Thou shalt love thy neighbor as thyself."

Love, not force, was the weapon of the Nazarene; sacrifice for others, not the exploitation of them, was His method of reaching the human heart. A missionary recently told me that the Stars and Stripes once saved his life because his assailant recognized our flag as a flag that had no blood upon it.

Let it be known that our missionaries are seeking souls instead of sovereignty; let it be known that instead of being the advance guard of conquering armies, they are going forth to help and uplift, having their loins girt about with truth and their feet shod with the preparation of the gospel of peace, wearing the breastplate of righteousness and carrying the sword of the spirit; let it be known that they are citizens of a nation which respects the rights of the citizens of other nations as carefully as it protects the rights of its own citizens, and the welcome given to our missionaries will be more cordial than the welcome extended to the missionaries of any other nation.

The argument made by some that it was unfortunate for the nation that it had anything to do with the Philippine Islands, but that the naval victory at Manila made the permanent acquisition of those islands necessary, is also unsound. We won a naval victory at Santiago, but that did not compel us to hold Cuba.

The shedding of American blood in the Philippine Islands does not make it imperative that we should retain possession forever; American blood was shed at San Juan Hill and El Caney, and yet the President has promised the Cubans independence. The fact that the American flag floats over Manila does not compel us to exercise perpetual sovereignty over the islands; the American flag waves over Havana to-day, but the President has promised to haul it down when the flag of the Cuban Republic is ready to rise in its place. Better a thousand times that our flag in the Orient give way to a flag representing the idea of self-government than that the flag of this Republic should become the flag of an empire.

There is an easy, honest, honorable solution of the Philippine question. It is set forth in the Democratic platform and it is submitted with confidence to the American people. This plan I unreservedly indorse. If elected, I will convene Congress in extraordinary session as soon as inaugurated and recommend an immediate declaration of the nation's purpose, first, to establish a stable form of government in the Philippine Islands, just as we are now establishing a stable form of government in Cuba; second, to give independence to the Filipinos as we have promised to give independence to the Cubans; third, to protect the Filipinos from outside interference while they work out their destiny, just as we have protected the republics of Central and South America, and are, by the Monroe doctrine, pledged to protect Cuba.

A European protectorate often results in the plundering of the ward by the guardian. An American protectorate gives to the nation protected the advantage of our strength, without making it the victim of our greed. For three-quarters of a century the Monroe doctrine has been a shield to neighboring republics and yet it has imposed no pecuniary burden upon us. After the Filipinos had aided us in the war against Spain, we could not honorably turn them over to their former masters; we could not leave them to be the victims of the ambitious designs of European nations, and since we do not desire to make them a part of us or to hold them as subjects, we propose the only alternative, namely, to give them independence and guard them against molestation from without.

When our opponents are unable to defend their position by argument they fall back upon the assertion that it is destiny, and insist that we must submit to it, no matter how much it violates our moral precepts and our principles of government. This is a complacent philosophy. It obliterates the distinction between right and wrong and makes individuals and nations the helpless victims of circumstance.

Destiny is the subterfuge of the invertebrate, who, lacking the courage to oppose error, seeks some plausible excuse of supporting it. Washington said that the destiny of the republican form of government was deeply, if not finally, staked on the experiment entrusted to the American people. How different Washington's definition of destiny from the Republican definition!

The Republicans say that this nation is in the hands of destiny; Washington believed that not only the destiny of our own nation but the destiny of the republican form of government throughout the world was entrusted to American hands. Immeasurable responsibility! The destiny of this republic is in the hands of its own people, and upon the success of the experiment here rests the hope of humanity. No exterior force can disturb this republic, and no foreign influence should be permitted to change its course. What the future has in store for this nation no one has authority to declare, but each individual has his own idea of the nation's mission, and he owes it to his country as well as to himself to contribute as best he may to the fulfilment of that mission.

Mr. Chairman and Gentlemen of the Committee: I can never fully discharge the debt of gratitude which I owe to my countrymen for the honors which they have so generously bestowed upon me; but, sirs, whether it be my lot to occupy the high office for which the convention has named me, or to spend the remainder of my days in private life, it shall be my constant ambition and my controlling purpose to aid in realizing the high ideals of those whose wisdom and courage and sacrifices brought this republic into existence.

I can conceive of a national destiny surpassing the glories of the present and the past—a destiny which meets the responsibilities of to-day and measures up to the possibilities of the future. Behold a republic, resting securely upon the foundation stones quarried by revolutionary patriots from the mountain of eternal truth—a republic applying in practise and proclaiming to the world the self- evident propositions that all men are created equal; that they are endowed by their Creator with inalienable rights; that governments are instituted among men to secure these rights, and that governments derive their just powers from the consent of the governed. Behold a republic in which civil and religious liberty stimulate all to earnest endeavor and in which the law restrains every hand uplifted for a neighbor's injury—a republic in which every citizen is a sovereign, but in which no one cares or dares to wear a crown. Behold a republic standing erect while empires all around are bowed beneath the weight of their own armaments—a republic whose flag is loved while other flags are only feared. Behold a republic increasing in population, in wealth, in strength and in influence, solving the problems of civilization and hastening the coming of an universal brotherhood—a republic which shakes thrones and dissolves aristocracies by its silent example and gives light and inspiration to those who sit in darkness. Behold a republic gradually but surely becoming the supreme moral factor in the world's progress and the accepted arbiter of the world's disputes—a republic whose history, like the path of the just, "is as the shinning light that shineth more and more unto the perfect day."

Source:

James Andrews and David Zarefsky, eds., *American Voices: Significant Speeches in American History, 1640–1945*. Reading, Mass.: Longman, 1989.

SUGGESTED READING

The Rise of Corporations, Heavy Industry, and Mechanized Farming

David A. Hounshell, *From the American System to Mass Production, 1800–1932: The Development of Manufacturing Technology in the United States*. Baltimore: Johns Hopkins University Press, 1984.

Thomas J. Misa, *American Genesis: A Century of Invention and Technological Enthusiasm, 1870–1970*. New York: Penguin, 1993.

Martin J. Sklar, *The Corporate Reconstruction of American Capitalism, 1890–1916*. New York: Cambridge University Press, 1988

Mark Wahlgren Summers, *The Gilded Age, Or the Hazard of New Functions*. Upper Saddle River, N.J.: Prentice-Hall, 1996.

Growth of the West and Federal Indian Policy

Frederick E. Hoxie, *A Final Promise: the Campaign to Assimilate the Indians, 1880–1920*. Lincoln: University of Nebraska Press, 1989.

Patricia Nelson Limerick, *The Legacy of Conquest: the Unbroken Past of the American West*. New York: W.W. Norton, 1987.

Joseph G. Rosa and Robin May, *Buffalo Bill and His Wild West*. Lawrence: University of Kansas Press, 1989.

Richard White, *"Its Your Misfortune and None of My Own": A New History of the American West*. Norman: University of Oklahoma Press, 1991.

Daniel Worster, *Under Western Skies: Nature and History in the American West*. New York: Oxford University Press, 1992.

Cultural Diversity and National Unity

Henry Adams, *The Education of Henry Adams, An Autobiography* (privately printed). 1907.

John Bodnar, *The Transplanted: A History of Immigrants in Urban America*. Bloomington: Indiana University Press, 1985.

Raymond A. Mohl, *The New City: Urban America in the Industrial Age, 1860–1920*. Wheeling, Ill,: Harlan Davidson, 1985.

Nell Irvin Painter, *Standing at Armageddon: The United States, 1877–1919*. New York: W.W. Norton, 1987.

Ronald Takaki, *Strangers from a Different Shore: A History of Asian Americans*. New York: Little, Brown, 1989.

C. Vann Woodward, with an Afterword by William S. McFeely, *The Strange Career of Jim Crow*. New York: Oxford University Press, 2001.

The Rise of the American Labor Movement

Paul Avrich, *The Haymarket Tragedy*. Princeton, N.J.: Princeton University Press, 1984.

Leon Fink, *Workingman's Democracy: The Knights of Laor and American Politics*. Champaign: University of Illinois Press, 1983.

David Montgomery, *The Fall of the House of Labor: The Workplace, the State, and American Labor Activism, 1865–1925*. New York: Cambridge University Press, 1987.

Elizabeth Anne Payne, *Reform, Labor, and Feminism*. Champaign: University of Illinois Press, 1988

Politics, Economy, and Society

William Leach, *Land of Desire: Merchants, Power, and the Rise of a New American Culture*. New York: Pantheon, 1993.

David Nasaw, *Going Out: The Rise and Fall of Public American Amusements*. New York: Basic Books, 1993.

Gretchen Ritter. *Goldbugs and Greenbacks: The Antimonopoly Tradition and the Politics of Finance in America*. New York: Cambridge University Press, 1997.

Theda Skocpol, *Protecting Soldiers and Mothers: the Political Origins of Social Policy in the United States*. Cambridge, Mass.: Belknap Press, 1992.

Mark W. Summers, *Railroads, Reconstruction and the Gospel of Prosperity*. Princeton, N.J.: Princeton University Press, 1984.

The Development of an Expansionist Foreign Policy

David McCullough. *The Path Between the Seas: The Creation of the Panama Canal, 1870–1914*. New York: Simon & Schuster, 1978.

David F. Trask. *The War with Spain in 1898*. New York: Free Press, 1981.

Index

Boldface page numbers denote extensive treatment of a topic.